THE BRITISH MEDICAL ASSOCIATION

NEW GUIDE TO

Medicines & Drugs

THE BRITISH MEDICAL ASSOCIATION

NEW GUIDE TO
Medicines & Drugs

Chief Medical Editor
Dr John Henry MB FRCP
Consultant Physician
Guy's and St Thomas's Hospital,
London

Dorling Kindersley
London • New York • Stuttgart

A DORLING KINDERSLEY BOOK

BRITISH MEDICAL ASSOCIATION

Chairman of the Council Dr A.W.Macara
Treasurer Dr J.A.Riddell
Chairman of the BMA Journal Committee Sir Anthony Grabham
Medical Editor, Family Doctor Publications Dr Tony Smith

Chief Medical Editor Dr John Henry MB FRCP
Drug Information Reviewer Mr Charles Tugwell BPharm, MSc, MRPharmS, MIInfSc
Contributors Dr Kiran Bhagat MSc, MRCP, Caroline Dunmore BPharm, MRPharmS, Miss Susanna Gilmour-White BPharm, MRPharmS, Dr Sandro Lanzon-Miller MD, MRCP, Dr Michael Polkey MB, MRCP, Michael Rogers BPharm, MRPharmS, DipInfSc, MIInfSc, Dr Maxwell Summerhayes BPharm, PhD, MRPharmS, Nick Thompson MSc(MedSci), DipInfSci, Susanna Ward MBBS, BSc, MRCP, Ms Heather Wiseman BSc, MSc
Dorling Kindersley would like to thank John Ramsey of St George's Hospital Toxicology Unit, London for supplying drugs for photography in the Colour Identification Guide

DORLING KINDERSLEY LIMITED

THIRD EDITION
Project Editor Mary Lindsay
Editorial Assistant Teresa Pritlove
Additional Editorial Assistance Fiona Courtenay-Thompson, David Harding, Martyn Page, Susan Sturrock
Indexer Kay Wright
Art Editor Clare Shedden
Designer Christina Betts
Additional Design Assistance Sue Knight
Illustrators Karen Cochrane, Tony Graham, Kevin Marks, Coral Mula, Lynda Payne, Andrew Popkiewicz
Photography Tim Ridley
Production Sarah Fuller

PREVIOUS EDITIONS
Senior Project Editor Cathy Meeus; Editors Marian Broderick, Deirdre Clark, Christiane Gunzi, Stephanie Jackson, Terence Monaighan, Penny Gray, David Bennett; Art Editor Chez Picthall; Designers Debra Lee, Gail Jones, Sandra Schneider; Dorling Kindersley would also like to thank Dr Sheila Bingham, Stephen and Nikki Carroll, Peter Cooling, and Guy's Hospital Pharmacy.

First published in Great Britain in 1988
by Dorling Kindersley Limited,
9 Henrietta Street, London WC2E 8PS
First published in paperback 1989, reprinted 1990
Second edition 1991, reprinted 1992, 1993
Third edition 1994, reprinted 1995

A CIP catalogue record for this book is available from the British Library.

ISBN 0-7513-0102-7

Computer page make-up by Deborah Rhodes
Colour reproduction by Llovet SPA, Barcelona
Printed in Singapore

Yamanouchi

FLOMAX® MR

(Tamsulosin hydrochloride modified release capsules)

GlaxoWellcome

20503325/1
(170500)

What is Flomax MR?

Flomax MR contains 400 micrograms tamsulosin hydrochloride in each modified release capsule, equivalent to 367 micrograms tamsulosin. The capsules also contain microcrystalline cellulose, methylacrylic acid copolymer, polysorbate, sodium lauryl sulphate, triacetin, calcium stearate and talc. These all help to make the granules which are in the capsule. The capsule shell contains gelatin, and is coloured with indigotin (E132), titanium dioxide (E171), and yellow and red iron oxide (E172).

Flomax MR capsules have an orange body and an olive-green cap. The capsules are supplied in blister packs of 30.

Tamsulosin hydrochloride, the active ingredient of Flomax MR, is an alpha$_{1A}$-adreno-ceptor blocker. It relaxes the muscles in the prostate and urethra, and lets urine pass more readily through the urethra and aids urination.

The product licence for Flomax MR is held by Yamanouchi Pharma Ltd, Yamanouchi House, Pyrford Road, West Byfleet, Surrey KT14 6RA. The capsules are manufactured by Yamanouchi Europe B.V., Elisabethhof 19, Leiderdorp, The Netherlands, at their site at Hogemaat 2, Meppel, The Netherlands.

What is Flomax MR used for?

Flomax MR is used to treat the symptoms associated with benign prostatic hyperplasia (BPH). These symptoms include difficulty in starting to pass water, frequent trips to the toilet to pass water, a feeling of not completely emptying your bladder and having to get up several times in the night to pass water.

In the prostate gland, bladder and urethra there are specialised cells containing alpha$_{1A}$-receptors that cause the muscles in the urethra to tighten. Flomax MR is an alpha$_{1A}$-adrenoceptor blocker, which reduces the action of these specialised cells and relaxes the muscles making it easier to pass water.

Before using Flomax MR

You should not use Flomax MR if you are allergic to tamsulosin or any of the inactive ingredients, or if you have a severe liver condition.

If you have ever fainted or felt dizzy when suddenly sitting or standing up, you should not take Flomax MR.

Dizziness can sometimes occur when taking Flomax MR, particularly if you are also taking other alpha$_1$- blockers.

If you do feel weak or dizzy make sure you sit or lie down straight away until the symptoms have disappeared.

⇒

FREE CONFIDENTIAL INFORMATION SERVICE

Dear Patient,

Your doctor has prescribed Flomax® MR to help treat your prostate symptoms.

To help ensure you have the best possible information about your condition, you can request any of a number of items from our Information Service. This service is **completely confidential and free of charge**. No personal details will be kept.

Just fill in the form overleaf and send it to the address given or ring our FREEPHONE HELPLINE on 0800 068 8068.

May we take this opportunity of wishing you the very best of health.

Yamanouchi Pharma Ltd.

You should not drive or operate machinery if you do feel faint or dizzy until the symptoms have passed.

Make sure you tell your doctor about all other medicines you are taking.

Taking Flomax MR

For adults and the elderly, the dose is one capsule each morning after breakfast. Swallow the capsule whole with a drink of water (about half a tumblerful) while sitting or standing.

Do not chew or crunch the capsule.

Your doctor may want to examine you from time to time whilst you are taking this medicine.

If you have missed your dose of Flomax MR

You may take your capsule later the same day after food if you have forgotten to take it after breakfast.

If you have missed a day, just continue to take your daily capsule from the next day.

If you have taken too many capsules, tell your doctor straight away.

After taking Flomax MR

A small number of people may show side-effects after taking Flomax MR. The following have been reported: Runny or blocked nose, fainting, dizziness, abnormal ejaculation (i.e. less, or no notice-able, semen ejaculated), dizziness as you sit or stand up, weakness, headache or palpitations (rapid or irregular heart beat).

The following side-effects have been reported less often:
Gastro-intestinal symptoms such as nausea and vomiting (feeling or being sick), diarrhoea or constipation and hypersensitivity reactions such as rash, itching, redness or local swelling.

Tell your doctor if any of these symptoms become troublesome.

There have been very rare reports of angioedema (swelling of the hands or feet) and priapism (persistent painful erection usually unrelated to sexual activity). Consult your doctor immediately if these occur. You should also tell your doctor or pharmacist if you have any other side-effects after taking Flomax MR.

General information

Keep all medicines out of the reach of children.

Do not use the capsules after the expiry date printed on the pack. They may be kept at temperatures of up to 30°C in the pack in which they are supplied.

Remember your medicines have been prescribed for you. Never give your medicines to others, even if it does seem that they have the same condition as you.

This leaflet was last revised in April 2000.

Yamanouchi Pharma Ltd.
Yamanouchi House, Pyrford Road
West Byfleet, Surrey KT14 6RA

© Yamanouchi Pharma Ltd.

- Video: "What you Really need to know about Enlarged Prostate" featuring John Cleese and Dr. Rob Buckman . . . . ( )   Please tick your choice!

- Video: "Talk About the Prostate" featuring the experiences of three men with prostate problems. . . ( )

- Audiocassette on "Enlarged Prostate" featuring Dr. Hilary Jones . . . . ( )

- Booklet: "The Complete Prostate Guide" by Anne Charlish . . . . ( )

Send this form in an envelope to **Yamanouchi Pharma Ltd., P.O. Box 448, Guildford, Surrey GU1 4GP** or ring our helpline free-of-charge on 0800 068 8068.

- Further general information on prostate health may be obtained by writing to The Prostate Help Association, Langworth, Lincoln, LN3 5DF. Please send two first-class stamps.

Your name . . . . Address . . . .
. . . .

PREFACE

Doctors no longer hand out prescriptions without any explanation, and the days are long gone when pharmacists solemnly handed patients bottles labelled "the mixture" or "the tablets" and expected no questions. Most patients today are critical consumers; they want to know what drugs they are taking, the actions of these drugs, their side effects, and their possible risks.

But information given by word of mouth at the end of a consultation may be difficult to remember. Researchers have shown that the most effective way of providing information about drugs is in the form of printed notes or data sheets. However, leaflets of this kind are not yet generally available in Britain, and there is, therefore, a need for more written information about the drugs that people commonly take.

The main section of this book consists of structured information on 235 of the most widely used drugs, presented in a clear, easy-to-understand format. These drug profiles provide the essential information for the patient, including what effects the drug has, potential problem areas, and what to do if a dose is forgotten. But these basic facts are not enough for an understanding of how the drug works. The first two sections of this book give a fuller account of the way drugs affect body systems, and outline the actions of the main classes of drugs. Other sections include a comprehensive directory of drugs and brand names, a colour identification guide to tablets and capsules, and information on vitamins, minerals, drugs of abuse, and drugs in sport.

The British Medical Association NEW GUIDE TO MEDICINES AND DRUGS has been compiled by doctors and pharmacists familiar with the sorts of questions patients ask. The detailed, factual content has been checked and verified by specialists. The book is not intended to supersede the information given to the individual patient by his or her doctor. Choosing the most suitable drug and advising on use depends on the doctor's knowledge of your previous health and medical background.

This guide should, however, help patients and their families to understand more about the treatment they have been prescribed, should alert them to early warning signs of adverse effects, and should act as a ready reference source for information that might otherwise have been forgotten. We believe it will improve relationships between patients and their doctors, and contribute to the effectiveness and safety of the drugs people take.

Dr Tony Smith
Medical Editor
BMA Family Doctor Publications

CONTENTS

4 A-Z OF DRUGS

5 GLOSSARY AND INDEX

INTRODUCTION

The British Medical Association New Guide to Medicines and Drugs has been planned and written to provide clear information and practical advice on drugs and medicines in a way that can be readily understood by a non-medical reader. The text reflects current medical knowledge and standard medical practice in this country. It is intended to complement and reinforce the advice of your doctor.

How the book is structured

The book is divided into five parts. The first part, Understanding and Using Drugs, provides a general introduction to the effects of drugs and gives general advice on practical questions such as the administration and storage of drugs. The second part, the Drug Finder, provides the means of locating information on specific drugs. Part 3, Major Drug Groups, will help you to understand the uses and mechanisms of action of the principal classes of drugs. Part 4, the A – Z of Drugs, consists of detailed profiles of all commonly prescribed drugs, and also includes special profiles on vitamins and minerals, drugs of abuse, and drugs in sport. Part 5 contains a glossary of drug-related terms (italicized in the text) and a general index.

Finding your way into the book

The information you require, whether on the specific characteristics of an individual drug or on the general effects and uses of a group of drugs, can be easily obtained without prior knowledge of the medical names of drugs or drug classification through one of two sources: the Drug Finder or the General Index. The diagram on the facing page shows how you can obtain information throughout the book on the subject concerning you from each of these starting points.

1 UNDERSTANDING AND USING DRUGS

The introductory part of the book on Understanding and Using Drugs gives a grounding in the fundamental principles underlying the medical use of drugs. Covering such topics as the classifications of drugs, mechanisms of action, and the proper use of medications, it provides valuable background information that backs up the more detailed descriptions and advice given in Parts 3 and 4. Read this section before seeking further specific information.

2 DRUG FINDER INDEX

This is comprised of two elements. The Colour Identification Guide contains photographs of over 200 brand-name tablets and capsules to help you identify medications. The Drug Finder helps you to find information on specific brand-name drugs and generic substances.

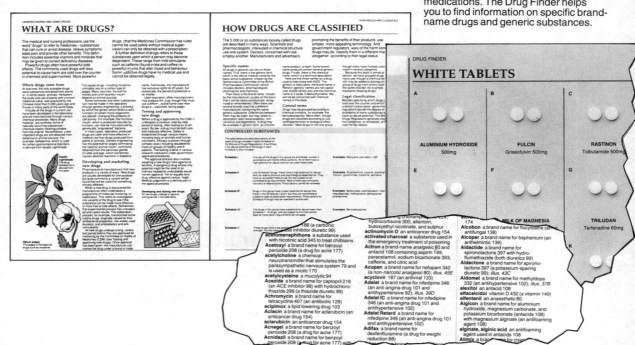

Finding your information

Whether you start by looking up an individual drug or a group of drugs, you will be led by cross-references to relevant information in all parts of the book.

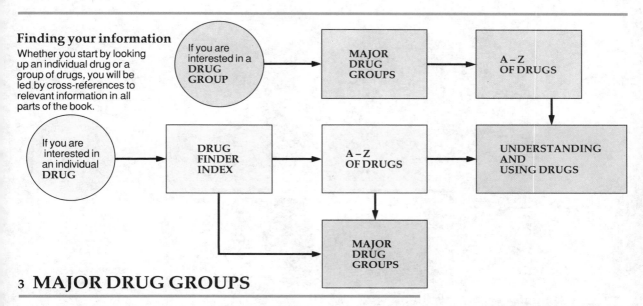

If you are interested in a DRUG GROUP → **MAJOR DRUG GROUPS** → **A – Z OF DRUGS**

If you are interested in an individual DRUG → **DRUG FINDER INDEX** → **A – Z OF DRUGS** → **UNDERSTANDING AND USING DRUGS**

MAJOR DRUG GROUPS

---

3 MAJOR DRUG GROUPS

Subdivided into sections dealing with each body system (for example, heart and circulation) or major disease grouping (for example, malignant and immune disease), this part of the book contains descriptions of the principal classes of drugs. Information is given on the uses, actions, effects and risks associated with each group of drugs and is backed up by helpful illustrations and diagrams. Individual drugs in each group are listed to allow cross-reference to Part 4.

4 A – Z OF DRUGS

This part contains a main listing of 235 profiles of generic drugs, written to a standard format to help you find specific informaion quickly and easily; cross-references to the relevant major drug groups are provided. Supplementary sections profile vitamins and minerals, drugs of abuse, and drugs in sport.

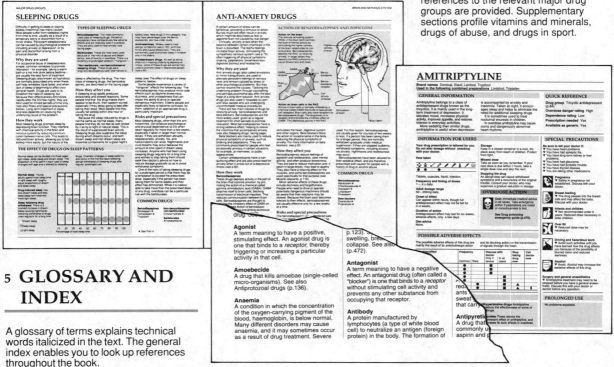

5 GLOSSARY AND INDEX

A glossary of terms explains technical words italicized in the text. The general index enables you to look up references throughout the book.

PART

1

UNDERSTANDING AND USING DRUGS

WHAT ARE DRUGS?

The medical and nursing professions use the word "drugs" to refer to medicines – substances that can cure or arrest disease, relieve symptoms, ease pain and provide other benefits. This definition includes essential vitamins and minerals that may be given to correct deficiency diseases.

Powerful drugs often have powerful side effects. The commonly used drugs with less potential to cause harm are sold over the counter in chemists and supermarkets. More powerful drugs, (that the Medicines Commission has ruled cannot be used safely without medical supervision) can only be obtained with a prescription.

A further definition of drugs refers to those substances upon which a person may become dependent. These range from mild stimulants such as caffeine (found in tea and coffee) to powerful agents that alter mood and behaviour. Some addictive drugs have no medical use and cannot be obtained legally.

Where drugs come from

At one time, the only available drugs were substances extracted from plants, or, in some cases, animals. Herbalism, the study and use of plants with a known medicinal value, was practised by the Chinese more than 5,000 years ago and thrives in many parts of the world today.

Virtually all the drugs in current use have been developed in the laboratory and are manufactured through various chemical processes. Many drugs, however, are synthetic forms of naturally occurring substances – chemical copies indistinguishable from the original. Nevertheless, a few important drugs are still obtained from botanical or animal sources. For example, belladonna, which is used for certain gastrointestinal disorders, is derived from deadly nightshade.

Deadly nightshade
The drug belladonna is derived from this plant.

Opium poppy
This poppy is the basis for drugs such as morphine.

The opiate drugs, including morphine, ultimately rely on a certain type of poppy. Many vaccines, thyroid hormones and (until recently) insulin depend on animal sources.

Some hormones and other substances can now be made in the laboratory through genetic engineering, a process by which the genes (which direct a cell's function) of certain micro-organisms are altered, changing the products of cell activity. For example, the hormone insulin, which is produced naturally by humans, can now be manufactured by genetically "engineered" bacteria.

In most cases, laboratory-produced drugs are safer and more effective in medical use than drugs produced from plants or animals. Genetic engineering has the potential for largely eliminating the need for animal insulin, commonly obtained from the pancreas glands of cattle and pigs, which sometimes causes adverse reactions in diabetics.

Developing and marketing new drugs

Pharmaceutical manufacturers find new products in a variety of ways. New drugs are usually developed for one purpose but quite commonly a variant will be found that will be useful for something entirely different.

When a new drug is discovered the manufacturer often undertakes a programme of molecular tincturing, or elaboration. This refers to investigation into variants of the drug to see if the substance can be made more effective or more free of side effects. Sometimes that experimental process has unexpected and useful results. The elaboration process, for example, transformed some sulpha drugs, originally valued for their antibacterial properties, into widely-used diuretics, oral antidiabetics and anticonvulsants.

All new drugs undergo a long, careful test period before they are approved for marketing by the Committee on Safety of Medicines (CSM) (see Testing and approving new drugs). Once approval has been given, the manufacturer can market the drug under a brand or trade name. Technically, the manufacturer has exclusive rights for 20 years; but realistically, the period of protection is far shorter.

Upon expiration, other manufacturers may produce the drug, though they must use a different brand name (see How drugs are classified, facing page).

Testing and approving new drugs

Before a drug is approved by the CSM, it undergoes a cautious, step-by-step period of testing, often lasting six to ten years. By law, a drug must be both safe and medically effective. Safety is established through various means, including tests on animals and human volunteers. Efficacy is proven through complex tests (including *double blind* trials) on groups of healthy and ill patients. The testing is done in various research institutions under government approved procedures.

The approval process also involves weighing a new drug's risks against its benefits. A dangerous drug whose only potential might be the relief of an ordinary headache undoubtedly would not win approval. Yet an equally *toxic* drug, effective against cancer, might. Medical judgement is a definite part of the approval process.

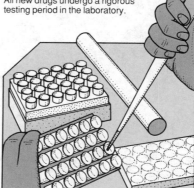

Developing and testing new drugs
All new drugs undergo a rigorous testing period in the laboratory.

HOW DRUGS ARE CLASSIFIED

The 5,000 or so substances loosely called drugs are described in many ways. Scientists and pharmacologists, interested in chemical structure, use one system. Doctors, concerned with use, employ another. Manufacturers and advertisers, promoting the benefits of their products, use simpler, more appealing terminology. And government regulators, wary of the harm some drugs may do, classify them in a different manner altogether, according to their legal status.

Specific names

All drugs in general use rely on three names. First, there is the generic term, which is the official medical name for the basic active substance, chosen by the Nomenclature Committee of the British Pharmacopoeia Commission (which includes doctors, pharmacologists, pharmacists, and chemists).

Then there is the brand name, chosen by the manufacturer usually on the basis that it can be easily pronounced, recognized, or remembered. Often there are several brands (each by a different manufacturer) containing the same generic substance. Differences between them may be slight but may relate to absorption rates (bioavailability), convenience, and digestibility. A drug may be available in generic form, as a brand-name product, or both. Some brand-name products contain several generic drugs. Finally, there is the chemical name, which is a technical description.

Here are the three names for a drug used to help those with AIDS. The generic is zidovudine, the brand name is Retrovir (generic names are not capitalized; brand names are) and the chemical name is 3-azido-3-deoxythymidine. We will not be concerned with chemical names in this book.

General terms

Drugs may be grouped according to chemical similarity, for example, the benzodiazepines. More often, though, drugs are classified according to use (antihypertensive) or biological effect (diuretic). Most drugs fit into one group, though many have multiple uses and are listed in several categories.

Because this book is aimed at the lay person, we have grouped drugs according to use, though a chemical description may be added to distinguish one group of drugs from others used to treat the same disorder (for example, benzodiazepine sleeping drugs).

Legal classification

Besides specifying which drugs can be sold over-the-counter and which require a doctor's prescription, government regulations decide the degree of availability of many substances which have an abuse potential. The Misuse of Drugs Regulations generally establish five categories, or schedules, of drugs (see the box below).

CONTROLLED SUBSTANCES

The table below provides descriptions of the types of drugs included in each schedule of the Misuse of Drugs Regulations. A summary of the abuse potential of the drugs in each schedule is also included.

Schedule I	Virtually all the drugs in this group are prohibited, except in accordance with Home Office authority. All of them have a high potential for abuse and are not used medicinally.	**Examples** Marijuana (cannabis), LSD.
Schedule II	Like Schedule I drugs, these have a high potential for abuse and can lead to physical and psychological dependence. They have an accepted medical use, but are subject to full controlled drug requirements. Most of them are stimulants, narcotics, or depressants. Prescriptions cannot be renewed.	**Examples** Amphetamine, cocaine, diamorphine (heroin), glutethimide, morphine, pethidine.
Schedule III	Drugs in this group have a lower potential for abuse than those in Schedules I and II, but they are nevertheless subject to special prescription requirements. Prescriptions for Schedule III drugs may be repeated if authorized.	**Examples** Barbiturates, diethylpropion, mazindol, meprobamate, methyprylone, pentazocine, phentermine.
Schedule IV	The drugs in this group have a potential for abuse lower than Schedule I – III drugs, and are subject to minimal control. Special prescription requirements do not apply.	**Examples** Benzodiazepines.
Schedule V	These drugs have a low potential for abuse because of their strength. For the most part, they are preparations that contain small amounts of narcotics, but are exempt from controlled drug requirements.	**Examples** Kaolin and morphine (an antidiarrhoeal), codeine linctus (a cough suppressant), DF118 tablets (a narcotic analgesic containing dihydrocodeine).

HOW DRUGS WORK

Before the discovery of the sulpha drugs in 1935, medical knowledge of drugs was limited. At that time, possibly only a dozen or so drugs had a clear medical value. Most of these were the extracts of plants (such as digitalis, which is extracted from foxgloves) while other drugs, such as aspirin, were chemically closely related to plant extracts (in this case, salicylic acid, which is extracted from the willow tree).

In the past 50 years that picture has changed dramatically. Not only is an impressive variety of effective drugs now available for medical use, but scientific knowledge in the drug field has virtually exploded.

Today's doctor understands far better than his or her predecessors the complexity of drug actions in the body and the wide range of effects drugs can have on it, both of a beneficial and of an adverse nature.

He or she can also recognize that some drugs interact harmfully with other drugs, or with certain foods and alcohol.

DRUG ACTIONS

While the exact workings of some drugs are not fully understood, medical science provides clear knowledge as to what most of them do once they enter or are applied to the human body. Drugs, of course, serve different purposes, sometimes curing a disease, sometimes only alleviating symptoms. Their impact occurs in various parts of the anatomy. But although different drugs act in different ways, their actions generally fall into one of three categories.

Replacing chemicals that are deficient

To function normally, the body requires sufficient levels of certain chemical substances. These include vitamins and minerals, which the body obtains from food. A balanced diet usually supplies what is needed. But when deficiencies occur, various deficiency diseases result. Lack of vitamin C causes scurvy; lack of vitamin D leads to rickets; and iron deficiency causes anaemia.

Other deficiency diseases arise from a lack of various *hormones*, chemical substances produced by glands which act as internal "messengers". Diabetes mellitus, Addison's disease, and hypothyroidism all result from deficiencies of different hormones.

Deficiency diseases are treated with drugs that replace the substances that are missing, or, in the case of some hormone deficiencies, with animal or synthetic replacements.

Interfering with cell function

Many drugs can change the way cells work by stimulating or reducing the normal level of activity. Inflammation, for example, is due to the action on blood vessels and blood cells of certain natural hormones and other chemicals. Anti-inflammatory drugs block the action of the hormones or slow their production. Drugs that act in a similar way are used in the treatment of a variety of conditions: hormone disorders, blood clotting problems, heart and kidney diseases.

Many such drugs do their work by altering the transmission system by which messages are sent from one part of the body to another.

A message – to contract a muscle, say – originates in the brain and enters a nerve cell through its receiving end. The message, in the form of an electrical impulse, travels the nerve to the sending end. Here a chemical substance called a *neurotransmitter* is released, conducting the message across the gap separating it from an adjacent nerve cell. That process is repeated until the message reaches the appropriate muscle.

Many drugs can alter this process, often by their effect on receptor sites on cells (see the box, left). Some drugs (*agonists*) intensify cell activity, while other drugs (*antagonists*) reduce activity in the cells.

Acting against invading organisms or abnormal cells

Infectious diseases are caused by viruses, bacteria, protozoa, and fungi invading the body. We now have a wide choice of drugs that destroy these micro-organisms, either by halting their multiplication or by killing them directly. Other drugs treat disease by killing abnormal cells – cancer cells, for example.

RECEPTOR SITES

Many drugs are thought to produce their effects by their action on special sites called *receptors* on the surface of body cells. Natural body chemicals such as *neurotransmitters* bind to these sites initiating a response in the cell. Cells may have many types of receptor, each of which has an affinity for a different chemical in the body. Drugs may also bind to receptors, either adding to the effect of the body's natural chemicals and enhancing cell response (agonist drugs) or preventing such a chemical from binding to its receptor, and thereby blocking a particular cell response (antagonist drugs).

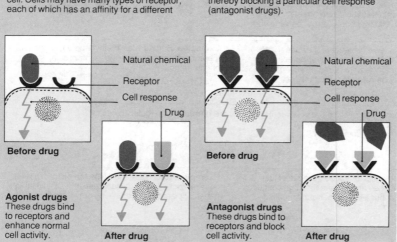

Before drug

Agonist drugs
These drugs bind to receptors and enhance normal cell activity.

After drug

Before drug

Antagonist drugs
These drugs bind to receptors and block cell activity.

After drug

Natural chemical
Receptor
Cell response
Drug

THE EFFECTS OF DRUGS

Before a doctor selects a drug to be used in the treatment of a sick person, he or she carefully weighs the benefits and the risks. Obviously, the doctor expects a positive result from the drug, a cure of the condition or at least the relief of symptoms. At the same time, consideration has to be given to the risks, for all drugs are potentially harmful, some of them considerably more than others.

Reaction time

Some drugs can produce rapid and spectacular relief from the symptoms of disease. Glyceryl trinitrate frequently provides almost immediate relief from the pain of angina; other drugs can quickly alleviate the symptoms of an asthmatic attack. Conversely, some drugs take much longer to produce a response. It may, for example, require several weeks of treatment with an antidepressant drug before a person experiences maximum benefit. This can add to anxiety unless the doctor has warned of the possibility of a delay in the onset of beneficial effects.

Side effects

The side effects of a drug are the known and frequently experienced, expected reactions to a drug. The old concept of a drug as a "magic bullet" that could be targeted to a specific type of cell is now recognized as inaccurate. Whether a drug is taken by mouth, by injection, or by inhalation, it will be distributed throughout the body, and its effects are unlikely to be restricted to one particular type of tissue or organ.

For example, *anticholinergic* drugs, which are prescribed to relieve spasm in the wall of the intestine, may also affect the eyes, causing blurred vision, the mouth, causing dryness, and the bladder, causing retention of urine. Such side effects may gradually disappear as the body becomes used to the drug. But if side effects persist, the dose of the drug may have to be reduced, or the

DOSE AND RESPONSE

Not everyone responds in the same way to a drug, and in many cases the dose has to be adjusted to allow for such factors as the age, weight, or general health of the patient.

The dose of any drug should be sufficient to produce a beneficial response but not so great that it will cause excessive adverse effects. If the dose is too low, the drug may not have any effect, either beneficial or adverse; if it is too high, it will not produce any additional benefits and may produce adverse effects. The aim of drug treatment, therefore, is to achieve a concentration of drug in the blood or tissue that lies somewhere between the minimum effective level and the maximum safe concentration. This is known as the therapeutic range.

For some drugs, such as digitalis drugs, the therapeutic range is quite narrow, so the margin of safety/effectiveness is small. Other drugs, such as penicillin antibiotics, have a much wider therapeutic range.

Wide therapeutic range

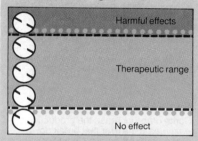

Dosage of drugs with a wide therapeutic range can vary considerably without altering the drug's effects.

Narrow therapeutic range

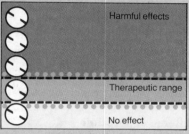

Dosage of drugs with a narrow therapeutic range has to be carefully calculated to achieve the desired effect.

length of time between doses may need to be increased.

The side effects of certain drugs, especially some anticancer drugs, can often be quite serious. Such drugs are administered only because they may be the only agents available for the treatment of a disease that might otherwise prove fatal. But all drugs, even the mildest, should be regarded as chemicals with a potential for producing serious, *toxic* reactions, especially if they are misused or abused.

Adverse reactions

Adverse reactions are unexpected, unpredictable reactions that are not related to the usual effects of a normal dose of a drug. Unpredictable drug reactions may be caused by conditions in the patient such as an allergy or a genetic disorder, such as the absence of an enzyme that usually inactivates the drug. Common adverse reactions of this type include a rash, swelling of the face, or jaundice. They may also be due to interactions with other drugs. Unpredictable drug reactions usually necessitate withdrawal of the drug under medical supervision.

Beneficial vs adverse effects

In evaluating the risk/benefit ratio of a drug which he or she may prescribe, a doctor has to weigh the therapeutic benefit to the sick person against the possible adverse effects. For example, such side effects as nausea, headache, and diarrhoea may result from taking an antibiotic. But they will certainly be considered acceptable risks if the problem is a life-threatening infection requiring immediate treatment. On the other hand, such side effects would be considered unacceptable for an oral contraceptive that is taken over a number of years by a healthy patient.

Because some people are more at risk from adverse drug reactions than others (particularly those with a history of drug allergy), the doctor normally checks whether there is any reason why a particular drug should not be given (see Drug treatment in special risk groups, p.20).

PLACEBO RESPONSE

The word placebo – Latin for "I will please" – is used to describe any chemically inert substance given as a substitute for a drug. Any benefit gained from taking a placebo occurs because the person taking it believes that it will produce good results.

New drugs are almost always tested against a placebo preparation in clinical trials as a way to assess the efficacy of a drug before it is marketed. The placebo is made to look identical to the active preparation, and volunteers are not told whether they have been given the active drug or the placebo. Sometimes the doctor is also unaware of which preparation an individual has been given. This is known as a *double blind* trial. In this way, the purely placebo effect can be eliminated and the effectiveness of the drug determined more realistically.

Sometimes the mere taking of a medicine has a psychological effect that produces a beneficial physical response. This type of placebo response can make an important contribution to the overall effectiveness of a chemically active drug, and is most commonly seen with analgesics, antidepressants, and anti-anxiety drugs. Some people, known as placebo responders, are more likely to experience this sort of reaction than the rest of the population.

DRUG INTERACTIONS

When two different drugs are taken together, or when a drug is taken in combination with certain foods or with alcohol, this may produce effects different from those produced when the drug is taken alone. In many cases, this is beneficial, and doctors frequently make use of interactions to increase the effectiveness of a treatment. Very often, more than one drug may be prescribed to treat cancer or high blood pressure (hypertension).

Other interactions, however, are unwanted and may be harmful. They may occur not only between prescription drugs, but also between prescription and over-the-counter drugs. It is therefore important to read warnings on drug labels and tell your doctor if you are taking any drug preparations – both prescription and over-the-counter – that the doctor does not know about.

A drug may interact with another drug or with food or alcohol for a number of reasons. The main types of interaction are discussed below.

Altered absorption

Alcohol and some drugs (especially narcotics) slow down the digestive process that empties the stomach contents into the intestine. This may delay the absorption, and therefore the effect, of another drug taken at the same time. Other drugs (for example, metoclopramide, an anti-emetic drug) may speed the rate at which the stomach empties and therefore may increase the rate at which another drug is absorbed and takes effect.

Some drugs also combine with another drug or a food in the intestine to form a compound that is not so readily absorbed. This occurs when tetracycline and iron tablets or antacids are taken together. Milk also reduces the absorption of certain drugs in this way.

Reduced absorption in the intestine

Absorption of drug (A) through the intestinal wall may be reduced if it combines with another drug (B).

Drug A

Drug B

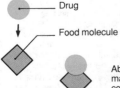

Drug

Food molecule

Absorption of a drug may be reduced if it combines with a food molecule.

EXAMPLES OF IMPORTANT INTERACTIONS

Adverse interactions between drugs may vary from a simple blocking of a drug's beneficial effect to a serious reaction between two drugs which may be life-threatening. Some of the more threatening adverse interactions occur between the following:

Drugs that depress the central nervous system (sleeping drugs, narcotics, antihistamines and alcohol). The effects of two or more of these drugs in combination may be additive, causing dangerous oversedation.

Drugs that lower blood sugar levels and such drugs as sulphonamides and alcohol. The drug interaction increases the effect of blood sugar-lowering drugs, thus further depressing blood sugar levels.

Oral anticoagulants and other drugs, particularly aspirin and antibiotics. Because these drugs may increase the tendency to bleed, it is essential to check the effects in every case.

Monoxamine oxidase inhibitors (MAOIs). Many drugs and foods can produce a severe rise in blood pressure when taken with these drugs. Dangerous drugs include amphetamines and decongestants. Foods that interact include cheese, herring, red wine, beer, and chocolate. However, newer monoamine oxidase inhibitors have been developed which are much less likely to interact with food and drugs.

Enzyme effects

Some drugs increase the production of *enzymes* in the liver that break down drugs, while others may inhibit or reduce enzyme production. They therefore affect the rate at which other drugs are activated or inactivated.

Excretion in the urine

A drug may reduce the kidney's ability to excrete another drug, thereby raising the level of the drug in the blood and increasing its effect.

Receptor effects

Drugs that act on the same *receptors* (p.14) sometimes redouble each other's stimulating effect on the body. Or they may compete with each other in occupying particular receptor sites. Naloxone, for instance, blocks the receptors used by narcotic drugs, thereby helping to reverse the effects of narcotic poisoning.

Similar effects

Drugs that produce similar effects (even though they do not act on the same receptor) may be given together so that a smaller dose of each is required, reducing the side effects of each. This is common practice in the treatment of high blood pressure, in giving anticancer drugs, and also in treating pain. Sometimes two antibiotics may be given simultaneously. Though their effects may be similar, the infecting organisms are less likely to develop resistance.

Reduced protein binding

Some drugs circulate around the body in the bloodstream with a proportion of the drug attached to the proteins of the blood plasma. This means that the amount of the drug attached to plasma proteins is inactive. If another drug is taken, some of the second drug may also attach itself to the plasma proteins and displace the first drug; more of the first drug is then active in the body.

Interaction between protein-bound drugs

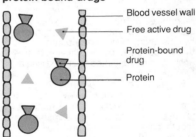

Blood vessel wall

Free active drug

Protein-bound drug

Protein

Protein-bound drug taken alone
Drug molecules that are bound to proteins in the blood are unable to pass into body tissues. Only free drug molecules are active.

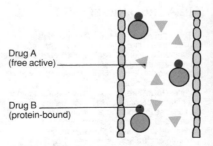

Drug A (free active)

Drug B (protein-bound)

Taken with another protein-bound drug
If a drug (B) with a greater ability to bind with proteins is also taken, the first drug (A) is displaced, increasing the amount of active drug.

METHODS OF ADMINISTRATION

The majority of drugs must be absorbed into the bloodstream in order to reach the site where their effects are needed. The method of administering a drug determines the route it takes to get into the bloodstream and the speed at which it is absorbed into the blood.

When a drug is meant to enter the bloodstream it is usually administered in one of the following ways: through the mouth or rectum, by injection, or inhalation. Drugs implanted under the skin or enclosed in a skin patch also enter the bloodstream. These are discussed under Slow-release preparations (p.18).

When it is unnecessary or undesirable for a drug to enter the bloodstream in large amounts, it may be applied *topically* so that its effect is limited mainly to the site of the disorder such as the surface of the skin or mucous membranes (the membranes of the nose, eyes and ears, vagina, or rectum). Drugs are administered topically in a variety of preparations, including creams, sprays, drops, and suppositories. Most inhaled drugs also have a local effect on the respiratory tract.

Very often, a particular drug may be available in different forms. Many drugs are available as tablets and injectable fluid. The choice between a tablet or injection depends upon a number of factors, including the severity of the illness, the urgency with which the drug effect is needed, the part of the body requiring treatment, and the patient's general state of health, in particular his or her ability to swallow.

The various routes of administration are discussed in greater detail below. For a description of the different forms in which drugs are given, see Drug forms (p.19).

ADMINISTRATION BY MOUTH

Giving drugs by mouth is the most frequently used method of administration. Most drugs that are given by mouth are absorbed into the bloodstream through the walls of the intestine. The speed at which the drug is absorbed and the amount of active drug that is available for use depends on several factors, including the form in which it is given (for example, as a tablet or a liquid) and whether it is taken with food or on an empty stomach. If a drug is taken when the stomach is empty (before meals, for example), it may act more quickly than a drug that is taken when the stomach is full.

Some drugs (like antacids which neutralize stomach acidity) are taken by mouth to produce a direct effect on the stomach or digestive tract.

Sublingual tablets
Tablets are available which are placed in the mouth but not swallowed. They are absorbed quickly into the bloodstream through the lining of the mouth, which has a rich supply of blood vessels. Both sublingual and buccal tablets act in this way. Sublingual tablets are placed under the tongue; buccal tablets are placed in the pouch between the cheek and teeth.

HOW DRUGS PASS THROUGH THE BODY

Most drugs taken by mouth reach the bloodstream by absorption through the small intestine wall. Blood vessels supplying the intestine then carry the drug to the liver where it may be broken down into a form that can be used by the body. The drug (or its breakdown product) then enters into the general circulation, which carries it around the body. It may pass back into the intestine before it is reabsorbed into the bloodstream. Some drugs are rapidly excreted via the kidneys; others may build up in fatty tissues in the body.

Certain insoluble drugs cannot be absorbed through the intestine and pass through the digestive tract unchanged. They are useful for treating bowel disorders, but if they are intended to have *systemic* effects elsewhere they must be given by intravenous injection.

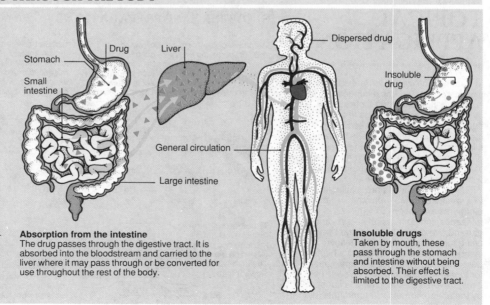

Absorption from the intestine
The drug passes through the digestive tract. It is absorbed into the bloodstream and carried to the liver where it may pass through or be converted for use throughout the rest of the body.

Insoluble drugs
Taken by mouth, these pass through the stomach and intestine without being absorbed. Their effect is limited to the digestive tract.

RECTAL ADMINISTRATION

Drugs intended to have a *systemic* effect may be given in the form of suppositories inserted into the rectum, from where they are absorbed into the bloodstream. This method may be used to give drugs that might be destroyed by the stomach's digestive juices. It is also sometimes used to administer drugs to people who cannot take medication by mouth, such as those suffering from nausea and vomiting.

Drugs may also be given rectally for local effect, either as suppositories (to relieve haemorrhoids) or as enemas for ulcerative colitis.

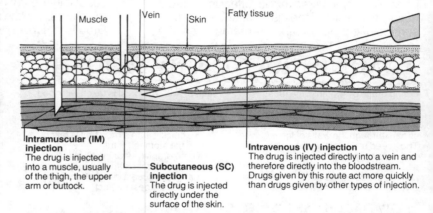

Rectum
Suppository

INHALATION

Drugs may be inhaled to produce a *systemic* effect or a local effect on the respiratory tract.

Gases to produce general anaesthesia are administered by inhalation and are absorbed into the bloodstream through the lungs, to produce a general effect on the body, particularly the brain.

Bronchodilators used to treat certain types of asthma, emphysema and bronchitis are a common example of drugs administered by inhalation for their direct effect on the respiratory tract, although some of the drug also reaches the bloodstream. (See also p.92.)

ADMINISTRATION BY INJECTION

Drugs may be injected into the body to produce a *systemic* effect. One reason for injecting drugs is the rapid response that follows. Other circumstances which call for injection are: a person's intolerance to a drug when taken by mouth; a drug's inability to resist inactivation by stomach acids (insulin is an example); the inability of the drug to pass through the intestinal walls into the bloodstream.

Drug injections may also be given to produce a local effect, as is often done to relieve the pain of arthritis.

The main types of injection – intramuscular, intravenous and subcutaneous – are described in the illustration (see right). The type of injection used depends on the nature of the drug and the condition being treated.

Muscle   Vein   Skin   Fatty tissue

Intramuscular (IM) injection
The drug is injected into a muscle, usually of the thigh, the upper arm or buttock.

Subcutaneous (SC) injection
The drug is injected directly under the surface of the skin.

Intravenous (IV) injection
The drug is injected directly into a vein and therefore directly into the bloodstream. Drugs given by this route act more quickly than drugs given by other types of injection.

TOPICAL APPLICATION

In treating localized disorders such as skin infections and nasal congestion, it is often preferable when a choice is available to prescribe drugs in a form that has a *topical* or localized rather than a *systemic* effect. This is because it is much easier to control the effects of drugs administered locally and to ensure that they produce the maximum benefit with minimum side effects.

Topical preparations are available in a variety of forms, from skin creams, ointments and lotions to vaginal pessaries, inhalers, nasal sprays, and ear and eye drops. It is important when using topical preparations to follow instructions carefully, avoiding a higher dose than recommended or application for longer than necessary. This will help avoid adverse systemic effects caused by the absorption of larger amounts into the bloodstream.

SLOW-RELEASE PREPARATIONS

A number of disorders can be treated with drug preparations that have been specially formulated to release their active drug slowly over a given period of time. Such preparations may be beneficial when it is inconvenient for a person to visit the doctor on a regular basis to receive treatment by injection, or when it is necessary accurately to control the release of small amounts of the drug into the body. Slow release of drugs can be achieved by *depot injections, transdermal patches,* slow-release capsules and tablets, and implants.

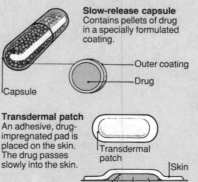

Slow-release capsule
Contains pellets of drug in a specially formulated coating.

Capsule
Outer coating
Drug

Transdermal patch
An adhesive, drug-impregnated pad is placed on the skin. The drug passes slowly into the skin.

Transdermal patch
Skin
Drug

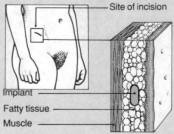

Site of incision
Implant
Fatty tissue
Muscle

Implants
A pellet containing the drug is implanted under the skin. By this rarely used method, a drug (usually a hormone) is slowly released into the bloodstream over a period of months.

DRUG FORMS

Most drugs are specially prepared in a form designed for convenience of administration. This helps to ensure that dosages are accurate and that taking the medication is as easy as possible. Inactive ingredients (those with no therapeutic effect) are sometimes added to flavour or colour the medicine, or to improve its chemical stability, extending the period during which it is effective.

The more common drug forms are described in detail below.

Tablet
This contains the drug compressed into a solid dosage form, often round in shape. Other ingredients are added to the powder before compression, often including an agent to bind the tablet together (see right). In some tablets, the active ingredient is released slowly after the tablet has been swallowed whole, to produce a prolonged (sustained) effect.

Capsule
The drug is contained in a cylindrically shaped gelatin shell that breaks open after the capsule has been swallowed, releasing the drug. Slow-release capsules contain pellets that dissolve in the gastrointestinal tract, releasing the drug slowly (facing page).

Liquids
Some drugs are available in liquid form, the active substance being combined in a solution, suspension or emulsion with other ingredients – solvents, preservatives, and flavouring or colouring agents. Many liquid preparations should be shaken before use to ensure that the active drug is evenly distributed. If it is not, inaccurate dosages will result.

A mixture
A mixture contains one or more drugs, either dissolved to form a solution or suspended in a liquid (often water).

An elixir
An elixir is a solution of a drug in a sweetened mixture of alcohol and water. It is often highly flavoured.

An emulsion
An emulsion is a drug dispersed in oil and water. An emulsifying agent is often included to stabilize the product.

A syrup
A syrup is a concentrated solution of sugar containing the active drug, with flavouring and stabilizing agents added.

Topical skin preparations
These are preparations designed for application to the skin and other surface tissues of the body. Preservatives are usually included to reduce the growth of

WHAT A TABLET CONTAINS

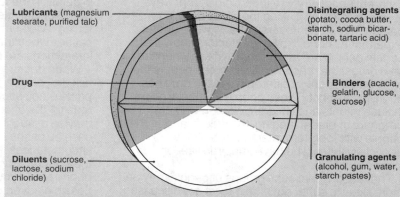

Lubricants (magnesium stearate, purified talc)

Drug

Diluents (sucrose, lactose, sodium chloride)

Disintegrating agents (potato, cocoa butter, starch, sodium bicarbonate, tartaric acid)

Binders (acacia, gelatin, glucose, sucrose)

Granulating agents (alcohol, gum, water, starch pastes)

Diluents add bulk. Granulating agents and binders form the ingredients into a tablet. Lubricants or a sugar coating ensure a smooth surface, and disintegrating agents dissolve the medication. In addition, colouring agents, dyes, and imprints are used to make the drug recognizable. The proportions of each ingredient may vary.

bacteria. The most commonly used types of skin preparations are described below. For a more detailed discussion of the various preparations, see Bases for skin preparations, p.175.

A cream
A cream is a non-greasy preparation used to apply drugs to an area of the body or to cool or moisten the skin. It is less noticeable than an ointment.

An ointment
An ointment is a greasy preparation used to apply drugs to an area of the body, or acts as a protective or lubricant layer for the relief of dry skin conditions.

A lotion
A lotion is a solution or suspension applied to unbroken skin to cool and dry the affected area. Some are more suitable for use in hairy areas since they are not as sticky as creams or ointments.

Injection solutions
Solutions for injections are sterile (germ-free) preparations of a drug dissolved or suspended in a liquid. Other agents, (anti-oxidants), are often added to preserve the stability of the drug or to regulate the acidity or alkalinity of the solution. Most injectable drugs used today are packaged in sterile, disposable syringes. This reduces chances of contamination. Certain drugs are still available in multiple-dose vials, and a chemical bactericide is added to prevent the growth of bacteria when the needle is reinserted through the rubber seal. For details on types of injection, see Administration by injection, facing page.

Suppositories and pessaries
Suppositories and pessaries are solid, bullet-shaped drug forms specially designed for easy insertion into the rectum (rectal suppository) or vagina (pessary). They contain a drug and an inert (chemically inactive) substance that is often derived from cocoa butter or another type of vegetable oil. The active drug is gradually released in the rectum or vagina as the suppository or pessary dissolves at body temperature.

Eye drops
A sterile drug solution (or suspension) dropped behind the eyelid to produce an effect on the eye.

Ear drops
A solution (or suspension) containing a drug introduced into the ear by dropper. Ear drops are usually given to produce an effect on the outer-ear canal.

Nasal drops/spray
A solution of a drug, usually in water, for introduction into the nose to produce a local effect.

Inhalers
Aerosol inhalers contain a solution or suspension of a drug under pressure. A valve mechanism ensures the delivery of the recommended dosage when the inhaler is activated. A mouthpiece fixed to the device facilitates inhalation of the drug as it is released from the canister. The correct technique is important; printed instructions should be followed carefully. Aerosol inhalers are used for respiratory conditions such as asthma (see also p.92).

DRUG TREATMENT IN SPECIAL RISK GROUPS

Different people may respond in different ways to drug treatment. Taking the same drug, one person may suffer adverse effects while another experiences none. However, doctors know that certain people are always more at risk when they take drugs; the reason is that in those people the body handles drugs differently, or the drug has an atypical effect. Those people at special risk include infants and children, women who are pregnant or breast feeding, the elderly and people with long-term medical conditions, especially those who have impaired liver or kidney function.

The reasons that such groups of people may be more likely to suffer adverse effects are discussed in detail on the following pages. Others who may need special attention include those already taking regular medication who may risk complications when they take another drug. Drug interactions are discussed more fully on p.16.

When doctors prescribe drugs for special risk groups they take extra care to select appropriate medication, adjust dosages and closely monitor the effects of treatment. If you think you may be at special risk, be sure to tell your doctor in case he or she is not fully aware of your particular circumstances. Similarly, if you are buying over-the-counter drugs you should ask your doctor or pharmacist if you think you may be at risk from any possible adverse effects.

INFANTS AND CHILDREN

Infants and children need a lower dosage of drugs than adults because children have a relatively low body weight. Moreover, because of differences in body composition, as well as the distribution and amount of body fat, and differences in the state of development and function of organs such as the liver and kidneys at different ages, children cannot simply be given a proportion of an adult dose as if they were small adults. Dosages need to be calculated in a more complex way, taking account of both age and weight. Although newborn babies often have to be given very small doses of drugs, older children may need relatively large doses of some drugs.

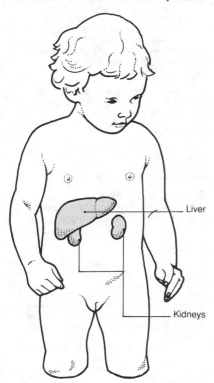

The liver
The liver's enzyme systems are not fully developed when a baby is born. This means that drugs are not broken down as rapidly as in an adult, and may become dangerously concentrated in the baby's body. For this reason, many drugs are not prescribed for babies or are prescribed in very reduced doses. In older children, because the liver is relatively large compared to the rest of the body, some drugs may need to be given in proportionately larger doses.

The kidneys
During the first six months, a baby's kidneys are unable to excrete drugs as efficiently as those of an adult. This, too, may lead to a dangerously high concentration of a drug in the blood. The dose of certain drugs may therefore need to be reduced. Between one and two years of age, kidney function improves, and higher doses of some drugs may then be needed.

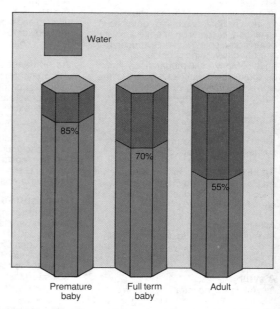

Water

85%

70%

55%

| Premature baby | Full term baby | Adult |

Body composition
The proportion of water in the body of a premature baby is about 85 per cent of its body weight, that of a full term baby is 70 per cent, and that of an adult is only 55 per cent. This means that certain drugs are not as concentrated in an infant's body as in an adult's, and higher doses relative to weight may need to be given initially.

PREGNANT WOMEN

Great care is needed during pregnancy to protect the fetus so that it develops into a healthy baby. Drugs taken by the mother can cross the placenta and enter the baby's bloodstream. With certain drugs, and at particular stages of pregnancy, there is a risk of developmental abnormalites, retarded growth, or post-delivery problems affecting the baby. In addition, some drugs may affect the health of the mother during pregnancy.

Many drugs are known to have adverse effects during pregnancy; others are known to be safe, but in a large number of cases there is no firm evidence to decide on risk or safety. Therefore, the most important rule if you are pregnant or trying to conceive is to consult your doctor before taking any prescribed or over-the-counter medication. Drugs such as marijuana, nicotine or alcohol should also be avoided. Your doctor will balance the potential benefits of drug treatment against any possible risks to decide whether or not a drug should be taken. This is particularly important if you need to take regular medication for a chronic condition such as epilepsy, high blood pressure or diabetes.

Drugs and the stages of pregnancy

Pregnancy is divided into three three-month stages called trimesters. Depending on the trimester in which they are taken, drugs can have different effects on the mother or the fetus or both. Some drugs may be considered safe during one trimester, but not another. Doctors, therefore, often need to change regular medications given during the course of pregnancy.

The trimesters of pregnancy

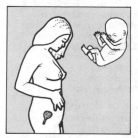  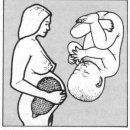

First trimester
During the first three months of pregnancy, the most critical period, drugs may affect the development of fetal organs, leading to congenital malformations. Very severe defects may result in miscarriage.

Second trimester
From the fourth until the sixth month some drugs may retard the growth of the fetus. This may also result in a low birthweight.

Third trimester
During the last three months of pregnancy, major risks include breathing difficulties in the newborn baby. Some drugs may also affect labour, causing it to be premature, delayed or prolonged.

How drugs cross the placenta

The placenta acts as a filter between the mother's bloodstream and that of the baby. It allows small molecules of nutrients to pass into the baby's blood, while preventing larger particles such as blood cells from doing so. Drug molecules are comparatively small and pass easily through the placental barrier.

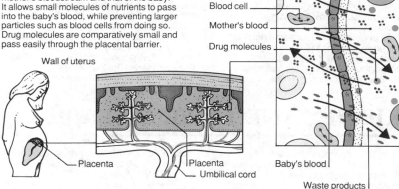

Wall of uterus
Nutrients
Blood cell
Mother's blood
Drug molecules
Placenta
Placenta
Umbilical cord
Baby's blood
Waste products

BREAST FEEDING

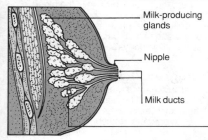

How drugs pass into breast milk
The milk-producing glands in the breast are surrounded by a network of fine blood vessels. Small molecules of substances such as drugs pass from the blood into the milk. Drugs that dissolve easily in fat may pass across in greater concentrations than other drugs.

Milk-producing glands
Nipple
Milk ducts

Just as drugs may cross from the mother's bloodstream into the baby's through the placenta, they may also pass to the baby from the mother's milk.

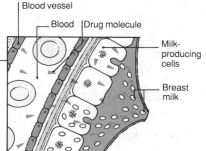

Blood vessel
Blood
Drug molecule
Milk-producing cells
Breast milk

This means that a breastfed baby may receive small doses of whatever drugs the mother is taking. In many cases this is not a problem because the amount of drug that passes into the milk is too small to have any significant effect on the baby. However, some drugs can produce unwanted effects on the baby. Antibiotics may sensitize the infant and consequently prevent their use later in life. Sedative drugs may make the baby drowsy and cause feeding problems. Moreover, some drugs may reduce the amount of milk produced by the mother.

Doctors usually advise breast-feeding women to take only essential drugs. When a mother needs to take regular medication while breast feeding, her baby may also need to be closely monitored for possible adverse effects.

THE ELDERLY

Older people are particularly at risk when taking drugs. This is partly due to the physical changes associated with ageing, and partly to the need for some elderly people to take several different drugs at the same time. They may also be at risk because they may be unable to manage their treatment properly, or lack the necessary information to do so.

Physical changes

Elderly people have a greater risk of accumulating drugs in their bodies because the liver is less efficient at breaking drugs down and the kidneys are less efficient at excreting them. Because of this, in some cases, the normal adult dose will produce side effects, and a half dose may be sufficient to produce a therapeutic effect without the side effects. (See also Kidney and liver disease, below.)

Older people, too, take more drugs than younger people – many take two or more drugs at the same time. Apart from increasing the number of drugs in their systems, taking more than one drug at a time can cause adverse drug interactions (see p.16).

As people grow older some parts of the body, such as the brain and nervous system, become more sensitive to drugs, thus increasing the likelihood of adverse reactions from drugs acting on

those sites (see right). A similar problem may occur due to changes in the body's ratio of body fat. Although allergic reactions (see p.123) are rarely a function of age, changes in the immune system may account for some unexpected reactions. Accordingly, doctors prescribe more conservatively for older people, particularly those with disorders likely to correct themselves in time.

Incorrect use of drugs

Elderly people often suffer harmful effects from their drug treatment because they fail to take their medication regularly or correctly. This may happen because they have been misinformed about how to take it or receive vague instructions. Problems arise sometimes because the elderly person forgets whether he or she has taken a drug and takes a double dose (see Exceeding the dose, p.30). Problems may also occur because the person is confused; this is not necessarily due to senility, but can arise as a result of drug treatment, especially if an elderly person is taking a number of different drugs or a sedative drug.

All prescriptions for the elderly should be especially clearly and fully labelled, and/or information about the drug and its use provided in the form of leaflets, either for the individual's use or that of

Effect of drugs that act on the brain

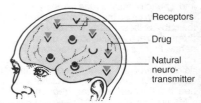

In young people
There are plenty of receptors to take up the drug as well as natural *neurotransmitters*.

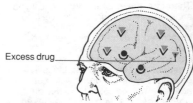

In older people
There are fewer receptors so that even a reduced drug dose may be excessive.

the person taking care of him or her. Where appropriate, special containers with memory aids should be used for dispensing the medication in single doses.

KIDNEY AND LIVER DISEASE

Long-term illnesses affect the way in which people respond to drug treatment. This is especially true of kidney and liver problems. The liver alters the chemical structure of many of the drugs that enter the body (see How drugs pass through the body, p.17), by breaking them down into simpler substances, while the kidneys excrete drugs in the urine. If the effectiveness of the liver or kidneys is curtailed or interfered with by illness, the

action of drugs on the individual can be significantly altered. In most cases, people with kidney and liver disease will be prescribed a smaller number of drugs and in lower doses. In addition, certain drugs may, in rare cases, damage the liver or kidneys. A doctor may therefore be reluctant to prescribe such a drug to someone with already reduced liver or kidney function to avoid the risk of further damage.

Drugs and kidney disease

People with poor kidney function are at greater risk from drug side effects. There are two reasons for this. First, drugs build up in the system because smaller amounts are excreted in urine. Secondly, kidney disease can cause protein loss through the urine, which lowers the level of protein in the blood. Some drugs bind to blood proteins, and if there are fewer proteins, a greater proportion of drug becomes free and active in the body (see Effects of protein loss, left).

Drugs and liver disease

Severe liver diseases such as cirrhosis of the liver and hepatitis affect the way the body breaks down drugs. This can lead to dangerous accumulation of certain drugs in the body. People suffering from these diseases or anything similar should consult their doctor before taking any medication (including over-the-counter drugs) or alcohol. Many drugs must be avoided completely since they can cause coma in someone with a damaged or poorly functioning liver.

Effects of protein loss

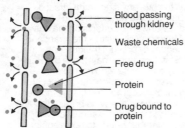

Blood passing through kidney

Waste chemicals

Free drug

Protein

Drug bound to protein

Normal kidney
Some drugs bind to proteins in the blood and are inactive; only free drugs affect the body.

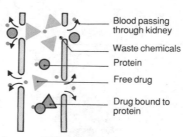

Blood passing through kidney

Waste chemicals

Protein

Free drug

Drug bound to protein

Damaged kidney
Loss of protein increases the amount of active drug, and therefore its overall effect.

DRUG DEPENDENCE

The term, drug dependence, applies far more widely than most people realize. It is usually thought of in association with use of drugs taken illegally such as heroin or with excessive intake of alcohol. But millions of people are dependent on other drugs, including stimulants, such as caffeine found in coffee and tea, and nicotine in tobacco, and certain prescription medicines, such as analgesics, sleeping drugs and tranquillizers (anti-anxiety drugs).

Psychological and physical dependence

Drug dependence, implying a person's inability to control use of a substance with abuse potential, is of two types. Psychological dependence is an emotional state of craving for a drug whose presence in the body has a desired effect or whose absence has an undesired effect. Physical dependence, which often includes psychological dependence, involves physiological adaptation to a drug or alcohol, characterized by severe physical disturbances – withdrawal symptoms – during a prolonged period of abstinence.

Physical dependence on a drug is further characterized by a developing *tolerance* to the drug's effects; the line between tolerance and lethal dosage is sometimes extremely fine (see Drug tolerance, below).

Drug dependence is now widely preferred to the word addiction, defined as the compulsive use of a substance resulting in physical, psychological or social harm to the user, with continued use despite the harm.

Drugs which cause dependence

Many people who need to take regular medication worry that they may become dependent on their drugs. In fact, only a few groups of drugs produce physical dependence, most of them substances that alter mood or behaviour. Such drugs include heroin and the narcotic analgesics (morphine, pethidine and other similar drugs), sleeping drugs and anti-anxiety drugs (benzodiazepines and barbiturates), depressants (alcohol) and nervous system stimulants (amphetamines, cocaine and nicotine). Consult the relevant drug profile in Part 4 of this book to discover the dependence rating of any drug you are taking.

The use of nicotine in the form of tobacco and the controlled or uncontrolled use of narcotic analgesics invariably produce physical dependence if taken

DRUG TOLERANCE

Drug tolerance occurs as the body adapts to the actions of a drug. Although people can develop a tolerance to many drugs, it is a dangerous characteristic of virtually all of the drugs of dependence. A person taking them needs larger and larger doses to achieve the original effect; as the dose increases, so do the risks of *toxic* effects and dependence.

The explanation of tolerance, still not fully understood, is highly complex. It stems from one (or both) of two actions. One is the liver increasing its capacity to break down and dispose of the drug, giving lower concentrations of it in the bloodstream and a shorter duration of action. The other potential action involves adaptation by the cells of the central nervous system, including the brain, to the drug, with lowered responsiveness to it.

Brain tolerance can also lead to cross-tolerance, a person's tolerance to one drug leading to tolerance of similar drugs. For example, the regular drinker who can tolerate high levels of alcohol (a depressant) can have a dangerous tolerance to other depressants such as sleeping drugs and anti-anxiety drugs. While cross-tolerance raises problems, it does allow a substance with a less addictive potential to replace the original. The symptoms of alcohol withdrawal can thus be controlled by the anti-anxiety drug diazepam, which is also a depressant.

Tolerance to some drugs has its benefits. A person can, for example, develop tolerance to the side effects of a drug but remain responsive to its curative powers. Many people taking antidepressants find that side effects such as dry mouth, constipation and blurred vision slowly disappear with the primary action of the drug continuing.

Increasing tolerance, however, does have its dangers. A person with a developed tolerance tends to increase dosage, sometimes to the toxic level.

Dosage and effect in drug tolerance
The chart below shows how some effects (these may be intended or unintended) of a fixed dose of tolerance-producing drugs gradually diminish over a period of time. If after this time the dose is significantly increased, the drug effect is restored. Remember, dosage of prescribed drugs should never be increased except on your doctor's instructions.

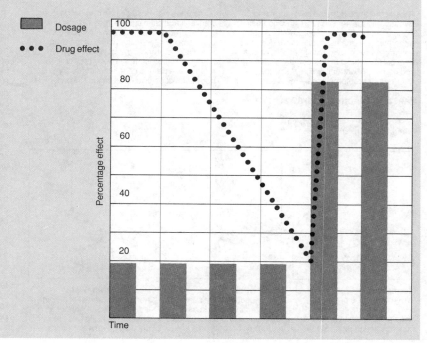

Dosage

● ● ● Drug effect

DRUG DEPENDENCE continued

regularly over a period of time. However, it is equally true that not all regular users of alcohol become alcoholics. There is much argument over the definition of an alcoholic. A widely used definition is: a person who has experienced physical, psychological, social or occupational impairment as a consequence of habitual, excessive consumption of alcohol.

Recognizing the dangers of drug dependence

Factors that determine the risk of developing physical dependence include the characteristics of the drug itself, the strength and frequency of doses and duration of use. However, the presence of these factors does not always result in dependence. Psychological and physiological factors unique to each individual also enter the equation, and there may be other, as yet unknown, factors involved.

For example, when the use of narcotic analgesics is restricted to the immediate short-term relief of severe pain in a medical setting, long-term dependence is rare. Yet there is a high risk of physical dependence when narcotic analgesics, or other drugs of abuse, are taken for non-medical reasons. There is also a risk in some cases of low-dose use when this is continued over a long

DRUG ABUSE

The term is defined as any use of drugs that cause physical, psychological, economic, legal or social harm to the user, or to persons who may be affected by the user's behaviour. Drug abuse commonly refers to taking drugs obtained illegally (such as heroin), but may also be used to describe the misuse of drugs generally obtainable legally (nicotine, alcohol), and to drugs obtainable through a doctor's prescription only (everything from sleeping drugs and tranquillizers to analgesics and stimulants).

The abuse of prescription drugs deserves more attention than it usually receives. The practice can include the personal use of drugs left over from a previous course of treatment, the sharing with others of drugs prescribed for yourself, the deliberate deception of doctors, the forgery of prescriptions and the theft of drugs from pharmacies. All of these practices can have dangerous consequences. Careful

attention to the advice in the section on Managing your drug treatment (p.25) will help to avoid inadvertent misuse of drugs. The dangers associated with abuse of individual drugs are discussed under Drugs of abuse (pp.434-443).

Common drugs of abuse
Alcohol
Amphetamines (including "ecstasy")
Amyl nitrite and similar drugs
Cocaine (including "crack")
Heroin
LSD
Marijuana (cannabis)
Nicotine
Pethidine
Solvents

period of time for the treatment of chronic pain.

No one can say for sure just what leads an individual to drug dependent behaviour. A person's physical and psychological make-up are thought to be factors, as well as his social environment, occupational pressures and outlook on life. Motivation and setting play major roles.

The indiscriminate use of certain prescription drugs can also cause drug dependence. Benzodiazepine drugs can produce dependence and this is one reason why doctors nowadays discourage the use of any drug to induce sleep or calm anxiety for more than a few weeks. Appetite suppressants require close medical supervision. Similarly, amphetamines are no longer prescribed as appetite suppressants because of the frequency with which they are abused.

Treating drug dependence

When a person is dependent on a drug, the cells in the body have adapted to a new chemical environment. To move someone from that condition to a drug-free state is a complex medical process. But a patient must become completely drug-free before long-term rehabilitation can occur.

The first step, detoxification, can take different forms. In cases of alcohol dependence, abstinence may often be abruptly imposed. With other substances, the drug may be gradually withdrawn, or other safer substances substituted. There are, however, differing schools of thought, and some treatment centres argue for the abrupt cessation method of detoxification for substances besides alcohol.

Withdrawal can be mild, violent, and occasionally fatal, and expert medical supervision is required. Drugs may be given to provide symptomatic relief.

Once a person is drug-free, rehabilitation measures begin. Drug therapy – such as the use of disulfiram (Antabuse) for alcoholism – psychotherapy, personal counselling and the work of support organizations like Alcoholics Anonymous play an important role.

SYMPTOMS OF WITHDRAWAL

These can range from the mild (sneezing, sweating) to the serious (vomiting, confusion) to the extremely serious (fits, coma). Alcohol withdrawal may be associated with delerium tremens, very occasionally fatal. Withdrawal from barbiturates can sometimes involve fits and coma. But under medical guidance, withdrawal symptoms can be relieved,

sometimes with doses of the original drug, or with less addictive substitutes.

Withdrawal symptoms occur because the body has adapted to the action of the drug (see Drug tolerance, p.23). When a drug is continuously present, the body may stop the release of a natural chemical necessary to normal function, like endorphins (below).

Pain and heroin withdrawal

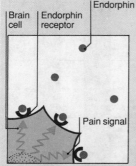

Normal brain
When no drug is present, natural substances called endorphins inhibit the transmission of pain signals.

Effect of heroin
Heroin occupies the same receptors in the brain as endorphins and suppresses endorphin production.

Heroin withdrawal
Abrupt withdrawal of heroin leaves the brain without a buffer to pain signals produced by even minor stimuli.

MANAGING YOUR DRUG TREATMENT

A prescribed drug does not automatically produce a beneficial response. For a drug to have maximum benefit, it must be taken as directed by the doctor or manufacturer. It is estimated that two out of every five people for whom a drug is prescribed do not take it properly, if at all. Reasons include failure to understand instructions, fear of adverse reactions, and lack of motivation, often arising from the disappearance of symptoms.

It is your responsibility to take a prescribed drug at the correct time, and in the manner stipulated. To do this, you need to know where to obtain information about the the drug (see Questions to ask your doctor, p.26) and to make certain that you understand the instructions.

The following pages describe the practical aspects of drug treatment, from getting a prescription and buying over-the-counter drugs to storing drugs and disposing of old medications safely. Problems caused by mismanaging drug treatment – overdosing, underdosing or stopping the drug altogether – and long-term drug treatment are dealt with on pp. 28 – 30. Information about managing specific drugs is given in Part 4.

OVER-THE-COUNTER DRUGS

Over-the-counter drugs are those for which a prescription is not required. They are sold widely in a variety of outlets (including supermarkets), although some are available only at chemists.

Since they are sold in this way, over-the-counter drugs are obviously suitable for self-treatment and are unlikely to produce adverse reactions if taken as directed. But as with all medicines, they can be harmful if they are misused. The ease with which they can be purchased is no guarantee of their absolute safety. For this reason, when using any over-the-counter medication, the same precautions should be taken as when using a prescription drug.

Using over-the-counter drugs

A number of minor ailments and problems, from coughs and colds to minor cuts and bruises, can be adequately dealt with by taking or using over-the-counter medicines. However, you must be sure to read the directions on the label and follow them carefully, particularly those advising on dosage and on when to see your doctor. Most over-the-counter drugs are clearly labelled. They may warn of conditions under which the drug should not be taken, or advise you to consult a doctor if symptoms persist.

The pharmacist is usually a good source of information about over-the-counter drugs. He or she cannot make a diagnosis or a decision about therapy, but can tell what is suitable for your complaint. The pharmacist can also tell you when an over-the-counter drug will probably not be effective, and can warn you if self-treatment or prolonged treatment is inadvisable. You should also tell your pharmacist about any prescription drugs you are taking.

It is particularly important to speak to your doctor before buying over-the-counter drugs for children. Children can become seriously ill very quickly, and if in any doubt you should call your doctor for advice.

Buying over-the-counter medications
Various drugs are available over-the-counter, ranging from cough medicines to eye drops. Your pharmacist can often help you to select the appropriate medication.

Eye preparations

Medicated creams, lotions and powders

Cough and cold treatments

Laxatives

Analgesics

Antacids

PRESCRIPTION DRUGS

Drugs prescribed by your doctor are not necessarily "stronger" or more likely to have side effects than those you can buy without prescription. Indeed doctors often prescribe drugs that are also available over the counter. Drugs available only on prescription are those for which it is not possible to write labelling that will ensure the drug will be used safely without medical supervision.

When a doctor prescribes a drug, he or she usually starts treatment at the normal dosage for the disorder being treated. The dosage may later be adjusted (lowered or increased) if the drug is not producing the desired effect or if there are adverse effects and the doctor may also switch to an alternative drug that may be more effective.

Prescribing generic and brand-name drugs

When writing a prescription for a drug, the doctor often has a choice between a generic and a brand-name product. Although the active ingredient is the same, two versions of the same drug may act in slightly different ways, because each manufacturer may formulate their product differently. They may also look different. Generic drugs are sometimes cheaper than brand-name products. For this reason, certain brand-name products are not available on the National Health Service. For example, Valium, a well known brand-name tranquillizer, is not prescribable on the NHS and a generic version of diazepam, the active drug, is always substituted. These are factors that a doctor must consider when writing a prescription.

Pharmacists in high street chemists are obliged to dispense precisely what the doctor has written on the prescription form and are not allowed to substitute a generic drug when a brand-name has been specified. However, if you are prescribed a generic drug, the pharmacist is free to dispense whatever version of this drug is available. This means that your regular medication may vary in appearance each time you renew your prescription.

Hospital pharmacies often dispense only generic versions of certain drugs. Therefore, if you are in hospital, the regular medication you receive may look different from that which you are used to at home.

Your prescription

It is advisable to order all your prescription drugs from the same pharmacist or at least from the same pharmacy, so that your pharmacist can advise you about any particular problems you may have, and keep supplies of any unusual drugs you may be taking.

If you need to take drugs prescribed by more than one doctor, or from your dentist in addition to your doctor, the pharmacist is able to call attention to possible harmful interactions. Doctors do ask if you are taking other medicines, but your regular pharmacist provides valuable additional advice.

Questioning your doctor

Countless surveys unmistakably point to lack of information as the most common reason for drug failure. Responses like "The doctor is too busy to be bothered with a lot of questions", or "The doctor will think I'm stupid if I ask that" recur over and over. Be certain you understand the instructions for a drug before leaving the doctor, and don't leave with any questions unanswered.

It is a good idea to make a list of the questions you may want to ask before your visit, and to make a few notes while you are there about what you are told. It is not uncommon to forget some of the instructions your doctor gives you during a consultation.

Know what you are taking

Although most of the important information you need will be written on the prescription and on the drug label, you should obtain any additional information as necessary from your doctor.

Your doctor should tell you the generic or brand name of the drug he or she is prescribing, and exactly what condition or symptom the drug has been prescribed to treat.

As well as knowing the name of the drug prescribed, you should know what dose to take, how often to take it, and whether you should have your prescription repeated. Be certain you understand fully the instructions about how and when to take the drug (see also Taking your medication, facing page). For example, exactly how much is a teaspoon, and does four times a day mean four times during the time you are awake, or four times in twenty-four hours? Ask your doctor how long treatment should last; some drugs cause harmful effects if you abruptly stop taking them, or do not have beneficial effects unless the course is completed.

Risks and special precautions

All drugs have side effects (see Effects of drugs, p.15), and you should know what these are. Ask your doctor what the possible adverse reactions of the drug are and what you should do if they occur. You should also ask if there are any foods or any other drugs you should avoid during treatment and if you can drink alcohol while taking the drug.

Your prescription

Your prescription tells the pharmacist the type and amount of drug to supply, and gives the information which will appear on the container label. Some people like to read prescriptions, to compare instructions written by your doctor with those on the label. If there are differences, you may discuss them with the pharmacist.

It is a good idea to ask the pharmacist to include several other facts on the drug label: the name of the drug, the number of tablets or capsules in the container, and how long the drug can be stored.

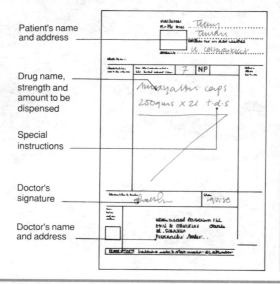

Patient's name and address

Drug name, strength and amount to be dispensed

Special instructions

Doctor's signature

Doctor's name and address

PRESCRIPTION TERMS

ac before meals	**pc** after meals
ad lib freely	**PM** evening
AM morning	**po** by mouth
bid twice a day	**prn** as needed
c with	**qd** once a day
cap capsule	**qds** four times
cc cubic centimetre	a day
ext for external use	**s** without
gtt drops	**sig ut dict** take as
mg milligrams	directed
ml millilitres	**stat** at once
nocte at night	**tab** tablet
od each day	**tds** three times a day
om each morning	**top** apply topically
on each night	**x** times

TAKING YOUR MEDICATION

Among the most important aspects of managing your drug treatment is knowing how often the drug is to be taken. On an empty stomach? With food? Mixed with something? Specific instructions on such points are given in the individual drug profiles in Part 4.

When to take your drugs

Certain drugs, analgesics and drugs for migraine, for example, are taken only as necessary, as warning symptoms occur. Others are meant to be taken regularly at specified intervals. The prescription or label instructions can be confusing, however. For instance, does four times a day mean four times every six hours out of 24 – for example, at 8 a.m., 2 p.m., 8 p.m. and 2 a.m.? Or does it mean take at four equal intervals during waking hours – morning, lunchtime, late afternoon and bedtime? The latter is usually the case but you need to ask your doctor for precise directions.

The actual time of day that you take a drug is generally flexible, so you can normally schedule your doses to fit your daily routine. This has the additional advantage of making it easier for you to remember to take your drugs. For example, if you are to take the drug three times during the day, it may be most convenient to take the first dose at 7 a.m., the second at 3 p.m. and the third at 11 p.m., while it may be more suitable for another person on the same regime to take the first dose at 8 a.m., and so on. You must, however, establish with your pharmacist or your doctor whether the drug should be taken with food, in which case you would probably need to take it with your breakfast, lunch and dinner. Try to take your dose at the

Four times a day?

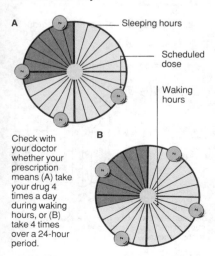

Check with your doctor whether your prescription means (A) take your drug 4 times a day during waking hours, or (B) take 4 times over a 24-hour period.

A — Sleeping hours

— Scheduled dose

— Waking hours

B

TIPS ON TAKING MEDICINES

● Whenever possible, take capsules and tablets while standing, or at least when you are in an upright sitting position, and take them with water. If you take them when you are lying down, or without fluid, it is possible for capsules and tablets to become stuck in the oesophagus. This can delay the action of the drug and may damage the oesophagus.

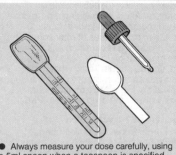

● Always measure your dose carefully, using a 5ml spoon when a teaspoon is specified, or an accurate measure such as a dropper, children's medicine spoon, or oral syringe.

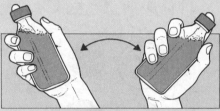

● When taking liquid medicines shake the bottle before measuring each dose, or you may give yourself improper dosages if the active substance has risen to the top or settles at the bottom of the bottle.

● A drink of cold water taken straight after an unpleasantly-flavoured medicine will often hide the taste.

recommended intervals; taking them too close together increases the risk of side effects occurring.

If you are taking several different drugs, ask your doctor if they can be taken together, or if they must be taken at different times in order to avoid any adverse effects or a reduction in effectiveness caused by an interaction between them.

How to take your drugs

If your prescription specifies taking your drug with food – or without food – it is very important to follow this instruction if you are to get the maximum benefit from your treatment.

Certain drugs should be taken on an empty stomach (usually one to two hours before eating) so they will be absorbed more quickly into the bloodstream; others should be taken with food to avoid stomach irritation. Similarly, you should comply with any instructions to avoid particular foods. Milk and dairy products may inhibit the absorption of some drugs; fruit juices can break down certain antibacterial drugs in the stomach and thereby reduce their action; alcohol is best avoided with many drugs. (See also Drug interactions, p.16.)

In some cases, when taking diuretics, for example, you may be advised to eat foods rich in potassium. But do not take potassium supplements unless you are advised to do so by your doctor (see Potassium, p.427). If you use salt substitutes (all of which contain potassium) remember to tell your doctor.

GIVING MEDICINES TO CHILDREN

A number of over-the-counter medicines are specifically prepared for children. Many other medicines have labels that give both adult and children's dosages. For the purposes of drug labelling, anyone 12 years of age or under is considered a child.

When giving over-the-counter medicines to children, you should follow the instructions on the label exactly and under no circumstances exceed the dosage recommended for a child. Never give a child even a small proportion of a medicine intended for adult use without the advice of your doctor.

Never deceive your child about what you are giving, pretending that tablets are sweets or that liquid medicines are soft drinks. Never leave a child's medicine within reach. He or she may be tempted to take an extra dose in order to hasten recovery.

MISSED DOSES

Missing a dose of your medication can be a problem only if you are taking the drug as part of a regular course of treatment. Although missing a drug dose is not uncommon, it is not a cause for concern in most cases. It may sometimes produce a recurrence of symptoms or a change in the action of the drug, so you should know what to do when you have forgotten to take your medication. For advice on individual drugs, consult the drug profile in Part 4.

Additional measures

With some drugs, the timing of dose depends on how long their actions last. When you miss a dose, the amount of drug in your body is lowered, and the effect of the drug may be diminished. You may therefore have to take other steps to avoid unwanted consequences. For example, if you are taking an oral contraceptive containing progesterone only, and forget to take one pill, you should take one as soon as you remember, and for the next 48 hours use another form of contraception.

If you miss more than one dose of any drug you are taking regularly, tell your doctor. Missed doses are especially important with insulin and drugs for epilepsy.

If you frequently forget to take your medication, you should tell your doctor. He or she may be able to simplify your treatment schedule by prescribing a multi-ingredient preparation that contains several drugs, or a preparation that releases the drug slowly into the body over a period of time, and only needs to be taken once or twice daily.

REMEMBERING YOUR MEDICATION

If you take several different drugs, it is useful to draw up a chart to remind yourself of when to take each drug. This will also help anyone who looks after you, or a visiting doctor unfamiliar with your treatment.

Bumetanide (a diuretic to counter fluid retention), one 1mg tablet in the morning (oval tablet).

Amiloride (another diuretic to counter potassium loss caused by bumetanide), two 5mg tablets in the morning (small round tablet).

The example given here is of a dosage chart made for an older woman suffering from arthritis and a heart condition who has trouble sleeping. Her doctor has prescribed the following treatment:

Ibuprofen (for arthritis), three 400mg tablets daily with meals (large round tablet).

Nifedipine (to treat her heart condition), three 10mg capsules a day (one-colour capsule).

Nitrazepam (a sleeping drug), one 5mg capsule at bedtime (two-colour capsule).

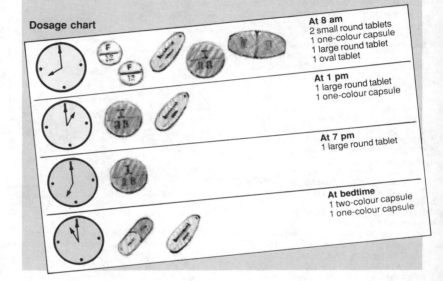

Dosage chart

At 8 am
2 small round tablets
1 one-colour capsule
1 large round tablet
1 oval tablet

At 1 pm
1 large round tablet
1 one-colour capsule

At 7 pm
1 large round tablet

At bedtime
1 two-colour capsule
1 one-colour capsule

ENDING DRUG TREATMENT

As with missed doses, ending drug treatment too soon can be a problem when you are taking a regular course of drugs. With medication that you take as required, you can stop treatment as soon as you feel better.

Advice on stopping individual drugs is given in the drug profiles in Part 4. Some general guidelines to ending drug treatment are given below.

Risks of stopping too soon

Suddenly stopping drug treatment before completing your course of medication may cause the original condition to recur or lead to other complications. The disappearance of the symptoms does not necessarily mean that a disorder is cured. Even if you begin to feel better, you still should not stop taking your medication unless your doctor advises you to do so. People

taking antibiotics often make this mistake. The full course of treatment prescribed should always be followed.

Adverse effects

Do not stop taking a drug simply because it produces unpleasant side effects. Many adverse effects disappear or become bearable after a while. But if they do not, check with your doctor who may want to reduce the dosage of the drug gradually or, alternatively, substitute another drug which does not produce the same side effects.

Gradual reduction

While many drugs can be stopped abruptly, others must be reduced gradually to avoid a reaction when treatment ends. This is the case with long-term corticosteroid treatment (see right) and with *dependence*-inducing drugs.

Phased reduction of corticosteroids

▨ Corticosteroid drug

☐ Natural adrenal hormone

Normal hormone level

Corticosteroid drugs suppress production in the body of natural adrenal hormones. A phased reduction of the drug dosage allows levels of the natural hormones to revert to normal gradually.

STORING DRUGS

Once you have completed a medically directed course of treatment, you should not keep any unused drugs. But most families will want to keep a store of remedies for headaches, colds, indigestion and so forth. Such drugs should not be used if they show signs of deterioration or if their period of effectiveness has expired (see When to dispose of drugs, right).

How to store drugs

Over-the-counter and prescription drugs should normally be stored in the container in which you purchased them. If you need to put them into other containers, say, special containers designed for the elderly, remember to keep the original container with the label and separate instructions for future reference.

Make certain that caps and lids are replaced and tightly closed after use; loose caps may leak and spill, or hasten deterioration of the drug.

Where to store drugs

The majority of drugs should be stored in a cool, dry place out of direct sunlight, even those in plastic containers or tinted glass. Room temperature, away from sources of direct heat, is suitable for most drugs. A few drugs should be stored in the refrigerator. Storage information for individual drugs is given in the drug profiles in Part 4.

All drugs including cough medicines, iron tablets and oral contraceptives should be kept out of the reach of children. If you are in the habit of keeping your medicines where you will see them as a reminder to take them, leave an empty medicine container out instead, and put the medicine itself safely out of reach.

Wall cabinets that can be locked are ideal for storing drugs, as long as the cabinet itself is in a cool, dry place and not, as often happens, in the bathroom, which is frequently warm and humid.

WHEN TO DISPOSE OF DRUGS

Old medications should be flushed down the toilet or returned to the pharmacist, but not put in the dustbin. Always dispose of:

● Aspirin and paracetamol tablets that smell of vinegar.

● Tablets that are chipped, cracked, or discoloured, and capsules that have softened, cracked or stuck together.

● Liquids that have thickened or discoloured, or that taste or smell different in any way from the original product.

● Tubes that are cracked, leaky or hard.

● Ointments and creams that have changed odour, or changed appearance by discolouring, hardening or separating.

● Any liquid needing refrigeration that has been kept for over two weeks.

● Tablets or capsules over two years old.

LONG-TERM DRUG TREATMENT

Many people require regular, prolonged treatment with one or more drugs. People suffering from chronic or recurrent disorders often need lifelong treatment with drugs to control symptoms or prevent complications. Antihypertensive drugs for high blood pressure and insulin or oral antidiabetic drugs for diabetes mellitus are familiar examples. Many other disorders take a long time to cure; people with tuberculosis, for example, usually need at least six months therapy with antituberculous drugs. Long-term treatment may also be necessary to prevent a condition from occurring, and will have to be taken for as long as the individual is at risk. Antimalarial drugs are a good example.

Possible adverse effects

You may worry that taking a drug for a long period will reduce its effectiveness or that you will become dependent on it. However, *tolerance* develops with only a few drugs; most drugs continue to have the same effect indefinitely. Similarly, taking a drug for more than a few weeks does not normally create dependence.

Changing drug treatment

If you are taking a drug regularly, you will need to know what to do if something else occurs to affect your health. If you wish to become pregnant, for example, you should ask your doctor right away if it is preferable to continue on your regular medicine or switch to another less likely to affect your pregnancy. If you contract a new illness, for

which an additional drug is prescribed, your regular medication may be altered.

There are a number of other reasons for changing drug. You may have had an adverse reaction, or an improved preparation may have become available.

Adjusting to long-term treatment

You should establish a daily routine for taking your medication in order to reduce the risk of a missed dose. Usually you should not stop taking your medication, even if there are side effects, without consulting your doctor (see Ending drug treatment, p.28). If you fear possible adverse effects from the drug, discuss this with your doctor.

Many people deliberately stop their drugs because they feel well or their symptoms disappear. This can be dangerous, especially with a disease like high blood pressure which has no noticeable symptoms. Stopping treatment may lead to a recurrence or worsening of a disease. If you are uncertain about why you have to keep taking a drug, ask your doctor. Only a few drugs require an alteration in habits. Some drugs should not be taken with alcohol; with one or two drugs you should avoid certain foods. If you require a drug that makes you drowsy, you should not drive a car or operate dangerous equipment.

If you are taking a drug that should not be stopped suddenly or that may interact with other drugs, it is a good idea to carry a warning card or bracelet, a Medic Alert for example. Such information might be

essential for emergency medical treatment in an accident.

Monitoring treatment

If you are on long-term treatment, you need to visit your doctor for periodic check-ups. He or she will check your underlying condition and monitor any adverse effects of treatment. Levels of the drug in the blood may be measured. With insulin, in addition to checks with the doctor, you need to monitor blood or urine levels each day.

If a drug is known to cause damage to an organ, tests may be done to check the function of the organ. For example, blood and urine tests to check kidney function, or a blood count to check the bone marrow may be indicated.

Medical check-ups
Blood pressure is commonly checked in people on regular drug treatment.

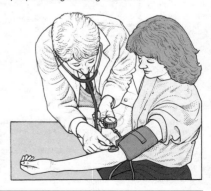

EXCEEDING THE DOSE

Most people associate drug overdoses with attempts at suicide or the fatalities and near fatalities brought on by abuse of street drugs. However, drug overdoses can also occur among people who deliberately or inadvertently exceed the stated dose of a drug that has been prescribed for them by their doctor.

A single extra dose of most drugs is unlikely to be a cause for concern, although accidental overdoses of several doses can create anxiety in the individual and his or her family, and may cause overdose symptoms which appear in a variety of different forms.

Overdose of some drugs, however, is potentially dangerous even when the dose has been exceeded by only a small amount. Each of the drug profiles in Part 4 of this book gives detailed information on the consequences of exceeding the dose, symptoms to look out for and what to do. Each drug has been given an overdose danger rating of low, medium, or high, which are described fully on p.184.

Taking an extra dose

People sometimes exceed the stated dose in the mistaken belief that by increasing dosage they will obtain more

Effects of repeated overdose
Repeated overdose of a drug over an extended period may lead to a build-up of high levels of the drug in the body, especially if liver or kidney function is reduced.

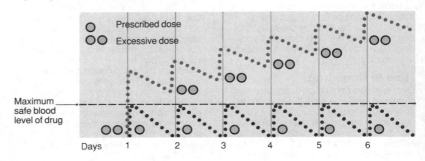

immediate action or a more effective cure. This is a particular risk with *tolerance* inducing drugs (see Drug dependence, p.23). Others exceed their dose accidentally, by miscalculating the amount or forgetting that the dose has already been taken.

Taking extra doses is often a problem in the elderly, who may double their dose through forgetfulness or confusion. This

is a special risk with medicines that cause drowsiness (see also p.22).

In some cases, especially when liver or kidney function is impaired, the drug builds up in the blood because the body cannot break down and excrete the extra dose quickly enough, so that symptoms of poisoning may result (see below left). Symptoms of excessive drug intake may not be apparent for many days.

When and how to get help

If you are not sure whether or not you have taken your tablets or medicine, think back and check again. If you honestly cannot remember, assume that you have missed the dose and follow the advice given in the individual drug profiles in Part 4 of this book. If you cannot find your drug there, consult your doctor. Make a note to use some system in the future which will help you remember to take your medication.

If you are looking after an elderly person on regular medication who suddenly develops unusual symptoms such as confusion, drowsiness, or unsteadiness, consider the possibility of an inadvertent drug overdose and call the family doctor as soon as possible.

Deliberate overdose

While many cases of drug overdose are accidental or the result of a mistaken belief that increasing the dose will enhance the benefits of drug treatment, sometimes an excessive amount of a drug is taken with the intention of causing harm or even as a suicide attempt. Whether or not you think a dangerous amount of a drug has been taken, deliberate overdoses of this kind should always be brought to the attention of your doctor. Not only is it necessary to ensure that no physical harm has occurred as a result of the overdose, but the psychological condition of a person who takes such action may require additional medical help.

HOW DRUGS ACCUMULATE

In most people liver and kidneys are able to cope with an occasional extra dose of a drug. But if they are functioning below normal efficiency, excessive doses may accumulate in the body.

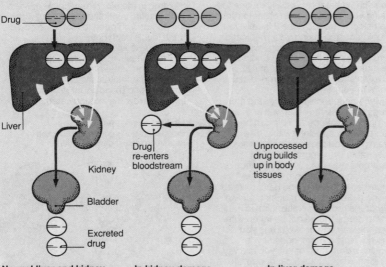

Normal liver and kidney
Drugs taken by mouth are processed in the liver and later excreted by the kidneys.

In kidney damage
The kidneys cannot eliminate excess drug in the urine; drug levels in the blood may rise.

In liver damage
The liver cannot process the excess drug which may build up in the body tissues.

DOs AND DON'Ts

On this page you will find a summary of the most important practical points concerning the management of your drug treatment. The advice is arranged under general headings, explaining the safest methods of storing drugs and following treatment, whether it is a prescribed medication or an over-the-counter drug. This information is equally applicable whether you are taking medication yourself or supervising the drug treatment of someone in your care.

At the doctor's

DO
● Tell your doctor about any medications you are already taking, both prescription and over-the-counter.
● Tell your doctor if you are pregnant, intending to become pregnant or breast feeding.
● Tell your doctor about any allergic reactions you have experienced to past drug treatments.
● Tell your doctor if you have a specific current health problem, such as liver or kidney disease, or if you think you might be at special risk from drug treatment for any other reason.

● Discuss your drug treatment with your doctor and make sure you understand the reasons why you have been prescribed a particular drug and what benefits you can expect. People who do not understand the reasons for their treatment often fail to take their medication correctly.

DON'T
▼ Leave your doctor's surgery without a clear understanding of how and when to take your medication.

At the chemist

DO
● Ask your pharmacist's advice about over-the-counter drugs if you are not sure what you should buy, or if you think you may react adversely to a drug.
● Try to see the same pharmacist or use the same chemist to obtain your regular prescriptions.
● Be sure you know the name and strength of the drug you have been prescribed. Check the label on your medication when it has been dispensed to ensure that you are receiving the correct drug.

● Make sure you understand what is on the drug label.
● Ask the pharmacist to put your medication in a container with an easy-to-remove cap if you have difficulty using child-resistant containers.

DON'T
▼ Send children to the chemist to get your medication for you.

Giving medicines to children

DO
● Check the dose on the label carefully before giving medicines to children.
● Make sure over-the-counter preparations you give to children for viral infections or fevers of unknown cause do not contain aspirin.

DON'T
▼ Pretend to children that medicinal preparations are sweets or soft drinks.

▼ Give any medicines to children under the age of five, except on the advice of your doctor.

Taking your medication

DO
● Make sure that your medication will not make you drowsy or otherwise affect your ability before you drive or perform difficult or dangerous tasks.
● Read the label and follow the instructions carefully. This is equally important with all types of drug – creams and lotions as well as drugs taken by mouth.
● Finish the drug treatment your doctor prescribes for you.
● Consult your doctor for advice if you experience side effects.

DON'T
▼ Take any prescribed or over-the-counter drugs without first consulting your doctor if you are pregnant or trying to conceive.
▼ Offer your medication to other people or take medication that has been prescribed for someone else (even if the symptoms are the same).

Food, drink and drugs of abuse

DO
● Check that it is safe to take alcohol with the drugs you have been prescribed and that there are no foods you should avoid.

DON'T
▼ Take medication (except that precribed by your doctor), drugs of abuse or alcohol if you are pregnant or trying to conceive. They may adversely affect the unborn baby.

Storing

DO
● Take care to store medications in a cool, dry place and protect them from light or refrigerate them, if advised to do so.
● Keep all drugs, including seemingly harmless medications such as cough preparations, locked away out of the reach of children.
● Check your medicine chest regularly in case other members of the family have left their unwanted drugs in it, and to make sure that none of the normal supplies are out of date.

● Keep all drugs in their original containers with the original instructions to avoid confusion.

DON'T
▼ Hoard drugs at home. When you have stopped taking a prescribed drug, dispose of it unless it is part of your family first aid kit.

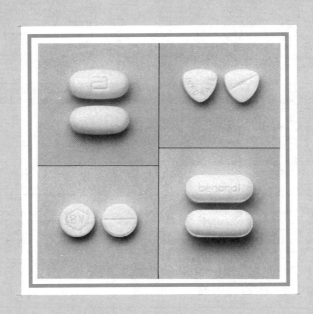

PART

2

DRUG FINDER

COLOUR IDENTIFICATION GUIDE
THE DRUG FINDER

COLOUR IDENTIFICATION CHART

The following pages contain photographs of 235 brand-name drugs. The guide is divided into six sections: one-colour tablets, multicolour tablets, one-colour and white capsules, multicolour capsules, white tablets, and nicotine chewing gum and patches. Within each section the products are arranged according to colour and size. The fact that a particular product is included in no way implies BMA endorsement of that brand.

The products included on these pages represent a selection of the most popular brand names in use in Britain. Several dosage strengths of some of the more widely prescribed brand names have been included. Each drug is photographed approximately life-size. Beneath each photograph you will find the name of the tablet or capsule with details of its main generic ingredients and their amounts in grams (g) or milligrams (mg). The drugs are laid out in a grid format. Each entry can be located from the Drug Finder by reference to the page number and the letter in the top left-hand corner of each square of the grid.

To enable you to locate the photograph of a particular medication, consult the chart, which will direct you to the relevant colour section. You will find an example of an entry in this section below.

HOW TO LOCATE YOUR MEDICATION

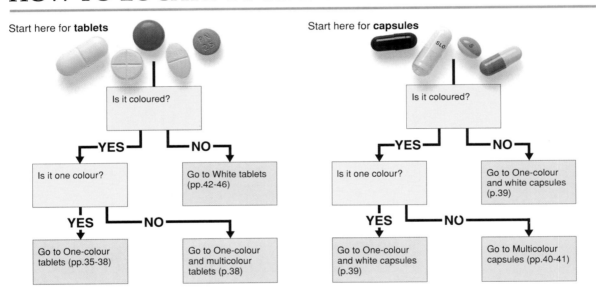

Start here for **tablets**

Is it coloured?

YES — Is it one colour?

NO — Go to White tablets (pp.42-46)

YES — Go to One-colour tablets (pp.35-38)

NO — Go to One-colour and multicolour tablets (p.38)

Start here for **capsules**

Is it coloured?

YES — Is it one colour?

NO — Go to One-colour and white capsules (p.39)

YES — Go to One-colour and white capsules (p.39)

NO — Go to Multicolour capsules (pp.40-41)

HOW TO UNDERSTAND THE ENTRIES

This example explains the significance of the text accompanying each photograph that will help you to identify a particular drug.

Identifying marks
These are unique to each product, but they may include the name of the manufacturer, brand name of the drug or a reference number.

Brand name
The brand name of the drug.

INDERAL

Propranolol 40mg

Grid letter
This letter refers to the tablet's position on the page. References given in the Drug Finder give the page number and the individual grid letter.

Generic ingredients
These are usually listed in order of their amount in each medication. Many products have several ingredients.

ONE-COLOUR TABLETS

A

BUTACOTE
Phenylbutazone 100mg

B

WELLDORM
Chloral hydrate 414mg

C

M.S.T. CONTINUS
Morphine sulphate 30mg

D

VENTOLIN
Salbutamol 4mg

E

VENTOLIN
Salbutamol 2mg

F

CELEVAC
Methyl cellulose 500mg

G

APRESOLINE
Hydralazine 50mg

H

SPARINE
Promazine 100mg

I

INDERAL
Propranolol 40mg

J

DELTACORTRIL
Prednisolone 5mg

K

PROTHIADEN
Dothiepin 75mg

L

PREMARIN
Conjugated oestrogens 0.625mg

M

ERYTHROMID
Erythromycin 250mg

N

TENORETIC
Atenolol 10mg
Chlorthalidone 25mg

O

GAMANIL
Lofepramine 70mg

P

NYSTAN
Nystatin 500,000 units

Q

TOFRANIL
Imipramine 25mg

R

KWELLS
Hyoscine 300mcg

S

NEO-MERCAZOLE
Carbimazole 5mg

T

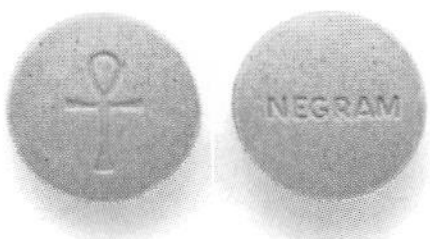

NEGRAM
Nalidixic acid 500mg

ONE-COLOUR TABLETS continued

A

MOLIPAXIN

Trazodone 150mg

B

ZOCOR

Simvastatin 20mg

C

MODURETIC

Hydrochlorothiazide 50mg
Amiloride 5mg

D

PALFIUM

Dextromoramide 10mg

E

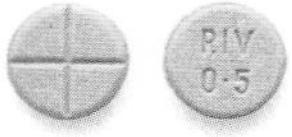

RIVOTRIL

Clonazepam 0.5mg

F

TENORMIN LS

Atenolol 50mg

G

TENORMIN

Atenolol 100mg

H

NARDIL

Phenelzine 15mg

I

PERSANTIN

Dipyridamole 25mg

J

CHENDOL

Chenodeoxycholic acid 250mg

K

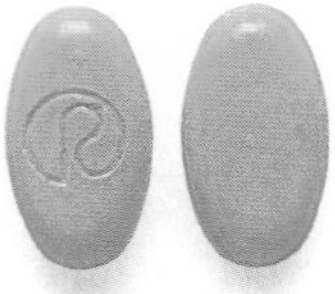

SALAZOPYRIN

Sulphasalazine 500mg

L

VOLTAROL

Diclofenac 25mg

M

SALOFALK

Mesalazine 250mg

N

DISIPAL

Orphenadrine 50mg

O

ZOFRAN

Ondansetron 4mg

P

YUTOPAR

Ritodrine 10mg

Q

NIVAQUINE

Chloroquine 200mg

R

MANERIX

Moclobemide 150mg

S

PIRITON

Chlorpheniramine 4mg

T

CLOMID

Clomiphene 50mg

A

CORDILOX
Verapamil 40mg

B

ALDOMET
Methyldopa 250mg

C

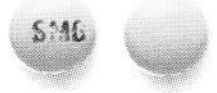

SANOMIGRAN
Pizotifen 0.5mg

D

MYAMBUTOL
Ethambutol 100mg

E

TRYPTIZOL
Amitriptyline 25mg

F

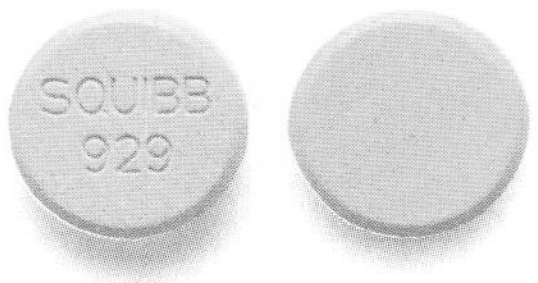

FUNGILIN
Amphotericin 10,000 units

G

VALIUM
Diazepam 5mg

H

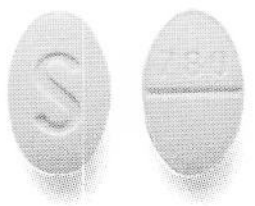

SORBITRATE
Isosorbide dinitrate 10mg

I

HALDOL
Haloperidol 1.5mg

J

RIDAURA
Auranofin 3mg

K

MIDAMOR
Amiloride 5mg

L

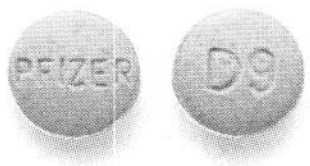

VIBRAMYCIN-D
Doxycycline 100mg

M

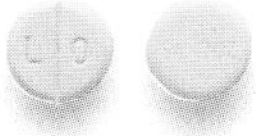

CLOZARIL
Clozapine 25mg

N

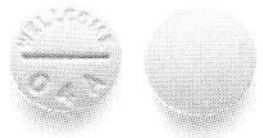

PURI-NETHOL
Mercaptopurine 50mg

O

IMURAN
Azathioprine 50mg

P

TAGAMET
Cimetidine 400mg

Q

TAGAMET
Cimetidine 200mg

R

CEDOCARD
Isosorbide dinitrate 40mg

S

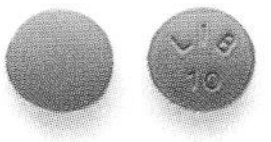

LIBRIUM
Chlordiazepoxide 10mg

T

LIBRIUM
Chlordiazepoxide 25mg

ONE-COLOUR AND MULTICOLOUR TABLETS

A

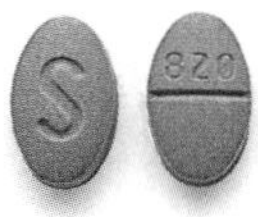

SORBITRATE

Isosorbide dinitrate 20mg

B

BLOCADREN

Timolol 10mg

C

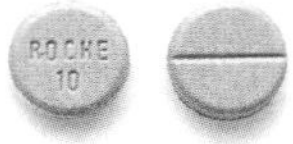

VALIUM

Diazepam 10mg

D

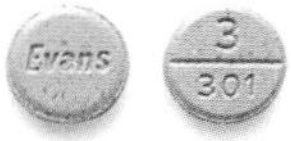

WARFARIN

3mg

E

ZOVIRAX

Acyclovir 200mg

F

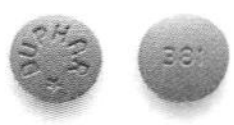

ZUMENON

Oestradiol 2mg

G

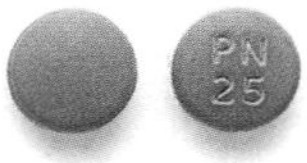

PHENERGAN

Promethazine 25mg

H

DIXARIT

Clonidine 25mcg

I

DISTACLOR MR

Cefaclor 375mg

J

NEO-NACLEX-K

Bendrofluazide 2.5mg
Potassium 8.4mmol

K

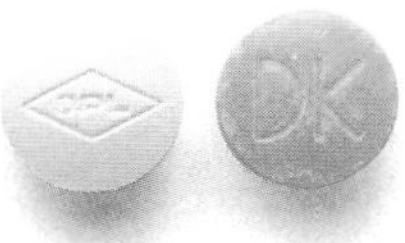

DIUMIDE-K

Frusemide 40mg
Potassium 8mmol

ONE-COLOUR AND WHITE CAPSULES

A

DYTAC

Triamterene 50mg

B

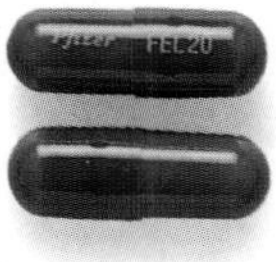

FELDENE

Piroxicam 20mg

C

SYMMETREL

Amantadine 100mg

D

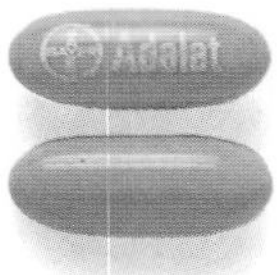

ADALAT

Nifedipine 10mg

E

EMESIDE

Ethosuximide 250mg

F

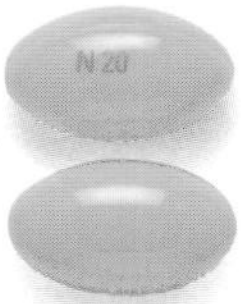

NORMISON

Temazepam 20mg

G

EFAMAST

Gamolenic acid 40mg

H

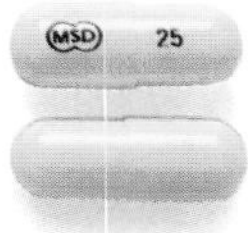

INDOCID

Indomethacin 25mg

I

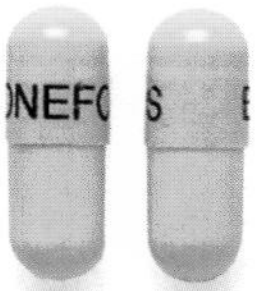

BONEFOS

Sodium clodronate 400mg

J

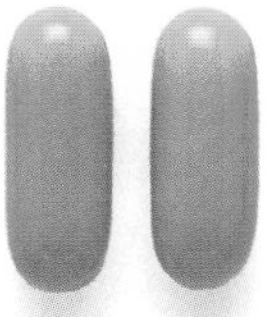

SANDIMMUN

Cyclosporin 50mg

K

RESTANDOL

Testosterone 40mg

L

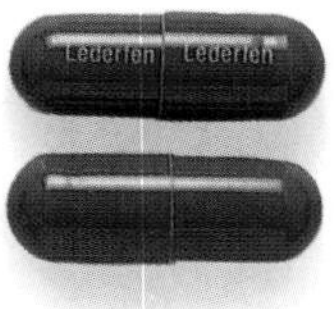

LEDERFEN

Fenbufen 300mg

M

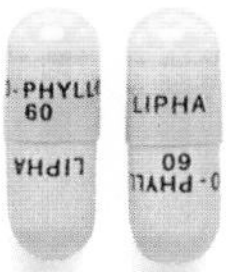

SLO-PHYLLIN

Theophylline 60mg

N

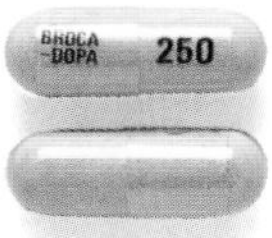

BROCADOPA

Levodopa 250mg

MULTICOLOUR CAPSULES

A

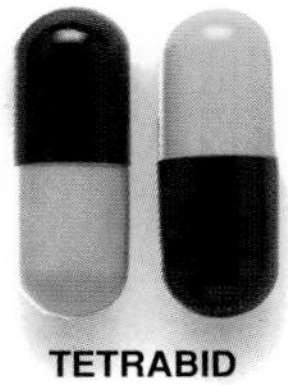

TETRABID

Tetracycline 250mg

B

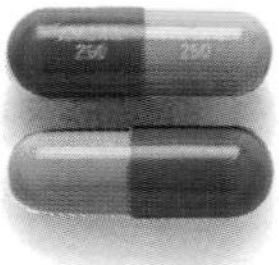

AMOXIL

Amoxycillin 250mg

C

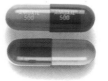

AMOXIL

Amoxycillin 500mg

D

RIFADIN

Rifampicin 150mg

E

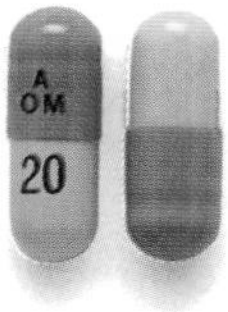

LOSEC

Omeprazole 20mg

F

ROACCUTANE

Isotretinoin 5mg

G

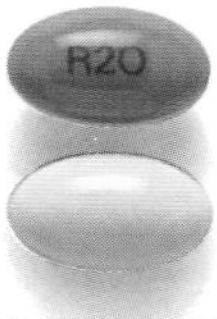

ROACCUTANE

Isotretinoin 20mg

H

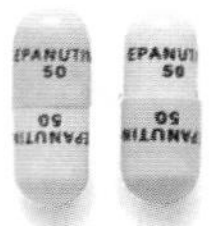

EPANUTIN

Phenytoin 50mg

I

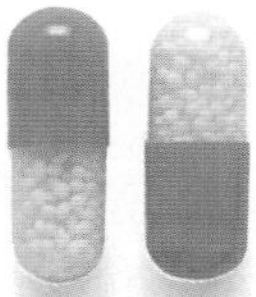

PROFLEX SR

Ibuprofen 300mg

J

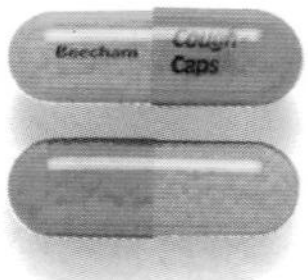

BEECHAM COUGHCAPS

Dextromethorphan 40.2mg

K

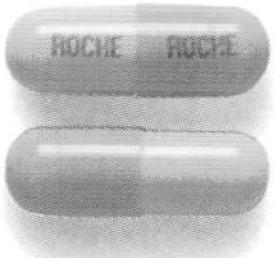

TIGASON

Etretinate 25mg

L

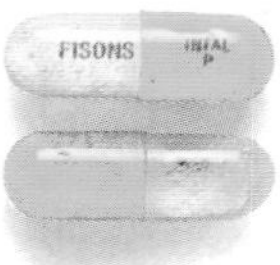

INTAL SPINCAP

Sodium cromoglycate 20mg

M

BECOTIDE ROTACAP

Beclomethasone 200mcg

N

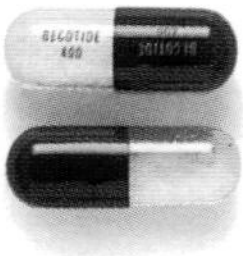

BECOTIDE ROTACAP

Beclomethasone 400mcg

O

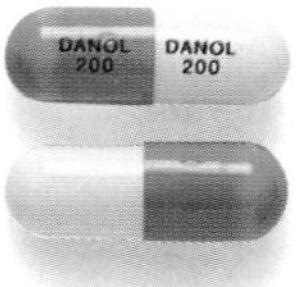

DANOL

Danazol 200mg

P

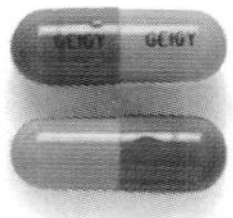

ANAFRANIL

Clomipramine 25mg

Q

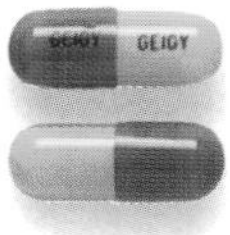

ANAFRANIL

Clomipramine 10mg

R

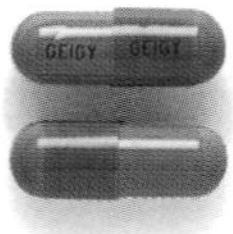

ANAFRANIL

Clomipramine 50mg

S

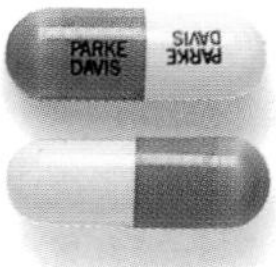

CHLOROMYCETIN

Chloramphenicol 250mg

T

IMODIUM

Loperamide 2mg

A

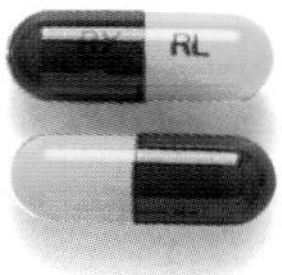

RYTHMODAN

Disopyramide 100mg

B

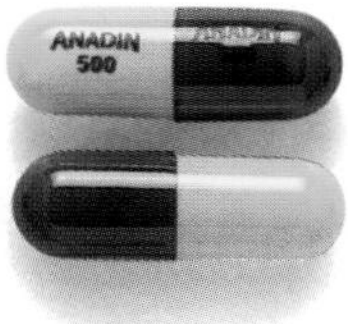

ANADIN 500

Aspirin 500mg
Caffeine 32mg

C

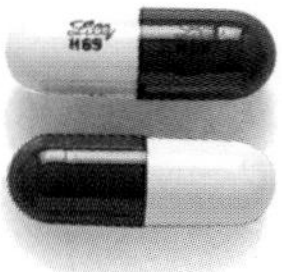

KEFLEX

Cephalexin 250mg

D

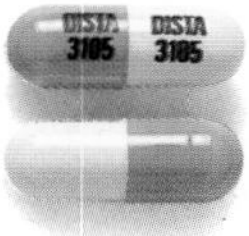

PROZAC

Fluoxetine 20mg

E

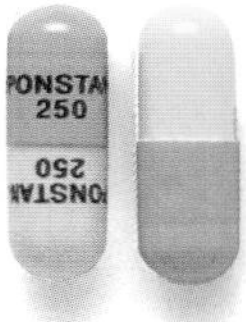

PONSTAN

Mefenamic acid 250mg

F

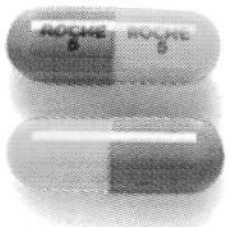

VALIUM

Diazepam 5mg

G

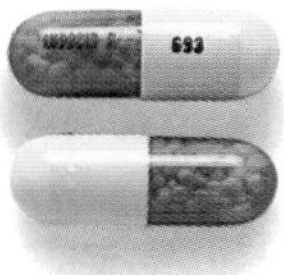

INDOCID R

Indomethacin 75mg

H

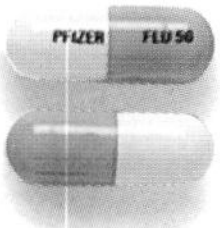

DIFLUCAN

Fluconazole 50mg

I

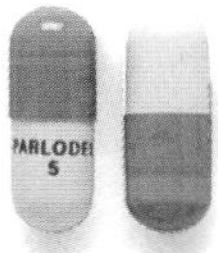

PARLODEL

Bromocriptine 5mg

J

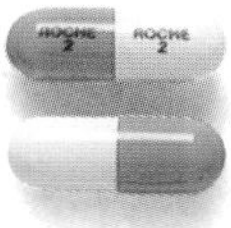

VALIUM

Diazepam 2mg

K

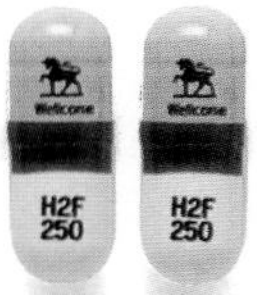

RETROVIR

Zidovudine 250mg

L

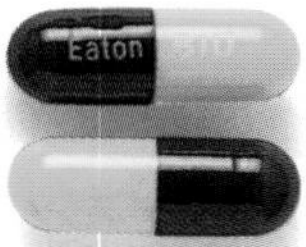

MACROBID

Nitrofurantoin 100mg

M

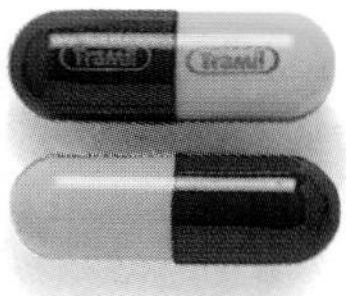

TRAMIL

Paracetamol 500mg

N

MOGADON

Nitrazepam 5mg

O

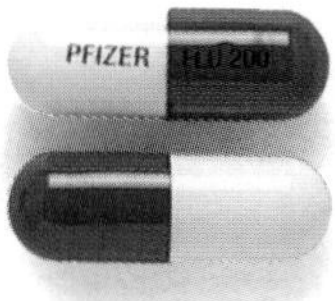

DIFLUCAN

Flucanazole 200mg

WHITE TABLETS

A

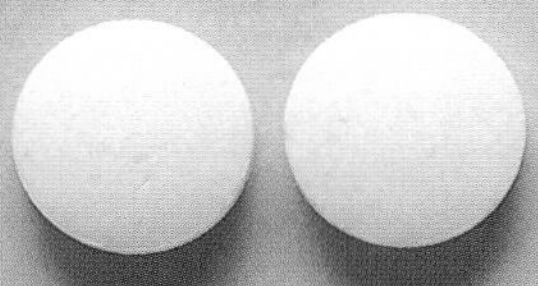

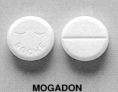

ALUMINIUM HYDROXIDE

500mg

B

FULCIN

Griseofulvin 500mg

C

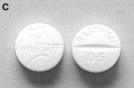

RASTINON

Tolbutamide 500mg

D

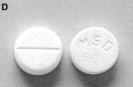

BENEMID

Probenecid 500mg

E

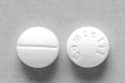

MOGADON

Nitrazepam 5mg

F

MILK OF MAGNESIA

Magnesium hydroxide 300mg

G

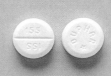

TRILUDAN

Terfenadine 60mg

H

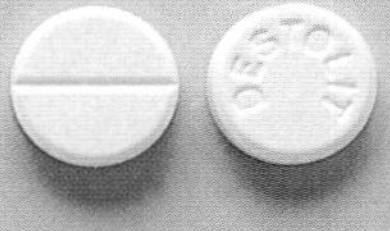

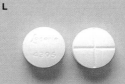

DESTOLIT

Ursodeoxycholic acid 150mg

I

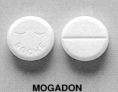

CAMCOLIT

Lithium carbonate 250mg

J

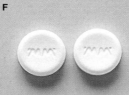

URISPAS

Flavoxate 200mg

K

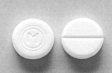

DUPHASTON

Dydrogesterone 10mg

L

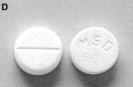

DIAMOX

Acetazolamide 250mg

M

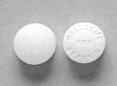

SEPTRIN

Co-trimoxazole 480mg

N

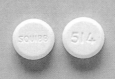

IPRAL

Trimethoprim 200mg

O

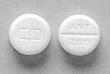

ANTABUSE

Disulfiram 200mg

P

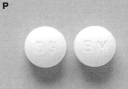

BEZALIP MONO

Bezafibrate 400mg

Q

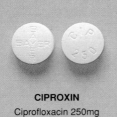

CIPROXIN

Ciprofloxacin 250mg

R

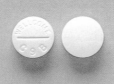

ZYLORIC

Allopurinol 300mg

S

GLUCOPHAGE

Metformin 500mg

T

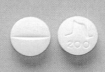

CORDARONE X

Amiodarone 200mg

A

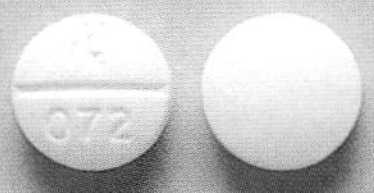

ASPIRIN

300mg

B

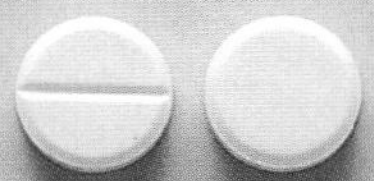

STABILLIN-VK

Phenoxymethylpenicillin 250mg

C

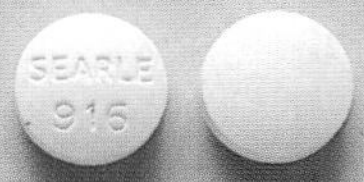

ALDACTONE

Spironolactone 50mg

D

FLAGYL

Metronidazole 200mg

E

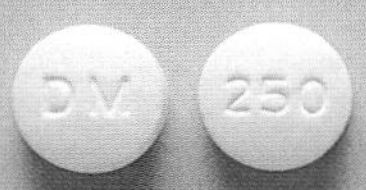

DISTAMINE

Penicillamine 250mg

F

CAFERGOT

Caffeine 100mg
Ergotamine 1mg

G

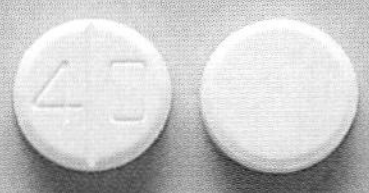

MEGACE

Megestrol 40mg

H

MYSOLINE

Primidone 250mg

I

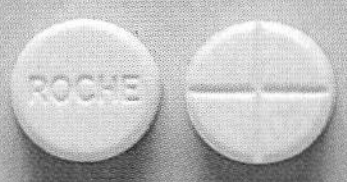

MESTINON

Pyridostigmine 60mg

J

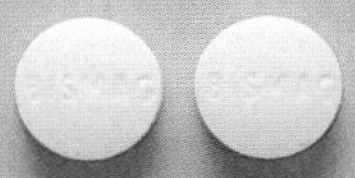

BISMAG

Sodium bicarbonate 149mg
Magnesium carbonate 156mg

K

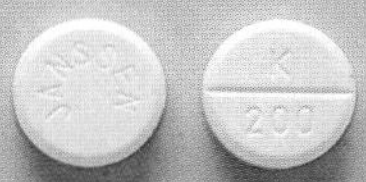

NIZORAL

Ketoconazole 200mg

L

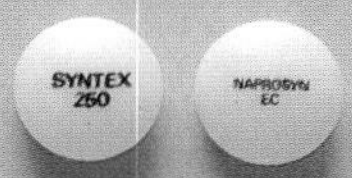

NAPROSYN

Naproxen 250mg

M

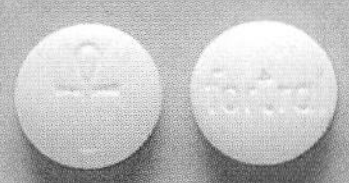

FORTRAL

Pentazocine 25mg

N

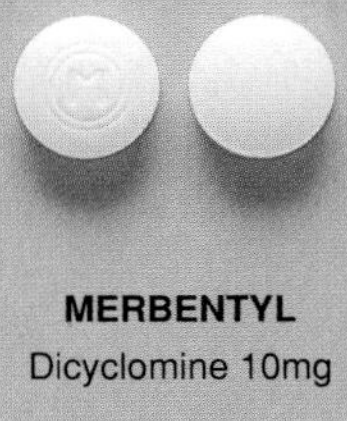

MERBENTYL

Dicyclomine 10mg

O

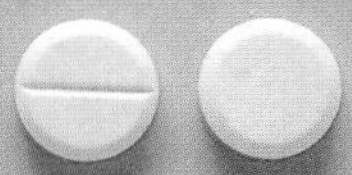

EPILIM

Sodium valproate 100mg

P

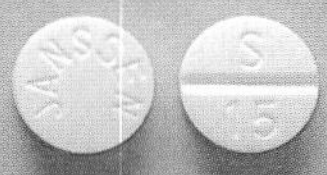

STUGERON

Cinnarizine 15mg

Q

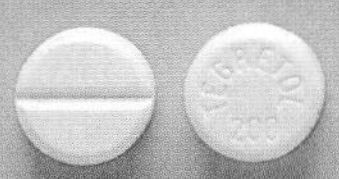

TEGRETOL

Carbamazepine 200mg

R

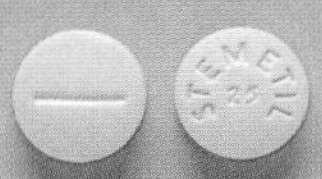

STEMETIL

Prochlorperazine 25mg

S

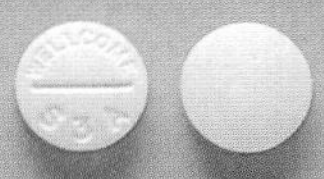

KEMADRIN

Procyclidine 5mg

T

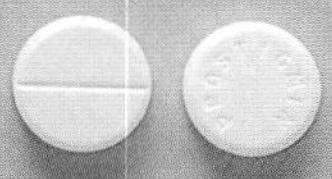

PROSTIGMIN

Neostigmine 15mg

WHITE TABLETS continued

A

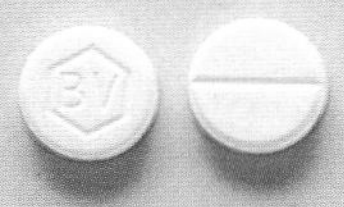

ANDROCUR

Cyproterone acetate 50mg

B

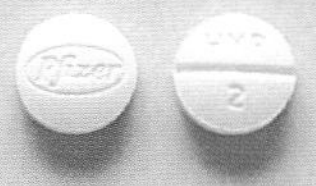

HYPOVASE

Prazosin 2mg

C

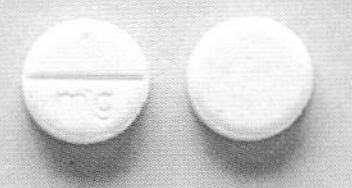

BURINEX

Bumetanide 1mg

D

PALUDRINE

Proguanil 100mg

E

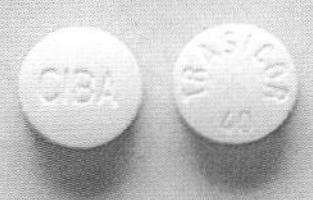

TRASICOR

Oxprenolol 40mg

F

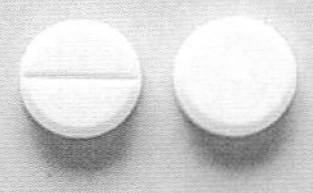

JUNIOR KWELLS

Hyoscine 150mcg

G

TILDIEM

Diltiazem 60mg

H

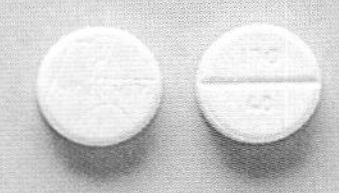

LASIX

Frusemide 40mg

I

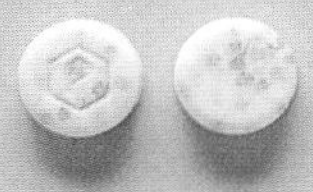

SAVENTRINE

Isoprenaline 30mg

J

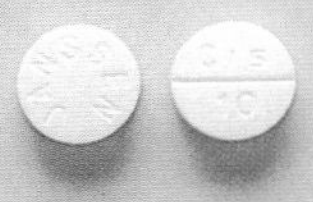

PREPULSID

Cisapride 10mg

K

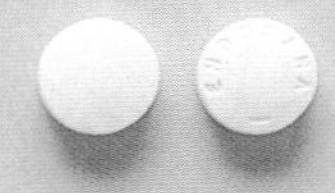

ENDOXANA

Cyclophosphamide 10mg

L

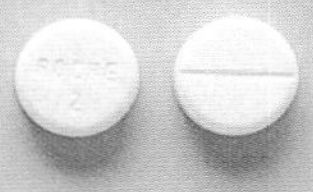

VALIUM

Diazepam 2mg

M

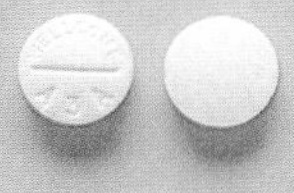

DARAPRIM

Pyrimethamine 25mg

N

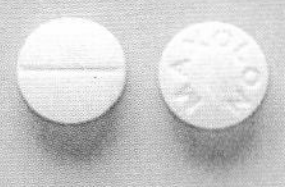

MAXOLON

Metoclopramide 10mg

O

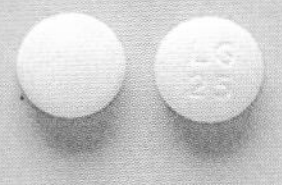

LARGACTIL

Chlorpromazine 25mg

P

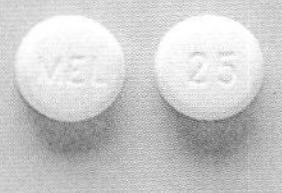

MELLERIL

Thioridazine 25mg

Q

BUSCOPAN

Hyoscine butylbromide 10mg

R

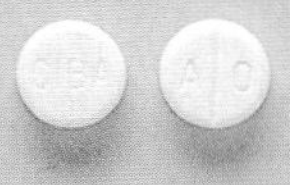

NAVIDREX

Cyclopenthiazide 0.5mg

S

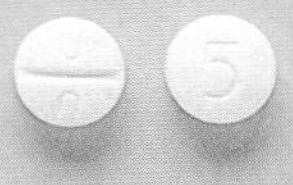

LONITEN

Minoxidil 5mg

T

MOTILIUM

Domperidone 10mg

A

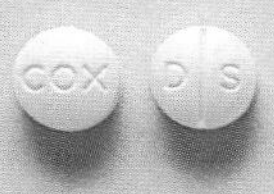

DAPSONE

100mg

B

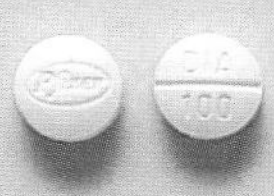

DIABINESE

Chlorpropamide 100mg

C

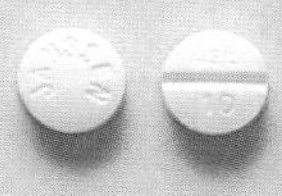

HISMANAL

Astemizole 10mg

D

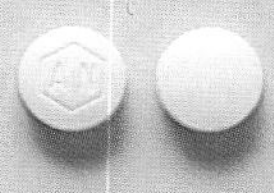

PRIMOLUT N

Norethisterone 5mg

E

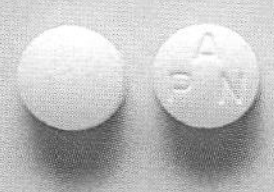

ACUPAN

Nefopam 30mg

F

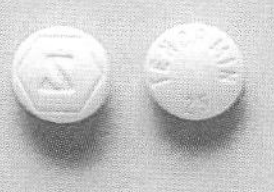

TENORMIN

Atenolol 25mg

G

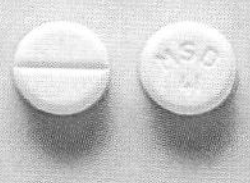

DECADRON

Dexamethasone 0.5mg

H

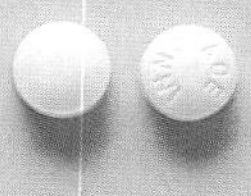

INNOVACE

Enalapril 2.5mg

I

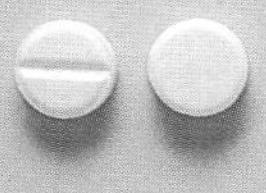

APRINOX

Bendrofluazide 5mg

J

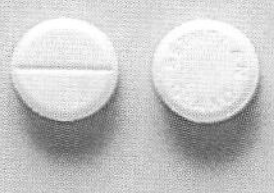

BETNELAN

Betamethasone 0.5mg

K

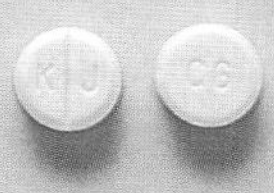

LIORESAL

Baclofen 10mg

L

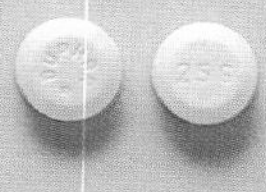

SERC

Betahistine 8mg

M

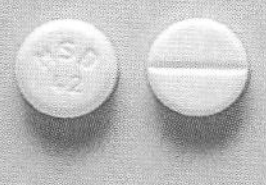

HYDROSALURIC

Hydrochlorothiazide 25mg

N

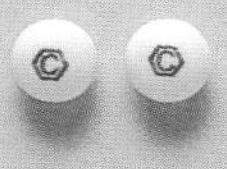

EUGYNON 30

Ethinyloestradiol 30mcg
Levonorgestrel 250mcg

O

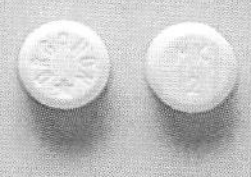

LIVIAL

Tibolone 2.5mg

P

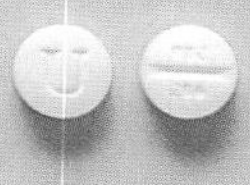

PROVERA

Medroxyprogesterone 5mg

Q

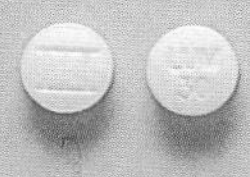

LUMINAL

Phenobarbitone 30mg

R

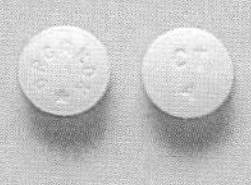

BOLVIDON

Mianserin 10mg

S

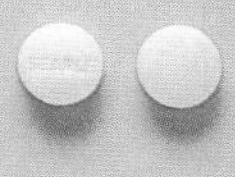

LOMOTIL

Diphenoxylate 2.5mg
Atropine 25mcg

T

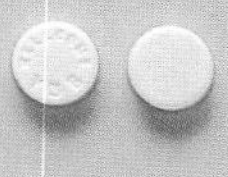

LANOXIN

Digoxin 0.125mg

WHITE TABLETS continued

A

MICROVAL
Levonorgestrel 30mcg

B

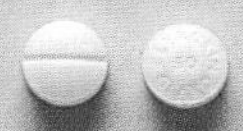

ELTROXIN
Thyroxine 0.05mg

C

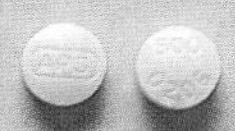

GLYCERYL TRINITRATE
500mcg

D

CORLAN
Hydrocortisone 2.5mg

E

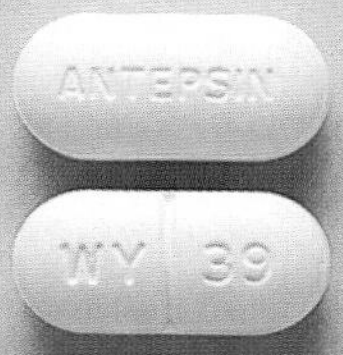

ANTEPSIN
Sucralfate 1g

F

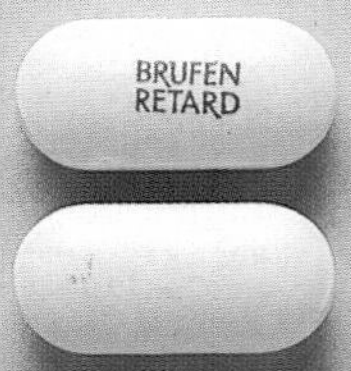

BRUFEN RETARD
Ibuprofen 800mg

G

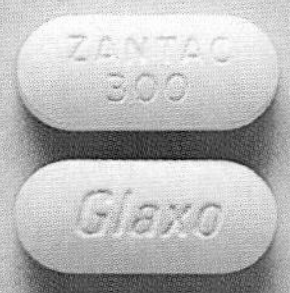

ZANTAC
Ranitidine 300mg

H

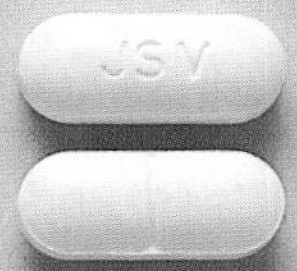

PARACETAMOL
500mg

I

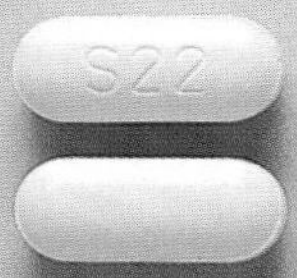

BENORYLATE
750mg

J

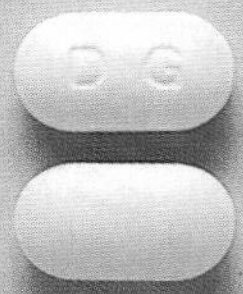

CO-PROXAMOL
Paracetamol 325mg
Dextropropoxyphene 32.5mg

K

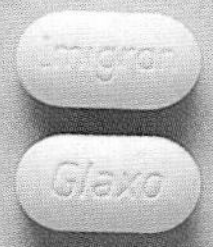

IMIGRAN
Sumatriptan 100mg

L

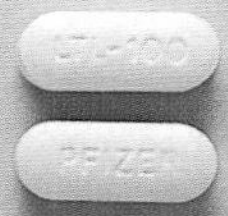

LUSTRAL
Sertraline 100mg

M

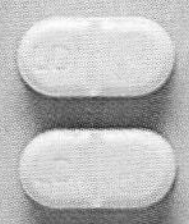

DAONIL
Glibenclamide 5mg

N

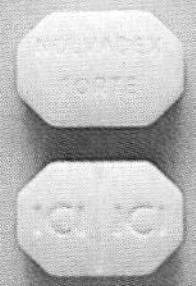

NOLVADEX FORTE
Tamoxifen 20mg

O

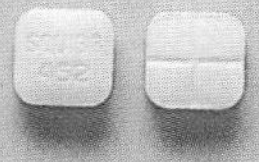

CAPOTEN
Captopril 25mg

P

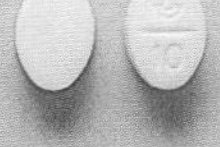

CLARITYN
Loratidine 10mg

Q

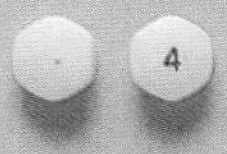

VOLMAX
Salbutamol 4mg

NICOTINE PRODUCTS

Smoking is considered an antisocial habit and is responsible for approximately 100,000 deaths in Britain each year, approximately one-third each from lung cancer, heart attacks, and chronic bronchitis. Many people would like to give up smoking but find it very difficult. The only proven drug remedy is nicotine.

Nicotine is the main active ingredient in tobacco, and is largely responsible for the addictive nature of the smoking habit. Pharmacologists have produced various formulations of nicotine in order to help smokers wean themselves from their habit.

The most widely used of these aids to giving up smoking – nicotine chewing gum and nicotine transdermal patches – are now available over the counter. Nicotine formulations are currently sold in

Britain under the brand names Nicorette, Nicabate, and Nicotinell-TTS. The products illustrated on this page are included only as examples of the types of formulations available and do not indicate BMA endorsement. Detailed information about doses and methods of use is given on p.344.

Although a prescription is not needed for nicotine chewing gum or nicotine transdermal patches, you may still find it useful to talk to your doctor about the hazards of smoking and about strategies that might help you break your smoking habit. It is important to remember that nicotine formulations should never be used while you continue to smoke. Ignoring this advice could lead to an excess build-up of nicotine that could cause dangerous adverse effects.

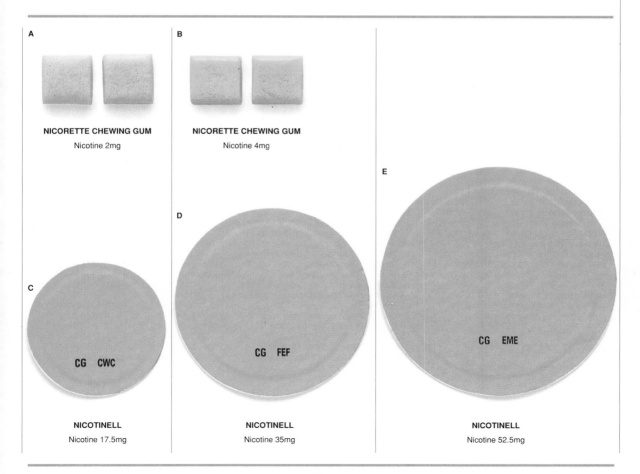

A

NICORETTE CHEWING GUM

Nicotine 2mg

B

NICORETTE CHEWING GUM

Nicotine 4mg

C

CG   CWC

NICOTINELL

Nicotine 17.5mg

D

CG   FEF

NICOTINELL

Nicotine 35mg

E

CG   EME

NICOTINELL

Nicotine 52.5mg

THE DRUG FINDER

This section contains the names of approximately 2,500 individual drug products and substances. It provides a quick and easy reference point for readers interested in learning about a specific drug or medication. There is no need for you to know before using the Drug Finder whether the item you want to look up has a brand name or a generic name, or whether it is a prescription or over-the-counter drug; all types of drug are listed.

What it contains
The drugs are listed alphabetically and include all major generic drugs and many less widely used substances. A broad range of brand names is included. The Drug Finder also contains the names of many vitamins and minerals. This comprehensive selection is designed to reflect the wide diversity of products available for the treatment and prevention of disease. Inclusion of a drug or product does not imply BMA endorsement of that drug or product, nor does the exclusion of a particular drug or product indicate BMA disapproval.

How the references work
References are to the pages in Part 4 containing the drug profiles of each principal generic ingredient and the section in Part 3 that describes the relevant drug group, as appropriate. Some entries for generic drugs that have not been given a full profile contain a brief description here. Certain technical terms within the entries appear in *italics* to indicate that they are defined in the Glossary (pp.446-451).

Colour identification guide
Brand-name products pictured in the Colour Identification Guide (pp.34-47) contain a reference in *italic* type to the page and grid letter where the photograph of that product may be found.

A

Abidec a brand-name multivitamin 149
Accupro a brand name for quinapril (an ACE inhibitor 98)
Accuretic a brand name for quinapril (an ACE inhibitor 98) with hydrochlorothiazide 299 (a diuretic 99)
acebutolol a beta blocker 97
acemetacin a non-steroidal anti-inflammatory 116)
Acepril a brand name for captopril 216 (an ACE inhibitor 98)
acetazolamide 186 (a carbonic anhydrase inhibitor diuretic 99)
acetomenaphthone a substance used with nicotinic acid 345 to treat chilblains
Acetoxyl a brand name for benzoyl peroxide 208 (a drug for acne 177)
acetylcholine a chemical *neurotransmitter* that stimulates the parasympathetic nervous system 79 and is used as a *miotic* 170
acetylcysteine a *mucolytic* 94
Acezide a brand name for captopril 216 (an ACE inhibitor 98) with hydrochlorothiazide 299 (a thiazide diuretic 99)
Achromycin a brand name for tetracycline 407 (an antibiotic 128)
acipimox a lipid lowering drug 103
Aclacin a brand name for aclarubicin (an anticancer drug 154)
aclarubicin an anticancer drug 154
Acnegel a brand name for benzoyl peroxide 208 (a drug for acne 177)
Acnidazil a brand name for benzoyl peroxide 208 (a drug for acne 177) with miconazole (an antifungal 138)

Acriflex a brand-name *topical antiseptic* containing chlorhexidine 179
Acrivastine an antihistamine 124
acrosoxacin an antibacterial 131
Actifed Compound a brand name for dextromethorphan 256 (a cough suppressant 94) with pseudoephedrine (a decongestant 93) and triprolidine (an antihistamine 124)
Actifed Exporant a brand name for guaiphenesin (an expectorant 98), with pseudoephedrine (a decongestant 93) and tripolidine (an antihistamine 124)
Actinac a brand-name acne preparation 177 containing chloramphenicol 224, hydrocortisone 300, allantoin, butoxyethyl nicotinate, and sulphur
actinomycin D an anticancer drug 154
activated charcoal a substance used in the emergency treatment of poisoning
Actron a brand-name *analgesic* 80 and antacid 108 containing aspirin 199, paracetamol, sodium bicarbonate 393, caffeine, and citric acid
Acupan a brand name for nefopam 342 (a non-*narcotic analgesic* 80); *illus. 45E*
acyclovir 187 (an antiviral 133)
Adalat a brand name for nifedipine 346 (an anti-angina drug 101 and antihypertensive 92); *illus. 39D*
Adalat IC a brand name for nifedipine 346 (an anti-angina drug 101 and antihypertensive 102)
Adalat Retard a brand name for nifedipine 346 (an anti-angina drug 101 and antihypertensive 102)
Adifax a brand name for dexfenfluramine (a drug for weight reduction 88)
Adizem-XL a brand name for diltiazem (an anti-angina drug 101)

adrenaline 188 (a *bronchodilator* 92 and drug for glaucoma 168)
Aerobec a brand name for beclomethasone (a corticosteroid 141)
Aerolin a brand name for salbutamol 389 (a *bronchodilator* 92)
Afrazine a brand name for oxymetazoline (a *topical* decongestant 93)
Agarol a brand-name laxative 111 containing liquid paraffin and phenolphthalein
Akineton a brand name for biperiden (an *anticholinergic* for *parkinsonism* 87)
alclometasone a *topical* corticosteroid 174
Alcobon a brand name for flucytosine (an antifungal 138)
Alcopar a brand name for bephenium (an anthelmintic 139)
Aldactide a brand name for spironolactone 397 with hydro-flumethiazide (both diuretics 99)
Aldactone a brand name for spirono-lactone 397 (a potassium-sparing diuretic 99); *illus. 43C*
Aldomet a brand name for methyldopa 332 (an antihypertensive 102); *illus. 37B*
alexitol an antacid 108
alfacalcidol vitamin D 432 (a vitamin 149)
alfentanil an *anaesthetic* 80
Algicon a brand name for aluminium hydroxide, magnesium carbonate, and potassium bicarbonate (antacids 108) with magnesium alginate (an antifoaming agent 108)
alginate, alginic acid an antifoaming agent used in antacids 108
Alimix a brand name for cisapride (a gastrointestinal motility regulator and antacid 108)
Alka-Seltzer a brand-name *analgesic* 80 and antacid 108 containing aspirin 199, sodium bicarbonate 393, and citric acid

Alkeran a brand name for melphalan (an anticancer drug 154)

allantoin a mild antibacterial 131

Allbee with C a brand-name multi-vitamin 149

Allegron a brand name for nortriptyline (a tricyclic antidepressant 84)

Aller-eze a brand name for clemastine (an antihistamine 124)

allopurinol 189 (a drug for gout 119)

allyloestrenol a progestogen 147

Almodan a brand name for amoxycillin 196 (a penicillin antibiotic 128)

Alomide a brand name for lodoxamide (an anti-allergic drug 124)

Alophen a brand name for aloin and phenolphthalein 68 (both stimulant laxatives 111)

Alphaderm a brand name for hydrocortisone 300 (a corticosteroid 141) with urea (a hydrating agent)

alpha tocopheryl acetate vitamin E 432 (a vitamin 149)

Alphosyl a brand-name drug for eczema 175 and psoriasis 178 containing coal tar and allantoin

alprazolam a benzodiazepine anti-anxiety drug 83

Alrheumat a brand name for ketoprofen (a non-steroidal anti-inflammatory 116)

Altacite Plus a brand name for hydrotalcite (an antacid 108) with dimethicone (an antifoaming agent 108)

Alteplase 90 (a thrombolytic 105)

Alu-Cap a brand name for aluminium hydroxide 191 (an antacid 108)

Aludrox gel a brand name for aluminium hydroxide 191 (an antacid 108)

Aludrox SA a brand name for ambutonium bromide (an *antispasmodic* for irritable bowel syndrome 110) with aluminium hydroxide 191 and magnesium hydroxide 323 (both antacids 108)

Aluhyde a brand name for aluminium hydroxide 191 and magnesium trisilicate (both antacids 108) with belladonna (an *antispasmodic* for irritable bowel 110)

aluminium acetate an *astringent* used for inflammation of the skin or outer ear canal 175; also used in rectal preparations 113

aluminium hydroxide 191 (an antacid 108); *illus. 42A*

Alupent a brand name for orciprenaline (a *bronchodilator* 92)

Alvedon a brand name for paracetamol 356 (a non-*narcotic analgesic* 80)

alverine an *antispasmodic* for irritable bowel 110

amantadine 192 (a drug used for *parkinsonism* 87 and as an antiviral 131)

Ambaxin a brand name for bacampicillin (a penicillin antibiotic 128)

amethocaine a local *anaesthetic* 80

Amfipen a brand name for ampicillin (a penicillin antibiotic 128)

amikacin an aminoglycoside antibiotic 128

Amikin a brand name for amikacin (an aminoglycoside antibiotic 128)

Amilco a brand name for amiloride 193 with hydrochlorothiazide 299 (both diuretics 99)

amiloride 193 (a potassium-sparing diuretic 99)

aminobenzoic acid an ingredient of sunscreens 179

aminoglutethimide a drug for advanced breast cancer 154 and Cushing's syndrome (an adrenal disorder)

aminophylline a *bronchodilator* 92 related to theophylline 408

amiodarone 194 (an anti-arrhythmic 100)

amitriptyline 195 (a tricyclic antidepressant 84)

amlodipine a calcium channel blocker 101

ammonium chloride a drug that increases urine acidity and speeds excretion of poisons 166, and is an expectorant 94

Amoram a brand name for amoxycillin (a penicillin antibiotic 128)

amoxapine a tricyclic antidepressant 84

Amoxil a brand name for amoxycillin 196 (a penicillin antibiotic 124); *illus. 40B, 40C*

amoxycillin 196 (a penicillin antibiotic 128)

amphotericin 197 (an antifungal 138)

ampicillin a penicillin antibiotic 128

Ampiclox a brand name for ampicillin with flucloxacillin (both penicillin antibiotics 128)

amsacrine an anticancer drug 154

Amsidine a brand name for amsacrine (an anticancer drug 154)

amylobarbitone a barbiturate sleeping drug 82

Amytal a brand name for amylobarbitone (a barbiturate sleeping drug 82)

Anacal a brand-name preparation for haemorrhoids 113 containing heparinoid

Anadin 500 a brand-name *analgesic* 80 containing aspirin 199 and caffeine; *illus. 41B*

Anadin Extra a brand-name *analgesic* 80 containing aspirin 199, paracetamol 356, and caffeine

Anadin Paracetamol a brand name for paracetamol 356 (a non-*narcotic analgesic* 80)

Anafranil a brand name for clomipramine 239 (a tricyclic antidepressant 84); *illus. 40P, 40Q, 40R*

Anafranil SR a brand name for clomipramine 239 (a tricyclic antidepressant 84)

Anbesol a brand-name *topical* liquid for mouth ulcers and teething pain, containing lignocaine (a local *anaesthetic* 80), cetylpyridinium, and chlorocresol (both *topical antiseptics*)

Andrews Antacid a brand name for calcium carbonate and magnesium carbonate (both antacids 108)

Androcur a brand-name drug for the control of sexual deviation in males containing cyproterone acetate 252; *illus. 44A*

Anestan Bronchial Tablets a brand-name *bronchodilator* 92 and decon-gestant 93 containing ephedrine 277 and theophylline 408

Anethaine a brand name for amethocaine (a local *anaesthetic* 80)

Angettes a brand name antiplatelet drug containing aspirin 199

Angilol a brand name for propranolol 380 (a beta blocker 97)

Anhydrol Forte a brand name for aluminium chloride (an *antiperspirant*)

Anodesyn suppositories a brand-name preparation for haemorrhoids containing allantoin (a mild antibacterial 131), lignocaine (a local *anaesthetic* 80) and ephedrine 277

Anquil a brand name for benperidol (an antipsychotic 85)

Antabuse a brand name for disulfiram 268 (an alcohol abuse deterrent); *illus. 42 O*

antazoline 198 (an antihistamine 124)

Antepsin a brand name for sucralfate 400 (an ulcer-healing drug 109); *illus. 46E*

Anthisan a brand name for mepyramine (an antihistamine cream 124)

Anthranol a brand name for dithranol 269 (a drug for psoriasis 178)

anti-D immunoglobulin a drug used to prevent sensitization to Rhesus antigen

antihaemophilic factor a blood protein used to promote blood clotting in haemophilia 104

Antipressan a brand name for atenolol 200 (a beta blocker 97)

Anturan a brand name for sulphin-pyrazone (a drug for gout 119)

Anugesic HC a brand name preparation for haemorrhoids containing hydrocorti-sone 300, benzyl benzoate, bismuth, Peru balsam, pramoxine, and zinc oxide

Anusol-HC a brand name preparation for haemorrhoids containing hydrocortisone 300, benzyl benzoate, bismuth, Peru balsam, and zinc oxide

Anusol suppositories a brand-name preparation for haemorrhoids 113 containing zinc oxide, bismuth, and Peru balsam

Apisate a brand name for diethylproprion (an appetite suppressant 88) with several B vitamins 149

APP a brand name for homatropine (an *antispasmodic* 110), with bismuth (an anti-ulcer drug 109), and calcium carbonate, magnesium carbonate, magnesium trisilicate, and aluminium hydroxide 191 (all antacids 108)

Apresoline a brand name for hydralazine 298 (an antihypertensive 102); *illus. 35G*

Aprinox a brand name for bendrofluazide 206 (a thiazide diuretic 99); *illus. 45 I*

aprotinin an antifibrinolytic 104 used to promote blood clotting

Apsifen a brand name for ibuprofen 302 (a non-steroidal anti-inflammatory 116)

Apsin VK a brand name for phenoxymethyl-penicillin 362 (a penicillin antibiotic 128)

APSOLOL – CALPOL

Apsolol a brand name for propranolol 380 (a beta blocker 97)

Apsolox a brand name for oxprenolol 355 (a beta blocker 97)

Aqua-Ban a brand name for caffeine with ammonium chloride used as a mild diuretic 99

Aquadrate a brand name for urea (a hydrating agent)

Arelix a brand name for piretanide (a loop diuretic 99)

argipressin synthetic vasopressin (a drug for diabetes insipidus 145)

Arpicolin a brand name for procyclidine 376 (a drug for *parkinsonism* 87)

Arpimycin a brand name for erythromycin 280 (an antibiotic 128)

Arret a brand name for loperamide 320 (an antidiarrhoeal 110)

Artane a brand name for benzhexol (a drug for *parkinsonism* 87)

Arthrotec a brand name for an antirheumatic drug containing diclofenac (a non-steroidal anti-inflammatory 116) with misoprostol (an anti-ulcer drug 109)

Artracin a brand name for indomethacin 305 (a non-steroidal anti-inflammatory 116 and drug for gout 119)

Arythmol a brand name for propafenone (an anti-arrhythmic 100)

Asacol a brand name for mesalazine (a drug for ulcerative colitis 112)

Ascabiol a brand name for topical benzyl benzoate (an antiparasitic 176)

ascorbic acid vitamin C 431 (a vitamin 149)

Asendis a brand name for amoxapine (a tricyclic antidepressant 84)

Asilone a brand name for aluminium hydroxide 191 and magnesium oxide (both antacids 108) with dimethicone (an antifoaming agent)

asparaginase a drug for leukaemia 154

Aspav a brand-name *analgesic* 80 containing aspirin 199 and papaveretum

aspirin 199 (a non-*narcotic analgesic* 80 and antiplatelet drug 104); *illus. 43A*

Aspro Clear a brand name for soluble aspirin 199 (a non-*narcotic analgesic* 80)

astemizole an antihistamine 124

Atarax a brand name for hydroxyzine (an anti-anxiety drug 83)

atenolol 200 (a beta blocker 97)

Ativan a brand name for lorazepam (a benzodiazepine anti-anxiety drug 83 and sleeping drug 82)

atracurium a drug used to relax the muscles in general *anaesthesia* 80

atropine 201 (an *anticholinergic* for irritable bowel syndrome 110 and *mydriatic* drug 170)

Atrovent a brand name for ipratropium bromide 308 (a *bronchodilator* 92)

Audicort a brand-name anti-infective ear preparation 171 containing benzocaine, neomycin, and triamcinolone

Augmentin a brand name for amoxycillin 196 (a penicillin antibiotic 128) with clavulanic acid (a substance which increases its effectiveness)

auranofin 202 (an antirheumatic 117)

Aureocort a brand name for chlortetra-cycline (a tetracycline antibiotic 128) with triamcinolone (a corticosteroid 141)

Aureomycin a brand name for chlortetracycline (a tetracycline antibiotic 128)

Avloclor a brand name for chloroquine 226 (an antimalarial 137 and antirheumatic 117)

Avomine a brand name for promethazine 379 (an antihistamine 124 and anti-emetic 90)

Azactam a brand name for aztreonam (an antibiotic 128)

Azamune a brand name for azathioprine 203 (an antirheumatic 117 and immunosuppressant 156)

azapropazone a non-steroidal anti-inflammatory 116

azatadine an antihistamine 124

azathioprine 203 (an antirheumatic 117 and immunosuppressant 156)

azelastine an antihistamine 124

azidothymidine zidovudine 420 (an antiviral for AIDS 157)

azithromycin an antibiotic 128

azlocillin a penicillin antibiotic 128

AZT zidovudine 420 (an antiviral drug for AIDS 157)

aztreonam an antibiotic 128

B

bacampicillin a penicillin antibiotic 128

baclofen 204 (a muscle relaxant 120)

Bactrim a brand name for co-trimoxazole 248 (an antibacterial 127)

Bactroban a brand name for mupirocin (an anti-infective 175)

Bambec a brand name for bambuterol (a *sympathomimetic bronchodilator* 92)

bambuterol a *sympathomimetic bronchodilator* 92

Baratol a brand name for indoramin (an antihypertensive 102)

Baxan a brand name for cefadroxil (a cephalosporin antibiotic 128)

Becloforte a brand name for beclomethasone 205 (a corticosteroid 137)

beclomethasone 205 (a corticosteroid 141)

Beconase a brand name for beclomethasone 205 (a corticosteroid 141)

Becosym a brand-name vitamin B complex preparation 149

Becotide a brand name for beclomethasone 205 (a corticosteroid 141); *illus. 40M, 40N*

Beechams Pills a brand name for aloin (a stimulant laxative 111)

Beechams Powders a brand name for paracetamol 356 (a non-*narcotic analgesic* 80) and pseudoephedrine (a decongestant 93)

Beechams Powders Capsules a brand name for paracetamol 356 (a non-*narcotic*

analgesic 80) with phenylephrine 364 (a decongestant 93) and caffeine (a stimulant 88)

belladonna an *antispasmodic anticholinergic* for irritable bowel syndrome 110

Benadon a brand name for pyridoxine 428 (a vitamin 149)

bendrofluazide 206 (a thiazide diuretic 99)

Benemid a brand name for probenecid 374 (a drug for gout 119); *illus. 42D*

benethamine penicillin an antibiotic 128

Benoral a brand name for benorylate 207 (a non-steroidal anti-inflammatory 116)

benorylate 207 (a non-steroidal anti-inflammatory 116); *illus. 46 I*

Benoxyl a brand name for benzoyl peroxide 208 (a drug for acne 177)

benperidol an antipsychotic 85

benserazide a drug used to enhance the effect of levodopa 315 (a drug for *parkinsonism* 87)

Benylin Children's Cough a brand name for diphenhydramine 264 (an antihistamine 124) with menthol (an alcohol)

Benylin with codeine a brand-name cough suppressant 94 containing diphenhydramine 264 (an antihistamine 124) codeine (a *narcotic analgesic* 80) and menthol

Benzagel a brand name for benzoyl peroxide 208 (a drug for acne 177)

benzalkonium chloride a skin *antiseptic* 175

benzathine penicillin an antibiotic 128

benzhexol a drug for *parkinsonism* 87

benzocaine a local *anaesthetic* 80

benzoin tincture a resin used in inhalations for sinusitis and nasal congestion 93

benzoyl peroxide 208 (a drug for acne 177)

benztropine an *anticholinergic* for *parkinsonism* 87

benzydamine an analgesic 80 used in mouthwash and throat spray

benzyl benzoate an antiparasitic 176 for scabies

benzylpenicillin a penicillin antibiotic 128

Berkatens a brand name for verapamil 418 (an anti-angina drug 101 and anti-arrhythmic 100)

Berkmycen a brand name for oxytetra-cycline (a tetracycline antibiotic 128)

Berkolol a brand name for propranolol 380 (a beta blocker 97)

Berkozide a brand name for bendrofluazide 206 (a thiazide diuretic 99)

Berotec a brand name for fenoterol (a *sympathomimetic bronchodilator* 92)

Beta-Adalat a brand name for nifedipine 346 (an anti-angina drug 101 and antihypertensive 102) with atenolol 200 (a beta blocker 97)

Beta-Cardone a brand name for sotalol (a beta blocker 97)

beta-carotene vitamin A 430 (a vitamin 149 and food additive)

Betadur a brand name for propranolol (a beta blocker 97)

Betagan a brand name for levobunolol (a beta blocker 97 and drug for glaucoma 169)

betahistine 209 (a drug for Ménière's disease 90)

Betaloc a brand name for metoprolol (a beta blocker 97)

betamethasone 210 (a corticosteroid 141)

Beta-Prograne a brand name for propranolol (a beta blocker 97)

Betasept Shampoo a brand-name shampoo containing povidone iodine (an *antiseptic* 175)

betaxolol a beta blocker 97 also used in glaucoma 168

bethanechol a *parasympathomimetic* for urinary retention 166 and paralytic ileus

Betim a brand name for timolol 412 (a beta blocker 97)

Betnelan a brand name for betamethasone 210 (a corticosteroid 141); *illus. 45J*

Betnesol a brand name for beta-methasone 210 (a corticosteroid 141)

Betnesol-N a brand name for betamethasone 210 (a corticosteroid 141) with neomycin (an aminoglycoside antibiotic 128)

Betnovate a brand name for beta-methasone 210 (a corticosteroid 141)

Betnovate-C a brand name for beta-methasone 210 (a corticosteroid 141) with clioquinol (an anti-infective 175)

Betnovate-N a brand name for betamethasone 210 (a corticosteroid 141) with neomycin (an aminoglycoside antibiotic 128)

Betoptic a brand-name drug for glaucoma 168 containing betaxolol

bezafibrate 211 (a lipid-lowering drug 103)

Bezalip a brand name for bezafibrate 211 (a lipid-lowering drug 103); *illus. 42P*

Bicillin a brand name for procaine penicillin and penicillin (both antibiotics 128)

BiNovum a brand-name oral contraceptive 161 containing ethinyloestradiol 282 and norethisterone 349

Biogastrone a brand name for carben-oxolone 218 (an anti-ulcer drug 109)

Biophylline a brand name for theophylline 408 (a *bronchodilator* 92)

Bioplex a brand-name drug for mouth ulcers containing carbenoxolone 218

Bioral Gel a brand-name drug for mouth ulcers containing carbenoxolone 218

Biorphen a brand name for orphenadrine 354 (a drug for *parkinsonism* 87)

biotin 422 (a vitamin 149)

biperiden an *anticholinergic* for *parkinsonism* 87

bisacodyl a stimulant laxative 111

Bismag a brand name for sodium bicarbonate 393 with magnesium carbonate (both antacids 108); *illus. 43J*

bismuth a metal given in compound form for gastric and duodenal ulcers 109 and haemorrhoids 113

Bisodol a brand name for sodium bicarbonate 393 with calcium carbonate and magnesium carbonate (all ant-acids 108)

bisoprolol a beta blocker 97

bleomycin a *cytotoxic* antibiotic for cancer 154

Blocadren a brand name for timolol 412 (a beta blocker 97); *illus. 38B*

Bolvidon a brand name for mianserin 335 (an antidepressant 84); *illus. 45R*

Bonefos a brand name for sodium clodronate for low blood calcium in cancer patients; *illus. 39 I*

Bonjela gel a brand name for choline salicylate (a drug similar to aspirin 199)

Bonjela pastilles a brand name for pastilles for mouth ulcers containing lignocaine (a local *anaesthetic*) and aminacrine (a skin *antiseptic* 175)

botulinum *toxin* used as a muscle relaxant 120

Bradilan a brand name for nicofuranose (a lipid-lowering drug 103 and *vasodilator* 98)

Brelomax a brand name for tulobuterol (a bronchodilator 92)

Bretylate a brand name for bretylium (an anti-arrhythmic 100)

bretylium tosylate an anti-arrhythmic 100

Brevibloc a brand name for esmolol (a beta blocker 97)

Brevinor a brand-name oral contraceptive 161 containing ethinyloestradiol 282 and norethisterone 349

Bricanyl a brand name for terbutaline (a *bronchodilator* 92 and drug used in premature labour 165)

Britiazim a brand name for diltiazem (an anti-angina drug 101)

Britlofex a brand name for lofexidine (a drug to treat opioid *withdrawal symptoms*)

Brocadopa a brand name for levodopa 315 (a drug for *parkinsonism* 87); *illus. 39N*

Broflex a brand name for benzhexol (a drug for *parkinsonism* 87)

Brolene a brand name for propamidine isethionate (an antibacterial 131) for eye infections

bromocriptine 212 (a pituitary agent 145 and drug for *parkinsonism* 87)

brompheniramine an antihistamine 124

Bronchodil a brand name for reproterol (a *bronchodilator* 92)

Brufen a brand name for ibuprofen 302 (a non-steroidal anti-inflammatory 116); *illus. 46F*

Buccastem a brand name for prochlor-perazine 375 (an anti-emetic 90)

buclizine an antihistamine 124 and anti-emetic 90 used for motion sickness

budesonide a corticosteroid 141

bufexamac a drug for skin inflammation 174

bumetanide 213 (a loop diuretic 99)

bupivacaine a long-lasting local *anaesthetic* 80 used in labour 165

buprenorphine a *narcotic analgesic* 80

Burinex a brand name for bumetanide 213 (a loop diuretic 99); *illus. 44C*

Burinex-K a brand name for bumetanide 213 (a loop diuretic 99) with potassium 427

Burneze a brand name for benzocaine (a local *anaesthetic* 80)

Buscopan a brand name for hyoscine 301 (an *antispasmodic* for irritable bowel syndrome 110); *illus. 44Q*

buserelin a drug for menstrual disorders 160

Buspar a brand name for buspirone (an anti-anxiety drug 83)

buspirone a non-benzodiazepine anti-anxiety drug 83

busulphan an alkylating agent for certain leukaemias 154

Butacote a brand name for phenylbutazone 363 (a non-steroidal anti-inflammatory 116); *illus. 35A*

butobarbitone a barbiturate sleeping drug 82

butoxyethyl nicotinate a *topical vasodilator* 98

C

Cafadol a brand name for paracetamol 356 (a non-*narcotic analgesic* 80) with caffeine (a stimulant 88)

Cafergot a brand name for ergotamine 279 (a drug for migraine 89) with caffeine (a stimulant 88); *illus. 43F*

caffeine a stimulant 88 in coffee, tea, and cola, sometimes added to *analgesic* preparations 80

Caladryl a brand name for diphenhydra-mine 264 (an antihistamine 124) with calamine lotion (an antipruritic 169)

calamine a substance containing zinc carbonate (an antipruritic 173) used to soothe irritated skin

calcifediol vitamin D 432 (a vitamin 149)

calciferol vitamin D 432 (a vitamin 149)

Calcilat a brand name for nifedipine 346 (an anti-angina drug 101 and antihypertensive 102)

calcipotriol 214 a drug derived from vitamin D 432 that is used to treat psoriasis 178

Calcitare a brand name for calcitonin 215 (a drug for bone disorders 122)

calcitonin 215 (a drug for bone disorders 122)

calcitriol vitamin D 432 (a vitamin 149)

calcium 422 (a mineral 150)

calcium acetate calcium 422 (a mineral 150)

calcium carbonate a calcium salt (a mineral 150) used as an antacid 108

calcium chloride calcium 422 (a mineral 150)

calcium gluconate calcium 422 (a mineral 150)

Calmurid HC a brand-name substance for eczema 175 containing hydro-cortisone 300, lactic acid, and urea

Calpol a brand name for paracetamol 356 (a non-*narcotic analgesic* 80)

CALPOL EXTRA – COSALGESIC

Calpol Extra a brand-name *analgesic* 80 containing paracetamol 356, codeine 244, and caffeine

CAM a brand name for ephedrine 277 with butethamate (both *bronchodilators* 92)

Camcolit a brand name for lithium 318 (an antimanic drug 85); *illus. 42 I*

camphor a *topical* antipruritic 173

Canesten a brand name for clotrimazole 242 (an antifungal 138)

Canesten HC a brand name for clotrimazole 242 (an antifungal 138) with hydrocortisone 300 (a corticosteroid 141)

Cantil a brand name for mepenzolate (an *anticholinergic antispasmodic* for irritable bowel syndrome 110)

Capastat a brand name for capreomycin sulphate (an antituberculous drug 132)

Capitol a brand name shampoo containing benzalkonium chloride (an antiseptic 175)

Caplenal a brand name for allopurinol 189 (a drug for gout 119)

Capoten a brand name for captopril 216 (an ACE inhibitor 98); *illus. 46 O*

Capozide a brand name for captopril 216 (an ACE inhibitor 98) with hydrochlorothiazide 299 (a thiazide diuretic 99)

capreomycin sulphate an antituberculous drug 132

Caprin a brand name for aspirin 199 (a non-*narcotic analgesic* 80 and antiplatelet drug 104)

captopril 216 (an ACE inhibitor 98)

Carace a brand name for lisinopril (an ACE inhibitor 98)

carbachol a drug used for its *miotic* effect in glaucoma 168 and *parasympathomimetic* effect in urinary retention 166

Carbalax sodium acid phosphate and sodium bicarbonate (both laxatives 111)

carbamazepine 217 (an anticonvulsant 86)

carbaryl an antiparasitic 176 for head lice

Carbellon a brand name for magnesium hydroxide 323 (an antacid 108 and laxative 111) with charcoal (an adsorbent) and peppermint oil (both substances for bowel spasm 110)

carbenicillin a penicillin antibiotic 128

carbenoxolone 218 (an anti-ulcer drug 109)

carbidopa a substance that enhances the therapeutic effect of levodopa 315 (a drug for *parkinsonism* 87)

carbimazole 219 (an anti-thyroid drug 144)

carbocysteine a *mucolytic* 93

Carbo-Dome a brand name for coal tar (a substance for psoriasis 178)

carboplatin an anticancer drug 154

Cardene a brand name for nicardipine (a calcium channel blocker 101)

Cardura a brand name for doxazosin (a *sympatholytic* antihypertensive 102)

Carisoma a brand name for carisoprodol (a muscle relaxant 120 related to meprobamate)

carisoprodol a muscle relaxant 120 related to meprobamate

carmustine an alkylating agent for Hodgkin's disease and solid tumours 154

carteolol a beta blocker 97 for glaucoma 168 and angina 101

Carylderm a brand name for carbaryl (an antiparasitic 176 for head lice)

cascara a stimulant laxative 111

castor oil a stimulant laxative 111

Catapres a brand name for clonidine 241 (an antihypertensive 102)

Catarrh-Ex a brand-name decongestant 93 containing pseudoephedrine and paracetamol 356 (a non-*narcotic analgesic* 80)

Caved-S a brand name for aluminium hydroxide 191 with sodium bicarbonate 368 and magnesium carbonate (all antacids 108), and liquorice and bismuth sulphate (both anti-ulcer drugs 109)

Cedocard a brand name for isosorbide dinitrate 311 (a nitrate *vasodilator* 98 and anti-angina drug 101); *illus. 37R*

cefaclor 220 (an antibiotic 128)

cefadroxil a cephalosporin antibiotic 128

cefamandole a cephalosporin antibiotic 128

cefixime a cephalosporin antibiotic 128

Cefizox a brand name for ceftizoxime (a cephalosporin antibiotic 128)

cefodizime a cephalosporin antibiotic 128

cefotaxime a cephalosporin antibiotic 128

cefoxitin a cephalosporin antibiotic 128

cefpodoxime a cephalosporin antibiotic 128

cefsulodin a cephalosporin antibiotic 128

ceftazidime a cephalosporin antibiotic 128

ceftizoxime a cephalosporin antibiotic 128

cefuroxime a cephalosporin antibiotic 128

Celance a brand name for pergolide (a drug for *parkinsonism* 87)

Celbenin a brand name for methicillin (a penicillin antibiotic 128)

Celectol a brand name for celiprolol (a beta blocker 97)

Celevac a brand name for methylcellulose 331 (a laxative 111 and antidiarrhoeal 110); *illus. 35F*

celiprolol a beta blocker 97

Centyl K a brand name for bendrofluazide 206 (a thiazide diuretic 99) and potassium 427 (a mineral 150)

cephalexin 221 (a cephalosporin antibiotic 128)

cephazolin a cephalosporin antibiotic 128

cephradine a cephalosporin antibiotic 128

Ceporex a brand name for cephalexin 221 (a cephalosporin antibiotic 128)

Cerumol a brand-name preparation for ear wax removal

Cesamet a brand name for nabilone (an anti-emetic 90 derived from marijuana for nausea and vomiting induced by anticancer drugs 154)

cetirizine an antihistamine 124

cetrimide a skin *antiseptic* 175

Chemotrim a brand name for co-trimoxazole 248 (an antibacterial 131)

Chendol a brand name for chenodeoxycholic acid 222 (a drug for gallstones 114); *illus. 36J*

chenodeoxycholic acid 222 (a drug for gallstones 114)

Chenofalk a brand name for chenodeoxycholic acid 222 (a drug for gallstones 114)

Chloractil a brand name for chlorpromazine 228 (a phenothiazine antipsychotic 85 and anti-emetic 90)

chloral betaine a sleeping drug 82

chloral hydrate 223 (a sleeping drug 82)

chlorambucil an anticancer drug 154 used for chronic lymphocytic leukaemia and lymphatic and ovarian cancers, and as an immunosuppressant 156 for rheumatoid arthritis 117

chloramphenicol 224 (an antibiotic 128)

chlordiazepoxide 225 (a benzodiazepine anti-anxiety drug 83)

chlorhexidine a skin *antiseptic* 175

chlormethiazole a non-benzodiazepine, non-barbiturate sleeping drug 82

chlormezanone an anti-anxiety drug 83 and muscle relaxant 120

Chloromycetin a brand name for chloramphenicol 224 (an antibiotic 128); *illus. 40S*

Chloromycetin Hydrocortisone a brand name for chloramphenicol 224 (an antibiotic 128) with hydrocortisone 300 (a corticosteroid 141)

chloroquine 226 (an antimalarial 137 and antirheumatic 117)

chlorothiazide a thiazide diuretic 99

chloroxylenol a skin *antiseptic* 175

chlorpheniramine 227 (an antihistamine 124)

chlorpromazine 228 (a phenothiazine antipsychotic 85 and anti-emetic 90)

chlorpropamide 229 (an antidiabetic 142)

chlortetracycline a tetracycline antibiotic 128

chlorthalidone a thiazide diuretic 99

cholecalciferol vitamin D 432 (a vitamin 149)

Choledyl a brand name for choline theophyllinate (a xanthine *bronchodilator* 92)

cholestyramine 230 (a lipid-lowering drug 103)

choline magnesium trisalicylate a drug similar to aspirin 199 used in arthritic conditions 117

choline salicylate a drug similar to aspirin 199 used in pain-relieving mouth gels 80

choline theophyllinate a xanthine *bronchodilator* 92

chromium 423 (a mineral 150)

Cicatrin a brand name for bacitracin with neomycin (both antibiotics 128)

Cidomycin a brand name for gentamicin 292 (an aminoglycoside antibiotic 128)

cilazapril an ACE inhibitor 98

Cilest a brand name oral contraceptive containing ethinyloestradiol 282 and norgestimate

cimetidine 232 (an anti-ulcer drug 109)

cinchocaine a local *anaesthetic* 80
cinnarizine 233 (an antihistamine anti-emetic 90)
Cinobac a brand name for cinoxacin (a urinary tract antibiotic 128)
cinoxacin a urinary tract antibiotic 128
ciprofibrate a lipid lowering drug 103
ciprofloxacin 234 (an antibacterial 131)
Ciproxin a brand name for ciprofloxacin (an antibacterial 131); *illus. 42Q*
cisapride a gastrointestinal motility regulator 110
cisplatin 236 (an anticancer drug 154)
Citramag a brand name for magnesium citrate (an osmotic laxative 111)
Claforan a brand name for cefotaxime (a cephalosporin antibiotic 128)
clarithromycin a macrolide antibiotic 128
Clarityn a brand name for loratadine (an antihistamine 124); *illus. 46P*
clavulanic acid a substance given with amoxycillin 196 (a penicillin antibiotic 128) to make it more effective
clemastine an antihistamine 124
Clexane a brand name for enoxaparin (a drug to prevent blood clotting 104)
clindamycin a lincosamide antibiotic 128
Clinicide a brand name for carbaryl (an antiparasitic 176)
Clinitar a brand name for coal tar (a sub-stance for psoriasis 178 and dandruff 179)
Clinoril a brand name for sulindac (a non-steroidal anti-inflammatory 116)
clioquinol an antibacterial 131 antifungal 138 for outer ear infections 171
clobazam a benzodiazepine anti-anxiety drug 83
clobetasol a topical corticosteroid 174
clobetasone a topical corticosteroid 174
clofazimine a drug for leprosy 131
Clomid a brand name for clomiphene 238 (a drug for infertility 164); *illus. 36T*
clomiphene 238 (a drug for infertility 164)
clomipramine 239 (a tricyclic antidepressant 84)
clonazepam 240 (a benzodiazepine anticonvulsant 86)
clonidine 241 (an antihypertensive 102 and drug for migraine 89)
clopamide a thiazide diuretic 99
Clopixol a brand name for zuclopenthixol (an antipsychotic 85)
clorazepate a benzodiazepine anti-anxiety drug 83
clotrimazole 242 (an antifungal 138)
cloxacillin a penicillin antibiotic 128
clozapine 243 (an antipsychotic 85)
Clozaril a brand name for clozapine 243 (an antipsychotic 85); *illus. 37M*
coal tar a substance for psoriasis 178 and eczema 175
co-amilofruse a generic substance containing amiloride 193 with frusemide 290 (both diuretics 99)
co-amilozide a generic substance containing amiloride 193 with hydrochlorothiazide 299 (both diuretics 99)
co-amoxiclav a generic substance containing amoxycillin 196 (a penicillin

antibiotic 128) with clavulanic acid (a substance that increases the effectiveness of amoxycillin)
co-beneldopa a generic substance containing levodopa 315 (a drug for *parkinsonism* 87) with benserazide (a drug that enhances the effect of levodopa)
Co-Betaloc a brand name for hydro-chlorothiazide 299 (a thiazide diuretic 99) with metoprolol (a beta-blocker 97)
co-careldopa a generic substance containing carbidopa with levodopa 315 (both drugs for *parkinsonism* 87)
co-codamol a generic substance containing codeine 244 with paracetamol 356 (both analgesics 80)
co-codaprin a generic substance containing aspirin 199 with codeine 244 (both analgesics 80)
Codafen continus a brand name for codeine 244 (a *narcotic* analgesic 80) and ibuprofen (a non-steroidal anti-inflammatory 116)
Coda-Med a brand-name *analgesic* 80 containing codeine 244, aspirin 199, and caffeine
co-danthramer a generic substance containing danthron with poloxamer (both stimulant laxatives 111)
co-danthrusate a generic substance containing danthron with docusate (both stimulant laxatives 111)
codeine 244 (a *narcotic* analgesic 80, antidiarrhoeal 110, and cough suppressant 94)
co-dergocrine mesylate a *vasodilator* 98 used to improve blood flow to the brain in senile dementia
Codis a brand name for aspirin 199 with codeine 244 (both analgesics 80)
co-dydramol a generic substance containing paracetamol 356 with dihydrocodeine (both *analgesics* 80)
co-fluampicil a generic substance containing flucloxacillin with ampicillin (both penicillin antibiotics 128)
co-flumactone a generic substance containing hydroflumethiazide with spironolactone 397(both diuretics 99)
Cogentin a brand name for benztropine (an *anticholinergic* for *parkinsonism* 87)
Cojene a brand-name *analgesic* 80 containing codeine 244, aspirin 199, and caffeine
colchicine 245 (a drug for gout 119)
Colestid a brand name for colestipol (a lipid-lowering drug 103)
colestipol a lipid-lowering drug 103
Colifoam hydrocortisone 300 (a corticosteroid 141)
colistin an antibiotic 128
collodion a substance that dries to form a sticky film, protecting broken skin 175
Colofac a brand name for mebeverine (an *antispasmodic* for irritable bowel syndrome 110)
Colomycin a brand name for colistin (an antibiotic 128)

Colpermin a brand name for peppermint oil (a substance for indigestion 108 and spasm of the bowel 110)
Colven a brand name for ispaghula husk (a bulk-forming agent used as a laxative 111 and antidiarrhoeal 110) with mebeverine (an *antispasmodic* 110)
co-magaldrox a generic substance containing aluminium hydroxide 191 with magnesium hydroxide 323 (both antacids 108)
Combantrin a brand name for pyrantel (an anthelmintic 139)
Comox a brand name for co-trimoxazole 248 (an antibacterial 131)
Compliment Continus a brand name for pyridoxine 428 (a vitamin 149)
Compound W a brand-name keratolytic treatment for warts containing salicylic acid
Concavit a brand-name multivitamin 149
Concordin a brand name for protriptyline (a tricyclic antidepressant 84)
conjugated oestrogens 246 (a female sex *hormone* 147)
Conotrane a brand name for benz-alkonium chloride (a skin *antiseptic* 175) with dimethicone (a base for skin preparations 175)
Conova 30 a brand-name oral contracep-tive containing ethinyloestradiol 282 and ethynodiol
Contac 400 a brand name for chlorpheniramine 227 (an antihistamine 124) with phenylpropanolamine 365 (a decongestant 93)
co-phenotrope a generic substance containing diphenoxylate 265 with atropine 201
copper 423 (a mineral 150)
co-prenozide a generic substance containing oxprenolol 355 (a beta blocker 97) with cyclopenthiazide 249 (a thiazide diuretic 99)
co-proxamol 247 (a *narcotic analgesic* 80); *illus. 46J*
Coracten a brand name for nifedipine (an anti-angina drug 101 and antihypertensive 102)
Cordarone X a brand name for amiodarone 194 (an anti-arrhythmic 100); *illus. 42T*
Cordilox a brand name for verapamil 418 (an anti-angina drug 101 and anti-arrhythmic 100); *illus. 37A*
Corgard a brand name for nadolol (a beta blocker 97)
Corgaretic a brand name for bendrofluazide 206 (a thiazide diuretic 99) with nadolol (a beta blocker 97)
Corlan a brand name for hydrocortisone 300 (a corticosteroid 141); *illus. 46D*
Coro-Nitro a brand name for glyceryl trinitrate 294 (an anti-angina drug 101)
corticotrophin a pituitary *hormone* 145
cortisone a corticosteroid 141
Cortistab a brand name for cortisone (a corticosteroid 141)
Cortisyl a brand name for cortisone (a corticosteroid 141)
Cosalgesic a brand name for co-proxamol 247 (a *narcotic analgesic* 80)

CO-SIMALCITE – DITHROCREAM

co-simalcite a generic substance containing hydrotalcite (an antacid 108) with dimethicone (an antifoaming agent)

Cosmegen Lyovac a brand name for actinomycin (an anticancer drug 154)

Cosuric a brand name for allopurinol 189 (a drug for gout 119)

co-tenidone a generic substance containing atenolol 200 (a beta blocker 97) with chlorthalidone (a thiazide diuretic 99)

co-triamterzide a generic substance containing hydrochlorthiazide 299 with triamterene 415 (both diuretics 99)

co-trimoxazole 248 (an antibacterial 131)

Coversyl a brand name for perindopril (an ACE inhibitor 98)

Cremalgin Balm a brand name for a *topical* preparation for muscular pain relief containing glycol monosalicylate, methyl nicotinate, and capiscum oleoresin

Creon a brand name for pancreatin (a preparation of pancreatic *enzymes* 114)

Cromogen a brand name for sodium cromoglycate (an anti-allergy drug 394)

crotamiton an antipruritic 173 and antiparasitic 176 for scabies

crystal violet a dye for skin infections 175

Crystapen a brand name for penicillin G (a penicillin antibiotic 128)

Cupanol a brand name for paracetamol 356 (a non-*narcotic analgesic* 80)

Cuplex a brand-name wart preparation containing copper acetate, lactic acid, and salicylic acid

Cuprofen a brand name for ibuprofen 302 (a non-steroidal anti-inflammatory 116)

cyanocobalamin vitamin B_{12} 431 (a vitamin 149)

Cyclimorph a brand name for morphine 339 (a *narcotic analgesic* 80) with cyclizine (an anti-emetic 90)

cyclizine an antihistamine 124 used as an anti-emetic 90

cyclobarbitone a barbiturate sleeping drug 82

Cyclobral a brand name for cyclandelate (a *vasodilator* 98)

Cyclocaps a brand name for salbutamol (a *bronchodilator* 92)

cyclofenil a drug similar to clomiphene 238 used for infertility 164

Cyclogest a brand name for progesterone (a female sex *hormone* 147)

cyclopenthiazide 249 (a thiazide diuretic 99)

cyclopentolate an *anticholinergic mydriatic* 170

cyclophosphamide 250 (an anticancer drug 154)

Cyclo-Progynova a brand name for oestradiol with norgestrel (both female sex *hormones* 147)

cycloserine an antibiotic 128 for tuberculosis 132

cyclosporin 251 (an immunosuppressant 156)

Cyklokapron a brand name for tranexamic acid (an antifibrinolytic used to promote blood clotting 104)

Cymalon a brand-name preparation for cystitis containing sodium bicarbonate, citric acid, sodium citrate, and sodium carbonate

Cymevene a brand name for ganciclovir (an antiviral 133)

cyproheptadine an antihistamine 124 used to stimulate the appetite 88

Cyprostat a brand name for cyproterone acetate 252 (a synthetic sex *hormone* used for acne 177 and cancer of the prostate 154)

cyproterone acetate 252 (a synthetic sex *hormone* used for acne 177, cancer of the prostate 154, and male sexual disorders)

Cystoleve a brand name for sodium citrate used for cystitis

Cystopurin a brand name for potassium citrate used for cystitis

Cystrin a brand name for oxybutynin (an *anticholinergic* and *antispasmodic* for urinary disorders 166)

Cytamen a brand name for cyanocobalamin (vitamin B_{12} 431)

cytarabine a drug for leukaemia 154

Cytotec a brand name for misoprostol 337 (an anti-ulcer drug 109)

D

dacarbazine a drug for malignant melanoma and cancer of soft tissues 154

dactinomycin a *cytotoxic* antibiotic for cancer 154

Daktacort a brand name for hydro-cortisone 300 (a corticosteroid 141) with miconazole (an antifungal 138)

Daktarin a brand name for miconazole (an antifungal 138)

Dalacin C a brand name for clindamycin (a lincosamide antibiotic 128)

Dalmane a brand name for flurazepam (a benzodiazepine sleeping drug 82)

danazol 253 (a drug for menstrual disorders 160)

Daneral-SA a brand name for pheniramine (an antihistamine 124)

Danol a brand name for danazol 253 (a drug for menstrual disorders 160); *illus. 40 O*

Danol-1/2 a brand name for danazol 253 (a drug for menstrual disorders 160)

danthron a stimulant laxative 111

Dantrium a brand name for dantrolene (a muscle relaxant 120)

dantrolene a muscle relaxant 120

Daonil a brand name for glibenclamide 293 (an oral antidiabetic 142); *illus. 46M*

dapsone 254 (an antibacterial 131); *illus. 45A*

Daranide a brand name for dichlorphen-amide (a carbonic anhydrase inhibitor for glaucoma 168)

Daraprim a brand name for pyrimethamine 383 (an antimalarial 137); *illus. 44M*

Davenol a brand name for ephedrine 277 (a *bronchodilator* 92 and decongestant 93) with carbinoxamine (an antihistamine 124) and pholcodine (a cough suppressant 94)

Day Nurse Capsules a brand name for dextromethorphan 256 (a cough suppressant 94) with paracetamol 356 (a non-*narcotic analgesic* 80) and phenylpropanolamine 365 (a decongestant 93)

Decadron a brand name for dexamethasone 255 (a corticosteroid 141); *illus. 45G*

Deca-Durabolin-100 a brand name for nandrolone (an anabolic steroid 146)

Decortisyl a brand name for prednisone (a corticosteroid 141)

Delfen brand name for nonoxinol 9 (a spermicidal agent)

Deltacortril a brand name for prednisolone 372 (a corticosteroid 141); *illus. 35J*

Deltastab a brand name for prednisolone 372 (a corticosteroid 141)

demeclocycline a tetracycline antibiotic 128

De-Nol a brand name for bismuth (a substance for gastric and duodenal ulcers 109)

De-Noltab a brand name for bismuth (a substance for gastric and duodenal ulcers 109)

Depixol a brand name for flupenthixol (an antipsychotic 85 and antidepressant 84)

Depo-Medrone a brand name for methyl-prednisolone (a corticosteroid 141)

Deponit a brand name for glyceryl trinitrate 294 (an anti-angina drug 101)

Depo-Provera a brand name for medroxyprogesterone 324 (a female sex *hormone* 147)

Depostat a brand name for gestronol (a progestogen 147)

Dequacaine a brand name for benzocaine (a local *anaesthetic* 80) with dequalinium (an antibacterial 131)

Dequadin a brand name for dequalinium (an antibacterial 131)

dequalinium an antibacterial 131 used for mouth infections

Derbac-C a brand-name shampoo containing carbaryl (an antiparasitic 176)

Derbac-M a brand-name shampoo containing malathion (an anti-parasitic 176)

Dermacort a brand-name preparation for hydrocortisone cream 300

Dermidex Cream a brand-name topical preparation for skin irritation containing chlorbutol, lignocaine, cetrimide, and aluminium chlorhydroxyallantoinate

Dermovate a brand name for clobetasol (a *topical* corticosteroid 174)

Dermovate NN a brand name for nystatin 350 (an antifungal 138) with clobetasol (a *topical* corticosteroid 174) and neomycin (an aminoglycoside antibiotic 128)

Deseril a brand name for methysergide (a drug used to prevent migraine 89)

desipramine a tricyclic antidepressant 84

desmopressin a drug similar to vasopressin (a pituitary *hormone* 145) used for diabetes insipidus 142

desogestrel a progestogen 147

desoxymethasone a *topical* corticosteroid 174

Destolit a brand name for ursodeoxycholic acid 417 (a drug for gallstones 114); *illus. 42H*

Deteclo a brand name for tetracycline 407 with chlortetracycline and demeclocycline (all tetracycline antibiotics 128)

Dettol a brand-name liquid skin *antiseptic* 175 containing chloroxylenol

dexamethasone 255 (a corticosteroid 141)

dexamphetamine an amphetamine 436

Dexa-Rhinaspray a brand name for dexamethasone 255 (a corticosteroid 141) with neomycin (an aminoglycoside antibiotic 128) and tramazoline (a nasal decongestant 93)

Dexedrine a brand name for dexamphetamine (an amphetamine 436)

Dexfenfluramine a drug for weight reduction

dextromethorphan 256 (a cough suppressant 94)

dextromoramide 257 (a *narcotic analgesic* 80)

dextropropoxyphene a constituent of co-proxamol (247) (a *narcotic analgesic* 80)

DF 118 a brand name for dihydrocodeine (a *narcotic analgesic* 80)

DHC Continus a brand name for dihydrocodeine (a *narcotic analgesic* 80)

Diabinese a brand name for chlorpropamide 229 (an oral antidiabetic 142); *illus. 45B*

Diamicron a brand name for gliclazide (an oral antidiabetic 142)

diamorphine 258 (a *narcotic analgesic* 80)

Diamox a brand name for acetazolamide 186 (a carbonic anhydrase inhibitor diuretic 99); *illus. 42L*

Dianette a brand name for cyproterone 252 (a synthetic sex *hormone* used for acne 177) with ethinyloestradiol 282 (a female sex *hormone* 147)

Diarrest a brand-name antidiarrhoeal 110 containing dicyclomine 261 and codeine 244

Diazemuls a brand name for diazepam 259 (a benzodiazepine anti-anxiety drug 83, muscle relaxant 120, and anticonvulsant 86)

diazepam 259 (a benzodiazepine anti-anxiety drug 83, muscle relaxant 120, and anticonvulsant 86)

diazoxide an antihypertensive 102 also used for hypoglycaemia 142

Dibenyline a brand name for phenoxy-benzamine (a *sympathomimetic* vasodilator 98 used for hypertension 102)

dichloralphenazone a form of chloral hydrate 223

dichlorphenamide a carbonic anyhdrase inhibitor for glaucoma 168

diclofenac 260 (a non-steroidal anti-inflammatory 116)

Diclomax Retard a brand name for diclofenac sodium 260 (a non-steroidal anti-inflammatory 116)

dicobalt edetate an *antidote* to cyanide poisoning

Diconal a brand name for dipipanone (a *narcotic analgesic* 80)

dicyclomine 261 (a drug for irritable bowel syndrome 110)

Dicynene a brand name for ethamsylate (an antifibrinolytic used to promote blood clotting 104)

Didronel a brand name for etidronate 284 (a drug for bone disorders 122)

dienoestrol a female sex *hormone* 147 applied as a cream for vaginal dryness

diethylcarbamazine an anthelmintic 139

diethylpropion an appetite suppressant 88

Difflam a brand name for benzydamine (an *analgesic* 80)

Diflucan a brand name for fluconazole (an antifungal 138); *illus. 41H, 41 O*

diflucortolone a *topical* corticosteroid 174

diflunisal a non-steroidal anti-inflammatory 116

digitoxin a digitalis drug 96

digoxin 262 (a digitalis drug 96)

Dihydergot a brand name for dihydro-ergotamine (a drug for migraine and cluster headaches 89)

dihydrocodeine a *narcotic analgesic* 80

dihydroergotamine a drug for migraine and cluster headaches 89

dihydrotachysterol vitamin D 432 (a vitamin 149)

Dijex a brand name for aluminium hydroxide 191 with magnesium hydroxide 323 (both antacids 108)

diloxanide furoate an antiprotozoal 136 for amoebic dysentery

diltiazem 263 (an antihypertensive 106 and anti-angina drug 101)

dimenhydrinate an antihistamine 124 used as an anti-emetic 90

dimethicone a silicone-based substance used in barrier creams 175 and as an antifoaming agent 108

dimethindene an antihistamine 124

Dimetriose a brand name for gestrinone (a drug for menstrual disorders 160)

Dimotane a brand name for brompheniramine (an antihistamine 124)

Dimotapp a brand name for phenylephrine 364 with phenyl-propanolamine 380 (both deconges-tants 93) and brompheniramine (an antihistamine 124)

Dimyril a brand name for isoaminile (a cough suppressant 94)

Dindevan a brand name for phenindione (an oral anticoagulant 104)

dinoprost a prostaglandin used to terminate pregnancy 165

dinoprostone a prostaglandin used to terminate pregnancy 165

Diocalm a brand-name antidiarrhoeal 110 containing attapulgite and morphine 339

Diocalm Ultra a brand name for loperamide 320 (an antidiarrhoeal 110)

Dioctyl a brand name for docusate (a stimulant laxative 111)

Dioderm a brand name for hydrocortisone 300 (a corticosteroid 141)

Dioralyte a brand name for rehydration salts containing sodium bicarbonate 393, glucose, potassium chloride, and sodium chloride

Diovol a brand-name antacid 108 containing aluminium hydroxide 191, magnesium hydroxide 323, and dimethicone

Dipentum a brand name for olsalazine (a drug for ulcerative colitis 112)

diphenhydramine 264 (an antihistamine 124 and anti-emetic 90)

diphenoxylate 265 (a *narcotic* antidiarrhoeal 110)

diphenylpyraline an antihistamine 124

dipipanone a *narcotic analgesic* 80

dipivefrin a *sympathomimetic* for glaucoma 168

Diprosalic a brand-name skin preparation containing betamethasone 210 (a corticosteroid 141) and salicylic acid (a keratolytic)

Diprosone a brand name for beta-methasone 210 (a corticosteroid 141)

dipyridamole 266 (an antiplatelet drug 104)

Dirythmin SA a brand name for disopyramide 267 (an anti-arrhythmic 100)

Disalcid a brand name for salsalate (a non-steroidal anti-inflammatory 116 similar to aspirin 199)

Disipal a brand name for orphenadrine 354 (a drug for *parkinsonism* 87); *illus. 36N*

disopyramide 267 (an anti-arrhythmic 100)

Disprin a brand name for soluble aspirin 199 (a non-*narcotic analgesic* 80)

Disprin Extra a brand-name soluble *analgesic* 80 containing aspirin 199 and paracetamol 356

Disprol a brand name for paracetamol 356 (a non-*narcotic analgesic* 80)

Distaclor a brand name for cefaclor 220 (a cephalosporin antibiotic 128); *illus. 38 I*

Distalgesic a brand name for co-proxamol 247 (a *narcotic analgesic* 80)

Distamine a brand name for penicillamine 357 (an antirheumatic 117); *illus. 43E*

Distaquaine V-K a brand name for phenoxymethylpenicillin 362 (a penicillin antibiotic 128)

distigmine a *parasympathomimetic* for urinary retention 166 and myasthenia gravis 121

disulfiram 268 (an alcohol abuse deterrent)

dithranol 269 (a drug for psoriasis 178)

Dithrocream a brand name for dithranol 269 (a drug for psoriasis 178)

DITHROLAN – FLORINEF

Dithrolan a brand name for dithranol 269 with salicylic acid (both drugs for psoriasis 178)

Ditropan a brand name for oxybutynin (an *anticholinergic* and *antispasmodic* for urinary disorders 166)

Diumide-K a brand name for frusemide 290 (a loop diuretic 99 and antihypertensive 102) with potassium 427; *illus. 38K*

Diurexan a brand name for xipamide (a thiazide diuretic 99)

Dixarit a brand name for clonidine 241 (a drug for migraine 89); *illus. 38H*

Doans Backache Pills a brand name for paracetamol 356 and sodium salicylate (both non-*narcotic analgesics* 80)

dobutamine a drug for heart failure and shock

docusate a faecal softener, stimulant laxative 111, and ear wax softener

Do-Do Tablets a brand-name bronchodilator 92 and decongestant 93 containing ephedrine 277, theophylline 408, and caffeine

Dolmatil a brand name for sulpiride (an antipsychotic 85)

Dolobid a brand name for diflunisal (a non-steroidal anti-inflammatory 116)

Doloxene a brand name for dextropropoxyphene (a *narcotic analgesic* 80)

Domical a brand name for amitriptyline 195 (a tricyclic antidepressant 84)

domperidone 270 (an anti-emetic 90)

Dopamet a brand name for methyldopa 332 (an antihypertensive 102)

Doralese a brand name for indoramin (an antihypertensive 102)

dothiepin 271 (a tricyclic antidepressant 84)

Dovonex a brand name for calcipotriol 214

doxapram a respiratory stimulant 88

doxazosin a *sympatholytic* antihypertensive 102

doxepin a tricyclic antidepressant 84

doxorubicin 272 (a *cytotoxic* anticancer drug 154)

doxycycline 273 (a tetracycline antibiotic 128)

doxylamine an antihistamine 124

Dozic a brand name for haloperidol 296 (a butyrophenone antipsychotic 85)

Dramamine a brand name for dimenhydrinate (an antihistamine 124 used as an anti-emetic 90)

Drapolene a brand name for benzalkonium chloride with cetrimide (both *antiseptics* 175)

Driclor a brand name for aluminium chloride (an *antiperspirant* 446)

Dristan Nasal Spray a brand name for oxymetazoline hydrochloride (a *topical* decongestant 93)

Drogenil a brand name for flutamide (an anticancer drug 154)

Droleptan a brand name for droperidol (a butyrophenone antipsychotic 85)

droperidol a butyrophenone antipsychotic 85

Dryptal a brand name for frusemide 290 (a loop diuretic 99 and antihypertensive 102)

Dulco-Lax a brand name for bisacodyl (a stimulant laxative 111)

Duofilm a brand-name wart preparation containing lactic acid, salicylic acid, and collodion

Duovent a brand name for fenoterol with ipratropium (both *bronchodilators* 92)

Duphalac a brand name for lactulose 314 (a laxative 111)

Duphaston a brand name for dydrogesterone 274 (a female sex *hormone* 147); *illus. 42K*

Durabolin a brand name for nandrolone (an anabolic steroid 146)

Duracreme a brand name for nonoxinol 11 (a spermicidal agent)

Duragel a brand name for nonoxinol 11 (a spermicidal agent)

Duromine a brand name for phentermine (an appetite suppressant 88)

Duvadilan a brand name for isoxsuprine (a uterine muscle relaxant 165)

Dyazide a brand name for hydrochlorothiazide 299 with triamterene 415 (both diuretics 99)

dydrogesterone 274 (a female sex *hormone* 147)

Dynese a brand name for magaldrate (an antacid 108)

Dyspamet a brand name for cimetidine 232 (an anti-ulcer drug 109)

Dysport a brand name for botulinum *toxin* (used as a muscle relaxant 120)

Dytac a brand name for triamterene 415 (a potassium-sparing diuretic 99); *illus. 39A*

Dytide a brand name for benzthiazide with triamterene 415 (both diuretics 99)

E

Earex Ear Drops a brand-name preparation for removal of ear wax

Ebufac a brand name for ibuprofen 302 (a non-steroidal anti-inflammatory 116)

Econacort a brand name for econazole 275 (an antifungal 138) with hydrocortisone 300 (a corticosteroid 141)

econazole 275 (an antifungal 138)

Economycin a brand name for tetracycline 407 (an antibiotic 128)

Ecostatin a brand name for econazole 275 (an antifungal 138)

Eczederm a brand name for arachis oil (an *emollient*) with calamine (an antipruritic 173)

Edecrin a brand name for ethacrynic acid (a loop diuretic 99)

Efamast a brand name for gamolenic acid (a drug used to treat breast pain); *illus. 39G*

Efcortelan a brand name for hydrocortisone 300 (a corticosteroid 141)

Efcortesol a brand name for hydrocortisone 300 (a corticosteroid 141)

Effercitrate a brand name for potassium 427

Efudix a brand name for fluorouracil (an anticancer drug 154)

Elantan a brand name for isosorbide mononitrate (a nitrate *vasodilator* 98 and anti-angina drug 101)

Elavil a brand name for amitriptyline 195 (a tricyclic antidepressant 84)

Eldepryl a brand name for selegiline (a drug for *parkinsonism* 87)

Electrolade a brand name for oral rehydration salts containing potassium 427, sodium bicarbonate 393, sodium chloride 429, and glucose

Elocon a brand name for mometasone (a *topical* corticosteroid 174)

Eltroxin a brand name for thyroxine 410 (a thyroid hormone 144); *illus. 46B*

Emcor a brand name for bisoprolol (a beta blocker 97)

Emeside a brand name for ethosuximide 283 (an anticonvulsant 86); *illus. 39E*

Emflex a brand name for acemetacin (a non-steroidal anti-inflammatory 116)

enalapril 276 (a *vasodilator* 98 and antihypertensive 102)

En-De-Kay a brand name for fluoride 424 (a mineral 150)

Endoxana a brand name for cyclophosphamide 250 (an anticancer drug 154); *illus. 44K*

Enduron a brand name for methyclothiazide (a thiazide diuretic 99)

ENO a brand-name antacid 108 containing sodium bicarbonate, sodium carbonate, and citric acid

enoxaparin a drug to prevent blood clotting 104

Entamizole a brand name for diloxanide furoate (an antiprotozoal 136)

Epanutin a brand name for phenytoin 366 (an anticonvulsant 86); *illus. 40H*

Epelix Worm Elixir a brand name for piperazine 368 (an anthelmintic 139)

ephedrine 277 (a *bronchodilator* 92 and decongestant 93)

Epifoam a brand name for hydrocortisone 300 (a corticosteroid 141) with pramoxine (a local *anaesthetic* 80)

Epifrin a brand name for adrenaline 188 (a drug for glaucoma 168)

Epilim a brand name for sodium valproate 395 (an anticonvulsant 86); *illus. 43 O*

epirubicin a *cytotoxic* anticancer drug 154

epoetin alfa a name for erythropoietin 278 (a kidney hormone 140)

Epogam a brand name for gamolenic acid (a drug for eczema 291)

Eppy a brand name for adrenaline 188 (a drug for glaucoma 168)

Eprex a brand name for erythropoietin 278 (a kidney hormone 140 used for anaemia due to kidney failure)

Equagesic a brand name for aspirin 199 with ethoheptazine (*analgesics* 80) and meprobamate (an anti-anxiety drug 83)

Eradacin a brand name for acrosoxacin (an antibacterial 131)

ergocalciferol vitamin D 432 (a vitamin 149)

ergometrine a uterine stimulant 165
ergotamine 279 (a drug for migraine 89)
Erycen a brand name for erythromycin 280 (an antibiotic 128)
Erymax a brand name for erythromycin 280 (an antibiotic 128)
Erythrocin a brand name for erythromycin 280 (an antibiotic 128)
Erythromid a brand name for erythromycin 280 (an antibiotic 128); *illus. 35M*
erythromycin 280 (an antibiotic 128)
Erythroped a brand name for erythromycin 280 (an antibiotic 128)
erythropoietin 278 (a kidney hormone 140 used for anaemia due to kidney failure)
Esidrex a brand name for hydrochlorothiazide 299 (a thiazide diuretic 99)
Eskamel a brand name for resorcinol (a drug for acne 177) with sulphur (a *topical* antibacterial 131 and antifungal 138)
Eskornade a brand name for phenylpropanolamine 365 (a decongestant 93) with diphenylpyraline (an antihistamine 124)
esmolol a beta blocker 97
Estracyt a brand name for estramustine (an alkylating agent 154)
estramustine an alkylating agent for cancer of the prostate 154
ethacrynic acid a loop diuretic 99
ethambutol 281 (an antituberculous drug 132)
ethamsylate an antifibrinolytic used to promote blood clotting 104
ethinyloestradiol 282 (a female sex *hormone* 147)
ethionamide a drug for leprosy 131
ethoheptazine a *narcotic analgesic* 80
ethosuximide 283 (an anticonvulsant 86)
ethynodiol diacetate a progestogen 147
etidronate 284 (a drug for bone disorders 122)
etodolac a non-steroidal anti-inflammatory 116
etomidate a drug for induction of general *anaesthesia* 80
etoposide a drug for cancers of the lung, lymphatic system, and testicles 154
Eudemine a brand name for diazoxide (an antihypertensive 102 also used for hypoglycaemia 142)
Euglucon a brand name for glibenclamide 293 (an oral antidiabetic 142)
Eugynon 30 a brand-name oral contraceptive containing ethinyloestradiol 282 and levonorgestrel 316; *illus. 45N*
Eumovate a brand name for clobetasone (a *topical* corticosteroid 174)
Eumovate-N a brand name for clobetasone (a *topical* corticosteroid 174) with neomycin (an aminoglycoside antibiotic 128)
Eurax a brand name for crotamiton (an antipruritic 173)
Eurax-Hydrocortisone a brand name for hydrocortisone 300 (a corticosteroid 141) with crotamiton (an antipruritic 173)
Evadyne a brand name for butriptyline (a tricyclic antidepressant 84)

Evorel a brand name for oestradiol (an oestrogen 351)
Exelderm a brand name for sulconazole (an antifungal 138)
Exirel a brand name for pirbutolol (a bronchodilator 92)
Ex-Lax a brand name for phenolphthalein (a stimulant laxative 111)
Exolan a brand name for dithranol 269 (a drug for psoriasis 178)
Expulin a brand-name cough preparation 94 containing chlorpheniramine 227, menthol, pholcodine, and pseudoephedrine
Expurhin a brand-name decongestant 93 containing chlorpheniramine 227, ephedrine 277, and menthol

F

Fabahistin a brand name for mebhydrolin (an antihistamine 124)
Fabrol a brand name for acetylcysteine (a *mucolytic* 94)
factor VIII a blood extract to promote blood clotting 104
famotidine an anti-ulcer drug 109
Fansidar a brand-name antimalarial 137 containing pyrimethamine 383 and sulfadoxine
Farlutal a brand name for medroxyprogesterone 324 (a female sex *hormone* 147)
Fasigyn a brand name for tinidazole (an antibacterial 131)
Faverin a brand name for fluvoxamine (an antidepressant 84)
Fectrim a brand name for co-trimoxazole 248 (an antibacterial 131)
Fefol a brand name for folic acid 424 (a vitamin 149) with iron 425 (a mineral 150)
Fefol-Vit a brand name for folic acid 424 (a vitamin 149) with iron 425 (a mineral 150) and several B vitamins
Fefol Z a brand name for folic acid 424 (a vitamin 149) with iron 425 and zinc 433 (both minerals 150)
Feldene a brand name for piroxicam 369 (a non-steroidal anti-inflammatory 116 and drug for gout 119); *illus. 39B*
felodipine a calcium channel blocker 101
Femeron a brand name for miconazole (an antifungal 142)
Femigraine a brand-name drug for migraine containing aspirin 199 (a non-*narcotic analgesic* 80) with cyclizine (an anti-emetic 90)
Feminax a brand-name analgesic 80 for dysmenorrhoea containing paracetamol 356, codeine 244, hyoscine 301, and caffeine
Femodene a brand-name oral contraceptive 161 containing ethinyloestradiol 282 and gestodene

Femulen a brand-name oral contraceptive 161 containing ethynodiol diacetate
Fenbid a brand name for ibuprofen 302 (a non-steroidal anti-inflammatory 116)
fenbufen 285 (a non-steroidal anti-inflammatory 116)
fenfluramine an appetite suppressant 88 related to amphetamine 436
fenofibrate a lipid-lowering drug 103
fenoprofen a non-steroidal anti-inflammatory 116
Fenopron a brand name for fenoprofen (a non-steroidal anti-inflammatory 116)
Fenostil Retard a brand name for dimethindene (an antihistamine 124)
fenoterol a *sympathomimetic bronchodilator* 92
fentanyl a *narcotic analgesic* 80 used in general *anaesthesia*
Fentazin a brand name for perphenazine (an antipsychotic 85 and anti-emetic 90)
Feospan a brand name for iron 425 (a mineral 150)
Fergon a brand name for iron 425 (a mineral 150)
ferric ammonium citrate iron 425 (a mineral 150)
Ferrocap F 350 a brand name for folic acid 424 (a vitamin 149) with iron 425 (a mineral 150)
Ferrograd a brand name for iron 425 (a mineral 150)
Ferrograd C a brand name for iron 425 (a mineral 150) with vitamin C 431 (a vitamin 149)
Ferrograd Folic a brand name for folic acid 424 (a vitamin 149) with iron 425 (a mineral 150)
Ferromyn a brand name for ferrous succinate iron 425 (a mineral 150)
ferrous fumarate iron 425 (a mineral 150)
ferrous gluconate iron 425 (a mineral 150)
ferrous succinate iron 425 (a mineral 150)
ferrous sulphate iron 425 (a mineral 150)
Fersaday a brand name for iron 425 (a mineral 150)
Fersamal a brand name for iron 425 (a mineral 150)
fibrinolysin a thrombolytic *enzyme* used to break down blood clots 104 and aid healing of skin ulcers 109
finasteride a drug for benign prostatic hypertrophy
Flagyl a brand name for metronidazole 334 (an antibacterial 131 and antiprotozoal 136); *illus. 43D*
Flamazine a brand name for silver sulphadiazine (a *topical* antibacterial 131)
flavoxate 286 (a urinary *antispasmodic* 166)
flecainide an anti-arrhythmic 100
Flemoxin a brand name for amoxycillin (a penicillin antibiotic 128)
Flexin Continus brand name for indomethacin (a non-steroidal anti-inflammatory 116)
Flixonase a brand name for fluticasone 289 (a corticosteroid 141)
Florinef a brand name for fludrocortisone (a corticosteroid 141)

FLOXAPEN – HYDROCORTISONE

Floxapen a brand name for flucloxacillin (a penicillin antibiotic 128)

Flu-Amp a brand name for ampicillin with flucloxacillin (both penicillin antibiotics 128)

Fluanxol a brand name for flupenthixol (an antipsychotic 85 used in depression 84)

fluclorolone a *topical* corticosteroid 174

flucloxacillin a penicillin antibiotic 128

fluconazole 287 (an antifungal 138)

flucytosine an antifungal 138

fludrocortisone a corticosteroid 141

flumethasone a corticosteroid 141

flunisolide a corticosteroid 141

flunitrazepam a benzodiazepine sleeping drug 82

fluocinolone a *topical* corticosteroid 174

Fluor-a-day a brand name for fluoride 424 (a mineral 150)

fluoride 424 (a mineral 150)

Fluorigard a brand name for fluoride 424 (a mineral 150)

fluorometholone a corticosteroid 141 for eye disorders

fluorouracil an antimetabolite for various tumours 154

fluoxetine 288 (an antidepressant 84)

flupenthixol an antipsychotic 85 used in depression 84

fluphenazine an antipsychotic 85 used in depression 84

flurandrenolone a *topical* corticosteroid 174

flurazepam a benzodiazepine sleeping drug 82

flurbiprofen a non-steroidal anti-inflammatory 116

Flurex Capsules a brand name for paracetamol 356 (a non-narcotic analgesic 80) with phenylephrine 364 (a decongestant 93) and dextromethorphan 256 (a cough suppressant 94)

fluspirilene an antipsychotic 85

flutamide an anticancer drug 154

fluticasone 289 (a corticosteroid 141)

fluvoxamine an antidepressant 84

FML a brand name for fluorometholone (a corticosteroid 141)

folate sodium folic acid 424 (a vitamin 149)

Folex-350 a brand name for folic acid 424 (a vitamin 149) with iron 425 (a mineral 150)

folic acid 424 (a vitamin 149)

Folicin a brand name for folic acid 424 (a vitamin 149) with minerals

follicle-stimulating hormone a natural *hormone* for infertility 164

formestane a drug for breast cancer 154

Fortral a brand name for pentazocine 358 (a *narcotic analgesic* 80); *illus. 43M*

Fortum a brand name for ceftazidime (a cephalosporin antibiotic 128)

foscarnet an antiviral 133

Foscavir a brand name for foscarnet (an antiviral 133)

fosfestrol a female *sex hormone* 147 and anticancer drug 154

fosinopril an ACE inhibitor 98

framycetin a *topical* aminoglycoside antibiotic 128 for ear, eye, and skin infections

frangula a mild stimulant laxative 111

Franol a brand-name *bronchodilator* 92 containing ephedrine 277 and theophylline 408

Franol Plus a brand-name *bronchodilator* 92 containing ephedrine 277 and theophylline 408

Franolyn for Chesty Coughs a brand-name decongestant 93 and expectorant 94 containing guaiphenesin, theophylline 408, and ephedrine 277

Frisium a brand name for clobazam (a benzodiazepine anti-anxiety drug 83)

Froben a brand name for flurbiprofen (a non-steroidal anti-inflammatory drug 116)

Fru-Co a brand name for amiloride 193 with frusemide 290 (both diuretics 99)

Frumil a brand name for amiloride 193 with frusemide 290 (both diuretics 99)

frusemide 290 (a loop diuretic 99)

Frusene a brand name for frusemide 290 with triamterene 415 (both diuretics 99)

Frusetic a brand name for frusemide 290 (a loop diuretic 99)

Frusid a brand name for frusemide 290 (a loop diuretic 99)

FSH follicle-stimulating hormone (a natural *hormone* for infertility 164)

Fucibet a brand name for betamethasone 210 (a corticosteroid 141) with fusidic acid (an antibiotic 128)

Fucidin a brand name for fusidic acid (an antibiotic 128)

Fucidin H a brand name for fusidic acid (an antibiotic 128) and hydrocortisone 300 (a corticosteroid 141)

Fulcin a brand name for griseofulvin 295 (an antifungal 138); *illus. 42B*

Fungilin a brand name for amphotericin 197 (an antifungal 138); *illus. 37F*

Fungizone a brand name for amphotericin 197 (an antifungal 138)

Furadantin a brand name for nitrofurantoin 348 (an antibacterial 131)

Furamide a brand name for diloxanide furoate (an antiprotozoal 136)

fusidic acid an antibiotic 128

Fybogel a brand name for ispaghula (a bulk-forming agent used as a laxative 111 and antidiarrhoeal 110)

Fynnon Salt a brand name for sodium sulphate (an osmotic laxative 111)

G

Galcodine a brand name for codeine 244 (a cough suppressant 94)

Galenamox a brand name for amoxycillin (a penicillin antibiotic 128)

Galenphol a brand name for pholcodine (a cough suppressant 94)

Galfer a brand name for iron 425 (a mineral 150)

Galfer FA a brand name for folic acid 424 (a vitamin 149) with iron 425 (a mineral 150)

Galpseud a brand name for pseudo-ephedrine (a *sympathomimetic* decongestant 93)

Gamanil a brand name for lofepramine 319 (a tricyclic antidepressant 84); *illus. 35 O*

gamma globulin immune globulin 134

gamolenic acid an extract of evening primrose used to treat breast pain and eczema 291

ganciclovir an antiviral 129

Ganda a brand-name preparation for glaucoma 168 containing adrenaline 188 and guanethidine

Garamycin a brand name for gentamicin 292 (an aminoglycoside antibiotic 128)

Gardenal a brand name for phenobarbitone 361 (a barbiturate anticonvulsant 86)

Gastrils a brand name for aluminium hydroxide 191 with magnesium carbonate (both antacids 108)

Gastrobid Continus a brand name for metoclopramide 333 (a gastrointestinal motility regulator and anti-emetic 90)

Gastrocote a brand-name antacid 108 containing aluminium hydroxide 191, sodium bicarbonate 393, magnesium trisilicate, and alginic acid

Gastromax a brand name for metoclopramide 333 (a gastrointestinal motility regulator and anti-emetic 90)

Gastron a brand-name antacid 108 containing aluminium hydroxide 191, sodium bicarbonate 393, magnesium trisilicate, and alginic acid

Gastrozepin a brand name for pirenzepine (an *anticholinergic* anti-ulcer drug 109)

Gaviscon a brand-name antacid 108 containing aluminium hydroxide 191, sodium bicarbonate 393, magnesium trisilicate, and alginic acid

Gelcosal a brand-name preparation for eczema 175 and psoriasis 178 containing coal tar and salicylic acid

Gelcotar a brand name for coal tar (a substance for dandruff 179, eczema 175, and psoriasis 178)

Gelusil a brand name for aluminium hydroxide 191 with magnesium trisilicate (both antacids 108)

gemfibrozil a lipid-lowering drug 103

Genisol a brand name for coal tar (a substance for dandruff 179, eczema 175, and psoriasis 178)

Genotropin a brand name for somatropin (a synthetic pituitary *hormone* 145)

gentamicin 292 (an aminoglycoside antibiotic 128)

gentian mixture, acid and **alkaline** an appetite stimulant 88

gentian violet crystal violet (an *antiseptic* 175)

Genticin a brand name for gentamicin 292 (an aminoglycoside antibiotic 128)

Genticin HC a brand name for gentamicin 292 (an aminoglycoside antibiotic 128) with hydrocortisone 300 (a cortico-steroid 141)

Gentisone HC a brand name for gentamicin 292 (an aminoglycoside antibiotic 128) with hydrocortisone 300 (a corticosteroid 141)

Gestanin a brand name for allyloestrenol (a progestogen 147)

gestodene a progestogen 147

gestrinone a drug for menstrual disorders 160

gestronol a progestogen 147

Glandosane a brand name for artificial saliva

glibenclamide 293 (an oral anti-diabetic 142)

Glibenese a brand name for glipizide (an oral antidiabetic 142)

gliclazide an oral antidiabetic 142

glipizide an oral antidiabetic 142

gliquidone an oral antidiabetic 142

glucagon a pancreatic *hormone* for hypoglycaemia 142

Gluco-lyte a brand name for oral rehydration salts containing sodium bicarbonate 393, potassium 427, sodium chloride, and glucose

Glucophage a brand name for metformin 329 (an oral antidiabetic 142); *illus. 42S*

Glurenorm a brand name for gliquidone (an oral antidiabetic 142)

Glutarol a brand name for glutaraldehyde (a *topical* wart preparation)

glycerol a drug used to reduce pressure inside the eye 168, and an ingredient in cough mixtures 94, skin preparations 175, laxative suppositories 111, and ear-wax softening drops 171

glyceryl trinitrate 294 (an anti-angina drug 101); *illus. 46C*

glycopyrronium bromide an *anticholinergic* used in general *anaesthesia* 80

Glytrin a brand name for glyceryl trinitrate (an anti-angina drug 101)

gold a metal for rheumatoid arthritis 117

Gonadotraphon LH a brand name for chorionic gonadotrophin 231 (a drug for infertility 164)

gonadotrophin, chorionic 231 (a drug for infertility 164)

goserelin a female *sex hormone* 147 and anticancer drug 154

gramicidin an aminoglycoside antibiotic 128 for eye, ear, and skin infections

Graneodin a brand name for gramicidin with neomycin (both aminoglycoside antibiotics 128)

granisetron an anti-emetic 90

Gregoderm a brand name for hydrocortisone 300 (a corticosteroid 141) with nystatin 350 (an antifungal 138), neomycin (an aminoglycoside antibiotic 128), and polymyxin B (an antibiotic)

griseofulvin 295 (an antifungal 138)

Grisovin a brand name for griseofulvin 295 (an antifungal 138)

growth hormone somatrem 396

GTN 300mcg a brand name for glyceryl trinitrate 294 (an anti-angina drug 101)

guaiphenesin an *expectorant* 94

guanethidine an antihypertensive 102 also used for glaucoma 168

Guanor Expectorant a brand-name cough preparation 94 containing diphenhydramine 264, ammonium chloride, and menthol

Guarem a brand name for guar gum (a drug used to control blood sugar levels 142)

guar gum a drug used to control blood sugar levels 142

Guarina a brand name for guar gum (a drug used to control blood sugar levels 142)

Gyno-Daktarin a brand name for miconazole (an antifungal 138)

Gynol II a brand name for nonoxinol 9 (a spermicidal agent)

Gyno-Pevaryl a brand name for econazole 275 (an antifungal 138)

H

Haelan a brand name for fluran-drenolone (a *topical* corticosteroid 174)

Halciderm Topical a brand name for halcinonide (a *topical* corticosteroid 174)

halcinonide a *topical* corticosteroid 174

Halcion a brand name for triazolam (a benzodiazepine sleeping drug 82)

Haldol a brand name for haloperidol 296 (a butyrophenone antipsychotic 85); *illus. 37I*

halibut liver oil a natural fish oil rich in vitamin A 430 and vitamin D 432 (both vitamins 149)

haloperidol 296 (a butyrophenone antipsychotic 85)

halothane a gas used to induce general *anaesthesia* 80

Halycitrol a brand name for vitamin A 430 with vitamin D 432 (both vitamins 149)

hamamelis an *astringent* in rectal preparations 113

Hamarin a brand name for allopurinol 189 (a drug for gout 119)

Harmogen a brand name for piperazine oestrogen sulphate (a drug for *hormone* replacement therapy)

Haymine a brand name for chlorphenir-amine 227 (an antihistamine 124) with ephedrine 277 (a *bronchodilator* 92 and decongestant 93)

HCG human chorionic gonadotrophin 231 (a drug for infertility 164)

Hedex a brand name for paracetamol 356 (a non-*narcotic analgesic* 80)

Hedex Extra a brand name for paracetamol 356 (a non-*narcotic analgesic* with caffeine)

Hemabate a brand name for carboprost (a prostaglandin 165)

Heminevrin a brand name for chlorme-thiazole (a non-benzodiazepine, non-barbiturate sleeping drug 82)

heparin 297 (an anticoagulant 104)

heparinoid a drug applied *topically* to reduce inflammation of the skin 174

Hep-Flush a brand name for heparin 297 (an anticoagulant 104)

Hepsal a brand name for heparin 297 (an anticoagulant 104)

heroin diamorphine 258 (a *narcotic* 439 and *analgesic* 80)

Herpid a brand name for idoxuridine 303 (an antiviral 133)

hexachlorophane a skin *antiseptic* 175

hexamine a drug for urinary tract infections 166

Hexopal a brand name for nicotinic acid 345 (a *vasodilator* 98)

Hibitane a brand name for chlorhexidine (a skin *antiseptic* 175)

Hioxyl a brand name for hydrogen peroxide (an *antiseptic* 175)

Hiprex a brand name for hexamine (a drug for urinary tract infections 166)

Hirudoid a brand name for heparinoid (a *topical* anti-inflammatory)

Hismanal a brand name for astemizole (an antihistamine 124); *illus. 45C*

Histalix a brand-name cough preparation 94 containing diphenhydramine 264, ammonium chloride, and menthol

Histryl a brand name for diphenylpyraline (an antihistamine 124)

homatropine a *mydriatic* 170

Honvan a brand name for fosfestrol (a female *sex hormone* 147 and anticancer drug 154)

Hormonin oestradiol (a female sex *hormone* 147)

Human Actraphane a brand name for insulin 306 (a drug for diabetes 142)

Human Actrapid a brand name for insulin 306 (a drug for diabetes 142)

Human Initard a brand name for insulin 306 (a drug for diabetes 142)

Human Insulatard a brand name for insulin 306 (a drug for diabetes 142)

Human Mixtard a brand name for insulin 306 (a drug for diabetes 142)

Human Monotard a brand name for insulin 306 (a drug for diabetes 142)

Human Protaphane a brand name for insulin 306 (a drug for diabetes 142)

Human Ultratard a brand name for insulin 306 (a drug for diabetes 142)

Human Velosulin a brand name for insulin 306 (a drug for diabetes 142)

Humatrope a brand name for somatropin (a synthetic pituitary *hormone* 145)

Humulin a brand name for insulin 306 (a drug for diabetes 142)

Hydergine a brand name for codergocrine mesylate (a *vasodilator* 98)

hydralazine 298 (an antihypertensive 102)

Hydrea a brand name for hydroxyurea (an anticancer drug 154)

Hydrenox a brand name for hydro-flumethiazide (a thiazide diuretic 99)

hydrochlorothiazide 299 (a thiazide diuretic 99)

hydrocortisone 300 (a corticosteroid 141)

HYDROCORTISTAB – LEMSIP

Hydrocortistab a brand name for hydrocortisone 300 (a corticosteroid 141)
Hydrocortisyl a brand name for hydrocortisone 300 (a corticosteroid 141)
Hydrocortone a brand name for hydrocortisone 300 (a corticosteroid 141)
hydroflumethiazide a thiazide diuretic 99
Hydromet a brand name for hydrochlorothiazide 299 (a thiazide diuretic 99) with methyldopa 332 (an antihypertensive 102)
HydroSaluric a brand name for hydro-chlorothiazide 299 (a thiazide diuretic 99); *illus. 45M*
hydrotalcite an antacid 108
hydroxocobalamin vitamin B$_{12}$ 431 (a vitamin 149)
hydroxychloroquine an antimalarial 137 and antirheumatic drug 117
hydroxyprogesterone a progestogen 147 used to prevent miscarriage
hydroxyurea a drug for chronic myeloid leukaemia 154
hydroxyzine an anti-anxiety drug 83
Hygroton a brand name for chlorthalidone (a thiazide diuretic 99)
Hygroton-K a brand name for potassium 427 (a mineral 150) with chlorthalidone (a thiazide diuretic 99)
hyoscine 301 (a drug for irritable bowel syndrome 110 and affecting the pupil 170)
Hypertane 50 a brand name for amiloride 193 with hydrochlorothiazide 299 (both diuretics 99)
Hypon a brand-name *analgesic* 80 containing aspirin 199, codeine 244, and caffeine
Hypovase a brand name for prazosin 371 (an antihypertensive 102); *illus. 44B*
hypromellose a substance in artificial tear preparations 170
Hypurin a brand name for insulin 306 (a drug for diabetes 142)
Hytrin a brand name for terazosin (a *sympatholytic* antihypertensive 102)

I

Ibugel a brand name for ibuprofen (a non-steroidal anti-inflammatory 116)
Ibuleve a brand name for gel for muscular pain relief containing ibuprofen 302 (a non-steroidal anti-inflammatory 116)
ibuprofen 302 (a non-*narcotic analgesic* 80 and non-steroidal anti-inflammatory 116)
ichthammol a substance in skin preparations for eczema 175
Idoxene a brand name for idoxuridine 303 (an antiviral 133)
idoxuridine 303 (an antiviral 133)
Iduridin a brand name for idoxuridine 303 (an antiviral 133)
ifosfamide an alkylating agent for chronic lymphocytic leukaemia, cancers of

the lymphatic system, and solid tumours 154
Ilosone a brand name for erythromycin 280 (an antibiotic 128)
Ilube a brand name for acetylcysteine (a *mucolytic* 94) with hypromellose (a substance in artificial tear preparations 170)
Imbrilon a brand name for indomethacin 305 (a non-steroidal anti-inflammatory 116 and drug for gout 119)
Imdur a brand name for isosorbide mononitrate (a nitrate *vasodilator* 98 and anti-angina drug 101)
Imferon a brand name for iron 425 (a mineral 150)
Imigran a brand name for sumatriptan (a drug for migraine 89); *illus. 46K*
imipenem an antibiotic 128
imipramine 304 (a tricyclic antidepressant 84)
immune globulin a preparation injected to prevent infectious diseases 134
Imodium a brand name for loperamide 320 (an antidiarrhoeal 110); *illus. 40T*
Imperacin a brand name for oxytetra-cycline (a tetracycline antibiotic 128)
Imtak a brand name for isosorbide dinitrate (a nitrate *vasodilator* 98 and anti-angina drug 101)
Imunovir a brand name for inosine pranobex (an antiviral 133)
Imuran a brand name for azathioprine 203 (an antirheumatic 117 and immunosuppressant 156); *illus. 37 O*
indapamide a thiazide-like diuretic 99
Inderal a brand name for propranolol 380 (a beta blocker 97); *illus. 35 I*
Inderal LA a brand name for propranolol 380 (a beta blocker 97)
Inderetic a brand name for bendro-fluazide 206 (a thiazide diuretic 99) with propranolol 380 (a beta blocker 97)
Inderex a brand name for bendro-fluazide 206 (a thiazide diuretic 99) with propranolol 380 (a beta blocker 97)
Indocid a brand name for indomethacin 305 (a non-steroidal anti-inflammatory 116 and drug for gout 119); *illus. 39H*
Indocid R a brand name for indomethacin 305 (a non-steroidal anti-inflammatory 116 and drug for gout 119); *illus. 41G*
indomethacin 305 (a non-steroidal anti-inflammatory 116 and drug for gout 119)
Indomod a brand name for indomethacin 305 (a non-steroidal anti-inflammatory 116 and drug for gout 119)
indoramin an antihypertensive 102
Infacol a brand name for dimethicone (an antifoaming agent 108)
Initard a brand name for insulin 306 (a drug for diabetes 142)
Innovace a brand name for enalapril 276 (a *vasodilator* 98 and antihypertensive 102); *illus. 45H*

Innozide a brand name for enalapril (a *vasodilator* 98 and antihypertensive 102) with hydrochlorothiazide (a diuretic 99)
inosine pranobex an antiviral 133
inositol a drug related to nicotinic acid 345
Inoven a brand name for ibuprofen 302 (an *analgesic* 80 and non-steroidal anti-inflammatory 116)
Insulatard a brand name for insulin 306 (a drug for diabetes 142)
insulin 306 (a drug for diabetes 142)
Intal a brand name for sodium cromo-glycate 394 (an anti-allergy drug 124)
Intal Compound a brand name for isoprenaline 310 (a *bronchodilator* 92) with sodium cromoglycate 394 (an anti-allergy drug 124)
Integrin a brand name for oxypertine (an antipsychotic 85 and anti-anxiety drug 83)
interferon 307 (an antiviral 133 and anticancer drug 154)
Intron A a brand name for interferon 307 (an antiviral 133 and anticancer drug 154)
Intropin a brand name for dopamine (a *neurotransmitter* for shock)
iodine 425 (a mineral 150)
Ionamin a brand name for phentermine (an appetite suppressant 88)
Ionil T a brand-name dandruff shampoo 179 containing benzalkonium chloride, coal tar, and salicylic acid
ipecac, syrup of a drug used to induce vomiting in drug overdose and poisoning 470
ipecacuanha a drug used to induce vomiting in drug overdose and poisoning 470, also used as an *expectorant* 94
Ipral a brand name for trimethoprim 416 (an antibacterial 131); *illus. 42N*
ipratropium bromide 308 (a *bronchodilator* 92)
iprindole an antidepressant 84
iron 425 (a mineral 150)
Ismelin a brand name for guanethidine (an antihypertensive 102 also used for glaucoma 168)
Ismo a brand name for isosorbide mononitrate (a nitrate *vasodilator* 98 and anti-angina drug 101)
isoaminile a cough suppressant 94
isocarboxazid an MAOI antidepressant 84
isoconazole an antifungal 138
isoflurane a volatile liquid inhaled as a general *anaesthetic* 80
Isogel a brand name for ispaghula (a laxative 111 and antidiarrhoeal 110)
Isoket a brand name for isosorbide dinitrate (a nitrate *vasodilator* 98 and anti-angina drug 101)
isometheptene mucate a drug for migraine 89
Isomide a brand name for disopyramide (an antiarrhythmic 100)
isoniazid 309 (an antituberculous drug 132)
isoprenaline 310 (a *bronchodilator* 92)
Isopto Alkaline, Isopto Plain a brand

name for hypromellose (a substance in artificial tear preparations 170)

Isopto Atropine a brand name for atropine 201 (an *anticholinergic mydriatic* 170) with hypromellose (a substance in artificial tear preparations 170)

Isopto Carpine a brand name for pilocarpine 367 (a *miotic* for glaucoma 168) with hypromellose (a substance in artificial tear preparations 170)

Isordil a brand name for isosorbide dinitrate 311(a nitrate *vasodilator* 98 and anti-angina drug 101)

isosorbide dinitrate 311 (a nitrate *vasodilator* 98 and anti-angina drug 101)

isosorbide mononitrate a nitrate *vasodilator* 98 and anti-angina drug 101

Isotrate a brand name for isosorbide mononitrate (a nitrate *vasodilator* 98 and anti-angina drug 101)

isotretinoin 312 (a drug for acne 177)

isoxsuprine a *vasodilator* 98 and uterine muscle relaxant 165

ispaghula a bulk-forming agent for constipation 111 and diarrhoea 110

isradipine a calcium channel blocker 101

Istin a brand name for amlodipine (a calcium channel blocker 101)

itraconazole an antifungal 138

ivermectin an anthelmintic 139

J

Joy-rides a brand name for hyoscine 301 used to prevent motion sickness

Junifen a brand name for ibuprofen 302 (a non-steroidal anti-inflammatory drug 116)

Junior Kwells a brand name for hyoscine 301 used to prevent motion sickness; *illus. 44F*

K

Kabikinase a brand name for strepto-kinase 399 (a thrombolytic 105)

Kalspare a brand name for triamterene 415 with chlorthalidone (both diuretics 99)

Kalten a brand name for amiloride 193 with hydrochlorothiazide 299 (both diuretics 99) and atenolol 200 (a beta blocker 97)

kanamycin an aminoglycoside antibiotic 128

Kannasyn a brand name for kanamycin (an aminoglycoside antibiotic 128)

kaolin an adsorbent used as an antidiarrhoeal 110

Kaopectate a brand name for kaolin (an antidiarrhoeal 110)

Karvol a brand name for menthol (a decongestant 93 *inhalant*)

Kay-Cee-L a brand name for potassium 427 (a mineral 150)

Kefadol a brand name for cefamandole (a cephalosporin antibiotic 128)

Keflex a brand name for cephalexin 221(a cephalosporin antibiotic 128); *illus. 41C*

Kefzol a brand name for cephazolin (a cephalosporin antibiotic 128)

Kelfizine W a brand name for sulfameto-pyrazine (a sulphonamide antibacterial 131)

Kelocyanor a brand name for dicobalt edetate (an *antidote* to cyanide poisoning)

Kemadrin a brand name for procyclidine 376 (an *anticholinergic* for *parkinsonism* 87); *illus. 43S*

Kemicetine a brand name for chloramphenicol 224 (an antibiotic 128)

Kenalog a brand name for triamcinolone (a corticosteroid 141)

Kerlone a brand name for betaxolol (a beta blocker 97)

Kest a brand name for magnesium sulphate with phenolphthalein (both stimulant laxatives 111)

ketamine a drug used to induce general *anaesthesia* 80

ketoconazole 313 (an antifungal 138)

ketoprofen a non-steroidal anti-inflammatory 116

ketorolac a non-steroidal anti-inflammatory 116 used as an analgesic 80

ketotifen a drug similar to sodium cromoglycate 394 for allergies and asthma 124

Kiditard a brand name for quinidine (an anti-arrhythmic 100)

Kinidin Durules a brand name for quinidine (an anti-arrhythmic 100)

Klaracid a brand name for clarithromycin (an antibiotic 128)

Kolanticon a brand name for aluminium hydroxide 191 and magnesium oxide (both antacids 108) with dicyclomine 261 (an *anticholinergic antispasmodic* 110) and dimethicone (an antifoaming agent)

Konakion a brand name for phytomenadione (vitamin K 433)

Kwells a brand name for hyoscine 301 used to prevent motion sickness; *illus. 35R*

Kytril a brand name for granisetron (an anti-emetic 90)

L

labetalol a beta blocker 97

Laboprin a brand name for aspirin 199 (a non-*narcotic analgesic* 80)

Labrocol a brand name for labetalol (a beta blocker 97)

lactic acid an ingredient in preparations for warts, *emollients* 175, and *pessaries*

lactulose 314 (a laxative 111)

Ladropen a brand name for flucloxacillin (a penicillin antibiotic 128)

Lamictal a brand name for lamotrigine (an anticonvulsant 86)

Lamisal a brand name for terbinafine (an antifungal 134)

lamotrigine an anticonvulsant 86

Lamprene a brand name for clofazimine (a drug for leprosy 131)

lanatoside C an anti-arrhythmic 100

Lanoxin a brand name for digoxin 262 (a digitalis drug 96); *illus. 45T*

Lanoxin-PG a brand name for digoxin 262 (a digitalis drug 96)

Lanvis a brand name for thioguanine (an anticancer drug 154)

Laractone a brand name for spirono-lactone 397 (a potassium-sparing diuretic 99)

Laraflex a brand name for naproxen 341 (a non-steroidal anti-inflammatory 116 and drug for gout 119)

Largactil a brand name for chlorpromazine 228 (a phenothiazine antipsychotic 85 and anti-emetic 90); *illus. 44 O*

Lariam a brand name for mefloquine (an antimalarial 137)

Larodopa a brand name for levodopa 315 (a drug for *parkinsonism* 87)

Lasikal a brand name for frusemide 290 (a loop diuretic 99) with potassium 427 (a mineral 150)

Lasilactone a brand name for frusemide 290 with spironolactone 397 (both diuretics 99)

Lasipressin a brand name for frusemide 290 (a loop diuretic 99) with penbutolol (a beta blocker 97)

Lasix a brand name for frusemide 290 (a loop diuretic 99); *illus. 44H*

Lasma a brand name for theophylline 408 (a *bronchodilator* 92)

Lasonil a brand name for heparinoid (a *topical* anti-inflammatory 174)

Lasoride a brand name for amiloride 193 (a potassium-sparing diuretic 99) with frusemide 290 (a loop diuretic 99 and antihypertensive 102)

Ledclair a brand name for sodium calcium edetate (an *antidote* to poisoning with lead and heavy metals)

Ledercort a brand name for triamcinolone (a corticosteroid 141)

Lederfen a brand name for fenbufen 285 (a non-steroidal anti-inflammatory 116); *illus. 39L*

Lederfen F a brand name for fenbufen 285 (a non-steroidal anti-inflammatory 116)

Ledermycin a brand name for demeclo-cycline (a tetracycline antibiotic 128)

Lederspan a brand name for triamcinolone (a corticosteroid 141)

Lemsip a brand name for paracetamol 356 (a non-*narcotic analgesic* 80) with phenylephrine 364 (a decongestant 93), and caffeine

LENIUM – MINOCIN

Lenium a brand-name dandruff 179 shampoo containing selenium

Lentard MC a brand name for insulin 306 (a drug for diabetes 142)

Lentaron a brand name for formestane (a drug for breast cancer 154)

Lentizol a brand name for amitriptyline 195 (a tricyclic antidepressant 84)

Leo K a brand name for potassium 427 (a mineral 150)

Leukeran a brand name for chlorambucil (an anticancer drug 154)

leuprorelin a drug for menstrual disorders 160

levamisole an anthelmintic 139

levobunolol a beta blocker 97 and drug for glaucoma 168

levodopa 315 (a drug for *parkinsonism* 87)

levonorgestrel 316 (a female sex *hormone* 147 and oral contraceptive 161)

Lexotan a brand name for bromazepam (a benzodiazepine anti-anxiety drug 83)

Lexpec a brand name for folic acid 424 (a vitamin 149)

Libanil a brand name for glibenclamide 293 (an oral antidiabetic 142)

Librium a brand name for chlordiazepoxide 225 (a benzodiazepine anti-anxiety drug 83); *illus. 37S, 37T*

lignocaine a local *anaesthetic* 80 and anti-arrhythmic 100

Li-liquid a brand name for lithium 318 (an antimanic drug 85)

Limbitrol a brand name for amitriptyline 195 (a tricyclic antidepressant 84) with chlordiazepoxide 225 (a benzodiazepine anti-anxiety drug 83)

lindane 317 (a *topical* antiparasitic 176)

Lingraine a brand name for ergotamine 279 (a drug for migraine 89)

Lioresal a brand name for baclofen 204 (a muscle relaxant 120); *illus. 45K*

liothyronine thyroid *hormone* 144

Lipantil a brand name for fenofibrate (a lipid-lowering drug 103)

Lipostat a brand name for pravastatin (a cholesterol-lowering agent 103)

liquid paraffin a lubricating agent used as a laxative 111 and in artificial tear preparations 170

liquorice a substance for peptic ulcers 109

lisinopril an ACE inhibitor 98

Liskonum a brand name for lithium 318 (an antimanic drug 85)

Litarex a brand name for lithium 318 (an antimanic drug 85)

lithium 318 (an antimanic drug 85)

Livial a brand name for tibolone (a female sex *hormone* 147); *illus. 45 O*

Lobak a brand name for paracetamol 356 (a non-*narcotic analgesic* 80) with chlormezanone (a muscle relaxant 120)

Locoid a brand name for hydrocortisone 300 (a corticosteroid 141)

Locorten-Vioform a brand name for clioquinol (an anti-infective skin preparation 175) with flumethasone (a corticosteroid 141)

Lodine a brand name for etodolac (a non-steroidal anti-inflammatory 116)

lodoxamide an anti-allergic drug 123

Loestrin 20 a brand-name oral contraceptive 161 containing ethinyl-oestradiol 282 and norethisterone 349

lofepramine 319 (a tricyclic antidepressant 84)

lofexidine a drug to treat opioid *withdrawal symptoms*

Logynon a brand-name oral contraceptive 161 containing ethinyloestradiol 282 and levonorgestrel 316

Lomotil a brand-name antidiarrhoeal 110 containing atropine 201 and diphenoxylate 265; *illus. 45S*

lomustine an alkylating agent for Hodgkin's disease 154

Loniten a brand name for minoxidil 336 (an antihypertensive 102); *illus. 44S*

loperamide 320 (an antidiarrhoeal 110)

Lopid a brand name for gemfibrozil (a lipid-lowering drug 103)

loprazolam a benzodiazepine sleeping drug 82

Lopresor a brand name for metoprolol (a cardioselective beta blocker 97)

Lopresoretic a brand name for chlorthalidone (a thiazide-like diuretic 99) with metoprolol (a cardioselective beta blocker 97)

loratadine 321 (an antihistamine 124)

lorazepam a benzodiazepine anti-anxiety drug 83 and sleeping drug 82

lormetazepam a benzodiazepine sleeping drug 82

Loron a brand name for sodium clodronate (to treat hypercalcaemia in cancer)

Losec a brand name for omeprazole 352 (an anti-ulcer drug 109); *illus. 40E*

Loxapac a brand name for loxapine (an antipsychotic 85)

loxapine an antipsychotic 85

Luborant a brand name for artificial saliva

Ludiomil a brand name for maprotiline (an antidepressant 84)

Lugol's solution an iodine 425 solution for overactive thyroid gland 144

Luminal a brand name for phenobarbitone 361 (a barbiturate anticonvulsant 86); *illus. 45Q*

Lurselle a brand name for probucol (a lipid-lowering drug 103)

Lustral a brand name for sertraline 390 (an antidepressant 84); *illus. 46L*

Lyclear a brand name for permethrin (a *topical* antiparasitic 176)

lymecycline a tetracycline antibiotic 128

lypressin 322 (a drug for diabetes insipidus 145)

lysuride a drug for *parkinsonism* 87

M

Maalox a brand-name antacid containing aluminium hydroxide 191 and magnesium hydroxide 323

Maalox Plus a brand-name antacid containing aluminium hydroxide 191, magnesium hydroxide 323, and dimethicone

Macrobid a brand name for nitrofurantoin 348 (an antibacterial 131); *illus. 41L*

Macrodantin a brand name for nitrofurantoin 348 (an antibacterial 131)

Madopar a brand name for levodopa 315 (a drug for *parkinsonism* 87) with benserazide (a drug that enhances the effect of levodopa)

magaldrate an antacid 108 that combines aluminium hydroxide 191 with magnesium hydroxide 323

Magnapen a brand name for ampicillin with flucloxacillin (both penicillin antibiotics 128)

magnesium 426 (a mineral 150)

magnesium carbonate an antacid 108

magnesium citrate an osmotic laxative 111

magnesium hydroxide 323 (an antacid 108 and laxative 111)

magnesium oxide an antacid 108

magnesium sulphate an osmotic laxative 111

magnesium trisilicate an antacid 108

malathion an antiparasitic 176 for head lice and scabies

Malix a brand name for glibenclamide 297 (an oral antidiabetic 142)

Maloprim a brand-name antimalarial 137 containing dapsone 254 and pyrimethamine 383

Manerix a brand name for moclobemide 338 (a reversible MAOI antidepressant 84); *illus. 36R*

Manevac a brand name for ispaghula (a bulk-forming agent) with senna (a stimulant laxative 111)

mannitol an osmotic diuretic 99

maprotiline an antidepressant 84

Marcain a brand name for bupivacaine (a local *anaesthetic* 80 used in labour 165)

Marevan a brand name for warfarin 419 (an anticoagulant 104)

Marplan a brand name for isocarboxazid (an MAOI antidepressant 84)

Marvelon a brand-name oral contraceptive 161 containing ethinyloestradiol 282 and desogestrel

Maxepa a brand name for concentrated fish oils (used to reduce fats in the blood 103)

Maxidex a brand name for dexamethasone 255 (a corticosteroid 141) with hypromellose (a substance in artificial tear preparations 170)

Maxitrol a brand name for dexamethasone 255 (a corticosteroid 141) with hypromellose (a substance used in artificial tear preparations 170), and neomycin and polymyxin B (both antibiotics 128)

Maxolon a brand name for metoclopramide 333 (a gastrointestinal motility regulator and anti-emetic 90); *illus. 44N*

Maxtrex a brand name for methotrexate (an antimetabolite anticancer drug 154)

mazindol an appetite suppressant 88

MCR-50 a brand name for isosorbide mononitrate (a nitrate *vasodilator* 98 and anti-angina drug 101)

mebendazole an anthelmintic 139

mebeverine an *antispasmodic* for irritable bowel syndrome 110

mebhydrolin an antihistamine 124

medazepam a benzodiazepine antianxiety drug 83

Medihaler-epi a brand name for adrenaline 188 (a *bronchodilator* 92)

Medihaler-Ergotamine a brand name for ergotamine 279 (a drug for migraine 89)

Medihaler-Iso a brand name for isoprenaline 310 (a *bronchodilator* 92)

Medijel gel a brand name for a pain relieving mouth gel containing lignocaine (a local *anaesthetic* 80) and aminacrine (a skin *antiseptic* 179)

Medised a brand name for paracetamol 356 (a non-*narcotic analgesic* 80) with promethazine 379 (an antihistamine 120 and anti-emetic 90)

Medrone tablets a brand name for methylprednisolone (a corticosteroid 141)

medroxyprogesterone 324 (a female sex *hormone* 147)

mefenamic acid 325 (a non-steroidal anti-inflammatory 116)

mefloquine an antimalarial 137

Mefoxin a brand name for cefoxitin (a cephalosporin antibiotic 128)

mefruside a thiazide-like diuretic 99

Megace a brand name for megestrol 326 (a female sex *hormone* 147 and anticancer drug 154); *illus. 43G*

megestrol 326 (a female sex *hormone* 147 and anticancer drug 154)

Melleril a brand name for thioridazine 409 (a phenothiazine antipsychotic 85); *illus. 44P*

melphalan an alkylating agent for multiple myeloma 154

menadiol vitamin K 433 (a vitamin 149)

menadione vitamin K 433 (a vitamin 149)

Menophase a brand name for mestranol and norethisterone (female sex *hormones* 147)

menotrophin a drug for infertility 164

menthol an alcohol from mint oils used as an *inhalation* and *topical* antipruritic 173

Menzol a brand name for norethisterone (a female sex *hormone* 147)

mepacrine an antiprotozoal 136 for giardiasis

mepenzolate an *anticholinergic antispasmodic* for irritable bowel syndrome 110

meprobamate an anti-anxiety drug 83

meptazinol a *narcotic analgesic* 80

Meptid a brand name for meptazinol (a *narcotic analgesic* 80)

mequitazine an antihistamine 124

Merbentyl a brand name for dicyclomine 261 (a drug for irritable bowel syndrome 110); *illus. 43N*

mercaptopurine 328 (an anticancer drug 154)

Merocaine Lozenges a brand-name preparation for sore throat and minor mouth infections containing benzocaine (a local *anaesthetic* 80) and cetylpyridinium (an *antiseptic* 179)

mesalazine 327 (a drug for ulcerative colitis 112)

mesterolone a male sex *hormone* 146

Mestinon a brand name for pyridostigmine 382 (a drug for myasthenia gravis 121); *illus. 43 I*

mestranol an oestrogen 147

Metamucil a brand name for ispaghula (a bulk-forming agent used as a laxative 111 and antidiarrhoeal 110)

Metenix 5 a brand name for metolazone (a thiazide-like diuretic 99)

Meterfolic a brand name for folic acid 424 (a vitamin 149) with iron 425 (a mineral 150)

metformin 311 (an antidiabetic 142)

methadone a *narcotic* 439 used as an *analgesic* 80 and to ease heroin withdrawal

methicillin a penicillin antibiotic 128

methionine an *antidote* to paracetamol 356 poisoning

methixene an *anticholinergic* for *parkinsonism* 87

methocarbamol a muscle relaxant 120

methohexitone a barbiturate used to induce general *anaesthesia* 80

methotrexate an antimetabolite anticancer drug 154

methotrimeprazine an antpsychotic 85

methoxsalen 330 (a drug for psoriasis 180)

methyclothiazide a thiazide diuretic 99

methylcellulose 331 (a laxative 111, antidiarrhoeal 110, and artificial tear preparation 170)

methylcysteine a *mucolytic* for coughs 94

methyldopa 332 (an antihypertensive 102)

methylphenobarbitone a barbiturate anticonvulsant 86

methylprednisolone a corticosteroid 141

methyl salicylate an *analgesic* 80 for muscle and joint pain

methyltestosterone a male sex *hormone* 146

methysergide a drug used to prevent migraine 89

metipranolol a beta blocker 97 for glaucoma 168

metirosine a drug for phaeochromocytoma (tumour of the adrenal glands)

metoclopramide 333 (a gastrointestinal motility regulator and anti-emetic 90)

metolazone a thiazide-like diuretic 99

metoprolol a beta blocker 97

Metosyn a brand name for fluocinonide (a *topical* corticosteroid 174)

Metrodin a brand name for urofollitrophin (a drug for pituitary disorders 145)

Metrolyl a brand name for metronidazole 334 (an antibacterial 131 and antiprotozoal 136)

metronidazole 334 (an antibacterial 131 and antiprotozoal 136)

Metrozol a brand name for metronidazole (an antibacterial 131 and antiprotozoal 136)

mexiletine an anti-arrhythmic 100

Mexitil a brand name for mexiletine (an anti-arrhythmic 100)

mianserin 335 (an antidepressant 84)

miconazole an antifungal 134

Microgynon 30 a brand-name oral contraceptive 161 containing ethinyloestradiol 282 and levonorgestrel 316

Micronor a brand-name oral contraceptive 161 containing norethisterone 349

Microval a brand-name oral contraceptive 161 containing levonorgestrel 316; *illus. 46A*

Mictral a brand-name drug for urinary tract infections 166 containing nalidixic acid 340

Midamor a brand name for amiloride 193 (a potassium-sparing diuretic 99); *illus. 37K*

midazolam a benzodiazepine 82 used as *premedication*

Midrid a brand-name drug for migraine 89 containing paracetamol 356 and isometheptene mucate

Migraleve a brand-name drug for migraine 89 containing codeine 244, paracetamol 356, and buclizine

Migravess a brand-name drug for migraine 89 containing aspirin 199 and metoclopramide 333

Migril a brand-name drug for migraine 89 containing ergotamine 279, caffeine, and cyclizine

Milk of Magnesia a brand name for magnesium hydroxide 323 (an antacid 108 and laxative 111); *illus. 42F*

Mil-Par a brand-name laxative 111 containing magnesium hydroxide 323 with liquid paraffin

Minihep a brand name for heparin 297 (an anticoagulant 104)

Minims Atropine a brand name for atropine 201 (a *mydriatic* 170)

Minims Chloramphenicol a brand name for chloramphenicol 224 (an antibiotic 128)

Minims cyclopentolate a brand name for cyclopentolate (an *anticholinergic mydriatic* 170)

Minims Pilocarpine a brand name for pilocarpine 367 (a *miotic* for glaucoma 168)

Minocin a brand name for minocycline (a tetracycline antibiotic 128)

minocycline a tetracycline antibiotic 128

Minodiab a brand name for glipizide (an oral antidiabetic 142)

minoxidil 336 (an antihypertensive 102)

Mintec a brand name for peppermint oil (a substance for irritable bowel syndrome 110)

Mintezol a brand name for thiabendazole (an anthelmintic 139)

Miraxid a brand name for pivampicillin and pivmecillinam (both penicillin antibiotics 128)

misoprostol 337 (an anti-ulcer drug 109)

Mithracin a brand name for plicamycin (a *cytotoxic* anticancer drug 154)

mitobronitol an alkylating agent for chronic myeloid leukaemia 154

mitomycin a *cytotoxic* antibiotic for breast and stomach cancer 154

mitozantrone an anticancer drug 154

Mixtard a brand name for insulin 306 (an antidiabetic 142)

Mobiflex a brand name for tenoxicam (a non-steroidal anti-inflammatory 116)

Mobilan a brand name for indomethacin 305 (a non-steroidal anti-inflammatory 116 and drug for gout 119)

moclobemide 338 (a reversible MAOI antidepressant 84)

Modalim a brand name for ciprofibrate (a lipid-lowering drug 103)

Modecate a brand name for fluphenazine (an antipsychotic 85)

Moditen a brand name for fluphenazine (an antipsychotic 85)

Modrasone a brand name for alclometasone (a *topical* corticosteroid 174)

Moducren a brand-name antihypertensive 102 containing amiloride 193, hydrochlorothiazide 299, and timolol 412

Moduret-25 a brand name for amiloride 193 with hydrochlorothiazide 299 (both diuretics 99)

Moduretic a brand name for amiloride 193 with hydrochlorothiazide 299 (both diuretics 99); *illus. 36C*

Mogadon a brand name for nitrazepam 347 (a benzodiazepine sleeping drug 82); *illus. 41N, 42E*

Molipaxin a brand name for trazodone 414 (an antidepressant 84); *illus. 36A*

molybdenum a mineral 150 required in minute amounts in the diet, poisonous if ingested in large quantities

mometasone a *topical* corticosteroid 174

Monaspor a brand name for cefsulodin (a cephalosporin antibiotic 128)

Monit a brand name for isosorbide mononitrate (a nitrate *vasodilator* 98 and anti-angina drug 101)

Mono-Cedocard a brand name for isosorbide mononitrate (a nitrate *vasodilator* 98 and anti-angina drug 101)

Monoclate P a brand name for factor VIII (a blood extract used to promote blood clotting 104)

Monocor a brand name for bisoprolol (a beta blocker 97)

Monoparin, Monoparin CA brand names for heparin 297 (an anti-coagulant 104)

monosulfiram an antiparasitic 176 for scabies

Monotrim a brand name for trimethoprim 416 (an antibacterial 131)

morphine 339 (a *narcotic analgesic* 80)

Motilium a brand name for domperidone 270 (an anti-emetic 90); *illus. 44T*

Motipress a brand name for fluphenazine (an antipsychotic 85) with nortriptyline (a tricyclic antidepressant 84)

Motival a brand name for fluphenazine (an antipsychotic 85) with nortriptyline (a tricyclic antidepressant 84)

Motrin a brand name for ibuprofen 302 (a non-steroidal anti-inflammatory 116)

Movelat a brand-name *topical* anti-inflammatory 175 containing mucopolysaccharide and salicylic acid

MST Continus a brand name for morphine 339 (a *narcotic analgesic* 80); *illus. 35C*

Mucaine a brand-name antacid 108 containing aluminium hydroxide 191, magnesium hydroxide 323, and oxethazaine

Mucodyne a brand name for carbocisteine (a *mucolytic* decongestant 94)

Mucogel a brand-name antacid 108 containing aluminium hydroxide 191 and magnesium hydroxide 323

Mu-Cron Tablets a brand name for phenylpropanolamine 365 (a decongestant 93) with paracetamol 356 (an analgesic 80)

Multiparin a brand name for heparin 297 (an anticoagulant 104)

mupirocin an antibacterial for skin infections 175

mustine a drug for Hodgkin's disease 154

Myambutol a brand name for ethambutol 281 (an antituberculous drug 132); *illus. 37D*

Mycardol a brand name for penta-erythritol tetranitrate (a nitrate anti-angina drug 101)

Mycota a brand name for undecanoate acid (an antifungal 138)

Mydrilate a brand name for cyclopentolate (an *anticholinergic mydriatic* 170)

Myelobromol a brand name for mitobronitol (an alkylating agent 154)

Myleran a brand name for busulphan (an alkylating agent 154)

Mynah a brand-name antituberculous drug 132 containing ethambutol 281 and isoniazid 309

Myocrisin a brand name for sodium aurothiomalate 392 (an antirheumatic 117)

Myotonine a brand name for bethanechol (a *parasympathomimetic* for urinary retention 166)

Mysoline a brand name for primidone 373 (an anticonvulsant 86); *illus. 43H*

Mysteclin tablets a brand name for nystatin 350 (an antifungal 138) with tetracycline 407 (an antibiotic 128)

N

nabilone an anti-emetic 90 derived from marijuana for nausea and vomiting induced by anticancer drugs 154

nabumetone a non-steroidal anti-inflammatory 116

Nacton a brand name for poldine methylsulphate (an *anticholinergic* 110)

nadolol a beta blocker 97

nafarelin a drug for menstrual disorders 160

naftidrofuryl a *vasodilator* 98

nalbuphine a *narcotic* analgesic 80

Nalcrom a brand name for sodium cromoglycate 394 (an anti-allergy drug 124)

nalidixic acid 340 (an antibacterial 131)

Nalorex a brand name for naltrexone (a drug for maintenance of opioid *withdrawal* 24)

naloxone an antidote to *narcotic* 439 poisoning 470

naltrexone a drug for maintenance of opioid *withdrawal* 24

nandrolone an anabolic steroid 146

naphazoline a *sympathomimetic* decongestant 93

Napratec a brand name for an antirheumatic drug containing naproxen 341 (a non-steroidal anti-inflammatory 116 and drug for gout 119) with misoprostol (an anti-ulcer drug 109)

Naprosyn a brand name for naproxen 341 (a non-steroidal anti-inflammatory 116 and drug for gout 119); *illus. 43L*

naproxen 341 (a non-steroidal anti-inflammatory 116 and drug for gout 119)

Narcan a brand name for naloxone (an antidote to *narcotic* 439 poisoning 470)

Nardil a brand name for phenelzine 360 (an MAOI antidepressant 84); *illus. 36H*

Narphen a brand name for phenazocine (a *narcotic analgesic* 80)

Naseptin a brand name for chlorhexidine (a skin *antiseptic* 175) with neomycin (an aminoglycoside antibiotic 128)

Natrilix a brand name for indapamide (a thiazide-like diuretic 99)

Natulan a brand name for procarbazine (an anticancer drug 154)

Navidrex a brand name for cyclopenthiazide 249 (a thiazide diuretic 99); *illus. 44R*

Navispare a brand name for cyclopenthiazide 249 with amiloride 193 (both diuretics 99)

Navoban a brand name for tropisetron (an anti-emetic 90)

Nebcin a brand name for tobramycin (an aminoglycoside antibiotic 128)

nedocromil a drug similar to sodium cromoglycate 394 used to prevent asthma attacks

nefopam 342 (a non-*narcotic analgesic* 80)

Negram a brand name for nalidixic acid 340 (an antibacterial 131); *illus. 35T*

Neocon 1/35 a brand-name oral contraceptive containing ethinyloestradiol 282 and norethisterone 349

Neo-Cortef a brand name for hydrocortisone 300 (a corticosteroid 141) with neomycin (an aminoglycoside antibiotic 128)

Neo-Cytamen a brand name for hydroxocobalamin (vitamin B$_{12}$ 431)

Neogest a brand name for norgestrel (a female sex *hormone* 147)

Neo-Medrone Cream a brand name for methylprednisolone (a corticosteroid 141) with neomycin (an aminoglycoside antibiotic 128)

Neo-Mercazole 5 a brand name for carbimazole 219 (an antithyroid drug 144); *illus. 35S*

Neo-Mercazole 20 a brand name for carbimazole 219 (an anti-thyroid drug 144)

neomycin an aminoglycoside antibiotic 128

Neo-NaClex a brand name for bendrofluazide 206 (a thiazide diuretic 99)

Neo-NaClex-K a brand name for bendrofluazide 206 (a thiazide diuretic 99) with potassium 427; *illus. 38J*

Neosporin a brand name for gramicidin with neomycin and polymyxin B (all antibiotics 128)

neostigmine 343 (a drug for myasthenia gravis 121)

Nepenthe a brand name for morphine 339 (a *narcotic analgesic* 80)

Nephril a brand name for polythiazide (a thiazide diuretic 99)

Nericur a brand name for benzoyl peroxide 208 (a drug for acne 177)

Nerisone a brand name for diflucortolone (a *topical* corticosteroid 174)

Netillin a brand name for netilmicin (an aminoglycoside antibiotic 128)

netilmicin an aminoglycoside antibiotic 128

Neulactil a brand name for pericyazine (an antipsychotic 85)

niacin 426 (a vitamin 149)

niacinamide niacin 426 (a vitamin 149)

Nicabate a brand name for nicotine 344 given as a drug for relief of smoking *withdrawal symptoms*

nicardipine a calcium channel blocker 101

niclosamide an anthelmintic 139 for tapeworms

nicofuranose a lipid-lowering drug 103 and *vasodilator* 98

Nicorette a brand name for nicotine 344 given as a drug for relief of smoking *withdrawal symptoms*

nicotinamide niacin 426 (a vitamin 149)

nicotine 344 (a nervous system stimulant 88)

Nicotinell a brand name for nicotine 344 given as a drug for relief of smoking *withdrawal symptoms*

nicotinic acid 345 (a *vasodilator* 98, lipid-lowering drug 103, and vitamin supplement 149)

nicotinyl alcohol tartrate niacin 426 (a vitamin 149)

nicoumalone an anticoagulant 104

nifedipine 346 (a calcium channel blocker 98)

Nifensar XL a brand name for nifedipine 346 (a calcium channel blocker 98)

Night Nurse a brand-name preparation for relief of cold symptoms containing paracetamol 356 (a non-*narcotic analgesic* 80) with promethazine 379

nikethamide a respiratory stimulant 88

Nilstim a brand-name appetite suppressant containing methylcellulose 331 and cellulose (both bulk-forming agents)

nimodipine a calcium channel blocker 98

Nimotop a brand name for nimodipine (a calcium channel blocker 98)

Nitoman a brand name for tetrabenazine (a drug for movement disorders)

nitrazepam 347 (a benzodiazepine sleeping drug 82)

Nitrocine a brand name for glyceryl trinitrate 294 (an anti-angina drug 101)

Nitrocontin a brand name for glyceryl trinitrate 294 (an anti-angina drug 101)

Nitro-dur a brand name for glyceryl trinitrate 294 (an anti-angina drug 101)

nitrofurantoin 348 (an antibacterial 131)

Nitrolingual a brand name for glyceryl trinitrate 294 (an anti-angina drug 101)

Nitronal a brand name for glyceryl trinitrate 294 (an anti-angina drug 101)

Nivaquine a brand name for chloroquine 226 (an antimalarial 137 and antirheumatic 117); *illus. 36Q*

Nivemycin a brand name for neomycin (an aminoglycoside antibiotic 128)

nizatidine an anti-ulcer drug 109

Nizoral a brand name for ketoconazole 313 (an antifungal 138); *illus. 43K*

Nobrium a brand name for medazepam (a benzodiazepine anti-anxiety drug 83)

Noctec a brand name for chloral hydrate 223 (a sleeping drug 82)

Noltam a brand name for tamoxifen 403 (an anticancer drug 154)

Nolvadex a brand name for tamoxifen 403 (an anticancer drug 154)

Nolvadex Forte a brand name for tamoxifen 403 (an anticancer drug 154); *illus. 46N*

Nordiject a brand name for somatropin (a synthetic pituitary *hormone* 145)

Norditropin a brand name for somatropin (a synthetic pituitary *hormone* 145)

Nordox a brand name for doxycycline 273 (a tetracycline antibiotic 128)

norethisterone 349 (a female sex *hormone* 147)

Norflex a brand name for orphenadrine 354 (an *anticholinergic* muscle relaxant 120)

norfloxacin an antibiotic 128

norgestimate an oral contraceptive 161

Norgeston a brand-name oral contraceptive 161 containing levonorgestrel 316

norgestrel a progestogen 147

Noriday a brand-name oral contraceptive 161 containing norethisterone 349

Norimin a brand-name oral contraceptive 161 containing ethinyloestradiol 282 and norethisterone 349

Norinyl-1 a brand-name oral contraceptive 161 containing norethisterone 349 and mestranol

Noristerat a brand-name injectable contraceptive containing norethisterone 349 (a female sex hormone 147)

Normacol plus a brand name for frangula with sterculia (both laxatives 111)

Normax a brand name for danthron and docusate (both laxatives 111)

Normison a brand name for temazepam 404 (a benzodiazepine sleeping drug 82); *illus. 39F*

Noroxin a brand name for norfloxacin (an antibiotic 128)

nortriptyline a tricyclic antidepressant 84

Norval a brand name for mianserin 335 (an antidepressant 84)

noscapine a cough suppressant 94

Novantrone a brand name for mitozantrone (an anticancer drug 154)

Noxyflex S a brand name for noxythiolin (an *antiseptic* for bladder or abdominal cavity infection)

Nozinan a brand name for methotrimeprazine (an antipsychotic 85)

Nubain a brand name for nalbuphine (a *narcotic analgesic* 80)

Nuelin a brand name for theophylline 408 (a *bronchodilator* 92)

Nu-K a brand name for potassium 427

Nulacin a brand-name antacid 108 containing calcium carbonate, magnesum carbonate, magnesium trisilicate, and magnesium oxide

Nurofen a brand name for ibuprofen 302 (a non-*narcotic analgesic* 80 and non-steroidal anti-inflammatory 116)

Nu-Seals Aspirin a brand name for aspirin 199 (a non-*narcotic analgesic* 80 and antiplatelet drug 104)

Nutraplus a brand name for urea (an *emollient*)

Nutrizym GR a brand name for pancreatin (a preparation of pancreatic *enzymes* 114)

Nuvelle a brand name for oestradiol and levonorgestrel (female sex *hormones* 147)

Nycopren a brand name for naproxen (a non-steroidal anti-inflammatory 116)

Nylax a brand-name stimulant laxative 111 containing bisacodyl, phenolpthalein, and senna

Nystadermal a brand name for nystatin 350 (an antifungal 138) with triamcinolone (a corticosteroid 141)

NYSTAFORM – PONDOCILLIN PLUS

Nystaform a brand name for nystatin 350 (an antifungal 138) with chlorhexidine (a skin *antiseptic* 175)

Nystaform-HC a brand name for hydrocortisone 300 (a corticosteroid 141) with nystatin 350 (an antifungal 138) and chlorhexidine (a skin *antiseptic* 175)

Nystan a brand name for nystatin 350 (an antifungal 138); *illus. 35P*

nystatin 350 (an antifungal 138)

Nystatin-Dome a brand name for nystatin 350 (an antifungal 138)

Nytol a brand-name preparation for sleep disturbance containing diphenhydramine 264 (an antihistamine 124)

O

octoxynol a spermicidal agent

octreotide a synthetic pituitary *hormone* 145 used to relieve symptoms of cancer of the pancreas 154

Ocusert Pilo a brand name for pilocarpine 367 (a *miotic* for glaucoma 168)

oestradiol 351 (an oestrogen 147)

oestriol an oestrogen 147

oestrogen a female sex *hormone* 147

oestrone an oestrogen 147

ofloxacin an antibiotic 128

Oilatum Emollient a brand-name bath additive for dry skin conditions containing liquid paraffin

Oilatum Gel a brand name for a shower gel containing liquid paraffin for dry skin conditions

Olbetam a brand name for acipimox (a lipid-lowering drug 103)

olsalazine a drug for ulcerative colitis 112

omeprazole 352 (an anti-ulcer drug 109)

Oncovin a brand name for vincristine (an anticancer drug 154)

ondansetron 353 (an anti-emetic 90)

Opilon a brand name for thymoxamine (a *vasodilator* 98)

opium tincture morphine 339 (a *narcotic analgesic* 80)

Opticrom a brand name for sodium cromoglycate 394 (an anti-allergy drug 124)

Optimine a brand name for azatadine (an antihistamine 124)

Optrex Eye Lotion a brand-name preparation containing witch hazel (an *astringent*)

Opulets Chloramphenicol a brand name for chloramphenicol 224 (an antibiotic 128)

Opulets Pilocarpine a brand name for pilocarpine 367 (a *miotic* for glaucoma 168)

Orabet a brand name for metformin 329 (an antidiabetic 142)

Oramorph a brand name for morphine sulphate (a *narcotic* analgesic 80)

Orap a brand name for pimozide (an antipsychotic 85)

Orbenin a brand name for cloxacillin (a penicillin antibiotic 128)

orciprenaline a *sympathomimetic* used as a *bronchodilator* 92

Orelox a brand name for cefpodoxime (a cephalosporin antibiotic 130)

Orimeten a brand name for aminoglutethimide (an anticancer drug 154)

orphenadrine 354 (an *anticholinergic* muscle relaxant 120 and drug for *parkinsonism* 87)

Ortho-Creme a brand name for nonoxinol 9 (a spermicidal agent)

Ortho-Dienoestrol a brand name for dienoestrol (a female sex *hormone* 147)

Orthoforms a brand name for nonoxinol 9 (a spermicidal agent)

Ortho-Gynest a brand name for oestriol (an oestrogen 147)

Ortho-Novin 1/50 a brand-name oral contraceptive 161 containing norethisterone 349 and mestranol

Orudis a brand name for ketoprofen (a non-steroidal anti-inflammatory 116)

Oruvail a brand name for ketoprofen (a non-steroidal anti-inflammatory 116)

Ossopan a brand name for hydroxyapatite (a calcium 422 supplement)

Otosporin a brand name for hydrocortisone 300 (a corticosteroid 141) with neomycin and polymyxin B (both antibiotics 128)

Otrivine a brand name for xylometazoline (a decongestant 93)

Otrivine-Antistin a brand name for antazoline 198 (an antihistamine 124) with xylometazoline (a decongestant 93)

ouabain a digitalis-like drug 96

Ovestin a brand name for oestriol (an oestrogen 147)

Ovex a brand name for mebendazole (an anthelmintic 139)

Ovran a brand-name oral contraceptive 161 containing ethinyloestradiol 282 and levonorgestrel 316

Ovranette a brand-name oral contraceptive 161 containing ethinyloestradiol 282 and levonorgestrel 316

Ovysmen a brand-name oral contraceptive 161 containing ethinyloestradiol 282 and norethisterone 349

oxatomide an antihistamine 124

oxazepam a benzodiazepine anti-anxiety drug 83

oxethazaine a local *anaesthetic* 80 used with antacids 108 for reflux oesophagitis

oxitropium a *bronchodilator* 92

Oxivent a brand name for oxitropium (a *bronchodilator* 92)

oxpentifylline a *vasodilator* 98 used to improve blood flow to the limbs in peripheral vascular disease

oxprenolol 355 (a beta blocker 97)

oxybenzone a sunscreening agent 179

oxybuprocaine a local *anaesthetic* 80

oxybutynin an *anticholinergic* and *antispasmodic* for urinary disorders 166

oxycodone a *narcotic analgesic* 80

oxymetazoline a *topical* decongestant 93

oxymetholone an anabolic steroid 146 for aplastic anaemia

Oxymycin a brand name for oxytetracycline (a tetracycline antibiotic 128)

oxypertine an antipsychotic 85

oxyphenbutazone a non-steroidal anti-inflammatory 116

oxytetracycline a tetracycline antibiotic 128

oxytocin a uterine stimulant 165

P

padimate-O a sunscreening agent 179

Palaprin Forte a brand name for aloxiprin (a buffered form of aspirin 199)

Paldesic a brand name for paracetamol 356 (a non-*narcotic analgesic* 80)

Palfium a brand name for dextromoramide 257 (a *narcotic analgesic* 80); *illus. 36D*

Paludrine a brand name for proguanil 377 (an antimalarial 137); *illus. 44D*

Pamergan a brand name for pethidine 359 (a *narcotic analgesic* 80) with promethazine 379 (an antihistamine 124 and anti-emetic 90)

Pameton a brand name for paracetamol 356 (a non-*narcotic analgesic* 80) with methionine (an *antidote* to paracetamol poisoning)

Panadol a brand name for paracetamol 356 (a non-*narcotic analgesic* 80)

Panadol Extra a brand name for paracetamol 356 (a non-*narcotic analgesic* 80) with caffeine

Panaleve a brand name for paracetamol 356 (a non-*narcotic analgesic* 80)

Pancrease a brand name for pancreatin (a preparation of pancreatic *enzymes* 114)

pancreatin a preparation of pancreatic *enzymes* 114

Pancrex a brand name for pancreatin (a preparation of pancreatic *enzymes* 114)

pancuronium a muscle relaxant 120 used during general *anaesthesia* 80

Panoxyl a brand name for benzoyl peroxide 208 (a drug for acne 177)

panthenol pantothenic acid 427 (a vitamin 149)

pantothenic acid 427 (a vitamin 149)

papaveretum a *narcotic analgesic* 80

papaverine a muscle relaxant 120

paracetamol 356 (a non-*narcotic analgesic* 80); *illus 46H*

Paracodol a brand-name *analgesic* 80 containing codeine 244 and paracetamol 356

Parake a brand-name *analgesic* 80 containing codeine 244 and paracetamol 356

paraldehyde an anticonvulsant 86 used for status epilepticus

Paramax a brand-name migraine drug 89 containing paracetamol 356 and metoclopramide 333

Paramol a brand name for paracetamol 356 with dihydrocodeine (both *analgesics* 80)

Paraplatin a brand name for carboplatin (an anticancer drug 154)

Parfenac a brand name for bufexamac (a drug for skin inflammation)

Parlodel a brand name for bromocriptine 212 (a pituitary agent 145 and drug for *parkinsonism* 87); *illus. 41 I*

Parnate a brand name for tranylcypromine (an MAOI antidepressant 84)

paroxetine an antidepressant 84

Parstelin a brand name for tranylcypromine (an MAOI antidepressant 84) with trifluoperazine (a phenothiazine antipsychotic 85)

Partobulin a brand name for anti-D immunoglobulin (a drug used to prevent sensitization to Rhesus antigen)

Pavacol-D a brand name for pholcodine (a cough suppressant 94)

Pecram a brand name for aminophylline (a drug used for heart failure)

pemoline a nervous system stimulant 88

Penbritin a brand name for ampicillin (a penicillin antibiotic 128)

penbutolol a beta blocker 97

Pendramine a brand name for penicillamine 357 (an antirheumatic 117)

penicillamine 357 (an antirheumatic 117)

penicillin G a name for benzylpenicillin (a penicillin antibiotic 128)

penicillin V a name for phenoxymethyl-penicillin 362 (a penicillin antibiotic 128)

Penidural a brand name for benzathine penicillin (an antibiotic 128)

Pentacarinat a brand name for pentamidine (an antiprotozoal 136)

pentaerythritol tetranitrate a nitrate anti-angina drug 101

pentamidine an antiprotozoal 136

pentazocine 358 (a *narcotic analgesic* 80)

Pepcid PM a brand name for famotidine (an anti-ulcer drug 109)

peppermint oil a substance for indigestion and bowel spasm 110

Pepto-Bismol a brand-name preparation for diarrhoea and upset stomach containing bismuth

Percutol a brand name for glyceryl trinitrate 294 (an anti-angina drug 101)

pergolide a drug for *parkinsonism* 83

Pergonal a brand name for menotrophin (a drug for infertility 160)

Periactin a brand name for cyproheptadine (an antihistamine 124 used as an appetite stimulant 88)

pericyazine an antipsychotic 85

perindopril an ACE inhibitor 98

permethrin a *topical* antiparasitic 176

perphenazine an antipsychotic 85 and anti-emetic 90

Persantin a brand name for dipyridamole 266 (an antiplatelet drug 104); *illus. 36 I*

Pertofran a brand name for desipramine (a tricyclic antidepressant 84)

Peru balsam an *antiseptic* 175 for haemorrhoids 113

pethidine 359 (a *narcotic analgesic* 80)

Pevaryl a brand name for econazole 275 (an antifungal 138)

Pharmorubicine a brand name for epirubicin (a *cytotoxic* anticancer drug 154)

Phasal a brand name for lithium 318 (an anti-manic drug 85)

phenazocine a *narcotic analgesic* 80

phenelzine 360 (an MAOI antidepressant 84)

Phenergan a brand name for promethazine 379 (an antihistamine 124 and anti-emetic 90); *illus. 38G*

phenindamine an antihistamine 124

phenindione an oral anticoagulant 104

pheniramine an antihistamine 124

phenobarbitone 361 (a barbiturate anticonvulsant 86)

phenol an *antiseptic* used in throat lozenges and sprays 175

phenolphthalein a stimulant laxative 111

phenoxybenzamine a drug for phaeochromocytoma (tumour of the adrenal glands)

phenoxymethylpenicillin 362 (a penicillin antibiotic 128)

Phensedyl a brand-name cough preparation 94 containing codeine 244 and promethazine 379

Phensic a brand-name *analgesic* 84 containing aspirin 199 and caffeine

phentermine an appetite suppressant 84

phenylbutazone 363 (a non-steroidal anti-inflammatory 116)

phenylephrine 364 (a decongestant 93)

phenylpropanolamine 365 (a decongestant 93)

phenytoin 366 (an anticonvulsant 86)

pholcodine a cough suppressant 94

Pholcomed a brand-name cough preparation 94 containing papaverine and pholcodine

Phyllocontin Continus a brand name for aminophylline (a *bronchodilator* 92)

Physeptone a brand name for methadone (a *narcotic* 439 used as an *analgesic* 80 and to ease heroin withdrawal)

physostigmine a *miotic* for glaucoma 168

Phytex a brand-name antifungal 138 containing salicyclic acid

Phytocil a brand name *topical* antifungal 138

phytomenadione vitamin K 433 (a vitamin 149)

Picolax a brand name for sodium picosulphate and magnesium citrate (both laxatives 111)

pilocarpine 367 (a *miotic* for glaucoma 168)

pimozide an antipsychotic 85 also used for movement disorders

pindolol a beta blocker 97

pipenzolate an *antispasmodic* for irritable bowel syndrome 110

piperacillin a penicillin antibiotic 128

piperazine 368 (an anthelmintic 139)

Piportil Depot a brand name for pipothiazine palmitate (an antipsychotic 85)

pipothiazine palmitate an antipsychotic 85

Pipril a brand name for piperacillin (a penicillin antibiotic 128)

Piptal a brand name for pipenzolate (an *antispasmodic* for irritable bowel syndrome 110)

Piptalin a brand name for pipenzolate (an *antispasmodic* for irritable bowel syndrome 110) with dimethicone

pirbuterol a *sympathomimetic bronchodilator* 92

pirenzepine an *anticholinergic* for peptic ulcers 109

piretanide a loop diuretic 99

Piriton a brand name for chlorpheniramine 227 (an antihistamine 124); *illus. 36S*

piroxicam 369 (a non-steroidal anti-inflammatory 116 and drug for gout 119)

pivampicillin a penicillin antibiotic 128

pivmecillinam a penicillin antibiotic 128

pizotifen 370 (a drug for migraine 89)

Plaquenil a brand name for hydroxychloroquine (an anti-malarial 137)

Platet 300 a brand name antiplatelet drug containing aspirin 199

Plendil a brand name for felodipine (a calcium channel blocker 101)

plicamycin a *cytotoxic* antibiotic 128

poldine methylsulphate an *antispasmodic* for irritable bowel syndrome 110

Pollon-Eze a brand name for astemizole (an antihistamine 124)

Polybactrin a brand name for bacitracin with neomycin and polymyxin B (all antibiotics 128)

Polyfax a brand name for bacitracin with polymyxin B (both antibiotics 128)

polymyxin B an antibiotic 128

polynoxylin an antifungal 138 and antibacterial 131

Polytar a brand name for coal tar (a substance used for eczema 174, psoriasis 178, and dandruff 179)

polythiazide a thiazide diuretic 99

Polytrim a brand-name antibacterial 131 containing trimethoprim 416 and polymyxin B

polyvinyl alcohol an ingredient of artificial tear preparations 170

Ponderax a brand name for fenfluramine (an appetite suppressant 88)

Pondocillin a brand name for pivampicillin (a penicillin antibiotic 128)

Pondocillin Plus a brand name for pivampicillin with pivmecillinam (both penicillin antibiotics 128)

PONSTAN – RONICOL

Ponstan a brand name for mefenamic acid 325 (a non-steroidal anti-inflammatory 116); *illus. 41E*

Posalfilin a brand name for podophyllin with salicylic acid (both drugs for warts)

potassium 427 (a mineral 150)

potassium acetate potassium 427 (a mineral 150)

potassium bicarbonate an antacid 108

potassium chloride potassium 427 (a mineral 150)

potassium citrate a drug for cystitis that reduces the acidity of urine 166

potassium clavulanate a name for clavulanic acid (a substance given with amoxycillin 196 to make it more effective)

potassium hydroxyquinolone sulphate an agent with antibacterial 131, anti-fungal 138, and deodorant properties, used for skin infections 175 and acne 177

potassium iodide a drug used for overactive thyroid before surgery 144

potassium permanganate a skin *antiseptic* 175

povidone-iodine a skin *antiseptic* 175

practolol a beta blocker 97

Pragmatar a brand-name preparation for eczema 175, psoriasis 178, and dandruff 179 containing coal tar, salicylic acid, and sulphur

Pranoxen Continus a brand name for naproxen (a non-steroidal anti-inflammatory 116)

pravastatin a cholesterol-lowering agent 103

Praxilene a brand name for naftidrofuryl (a *vasodilator* 98)

praziquantel an anthelmintic 139 for tapeworms

prazosin 371 (an antihypertensive 102 also used to relieve urinary retention)

Precortisyl a brand name for prednisolone 372 (a corticosteroid 141)

Predenema a brand name for prednisolone 372 (a corticosteroid 141)

Predfoam a brand name for prednisolone 372 (a corticosteroid 141)

Prednesol a brand name for prednisolone 372 (a corticosteroid 141)

prednisolone 372 (a corticosteroid 141)

prednisone a corticosteroid 141

Predsol a brand name for prednisolone 372 (a corticosteroid 141)

Predsol-N a brand name for prednisolone 372 (a corticosteroid 141) with neomycin (an aminoglycoside antibiotic 128)

Prefil a brand name for sterculia (a bulk-forming agent 110 used as an appetite suppressant)

Pregaday a brand name for folic acid 424 (a vitamin 149) with iron 425 (a mineral 150)

Pregnavite Forte F a brand-name multivitamin 149 with iron 425 (a mineral 150)

Pregnyl a brand name for human chorionic gonadotrophin (a drug for infertility 164)

Premarin a brand name for conjugated oestrogens 246 (a female sex *hormone* 147); *illus. 35L*

Prempak-C a brand-name drug for menopausal symptoms 147 containing conjugated oestrogens 246 and norgestrel

Prepulsid a brand name for cisapride (a gastrointestinal motility regulator and antacid 108); *illus. 44J*

Prescal a brand name for isradipine (a calcium channel blocker 101)

Prestim a brand name for bendrofluazide 206 (a thiazide diuretic 99) with timolol 412 (a beta blocker 97)

Priadel a brand name for lithium 318 (an antimanic drug 85)

prilocaine a local *anaesthetic* 80

Primalan a brand name for mequitazine (an antihistamine 124)

primaquine an antimalarial 137

Primaxin a brand name for cilastatin and imipenem (both antibiotics 128)

primidone 373 (an anticonvulsant 86)

Primolut N a brand name for norethisterone 349 (a female sex *hormone* 147); *illus. 45D*

Primoteston Depot a brand name for testosterone 406 (a male sex *hormone* 146)

Primperan a brand name for metoclopramide 333 (a gastrointestinal motility regulator and anti-emetic 90)

Prioderm a brand name for malathion (a *topical* antiparasitic 176)

Pripsen a brand name for piperazine 368 (an anthelmintic 139) with senna (a stimulant laxative 111)

Pro-Actidil a brand name for triprolidine (an antihistamine 124)

Pro-Banthine a brand name for propantheline (an *anticholinergic anti-spasmodic* for irritable bowel syndrome 110 and urinary incontinence 166)

probenecid 374 (a uricosuric for gout 119)

probucol a lipid-lowering drug 103

procainamide an anti-arrhythmic 100

Procainamide Durules a brand name for procainamide (an anti-arrhythmic 100)

procaine a local *anaesthetic* 80

procaine penicillin a penicillin antibiotic 128

procarbazine a drug for lymphatic cancers and small-cell cancer of the lung 154

prochlorperazine 375 (a phenothiazine anti-emetic 90 and antipsychotic 85)

Proctofoam HC a brand name for hydrocortisone 300 (a corticosteroid 141) with pramoxine (a local *anaesthetic* 80)

Proctosedyl a brand name for hydrocortisone 300 (a corticosteroid 141) with cinchocaine (a local *anaesthetic* 80)

procyclidine 376 (an *anticholinergic* for *parkinsonism* 87)

Profasi a brand name for human chorionic gonadotrophin 231 (a drug for infertility 164)

Proflex a brand name for ibuprofen 302 (a non-steroidal anti-inflammatory 116)

Progesic a brand name for fenoprofen (a non-steroidal anti-inflammatory 116)

progesterone a female sex *hormone* 147

proguanil 377 (an antimalarial 137)

Progynova a brand name for oestradiol (an oestrogen 147)

prolintane a nervous system stimulant 88

Proluton Depot a brand name for hydroxyprogesterone (a progestogen 147 used to prevent miscarriage)

promazine 378 (a phenothiazine antipsychotic 85)

promethazine 379 (an antihistamine 124 and anti-emetic 90)

Prominal a brand name for methylphenobarbitone (a barbiturate anticonvulsant 86)

Prondol a brand name for iprindole (an antidepressant 84)

Pronestyl a brand name for procainamide (an anti-arrhythmic 100)

Propaderm a brand name for beclo-methasone 205 (a corticosteroid 141)

Propaderm-A a brand name for beclomethasone 205 (a corticosteroid 141) with chlortetracycline (a tetracycline antibiotic 128)

propafenone an anti-arrhythmic 100

Propain a brand-name analgesic 80 containing codeine 244, diphen-hydramine 264, paracetamol 356, and caffeine

propamidine isethionate an antibacterial 131 for eye infections

propantheline an *anticholinergic anti-spasmodic* for irritable bowel syndrome 110 and urinary incontinence 166

Propine a brand name for dipivefrin (a *sympathomimetic* for glaucoma 166)

Pro-Plus a brand name for caffeine (a stimulant 92)

propranolol 380 (a beta blocker 97)

propylthiouracil 381 (an antithyroid drug 144)

Proscar a brand name for finasteride

Prostap SR a brand name for leuprorelin (a drug for menstrual disorders 160)

Prostigmin a brand name for neo-stigmine 343 (a drug for myasthenia gravis 121); *illus. 43T*

Prothiaden a brand name for dothiepin 271 (a tricyclic antidepressant 84); *illus. 35K*

protriptyline a tricyclic anti-depressant 84

Pro-Vent a brand name for theophylline 408 (a *bronchodilator* 92)

Provera a brand name for medroxy-progesterone 324 (a female sex *hormone* 147); *illus. 45P*

Pro-Viron a brand name for mesterolone (a male sex *hormone* 146)

Prozac a brand name for fluoxetine 288 (an antidepressant 84); *illus. 41D*

pseudoephedrine a *sympathomimetic* decongestant 93

Psoradrate a brand name for dithranol 269 (a drug for psoriasis 178) with urea (an *emollient*)

Psorin a brand-name drug for psoriasis 178 containing dithranol 269, coal tar, and salicylic acid

Pulmadil a brand name for rimiterol (a *sympathomimetic bronchodilator* 92)

Pulmicort a brand name for budesonide (a corticosteroid 141)

Puri-Nethol a brand name for mercaptopurine 328 (an anticancer drug 154); *illus. 37N*

Pyopen a brand name for carbenicillin (a penicillin antibiotic 128)

pyrantel an anthelmintic 139

pyrazinamide an antituberculous drug 132

pyridostigmine 382 (a drug for myasthenia gravis 121)

pyridoxine 428 (a vitamin 149)

pyrimethamine 383 (an antimalarial 137)

pyrithione zinc an antimicrobial for dandruff 179

Pyrogastrone a brand name for aluminium hydroxide 191, magnesium trisilicate, and sodium bicarbonate 393 (all antacids 108), carbenoxolone 218 (an anti-ulcer drug 109) and alginic acid (an antifoaming agent)

Q

Quellada a brand name for lindane 317 (a *topical* antiparasitic 176)

Questran a brand name for cholestyramine 230 (a lipid-lowering drug 103)

quinalbarbitone a barbiturate sleeping drug 82

quinapril an ACE inhibitor 98

quinestrol an oestrogen 147

quinine 384 (an antimalarial 137)

Quinocort a brand name for hydrocortisone 300 (a corticosteroid 141) with potassium hydroquinoline sulphate (an agent for skin infections 175)

Quinoderm a brand-name preparation for acne 177 containing benzoyl peroxide 208 and potassium hydroquinoline sulphate

Quinoped a brand-name antifungal 138 containing benzoyl peroxide 208 and potassium hydroquinoline sulphate (an agent for skin infections 175)

R

ramipril an ACE inhibitor 98

ranitidine 385 (an anti-ulcer drug 109)

Rapitard a brand name for insulin 306 (an antidiabetic 142)

Rastinon a brand name for tolbutamide 413 (an antidiabetic 142); *illus. 42C*

razoxane a *cytotoxic* anticancer drug 154

Razoxin a brand name for razoxane (a *cytotoxic* anticancer drug 154)

R.B.C. a brand name for antazoline 198 (an antihistamine 124) with calamine and camphor (both antipruritics 173), and cetrimide (a skin *antiseptic* 175)

Recormon a brand name for epoietin 278 (a kidney hormone 140)

Redeptin a brand name for fluspirilene (an antipsychotic 85)

Redoxon a brand name for vitamin C 431 (a vitamin 149)

Regaine a brand name for minoxidil 336 (for treatment of male pattern baldness 179)

Regulan a brand name for ispaghula (a bulk-forming agent used as a laxative 111)

Rehibin a brand name for cyclofenil (a drug used to treat infertility 164)

Rehidrat a brand name for oral rehydration salts containing potassium 427, sodium chloride 429, sodium bicarbonate 393, and glucose

Relifex a brand name for nabumetone (a non-steroidal anti-inflammatory 116)

Remediene a brand name for paracetamol 356 (a non-*narcotic analgesic* 80) with dihydrocodeine (a *narcotic analgesic* 80)

Remnos a brand name for nitrazepam 347 (a benzodiazepine sleeping drug 82)

remoxipride an antipsychotic 85

Rennie Digestif a brand-name antacid 108 containing calcium carbonate with magnesium carbonate

reproterol a *bronchodilator* 92

reserpine a centrally-acting antihypertensive 102

Resolve a brand-name *analgesic* 80 and antacid 108 containing paracetamol 356, sodium bicarbonate 393, calcium carbonate, potassium bicarbonate, citric acid, and vitamin C 431

resorcinol a keratolytic agent used mainly in acne preparations 177

Respacal a brand name for tulobuterol (a *bronchodilator* 92)

Restandol a brand name for testosterone 406 (a male sex *hormone* 146); *illus. 39K*

Retin A a brand name for tretinoin (a drug for acne 177)

retinoic acid vitamin A 430 (a vitamin 149)

retinoids vitamin A 430 (a vitamin 149)

retinol vitamin A 430 (a vitamin 149)

Retrovir a brand name for zidovudine 420 (an antiviral for HIV infection and AIDS 157); *illus. 41K*

Revanil a brand name for lysuride (a drug for *parkinsonism* 87)

Rheumacin LA a brand name for indomethacin 305 (a non-steroidal anti-inflammatory 116 and drug for gout 119)

Rheumox a brand name for azapropazone (a non-steroidal anti-inflammatory 116)

Rhinocort a brand name for budesonide (a corticosteroid 141)

Rhinolast a brand name for azelastine (an antihistamine 124)

Rhumalgan a brand name for diclofenac (a non-steroidal anti-inflammatory 116)

ribavirin an antiviral 133 used for certain lung infections in infants and children

riboflavin 428 (a vitamin 149)

Ridaura a brand name for auranofin 202 (an antirheumatic 117); *illus. 37J*

Rifadin a brand name for rifampicin 386 (an antituberculous drug 132); *illus. 40D*

rifampicin 386 (an antituberculous drug 132)

Rifater a brand name for isoniazid 309 with rifampicin 386 and pyrazinamide (all antituberculous drugs 132)

Rifinah 150 a brand name for isoniazid 309 with rifampicin 386 (both antituberculous drugs 132)

Rifinah 300 a brand name for isoniazid 309 with rifampicin 386 (both antituberculous drugs 132)

Rimactane a brand name for rifampicin 386 (an antituberculous drug 132)

Rimactazid a brand name for isoniazid 309 with rifampicin 386 (both antituberculous drugs 132)

Rimifon a brand name for isoniazid 309 (an antituberculous drug 132)

rimiterol a *sympathomimetic bronchodilator* 92

Rimso-50 a brand name for dimethyl sulphoxide (a drug for urinary infection 166)

Rinatec a brand name for ipratropium bromide 308 (a *bronchodilator* 92)

Risperdal a brand name for risperidone 387 (an antipsychotic 85)

risperidone 387 (an antipsychotic 85)

ritodrine 388 (a uterine muscle relaxant 165)

Rivotril a brand name for clonazepam 240 (a benzodiazepine anticonvulsant 86); *illus. 36E*

Roaccutane a brand name for isotretinoin 312 (a drug for acne 177); *illus. 40F, 40G*

Ro-A-Vit a brand name for vitamin A 430 (a vitamin 149)

Robaxin a brand name for methocarbamol (a muscle relaxant 120)

Robaxisal Forte a brand name for aspirin 199 (a non-*narcotic analgesic* 80) with methocarbamol (a muscle relaxant 120)

Robinul a brand name for glycopyrronium bromide (an *anticholinergic* used in general *anaesthesia* 80)

Robitussin Chesty Cough a brand name for guaiphenesin (an expectorant 94)

Roferon-A a brand name for interferon 307 (an antiviral 133 and anticancer drug 154)

Rohypnol a brand name for flunitrazepam (a benzodiazepine sleeping drug 82)

Ronicol a brand name for nicotinyl alcohol (a form of niacin 426)

Roter a brand-name antacid 108 containing sodium bicarbonate 393, magnesium carbonate, frangula, and bismuth

Rotersept a brand name for chlorhexidine (a skin *antiseptic* 175)

Rowachol a brand-name preparation of essential oils for gallstones 114

Roxiam a brand name for remoxipride (an antipsychotic 85)

Rynacrom a brand name for sodium cromoglycate 394 (an anti-allergy drug 124)

Rynacrom Compound a brand name for sodium cromoglycate 394 (an anti-allergy drug 124) with xylometazoline (a decongestant 93)

Rythmodan a brand name for disopyramide 267 (an anti-arrhythmic 100); *illus. 41A*

S

Sabril a brand name for vigabatrin (an anticonvulsant 82)

Sabidal SR 270 a brand name for choline theophyllinate (a xanthine *bronchodilator* 92)

Saizen a brand name for somatropin (a synthetic pituitary *hormone* 145)

Salactol a brand-name wart preparation containing salicylic acid, lactic acid, and collodion

Salazopyrin a brand name for sulphasalazine 401 (a drug for inflammatory bowel disease 110 and an antirheumatic 117); *illus. 36K*

Salbulin a brand name for salbutamol 389 (a *bronchodilator* 92)

salbutamol 389 (a *bronchodilator* 92 and drug used in labour 165)

salcatonin a drug for bone disorders 122

salicylic acid a keratolytic for acne 177, dandruff 179, psoriasis 178, and warts

salmeterol a *bronchodilator* 92

Salofalk a brand name for mesalazine 327 (a drug for ulcerative colitis 112); *illus. 36M*

salsalate a drug similar to aspirin 199 used for arthritic disorders 117

Saluric a brand name for chlorothiazide (a thiazide diuretic 99)

Salzone a brand name for paracetamol 356 (a non-*narcotic analgesic* 80)

Sandimmun a brand name for cyclosporin (an immunosuppressant 156); *illus. 39J*

Sandocal a brand name for calcium 422 (a mineral 150)

Sando-K a brand name for potassium 427 (a mineral 150)

Sandostatin a brand name for octreotide (a synthetic pituitary *hormone* 145 used to relieve symptoms of cancer of the pancreas 154)

Sanomigran a brand name for pizotifen (a drug for migraine 89); *illus. 37C*

Saventrine a brand name for isoprenaline 310 (a *bronchodilator* 92); *illus. 44 I*

Savlon Liquid Antiseptic Disinfectant a brand name fo chlorhexidine with cetrimide (both skin *antiseptics* 175)

Schering PC4 a brand-name postcoital contraceptive containing ethinyloestradiol 282 and levonorgestrel 316

Scheriproct a brand name for prednisolone 372 (a corticosteroid 141) with cinchocaine (a local *anaesthetic* 80)

Scopoderm a brand name anti-emetic drug containing hyoscine 301

Sea Legs a brand name for meclozine (an antihistamine 124 used to prevent motion sickness)

Secadrex a brand name for hydrochlorothiazide 299 (a thiazide diuretic 99) with acebutolol (a beta blocker 97)

Seconal Sodium a brand name for quinalbarbitone (a barbiturate sleeping drug 82)

Sectral a brand name for acebutolol (a beta blocker 97)

Securon a brand name for verapamil 418 (an anti-angina drug 101 and anti-arrhythmic 100)

Securopen a brand name for azlocillin (a penicillin antibiotic 128)

Seldane a brand name for terfenadine 405 (an antihistamine 124)

selegiline a drug for severe *parkinsonism* 87

selenium 429 (a mineral 150)

selenium sulphide a substance for skin inflammation 175 and dandruff 179

Selexid a brand name for pivmecillinam (a penicillin antibiotic 128)

Selsun a brand-name dandruff shampoo 179 containing selenium sulphide

Semi-Daonil a brand name for glibenclamide 293 (an oral antidiabetic 142)

Semitard MC a brand name for insulin 306 (a drug for diabetes 142)

Semprex a brand name for acrivastine (an antihistamine 124)

Senlax a brand name for senna (a stimulant laxative 111)

senna a stimulant laxative 111

Senokot a brand name for senna (a stimulant laxative 111)

Sential HC a brand name for hydrocortisone 300 (a corticosteroid 141) with urea (an *emollient*)

Septrin a brand name for co-trimoxazole 248 (an antibacterial 131); *illus. 42M*

Serc a brand name for betahistine 209 (a drug for Ménière's disease 90); *illus. 45L*

Serenace a brand name for haloperidol 296 (a butyrophenone antipsychotic 85)

Serevent a brand name for salmeterol (a *bronchodilator* 92)

Serophene a brand name for clomiphene 238 (a drug for infertility 164)

Seroxat a brand name for paroxetine (an antidepressant 84)

sertraline 390 (an antidepressant 84)

Setlers a brand-name antacid 108 containing calcium carbonate and magnesium hydroxide 323

Sevredol a brand name for morphine sulphate (a *narcotic analgesic* 80)

SH-420 a brand name for norethisterone 349 (a female sex *hormone* 147)

silver nitrate a skin disinfectant 175

silver sulphadiazine a *topical* antibacterial 131 used to prevent infection in burns 175

Simeco suspension a brand-name antacid 108 containing aluminium hydroxide 191, dimethicone, magnesium carbonate, and magnesium hydroxide

Simeco tablets a brand-name antacid 108 containing aluminium hydroxide 191, dimethicone, magnesium carbonate, and magnesium hydroxide 323

Simplene a brand name for adrenaline 188 (a drug for glaucoma 168)

simvastatin 391 (a lipid-lowering drug 103)

Sinemet a brand name for levodopa 315 with carbidopa (both drugs for *parkinsonism* 87)

Sinequan a brand name for doxepin (a tricyclic antidepressant 84)

Sinthrome a brand name for nicoumalone (an anticoagulant 104)

Sinutab a brand name for paracetamol 356 (a non-*narcotic analgesic* 80) with phenylpropanolamine 356 (a decongestant 93)

Siopel a brand-name barrier cream containing cetrimide and dimethicone

Slo-Indo a brand name for indomethacin 305 (a non-steroidal anti-inflammatory 116 and drug for gout 119)

Slo-Phyllin a brand name for theophylline 408 (a *bronchodilator* 92); *illus. 39M*

Sloprolol a brand name for propranolol 380 (a beta blocker 97)

Slow-Fe a brand name for iron 425 (a mineral 150)

Slow-Fe Folic a brand name for folic acid 424 (a vitamin 149) with iron 425 (a mineral 150)

Slow-K a brand name for potassium 427 (a mineral 150)

Slow-Trasicor a brand name for oxprenolol 355 (a beta blocker 97)

Sno Phenicol a brand name for eye drops containing chloramphenicol 224 (an antibiotic 128)

Sno Pilo a brand name for pilocarpine 367 (a *miotic* for glaucoma 168)

Sno Tears a brand name for polyvinyl alcohol (an ingredient of artificial tear preparations 170)

soda mint tablets sodium bicarbonate 393 (an antacid 108)

sodium 429 (a mineral 150)

sodium acid phosphate a laxative 111

Sodium Amytal a brand name for amylobarbitone (a barbiturate sleeping drug 82)

sodium aurothiomalate 392 (an antirheumatic 117)

sodium bicarbonate 393 (an antacid 108)

sodium calcium edetate an *antidote* to poisoning by lead and other heavy metals

sodium cellulose phosphate an agent used to reduce levels of calcium 422 in the blood

sodium chloride common salt, contains sodium 429 (a mineral 150)

sodium citrate a drug for urinary tract infections 166

sodium clodronate an agent used to treat low blood calcium in cancer patients

sodium cromoglycate 394 (an anti-allergy drug 124)

sodium fluoride fluoride 424 (a mineral 150)

sodium fusidate an antibiotic 128

sodium ironedetate iron 425 (a mineral 150)

sodium nitroprusside a *vasodilator* 98

sodium picosulphate a stimulant laxative 111

sodium valproate 395 (an anti-convulsant 86)

Sofradex a brand name for dexametha-sone 255 (a corticosteroid 141) with framycetin and gramicidin (both antibiotics 128)

Soframycin a brand name for framycetin (an antibiotic 128)

Solarcaine a brand name for benzocaine (a local *anaesthetic* 80) with triclosan (an antimicrobial 175)

Solpadeine a brand-name *analgesic* 80 containing codeine 244, paracetamol 356, and caffeine

Solpadol a brand name for paracetamol 356 (a non-*narcotic analgesic* 80) with codeine 244 (a *narcotic analgesic* 80)

Solu-Cortef a brand name for hydro-cortisone 300 (a corticosteroid 141)

Solu-Medrone a brand name for methylprednisolone (a cortico-steroid 141)

Solvazinc a brand name for zinc 433 (a mineral 150)

somatropin a synthetic pituitary *hormone* 145

Sominex a brand-name sleeping drug 82 containing promethazine 379

Somnite a brand name for nitrazepam 347 (a benzodiazepine sleeping drug 82)

Soneryl a brand name for butobarbitone (a benzodiazepine sleeping drug 82)

Soni-Slo a brand name for isosorbide dinitrate 311 (a nitrate *vasodilator* 98 and anti-angina drug 101)

Sorbichew a brand name for isosorbide dinitrate 311 (a nitrate *vasodilator* 98 and anti-angina drug 101)

Sorbid SA a brand name for isosorbide dinitrate 311 (a nitrate *vasodilator* 98 and anti-angina drug 101)

sorbitol a sweetening agent used in diabetic foods, and included in skin creams as a moisturizer 175

Sorbitrate a brand name for isosorbide dinitrate 311 (a nitrate *vasodilator* 98 and anti-angina drug 101); *illus. 37H, 38A*

Sotacor a brand name for sotalol (a beta blocker 97)

sotalol a beta blocker 97

Sotazide a brand name for hydrochloro-thiazide 299 (a thiazide diuretic 99) with sotalol (a beta blocker 97)

Sparine a brand name for promazine 378 (a phenothiazine antipsychotic 85); *illus. 35H*

Spasmonal a brand name for alverine citrate (an *antispasmodic* for irritable bowel syndrome 110)

spectinomycin an aminoglycoside antibiotic 128

Spectraban 4 lotion a brand name for padimate-O (a sunscreening agent 179)

Spectraban 15 lotion a brand name for aminobenzoic acid with padimate-O (both sunscreening agents 179)

Spiroctan a brand name for spironolactone 397 (a potassium-sparing diuretic 99)

Spirolone a brand name for spirono-lactone 397 (a potassium-sparing diuretic 99)

spironolactone 397 (a potassium-sparing diuretic 99)

Sporanox a brand name for itraconazole (an antifungal 138)

Sprilon a brand-name skin preparation containing dimethicone and zinc oxide

SRM Rhotard a brand name for morphine sulphate (a *narcotic analgesic* 80)

Stabillin V-K a brand name for phenoxymethylpenicillin 362 (a penicillin antibiotic 128); *illus. 43B*

Stafoxil a brand name for flucloxacillin (a penicillin antibiotic 128)

stanozolol an anabolic steroid 146

Staril a brand name for fosinopril (an ACE inhibitor 98)

Staycept Jelly a brand name for octoxynol (a spermicidal agent)

Staycept pessaries a brand name for nonoxinol 9 (a spermicidal agent)

Stelazine a brand name for trifluoperazine (a phenothiazine antipsychotic 85 and anti-emetic 90)

Stemetil a brand name for prochlor-perazine 375 (a phenothiazine anti-emetic 90 and antipsychotic 85); *illus. 43R*

sterculia a bulk-forming agent used as an antidiarrhoeal 110 and laxative 111

Ster-Zac Bath Concentrate a brand name for triclosan (an antimicrobial 175)

Ster-Zac Powder a brand name for hexachlorophane (a skin *antiseptic* 175) with zinc oxide (an agent used in skin preparations 175)

Stesolid a brand name for diazepam 259 (a benzodiazepine anti-anxiety drug 83, muscle relaxant 120, and anti-convulsant 86)

Stiedex a brand name for desoxy-methasone (a *topical* corticosteroid 174)

Stiedex LPN a brand name for desoxy-methasone (a *topical* corticosteroid 174) with neomycin (an aminoglycoside antibiotic 128)

stilboestrol 398 (a female sex *hormone* 147)

Strepsils a brand-name preparation for mouth and throat infections containing amymetacresol and dichlorobenzyl alcohol (both *antiseptics* 179)

Streptase a brand name for streptokinase 399 (a thrombolytic 105)

streptokinase 399 (a thrombolytic agent 105)

streptomycin an antituberculous drug 132

Stromba a brand name for stanozolol (an anabolic steroid 146)

Stugeron a brand name for cinnarizine 233 (an antihistamine anti-emetic 90); *illus. 43P*

sucralfate 400 (an ulcer-healing drug 109)

Sudafed a brand name for pseudo-ephedrine (a decongestant 93)

Sudafed Co a brand name for paracetamol 356 (a non-*narcotic analgesic* 80) and pseudoephedrine (a decongestant 93)

Sudafed Expectorant a brand name for guaiphenesin (an expectorant 94) with pseudoephedrine (a decong-estant 93)

Sudafed SA a brand name for pseudo-ephedrine (a decongestant 93)

Sudocrem a brand-name skin preparation containing benzyl benzoate and zinc oxide

sulconazole an antifungal 138

Suleo-C a brand name for carbaryl (an antiparasitic 176)

Suleo-M a brand name for malathion (an antiparasitic 176)

sulfadoxine a drug used with pyrimeth-amine 383 for malaria 137

sulfametopyrazine a sulphonamide antibacterial 131

sulindac a non-steroidal anti-inflammatory 116

sulphabenzamide a sulphonamide antibacterial 131

sulphacetamide a sulphonamide antibacterial 131

sulphadiazine a sulphonamide antibacterial 131

sulphadimidine a sulphonamide antibacterial 131

sulphamethoxazole a sulphonamide antibacterial 131

sulphasalazine 401 (a drug for inflammatory bowel syndrome 112 and an antirheumatic 117)

sulphathiazole a sulphonamide antibacterial 131

sulphinpyrazone a uricosuric for gout 119

sulphur a *topical* antibacterial 131 and antifungal 138 for acne 177 and dandruff 179

sulpiride an antipsychotic 85

Sulpitil a brand name for sulpiride (an antipsychotic 85)

Sultrin a brand name for sulphathiazole with sulphacetamide and sulpha-benzamide (all sulphonamide antibacterials 131)

sumatriptan 402 (a drug for migraine 89)

Suprax a brand name for cefixime (a cephalosporin antibiotic 128)

Suprecur a brand name for buserelin (a drug for menstrual disorders 160)

Suprefact a brand name for buserelin (a drug for menstrual disorders 160)

Surgam a brand name for tiaprofenic acid (a non-steroidal anti-inflammatory 116)

Surmontil a brand name for trimipramine (a tricyclic antidepressant 84)

Suscard a brand name for glyceryl trinitrate 294 (an anti-angina drug 101)

Sustac a brand name for glyceryl trinitrate 294 (an anti-angina drug 101)

Sustamycin a brand name for tetracycline 407 (an antibiotic 128)

Sustanon a brand name for testosterone 406 (a male sex *hormone* 146)

Symmetrel a brand name for amantadine 192 (an antiviral 133 and drug for *parkinsonism* 87); *illus. 39C*

Synacthen a brand name for tetracosactrin (a drug used to assess adrenal gland function)

Synalar a brand name for fluocinolone (a *topical* corticosteroid 174)

Synalar C a brand name for fluocinolone (a *topical* corticosteroid 174) with clioquinol (an *antiseptic* 175)

Synalar N a brand name for fluocinolone (a *topical* corticosteroid 174) with neomycin (an aminoglycoside anti-biotic 128)

Synarel a brand name for nafarelin (a drug for menstrual disorders 160)

Syndol a brand name for codeine 244 and paracetamol 356 (both *analgesics* 80), with caffeine (a stimulant 88) and doxylamine (an antihistamine 124)

Synflex a brand name for naproxen 341 (a non-steroidal anti-inflammatory 116 and drug for gout 119)

Synkavit a brand name for menadiol sodium phosphate (vitamin K 433)

Synphase a brand-name oral contra-ceptive 161 containing ethinyloestradiol 282 and norethisterone 349

Syntaris a brand name for flunisolide (a corticosteroid 141)

Syntex Menophase a brand name for norethisterone 349 with mestranol (both female sex *hormones* 147)

Syntocinon a brand name for oxytocin (a uterine stimulant 165)

Syntometrine a brand name for ergometrine with oxytocin (both uterine stimulants 165)

Syntopressin a brand name for lypressin 322 (a drug for diabetes insipidus 145)

Synuretic a brand name for amiloride 193 with hydrochlorothiazide 299 (both diuretics 99)

Sytron a brand name for sodium ironedetate (iron 425)

T

Tagamet a brand name for cimetidine 232 (an anti-ulcer drug 109); *illus. 37P, 37Q*

talampicillin a penicillin antibiotic 128

Talpen a brand name for talampicillin (a penicillin antibiotic 128)

Tambocor a brand name for flecainide (an anti-arrhythmic 100)

Tamofen a brand name for tamoxifen 403 (an anticancer drug 154)

tamoxifen 403 (an anticancer drug 154)

Tampovagan a brand name for stilboestrol (a female sex *hormone* 147) and lactic acid

Tancolin a brand-name cough preparation 94 containing dextro-methorphan 256, and glycerol

Tanderil a brand name for oxyphenbutazone (a non-steroidal anti-inflammatory 116)

Tarcortin a brand name for hydrocortisone 300 (a corticosteroid 141) with coal tar (a substance for psoriasis 178 and eczema 175)

Targocid a brand name for teicoplanin (an antibiotic 128)

Tarivid a brand name for ofloxacin (an antibiotic 128)

Tavegil a brand name for clemastine (an antihistamine 124)

Tazocin a brand name for piperacillin (an antibiotic 128) with tazobactam (a substance that increases the effectiveness of piperacillin)

TCP Liquid Antiseptic a brand-name *antiseptic* 179 containing phenol, chlorophenol, and 2-iodophenol

Tears Naturale a brand-name artificial tear preparation 170 containing hypromellose

Teejel a brand name for choline salicylate (a drug similar to aspirin 199)

Tegretol a brand name for carbamazepine 217 (an anticonvulsant 86); *illus. 43Q*

teicoplanin an antibiotic 128

temazepam 404 (a benzodiazepine sleeping drug 82)

Temgesic a brand name for buprenorphine (a *narcotic analgesic* 80)

temocillin an antibiotic 128

Temopen a brand name for temocillin (an antibiotic 128)

Tenif a brand name for atenolol 200 (a beta blocker 97) with nifedipine 346 (an anti-angina drug 101 and antihypertensive 102)

Tenoret-50 a brand name for atenolol 200 (a beta blocker 97) with chlorthalidone (a thiazide diuretic 99)

Tenoretic a brand name for atenolol 200 (a beta blocker 97) with chlorthalidone (a thiazide diuretic 99); *illus. 35N*

Tenormin a brand name for atenolol 200 (a beta blocker 97); *illus. 36G, 45F*

tenoxicam a non-steroidal anti-inflammatory 116

Tensium a brand name for diazepam 259 (a benzodiazepine anti-anxiety drug 83 and muscle relaxant 120)

Tenuate Dospan a brand name for diethylpropion (an appetite suppressant 88)

Teoptic a brand name for carteolol (a beta blocker 97 for glaucoma 168)

terazosin a *sympatholytic* antihypertensive 102

terbinafine an antifungal 138

terbutaline a *sympathomimetic bronchodilator* 92 and uterine muscle relaxant 165

terfenadine 405 (an antihistamine 124)

Teronac a brand name for mazindol (an appetite suppressant 88)

Terpoin a brand-name cough preparation 94 containing codeine 244, cineole, and menthol

Terra-Cortril a brand name for hydrocortisone 300 (a corticosteroid 141) with oxytetracycline (a tetracycline antibiotic 128)

Terra-Cortril Nystatin a brand name for hydrocortisone 300 (a corticosteroid 141) with nystatin 350 (an antifungal 138) and oxytetracycline (a tetracycline antibiotic 128)

Terramycin a brand name for oxytetra-cycline (a tetracycline antibiotic 128)

Tertroxin a brand name for liothyronine (a thyroid *hormone* 144)

testosterone 406 (a male sex *hormone* 146)

Tetmosol a brand name for monosulfiram (an antiparasitic 176)

tetrabenazine a drug for movement disorders

Tetrabid a brand name for tetracycline 407 (an antibiotic 128); *illus. 40A*

Tetrachel a brand name for tetracycline 407 (an antibiotic 128)

tetrachlorethylene an anthelmintic 139

tetracosactrin a drug similar to corticotrophin used to assess adrenal gland function 145

tetracycline 407 (an antibiotic 128)

Tetralysal 300 a brand name for lymecycline (a tetracycline anti-biotic 128)

T-Gel a brand name for coal tar (an agent for dandruff 179 and psoriasis 178)

Theo-Dur a brand name for theophylline 408 (a *bronchodilator* 92)

theophylline 408 (a *bronchodilator* 92)

Thephorin a brand name for phenindamine (an antihistamine 124)

thiabendazole an anthelmintic 139

thiamine 414 (a vitamin 149)

thiethylperazine an anti-emetic 90

thioguanine an antimetabolite for acute leukaemia 154

thiopentone a fast-acting barbiturate used to induce general *anaesthesia* 80

thioridazine 409 (a phenothiazine antipsychotic 85)

thymoxamine a drug used to reduce the size of the pupil after examination 170 and as a *vasodilator* 98 to improve blood supply to the limbs

thyroid hormones synthetic thyroid *hormones* used for hypothyroidism 144

thyroxine 410 (a thyroid *hormone* 144)

tiaprofenic acid a non-steroidal anti-inflammatory 116

tibolone 411 (a female sex *hormone* 147)

Ticar a brand name for ticarcillin (a penicillin antibiotic 128)

ticarcillin a penicillin antibiotic 128

Tigason a brand name for etretinate (a drug for psoriasis 178); *illus. 40K*

Tilade a brand name for nedocromil (a *bronchodilator* 92)

Tildiem a brand name for diltiazem 263 (an anti-angina drug 101); *illus. 44G*

Timecef a brand name for cefodizime (a cephalosporin antibiotic 128)

Timentin a brand name for ticarcillin (a penicillin antibiotic 128) with clavulanic acid (a substance that increases the effectiveness of ticarcillin)

Timodine a brand name for hydro-cortisone 300 (a corticosteroid 141) with nystatin 350 (an antifungal 138), benzalkonium chloride (an *antiseptic* 175), and dimethicone (a base for skin preparations 175)

timolol 412 (a beta blocker 97 and drug for glaucoma 168)

Timoptol a brand name for timolol 412 (a beta blocker 97 and drug for glaucoma 168)

Tinaderm-M a brand name for nystatin 350 with tolnaftate (both antifungals 138)

tinidazole an antibacterial 131

Tinset a brand name for oxatomide (an antihistamine 124)

tioconazole an antifungal 138

tissue plasminogen activator another name for alteplase 190 (a thrombolytic 105)

Titralac a brand name for calcium carbonate (a substance used to reduce blood phosphate levels) and glycine

Tixylix a brand name for promethazine 379 (an antihistamine 124) with pholcodine (a cough suppressant 94)

Tixylix Cough and Cold a brand-name cough suppressant 94 and decon-gestant 93 containing chlorpheniramine 227, pseudoephedrine, and pholcodine

Tobralex a brand name for tobramycin (an aminoglycoside antibiotic 128)

tobramycin an aminoglycoside anti-biotic 128

tocainide an anti-arrhythmic 100

tocopherols, tocopheryl vitamin E 432 (a vitamin 149)

Tofranil a brand name for imipramine 304 (a tricyclic antidepressant 84); *illus. 35Q*

Tolanase a brand name for tolazamide (an oral antidiabetic 142)

tolazamide an oral antidiabetic 142

tolbutamide 413 (an antidiabetic 142)

Tolectin a brand name for tolmetin (a non-steroidal anti-inflammatory 116)

Tolerzide a brand name for hydro-chlorothiazide 299 (a thiazide diuretic 99) with sotalol (a beta blocker 97)

tolmetin a non-steroidal anti-inflammatory 116

tolnaftate an antifungal 138

Tonocard a brand name for tocainide (an anti-arrhythmic 100)

Topal a brand-name antacid 108 containing aluminium hydroxide 191, magnesium carbonate, and alginic acid

Topicycline a brand name for tetracycline 407 (an antibiotic 128)

Topilar a brand name for fluclorolone (a *topical* corticosteroid 174)

Toradol a brand name for ketorolac (a non-steroidal anti-inflammatory 116 used as an *analgesic* 80)

Torecan a brand name for thiethylperazine (an anti-emetic 90)

Totamol a brand name for atenolol 200 (a beta blocker 97)

tramazoline a nasal decongestant 93

Tramil a brand name for paracetamol 356 and caffeine 88; *illus. 41M*

Tramil 500 a brand name for paracetamol 356 (a non-*narcotic analgesic* 80)

Trancopal a brand name for chlor-mezanone (an anti-anxiety drug 83)

Trandate a brand name for labetalol (a beta blocker 97)

tranexamic acid an antifibrinolytic used to promote blood clotting 104

Transiderm-Nitro a brand name for glyceryl trinitrate 294 (an anti-angina drug 101)

Tranxene a brand name for clorazepate (a benzodiazepine anti-anxiety drug 83)

tranylcypromine an MAOI antidepressant 84

Trasicor a brand name for oxprenolol 355 (a beta blocker 97); *illus. 44E*

Trasidrex a brand name for cyclo-penthiazide 249 (a thiazide diuretic 99) with oxprenolol 355 (a beta blocker 97)

Trasylol a brand name for aprotinin (an antifibrinolytic 104 used to promote blood clotting)

Travogyn a brand name for isoconazole (an antifungal 138)

trazodone 414 (an antidepressant 84)

Tremonil a brand name for methixene (an *anticholinergic* for *parkinsonism* 87)

Trental a brand name for oxpentifylline (a *vasodilator* 98)

treosulfan a drug for ovarian cancer 154

tretinoin a drug for acne 177

Tri-Adcortyl a brand name for nystatin 350 (an antifungal 138) with gramicidin and neomycin (both aminoglycoside antibiotics 128) and triamcinolone (a corticosteroid 141)

triamcinolone a corticosteroid 141

Triamco a brand name for hydrochloro-thiazide 299 with triamterene 415 (both diuretics 99)

triamterene 415 (a potassium-sparing diuretic 99)

triazolam a benzodiazepine sleeping drug 82

tribavirin ribavirin (an antiviral 133 used for certain lung infections in infants and children)

Tribiotic a brand name for neomycin with polymyxin and bacitracin (all antibiotics 128)

Tri-Cicatrin a brand name for neomycin with bacitracin (both antibiotics 128), hydrocortisone 300 (a corticosteroid 141), and nystatin 350 (an antifungal 138)

triclofos a non-benzodiazepine, non-barbiturate sleeping drug 82

triclosan an antimicrobial in skin preparations 175

Tridil a brand name for glyceryl trinitrate 294 (an anti-angina drug 101)

trifluoperazine a phenothiazine anti-psychotic 85 and an anti-emetic 90

trifluperidol an antipsychotic 85

Trilisate a brand name for choline magnesium trisalicylate (a drug similar to aspirin 199 used in arthritic conditions 117)

trilostane an adrenal *antagonist* for Cushing's syndrome and breast cancer

Triludan a brand name for terfenadine 405 (an antihistamine 124); *illus. 42G*

trimeprazine an antihistamine 124

trimethoprim 416 (an antibacterial 131)

trimipramine a tricyclic antidepressant 84

Trimogal a brand name for trimethoprim 416 (an antibacterial 131)

Trimopan a brand name for trimethoprim 416 (an antibacterial 131)

Trimovate a brand name for clobetasone (a *topical* corticosteroid 174) with nystatin 350 (an antifungal 138) and oxytetracycline (a tetracycline anti-biotic 128)

Trinordiol a brand-name oral contra-ceptive 161 containing ethinyloestradiol 282 and levonorgestrel 316

TriNovum a brand-name oral contraceptive 161 containing ethinyloestradiol 282 with norethisterone 349

Triogesic a brand name for paracetamol 356 (a non-*narcotic analgesic* 80) with phenylpropanolamine 365 (a decongestant 93)

Triominic a brand name for phenylpro-panolamine 365 (a decongestant 93) with pheniramine (an antihistamine 124)

Triperidol a brand name for trifluperidol (an antipsychotic 85)

Triplopen a brand name for benethamine penicillin, procaine penicillin, and benzylpenicillin (all penicillin antibiotics 128)

tripotassium dicitratobismuthate a bismuth compound used to treat peptic ulcers 109

triprolidine an antihistamine 124

Triptafen a brand name for amitriptyline 195 (a tricyclic antidepressant 84) with perphenazine (an antipsychotic 85)

Trisequens a brand name for oestradiol and oestriol (female sex *hormones* 147)

TRITACE – ZYMAFLUOR

Tritace a brand name for ramipril (an ACE inhibitor 98)

Trobicin a brand name for spectinomycin (an aminoglycoside antibiotic 128)

tropicamide a *mydriatic* 170

tropisetron an anti-emetic 90

Tropium a brand name for chlordiazepoxide 225 (a benzodiazepine anti-anxiety drug 83)

Trosyl a brand name for tioconazole (an antifungal 138)

Tryptizol a brand name for amitriptyline 195 (a tricyclic antidepressant 84); *illus.37E*

tubocurarine a drug used to relax muscles in general *anaesthesia* 80

Tuinal a brand name for amylobarbitone with quinalbarbitone (both barbiturate sleeping drugs 82)

tulobuterol a *bronchodilator* 92

Two's Company a brand name for nonoxinol 9 (a spermicidal agent)

Tylex a brand-name *analgesic* 80 containing codeine 244 and paracetamol 356

Tyrozets a brand name for benzocaine (a local *anaesthetic* 80) with tyrothricin (an antibiotic 128)

U

Ubretid a brand name for distigmine (a *parasympathomimetic* for urinary retention 166 and myasthenia gravis 121)

Ucerax a brand name for hydroxyzine (an anti-anxiety drug 83)

Ukidan a brand name for urokinase (a thrombolytic 105)

Ultralanum Plain a brand name for fluocortolone (a *topical* corticosteroid 174)

Ultraproct a brand name for fluocortolone (a *topical* corticosteroid 174) with cinchocaine (a local *anaesthetic* 80)

undecenoic acid an antifungal 138 for athlete's foot

Uniflu a brand name for codeine 244 (a *narcotic analgesic* 80 and cough suppressant) with diphenhydramine 264 (an antihistamine 128), paracetamol 356 (a non-*narcotic analgesic* 80), phenylephrine 364 (a decongestant 93), and caffeine (a stimulant 88)

Unigest a brand name for aluminium hydrochloride (an antacid 108) with dimethicone (an antifoaming agent)

Unihep a brand name for heparin 297 (an anticoagulant 104)

Uniparin, Uniparin CA (calcium) a brand name for heparin 297 (an anticoagulant 104)

Uniphyllin Continus a brand name for theophylline (a *bronchodilator* 92)

Uniroid a brand-name anal preparation 113 containing hydrocortisone 300, cinchocaine, neomycin, and polymyxin B

Unisomnia a brand name for nitrazepam 347 (a benzodiazepine sleeping drug 82)

Univer a brand name for verapamil 418 (an anti-arrhythmic 100 and anti-angina drug 101)

Uriben a brand name for nalidixic acid 346 (an antibacterial 131)

Urispas a brand name for flavoxate 286 (a urinary *antispasmodic* 166); *illus. 42J*

urofollitrophin a drug for pituitary disorders 145

urokinase a thrombolytic 105

ursodeoxycholic acid 417 (a drug for gallstones 114)

Ursofalk a brand name for ursodeoxy-cholic acid 417 (a drug for gallstones 114)

Uticillin a brand name for carfecillin (a penicillin antibiotic 128)

Utinor a brand name for norfloxacin (an antibiotic 128)

Utovlan a brand name for norethisterone 349 (a female sex *hormone* 147)

V

Vagifem a brand name for oestradiol (a female sex *hormone* 147)

Vaginyl a brand name for metronidazole 334 (an antibacterial 131 and antiprotozoal 136)

Valderma Active Gel a brand-name preparation for acne 177 containing benzoyl peroxide 208

Valderma Cream a brand-name preparation for minor skin troubles containing potassium hydroxyquinoline sulphate (an agent with antibacterial 131 and antifungal 138 properties) and chlorocresol

Valium a brand name for diazepam 259 (a benzodiazepine anti-anxiety drug 83, muscle relaxant 120, and anticonvulsant 86); *illus. 37G, 38C, 41F, 41J, 44L*

Vallergan a brand name for trimeprazine (an antihistamine 124)

Valoid a brand name for cyclizine (an antihistamine 124 used as an anti-emetic 90)

Vancocin a brand name for vancomycin (an antibiotic 128)

vancomycin an antibiotic 128 for serious infections

Varidase a brand name for streptokinase 399 (a thrombolytic agent 105) with streptodornase (a fibrinolytic *enzyme*)

Vascace a brand name for cilazapril (an ACE inhibitor 98)

Vascardin a brand name for isosorbide dinitrate 311 (a nitrate *vasodilator* 98 and anti-angina drug 101)

Vasocon A a brand name for antazoline 198 (an antihistamine 124) with naphazoline (a *sympathomimetic* decongestant 93)

Vasogen a brand-name barrier cream containing calamine, dimethicone, and zinc oxide

vasopressin a *hormone* produced in the pituitary gland given for diabetes insipidus 145

V-Cil-K a brand name for phenoxy-methylpenicillin 362 (a penicillin antibiotic 128)

vecuronium a drug used in general *anaesthesia* 80

Veganin a brand-name *analgesic* 80 containing aspirin 199, paracetamol 356, and codeine 244

Velbe a brand name for vinblastine (an anticancer drug 154)

Velosef a brand name for cephradine (a cephalosporin antibiotic 128)

Velosulin a brand name for insulin 306 (an antidiabetic 142)

Ventide a brand name for beclo-methasone 205 (a corticosteroid 141) with salbutamol 389 (a *broncho-dilator* 92)

Ventolin a brand name for salbutamol 389 (a *bronchodilator* 92 and drug used in labour 165); *illus. 35D, 35E*

Vepesid a brand name for etoposide (an anticancer drug 154)

Veracur a brand name for formaldehyde (a substance for warts)

verapamil 418 (an anti-angina drug 101 and anti-arrhythmic 100)

Vermox a brand name for mebendazole (an anthelmintic 139)

Verrugon a brand name for salicylic acid (a keratolytic for warts)

Vertigon a brand name for prochlorperazine 375 (a phenothiazine anti-emetic 90 and antipsychotic 85)

Verucasep a brand name for glutaralde-hyde (a *topical* wart preparation)

Vibramycin a brand name for doxycycline 273 (a tetracycline antibiotic 128)

Vibramycin-D a brand name for doxycycline 273 (a tetracycline antibiotic 128); *illus. 37L*

Vibrocil a brand name for phenyl-ephrine 364 (a decongestant 93) with dimethindene (an antihistamine 124) and neomycin (an aminoglycoside antibiotic 128)

Vicks Coldcare a brand name for dextro-methorphan 256 (a cough suppressant 94) with paracetamol 356 (a non-*narcotic analgesic* 80) and phenylpropanolamine 365 (a decongestant 93)

Vicks Medinite a brand name for paracetamol 356 (a non-*narcotic analgesic* 80), dextromethorphan 256 (a cough suppressant 94) and pseudoephedrine (a decongestant 93)

Videne a brand name for povidone-iodine (a skin *antiseptic* 175)

Vidopen a brand name for ampicillin (a penicillin antibiotic 128)

vigabatrin an anticonvulsant 86

Vigranon B a brand-name B vitamin complex preparation 149

viloxazine an antidepressant 84
vinblastine an anticancer drug 154
vincristine an anticancer drug 154
vindesine an anticancer drug 154
Vioform-Hydrocortisone a brand name for hydrocortisone 300 (a corticosteroid 141) with clioquinol (an anti-infective skin preparation 175)
Virazid a brand name for ribavirin (an antiviral 133)
Virormone a brand name for testosterone 406 (a male sex *hormone* 146)
Virudox a brand name for idoxuridine 303 (an antiviral 133)
Visclair a brand name for methylcysteine (a *mucolytic* for coughs 94)
Viskaldix a brand name for clopamide (a thiazide diuretic 99) with pindolol (a beta blocker 97)
Visken a brand name for pindolol (a beta blocker 97)
Vista-Methasone a brand name for betamethasone 210 (a corticosteroid 141)
vitamin A 430 (a vitamin 149)
vitamin B$_{12}$ 431 (a vitamin 149)
vitamin C 431 (a vitamin 149)
vitamin D 432 (a vitamin 149)
vitamin E 432 (a vitamin 149)
vitamin K 433 (a vitamin 149)
Vitathone Chilblain Ointment a brand name for methyl nicotinate (a topical vasodilator 98)
Vivalan a brand name for viloxazine (an antidepressant 84)
Volital a brand name for pemoline (a nervous system stimulant 88)
Volmax a brand name for salbutamol (a *bronchodilator* 92); *illus. 46Q*
Volraman a brand name for diclofenac (a non-steroidal anti-inflammatory 116)
Voltarol a brand name for diclofenac (a non-steroidal anti-inflammatory 116); *illus. 36L*

W

warfarin 419 (an anticoagulant 104); *illus. 38D*
Wasp-eze a brand-name aerosol preparation for insect bites and stings containing benzocaine (a local *anaesthetic* 80) and mepyramine (an antihistamine 124)
Waxsol a brand name for docusate (an ear wax softener)
Welldorm a brand name for chloral hydrate 223 (a non-benzodiazepine, non-barbiturate sleeping drug 82); *illus. 35B*
Wellferon a brand name for interferon 307 (an anticancer drug 154)
witch hazel an *astringent* used in *topical* 175 and rectal preparations 113

Woodwards Gripe Water a brand-name preparation for wind pain in infants, containing sodium bicarbonate 393 and dill seed oil

X

Xanax a brand name for alprazolam (a benzodiazepine anti-anxiety drug 83)
xipamide a thiazide-like diuretic 99
Xuret a brand name for metolazone (a thiazide-like diuretic 99)
Xylocaine a brand name for lignocaine (a local *anaesthetic* 80)
xylometazoline a decongestant 93
Xyloproct a brand-name anal preparation 113 containing hydrocortisone 300, aluminium acetate, lignocaine, and zinc oxide

Y

Yomesan a brand name for niclosamide (an anthelmintic 139 for tapeworms)
Yutopar a brand name for ritodrine 388 (a uterine muscle relaxant 165); *illus. 36P*

Z

Zaditen a brand name for ketotifen (a drug used to prevent asthma)
Zadstat a brand name for metronidazole 334 (an antibacterial 131 and antiprotozoal 136)
Zantac a brand name for ranitidine 385 (an anti-ulcer drug 109) *illus. 46G*
Zarontin a brand name for ethosuximide 283 (an anticonvulsant 86)
Zestoric a brand name for lisinopril (an ACE inhibitor 94) with hydrochlorothiazide 299 (a diuretic 99)
Zestril a brand name for lisinopril (an ACE inhibitor 94)
zidovudine 420 (an antiviral for HIV infection and AIDS 157)
Zimovane a brand name for zopiclone (a sleeping drug 82)
Zinacef a brand name for cefuroxime (a cephalosporin antibiotic 128)
Zinamide a brand name for pyrazinamide (an antituberculous drug 132)
zinc 433 (a mineral 150)
Zincomed a brand name for zinc 433 (a mineral 150)
zinc oxide a soothing agent 175
zinc pyrithione an antimicrobial with antibacterial 131 and anti-

fungal 138 properties used for dandruff 179
zinc sulphate zinc 433 (a mineral 150)
Zinnat a brand name for cefuroxime (a cephalosporin antibiotic 128)
Zirtek a brand name for cetirizine (an antihistamine 124)
Zithromax a brand name for azithromycin (an antibiotic 128)
Zocor a brand name for simvastatin 391 (a lipid-lowering drug 103); *illus. 36B*
Zofran a brand name for ondansetron 353 (an anti-emetic 90); *illus. 36 O*
Zoladex a brand name for goserelin (a female sex *hormone* 147 and anticancer drug 154)
zopiclone a sleeping drug 82
Zovirax a brand name for acyclovir 187 (an antiviral 133); *illus. 38E*
Z Span a brand name for zinc 433 (a mineral 150)
zuclopenthixol an antipsychotic 85
Zumenon a brand name for oestradiol (a female sex *hormone* 147); *illus. 38F*
Zyloric a brand name for allopurinol 189 (a drug for gout 119); *illus. 42R*
Zymafluor fluoride 424 (a mineral 150)

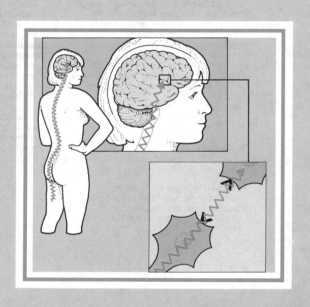

BRAIN AND NERVOUS SYSTEM

The human brain contains over 500 billion nerve cells (neurons). The brain cells receive electro-chemical impulses from everywhere in the body. They interpret these impulses and send responsive signals back to various glands and muscles. The brain functions continuously as a switchboard for the human communications system. At the same time, it serves as the seat of emotions and mood, of memory, personality, and thought. Extending from the brain is an additional cluster of nerve cells that forms the spinal cord. Together these two elements comprise the central nervous system.

Radiating from the central nervous system is the peripheral nervous system, which has three parts. One branches off the spinal cord and extends to skin and muscles throughout the body. Another, in the head, links the brain to the eyes, ears, nose, and taste buds. The third is a semi-independent network called the autonomic, or involuntary, nervous system. This is the part of the nervous system that controls unconscious body functions such as breathing, digestion, and glandular activity (see facing page).

Signals traverse the nervous system by electrical and chemical means. Electrical impulses carry signals from one end of a nerve cell to the other. To cross the gap between cells, chemical *neurotransmitters* are released from one cell to bind onto the receptor sites of nearby cells. *Excitatory* transmitters stimulate action; *inhibitory* transmitters reduce it.

What can go wrong

Disorders of the brain and nervous system range from conditions that are generally understood and frequently respond well to drug treatment (for example, epilepsy) to others (including serious mental illnesses such as schizophrenia) whose origins remain mysterious and yield to medical intervention only marginally.

Many authorities believe that an imbalance between the excitatory and inhibitory neuro-transmitters explains, in most cases, such conditions as depression, anxiety, and prolonged insomnia. The same may be said about Parkinson's disease, which is caused by a deficiency of dopamine, an excitatory neuro-transmitter. Poor circulation of blood to the brain hastens the death of neurons and leads to a wide range of conditions, including anything from absentmindedness to certain forms of dementia and senility. Temporary changes to blood circulation within and around the brain are thought

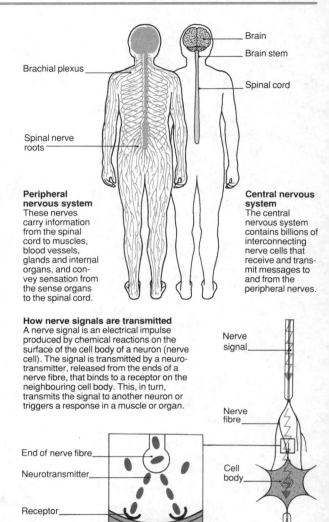

Brachial plexus

Spinal nerve roots

Brain

Brain stem

Spinal cord

Peripheral nervous system
These nerves carry information from the spinal cord to muscles, blood vessels, glands and internal organs, and convey sensation from the sense organs to the spinal cord.

Central nervous system
The central nervous system contains billions of interconnecting nerve cells that receive and trans-mit messages to and from the peripheral nerves.

How nerve signals are transmitted
A nerve signal is an electrical impulse produced by chemical reactions on the surface of the cell body of a neuron (nerve cell). The signal is transmitted by a neuro-transmitter, released from the ends of a nerve fibre, that binds to a receptor on the neighbouring cell body. This, in turn, transmits the signal to another neuron or triggers a response in a muscle or organ.

Nerve signal

Nerve fibre

End of nerve fibre

Neurotransmitter

Receptor

Cell body of neighbouring neuron

Cell body

Electric impulse to target

Nerve signal

to be the principal cause of migraine headache.

Why drugs are used

By and large, the drugs described in this section do not eliminate nervous system disorders. Their function is to correct or modify the communication of the signals that traverse the nervous system. By doing so they can relieve symptoms or restore normal functioning and behaviour.

In some cases, such as anxiety and insomnia, drugs encourage the action of inhibitory neuro-

AUTONOMIC NERVOUS SYSTEM

The autonomic, or involuntary, nervous system governs the actions of the muscles of the organs and glands. Such vital functions as heartbeat, salivation, and digestion continue without conscious direction, whether we are awake or asleep.

The autonomic system is divided into two parts, the effects of one generally balancing those of the other. The *sympathetic* nervous system has an *excitatory* effect. It widens the airways to the lungs, for example, and increases the flow of blood to the arms and legs. The *parasympathetic* system, by contrast, has an opposing effect. It slows the heart rate and stimulates the flow of the digestive juices.

Although the functional pace of most organs results from the interplay between the two systems, the muscles surrounding the blood vessels respond only to the signals of the sympathetic system. What decides between the constriction and dilation of the vessels is the relative stimulation of two sets of receptor sites: alpha sites and beta sites.

Neurotransmitters
The parasympathetic nervous system depends on the neurotransmitter, acetylcholine, to transmit signals from one cell to another. The sympathetic nervous system relies on adrenaline and noradrenaline, products of the adrenal glands that act as both hormones and neurotransmitters.

Drugs that act on the sympathetic nervous system
Drugs that stimulate the sympathetic nervous system are called adrenergics (or sympathomimetics, see chart). They either promote the release of adrenaline and noradrenaline or mimic their effects. Drugs which interfere with the action of the sympathetic nervous system are called sympatholytics. Alpha blockers act on alpha receptors; beta blockers act on beta receptors (see also Beta blockers, p.97).

Drugs that act on the parasympathetic nervous system
Drugs that stimulate the parasympathetic nervous system are called cholinergics (or parasympathomimetics), and drugs which oppose its action are called anticholinergics. Many drugs prescribed medically have anticholinergic properties (see chart, right).

Effects of stimulation of the autonomic nervous system

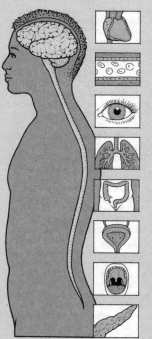

	Sympathetic	Parasympathetic
Heart	The rate and strength of the heart beat are increased.	The rate and strength of the heart beat are reduced.
Blood vessels in skin	These are constricted by stimulation of alpha receptors.	No effect.
Pupils	The pupils are dilated.	The pupils are constricted.
Airways	The bronchial muscles relax and widen the airways.	The bronchial muscles contract and narrow the airways.
Intestines	Activity of the muscles of the intestinal wall is reduced.	Activity of the muscles of the intestinal wall is increased.
Bladder	The bladder wall relaxes and the sphincter muscle contracts.	The bladder wall contracts and the sphincter muscle relaxes.
Salivary glands	Secretion of thick saliva increases.	Secretion of watery saliva increases.
Pancreas	Insulin secretion is increased (beta receptors) or reduced (alpha receptors).	Insulin secretion is increased.

Drugs that act on the autonomic nervous system

	Sympathetic	Parasympathetic
Stimulated by		
Natural neurotransmitters	Adrenaline Noradrenaline	Acetylcholine
Drugs	Adrenergic drugs (including alpha agonists, beta agonists) Sympathomimetics	Cholinergic drugs Parasympathomimetics
Blocked by		
Drugs	Alpha blockers (antagonists) Beta blockers (antagonists)	Anticholinergic drugs

transmitters, lowering the level of activity. In other disorders – depression, for example – the excitatory neurotransmitters are stimulated thereby encouraging the opposite effect.

Drugs that act on the nervous system are also used for conditions that outwardly have nothing to do with nervous system disorders. Migraine headaches, for example, are often treated with drugs that cause the autonomic nervous system to send out signals constricting the dilated blood vessels that cause the migraine.

MAJOR DRUG GROUPS

Analgesics	Anticonvulsant drugs
Sleeping drugs	Drugs for parkinsonism
Anti-anxiety drugs	Nervous system stimulants
Antidepressant drugs	Drugs for migraine
Antipsychotic drugs	Anti-emetics

ANALGESICS

Analgesics are drugs that relieve pain. Since pain is not a disease but a symptom, long-term relief depends on treatment of the underlying cause. For example, the pain of toothache can be relieved by drugs but can only be cured by appropriate dental treatment. When the underlying disorder is irreversible long-term analgesic treatment may be needed.

Damage to body tissue from disease or injury is detected by nerve endings that transmit signals to the brain. The interpretation of these sensations can be affected by the psychological state of the individual so that pain is worsened by anxiety and fear, for example. Often a reassuring explanation of the cause of discomfort can make pain easier to bear and may even relieve it altogether. Because of these psychological factors, sleeping drugs (p.82), anti-anxiety drugs (p.83) or antidepressant drugs (p.84) are often prescribed in addition to, or instead of, analgesics.

Types of analgesics

Narcotics and non-narcotics are the two principal types of analgesic. Another group of drugs that are commonly used to relieve pain are the local anaesthetics (see below). Narcotics are related to morphine and they are the most powerful analgesic drugs. Non-narcotic drugs are less powerful, and they include aspirin, paracetamol and non-steroidal anti-inflammatory drugs (NSAIDs).

SITES OF ACTION

Narcotic drugs (and paracetamol) act on the brain and spinal cord to reduce the perception of a painful stimulus. Non-narcotic drugs act at the site of pain to prevent the stimulation of nerve endings.

Narcotic drugs act on brain and spinal cord

Non-narcotic drugs act at the site of pain

Narcotics and paracetamol act directly on the brain and spinal cord to alter the perception of pain. Narcotics act like the endorphins, hormones naturally produced in the brain that stop the cell-to-cell transmission of pain sensation. Non-narcotics (except for paracetamol) prevent stimulation of the nerve endings at the site of the pain.

When pain is treated under medical supervision it is common to start with a non-narcotic, and if this provides inadequate relief, to change to a combination drug (a mixture of a mild narcotic and a non-narcotic), and finally to use a strong narcotic if the less powerful drugs are ineffective. More severe (e.g. post-operative) or long-lasting continuous pain may be treated by injections of narcotics.

When treating pain with an over-the-counter preparation, for example, taking aspirin for a headache, you should seek medical advice if pain persists for longer than 48 hours, recurs or is worse or different from previous pain.

Non-narcotic analgesics
Aspirin
Used for many years to relieve pain and reduce fever, aspirin also reduces inflammation, by blocking the production of chemicals called prostaglandins, which contribute to swelling and pain in inflamed tissue (see Action of analgesics, facing page). Aspirin is useful for headaches, toothaches, mild rheumatic pain, sore throat, and discomfort caused by feverish illnesses. Given regularly, it can also relieve the pain and inflammation of chronic rheumatoid arthritis (see Antirheumatic drugs, p.117).

Aspirin is often found in combination with other substances in a variety of medicines (see Cold cures, p.94). Another use is in the treatment of some blood disorders, since an important effect of aspirin is that it helps to prevent abnormal clotting of blood (see Drugs that affect blood clotting, p.104). For this reason, it is not suitable for people whose blood does not clot normally.

LOCAL ANAESTHETICS

These are used to prevent pain, usually in minor surgical procedures, for example, dental treatment and stitching cuts. They can also be injected into the space around the spinal cord to numb the lower half of the body. This is called spinal or epidural anaesthesia. Local anaesthetics block the passage of nerve impulses at the site of administration, so deadening all feeling at that site. They do not interfere with consciousness. Local anaesthetics are usually given by injection, but they can also be applied to the skin, mouth or eye to relieve pain.

Local anaesthetics occasionally cause the

ASPIRIN AND STOMACH IRRITATION

Standard aspirin can irritate the stomach, but buffered or coated aspirin may offer some protection against this. Buffered aspirin is released in the stomach like standard aspirin, but contains chemicals that reduce acidity and irritation. Coated preparations do not release aspirin until in the small intestine.

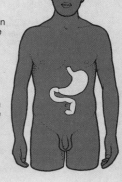

Standard and buffered aspirin released in the stomach

Coated aspirin released in the small intestine

Aspirin's major drawback is that it can cause irritation and even ulceration of the stomach and duodenum, possibly leading to bleeding. For this reason it is best taken after a meal. Specially formulated aspirin preparations designed to avoid irritating the stomach are available. These include buffered aspirin and coated aspirin. Buffered aspirin contains substances which reduce the acidity of the stomach contents and so may lessen the irritation. The same or similar effect may be obtained by taking regular aspirin with a standard dose of an antacid or a glass of milk. Coated aspirin preparations do not release the aspirin until they have passed through the stomach and have entered the small

skin at the site of application to become red and itchy, and if high doses of the anaesthetic enter the bloodstream it may cause a number of adverse effects – restlessness, nausea and tremors. Because such drugs may also lower blood pressure and disturb heart rhythm they are given carefully to people with heart problems.

In order to restrict the anaesthetic to the site of injection it is often given together with a *vasoconstrictor* drug such as adrenaline, which cuts down the blood supply at the site of injection and prevents the drug being carried away. This prolongs the action and minimizes the likelihood of side effects.

intestine (see Aspirin and stomach irritation, facing page). Aspirin in the form of soluble tablets, dissolved in water before being taken, is absorbed into the bloodstream quicker, thereby relieving pain faster than tablets. Soluble aspirin is not, however, less irritating to the stomach lining.

Aspirin is available in many formulations, all of which have a similar effect, but because the amount of aspirin in a tablet of each type varies, it is important to read the packet for the correct dosage. It is not recommended for children under 12 because its use has been linked to Reye's syndrome, a rare but potentially fatal liver and brain disorder.

Paracetamol

This is thought to act by reducing the production of prostaglandins in the brain but, unlike aspirin, it does not affect prostaglandin production in the rest of the body and so does not reduce inflammation. Paracetamol can be used for everyday aches and pains, such as headaches, toothache and joint pains. It is given as a liquid for treating pain and reducing fever in children.

It is one of the safest of all analgesics when taken correctly. It does not usually irritate the stomach and allergic reactions are rare. However, an overdose can cause severe and possibly fatal liver and kidney damage. Its toxic potential may be increased in heavy drinkers.

Non-steroidal anti-inflammatory drugs (NSAIDs)

These can relieve both pain and inflammation. NSAIDs are related to aspirin and also work by blocking the production of prostaglandins. They are most commonly used to treat muscle and joint pain and may also be prescribed for menstrual period pain. Like aspirin, NSAIDs can irritate the stomach lining and they are not usually given to people with stomach ulcers. For further information on these drugs, see p.116.

Narcotic analgesics

These are also called opioids and are related to opium, an extract of poppy seeds. They act directly on several sites in the central nervous system involved in pain perception and block the transmission of pain signals (see Action of analgesics, above). Because they act directly on the parts of the brain where pain is perceived, narcotics are the most effective analgesics and are used to treat the pain arising from surgery, serious injury and disease. These drugs are particularly valuable for alleviating severe pain during terminal illnesses.

Morphine is the best known narcotic analgesic. Others include diamorphine (heroin) and pethidine. The use of these

ACTION OF ANALGESICS

Cause of pain
Damage to tissue (due to injury or infection, for example), leads to the production of chemicals called prostaglandins, which act on nerve endings so that a signal is passed along a series of nerve cells to the brain where the signal is interpreted as pain by brain cells.

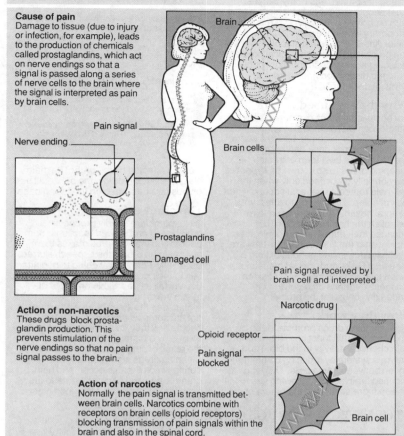

Brain

Pain signal

Nerve ending

Prostaglandins

Damaged cell

Brain cells

Pain signal received by brain cell and interpreted

Narcotic drug

Opioid receptor

Pain signal blocked

Brain cell

Action of non-narcotics
These drugs block prostaglandin production. This prevents stimulation of the nerve endings so that no pain signal passes to the brain.

Action of narcotics
Normally the pain signal is transmitted between brain cells. Narcotics combine with receptors on brain cells (opioid receptors) blocking transmission of pain signals within the brain and also in the spinal cord.

powerful narcotics is strictly controlled because they may produce euphoria, which can lead to abuse and addiction. When they are given under medical supervision to treat severe pain for a short period of time the risk of addiction is negligible.

Narcotic analgesics may cloud consciousness and prevent clear thought. Other drawbacks are that they can produce drowsiness, nausea, vomiting, constipation and depressed breathing. When taken in overdose, narcotics may induce a deep coma and produce fatal breathing difficulties.

In addition to the powerful narcotics, there are less powerful drugs in this group that are used to relieve mild to moderate pain. They include codeine and dextropropoxyphene.

Combined analgesics

Mild narcotics, such as codeine, are often found in combination preparations with

non-narcotics, such as aspirin or paracetamol. These mixtures may thus add the advantages of analgesics which act on the brain to the benefits of those acting at the site of pain. However, there is little evidence that preparations containing more than one analgesic are more effective than a single drug. A combined preparation may also combine the side effects of both classes of drug. For these reasons it is usually advisable to use a single ingredient preparation which you find effective.

COMMON DRUGS

Narcotics	**Non-narcotics**
Codeine *	Aspirin *
Co-proxamol *	Ibuprofen *
Diamorphine (heroin) *	Paracetamol *
Morphine *	NSAIDs (see p.116)
Pentazocine *	
Pethidine *	**Other drugs**
	Nefopam *
* See Part 4	

SLEEPING DRUGS

Difficulty in getting to sleep or staying asleep (insomnia) has many causes. Most people suffer from sleepless nights from time to time, usually as a result of a temporary worry or discomfort from a minor illness. Persistent sleeplessness can be caused by psychological problems including anxiety or depression, or by pain and discomfort arising from a physical disorder.

Why they are used

For occasional bouts of sleeplessness, simple, common remedies to promote relaxation – for example, taking a warm bath or a hot milk drink before bedtime – are usually the best form of treatment. Sleeping drugs (also known as hypnotics) are normally prescribed only when these self-help remedies have failed, and when lack of sleep is beginning to affect your general health. Drugs are used to re-establish the habit of sleeping, but because their effectiveness diminishes rapidly after the first few nights, they are best used for limited periods of time only (see also Risks and special precautions, below). Long-term treatment of sleep-lessness depends on resolving the underlying cause of the problem.

How they work

Most sleeping drugs promote sleep by depressing brain function. They interfere with chemical activity in the brain and nervous system by reducing communi-cation between nerve cells. This leads to reduced brain activity, allowing you to fall asleep more easily, but the nature of the

TYPES OF SLEEPING DRUGS

Benzodiazepines The most commonly used class of sleeping drugs, the benzo-diazepines have comparatively few adverse effects and are relatively safe in overdose. They are also used to treat anxiety (see facing page).

Barbiturates These are now rarely used because of the risks of abuse and depen-dence, and of toxicity in overdose. There is a tendency to prolonged sedation ("hangover").

"Non-barbiturate, non-benzodiazepine" sleeping drugs These drugs were originally developed as safer alternatives to

barbiturates. New drugs in this category, that may have advantages over the benzo-diazepines, are now available.

Antihistamines Widely used to treat allergic symptoms (see p.124), antihista-mines also cause drowsiness. They are sometimes used to promote sleep in children and in the elderly.

Antidepressant drugs As well as being effective in treating underlying depressive illness, some of these drugs are sometimes used to promote sleep in depressed people (see p.84).

sleep is affected by the drug. The main class of sleeping drugs, the benzodiaz-epines, are described on the facing page.

How they affect you

A sleeping drug rapidly produces drowsiness and slowed reactions. Some people find that the drug makes them appear to be drunk, their speech slurred, especially if they delay going to bed after taking their dose. Most people find they usually fall asleep within one hour of taking the drug.

Because the sleep induced by drugs is not the same as normal sleep, many people find they do not feel as well rested by it as by a night of natural sleep. This is the result of suppressed brain activity. Sleeping drugs also suppress the sleep during which dreams occur, and both dream sleep and non-dream sleep are essential components for a good night's

sleep (see The effect of drugs on sleep patterns, below).

Some people experience a variety of "hangover" effects the following day. Some benzodiazepines may produce minor side effects such as daytime drowsiness, dizziness, and unsteadiness that can impair the ability to drive or operate dangerous machinery. Elderly people are especially likely to become confused; for them, selection of an appropriate drug is particularly important.

Risks and special precautions

Most sleeping drugs, other than the antihistamines, can produce psycho-logical and physical dependence (p.23) when taken regularly for more than a few weeks, especially if taken in larger than normal doses. Zopiclone is less likely than benzodiazepines to lead to dependence. If sleeping drugs are withdrawn abruptly, sleeplessness, anxiety, fits, and hallucinations can arise. Nightmares and vivid dreams may occur because the amount of time spent in dream sleep increases. Any-one who has been using sleeping drugs regularly for a long time and wishes to stop taking them should seek their doctor's advice on how to reduce dosage gradually so as to avoid with-drawal symptoms.

One of the risks of taking sleeping drugs for a prolonged period is that there may be a temptation to exceed the prescribed dose, especially if the person has been taking them for some weeks and their effect has diminished.

THE EFFECT OF DRUGS ON SLEEP PATTERNS

Normal sleep can be divided into three types: light sleep, deep sleep and dream sleep. The proportion of time spent in each type of sleep changes with age and is altered by sleeping

drugs. Dramatic changes in sleep patterns also occur in the first few days following abrupt withdrawal of sleeping drugs after regular, prolonged use.

Normal sleep Young adults spend most sleep time in light sleep with roughly equal proportions of dream and deep sleep.

Drug-induced sleep has less dream sleep and less deep sleep with relatively more light sleep.

Sleep following drug withdrawal There is a marked increase in dream sleep causing nightmares following withdrawal of drugs used regularly for a long time.

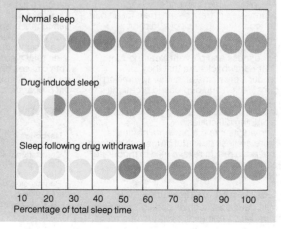

○ Dream sleep
● Deep sleep
◐ Light sleep

Normal sleep

Drug-induced sleep

Sleep following drug withdrawal

10 20 30 40 50 60 70 80 90 100
Percentage of total sleep time

COMMON DRUGS

Benzodiazepines
Nitrazepam ✳
Temazepam ✳
Triazolam

Non-benzodiazepines/ non-barbiturates
Chloral hydrate ✳
Chlormethiazole
Dichloralphenazone
Zopiclone

Barbiturates
Amylobarbitone

✳ See Part 4

ANTI-ANXIETY DRUGS

A certain amount of stress can be beneficial, providing a stimulus to action. But too much will often result in anxiety, which might be described as fear or apprehension not caused by real danger.

Clinically, anxiety arises when the balance between certain chemicals in the brain is disturbed. The fearful feelings increase brain activity, stimulating the sympathetic nervous system (see p.79), often triggering off physical symptoms: shaking, palpitations, breathlessness, digestive distress and headaches.

Why they are used

Anti-anxiety drugs (also called anxiolytics or minor tranquillizers) are used to alleviate persistent feelings of nervousness and tension caused by stress or other psychological problems. But they cannot resolve the causes. Tackling the underlying problem through counselling and perhaps psychotherapy offer the best hope of a long-term solution. Anti-anxiety drugs are also used in hospitals to calm and relax people who are undergoing uncomfortable medical procedures.

There are two main classes of drugs for relieving anxiety: benzodiazepines and beta blockers. Benzodiazepines are the most widely used, given as a regular treatment for short periods to promote relaxation. Most benzodiazepines have a strong sedative effect, helping to relieve the insomnia that accompanies anxiety (see also Sleeping drugs, facing page).

Beta blockers are mainly used to reduce physical symptoms of anxiety, such as shaking and palpitations. They are commonly prescribed for people who feel excessively anxious in certain situations, for example, at interviews, or public appearances.

Certain antidepressants have a tranquillizing effect and are also prescribed for anxiety when it arises out of a depressive illness (see p.84).

How they work
Benzodiazepines

These drugs depress activity in the part of the brain that controls emotion, by promoting the action of a chemical called gamma-aminobutyric acid (GABA). GABA attaches itself to brain cells, blocking transmission of electrical impulses. This reduces communication between brain cells. Benzodiazepines are thought to increase the inhibitory effect of GABA on brain cells (see Action of benzodiazepines, above), thus preventing excessive brain activity that causes anxiety.

Beta blockers

The physical symptoms of anxiety are produced by an increase in the activity of the sympathetic nervous system. Sympathetic nerve endings release a chemical transmitter called noradrenaline that

ACTION OF BENZODIAZEPINES AND ZOPICLONE

Action on the brain
The reticular activating system (RAS) in the brain stem controls the level of mental activity by stimulating the higher centres of the brain responsible for consciousness. Benzodiazepines and zopiclone depress the RAS, so relieving anxiety. In larger doses they depress the RAS sufficiently to cause drowsiness and sleep.

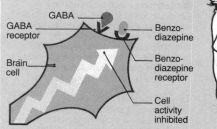

Action on brain cells in the RAS
Brain cell activity is normally inhibited by GABA, a chemical that binds to specialized cell *receptors*. Brain cells also have receptors for benzodiazepines. The drug binds to its receptor and promotes the inhibitory effect of GABA. This depresses activity in the RAS. Zopiclone, a new sleeping drug, promotes the inhibitory effect of GABA without binding to benzodiazepine receptors.

stimulates the heart, digestive system and other organs. Beta blockers block the action of noradrenaline in the body, reducing the physical symptoms of anxiety. For more information on beta blockers, see p.97.

How they affect you

Benzodiazepines reduce feelings of agitation and restlessness, slow mental activity, and often produce drowsiness. They are said to reduce motivation and, if taken in large doses, may lead to apathy. They also have a relaxing effect on the muscles, and some benzodiazepines are used specifically for that purpose (see Muscle relaxants, p.120).

Minor adverse effects of these drugs include dizziness and forgetfulness. People who need to drive or operate potentially dangerous machinery should be aware that their reactions may be slowed. Because the brain soon becomes tolerant to their effects, benzodiazepines are usually effective only for a few weeks at a time.

Risks and special precautions

The benzodiazepines are considered safe for most people. They are not likely to be fatal in overdose. The main risk is that people who take them regularly may become psychologically and physically dependent on them, particularly when larger-than-average doses have been

used. For this reason, benzodiazepines are usually given for courses of two weeks or less. If a person has been taking them for a longer period, they are normally withdrawn gradually under medical supervision. If they are stopped suddenly, withdrawal symptoms, including excessive anxiety, nightmares and restlessness may occur.

Benzodiazepines have been abused for their sedative effect, and are therefore prescribed with caution for people with a history of drug or alcohol abuse.

COMMON DRUGS

Benzodiazepines
Alprazolam
Chlordiazepoxide *
Diazepam *
Lorazepam
Oxazepam

Beta blockers
Atenolol *
Oxprenolol *
Propranolol *

Other drugs
Buspirone

* See Part 4

ANTIDEPRESSANT DRUGS

Occasional moods of sadness or discouragement are normal and usually pass quickly. But more severe depression, accompanied by despair, lethargy, loss of sex drive, apathy and often poor appetite may call for medical attention. Such depression can arise from life stresses such as the death of someone close, an illness, or sometimes from no apparent cause.

There are three main types of drug used to treat depression: tricyclics, monoamine oxidase inhibitors, and serotonin re-uptake inhibitors (see Types of antidepressant, below). Lithium, a metallic element that is used mainly to treat manic depression, is discussed under Antimanic drugs (facing page), but is also used as an antidepressant. Other antidepressant drugs that may be prescribed include maprotiline, mianserin, and trazodone.

Why they are used
Minor depression does not usually require drug treatment, and physicians usually avoid prescribing antidepressants when it is likely that the depression will soon lift. In such cases support and help in coming to terms with the cause is often more effective than drugs. Severe depression, however, may be helped by antidepressant drugs. Antidepressants may have to be taken for many months. However, they can sometimes be withdrawn gradually after prolonged treatment without relapse occurring.

How they work
Depression is thought to be caused by a reduction in the level of certain chemicals in the brain called *neurotransmitters* that affect mood by stimulating brain cells. Antidepressants increase the level of these *excitatory* neurotransmitters.

Tricyclics
When excitatory neurotransmitters are released by brain cells they are normally rapidly taken up again into the cells.

TYPES OF ANTIDEPRESSANT

Tricyclics
Some tricyclics, such as amitriptyline, are mainly sedative and will improve sleep at once, even before the depression is relieved. Other tricyclics, such as imipramine and lofepramine, lack this effect and are given to people who feel lethargic.

Monoamine oxidase inhibitors (MAOIs)
These are usually given if people do not respond to the tricyclics, or if tricyclics are not suitable. MAOIs are especially effective in people who are anxious as well as depressed, or who suffer from phobias.

Seratonin re-uptake inhibitors (SRIs)
These increase the activity of the neurotransmitter, serotonin. They often have fewer side effects, but may cause nausea.

Tricyclics block this re-uptake of neurotransmitters, and the level outside the brain cell therefore increases, so prolonging their stimulatory effect on the brain (see Action of antidepressants, right).

Seratonin re-uptake Inhibitors (SRIs)
These drugs block the re-uptake of one neurotransmitter, serotonin, raising its levels outside the nerve ending and thus increasing its effect (see Action of antidepressants, right).

Monoamine oxidase inhibitors
These drugs block the action of a brain enzyme that normally breaks down the excitatory neurotransmitters. By blocking this breakdown, MAOIs allow the neurotransmitters to build up to a high level and produce a greater stimulation of the brain (see Action of antidepressants, right).

How they affect you
The beneficial effect of antidepressants is not usually noticeable for 10 to 14 days after initial dose, and it may be 6 to 8 weeks before the full effect is felt. However, within the first day of treatment some of the tricyclics can produce drowsiness and a variety of *anticholinergic* effects, including difficulty urinating, dry mouth, and blurred vision.

Risks and special precautions
Overdose of tricyclics and MAOIs is dangerous: tricyclics can produce coma, cause fits, and disturb heart rhythm, which may be fatal; MAOIs can also cause fits and even death. Both are prescribed with caution for people with heart problems or epilepsy.

Monoamine oxidase inhibitors have numerous side effects because they deactivate enzymes in the body that normally break down certain chemicals (particularly tyramine) found in some foods. MAOIs taken with certain drugs or food rich in tyramine (e.g. cheese, meat or yeast extracts, and red wine) can produce a dramatic rise in blood pressure, with headache and vomiting, even two weeks after stopping the drug. People taking these drugs are given a treatment card listing prohibited drugs and foods.

A newer MAOI, moclobemide, has been developed which is much less likely to lead to unwanted symptoms when taken with food, and restrictions in diet are not usually needed.

COMMON DRUGS

SRIs	Tricyclics
Fluoxetine✳	Amitriptyline ✳
Fluvoxamine	Clomipramine ✳
Sertraline ✳	Dothiepin ✳
Paroxetine	Imipramine ✳
	Lofepramine ✳
MAOIs	
Phenelzine ✳	**Other drugs**
Moclobemide ✳	Maprotiline
	Mianserin✳
✳ See Part 4	Trazodone✳

ACTION OF ANTIDEPRESSANTS

Normally brain cells release sufficient quantities of excitatory chemicals (neurotransmitters) to stimulate neighbouring cells. The neurotransmitters are constantly reabsorbed into the brain cells where they are broken down by an enzyme called monoamine oxidase. In depression fewer neurotransmitters are released. Antidepressant drugs act to raise the levels of neurotransmitters in the brain.

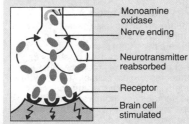

- Monoamine oxidase
- Nerve ending
- Neurotransmitter reabsorbed
- Receptor
- Brain cell stimulated

Normal brain activity
In a normal brain neurotransmitters are constantly being released, reabsorbed, and broken down.

Brain activity in depression
Fewer neurotransmitters than normal are released, leading to reduced stimulation.

- Brain cell poorly stimulated

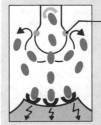

- Drug blocks reabsorption of neurotransmitter

Action of tricyclics and SRIs
Tricyclic and SRI drugs increase the levels of neurotransmitters by blocking their reabsorption.

- Drug blocks enzyme

Action of MAOIs
MAOIs increase the levels of neurotransmitters by blocking the action of the enzyme (monoamine oxidase) that breaks them down.

ANTIPSYCHOTIC DRUGS

Psychosis is a term used to describe mental disorders that prevent the sufferer from thinking clearly, recognizing reality, and acting rationally. These disorders include schizophrenia, manic depression and paranoia. The precise causes of these disorders are unknown, although a number of factors, including stress, heredity, and brain injury may be involved. Temporary psychosis can also arise as a result of alcohol withdrawal or the abuse of mind-altering drugs (see Drugs of abuse, p.434). A variety of drugs is used to treat psychotic disorders (see Common drugs, below), most of which have similar actions and effects. One exception is lithium, which is particularly useful for manic depression (see Antimanic drugs, right).

Why they are used

Because a person with a psychotic illness may recover spontaneously, a drug will not always be prescribed immediately. Long-term treatment is only started when normal life is seriously interfered with. Antipsychotic drugs (also called major tranquillizers or neuroleptics) do not cure the underlying disorder, but they can restore normal behaviour.

The drug given to a particular individual depends on the nature of his or her illness and the side effects experienced. Drugs differ in the amount of sedation that they produce; the need for sedation also influences the choice.

Antipsychotics may also be given to calm or sedate a highly agitated or aggressive person, whatever the cause. Some antipsychotic drugs also have a powerful action against nausea and vomiting (see p.90), and are sometimes used as premedication before surgery.

How they work

It is thought that some forms of mental illness are caused by an increase in communication between brain cells due to overactivity of a chemical called dopamine. This may disturb normal thought processes and produce abnormal behaviour. Dopamine combines with *receptors* on the brain cells. Antipsychotics reduce the transmission of nerve signals by binding to these receptors, thus making the brain cells less sensitive to dopamine (see Action of antipsychotics, below).

How they affect you

By modifying abnormal behaviour, the antipsychotics enable the sufferer to live outside mental institutions, where people with such mental illnesses were usually confined up until the 1950s.

Because antipsychotics depress the action of dopamine, they can disturb its balance with another chemical in the brain, acetylcholine. If that occurs, symptoms like those of parkinsonism can appear – an expressionless face and shaky hands (see Drugs for parkinsonism, p.87).

In these circumstances, a change in medication may be necessary. Rather than prescribe a drug specifically to counteract the adverse effects of the antipsychotic, a doctor will sometimes try treatment with drugs of a different class.

Antipsychotics may also block the action of another neurotransmitter in the brain, noradrenaline. This lowers the blood pressure, especially when you stand up, causing dizziness. It may also prevent ejaculation.

Risks and special precautions

It is important to continue taking these drugs even if all symptoms have gone, because symptoms are only controlled by taking the prescribed dose.

Because these drugs can have permanent as well as temporary side effects, the minimum necessary dosage is used.

ANTIMANIC DRUGS

Changes in mood are normal, but when a person's mood swings become grossly exaggerated, with peaks of elation or mania alternating with troughs of depression, it becomes an illness called manic depression. This is usually treated with lithium, a drug that reduces the intensity of the mania, lifts the depression and lessens the frequency of mood swings. Because it may take three weeks before the lithium starts to work, an antipsychotic may be prescribed with lithium at first to give immediate relief of symptoms.

Lithium can be toxic if levels of the drug in the blood rise too high. Checks on blood concentrations of lithium are therefore usually carried out regularly during treatment. Symptoms of lithium poisoning include blurred vision, twitching, vomiting and diarrhoea.

This is found by starting with a low dose and increasing it until symptoms are controlled. Sudden withdrawal of antipsychotics after more than a few weeks can cause nausea, vomiting, sweating, headache and restlessness. For this reason the dose is reduced gradually when drug treatment needs to be stopped.

The most serious long-term risk of antipsychotic treatment is a disorder known as *tardive dyskinesia*, which may develop after one to five years. This consists of repeated jerking movements of the mouth, tongue and face, and sometimes the hands and feet.

Some doctors have suggested that periodic withdrawal of the drug for several months may reduce the severity of this condition, but such "drug holidays" have no value and may lead to relapse.

How they are administered

Antipsychotics may be given by mouth as tablets, capsules or syrup, or by injection. They can also be given in the form of a *depot injection* that releases the drug slowly over several weeks. This is helpful for people who might forget to take their drugs or who might take an overdose.

ACTION OF ANTIPSYCHOTICS

Brain activity is partly governed by the action of a chemical called dopamine, which transmits signals between brain cells. In psychotic illness the brain cells release too much dopamine, causing excessive stimulation. Antipsychotic drugs help to reduce the adverse effects of excess dopamine.

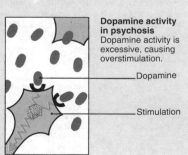

Dopamine activity in psychosis
Dopamine activity is excessive, causing overstimulation.

Dopamine

Stimulation

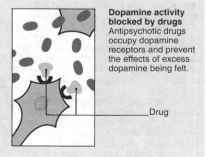

Dopamine activity blocked by drugs
Antipsychotic drugs occupy dopamine receptors and prevent the effects of excess dopamine being felt.

Drug

COMMON DRUGS

Phenothiazine antipsychotics
Chlorpromazine *
Fluphenazine
Perphenazine
Pipothiazine
Prochlorperazine *
Thioridazine *
Trifluoperazine

Butyrophenone antipsychotics
Haloperidol *

Other antipsychotics
Clozapine *
Fluspirilene
Loxapine
Remoxipride
Risperidone *
Sulpiride
Zuclopenthixol

Antimanic drugs
Lithium *

| * See Part 4 |

ANTICONVULSANT DRUGS

Electrical signals from nerve cells in the brain are normally finely coordinated to produce smooth movements of arms and legs, but these signals can become paroxysmal and chaotic, and trigger the disorderly muscular activity and mental changes which are characteristic of an epileptic fit (also called a seizure or convulsion). The most common cause of fits is the disorder known as epilepsy. However, they may also be brought on by outside stimuli such as flashing lights, or be caused by brain disease or injury, by the toxic effects of certain drugs, or, in young children, by a high temperature.

Anticonvulsant drugs are used to reduce the risk of an epileptic fit or to stop one that is in progress.

Why they are used
Isolated seizures seldom require drug treatment, but anticonvulsant drugs are the usual treatment for controlling epileptic seizures. They permit epileptics to lead a normal life, reducing the possibility of brain damage, that can result from recurrent seizures.

ACTION OF ANTICONVULSANTS

Normally there is a relatively low level of electrical activity in the brain. In an epileptic fit, excessive electrical activity builds up, causing uncontrolled stimulation of the brain. Anticonvulsant drugs have an inhibitory effect which neutralizes excessive electrical activity in the brain.

Normal brain activity

- Brain
- Normal electrical activity
- Spinal cord

Brain activity in a fit

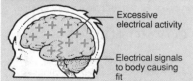

- Excessive electrical activity
- Electrical signals to body causing fit

Drug action on brain activity

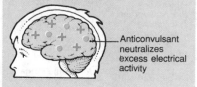

- Anticonvulsant neutralizes excess electrical activity

Most people with epilepsy need to take anticonvulsants on a regular basis to prevent fits. Usually a single drug is used, and treatment continues until there have been no attacks for at least two years. The particular drug prescribed depends on the kind of epilepsy (see Types of epilepsy, right).

If one drug alone is not effective, a combination of drugs may be given. Even when under treatment a person can suffer fits. A prolonged fit can be halted by injection of diazepam or a similar drug.

How they work
Brain cells bring about body movement by a form of electrical activity which passes through the nerves to the muscles. In an epileptic fit, excessive electrical activity starts in one part of the brain and spreads to other parts causing uncontrolled stimulation of brain cells. Most anticonvulsant drugs have an *inhibitory* effect on brain cells and damp down electrical activity, preventing the excessive build-up which causes epileptic fits (see Action of anticonvulsants, left).

How they affect you
Ideally, the only effect an anticonvulsant should have is to reduce or prevent fitting. Unfortunately, no drug prevents fits without potentially affecting normal brain function, leading to poor memory, inability to concentrate, lack of coordination, and lethargy. It is important, therefore, to find a dosage that is sufficient to prevent fits without causing unacceptable side effects. The dose has to be carefully tailored to the individual – there is no standard dose for anticonvulsants. It is usual to start with a low dose of a selected drug and to increase it gradually until a balance is achieved between the effective control of fitting and the occurrence of side effects, many of which wear off after the first few weeks of treatment.

Blood tests to monitor levels of the drug in the body are usually carried out periodically. Finding the correct dose may take several months.

Risks and special precautions
Each anticonvulsant drug has its own specific adverse effects and risks. In addition, most of them affect the liver's ability to break down other drugs (see Drug interactions, p.16) and so may influence the action of other drugs you are taking. Doctors try to use the minimum number of anticonvulsants in any one person in order to reduce the risk of such interactions occurring.

Most anticonvulsants have risks for the developing baby – if you are hoping to become pregnant, you should discuss the risks, and whether your medication should be changed, with your doctor.

People taking anticonvulsants need to

TYPES OF EPILEPSY

The selection of anticonvulsant drug depends on the type of epilepsy, although the age and particular response to drug treatment of the individual is also important.

Tonic/clonic (grand mal) seizures This type of fit is characterized by a warning sensation such as flashing lights or a noise, which is followed by a sudden loss of consciousness during which convulsions occur, and the sufferer may urinate uncontrolledly or foam at the mouth. The fit usually lasts for a few minutes only, but it can occasionally last longer. Prolonged attacks which last for over an hour are called status epilepticus.

The principal drugs used to prevent tonic/clonic seizures are phenytoin, phenobarbitone, primidone, and carbamazepine. Doctors try to avoid prescribing phenytoin in young children because of its unpleasant side effects which include overgrowth of the gums, acne and increased body hair. These effects are less prominent when the drug is prescribed in adults. Status epilepticus is usually treated by injection of a benzodiazepine drug such as diazepam.

Absence (petit mal) seizures This form of epilepsy most commonly affects children. The fits consist of a momentary loss of consciousness during which the child may seem to go 'blank'. Convulsions do not occur. The following drugs are used for the prevention of this type of fit: ethosuximide, sodium valproate and, less commonly, clonazepam.

Partial seizures There are a number of different variations of this form of epilepsy. Most partial seizures cause a sudden severe disturbance of the senses and/or muscle spasm without loss of consciousness. Phenytoin, phenobarbitone, and carbamazepine are the drugs most commonly used to prevent partial seizures.

be particularly careful to take their medication regularly as prescribed. If the levels of the anticonvulsant in the body are allowed to fall suddenly, fits are very likely to occur. The dose should not be reduced or the treatment stopped, except on the advice of a doctor.

If, for any reason, treatment with anticonvulsant drugs needs to be stopped, the dose should be reduced gradually. People on anticonvulsant therapy are advised to carry an identification tag giving full details of their condition and treatment.

COMMON DRUGS

Carbamazepine*	Neurontin
Clobazam	Phenobarbitone*
Clonazepam*	Phenytoin*
Diazepam*	Primidone*
Ethosuximide*	Sodium valproate*
Lamotrigine	Troxidone
	Vigabatrin

* See Part 4

DRUGS FOR PARKINSONISM

Parkinsonism is the general term used to describe shaking of the head and limbs, muscular stiffness, an expressionless face and inability to control or initiate movement. It is caused by an imbalance between the chemicals dopamine and acetylcholine in the brain. These chemicals are responsible for the transmission of nerve signals in the part of the brain that coordinates movement. They have opposing actions and are normally finely balanced. In parkinsonism there is a reduction in the action of dopamine so that the effect of acetylcholine is increased and an imbalance is created.

Parkinsonism has a variety of causes, but the most common is degeneration of the dopamine-producing cells in the brain, known as Parkinson's disease. Other causes include the side effects of certain drugs, notably antipsychotics (see p.85), brain damage, and narrowing of the blood vessels in the brain.

Why they are used

Drugs can help to relieve the symptoms of parkinsonism. Unfortunately, they cannot cure the underlying cause of the chemical imbalance. In particular, the degeneration of brain cells in Parkinson's disease cannot be halted, although drugs can minimize symptoms of the disease for many years.

How they work

Drugs used in the treatment of parkinsonism restore the balance between dopamine and acetylcholine. They fall into two main groups: those that act by reducing the effect of acetylcholine (*anticholinergic* drugs), and those that act by boosting the effect of dopamine.

Anticholinergic drugs

Acetylcholine acts by combining with *receptors* on brain cells and stimulating them. Anticholinergic drugs combine with these receptors and prevent acetylcholine from binding to them. This reduces acetylcholine's relative overactivity and restores the balance with dopamine.

Drugs that boost the effect of dopamine

Dopamine levels in the brain cannot be boosted by giving dopamine directly because it is poorly absorbed through the digestive tract, nor can it pass from the bloodstream into the brain. Levodopa (L-dopa), the chemical from which dopamine is naturally produced in the brain and that can be absorbed well through the digestive tract, increases the level of dopamine and so restores the balance with acetylcholine.

Because a high proportion of each dose of L-dopa is broken down in the body before it reaches the brain, it is usually combined with carbidopa to prevent this

ACTION OF DRUGS FOR PARKINSONISM

Normal movement depends on a balance in the brain between dopamine and acetylcholine which combine with receptors on brain cells. In parkinsonism there is less dopamine so that acetylcholine is relatively overactive. The balance between acetylcholine and dopamine may be restored by anticholinergic drugs, which combine with the receptor for acetylcholine and block acetylcholine's action on the brain cell, or by dopamine-boosting drugs, which increase the level of dopamine activity in the brain.

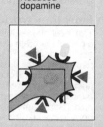

Normal chemical balance
Normally dopamine and acetylcholine are balanced.

Chemical imbalance in parkinsonism
When dopamine activity is reduced, acetylcholine is overactive.

Action of anticholinergic drugs
Anticholinergic drugs displace acetylcholine and restore balance.

Action of dopamine boosting drugs
These drugs increase dopamine activity and restore balance.

breakdown. Dopamine is broken down in the brain, and to reduce this breakdown L-dopa is sometimes given with selegiline to prolong the action of dopamine. Amantadine (also used as an antiviral agent, see p.133) boosts the levels of dopamine in the brain by stimulating its release. The action of dopamine can also be boosted by bromocriptine which mimics the natural chemical.

How they affect you

Each type of drug relieves some symptoms of parkinsonism better than others, although it is difficult to control symptoms in the more advanced stage of the disease. Anticholinergics improve stiffness more than shaking or the inability to initiate movement, and benefit is felt within a few days. They also reduce excessive salivation: dribbling is often a problem in Parkinson's disease.

Levodopa often produces a dramatic improvement in all symptoms. Side effects of levodopa include nausea, vomiting and flushing. When given in excess it can also cause involuntary movements in the face and the body. Although these problems may be alleviated by reducing the dose, as the disease progresses it becomes increasingly difficult to give sufficient levodopa to improve symptoms without causing side effects. Also, in the later stage of the disease the effect of each dose wears off before the next one is taken, and it may be necessary to take the drug more frequently.

Amantadine relieves all symptoms of parkinsonism in people with mild to

moderate disease. It has few side effects but the beneficial effect may wear off over a few months. The most common side effects of bromocriptine are the same as those produced by levodopa.

Choice of drug

The particular drug that is prescribed depends on both the severity of the disease and the potential adverse effects of the drug.

Anticholinergic drugs are often effective in the early stages of Parkinson's disease when they may control symptoms adequately without any other antiparkinson drugs. They are often used to treat parkinsonism caused by antipsychotic drugs, which have dopamine-blocking properties. Levodopa is usually prescribed when the disease impairs walking. The effectiveness of levodopa usually wanes after two to five years and if this happens bromocriptine or amantadine may be prescribed as well. People who do not benefit from levodopa or who cannot be given it because of side effects, may also be given one of the other drugs.

COMMON DRUGS

Anticholinergic drugs	Dopamine-boosting drugs
Benzhexol	Amantadine *
Benztropine	Bromocriptine *
Biperiden	Levodopa *
Orphenadrine *	Pergolide
Procyclidine *	Selegiline
	Lysuride

* See Part 4

NERVOUS SYSTEM STIMULANTS

A person's state of mental alertness varies throughout the day and is under the control of chemicals in the brain, some of which are depressant, causing drowsiness, and others that are stimulant, heightening awareness.

It is thought that an increase in the activity of the depressant chemicals may be responsible for a condition called narcolepsy, a tendency to fall asleep during the day for no obvious reason. Nervous system stimulants are administered to increase wakefulness. They include the amphetamines and related drugs, notably methylphenidate. The commonest home remedy for increasing alertness is caffeine, a mild stimulant. Respiratory stimulants, related to caffeine (found in coffee, tea and cola), are used to improve breathing (above right).

Why they are used

In adults who suffer from narcolepsy some of these drugs prevent excessive drowsiness during the day. Stimulants do not cure narcolepsy, and since the disorder usually lasts throughout the sufferer's lifetime, they may have to be taken indefinitely. Nervous system stimulants are also occasionally given to hyperactive children who have a short attention span.

Because reduced appetite is a side effect of amphetamines, they have also been used as part of the treatment for obesity. A newly introduced amphetamine drug, dexfenfluramine, helps weight loss especially during the first few months. This drug is particularly useful as it carries no risk of addiction.

Caffeine is sometimes added to analgesic preparations, but without any clear justification.

Unfortunately, apart from their use in narcolepsy, stimulants are not useful in the long term because the brain soon becomes *tolerant* to them.

How they work

The level of wakefulness is controlled by a part of the brain stem called the reticular activating system (RAS). Activity here depends on the balance between chemicals, some of which are *excitatory* (including noradrenaline) and some *inhibitory* (such as gamma aminobutyric acid). Stimulants promote the release of noradrenaline by brain cells, increasing activity in the RAS and other parts of the brain, so raising the level of alertness.

How they affect you

In adults, central nervous system stimulants taken in the prescribed dose for narcolepsy increase wakefulness, so allowing normal concentration and thought processes to occur. They may also reduce appetite and cause tremors. In hyperactive children they reduce the general level of activity to a more normal level and increase the attention span.

RESPIRATORY STIMULANTS

Some stimulants (for example, aminophylline, theophylline, and doxapram) act on the part of the brain – the respiratory centre – that controls respiration. They are sometimes used in hospitals to help people who have difficulty breathing, mainly very young babies or adults with severe chest infections.

Risks and special precautions

Some people, especially the elderly or those with previous psychiatric problems, are particularly sensitive to stimulants and may experience adverse effects, even when the drugs are given in comparatively low doses. They need to be used with caution in children because they can retard growth if taken for prolonged periods. An excess of these drugs given to a child may depress the nervous system, producing drowsiness or even loss of consciousness. Palpitations may also occur.

These drugs reduce the level of natural stimulants in the brain so that after regular use for a few weeks a person may become physically dependent on them for normal function. If they are abruptly withdrawn after regular use, the excess of natural inhibitory chemicals in the brain depresses activity in the central nervous system, producing withdrawal symptoms. These may include lethargy, depression, increased appetite and difficulty staying awake.

If used by adults inappropriately or in excess, stimulants can produce over-activity in the brain resulting in extreme restlessness, sleeplessness, and feelings of nervousness or anxiety. They also stimulate the sympathetic branch of the autonomic nervous system (see p.79), causing shaking, sweating and palpitations. More serious risks of exceeding the prescribed dose are fits and a major disturbance in mental functioning that may result in delusions and hallucinations. Because these drugs have been abused, they are classified as controlled drugs (see p.434).

ACTION OF NERVOUS SYSTEM STIMULANTS

Wakefulness is controlled by a part of the brain stem called the reticular activating system (RAS).

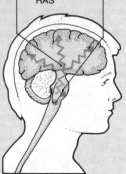

Stimulatory signals to brain

RAS

Signals to brain reduced

Signals to brain increased

Drug stimulates RAS

Brain stem

Normal brain activity
When the brain is functioning normally, signals from the RAS stimulate the upper parts of the brain which control thought processes and alertness.

Brain activity in narcolepsy
In narcolepsy the level of signals from the RAS is greatly reduced.

Normal brain activity restored
Central nervous system stimulants act on the RAS to increase the level of stimulatory signals to the brain.

COMMON DRUGS

Amphetamines
Dexamphetamine

Respiratory stimulants
Aminophylline
Doxapram
Nikethamide
Theophylline ✳

Other drugs
Caffeine
Dexfenfluramine
Methylphenidate

✳ See Part 4

DRUGS USED FOR MIGRAINE

Migraine is a term applied to recurrent severe headaches affecting only one side of the head and caused by changes in the blood vessels. They may be accompanied by nausea and vomiting and preceded by warning signs, usually flashing lights or numbness and tingling in the arms. Occasionally speech may be impaired, and the attack may be disabling. The exact cause of migraine is unknown, but an attack may be triggered by emotional factors including excitement, tension or shock, physical exertion, a blow to the head, some foods and some drugs. A family history of migraine also increases the likelihood that an individual will suffer from migraine.

Why they are used

Drugs are used either to relieve symptoms or to prevent attacks. Different drugs are used in each approach, but none cures the underlying disorder. However, a susceptibility to migraine can clear up spontaneously, and if you are taking drugs regularly, your doctor may recommend that you stop them after a few months to see if this has happened.

In most people migraine headaches can be relieved by a mild analgesic such as aspirin or paracetamol, or a stronger one like codeine (see Analgesics, p.80). But because the migraine may be accompanied by nausea and vomiting these drugs may not be absorbed sufficiently to provide relief. Injections of sumatriptan or suppository forms of other drugs may be used. Preparations containing caffeine have been used for decades to suppress the headache when the early warning symptoms are present but before the pain is manifest. Drugs such as sumatriptan or ergotamine are given once the headache begins.

When attacks occur more often than once a month, daily drug therapy for a period of weeks or months with propranolol, a beta blocker (see p.97) or clonidine, an antihypertensive (p.102) may be advised to prevent them.

Anxiety or depression which can accompany migraine may be treated with anti-anxiety drugs (p.83) or antidepressants, p.84). Nausea and vomiting may be controlled with an anti-emetic drug (see p.90).

Amitriptyline, an antidepressant, is sometimes prescribed regularly for a while to prevent migraine attacks, even for people who are not suffering from depression.

How they work

A migraine attack begins when blood vessels surrounding the brain constrict, producing the typical migraine warning signs. This is thought to be caused by certain chemicals in food or produced in the body. The neurotransmitter serotonin causes large blood vessels in the brain to constrict. Sumatriptan is closely related

ACTION OF DRUGS USED FOR MIGRAINE

Migraine is caused by the action of chemicals in the bloodstream on blood vessels surrounding the brain and in the scalp. In the first stage of a migraine attack, the blood vessels surrounding the brain constrict, causing warning signs (below left). In the second stage, the blood vessels in the scalp dilate, causing a severe headache (below right).

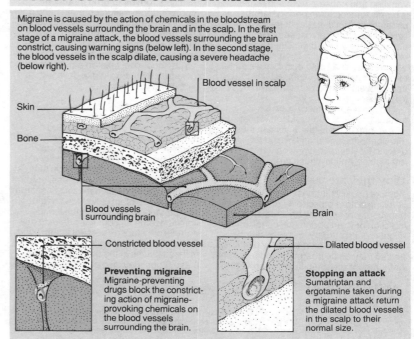

Preventing migraine
Migraine-preventing drugs block the constricting action of migraine-provoking chemicals on the blood vessels surrounding the brain.

Stopping an attack
Sumatriptan and ergotamine taken during a migraine attack return the dilated blood vessels in the scalp to their normal size.

to serotonin and reverses the dilatation of brain blood vessels which occurs in migraine. Methysergide and propranolol block the effect of chemicals on blood vessels and so prevent attacks (see Action of drugs used for migraine, above).

The next stage occurs when blood vessels in the scalp and around the eyes dilate. This causes the release of chemicals called prostaglandins which produce pain. Aspirin and paracetamol relieve pain by blocking the production of prostaglandins, whereas codeine acts directly on the brain to alter the perception of pain (see Action of analgesics, p.80). Both sumatriptan and ergotamine relieve pain by narrowing the dilated blood vessels.

How they affect you

All of these drugs have their own side effects. Sumatriptan may cause chest tightness. Ergotamine may cause drowsiness, tingling sensations in the skin (paresthesiae), cramps, and weakness in the legs.

For more information about the effects of propranolol, see Beta blockers (p.97), and for more information on the effects of analgesics, see p.80.

Risks and special precautions

Sumatriptan should not normally be used by those with high blood pressure, angina, or coronary heart disease. Ergotamine should be used with caution if you have

poor circulation as it can damage blood vessels through prolonged overconstriction. Frequent use can lead to dependence and numerous adverse effects, including headache. You should not take more than your doctor advises in any one week.

Methysergide taken long term can produce pain in the abdomen or lower back, and also shortness of breath due to an unusual type of damage to tissues.

How they are administered

They are usually taken by mouth as tablets or capsules. Sumatriptan is normally taken in tablet form, but if an attack is getting worse and vomiting has already taken hold, it can be administered by a self-injection device. Dihydroergotamine, a drug similar to ergotamine, may be given by injection. Ergotamine may also be taken by aerosol inhalation, or as tablets to be dissolved under the tongue.

COMMON DRUGS

Drugs to prevent migraine
Clonidine *
Methysergide *
Pizotifen *
Propranolol *

| * See Part 4 |

Drugs to relieve migraine
Aspirin *
Codeine *
Ergotamine *
Paracetamol *
Sumatriptan *

ANTI-EMETICS

Anti-emetics are drugs used to suppress vomiting and nausea. Vomiting (emesis) is a reflex action for expelling harmful substances, but it may also be a symptom of disease. Common causes of vomiting and nausea include digestive tract infection, pregnancy, motion sickness and vertigo. It can also occur as a side effect of a medication, general anaesthesia or drug or radiation therapy for cancer.

The main anti-emetic drugs are metoclopramide, domperidone, ondansetron, granisetron, the antihistamines, and phenothiazine drugs, which are also used to treat certain types of mental illness (see Antipsychotic drugs, p.85).

Why they are used

Doctors usually diagnose the cause of vomiting before prescribing an anti-emetic because vomiting may be a reaction to infection or to an abdominal condition that might require surgery. Suppressing vomiting and nausea may delay diagnosis, and so may delay treatment and recovery. Anti-emetics are often taken to prevent motion sickness (antihistamines), nausea resulting from other drug treatment (domperidone, metoclopramide and phenothiazines), to suppress nausea in vertigo (see right), and occasionally to relieve severe vomiting in pregnancy (antihistamines and phenothiazines).

You should not take an anti-emetic drug for longer than a couple of days without consulting your doctor.

How they work

Nausea and vomiting occur when a specialized part of the brain called the vomiting centre is stimulated by signals which may arise from various points in the brain and body: from the digestive system; from the part of the brain that is responsible for consciousness, or from the inner ear. Signals may also arise from an area of the brain called the chemoreceptor trigger, which stimulates the vomiting (emetic) centre if it detects any harmful substances present in the blood. Anti-emetic drugs may act at one or more of these places in the body. In addition, these drugs may also promote the normal

VERTIGO AND MÉNIÈRE'S DISEASE

Vertigo is a spinning sensation in the head often accompanied by nausea and vomiting. It is usually caused by disease of the organ of balance in the inner ear. Anti-emetic drugs are prescribed to relieve symptoms with modest effect.

Ménière's disease is a disorder in which excess fluid builds up in the inner ear causing vertigo, noises in the ear and gradual deafness. It is usually treated with an antihistamine, prochlorperazine or an anti-anxiety drug (see p.83). A diuretic (see p.99) may also be given in order to reduce the excess fluid in the ear.

emptying of the stomach contents into the intestine.

Each anti-emetic drug may act on one or more parts of the vomiting mechanism (see Action of anti-emetics, below left).

How they affect you

In addition to reducing or preventing vomiting and nausea, many anti-emetics may make you feel drowsy. Certain non-sedating antihistamines (see p.125) may therefore be preferred for the prevention of motion sickness.

Because the antihistamines block the parasympathetic system (see p.79) they can produce many *anticholinergic* side effects, including dry mouth, blurred vision and difficulty passing urine. Phenothiazine drugs can lower blood pressure, leading to dizziness.

Risks and special precautions

Because antihistamines can make you drowsy, it may be advisable not to drive while taking them.

Phenothiazines and metoclopramide can produce uncontrolled movements of the face and tongue, and for this reason they are used with caution in people who suffer from movement disorders such as *parkinsonism*.

ACTION OF ANTI-EMETICS

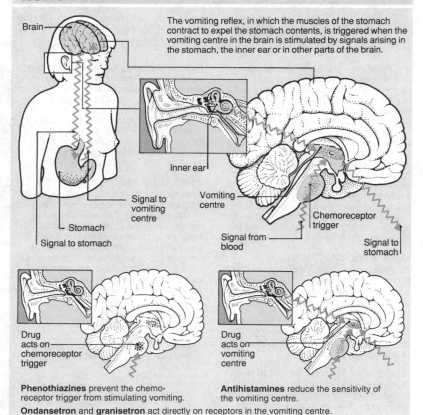

The vomiting reflex, in which the muscles of the stomach contract to expel the stomach contents, is triggered when the vomiting centre in the brain is stimulated by signals arising in the stomach, the inner ear or in other parts of the brain.

Brain
Inner ear
Signal to vomiting centre
Stomach
Signal to stomach
Vomiting centre
Signal from blood
Chemoreceptor trigger
Signal to stomach

Drug acts on chemoreceptor trigger

Drug acts on vomiting centre

Phenothiazines prevent the chemoreceptor trigger from stimulating vomiting.

Antihistamines reduce the sensitivity of the vomiting centre.

Ondansetron and **granisetron** act directly on receptors in the vomiting centre.

COMMON DRUGS

Antihistamines
Cinnarizine *
Dimenhydrinate
Meclozine
Promethazine *

Phenothiazines
Perphenazine
Prochlorperazine *

Other drugs
Domperidone *
Metoclopramide *
Ondansetron*
Granisetron
Tropisetron

* See Part 4

RESPIRATORY SYSTEM

The respiratory system consists of the lungs and the passageways by which air reaches them. Through the process of inhaling and exhaling air – breathing – the body is able to obtain the oxygen necessary to survival, and to expel carbon dioxide, which is the waste product of man's basic biological process.

What can go wrong

Difficulty in breathing may be due to narrowing of the air passages, from spasm (as in asthma and bronchitis), or from swelling of the linings of the air passages (as in bronchiolitis and bronchitis). Breathing difficulties may also be due to an infection of the lung tissue (as in pneumonia and bronchitis), or to damage to the small air sacs (alveoli) from emphysema or from inhaled dusts or moulds (as in pneumoconiosis and farmer's lung).

Sometimes difficulty in breathing may be due to congestion of the lungs from heart disease, to an inhaled object such as a peanut, or to infection or inflammation of the throat. Symptoms of breathing difficulties often include a cough and tight chest.

Why drugs are used

Drugs with a variety of actions are used to clear the air passages, soothe inflammation and reduce the production of mucus. Many of these can be bought without a prescription as single ingredients or combined ingredient preparations, often with an analgesic.

Decongestants (p.93) reduce the swelling inside the nose, so making it possible to breathe more freely. If the cause of congestion is an allergic response, an antihistamine (p.124) is often recommended to relieve symptoms or to prevent attacks. Infections of the respiratory tract, such as bronchitis or pneumonia, are usually treated with antibiotics.

Drugs that widen the bronchi are known as bronchodilators (p.92). They are used to relieve or prevent asthma attacks. This group of drugs includes drugs that relax the muscles surrounding the airways. They also include drugs such as corticosteroids (p.141) that widen the air passages by reducing inflammation of the mucous lining. These may also be of limited benefit in chronic respiratory problems such as chronic bronchitis, but they are not used for asthma attacks in progress.

A variety of drugs may be used to relieve coughs. Some of them make it easier to eliminate phlegm; others suppress the cough by inhibiting the cough reflex itself.

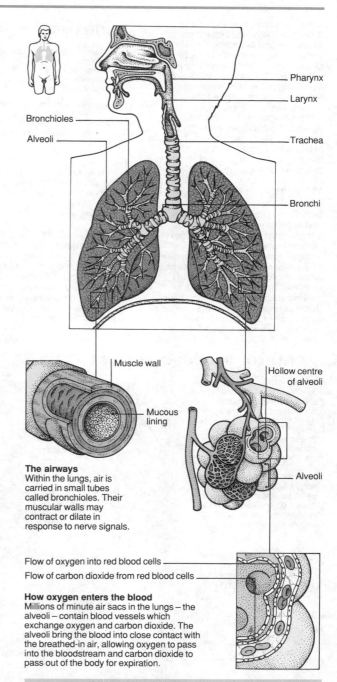

The airways
Within the lungs, air is carried in small tubes called bronchioles. Their muscular walls may contract or dilate in response to nerve signals.

Flow of oxygen into red blood cells
Flow of carbon dioxide from red blood cells

How oxygen enters the blood
Millions of minute air sacs in the lungs – the alveoli – contain blood vessels which exchange oxygen and carbon dioxide. The alveoli bring the blood into close contact with the breathed-in air, allowing oxygen to pass into the bloodstream and carbon dioxide to pass out of the body for expiration.

MAJOR DRUG GROUPS

Bronchodilators
Decongestants
Drugs to treat coughs

BRONCHODILATORS

When air enters the lungs it passes through narrow tubes called bronchioles. In asthma and bronchitis the bronchioles become narrower, either as a result of contraction of the muscles in their walls or as a result of mucus congestion. This tightening of the bronchioles obstructs the flow of air into and out of the lungs and causes breathlessness.

Bronchodilators are prescribed to widen the bronchioles and improve breathing. There are three main groups of bronchodilators: *sympathomimetic* drugs, *anticholinergics* and xanthine drugs, which are related to caffeine.

Why they are used

Bronchodilators help to dilate the bronchioles of people suffering from asthma and bronchitis. However, they are of little benefit to those suffering from severe chronic bronchitis.

Bronchodilators can either be taken when they are needed to relieve an attack of breathlessness that is in progress, or on a regular basis to prevent such attacks from occurring. Some people find it helpful to take an extra dose of their bronchodilator immediately before undertaking any activity that is likely to provoke an attack

INHALERS

Inhaling a bronchodilator drug directly into the lungs is the best way of getting benefit without excessive side effects. Devices for delivering the drug into the airways are described below.

Inhalers or puffers release a small dose when they are pressed, but require some skill to use effectively. A large hollow plastic "spacer" can help you to inhale your drug more easily.

Insufflation cartridges deliver larger amounts of drug than inhalers and are easier to use because the drug is taken in as you breathe normally.

Nebulizers pump compressed air through a solution of drug to produce a fine mist which is inhaled through a face mask. They deliver large doses of the drug to the lungs, rapidly relieving breathing difficulty.

of breathlessness. Sympathomimetic drugs are mainly used for the rapid relief of breathlessness; anticholinergic and xanthine drugs are more often used for the long-term prevention of attacks.

How they work

Bronchodilator drugs act by relaxing the muscles surrounding the bronchioles. Sympathomimetic and anticholinergic drugs achieve this by interfering with nerve signals passed to the muscles through the autonomic nervous system (see p.79). Xanthine drugs are thought to relax the muscle in the bronchioles by a direct effect on the muscle fibres, but their precise action is not known.

When taken for the immediate relief of breathlessness, bronchodilators usually improve breathing within a few minutes. Taken to prevent attacks, corticosteroids usually start to increase the sufferer's capacity for exercise within a few days, and most people find that the frequency of these attacks of breathlessness is reduced.

Because sympathomimetic drugs stimulate a branch of the autonomic nervous system that controls heart rate, they may sometimes cause palpitations and trembling. Typical side effects of anticholinergic drugs include dry mouth, blurred vision, and difficulty in passing urine. Xanthine drugs may cause headaches and nausea.

Risks and special precautions

Since most bronchodilators are not taken by mouth, but inhaled (see above), they do not commonly cause serious side effects. However, because of their possible effect on heart rate, sympathomimetic and xanthine drugs need to be prescribed with caution for those with heart problems, high blood pressure or an overactive thyroid gland. Anticholinergic drugs may not be suitable for people with urinary retention or who have a tendency to glaucoma.

ACTION OF BRONCHODILATORS

When the bronchioles are narrowed following contraction of the muscle layer and swelling of the mucous lining, the passage of air is impeded. Bronchodilators act on the nerve signals that govern muscle activity. Sympathomimetics enhance the action of neurotransmitters that encourage muscle relaxation. Anticholinergics block the neurotransmitters that trigger muscle contraction. Xanthines promote muscle relaxation by a direct effect on the muscles.

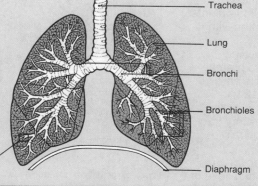

- Trachea
- Lung
- Bronchi
- Bronchioles
- Diaphragm

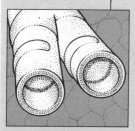

Normal bronchioles
The muscle surrounding the bronchioles is relaxed, leaving the airway open.

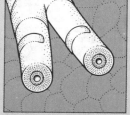

Asthmatic spasm
The muscle contracts and the lining swells, narrowing the airway.

After drug treatment
The muscles relax, opening the airway, but the mucous lining remains swollen.

COMMON DRUGS

Sympathomimetics	Xanthines
Adrenaline✱	Aminophylline
Bambuterol	Theophylline ✱
Ephedrine ✱	
Isoprenaline ✱	**Corticosteroids**
Salbutamol ✱	Fluticasone ✱
Salmeterol	Beclomethasone ✱
Terbutaline	
Tulobuterol	

Anticholinergics
Atropine ✱
Ipratropium bromide ✱
Oxitropium

✱ See Part 4

DECONGESTANTS

The usual cause of a blocked nose is swelling of the delicate mucous membrane that lines the nasal passages and excessive production of mucus as a result of inflammation. This may be caused by an infection (usually a common cold) or it may be caused by an allergy – for example, to pollen – a condition known as allergic rhinitis or hay fever. Congestion can also occur in the sinuses (the air spaces in the skull), resulting in sinusitis. Decongestants are drugs that reduce swelling of the mucous membrane and suppress the production of mucus, therefore helping to clear blocked nasal passages and sinuses. Antihistamines, which counter the allergic response in allergy-related conditions, are discussed on p.124.

Why they are used

Most common colds do not need to be treated with decongestants. Simple home remedies such as steam inhalation, possibly with the addition of an aromatic oil – such as menthol or eucalyptus is often effective. Decongestants are used when such measures are ineffective, or when there is a particular risk from untreated congestion – for example, in people who suffer from recurrent middle ear or sinus infections.

   Decongestants are available in the form of drops that are applied directly into the nose (*topical* decongestants), or they can be taken by mouth. Small quantities of decongestant drugs are often added to over-the-counter cold remedies (see p.94).

How they work

When the mucous membrane lining the nose is irritated by infection or allergy, the blood vessels supplying the membrane become enlarged. This leads to fluid accumulation in the surrounding tissue and encourages the production of larger than normal amounts of mucus.

   Most decongestants belong to the *sympathomimetic* group of drugs which stimulate the sympathetic branch of the autonomic nervous system (see p.79). One effect of this action is to constrict the blood vessels, so reducing swelling

ACTION OF DECONGESTANTS

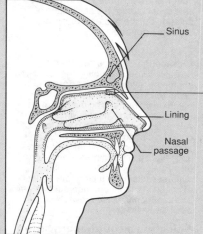

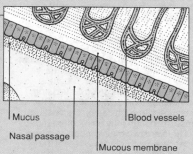

Sinus

Lining

Nasal passage

Normal nasal passages
The lining of the nasal passages consists of a layer of mucus-producing cells (mucous membrane) supplied by blood vessels. The walls of the blood vessels contain nerve endings that, when stimulated, cause the vessel to constrict.

Mucus

Nasal passage

Blood vessels

Mucous membrane

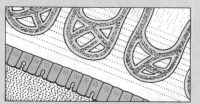

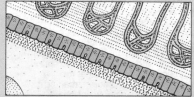

Congested nasal lining
When the blood vessels enlarge in response to infection or irritation, increased amounts of fluid pass into the mucous membrane which swells and produces more mucus.

Effect of decongestants
Decongestants enhance the action of chemicals that stimulate constriction of the blood vessels. Narrowing of the blood vessels reduces swelling and mucus production.

of the lining of the nose and sinuses.

How they affect you

When applied topically in drops these drugs start to relieve congestion within a few minutes. Decongestants by mouth take a little longer to act, but their effect may last longer.

   Topical decongestants used in moderation have few adverse effects because they are not absorbed by the

body in large amounts. Decongestants taken by mouth are more likely to cause symptoms related to their action on the sympathetic nervous system, including increased heart rate and trembling. For these reasons they should be used with caution by those with heart problems, high blood pressure or an overactive thyroid gland.

   Used for too long or in excess, decongestants can, after giving initial relief, do more harm than good, causing a "rebound congestion" (see left). This can be avoided by taking the minimum effective dose and by using decongestant preparations only when absolutely necessary.

REBOUND CONGESTION

This can happen when decongestants are suddenly withdrawn after an extended period of treatment, or when decongestant nose drops are overused. The result is a sudden increase in congestion due to widening of the blood vessels in the nasal lining because blood vessels are no longer constricted by the decongestant.

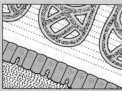

Congestion before drug treatment

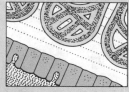

Congestion after stopping drug treatment

COMMON DRUGS

Ephedrine ✻
Ipratropium bromide ✻

Oxymetazoline
Phenylephrine ✻
Phenylpropanolamine ✻
Xylometazoline

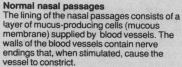

✻ See Part 4

DRUGS TO TREAT COUGHS

Coughing is a natural response to irritation of the lungs and air passages, designed to expel harmful substances from the respiratory tract. Common causes of coughing include infection of the respiratory tract (for example, bronchitis or pneumonia), inflammation of the airways caused by asthma, or exposure to certain irritant substances such as smoke or chemical fumes. Depending on their cause, coughs may be productive – that is, phlegm-producing – or they may be dry.

In most cases coughing is a helpful reaction that assists the body to get rid of excess phlegm or irritant substances; suppressing the cough may actually delay recovery. However, repeated bouts of coughing can be distressing, sometimes increasing irritation of the air passages. In such cases, medication to ease the cough may be recommended.

There are two main groups of cough remedies, according to whether the cough is productive or dry.

Productive coughs

Mucolytics and expectorants are the groups of drugs most commonly recommended for productive coughs when simple home remedies such as steam inhalation have failed to "loosen" the cough and make it easier to cough up phlegm. Mucolytics alter the consistency of the phlegm, making it less sticky and easier to cough up. These are often given by inhalation.

Expectorants are drugs that are frequently included in over-the-counter cough and cold remedies. These are said to encourage the production of phlegm, but the overall benefits of such drugs are doubtful.

Dry coughs

In dry coughs there is no advantage to be gained from promoting the expulsion of phlegm. Drugs used for dry coughs are given to suppress the coughing mechanism by calming the part of the brain that governs the coughing reflex. Antihistamines are often given for mild coughs, particularly in children. For persistent coughs, mild narcotic drugs such as codeine are prescribed (see also Analgesics, p.80). All cough suppressants have a generally sedating effect on the brain and nervous system and commonly cause 'drowsiness and other side effects.

Selecting a cough medication

There is a bewildering variety of over-the-counter medications available for treating coughs. Most consist of a syrupy base to which active ingredients and flavourings are added. Many contain a number of different active ingredients, sometimes with contradictory effects: it is not uncommon to find an expectorant (for a productive cough) and a cough suppressant (for a dry cough) included in the same preparation.

It is important to select the correct

type of medication for your cough to avoid the risk that you may make your condition worse. For example, using a cough suppressant for a productive cough may prevent you from getting rid of excess infected phlegm and may delay your recovery. It is best to choose a preparation with a single active ingredient that is appropriate for your type of cough. Diabetics may need to select a sugar-free product. If you are in any doubt ask your doctor or pharmacist for advice. Because there is a danger that use of over-the-counter cough remedies to alleviate symptoms may delay the diagnosis of a more serious underlying disorder, it is important to seek medical advice for any cough that persists for longer than a few days or if a cough is accompanied by additional symptoms such as fever or blood in the phlegm.

ACTION OF COUGH REMEDIES

Cough remedies are divided into two main groups: those that alter the consistency or production of phlegm (mucolytics and expectorants); and those that suppress the coughing reflex (narcotic and non-narcotic cough suppressants). Mucolytics are usually given by inhalation and act directly on the lungs and airways. Expectorants are taken by mouth, and are supposed to help bring up phlegm. Cough suppressants are taken by mouth and they act on the coughing centre in the brain.

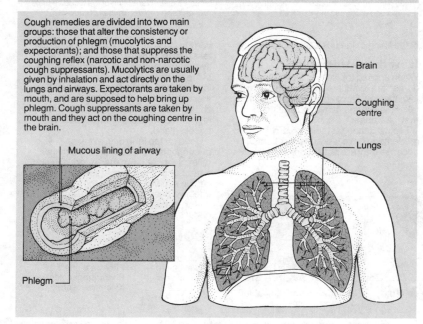

Mucous lining of airway

Phlegm

Brain

Coughing centre

Lungs

COMMON DRUGS

Expectorants
Ammonium chloride

Mucolytics
Acetylcysteine
Carbocysteine

Narcotic cough suppressants
Codeine *
Dextromethorphan *
Hydrocodone

Non-narcotic cough suppressants
Antihistamines (see p.124)

* See Part 4

HEART AND CIRCULATION

The blood transports oxygen, nutrients, and heat, contains chemical messages in the form of drugs and hormones, and carries away waste products for excretion by the kidneys. It is pumped by the heart to and from the lungs, and then in a separate circuit to the brain, digestive organs, muscles, kidneys, and skin.

What can go wrong

The efficiency of the circulation may be impaired by weakening of the heart's pumping action (heart failure) or irregularity of heart rate (arrhythmia). In addition, the blood vessels may be narrowed and obstructed by fatty deposits (atherosclerosis). This may reduce blood supply to the brain, the extremities (peripheral vascular disease) or to the heart muscle (coronary heart disease) causing angina. These last disorders can be complicated by the formation of clots which may block a blood vessel. A clot in the arteries supplying the heart muscle is known as coronary thrombosis; a clot in an artery inside the brain is the most frequent cause of stroke.

One common circulatory disorder is abnormally high blood pressure (hypertension) where the pressure of circulating blood on the vessel walls is increased for reasons not fully understood. One factor may be loss of elasticity of the vessel walls (arteriosclerosis). Several other conditions, such as migraine and Raynaud's disease, are caused by temporary alterations to blood vessel size.

Why drugs are used

Because those suffering from heart disease often have more than one problem, several drugs may be prescribed at once. Many act directly on the heart to alter the rate and rhythm of the heartbeat. These are known as anti-arrhythmics and include beta blockers and digoxin.

Other drugs affect the blood vessel diameter, either dilating them (vasodilators) to improve blood flow and reduce blood pressure, or constricting them (vasoconstrictors).

Drugs may also reduce blood volume and cholesterol levels, and alter clotting ability. Diuretics (used in the treatment of hypertension and heart failure) increase the body's excretion of water. Lipid-lowering drugs reduce blood cholesterol levels, thereby minimizing the risk of atherosclerosis. Drugs to reduce blood clotting are administered when there is a risk of abnormal blood clots forming in the heart, veins, or arteries. Drugs that increase clotting are given when the body's natural clotting mechanism is defective.

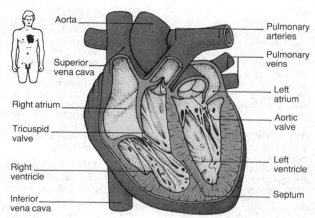

Labels: Aorta · Pulmonary arteries · Pulmonary veins · Superior vena cava · Left atrium · Right atrium · Aortic valve · Tricuspid valve · Right ventricle · Left ventricle · Inferior vena cava · Septum

The heart
The heart is a pump containing four chambers. The atrium and ventricle on the left side pump oxygenated blood, while the corresponding chambers on the right pump de-oxygenated blood. Backflow of blood is prevented by valves at the chamber exits.

How blood circulates
De-oxygenated blood is carried to the heart from all parts of the body. It is then pumped to the lungs where it becomes oxygenated. The oxygenated blood returns to the heart and from there is pumped throughout the body.

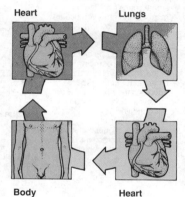

Heart · Lungs · Body · Heart

☐ De-oxygenated blood
☐ Oxygenated blood

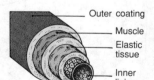

Labels: Outer coating · Muscle · Elastic tissue · Inner lining

Arteries
Arteries carry blood away from the heart. Muscle walls contract and dilate in response to nerve signals.

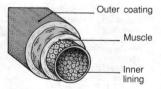

Labels: Outer coating · Muscle · Inner lining

Veins
Veins carry de-oxygenated blood back to the heart. The walls are less elastic than artery walls.

MAJOR DRUG GROUPS

Digitalis drugs
Beta blockers
Vasodilators
Diuretics
Anti-arrhythmics

Anti-angina drugs
Antihypertensive drugs
Lipid-lowering drugs
Drugs that affect blood clotting

DIGITALIS DRUGS

Digitalis is the collective term for a number of naturally-occurring substances (also called cardiac glycosides) that are found in the leaves of plants of the foxglove family and used for certain heart disorders. The principal drugs in this group are digoxin and digitoxin. Digoxin is more commonly used because it is shorter acting and dosage is easier to adjust (see also Risks and special precautions, below).

Why they are used

Digitalis drugs do not cure heart disease but improve the heart's pumping action and so relieve many of the symptoms that result from poor heart function. They are useful for treating conditions in which the heart beats irregularly or too rapidly (notably in atrial fibrillation, see Anti-arrhythmics, p.100), or when it pumps too weakly (in congestive heart failure), or when the heart muscle is damaged and weakened following a heart attack.

Digitalis drugs can be used for a short period when the heart is working poorly, but in many cases they have to be taken indefinitely. Their effect does not diminish with time. In heart failure, digitalis drugs are often given together with a diuretic (see p.99).

How they work

The normal heart beat results from electrical impulses generated in nerve tissue within the heart. These cause the heart muscle to contract and pump blood. By reducing the flow of electrical impulses in the heart, digitalis makes the heart beat more slowly.

The force with which the heart muscle contracts depends on chemical changes in the muscle. By promoting these chemical changes, digitalis increases the force of muscle contraction each time the heart is stimulated. This compensates for the loss of power that occurs when some of the muscle is damaged following a heart attack. The stronger heart beat increases the flow of blood to the kidneys. This increases urine production and helps to remove the excess fluid that often accumulates as a result of heart failure.

How they affect you

Digitalis relieves symptoms of heart failure – fatigue, breathlessness, and swelling of the legs – and increases your capacity for exercise. The frequency with which you need to pass urine is also increased initially.

Risks and special precautions

Digitalis drugs can be toxic and, if blood levels rise too high, may produce symptoms of digitalis poisoning. These include excessive tiredness, confusion, loss of appetite, nausea, vomiting, and diarrhoea. If such symptoms occur, it is important to report them to your doctor promptly.

Digoxin is normally removed from the body by the kidneys; if kidney function is impaired, the drug is more likely to accumulate in the body and cause toxic effects. Digitoxin, which is broken down in the liver, is sometimes preferred in such cases. Digitoxin can accumulate after repeated dosage, especially if liver function is reduced.

Both digoxin and digitoxin are more toxic when blood potassium levels are low. Potassium deficiency is commonly caused by diuretic drugs so that people taking these along with digitalis drugs need to have the effects of both drugs and blood potassium levels carefully monitored. Potassium supplements may be required.

ACTION OF DIGITALIS DRUGS

The heart beat is triggered by electrical impulses that are generated by the pacemaker, a small mass of nerve tissue in the right atrium. Electrical signals pass from the pacemaker to the atrio-ventricular node. From here a wave of impulses spreads through the heart muscle causing it to contract and pump blood to the body. The pumping action of the heart can become weak if the heart muscle is damaged or if the heart beat is too fast, as in atrial fibrillation. In this condition (shown right), rapid signals from the pacemaker trigger off fast and inefficient contractions of both the atria and the ventricles.

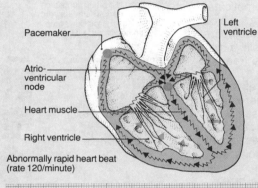

Pacemaker
Atrio-ventricular node
Heart muscle
Right ventricle
Left ventricle

Abnormally rapid heart beat (rate 120/minute)

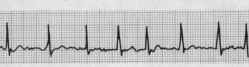

The effect of digitalis
Digitalis drugs reduce the flow of electrical impulses through the atrio-ventricular node so that the ventricles contract less often. In addition, by promoting the chemical changes in muscle cells necessary for muscular contraction, these drugs increase the force with which the heart muscle contracts and so improve the efficiency of each heart beat.

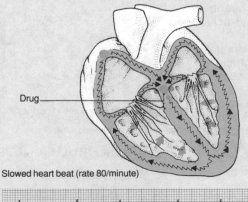

Drug

Slowed heart beat (rate 80/minute)

COMMON DRUGS

Digoxin *
Digitoxin

* See Part 4

BETA BLOCKERS

Beta blockers are drugs that interrupt the transmission of stimuli through the beta *receptors* of the body. Since the actions they block originate in the adrenal glands (and elsewhere) they are also sometimes called beta adrenergic blocking agents. Used mainly in heart disorders, they are occasionally prescribed for other conditions.

Why they are used

Beta blockers are used in the treatment of angina (see p.101), hypertension (see p.102), and irregular heart rhythms (see p.100). They are sometimes given after a heart attack to reduce the likelihood of abnormal heart rhythms or further damage to the heart muscle. These drugs are also prescribed to improve heart function in heart muscle disorders – cardiomyopathies.

Beta blockers may also be given to prevent migraine headaches (see p.89) or to reduce the physical symptoms of anxiety (see p.83). They may also be given to control symptoms of an over-active thyroid gland (see p.144). A beta blocker is sometimes given in the form of eye drops in glaucoma to lower fluid pressure inside the eye (see p.168).

How they work

By occupying the beta receptors, beta blockers nullify the stimulating action of noradrenaline, the main "fight or flight" hormone. Thus they reduce the force

THE USES AND EFFECTS OF BETA BLOCKERS

The blockade of the transmission of signals through beta receptors in different parts of the body produces a wide variety of benefits and side effects according to the disease being treated. The illustration (right) shows the main areas and body systems affected by the action of beta blockers.

Brain
Dilatation of the blood vessels surrounding the brain is inhibited, so preventing migraine.

Eyes
Beta blocker eye drops reduce fluid production and so lower pressure inside the eye.

Heart
Slowing of the heart rate and reduction of the force of the heart beat reduces the workload of the heart, helping to prevent angina and abnormal heart rhythms. But this action may worsen heart failure.

Lungs
Constriction of the airways may provoke breathless attacks in asthmatics or those with chronic bronchitis.

Blood vessels
Constriction of the blood vessels may cause coldness of the hands and feet.

Muscles
Muscle tremor in anxiety and overactivity of the thyroid gland is reduced.

Blood pressure
This is lowered because the rate and force at which the heart pumps blood into the circulatory system is reduced.

BETA RECEPTORS

Signals from the sympathetic nervous system are carried by noradrenaline, a *neurotransmitter* produced in the adrenal glands and at the ends of sympathetic nerve fibers. Beta blockers stop the signals from the neurotransmitter.

Neurotransmitter

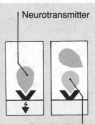

Beta blocker

Types of beta receptor

There are two types of beta receptor: beta 1 and beta 2. Beta 1 receptors are located mainly in the heart muscle; beta 2 receptors are found in the airways and blood vessels. Cardioselective drugs act mainly on beta 1 receptors; non-cardioselective drugs act on both types.

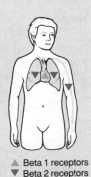

▲ Beta 1 receptors
▼ Beta 2 receptors

and speed of the heart beat and prevent the dilatation of the blood vessels surrounding the brain and leading to the extremities. The effect of this "beta blockade" in a variety of disorders is shown in the box above.

How they affect you

Taken to treat angina, beta blockers reduce the frequency and severity of attacks. As part of the treatment for hypertension, they help to lower blood pressure and thus reduce the risks that are associated with this condition. Beta blockers help to prevent severe attacks of arrhythmia or wild, uncontrolled heart beats.

Because beta blockers affect many parts of the body, they commonly produce minor side effects. By reducing heart rate and air flow to the lungs, they may reduce capacity for strenuous exercise, although this is unlikely to be noticed by somebody whose physical activity was previously limited by heart problems. Many people experience cold hands and feet while taking these drugs, owing to the reduction in blood supply to the limbs. Reduced circulation can also lead to temporary impotence during beta blocker treatment.

Risks and special precautions

The main risk of beta blockers is that of provoking breathing difficulties as a result of their blocking effect on beta receptors in the lungs. Cardioselective beta blockers which act principally on the heart are thought to be less likely than non-cardioselective ones to cause

such problems. But all beta blockers are prescribed with caution in people with asthma, bronchitis, or other forms of respiratory disease.

Beta blockers are not usually prescribed for people who have poor circulation in the limbs because they reduce the flow of blood and may aggravate such conditions. They are not normally given to people who are subject to heart failure because they may further reduce the force of the heart beat. Diabetics who need to take beta blockers should be aware that they may notice a change in the warning signs of low blood sugar – in particular, symptoms such as palpitations and tremor may be suppressed.

Beta blockers should not be stopped suddenly after prolonged use; this may provoke a sudden and severe recurrence of symptoms of the original disorder, even a heart attack. Blood pressure may also rise markedly. When the treatment needs to be stopped, it should be withdrawn gradually under medical supervision.

COMMON DRUGS

Non-cardioselective	Cardioselective
Acebutolol	Atenolol *
Labetalol	Metoprolol
Nadolol	Celiprolol
Oxprenolol *	
Propranolol *	
Timolol	

* See Part 4

VASODILATORS

Vasodilators are drugs that widen blood vessels. Their most obvious use is to reverse narrowing of the blood vessels when this leads to reduced blood flow and, consequently, a lower oxygen supply to parts of the body. This occurs in angina, when narrowing of the coronary arteries reduces blood supply to the heart muscle. Vasodilators are also often used to treat high blood pressure (hypertension).

Several classes of drug are prescribed for their vasodilator effect: nitrates, *sympatholytics*, calcium channel blockers, and ACE (angiotensin-converting enzyme) inhibitors.

Why they are used

Vasodilators improve blood flow and oxygen supply to areas of the body where they are most needed. In angina, dilatation of the blood vessels throughout the body reduces the force with which the heart needs to pump and therefore eases its workload (see also Anti-angina drugs, p.101). This is also sometimes helpful in treating congestive heart failure when other treatments are not effective.

Because blood pressure depends partly on the diameter of the blood vessels, vasodilators are often helpful in treating hypertension (see p.102).

In peripheral vascular disease, narrowed blood vessels in the legs cannot supply sufficient blood to the extremities, often leading to pain in the legs during exercise. Unfortunately, because the vessels are narrowed by atherosclerosis, vasodilators have little effect.

Vasodilator drugs have also been used for senile dementia, in the hope of increasing the supply of oxygen to the brain. The benefits of this treatment have not yet been proved.

How they work

Vasodilators widen the blood vessels by relaxing the muscles surrounding

ACTION OF VASODILATORS

The diameter of blood vessels is governed by the contraction of the surrounding muscle. The muscle contracts in response to signals from the sympathetic nervous system (p.79). Vasodilators encourage the muscles to relax, thus increasing the size of blood vessels.

Constricted blood vessel   **Dilated blood vessel**

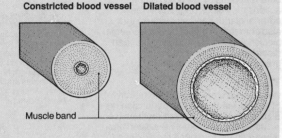

Muscle band

Where they act
Each type of vasodilator acts on a different part of the mechanism controlling blood vessel size to prevent contraction of the surrounding layer of muscles.

Nerves – Sympatholytics interfere with nerve signals to the muscles.

Muscle layer – Nitrates and calcium channel blockers act directly on the muscle to inhibit contraction.

Blood – ACE inhibitors block enzyme activity in the blood (see box below).

them. They achieve this either by affecting the action of the muscles directly (nitrates and calcium channel blockers) or by interfering with the nerve signals that govern contraction of the blood vessels (sympatholytics). ACE inhibitors act by blocking the activity of an enzyme in the blood. The enzyme is responsible for producing a substance (angiotensin II) which is a powerful vasoconstrictor (see the box below).

How they affect you

As well as relieving the symptoms of the disorders for which they are taken, vasodilators can have many minor side

effects related to their action on the circulation. Flushing and headaches are common at the start of treatment. Dizziness and fainting may also occur as a result of lowered blood pressure. Dilatation of the blood vessels can also cause fluid build-up leading to swelling, particularly of the ankles.

Risks and special precautions

The major risk is that blood pressure may sometimes fall too low. Therefore, vasodilator drugs are prescribed with caution for people with unstable blood pressure. It is also advisable to take the first dose of vasodilator drugs at a time when it is possible for you to sit or lie down afterwards.

ACE INHIBITORS

ACE (angiotensin-converting enzyme) inhibitors are powerful vasodilators. They act by blocking the action of an enzyme in the bloodstream that is responsible for converting a chemical called angiotensin I into angiotensin II. Angiotensin II encourages constriction of the blood vessels and its absence permits them to dilate (see right).

Angiotensin II
Angiotensin I   ACE   Drug

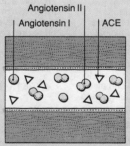

Before drug
Angiotensin I is converted by the enzyme into angiotensin II. The blood vessel constricts.

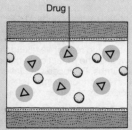

Drug action
ACE inhibitors block enzyme activity thereby preventing the formation of angiotensin II. The blood vessel dilates.

COMMON DRUGS

Nitrates
Glyceryl trinitrate *
Isosorbide
dinitrate *

ACE inhibitors
Captopril *
Enalapril*
Cilazapril
Fosinoprill
Lisinopril
Perindopril
Quinapril
Rimapril

Calcium channel blockers
Diltiazem *
Nifedipine *
Verapamil *

Sympatholytics
Hydralazine *
Prazosin *

Other drugs
Minoxidil *

| * See Part 4 |

DIURETICS

Diuretic drugs help to turn excess body water into urine. As the urine is expelled, two disorders are relieved: tissues become less water-swollen (oedema) and heart action improves because a smaller volume of blood is circulating. There are several classes of diuretics, each of which has different uses, modes of action, and effects (see Types of diuretic, below). But all act on the kidneys, the organs that govern the water content of the body.

Why they are used

One of the most common uses of diuretics is in the treatment of high blood pressure (hypertension). By removing larger than usual amounts of water from the bloodstream, the kidneys reduce the total volume of blood circulating. This in turn reduces the pressure within the blood vessels (see Antihypertensive drugs, p.102).

Diuretics are also widely used to treat heart failure in which the heart's pumping mechanism has become weak. In this disorder they remove fluid that has accumulated in the tissues and lungs. The resulting drop in blood volume reduces the work of the heart.

Other conditions for which diuretics are often prescribed include nephrotic syndrome (a kidney disorder that causes oedema), cirrhosis of the liver (in which fluid may accumulate in the abdominal cavity), and premenstrual syndrome (when hormonal activity can lead to fluid retention and bloating).

Less common uses for diuretics include glaucoma (see p.168) and Ménière's disease (see p.90).

How they work

The normal filtration process of the kidneys takes water, salts (mainly potassium and sodium), and waste products out of the bloodstream. Most of the salts and water are returned to the bloodstream, but certain amounts are expelled from the body together with the waste products in the urine. Diuretics interfere with this normal kidney action

ACTION OF DIURETICS

As blood passes through the kidney, water, sodium and potassium salts, and waste products are filtered out of the bloodstream. Most of the water and filtered salts are then reabsorbed by the bloodstream from the tubule and the remainder is excreted as urine.

By blocking the movement of sodium back into the bloodstream, diuretics prevent the reabsorption of water so that more is expelled from the body as urine. Different diuretic drugs act on different parts of the tubule (see right).

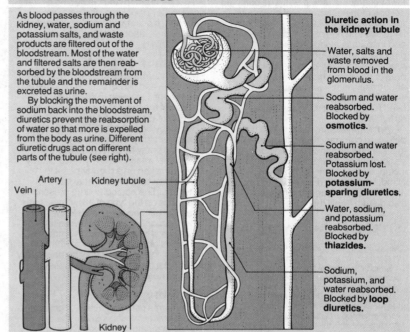

Artery   Kidney tubule

Vein

Kidney

Diuretic action in the kidney tubule

Water, salts and waste removed from blood in the glomerulus.

Sodium and water reabsorbed. Blocked by **osmotics**.

Sodium and water reabsorbed. Potassium lost. Blocked by **potassium-sparing diuretics**.

Water, sodium, and potassium reabsorbed. Blocked by **thiazides**.

Sodium, potassium, and water reabsorbed. Blocked by **loop diuretics**.

by reducing the amounts of sodium and water taken back into the bloodstream, thus increasing the volume of urine produced. In this way the water content of the blood is reduced and excess water is drawn out of the tissues for elimination as urine.

How they affect you

All diuretics increase the frequency with which you need to pass urine. This is most noticeable at the start of treatment. People who have suffered from oedema may notice that swelling – particularly of the ankles – is reduced, and those with heart failure may find that breathlessness is relieved.

Risks and special precautions

Diuretics can cause chemical imbalances in the blood. Most common of these is a fall in potassium levels in the blood (hypokalaemia) that can cause weakness and confusion, particularly in the elderly. Low potassium can also trigger abnormal heart rhythms, especially in those taking digitalis drugs. The imbalance can usually be corrected by potassium supplements (see p. 427) or by a potassium-sparing diuretic. A diet that is rich in potassium (containing plenty of fresh fruits and vegetables) may be helpful.

Some types of diuretic may increase levels of uric acid in the blood and thus the risk of gout in susceptible people. They may also raise blood sugar level which can cause problems for diabetics.

TYPES OF DIURETIC

Thiazides The type most commonly prescribed, thiazides may lead to potassium deficiency and they are, therefore, often given together with a potassium supplement or in conjunction with a potassium-sparing diuretic (see right).

Loop diuretics These fast-acting, powerful drugs increase the output of urine for a few hours and they are sometimes used in emergencies. They may cause excessive loss of potassium which may need to be countered as for thiazides. Large doses may disturb hearing.

Potassium-sparing diuretics These mild diuretics are usually used in conjunction with a thiazide or a loop diuretic to prevent excessive potassium loss.

Osmotic diuretics Prescribed only rarely, these are used to maintain the flow of urine through the kidneys after surgery or injury, and to reduce pressure rapidly within fluid-filled cavities.

Acetazolamide This mild diuretic drug is used principally in the treatment of glaucoma (see p.168).

COMMON DRUGS

Thiazides	Loop diuretics
Bendrofluazide *	Bumetanide *
Chlorthalidone	Co-amilofruse
Co-amilozide	Frusemide *
Co-flumactone	
Co-triamterzide	**Potassium-sparing diuretics**
Cyclopenthiazide *	
Hydrochlorthiazide *	Amiloride *
Metolazone	Spironolactone *
	Triamterene *

* See Part 4

ANTI-ARRHYTHMICS

The heart contains two upper and two lower chambers (see p.95). The pumping actions of these two sets of chambers are normally coordinated by electrical impulses that originate in the pacemaker and then pass along conducting pathways so that the heart beats with a regular rhythm. If this coordination breaks down, the heart may beat abnormally, either irregularly, or faster or slower than usual. The general term used for abnormal heart rhythm is arrhythmia.

Arrhythmias may be due to a birth defect, to coronary heart disease, and to other less common heart disorders. Various more general conditions, including overactivity of the thyroid gland, and certain drugs – for example, *anticholinergic* drugs and caffeine – can also disturb heart rhythm.

SITES OF DRUG ACTION

Anti-arrhythmic drugs either slow the flow of electrical impulses to the heart muscle, or inhibit the ability of the muscle to contract. Beta blockers reduce the ability of the pacemaker to pass electrical signals to the atria. Digitalis drugs reduce the passage of signals from the atrio-ventricular node. Calcium channel blockers interfere with the ability of the heart muscle to contract by impeding the flow of calcium into muscle cells. Other drugs such as quinidine and disopyramide reduce the sensitivity of muscle cells to electrical impulses.

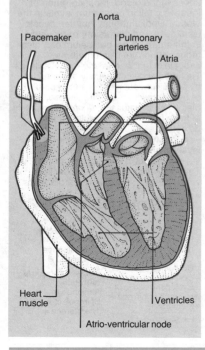

Aorta

Pacemaker

Pulmonary arteries

Atria

Heart muscle

Ventricles

Atrio-ventricular node

A broad range of drugs are used to regulate heart rhythm, including digitalis drugs, beta blockers, and calcium channel blockers. Other drugs used are lignocaine, disopyramide, procainamide, and quinidine.

Why they are used

Minor disturbances of heart rhythm are common and do not usually require drug treatment. However, if the pumping action of the heart is seriously affected, the circulation of blood throughout the body may become inefficient, and drug treatment may be necessary.

Drugs may be taken either to treat individual attacks of arrhythmia or they may be taken on a regular basis to prevent or control abnormal heart rhythms. The particular drug prescribed depends on the type of arrhythmia to be treated, but because people differ in their response, it may be necessary to try several in order to find the most effective one. When the arrhythmia is sudden and severe, it may be necessary to inject a drug immediately to restore normal heart function.

How they work

The heart's pumping action is governed by electrical impulses under the control of the sympathetic nervous system (see Autonomic nervous system, p.79). These signals pass through the heart muscle and cause each of the two pairs of heart chambers – the atria and the ventricles – to contract in turn (see Sites of drug action, left).

All anti-arrhythmic drugs alter the conduction of electrical signals in the heart, but each drug or drug group affects this sequence of events in a different way. Some block the transmission of signals to the heart (beta blockers); some affect the way signals are conducted within the heart (digitalis drugs); others affect the response of the heart muscle to the signals received (calcium channel blockers, disopyramide, procainamide, and quinidine).

How they affect you

These drugs usually prevent symptoms of arrhythmia and may restore a regular heart rhythm. Although they do not prevent all arrhythmias, they usually reduce the frequency and severity of any symptoms.

Unfortunately, as well as suppressing arrhythmias, many of these drugs tend to depress normal heart function, and may produce dizziness on standing up, or increased breathlessness on exertion. Mild nausea and visual disturbances are also fairly frequent. Verapamil can cause constipation, especially in high doses. Disopyramide

TYPES OF ARRHYTHMIA

Atrial fibrillation In this common arrhythmia, the atria contract irregularly at such a high rate that the ventricles cannot keep pace. It is treated with digoxin, sometimes in combination with quinidine.

Ventricular tachycardia This arises from abnormal electrical activity in the ventricles that causes the ventricles to contract rapidly. Regular treatment with disopyramide, procainamide or quinidine is usually given.

Supraventricular tachycardia This occurs when extra electrical impulses arise in the pacemaker or atria. These extra impulses stimulate the ventricles to contract rapidly. Attacks may disappear on their own without treatment, but drugs such as digoxin, verapamil or propranolol may be given.

Heart block When signals are not conducted from the atria to the ventricles, the ventricles start to beat at a slower rate. Some cases of heart block do not require treatment. For more severe heart block accompanied by dizziness and fainting, doctors sometimes give colchicine to provide temporary relief, but in the long term it is usually necessary to fit an artificial pacemaker.

may interfere with the parasympathetic nervous system (see p.79), resulting in a number of *anticholinergic* effects.

Risks and special precautions

These drugs may further disrupt heart rhythm under certain circumstances and therefore they are used only when the likely benefit outweighs the risks.

Quinidine can be toxic in overdose, resulting in a syndrome called cinchonism, which includes disturbed hearing, giddiness, and impaired vision (even blindness). Because some people are particularly sensitive to this drug, a test dose is usually given before regular treatment is started.

COMMON DRUGS

Beta blockers
(See p.97)

Calcium channel blockers
Diltiazem *
Verapamil *

Digitalis drugs
Digoxin
Digitoxin

Other drugs
Amiodarone *
Disopyramide *
Lignocaine
Procainamide
Quinidine
Propafenone

* See Part 4

ANTI-ANGINA DRUGS

Angina is chest pain produced when insufficient oxygen reaches the heart muscle. This is usually caused by a narrowing of the blood vessels (coronary arteries) that carry blood and oxygen to the heart muscle. In the most common type of angina (classic angina), pain typically occurs during exertion or emotional stress. In variant angina, pain may also occur at rest. In classic angina, narrowing of the coronary arteries results from deposits of fat – called atheroma – on the walls of the arteries, whereas in variant angina it is caused by contraction (spasm) of muscle fibres in the artery wall.

Atheroma deposits build up more rapidly in the arteries of smokers and people who eat a high-fat diet. This is why, as a basic part of angina treatment, doctors recommend that you stop smoking and change your diet. Overweight people are also advised to lose weight in order to reduce the demands placed on their hearts. While such changes in lifestyle often produce an improvement in symptoms, drug treatment to relieve angina is also frequently necessary.

Three types of drugs are used to treat angina: beta blockers, nitrates, and calcium channel blockers.

Why they are used

Frequent episodes of angina can be disabling, and if left untreated can lead to an increased risk of a heart attack. Drugs can be used both to relieve angina attacks and to reduce their frequency. People who suffer from only occasional episodes are usually prescribed a rapid-acting drug to take at the first signs of an attack, or before an activity that is known to bring on pain. A rapid-acting nitrate – glyceryl trinitrate – is usually prescribed for this purpose.

If attacks become more frequent or more severe, regular preventative treatment may be advised. Beta blockers, long-acting nitrates and calcium channel blockers are used as regular medication to prevent attacks. The introduction of adhesive patches for administering nitrates through the skin has extended the duration of action of glyceryl trinitrate, making treatment easier.

Drugs can often control angina for many years, but they cannot cure the disorder. When severe angina cannot be controlled by drugs, then angioplasty or surgery to increase the blood flow to the heart may be recommended.

How they work

Nitrates and calcium channel blockers dilate blood vessels by relaxing the muscle layer in the blood vessel wall (see also Vasodilators, p.98). This reduces strain on the heart by making it easier to pump blood.

Beta blockers interrupt the transmission of signals in the heart and so reduce stimulation of the heart muscle during exercise or stress. This also reduces the oxygen requirement of the heart muscle and makes angina attacks less likely to occur. For further information on beta blockers, see p.97.

How they affect you

Treatment with one or more of these drugs is usually effective in controlling angina. Drugs to prevent attacks allow sufferers to undertake more strenuous activities without provoking pain, and if an attack does occur, nitrates usually provide effective relief.

These drugs do not usually cause serious adverse effects, but they can produce a variety of minor symptoms. By dilating blood vessels throughout the body, nitrates and calcium channel blockers can cause dizziness (especially when standing) and sometimes fainting. Other possible side effects are headaches at the start of treatment, flushing of the skin – especially of the face – and ankle swelling. Beta blockers often cause cold hands and feet, and can produce tiredness and a feeling of heaviness in the legs.

ACTION OF ANTI-ANGINA DRUGS

ACTION OF ANTI-ANGINA DRUGS

The pain of angina arises when the heart muscle runs short of oxygen as it pumps blood through the circulatory system. Nitrates and calcium channel blockers reduce the heart's work by dilating blood vessels. Beta blockers impede the stimulation of heart muscle, reducing its oxygen requirement, thus relieving or preventing angina.

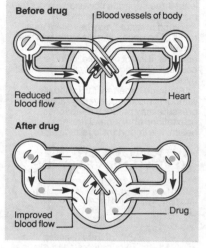

Before drug
Blood vessels of body
Reduced blood flow
Heart

After drug
Improved blood flow
Drug

COMMON DRUGS

Beta blockers (See p.97)	Nitrates
	Glyceryl trinitrate *
Calcium channel blockers	Isosorbide dinitrate *
Diltiazem *	Isosorbide mononitrate
Felodipine	
Isradipine	
Nifedipine *	
Nimodipine	
Verapamil *	

* See Part 4

CALCIUM CHANNEL BLOCKERS

The passage of calcium through special channels into muscle cells is an essential part of the mechanism of muscle contraction (see right). This relatively new class of drugs prevents movement of calcium in the muscles of the blood vessels and so encourages them to dilate (see far right). The action helps to reduce blood pressure and relieves the strain on the heart muscle in angina by making it easier for the heart to pump blood throughout the body (see the box above right). Calcium channel blockers also slow the passage of nerve signals through the heart muscle. This can be helpful for correcting certain types of abnormal heart rhythm.

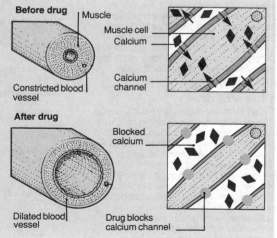

Before drug
Muscle
Constricted blood vessel
Muscle cell
Calcium
Calcium channel

After drug
Dilated blood vessel
Blocked calcium
Drug blocks calcium channel

ANTIHYPERTENSIVE DRUGS

Blood pressure is a measurement of the force exerted by the blood circulating in the arteries. Two readings are taken: one indicates force while the heart's ventricles are contracting (systolic pressure). It is a higher figure than the other reading, which measures the blood pressure during ventricle relaxation (diastolic pressure). Blood pressure varies among individuals and normally increases with age. If a person's blood pressure is higher than normal on at least three separate occasions, a doctor may diagnose hypertension.

Blood pressure may be raised as a result of an underlying disorder, which a doctor will try to identify. Usually, however, it is not possible to find a cause. This condition is called essential hypertension.

Although hypertension is usually without symptoms, severely raised pressure may produce headaches, palpitations and general feelings of ill-health. It is important to reduce high blood pressure, because it can have serious consequences, including stroke, heart attack, heart failure, and kidney damage. Certain groups are particularly at risk from high blood pressure. These include diabetics, smokers, people with pre-existing heart damage and those whose blood contains a high level of fat. High blood pressure is more common among black people than among whites.

A small reduction in blood pressure may be brought about by reducing weight, exercising regularly, and keeping to a low-salt diet. But for more severely raised blood pressure, one or more antihypertensive drugs may be prescribed. Several different classes of drugs have antihypertensive properties, including centrally-acting antihypertensives, diuretics (p.99), beta blockers (p.97), calcium channel blockers, ACE (angiotensin-converting enzyme) inhibitors, and *sympatholytics*. See also Vasodilators, p.98.

Why they are used

These drugs are prescribed when diet, exercise and other simple remedies have not brought about an adequate reduction in blood pressure, and your doctor sees a risk of serious consequences if the condition is not treated. Antihypertensive drugs do not cure hypertension and may have to be taken indefinitely. However, it is sometimes possible to taper off drug treatment when blood pressure has been reduced to a normal level for a year or more.

How they work

Blood pressure depends not only on the force with which the heart pumps blood, but also on the diameter of blood vessels and the volume of blood in circulation: blood pressure is increased if the vessels are narrow, or the volume of blood is high. Antihypertensive drugs lower blood pressure either by dilating the blood vessels or by reducing blood volume. Antihypertensive drugs work in different ways and some have more than one action (see Action of antihypertensive drugs, left).

Choice of drug

Drug treatment depends on the severity of hypertension. At the beginning of treatment for mild or moderately high blood pressure a single drug is used. A thiazide diuretic is often chosen for initial treatment, but it is also increasingly common to use a beta blocker, a calcium channel blocker, or an ACE inhibitor. If a single drug does not reduce the blood pressure sufficiently, a diuretic in combination with one of the other drugs may be used. Some people with moderate hypertension require a third drug, in which case a sympatholytic or centrally-acting antihypertensive may also be given.

Severe hypertension is usually controlled with a combination of several drugs, which may need to be given in high doses. A doctor may need to try a number of drugs before finding a combination that controls blood pressure without unacceptable side effects.

How they affect you

Treatment with antihypertensive drugs relieves symptoms such as headache and palpitations. However, since most people with hypertension have few, if any symptoms, side effects may be more noticeable than any immediate beneficial effect. Some antihypertensive drugs may cause dizziness and fainting at the start of treatment because they can sometimes produce an excessive fall in blood pressure. It may take a while for the doctor to determine a dosage that avoids such effects. For detailed information on the adverse effects of drugs used to treat hypertension, consult the individual drug profiles in Part 4.

Risks and special precautions

Since your doctor needs to know exactly how treatment with a particular drug affects your hypertension – the benefits as well as side effects, it is important to keep using antihypertensive medication as prescribed, even though you may feel the problem is under control. Sudden withdrawal of some of these drugs may cause a potentially dangerous rebound increase in blood pressure; when treatment is stopped the dose needs to be reduced gradually under medical supervision.

ACTION OF ANTI-HYPERTENSIVE DRUGS

Each type of antihypertensive drug acts on a different part of the body to lower blood pressure.

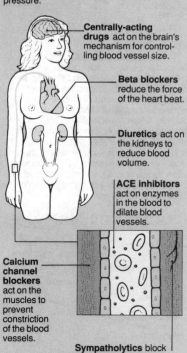

Centrally-acting drugs act on the brain's mechanism for controlling blood vessel size.

Beta blockers reduce the force of the heart beat.

Diuretics act on the kidneys to reduce blood volume.

ACE inhibitors act on enzymes in the blood to dilate blood vessels.

Calcium channel blockers act on the muscles to prevent constriction of the blood vessels.

Sympatholytics block nerve signals that trigger constriction of blood vessels.

COMMON DRUGS

ACE inhibitors
(see p.98)

Beta blockers
(see p.97)

Calcium channel blockers
(See p.101)

Centrally-acting antihypertensives
Clonidine *
Methyldopa *

Diuretics
(see p.99)

Sympatholytics
Doxazosin
Prazosin *
Terazosin

Vasodilators
(See p.98)

✳ See Part 4

LIPID-LOWERING DRUGS

The blood contains several types of fats, or lipids. They are necessary for normal body function but can be damaging if present in excess, particularly saturated fats such as cholesterol. The main risk is atherosclerosis, in which fatty deposits called atheroma build up in the arteries, restricting and disrupting the flow of blood. This can lead to a greater likelihood of the formation of abnormal blood clots, leading to potentially fatal disorders such as stroke and heart attack.

For most people, cutting down the amount of fat in the diet is sufficient to reduce the risk of atherosclerosis. However, for those with an inherited tendency to high levels of fat in the blood (hyperlipidaemia), lipid-lowering drugs may also be recommended.

Why they are used

Lipid-lowering drugs are generally prescribed only when dietary measures have failed to control hyperlipidaemia. They may be given at an earlier stage to individuals at increased risk of atherosclerosis – such as diabetics and people already suffering from circulatory disorders. Drugs may remove existing atheroma in the blood vessels and prevent the accumulation of new deposits.

For maximum benefit, these drugs are used in conjunction with a low-fat diet and a reduction in other risk factors such as obesity and smoking. As the choice of drug depends on the type of lipid causing problems, a full medical history, examination, and laboratory analysis of blood samples are needed before drug treatment is prescribed.

How they work

Cholesterol and triglycerides are two of the major fats in the blood. One or both may be raised, influencing the choice of lipid-lowering drug. Drugs that act on bile salts reduce cholesterol levels. They act via bile salts which contain large amounts of cholesterol and are normally released into the bowel to aid digestion before being reabsorbed into the bloodstream. However, these drugs block the reabsorption, increasing the loss of cholesterol from the body. Fibrate drugs act on the liver and can reduce the amount of both cholesterol and triglycerides in the blood. A new group called statins have been developed. These inhibit an enzyme which produces cholesterol in the liver, so reducing cholesterol levels.

Lipid-lowering drugs do not correct the underlying cause of raised levels of fat in the blood, so it is usually necessary to continue with diet and drug treatment indefinitely. Withdrawal of treatment usually leads to a return of high blood lipid levels.

ACTION OF LIPID-LOWERING DRUGS

Lipid-lowering drugs reduce the levels of fats in the blood by interfering with the absorption of bile salts in the bowel, or by altering the way in which the liver converts fatty acids in the blood into different types of lipids.

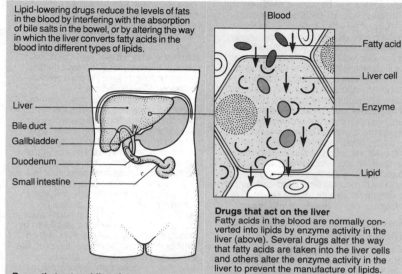

Liver
Bile duct
Gallbladder
Duodenum
Small intestine

Blood
Fatty acid
Liver cell
Enzyme
Lipid

Drugs that act on the liver
Fatty acids in the blood are normally converted into lipids by enzyme activity in the liver (above). Several drugs alter the way that fatty acids are taken into the liver cells and others alter the enzyme activity in the liver to prevent the manufacture of lipids.

Drugs that act on bile salts
Bile is produced by the liver and released into the small intestine via the bile duct to aid digestion. Salts in the bile carry large amounts of cholesterol and are normally reabsorbed into the bloodstream from the intestine during digestion (right). Some drugs combine with bile salts in the intestine and prevent their reabsorption (far right). This action reduces the levels of bile salts in the blood, and triggers the liver to convert more cholesterol into bile salts, thus reducing cholesterol levels in the blood.

Before drug
After drug

Bile salts
Small intestine
Blood vessel
Bile salt combined with drug

How they affect you

Because hyperlipidaemia and atherosclerosis are usually without symptoms, you are unlikely to notice any short-term benefits from these drugs. Rather, the aim of treatment is to reduce long-term complications. There may be minor side effects from some of these drugs.

By increasing the amount of bile in the digestive tract, several drugs can cause gastrointestinal disturbances such as nausea and constipation or diarrhoea, especially at the start of treatment. The newly introduced statin drugs seem well-tolerated. Because long-term safety is not yet fully established, they are reserved for severe or resistant cases.

Risks and special precautions

Drugs that act on bile salts can limit absorption of some fat soluble vitamins, so vitamin supplements may be needed. The fibrate drugs can increase susceptibility to gallstones and occasionally upset the balance of fats in the blood. Statins are used with caution in those with reduced liver function, and monitoring of blood samples is often advised.

COMMON DRUGS

Drugs that act act on the liver
Acipimox
Bezafibrate
Ciprofibrate
Clofibrate *
Fenofibrate

Gemfibrozil
Nicotinic acid *
Pravastatin
Probucol

Drugs that act on bile salts
Cholestyramine *
Colestipol

* See Part 4

DRUGS THAT AFFECT BLOOD CLOTTING

When bleeding occurs from injury or surgery, the body normally acts swiftly to stem the flow by sealing the breaks in the blood vessels. This occurs in two stages – first when cells called platelets accumulate as a plug at the opening in the blood vessel wall, and then when these platelets produce chemicals that activate clotting factors in the blood to form a protein called fibrin. Vitamin K plays an important role in this process (see The clotting mechanism, below). An enzyme in the blood called plasmin ensures that clots are broken down when the injury has been repaired.

Some disorders interfere with this process, either preventing clot formation or creating clots uncontrolledly. There is a danger that a lack of blood clotting will result in excessive blood loss; inappropriate development of clots can lead to blockage of the blood to a vital organ.

Drugs used to promote blood clotting

Fibrin formation depends on the presence in the blood of several clotting-factor proteins. When Factor VIII is absent or at low levels, an inherited disease called haemophilia exists – the symptoms almost always appearing only in males. Factor IX deficiency causes another bleeding condition called Christmas disease, named after the person in whom it was first identified. Lack of these clotting factors can lead to uncontrolled bleeding or excessive bruising following injury.

Regular drug treatment for haemophilia is not normally required. But if severe bleeding or bruising occurs, a concentrated form of the missing factor, extracted from normal blood, may be injected in order to promote clotting and so halt bleeding. Injections may need to be repeated for several days after injury.

It is sometimes useful to promote blood clotting in non-haemophiliacs when bleeding is difficult to stop (for example, after surgery). In such cases, blood clots are sometimes stabilized by reducing the action of plasmin with an antifibrinolytic (or haemostatic) drug like aminocaproic acid; this is also occasionally given to haemophiliacs before minor surgery such as tooth-extraction.

A tendency to bleed may also occur as a consequence of vitamin K deficiency (see the box below).

Drugs used to prevent abnormal blood clotting

Blood clots normally form only in response to injury. In some people, however, there is a tendency for clots to form in the blood vessels without apparent cause. Disturbed blood flow as a result of the presence of fatty deposits – atheroma – inside the blood vessels increases the risk of the formation of this type of abnormal clot (or thrombus). In addition, a portion of a blood clot (known as an embolus) formed in response to injury or surgery may sometimes break off and be carried away in the bloodstream. The likelihood of this occurring is increased by long periods of little or no activity. When an abnormal clot forms, there is a risk that it may become lodged in a blood vessel,

ACTION OF ANTIPLATELET DRUGS

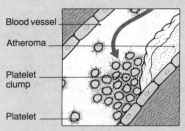

Blood vessel
Atheroma
Platelet clump
Platelet

Before drug
When blood flow is disrupted by atheroma in the blood vessels, platelets tend to clump together.

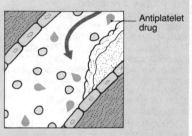

Antiplatelet drug

After drug
Antiplatelet drugs reduce the ability of platelets to stick together and so prevent clot formation.

thus blocking the blood supply to a vital organ such as the brain or heart.

Three main types of drug are used to prevent and disperse clots: antiplatelet drugs, anticoagulant drugs, and thrombolytic drugs.

Antiplatelet drugs

Taken regularly by people with a tendency to form clots in the fast-flowing blood of the heart and arteries, these are also given to prevent clots from forming after heart surgery. They reduce the tendency of platelets to stick together when blood flow is disrupted (see Action of antiplatelet drugs, above).

The most widely used antiplatelet drug is aspirin (see also Analgesics, p.80). Aspirin has an antiplatelet action even when given in much lower doses than would be necessary to reduce pain. In these low doses adverse effects that may occur when the drug is given in pain-relieving doses are unlikely. Other less common antiplatelet drugs include dipyridamole and sulphinpyrazone.

Anticoagulants

Anticoagulant drugs help to maintain normal blood flow in people who are at

THE CLOTTING MECHANISM

When a blood vessel wall is damaged, platelets accumulate at the site of damage and form a plug (1). Platelets clumped together release chemicals that activate blood clotting factors (2). These factors together with vitamin K act on a substance called fibrinogen and convert it to fibrin (3). Strands of fibrin become enmeshed in the platelet plug to form a blood clot (4).

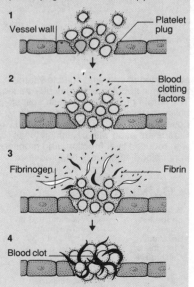

1
Vessel wall — Platelet plug

2 — Blood clotting factors

3
Fibrinogen — Fibrin

4
Blood clot

VITAMIN K

Vitamin K is required for the production of several blood clotting factors. It is absorbed from the intestine in fats, but in some diseases of the small intestine or pancreas in which fat is poorly absorbed, the level of vitamin K in the circulation is low, resulting in impaired blood clotting. A similar problem sometimes occurs in newborn babies due to an absence of the vitamin. Injections of a vitamin K preparation called phytomenadione are used to restore normal levels.

risk from clot formation. They can either prevent the formation of blood clots in the veins, or stabilize an existing clot so that it does not break away and become a circulation-stopping embolism. All anticoagulant drugs reduce the activity of certain blood clotting factors, although the precise mode of action of each drug differs (see Action of anticoagulants, right). They do not, however, dissolve clots that have already formed; these are treated with thrombolytics (below).

Anticoagulants fall into two groups: those that are given by intravenous injection and act immediately, and those that are given by mouth and take effect after a few days.

Intravenous anticoagulants
Heparin is the most widely used drug of this type and it is used mainly in hospital during or after surgery. In addition, it is also given during kidney dialysis to prevent clots from forming in the dialysis equipment. Because heparin cannot be given by mouth, it is an unsuitable drug for long-term treatment in the home.

Heparin is sometimes given prior to starting regular treatment with an oral anticoagulant.

Oral anticoagulants
These drugs are mainly used to prevent the formation of clots in veins – they are less likely to prevent the formation of blood clots in arteries. Oral anticoagulants may be given following injury or surgery (in particular, heart valve replacement) when there is a high risk of embolism. They are also given as a preventive treatment to people who are at risk from strokes.

ACTION OF ANTICOAGULANT DRUGS

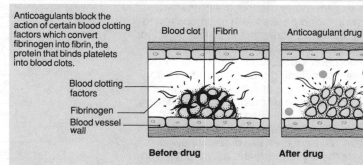

Anticoagulants block the action of certain blood clotting factors which convert fibrinogen into fibrin, the protein that binds platelets into blood clots.

Blood clot | Fibrin

Anticoagulant drug

Blood clotting factors

Fibrinogen

Blood vessel wall

Before drug

After drug

A common problem with these drugs is that overdosage may lead to bleeding from the nose, gums or in the urinary tract. For this reason the dosage needs to be carefully calculated; regular blood tests are performed to ensure that the clotting mechanism is correctly adjusted. Warfarin is the most widely used drug of this type.

The action of oral anticoagulant drugs may be affected by many other drugs, and it may therefore be necessary to alter the dosage of anticoagulant when other drugs also need to be given. People who have been prescribed anticoagulants should carry a warning list of drugs which should not be administered. Aspirin in particular should not be taken together with anticoagulants except on the direction of a doctor.

Thrombolytics
Also known as fibrinolytics, these drugs are used to dissolve clots that have

already formed. They are usually administered in hospital by intravenous injection to clear a blocked blood vessel – for example, in coronary thrombosis. Thrombolytic drugs may be administered either intravenously or directly into the blocked blood vessel.

The main thrombolytic drugs are streptokinase and the recently introduced tissue plasminogen activator (tPA), both of which act by increasing the blood level of plasmin, the naturally occurring enzyme that normally breaks down fibrin (see Action of thrombolytic drugs, below). When administered promptly, tPA appears to be tolerated better and is quite effective.

The most common problems with the use of these drugs are increased susceptibility to bleeding and bruising, and allergic reactions (with streptokinase) which often take the form of rashes, breathing difficulty, or general weakness or discomfort.

ACTION OF THROMBOLYTIC DRUGS

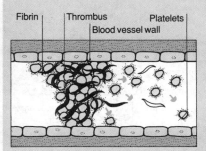

Fibrin | Thrombus | Platelets
Blood vessel wall

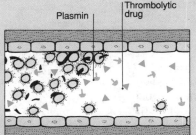

Plasmin

Thrombolytic drug

Before drug
When platelets accumulate in a blood vessel and are reinforced by strands of fibrin, the resultant blood clot, called a thrombus, cannot be dissolved either by antiplatelet drugs or anticoagulant drugs.

After drug
Thrombolytic drugs boost the action of plasmin, an enzyme in the blood that breaks up the strands of fibrin that bind the clot together. This allows the accumulated platelets to disperse, and restores normal blood flow.

COMMON DRUGS

Normal blood extracts	**Thrombolytic drugs**
Antihaemophilic factor	Streptokinase *
Factor VIII	Alteplase *
Factor IX complex	
Antifibrinolytic drugs	
Aminocaproic acid	
Vitamin K	
Phytomenadione	
Antiplatelet drugs	
Aspirin *	
Dipyridamole *	
Sulphinpyrazone	
Anticoagulant drugs	
Enoxaparin	
Heparin *	
Warfarin *	

* See Part 4

GASTROINTESTINAL TRACT

The gastrointestinal tract (also known as the digestive or alimentary tract) is the pathway through which food passes as it is processed to enable the nutrients it contains to be absorbed for use by the body. It consists of the mouth, oesophagus, stomach, duodenum, small intestine, large intestine (including the colon and rectum), and anus. In addition, a number of other organs are involved in the digestion of food; the salivary glands in the mouth, the liver, pancreas, and gallbladder. These organs, together with the gastrointestinal tract form the digestive system.

The digestive system breaks down large complex chemicals – proteins, fats, carbohydrates – present in the food we eat into simpler molecules that can be used by the body (see also Nutrition, p.148). Undigested or indigestible material, together with some of the body's waste products pass to the large intestine, and when a sufficient mass of such matter has accumulated it is expelled from the body as faeces.

What can go wrong

Inflammation of the lining of the stomach or intestine (gastroenteritis) is usually the result of an infection or parasitic infestation. Damage may also be done by the inappropriate production of digestive juices leading to minor complaints like acidity and major disorders like peptic ulcers. The lining of the intestine can be damaged by abnormal functioning of the immune system (inflammatory bowel disease). The rectum and anus can become painful and irritated by damage to the lining, tears in the skin at the opening of the anus, or enlarged veins (haemorrhoids).

The most frequent gastrointestinal disorders, constipation, irritable bowel syndrome, and diarrhoea, occur when something disrupts the normal muscle contractions that propel food residue through the bowel.

Why drugs are used

Many drugs for gastrointestinal disorders are taken by mouth and act directly on the digestive tract without first entering the bloodstream. Such drugs include certain antibiotics and other drugs to treat infestation. Some antacids for peptic ulcers and excess stomach acidity, and bulk-forming agents for constipation and diarrhoea also pass through the system unabsorbed.

However, for any disorders drugs with a *systemic* effect are required, including anti-ulcer drugs, narcotic antidiarrhoeal drugs, and some of the drugs for inflammatory bowel disease.

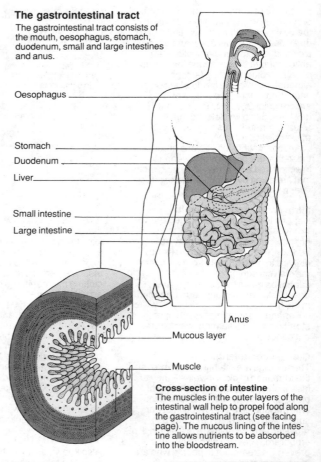

The gastrointestinal tract
The gastrointestinal tract consists of the mouth, oesophagus, stomach, duodenum, small and large intestines and anus.

Oesophagus

Stomach

Duodenum

Liver

Small intestine

Large intestine

Anus

Mucous layer

Muscle

Cross-section of intestine
The muscles in the outer layers of the intestinal wall help to propel food along the gastrointestinal tract (see facing page). The mucous lining of the intestine allows nutrients to be absorbed into the bloodstream.

Pancreas
The pancreas produces *enzymes* that digest fats, proteins and carbohydrates into simpler substances. Pancreatic juices neutralize acidity of the stomach contents.

Gallbladder
Bile produced by the liver is stored in the gallbladder and released into the small intestine. Bile improves the digestion of fats by reducing them to smaller units that are more easily acted upon by digestive enzymes.

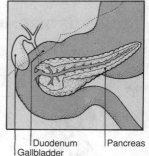

Duodenum

Gallbladder

Pancreas

MAJOR DRUG GROUPS

Antacids
Anti-ulcer drugs
Antidiarrhoeal drugs
Laxatives
Drugs for inflammatory
 bowel disease

Drugs for rectal and
 anal disorders
Drug treatment for
 gallstones

The lining of the gastrointestinal tract

The internal lining of the different sections of the gastro-intestinal tract varies according to the function of that part, depending, for example, on whether its principal role is to secrete digestive juices or to absorb nutrients.

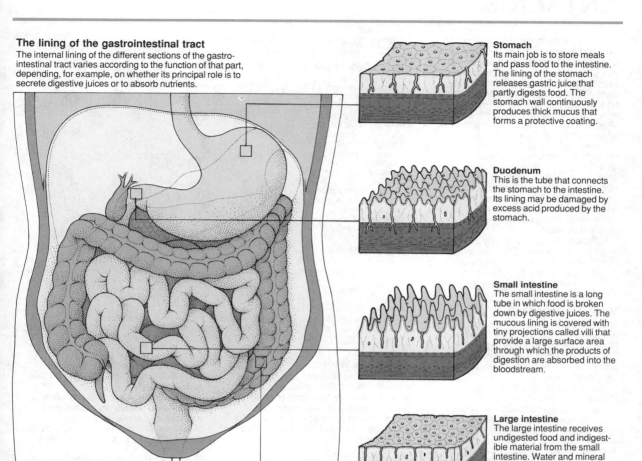

Stomach
Its main job is to store meals and pass food to the intestine. The lining of the stomach releases gastric juice that partly digests food. The stomach wall continuously produces thick mucus that forms a protective coating.

Duodenum
This is the tube that connects the stomach to the intestine. Its lining may be damaged by excess acid produced by the stomach.

Small intestine
The small intestine is a long tube in which food is broken down by digestive juices. The mucous lining is covered with tiny projections called villi that provide a large surface area through which the products of digestion are absorbed into the bloodstream.

Large intestine
The large intestine receives undigested food and indigestible material from the small intestine. Water and mineral salts pass through the lining into the bloodstream.

MOVEMENT OF FOOD THROUGH THE GASTROINTESTINAL TRACT

Food is propelled through the gastrointestinal tract by rhythmic waves of muscular contraction known as peristalsis. The illustration (right) shows how peristaltic contractions of the bowel wall push food through the intestine.

Muscle contraction in the tract is controlled by the autonomic nervous system (p.79), and is therefore easily disrupted by drugs that either stimulate or inhibit the activity of the autonomic nervous system. Excessive peristaltic action may cause diarrhoea; slowed peristalsis may cause constipation.

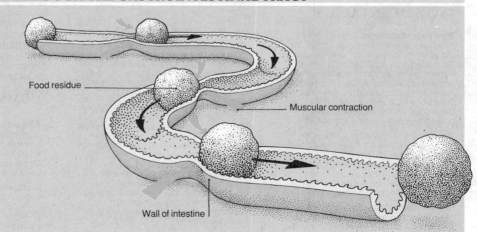

Food residue

Muscular contraction

Wall of intestine

ANTACIDS

Digestive juices in the stomach contain acid and enzymes that break down food before it passes into the intestine. The wall of the stomach is normally protected from the action of digestive acid by a layer of mucus that is constantly secreted by the stomach lining. Problems arise when the stomach lining is damaged or when too much acid is produced and eats away at the mucous layer.

Excess acid leading to discomfort, commonly referred to as indigestion, may result from overeating, coffee, alcohol, smoking, anxiety, or, in some people, from eating certain foods. Some drugs, notably aspirin and non-steroidal anti-inflammatory drugs, can also irritate the stomach lining and even cause ulcers to develop.

Antacids are used to neutralize acid and thus relieve pain. They are simple chemical compounds that are mildly alkaline and some also act as chemical buffers. Their chalky taste is often disguised with flavourings.

Why they are used

Antacids may be needed where simple remedies such as a change in diet or a glass of milk fail to relieve indigestion. They are especially useful one to three hours after meals to neutralize after-meal acid surge.

Doctors prescribe these drugs to relieve dyspepsia (pain in the chest or upper abdomen caused by, or aggravated by acid) in disorders such as inflammation or ulceration of the oesophagus, stomach lining and duodenum. Antacids usually relieve pain resulting from ulcers in the oesophagus, stomach or duodenum within a few minutes. Regular treatment with antacids reduces the acidity of the stomach and thereby encourages the healing of any ulcers that may have formed.

ACTION OF ANTACIDS

Excess acid in the stomach may eat away at the protective layer of mucus that lines the stomach. When this occurs, or when the mucous lining is damaged, for example, by an ulcer, stomach acid comes into contact with the underlying tissues causing pain and inflammation (right). Antacids combine with stomach acid to reduce the acidity of the digestive juices. This helps to prevent pain and inflammation and allows the mucous layer to repair itself (far right).

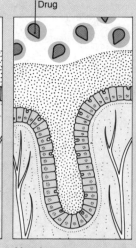

Mucus
Mucous lining
Stomach wall

Before drug
Acid damages mucous layer of stomach lining.

After drug
Acid is neutralized by antacid action.

How they work

By neutralizing stomach acid, antacids prevent inflammation, relieve pain and allow the mucous layer and lining to mend. When used in the treatment of ulcers, they prevent acid from attacking damaged stomach lining and so allow the ulcer to heal.

How they affect you

If antacids are taken according to instructions, they are usually effective in relieving abdominal discomfort caused by acid. The speed of action, dependent on the ability to neutralize acid, varies.

Their duration of action also varies; short-acting drugs may have to be taken quite frequently.

Although most antacids have few serious side effects when used only occasionally, some may cause diarrhoea, and others may cause constipation (see Types of antacids, below).

Risks and special precautions

Antacids should not be taken to prevent abdominal pain on a regular basis except under medical supervision, as they may suppress the symptoms of stomach cancer. Your doctor is likely to want to arrange tests such as endoscopy or barium X-rays before prescribing long-term treatment.

All antacids can interfere with the absorption of other drugs. For this reason, if you are taking a prescription medicine, you should check with your doctor before taking an antacid.

TYPES OF ANTACIDS

Aluminium compounds These have a prolonged action and are widely used, especially for the treatment of peptic ulcers. They may cause constipation, but this is often countered by combining this type of antacid with one that contains magnesium. Aluminium compounds can interfere with the absorption of phosphate from the diet, causing weakness and bone damage if taken in high doses over a long period.

Magnesium compounds Like the aluminium compounds, these have a prolonged action. In large doses they can cause diarrhoea, and in people who have impaired kidney function, a high blood magnesium level may build up, causing weakness, lethargy and drowsiness.

Sodium bicarbonate Sodium bicarbonate, the only sodium compound used as an antacid, acts quickly, but its effect soon passes. It reacts with stomach acids to produce gas, which may cause bloating and belching. This antacid is not advised for people with heart or kidney disease, as it can lead to the accumulation of water (oedema) in the legs and lungs, or serious changes in the acid-base balance of the blood.

Combined preparations Antacids may be combined with other substances called alginates and antifoaming agents. Alginates are intended to float on the contents of the stomach and produce a neutralizing layer to subdue acid that can rise into the oesophagus, causing heartburn.

Antifoaming agents, usually dimethicone, are intended to relieve flatulence. In some preparations a local anaesthetic is combined with the antacid to relieve discomfort in oesophagitis. None of those additives is of primary benefit.

COMMON DRUGS

Antacids
Aluminium hydroxide ✴
Calcium carbonate
Hydrotalcite
Magnesium hydroxide ✴
Sodium bicarbonate ✴

Antifoaming agent
Dimethicone

Other drugs
Cisapride ✴

✴ See Part 4

ANTI-ULCER DRUGS

Normally, the linings of the oesophagus, stomach, and duodenum are protected from the irritant action of stomach acids or bile by mucus. If this is damaged, or if large amounts of stomach acid are formed, the underlying tissue may become eroded, causing a peptic ulcer. A peptic ulcer often leads to episodes of abdominal pain, vomiting, and loss of appetite. The most common type occurs in the outlet of the stomach, the duodenum. The exact cause of peptic ulcers is not understood, but a number of predisposing risk factors have been identified; these include heavy smoking, the regular use of aspirin or similar drugs, and family history. An organism called *Helicobacter pylori* is found in 90 per cent of patients with duodenal ulcers and is now thought to be a causative agent.

Symptoms may be relieved by an antacid (see facing page), but healing will be slow. The usual first-line treatment is with an anti-ulcer drug, like an H₂ blocker. Bismuth, sucralfate,

SITES OF PEPTIC ULCERS

Peptic ulcers most commonly occur in the walls of the stomach or duodenum when damage to the mucous lining allows stomach acid to erode the underlying tissue. Ulcers may also form in the oesophagus if acid backs up into the oesophagus. Peptic ulcers also occur at the margin where the stomach has been sewn to the intestine after ulcer surgery. Similar drugs are prescribed for all three types of peptic ulcer.

Oesophagus

Stomach

Duodenum

or the newly-introduced misoprostol or omeprazole may be used.

Why they are used

Anti-ulcer drugs are used to relieve symptoms and heal the ulcer. Untreated ulcers may erode blood vessel walls or perforate the stomach or duodenum. Until recently, drugs could heal but not cure ulcers; but eradication of *Helicobacter pylori* by bismuth combined with two antibiotics (triple therapy) may

provide a cure for such ulcers. Surgery is reserved for complications such as obstruction, perforation, and haemorrhage, and when there is a possibility of malignancy in the case of stomach ulcers.

How they work

Drugs protect ulcers from the action of stomach acid, thereby allowing the underlying tissue to heal. H₂ blockers, misoprostol, and omeprazole reduce the amount of acid released, whereas bismuth and sucralfate form a protective coating over the ulcer. Bismuth, used with antibiotics, can eradicate the growth of *Helicobacter pylori*.

How they affect you

These drugs begin to reduce pain in a few hours and usually allow the ulcer to heal in four to eight weeks. They produce few side effects, though H₂ blockers can cause confusion in the elderly. Bismuth and sucralfate may cause constipation; misoprostol, diarrhoea; and omeprazole, either. As they may mask symptoms of stomach cancer, they are normally prescribed only when tests have ruled out this disorder.

Risks and special precautions

The H₂ blockers cimetidine and ranitidine have both been prescribed for millions of patients and seem safe. They are usually given initially for six to eight weeks with repeat courses or a lower maintenance dose if there is recurrent ulceration. Sucralfate is prescribed for up to 12 weeks, and bismuth, misoprostol, and omeprazole usually for four to six weeks at a time. Bismuth must be taken with plenty of water.

ACTION OF ANTI-ULCER DRUGS

H₂ blockers

Histamine is a chemical released by mast cells (see Allergies, p.123). It can produce a number of effects, including dilation of the blood vessels in the nose and eyes, constriction of the airways, skin rashes (hives), and increased secretion of stomach acid. Antihistamines (p.124), used medically for many years to block the effects of histamine

in allergic disorders, act only on *receptors* known as H₁ receptors, and do not block the effect of histamine on stomach acid production which is triggered by the action of histamine on H₂ receptors. A new type of drug was therefore developed to block this action. Since their introduction in the 1970s, the H₂ blockers have been among the most widely prescribed drugs around the world.

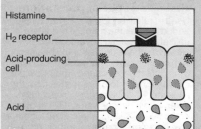

Histamine

H₂ receptor

Acid-producing cell

Acid

The action of histamine on the stomach
Histamine binds to specialized H₂ receptors and stimulates acid-producing cells in the stomach wall to release acid.

H₂ blocker

Acid

Mucus

The action of H₂ blockers
H₂ blockers occupy H₂ receptors, preventing histamine from triggering the production of acid. This allows the mucous lining to heal.

Bismuth and sucralfate

These drugs form a coating over the ulcer, protecting it from the action of stomach acid, thus allowing it to heal. Bismuth also kills bacteria, which are believed to aggravate duodenal ulcers.

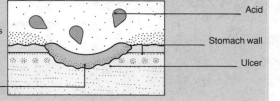

Acid

Stomach wall

Ulcer

Drug

COMMON DRUGS

H₂ blockers	Other drugs
Cimetidine *	Antacids (see p.108)
Famotidine	
Nizatidine	Bismuth
Ranitidine *	Carbenoxolone *
	Misoprostol *
	Omeprazole *
* See Part 4	Sucralfate *

ANTIDIARRHOEAL DRUGS

Diarrhoea is an increase in the fluidity and frequency of bowel movements. In some cases diarrhoea protects the body from harmful substances in the intestine by hastening their removal. The most common causes of diarrhoea are viral infection, food poisoning or parasites. But diarrhoea also occurs in other illnesses. It can be a side effect of some drugs and may follow radiation therapy for cancer. Diarrhoea may also be caused by anxiety.

An attack of diarrhoea usually clears up quickly without medical attention. The best treatment is to abstain from food and drink plenty of clear fluids. Rehydration solutions containing sugar and potassium and sodium salts are widely recommended for preventing dehydration and chemical imbalances, particularly in children. You should consult your doctor if: the condition does not improve within 48 hours; the diarrhoea contains blood; there is severe abdominal pain and vomiting; you have just returned from a foreign country; or if the diarrhoea occurs in a small child or an elderly person.

Severe diarrhoea can impair absorption of drugs, and anyone taking a prescription medicine should call a doctor. A woman taking oral contraceptives may need to take additional contraceptive measures (see p.163).

The main types of drug used to relieve non-specific diarrhoea are narcotics, and bulk-forming and *adsorbent* agents. Antispasmodic drugs may also be used to relieve accompanying pain (see Drugs for irritable bowel syndrome, below).

Why they are used

An antidiarrhoeal drug may be prescribed to provide relief when simple remedies are not effective, and once it is certain that the diarrhoea is neither infectious nor toxic.

ACTION OF ANTIDIARRHOEAL DRUGS

Narcotic antidiarrhoeals
Narcotics reduce the transmission of nerve signals to the intestinal muscles, thus reducing muscle contraction. This allows more time for water to be absorbed from the food residue and therefore reduces the fluidity as well as the frequency of bowel movements.

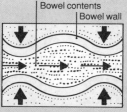 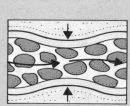

Bowel contents
Bowel wall

Before drug
Rapid bowel contraction prevents water from being absorbed.

After drug
Slowed bowel action allows more water to be absorbed.

Bulk-forming agents
These preparations contain particles that swell up as they absorb water from the large intestine. This makes the faeces firmer and less fluid. It is thought that these agents may absorb irritants and harmful chemicals along with excess water.

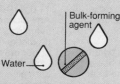 

Bulk-forming agent

Water

Water is attracted by bulk-forming agent.

Bulk-forming agent swells as water is absorbed.

Narcotics are the most effective antidiarrhoeals. They are used when diarrhoea is severe and debilitating. Bulking and adsorbent agents have a milder effect and are often used when it is necessary to regulate bowel action over a prolonged period – for example, in those with colostomies or ileostomies.

How they work

Each type of antidiarrhoeal drug works differently. Narcotic drugs decrease the propulsive activity of the muscles so that faecal matter passes more slowly through the bowel.

Bulk-forming agents and adsorbents absorb water and irritants present in the bowel so producing larger and firmer stools less frequently.

How they affect you

Drugs used to treat diarrhoea reduce the urge to move the bowels. Narcotic drugs and antispasmodics may relieve abdominal pain. All antidiarrhoeals may cause constipation if used in excess.

Risks and special precautions

Used in relatively low doses for a limited period of time, the narcotic drugs are unlikely to produce adverse effects. However, these drugs should be used with caution when diarrhoea is caused by an infection, since they may slow the elimination of micro-organisms from the intestine. All antidiarrhoeals should be taken with plenty of water. It is important not to take a bulk-forming agent together with a narcotic or antispasmodic drug, because a bulky mass could form and obstruct the bowel.

DRUGS FOR IRRITABLE BOWEL SYNDROME

Irritable bowel syndrome is a common stress-related condition in which the normal coordinated waves of muscular contraction responsible for moving the bowel contents smoothly through the intestines become strong and irregular, often causing pain, and associated with diarrhoea or constipation.

Symptoms are often relieved by adjusting the amount of fibre in the diet, but medication may also be required. Bulk-forming agents may be given to regulate the consistency of the bowel contents. If pain is severe, an antispasmodic drug may be prescribed. These *anticholinergic* drugs reduce the transmission of nerve signals to the bowel wall, thus preventing spasm. Because irritable bowel is often made worse by anxiety, an anti-anxiety drug (p.83) may also be prescribed.

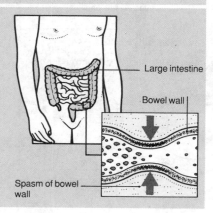

Large intestine

Bowel wall

Spasm of bowel wall

COMMON DRUGS

Antispasmodics
Atropine *
Dicyclomine *

Narcotics
Codeine *
Diphenoxylate *
Loperamide *

Bulk-forming and adsorbent agents
Isphagula
Kaolin
Methylcellulose *

| * See Part 4 |

LAXATIVES

When your bowels do not move as frequently as usual and the faeces are hard and difficult to pass, you are suffering from constipation. The most common cause is the lack of sufficient fibre in your diet, fibre supplying the bulk that makes the faeces soft and easy to pass. The simple remedy is more fluid and a diet that contains plenty of foods that are high in fibre, but laxative drugs may also be used.

Ignoring the urge to defecate can also cause constipation, the faeces becoming dry, hard to pass and too small to stimulate the muscles that propel them through the intestine.

Certain drugs may be constipating: narcotic analgesics, tricyclic anti-depressants and antacids containing aluminium. Some diseases, such as hypothyroidism, and scleroderma, a rare disorder of the connective tissues characterized by hardening of the skin, can lead to constipation.

The onset of constipation in a middle-aged or elderly person may be an early symptom of bowel cancer. Consult your doctor about any persistent change in bowel habit.

Why they are used

Since prolonged use is harmful, laxatives should be used for short periods only. They may prevent pain and straining in people with hernias or haemorrhoids (p.113). Doctors may prescribe laxatives for the same reason after childbirth or abdominal surgery. Laxatives are also used to clear the bowel before investigative procedures such as colonoscopy. They may also be given to the elderly and bedridden, because lack of exercise can lead to constipation.

How they work

Laxatives act on the large intestine – by increasing the speed with which faecal matter passes through the bowel, or

ACTION OF LAXATIVES

Bulk-forming agents
Taken after a meal, these agents are not absorbed as they pass through the digestive tract. They contain particles that absorb many times their own volume of water. By doing so they increase the bulk of the faeces and thus encourage bowel action.

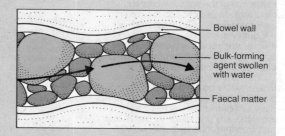

- Bowel wall
- Bulk-forming agent swollen with water
- Faecal matter

Stimulant laxatives
These laxatives are thought to encourage bowel movement by acting on nerve endings in the wall of the intestines that trigger contraction of the intestinal muscles. This speeds the passage of faecal matter through the large intestine, allowing less time for water to be absorbed. Thus faeces become more liquid and are passed more frequently.

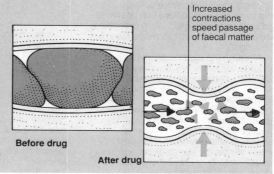

Increased contractions speed passage of faecal matter

Before drug

After drug

increasing its bulk and/or water content.

Stimulants cause the bowel muscle to contract, increasing the speed at which faecal matter passes through the intestine. Bulk-forming laxatives absorb water in the bowel, thereby increasing the volume of faeces, making them softer and easier to pass. Lactulose also causes fluid to accumulate in the intestine. Osmotic laxatives prevent the body from drawing water out of the bowel because they have an osmotic effect. This increases the bulk of the faeces and enables them to be passed more easily. Lubricant liquid paraffin preparations make bowel

movements softer and easier to pass without increasing their bulk. Prolonged use can interfere with absorption of some essential vitamins.

Risks and special precautions

Laxatives can cause diarrhoea if taken in overdose, and constipation if overused. The most serious risk of prolonged use of most laxatives is developing dependence on the laxative for normal bowel action. Use of a laxative should therefore be discontinued as soon as normal bowel movements have been re-established. Children should not be given laxatives except in special circumstances on the advice of a doctor.

TYPES OF LAXATIVES

Bulk-forming agents These are relatively slow acting, but are less likely than other laxatives to interfere with normal bowel action. Only after consultation with your doctor should they be taken for constipation accompanied by abdominal pain because of the risk of intestinal obstruction.

Stimulant (contact) laxatives These are suitable for occasional use when other treatments have failed or when a rapid onset of action is required. Stimulant laxatives should not normally be used for longer than a week as they can cause abdominal cramps and diarrhoea.

Lubricants Liquid paraffin is used as a faecal softener when hard bowel movements cause

pain on defecation – for example, if haemorrhoids are present. Lubricant preparations are often recommended for elderly or debilitated people and for the relief of faecal impaction (blockage of the bowel by faecal material).

Osmotic laxatives Salts such as Epsom salts (magnesium sulphate) may be used to evacuate the bowel before surgery or investigative procedures. They are not normally used for the long-term relief of constipation because they can cause chemical imbalances in the blood.

Lactulose is an alternative to bulk-forming laxatives for the long-term treatment of chronic constipation. It may cause stomach cramps and flatulence, but is usually well tolerated.

COMMON DRUGS

Stimulant laxatives
Bisacodyl
Co-danthramer
Docusate
Frangula
Phenolphthalein
Senna

Bulk-forming laxatives
Isphagula
Methylcellulose *
Sodium alginate

Lubricant laxatives
Liquid paraffin

Osmotic laxatives
Lactulose *
Magnesium hydroxide *
Magnesium sulphate
Magnesium citrate
Sodium acid phosphate

* See Part 4

DRUGS FOR INFLAMMATORY BOWEL DISEASE

Inflammatory bowel disease is the term used for disorders in which inflammation of the wall of the intestine causes recurrent attacks of abdominal pain, general feelings of ill-health and frequently diarrhoea, with blood and mucus present in the faeces. Loss of appetite and poor absorption of food often result in weight loss.

Doctors identify two main types of inflammatory bowel disease: Crohn's disease and ulcerative colitis. In Crohn's disease (also known as regional enteritis), any part of the digestive tract may become inflamed, although the small intestine is the most commonly affected site. In ulcerative colitis, it is the large intestine (colon) that becomes inflamed and ulcerated, often producing violent blood-stained diarrhoea (see the box, right).

Although the exact cause of these disorders is unknown, the risks and severity of attacks are increased by some infections, antibiotics and excessive stress.

Establishing a proper diet and a less stressful lifestyle may help to alleviate these conditions. Bed rest during attacks is also advisable. However, these simple measures alone do not usually relieve or prevent attacks, and drugs are often necessary.

Three types of drug are used to treat inflammatory bowel disease: cortico-steroids (p.141), immunosuppressants (p.156) and sulphasalazine. Safer deriv-atives of sulphasalazine are currently under investigation. Other drugs that may be given to treat inflammatory bowel

SITES OF BOWEL INFLAMMATION

The two main types of bowel inflammation are called ulcerative colitis and Crohn's disease. The former occurs in the large intestine. Crohn's disease can occur any-where along the gastrointestinal tract, but most often affects the small intestine.

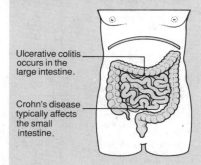

Ulcerative colitis occurs in the large intestine.

Crohn's disease typically affects the small intestine.

disease include nutritional supplements (used especially for Crohn's Disease) and antidiarrhoeal drugs (p.110). In very severe cases surgery may be necessary in order to remove damaged areas of the intestine.

Why they are used

Drugs cannot cure inflammatory bowel disease, but treatment is needed, not only to control symptoms, but to prevent complications, especially severe anae-mia and perforation of the intestinal wall.

Sulphasalazine is used both to treat attacks and to prevent ulcerative colitis. People who suffer from severe bowel inflammation are usually prescribed a course of corticosteroids, particularly during a sudden flare-up. Once the disease is under control an immuno-suppressant drug may be given to prevent a relapse.

How they work

Corticosteroids and sulphasalazine damp down the inflammatory process, allowing the damaged tissue to recover. They act in different ways to prevent migration of white blood cells into the bowel wall, which may be responsible in part for the inflammation of the bowel.

How they affect you

Taken to treat attacks, these drugs relieve symptoms within a few days and general health improves gradually over a few weeks. Sulphasalazine is usually effective in providing longer-term relief from symptoms of ulcerative colitis.

The first course of treatment with an immunosuppressant drug may take several months before improving the condition. However, they act more quickly in treating subsequent attacks.

Risks and special precautions

Immunosuppressant and corticosteroid drugs can cause serious adverse eff-ects, and they are thus only prescribed when potential benefits outweigh the risks involved.

It is important to continue taking these drugs as instructed because stopping them suddenly may cause a sudden flare-up of the disorder. Doctors usually supervise a gradual reduction in dosage when stopping such drugs, even when they are given as a short course for an attack. Antidiarrhoeal drugs should not be taken on a routine basis because they may mask signs of deterioration or aid sudden bowel dilation or rupture.

How they are administered

These drugs are usually taken in tablet form, although mild ulcerative colitis in the last part of the large intestine may be treated with suppositories or an enema containing a corticosteroid.

ACTION OF DRUGS IN ULCERATIVE COLITIS

Ulcerative colitis is the most common form of inflamma-tory bowel disease. It affects the large intestine, causing ulceration of the lining and producing pain and violent blood-stained diarrhoea. It is often treated with cortico-steroids and sulphasalazine.

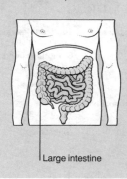

Large intestine

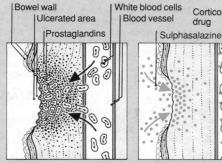

Bowel wall
Ulcerated area
Prostaglandins
White blood cells
Blood vessel
Corticosteroid drug
Sulphasalazine

Before drug
Damage to the intestinal lining provokes the formation of chemicals known as prostaglandins which trigger the migration of white blood cells into the ulcerated area. The accumulation of white blood cells in the bowel wall causes inflammation.

Drug action
Sulphasalazine passes into the ulcerated area from inside the bowel. It prevents prostaglandins forming around the damaged tissue. Corticosteroids act in the bloodstream to reduce the ability of white blood cells to pass into the bowel wall.

COMMON DRUGS

Corticosteroids
Hydrocortisone *
Prednisolone *

Immunosuppressants
Azathioprine *
Mercaptopurine *

Other drugs
Mesalazine *
Sulphasalazine *
Osalazine

* See Part 4

DRUGS FOR RECTAL AND ANAL DISORDERS

The most common disorder affecting the rectum (the last part of the large intestine) and anus (the opening from the rectum) is haemorrhoids, commonly known as piles. They occur when haemorrhoidal veins become swollen or irritated, often the result of prolonged, local pressure such as that caused by a pregnancy or a job requiring long hours of sitting. Haemorrhoids may cause irritation and pain, especially on defecation. The condition is aggravated by constipation and straining during defecation. Sometimes haemorrhoids may bleed and occasionally clots may form in the swollen veins, leading to severe pain, a condition known as thrombosed haemorrhoids.

Other common disorders affecting the anus include anal fissure (painful cracks in the anus), and pruritus ani (itching around the anus). Anal disorders of all kinds occur less frequently in those who have soft and bulky stools.

A number of over-the-counter and prescription-only preparations are available for the relief of such disorders.

Why they are used

Preparations for relief of haemorrhoids and anal discomfort fall into two main groups: creams or suppositories that act locally to relieve inflammation and irritation; and measures that relieve constipation, which contributes to the formation of, and discomfort from, haemorrhoids and anal fissure.

Preparations from the first group often contain a soothing agent with *antiseptic*, *astringent* or *vasoconstrictor* properties. Ingredients of this type include zinc oxide, bismuth, hamamelis (witch hazel), Peru balsam and ephedrine. Some products also include a mild local anaesthetic such as lignocaine (see p.80). In some cases a doctor may prescribe an ointment containing a corticosteroid to relieve inflammation around the anus (see Topical corticosteroids, p.174).

People who suffer from haemorrhoids or anal fissure are generally advised to include plenty of fluids and fibre-rich foods in their diet, such as fresh fruit, vegetables and whole grain products, to prevent constipation and to ease defecation. A mild bulk-forming or lubricant laxative may also be prescribed (see p.111).

Neither type of treatment can shrink large haemorrhoids, although they may provide relief while healing occurs naturally in anal fissure. Severe, persistently painful haemorrhoids that continue to be troublesome in spite of these measures may need to be removed surgically or, more commonly, by banding with specially applied small rubber bands (see below left).

How they affect you

The treatments described above usually relieve discomfort, especially during defecation. Most people experience no adverse effects, although preparations containing local anaesthetics may cause irritation or even a rash in the anal area. It is rare for ingredients in locally-acting preparations to be absorbed into the body in sufficient quantities to cause generalized side effects.

The main risk is that self-treatment of haemorrhoids may delay diagnosis of bowel cancer. It is therefore always wise to consult your doctor if you have symptoms of haemorrhoids, especially if you have noticed bleeding from the rectum or a change in bowel habits.

DISORDERS OF THE RECTUM AND ANUS

The rectum and anus form the last part of the digestive tract. Common conditions affecting the area include swelling of the veins around the anus (haemorrhoids), cracks in the anus (anal fissure), and inflammation and irritation of the anus and surrounding area (pruritus ani).

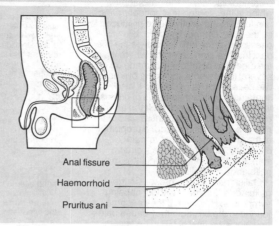

Anal fissure
Haemorrhoid
Pruritus ani

COMMON DRUGS

Soothing and astringent agents	Topical corticosteroids
Aluminium acetate	Hydrocortisone *
Bismuth	
Hamamelis	Local anaesthetics
Peru balsam	(See p.80)
Zinc oxide	
	Laxatives
Vasoconstrictors	(See p.111)
Ephedrine *	

SITES OF DRUG ACTION

The illustration below shows how and where drugs for the treatment of rectal disorders act to relieve symptoms.

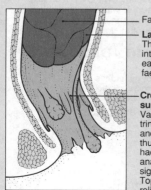

Faecal matter

Laxatives
These act in the large intestine to soften and ease the passage of faeces.

Creams and suppositories
Vasoconstrictors and astringents reduce swelling and restrict blood supply, thus helping to relieve haemorrhoids. Local anaesthetics numb pain signals from the anus. Topical corticosteroids relieve inflammation.

Banding treatment
A small rubber band is tightly applied to a haemorrhoid thereby blocking off its blood supply. The haemorrhoid will eventually wither away.

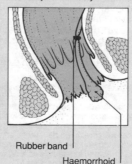

Rubber band
Haemorrhoid

*See Part 4

DRUG TREATMENT FOR GALLSTONES

The formation of gallstones is the most common disorder of the gallbladder, which is the storage and concentrating unit for bile, a digestive juice produced by the liver. During digestion, bile passes from the gallbladder via the bile duct into the small intestine where it aids the digestion of fats. Bile is made up of several ingredients, including bile acids, bile salts, and bile pigments. It also contains significant amounts of cholesterol dissolved in bile acid. If the amount of cholesterol in the bile increases or if that of bile acid is reduced, a proportion of the cholesterol cannot remain dissolved, and under certain circumstances this excess accumulates in the gallbladder as gallstones.

Gallstones may be present in the gallbladder for years without causing symptoms. However, if they become lodged in the bile duct they cause pain and block the flow of bile. The accumulation of bile in the blood may cause an attack of jaundice, or the gallbladder may become infected and inflamed.

Drugs can be used to dissolve stones that are made principally of cholesterol. However, when they contain other material, such as calcium, or if a stone lodges in the bile duct, surgery or ultrasound treatment may be needed. The most common gallstone-dissolving drug is chenodeoxycholic acid, but ursodeoxycholic acid is also used.

Why they are used
Even if you do not have any symptoms, once gallstones have been diagnosed your doctor may advise treatment because of the risk of blockage of the bile duct. Drug treatment is preferred to surgery for small cholesterol stones when it is considered that surgery may be risky.

How they work
Chenodeoxycholic acid is a substance that is naturally present in bile. It acts on chemical processes in the liver to regulate the amount of cholesterol in the blood, by controlling the amount that passes into the bile. Once the level of cholesterol in the bile is reduced, the bile acids are able to start dissolving the stones in the gallbladder. For maximum

DIGESTION OF FATS

The digestion of fats (or lipids) in the small intestine is assisted by the action of bile, a digestive juice produced by the liver and stored in the gallbladder. A complex sequence of chemical processes enables fats to be absorbed through the intestinal wall, broken down in the liver and converted for use in the body. Cholesterol, a lipid present in bile, plays an important part in this chain.

2 Bile salts act on fats to enable them to pass from the small intestine into the bloodstream, either directly or via the lymphatic system.

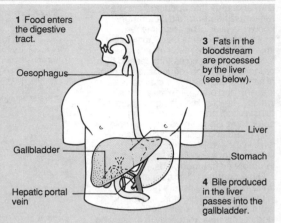

1 Food enters the digestive tract.

3 Fats in the bloodstream are processed by the liver (see below).

Oesophagus

Liver

Gallbladder

Stomach

Hepatic portal vein

4 Bile produced in the liver passes into the gallbladder.

How fats are processed in the liver

Fat molecules are broken down in the liver into fatty acids and glycerol. Glycerol and some of the fatty acids pass back into the bloodstream. Other fatty acids are used to form cholesterol, some of which in turn is used to make bile salts. Unchanged cholesterol is dissolved in the bile which then passes into the gallbladder.

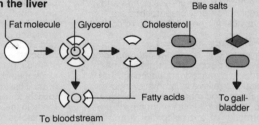

Fat molecule | Glycerol | Cholesterol | Bile salts

Fatty acids

To blood stream

To gallbladder

effect, chenodeoxycholic acid treatment needs to be accompanied by adherence to a low-cholesterol high-fibre diet.

How they affect you
Drug treatment often takes years to dissolve gallstones completely. You will not, therefore, feel any immediate benefit from the drugs, but you may have some minor side effects, the most usual of which is diarrhoea. If this occurs, your doctor may adjust the dosage. The effects of drug treatment on the gallstones is usually monitored at regular intervals by means of ultrasound or X-ray examinations.

Even after successful treatment with drugs, gallstones can recur when the

drug is stopped. In some cases drug treatment and dietary restrictions may be continued after the gallstones have dissolved, in order to prevent a recurrence of the problem.

Although these drugs reduce the amount of cholesterol in the gallbladder, they increase the level of cholesterol in the blood. Doctors therefore prescribe them with caution to people with atherosclerosis (fatty deposits in the blood vessels). They are not usually given to people with liver disorders because they can interfere with the normal liver function.

COMMON DRUGS

Drugs for gallstones
Chenodeoxycholic acid *
Ursodeoxycholic acid *

Pancreatic enzymes
Pancreatin

AGENTS USED IN DISORDERS OF THE PANCREAS

The pancreas releases certain *enzymes* into the small intestine which are necessary for digestion of a range of foods. If the release of pancreatic enzymes is impaired, for example by chronic pancreatitis or cystic fibrosis, enzyme replacement therapy may be necessary. Replacement of enzymes does not cure the underlying disorder, but restores normal digestion. Pancreatic enzymes should

be taken just before or with meals, and usually take effect immediately. Your doctor will probably advise you to eat a diet that is high in protein and carbohydrate and low in fat.

Pancreatin, the general name for preparations containing pancreatic enzymes, is extracted from pig pancreas. Treatment must be continued indefinitely as long as the pancreatic disorder persists.

*See Part 4

MUSCLES, BONES AND JOINTS

The basic architecture of the human body relies on bones (206 of them), over 600 muscles and a complex assortment of other tissues – ligaments, tendons and cartilage – that enables the body to move with remarkable efficiency.

What can go wrong

Though tough, these structures often suffer damage. Muscles, tendons and ligaments can be strained or torn by violent movement. Such injury may cause inflammation, making the affected tissue swollen and painful. Joints, especially those that bear the body's weight – hips, knees, ankles and vertebrae – are prone to wear and tear. The cartilage covering the bone ends may tear, causing pain and inflammation. Joint damage also occurs in rheumatioid arthritis, thought to be a form of auto-immune disorder. Gout, in which uric acid crystals form in some joints, may also cause inflammation, a condition known as gouty arthritis.

Other problems affecting the muscles, bones and joints include those in which nerve control over muscle contraction is altered due to injury or a neurological disorder, or by poor nerve signals as in myasthenia gravis. The mineral composition of bone may be weakened by vitamin, mineral or hormone deficiencies.

Why drugs are used

A simple analgesic drug or one that has an anti-inflammatory effect will provide pain relief in most of the above conditions. For more severe inflammation a doctor may inject a drug with a more powerful anti-inflammatory effect – such as a corticosteroid – into the affected site. In cases of severe progressive rheumatoid arthritis, anti-rheumatic drugs may halt the disease process as well as relieving symptoms.

Drugs that help to eliminate excess uric acid from the body are often prescribed to treat gout. Muscle relaxants that inhibit transmission of nerve signals to the muscles are used to treat muscle spasm. Drugs that increase nervous stimulation of the muscle are prescribed for myasthenia gravis. Bone disorders in which the mineral content of the bone is reduced are treated with supplements of minerals, vitamins and hormones.

MAJOR DRUG GROUPS

Non-steroidal anti-inflammatory drugs	Muscle relaxants
Antirheumatic drugs	Drugs used for myasthenia gravis
Locally-acting corticosteroids	Drugs for bone disorders
Drugs for gout	

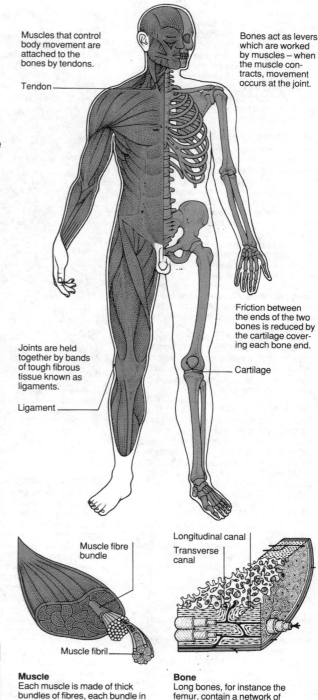

Muscles that control body movement are attached to the bones by tendons.

Tendon

Bones act as levers which are worked by muscles – when the muscle contracts, movement occurs at the joint.

Friction between the ends of the two bones is reduced by the cartilage covering each bone end.

Cartilage

Joints are held together by bands of tough fibrous tissue known as ligaments.

Ligament

Muscle fibre bundle

Muscle fibril

Longitudinal canal

Transverse canal

Muscle
Each muscle is made of thick bundles of fibres, each bundle in turn is made of fibrils. Tiny nerves and blood vessels enable the muscle to function.

Bone
Long bones, for instance the femur, contain a network of longitudinal and transverse canals to carry blood, nerves and lymph vessels through the bone.

NON-STEROIDAL ANTI-INFLAMMATORY DRUGS

Drugs in this group are used to relieve pain, stiffness, and inflammation of painful conditions affecting the muscles, bones and joints. NSAIDs are called "nonsteroidal" to distinguish them from corticosteroid drugs (see p.141), which also damp down inflammation.

Many NSAIDs are currently available; and others are being investigated in the hope of finding new compounds with fewer side effects.

Why they are used

NSAIDs are widely prescribed in the treatment of rheumatoid arthritis, osteoarthritis and other rheumatic conditions. They do not alter the progress of these diseases, but reduce inflammation and thus relieve pain and swelling of joints.

The response to the various drugs in this group varies between individuals and the first drug chosen may not be effective. It is sometimes necessary for the doctor to prescribe a number of different NSAIDs before finding the one which best suits a particular individual.

Because NSAIDs do not change the progress of the disease, additional treatment may be required, particularly in the case of rheumatoid arthritis (see facing page).

NSAIDs are also commonly prescribed to relieve back pain, gout (p.119), menstrual pain (p.160), headaches, mild pain following surgery, and pain from soft tissue injuries such as sprains and strains (see also Analgesics, p.80).

How they work

Prostaglandins are chemicals released by the body at the site of injury. They are responsible for producing pain and inflammation following tissue damage and in immune reactions. All types of NSAIDs block the production of prostaglandins and thus reduce pain and inflammation (see p.81).

How they affect you

NSAIDs are usually effective in reducing joint pain and swelling. They are rapidly absorbed from the digestive system and most start to relieve symptoms within an hour. When used regularly for long term treatment, they reduce stiffness and may restore or improve the function of a joint if this has been impaired.

Common side effects include nausea, indigestion and altered bowel action. However, the potential of most NSAIDs to irritate the stomach is less than that of aspirin.

A majority of the NSAIDs are short acting and need to be taken a few times a day in order to provide optimal relief of pain. Some need to be taken only twice daily. Others such as piroxicam are very slowly eliminated from the body and are effective when taken once a day.

ACTION OF NSAIDs IN OSTEOARTHRITIS

Non-steroidal anti-inflammatory drugs are commonly prescribed to diminish the pain and stiffness associated with osteoarthritis, a disorder in which, typically, a weight-bearing joint such as the hip is damaged by wear and tear or other factors.

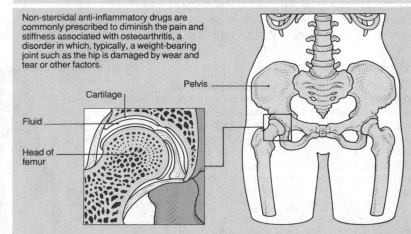

Cartilage
Pelvis
Fluid
Head of femur

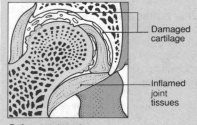

Damaged cartilage

Inflamed joint tissues

Before treatment
The protective layers of cartilage surrounding the joint are worn away and the joint becomes inflamed and painful.

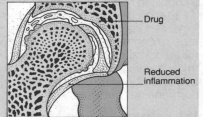

Drug

Reduced inflammation

Effect of NSAIDs
NSAIDs reduce inflammation and may thus relieve pain, but damage to the joint remains and symptoms are likely to worsen or recur if the drug is stopped.

Risks and special precautions

With a few exceptions, most NSAIDs are free from serious adverse effects. The main danger is that they can occasionally cause bleeding in the stomach or duodenum. They should normally be avoided by people who have suffered from peptic ulcers.

Most are not recommended during pregnancy or for nursing mothers. Caution is also advised for those with kidney or liver abnormalities or with a history of hypersensitivity to other drugs.

NSAIDs may impair blood clotting and are, therefore, prescribed with caution for people with bleeding disorders or who are taking drugs that reduce blood clotting. One of the first NSAIDs, phenylbutazone, can impair the bone marrow's ability to produce blood cells. Early signs of this include sore throat or fever and need to be reported. Phenylbutazone is prescribed only for ankylosing spondylitis, and regular blood tests are carried out.

Misoprostol

The NSAIDs' side effect of bleeding is due to their antiprostaglandin action occurring where it is not wanted. To protect against this, a prostaglandin-like drug called misoprostol is sometimes prescribed with the NSAID. Misoprostol can also help peptic ulcers to heal.

COMMON DRUGS

Acemetacin	Flurbiprofen
Aspirin *	Ibuprofen *
Azapropazone	Indomethacin *
Benorylate *	Ketoprofen
Benzydamine	Mefenamic acid *
Diclofenac	Nabumetone
Diflunisal	Naproxen *
Etodolac	Phenylbutazone *
Felbinac	Piroxicam *
Fenbufen *	Sulindac
Fenoprofen	Tenoxicam
	Tiaprofenic acid
* See Part 4	Tolmetin

ANTIRHEUMATIC DRUGS

These drugs are used in the treatment of various rheumatic disorders, the most crippling and deforming of which is rheumatoid arthritis, an autoimmune disease in which the body's mechanism for fighting infection contributes to the damage of its own joint tissue. The disease causes pain, stiffness and swelling of the joints that over many months can lead to deformity. Flare-ups of rheumatoid arthritis also cause generalized feelings of being unwell, such as tiredness and loss of appetite.

Treatments include drugs, rest, changes in diet, immobilization of joints and physiotherapy. Rheumatoid arthritis cannot yet be cured, although in many cases it does not progress far enough to cause permanent disability. The disease may subside spontaneously for prolonged periods.

Why they are used

The aim of drug treatment is to relieve pain and stiffness, maintain mobility, and prevent deformity. There are two main forms of drug treatment for rheumatoid arthritis: the first alleviates symptoms and the second modifies, halts, or slows the underlying disease process. Drugs in the first category include aspirin (p.199) and the non-steroidal anti-inflammatory drugs (NSAIDs, facing page). These drugs are usually prescribed as a first treatment.

However, if the rheumatoid arthritis is severe or the initial drug treatment has proved to be ineffective, the second category of drugs may be given. These drugs may impede any further joint damage and disability. They are not prescribed routinely because they have potentially severe adverse effects (see Types of antirheumatic drugs, below, for further information on individual drugs), and because the disease may stop spontaneously.

Corticosteroids (p.141) are sometimes used in the treatment of rheumatoid arthritis, but only for limited periods.

THE EFFECTS OF ANTIRHEUMATIC DRUGS

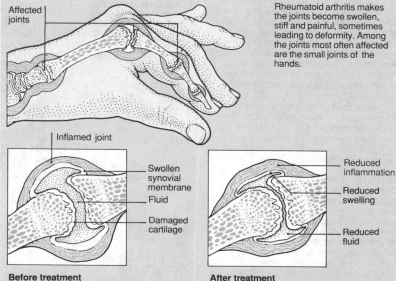

Rheumatoid arthritis makes the joints become swollen, stiff and painful, sometimes leading to deformity. Among the joints most often affected are the small joints of the hands.

Before treatment
The synovial membrane surrounding the joint is inflamed and thickened, producing increased fluid within the joint. The surrounding tissue is inflamed and joint cartilage damaged.

After treatment
Treatment with antirheumatic drugs relieves pain, swelling and inflammation. Damage to cartilage and bone may be halted so that further deformity is minimized.

How they work

It is not known precisely how most antirheumatic drugs stop or slow the disease process. Some may reduce the body's immune response, which is thought to be partly responsible for the disease (see also Immunosuppressants, p.156). When effective, such drugs prevent damage to the cartilage and bone, thereby reducing progressive deformity and disability. The effectiveness of each drug varies depending on the individual response.

How they affect you

These drugs are generally slow-acting; it may be weeks or months before benefit is noticed. Therefore treatment with NSAIDs or aspirin is usually continued. Prolonged treatment with antirheumatic drugs can cause a marked improvement in symptoms. Pain is reduced, joint mobility increased and generalized symptoms of ill-health fade. Side effects (these vary between individual drugs) may be noticed before any beneficial effect, so patience is required. Severe side effects may occasionally necessitate abandoning the treatment.

TYPES OF ANTIRHEUMATIC DRUGS

Chloroquine Originally developed to treat malaria (see p.137), chloroquine and related drugs are less effective than penicillamine or gold. Since prolonged use may cause eye damage, regular eye checks are needed.

Immunosuppressants These may be prescribed if other drugs do not provide relief, and if rheumatoid arthritis is severe and disabling. Regular observation and blood tests must be carried out because immunosuppressants can cause severe complications.

Sulphasalazine Used mainly for ulcerative colitis (p.112), this drug was originally introduced to treat rheumatoid arthritis and is effective in some cases.

Gold-based drugs These are believed to be the most effective, and may be given orally or by injection for many years. Side effects can include a rash and digestive disturbances. Gold may sometimes damage the kidneys, which recover on stopping treatment; regular urine tests are usually carried out. It can also suppress blood cell production in bone marrow, so periodic blood tests are carried out.

Penicillamine This drug (not an antibiotic) may be used when rheumatoid arthritis is worsening, or when gold cannot be used. Symptoms may take 3 – 6 months to improve. It has similar side effects to gold, so periodic blood and urine tests are usually performed.

COMMON DRUGS

Immunosuppressants
Azathioprine *
Chlorambucil
Cyclophosphamide *
Cyclosporin
Methotrexate

Gold-based drugs
Auranofin *

Sodium
aurothiomalate *

Other drugs
Chloroquine *
Hydroxychloroquine
Penicillamine *
Sulphasalazine *

| * See Part 4 |

LOCALLY-ACTING CORTICOSTEROIDS

The adrenal glands lie on the upper part of the kidneys. They produce a number of important hormones, among which are the corticosteroids, so named because they are made in the outer part (cortex) of the glands. These hormones play an important role, influencing the immune system and regulating the carbohydrate and mineral *metabolism* of the body. A number of drugs that mimic the effects of natural corticosteroid hormones have been developed.

These drugs have many uses and are discussed in more detail under Corticosteroids (p.141). This section concentrates on corticosteroids given by injection into an affected site to treat various joint disorders.

Why they are used
Corticosteroids given by injection are particularly useful for treating joint disorders – notably rheumatoid arthritis and osteoarthritis – when one or only a few joints are involved and pain and inflammation have not been relieved by other drugs. In such cases it is possible to relieve symptoms by injecting each of the affected joints individually. Corticosteroids may also be injected to reduce pain and inflammation caused by strained or contracted muscles, ligaments and/or tendons – for example, in frozen shoulder or tennis elbow. They may also be given for bursitis, tendinitis or swelling that may be compressing a nerve. Corticosteroid injections are sometimes used to relieve pain and stiffness sufficiently to allow physiotherapy to be undertaken.

How they work
These drugs have two main actions that are thought to account for their effective-

ness. They depress the activity of the white blood cells that are responsible for inflammation (below) and also block the production of chemicals called prostaglandins, which are responsible for triggering pain and inflammation. Administration by injection concentrates the effects of the corticosteroids at the site of the problem, producing maximum benefit where it is most needed.

COMMON INJECTION SITES

Corticosteroids are often injected into joints affected by osteo- and rheumatoid arthritis. Joints commonly treated in this way are knee, shoulder and finger joints.

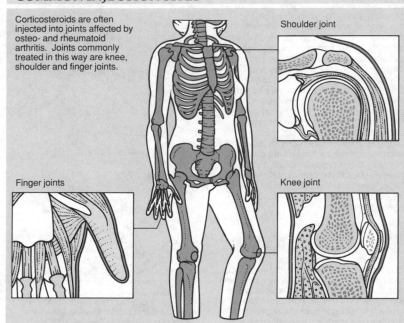

Shoulder joint

Finger joints

Knee joint

How they affect you
Corticosteroids usually produce dramatic relief from symptoms when they are injected into a joint. Often a single injection is sufficient to relieve pain and swelling, and to improve mobility. When used to treat muscle or tendon pain they may not always be effective because it is difficult to position the needle so that the drug reaches the right spot. In some cases repeated injections are necessary.

Because these drugs are concentrated in the affected area, and are not dispersed in significant amounts in the body, generalized adverse effects that may occur with corticosteroids taken by mouth are unlikely. Minor side effects such as loss of skin pigment at the injection site are uncommon. Occasionally, a temporary increase in pain (steroid flare) may occur. In such cases, local application of ice, rest and analgesic medication may relieve the condition. Sterile injection technique is critically important.

ACTION OF CORTICOSTEROIDS ON INFLAMED JOINTS

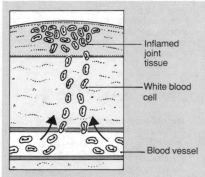

Inflamed joint tissue

White blood cell

Blood vessel

Reduced inflammation

Drug

Inflamed tissue
Inflammation occurs when disease or injury causes large numbers of white blood cells to accumulate in the affected area. In joints this leads to swelling and stiffness.

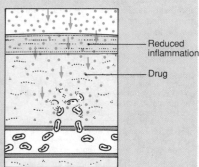

Action of corticosteroids
Corticosteroids injected into the area permeate the joint lining (synovial membrane) and prevent white blood cells accumulating.

COMMON DRUGS

Betamethasone *
Dexamethasone *

Hydrocortisone *
Prednisolone *

* See Part 4

DRUGS FOR GOUT

Gout is a disorder that arises when the blood contains increased levels of uric acid, a by-product of the *metabolism* excreted in the urine. When its concentration in the blood is excessive, uric acid crystals may form in various parts of the body, especially in the joints of the foot (most often the big toe), the knee and hand, causing intense pain and inflammation known as gouty arthritis. Crystals may form as white masses, known as tophi, in soft tissue, and in the kidneys as stones. Attacks of gouty arthritis can recur, and may lead to damaged joints and deformity. Kidney stones can cause kidney damage.

An excess of uric acid can be caused either by increased production or by an impairment in the kidney function that removes it from the body. The disorder tends to run in families and is far more common in men. The risk of attack is increased by high alcohol intake, the consumption of certain foods (red meat, sardines, anchovies, offal such as liver, brains and sweetbreads) and obesity. An attack may be triggered by drugs such as thiazide diuretics (see p.99), anticancer drugs (see p.154), or excessive drinking. Changes in diet and a reduction in alcohol consumption may be an important part of treatment.

Drugs used to treat acute attacks of gouty arthritis include non-steroidal anti-inflammatory drugs (NSAIDs, see p.116) and colchicine. Other drugs which lower the blood level of uric acid are used for the long-term prevention of gout. These include allopurinol and the uricosuric drugs, probenecid and sulphinpyrazone. Aspirin is not prescribed for pain relief because it slows the excretion of uric acid.

Why they are used

Drugs may be prescribed to treat an attack of gout or to prevent recurrent attacks that could lead to deformity of affected joints and kidney damage. Colchicine can halt an attack of gout; NSAIDs may also ease the symptoms. Either type of drug should be taken as soon as an attack begins. Because colchicine is relatively specific in relieving the pain and inflammation arising from gout, doctors sometimes administer it in order to confirm their diagnosis of the condition before prescribing an NSAID.

If symptoms recur, your doctor may advise long-term treatment with allopurinol or uricosuric drugs.

These drugs usually have to be taken indefinitely. Since they can trigger attacks of gout at the beginning of treatment, colchicine is sometimes given with these drugs for a few months.

How they work

Allopurinol reduces the level of uric acid in the blood by interfering with the activity of xanthine oxidase, an *enzyme* that is involved in the production of uric acid in the body. Probenecid and sulfinpyrazone, the uricosuric drugs, increase the rate at which uric acid is excreted by the kidneys. It is not known how colchicine reduces inflammation and relieves pain. The actions of NSAIDs are described on p.116.

How they affect you

Drugs used in the long-term treatment of gout are usually successful in preventing attacks and joint deformity. However, response may be slow.

Colchicine can disturb the digestive system, causing abdominal pain and diarrhoea, which your doctor can control.

Risks and special precautions

Since they increase the output of uric acid through the kidneys, uricosuric drugs can cause uric acid crystals to form in the kidneys. They are not, therefore, usually prescribed for those who already have kidney problems. In such cases allopurinol may be preferred. It is always important to drink plenty of fluids while taking anti-gout drugs to prevent kidney crystals from forming. Regular blood tests to monitor levels of uric acid in the blood may be required.

ACTION OF URICOSURIC DRUGS

Uric acid is removed from the blood by the kidneys and excreted in the urine. Excess uric acid, caused by increased production or impaired kidney function, requires treatment with uricosuric drugs, which increase the rate at which uric acid is expelled.

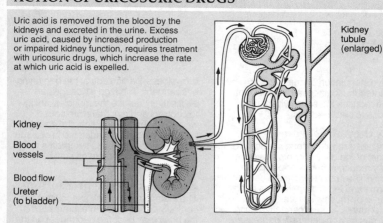

Kidney tubule (enlarged)

Kidney

Blood vessels

Blood flow

Ureter (to bladder)

Uric acid and gouty arthritis

Gouty arthritis occurs when uric acid crystals form in a joint, often in the toe, the knee or hand, causing inflammation and pain. This is the result of excessively high levels of uric acid in the blood. In some cases this is caused by over-production of uric acid, while in others it is the result of reduced excretion of uric acid by the kidneys.

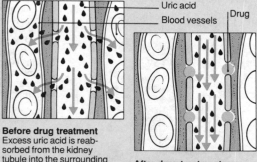

Uric acid

Blood vessels

Drug

Before drug treatment
Excess uric acid is reabsorbed from the kidney tubule into the surrounding blood vessels. This leads to the formation of uric acid crystals, which can cause gouty arthritis.

After drug treatment
By blocking the reabsorption of uric acid into the blood vessels, the amount of uric acid excreted in the urine is increased.

COMMON DRUGS

Drugs to treat attack	Drugs to prevent attacks
Colchicine *	Allopurinol *
NSAIDs (see p.116)	Azapropazone
	Probenecid *
	Sulphinpyrazone

* See Part 4

MUSCLE RELAXANTS

Several drugs are available to treat muscle spasm, the involuntary, painful contraction of a muscle or a group of muscles that can stiffen an arm or leg, or make it nearly impossible to straighten your back. There are various causes. It can follow an injury, or come on without warning. It may also be brought on by a disorder like osteoarthritis, the pain in the affected joint triggering abnormal tension in a nearby muscle.

Spasticity is another form of muscle tightness seen in some neurological disorders such as multiple sclerosis, stroke or cerebral palsy. This can sometimes be helped by physiotherapy but in severe cases drugs may be used to relieve symptoms.

Why they are used
Painful muscle spasm resulting from direct injury is usually and most effectively treated with an analgesic or non-steroidal anti-inflammatory drug (see p.80). However, if the spasm is severe, as it may be following a back injury, a muscle relaxant may be tried for a short period to relieve the symptoms. Muscle relaxants are frequently added to analgesic preparations for the relief of spasm caused by painful conditions of this type.

In spasticity, the sufferer's legs may become so stiff and uncontrollable that it is impossible for them to walk unaided. In such cases a drug may be prescribed which relieves symptoms without taking all the strength away from the muscles. Relaxation of the muscles often permits physiotherapy to be given for longer term relief in certain spastic conditions.

How they work
Muscle relaxant drugs work in one of two ways: the centrally-acting drugs damp down the passage of the nerve signals from the brain and spinal cord that cause muscles to contract, thus reducing ex-

SITES OF ACTION OF MUSCLE RELAXANTS

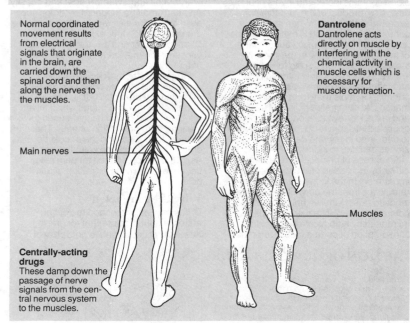

Normal coordinated movement results from electrical signals that originate in the brain, are carried down the spinal cord and then along the nerves to the muscles.

Dantrolene
Dantrolene acts directly on muscle by interfering with the chemical activity in muscle cells which is necessary for muscle contraction.

Main nerves

Muscles

Centrally-acting drugs
These damp down the passage of nerve signals from the central nervous system to the muscles.

cessive stimulation of muscles and unwanted muscular contraction. Dantrolene reduces the sensitivity of the muscles to nerve signals.

How they affect you
Drugs taken regularly for a spastic disorder of the central nervous system usually reduce stiffness and improve mobility. They may restore the use of the arms and legs when this has been impaired by muscle spasm.

Unfortunately, most centrally-acting drugs can have a generally depressant effect on nervous activity and produce

drowsiness, particularly at the beginning of treatment. Too high a dosage can excessively reduce the muscles' ability to contract and can therefore cause weakness. For this reason, the dosage needs to be carefully adjusted in order to find a level that controls symptoms and at the same time maintains sufficient muscular strength.

Risks and special precautions
The main long-term risk associated with centrally-acting muscle relaxants is that the body may become dependent on the drug for depressing the excessive nervous activity responsible for muscle spasm. If the drug is withdrawn suddenly, the stiffness may become worse than it was before drug treatment began.

Dantrolene can, in rare cases, cause serious liver damage and for this reason anyone taking this drug should have their blood tested regularly to assess liver function.

ACTION OF CENTRALLY-ACTING DRUGS

Centrally-acting muscle relaxants restrict the passage of nerve signals to the muscles by occupying a proportion of the *receptors* in the central nervous system that are normally used by chemical *neurotransmitters* to transmit such impulses. Reduced nervous stimulation allows the muscles to relax; however, if the dose of the drug is too high this action may give rise to excessive muscle weakness.

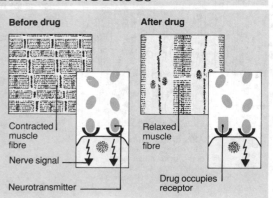

Before drug

After drug

Contracted muscle fibre

Relaxed muscle fibre

Nerve signal

Drug occupies receptor

Neurotransmitter

COMMON DRUGS

Centrally-acting drugs
Baclofen *
Carisoprodol
Cyclobenzaprine
Diazepam *

Methocarbamol
Orphenadrine *

Others
Botulinum toxin
Dantrolene
Quinine *

* See Part 4

DRUGS USED FOR MYASTHENIA GRAVIS

Myasthenia gravis is a disorder that occurs when the immune system (see p.152) becomes defective and produces antibodies that disrupt the signals being transmitted between the nervous system and the muscles under voluntary control. The result is a progressive weakening of muscular response, the muscles first affected being those controlling the eyes, eyelids, face, throat and voice, with muscles in the arms and legs becoming involved as the disease progresses. The disease is often linked to a disorder of the thymus gland, the source of the destructive antibodies concerned.

Treatment of myasthenia gravis can take several forms. It may involve the removal of the thymus gland (thymectomy). Temporary relief may be obtained by clearing the blood of antibodies, a procedure known as plasmapheresis. Drugs are available that improve muscle function, principally neostigmine and pyridostigmine. They may be used alone or together with other drugs that depress the immune system – usually corticosteroids (see p.141) or azathioprine (see Immunosuppressants, p.156).

THE EFFECTS OF MYASTHENIA GRAVIS

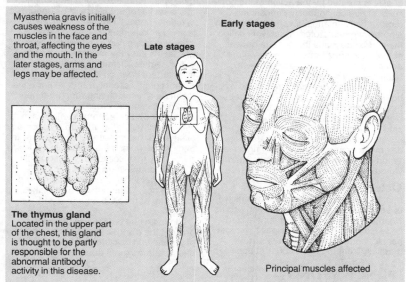

Myasthenia gravis initially causes weakness of the muscles in the face and throat, affecting the eyes and the mouth. In the later stages, arms and legs may be affected.

Late stages

Early stages

The thymus gland
Located in the upper part of the chest, this gland is thought to be partly responsible for the abnormal antibody activity in this disease.

Principal muscles affected

Why they are used

Drugs may be given when it is not feasible to remove the thymus gland, or when surgery does not provide adequate relief. Drugs may be taken in the long-term to improve muscular strength, but these have no effect on the disease process itself. One of these, edrophonium, acts very rapidly and is used to confirm the diagnosis. When administered, it brings about a dramatic improvement in symptoms, but, as the benefits last for only a few minutes, it is not prescribed for regular treatment.

These drugs may also be given following surgery to counteract the effects of a muscle relaxant drug given prior to certain surgical procedures.

How they work

Normal muscle action occurs when a nerve impulse triggers a nerve ending to release a *neurotransmitter*, which combines with a specialized *receptor* on the muscle cells and causes the muscles to contract. In myasthenia gravis, the body's immune system destroys many of these receptors so that the muscle is less responsive to nervous stimulation. Drugs used to treat the disorder, like neostigmine, increase the amount of neurotransmitter at the nerve ending by blocking the action of an *enzyme* which normally breaks it down. Increased levels of the neurotransmitter permit the remaining receptors to function more efficiently (see

Action of drugs used for myasthenia gravis, below left).

How they affect you

These drugs usually restore muscle function to a normal, or near normal level, particularly when the disease takes a mild form. Unfortunately, they can produce unwanted muscular activity by enhancing the transmission of nerve impulses elsewhere in the body.

Common side effects include vomiting, nausea, diarrhoea, and cramps in the muscles of the arms, legs and abdomen.

Risks and special precautions

Muscle weakness can suddenly worsen even when it is being treated with drugs. Should this occur, it is important not to take larger doses of the drug treatment in an attempt to relieve the symptoms, because excessive levels can interfere with the transmission of nerve impulses to muscles, causing further weakness. The administration of other drugs, including some antibiotics, can also markedly increase the symptoms of myasthenia gravis. If your symptoms suddenly become worse, consult your doctor.

ACTION OF DRUGS USED FOR MYASTHENIA GRAVIS

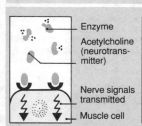

Enzyme
Acetylcholine (neurotransmitter)
Nerve signals transmitted
Muscle cell

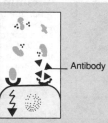

Antibody

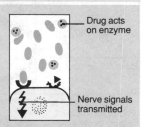

Drug acts on enzyme
Nerve signals transmitted

Normal nerve transmission
Muscles contract when a neurotransmitter (acetylcholine) binds to receptors on muscle cells. An enzyme breaks down acetylcholine.

In myasthenia gravis
Abnormal antibody activity destroys many receptors, reducing stimulation of muscle cells and weakening muscle action.

Drug action
Drugs block enzyme action, increasing acetylcholine, and prolonging the muscle cell response to nervous stimulation.

COMMON DRUGS

Neostigmine *
Pyridostigmine *

* See Part 4

DRUGS FOR BONE DISORDERS

Bone is a living structure. Its hard, mineral quality is created by the action of the bone cells. These continuously deposit and remove calcium and phosphorus stored in a honeycombed protein framework called the matrix. Because the rates of deposit and removal (the bone *metabolism*) are about equal in adults, the bone mass remains fairly constant.

Removal and renewal is regulated by hormones and influenced by a number of factors, notably the level of calcium in the blood. This depends on the intake of calcium and vitamin D from the diet, the actions of various hormones, plus every-day movement and weight-bearing stress. When normal bone metabolism is altered, various bone disorders result.

Osteoporosis

In osteoporosis the strength and density of bone are reduced. Such wasting occurs when the rate of removal of mineralized bone exceeds the rate of deposit. In most people, bone density decreases very gradually from the age of 30. But bone loss can dramatically increase when a person is immobilized for a period, and this is an important cause of osteoporosis in elderly people. Hormone deficiency is another important cause, commonly occurring in women with lowered oestrogen levels after the menopause or removal of the ovaries. Osteoporosis also occurs in disorders in which there is excess production of adrenal or thyroid hormones. It can be a result of long-term treatment with corticosteroid drugs.

People with osteoporosis often have no symptoms, but, if the vertebrae become so weakened that they are unable to bear the body's weight, or if the person is injured in a fall, they may collapse. Subsequently, the individual suffers from back pain, reduced height and a round-shouldered appearance. Osteoporosis also makes a fracture or break of an arm or leg more likely.

Most doctors emphasize the need to prevent the disorder by an adequate intake of protein and calcium and by regular exercise throughout adult life. If lack of calcium in the diet is a major cause, supplements are usually prescribed, possibly with vitamin D. Oestrogen supplements during and after the menopause may be used to prevent osteoporosis in older women. For discussion of such hormone replacement therapy, see p.147.

The condition of bones damaged by osteoporosis cannot usually be improved, although drug treatment can help prevent further deterioration and help fractures heal. The hormone calcitonin is involved with regulation of bone turnover and calcium balance; a synthetic derivative called salcatonin is more suitable for long-term use and is prescribed with dietary calcium and vitamin D. A group of drugs called biphosphonates reduce the rate of bone turnover; one of them, etidronate, is used with calcium carbonate tablets for vertebral osteoporosis.

Osteomalacia and rickets

In osteomalacia – called rickets when it affects children – lack of vitamin D leads to loss of calcium, resulting in softening of the bones. Sufferers experience pain and tenderness and there is a risk of fracture and bone deformity. In children, growth is retarded.

The commonest cause of osteomalacia is lack of vitamin D. This can be caused by inadequate diet, inability to absorb the vitamin, or by insufficient exposure of the skin to sunlight (the action of the sun on the skin produces vitamin D inside the body). People at special risk include those whose absorption of vitamin D is impaired by an intestinal disorder, like Crohn's disease or coeliac disease. People with dark skins living in Northern Europe are also susceptible. Chronic kidney disease is an important cause of rickets in children and of osteomalacia in adults, since healthy kidneys play an essential role in the body's metabolism of vitamin D.

Long-term relief depends on treating the underlying disorder where possible. Treatment may in rare cases be lifelong.

Vitamin D

A number of substances related to vitamin D may be used in the treatment of some bone disorders. Examples are alfacalcidol, calcitriol, and ergocalciferol (calciferol); the prescribed substance depends on the underlying problem.

BONE WASTING

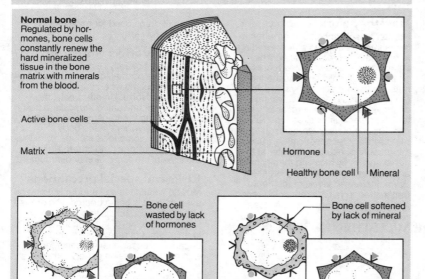

Normal bone
Regulated by hormones, bone cells constantly renew the hard mineralized tissue in the bone matrix with minerals from the blood.

Active bone cells

Matrix

Hormone

Healthy bone cell   Mineral

Bone cell wasted by lack of hormones

Damage to bone cell halted by drug

Drug

Bone cell softened by lack of mineral

Bone cell restored by drug

Drug

In osteoporosis
Hormonal disturbance leads to wasting of active bone cells. The bones become less dense and more fragile. Drug treatment with hormone and mineral supplements usually only prevents further bone loss.

In osteomalacia
Deficiency of calcium or vitamin D causes softening of the bone tissue. The bones become weaker and sometimes deformed. Drug treatment with vitamin and minerals usually restores bone strength.

COMMON DRUGS

Calcitonin *
Calcium carbonate *
Conjugated oestrogens *
Etidronate *
Fluoride *
Vitamin D *

* See Part 4

ALLERGY

Allergy – a hypersensitivity to certain substances – reflects an excessive reaction of the body's immune system. Acting by means of a variety of mechanisms (see Malignant and immune disease, p.152), the immune system protects the body by trying to eliminate foreign substances that it does not recognize, such as micro-organisms (bacteria or viruses).

One way in which it acts is through the production of *antibodies*. When a particular foreign substance (or allergen) is encountered for the first time, white blood cells known as lymphocytes produce antibodies that attach themselves to other white blood cells known as mast cells. If the same substance is encountered again, the allergen binds to the antibodies on the mast cells causing the release of chemicals called mediators, which help destroy the invader if it is a micro-organism.

The most important of the mediators is histamine. This chemical can produce rash, swelling, narrowing of the airways, and a drop in blood pressure. These effects are important in protecting against infection but they may also be triggered inappropriately in allergy.

What can go wrong

One of the most common allergic disorders, hay fever, is caused by an allergic reaction to inhaled grass pollen leading to allergic rhinitis – swelling and irritation of the nasal passages and watering of the nose and eyes. Other substances such as house-dust mites, animal fur, and feathers may cause a similar reaction in susceptible people. Asthma, another allergic disorder, may result from the action of mediators other than histamine. Other allergic conditions include urticaria (hives) or other rashes (sometimes in response to a drug), some forms of eczema and dermatitis, and allergic alveolitis (farmer's lung).

Why drugs are used

Antihistamines and drugs that inhibit mast-cell activity are used to prevent and treat allergic reactions. Other drugs are useful for treating allergic symptoms, for example, decongestants (p.93) to clear the nose in allergic rhinitis, bronchodilators (p.92) to widen the airways of those with asthma, and corticosteroids applied to the skin in eczema (p.174).

MAJOR DRUG GROUPS

Antihistamines

Allergic response

Lymphocytes produce antibodies to allergens, which attach to mast cells. If the allergen enters the body again, it binds to the antibodies, and the mast cells release histamine.

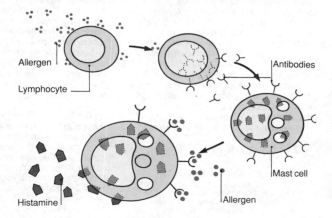

Allergen
Lymphocyte
Antibodies
Mast cell
Allergen
Histamine

Histamine and histamine receptors

Histamine, released in response to injury or the presence of allergens, acts on H_1 *receptors* in the skin, blood vessels, nasal passages and airways, and on H_2 receptors in the stomach lining, salivary and lacrimal (tear) glands. It provokes dilation of blood vessels, inflammation and swelling of tissues and narrowing of the airways. Sometimes a reaction termed anaphylactic shock occurs, caused by a dramatic fall in blood pressure and leading to collapse. Antihistamine drugs block H_1 receptors and H_2 antagonists block H_2 receptors (see also Antihistamines, p.124 and Anti-ulcer drugs, p.105).

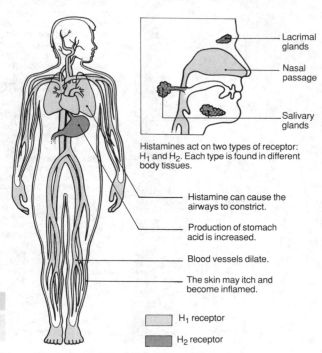

Lacrimal glands
Nasal passage
Salivary glands

Histamines act on two types of receptor: H_1 and H_2. Each type is found in different body tissues.

Histamine can cause the airways to constrict.

Production of stomach acid is increased.

Blood vessels dilate.

The skin may itch and become inflamed.

H_1 receptor

H_2 receptor

ANTIHISTAMINES

Antihistamines are the most widely used drugs in the treatment of allergic reactions of all kinds. They can be sub-divided according to chemical structure, each subgrouping with slightly different actions and characteristics (see the table on the facing page). Their main action is to counter the effects of histamine, one of the chemicals released in the body when there is an allergic reaction. (For a full explanation of the allergy mechanism, see p.123).

Histamine is also involved in a number of other body functions, including blood vessel dilation and constriction, the contraction of the muscles of the respiratory and gastrointestinal tracts,

and the release of digestive juices in the stomach. The antihistamine drugs described here are also known as H_1 blockers because they only block the action of histamine on certain *receptors*, known as H_1 receptors. Another group of antihistamines, known as H_2 blockers, are used in the treatment of peptic ulcers (see Anti-ulcer drugs, p.109).

Some antihistamines have a significant *anticholinergic* action. This is used to advantage in a variety of conditions, but it also accounts for certain undesired side effects.

Why they are used
Antihistamines relieve allergy-related symptoms when it is not possible or practical to prevent exposure to the substance that has provoked the re-action. Their most common use is in the prevention of allergic rhinitis (hay fever), inflammation of the nose and upper airways resulting from an allergic reaction to a substance such as pollen, house dust or animal fur. They are more effective when taken before the start of an attack. If they are taken only after an attack has already started, beneficial effects may be delayed.

Antihistamines are not generally effective in asthma caused by similar allergens because the symptoms of this allergic disorder are not solely caused by the action of histamine, but are likely to be the result of more complex mech-anisms. Antihistamines are usually the first drugs to be tried in the treatment of allergic disorders but alternatives can be prescribed (see below).

Antihistamines are also useful for relieving the itching, swelling and red-ness characteristic of allergic reactions

involving the skin – for example, urti-caria (hives), infantile eczema and other forms of dermatitis. Irritation from chickenpox may be reduced by these drugs. In addition, allergic reactions to insect stings may also be reduced by antihistamines. In such cases the drug may be taken by mouth or applied *topically*. Applied as drops, antihist-amines also reduce inflammation and irritation of the eyes and eyelids in allergic conjunctivitis.

An antihistamine is often included as an ingredient in cough and cold prepara-tions (see p.94), when the anti-cholinergic effect of drying mucus secretions and their sedative effect on the coughing mechanism may be helpful.

Because most antihistamines have a depressant effect on the brain, they are sometimes used to promote sleep, especially when discomfort from itching is disturbing sleep (see also Sleeping drugs, p.82). The depressant effect of antihistamines on the brain also extends to the centres that control nausea and vomiting. Antihistamines are therefore often effective for preventing and controlling these symptoms (see Anti-emetics, p.90).

Occasionally, antihistamines are used to treat fever, rash and breathing difficulties that may occur in adverse reactions to blood transfusions and allergic reactions to drugs. Prome-thazine and trimeprazine are also used as *premedication* to provide sedation and to dry secretions during surgery, particularly in children.

How they work
Antihistamines block the action of hist-amine on H_1 receptors. These are found

SITES OF ACTION

Antihistamines act on a variety of sites and systems throughout the body. Their main action is on the muscles surrounding the small blood vessels that supply the skin and mucous membranes. They also act on the airways in the lung and on the brain.

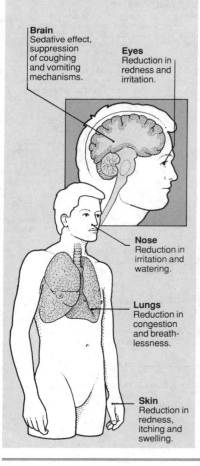

Brain
Sedative effect, suppression of coughing and vomiting mechanisms.

Eyes
Reduction in redness and irritation.

Nose
Reduction in irritation and watering.

Lungs
Reduction in congestion and breath-lessness.

Skin
Reduction in redness, itching and swelling.

OTHER ALLERGY TREATMENTS

Other drugs can replace antihistamines if they are unsuitable or may be added if the symptoms are not adequately controlled.

Sodium cromoglycate
This drug is a mast cell inhibitor that prevents release of histamine from mast cells (see p. 123) in response to exposure to an allergen, thus preventing the physical symptoms of allergies. It is commonly given by inhaler for the prevention of allergy-induced rhinitis or asthma attacks and by drops for the treatment of allergic eye disorders. For further information on this drug, see p.394.

Corticosteroids are used to treat allergic rhinitis and asthma, usually by inhalers using doses much lower than given in tablet form.

Desensitization
This may be tried in such allergic conditions as allergic rhinitis due to pollen sensitivity and insect venom hypersensitivity, when antihistamines and other treatments have not been effective and tests have shown one

or two specific allergens to be responsible.
Because desensitization often provides only incomplete relief and can be time consuming it is attempted only when simpler measures such as avoidance of the allergen have been unsuccessful.

The treatment involves giving a series of injections containing gradually increasing doses of an extract of the allergen. The precise mechanism by which this prevents allergic reactions is not fully understood. One explanation is that such controlled exposure to the substance triggers the immune system to produce increasing levels of antibodies to the allergen so that the body no longer responds dramati-cally when the allergen is encountered naturally.

Desensitization must be carried out under specialist medical supervision because it can occasionally provoke a severe allergic response. It is important to remain within close range of emergency medical facilities for at least 60 minutes after each injection.

COMPARISON OF ANTIHISTAMINES

Although antihistamines have broadly similar effects and uses, differences in their strength of anticholinergic action and the amount of drowsiness they produce, and also in their duration of action affects the uses for which each drug is commonly selected. The table below indicates the main uses of each of the common antihistamines and gives an indication of the relative strengths of their anticholinergic and sedative effect and of their duration of action.

■ Strong

◩ Medium

□ Minimal

▲ Long (over 12 hours)

◭ Medium (6 – 12 hours)

△ Short (4 – 6 hours)

Drugs	Common uses					Action and effects		
	Allergic rhinitis	Skin allergy	Sedation	Premedication	Nausea/vomiting	Drowsiness	Anticholinergic action	Duration of action
Astemizole	●	●				□	□	▲
Azatadine	●	●				■	◩	▲
Brompheniramine	●	●				◩	□	△
Cetirizine	●	●				□	□	▲
Chlorpheniramine	●	●				◩	□	◭
Dimenhydrinate					●	◩	◩	△
Diphenhydramine			●		●	■	◩	△
Hydroxyzine		●	●			◩	□	△
Loratadine	●	●				□	□	▲
Promethazine	●	●	●	●		■	◩	△
Terfenadine	●	●				□	□	▲
Trimeprazine		●	●	●		■	◩	◭
Triprolidine	●	●				◩	□	◭

in various body tissues, particularly the small blood vessels in the skin, nose and eyes. This helps prevent the dilation of the vessels, thus reducing the redness and swelling. The anticholinergic action of these drugs also contributes to this effect.

Antihistamines pass from the blood into the brain where their blocking action on histamine activity produces general sedation, and depression of various brain functions, including the vomiting and coughing mechanisms.

How they affect you

Antihistamines frequently cause a degree of drowsiness and may adversely affect coordination, leading to clumsiness. Some of the newer drugs have little or no sedative effect (see table above).

Anticholinergic side effects including dry mouth, blurred vision, and difficulty passing urine are common. Most side effects diminish with continued use and can often be helped by an adjustment in dosage or a change to a different drug.

Risks and special precautions

Because of their sedative effects it may be advisable to avoid driving or operating potentially dangerous machinery whilst taking antihistamines. The sedative effects of alcohol, sleeping drugs, narcotic analgesics, and anti-anxiety drugs which have a depressant effect on the central nervous system can also be increased by antihistamines.

In high doses or in children some antihistamines can cause excitement. Abnormal heart rhythms have been seen after high doses with some antihistamines or when some drugs such as anti-fungals or antibiotics have been taken at the same time or in people with liver disease, electrolyte disturbances, or heart trace changes. People with these conditions, or with glaucoma or prostate trouble, should seek medical advice before taking antihistamines because their various drug actions may make such conditions worse.

ANTIHISTAMINES AND ALLERGIC RHINITIS

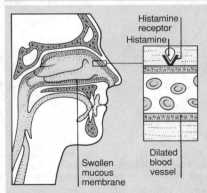

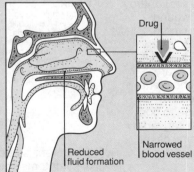

Before drug treatment
In allergic rhinitis, histamine released in response to an allergen acts on histamine receptors and produces dilation of the blood vessels supplying the lining of the nose, leading to swelling and increased mucus production. There is also irritation that causes sneezing, and often redness and watering of the eyes.

After drug treatment
Antihistamine drugs prevent histamine from attaching to histamine receptors, thereby preventing the body from responding to allergens. Over a period of time, the swelling, irritation, sneezing and watery discharge are reduced.

COMMON DRUGS

Acrivastine
Azatadine
Azelastine
Brompheniramine
Cetirizine
Chlorpheniramine *

Dimenhydrinate
Diphenhydramine *
Hydroxyzine
Loratadine *
Promethazine *
Terfenadine *
Trimeprazine
Triprolidine

* See Part 4

INFECTIONS AND INFESTATIONS

The human body provides a setting for the growth of many different types of micro-organism, including bacteria, viruses, fungi, yeasts, and protozoa. It may also become the host for animal parasites such as insects, worms, and flukes.

Micro-organisms (microbes) exist all around us and can be transmitted from person to person in many ways: direct contact, inhalation of infected air, and consumption of contaminated food or water (see Transmission of infection, facing page). Not all micro-organisms cause disease; many types of bacteria exist on the skin surface or in the bowel without causing ill-effects, while others cannot live either in or on the body.

Normally the immune system protects the body from infection. Invading microbes are killed before they can multiply in sufficient numbers to produce symptoms of disease. (See also Malignant and immune disease, p.152.)

What can go wrong

Infectious diseases occur when the body is invaded by microbes against which its natural defences are ineffective. This may be because the body has little or no natural immunity to the infection in question, or because the number of invading microbes is too great for the immune system to overcome. Serious infections can occur when the immune system does not function properly or when a disease weakens or destroys the immune system. That is what happens in AIDS (acquired immune deficiency syndrome).

Infections can be generalized (such as flu-like viruses and childhood infectious diseases) or they may affect one part of the body (as in wound infections). Some parts of the body are more susceptible to infection than others: respiratory tract infections are relatively common, whereas infections of the bones and muscles are rare.

Symptoms and consequences depend on the infecting organism and the parts of the body affected. Some are the result of damage to body tissues by the infection; others may be caused by *toxins* released by the microbes. In many cases, symptoms are the result of the activity of the body's immune system.

Most bacterial and viral infections cause fever. Bacterial infections may also cause inflammation and pus formation in the affected area.

Why drugs are used

Antibacterial and antibiotic drugs are frequently used to treat bacterial infections. They either kill the bacteria or prevent them from multiplying.

Types of infecting organism

Bacteria

A typical bacterium (right) consists of a single cell with a protective wall. Some bacteria are aerobic – that is, they require oxygen and therefore are more likely to infect surface areas such as the skin or respiratory tract. Others are anaerobic and multiply in oxygen-free surroundings such as the bowel or deep puncture wounds.

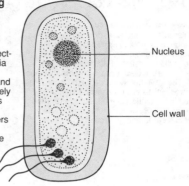

Nucleus

Cell wall

Cocci (spherical)
Streptococcus (above) can cause sore throats and pneumonia.

Bacilli (rod-shaped)
Mycobacterium tuberculosis (illustrated above) causes tuberculosis.

Spirochete (spiral-shaped) This group includes those bacteria that cause syphilis and infections of the gums.

Viruses

The smallest known infectious agents, viruses consist simply of a core of genetic material (RNA) surrounded by a protein coat. A virus can multiply only in a living cell, using the host tissue's own replicating material (DNA).

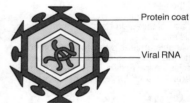

Protein coat

Viral RNA

Protozoa

These single-celled parasites are slightly bigger than bacteria. Many live in the human intestine and are harmless. However, some types cause malaria, sleeping sickness and dysentery.

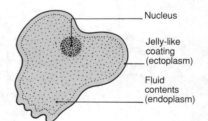

Nucleus

Jelly-like coating (ectoplasm)

Fluid contents (endoplasm)

Treatment is necessary because the appearance of symptoms shows that the immune system has failed to overcome the infection. Many antibiotics can be used for a broad range of applications while others have a specific effect against a particular type of bacteria.

Antiviral drugs are usually less effective than those used for bacterial infection. They are used in *topical* preparations for the skin and eyes and some can be given by mouth. Luckily, many viral

How bacteria affect the body

Bacteria can cause symptoms of disease in two principal ways: first by releasing toxins that harm body cells; secondly, by provoking immune system activity that leads to inflammation.

Effects of toxins

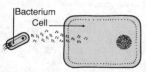

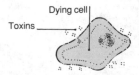

The invading bacterium gives off poisons (toxins) which attack the body cell.

The toxins emanating from the bacterium break through the cell structure and destroy the cell.

Immune system reactions

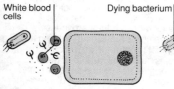

White blood cells of the immune system attack the bacterium directly by releasing inflammatory substances and, later, antibodies.

A side-effect of this attack of the immune system on the bacterium is damage and inflammation to the body's own cells.

Transmission of infection

Infecting organisms can enter the human body through a variety of routes including direct contact between an infected person and another, and eating or breathing in infected material.

Droplet infection
Coughing and sneezing spreads infected secretions.

Insects
Insect bites may transmit infection.

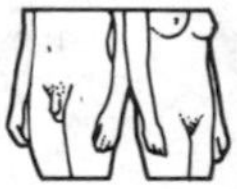

Physical contact
Everyday contact may spread infection.

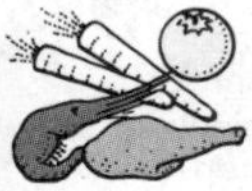

Sexual contact
Certain infections and infestations may be spread by genital contact.

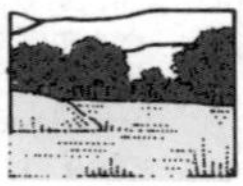

Food
Many infecting organisms can be ingested in food.

Water
Infections can be spread in polluted water.

infections do not require drug treatment; they get better in their own time.

Other groups of drugs used in the fight against infection include antiprotozoal drugs (including antimalarials) used for protozoal infections, antifungal drugs used for infection by fungi and yeasts, and anthelmintics that eradicate worm and fluke infestation. Infestation by skin parasites is usually treated with topical application of insecticides (see p.176).

INFESTATIONS

Invasion by parasites that live on the body (such as lice) or in the body (such as tapeworm) is known as infestation. Because the body does not have strong natural defences against infestation, antiparasitic treatment is necessary. Infestations are associated with tropical climates and poor standards of hygiene.

Tapeworms and roundworms live in the intestines and may cause diarrhoea and anaemia. Roundworm eggs may be passed in faeces. Larvae in infected soil penetrate the skin and grow into hookworms. Tapeworms may grow to 30 feet and are passed through undercooked meat containing larvae.

Flukes are of various types. The liver fluke (acquired from infected vegetation) lives in the bile duct in the liver and can lead to jaundice. Another, more serious type (which lives in small blood vessels supplying the bladder or intestines) causes schistosomiasis, and is acquired from swimming in infected water.

Lice and scabies spread by direct contact. Head, clothing and pubic lice need human blood to survive and die away from the body. The dried faeces of clothing lice spread typhus by being inhaled or infecting wounds. Scabies (caused by a tiny mite which does not carry disease) makes small, itchy tunnels in the skin.

Life cycle of a worm

Many worms have a complex life cycle. The life cycle of the worm that causes the group of diseases known as filariasis is illustrated below.

A mosquito ingests the filarial larvae and bites a human, thereby transmitting the larvae.

The mature larvae enter the lymph glands and vessels and reproduce there, often causing no ill effects.

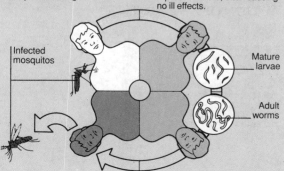

Infected mosquitos

Mature larvae

Adult worms

The infestation is spread by mosquitos biting infected people, and restarting the cycle.

The larvae grow into adult worms which release larvae into the bloodstream.

MAJOR DRUG GROUPS

Antibiotics
Antibacterials
Antituberculous drugs
Antiviral drugs
Vaccines and immunizations

Antiprotozoal drugs
Antimalarial drugs
Antifungal drugs
Anthelmintics

ANTIBIOTICS

One in every six prescriptions that British doctors write each year is for antibiotics. These drugs are usually both safe and effective in the treatment of bacterial disorders ranging from minor infections, like conjunctivitis, to life-threatening diseases, like pneumonia, meningitis, and septicaemia. They are similar in function to the antibacterial drugs (see p.131), but the early antibiotics all had a botanical origin in moulds and fungi, although most are now synthesized.

Since 1941 when the first antibiotic, penicillin, was introduced, many different classes have been developed. Each one has a different chemical composition and is effective against a particular range of bacteria. None is effective against virus infections (see Antiviral drugs, p.133).

Some antibiotics have a broad spectrum of activity against a wide variety of bacteria. Others are used in the treatment of infection by only a few specific organisms. For a description of each class of antibiotic, see the box on page 130.

Why they are used

We are surrounded by bacteria – in the air we breathe, in the mucous membranes of the mouth and nose, on the skin, in the intestines. But we are protected, most of the time, by our immunological defences. When these

ANTIBIOTIC RESISTANCE

The increasing use of antibiotics in the treatment of infection over the past half century has led to the development of resistance in certain types of bacteria to the effects of particular antibiotics. This resistance to the drug usually occurs when bacteria develop mechanisms of growth and reproduction that are not disrupted by the effects of the antibiotics. In other cases, bacteria produce *enzymes* that neutralize the antibiotics.

Antibiotic resistance may develop in an individual during prolonged treatment when a drug has failed to eliminate the infection

quickly, sometimes because the drug was not taken regularly. The resistant strain of bacteria is able to multiply, thereby prolonging the illness. It may also infect other people, causing the spread of resistant infection within a community.

Doctors try to prevent the development of antibiotic resistance by selecting the drug most likely to eliminate the bacteria present in each individual case as quickly and as thoroughly as possible. Failure to complete a course of antibiotics as prescribed by your doctor increases the likelihood that the infection will recur in a resistant form.

break down, or when bacteria already present migrate to a vulnerable new site, or when harmful bacteria not usually present invade the body, infectious disease sets in.

The bacteria multiply rapidly, destroying tissue, releasing toxins and, in some cases, threatening to spread via the bloodstream to such vital organs as the heart, brain, lungs and kidneys. The symptoms of infectious disease, although they almost always include fever, vary widely, depending on the site of the infection and the type of bacteria.

Confronted with a sick person and suspecting a bacterial infection, the doctor ideally should identify the organism causing the disease before prescribing any drug. But tests to

analyse the blood, sputum, urine, stool or pus usually take 24 hours or more. In the meantime, especially if the person is in discomfort or pain, the doctor usually makes a preliminary drug choice, something of an educated guess as to the causative organism. In starting this "empirical" treatment, as it is called, the doctor is guided by the site of the infection, the nature and severity of the symptoms, the likely source of infection and the degree of prevalence of any similar illnesses in the community at that time.

In such circumstances, pending laboratory identification of the trouble-making bacteria, the doctor may initially prescribe a broad-spectrum antibiotic, that is, one effective against a wide variety of bacteria. As soon as tests provide more exact information, the doctor may then switch you to an antibiotic that is the recommended treatment for the identified bacteria. Sometimes more than one antibiotic is prescribed to be sure of eliminating all strains of bacteria.

In most cases, antibiotics can be given by mouth. However, in serious infections when high blood levels of the drug are needed rapidly, or when a type of antibiotic is needed that cannot be given by mouth, the drug may be given by injection. Antibiotics are also included in *topical* preparations for localized skin, eye, and ear infections (see also Anti-infective skin preparations, p.175, and Drugs for ear disorders, p.171).

How they work

Depending on the type of drug and the dosage, antibiotics are either bactericidal, killing organisms directly, or bacteriostatic, halting the multiplication of bacteria, and enabling the body's natural defences to overcome the remaining infection.

There are two main mechanisms of action: penicillins and cephalosporins destroy bacteria by preventing them from making normal cell walls; most

ACTION OF ANTIBIOTICS

Penicillins and cephalosporins
Drugs from these groups are bactericidal, that is, they kill bacteria. They interfere with the chemicals that bacteria need to form normal cell walls (right). As the cell swells, its outer lining disintegrates and the bacterium dies (far right).

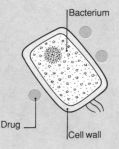

Drug

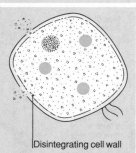

Bacterium

Cell wall

Disintegrating cell wall

Other antibiotics
These alter chemical activity inside the bacteria, thereby preventing the production of proteins that the bacteria need in order to multiply and survive (right). This may have a lethal effect in itself, or it may prevent reproduction (bacteriostatic action) (far right).

Drug

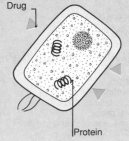

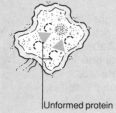

Protein

Unformed protein

THE USES OF ANTIBIOTICS

The table below shows which common drugs in each class of antibiotic are used for the treatment of infections in different parts of the body. For the purposes of comparison, the table also includes at the bottom some of the antibacterial drugs discussed on p.131.

This is not intended to be used as a guide to prescribing, but broadly to indicate the range of applications of each drug.

Some drugs have a wide range of theoretical applications, but this table concentrates on the most common uses of each drug. Selection of

the most suitable antibiotic for any individual is determined by the doctor's assessment of the condition, the medical history of the person concerned, and also by the results of laboratory findings (see Why they are used, facing page).

Antibiotic / Site of infection	Ear, nose, throat, and mouth	Respiratory tract	Skin and soft tissue	Gastrointestinal tract	Eye	Kidney and urinary tract	Brain and nervous system	Heart	Bones and joints	Genital tract
Penicillins										
Amoxycillin	●	●	●			●			●	●
Ampicillin	●	●	●			●	●		●	●
Benzylpenicillin	●	●	●				●	●	●	●
Co-amoxiclav	●	●	●			●			●	
Flucloxacillin			●						●	
Phenoxymethylpenicillin	●	●	●							
Cephalosporins										
Cefaclor	●					●				
Cefoxitin		●	●			●				●
Cephalexin		●	●			●				
Aminoglycosides										
Gentamicin		●	●	●	●	●	●	●	●	
Neomycin		●	●	●						
Netilmicin		●	●	●		●	●		●	
Streptomycin		●						●		
Tobramycin		●	●	●					●	
Tetracyclines										
Doxycycline	●	●				●				●
Oxytetracycline	●	●								
Tetracycline	●	●			●	●				●
Sulphonamides										
Sulphafurazole	●	●				●				
Sulphamethoxazole						●				
Lincosamides										
Clindamycin		●	●	●					●	
Lincomycin		●	●						●	
Other drugs										
Azithromycin	●	●	●							●
Chloramphenicol	●			●	●		●			
Ciprofloxacin		●		●		●				
Colistin		●				●				
Co-trimoxazole	●	●		●		●				
Dapsone			●							
Erythromycin	●	●	●		●				●	●
Fusidic acid			●						●	
Metronidazole	●		●	●			●	●	●	●
Nalidixic acid						●				
Nitrofurantoin						●				
Trimethoprim	●					●				
Vancomycin				●				●		

ANTIBIOTICS continued

other antibiotics act inside the bacteria, interfering with the chemical activities essential to their life cycle.

How they affect you

Antibiotics stop most common types of infection within days. Because they do not relieve symptoms directly, your doctor may advise additional medication such as analgesics (see p. 80) to relieve pain and fever until the antibiotics start to take effect.

It is important to complete the course of medication as prescribed by your doctor, even if all symptoms seem to have disappeared. Failure to do this can lead to a resurgence of the infection in an antibiotic-resistant form (see Antibiotic resistance, p.128).

Most antibiotics used in the home do not cause side effects if taken in the recommended dosage. But digestive disturbances such as nausea and diarrhoea are among the more common reactions. Some people may be sensitive to particular types of antibiotics, and this can lead to serious adverse reactions.

Risks and special precautions

Most antibiotics prescribed for short periods outside a hospital setting are safe for the majority of people. The most common risk, particularly with penicillins and cephalosporins, is a severe allergic reaction to the drug that can cause rashes and sometimes swelling of the face and throat. If this happens the drug should be stopped and immediate medical advice sought. A previous allergic reaction to an antibiotic may mean that all other drugs in that class and related classes should be avoided. It is therefore important to inform your doctor if you have previously suffered an adverse reaction to an antibiotic treatment (except minor bowel disturbances).

Another risk of antibiotic treatment, especially if it is prolonged, is that the balance of micro-organisms normally inhabiting the body may be disturbed. In particular, antibiotics may destroy bacteria that limit the growth of Candida, a yeast often present in the body in small amounts. This can lead to overgrowth of Candida (also known as thrush) in the mouth, vagina, or bowel. In such cases an antifungal drug (p.138) may need to be prescribed.

A rarer, but more serious consequence of disruption of normal bacterial activity in the body, is a disorder called pseudomembranous colitis, in which bacteria that are resistant to the antibiotic multiply in the bowel, causing violent, bloody diarrhoea. Although this potentially fatal disorder can occur with any antibiotic, it is most common with the lincosamides.

Most antibiotics taken by mouth or injection are changed in the liver and eliminated from the body through the kidneys. Therefore, like many drugs, they should be prescribed with caution for those people with reduced kidney or liver function. Less common risks associated with particular types of antibiotics are described under Classes of antibiotics, below.

COMMON DRUGS

Penicillins
Amoxycillin *
Ampicillin
Aztreonam
Benzylpenicillin
Cloxacillin
Co-amoxiclav
Co-fluampicil
Imipenem
Phenoxy-
methylpenicillin *
Sultamicillin

Cephalosporins
Cefaclor *
Cefamandole
Cefixime
Cefodizime
Cefoxitin
Cefpodoxime
Cefsulodin
Cephalexin *
Cephazolin

Aminoglycocides
Gentamicin *
Neomycin
Netilmicin
Streptomycin
Tobramycin

Tetracyclines
Doxycycline *
Oxytetracycline
Tetracycline *

Macrolides
Azithromycin
Clarithromycin
Erythromycin *

Lincosamides
Clindamycin
Lincomycin

Other drugs
Chloramphenicol *
Ciprofloxacin
Norfloxacin
Ofloxacin
Spectinomycin
Teicoplanin

* See Part 4

CLASSES OF ANTIBIOTICS

Penicillins The first antibiotic drugs to be developed, penicillins are still widely used to treat many common infections. Some penicillins are not effective when they are taken by mouth and therefore have to be given by injection in hospital. Unfortunately, certain strains of bacteria are resistant to penicillin treatment, and other drugs may have to be substituted. Penicillins often cause allergic reactions.

Cephalosporins These are broad spectrum antibiotics similar to the penicillins. They are often used when penicillin treatment has proved ineffective. Some cephalosporins can be given by mouth, but others are only given by injection. About 5% of people who are allergic to penicillins are also potentially allergic to cephalosporins. Another serious, although rare, adverse effect of a few cephalosporins is their occasional interference with normal blood clotting and consequent bleeding, especially in the elderly.

Macrolides Erythromycin is the only common drug in this group. It is a broad spectrum antibiotic that is often prescribed as an alternative to penicillins or cephalo-sporin antibiotics. Erythromycin is also effective for some diseases such as Legionnaires' disease (a rare type of pneumonia) that cannot be treated with other antibiotics. The main risk with erythromycin is that it can occasionally impair liver function.

Tetracyclines These have a broader spectrum of activity than any other class of antibiotic. However, increasing bacterial resistance to their effects (see antibiotic resistance, p.128) has limited their use, although they remain widely prescribed. In addition to the treatment of infections, tetracyclines are also used in the long-term treatment of acne, although this application is probably not related to their antibacterial action. A major drawback to the use of tetracycline antibiotics in young children and in pregnant women is that they can discolour developing teeth.

With the exception of doxycycline, these drugs are poorly absorbed through the intestines, and when given by mouth they have to be administered in high doses in order to reach effective levels in the blood. Such high doses increase the likelihood of diarrhoea as a side effect. The absorption of tetracyclines can be further reduced by interaction with calcium and other minerals. Drugs from this group should not therefore be taken with iron tablets or milk products. Tetracyclines deteriorate and may become poisonous with time. Leftover tablets or capsules should therefore always be discarded.

Aminoglycosides These potent drugs are effective against a broad range of bacteria, but they are not as widely used as some other antibiotics because they have to be given by injection, and they also have potentially serious side effects. Their use is therefore limited to hospital treatment of serious infections. They are often given in conjunction with other antibiotics.

Possible adverse effects include damage to the nerves in the ear, damage to the kidneys and severe skin rashes.

Lincosamides These drugs are not commonly used because they are more likely to cause serious disruption of bacterial activity in the bowel than other antibiotics. They are mainly reserved for the treatment of bone, joint and abdominal infections that do not respond well to safer antibiotics.

ANTIBACTERIALS

This broad classification of drugs comprises agents that are similar to the antibiotics (p.128) in function but dissimilar in origin. The original antibiotics were derived from moulds and fungi, whereas antibacterials were developed from chemicals. The early antibacterials (the so-called sulpha drugs) were derived from a deep red industrial dye called prontosil that is metabolized by the body into sulphanilamide, the active antibacterial ingredient. The sulpha drugs, introduced in the 1930s, quickly proved to be effective against many bacterial infections.

Why they are used

Sulphonamides, the largest group of drugs within the antibacterial group, are today's successors to the original sulpha drugs. Because of the appearance of strains of bacteria resistant to their actions (see Antibiotic resistance, p.128), sulphonamides have in many cases been superseded by antibiotics that are more effective and safe. Yet there are many circumstances in which doctors believe the sulphonamide antibacterials to be more effective than antibiotics.

Because they reach high concentrations in the urine, sulphonamides are particularly useful in treating many infections of the urinary tract. They are frequently used for chlamydia pneumonia and for some middle ear infections; sulphacetamide is often included in *topical* preparations for skin, eye and outer-ear infections. Sulphamethoxazole, in combination with trimethoprim, often in a single large dose, is used for bladder infections, certain types of bronchitis and some gastrointestinal infections. Not all

ACTION OF SULPHONAMIDES

Before drug treatment
Folic acid, a chemical that is necessary for growth of bacteria, is produced within bacterial cells by the action of an *enzyme* on a chemical called para-aminobenzoic acid.

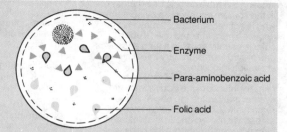

- Bacterium
- Enzyme
- Para-aminobenzoic acid
- Folic acid

After drug treatment
Sulphonamides interfere with the release of the enzyme. This prevents folic acid from being formed. The bacterium is thus unable to function properly and dies.

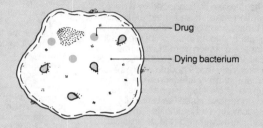

- Drug
- Dying bacterium

antibacterials are sulphonamides, of course. The antibacterials used for tuberculosis are discussed on p.128. Other antibacterials are used against protozoal infections (see Antiprotozoal drugs, p.136. Others, sometimes classified as antimicrobials, include metronidazole, prescribed for a variety of genital infections, and some serious infections in the abdomen, pelvic region, the heart and central nervous system. Nalidixic acid and nitrofurantoin are effective as antiseptics for the urinary tract, and are used to cure or prevent recurrent infections.

How they work

Most antibacterials rid the body of bacteria by preventing the growth and multiplication of the organisms (see also Action of antibiotics, p.128, and Action of sulphonamides, above).

How they affect you

Antibacterials usually take several days to eliminate bacteria. During this time your doctor may recommend additional medication to alleviate pain and fever. Sulphonamides can cause loss of appetite, rash, nausea and drowsiness.

Risks and special precautions

Like antibiotics, most antibacterials can cause allergic reactions in susceptible people. Possible symptoms that should always be brought to your doctor's attention include rashes and fever. If such a reaction occurs, a change to another drug is likely to be necessary.

Treatment with sulphonamides carries a number of serious, but rare risks. Some drugs in this group can cause crystals to form in the kidneys, a risk that can be reduced by drinking adequate amounts of fluid during prolonged treatment. Because sulphonamides may also occasionally damage the liver, they are not usually prescribed for people with impaired liver function. There is also a slight risk of damage to bone marrow, lowering the production of white blood cells and increasing the chances of infection. Doctors therefore try to avoid prescribing sulphonamides for prolonged periods. Liver function and blood composition are often monitored during unavoidable long-term treatment.

COMMON DRUGS

Sulphonamides
Co-trimoxazole *
Sulphacetamide

Urinary antiseptics
Nalidixic acid *
Nitrofurantoin *

Other drugs
Dapsone *
Metronidazole *
Trimethoprim *

* See Part 4

DRUG TREATMENT FOR LEPROSY

Hansen's disease, formerly known as leprosy, is a bacterial infection caused by an organism called Mycobacterium leprae. It is rare in the United Kingdom, but relatively common in parts of Africa, Asia and Latin America.

The disease progresses slowly, first affecting the peripheral nerves, and causing loss of sensation in the hands and feet. This leads to frequent unnoticed injuries, and consequent scarring. Later, the nerves of the face may also be affected.

Treatment with dapsone, an antibacterial drug related to the sulphonamides, rapidly halts infectivity and eventually eradicates the disease (courses of treatment usually last about two years). However, because resistance to this drug is increasing, other drugs such as the antituberculous drugs rifampicin and ethionamide may also be prescribed.

ANTITUBERCULOUS DRUGS

Tuberculosis is a contagious bacterial disease acquired, often in childhood, by inhaling the tuberculosis bacilli present in the sputum coughed up by someone who is actively infected. It may also be acquired from infected milk. Tuberculosis usually starts in a lung and takes one of two forms: primary infection or re-activation infection.

In 90 – 95 per cent of those with primary infection, the body's immune system inactivates the bacilli. They remain alive, however, and they may spread via the lymphatic system and the bloodstream throughout the body (see Sites of infection below).

The disease is diagnosed by a doctor detecting scarring and inflammation of the lungs. Another indication of infection is a reaction to an injection of tuberculin, a sterile extraction from the tuberculosis bacilli. When this is injected into or under the skin, only those people who have the dormant, primary infection show a reaction. Preventative measures are then undertaken (see the box, right).

Reactivation tuberculosis – the gradual emergence of the destructive, progressive and sometimes fatal disease in adults – occurs in 5 – 10 per cent of those with a primary infection. The cause is not known. A clinically identical form of the disease, called reinfection tuberculosis, occurs when someone with the dormant, primary form of the disease is reinfected. The

SITES OF INFECTION

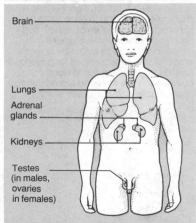

Brain

Lungs

Adrenal glands

Kidneys

Testes (in males, ovaries in females)

Tuberculosis usually affects only part of the lung at first. However, later outbreaks generally spread to both lungs and may also affect the kidneys, leading to pyelo-nephritis, the adrenal glands, causing Addison's disease, and the membranes surrounding the brain, which may lead to meningitis. The testes (in men) and the ovaries (in women) may also be affected.

symptoms of reactivation (or reinfection) tuberculosis can be deceiving, for the disease may start in any part of the body originally seeded with bacilli. It is most often first seen in the upper lobes of the lung, and is frequently diagnosed after a chest X-ray. The early symptoms appear gradually and often include generally poor health, loss of appetite and weight, night sweats, recurrent fever and cough.

Why they are used

Left untreated, tuberculosis continues to destroy tissue, spreading, and eventually causing death. It remained one of the most common causes of death in the United Kingdom until the 1940s.

Antituberculous drugs can success-fully eradicate the infection from the body but cannot restore destroyed tissue or scarring that has occurred as result of the disease.

A person diagnosed as having tuberculosis is likely to be treated with three or four antituberculous drugs. This helps overcome the danger that the bacteria may develop resistance to one of the drugs (see Antibiotic resistance, p.128).

Initially, rifampicin, isoniazid, and pyrazinamide are likely to be prescribed, but the choice of drug is determined by the areas of the body affected, and by the results of sensitivity tests. These tests may take up to two months to confirm whether the infection is sensitive or resistant to the drugs initially used. If it is found to be resistant, or the initial treatment fails, or if serious adverse effects are experi-enced, the treatment may be changed. After two months, if all is well, treatment is continued with only two drugs for a further four months.

Short, six-month courses are some-times given for otherwise healthy people suffering from uncomplicated disease, but courses of treatment for up to two years are required for those with reduced resistance to infection, or diabetes or silicosis. Patients who are HIV positive are recommended to remain on one drug, which is usually isoniazid, for life to prevent relapse.

How they work

Antituberculous drugs act in the same way as antibiotics, either by directly killing the bacteria or by preventing them from multiplying (see Action of antibiotics, p.128).

How they affect you

Although the drugs start to combat the disease within days, benefits of drug treatment are not likely to be noticeable for a few weeks. As the infection is gradually eradicated, the body's healing processes repair the damage caused by the disease. Symptoms such as fever

TUBERCULOSIS PREVENTION

A vaccine prepared from an artificially weakened strain of cattle tuberculosis bacteria can provide immunity from tuberculosis by provoking the develop-ment of natural resistance to the disease (see Vaccines and immunization, p.134). The vaccine known as BCG (Bacille Calmette-Guérin) is usually given to children between the ages of 10 and 14 years who are shown to have no natural immunity when given a skin test. BCG vaccination is sometimes given to new-born babies if, for example, someone in the family has tuberculosis.

How it is done
The vaccine is usually injected into the upper arm. A small pustule appears six to twelve weeks later.

and coughing gradually subside, and weight is gained as appetite and general health improve.

Risks and special precautions

Some antituberculous drugs may cause adverse effects (nausea, vomiting and abdominal pain), and they occasionally lead to serious allergic reactions. These are most likely to occur during the second month of treatment and may parallel the symptoms of the disease itself – fever and general ill-health, for instance. When this happens, another drug is substituted.

Some drugs may affect liver function (rifampicin and isoniazid); others may adversely affect the nerves (isoniazid). Ethambutol can cause changes in colour vision, and for this reason is not generally prescribed for young children because they are unable to report the warning symptoms. Isoniazid can cause pyridoxine deficiency, and this vitamin is usually given with the drug.

Because the occurrence of adverse effects is usually related to levels of the drug in the bloodstream, dosage is carefully monitored. Special care is needed for children, the elderly and those with reduced kidney function.

COMMON DRUGS

Ethambutol *
Isoniazid *
Pyrazinamide
Rifampicin *
Streptomycin

* See Part 4

ANTIVIRAL DRUGS

Viruses are simpler and smaller organisms than bacteria and are less able to sustain themselves. They can survive and multiply only by penetrating body cells (see box, right). Because viruses perform few functions independently, medicines that disrupt or halt their life cycle without harming human cells have been difficult to develop.

There are many different types of virus, and viral infections cause illnesses with various symptoms and degrees of severity. Common viral illnesses include the cold, influenza and flu-like illnesses, and the usual childhood diseases such as mumps and chickenpox. Throat infections, acute bronchitis, pneumonia, gastroenteritis and meningitis are often, but not always, caused by a virus.

Fortunately, the body's natural defences are usually strong enough to overcome infections such as these, with drugs given to ease pain and lower fever. However, the more serious viral diseases, such as pneumonia and meningitis, require close medical supervision.

Another difficulty with viral infections is the speed with which the virus multiplies. By the time symptoms appear, the viruses are so numerous that antiviral drugs have little effect. Antiviral agents must be given early in the course of an infection or used prophylactically, i.e. as a preventive. Some viral infections can be prevented by vaccination (see p.134).

In recent years, a few drugs have been introduced that have a partial effect against certain specific viruses.

Why they are used
The main area where antiviral drugs are helpful is in the treatment of various conditions caused by the herpes virus: cold sores, encephalitis, genital herpes, chickenpox and shingles.

Some drugs are applied *topically* to treat outbreaks of cold sores, herpes eye infections and genital herpes. They can reduce the severity and duration of an outbreak, but they do not eliminate the infection permanently. Other antiviral drugs are given by mouth or injection under exceptional circumstances to prevent chickenpox or severe, recurrent attacks of the herpes virus infections in those who are weakened by other conditions.

Antiviral agents are also given to prevent influenza A, as is a drug for parkinsonism, amantadine, which has antiviral properties.

AIDS (acquired immune deficiency syndrome) is a virus infection that reduces the body's resistance to infection by other viruses, bacteria and protozoa, as well as some types of

ACTION OF ANTIVIRAL DRUGS

In order to reproduce, a virus requires a living cell. The invaded cell eventually dies and the new viruses are released, spreading and infecting other cells. Most antiviral drugs act to prevent the virus from using the cell's genetic material, DNA, to multiply. Unable to divide, the virus therefore dies and the spread of infection is halted.

Before drug

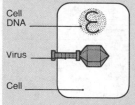

Cell
DNA

Virus

Cell

Virus enters body cell.

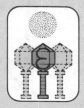

Virus uses cell DNA in order to reproduce.

Cell dies and new viruses are released.

After drug

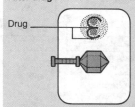

Drug

Virus enters cell that has absorbed antiviral drug.

Cell DNA is altered by drug action and virus cannot use it.

Virus dies and spread of infection is halted.

cancer. Some antiviral drugs may be effective in limiting the progress of this disease. Drug treatment for AIDS is discussed more fully on p.157.

How they work
Some antiviral drugs such as idoxuridine act by altering the cell's genetic material (a protein called DNA) so that the virus cannot use it to multiply. Other drugs prevent viruses from multiplying by blocking enzyme activity within the host cell. Halting multiplication of the virus prevents its spread to uninfected cells and improves symptoms rapidly, but in the case of herpes infections, does not completely eradicate the virus from the body. Infection may therefore flare up again on another occasion.

Amantadine has a different action: it prevents the influenza virus from entering the cells. It is therefore most effective when given before the infection has spread widely.

How they affect you
Topical antiviral drugs usually start to act at once. Providing that the treatment is applied early enough, an outbreak of herpes can be cut short. Symptoms

usually clear up within two to four days. Antiviral ointments may cause irritation and redness. Antiviral drugs given by mouth or injection can occasionally cause nausea and dizziness.

Risks and special precautions
Because some of these drugs may affect the kidneys adversely, they are prescribed with caution for people with reduced kidney function. Some antiviral drugs can adversely affect the activity of normal body cells, particularly those in the bone marrow. Idoxuridine is, for this reason, available only for topical application.

COMMON DRUGS

Acyclovir ✳
Amantadine ✳
Foscarnet
Ganciclovir
Idoxuridine ✳
Inosine pranobex

Interferon ✳
Vidarabine
Zidovudine ✳

✳ See Part 4

VACCINES AND IMMUNIZATION

Many infectious diseases, including most of the common viral infections, occur only once during a person's lifetime. The reason for this is that the antibodies produced in response to the disease remain afterwards, prepared to repel any future invasion as soon as the first infectious germs appear. The duration of such natural immunity varies, but it can last a lifetime.

Protection against many infections can now be provided artificially by the use of vaccines derived from altered forms of the infecting organism. These vaccines stimulate the immune system in the same way as a genuine infection, and provide lasting, active immunity. Because each type of microbe stimulates the production of a specific type of antibody, a different vaccine must be given for each disease.

Another type of immunization, called passive immunization, relies on the introduction of antibodies from someone who has recovered from a particular infectious disease. The transfer is made by means of serum (a part of the blood) containing antibodies (see Immune globulins, below).

Why they are used
Some infectious diseases cannot be treated effectively or are potentially so serious that prevention is the best treatment. The aim of routine immunization is not only to protect the individual, but gradually to eradicate the disease completely, as has been achieved with smallpox. Most children between the ages of 3 months and 15 years are routinely vaccinated against the common childhood infectious diseases. Newborn babies receive antibodies for many diseases from their mother, but this protection only lasts for about three months. In addition, travellers to many underdeveloped countries, especially those in the tropics, are often urged to be vaccinated against the diseases common in those regions.

ACTIVE AND PASSIVE IMMUNIZATION

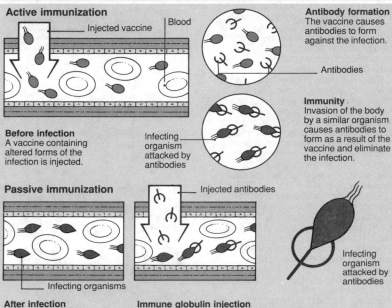

Active immunization
Injected vaccine | Blood

Before infection
A vaccine containing altered forms of the infection is injected.

Antibody formation
The vaccine causes antibodies to form against the infection.

Antibodies

Immunity
Invasion of the body by a similar organism causes antibodies to form as a result of the vaccine and eliminate the infection.

Infecting organism attacked by antibodies

Passive immunization
Injected antibodies

Infecting organisms

After infection
Passive immunization is needed when the infection has entered the blood.

Immune globulin injection
A serum containing antibodies (immune globulin) extracted from donated blood is injected. This helps the body to fight the infection.

Infecting organism attacked by antibodies

Effective lifelong immunization can sometimes be achieved by a single dose of the vaccine. However, in many cases reinforcing doses, commonly called booster shots, are needed later in order to maintain reliable immunity.

Vaccines do not provide immediate protection against infection, and it may be up to four weeks before full immunity develops. When immediate protection from a disease is needed, for example, following exposure to infection, it may be necessary to establish passive immunity with immune globulins.

How they work
Vaccines provoke the immune system into creating antibodies that help the body to resist specific infectious diseases. Many vaccines are made from artificially weakened forms of the disease-causing germ (live vaccine). But these weak germs are nevertheless effective in stimulating sufficient growth of antibodies. Other vaccines rely on inactive (or killed) disease-causing germs, or inactive derivatives. But their effect on the immune system remains the same. Effective antibodies are created; active immunity is established.

How they affect you
The degree of protection varies among different vaccines. Some provide reliable lifelong immunity, others may not give full protection against a disease and the effects may last for as little as six months. Any vaccine may cause side effects, but when these occur they are usually mild and soon disappear. The most common reactions are a red, slightly raised tender area at the site of injection, and a slight fever or a flu-like illness lasting for one or two days.

Risks and special precautions
Serious reactions with vaccines are rare, and for most children the risk is far

IMMUNE GLOBULINS

Antibodies, which can result from snake and insect venom as well as infectious disease, permeate the serum of the blood (the part remaining after the red cells and clotting agents are removed). The concentrated serum of people who have survived diseases or poisonous bites is called immune globulin, and given by injection, creates passive immunity. Immune globulin from blood donated by a wide cross-section of donors is likely to contain antibodies to most common diseases. Specific immune globulins against rare diseases or toxins are derived from the blood of selected donors likely to have high levels of antibodies to that disease. These are called hyperimmune

globulins. Some immune globulins are extracted from horse blood.

Because immune globulins do not stimulate the body to produce its own antibodies, their effect is not long-lasting and diminishes progressively over three or four weeks. Continued protection requires repeated injections.

Adverse effects from immune globulins are uncommon. Some people are sensitive to horse globulins, and about a week after the injection may experience a reaction known as serum sickness, with fever, rash, joint swelling and pain. This usually ends in a few days, but should be reported to your doctor before any further immunization.

outweighed by the value of the protection given. Children who have had seizures in the past or who have a family history of epilepsy may be advised against vaccinations for whooping cough or measles. Children who have an infectious illness will not be given any routine vaccination until they have recovered.

Live vaccines should not be given during pregnancy since they can affect the developing baby, nor should they be given to people whose immune systems are weakened by disease or drug treatment. It is also advisable for those taking corticosteroid drugs (p.141) to delay their vaccination until the end of drug treatment.

COMMON VACCINATIONS

Disease	Approximate age given	How taken	General information
Diphtheria	2 months, 3 months, 4 months, 3 – 5 years.	Injection	Usually given routinely in infancy as a combined injection with tetanus and whooping cough vaccines. Immunity may diminish in later life.
Tetanus	2 months, 3 months, 4 months, 3 – 5 years. Boosters on leaving school and every 5 –10 years thereafter.	Injection	Given routinely in infancy, this gives protection for five to 10 years. Injury likely to result in tetanus infection in a person who has not been vaccinated within the last five years is usually treated immediately with immune globulin (see facing page), usually with a course of booster injections of the active vaccine.
Whooping cough (pertussis)	2 months, 3 months, 4 months.	Injection	The pertussis vaccine may not give complete protection against whooping cough, but it reduces the severity of symptoms that may develop following infection. Pertussis vaccine may cause mild fever, irritability, and, rarely, fits. Children known to be at special risk from fits are not usually given this vaccine.
Polio	2 months, 3 months, 4 months, 3 – 5 years. Booster 15 –19 years.	By mouth	Many doctors recommend a booster every ten years, especially for people likely to be travelling to countries where polio is still prevalent.
Rubella (German measles)	12 – 18 months, 10 – 14 years (girls).	Injection	This is given as a combined injection with measles and mumps vaccine in infancy (MMR). Immunization against rubella is important because it can damage the developing baby if it affects a woman in early pregnancy. Adult women who have received the vaccine should avoid becoming pregnant for at least three months following the injection.
Measles	12 – 18 months.	Injection	Given together with mumps and rubella vaccine in infancy (MMR). It may cause a brief fever or rash, and there is a possibility of fits. Measles vaccine does not always provide complete protection against the disease, but it does reduce the severity of illness.
Mumps	12 – 18 months.	Injection	Given in infancy together with measles and rubella vaccines (MMR).
Tuberculosis (BCG)	13 years.	Injection	See p.132.
Influenza	People of any age who are at risk.	Injection	It is impossible to confer long-term immunity against all forms of this disease, but protection against some types may be given to people especially at risk from complications. Protection develops within four weeks, and side effects are rare. Annual booster vaccinations may be needed.
Hib	2 months, 3 months, 4 months.	Injection	Recommended for newborns to prevent serious disease up to the age of 4 years.
Hepatitis B	3 inoculations 1 and 5 months apart.	Injection	Efficacy is checked by a blood test. Recommended for 'at risk' groups, such as health-care professionals, travellers to tropical countries, and intravenous drug users.

ANTIPROTOZOAL DRUGS

Protozoa are single-celled organisms that are often present in soil. They may be transmitted to or between humans through contaminated food or water, sexual contact, or bites from insects. There are many types of protozoal infection, each causing a different disease, depending on the organism involved. Trichomoniasis, giardiasis and pneumocystis pneumonia are probably the most common protozoal infections seen in the United Kingdom. The rarer infections are usually contracted as a result of exposure to infection in another part of the world.

Many types of protozoa infect the bowel, causing diarrhoea and generalized symptoms of ill-health. Others may infect the genital tract or skin. Some may penetrate vital organs such as the lungs, brain and liver. Prompt diagnosis and treatment are important in order to limit the spread of the infection within the body and, in some cases, to others. In many cases, increased attention to hygiene is an important factor in controlling the spread of the disease.

A variety of drugs are used in the treatment of these diseases. Some, such as metronidazole and tetracycline are also commonly used for their antibacterial action. Others, such as pentamidine are rarely used except in specific protozoal infections.

How they affect you

Protozoa are often difficult to eradicate from within the body. Drug treatment may therefore need to be continued for months in order to eliminate the infecting organisms completely, and thus prevent recurrence of the disease. In addition, unpleasant side effects such as nausea, diarrhoea and abdominal cramps are often unavoidable because of the limited choice of drugs and the need to maintain dosage levels that will effectively cure the disease. For detailed information on the risks and adverse effects of individual anti-protozoal drugs, consult the appropriate drug profile in Part 4.

The table below describes the principal protozoal infections and the drugs used in their treatment. Malaria, probably the most common protozoal disease world-wide, is discussed on the facing page.

SUMMARY OF PROTOZOAL DISEASES

Disease	Protozoa	Description	Drugs
Amoebiasis (amoebic dysentery)	Entamoeba histolytica	Infection of the bowel by an organism called Entamoeba histolytica. Usually transmitted in contaminated food or water. Major symptom is violent, sometimes bloody diarrhoea.	Diloxanide Metronidazole Chloroquine
Balantidiasis	Balantidium coli	Infection of the bowel by Balantidium coli, usually transmitted through contact with infected pigs. Possible symptoms include diarrhoea and abdominal pain.	Tetracycline
Dientamoebiasis	Dientamoeba fragilis	A form of amoebic dysentery caused by Dientamoeba fragilis, possibly transmitted in the threadworm egg. Causes diarrhoea and flu-like symptoms.	Tetracycline
Giardiasis (lambliasis)	Giardia lambia	Infection of the bowel by Giardia lambia, usually transmitted in contaminated food or water, but may also be spread by some types of sexual contact. Major symptoms are general ill-health, diarrhoea, flatulence and abdominal pain.	Metronidazole Mepacrine Tinidazole
Leishmaniasis	Leishmania	A mainly tropical and subtropical disease caused by organisms (Leishmania) spread by sandflies. It affects the mucous membranes of the mouth, nose and throat, and may in its severe form invade organs such as the liver.	Sodium stibogluconate
Pneumocystis pneumonia	Pneumocystis carinii	Potentially fatal lung infection caused by Pneumocystis carinii. It usually affects only those with reduced resistance to infection, such as AIDS victims. Symptoms include cough, breathlessness, fever and chest pain.	Co-trimoxazole Pentamidine
Toxoplasmosis	Toxoplasmosis gondii	Infection by Toxoplasma gondii usually spread via contact with cat faeces or by eating undercooked meat. It may also be transmitted from mother to baby during pregnancy. May be symptomless, but sometimes causes generalized ill-health, low fever, and may affect vision.	Pyrimethamine/ sulphadiazine
Trichomoniasis	Trichomonas vaginalis	Infection by Trichomonas vaginalis most commonly affects the vagina, causing irritation and an offensive discharge. In men infection may occur in the urethra. The disease is usually sexually transmitted.	Metronidazole Nimorazole
Trypanosomiasis	Trypanosoma	African trypanosomiasis (sleeping sickness) is spread by the tsetse fly and causes fever, swollen glands and drowsiness. South American trypanosomiasis (Chagas disease) is spread by cone-nosed bugs. It causes inflammation, enlargement of internal organs and infection of the brain.	Pentamidine (sleeping sickness) Primaquine (Chagas disease)

ANTIMALARIAL DRUGS

Malaria is one of the main killing diseases in the tropics (see map below). It is only likely to affect people who live in or travel to such places.

The disease is caused by single-cell protozoa whose life cycle is far from simple. A parasite, the malaria plasmodium, lives in and depends on the female anopheles mosquito during one part of its life. It lives in and depends on human beings during other parts of its life cycle.

Transferred to man in the saliva of the mosquito as she penetrates ("bites") the skin, the malaria parasite enters the bloodstream and settles in the liver. At that time no symptoms appear, but the malaria parasite multiplies.

Following its stay in the liver, the parasite enters another phase of its life cycle, circulating in the bloodstream, penetrating and destroying red blood cells, and reproducing again. If the plasmodia then transfer back to a female anopheles mosquito via another "bite", they breed once more, and are again ready to start a human infection.

It is after the emergence from the liver, when the plasmodia are entering and rupturing the red blood cells, that malaria appears in its symptomatic form, with high fever and profuse sweating, alternating with equally agonizing episodes of shivering and chills. One strain of malaria (there are four) produces a single severe attack, which can be fatal. The others cause recurrent attacks, sometimes extending over many years.

A number of drugs are available for malaria, the choice depending on many factors, such as the region in which the disease may have been contracted and whether it is thought that the type of malaria plasmodium prevailing in that area is resistant to any of the commonly used drugs. Certain forms of malaria, for example, are resistant to chloroquine (see Choice of drugs, below).

Why they are used

The medical response to malaria takes three forms: prevention, the treatment of symptomatic attacks, and the eradication of the plasmodia (radical cure).

For someone planning a trip to an area where malaria is prevalent, drugs are given that destroy the parasites before they can reach the liver. Treatment begins the week before arrival in the malarial area and should continue for 4 to 6 weeks after return.

The same drugs are effective during the symptomatic period, relieving the episodes of fever and chills. However, these medicines do not destroy the plasmodia remaining in the liver. Future malarial attacks are probable, sometimes occurring many years later.

To rid someone of the infection completely, a 14-day course of primaquine is administered. Although highly effective in destroying the plasmodia in the liver, the drug is curiously weak against those in the cell-bursting stage. Primaquine treatment is recommended only after a person leaves the malarial area because of the high risk of re-infection. This treatment is advisable whether or not an individual has suffered attacks of malaria because the infection can be present for several weeks without causing symptoms.

How they work

Most antimalarial drugs act by rapidly killing plasmodia in the bloodstream. Taken to prevent the disease, the drugs kill the plasmodia before they enter the liver, so stopping them from multiplying. Once the plasmodia have multiplied in the liver, the same drugs given in higher doses kill the parasites that re-enter the bloodstream. Only primaquine destroys the plasmodia in the liver, and it is thus the only drug effective as a radical cure.

How they affect you

The low doses of antimalarial drugs taken to prevent the disease rarely cause noticeable effects. Drugs taken for an attack usually begin to relieve symptoms within a few hours. Most of them can cause nausea, vomiting, and diarrhoea. More seriously, quinine can produce giddiness, noises in the ear, and disturbances in vision and hearing.

Risks and special precautions

When drugs are given to prevent or cure malaria the full course of treatment must be taken. No drugs give long-term protection; new treatment is needed for each journey. Because no drug is effective against every type of malaria, a change of antimalarial drug may be necessary when travelling from one malarial area to another where a different form of malaria may be prevalent.

Most of these drugs do not produce severe adverse effects, but primaquine can cause the blood disorder, haemolytic anaemia, particularly in people with glucose-6-phosphate dehydrogenase (G6PD) deficiency. Hence, blood tests are usually taken during treatment.

CHOICE OF DRUGS

The parts of the world in which malaria is prevalent (illustrated on the map right), and travel to which may make antimalarial drug treatment advisable, can be divided into three groups: zones A, B and C. The table below indicates the drug(s) currently recommended for the prevention and treatment of malaria in each zone. It is, however, advisable to take specific medical advice before travelling to these areas. Pregnant women and women of childbearing age may need alternative drug treatment.

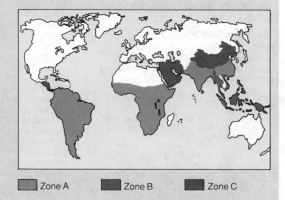

Zone A ■   Zone B ■   Zone C ■

Zone	Countries	Recommended antimalarial drugs
A	Africa (south of the Sahara), Indian subcontinent, South America, southern China	*Prevention:* chloroquine *and* proguanil *or* mefloquine *Treatment:* amodiaquine, chloroquine *or* quinine
B	South East Asia and Oceania	*Prevention:* chloroquine *and* pyrimethamine/dapsone (Maloprim) *or* mefloquine *Treatment:* amodiaquine, chloroquine *or* quinine
C	Central America, central and northern China, Maldives, and Mauritius	*Prevention:* chloroquinine *or* proguanill *Treatment:* amodiaquine, chloroquine *or* quinine

COMMON DRUGS

Amodiaquine	Primaquine ✱
Chloroquine ✱	Proguanil ✱
Dapsone	Pyrimethamine ✱
Mefloquine	Quinine ✱

✱ See Part 4

ANTIFUNGAL DRUGS

We are continually exposed to fungi – in the air we breathe, the food we eat and the water we drink. Fortunately, most of them cannot live in the body, and few are harmful. But some can grow in the mouth, skin, hair or nails, causing irritating or unsightly changes, and a few can cause serious and possibly fatal disease. The most common fungal infections are caused by the tinea group of infections. These include tinea pedis (athlete's foot), tinea cruris (jock itch), and tinea capitis (scalp ringworm). They are caused by a variety of organisms and may be spread by direct or indirect contact with infected humans or animals. Infection is encouraged by warm, moist conditions.

Problems may also result from the proliferation of a fungus normally present in the body; the most common example is excessive growth of Candida, a yeast which causes thrush infection of the mouth, vagina and bowel. It can also infect other organs if it spreads through the body via the bloodstream. Overgrowth of Candida may occur in people taking antibiotics (p.128) or oral contraceptives (p.161), or in pregnant women, or those with diabetes or immune system disorders such as AIDS.

Superficial fungal infections – those that attack only the outer layer of the skin and mucous membranes – are common and although irritating are not . usually a threat to general health. Internal fungal infections – for example, of the lungs, heart or other organs – are rare, but may be serious and prolonged.

Because antibiotics and other antibacterial drugs have no effect on fungi and yeasts, a different type of drug is needed. Drugs for fungal infections are either applied *topically* to treat minor infections of the skin and mucous membranes, or given by mouth or injection to eliminate serious fungal infections of the internal organs and nails.

Why they are used

Drug treatment is necessary for most fungal infections since they rarely improve alone. Measures such as careful washing and drying of affected areas may help, but are not a substitute for antifungal drugs. The use of over-the-counter preparations to increase the acidity of the vagina is not usually effective except when accompanied by drug treatment.

Fungal infections of the skin and scalp are usually treated with an antifungal cream. Drugs for vaginal thrush are most commonly applied in the form of vaginal pessaries or cream applied with a special applicator. Some preparations may be effective after a single dose; others require repeated applications. Mouth infections are usually eliminated by lozenges dissolved in the mouth or an antifungal solution applied directly to the affected areas. When Candida infects the bowel, an antifungal drug that is not absorbed into the bloodstream, such as nystatin, is given in tablet form.

In the rare cases in which fungal infections affect internal organs, or when the nails are severely affected by persistent tinea infection, drugs such as griseofulvin and amphotericin that pass into the bloodstream are given by mouth or injection.

How they work

Most of these drugs alter the permeability of the fungal cell's walls. The chemicals essential for cell life leak out and the cell dies.

ACTION OF ANTIFUNGAL DRUGS

Drug

Cell wall

Stage one
The drug acts on the wall of the fungal cell.

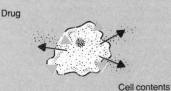

Drug

Cell contents

Stage two
The drug damages the cell wall and the cell contents leak out. The cell dies.

How they affect you

The speed with which antifungal drugs provide benefit varies with the type of infection. Thrush and most other fungal or yeast infections of the skin, mouth and vagina improve within a week. The condition of nails affected by fungal infections only improves when new nail growth occurs, and this takes many months. *Systemic* infections of the internal organs can take weeks to cure.

Antifungal drugs applied topically rarely cause side effects, although they may irritate the skin. However, treatment by mouth or injection for systemic and nail infections may produce more serious side effects. Amphotericin, injected in cases of life-threatening, systemic infections, often causes unpleasant and potentially dangerous effects, notably a severe fever that may require other drugs. Because this drug may also cause kidney damage, sufferers need regular blood tests. Griseofulvin, given for persistent nail infections, carries a risk of liver damage. For this reason it is prescribed only when topical treatments have failed and nail damage is severe.

CHOICE OF ANTIFUNGAL DRUG

The table below shows the range of uses for each antifungal drug. The particular drug chosen in each case depends on the precise nature and site of the infection. The usual route of administration for each drug is also indicated.

Drug	Infection									Administration		
	Oesophagal thrush	Cryptococcal meningitis	Skin ringworm	Scalp ringworm	Nail infection	Mouth thrush	Vaginal thrush	Candida of the skin	Systemic candida	Topical	Injection	Oral
Amphotericin B	●	●				●	●	●	●	●	●	
Clotrimazole			●	●		●	●	●		●		
Fluconazole	●	●						●	●			●
Flucytosine	●	●							●		●	●
Griseofulvin			●	●	●							●
Ketoconazole			●	●		●	●	●	●	●	●	●
Miconazole					●	●	●	●	●	●	●	●
Nystatin						●	●	●	●	●	●	●
Terbinafine			●	●	●							●

COMMON DRUGS

Amphotericin *
Clotrimazole *
Econazole *
Fluconazole *

Griseofulvin
Itraconazole
Ketoconazole *
Nystatin *
Terbinafine
Tioconazole

* See Part 4

ANTHELMINTICS

Anthelmintics are drugs that are used to eliminate the many types of worm (helminths) that can enter the body and live there as parasites, producing a general weakness in some cases and serious harm in others. The body may be host to many different worms (see Choice of drug, below). Most species spend part of their life cycle in another animal, and the infestation is often passed on to humans in food contaminated with the eggs or larvae. In some cases, such as hookworm, larvae enter the body through the skin. Larvae or adults may attach themselves to the intestinal wall and feed on the bowel contents; others feed off the intestinal blood supply, causing anaemia. Worms can also infest the bloodstream or lodge in muscle or internal organs.

Many people have worms at some time during their life, especially during childhood: most can be effectively eliminated with anthelmintic drugs.

Why they are used

Most worms common in the United Kingdom cause only mild symptoms and generally do not pose any threat to general health. Anthelmintic drugs are usually necessary, however, because the body's natural defences against infection are not effective against most worm infestations. Certain types of worm infestation must always be treated since they can cause serious complications. In some cases, such as threadworm infestation, doctors may advise anthelmintic treatment for the whole family, to prevent reinfection. If worms that have invaded tissues have formed cysts, they may need to be removed surgically. Laxatives are given with some anthelmintics to hasten expulsion of worms from the bowel. Other drugs may be prescribed to ease symptoms or to compensate for any blood loss or nutritional deficiency.

How they work

The anthelmintic drugs act in several ways. Many of them kill or paralyse the worms, and they pass out of the body in the faeces. Others, that act *systemically*, are used to treat infection in the tissues.

Many anthelmintics are specific for particular worms, and the doctor must identify the worm before selecting the most appropriate treatment (see Choice of drug). Most common infestations of the intestine are easily treated, often with only one or two doses of the drug. However, tissue infections may require more prolonged treatment.

How they affect you

Once the drug has eliminated the worms, symptoms caused by infestation rapidly disappear. Taken as a single dose, or a short course, anthelmintics do not usually produce side effects. However, treatment can disturb the digestive system, causing abdominal pain, nausea and vomiting.

COMMON DRUGS

Bephenium
Diethylcarbamazine
Mebendazole
Niclosamide
Piperazine *
Praziquantel
Pyrantel
Thiabendazole

* See Part 4

CHOICE OF DRUG

Threadworm (*enterobiasis*)
The most common worm infection in the United Kingdom. Commonly affects children. Eggs are usually swallowed in contaminated food or from sucking contaminated fingers or objects. Worms infect the intestines and lay eggs around the skin of the anus, often causing irritation.
Drugs Mebendazole, piperazine

Common roundworm (*ascariasis*)
The most common worm infection worldwide – transmitted in contaminated raw food or in soil. Infects the intestine. The worms are large and can block the intestine.
Drugs Mebendazole, piperazine

Strongyloidiasis (tropical threadworm)
Mainly occurs in southern Europe. Larvae penetrate skin in contact with contaminated soil, pass into the lungs and later are swallowed into the digestive tract.
Drugs Thiabendazole

Whipworm (*trichuriasis*)
Mainly occurs in tropical areas as a result of eating contaminated raw vegetables. Worms infest the intestines.
Drugs Mebendazole

Hookworm (*uncinariasis*)
Mainly found in tropical areas. Worm larvae penetrate skin and pass via the lymphatic system and bloodstream to the lungs. They then travel up the airways, are swallowed and attach themselves to the intestinal wall.
Drugs Bephenium, mebendazole, pyrantel

Pork roundworm (*trichinosis*)
Transmitted in infected undercooked pork. Initially worms lodge in the intestines, but larvae may invade muscle to form cysts that are often resistant to drug treatment.
Drugs Mebendazole, thiabendazole

Toxocariasis (*visceral larva migrans*)
Usually occurs as a result of eating soil contaminated by dog or cat faeces. Eggs hatch in the intestine and may travel in the bloodstream to the lungs, liver, kidney, brain and eyes.
Drugs Mebendazole, thiabendazole

Creeping eruption (*cutaneous larva migrans*)
Mainly occurs in tropical areas and coastal areas of southeastern United States as a result of skin contact with larvae from cat and dog faeces. Infestation is usually confined to skin.
Drugs Thiabendazole

Filariasis (including onchocerciasis and loiasis)
Tropical areas only. Infection by this group of worms is spread by bites of insects that are carriers of worm larvae or eggs. May affect lymphatic system, blood, eyes and skin.
Drugs Diethylcarbamazine

Flukes
Sheep liver fluke (fascioliasis) is indigenous to the United Kingdom. Infestation usually results from eating watercress grown in contaminated water. Mainly affects the liver and biliary tract. Other flukes only found abroad may infect the lungs, intestines or blood.
Drugs Praziquantel

Tapeworms (including beef, pork, fish and dwarf tapeworms)
Depending on type, may be carried by pigs, cattle or fish and transmitted to humans in undercooked meat. Most types affect the intestines. Larvae of the pork tapeworm may form cysts in muscle and other tissues.
Drugs Niclosamide, praziquantel

Hydatid disease (*echinococciasis*)
Eggs are transmitted in dog faeces. Larvae may form cysts over years, commonly in the liver. Surgery is the usual treatment for cysts.
Drugs Mebendazole

HORMONES AND ENDOCRINE SYSTEM

The endocrine system is a collection of glands located throughout the body that produce *hormones* and release them into the bloodstream. Each endocrine gland produces one or more hormones, each of which governs a particular body function, including growth and repair of tissues, sexual development, and reproductive function, and the body's response to stress.

Most hormones are released continuously from birth, but the amount produced fluctuates with the body's needs. Others are produced mainly at certain times: growth hormone is released principally during childhood and adolescence. Sex hormones are produced by the testes and ovaries from puberty onwards (see p.158).

Many endocrine glands release hormones in response to triggering hormones produced by the pituitary gland. The activity of the pituitary gland is partly controlled by the brain through the hypothalamus, which produces "releasing" hormones that stimulate the release of a particular pituitary hormone that in turn stimulates hormone production by the appropriate endocrine gland.

A "feedback" system usually regulates blood hormone levels: if the level rises too high the pituitary releases another hormone that inhibits endocrine gland activity.

What can go wrong

Endocrine disorders, usually resulting in too much or too little of a particular hormone, have a variety of causes. Some are congenital in origin; others may be caused by cancer, autoimmune disease (including some forms of diabetes mellitus), injury, and certain drugs.

Why drugs are used

Natural hormone preparations or their synthetic versions are often prescribed to treat deficiency. Sometimes drugs are given to stimulate increased hormone production in the endocrine gland, such as oral antidiabetic drugs. When too much hormone is produced, drug treatment may reduce the activity of the gland.

Hormones or related drugs are also used to treat other conditions. Corticosteroids are related to adrenal hormones and are used to relieve inflammation, and to suppress immune system activity (see p.156). Several types of cancer are treated with sex hormones (see p.154). Female sex hormones are given as contraceptives (see p.161) and to treat menstrual disorders (p.160).

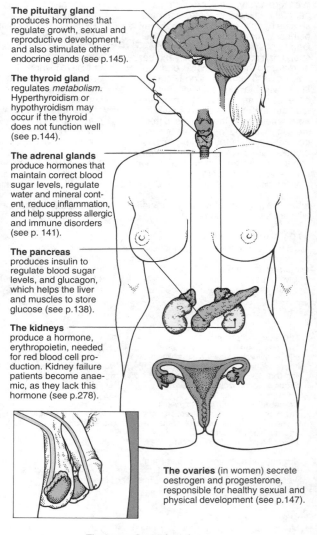

The pituitary gland produces hormones that regulate growth, sexual and reproductive development, and also stimulate other endocrine glands (see p.145).

The thyroid gland regulates *metabolism*. Hyperthyroidism or hypothyroidism may occur if the thyroid does not function well (see p.144).

The adrenal glands produce hormones that maintain correct blood sugar levels, regulate water and mineral content, reduce inflammation, and help suppress allergic and immune disorders (see p. 141).

The pancreas produces insulin to regulate blood sugar levels, and glucagon, which helps the liver and muscles to store glucose (see p.138).

The kidneys produce a hormone, erythropoietin, needed for red blood cell production. Kidney failure patients become anaemic, as they lack this hormone (see p.278).

The ovaries (in women) secrete oestrogen and progesterone, responsible for healthy sexual and physical development (see p.147).

The testes (in men) produce testosterone, which controls the development of male sexual and physical characteristics (see p.146).

MAJOR DRUG GROUPS

Corticosteroids
Drugs used in diabetes
Drugs for thyroid disorders
Drugs for pituitary disorders
Male sex hormones
Female sex hormones

CORTICOSTEROIDS

Corticosteroid drugs – often referred to simply as steroids – are derived from, or are synthetic variants of, the natural corticosteroid *hormones* formed in the outer part (cortex) of the adrenal glands, situated on top of each kidney. Release of these hormones is governed by the pituitary gland (see p.145).

Corticosteroids have two types of effect: glucocorticoid and mineralocorticoid. The glucocorticoid effects include the maintenance of normal levels of sugar in the blood and the promotion of recovery from injury and stress. The main mineralocorticoid effects are the regulation of the balance of mineral salts and the water content of the body. When present in large amounts, corticosteroids reduce inflammation and suppress allergic reactions and immune system activity. They are distinct from another group of hormones, the anabolic steroids (p.146).

Although corticosteroids have broadly similar actions, they vary in their relative strength and duration of action. The

ADVERSE EFFECTS OF CORTICOSTEROIDS

Corticosteroids are effective and useful drugs that often provide benefit when other drugs are ineffective. However, long-term use of high doses can lead to a variety of unwanted effects on the body as shown below.

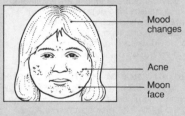

Mood changes

Acne

Moon face

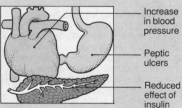

Increase in blood pressure

Peptic ulcers

Reduced effect of insulin

Fat pad on back

Osteoporosis (p.122)

strength of mineralocorticoid effects also varies.

Why they are used
Corticosteroid drugs are used primarily for their effect in damping down inflammation, whatever its cause. *Topical* preparations containing corticosteroids are frequently used for the treatment of many inflammatory skin disorders (see p.174). These drugs may also be injected directly into a joint or around a tendon to relieve inflammation caused by injury or disease (see p.118). However, when local administration of the drug is not possible or effective, corticosteroids may be given *systemically*, either by mouth or by intravenous injection.

An important use of oral corticosteroids is to replace the natural hormones that are deficient when adrenal gland function is reduced, as in Addison's disease. In these cases, drugs that most closely resemble the actions of the natural hormones are selected and a combination of these may be used.

Corticosteroids are commonly part of the treatment of many disorders in which inflammation is thought to be caused by excessive or inappropriate activity of the immune system. Such disorders include rheumatoid arthritis (p.117), inflammatory bowel disease (p.112), glomerulonephritis (a kidney disease), and some rare connective tissue disorders such as systemic lupus erythematosus. In these conditions they relieve symptoms and may temporarily halt the disease.

Corticosteroids may be given regularly by mouth or inhaler to treat asthma, although they are not effective for the relief of asthma attacks in progress.

Some cancers of the blood (leukaemias) and of the lymphatic system (lymphomas) may also respond to corticosteroid treatment. These drugs are also widely used to prevent or treat rejection of organ transplants, usually in conjunction with other drugs (see Immunosuppressants, p.156).

How they work
Given in high doses, corticosteroid drugs reduce inflammation by blocking the action of chemicals called prostaglandins that are responsible for triggering the inflammatory response. They also temporarily depress the immune system by reducing the activity of certain types of white blood cell.

How they affect you
Corticosteroid drugs often produce a dramatic improvement in symptoms. Given systemically, corticosteroids may also act on the brain to produce

a heightened sense of well-being and, in some people, a sense of euphoria.

Troublesome day-to-day side effects are rare. However, long-term corticosteroid treatment carries a number of serious risks.

Risks and special precautions
Given in low doses by mouth for the treatment of Addison's disease, there are few risks associated with these drugs. Expected adverse effects from higher doses depend on the drug used and the duration of treatment.

Drugs with strong mineralocorticoid effects such as hydrocortisone may cause water retention, swelling, particularly of the ankles, and an increase in blood pressure. Because corticosteroids reduce the effect of insulin, they create problems in diabetics. They may even give rise to diabetes in susceptible individuals. They can also cause peptic ulcers.

Since corticosteroids suppress the immune system, they increase susceptibility to infection. They also suppress symptoms of infectious disease. With long-term use, corticosteroids may cause a variety of adverse effects as described in the box on the left. Doctors try to avoid long-term prescription of corticosteroid drugs to children because prolonged use may retard growth.

Long-term use of corticosteroids suppresses the production of the body's own corticosteroid hormones. For this reason, treatment lasting for more than a few weeks should be withdrawn gradually to give the body time to adjust. If the drug is stopped abruptly, the lack of corticosteroid hormones may lead to sudden collapse.

People taking corticosteroids by mouth for longer than one month are advised to carry a warning card for two years. In the case of an accident, their defences against shock may need to be quickly strengthened with extra hydrocortisone.

COMMON DRUGS

Beclomethasone ✱
Betamethasone ✱
Cortisone
Dexamethasone ✱
Fluocinolone
Hydrocortisone ✱
Fluticasone ✱
Methylprednisolone
Mometasone
Prednisolone ✱
Triamcinolone

✱ See Part 4

DRUGS USED IN DIABETES

The body obtains most of its energy from glucose, a simple form of sugar formed in the intestine from the breakdown of starch and other sugars. Insulin is a hormone produced by the pancreas, which enables body tissues to take up glucose from the blood, either to use it for energy or to store it. In diabetes mellitus (or sugar diabetes) insulin production is defective. This results in reduced uptake of glucose by the tissues and hence the glucose level in the blood rises abnormally: a high blood glucose level is called hyperglycaemia.

There are two main types of diabetes mellitus. Insulin dependent (Type 1) diabetes usually appears in young people, fifty percent of cases occurring around the time of puberty. The insulin-secreting cells in the pancreas are gradually destroyed. The initiating cause of this process is unknown. However, childhood viral infections or an autoimmune condition, (where the body recognises its pancreas as "foreign" and tries to eliminate it) are the most likely candidates. The decline in insulin production is slow but the condition usually presents suddenly at times of stress, e.g. infection, puberty, when the body's insulin requirements are high. Symptoms of Type 1 diabetes include extreme thirst, increased urination, lethargy, and weight loss. The condition is fatal if left untreated.

Non-insulin dependent diabetes mellitus (NIDDM), Type 2 or maturity-onset diabetes, appears at an older age (usually over 40) and tends to come on much more gradually. In this type of diabetes, the levels of insulin in the blood are high. However, the cells of the body are resistant to the effects of insulin and have a reduced glucose uptake despite the high insulin levels. This results in hyperglycaemia. Obesity is the commonest cause of Type 2 diabetes.

In both types of diabetes an alteration in diet is vital. A healthy diet consisting of a low fat, high fibre, low simple sugar (cakes, sweets) and high complex sugar

ADMINISTRATION OF INSULIN

The body produces a constant background level of insulin, with additional insulin being produced as required during meals. The aim of insulin treatment is to mimic this pattern. In young diabetics this is best achieved by the injection of long-acting insulin twice daily to provide the background level and the injection of short-acting insulin before meals. Insulin pen injectors that contain the short-acting insulin make this regime more acceptable. The pen is discreet and easy to carry and contains a dial enabling selection of the appropriate dose. Older diabetics may be given a mixture of long and short-acting insulins twice daily. A device that delivers continuous subcutaneous insulin may be required for unstable diabetics to produce a finer control.

Duration of action of types of insulin

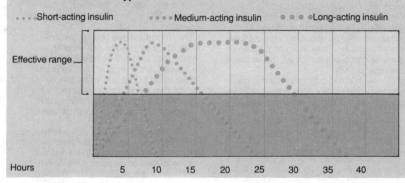

Short-acting insulin   Medium-acting insulin   Long-acting insulin

Effective range

Hours   5   10   15   20   25   30   35   40

(pasta, rice, potatoes) intake is recommended. In NIDDM, a reduction in weight alone may be sufficient to lower the body's energy requirements and restore blood glucose to normal levels. If diet fails, oral antidiabetic drugs, e.g. metformin or sulphonylureas, are prescribed. Insulin may need to be given to patients with NIDDM if the above treatments fail or in special circumstances when the "tight" control of blood glucose is advantageous. These situations arise in pregnancy, during severe illness, and before undergoing surgery. In insulin dependent diabetes, insulin treatment is essential to prevent death and is the only treatment option. It

has to be continued for the rest of the patient's life.

Several types of insulin are available. Some have a long duration of action; others are short-acting. Sometimes more than one type of insulin is given to provide steady diabetic control (see administration of insulin above).

Importance of treating diabetes

If diabetes is left untreated, the continuous high blood glucose levels cause damage to the body. The major problems arise secondary to the build up of atherosclerosis in arteries, which narrows the vessels to reduce the flow of blood. This can result in heart attacks, blindness, kidney failure, reduced circulation in the legs, and even gangrene. Although well-controlled diabetics remain at risk of these conditions, the risk is greatly reduced with treatment. Careful control of diabetes in the young is therefore of great importance in reducing long-term complications; in older diabetics who require insulin, a simpler regime is usually employed (see administration of insulin, above).

How antidiabetic drugs work

Sulphonylurea oral antidiabetic drugs encourage the pancreas to produce insulin. They are therefore only effective when some insulin-secreting cells remain active and this is why they are

ACTION OF SULPHONYLUREA DRUGS

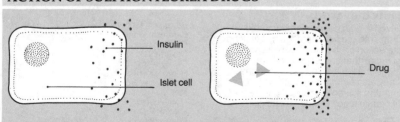

Insulin

Islet cell

Drug

Before drug treatment
In type 2 diabetes the islet cells of the pancreas secrete insufficient insulin to meet the body's needs.

After drug treatment
The drug stimulates the islet cells to release increased amounts of insulin.

ineffective in Type 1 diabetes. Biguanides such as metformin alter the way in which the body *metabolizes* sugar. Insulin treatment directly replaces the natural hormone that is deficient in diabetes mellitus.

All drugs for diabetes promote the uptake of glucose into body tissues and help to prevent an excessive rise in the level of glucose in the blood.

Unfortunately, insulin cannot be given by mouth because it is broken down in the digestive tract before it reaches the bloodstream. Regular injections are therefore necessary (see Administration of insulin, facing page).

Antidiabetic drugs and you

Oral antidiabetic drugs relieve the symptoms of diabetes by returning the blood glucose to normal. A normal, healthy, active lifestyle should be encouraged, However, occasionally, drug treatment may produce side-effects. The sulphonylureas may lower the blood glucose too much, a condition called hypoglycaemia. This can be avoided by starting treatment with low doses and ensuring a regular food intake. Rarely, these drugs cause skin rashes, upset in the blood count, intestinal or liver disturbances. Interactions may occur with other drugs and hence your doctor should be informed of your treatment before prescribing any medicines for you.

Metformin does not cause hypoglycaemia. Its most common side effects are nausea, weight loss, abdominal distension and diarrhoea.

Insulin treatment and you

The insulin requirements in diabetes vary greatly between individuals and within an individual with alteration in physical activity and calorie intake. Hence insulin regimens are tailored to each individual's particular needs. Each diabetic is encouraged to take an active role in his or her own management.

Regular records of home blood glucose monitoring should be kept. This forms the basis on which insulin doses are adjusted, either by the doctor or by diabetics themselves.

A diabetic should be taught how to recognise a hypoglycaemia event. This may be induced by giving insulin under a doctor's supervision. The symptoms of sweating, faintness, or palpitations are produced. These resolve with the administration of glucose, hence a diabetic should always carry glucose tablets or sweets. The occasional "hypo" may require a reduction of insulin dose. Rarely, unrecognised low glucose levels may lead to coma. The injection of glucagon (a substance that raises blood glucose) rapidly reverses this. A relative may be instructed how to perform this procedure.

Other complications may arise from insulin injection. Insulin is commonly extracted from the pancreas of the pig or cattle and some individuals are allergic to this. Nowadays, human insulin is available

SITES OF INJECTION

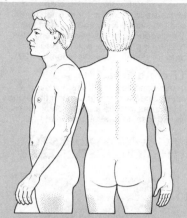

The shaded areas indicate suitable sites for the injection of insulin.

and may be prescribed as an alternative. Repeated injection at the same site may disturb the fat layer beneath the skin, producing either swelling or dimpling. This alters the rate of insulin absorption and can be avoided by the regular rotation of injection sites.

Insulin requirements are increased during illness and pregnancy. More frequent glucose monitoring is necessary and insulin injections should not be omitted. During an illness, the urine should be checked for ketones. Ketones are produced from proteins when there is insufficient insulin to permit the normal uptake of glucose by the tissues. They indicate that the tissues are being deprived of glucose despite a high blood glucose. If high ketone levels occur in a diabetic's urine during an illness, urgent medical advice should be sought.

Exercise increases the body's need for glucose and therefore extra calories should be taken prior to exertion.

It is advisable for diabetics to carry a warning card or bracelet that details their diabetic treatment. This may be useful in an emergency.

MONITORING BLOOD GLUCOSE

Diabetics need to check either their blood or urine glucose level at home. Blood tests give the most accurate results. The kit illustrated right consists of a programmable meter that reads the glucose levels of blood samples applied to a special card testing strip.

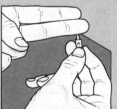

1 Prick your finger to produce a large drop of blood.

2 Touch the blood onto the test pads of the testing strip.

3 Press the time button on the meter. After 60 seconds wipe the blood from the test pads with a clean, dry cotton ball.

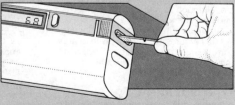

4 Within 120 seconds insert the test strip into the meter as shown. Your reading will appear after 120 seconds.

COMMON DRUGS

Sulphonylurea drugs	Other drugs
Glibenclamide *	Glucagon
Gliclazide	Insulin *
Glipizide	Metformin *
Tolbutamide *	

* See Part 4

DRUGS FOR THYROID DISORDERS

The thyroid gland produces the *hormone* thyroxine which regulates the body's *metabolism*. During childhood, thyroxine is essential for normal mental and physical development. Calcitonin, also produced by the thyroid, regulates calcium metabolism, and is used as a drug for certain bone disorders (p.122)

Thyrotoxicosis

In this condition, the thyroid is over-active and produces too much thyroxine. Symptoms include anxiety, palpitations, weight loss, increased appetite, heat intolerance, diarrhoea, and menstrual disturbances. Graves' disease is the commonest cause of thyrotoxicosis. It is an autoimmune disease in which the body produces antibodies that stimulate the thyroid to produce excess thyroxine. Patients with Graves' disease may develop abnormally protuberant eyes (exophthalmos) or a swelling involving the skin over the shins (pretibial myxoedema). These features are unique to Graves' disease. Thyrotoxicosis can be caused by a benign single tumour of the thyroid but may arise in older women with a pre-existing multinodular goitre. Rarely, an overactive thyroid may follow a viral infection, a condition called thyroiditis. Inflammation of the gland leads to the release of stored thyroxine. This is associated with a painful goitre and is a transient condition.

Management of thyrotoxicosis

There are three possible treatments: anti-thyroid drugs, radio-iodine and surgery. The most commonly used antithyroid drug is carbimazole. This drug inhibits the formation of thyroid hormones and reduces their levels to normal over a period of about three weeks. In the early stage of treatment a beta blocker (p.97) may be prescribed to control symptoms. This should be stopped once thyroid function returns to normal. The required dose of carbimazole is adjusted depending upon the patient's response. Long-term use of carbimazole for up to two years may be required to prevent relapse.

Carbimazole may produce minor side effects such as nausea, vomiting, headaches, or skin rashes. Rarely, the drug may reduce the white blood cell count. Hence, patients should seek medical advice if they develop either an unexplained fever or a sore throat. If necessary, propylthiouracil may be used as an alternative antithyroid drug.

Radio-iodine (radioactive iodine) is frequently chosen as a first-line therapy, especially in the elderly, and is the second choice if thyrotoxicosis recurs following use of carbimazole. It works by destroying thyroid tissue. Hypothyroidism occurs in up to 80 per cent of people in a 20 year period after treatment. Long-term studies show radio-iodine to be safe, although its use is to be avoided during pregnancy.

Surgery is a third-line therapy. Its use may be favoured for patients with a large goitre. Exophthalmus does not respond to the above treatments; corticosteroids (p.141) may be required.

Hypothyroidism

This is a condition resulting from too little thyroxine. It may be caused by an autoimmune disorder (in which the body's immune system attacks the thyroid) or it

ACTION OF DRUGS FOR THYROID DISORDERS

Thyroid hormone production
Iodine combines with other chemicals (precursors) in the thyroid gland to make thyroid hormones.

Iodine
Thyroid precursor
Thyroid hormone

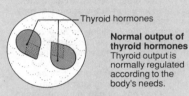

Thyroid hormones

Normal output of thyroid hormones
Thyroid output is normally regulated according to the body's needs.

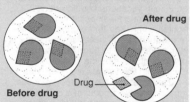

After drug

Drug

Before drug

Action of antithyroid drugs
In thyrotoxicosis, antithyroid drugs reduce the production of thyroid hormones, by preventing iodine from combining with thyroid precursors in the thyroid gland.

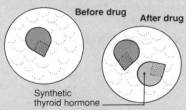

Before drug

After drug

Synthetic thyroid hormone

Action of thyroid hormones
In hypothyroidism when the thyroid gland is underactive, supplements of synthetic or (rarely) natural thyroid hormones restore hormone levels to normal.

TREATMENT FOR GOITRE

A goitre is a swelling of the thyroid gland. It may occur temp-orarily during puberty or pregnancy, or may be due to an abnormal growth of thyroid tissue that requires surgical removal. It may rarely be brought about by iodine deficiency. This last cause is treated with iodine supplements (see also p.425).

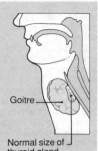

Goitre

Normal size of thyroid gland

may arise after treatment for thyro-toxicosis. In the newborn, it may result from an inborn enzyme disorder, and in the past, it arose from a deficiency of iodine in the diet. Symptoms of hypo-thyroidism develop slowly and include weight gain, mental slowness, dry skin, hair loss, cold intolerance, and heavy menstual periods. In babies, low thyroxine levels cause permanent mental and physical retardation (cretinism).

Management of hypothyroidism

Lifelong oral treatment with synthetic thyroxine is the only option. Blood tests are performed regularly to monitor treatment and permit dosage adjustments. In those with heart disease and the elderly, more gradual introduction of thyroxine is undertaken to prevent heart strain.

In severely ill patients, thyroxine may be given by injection. This method of administration may also be used to treat newborn infants with low levels of thyroxine.

Symptoms of thyrotoxicosis may appear if excess thyroxine replacement is given. Otherwise, no adverse events occur since treatment is adjusted to replace the natural hormone that the body should produce itself.

COMMON DRUGS

Drugs for thyrotoxicosis
Carbimazole *
Propylthiouracil *

Drugs for hypothyroidism
Liothyronine
Thyroxine *

Other drugs
Iodine *

* See Part 4

DRUGS FOR PITUITARY DISORDERS

The pituitary gland, which lies at the base of the brain, produces a number of *hormones* that regulate physical growth, *metabolism*, sexual development and reproductive function. Many of these hormones act indirectly by stimulating other glands, such as the thyroid, adrenal glands, ovaries and testes to release their own hormones. A summary of the actions and effects of each pituitary hormone is given below.

An excess or a lack of a pituitary hormone may produce serious effects, the nature of which depends on the hormone involved. Abnormal levels of a particular hormone may be caused by a pituitary tumour, usually treated surgically. In other cases, drugs may be used to correct the hormonal imbalance.

The more common pituitary disorders that can be treated with drugs are those involving growth hormone, antidiuretic hormone, prolactin, adrenal hormones and the gonadotrophins. The first three are discussed below. For information on the use of drugs to treat infertility arising from inadequate levels of gonadotrophins (see p.164). The lack of corticotrophin, which leads to inadequate production of adrenal hormones, is usually treated with corticosteroid drugs (see p.141).

Drugs for growth hormone disorders

Growth hormone (somatotrophin) is the principal hormone required for normal growth in childhood and adolescence.

Lack of growth hormone impairs normal physical growth, a condition known as pituitary dwarfism. Doctors administer hormone treatment only after tests have shown that a lack of this hormone is the cause of the disorder. If treatment begins early, regular injections of somatrem, a synthetic form of natural growth hormone, until the end of adolescence usually allows normal growth and development to take place.

Less often, the pituitary produces an excess of growth hormone. In children this can result in pituitary gigantism; in adults, it can produce a condition known as acromegaly. Acromegaly is usually the result of a pituitary tumour, and is characterized by thickening of the skull, face, hands and feet, and the enlargement of some internal organs.

Although these conditons are irreversible, treatment is necesary to halt gigantism and to prevent premature death. The pituitary tumour may either be surgically removed or destroyed by radiotherapy. In the frail or elderly, drugs such as bromocriptine and octreotide are used in order to reduce growth hormone levels.

Drugs for diabetes insipidus

Antidiuretic hormone (also known ADH or vasopressin) acts on the kidneys, controlling the amount of water retained in the body and returned to the blood. A lack of ADH is usually caused by damage to the pituitary, and this in turn causes diabetes insipidus. In this rare condition, the kidneys cannot retain water and large quantities pass into the urine. The chief symptoms of diabetes insipidus are constant thirst and the production of large volumes of urine.

Diabetes insipidus is treated with vasopressin or a related synthetic drug, lypressin. These replace the brain's output and may be given by injection or as an intranasal spray. Chlorpropamide (p.229) may be used to treat mild cases; it acts by increasing ADH release from the pituitary and by sensitising the kidney to the effect of ADH.

Alternatively, a thiazide diuretic (such as chlorthalidone) may be prescribed for mild cases (see Diuretics, p.99). The usual effect of such drugs is to increase urine production, but in diabetes insipidus they have the opposite effect, reducing water loss from the body.

Drugs used to reduce prolactin levels

Prolactin, or lactogenic hormone, is produced in both men and women. In women, prolactin controls the secretion of breast milk following childbirth; its function in men is not understood, although it appears to be necessary for normal sperm production.

The disorders associated with prolactin are all concerned with overproduction. High levels of prolactin in women can cause lactation unassociated with pregnancy and birth (galactorrhoea), lack of menstruation (amenorrhoea) and infertility. If excessive amounts are produced in men, the result may be galactorrhoea and/or infertility.

Some drugs, notably phenothiazine antipsychotics, oestrogen and methyldopa, can raise the level of prolactin in the blood. More often, however, increased prolactin results from a pituitary tumour that is usually treated surgically. Bromocriptine inhibits the production of prolactin and is also used in the short term to relieve breast symptoms prior to surgery.

THE EFFECTS OF PITUITARY HORMONES

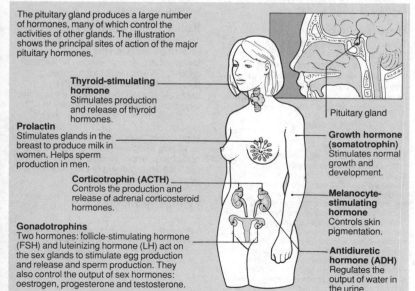

The pituitary gland produces a large number of hormones, many of which control the activities of other glands. The illustration shows the principal sites of action of the major pituitary hormones.

Thyroid-stimulating hormone
Stimulates production and release of thyroid hormones.

Prolactin
Stimulates glands in the breast to produce milk in women. Helps sperm production in men.

Corticotrophin (ACTH)
Controls the production and release of adrenal corticosteroid hormones.

Gonadotrophins
Two hormones: follicle-stimulating hormone (FSH) and luteinizing hormone (LH) act on the sex glands to stimulate egg production and release and sperm production. They also control the output of sex hormones: oestrogen, progesterone and testosterone.

Pituitary gland

Growth hormone (somatotrophin)
Stimulates normal growth and development.

Melanocyte-stimulating hormone
Controls skin pigmentation.

Antidiuretic hormone (ADH)
Regulates the output of water in the urine.

COMMON DRUGS

Drugs for growth hormone disorders
Bromocriptine *
Somatropin *
Octreotide

Drugs for diabetes insipidus
Chlorpropamide *
Lypressin *

Drugs to reduce prolactin levels
Bromocriptine *

MALE SEX HORMONES

Male sex hormones – androgens – are responsible for the development of male sexual characteristics. The principal androgen is testosterone, which in men is produced by the testes from puberty onwards. Women also produce testosterone in small amounts in the adrenal glands, but its exact function in the female body is not known.

Testosterone has two major effects: an androgenic effect and an anabolic effect. Its androgenic effect is to stimulate the appearance of secondary sexual characteristics at puberty, such as the growth of body hair, deepening of the voice, and an increase in the size of the genitals. Its anabolic effect is to increase muscle bulk and accelerate rate of growth.

There are a number of synthetically produced derivatives of testosterone that produce varying degrees of the androgenic and anabolic effects mentioned above. Those having a mainly anabolic effect are known as anabolic steroids (see box below).

Testosterone and its derivatives have been used in both men and women to treat a number of conditions.

Why they are used

Male sex hormones are mainly given to men to promote the development of male sexual characteristics when hormone production is deficient. This may be the result of an abnormality of the testes or from inadequate production of the pituitary hormones that stimulate the testes to release testosterone.

A course of treatment with male sex hormones is sometimes prescribed for adolescent boys in whom the onset of puberty is delayed by pituitary problems. This treatment may also help to stimulate the development of secondary male sexual characteristics and to increase sex drive (libido) in adult men who are producing inadequate levels of testosterone. However, this type of hormone treatment reduces the production of sperm. (For information

on the drug treatment of male infertility, see p.164.)

Male sex hormones and mainly some of their synthetic variants may also be prescribed for women to treat certain types of cancer of the breast and uterus (see Anticancer drugs, p.154).

How they work

Taken in low doses as part of replacement therapy when natural production is low, male sex hormones act in the same way as the natural hormones. In adolescents suffering from delayed puberty, hormone treatment produces androgenic and anabolic effects (above), initiating

the development of secondary sexual characteristics over a few months; full sexual development usually takes place over three to four years. Given to adult men, the effects on physical appearance and libido may begin to be felt within a few weeks.

Risks and special precautions

The main risks with these drugs occur when they are given to boys with delayed puberty and to women with breast cancer. Given to initiate the onset of puberty, they may stunt growth by prematurely sealing the growing ends of the long bones. Doctors normally try to avoid prescribing hormones in these circumstances until growth is complete. High doses given to women have masculinizing effects – increased facial and body hair, deeper voice. They may also produce enlargement of the clitoris, acne and changes in libido.

EFFECTS OF MALE SEX HORMONES

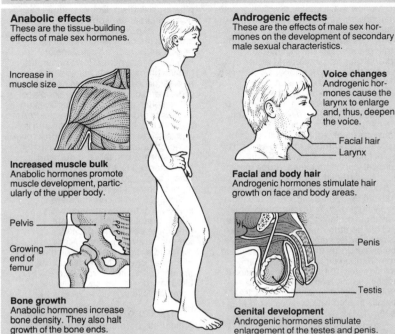

Anabolic effects
These are the tissue-building effects of male sex hormones.

Increase in muscle size

Increased muscle bulk
Anabolic hormones promote muscle development, particularly of the upper body.

Pelvis

Growing end of femur

Bone growth
Anabolic hormones increase bone density. They also halt growth of the bone ends.

Androgenic effects
These are the effects of male sex hormones on the development of secondary male sexual characteristics.

Voice changes
Androgenic hormones cause the larynx to enlarge and, thus, deepen the voice.

Facial hair
Larynx

Facial and body hair
Androgenic hormones stimulate hair growth on face and body areas.

Penis

Testis

Genital development
Androgenic hormones stimulate enlargement of the testes and penis.

ANABOLIC STEROIDS

Anabolic steroids are synthetically produced variants that mimic the anabolic effects of the natural hormones. They increase muscle bulk and body growth.

Doctors occasionally prescribe anabolic steroids and a high protein diet to promote recovery after serious illness or major surgery. The steroids may also help to increase the production of blood cells in some forms of anaemia. They have also been used in the treatment of the bone-wasting disorder osteoporosis (see p.122) in post menopausal women but because of the risk of serious side effects alternative forms of treatment are usually given.

Anabolic steroids have been widely abused by athletes because they speed up the recovery of muscles after a session of intense exercise. This enables the athlete to go through a more demanding daily exercise programme, resulting in a significant improvement in muscle power. The use of anabolic steroids by athletes to improve their performance is condemned by doctors and athletic organizations because of the risks to health, particularly for women. Side effects range from acne and baldness to fluid retention, reduced fertility in men and women, hardening of the arteries, a long-term risk of liver disease, and certain forms of cancer.

COMMON DRUGS

Primarily androgenic
Testosterone *
Mesterolone

Primarily anabolic
Nandrolone
Oxymetholone

* See Part 4

FEMALE SEX HORMONES

There are two types of female sex hormones, oestrogens and progesterone. In women these are secreted by the ovaries from puberty until after the menopause. Each month, levels of oestrogens and progesterone fluctuate, producing the menstrual cycle (see p.158). During pregnancy, the placenta produces extra oestrogens and progesterone. The adrenal gland also makes small amounts of oestrogens. The production of these hormones is regulated by two gonadotrophin hormones produced by the pituitary gland (see p.145).

Oestrogens are responsible for the development of female sexual characteristics, including breast development, growth of pubic hair, and widening of the pelvis. Progesterone prepares the lining of the uterus for implantation of a fertilized egg. It is also important for the maintenance of pregnancy.

Oestrogens and progesterone and synthetic variants of these hormones (synthetic progesterone-like drugs are known as progestogens) are used medically to treat a number of conditions.

Why they are used
The best known use of these drugs is in oral contraceptive preparations. These are discussed on p.161. Other uses include the treatment of menstrual disorders (p.160) and certain hormone sensitive cancers (p.154). This page discusses the treatment of natural hormone deficiency.

Hormone deficiency
Deficiency of female sex hormones may occur as a result of deficiency of gonadotrophins caused by a pituitary disorder or by abnormal development of the ovaries (ovarian failure). This may lead to the absence of menstruation and lack of sexual development. If tests show a deficiency of gonadotrophins, preparations of these hormones may be prescribed (see p.164). These trigger the release of oestrogens and progesterone from the ovaries. If pituitary function is normal and ovarian failure is diagnosed as the cause of hormone deficiency, oestrogen and progesterone supplements may be given. In this situation, hormone supplements ensure development of normal female sexual characteristics, but cannot stimulate ovulation.

Menopause
A fall in levels of oestrogens and progesterone occurs naturally after the menopause, when the menstrual cycle ceases. The sudden reduction in levels of oestrogen often causes distressing symptoms including sweating, hot flushes, dryness of the vagina and mood changes. Many doctors advocate the use of hormone supplements following the menopause. Such hormone replacement therapy (HRT) helps to reduce the symptoms of the menopause

and also helps to delay some of the long-term consequences of reduced oestrogen levels in old age, including osteoporosis (p.122) and deposition of fat in the arteries (atherosclerosis). When dryness of the vagina is a particular problem, oestrogen cream may be prescribed. Hormone replacement therapy is usually maintained for 18 to 24 months, after which the dose is gradually reduced unless the woman is assessed as having a high risk of osteoporosis. Hormone replacement therapy may also be prescribed for women who have undergone a premature menopause as a result of surgical removal of the ovaries or radiotherapy for ovarian cancer.

How they affect you
Hormones given to treat ovarian failure or delayed puberty take three to six months to produce a noticeable effect on sexual development. Taken for menopausal symptoms, they can dramatically reduce hot flushes within a week.

Both oestrogens and progestogens can cause fluid retention, and oestrogens may cause nausea, vomiting, breast tenderness, headache, dizziness and depression. Progestogens may cause "breakthrough" bleeding between menstrual periods. In the comparatively low doses used to treat these disorders, side effects are unlikely.

Risks and special precautions
Treatment with oestrogens and progestogens for ovarian failure carries few risks for otherwise healthy young women, though there are risks linked to long-term oestrogen treatment in older women. Oestrogens increase the risk of abnormal blood clotting (thrombosis) and raised blood pressure (hypertension). Therefore, oestrogen treatment is used with caution in women with heart or circulatory disorders, or who are overweight or smoke. Oestrogens may also trigger diabetes mellitus in susceptible people. The risks of oestrogen hormones are reduced by prescribing them with progestogens, which oppose some of the harmful effects. Tibolone has oestrogen and progestogen properties and can be used on its own.

COMPARATIVE HORMONE LEVELS DURING THE MENSTRUAL CYCLE AND PREGNANCY

In an adult woman of child-bearing years the production of female sex hormones fluctuates during a monthly cycle. During pregnancy the levels of both oestrogen and progesterone rise dramatically. After the menopause hormone production falls to a level similar to that which occurs during menstruation.

The large graph (right) shows the rise in hormone levels during the 40 weeks of pregnancy. The smaller graph (inset) illustrates hormone levels in a typical 28-day menstrual cycle. The hormone levels in pregnancy are much greater than in the menstrual cycle, each step of measurement on the pregnancy graph is equivalent to 100 units in the menstrual cycle graph.

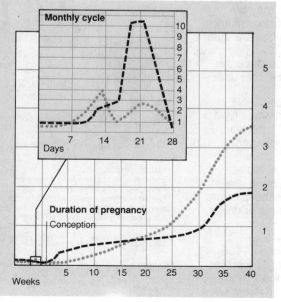

Monthly cycle

Days 7 14 21 28

Duration of pregnancy
Conception

Weeks 5 10 15 20 25 30 35 40

······ Oestrogen
- - - - Progesterone

COMMON DRUGS

Progestogens
Allyloestrenol
Desogestrel
Dydrogesterone
Ethynodiol
Gestodene
Hydroxyprogesterone
Levonorgestrel *

Medroxyprogesterone *
Norethisterone *
Progesterone

Oestrogens
Conjugated
  oestrogens *
Ethinyloestradiol *
Mestranol
Oestradiol
Oestriol

* See Part 4

NUTRITION

Food provides energy (as calories) and materials called nutrients needed for growth and renewal of tissues. Protein, carbohydrate, and fat are the three major nutrient components of food. Vitamins and minerals are found only in small amounts in food, but are just as important for normal function of the body. Fibre, found only in foods from plants, is needed for a healthy digestive system.

During digestion, large molecules of food are broken down into smaller molecules, releasing nutrients that can be absorbed into the bloodstream. Carbohydrate and fat are then *metabolized* by body cells to produce energy. They may also be incorporated with protein into cell structure. Each metabolic process is promoted by a specific *enzyme* and often requires the presence of a particular vitamin or mineral.

Why drugs are used

Dietary deficiency of essential nutrients can lead to illness. In poorer countries where there is a shortage of food, marasmus resulting from lack of food energy and kwashiorkor from lack of protein are common. In the developed world, however, excessive food intake leading to obesity is more common. Nutritional deficiencies in developed countries result from poor food choices and usually stem from lack of a specific vitamin or mineral such as in iron-deficiency anaemia.

Some nutritional deficiencies may be caused by an inability of the body to absorb nutrients from food (malabsorption) or to utilize them once they have been absorbed, Malabsorption may be caused by lack of an enzyme or an abnormality of the digestive tract. Errors of metabolism are often inborn and are not yet fully understood. They may be caused by failure of the body to produce the chemicals required to process nutrients for use.

Why supplements are used

Deficiencies of the kwashiorkor-marasmus type are not usually treated by drugs, but by dietary improvement, and perhaps food supplements. Vitamin and mineral deficiencies are usually treated with appropriate supplements. Malabsorption disorders may require continued use of supplements or changes in diet. Metabolic errors are not easily treated with supplements or drugs. Dietary changes may be tried.

Obesity has been treated with appetite-suppressants related to amphetamines (p.436), the use of which is now discouraged. The preferred treatment includes reduction of food intake, altered eating patterns, and increased exercise.

Major food components

Proteins
Vital for growth and repair of tissue. In meat and dairy products, cereals and pulses.

Carbohydrates
A major energy source, stored as fat when taken in excess. In cereals, sugar and vegetables.

Fats
A concentrated energy form but needed only in small quantities. In animal products and oils.

Fibre
The indigestible part of any plant product which, though it contains no nutrients, adds bulk to faeces.

Absorption of nutrients
Food passes through mouth, oesophagus and stomach to the small intestine, whose lining secretes many enzymes and is covered by tiny projections (villi) which enable nutrients to pass into the blood.

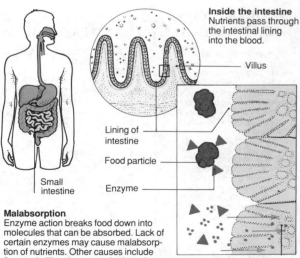

Inside the intestine
Nutrients pass through the intestinal lining into the blood.

Villus

Lining of intestine

Food particle

Enzyme

Small intestine

Food molecules absorbed

Malabsorption
Enzyme action breaks food down into molecules that can be absorbed. Lack of certain enzymes may cause malabsorption of nutrients. Other causes include flattened villi and scars on the intestine.

MAJOR DRUG GROUPS

Vitamins

VITAMINS

Vitamins are complex chemicals that are essential for a variety of body functions. The body is unable to manufacture these substances itself and therefore we need to take them in in the diet. There are 13 major vitamins: A, C, D ,E, K, and the eight B complex vitamins – thiamin (B_1), riboflavin (B_2), niacin (B_3), folic acid, biotin (Vitamin H), pantothenic acid (B_5), pyridoxine (B_6), and cobalamin (B_{12}). Most are required in extremely small amounts and each vitamin is present in one or more foods (see Main food sources of vitamins, p.150). Vitamin D is also produced in the body when the skin is exposed to sunlight. Vitamins fall into two groups: those that dissolve in fat and those that dissolve in water (see Fat-soluble and water-soluble vitamins, p.151).

A balanced diet that includes a variety of different types of food is likely to contain adequate amounts of all the vitamins. Inadequate intake of any vitamin over an extended period can lead to symptoms of deficiency. The nature of these symptoms depends on the vitamin concerned.

A doctor may recommend supplements of one or more vitamins in a variety of circumstances: to prevent vitamin deficiency from occurring in people considered at special risk, to treat symptoms of deficiency, and in the treatment of certain medical conditions.

Why they are used
Preventing deficiency
Most people in the United Kingdom obtain sufficient quantities of vitamins in their diet, and it is therefore unnecessary in most cases to take additional vitamins in the form of supplements. People who are unsure as to whether their present diet is adequate are advised to look at the table on p.150 to check that foods that are rich in vitamins are eaten regularly. Vitamin intake can often be boosted simply by increasing the quantities of fresh foods and raw fruit and vegetables in the diet.

Certain groups in the population are, however, at increased risk of vitamin deficiency. These include those who have an increased need for certain vitamins that may not be met from dietary sources – in particular, women who are pregnant or nursing, and infants and young children. The elderly who may not be eating a varied diet may also be at risk. Strict vegetarians and others on restricted diets may not receive adequate amounts of all vitamins.

In addition, people being fed intravenously or by stomach tube on artificial nutrients for prolonged periods, those suffering from disorders in which absorption of nutrients from the bowel is impaired, or who need to take drugs (for example, lipid-lowering drugs) which reduce vitamin absorption, are usually given additional vitamins.

In these cases, a doctor is likely to advise supplements of one or more vitamins. Although most vitamin preparations are available without a prescription, it is important to seek specialist advice before starting a course of vitamin supplements, so that a proper assessment can be made of your individual requirements.

Vitamin supplements should not be used as a general tonic to improve well-being – they do not do so – nor should they be used as a substitute for a balanced diet.

Vitamin deficiency
It is rare for a diet to be completely lacking in a particular vitamin. But if

PRIMARY FUNCTIONS OF VITAMINS

The role of vitamins in the body is not yet fully understood; most of our knowledge is based on the evidence provided by symptoms that occur as a result of deficiency of a particular vitamin. Most vitamins have been found to have a number of important actions on one or more body systems or functions. Many are involved in the activity of *enzymes* (substances that promote biochemical reactions in the body). The illustration below indicates the organs and body systems on which each vitamin has its principal effect.

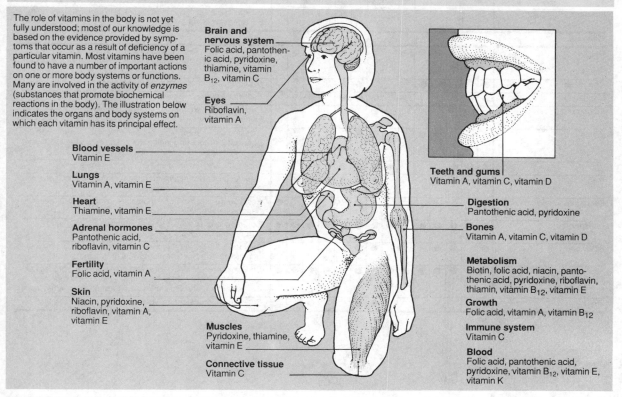

Brain and nervous system
Folic acid, pantothenic acid, pyridoxine, thiamine, vitamin B_{12}, vitamin C

Eyes
Riboflavin, vitamin A

Blood vessels
Vitamin E

Lungs
Vitamin A, vitamin E

Heart
Thiamine, vitamin E

Adrenal hormones
Pantothenic acid, riboflavin, vitamin C

Fertility
Folic acid, vitamin A

Skin
Niacin, pyridoxine, riboflavin, vitamin A, vitamin E

Muscles
Pyridoxine, thiamine, vitamin E

Connective tissue
Vitamin C

Teeth and gums
Vitamin A, vitamin C, vitamin D

Digestion
Pantothenic acid, pyridoxine

Bones
Vitamin A, vitamin C, vitamin D

Metabolism
Biotin, folic acid, niacin, pantothenic acid, pyridoxine, riboflavin, thiamin, vitamin B_{12}, vitamin E

Growth
Folic acid, vitamin A, vitamin B_{12}

Immune system
Vitamin C

Blood
Folic acid, pantothenic acid, pyridoxine, vitamin B_{12}, vitamin E, vitamin K

VITAMINS continued

MAIN FOOD SOURCES OF VITAMINS AND MINERALS

The table below indicates which foods are especially good sources of particular vitamins and minerals. Ensuring that you regularly select foods from a variety of categories helps to maintain adequate intake for most people, without any need for supplements. It is important to remember that processed and overcooked foods are likely to contain fewer vitamins than fresh, raw or lightly cooked foods.

Vitamins	Red meat	Poultry	Liver	Milk	Cheese	Butter/margarine	Eggs	Fish	Cereals and bread	Green vegetables	Root vegetables	Pulses/legumes	Nuts	Fruit	Other	
Biotin			●				●				●		●			Especially peanuts. Cauliflower is good vegetable source.
Folic acid			●				●			●					●	Wheat germ and mushrooms are rich sources.
Niacin as nicotinic acid	●	●	●					●	●		●	●				Protein-rich foods such as milk and eggs contain tryptophan which can be converted to niacin in the body.
Pantothenic acid			●					●	●							Each food group contributes some pantothenic acid.
Pyridoxine	●	●	●					●	●	●						Especially white meat (chicken, fish) and whole-grain cereals.
Riboflavin		●	●	●	●		●		●		●	●	●			Found in most foods.
Thiamin	●								●		●	●				Brewer's yeast, wheat germ and bran are also good sources.
Vitamin A			●	●	●	●	●			●					●	Fish liver oil, dark green leafy vegetables such as spinach, and orange or yellow-orange vegetables and fruits such as carrots, apricots and peaches, are especially good sources of vitamin A.
Vitamin B$_{12}$	●		●	●	●		●	●								Obtained only from animal products.
Vitamin C										●					●	Especially citrus fruits, tomatoes, potatoes, broccoli, strawberries and melon.
Vitamin D			●				●									Dietary products are the best source, but the vitamin is also obtained by the body when the skin is exposed to sunlight.
Vitamin E			●		●	●			●	●					●	Vegetable oils, whole grain cereals and wheat germ are the best sources.
Vitamin K										●						Found in small amounts in fruits, seeds, root vegetables, dairy and meat products.
Minerals																
Calcium				●	●					●		●	●			Dark green leafy vegetables, soya bean products and nuts are good non-dairy alternatives. Also present in "hard" or alkaline water supplies.
Chromium	●			●					●	●						Especially unrefined whole grain cereals.
Copper	●	●	●					●	●	●		●	●			Especially shellfish, whole grain cereals and mushrooms.
Fluoride								●								Primarily obtained from fluoridated water supplies. Also in seafood and tea.
Iodine				●	●			●	●							Provided by "iodized" table salt but adequate amounts can be obtained without using table salt from dairy products, saltwater fish and bread.
Iron	●	●	●				●	●	●	●						Especially liver, red meat and enriched or whole grains.
Magnesium				●				●	●	●		●	●			Dark green leafy vegetables such as spinach are rich sources. Also present in alkaline water supplies.
Potassium								●	●	●				●		Best sources are fruits and vegetables, especially oranges, bananas and potatoes.
Phosphorus	●	●	●	●	●		●	●	●	●		●	●			Common food additive. Large amounts found in some carbonated beverages.
Selenium	●		●	●				●	●							Seafood is the richest source. Amounts in most foods are variable depending on soil where plants were grown and animals grazed.
Sodium	●	●	●	●	●	●	●	●	●	●	●		●			Sodium is present in all foods, especially table salt, processed foods, potato crisps, crackers, and pickled, cured or smoked meats, seafood and vegetables. Also present in "softened" water.
Zinc	●						●	●		●						Sufficient amounts only in whole grain breads and cereals.

intake of a particular vitamin is regularly lower than the body's requirements, over a period of time the body's stores of vitamins may become depleted and symptoms of deficiency may begin to appear. In Britain vitamin deficiency disorders are most common among vagrants and alcoholics and those on low incomes who fail to eat an adequate diet. Deficiencies of water-soluble vitamins are more likely since most of these are not stored in large quantities in the body. For descriptions of individual deficiency disorders, see the appropriate vitamin profile in Part 4.

Dosages of vitamins prescribed to treat vitamin deficiency are likely to be larger than those used to prevent deficiency. Medical supervision is required in these cases.

Other medical uses of vitamins
A number of claims have been made for the value of vitamins in the treatment of a range of medical disorders other than vitamin deficiency. In particular, high doses of vitamin C have been said to be effective in the prevention and treatment of the common cold and in the prevention of coronary heart disease and cancer; these claims are unproven. Vitamin and mineral supplements do not improve IQ in well-nourished children, but quite small dietary deficiencies can cause poor academic performance.

Certain vitamins have recognized medical uses apart from their nutritional role. Vitamin D has long been used to treat bone-wasting disorders (p.122). Niacin is sometimes used (as nicotinic acid) as a lipid-lowering drug (p.103). Derivatives of vitamin A (retinoids) are an established part of the treatment for severe acne (p.177). Many sufferers of pre-

MINERALS

Minerals are elements – the simplest form of matter – many of which are essential in trace amounts for normal bodily processes. A balanced diet usually contains all of the minerals that the body requires; mineral deficiency diseases, except iron-deficiency anaemia, are uncommon.

Dietary supplements are necessary only as part of the treatment for a medical disorder or when a doctor has diagnosed a specific deficiency. Doctors commonly prescribe minerals for people with intestinal diseases that reduce the absorption of minerals from the diet. Iron supplements are often advised for women who are pregnant or nursing, and iron-enriched cereals are recommended for infants over 6 months.

Much of the general advice given for vitamins also applies to minerals: taking supplements unless under medical direction is not advisable, exceeding the body's daily requirements is not beneficial, and large doses may be harmful.

CALCULATING DAILY VITAMIN REQUIREMENTS

Guidelines for assessing the nutritional value of diets are called Reference Nutrient Intakes (RNI), and are based on the estimated requirement of individuals with the highest needs. For most people the RNI is several times their requirement.

RNI do not cover individual variation due to acquired or inherited diseases, but are designed to cover the needs of about 97 per cent of the population. Those consuming much less than the RNI may not be consuming less than their needs but the risk of doing so is increased.

The current RNI (see table below) were set by the UK Department of Health Committee on Medical Aspects of Food Policy (COMA) in 1991, and replace the Recommended Dietary Allowances (RDA). Where no RNI exists, the 1989 US RDA is given.

Daily reference nutrient intakes of vitamins for adults (aged 19–50)

Vitamin (unit)	RNI		
	Men	Women	Pregnancy and breast feeding
Biotin (mcg)	10–200*	10–200*	Not established
Folic acid as folate (mcg)	200	200	260–300
Niacin as nicotinic acid (mg)	17	13	13–15
Pantothenic acid (mg)	3–7*	3–7*	3–7*
Pyridoxine (mg)	1.4	1.2	1.2
Riboflavin (mg)	1.3	1.1	1.4–1.6
Thiamin (mg)	1.0	0.8	0.9–1.0
Vitamin A (mg)	0.7	0.6	0.7–0.95
Vitamin B$_{12}$ (mcg)	1.5	1.5	1.5–2.0
Vitamin C (mg)	40	40	50–70
Vitamin D (mcg)	Ø	Ø	10
Vitamin E (mg)	10†	8†	10–12†

* Estimated requirement; † US figure; Ø See Vitamin D p.432.

menstrual syndrome take supplements of pyridoxine (vitamin B$_6$). See also Drugs for menstrual disorders, p.160.)

Risks and special precautions
Vitamins are natural substances and supplements can be taken without risk by most people. It is, however, important to be careful not to exceed the recommended dosage, particularly in the case of fat-soluble vitamins that may accumulate in the body. Dosage needs to be carefully calculated, taking account of the degree of deficiency, dietary intake, and duration of treatment. Overdosage has at best no therapeutic value and at worst may incur the risk of serious harmful effects. Preparations containing several times the recommended daily intake are best avoided except on medical advice. "Multivitamin" preparations containing a large number of different vitamins are widely available. Fortunately, the amounts of each vitamin contained in each tablet are not usually large and are not likely to be harmful unless the dose is greatly exceeded. Single vitamin supplements can be harmful because an excess of one vitamin may increase requirements for others. For specific information on each vitamin, see Part 4, pp.395 – 407.

FAT-SOLUBLE AND WATER-SOLUBLE VITAMINS

Fat soluble vitamins
Vitamins A, D, and K are absorbed from the intestine into the bloodstream together with fat (see also The passage of drugs through the body, p.17). Deficiency of these vitamins may occur as a result of any disorder that affects the absorption of fat (for example, sprue). These vitamins are stored in the liver and reserves of some of them may last for several years. Taking an excess of a fat-soluble vitamin for a long period may cause it to build up to a harmful level in the body. Ensuring that foods rich in these vitamins are regularly included in the diet usually provides a sufficient supply without the risk of overdosage.

Water-soluble vitamins
Vitamin C and the B vitamins dissolve in water. Most are stored in the body for only a short period and are rapidly excreted by the kidneys if taken in higher amounts than the body requires. Vitamin B$_{12}$ is the exception; it is stored in the liver, which may hold up to four years' supply. For these reasons foods containing water-soluble vitamins need to be eaten daily. They are easily lost in cooking, so uncooked foods containing these vitamins should be eaten regularly. An overdose of water-soluble vitamins does not usually cause toxic effects, but adverse reactions to large dosages of vitamin C and pyridoxine (vitamin B$_6$) have been reported.

MALIGNANT AND IMMUNE DISEASE

New cells are continuously needed by the body to replace those that wear out and die naturally, and to repair injured tissue. In normal circumstances the rate at which cells are created and multiply is carefully regulated.

But sometimes abnormal cells are formed, and sometimes they multiply uncontrollably. They may form lumps, warts, or nodules of abnormal tissue. These tumours are most often confined to one place and cause few problems; these are benign growths. In other types of tumour the body cells may invade or destroy the structures around the tumour, and abnormal cells may also spread to other parts of the body forming satellite or metastatic tumours. These are malignant growths, also known as cancers.

Opposing such actions, often effectively, are the workings of the immune system. It can recognize unfamiliar cells, not only those of infectious bacteria and viruses, but also the cells of transplanted tissues. The immune system relies on different types of white blood cells produced in the lymph glands and the bone marrow. They respond to foreign cells in a variety of ways which are described on the facing page).

The activity of the immune system is also responsible for allergic reactions (see Allergy, p.123).

What can go wrong

Although medical science does not identify; a single "cause" of cancer, certain outside factors (carcinogens) can often provoke the formation of abnormal cells. Tobacco smoke, for example, is a factor in lung cancer; people with light complexions who have spent a lot of time in the sun have a higher-than-average incidence of skin cancer. In one form or another, cancer seems to catch up with nearly everyone who lives to old age, and many doctors now believe that genetic faults increase the risk of certain cancers.

Failure of the immune system can lead to increased susceptibility both to infections and to the development of some cancers. Such failure can result from infection by human immuno-deficiency virus (HIV), the virus that causes AIDS. Immune system function can also be reduce by some types of drug, either deliberately or as an unavoidable consequence of necessary drug treatment.

In some cases the immune system triggers an inappropriate attack on the body's own tissue, leading to a wide variety of disorders known collectively as autoimmune diseases. Common conditions that are thought to be caused by auto-

Types of cancer

Uncontrolled multiplication of cells leads to the formation of tumours that may be benign or malignant. Benign tumours do not spread to other tissues; malignant (cancerous) tumours do. Some of the main types of cancer are defined below.

Type of cancer	Tissues affected
Carcinoma	Skin and glandular tissue lining cells of internal organs
Sarcoma	Muscles, bones and fibrous tissues and lining cells of vessels
Leukaemia	White blood cells
Lymphoma	Lymph glands

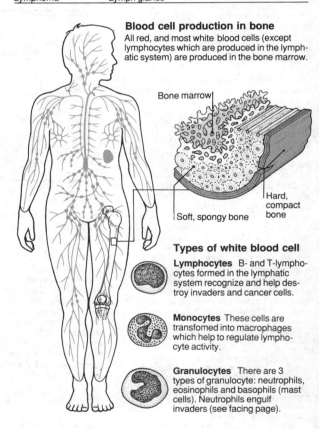

Blood cell production in bone
All red, and most white blood cells (except lymphocytes which are produced in the lymphatic system) are produced in the bone marrow.

Bone marrow

Hard, compact bone

Soft, spongy bone

Types of white blood cell

Lymphocytes B- and T-lymphocytes formed in the lymphatic system recognize and help destroy invaders and cancer cells.

Monocytes These cells are transfomed into macrophages which help to regulate lymphocyte activity.

Granulocytes There are 3 types of granulocyte: neutrophils, eosinophils and basophils (mast cells). Neutrophils engulf invaders (see facing page).

immune activity include rheumatoid arthritis, inflammatory skin disorders (lupus erythematosus), and some forms of hypothyroidism.

Immune system activity can also be troublesome following an organ or tissue transplant when it may lead to rejection of the foreign tissue.

Why drugs are used

Drugs act on the mechanisms that lead to malignant and immune disease in a variety of ways. Cytotoxic (cell-killing) drugs are used to

Types of immune response

A specific response occurs when the immune system recognizes an invader. Two types of specific response, humoral and cellular, are described below. Phagocytosis, a non-specific response that does not depend on recognition of the invader, is also described.

Humoral response

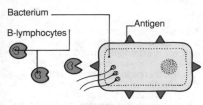

B-lymphocytes are activated by unfamiliar proteins (antigens) on the surface of the invading bacterium.

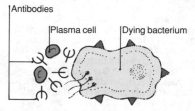

The activated B-lymphocytes form plasma cells which release antibodies that bind to the the invader and kill it.

Cellular response

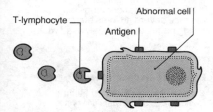

T-lymphocytes recognize the antigens on abnormal or invading cells.

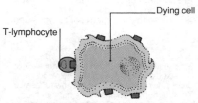

The T-lymphocytes bind to the abnormal cell and destroy it by altering chemical activity within the cell.

Engulfing invaders (phagocytosis)

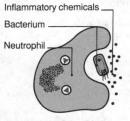

Certain cells such as neutrophils are attracted by inflammatory chemicals to an area of bacterial infection.

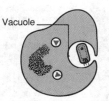

The neutrophil flows around the bacterium enclosing it within a fluid-filled space called a vacuole.

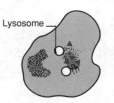

When the vacuole is formed, enzymes from areas called lysosomes within the neutrophil destroy the bacterium.

INTERFERON

Interferons are natural proteins that limit viral infection by inhibiting viral replication within body cells. These substances also assist in the destruction of cancer cells.

Effect on viral infection

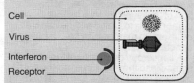

Interferon binds to receptors on a virus-infected cell.

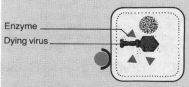

The presence of interferon triggers the release of enzymes that block viral replication. The virus is thus destroyed.

Effect on cancer cells

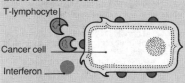

Interferon produced in response to an cancer cell activates T-lymphocytes.

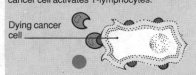

T-lymphocytes attack and destroy the cancer cell.

eliminate abnormally-dividing cells in cancer. Because these drugs act against all rapidly dividing cells, they also reduce the numbers of blood cells being produced by the bone marrow. This action can produce serious adverse effects, like anaemia, but can also be useful for limiting white blood cell activity in autoimmune disorders.

Other drugs also have immunosuppressant effects including corticosteroids and cyclosporin, used following transplant surgery. No drugs are yet available that directly stimulate immune system activity for use in the treatment of immune-deficiency diseases. Deficient plasma factors may be replaced, however, and drugs may also be used to treat the infections and other consequences of immune deficiency.

MAJOR DRUG GROUPS

Anticancer drugs
Immunosuppressants
Drugs for AIDS and immune deficiency

ANTICANCER DRUGS

Cancer is a general term that covers a wide range of disorders ranging from the leukaemias (blood cancers) to solid tumours of the lung, breast, and other organs. What all cancers have in common is that part of the body is ignoring the normal controls on cell growth and multiplication. As a result, the cells of the cancerous tissue (which may be blood cells, the cells of the skin, part of the digestive tract, or indeed any organ) begin to crowd out the normal cells, and in many cases an obvious tumour develops.

A cancerous or malignant tumour will spread in to the structures around it, blocking blood vessels and compressing nerves and other structures. Fragments of the tumour may become detached and be carried in the bloodstream to other parts of the body, where they form secondary growths (metastases).

Cancerous cells are frequently unable to perform their usual functions, and this may lead to progressively impaired function of the organ or area concerned.

Many different factors can provoke cancerous changes in cells. A combination of factors may be involved, notably an individual's genetic background, immune system failure, and overexposure to cancer-causing substances (carcinogens). Known carcinogens include strong sunlight (for those who are fair-skinned), tobacco smoke, radiation, and certain chemicals, viruses and dietary factors.

Treating cancer is a complicated process that depends on the type of cancer, its stage of development, and the patient's condition and wishes. Any of the following treatments may be used on its own or in combination: surgical removal of the cancer, radiation treatment, and chemotherapy, that is, the use of anticancer drugs.

Anticancer drugs that kill cancer cells are sometimes referred to as cytotoxic drugs. They fall into several classes, according to their chemical composition and principal mode of action. Alkylating agents, antimetabolites and cytotoxic antibiotics are among the most widely used classes. In addition to these drugs, sex hormones and related substances are also used to treat some types of cancer.

Why they are used

Anticancer drugs are the treatment of choice for leukaemias, lymphatic cancers and certain forms of cancer of the testis. They are particularly useful for rapidly spreading cancers, but are less effective in the treatment of solid tumours. A fuller listing of cancers in which treatment with drugs may be of benefit is included in the box below. Hormone treatment is offered in most cases of hormone-sensitive cancer, including some forms of breast cancer and cancer of the uterus.

Since all anticancer drugs may produce severe adverse effects (see facing page), they are only used when

SUCCESSFUL CHEMOTHERAPY

Not all cancers respond to treatment with anticancer drugs. Some cancers can be cured by drug treatment. In others, drug treatment can slow or temporarily halt the progress of the disease. In a certain number of cases, drug treatment has no beneficial effect, although in some of these cases other treatments, such as surgery, often produce significant benefits. The table right summarizes the main cancers that fall into each of the three groups described.

Successful drug treatment of cancer normally requires repeated courses of

anticancer drugs because treatment needs to be halted periodically to allow the blood-producing cells in the bone marrow to recover. The diagram below shows the number of cancer cells and normal blood cells before and after each course of treatment with cytotoxic anticancer drugs during successful chemotherapy. Both cancer cells and blood cells are reduced, but the blood cells recover quickly between courses of drug treatment. When treatment is effective, the number of cancer cells is reduced so that they no longer cause symptoms.

Response to chemotherapy

Cancers that can be cured by drugs
Some cancers of the lymphatic system (including Hodgkin's disease)
Acute lymphoblastic leukaemia (a form of blood cancer)
Choriocarcinoma (cancer of the placenta)
Germ cell tumours (cancers affecting sperm and egg cells)
Wilms' tumour (a rare form of kidney cancer that affects children)
Cancer of the testis

Cancers in which drugs produce worthwhile benefits
Breast cancer
Ovarian cancer
Some leukaemias
Multiple myeloma (a bone marrow cancer)
Many types of lung cancer
Cancer of the stomach
Head and neck cancers
Cancer of the prostate
Some cancers of the lymphatic system
Bladder cancer
Cancer of the islet cells of the pancreas
Endometrial cancer (cancer affecting the lining of the uterus)
Cancer of the large intestine
Cancer of the oesophagus

Cancers in which drugs are unlikely to be of benefit
Thyroid cancer
Brain cancer in adults
Malignant melanoma (a form of skin cancer)
Cancer of the soft tissues
Liver cancer
Cancer of the pancreas
Cancer of the cervix
Kidney cell cancer

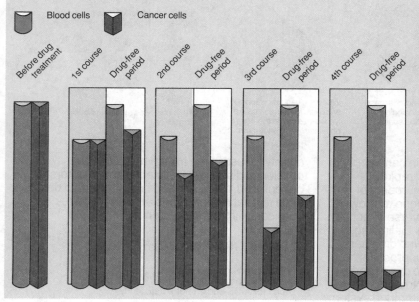

Blood cells   Cancer cells

Before drug treatment | 1st course | Drug-free period | 2nd course | Drug-free period | 3rd course | Drug-free period | 4th course | Drug-free period

there is a reasonable chance of achieving a complete cure, significantly prolonging life, or relieving distressing symptoms. Their effectiveness varies a great deal, depending primarily on the type of cancer and the extent of its spread.

Chemotherapy can also be useful after surgical removal of a tumour, or following radiation treatment, in order to kill any cancer cells that remain.

The choice of anticancer drug depends on the type of cancer and the condition of the person being treated. No class of anticancer drugs is used specifically for a particular cancer; individual drugs have separate properties and uses. Often several different drugs are used, either simultaneously or successively.

Certain anticancer drugs are also used for their effect in suppressing immune system activity (see p.156).

How they work

All cytotoxic anticancer drugs kill cancer cells by preventing them from growing or dividing. Cells grow and divide in several stages. Most anticancer drugs act on one specific stage. During treatment, several drugs may be given in sequence in order to eliminate abnormal cells at all stages of development.

Hormone treatments work by opposing the hormone that encourages the growth of the cancer. For example, some breast cancers are stimulated by the female sex hormone oestrogen. Spread of the cancer may thus be limited by a drug such as tamoxifen that opposes the effects of oestrogen. Other hormone-sensitive cancers are damaged by high doses of a particular sex hormone. Medroxyprogesterone, a progesterone, often halts the spread of endometrial cancer.

How they affect you

At the start of treatment adverse effects of cytotoxic anticancer drugs may be more noticeable than benefits. The most common side effect is nausea and vomiting, for which an anti-emetic drug (see p.90) may be prescribed. Diarrhoea is also a common side effect. Many anticancer drugs cause hair loss because of their effect on the activity of the cells of the hair follicles, but the hair usually starts to regrow after chemotherapy has been completed. Individual drugs may produce other side effects which doctors monitor.

Anticancer drugs are usually administered in the highest doses that can be tolerated in order to kill as many cancer cells as quickly as possible, and therefore to reduce the risk of the cancer spreading to other parts of the body and forming metastases.

Beneficial effects on the underlying

ACTION OF CYTOTOXIC ANTICANCER DRUGS

Each type of cytotoxic drug affects a separate stage of the cancer cell's development, and each type of drug kills the cell by a different mechanism of action. The action of some of the principal classes of cytotoxic drugs is described below.

Alkylating agents and cytotoxic antibiotics
These act within the cell's nucleus to damage the cell's genetic material, DNA. This prevents the cell from growing and dividing.

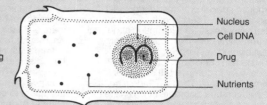

Nucleus
Cell DNA
Drug
Nutrients

Antimetabolites
These drugs prevent the cell from *metabolizing* (processing) nutrients and other substances that are necessary for normal activity in the cell.

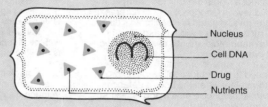

Nucleus
Cell DNA
Drug
Nutrients

disease may not be apparent for several weeks. The unpleasant side effects of intensive cancer chemotherapy combined with the lack of immediate response to the treatment often leads to depression among those receiving anticancer drugs. Specialist counselling may be helpful.

Risks and special precautions

All cytotoxic anticancer drugs interfere with the activity of non-cancerous cells, and for this reason they often produce serious adverse effects during long-term treatment. In particular, these drugs often adversely affect the blood producing cells in the bone marrow. The numbers of both red and white cells and the number of platelets (particles in the blood which are responsible for clotting) may all be reduced. In some cases, symptoms of *anaemia* (weakness and fatigue) and an increased risk of abnormal or excessive bleeding may develop as a result of treatment. In addition, wounds may take longer to heal and susceptible people can develop gout as a result of increased release of uric acid as a by-product of cell destruction. Reduction in the number of white blood cells may result in an increased susceptibility to infection.

Because of these problems, anticancer chemotherapy is often given in hospital where the effects can be closely monitored. Several short courses of drug treatment are often given, thus allowing the bone marrow time to recover in the intervening period

(see Successful chemotherapy, facing page). Blood tests are performed regularly. Where necessary, blood transfusions, antibiotics or other forms of treatment are used to overcome the adverse effects. Where relevant, contraceptive advice is given early in treatment, because most anticancer drugs can damage a developing baby.

In addition to these general effects, individual drugs may have adverse effects on particular organs. These are described in the drug profiles in Part 4.

COMMON DRUGS

Alkylating agents
Chlorambucil
Cyclophosphamide ✱
Melphalan

Antimetabolites
Cytarabine
Fluorouracil
Mercaptopurine ✱
Methotrexate

Hormone treatments
Aminoglutethimide
Clodronate ✱
Flutamide
Formestane
Fosfestrol
Goserelin
Leuprorelin
Medroxyprogesterone ✱
Megestrol ✱
Stilboestrol ✱
Tamoxifen ✱

Cytotoxic antibiotics
Aclarubicin
Doxorubicin ✱
Epirubicin

Other drugs
Actinomycin
Amsacrine
Carboplatin
Cisplatin ✱
Etoposide
Interferon ✱
Procarbazine

✱ See Part 4

IMMUNOSUPPRESSANT DRUGS

The body is protected against attack from bacteria and viruses by the specialized cells and proteins in the blood and tissues that make up the immune system (see p.152). White blood cells known as lymphocytes either kill these invading organisms directly or produce special proteins (*antibodies*) to destroy them. These mechanisms are also responsible for eliminating abnormal or unhealthy cells that could otherwise multiply and develop into a cancer.

In certain conditions, it is medically necessary to dampen the activity of the immune system. These include a number of autoimmune disorders in which the immune system attacks normal body tissue. Autoimmune disorders may affect a single organ – for example, the kidneys in Goodpasture's syndrome or the thyroid gland in Hashimoto's disease – or may cause widespread damage, as in rheumatoid arthritis or systemic lupus erythematosus.

Immune system activity may also need to be reduced following an organ transplant when the body's defences would otherwise attack and reject the transplanted tissue.

Several types of drug are used as immunosuppressants: anticancer drugs (p.154), corticosteroids (p.141), and cyclosporin (p.251).

Why they are used
Immunosuppressant drugs are given in autoimmune disorders such as rheumatoid arthritis when symptoms are severe and other treatments have not provided adequate relief. Cortico-

steroids are usually prescribed initially. The pronounced anti-inflammatory effect of these drugs as well as their immunosuppressant action helps to promote healing of tissue damaged by abnormal immune system activity. Anti-cancer drugs such as azathioprine may be used in addition to corticosteroids if these do not produce sufficient improvement or if their effect wanes (see also Antirheumatic drugs, p.117).

Immunosuppressant drugs are given before and after organ and other tissue transplants. Treatment may have to continue permanently following the transplant to prevent rejection. A number of drugs and drug combinations are used, depending on the organ or tissue being transplanted and the underlying condition of the recipient. Until recently, the most widely used therapy was corticosteroids in conjunction with azathioprine. However, cyclosporin is now the most widely used drug for preventing organ rejection, and is currently being studied to evaluate its possible usefulness in the treatment of auto-immune disorders.

How they work
Immunosuppressant drugs reduce the effectiveness of the immune system, either by depressing the production of lymphocytes or by altering their activity.

How they affect you
When immunosuppressants are given to treat an autoimmune disorder they reduce the severity of the symptoms and in many cases temporarily halt the

progress of the disease. However, they cannot restore major tissue damage – such as damage to the joints in rheumatoid arthritis.

Corticosteroids often promote a general feeling of well-being, but given in doses high enough to produce an immunosuppressant effect, they may also produce unwanted effects. These are described in more detail on p.141. Anticancer drugs, when prescribed as immunosuppressants, are given in low doses that produce only mild side effects. They may cause nausea and vomiting, for which an anti-emetic drug (p.90) may be prescribed. Hair loss may occur, but hair growth usually resumes when the drug is discontinued. Cyclosporin may cause increased growth of facial hair, swelling of the gums, and tingling in the hands.

Risks and special precautions
All of these drugs may produce potentially serious adverse effects. By reducing immune system activity, immunosuppressant drugs can affect the body's ability to fight invading micro-organisms, thereby increasing the risk of serious infections, such as those described on the facing page. Because lymphocyte activity is also important for preventing the multiplication of abnormal cells, there is an increased risk of certain types of cancer. A major draw-back of anticancer drugs is that, in addition to their effect on the production of lymphocytes, they interfere with the growth and division of other blood cells in the bone marrow. Reduced production of red blood cells can cause *anaemia*; when the production of blood platelets is suppressed, blood clotting may be less efficient.

Because cyclosporin is more specific in its action than corticosteroids or anticancer drugs, it produces fewer troublesome side effects. However, it may cause kidney damage, and, in too high a dose, may affect the brain, causing hallucinations or fits. Cyclosporin also tends to raise blood pressure, and another drug may be required to counter-act this effect (see Antihypertensive drugs, p.102).

ACTION OF IMMUNOSUPPRESSANTS

Before treatment
Many types of blood cell, each with a distinct role, form in the bone marrow. Lymphocytes respond to infection and foreign tissue. B lymphocytes produce antibodies to attack invading organisms, whereas T lymphocytes directly attack Invading cells. Other blood cells help the action of the B and T cells.

Other blood cells

B lymphocytes

T lymphocytes

Antibodies

Anticancer drugs
Anticancer drugs slow the production of all cells in the bone marrow.

Corticosteroids
These reduce both B and T lymphocyte activity.

Cyclosporin
This inhibits the activity of T lymphocytes only, and not the activity of B lymphocytes.

COMMON DRUGS

Anticancer drugs
Azathioprine ✳
Chlorambucil
Cyclophosphamide ✳
Methotrexate

Corticosteroids
(See p.141)

Other drugs
Anti-lymphocyte globulin
Cyclosporin ✳

✳ See Part 4

DRUGS FOR AIDS AND IMMUNE DEFICIENCY

Immune deficiency is due to a failure of the body's immune system, which normally protects the body against infecting organisms and the development of cancer. Immune deficiency may be present from birth because the body's immune system has not developed normally, or, it may occur during drug treatment (for example, with corticosteroids or anticancer drugs), or as a result of cancer or infection.

AIDS (acquired immune deficiency syndrome) is a disorder caused by infection with the HIV virus. The virus invades certain types of cells, particularly the white blood cells known as T – helper lymphocytes. T – helper lymphocytes normally activate other cells in the immune system to produce antibodies to fight infection. Because the AIDS virus kills T – helper lymphocytes, the body is unable to fight the AIDS virus or any subsequent infection.

There may be a long interval between infection with the HIV virus and the development of AIDS. Not everybody who is HIV positive progresses to AIDS. Illnesses that commonly affect people with AIDS include candidiasis (thrush), herpes simplex infections, tuberculosis, pneumocystis carinii pneumonia (PCP, a rare form of pneumonia), cryptoccal meningitis, Kaposi's sarcoma (a rare form of skin cancer), lymphomas, and dementia.

Why they are used

Serious infections are the most common consequence of all immune deficiency disorders. These are treated with a variety of antibiotics (p.128), antibacterial drugs (p.131), antiviral drugs (133), and antifungal drugs (p.138). The antiprotozoal drug pentamidine may be used to treat PCP. Kaposi's sarcoma and other cancers are not consistently treated with anti-cancer drugs since there is an added risk of depressing the immune system. Radiation therapy may be given instead.

When serious AIDS-related infections have occurred, the new antiviral drug zidovudine, originally known as AZT (azidothymidine), may be prescribed. This does not provide a cure, but may prolong life expectancy. HIV positive patients may be given treatments to prevent some of these conditions (especially PCP and tuberculosis).

New drugs

Current research into new drug treatment for AIDS is proceeding along two principal lines. Scientists are searching for a vaccine that will provide immunity against the AIDS virus, and they are also trying to develop drugs to eradicate the HIV– 1 virus from the body once infection has occurred (see box, right).

AIDS INFECTION AND POSSIBLE TREATMENTS

The illustrations below show how the AIDS virus enters body cells and, once inside, replicates itself to produce new viruses. The stages at which drugs might in the future be used to block the action of AIDS viruses, or destroy them, are also indicated.

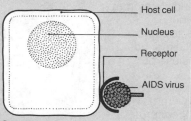

Stage 1
The virus binds to a specialized site (receptor) on a body cell.

Possible drug intervention
Binding could be blocked by the production of antibodies to destroy the virus or the cell's receptor.

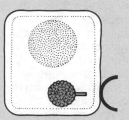

Stage 2
The virus enters the cell.

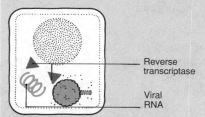

Stage 3
The virus loses its protective coat and releases RNA, its genetic material, and an enzyme known as reverse transcriptase.

Possible drug intervention
Drugs may be developed to prevent the virus from losing its protective coat. Amantadine has this effect on the influenza A virus but not on HIV–1.

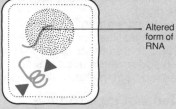

Stage 4
The enzyme reverse transcriptase converts the viral RNA into a form that can then enter the host cell's nucleus and may become integrated with the cell's genetic material.

Possible drug intervention
Zidovudine blocks the action of reverse transcriptase.

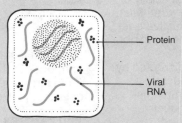

Stage 5
The host cell starts to produce new viral RNA and protein from the viral material that has been incorporated into its nucleus.

Possible drug intervention
There is a possibility that in the future drugs may be available to inhibit the production of new viral RNA and proteins by altering genes on the viral material.

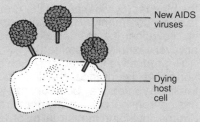

Stage 6
The new viral RNA and proteins are assembled to produce new viruses. These leave the host cell (which then dies) and are free to attack other cells in the body.

Possible drug intervention
The drug alpha interferon prevents the new viruses from leaving the cell. It is under investigation for limiting the spread of AIDS infection within the body.

REPRODUCTIVE & URINARY TRACTS

The reproductive systems of men and women consist of those organs which produce and release sperm (male), store and release eggs (female), and then nurture a fertilized egg until it becomes a baby (female).

The urinary system filters wastes and water from the blood, producing urine, which is then expelled from the body. The reproductive and urinary systems of men are partially linked, but those of women form two physically close but functionally separate systems.

The female reproductive organs comprise the ovaries, fallopian tubes, and uterus (womb). The uterus opens via the cervix (neck of the uterus) into the vagina. The principal male reproductive organs are the two sperm-producing glands, the testes (testicles) that lie within the scrotum, and the penis. Other structures in the male reproductive tract include the prostate gland and several tubular structures: the epididymis, the vas deferens, the seminal vesicles, and the urethra (see right).

The urinary organs in both sexes comprise the kidneys that filter urine from the blood (see also p.99), the ureters down which urine passes, and the bladder where urine is stored until it is released from the body via the urethra.

What can go wrong

The reproductive and urinary tracts are both subject to infection. Such infections (apart from those transmitted by sexual activity) are relatively uncommon in men because the long male urethra prevents bacteria and other organisms passing easily to the bladder and upper urinary tract, and to the male sex organs. The shorter female urethra allows urinary tract infections, especially of the bladder (cystitis) and of the urethra (urethritis), to occur commonly. The female reproductive tract is also vulnerable to infection, sometimes, but not always, sexually transmitted.

Reproductive function may also be disrupted by hormonal disturbances that lead to reduced fertility. Women may be troubled by symptoms arising from normal activity of the reproductive organs, including menstrual disorders and problems associated with childbirth.

The most common urinary problems apart from infection are those related to bladder function. Urine may be released involuntarily (incontinence) or it may be retained in the bladder. Such disorders are usually the result of abnormal nerve signals to the bladder or sphincter muscle. The filtering action of the kidneys may be disrupted by

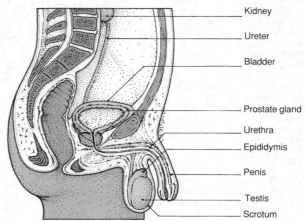

Male reproductive system
Sperm produced in each of the testes pass into the epididymis, a tightly-coiled tube in which the sperm mature before passing along the vas deferens to the seminal vesicle. Sperm are stored in the seminal vesicle until they are ejaculated from the penis via the urethra together with seminal fluid and secretions from the prostate gland.

Kidney
Ureter
Bladder
Prostate gland
Urethra
Epididymis
Penis
Testis
Scrotum

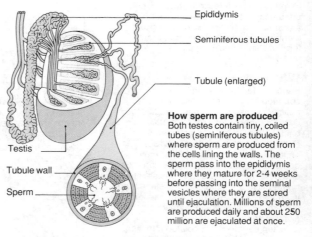

Epididymis
Seminiferous tubules
Tubule (enlarged)
Testis
Tubule wall
Sperm

How sperm are produced
Both testes contain tiny, coiled tubes (seminiferous tubules) where sperm are produced from the cells lining the walls. The sperm pass into the epididymis where they mature for 2-4 weeks before passing into the seminal vesicles where they are stored until ejaculation. Millions of sperm are produced daily and about 250 million are ejaculated at once.

alteration to the composition of the blood or the hormones that regulate urination, or by damage (from infection or inflammation) to the filtering units themselves.

Why drugs are used

Antibiotic drugs (p.128) are used to eliminate both urinary and reproductive tract infections (including sexually transmitted infections). Certain infections of the vagina are caused by fungi or yeasts and require antifungal drugs (p.138).

Hormone drugs are used both to reduce fertility deliberately (oral contraceptives) and to increase fertility in certain situations where it has not been

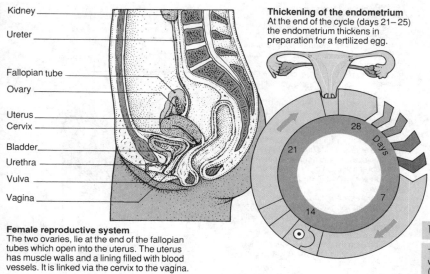

Kidney
Ureter
Fallopian tube
Ovary
Uterus
Cervix
Bladder
Urethra
Vulva
Vagina

Thickening of the endometrium
At the end of the cycle (days 21–25) the endometrium thickens in preparation for a fertilized egg.

28
21
Days
7
14

Menstrual cycle
A monthly cycle of hormone interactions allows an egg to be released and, if fertilized, creates the correct environment for it to implant in the uterus. Major body changes occur, most obviously, monthly vaginal bleeding (menstruation). The cycle usually starts between 11 and 14 years, and continues until the menopause which occurs at around 50. After the menopause, childbearing is no longer possible. The cycle is usually 28 days, but this varies with individuals.

Menstruation
If no egg is fertilized, the endometrium is shed (days 1–5).

Fertile period
Conception may take place in the two days after ovulation (days 14–16).

Female reproductive system
The two ovaries, lie at the end of the fallopian tubes which open into the uterus. The uterus has muscle walls and a lining filled with blood vessels. It is linked via the cervix to the vagina.

URINARY SYSTEM

The kidneys extract waste and excess water from the blood. The waste liquid (urine) passes into the bladder, from whichit is expelled via the urethra.

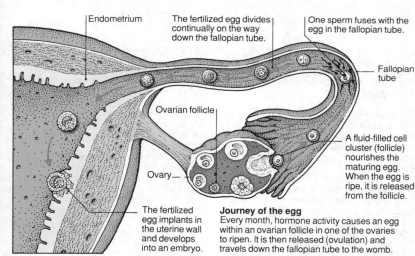

Endometrium

The fertilized egg divides continually on the way down the fallopian tube.

One sperm fuses with the egg in the fallopian tube.

Fallopian tube

Ovarian follicle

A fluid-filled cell cluster (follicle) nourishes the maturing egg. When the egg is ripe, it is released from the follicle.

Ovary

The fertilized egg implants in the uterine wall and develops into an embryo.

Journey of the egg
Every month, hormone activity causes an egg within an ovarian follicle in one of the ovaries to ripen. It is then released (ovulation) and travels down the fallopian tube to the womb.

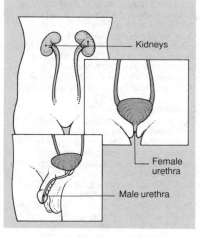

Kidneys

Female urethra

Male urethra

possible for a couple to conceive. Hormones may also be used to regulate menstruation when it is irregular or excessively painful or heavy. Analgesic drugs (p.80) are used to treat menstrual period pain and are also widely used for pain relief in labour. Other drugs used in labour include those that increase contraction of the muscles of the uterus and those that limit blood loss after the birth. Drugs may also be employed to halt premature labour.

Drugs that alter the transmission of nerve signals to the bladder muscles have an important role in the treatment of urinary incontinence and retention. Drugs that increase the filtering action

of the kidneys are commonly used to reduce blood pressure and fluid retention (see Diuretics, p.99). Other drugs may alter the composition of the urine, such as the uricosuric drugs used in the treatment of gout (p.119).

MAJOR DRUG GROUPS

Drugs used to treat menstrual disorders
Oral contraceptives
Drugs for infertility
Drugs used in labour
Drugs used for urinary disorders

DRUGS USED TO TREAT MENSTRUAL DISORDERS

The menstrual cycle results from the actions of female sex hormones that each month cause ovulation (release of an egg) and thickening of the endometrium (lining of the uterus) in preparation for pregnancy. Unless the egg is fertilized, the endometrium is shed about two weeks later during menstruation (see also p.158).

The main problems associated with menstruation that may require medical treatment are excessive blood loss (menorrhagia), pain during menstruation (dysmenorrhoea), and distressing symptoms prior to menstruation (pre-menstrual syndrome). Absence of periods (amenorrhoea) is discussed under Female sex hormones (p.147).

The drugs most commonly used to treat the menstrual disorders described above include oestrogens and pro-gesterone (or synthetic progesterone drugs known as progestogens), danazol, and analgesics.

Why they are used

Drug treatment for menstrual disorders is undertaken only when the doctor has ruled out the possibility of an underlying gynaecological disorder such as pelvic infection or fibroids. In some cases, especially in women over the age of 35, a D and C (dilatation and curettage) may be recommended. When no underlying reason for the problem has been found, drug treatment aimed primarily at the relief of symptoms is usually prescribed.

Dysmenorrhoea

Painful menstrual periods are usually treated initially with a simple analgesic (see also p.80). Aspirin and the nonsteroidal anti-inflammatory drug mefenamic acid are often most effective because they counter the effects of chemicals called prostaglandins, which are partly responsible for transmission of pain. Mefenamic acid is also used to reduce excessive blood loss in menorrhagia (see below).

When these drugs fail to provide sufficient relief of pain, hormonal drug treatment may be advised. If contra-ception is also required, treatment may take the form of an oral contraceptive pill containing an oestrogen and a pro-gestogen, or a progestogen alone. However, non-contraceptive pro-gestogen preparations may also be prescribed. These are usually taken for only a few days during each month. The treatment of dysmenorrhoea caused by endometriosis is described in the box above right.

Menorrhagia

Excessive blood loss during mens-truation can sometimes be reduced by mefenamic acid. But in many cases,

ENDOMETRIOSIS

Endometriosis is a condition in which fragments of endometrial tissue (uterine lining) occur outside the uterus in the pelvic cavity. This disorder causes severe pain during menstruation, often pain during intercourse and may sometimes lead to infertility.

Drugs used for this disorder are similar to those prescribed for heavy periods (menorrhagia). However, in this case the intention is to suppress endometrial development for an extended period so that the abnormal tissue eventually withers away. Progesterone supplements to suppress thickening of the endometrium may be prescribed throughout the mens-trual cycle. Alternatively, danazol, a drug that suppresses endometrial develop-ment by reducing oestrogen production, may be prescribed. Any drug treatment usually needs to be continued for a minimum of six months.

When drug treatment is unsuccessful, surgical removal of the abnormal tissue is usually necessary.

Sites of endometriosis

Ovary | Wall of uterus | Fallopian tube

Bladder wall | Bowel wall

☐ Endometrial tissue

hormone treatment as described under dysmenorrhoea is advised. Alter-natively, danazol, a drug that reduces production of the hormone oestrogen, may be prescribed.

Premenstrual syndrome

This is a collection of psychological and physical symptoms that affect many women to some degree in the days before menstruation. Psychological symptoms include mood changes such as increased irritability, depression and anxiety. The principal physical symp-toms are bloating, headache, and breast tenderness. Because many doctors believe the premenstrual syndrome to be the result of a drop in progesterone levels in the last half of the menstrual cycle, non-contraceptive supplements of this hormone may be given in the week or so before menstruation. Oral contraceptives may be considered as an alternative. Other drugs sometimes used include pyridoxine (vitamin B₆) for depression, diuretics (p.99) if bloating due to fluid retention is a problem, and bromocriptine when breast tenderness is the major symptom. Anti-anxiety drugs (p.83) may be prescribed in rare cases where severe premenstrual psychological disturbance is experienced.

How they work

Drugs used in menstrual disorders act in a variety of ways. Hormonal treatments are aimed at suppressing the pattern of hormonal changes that is causing troublesome symptoms. Contraceptive

preparations override the normal men-strual cycle. Ovulation does not occur and the endometrium does not thicken normally. Bleeding that occurs at the end of a cycle is less likely to be abnormally heavy, to be preceded by distressing symptoms, or to be accompanied by severe discomfort. For further information on oral contra-ceptives, see p.161.

Non-contraceptive progestogen preparations taken in the days before menstruation do not suppress ovulation. Increased progesterone during this time reduces premenstrual symptoms and prevents excessive thickening of the endometrium.

Danazol, a potent drug, prevents the thickening of the endometrium, thereby correcting excessively heavy periods. Blood loss is reduced; in some cases menstruation ceases altogether during treatment.

COMMON DRUGS

Oestrogens and progestogens
(See p.147)

Analgesics
Aspirin ✳
Mefenamic acid ✳

Diuretics
(See p.99)

Others
Bromocriptine ✳
Buserelin
Danazol ✳
Gestrinone
Leuprorelin
Nafarelin
Pyridoxine ✳

✳ See Part 4

ORAL CONTRACEPTIVES

There are many different means of ensuring that conception and pregnancy do not follow sexual intercourse, but for most women the oral contraceptive is the most effective method (see Comparison of reliability of different methods of contraception, right). It has the added advantage of being convenient and unobtrusive during lovemaking. About 25 per cent of women seeking contraceptive protection in Great Britain choose a form of oral contraceptive.

There are three main types of oral contraceptive: the combined pill, the progestogen-only pill and the phased pill. All types contain a progestogen (a synthetic form of the female sex hormone progesterone). Combined and phased pills also contain a natural or synthetic oestrogen (see also Female sex hormones, p.147). All types are taken in a monthly cycle.

COMPARISON OF RELIABILITY OF DIFFERENT METHODS OF CONTRACEPTION

The table (right) indicates the number of pregnancies that occur with each method of contraception among 100 women using that method in a year. The wide variation that occurs with some methods takes into account pregnancies that occur as a result of incorrect use of the method.

Method	Pregnancies*
Combined and phased pills	2 – 3
Progestogen-only pill	2.5 – 4
IUCD**	4 – 9
Condom/diaphragm	3 – 20
Rhythm	25 – 30
Contraceptive sponge	9 – 27
Vaginal spermicide alone	2 – 30
Norethisterone implant	Less than 1
No contraception	80 – 85

*Per 100 users per year.
** Intra-uterine contraceptive device.

Why they are used
The combined pill
The combined pill is the most widely prescribed form of oral contraceptive and that with the lowest failure rate in terms of unwanted pregnancies. It is referred to simply as the "pill" and is the type considered most suitable for young women who want to use a hormonal form of contraception. The combined pill is particularly suitable for those women who regularly experience exceptionally painful, heavy or prolonged periods (see Drugs for menstrual disorders, facing page).

There are many different products available containing a fixed dose of an oestrogen and a progestogen drug. They are generally divided into three groups according to their oestrogen content (see Hormone content of oral contraceptives, below). Low dose products are selected whenever possible in order to minimize the risk of adverse effects.

Progestogen-only pill
The progestogen-only pill is often recommended for women who react adversely to the oestrogen in the combined pill or for whom the combined pill is not considered suitable because of their age or medical history (see Risks and special precautions, p.163). It is also prescribed for women who are breast feeding since it does not reduce milk production. This form of pill is slightly less reliable than the combined pill and must be taken at precisely the same time each day for maximum contraceptive effect.

Phased pills
The newest form of oral contraceptive, each pack of products of this type contain pills divided into two or three groups or phases. Each phase contains a different proportion of an oestrogen and a progestogen. The aim is to provide a hormonal balance that more closely resembles the fluctuations of a normal menstrual cycle. Phased pills, taken in the same way as the combined pill, provide effective contraceptive protection for many women who suffer side effects from the other forms of oral contraceptive available.

How they work
In a normal menstrual cycle the ripening and release of an egg, and the preparation of the uterus for implantation of the fertilized egg are the result of a complex interplay between the natural female sex hormones, oestrogen and progesterone, and the pituitary hormones, follicle-stimulating hormone (FSH) and luteinizing hormone (LH) (see also p.147). Oestrogen and progestogens contained in oral contraceptives act in a variety of ways to disrupt the normal cycle in such a way as to make conception less likely.

With combined and phased pills, increased levels of oestrogen and progesterone produce similar effects as the hormonal changes of pregnancy. The actions of the hormones inhibit the production of FSH and LH, thereby preventing the egg from ripening in the ovary and from being released.

The progestogen-only pill has a slightly different action. It does not always prevent release of an egg; its main contraceptive effect may be on the

THE HORMONE CONTENT OF COMMON ORAL CONTRACEPTIVES

Oral contraceptive formulations vary according to their hormone content. Oestrogen-containing formulations are classified according to their oestrogen content. Those that contain less than 50 micrograms (mcg) of oestrogen are considered low oestrogen; those that contain 50mcg or above are high oestrogen. All phased pills are low oestrogen.

Type of pill (oestrogen content)	Brand names
Combined (30mcg and under)	Cosnova 30, Eugynon 30, Femodene, Femodene ED, Loestrin 20, Loestrin 30, Marvelon, Mercilon, Microgynon 30, Minulet, Ovran 30, Ovranette.
(35mcg)	Brevinor, Cilest, Neocon 1/35, Norimin, Ovysmen.
(50mcg)	Norinyl-1, Ortho-Novin 1/50, Ovran.
Phased (30 – 40mcg)	BiNovum, Logynon, Logynon ED, Synphase, Triadene, Tri-Minulet, Trinordial, TriNovum, TriNovum ED.
Progestogen-only (no oestrogen)	Femulen, Micronor, Microval, Neogest, Norgeston, Noriday.

ORAL CONTRACEPTIVES continued

BALANCING THE RISKS AND BENEFITS OF ORAL CONTRACEPTIVES

Oral contraceptives are safe for the vast majority of young women. However, every woman considering using this method of contraception should see her doctor to discuss the risks and possible adverse effects of these drugs

before deciding that a hormonal method is the most suitable in her case. A variety of factors must be taken into account, including the woman's age, her own medical history and that of her close relatives, and factors such as

whether she is a smoker. The importance of these factors varies according to the type of pill. The table below summarizes the main advantages and disadvantages of oestrogen-containing and progestogen-only pills.

Type of oral contraceptive	Oestrogen-containing (combined and phased)	Progestogen-only
Advantages	● Very reliable ● Convenient/unobtrusive ● Regularizes menstruation ● Reduced menstrual pain and blood loss ● Reduced risk of: ▼ benign breast disease ▼ endometriosis ▼ ectopic pregnancy ▼ ovarian cysts ▼ pelvic infection ▼ ovarian and endometrial cancer	● Reasonably reliable ● Convenient/unobtrusive ● Suitable during lactation ● Avoids oestrogen-related side effects and risks ● Allows rapid return to fertility
Side effects	● Weight gain ● Depression ● Breast swelling ● Reduced sex drive ● Headaches ● Increased vaginal discharge ● Nausea	● Irregular menstruation
Risks	● Thrombosis/embolism ● Heart disease ● High blood pressure ● Jaundice ● Cancer of the liver (rare) ● Gallstones	● Ectopic pregnancy ● Ovarian cysts
Factors that may prohibit use	● Previous thrombosis ● Heart disease ● High levels of fat in blood ● Liver disease ● Blood disorders ● High blood pressure ● Unexplained vaginal bleeding ● Migraine ● Otosclerosis ● Presence of several risk factors (below)	● Previous ectopic pregnancy ● Heart or circulatory disease ● Unexplained vaginal bleeding
Factors that increase risks	● Smoking ● Obesity ● Increasing age ● Diabetes mellitus ● Family history of heart or circulatory disease ● Current treatment with other drugs	● As for oestrogen-containing pills, but to a lesser degree

How to minimize your health risks while taking the pill

▼ Give up smoking.
▼ Maintain a healthy weight.
▼ Have regular blood pressure and blood fat checks.
▼ Have regular cervical smear tests.

▼ Remind your doctor that you are taking oral contraceptives before taking other prescription drugs.
▼ Stop taking oestrogen-containing oral contraceptives 4 weeks before planned major surgery (use alternative contraception).

mucus that lines the cervix which thickens and becomes impenetrable to sperm. This effect also occurs to a lesser extent with combined pills and phased pills.

How they affect you

Each course of combined and phased pills lasts for 21 days followed by a pill-free seven days during which menstruation occurs. Some brands contain seven additional inactive pills. This means that the new course directly follows the last so that the habit of taking the pill daily is not broken. Progestogen-only pills are taken for 28 days each month. Menstruation usually occurs during the last few days of the menstrual cycle.

Women taking oral contraceptives, especially those containing oestrogen, usually find that their menstrual periods are lighter and relatively pain-free. Some women cease to menstruate altogether. This is not a cause for concern in itself, providing no pills have been missed, but it may make it difficult to determine if pregnancy has occurred. An apparently missed period probably indicates a light one, rather than pregnancy. However, if you have missed two consecutive periods and you feel that you are pregnant, it is advisable to have a pregnancy test.

All forms of oral contraceptive may cause spotting of blood in mid-cycle ("breakthrough bleeding") especially at first, but this can be a particular problem of the progestogen-only pill.

Oral contraceptives containing oestrogen may produce any of a large number of mild side effects depending on the dose. Symptoms similar to those experienced early in pregnancy may occur, particularly in the first few months of pill use: some women complain of nausea and vomiting, weight gain, depression, altered libido, increased appetite, and cramps in the legs and abdomen. The pill may also affect the circulation, producing minor headaches and dizziness. All these effects usually disappear within a few months, but if they persist, it may be advisable to change to a brand containing a lower dose of oestrogen or to another contraceptive method.

Risks and special precautions

All oral contraceptives need to be taken regularly for maximum protection against pregnancy. Contraceptive protection can be reduced by missing a pill (see What to do if you miss a pill, below). It may also be reduced by vomiting or diarrhoea. If you suffer from either of these symptoms, it is advisable to act as if you had missed your last pill. Many drugs may also affect the action of oral contraceptives and it is essential to inform your doctor that you are taking oral contraceptives before taking additional prescribed medications.

Oral contraceptives, particularly those containing an oestrogen, have been found to carry a number of risks. These are summarized in the box on the facing page. One of the most serious potential

POSTCOITAL CONTRACEPTION

Pregnancy following intercourse without contraception may be avoided by taking a short course of postcoital ("morning after") contraceptive pills. The preparations used for this purpose usually contain an oestrogen and a progestogen and are usually taken in two doses within 72 hours following intercourse. Alternatively, a high dose of oestrogen alone may be used. These drugs postpone ovulation and act on the lining of the uterus to prevent implantation of the egg. However, the high doses required make them unsuitable for regular use.

adverse effects of oestrogen-containing pills is development of a thrombus (blood clot) in a vein or artery that may travel to the lungs or cause a stroke or heart attack. The risk of thrombus-formation increases with age and other factors, notably obesity, high blood pressure and smoking. Doctors assess these risk factors for each individual when prescribing oral contraceptives. A woman over 35 may be advised against taking a combined pill, especially if she smokes or has an underlying medical condition such as diabetes mellitus.

High blood pressure is a possible complication of oral contraceptives for some women. Measurement of blood pressure before the pill is prescribed and at six-monthly intervals thereafter is advised for all women taking oral contraceptives.

Despite frequent reports linking the use of oral contraceptives to certain forms of cancer, evidence supporting a direct relationship between the pill and cancer is not conclusive. Some very rare liver cancers have occurred in pill-users, but cancers of the ovaries and uterus are less common.

There is no evidence that oral contraceptives reduce a woman's fertility or that they damage babies conceived after they are discontinued, but doctors advise that you wait for at least one normal menstrual period before attempting to become pregnant.

COMMON DRUGS

Progestogens	Oestrogens
Desogestrel	Ethinyloestradiol *
Gestodene	Mestranol
Levonorgestrel *	
Norethisterone *	
Norgestimate	

| * See Part 4 |

WHAT TO DO IF YOU MISS A PILL

Contraceptive protection may be reduced if blood levels of the hormones in the body fall as a result of missing a pill. It is particularly important to ensure that the progestogen-only pills are taken punctually. If you miss a pill, the action you should take depends on the degree of lateness and the type of pill being used (see below).

	Combined and phased pills	Progestogen-only pills
3 – 12 hours late	Take now. No additional precautions necessary.	Take now. Take additional precautions for the next 7 days.
Over 12 hours late	Take the missed pill straight away and the next on time (even if on the same day). If more than one pill has been missed, take the latest missed pill now and the next on time. Take additional precautions for the next 7 days. If the 7 days extends into the pill-free (or inactive pill) period start the next packet without a break (or without taking the inactive pills).	Take the missed pill. Take the next on time. Take additional precautions for the next 7 days.

DRUGS FOR INFERTILITY

Conception and establishment of pregnancy require a healthy reproductive tract in both partners. The man must produce sufficient numbers of healthy sperm; the woman must be able to produce healthy eggs that are able to pass freely down the fallopian tubes to the uterus. The lining of the uterus must be in a condition that allows the implantation of the fertilized egg.

Although the cause of infertility sometimes remains undiscovered, in the majority of cases it is found to be due to one of the following factors: intercourse taking place at the wrong time during the menstrual cycle; the man producing too few or unhealthy sperm; the woman failing to ovulate (release an egg), or having blocked fallopian tubes as a result of previous pelvic infection.

The production of gonadotrophin hormones – follicle-stimulating hormone (FSH) and luteinizing hormone (LH) – necessary for ovulation and implantation of the egg may be disturbed by physical illness or psychological stress.

Doctors do not usually begin to investigate the cause of failure to conceive until normal sexual intercourse without contraception has been taking place regularly for over a year. If no simple explanation can be found, the man's semen will be analysed to find out if he is producing healthy sperm in sufficient quantity. If these tests show abnormally low numbers of sperm or if a large proportion of the sperm produced are unhealthy, some of the treatments described in the box below may be tried.

If no abnormality of sperm production is found, the woman will be given a thorough medical examination. Ovulation is monitored and blood tests may be performed to assess hormone levels. If ovulation does not occur, the woman may be offered drug treatment.

Why they are used

Drugs are useful in helping to achieve pregnancy only when a hormone defect

MALE INFERTILITY

When the quality of the sperm is normal, but the numbers produced insufficient, the cause may be under-production of FSH and LH by the pituitary gland. In such cases, regular treatment may be prescribed with a pituitary-stimulating drug such as clomiphene, or with FSH or human chorionic gonadotrophin which mimics the action of LH. Such drug treatment may need to be continued for many months before any increase in sperm production can be detected.

If, however, abnormal sperm production is due to an abnormality of the testes or another part of the genito-urinary tract, drug treatment is unlikely to be helpful.

ACTION OF FERTILITY DRUGS

Ovulation (release of an egg) and implantation are governed by hormones. FSH stimulates ripening of the egg follicle. LH triggers ovulation and ensures that progesterone is produced to prepare the uterus for the implantation of the egg. Drugs for female infertility boost these hormones.

FSH and HCG Additional FSH enhances

the action of the natural hormone early in the menstrual cycle. HCG mimics the action of natural LH at mid-cycle.

Clomiphene Normally, oestrogen suppresses the output of FSH and LH by the pituitary gland. Clomiphene opposes the action of oestrogen so that FSH and LH continue to be produced.

Comparison of normal hormone fluctuation and timing of drug treatment

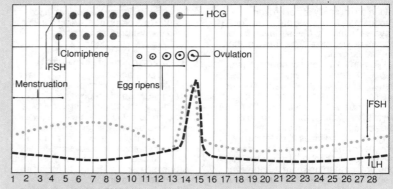

Days of menstrual cycle

that inhibits ovulation has been diagnosed. Treatment with fertility drugs may need to be continued for many months and does not always produce a pregnancy.

Women in whom the pituitary gland produces some FSH and LH may be given courses of clomiphene for several days during each month. An effective dose produces ovulation 5 to 10 days after the last tablet is taken. Couples are advised to have intercourse during this phase.

Clomiphene occasionally thickens the cervical mucus, thereby impeding the passage of sperm. If this happens, an oestrogen drug that counteracts this effect may be given prior to the course of clomiphene.

If treatment with clomiphene fails to produce ovulation, or if a disorder of the pituitary gland prevents the production of FSH and LH, treatment with FSH and human chorionic gonadotrophin (HCG) may be given.

FSH is given during the second week of the menstrual cycle, followed by an injection of HCG. It may be necessary to repeat the courses of these drugs several times before a pregnancy occurs.

How they work

Fertility drugs increase the chance of ovulation by boosting the levels of LH

and FSH, the pituitary hormones that govern ovulation.

Clomiphene stimulates the pituitary gland to increase its output of these hormones. FSH and HCG mimic the action of naturally-produced FSH and LH respectively. Both forms of treatment, when successful, stimulate ovulation and implantation of the fertilized egg.

How they affect you

Each of these drugs may produce minor adverse effects. Clomiphene may cause hot flushes, nausea and headache, while HCG can cause tiredness, headache and mood changes. FSH can make the ovaries enlarge, producing abdominal discomfort that may continue for several days.

All these drugs increase the likelihood of multiple births (usually twins). A less common adverse effect is an increased risk of ovarian cysts with clomiphene.

COMMON DRUGS

Chorionic gonadotrophin (HCG) *
Clomiphene *
Cyclofenil
Goserelin

Menotrophin (FSH plus LH)
Tamoxifen *
Urofollitrophin (FSH)

* See Part 4

DRUGS USED IN LABOUR

Normal labour has three stages. In the first stage the uterus begins to contract, first irregularly and then gradually more regularly and powerfully, while the cervix dilates until it is fully stretched. During the second stage, powerful contractions of the uterus push the baby down the birth canal and out of the body. The third stage is the delivery of the placenta.

Drugs may be required during one or more stages of labour for any of the following reasons: to induce or augment labour; to delay premature labour (see Uterine muscle relaxants, below right); and to relieve pain. The administration of some drugs may be viewed as part of normal obstetric care; for example, the uterine stimulant ergometrine may be injected routinely before the third stage of labour. Other drugs are administered only when the condition of the mother or baby requires intervention. The possible adverse effects of the drug on both parties are always carefully balanced against the benefits.

Drugs to induce or augment labour

Induction of labour may be advised when a doctor considers it risky for the health of the mother or baby for the pregnancy to continue – for example, if natural labour does not occur within two weeks of the due date or when a woman has pre-eclampsia. Other common reasons for inducing labour include premature rupture of the membrane surrounding the baby (breaking of the waters), slow growth of the baby due to poor nourishment by the placenta, or death of the fetus in the uterus.

When labour needs to be induced, oxytocin, a uterine stimulant, may be administered intravenously. Alternatively, a prostaglandin pessary may be given to soften and dilate the cervix. If these methods are ineffective or cannot be used because of potential adverse effects (see Risks and special precautions, above right), a caesarean delivery may have to be performed.

DRUGS USED TO TERMINATE PREGNANCY

Drugs may be used in a hospital or clinic to terminate pregnancy up to 20 weeks, or to empty the uterus after the death of the baby. Before the 14th week of pregnancy, a prostaglandin may be given as a vaginal pessary to dilate the cervix before removing the fetus under general anaesthetic.

After the 14th week, labour is induced with a prostaglandin drug in a vaginal pessary, injected into the uterus, or via a catheter placed through the cervix. These methods may be supplemented by oxytocin given by intravenous drip (see Drugs to induce or augment labour, above).

Oxytocin may also be used to strengthen the force of contractions in labour that has started spontaneously but is not progressing.

A combination of oxytocin and another uterine stimulant, ergometrine, is given to most women as the baby is being born or immediately following birth to prevent excessive bleeding after the delivery of the placenta. This combination encourages the uterus to contract after delivery, which restricts the flow of blood.

Risks and special precautions

When oxytocin is used to induce labour, the dosage is carefully monitored throughout to prevent the possibility of excessively violent contractions. It is administered to women who have had surgery of the uterus only with careful monitoring. The drug is not known to affect the baby adversely. Ergometrine is not given to women who have suffered from high blood pressure during the course of pregnancy.

Drugs used for pain relief

Narcotic analgesics

Narcotic drugs such as pethidine may be given once active labour has been established (see Analgesics, p.80). Possible side effects for the mother include drowsiness, nausea and vomiting. Narcotics may cause breathing problems for the new baby but these problems may be reversed by the antidote naloxone.

Epidural anaesthesia

This provides pain relief during labour and birth by numbing the nerves leading to the uterus and pelvic area. It is often used during a planned caesarean delivery thus enabling the mother to be fully conscious for the birth.

An epidural involves the injection of a local anaesthetic drug (see p.80) into the epidural space between the spinal cord and the vertebrae. An epidural may block the mother's urge to push during the second stage, and a forceps delivery may be necessary. Headaches may occasionally occur following epidural anaesthesia.

Oxygen and nitrous oxide

These gases are combined to produce a mixture that reduces the pain of contractions. During the first and second stages of labour it is self-administered by inhalation through a mask or mouthpiece. If it is used over too long a period it may produce nausea, confusion and dehydration in the mother.

Local anaesthetics

These drugs are injected inside the vagina or near the vaginal opening and are used to numb sensation during

WHEN DRUGS ARE USED IN LABOUR

The drugs used in each stage of labour are described below.

Before labour
Oxytocin
Prostaglandins

First stage
Epidural anaesthetics
Oxytocin
Pethidine

Second stage
Local anaesthetics
Nitrous oxide
Oxytocin

Third stage
Ergometrine
Oxytocin

forceps delivery, before an episiotomy (an incision made to enlarge the vaginal opening) and when stitches are necessary. Side effects are rare.

Uterine muscle relaxants

When contractions of the uterus start before the 34th week of pregnancy, doctors usually advise bed rest and may also administer a drug to relax the muscles of the uterus and thus halt labour. Initially the drug is given in hospital by injection, but may be continued orally at home. These drugs stimulate the sympathetic nervous system (see Autonomic nervous system, p.79) and may cause palpitations and anxiety in the mother. They have not been shown to have adverse effects on the baby.

COMMON DRUGS

Prostaglandins
Carboprost
Dinoprostone
Gemeprost
Mifepristone

Pain relief
Entonox® (oxygen
and nitrous oxide)

Narcotic analgesics
Pethidine *

Uterine muscle relaxants
Isoxuprine
Ritodrine *
Salbutamol *
Terbutaline

Uterine stimulants
Ergometrine
Oxytocin

Local anaesthetics
Bupivacaine
Lignocaine

＊ See Part 4

DRUGS USED FOR URINARY DISORDERS

Urine is produced by the kidneys and stored in the bladder. As urine accumulates, the bladder walls stretch, and pressure within the bladder increases. Eventually, the stretching stimulates nerve endings that produce the urge to urinate. The ring of muscle (sphincter) around the bladder neck normally keeps the bladder closed until it is consciously relaxed, allowing urine to pass via the urethra out of the body.

A number of disorders can affect the urinary tract. The most common are infection in the bladder (cystitis) and urethra (urethritis), and loss of reliable control over urination (urinary incontinence). A less common problem is inability to expel urine (urinary retention). Drugs used to treat these problems include antibiotics and antibacterial drugs, analgesics, drugs to increase the acidity of the urine, and drugs that act on nerve control over the muscles of the bladder and sphincter.

Drugs for urinary infection

Infections of the bladder are almost always caused by bacteria. Symptoms include a continual urge to urinate, although often nothing is passed, pain on urinating, and lower abdominal pain.

Antibiotic and antibacterial drugs are used to eradicate infection. Co-trimoxazole, sometimes in a single large dose or in longer courses lasting seven to fourteen days, is one of the most common treatments. A large number of other drugs are also effective in the treatment of infections (see Antibiotics, p.128, and Antibacterial drugs, p.131).

Measures are also sometimes taken to increase the acidity of the urine, making it hostile to bacteria. Ascorbic acid (vitamin C) powder in water, and acid fruit juices have this effect. Symptoms are commonly relieved within a few hours of the start of treatment.

For maximum effect, all drug treatments prescribed for urinary tract infections need to be accompanied by increased fluid intake.

Drugs for urinary incontinence

Urinary incontinence can occur for a number of reasons. A weak sphincter muscle allows the involuntary passage of urine when abdominal pressure is raised by coughing or physical exertion. This is known as stress incontinence and commonly affects women who have had children. Urgency – the sudden need to urinate – stems from increased sensitivity of the bladder muscle; small quantities of urine stimulate the urge to urinate frequently.

Incontinence can also occur due to loss of nerve control in neurological disorders such as multiple sclerosis. In children, inability to control urination at night (nocturnal enuresis) is also a form of urinary incontinence.

Drug treatment is not necessary or appropriate for all forms of incontinence. In stress incontinence, exercises to strengthen the pelvic floor muscles or surgery to tighten stretched ligaments may be effective. In urgency, regular emptying of the bladder can often avoid the need for medical intervention. Incontinence caused by loss of nerve control is unlikely to be helped by drug treatment. Stress incontinence may

sometimes be helped by *sympathomimetic* drugs such as ephedrine that help to constrict the sphincter muscle. Frequency of urination in urgency may be reduced by *anticholinergic* and *antispasmodic* drugs. These reduce nerve signals from the muscles in the bladder, allowing greater volumes of urine to accumulate without stimulating the urge to pass urine. Tricyclic antidepressants, such as imipramine, have a strong anticholinergic action, and have been prescribed for nocturnal enuresis in children, but many doctors believe the risk of overdosage is unacceptable. Desmopressin, a synthetic derivative of antidiuretic hormone (see p.145) is also used for nocturnal enuresis.

Drugs for urinary retention

Urinary retention is the inability to empty the bladder. This usually results in the failure of the bladder muscle to contract sufficiently to expel accumulated urine. Possible causes include an enlarged prostate gland or tumour, or a long-standing neurological disorder.

Most cases of urinary retention need to be relieved by inserting a tube (catheter) into the urethra, and surgery may be needed to prevent a recurrence of the problem. Finasteride, an anti-androgen, is sometimes used instead of surgery to shrink the prostate and relieve the obstruction; it may take several months to show benefit. Phenoxybenzamine, an alpha-adrenergic blocking agent (see Autonomic nervous system, p.79) that relaxes the sphincter, may be used to relieve urinary retention prior to surgery. Bethanechol, a *parasympathomimetic* drug that increases the strength of contraction of the bladder muscle, may relieve urinary retention following surgery. Neither drug is suitable for long-term treatment.

ACTION OF DRUGS ON URINATION

Normal bladder action
Urination occurs when the sphincter that keeps the exit from the bladder into the urethra closed is consciously relaxed in response to signals from the bladder indicating that it is full. As the sphincter opens, the bladder wall contracts and urine is expelled.

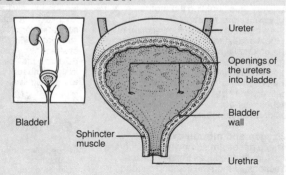

Bladder

Ureter

Openings of the ureters into bladder

Bladder wall

Sphincter muscle

Urethra

How drugs act to improve bladder control
Anticholinergic drugs relax the bladder muscle by interfering with the passage of nerve impulses to the muscle.

Sympathomimetics act directly on the sphincter muscle, causing it to contract.

How drugs act to relieve urinary retention
Parasympathomimetics (cholinergics) stimulate contraction of the bladder wall.

Alpha-adrenergic blocking agents relax the muscle of the sphincter.

COMMON DRUGS

Antibiotics and antibacterials
(See pp.128 – 131)

Anticholinergics
Flavoxate *
Oxybutynin

Sympathomimetics
Ephedrine *

Tricyclic antidepressants
Imipramine *

Parasympatho-mimetics
Bethanechol
Distigmine

Alpha-adrenergic blockers
Idoramin
Phenoxybenzamine
Prazosin *

Other drugs
Ascorbic acid
Desmopressin
Finasteride
Potassium citrate

* See Part 4

EYES AND EARS

The eye and ear are the two sense organs that provide us with most information about the world around us. The eye is the organ of vision that converts light images into nerve signals which are transmitted to the brain for interpretation.

The ear not only provides the means by which sound is detected and communicated to the brain, but it also contains the organ of balance that tells the brain about the position and movement of the body. It is divided into three parts – outer, middle, and inner ear.

What can go wrong

The most common eye and ear disorders are infection and inflammation (sometimes caused by allergy). Many parts of the eye may be affected, notably the conjunctiva (membrane that covers the front of the eye and lines the eyelids) and the iris. The middle and outer ear are more commonly affected by infection than the inner ear.

The eye may also be damaged by glaucoma, a disorder in which pressure of fluid within the eye builds up and may eventually threaten vision. Eye problems such as retinopathy (disease of the retina) or cataracts (clouding of the lens) may occur as a result of diabetes, but both are now treatable. Eye and ear disorders for which no drug treatment is appropriate are beyond the scope of this book.

Other disorders affecting the ear include build up of wax (cerumen) in the outer ear canal and disturbances to the balance mechanism (see Vertigo and Ménière's disease, p.90).

Why drugs are used

Doctors usually prescribe antibiotics (p.128) to clear ear and eye infections. These may be given by mouth or *topically*. Topical eye and ear preparations may contain a corticosteroid (p.141) to reduce inflammation. When inflammation has been caused by allergy, antihistamines (p.124) may also be taken. Decongestant drugs (p.93) are often prescribed to help clear the eustachian tube in middle ear infections.

A variety of drugs are used to reduce fluid pressure in glaucoma. These include diuretics (p.99), beta blockers (p.97), and *miotics* to narrow the pupil. In other cases, the pupil may need to be widened by *mydriatic* drugs.

MAJOR DRUG GROUPS

Drugs for glaucoma
Drugs affecting the pupil

Drugs for ear disorders

How the eye works
Light enters the eye through the cornea. The muscles of the iris control pupil size and thus the amount of light passing into the eye. The optic nerve carries signals received by the retina to be interpreted in the brain.

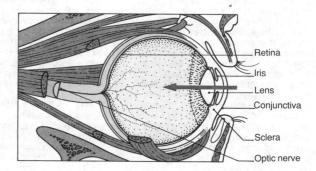

Retina
Iris
Lens
Conjunctiva
Sclera
Optic nerve

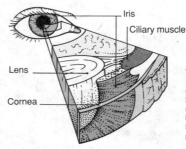

Iris
Ciliary muscle
Lens
Cornea

The eye muscles
Focusing and pupil size are governed by muscles controlled by the autonomic nervous system (p.79), which may be affected by many drugs. Disturbed vision is often a side effect of such drugs.

The ear
The outer ear canal is separated from the middle ear by the ear drum. Three bones in the middle ear connect it to the inner ear. This contains the cochlea (organ of balance) and the labyrinth (organ of hearing).

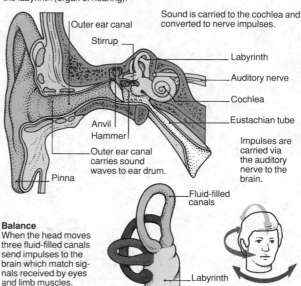

Sound is carried to the cochlea and converted to nerve impulses.

Outer ear canal
Stirrup
Labyrinth
Auditory nerve
Cochlea
Eustachian tube
Anvil
Hammer
Outer ear canal carries sound waves to ear drum.
Pinna
Impulses are carried via the auditory nerve to the brain.

Balance
When the head moves three fluid-filled canals send impulses to the brain which match signals received by eyes and limb muscles.

Fluid-filled canals
Labyrinth

DRUGS FOR GLAUCOMA

Glaucoma is the name given to a group of conditions in which the pressure in the eye builds up to an abnormally high level. This compresses the blood vessels supplying the nerve that connects the eye to the brain (optic nerve), and may lead to irreversible nerve damage and permanent loss of vision.

In the most common type of glaucoma, known as chronic (or open-angle) glaucoma, reduced drainage of fluid from the eye causes pressure inside the eye to build up slowly. Progressive reduction in the peripheral field of vision may take months or years to be noticed. Acute (or closed-angle) glaucoma occurs when drainage of fluid is suddenly blocked by the iris. Fluid pressure builds up quite suddenly, blurring vision in the affected eye (see the box below). The eye becomes red and painful, accompanied by a headache and sometimes vomiting. The main attack is often preceded by milder warning attacks such as seeing

haloes around lights in the previous weeks or months. Elderly, far-sighted people are particularly at risk of developing acute glaucoma. The angle may also narrow suddenly following injury or after taking certain drugs, for example, *anticholinergic* drugs. Closed angle glaucoma may develop more slowly (chronic closed angle glaucoma).

Drugs are used in the treatment of both types of glaucoma. These include miotics (see also Drugs affecting the pupil, p.170), beta blockers (p.97) and certain diuretics (carbonic anhydrase inhibitors and osmotics).

Why they are used
Chronic glaucoma
In this form of glaucoma, drugs are used to reduce pressure inside the eye and to maintain normal pressure thereafter (lifelong treatment is often necessary). This prevents further deterioration of vision, but cannot restore any damage that has already been sustained.

Initially drops containing a beta blocker (usually timolol) are given to reduce secretion of fluid within the eye. A miotic drug, such as pilocarpine, which improves drainage of fluid from the eye may also have to be given. Adrenaline or dipivefrine drops, which reduce secretion and increase the outflow, may also be helpful. If these measures fail to reduce pressure within the eye a carbonic anhydrase inhibitor such as acetazolamide tablets may be given to further reduce fluid production; treatment is usually continued only until laser treatment or surgery can be arranged.

Acute glaucoma
People with acute glaucoma need immediate medical treatment to prevent total loss of vision. Drugs are used initially to bring down blood pressure within the eye. Laser treatment or eye surgery is then carried out to prevent a recurrence of the problem. It is rare for drug treatment to be continued long term.

WHAT HAPPENS IN GLAUCOMA

Normal eye
The ciliary body, situated at the root of the iris, continuously produces aqueous humour – a watery fluid that helps maintain the normal shape of the eyeball. Aqueous humour drains via the angle between the cornea and iris through a mesh of fibres (the trabecular meshwork) into a channel in the sclera (white of the eye).

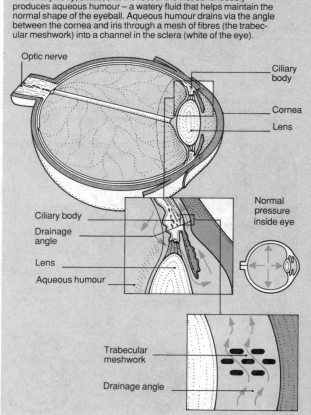

Optic nerve
Ciliary body
Cornea
Lens
Ciliary body
Drainage angle
Lens
Aqueous humour
Trabecular meshwork
Drainage angle

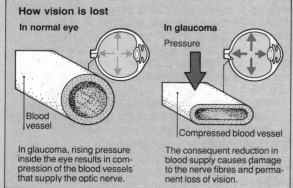

How vision is lost

In normal eye

In glaucoma
Pressure

Blood vessel

Compressed blood vessel

In glaucoma, rising pressure inside the eye results in compression of the blood vessels that supply the optic nerve.

The consequent reduction in blood supply causes damage to the nerve fibres and permanent loss of vision.

Normal pressure inside eye

Acute glaucoma
In acute glaucoma, the drainage angle between the cornea and the iris becomes completely closed – so that the pressure inside the eye rises rapidly. This may lead to permanent damage to the nerve fibres.

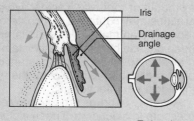

Iris
Drainage angle

Chronic glaucoma
In chronic glaucoma, the trabecular meshwork through which the aqueous humour normally drains gradually closes off, so that fluid pressure builds up slowly, gradually damaging the optic nerve.

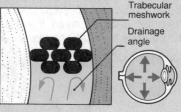

Trabecular meshwork
Drainage angle

Acetazolamide (see p.186) is usually the first drug administered when the condition is diagnosed. This is initially injected for rapid effect and thereafter administered by mouth. Frequent applications of eye drops containing pilocarpine, or another miotic drug are given. Occasionally, an osmotic diuretic is administered. This draws fluid out of all body tissues including the eye and reduces pressure within the eye.

How they work

The drugs used to treat glaucoma act in various ways to reduce the pressure of fluid in the eye. Miotics improve the drainage of the fluid out of the eye. In chronic glaucoma this is achieved by increasing the outflow of aqueous humour through the drainage channel called the trabecular meshwork. In acute glaucoma the pupil-constricting effect of miotics pulls the iris away from the drainage channel, allowing the aqueous humour to flow out normally. Beta blockers and carbonic anhydrase inhibitors act on the fluid-producing cells inside the eye to reduce the output of aqueous humour.

How they affect you

Drugs for acute glaucoma act quickly, relieving pain and other symptoms within a few hours. The benefits of drug treatment in chronic glaucoma may not be immediately apparent since they only halt a further deterioration of vision.

People receiving miotic eye drops are likely to notice darkening of vision and difficulty seeing in the dark. Increased short sightedness may be noticeable. Some miotics also cause irritation and redness of the eyes.

ACTION OF DRUGS FOR GLAUCOMA

Miotics
These act on the circular muscle in the iris to reduce the size of the pupil. In acute glaucoma this relieves any obstruction to the flow of aqueous humour by pulling the iris away from the cornea (right). In chronic glaucoma, miotic drugs act directly to increase the outflow of aqueous humour.

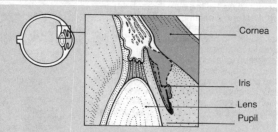

- Cornea
- Iris
- Lens
- Pupil

Beta blockers
The fluid-producing cells in the ciliary body are stimulated by signals passed through beta receptors. Beta blocking drugs prevent the transmission of signals through these receptors, thereby reducing the stimulus to produce fluid.

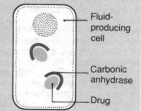

- Fluid-producing cell
- Carbonic anhydrase
- Drug

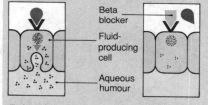

- Beta blocker
- Fluid-producing cell
- Aqueous humour

Before drug   **After drug**

Carbonic anhydrase inhibitors
These block carbonic anhydrase, an *enzyme* involved in the production of aqueous humour in the ciliary body.

Beta blocker eye drops have few day-to-day side effects but carry risks for a few people (see below). Acetazolamide usually causes an increase in frequency of urination and thirst. Nausea and general malaise are also common.

Risks and special precautions

Miotics are generally risk free. If beta blockers are absorbed into the body they can affect the lungs, heart, and circulation. For this reason, they are prescribed with caution to people with asthma or certain circulatory disorders, and in some cases they are withheld altogether. The amount of the drug absorbed into the body can be reduced by applying the eye drops carefully as described in the box (left). Acetazolamide is not normally prescribed for prolonged treatment because of its troublesome adverse effects, including painful tingling of the hands and feet. It may encourage the formation of kidney stones and may in rare cases cause kidney damage. People with existing kidney problems are not usually prescribed this drug.

APPLYING EYE DROPS IN GLAUCOMA

To reduce the amount of drug absorbed into the blood via the lacrimal (tear) duct, apply eye drops as described. This also improves the effectiveness of the drug.

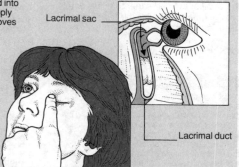

- Lacrimal sac
- Lacrimal duct

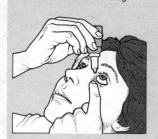

1 Press firmly on the lacrimal sac in the corner of the eye and apply the number of drops prescribed by your doctor.

2 Maintain pressure on the lacrimal sac for a few moments after applying the drops.

COMMON DRUGS

Miotics
Carbachol
Physostigmine
Pilocarpine *

Carbonic anhydrase inhibitors
Acetazolamide *
Dichlorphenamide

Beta blockers
Betaxolol
Carteolol
Levobunolol
Metipranolol
Timolol *

Other drugs
Adrenaline
Dipivefrine
Guanethidine

* See Part 4

DRUGS AFFECTING THE PUPIL

The pupil of the eye is the circular opening in the centre of the iris (the coloured part of the eye) through which light enters. It continually changes in size to adjust to variations in the intensity of light: in bright light it becomes quite small (constricts), but in dim light it enlarges (dilates).

Eye drops containing drugs that act on the pupil are widely used by eye specialists. They are of two types: those that dilate the pupil, known as *mydriatics;* and those that constrict the pupil, known as *miotics.*

Why they are used

Mydriatics are most often used to allow the doctor to view the inside of the eye – particularly the retina, the optic nerve head, and the blood vessels that supply the retina. Many of these drugs cause a temporary paralysis of the eye's focusing mechanism, a state known as cycloplegia. Cycloplegia is sometimes induced to help determine the presence of any focusing errors, especially in babies and young children. By producing cycloplegia it is possible to determine the precise optical prescription required for a small child, especially in the case of a squint.

Dilation of the pupil is part of the treatment for uveitis, an inflammatory disease of the iris and focusing muscle. In uveitis, the inflamed iris may stick to the lens, and thus cause severe damage to the eye. This can be prevented by early dilation of the pupil so that the iris is no longer in contact with the lens.

Constriction of the pupil with miotic drugs is often required in the treatment of glaucoma (see p.168). Miotics can also be used to restore the pupil to a normal size after dilation has been induced artificially.

How they work

The size of the pupil is controlled by two separate sets of muscles in the iris, the circular muscle and the radial muscle. Each set of muscles is governed by a separate branch of the autonomic nervous system (see p.79): the sympathetic nervous system controls the radial muscle, and the parasympathetic nervous system controls the circular muscle.

Individual mydriatic and miotic drugs take effect on different branches of the autonomic nervous system, and will cause the pupil of the eye either to dilate or to contract, depending on the type being used (see illustration above).

ACTION OF DRUGS AFFECTING THE PUPIL

The muscles of the iris
The pupil is made smaller and larger by the co-ordinated action of the circular and radial muscles in the iris. The circular muscle forms a ring around the pupil; when it contracts the pupil becomes smaller. The radial muscle is composed of fibres that run from the pupil to the base of the iris like the spokes of a wheel. Contraction of these fibres causes the pupil to become larger.

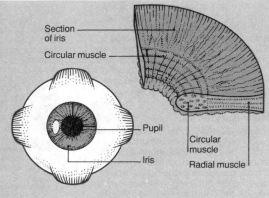

Section of iris
Circular muscle
Pupil
Iris
Circular muscle
Radial muscle

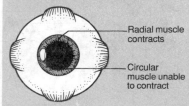

Radial muscle contracts
Circular muscle unable to contract

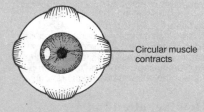

Circular muscle contracts

Mydriatics
Mydriatics enlarge the pupil in one of two ways. The *sympathomimetics* stimulate the radial muscle to contract. The *anticholinergics* prevent the circular muscle from contracting.

Miotics
Most miotics reduce the size of the pupil by stimulating the activity of the parasympathetic nervous system which causes the circular muscle to contract.

How they affect you

Mydriatic drugs – especially the long-acting types – impair the ability to focus the eye(s) for several hours after use. This interferes particularly with close activities such as reading. Bright light may cause discomfort. Miotics often interfere with night vision and may cause temporary short sight.

Normally, these eye drops produce few serious adverse effects. *Sympathomimetic* mydriatics may raise blood pressure and are used with caution in people with heart disease or hypertension. Miotics may irritate the eye, but rarely cause generalized effects.

ARTIFICIAL TEAR PREPARATIONS

Tears are continually produced to keep the front of the eye covered with a thin moist film. This is essential for clear vision and for keeping the front of the eye free from dirt and other irritants. In some conditions, known collectively as dry eye syndromes (for example, Sjögren's syndrome), inadequate tear production may make the eyes feel dry and sore. Sore eyes can also occur in disorders where the eyelids do not close properly, causing the eye to become dry.

Why they are used
Since prolonged deficiency of natural tears can damage the cornea, regular application of artificial tears in the form of eyedrops is recommended in all of the conditions described. Artificial tears may also be used to provide temporary relief from any feeling of discomfort and dryness in the eye caused by irritants, exposure to wind or sun, or the initial wearing of contact lenses.

Although artificial tears are non-irritating, the preparations containing them often include a preservative (for example, thimerosal or benzalkonium chloride) that may cause irritation. This risk is increased for wearers of soft contact lenses who should ask their optician for advice before using any type of eye drops.

COMMON DRUGS

Sympathomimetic mydriatics	Anticholinergic mydriatics
Adrenaline ✳	Atropine ✳
Phenylephrine ✳	Cyclopentolate
	Homatropine
Miotics	Hyoscine ✳
Carbachol	Tropicamide
Physostigmine	
Pilocarpine ✳	

✳ See Part 4

DRUGS FOR EAR DISORDERS

Inflammation and infection of the outer and the middle ear are the most common disorders affecting the ear that are treated with drugs. Drug treatment of Ménière's disease, which affects the inner ear, is described under Vertigo and Ménière's disease, p.90).

The type of drug treatment given for ear inflammation depends on the cause of the trouble and the site affected.

Inflammation of the outer ear

Inflammation of the external ear canal (otitis externa) can be caused by eczema, or by a bacterial or fungal infection. The risk of inflammation is increased by swimming in dirty water, the accumulation of wax in the ear, or by too frequent poking or scratching at the ear.

Symptoms vary, but often there is itching, pain (which may be severe if there is a boil in the ear canal), tenderness, and possibly some loss of hearing. If the ear is infected as well there will probably be a discharge.

Drug treatment

A weak corticosteroid (see p.141), in the form of ear drops, may be used to treat inflammation of the outer ear when there is no infection. Aluminium acetate solution, as drops or applied on a piece of gauze, may also be used. Relief is usually obtained within a day or two. Prolonged use of corticosteroids is not advisable because they may reduce the ear's resistance to infection.

If there is both inflammation and infection, your doctor may prescribe ear drops containing an antibiotic (see p.128) combined with a weak corticosteroid to relieve the inflammation. Usually a combination of antibiotics is prescribed to make the treatment effective against a wide range of bacteria. Commonly-used antibiotics include

EAR WAX REMOVAL

Ear wax (or cerumen) is a natural secretion from the outer ear canal that keeps it free from dust and skin debris. Occasionally, wax may build up in the outer ear canal and become hard, leading to irritation and/or hearing loss.

A number of over-the-counter products are available to soften ear wax and hasten its expulsion. Such products may contain irritating substances that can cause inflammation. Doctors advise instead application of oil or glycerine. A cotton plug should be inserted to retain the oil in the outer ear. When ear wax is not dislodged by such home treatment, your doctor may syringe the ear with warm water.

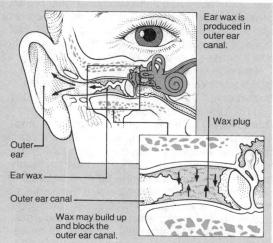

Ear wax is produced in outer ear canal.

Outer ear

Ear wax

Outer ear canal

Wax plug

Wax may build up and block the outer ear canal.

framycetin, neomycin and polymyxin B. These antibiotics are not usually taken for long periods, since prolonged use can irritate the skin lining the ear canal.

Sometimes an antibiotic given in the form of drops is not effective, and another type of antibiotic may also have to be taken by mouth.

Infection of the middle ear

Infection of the middle ear (otitis media) often causes severe pain and hearing loss. It is particularly common in young children in whom infecting organisms are able to spread easily into the middle ear from the nose or throat via the eustachian tube.

Viral infections of the middle ear usually cure themselves and are less serious than those caused by bacteria.

Bacterial infections often cause the eustachian tube to swell and become blocked. When a blockage occurs, pus builds up in the middle ear and puts pressure on the ear drum, which may then perforate.

Drug treatment

Doctors usually prescribe a decongestant (see p.93) or antihistamine (see p.124) to reduce swelling in the eustachian tube, thus allowing the pus to drain out of the middle ear. Usually, an antibiotic is also given by mouth to clear the infection.

Antibiotics are not effective against viral infections, but as it is often difficult to distinguish between a viral and a bacterial infection of the middle ear, your doctor may prescribe an antibiotic as a precautionary measure. Paracetamol, an analgesic (see p.80), may be given to relieve pain. When infection is recurrent, antibiotic treatment lasting several weeks may be prescribed.

HOW TO USE EAR DROPS

Ear drops for outer ear disorders are more easily and efficiently administered if you have someone to help you. Lie on your side while the other person drops the medication into the ear cavity ensuring that the dropper does not touch the ear. If possible, it is advisable to remain lying in that position for a few minutes in order to allow the drops to bathe the ear canal. Ear drops should be discarded when the course of treatment has been completed.

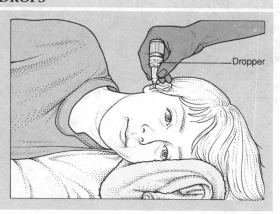

Dropper

COMMON DRUGS

Antibiotic and anti-bacterial ear drops
Chloramphenicol *
Clioquinol
Clotrimazole *
Framycetin
Gentamicin *
Neomycin
Polymyxin B
Tetracycline *

Corticosteroids
Betamethasone *
Prednisolone *

Decongestants
Ephedrine *
Oxymetazoline
Xylometazoline

Other drugs
Aluminium acetate
Antihistamines (see p.124)

* See Part 4

SKIN

The skin waterproofs, cushions, and protects the rest of the body and is, in fact, its largest organ. It provides a barrier against innumerable infections and infestations; it helps the body retain its vital fluids; it plays a major role in temperature control; and it houses the sensory nerves of touch.

The skin consists of two main layers: a thin, tough top layer, the epidermis, and below it a thicker layer, the dermis. The epidermis divides into two: the skin surface, or stratum corneum (horny layer) consisting of dead skin cells, and below, a layer of active cells. The active layer cells divide and eventually die, maintaining the horny layer. Living cells produce keratin, which toughens the epidermis and is the basic substance of hair and nails. Some living cells in the epidermis contain melanin, a pigment released following exposure to sunlight which protects the dermis.

The dermis contains different types of nerve endings for sensing pain, pressure, and temperature; sweat glands to cool the body; sebaceous glands that release an oil (sebum) that lubricates and waterproofs the skin; and white blood cells that help keep the skin clear of infection.

What can go wrong
Most skin complaints are not serious, but they may be distressing if visible. They include infection, inflammation, and irritation, infestation by skin parasites, and changes in skin structure and texture (psoriasis, eczema, and acne).

Why drugs are used
Skin problems often resolve themselves without drug treatment. Over-the-counter preparations containing active ingredients are available, but doctors generally advise against their use without medical supervision because they could aggravate some skin conditions if used inappropriately. Drugs prescribed by doctors are often highly effective: antibiotics (p.128) for bacterial infections; antifungal drugs (p.138) for fungal infections; anti-infestation agents for skin parasites (p.176); and corticosteroids (p.174) for inflammatory conditions. Specialized drugs are available for conditions like psoriasis and acne.

Although many drugs are *topical* medications, you must use them as carefully as drugs taken by mouth since they can also cause adverse effects.

Structure of the skin
The epidermis contains keratin and melanin, while the dermis contains sweat glands, sebaceous glands and nerve endings that sense pain, temperature and pressure.

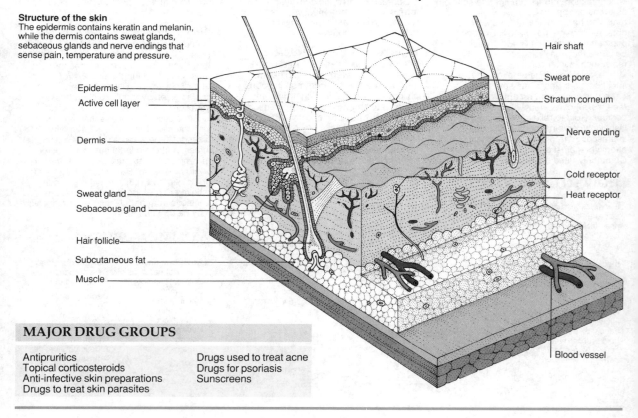

Epidermis
Active cell layer
Dermis
Sweat gland
Sebaceous gland
Hair follicle
Subcutaneous fat
Muscle

Hair shaft
Sweat pore
Stratum corneum
Nerve ending
Cold receptor
Heat receptor
Blood vessel

MAJOR DRUG GROUPS

Antipruritics
Topical corticosteroids
Anti-infective skin preparations
Drugs to treat skin parasites

Drugs used to treat acne
Drugs for psoriasis
Sunscreens

ANTIPRURITICS

Itching (irritation of the skin that creates the urge to scratch), also known as pruritus, most often occurs as a result of chemical changes in the skin caused by disease, allergy, inflammation or exposure to irritant substances. People differ in their tolerance of itching, and an individual's threshold can be altered by stress and other psychological factors.

Itching is a common symptom of many skin disorders, including eczema and allergic conditions such as urticaria (hives). It may also be caused by localized fungal infection or parasitic infestation. Diseases such as chickenpox and psoriasis may also cause itching. Less commonly, itching may also occur in diabetes mellitus, jaundice and kidney failure.

In many cases, generalized itching is caused by dry skin. Itching in particular parts of the body often has special causes: itching around the anus (pruritus ani) may result from haemorrhoids or worm infestation; genital itching in women (pruritus vulvae) may be caused by vaginal infection or, in older women, hormone deficiency.

Although scratching provides temporary relief, it often increases skin inflammation and thus may make the condition worse. In some cases, continued scratching of an area of irritated skin can lead to a vicious circle of scratching and itching that continues long after the original cause of the trouble has been removed.

A number of different types of medication are used for the relief of skin irritation. These include soothing preparations that are applied to the affected skin and drugs that are taken by mouth. The principal drugs used in antipruritic medications include corticosteroids (see Topical corticosteroids, p.174), local anaesthetics (p.80), and antihistamines (p.124). Plain *emollient* or cooling creams and ointments containing no active ingredients are often recommended.

Why they are used

For mild itching arising from sunburn, urticaria or insect bites, a cooling lotion such as calamine, perhaps containing menthol, phenol or camphor, may be the most appropriate treatment. Local anaesthetic creams are sometimes helpful for small areas of irritation such as insect bites, but are unsuitable for widespread itching. Itching from dry skin is often soothed by a simple emollient. Avoidance of excessive bathing and use of moisturizing bath oils may also help.

Severe itching from eczema or other inflammatory skin conditions may be treated with a topical corticosteroid preparation. Where the irritation prevents sleep, a doctor may prescribe an antihistamine drug to be taken at night which promotes sleep as well as relieving itching (see also Sleeping drugs, p.82). Antihistamines are also often included in topical preparations for the relief of skin irritation but their effectiveness when administered in this way is doubtful. For the treatment of pruritus ani, see Drugs for rectal and anal disorders (p.113). Post-menopausal pruritus vulvae may be helped by vaginal creams containing oestrogen. For further information, see Female sex hormones (p.147). Itching that is caused by an underlying illness cannot be helped by skin creams, and requires treatment for the principal disorder.

Risks and special precautions

The main risk with any of these preparations other than simple emollient and soothing preparations is that prolonged or heavy use may cause skin irritation, thereby aggravating itching. Antihistamine and local anaesthetic creams are especially likely to cause a reaction, and have to be stopped if they do so. Antihistamines taken by mouth to relieve itching are likely to cause drowsiness. The special risks of topical corticosteroids are discussed on p.174.

Because itching can be a symptom of many underlying conditions, self-treatment should be continued for no longer than a week before seeking medical advice.

ACTION OF ANTIPRURITICS

Irritation of the skin causes the release of substances from the blood that cause blood vessels to dilate and fluid to accumulate under the skin. This causes itching and inflammation. Antipruritic drugs act either by reducing inflammation and therefore irritation, or by numbing the nerve impulses that transmit sensation to the brain.

Corticosteroids applied to the skin surface reduce itching caused by allergy within a few days, although the soothing effect of the cream may produce an immediate improvement. They pass into the underlying tissues and blood vessels and reduce the release of histamine, the chemical that causes itching and inflammation.

Antihistamines act within a few hours to reduce allergy-related skin inflammation. Applied to the skin, they pass into the underlying tissue and block the effects of histamine on the blood vessels beneath the skin. Taken by mouth they also act on the brain to reduce the perception of irritation.

Local anaesthetics absorbed through the skin numb the transmission of signals from the nerves in the skin to the brain.

Soothing and emollient creams Calamine lotion and similar preparations applied to the skin surface reduce inflammation and itching by cooling the skin. Emollient creams lubricate the skin surface and prevent dryness.

Antihistamines by mouth
The action of these drugs on histamine in the brain reduces the response to signals from irritated skin.

Local anaesthetics numb nerve endings.

Nerve

Soothing creams act on the skin surface.

Histamine

Corticosteroids reduce histamine release.

Antihistamine creams block the effects of histamine on blood vessels.

Blood vessel

COMMON DRUGS

Corticosteroids
Hydrocortisone ✱
(see p.141)

Local anaesthetics
Amethocaine
Benzocaine
Lignocaine

Antihistamines
Antazoline ✱
Diphenhydramine ✱
Mepyramine
(see p.124)

Emollient and cooling preparations
Aqueous cream
Calamine lotion
Cold cream
Phenolated
    calamine lotion

Other drugs
Crotamiton

✱ See Part 4

TOPICAL CORTICOSTEROIDS

Corticosteroid drugs (often simply called steroids) are related to hormones produced by the adrenal glands. For a full description of these drugs, see p.141. *Topical* preparations containing a corticosteroid drug are often used to treat skin conditions in which inflammation is a prominent symptom.

Why they are used

Corticosteroid creams and ointments are most commonly given to relieve itching and inflammation associated with skin diseases such as eczema and dermatitis. These preparations may also be prescribed for psoriasis (see p.178). Corticosteroids do not affect the underlying cause of skin irritation, and the condition is therefore likely to recur unless the substance (allergen or irritant) that has provoked the irritation is itself removed, or the underlying condition treated.

A doctor may not prescribe a corticosteroid as the initial treatment, preferring to try a topical medicine that has fewer adverse effects (see Antipruritics, p.173).

In most cases treatment is started with a preparation containing a low concentration of a mild corticosteroid drug. A stronger preparation may be prescribed subsequently if the first product is ineffective.

How they affect you

Corticosteroids prevent the release of chemicals that trigger the symptoms of inflammation (see Action of corticosteroids on the skin, above right). Conditions for which topical corticosteroids are prescribed improve within a few days of starting treatment. Applied topically, corticosteroids rarely cause adverse effects, but the stronger drugs used in high concentrations carry certain risks.

ACTION OF CORTICOSTEROIDS ON THE SKIN

Skin inflammation
Irritation of the skin caused by allergens or irritant substances provokes the release by white blood cells of substances that dilate the blood vessels. This makes the skin hot, red and swollen.

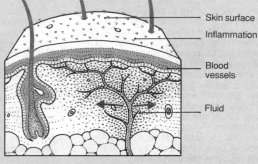

Skin surface
Inflammation
Blood vessels
Fluid

Drug action
Applied to the skin surface, corticosteroids are absorbed into the underlying tissue. There they inhibit the action of the substances that cause inflammation, thereby allowing the blood vessels to return to normal and reducing the swelling.

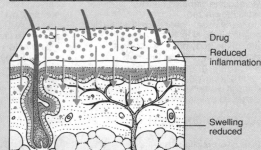

Drug
Reduced inflammation
Swelling reduced

Risks and special precautions

Prolonged use of potent corticosteroids in high concentrations can lead to permanent changes in the skin. The most common effect is thinning of the skin, sometimes resulting in stretch marks that may be permanent. Fine blood vessels under the surface of the skin may become prominent (a condition known as telangiectasia). The vessels may become damaged, resulting in a red rash beneath the skin. Because the skin on the face is especially vulnerable to such damage, topical corticosteroids are not usually prescribed for use on the face. Dark-skinned people sometimes suffer a temporary reduction in pigmentation at the site of application.

When powerful corticosteroid preparations have been used for a prolonged period, abrupt discontinuation of the treatment can result in a general reddening of the skin called "rebound erythroderma". This may be avoided by a gradual reduction in dosage. Corticosteroids suppress the body's immune system (see p.156), thus increasing the risk of infection. For this reason, they are not used alone to treat skin inflammation caused by bacterial or fungal infection. However, they may sometimes be included in a topical preparation that also contains an antibiotic or antifungal agent (see Anti-infective skin preparations, facing page).

LONG-TERM EFFECTS OF TOPICAL CORTICOSTEROIDS

Prolonged use of topical corticosteroids causes drying and thinning of the epidermis, so that tiny blood vessels close to the skin surface become visible. In addition, long-term use of these drugs weakens the underlying connective tissue of the dermis, leading to an increased susceptibility to stretch marks.

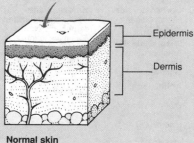

Epidermis
Dermis

Normal skin

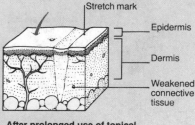

Stretch mark
Epidermis
Dermis
Weakened connective tissue

After prolonged use of topical corticosteroids

COMMON DRUGS

Potent
Beclomethasone *
Betamethasone *
Budesonide
Triamcinolone

Moderate
Clobetasone
Fluocinolone
Hydrocortisone *

Mild
Fluocinolone
Hydrocortisone *
Methylprednisolone

* See Part 4

ANTI-INFECTIVE SKIN PREPARATIONS

The skin is the body's first line of defence against infection. Yet it can also become infected itself, especially if the outer layer (epidermis) is damaged by a burn, cut, scrape, insect bite or an inflammatory skin condition such as eczema or dermatitis.

Several different types of organism may infect the skin including bacteria, viruses, fungi and yeasts. This page concentrates on drugs applied *topically* to treat bacterial skin infections. These include antiseptics, antibiotics and other antibacterial agents. Infection by other organisms is covered elsewhere (see Antiviral drugs, p.133, Antifungal drugs, p.138, and Drugs used to treat skin parasites, p.176).

Why they are used

Bacterial infection of a skin wound can usually be prevented by thorough cleansing of the area of damage and the application of antiseptic creams and lotions as described in the box (right). If infection does occur the wound usually becomes inflamed and swollen, and pus may form. If you develop these signs you should see your doctor. The usual treatment for a wound infection is an antibiotic taken orally, although often an antibiotic cream is also prescribed.

An antibiotic or antibacterial skin cream may also be used to prevent infection when your doctor considers this to be a particular risk – for example, in the case of severe burns.

Other skin disorders in which topical antibiotic treatment may be prescribed include impetigo and infected eczema, skin ulcers, bedsores and nappy rash. Usually, a preparation containing two or more antibiotics is used in order to ensure that all bacteria are eradicated. The antibiotics selected for inclusion in topical preparations are usually drugs

ANTISEPTICS

Antiseptics (sometimes called germicides or skin disinfectants) are chemicals that kill or prevent the growth of micro-organisms. They are weaker than household disinfectants which are irritating to the skin.

Antiseptic lotions, creams and solutions may be effective for preventing infection following surface wounds to the skin. Solutions can be added to water while bathing wounds

Soaps, shampoos, throat lozenges and mouthwashes, skin lotions, creams and ointments may contain antiseptic ingredients.

(used undiluted they may cause inflammation and increase the risk of infection). Creams may be applied to wounds after cleansing.

Antiseptics are also included in some soaps and shampoos for the prevention of acne and dandruff, but their benefits in these disorders is doubtful. They are also included as ingredients of some throat lozenges but their effectiveness in curing throat infections is unproven.

that are poorly absorbed through the skin (for example, the aminoglycosides). Thus the drug remains concentrated on the surface and in the skin's upper layers where it is intended that it should have its effect. However, if the infection is deep under the skin, or is causing fever and malaise, antibiotics may need to be administered by mouth or injection.

Risks and special precautions

Any topical antibiotic product can irritate the skin or cause an allergic reaction. Irritation is sometimes caused by

another ingredient of the preparation rather than the active drug, for example, a preservative contained in the preparation. An allergic reaction with swelling and reddening of the skin is more likely to be caused by the antibiotic drug itself. Any adverse reaction of this kind should be reported to your doctor, who may substitute another drug, or prescribe a different preparation.

Always follow your doctor's instructions on how long the treatment with antibiotic creams should be continued. Stopping too soon may cause the infection to flare up again.

Never use a skin preparation that has been prescribed for someone else as it may aggravate your condition. Always throw away any unused medication.

BASES FOR SKIN PREPARATIONS

Drugs that are applied to the skin are usually in a preparation known as a base (or vehicle), such as cream, lotion, ointment or paste. Many bases have beneficial effects of their own.

Creams These have an *emollient* effect. They are usually composed of an oil-in-water base and are used in the treatment of dry skin disorders, such as psoriasis and dry eczema. They may contain other ingredients such as camphor or menthol. Barrier creams protect the skin against water and irritating substances. They may be used in the treatment of nappy rash and to protect the skin around an open sore. They may contain powders and water-repellent substances, such as silicones.

Lotions Thin, semi-liquid preparations often used to cool and soothe inflamed skin. They are most suitable for use on large, hairy areas. Shake lotions contain fine powder which

remains on the surface of the skin when the liquid has evaporated. They are used to encourage scabs to form.

Ointments These are usually greasy and are suitable for treating wet (weeping) eczema.

Pastes Containing large amounts of finely powdered solids such as starch or zinc oxide, pastes protect the skin as well as absorb unwanted moisture and are used for skin conditions that affect clearly defined areas, such as psoriasis.

Collodions These are preparations that, when applied to damaged areas of the skin such as ulcers and minor wounds, dry to form a protective film. They are sometimes used to keep a dissolved drug in contact with the skin.

COMMON DRUGS

Antibiotics
Chlortetracycline
Colistin
Framycetin
Fusidic acid
Gentamicin *
Mupirocin
Neomycin
Tetracycline *

Antiseptics and other bacterials
Cetrimide
Chlorhexidine
Metronidazole *
Potassium permanganate
Silver sulphadiazine

* See Part 4

DRUGS TO TREAT SKIN PARASITES

Mites and lice are the most common parasites that live on the skin. One common mite causes the skin disease scabies. The mite burrows into the skin and lays eggs, causing intense itching. Scratching the affected area results in bleeding and scab formation, as well as increasing the risk of infection.

There are three types of lice, each of which infests a different part of the body: the head louse, the body or clothes louse, and the crab louse, which often infests the pubic areas, but is also sometimes found on other hairy areas such as the eyebrows. All of these lice cause itching and lay eggs (nits) that look like white grains attached to hairs.

Both mites and lice are passed on by direct contact with an infected person (during sexual intercourse in the case of pubic lice) or, particularly in the case of body lice, by contact with infected bedding or clothing.

The drugs most commonly used to eliminate skin parasites are insecticides that kill both the adult insects and their eggs. The most widely used drugs are malathion, permethrin, and lindane (both scabies and louse infestations), benzyl benzoate (scabies only), carbaryl and phenothrin (louse infestations only). Lindane is not often used for head lice because of resistant strains.

Why they are used

Skin parasites do not represent a serious threat to health, but require prompt treatment since they can cause severe irritation and spread rapidly if untreated. Drugs are used to eradicate the parasites from the body, but bedding and clothing may need disinfecting to avoid the possibility of reinfection.

How they are used

Lotions for the treatment of scabies are applied to the whole body – with the exception of the head and neck –

SITES AFFECTED BY SKIN PARASITES

Scabies
The female scabies mite burrows into the skin and lays its eggs under the skin surface. After hatching, the larvae travel to the skin surface where they mature for 10 – 17 days before starting the cycle again.

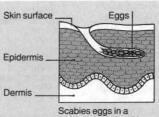

Skin surface   Eggs
Epidermis
Dermis

Scabies eggs in a burrow under the skin.

Scabies mite

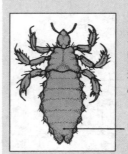

Head louse

Head lice
These tiny brown insects are transmitted from person to person (commonly among children). Their bites often cause itching.

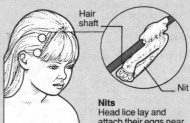

Hair shaft

Nit

Nits
Head lice lay and attach their eggs near the base of the hair shaft, especially around the ears.

---

following a bath or shower. Many people find these lotions messy to use, but they should not be washed off for 12 hours (malathion, lindane) or 48 hours (benzyl benzoate), otherwise they will not be effective. It is probably most convenient to apply malathion or lindane before going to bed. It may then be washed off the following morning.

One or two treatments are normally sufficient to remove the scabies mites. However, the itch associated with scabies may persist after the mite has been removed, so it may be necessary to use a soothing cream or medication containing an antipruritic drug (see p. 173) to ease this. People who have skin-to-skin

contact with a sufferer from scabies – family members and sexual partners – should also undergo treatment at the same time.

Head and pubic lice infestations are usually treated by applying a preparation of one of the products, and washing it off with water when and as instructed by the leaflet with the preparation. If the skin has become infected as a result of scratching, a *topical* antibiotic (see Anti-infective skin preparations p.175) may also be prescribed.

Risks and special precautions

Lotions prescribed to control parasites can cause irritation and stinging that may be intense if the medication is allowed to come into contact with the eyes, mouth or other moist membranes. Care is therefore needed when applying lotions and shampoos.

Because they are applied topically, antiparasitic drugs seldom have generalized effects. Nevertheless, it is important not to apply these preparations more often than directed.

ELIMINATING PARASITES FROM BEDDING AND CLOTHING

Most skin parasites may also infest bedding and clothing that has been next to the skin of an infected person. Therefore, to avoid reinfestation following removal of the parasites from the body, it is essential to eradicate insects and eggs that may be lodged in them.

Washing
Since all skin parasites are killed by heat, washing affected items of clothing and bedding in hot water and drying them in a hot drier is an effective and convenient method of dealing with the problem.

Non-washable items
Items that cannot be washed should be isolated in plastic bags. The insects and their eggs cannot survive long without their human

hosts and die within days. The length of time they can survive, and therefore the period of isolation, varies depending on the type of parasite (see the table below).

Parasite	Maximum survival time away from host		Isolation period
	Insects	Eggs	
Scabies	2 days	0 days	2 days
Head lice	2 days	10 days	10 days
Crab lice	1 day	10 days	10 days
Body lice	10 days	30 days	30 days

COMMON DRUGS

Benzyl benzoate	Permethrin
Carbaryl	Phenothrin
Lindane	
Malathion	

∗ See Part 4

DRUGS USED TO TREAT ACNE

Acne, known medically as acne vulgaris, is a common condition caused by an excess production of the skin's natural oil (sebum), which leads to blockage of hair follicles (see What happens in acne, right). Though it chiefly affects adolescents, acne may occur at any age as a result of taking certain drugs, exposure to industrial chemicals, oily cosmetics, or hot and humid conditions.

Acne primarily affects the skin on the face, neck, back, and chest. The principal skin symptoms are blackheads, papules (inflamed spots), and pustules (raised pus-filled spots with a white centre). Mild acne may produce only blackheads and an occasional papule or pustule. Moderate cases are characterized by larger numbers of pustules and papules. In severe cases of acne, painful, inflamed cysts also develop. These can cause permanent pitting and scarring.

Medication for acne can be divided into two groups: *topical* preparations applied directly to the skin and *systemic* treatments taken by mouth.

Why they are used

Mild acne does not normally require medical intervention. It can be controlled by regular washing and moderate exposure to sunlight or ultraviolet light. Over-the-counter antibacterial soaps and lotions have only a limited usefulness and may cause irritation.

CLEARING BLOCKED HAIR FOLLICLES

The most common treatment for acne is the application of keratolytic skin ointments. These encourage the layer of dead and hardened skin cells that form the skin surface to peel off. This action simultaneously clears blackheads that block hair follicles and give rise to the formation of acne spots.

Blackhead
Trapped sebum

Blocked hair follicle
A hair follicle blocked by a blackhead encourages acne spot formation.

Freed sebum

Cleared hair follicle
Once the follicle is unblocked, sebum can escape and air can enter, thereby limiting bacterial activity.

WHAT HAPPENS IN ACNE

In normal skin, sebum produced by a sebaceous gland attached to a hair follicle is able to flow out of the follicle along the hair. An acne spot forms when the flow of the sebum from the sebaceous gland is blocked by a plug of skin debris and hardened sebum, leading to an accumulation of sebum.

Acne papules and pustules
Bacterial activity leads to the formation of pustules and papules. Irritant substances may leak into the surrounding skin, causing inflammation.

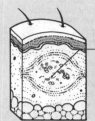

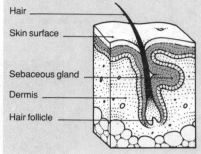

Hair
Skin surface
Sebaceous gland
Dermis
Hair follicle

Sebum
Blackhead
Cyst

Cystic acne
When acne is severe, cysts may form in the inflamed dermis. These are pockets of pus enclosed within scar tissue.

When a doctor or dermatologist thinks acne is severe enough to need medical treatment, he or she usually recommends a topical preparation containing benzoyl peroxide, sulphur or salicylic acid. If this does not produce an improvement, an ointment containing tretinoin, a drug related to vitamin A, azelaic acid, or tetracycline, an antibiotic, may be prescribed.

If acne is severe or does not respond to topical treatments, a doctor may prescribe a course of antibiotics by mouth. If these measures are unsuccessful, the more powerful vitamin A-like drug isotretinoin may be prescribed by mouth.

Oestrogen drugs may have a beneficial effect on acne. A woman suffering from acne who also needs contraception may be given an oestrogen-containing oral contraceptive (p.161). Alternatively, a preparation containing an oestrogen and cyproterone (a drug that opposes male sex hormones) may be prescribed.

How they work

Drugs used to treat acne act in different ways. Some have a keratolytic effect – that is they loosen the dead cells on the skin surface (see Clearing blocked hair follicles, left). Other drugs prevent bacterial activity in the skin or reduce sebum production.

Topical preparations such as benzoyl peroxide, salicylic acid, tretinoin, and sulphur have a keratolytic effect. Benzoyl peroxide and sulphur also have an antibacterial effect. Topical or systemic tetracyclines reduce bacteria, but may also have a direct anti-inflammatory effect on the skin. Isotretinoin reduces sebum production, soothes inflammation, and helps to unblock hair follicles.

How they affect you

Keratolytic preparations often cause soreness of the skin, especially at the start of treatment. If this persists, a change to a milder preparation may be recommended. Day-to-day side effects are rare with antibiotics.

Isotretinoin treatment often causes dryness and scaling of the skin, particularly on the lips. The skin may become itchy and some hair loss may occur.

Risks and special precautions

Antibiotic ointments may, in rare cases, provoke an allergic reaction requiring discontinuation of treatment. The tetracyclines, some of the most commonly used antibiotics for acne, are not suitable for use by mouth in pregnancy since they can discolour the teeth of the developing baby. Isotretinoin can increase levels of fat in the blood. More seriously, the drug is known to damage the developing baby if taken during pregnancy. Women taking this drug must be certain to use effective contraception during treatment.

COMMON DRUGS

Antibiotics
Clindamycin
Erythromycin ✳
Minocycline
Tetracycline ✳

Other oral drugs
Cyproterone ✳
Isotretinoin ✳

Topical treatments
Azelaic acid
Benzoyl peroxide ✳
Isotretinoin ✳
Salicylic acid
Sulphur
Tretinoin

Eczema
Gamolenic acid

✳ See Part 4

DRUGS FOR PSORIASIS

The skin is constantly being renewed; as fast as dead cells in the outermost layer (epidermis) are shed, they are replaced by cells from the base of the epidermis. Psoriasis occurs when the production of new cells increases, while the shedding of old cells remains normal. As a result, the live skin cells accumulate and produce patches of inflamed, thickened skin covered by silvery scales. In some cases, the area of skin affected is extensive and causes severe embarrassment and physical discomfort. Psoriasis may occasionally be accompanied by arthritis in which the joints become swollen and painful.

The underlying cause of psoriasis is unknown. It usually first occurs between the ages of 10 and 30, and recurs throughout life. Outbreaks may be triggered by emotional stress, skin damage, and physical illnesses. Psoriasis can also be a consequence of the withdrawal of corticosteroid drugs.

There is no complete cure for psoriasis. Simple measures such as careful sunbathing or using an ultraviolet lamp may help to clear mild psoriasis. An *emollient* cream (see Antipruritics, p.173) often soothes the irritation. When such measures fail to provide adequate relief, additional drug therapy is needed.

Why they are used

Drugs are used to reduce the size of areas of affected skin and to reduce inflammation and scaling. Mild or moderate psoriasis is usually treated with a *topical* preparation. Coal tar preparations in the form of creams, pastes and bath additives are often helpful, although some people dislike the smell. Dithranol is also widely used. Applied to the affected areas, it is then left for a few minutes or overnight (depending on preparation), after which it is washed off. Both dithranol and coal tar can stain clothes and bed linen.

If these agents alone do not produce adequate benefit, ultraviolet light therapy in the form of regulated exposure to natural sunlight or to ultraviolet lamps may be advised. Salicylic acid may be applied to help remove thick scale and crusts, especially from the scalp.

Topical corticosteroids (see p.174) may be used in difficult cases that do not respond to those treatments. They are particularly useful for the skinfold areas and may be given to counter irritation caused by dithranol.

For more severe psoriasis, not improved by any of these treatments, your dermatologist may recommend specialist treatment with more powerful drugs. These include acitretin and etretinate, vitamin A derivatives that are taken by mouth in courses lasting about 6 months, and methotrexate, an anticancer drug. Another

PUVA

PUVA is the combined use of a psoralen drug (methoxsalen) and ultraviolet A light (UVA). The drug is applied *topically* or taken by mouth some hours before exposure to UVA, which enhances the effect of the drug on skin cells.

This therapy is given two to three times a week, producing an improvement in skin condition within about four to six weeks.

Possible adverse effects include nausea, itching, and painful reddening of the normal areas of skin. More seriously, there is a risk of the skin ageing prematurely and a long-term risk of skin cancer, particularly in fair-skinned people. For these reasons, PUVA therapy is generally recommended only for severe psoriasis after other treatments have failed.

In psoriasis
Skin cells form at the base of the epidermis faster than they can be shed from the skin surface. This causes the formation of patches of thickened, inflamed skin covered by a layer of flaking dead skin.

Normal skin

Skin in psoriasis

Epidermis

Rapidly-dividing skin cells

Dermis

Skin cell

DNA

Drug

UVA rays

Drug

DNA restricted

Psoralen drugs
In PUVA, psoralen drugs administered by mouth or as ointment penetrate the skin cells.

Ultraviolet light
The drug is activated by exposure of the skin to ultraviolet light. It acts on the cell's genetic material (DNA) to regulate its rate of division.

form of treatment, PUVA, is described above.

How they work

Dithranol, etretinate, and methotrexate slow down the rapid rate of cell division that is responsible for skin thickening. Acitretin and etretinate reduce production of keratin, the hard protein that forms in the outer layer of skin. Salicylic acid and coal tar remove the layers of dead skin cells. Corticosteroids reduce inflammation of the underlying skin.

How they affect you

Appropriate treatment of psoriasis usually improves the appearance of the skin. However, because drugs cannot cure the underlying cause of the disorder, psoriasis tends to recur even after successful treatment.

Individual drugs may cause side effects. Topical preparations can cause stinging and inflammation, especially if applied to normal skin. Coal tar and methoxsalen increase the skin's sensitivity to sunlight;

excessive sunbathing or over-exposure to artificial ultraviolet light may damage skin and worsen the condition.

Acitretin and methotrexate have several serious side effects, including liver damage (acitretin, etretinate), gastro-intestinal upsets and bone marrow damage (methotrexate). All three are contraindicated in pregnancy and women are advised not to become pregnant for two years after completing treatment with acitretin or etretinate. Topical corticosteroids may cause rebound worsening of psoriasis when stopped.

COMMON DRUGS

Acitretin
Calcipotriol *
Coal tar
Cyclosporin *
Dithranol *

Etretinate *
Methotrexate
Methoxsalen *
Salicylic acid

Topical corticosteroids (see p.174)

* See Part 4

SUNSCREENS

Sunscreens are chemicals that protect the skin from the damaging effects of ultraviolet radiation from the sun, usually formulated as creams or oils.

People vary widely in their sensitivity to sunlight. Fair-skinned people generally have the least tolerance to direct sunlight and tend to burn easily, while people with darker skin can usually withstand exposure to the sun for much longer periods without noticeable harm.

In a few cases the skin is made more sensitive to sunlight by a disease such as pellagra (a form of malnutrition primarily due to niacin deficiency, see p.426) or herpes simplex infection. Certain drugs, such as the thiazide diuretics, phenothiazine antipsychotics, sulphonamide antibacterials, tetracycline antibiotics, psoralens, and nalidixic acid, can also increase the skin's sensitivity to sunlight.

Why they are used

Sunscreens are usually applied before sunbathing to prevent burning while allowing the skin to tan. Prolonged exposure of unprotected skin to strong sunlight can cause premature ageing of the skin. It also increases the risk of skin cancer especially among fair-skinned people, and those being treated long term with immunosuppressant drugs such as cyclosporin. A sunscreen is particularly advisable for people travelling to tropical and subtropical countries who are unaccustomed to strong sunlight.

Sunscreens are graded according to the degree of protection they offer; the

ACTION OF SUNSCREENS

Fair skin unprotected by a sunscreen suffers damage as ultraviolet rays pass through to the layers beneath, causing pain and inflammation. Sunscreens block out some of these ultraviolet rays, while allowing a proportion of them to pass through the skin surface to the epidermis to stimulate the activity of melanin, the pigment that gives the skin a tan and helps to protect it during further exposure to the sun.

Skin unprotected

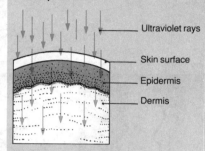

- Ultraviolet rays
- Skin surface
- Epidermis
- Dermis

Skin protected by sunscreen

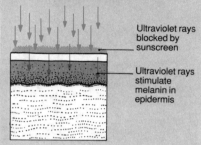

- Ultraviolet rays blocked by sunscreen
- Ultraviolet rays stimulate melanin in epidermis

sun protection factor (SPF). This is a measure of the amount of ultraviolet radiation that they absorb; the higher the number, the more ultraviolet radiation is prevented from reaching the skin. This allows people with different skin types to choose the most suitable sunscreen. People with fair skin should start with a sunscreen with an SPF of 10 to 15 while those with darker skin may use a screen with an SPF of 6 to 8. As the skin tans, a lower SPF may be adequate.

How they work

Sunlight is composed of different wavelengths of electromagnetic radiation. Of these, ultraviolet radiation can be particularly harmful to the skin. The chemical sunscreens absorb ultraviolet radiation, ensuring that a smaller proportion of it reaches the skin.

Risks and special precautions

Sunscreens only form a physical barrier to the passage of ultraviolet radiation. They do not alter the skin to make it more resistant to sunlight. Therefore a sunscreen lotion must be applied frequently to maintain protection.

Even sunscreens with the highest blocking effect, that is, a protection factor of 30, do not completely exclude radiation from the sun. Accordingly, people who are fair-skinned or very sensitive to sunlight should never expose themselves to direct sun, even if they are using a sunscreen.

Sunscreens can irritate the skin and some may cause an allergic rash. People who are sensitive to drugs such as procaine and benzocaine, certain hair dyes and sulphanilamide, may develop a rash following application of a sunscreen preparation containing aminobenzoic acid or a benzophenone chemical like oxybenzone.

TREATMENTS FOR HAIR LOSS AND DANDRUFF

Drugs used for hair loss
One of the most common causes of hair loss is male pattern baldness, in which hair lost from the temples and crown is initially replaced by fine downy hair, and is finally lost permanently. It is probably caused by hormonal changes and most commonly affects men, although women can also suffer this type of hair loss.

Traditionally, the response to male pattern baldness has included the use of wigs and toupees and hair transplants. Recently, however, minoxidil, a vasodilator and antihypertensive drug, has been found to stimulate hair growth in some people. A topical preparation of the drug is at present being investigated as a possible treatment for hair loss. It acts by increasing blood flow in the skin, and elongating the hair follicles as well as reducing the number of white cells around hair follicles. The drug may be absorbed through the scalp and in excessive concentrations can produce harmful effects.

Temporary thinning of the hair may be caused by fungal infection, stress, serious illness, childbirth, or following treatment with anticancer drugs (see p.154). In these cases drug treatment is not effective and hair growth returns to normal once the cause has been removed.

Dandruff treatments
The condition in which dead cells accumulate on the scalp and form white flaky scales is commonly referred to as dandruff. It is not a sign of ill health, but most people find it unsightly and want to get rid of it. In some cases frequent washing (four to six times a week) with a mild shampoo keeps the scalp free of dandruff. Many people, however, find that a medicated shampoo is more effective.

Medicated shampoos usually contain active ingredients such as tar, sulphur, or salicylic acid that soften the dead scales and make them easier to remove.

Shampoos that contain zinc pyrithione or selenium sulphide are often effective for more severe cases. These reduce the formation of dandruff by slowing down the growth of skin cells. They also have a mild antifungal action. (Some doctors believe that yeast infection is a cause of dandruff.)

If the dandruff is severe and does not respond to any of those treatments, some doctors may prescribe a weak corticosteroid lotion or gel (see also Topical corticosteroids, p.174).

COMMON DRUGS

Aminobenzoic acid	Ethylhexyl
Butyl methoxydi-	methoxycinnamate
benzoylmethane	Mexenone
Dibenzoylmethane	Minoxidil *
	Oxybenzone
* See Part 4	Padimate-O
	Titanium dioxide

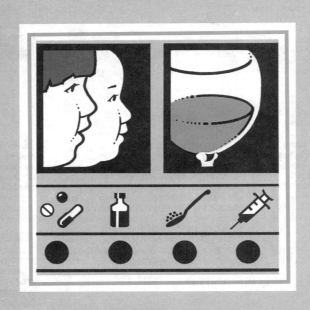

A – Z
OF DRUGS

A – Z OF MEDICAL DRUGS
A – Z OF VITAMINS AND MINERALS
DRUGS OF ABUSE
DRUGS IN SPORT

A - Z OF MEDICAL DRUGS

The drug profiles in this section provide information and practical advice on 235 individual drugs. It is intended that these profiles should provide reference and guidance for non-medical readers taking drug treatment. However, it is impossible for a book of this kind to take into account every variation in individual circumstances, and readers should always follow their doctor's instructions where these differ from the advice in this section.

The drugs have been selected to provide representative coverage of the principal classes of drugs in medical use today. For disorders where a number of drugs are available, the ones which are used most commonly have been selected.

Emphasis has also been placed on those drugs that are likely to be used in the home, although in a few cases those that are administered only in hospital have been included when it has been judged a drug is of sufficient general interest. At the end of this section, supplementary profiles are provided on vitamins and minerals (pp.421 – 433), drugs of abuse (pp.434 – 441), and drugs in sport (pp 441 – 442).

Each drug profile is organized in the same way using standard headings (see sample page, below). To help you make the most of the information provided, the terms used and the instructions given under each heading are discussed and explained on the following pages.

HOW TO UNDERSTAND THE PROFILES

For ease of reference, the information on each drug is arranged in a consistent format under standard headings.

Drug name
Tells you the drug's generic name, brand names under which the drug is marketed, and lists the combined preparations which contain the drug.

General information
Gives you a brief summary of the drug's important characteristics.

Information for users
Practical information on how and when to take the drug, the usual recommended dosage, how soon it takes effect, how long it is active, and advice on diet, storage and missed doses.

Possible adverse effects
Indicates any adverse effects that you may experience with the drug.

Interactions
Tells you how the drug may interact with other drugs or substances taken at the same time.

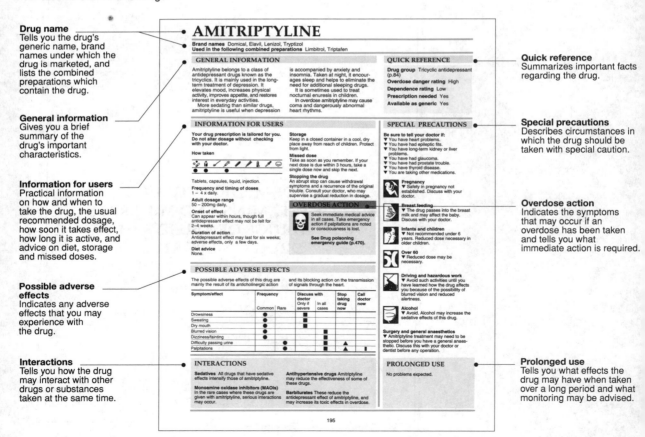

Quick reference
Summarizes important facts regarding the drug.

Special precautions
Describes circumstances in which the drug should be taken with special caution.

Overdose action
Indicates the symptoms that may occur if an overdose has been taken and tells you what immediate action is required.

Prolonged use
Tells you what effects the drug may have when taken over a long period and what monitoring may be advised.

DRUG NAME

Generic name
The main heading on the page is the shortest form of the drug's *generic* name, unless the short form causes confusion with another drug, in which case the full generic name is given. For example, proguanil hydrochloride, an antimalarial drug, is listed as proguanil, as there is no other generic drug of this name. However, magnesium hydroxide, an antacid, is listed under its full name to avoid confusing it with the mineral magnesium, or other compounds of the mineral, such as magnesium sulphate.

Brand names
Under the generic name are the brand names of products in which the drug is the major single active ingredient. If

there are many different brand names of the drug, because of limitations of space, only the most commonly-used ones are given. The names of the principal preparations, if any, in which the drug is combined with other drugs, are also listed. For more information about brand names and generic names, see p.13.

AMITRIPTY

Brand names Domical, Elavil, Lentizo
Used in the following combined pre

GENERAL INFORMATION

GENERAL INFORMATION

The information here builds up an overall picture of the drug. It may include notes on the drug's history (for example, when it was first introduced), and the principal disorders for which it is prescribed. This section also discusses the drug's major advantages and disadvantages.

Used in the following combined pr

GENERAL INFORMATION

Amitriptyline belongs to a class of antidepressant drugs known as the tricyclics. It is mainly used in the long-term treatment of depression. It

QUICK REFERENCE

The text in this box summarizes the important facts regarding your drug, and is organized under five headings which are explained in detail below.

Drug group
This tells you which of the major groups the drug belongs to, and the page on which you can find out more about the drugs in the group and the various disorders or conditions they are used to treat. Where a drug belongs to more than one group, each group included in the book is listed. For example, interferon is listed as an antiviral drug (p.133) and an anticancer drug (p.154).

Overdose danger rating
Gives a general indication of the seriousness of the drug's effects if the dosage prescribed by your doctor, or that recommended on the label of an over-the-counter drug is exceeded. The ratings – low, medium and high – are explained

QUICK REFERENCE

Drug group Tricyclic antidepressa (p.84)

Overdose danger rating High

Dependence rating Low

Prescription needed Yes

below. The rating also determines the advice given under Exceeding the dose.

- **Low** Symptoms unlikely. Death unknown.
- **Medium** Medical advice needed. Death rare.
- **High** Medical attention needed urgently. Potentially fatal.

If you do exceed the dose, advice is given under Exceeding the dose.

Dependence rating
Drugs are classified on the basis of the risk of dependence, and are given a rating of high, medium or low.

- **Low** Dependence unknown.
- **Medium** Rare possibility of dependence.
- **High** Dependence is likely in long-term use.

Prescription needed
This tells you whether or not a prescription is needed to obtain the drug. Some prescription drugs are currently having their status reviewed and may soon be available from the pharmacy counter. Certain other prescription drugs are subject to government regulations (see How drugs are classified p.13).

Available as generic
Tells you if a drug is available as a generic product.

INFORMATION FOR USERS

This section contains information on the following: methods of administration, frequency and amount of dosage, effects and actions, diet advice, practical advice on storage, missed doses, overdose and stopping drug treatment. All infomation is generalized and is in no way a recommendation for an individual dosing schedule. Always follow your doctor's instructions in the case of prescription drugs, and those of the manufacturer for over-the-counter medications.

How taken
The symbols in the box represent the various ways in which drugs can be administered. The dot that appears below

the symbol indicates the form in which the drug is available. This acts as a visual back-up to the written information which follows immediately below the box.

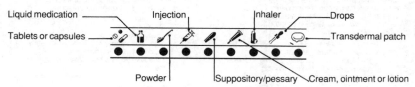

Liquid medication — Injection — Inhaler — Drops
Tablets or capsules —
Powder — Suppository/pessary — Cream, ointment or lotion

A – Z OF MEDICAL DRUGS continued

INFORMATION FOR USERS continued

Frequency and timing of doses
This refers to the standard number of times each day that the drug should be taken, and where relevant, whether it should be taken with liquid, with meals, or on an empty stomach.

> **Frequency and timing of doses**
> *Angina* 3 x daily. For rapid relief of pain an additional capsule may be bitten open and swallowed.
> *High blood pressure* 2 x daily.

> **Frequency and timing of doses**
> 2 x daily with meals.

Dosage range
This is generally given as the normal oral dosage range for an adult – dosages for injection are not usually given. In cases where the dosage for specific age groups vary significantly from the normal adult dosage, these will also be given. Where dosage varies according to use, the dosage for each is included.

The vast majority of drug dosages are expressed in metric units, usually milligrams (mg) or micrograms (mcg). In a few dosage is given in units (u) or international units (IU). See also Weights and measures, facing page.

> **Adult dosage range**
> *Prevention of gout attacks* 0.6 – 1.8mg daily.
> *Relief of gout attacks* 0.5 or 0.6mg per dose up to a maximum of 6mg daily until joint is better or gastrointestinal problems arise.

> **Dosage range**
> *Adults* 25mg per dose (prevention of malaria).
> *Children* Reduced dose necessary according to age and weight.

Onset of effect
The onset of effect is the time it takes for the drug to become active in the body. This sometimes coincides with the onset of beneficial effects, but there may sometimes be an interval between the time when a drug is pharmacologically active and when you start to notice improvement in your symptoms or your underlying condition.

> **Onset of effect**
> Adverse effects may be noticed within a few days, but full beneficial effects may not be felt for 1 – 3 weeks depending on the severity of the condition.

> **Onset of effect**
> 2 – 3 days. In rheumatoid arthritis, full effect may not be felt for up to 6 months.

Duration of action
The information given here refers to the length of time that one dose of the drug remains active in the body.

> **Duration of action**
> Up to 6 hours.

> **Duration of action**
> 8 hours (tablets, liquid, suppositories); 12 – 24 hours (slow-release tablets).

Diet advice
With some drugs, it is important to avoid certain foods, either because they reduce the effect of the drug or because they interact adversely. This section of the profile tells you what, if any, dietary changes are necessary.

> **Diet advice**
> A low fat diet may be recommended. Use of this drug may deplete levels of certain vitamins. Supplements may be advised.

Storage
Drugs will deteriorate and may become inactive if they are not stored under suitable conditions. The advice given in the profiles is usually to store in a cool, dry place out of the reach of children. Some drugs must also be protected from light. Some drugs, especially liquid medications, need to be kept in a refrigerator, but should not be frozen. For further advice on storing drugs, see p.29.

> **Storage**
> Keep in a closed container in a cool, dry place away from reach of children. Protect from light.

Missed dose
This section gives advice on what to do if you forget a dose of your drug, so that the effectiveness and safety of your treatment is maintained as far as possible. If you forget to take several doses in succession, consult your doctor. You can read more about missed doses on p.28.

> **Missed dose**
> No cause for concern, but take when you remember. If your next dose is due within 2 hours, take a single dose now and skip the next.

> **Missed dose**
> Take as soon as you remember. If your next dose is due within 24 hours (once weekly schedule), 6 hours (once or twice daily schedule) take a single dose now and skip the next.

Stopping the drug
If you are taking a drug regularly you should know how and when you can safely stop taking it. Some drugs can be safely stopped as soon as you feel better, or as soon as your symptoms have disappeared. Others must not be stopped until the full course of treatment has been completed, or they must be gradually withdrawn under the supervision of a doctor. Failure to comply with instructions for stopping a drug may lead to adverse effects. It may also cause your condition to worsen or your symptoms to reappear. See also Ending treatment, p.28.

> **Stopping the drug**
> Can be safely stopped as soon as you no longer need it.

> **Stopping the drug**
> Do not stop the drug without consulting your doctor; stopping the drug may lead to worsening of the underlying condition.

Exceeding the dose
The information in this section expands on that in the quick reference box on the drug's overdose danger rating. It explains the possible consequences of exceeding the dose and what to do if an overdose is taken. Examples of wordings used for low, medium or high overdose ratings are as follows:

Low
An occasional extra dose is unlikely to be a cause for concern, but if you notice unusual symptoms, or if a large overdose has been taken, notify your doctor.

Medium
An occasional extra dose is unlikely to cause problems. Large overdoses may cause [symptoms]. Notify your doctor.

High
Seek immediate medical advice in all cases. Take emergency action if [relevant symptoms] occur.

> **Exceeding the dose**
> An occasional unintentional extra dose is unlikely to be a cause for concern. But if you notice unusual symptoms, or if a large overdose has been taken, notify your doctor.

> **OVERDOSE ACTION**
>
>
>
> Seek immediate medical advice in all cases. Take emergency action if palpitations are noted or consciousness is lost.
>
> See **Drug poisoning emergency guide (p.470)**.

SPECIAL PRECAUTIONS

Many drugs need to be taken with care by people with a history of particular conditions. The profile lists conditions you should tell your doctor about when you are prescribed a drug, or about which you should consult your doctor or pharmacist before taking an over-the-counter drug. Certain groups of people (pregnant women, nursing mothers, children and the over 60s) may also be at special risk from drug treatment. Advice for these groups is given on every profile. Information is also included about drinking alcohol, driving and undertaking hazardous work.

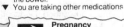

SPECIAL PRECAUTIONS

Be sure to tell your doctor if:
▼ You have long-term kidney or liver problems.
▼ You have heart problems.
▼ You have a blood disorder.
▼ You have stomach ulcers.
▼ You have chronic inflammation of the bowel.
▼ You are taking other medications

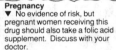

Pregnancy
▼ No evidence of risk, but pregnant women receiving this drug should also take a folic acid supplement. Discuss with your doctor.

Breast feeding
▼ The drug passes into the breast milk, but at normal doses adverse effects on the baby are unlikely. Discuss with your doctor.

Infants and children
▼ Not recommended under 2 years. Reduced dose necessary in older children.

Over 60
▼ Increased likelihood of adverse effects. Reduced dose may therefore be necessary.

Driving and hazardous work
▼ Avoid such activities until you have learned how the drug affects you because the drug may cause dizziness and drowsiness.

Alcohol
▼ Although this drug does not interact with alcohol, your underlying condition may make it inadvisable to take alcohol.

WEIGHTS AND MEASURES

Metric equivalents of measurements used in this book:

1000 mcg (microgram) = 1 mg (milligram)
1000 mg = 1g (gram)
1000 ml (millilitre) = 1 l (litre)

POSSIBLE ADVERSE EFFECTS

The adverse effects discussed in the drug profile are symptoms or reactions that may arise when taking the drug. The emphasis is on symptoms that you, the patient, are likely to notice, rather than on the findings of laboratory tests that your doctor may order. The bulk of the section is in the form of a table which lists the adverse effects and indicates whether they occur commonly or rarely, when to tell your doctor about them and when to stop taking the drug. The headings on the table are explained below.

Frequency
Tells you whether the adverse effect is common or rare. Common effects are listed first.

Discuss with doctor
The marker in this section indicates under what circumstances you need to inform your doctor about an adverse effect you are experiencing.

Only if severe A marker in this column means that the symptom is unlikely to be serious, but that if you are troubled by it to seek your doctor's advice.
In all cases Adverse effects marked in this column require prompt, but not necessarily emergency, medical attention. (See also Call doctor now, below.)

Stop taking the drug now
In cases where certain unpleasant or dangerous adverse effects of a drug may override its beneficial effects, you are advised to stop taking the drug immediately, if necessary before seeing your doctor.

Call doctor now
Effects marked in this column require immediate medical help. They indicate a potentially dangerous response to the drug treatment for which you should seek emergency medical attention.

Symptom/effect	Frequency		Discuss with doctor		Stop taking drug now	Call doctor now
	Common	Rare	Only if severe	In all cases		
Nausea	●		■			
Diarrhoea/abdominal pain	●		■			
Headache/dizziness		●	■			
Rash		●		■	▲	❘
Blurred vision		●		■	▲	❘

INTERACTIONS

The interactions discussed here are those that may occur between the drug under discussion and other drugs. Information includes the name of the interacting drug or drug groups and the effect of the interaction.

INTERACTIONS

Diuretics can lower levels of potassium in the body, and this increases the risk of adverse effects.

Quinidine and verapamil may increase

Sy
epi
incr
thes

Units or international units
Units (u) and international units (IU) are also used to express drug dosages. They represent the biological activity of a drug (its effect on the body). This ability cannot be measured in terms of weight or volume, but must be calculated in a laboratory.

PROLONGED USE

The information given here concerns the adverse, and sometimes beneficial effects, of the drug, which may occur during long-term use. These may differ from those listed under Possible Adverse Effects. This section of the profile also includes information on monitoring the effects of the drug during long-term treatment, explaining the tests you may be given if your doctor thinks they are necessary.

PROLONGED USE

Prolonged use of this drug may lead to hair loss, rashes, tingling in the hands and feet, muscle pain and weakness, and blood disorders.

Monitoring Periodic blood checks are usually required.

ACETAZOLAMIDE

Brand name Diamox
Used in the following combined preparations None

GENERAL INFORMATION

Acetazolamide is a carbonic anhydrase inhibitor, which acts as a diuretic by affecting chemical processes in the kidney and other parts of the body. One of the prinicipal actions of this drug is to reduce the volume of fluid in the anterior (front) chamber of the eye, making acetazolamide a valuable drug in the treatment of glaucoma. It is occasionally used with other drugs for certain types of epilepsy and to prevent or treat acute mountain (altitude) sickness. It is sometimes prescribed to prevent a rare hereditary disease (familial periodic paralysis) associated with changes in potassium levels and muscle weakness. It is rarely used as a diuretic to treat fluid retention in heart failure or liver disease.

QUICK REFERENCE

Drug group Carbonic anhydrase inhibitor diuretic (p.99)
Overdose danger rating Medium
Dependence rating Low
Prescription needed Yes
Available as generic Yes

INFORMATION FOR USERS

Your drug prescription is tailored for you. Do not alter dosage without checking with your doctor.

How taken

Tablets, capsules, injection.

Frequency and timing of doses
4 x daily (the drug is not necessarily taken every day) or 2 x daily (slow-release capsules, which should be swallowed whole).

Adult dosage range
250 – 1000mg daily.

Onset of effect
Within 30 minutes.

Duration of action
6 – 24 hours.

Diet advice
Use of this drug may reduce potassium in the body. Eat plenty of fresh fruit and vegetables. Also, drink plenty of fluids to help eliminate acetazolamide from the kidneys.

Storage
Keep in a closed container in a cool, dry place away from reach of children.

Missed dose
No cause for concern, but take as soon as you remember.

Stopping the drug
Do not stop the drug without consulting your doctor; symptoms may recur.

Exceeding the dose
An occasional unintentional extra dose is unlikely to cause problems. Large overdoses may cause nausea and confusion. Notify your doctor.

SPECIAL PRECAUTIONS

Be sure to tell your doctor if:
▼ You have long-term kidney problems.
▼ You have Addison's disease.
▼ You are taking other medications.

 Pregnancy
▼ Not usually prescribed. May cause abnormalities in the developing baby. Discuss with your doctor.

 Breast feeding
▼ The drug passes into the breast milk and may reduce your milk supply. Discuss with your doctor.

 Infants and children
▼ Not usually prescribed. Reduced dose necessary.

 Over 60
▼ Increased likelihood of adverse effects.

 Driving and hazardous work
▼ Do not undertake such activities until you know how the drug affects you because it can cause drowsiness and confusion.

 Alcohol
▼ Avoid. Dehydration after consumption of alcohol could occur.

POSSIBLE ADVERSE EFFECTS

There are a number of troublesome side effects associated with acetazolamide. In some cases, side effects can become severe enough to make stopping the drug necessary.

Symptom/effect	Frequency		Discuss with doctor		Stop taking drug now	Call doctor now
	Common	Rare	Only if severe	In all cases		
Lethargy	●		■			
Headache/dizziness	●		■			
Loss of appetite/weight loss	●		■			
Tingling hands and feet	●			■		
Confusion		●		■		
Rash		●		■	▲	

PROLONGED USE

Serious problems are unlikely, but levels of certain salts in the body may occasionally become disrupted during prolonged use.

Monitoring Periodic tests may be performed to check on kidney function, levels of body salts, and to detect any effects on the blood.

INTERACTIONS

Thiazide diuretics Excessive loss of potassium may occur when thiazide diuretics are taken with acetazolamide. The combination is usually avoided.

Aspirin may increase the levels of acetazolamide and increase the risk of adverse effects.

Lithium Acetazolamide may reduce blood levels of lithium.

ACYCLOVIR

Brand name Zovirax
Used in the following combined preparations None

GENERAL INFORMATION

Acyclovir is an antiviral drug used in the treatment of herpes infections of all types. Most commonly given in the form of an ointment, acyclovir reduces the severity of outbreaks of cold sores and herpes. Acyclovir may be given by injection or by mouth for severe or recurrent cases of genital herpes. Herpes zoster (shingles) infections are treated with acyclovir tablets. The drug is prescribed on a regular basis for people with reduced immunity. In addition, acyclovir is administered as an ointment for herpes infections of the eye.

The injected form is prescribed with caution to those with impaired kidney function because of the risk of acyclovir accumulating in the body.

INFORMATION FOR USERS

Your drug prescription is tailored for you. Do not alter dosage without checking with your doctor.

How taken

Tablets, liquid, injection, cream, eye ointment.

Frequency and timing of doses
2 – 5 x daily.

Dosage range
Tablets/liquid 1g daily, occasionally 4g daily (treatment); 800mg daily, occasionally 1.6g daily (prevention).
Cream and eye ointment As directed.

Onset of effect
Within 24 hours.

Duration of action
Up to 8 hours.

Diet advice
None.

Storage
Keep in a closed container in a cool, dry place away from reach of children. Protect from light.

Missed dose
Ointment Do not apply the missed dose. Apply your next dose as usual.
Tablets/liquid Take as soon as you remember.

Stopping the drug
Complete the full course as directed.

Exceeding the dose
An occasional unintentional extra dose is unlikely to be a cause for concern. But if you notice unusual symptoms, or if a large overdose has been taken, notify your doctor.

SPECIAL PRECAUTIONS

Be sure to tell your doctor if:
▼ You have a long-term kidney problem.
▼ You are taking other medications.

Pregnancy
▼ Topical preparations carry no known risk, but oral and injectable forms are not usually prescribed as the effects on the developing baby are unknown.

Breast feeding
▼ No evidence of risk with topical preparations. The drug passes into the breast milk following injections or oral administration. Discuss with your doctor.

Infants and children
▼ Reduced dose necessary in young children.

Over 60
▼ Reduced dose may be necessary.

Driving and hazardous work
▼ No known problems.

Alcohol
▼ No known problems.

POSSIBLE ADVERSE EFFECTS

Serious adverse effects are rare. Ointment commonly causes discomfort at the site of application. Confusion and hallucinations occur rarely with injections.

Symptom/effect	Frequency		Discuss with doctor		Stop taking drug now	Call doctor now
	Common	Rare	Only if severe	In all cases		
Topical preparations						
Burning/stinging/itching	●		■			
Rash		●		■	▲	
By mouth						
Nausea/vomiting		●	■			
Headache/dizziness		●	■			
Injection						
Kidney problems		●		■	▲	
Confusion/hallucinations		●		■	▲	

INTERACTIONS (by mouth or injection only)

General note Any drug that affects the kidney increases the risk of side effects with acyclovir.

Probenecid This drug increases the level of acyclovir in the blood.

PROLONGED USE

Acyclovir is usually given as single courses of treatment and is not given long term.

ADRENALINE

Brand names Eppy, Medihaler-Epi, Simplene
Used in the following combined preparations Brovon, Ganda, Marcain with adrenaline

GENERAL INFORMATION

Adrenaline is a *neurotransmitter* that is produced in the centre (medulla) of the adrenal glands that has been produced synthetically since 1900. Medically, adrenaline is used to stimulate heart activity. It also narrows blood vessels in the skin and intestine.

Adrenaline is injected to counteract cardiac arrest, or to relieve severe allergic reactions (anaphylaxis) to drugs or insect stings. Patients at risk of anaphylaxis from insect stings may be given adrenaline to self-inject.

Because it constricts blood vessels, adrenaline is used to control bleeding in surgery and to slow the dispersal and thereby prolong the effect of local anaesthetics.

As eye drops, it can lower the pressure within the eye, making it useful in glaucoma and eye surgery.

INFORMATION FOR USERS

Your drug prescription is tailored for you. Do not alter dosage without checking with your doctor.

How taken

Injection, inhaler, eye drops.

Frequency and timing of doses
As directed according to method of administration and underlying disorder.

Dosage range
As directed according to method of administration and underlying disorder.

Onset of effect
Within 5 minutes (injection, inhaler); within 1 hour (eye drops).

Duration of action
Up to 4 hours (inhaler); up to 4 hours (injection); up to 24 hours (eye drops).

Diet advice
None.

Storage
Keep in a closed container in a cool, dry place away from reach of children. Protect from light.

Missed dose
Do not take the missed dose. Take your next dose as usual.

Stopping the drug
Do not stop taking the drug without consulting your doctor; stopping the drug may lead to worsening of the underlying condition.

OVERDOSE ACTION

Seek immediate medical advice in all cases. Take emergency action if palpitations, breathing difficulties or loss of consciousness occur.

See Drug poisoning emergency guide (p.470).

SPECIAL PRECAUTIONS

Be sure to tell your doctor if:
▼ You have heart problems.
▼ You have diabetes.
▼ You have an overactive thyroid gland.
▼ You have nervous problems.
▼ You are taking other medicines.
▼ You have high blood pressure.

Pregnancy
▼ Not usually prescribed. Discuss with your doctor.

Breast feeding
▼ The drug passes into the milk, but at normal doses adverse effects on the baby are unlikely. Discuss with your doctor.

Infants and children
▼ Not usually prescribed for children. Reduced dose necessary.

Over 60
▼ Increased likelihood of adverse effects. Reduced dose may therefore be necessary.

Driving and hazardous work
▼ Eye drops may cause temporary blurred vision.

Alcohol
▼ No known problems

Surgery and general anaesthetics
▼ Adrenaline may need to be stopped before you have a general anaesthetic. Discuss this with your doctor or dentist before any surgery.

POSSIBLE ADVERSE EFFECTS

The principal adverse effects of this drug are related to its stimulant action on the heart and central nervous system. Eye drops cause local burning or inflammation.

Symptom/effect	Frequency		Discuss with doctor		Stop taking drug now	Call doctor now
	Common	Rare	Only if severe	In all cases		
Dry mouth	●		■			
Nervousness/restlessness	●		■			
Palpitations	●			■		
Headache/blurred vision	●			■		

PROLONGED USE

Long-term use of adrenaline eye drops with soft contact lenses is not recommended.

INTERACTIONS

General note A variety of drugs interact with adrenaline to increase the risk of palpitations and/or high blood pressure. Such drugs include tricyclic and monoamine oxidase inhibitor antidepressants.

Beta blockers Adrenaline can produce a dangerous rise in blood pressure with certain beta blockers such as propranolol.

Antidiabetic drugs The effectiveness of such drugs may be reduced by adrenaline.

ALLOPURINOL

Brand names Caplenal, Cosuric, Hamarin, Rimapurinol, Xanthomax, Zyloric
Used in the following combined preparations None

GENERAL INFORMATION

Allopurinol is prescribed as a long-term preventive of recurrent attacks of gout. It acts by halting the formation in the joint of uric acid crystals, which cause the inflammation characteristic of gout. It is also employed to lower high uric acid levels (hyperuricaemia) caused by other drugs, such as anticancer drugs.

Allopurinol is not effective in relieving the pain of an acute flare-up. In fact, gout attacks may increase initially, so an anti-inflammatory drug is often given as well.

Unlike the gout drugs that reduce uric acid levels by increasing the quantity excreted in the urine, allopurinol does not raise the risk of kidney stones. This makes it particularly suitable for those with poor kidney function or a tendency to form kidney stones.

QUICK REFERENCE

Drug group Drug for gout (p.119)
Overdose danger rating Medium
Dependence rating Low
Prescription needed Yes
Available as generic Yes

INFORMATION FOR USERS

Your drug prescription is tailored for you. Do not alter dosage without checking with your doctor.

How taken

Tablets.

Frequency and timing of doses
1 – 3 x daily with meals.

Adult dosage range
Gout 100 – 600mg daily, usually 300mg.
With anticancer drugs 600 – 900mg daily.

Onset of effect
Within 24 – 48 hours. Full effect may not be felt for several weeks.

Duration of action
Up to 30 hours. Effects may last for 1 – 2 weeks after the drug has been stopped.

Diet advice
A high fluid intake (2 litres of fluid daily) is recommended.

Storage
Keep in a closed container in a cool, dry place away from reach of children.

Missed dose
Take as soon as you remember. If your next dose is not due for another 12 hours or more, take a dose now and take the next one on time. Otherwise skip the missed dose, and take your next dose on schedule.

Stopping the drug
Do not stop the drug without consulting your doctor; symptoms may recur.

Exceeding the dose
An occasional unintentional extra dose is unlikely to cause problems. Large overdoses may cause nausea, vomiting, abdominal pain, diarrhoea, and dizziness. Notify your doctor.

POSSIBLE ADVERSE EFFECTS

Adverse effects of allopurinol are not very common. The most serious is an allergic rash that may require the drug to be stopped and an alternative treatment substituted. Nausea can be avoided by taking allopurinol with meals.

Symptom/effect	Frequency		Discuss with doctor		Stop taking drug now	Call doctor now
	Common	Rare	Only if severe	In all cases		
Nausea	●		■			
Rash/itching	●			■	▲	
Drowsiness		●	■			
Headache		●		■		
Fever		●		■	▲	
Metallic taste		●		■		
Fever and chills		●		■		

INTERACTIONS

Mercaptopurine and azathioprine Allopurinol blocks the breakdown of these drugs so they have to be given in reduced doses.

Anticoagulants Allopurinol may increase the effects of these drugs.

Chlorpropamide The hypoglycaemic effects of chlorpropamide may be increased .

SPECIAL PRECAUTIONS

Be sure to tell your doctor if:
▼ You have long-term liver or kidney problems.
▼ You have a current acute attack of gout.
▼ You are taking other medications.

Pregnancy
▼ Safety in pregnancy not established. Discuss with your doctor.

Breast feeding
▼ The drug passes into the breast milk and may affect the baby. Discuss with your doctor.

Infants and children
▼ Reduced dose necessary.

Over 60
▼ Reduced dose may be necessary.

Driving and hazardous work
▼ Avoid such activities until you have learned how the drug affects you because the drug can cause drowsiness.

Alcohol
▼ Avoid. Alcohol may increase the adverse effects of this drug.

PROLONGED USE

Apart from an increased risk of gout in the first weeks or months, no problems are expected.

Monitoring Periodic checks on uric acid levels in the blood are usually performed.

ALTEPLASE (tPA)

Brand name Actilyse
Used in the following combined preparations None

GENERAL INFORMATION

Alteplase, also known as tissue plasminogen activator (tPA) is an enzyme involved in the breakdown of blood clots. Manufactured or cloned by genetic engineering techniques, it is used in the treatment of heart attacks in which a blood clot (thrombus) forms in one of the blood vessels of the heart muscle, cutting off its blood supply.

Given by infusion into a vein, alteplase acts quickly to dissolve the clot and restore the blood supply to the heart muscle. Used within a few hours of an attack, it can dramatically reduce the amount of damage to the heart muscle. Infusion is usually continued for a few hours after the clot has dispersed to prevent further clot formation.

As with other thrombolytic drugs, there is a risk of internal bleeding, and bleeding or bruising at the injection site is common. As a naturally occurring substance, however, it is less likely to produce an allergic reaction than other thrombolytic drugs such as streptokinase.

INFORMATION FOR USERS

This drug is given only under medical supervision and is not for self-administration.

How taken

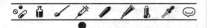

Injection.

Frequency and timing of doses
By continuous infusion over several hours.

Dosage range
Dosage is determined individually by condition and response.

Onset of effect
The blood clot begins to dissolve as soon as the drug reaches it.

Duration of action
The effect of the drug disappears a few minutes after it is stopped.

Diet advice
None.

Storage
Not applicable. This drug is not kept in the home.

Missed dose
Not applicable. This drug is given only in hospital under close medical supervision.

Stopping the drug
The drug is stopped under medical supervision a few hours after the clot has dispersed.

Exceeding the dose Overdosage is unlikely since treatment is carefully monitored in hospital.

POSSIBLE ADVERSE EFFECTS

There is a risk of internal bleeding with alteplase, particularly in the stomach and intestinal tract. All adverse effects are closely monitored under strict medical supervision.

Symptom/effect	Frequency		Discuss with doctor		Stop taking drug now	Call doctor now
	Common	Rare	Only if severe	In all cases		
Nausea/vomiting	●			■		▌
Abnormal bleeding	●			■		▌

INTERACTIONS

Anticoagulants There is an increased risk of bleeding when these are taken at the same time as alteplase.

SPECIAL PRECAUTIONS

tPA is prescribed only under close medical supervision, taking account of your present condition and medical history.

 Pregnancy
▼ Used only when the life of the mother is at risk.

 Breast feeding
▼ Used only when the life of the mother is at risk.

 Infants and children
▼ Not recommended.

 Over 60
▼ No special problems.

 Driving and hazardous work
▼ Not applicable.

 Alcohol
▼ Not applicable.

PROLONGED USE

The drug is not used long-term.

ALUMINIUM HYDROXIDE

Brand names Alu-Cap, Aludrox Gel
Used in the following combined preparations Asilone, Gaviscon, Gelusil, Maalox, Mucaine, Mucogel, Topol, and others

GENERAL INFORMATION

In use for over 50 years to neutralize stomach acid, aluminium hydroxide is the ingredient basic to many over-the-counter remedies for indigestion and heartburn. Because it is constipating (it is sometimes used for diarrhoea), aluminium hydroxide is usually combined with a magnesium-containing antacid with a balancing laxative effect.

The prolonged action of the drug makes it useful in preventing the pain of stomach and duodenal ulcers or reflux oesophagitis. It can also promote the healing of ulcers.

In the intestine, aluminium hydroxide inactivates phosphate. This makes it helpful in treating high blood phosphate (hyperphosphataemia), a condition of some people with impaired kidney function. Prolonged use can lead to phosphate deficiency causing weakening of the bones.

Some preparations include large amounts of sodium and should be used with caution by those on low sodium diets. Liquid preparations of the drug may be more effective as an antacid than tablets.

INFORMATION FOR USERS

Follow instructions on the label. Call your doctor if symptoms worsen.

How taken

Tablets, capsules, liquid (gel suspension). Tablets should be well chewed.

Frequency and timing of doses
As antacid 4 – 6 x daily as needed, or one hour before and after meals.
Peptic ulcer Every 1 – 2 hours while awake.
Hyperphosphataemia 3 – 4 x daily with meals.
Diarrhoea 3 – 6 x daily.

Dosage range
Adults Up to 100ml daily (liquid),1.5 – 9.5g daily (tablets or capsules).
Children over 6 years Reduced dose according to age and weight.

Onset of effect
Within 15 minutes.

Duration of action
2 – 4 hours.

Diet advice
For hyperphosphataemia, aluminium hydroxide may be given with a low phosphate diet.

Storage
Keep in a closed container in a cool, dry place away from reach of children.

Missed dose
Do not take the missed dose. Take your next dose as usual.

Stopping the drug
Can be safely stopped as soon as you no longer need it (indigestion). When given as ulcer treatment or for hyperphosphataemia, do not stop without consulting your doctor.

Exceeding the dose
An occasional unintentional extra dose is unlikely to be a cause for concern. But if you notice unusual symptoms, or if a large overdose has been taken, notify your doctor.

SPECIAL PRECAUTIONS

Be sure to consult your doctor or pharmacist before taking this drug if:
▼ You have long-term kidney problems.
▼ You have heart problems.
▼ You have high blood pressure.
▼ You suffer from constipation.
▼ You have a bone disease.
▼ You are taking other medications.

Pregnancy
▼ Safety in pregnancy not established. Discuss with your doctor.

Breast feeding
▼ No evidence of risk.

Infants and children
▼ Not recommended in children under 6 years except on the advice of a doctor.

Over 60
▼ Increased likelihood of adverse effects. Reduced dose may therefore be necessary.

Driving and hazardous work
▼ No known problems.

Alcohol
▼ No known problems.

POSSIBLE ADVERSE EFFECTS

Constipation is common with aluminium hydroxide; nausea and vomiting may occur due to the granular powdery nature of the drug. Bone pain only occurs when large doses have been taken regularly for months or years.

Symptom/effect	Frequency		Discuss with doctor		Stop taking drug now	Call doctor now
	Common	Rare	Only if severe	In all cases		
Constipation	●		■			
Nausea		●	■			
Vomiting		●			■	

PROLONGED USE

Aluminium hydroxide should not be used for longer than 4 weeks without consulting your doctor. Prolonged use in high doses may deplete blood phosphate and calcium levels, leading to weakening of the bones and fractures.

INTERACTIONS

General note Aluminium hydroxide may interfere with the absorption or excretion of oral anticoagulants, digoxin, antipsychotics, tetracyclines, and some other antibiotics, penicillamine, phenytoin and corticosteroids.

Enteric-coated tablets This drug may break up the enteric coating of tablets such as bisacodyl, causing stomach irritation.

AMANTADINE

Brand name Symmetrel
Used in the following combined preparations None

GENERAL INFORMATION

Amantadine was introduced in the 1960s as an antiviral drug, originally for the prevention and treatment of influenza A. As a preventive against influenza A, it protects some 70 per cent of those not receiving vaccination. As treatment, it is effective for reducing the severity of symptoms when given within 48 hours of the onset of flu.

In 1969 Amantadine was found to be helpful in parkinsonism, and this is now its most common use. Though amantadine usually produces symptomatic improvement during the first few weeks, its effectiveness wears off over a few months, requiring replacement by another drug. It is sometimes given with levodopa (see p.315), another antiparkinsonism drug.

QUICK REFERENCE

Drug group Drug for parkinsonism (p.87) and antiviral drug (p.133)
Overdose danger rating Low
Dependence rating Low
Prescription needed Yes
Available as generic No

INFORMATION FOR USERS

Your drug prescription is tailored for you. Do not alter dosage without checking with your doctor.

How taken

Capsules, liquid.

Frequency and timing of doses
1 – 2 x daily. The second dose should not be taken later than 4pm.

Adult dosage range
100 – 200mg daily.

Onset of effect
In Parkinson's disease full effect may not be felt for up to 2 weeks. In viral infections the severity and duration of symptoms is likely to be reduced during a 1 – 2 week course of treatment if the drug is begun within 48 hours of onset of symptoms.

Duration of action
Up to 24 hours.

Diet advice
None.

Storage
Keep in a closed container in a cool, dry place away from reach of children.

Missed dose
Take as soon as you remember. If your next dose is due within 2 hours, take a single dose now and miss the next.

Stopping the drug
Do not stop taking the drug without consulting your doctor; symptoms may recur.

Exceeding the dose
An occasional unintentional extra dose is unlikely to cause problems. But if you notice unusual symptoms, or if a large overdose has been taken, notify your doctor.

SPECIAL PRECAUTIONS

Be sure to tell your doctor if:
▼ You have long-term kidney or liver problems.
▼ You have a peptic ulcer.
▼ You have had epileptic fits.
▼ You suffer from eczema.
▼ You are taking other medications.

 Pregnancy
▼ Safety in pregnancy not established. Discuss with your doctor.

 Breast feeding
▼ The drug passes into the breast milk and may affect the baby. Discuss with your doctor.

 Infants and children
▼ Not usually prescribed. Reduced dose necessary.

 Over 60
▼ Increased likelihood of adverse effects. Reduced dose may therefore be necessary.

 Driving and hazardous work
▼ Avoid such activities until you have learned how the drug affects you because of the possibility of blurred vision, dizziness, and confusion.

 Alcohol
▼ Avoid in the first few days of treatment, thereafter keep consumption low.

POSSIBLE ADVERSE EFFECTS

Adverse effects are uncommon and often wear off during continued treatment. They are rarely serious enough to require treatment to be stopped.

Symptom/effect	Frequency		Discuss with doctor		Stop taking drug now	Call doctor now
	Common	Rare	Only if severe	In all cases		
Nervousness/agitation	●		■			
Confusion	●			■		
Insomnia		●	■			
Dizziness		●		■		
Blurred vision		●		■		
Loss of appetite		●		■		
Ankle swelling		●		■		
Rash		●		■	▲	

INTERACTIONS

Anticholinergic drugs Amantadine may add to the effects of *anticholinergic* drugs. In that event your doctor will probably reduce the dose of the anticholinergic drug.

PROLONGED USE

The beneficial effects of amantadine usually diminish during continuous treatment for parkinsonism. When this happens, another drug may be substituted or given together with amantadine. Sometimes the effectiveness of amantadine can be restored if it is withdrawn for a few weeks and later reintroduced.

AMILORIDE

Brand name Amilospare, Berkamil, Midamor
Used in the following combined preparations Frumil, Kalten, Lasoride, Moducren, Moduretic, Navispare, and others

GENERAL INFORMATION

Amiloride belongs to the class of drugs known as potassium-sparing diuretics. Combined with thiazide or loop diuretics, amiloride is used in the treatment of hypertension, and oedema (fluid retention), resulting from heart failure or liver disease.

Amiloride's effect on urine flow may be noticed for several hours. For this reason, it should be avoided after about 4p.m. Otherwise you may need to pass urine during the night. As with other potassium-sparing diuretics, amiloride can be risky when there are unusually high levels of potassium in the blood. The drug is prescribed with caution for people with kidney disorders.

INFORMATION FOR USERS

Your drug prescription is tailored for you. Do not alter dosage without checking with your doctor.

How taken

Tablets, liquid.

Frequency and timing of doses
Once daily, usually in the morning; sometimes twice daily.

Dosage range
5 – 20mg daily.

Onset of effect
Within 2 – 4 hours.

Duration of action
12 – 24 hours.

Diet advice
Avoid foods that are high in potassium – for example, dried fruit and salt substitutes.

Storage
Keep in a closed container in a cool, dry place away from reach of children. Protect from light.

Missed dose
Take as soon as you remember. However, if it is late in the day, do not take the missed dose, or you may need to get up at night to pass urine. Take the next scheduled dose as usual.

Stopping the drug
Do not stop the drug without consulting your doctor; symptoms may recur.

Exceeding the dose
An occasional unintentional extra dose is unlikely to be a cause for concern. But if you notice unusual symptoms, or if a large overdose has been taken, notify your doctor.

SPECIAL PRECAUTIONS

Be sure to tell your doctor if:
▼ You have long-term kidney problems.
▼ You have gout.
▼ You have diabetes.
▼ You are taking other medications.

 Pregnancy
▼ Not usually prescribed. May cause a reduction in the blood supply to the developing baby. Discuss with your doctor.

 Breast feeding
▼ The drug passes into the breast milk and could also reduce your milk supply. Discuss with your doctor.

 Infants and children
▼ Not recommended.

 Over 60
▼ Increased likelihood of adverse effects. Reduced dose may therefore be necessary.

 Driving and hazardous work
▼ Avoid such activities until you have learned how the drug affects you because the drug may cause confusion.

 Alcohol
▼ No special problems.

POSSIBLE ADVERSE EFFECTS

Amiloride has few adverse effects; the main problem is the possibility that potassium may be retained by the body causing muscle weakness and numbness.

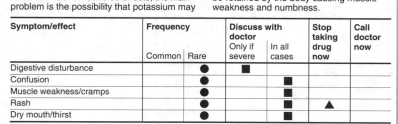

Symptom/effect	Frequency		Discuss with doctor		Stop taking drug now	Call doctor now
	Common	Rare	Only if severe	In all cases		
Digestive disturbance		●	■			
Confusion		●			■	
Muscle weakness/cramps		●			■	
Rash		●			■	▲
Dry mouth/thirst		●			■	

INTERACTIONS

Lithium Amiloride may increase the blood levels of lithium, leading to an increased risk of lithium poisoning.

ACE Inhibitors may increase the risk of potassium retention with amiloride.

PROLONGED USE

Serious problems are unlikely.

Monitoring Blood tests may be performed to check on kidney function and levels of body salts.

AMIODARONE

Brand name Cordarone X
Used in the following preparations None

GENERAL INFORMATION

Amiodarone was introduced in the 1950s and is used to treat a variety of abnormal heart rhythms (arrhythmias). It works by slowing nerve impulses in the heart muscle.

Amiodarone is given to prevent recurrent atrial and ventricular fibrillation and to treat ventricular and supraventricular tachycardias. It is also used to treat Wolff-Parkinson-White Syndrome. The drug is usually the last

choice because of its serious adverse effects, especially when used long term. These effects include liver damage, thyroid problems, and damage to the eyes and lungs.

Treatment should only be started under specialist supervision or in hospital and the dosage carefully controlled so as to achieve the desired effect using the lowest possible dose.

INFORMATION FOR USERS

Your drug prescription is tailored for you. Do not alter dosage without checking with your doctor.

How taken

Tablets, injection.

Frequency and timing of doses
3 x daily or by injection initially, then reduced to twice daily, then once daily or every other day (maintenance dose).

Adult dosage range
400 – 600mg daily (starting dose), reduced to 100 – 200mg daily (maintenance dose).

Onset of effect
Some effects may be noticed within 2 hours, but full benefits may not be felt for some weeks.

Duration of action
Up to 1 month.

Diet advice
None.

Storage
Keep in a closed container in a cool, dry place away from reach of children. Protect from light.

Missed dose
Take as soon as you remember. If your next dose is due within 12 hours, do not take the missed dose. Take your next scheduled dose as usual.

Stopping the drug
Do not stop the drug without consulting your doctor; symptoms may recur.

Exceeding the dose
An occasional unintentional extra dose is unlikely to cause problems. If a large overdose has been taken or you have unusual symptoms, notify your doctor.

SPECIAL PRECAUTIONS

Be sure to tell your doctor if:
▼ You have long-term liver or kidney problems.
▼ You have heart disease.
▼ You have eye disease.
▼ You have a lung disorder such as asthma or bronchitis.
▼ You have a thyroid disorder.
▼ You are taking other medications.

Pregnancy
▼ Not usually prescribed. May cause thyroid disease and slow heart beat in the newborn infant. Discuss with your doctor.

Breast feeding
▼ The drug passes into the breast milk and may affect the baby. Discuss with your doctor.

Infants and children
▼ Not recommended.

Over 60
▼ Increased likelihood of adverse effects. Reduced dose may therefore be necessary.

Driving and hazardous work
▼ No known problems.

Alcohol
▼ No known problems.

POSSIBLE ADVERSE EFFECTS

Amiodarone has a number of unusual side effects, including a metallic taste in the mouth, increased sensitivity of the skin to sunlight, and a greyish skin colour.

Symptom/effect	Frequency		Discuss with doctor		Stop taking drug now	Call doctor now
	Common	Rare	Only if severe	In all cases		
Nausea/vomiting	●		■			
Metallic taste	●		■			
Shortness of breath	●			■		
Headache	●			■		
Grey skin colour	●			■		
Light sensitve rash	●			■		
Weakness/fatigue	●			■		

INTERACTIONS

General note Amiodarone can interact with many drugs. Check with your doctor or pharmacist before taking other medication.

Loop diuretics The potassium loss caused by these drugs may increase *toxic* effects of amiodarone.

Other anti-arrhythmics Amiodarone is likely to increase the effects of drugs such as beta blockers, digoxin, diltiazem or verapamil.

Warfarin Amiodarone may increase the anticoagulant effect of warfarin.

PROLONGED USE

Prolonged use of this drug may cause a number of adverse effects on the eyes, lung, thyroid gland, and liver.

Monitoring Blood may be taken periodically to check hormone levels and liver function and to measure drug levels. Regular ophthalmic examination is recommended.

AMITRIPTYLINE

Brand names Domical, Elavil, Lentizol, Tryptizol
Used in the following combined preparations Limbitrol, Triptafen

GENERAL INFORMATION

Amitriptyline belongs to a class of antidepressant drugs known as the tricyclics. It is mainly used in the long-term treatment of depression. It elevates mood, increases physical activity, improves appetite, and restores interest in everyday activities.

More sedating than similar drugs, amitriptyline is useful when depression is accompanied by anxiety and insomnia. Taken at night, it encourages sleep and helps to eliminate the need for additional sleeping drugs.

It is sometimes used to treat nocturnal enuresis in children.

In overdose amitriptyline may cause coma and dangerously abnormal heart rhythms.

QUICK REFERENCE

Drug group Tricyclic antidepressant (p.84)
Overdose danger rating High
Dependence rating Low
Prescription needed Yes
Available as generic Yes

INFORMATION FOR USERS

Your drug prescription is tailored for you. Do not alter dosage without checking with your doctor.

How taken

Tablets, capsules, liquid, injection.

Frequency and timing of doses
1 – 4 x daily.

Adult dosage range
50 – 200mg daily.

Onset of effect
Can appear within hours, though full antidepressant effect may not be felt for 2–4 weeks.

Duration of action
Antidepressant effect may last for six weeks; adverse effects, only a few days.

Diet advice
None.

Storage
Keep in a closed container in a cool, dry place away from reach of children. Protect from light.

Missed dose
Take as soon as you remember. If your next dose is due within 3 hours, take a single dose now and skip the next.

Stopping the drug
An abrupt stop can cause withdrawal symptoms and a recurrence of the original trouble. Consult your doctor, who may supervise a gradual reduction in dosage.

OVERDOSE ACTION

 Seek immediate medical advice in all cases. Take emergency action if palpitations are noted or consciousness is lost.

See Drug poisoning emergency guide (p.470).

SPECIAL PRECAUTIONS

Be sure to tell your doctor if:
▼ You have heart problems.
▼ You have had epileptic fits.
▼ You have long-term kidney or liver problems.
▼ You have had glaucoma.
▼ You have had prostate trouble.
▼ You have thyroid disease.
▼ You are taking other medications.

 Pregnancy
▼ Safety in pregnancy not established. Discuss with your doctor.

 Breast feeding
▼ The drug passes into the breast milk and may affect the baby. Discuss with your doctor.

 Infants and children
▼ Not recommended under 6 years. Reduced dose necessary in older children.

 Over 60
▼ Reduced dose may be necessary.

 Driving and hazardous work
▼ Avoid such activities until you have learned how the drug affects you because of the possibility of blurred vision and reduced alertness.

 Alcohol
▼ Avoid. Alcohol may increase the sedative effects of this drug.

Surgery and general anaesthetics
▼ Amitriptyline treatment may need to be stopped before you have a general anaesthetic. Discuss this with your doctor or dentist before any operation.

POSSIBLE ADVERSE EFFECTS

The possible adverse effects of this drug are mainly the result of its *anticholinergic* action and its blocking action on the transmission of signals through the heart.

Symptom/effect	Frequency		Discuss with doctor		Stop taking drug now	Call doctor now
	Common	Rare	Only if severe	In all cases		
Drowsiness	●		■			
Sweating	●		■			
Dry mouth	●		■			
Blurred vision	●			■		
Dizziness/fainting	●			■		
Difficulty passing urine		●		■	▲	
Palpitations		●		■	▲	■

INTERACTIONS

Sedatives All drugs that have sedative effects intensify those of amitriptyline.

Monoamine oxidase inhibitors (MAOIs)
In the rare cases where these drugs are given with amitriptyline, serious interactions may occur.

Antihypertensive drugs Amitriptyline may reduce the effectiveness of some of these drugs.

Barbiturates These reduce the antidepressant effect of amitriptyline, and may increase its toxic effects in overdose.

PROLONGED USE

No problems expected.

AMOXYCILLIN

Brand names Amix, Almodan, Amoram, Amoxil, Amrit, Flemoxin, Galenamox, Rimoxallin
Used in the following combined preparation Augmentin

GENERAL INFORMATION

Amoxycillin is a penicillin antibiotic. It is prescribed to treat a variety of infections, but is particularly useful for treating ear, nose, and throat infections, respiratory tract infections, cystitis, uncomplicated gonorrhoea, and certain skin and soft tissue infections. Taken by mouth, amoxycillin is absorbed well by the body and it works quickly and effectively.

The most common side effect of amoxycillin is a blotchy skin rash, which does not mean that the patient has a penicillin allergy. It can also provoke a more severe allergic reaction with fever, swelling of the mouth and tongue, itching, and breathing difficulties. This usually means that the patient is allergic to all penicillin antibiotics.

INFORMATION FOR USERS

Your drug prescription is tailored for you. Do not alter dosage without checking with your doctor.

How taken

Tablets, capsules, sachets, liquid, injection.

Frequency and timing of doses
Normally 3 x daily.

Dosage range
Adults 750mg – 1.5g daily. In some cases, a short course of up to 6g daily is given.
Children Reduced dose according to age and weight.

Onset of effect
1 – 2 hours.

Duration of action
Up to 8 hours.

Diet advice
None.

Storage
Keep in a closed container in a cool, dry place away from reach of children.

Missed dose
Take as soon as you remember. Take your next dose at the scheduled time.

Stopping the drug
Take the full course. Even if you feel better, the original infection may still be present and symptoms may recur if treatment is stopped too soon.

Exceeding the dose
An occasional unintentional extra dose is unlikely to be a cause for concern. But if you notice any unusual symptoms, or if a large overdose has been taken, notify your doctor.

SPECIAL PRECAUTIONS

Be sure to tell your doctor if:
▼ You have a long-term kidney problem.
▼ You have an allergy (for example, asthma, hay fever, or eczema).
▼ You have had an allergic reaction after being given a penicillin or cephalosporin antibiotic.
▼ You have ulcerative colitis.
▼ You have glandular fever.
▼ You are taking other medications.

Pregnancy
▼ No evidence of risk.

Breast feeding
▼ The drug passes into the breast milk, but at normal doses adverse effects on the baby are unlikely. Discuss with your doctor.

Infants and children
▼ Reduced dose necessary.

Over 60
▼ No known problems.

Driving and hazardous work
▼ No known problems.

Alcohol
▼ No known problems.

POSSIBLE ADVERSE EFFECTS

If you develop a rash, wheezing, itching, fever, or joint swelling this may indicate an allergy. Call your doctor who may prescribe a different antibiotic.

Symptom/effect	Frequency		Discuss with doctor		Stop taking drug now	Call doctor now
	Common	Rare	Only if severe	In all cases		
Rash	●				■	
Nausea/vomiting		●	■			
Diarrhoea		●		■		
Wheezing		●		■	▲	▎
Itching		●		■	▲	▎
Swollen mouth/tongue		●		■	▲	▎

INTERACTIONS

Oral contraceptives Amoxycillin may reduce the effectiveness of the contraceptive pill and also increase the risk of breakthrough bleeding. Discuss with your doctor.

PROLONGED USE

Amoxycillin is usually given only for short courses of treatment.

AMPHOTERICIN

Brand names AmBisome, Fungilin, Fungizone
Used in the following combined preparation None

GENERAL INFORMATION

Since its introduction in the 1950s, amphotericin has come to be regarded as a highly effective and powerful antifungal drug. Administered in the form of injection, it is used in cases of serious *systemic* fungal infections. Amphotericin is also given by mouth to treat candida (thrush) infections of the mouth or intestines. It is not, however, used in vaginal candidiasis.

Treatment by injection is carefully supervised, usually in hospital, because of adverse effects. A new formulation of amphotericin has recently been introduced. This appears to be less toxic than the original injection. Adverse reactions to the oral forms are rare.

QUICK REFERENCE

Drug group Antifur.jal drug (p.138)
Overdose danger rating Low
Dependence rating Low
Prescription needed Yes
Available as generic No

INFORMATION FOR USERS

Your drug prescription is tailored for you. Do not alter dosage without checking with your doctor.

How taken

● ● ●

Tablets, lozenges, liquid, injection.

Frequency and timing of doses
Daily, usually over 6 hour period (injection); every 6 hours (by mouth).

Dosage range
400 – 800mg daily (tablets and liquid); 40 – 80mg daily (lozenges). The dosage for injection is determined individually.

Onset of effect
Improvement may be noticed after 2 – 4 days.

Duration of action
3 – 6 hours.

Diet advice
When given by injection, amphotericin may reduce the levels of potassium and magnesium in the blood. Mineral supplements may be recommended.

Storage
Keep in a closed container in a cool, dry place away from reach of children.

Missed dose
Take as soon as you remember. Take your next dose when scheduled.

Stopping the drug
Take the full course as prescribed. Even if symptoms improve, the original infection may still be present and symptoms may recur if treatment is stopped too soon.

Exceeding the dose
An occasional unintentional extra dose is unlikely to be a cause for concern. But if you notice unusual symptoms, notify your doctor.

SPECIAL PRECAUTIONS

Be sure to tell your doctor if:
▼ You have long-term kidney problems.
▼ You have previously had an allergic reaction to amphotericin.
▼ You are taking other medications.

 Pregnancy
▼ There is no evidence of risk from the oral forms of the drug. Injections are given only when the infection is very serious.

 Breast feeding
▼ No evidence of risk from the oral forms of the drug. Given by injection, the drug may pass into the breast milk. Discuss with your doctor.

 Infants and children
▼ Reduced dose may be necessary.

 Over 60
▼ No special problems.

 Driving and hazardous work
▼ No known problems.

 Alcohol
▼ No known problems.

POSSIBLE ADVERSE EFFECTS

Amphotericin is given by injection only under close medical supervision. Adverse effects are thus carefully monitored and promptly treated. Adverse effects from oral administration are rare.

Symptom/effect	Frequency		Discuss with doctor		Stop taking drug now	Call doctor now
	Common	Rare	Only if severe	In all cases		
Injection						
Nausea/vomiting	●				■	
Headache/fever	●				■	
Unusual bleeding		●			■	
Muscle and joint pain		●			■	
Pain at injecton site	●				■	

PROLONGED USE

Given by injection the drug may cause a reduction in blood levels of potassium and magnesium. It may also damage the kidneys and cause blood disorders.

Monitoring Regular blood tests to monitor kidney function are advised during treatment by injection.

INTERACTIONS (injection only)

Digitalis drugs Amphotericin may increase the toxicity of digoxin.

Diuretics Amphotericin increases the risk of low potassium levels with diuretics.

Aminoglycoside antibiotics Taken with amphotericin, these drugs increase the likelihood of kidney damage.

Corticosteroids may increase loss of potassium from the body caused by amphotericin.

Cyclosporin increases the likelihood of kidney damage.

ANTAZOLINE

Brand names None
Used in the following combined preparations Otrivine-Antistin, RBC, Vasocon-A

GENERAL INFORMATION

Antazoline is an antihistamine drug that can be bought over-the-counter as an ingredient of a variety of *topical* preparations. Eye drops containing the drug are used to relieve irritation caused by allergic conjunctivitis. The drug is also applied to the skin in the form of a cream for the relief of itching and irritation caused by insect bites or allergic rashes.

Adverse effects from the drug are rare. Continuous use for longer than a few days should be avoided.

QUICK REFERENCE

Drug group Antihistamine (p.124)
Overdose danger rating Low
Dependence rating Low
Prescription needed No
Available as generic No

INFORMATION FOR USERS

Follow instructions on the label. Call your doctor if symptoms worsen.

How taken

Cream, eye drops.

Frequency and timing of doses
Every 3 – 6 hours, depending on preparation.

Adult dosage range
Varies according to preparation.

Onset of effect
Within a few minutes.

Duration of action
Up to 6 hours.

Diet advice
None.

Storage
Keep in a closed container in a cool, dry place away from reach of children.

Missed dose
No cause for concern. Use only when needed.

Stopping the drug
Can be safely stopped as soon as you no longer need it.

Exceeding the dose
An occasional unintentional extra application is unlikely to be a cause for concern. But if you notice unusual symptoms, or if a large amount has been swallowed, notify your doctor.

POSSIBLE ADVERSE EFFECTS

Antazoline is less likely to cause irritation than other antihistamines used in topical preparations.

Symptom/effect	Frequency		Discuss with doctor		Stop taking drug now	Call doctor now
	Common	Rare	Only if severe	In all cases		
Irritation/discomfort		●	■			
Headache		●		■	▲	

INTERACTIONS

None.

SPECIAL PRECAUTIONS

Be sure to consult your doctor or pharmacist before taking this drug if:
▼ You have glaucoma.
▼ You have angina or high blood pressure.
▼ You are taking other medications.
▼ You wear contact lenses (eye drops).

 Pregnancy
▼ No evidence of risk to developing baby.

 Breast feeding
▼ No evidence of risk.

 Infants and children
▼ No special problems.

 Over 60
▼ No special problems.

 Driving and hazardous work
▼ No special problems.

 Alcohol
▼ No spercial problems.

PROLONGED USE

Regular long-term use is not recommended.

ASPIRIN

Brand names Caprin, Laboprin, Nu-Seals Aspirin
Used in the following combined preparations Anadin, Angettes, Aspav, Codis, Equagesic, Veganin, and others

GENERAL INFORMATION

Commonly used for over 80 years, aspirin is a non-narcotic analgesic that relieves pain, reduces fever, and alleviates the symptoms of arthritis. In small doses, it helps to prevent blood clots from forming.

It is present in many medicines for colds, menstrual period pains, headaches, and joint or muscular aches.

One disadvantage of aspirin is its tendency to irritate the stomach and even cause bleeding. Also there is a possibility that it can cause Reyes disease, a rare brain and liver disorder usually occurring in children. It should be given to children under 12 only under close medical supervision.

QUICK REFERENCE

Drug group Non-narcotic analgesic (p.80), antiplatelet drug (p.104), and antipyretic (p.446)

Overdose danger rating High

Dependence rating Low

Prescription needed No

Available as generic Yes

INFORMATION FOR USERS

Follow instructions on the label. Call your doctor if symptoms worsen.

How taken

Tablets, suppositories.

Frequency and timing of doses
Relief of pain and fever Every 4 – 6 hours, as necessary, with food or milk.
Prevention of blood clots Once daily.

Adult dosage range
Relief of pain and fever 300 – 900mg per dose.
Prevention of blood clots 75 – 300mg daily.

Onset of effect
30 – 60 minutes (regular aspirin); $1\,^1/_2$ – 8 hours (enteric coated tablets or slow-release capsules).

Duration of action
Up to 12 hours. Some effect may persist for several days when used to prevent blood clotting.

Diet advice
None.

Storage
Keep in a closed container in a cool, dry place away from reach of children.

Missed dose
Take as soon as you remember. If the next dose is due within 2 hours, take a single dose now and skip the next.

Stopping the drug
If you have been prescribed aspirin by your physician for a long-term condition, you should seek medical advice before stopping the drug. Otherwise it can be safely stopped

OVERDOSE ACTION

 Seek immediate medical advice in all cases. Take emergency action if there is restlessness, stomach pain, ringing noises in the ears, blurred vision, or vomiting.

See Drug poisoning emergency guide (p.470).

SPECIAL PRECAUTIONS

Be sure to consult your doctor or pharmacist before taking this drug if:
▼ You have long-term kidney or liver problems.
▼ You have asthma.
▼ You have a blood clotting disorder.
▼ You have had a stomach ulcer.
▼ You are taking other medications.

 Pregnancy
▼ Not usually recommended. An alternative drug may be safer. Discuss with your doctor.

 Breast feeding
▼ The drug passes into the breast milk. Discuss with your doctor.

 Infants and children
▼ Not recommended under 12 years.

 Over 60
▼ No special problems.

 Driving and hazardous work
▼ No special problems.

 Alcohol
▼ Avoid. Alcohol increases the likelihood of stomach irritation with this drug.

Surgery and general anaesthetics
▼ Regular treatment with aspirin may need to be stopped about one week before surgery. Discuss with your doctor or dentist before any operation.

PROLONGED USE

Aspirin should not be taken for longer than 2 days except on your doctor's advice. Prolonged use of aspirin may lead to bleeding in the stomach and to stomach ulcers.

POSSIBLE ADVERSE EFFECTS

Adverse effects are more likely to occur with high dosage of aspirin, but may be reduced by taking the drug with food or in buffered or enteric coated forms.

Symptom /effect	Frequency		Discuss with doctor		Stop taking drug now	Call doctor now
	Common	Rare	Only if severe	In all cases		
Nausea/vomiting		●		■		
Indigestion	●		■		▲	
Rash		●		■	▲	
Breathlessness/wheezing		●		■	▲	
Ringing in the ears		●	■		▲	■

INTERACTIONS

Anticoagulants Aspirin may add to the anticoagulant effect of such drugs leading to an increased risk of abnormal bleeding.

NSAIDs may increase the likelihood of stomach irritation when taken with aspirin.

Drugs for gout Aspirin may reduce the effect of these drugs, especially probenecid and sulphinpyrazone.

Oral antidiabetic drugs Aspirin may increase the effect of these drugs.

ATENOLOL

Brand name Antipressan, Atenix, Tenormin, Totamol, Vasaten
Used in the following combined preparation Beta-Adalat, Kalten, Tenchlor, Tenif, Tenoret, Tenoretic

GENERAL INFORMATION

Atenolol belongs to the class of drugs known as beta blockers (see p.93). It prevents the heart from beating too quickly and is mainly used to treat angina, high blood pressure, and abnormal heart rhythms.

Atenolol is sometimes given to people with lung problems because unlike some other beta blockers, it acts mainly on the heart rather than other parts of the body. It may also be given just after a heart attack to protect the heart from further damage.

Because atenolol does not cure heart disease, but only controls the symptoms, it may have to be taken continuously over a long period, even for the rest of a person's life. It only needs to be taken once a day, an advantage to people who have difficulty in remembering to take their drugs.

QUICK REFERENCE

Drug group Beta blocker (p.97)
Overdose danger rating Medium
Dependence rating Low
Prescription needed Yes
Available as generic Yes

INFORMATION FOR USERS

Your drug prescription is tailored for you. Do not alter dosage without checking with your doctor.

How taken

Tablets, liquid, injection.

Frequency and timing of doses
1 – 2 x daily.

Adult dosage range
50 – 100 mg daily.

Onset of action
2 – 4 hours.

Duration of action
20 – 30 hours.

Diet advice
None.

Storage
Keep in a tightly closed container in a cool, dry place away from reach of children. Protect from light.

Missed dose
Take as soon as you remember. If your next dose is due within 6 hours, do not take the missed dose but take the next scheduled dose as usual.

Stopping the drug
Do not stop taking the drug without consulting your doctor; withdrawal of the drug may lead to severe worsening of the underlying condition. It should be withdrawn gradually.

Exceeding the dose
An occasional unintentional extra dose is unlikely to be a cause for concern. But if you notice unusual symptoms, or if a large overdose has been taken, notify your doctor.

SPECIAL PRECAUTIONS

Be sure to tell your doctor if:
▼ You have long-term kidney problems.
▼ You have poor circulation.
▼ You have a lung disorder such as asthma or bronchitis.
▼ You are taking other medications.

Pregnancy
▼ No evidence of risk. Discuss with your doctor.

Breast feeding
▼ The drug passes into the breast milk. Discuss with your doctor.

Infants and children
▼ Not recommended.

Over 60
▼ No special problems. Reduced dose may be necessary if kidney function is impaired.

Driving and hazardous work
▼ No special problems.

Alcohol
▼ No special problems with small intake.

Surgery and general anaesthetics
▼ Atenolol may need to be stopped before you have a general anaesthetic. Discuss this with your doctor or dentist before any surgery.

POSSIBLE ADVERSE EFFECTS

Atenolol has adverse effects that are common to most beta blockers. Symptoms are usually temporary and diminish with long-term use.

Symptom/effect	Frequency		Discuss with doctor		Stop taking drug now	Call doctor now
	Common	Rare	Only if severe	In all cases		
Muscle ache	●		■			
Cold hands and feet		●	■			
Nightmares/sleeplessness		●	■			
Headache		●		■		
Rash		●	■			
Fatigue/depression/confusion		●	■			
Breathing difficulties		●		■		▮

INTERACTIONS

Anti-arrhythmic drugs When used together wih atenolol they may increase the risk of adverse effects on the heart.

Indomethacin may reduce the antihypertensive effect of atenolol.

PROLONGED USE

No special problems expected.

ATROPINE

Brand names Minims Atropine
Used in the following combined preparations Isopto-Atropine, Lomotil

GENERAL INFORMATION

Atropine is an *anticholinergic* drug. Because of its *antispasmodic* action which produces relaxation of the muscle wall of the intestine, it has been used to relieve abdominal cramps in irritable bowel syndrome. Atropine is also prescribed in combination with diphenoxylate, an antidiarrhoeal drug. Its unpleasant effects in overdose help to deter excessive dosage with diphenoxylate which is potentially a *dependence*-inducing drug.

Atropine eye drops are used to enlarge the pupil during eye examinations and in the treatment of uveitis. Atropine is commonly administered as part of the *premedication* before a general anaesthetic. It is occasionally injected to restore normal heartbeat in heart block (p.100).

(p.110)

QUICK REFERENCE

Drug group Anticholinergic drug for irritable bowel syndrome (p.110) and mydriatic drug (p.170)
Overdose danger rating High
Dependence rating Low
Prescription needed Yes
Available as generic Yes

INFORMATION FOR USERS

Your drug prescription is tailored for you. Do not alter dosage without checking with your doctor.

How taken

Tablets, injection, eye drops, ointment.

Frequency and timing of doses
Eye drops: 2 – 4 x daily. Other forms: as directed.

Adult dosage range
Eye drops: 1 – 2 drops as directed. Other forms: as directed.

Onset of effect
Varies according to method of administration.

Duration of action
Several hours.

Diet advice
None.

Storage
Keep in a closed container in a cool, dry place away from reach of children.

Missed dose
Take as soon as you remember. If your next dose is due within 2 hours, take a single dose now and skip the next.

Stopping the drug
Do not stop the drug without consulting your doctor.

OVERDOSE ACTION

Seek immediate medical advice in all cases. Take emergency action if palpitations, tremor, delirium, fits or loss of consciousness occur.

See Drug poisoning emergency guide (p.470).

POSSIBLE ADVERSE EFFECTS

The use of this drug is limited by the frequency of anticholinergic side effects.

In addition to these effects, atropine eye drops may cause stinging.

Symptom/effect	Frequency		Discuss with doctor		Stop taking drug now	Call doctor now
	Common	Rare	Only if severe	In all cases		
Blurred vision	●		■			
Flushing/dry skin	●			■		
Constipation	●		■			
Difficulty passing urine		●		■		
Eye pain and irritation		●		■	▲	▮
Palpitation/confusion		●		■	▲	▮

INTERACTIONS

Anticholinergic drugs Atropine increases the risk of side effects from drugs that also have anticholinergic effects.

Ketoconazole Atropine reduces the absorption of this drug from the digestive tract. Increased dose may be necessary.

SPECIAL PRECAUTIONS

Be sure to tell your doctor if:
▼ You have long-term liver or kidney problems.
▼ You have glaucoma.
▼ You have urinary difficulties.
▼ You have myasthenia gravis.
▼ You have ulcerative colitis.
▼ You wear contact lenses (eye drops).
▼ You have heart problems or high blood pressure.
▼ You are taking other medications.

Pregnancy
▼ Safety in pregnancy not established. Discuss with your doctor.

Breast feeding
▼ The drug passes into the breast milk and may affect the baby. Discuss with your doctor.

Infants and children
▼ Not usually prescribed for children under 2 years. Reduced dose necessary in older children.

Over 60
▼ Increased likelihood of adverse effects.

Driving and hazardous work
▼ Avoid such activities until you have learned how the drug affects you because the drug can cause blurred vision and may impair concentration.

Alcohol
▼ No special problems.

PROLONGED USE

No problems expected.

AURANOFIN

Brand name Ridaura
Used in the following combined preparations None

GENERAL INFORMATION

Introduced in 1987, auranofin is the only gold-based drug for rheumatoid arthritis that can be taken by mouth. The other gold drugs have to be injected, usually in hospital. Most of the drugs for rheumatoid arthritis ease the pain and soothe the inflammation (aspirin and non steroidal anti-inflammatory drugs). They do not change the course of the disease.

Auranofin and the other gold drugs, however, are able to arrest or slow the progression of the disease. The gold drugs are toxic, however, and so long as an arthritic condition remains stable,

most doctors prefer to keep a person on other treatment. But when early signs of deformity appear, signalling an increase in the pace of the disease, treatment by auranofin is appropriate. Since it can take 3 – 6 months to work, the use of analgesics and anti-inflammatory drugs is continued for that period.

Diarrhoea commonly occurs and may be severe enough for treatment to be stopped. More serious effects – blood disorders, rashes, and impaired kidney function – occur only rarely.

INFORMATION FOR USERS

Your drug prescription is tailored for you. Do not alter dosage without checking with your doctor.

How taken

Tablets.

Frequency and timing of doses
1 – 2 x daily, with food.

Dosage range
6mg daily. This may be increased up to a maximum of 9mg daily in some people.

Onset of effect
Adverse effects may be felt within 2 weeks. Beneficial effects may not be felt for 3 – 6 months.

Duration of action
Effects may last for several months after stopping the drug.

Diet advice
None.

Storage
Keep in a closed container in a cool, dry place away from reach of children.

Missed dose
Take as soon as you remember. If your next dose is due within 2 hours, take a single dose now and skip the next.

Stopping the drug
Do not stop the drug without consulting your doctor; stopping suddenly could lead to a flare-up of rheumatoid arthritis.

Exceeding the dose
An occasional unintentional extra dose is unlikely to cause problems. Large overdoses may cause vomiting. Notify your doctor.

SPECIAL PRECAUTIONS

Be sure to tell your doctor if:
▼ You have long-term liver or kidney problems.
▼ You have previously had an allergic reaction to gold treatment.
▼ You have inflammatory bowel disease.
▼ You have severe eczema.
▼ You have had a blood disorder.
▼ You are taking other medications.

Pregnancy
▼ Safety in pregnancy not established; may adversely affect the baby. Discuss with your doctor.

Breast feeding
▼ The drug may pass into the breast milk and may affect the baby. Discuss with your doctor.

Infants and children
▼ Not recommended.

Over 60
▼ No special problems.

Driving and hazardous work
▼ No known problems.

Alcohol
▼ No known problems.

POSSIBLE ADVERSE EFFECTS

The most common adverse effects of this drug include rashes that may sometimes be serious, nausea, and diarrhoea. Cloudy urine may be a sign of kidney problems.

Symptom/effect	Frequency		Discuss with doctor		Stop taking drug now	Call doctor now
	Common	Rare	Only if severe	In all cases		
Diarrhoea/nausea	●		■			
Indigestion/abdominal pain	●			■		
Conjunctivitis	●			■		
Mouth ulcers/soreness	●			■		
Cloudy urine		●		■		
Rash/itching	●			■	▲	■
Metallic taste	●		■			
Breathlessness		●		■		■

INTERACTIONS

None.

PROLONGED USE

Prolonged use may rarely lead to kidney damage and blood disorders.

Monitoring Periodic blood counts, urine examination, and tests of kidney function are necessary.

AZATHIOPRINE

Brand names Azamune, Berkaprine, Immunoprin, Imuran
Used in the following combined preparations None

GENERAL INFORMATION

Azathioprine is an immunosuppressant drug used to prevent immune system rejection of transplanted organs. The drug is also given for severe rheumatoid arthritis that has failed to respond to conventional drug therapy.

Autoimmune and collagen diseases, (including systemic lupus erythematosus, polymyositis, dermatomyositis, myasthenia gravis, and chronic inflammatory bowel disease) may also be treated with azathioprine.

Often prescribed when corticosteroids have proved insufficient, azathioprine boosts the effects of these drugs, thus allowing a reduction in the dose of corticosteroids in some cases.

Azathioprine is only given under close supervision because of the risk of serious adverse effects. These include suppression of the production of white blood cells, thereby increasing the risk of infection, and the risk of excessive or prolonged bleeding.

INFORMATION FOR USERS

Your drug prescription is tailored for you. Do not alter dosage without checking with your doctor.

How taken

Tablets, injection.

Frequency and timing of doses
Usually once daily with food.

Dosage range
Initially according to body weight and the condition being treated and then adjusted according to response.

Onset of effect
2 – 4 weeks. Antirheumatic effect may not be felt for 8 weeks or more.

Duration of action
Immunosuppressant effects may last for several weeks after the drug is stopped.

Diet advice
None.

Storage
Keep in a closed container in a cool, dry place away from reach of children. Protect from light.

Missed dose
Take as soon as you remember, then return to your normal schedule. If more than 2 doses are missed, consult your doctor.

Stopping the drug
Do not stop the drug without consulting your doctor. If taken to prevent graft transplant rejection, stopping treatment could provoke rejection of the transplant.

Exceeding the dose
An occasional unintentional extra dose is unlikely to cause problems. Large overdoses may cause nausea, vomiting, abdominal pains, and diarrhoea. Notify your doctor.

SPECIAL PRECAUTIONS

Be sure to tell your doctor if:
▼ You have long-term liver or kidney problems.
▼ You have recently had shingles or chickenpox.
▼ You have an infection.
▼ You have pancreatitis.
▼ You have a blood disorder.
▼ You are taking other medications.

 Pregnancy
▼ Not usually prescribed. But azathioprine has been taken in pregnancy without problems. Discuss with your doctor.

 Breast feeding
▼ It is not known whether the drug passes into the breast milk. Discuss with your doctor.

 Infants and children
▼ No special problems.

 Over 60
▼ Increased likelihood of adverse effects. Lower doses may be used.

 Driving and hazardous work
▼ No known problems.

 Alcohol
▼ No known problems.

POSSIBLE ADVERSE EFFECTS

Digestive disturbances and adverse effects on the blood which could lead to sore throat, fever, and weakness are common with azathioprine. Unusual bleeding or bruising while taking this drug may be a sign of reduced levels of platelets in the blood.

Symptom/effect	Frequency		Discuss with doctor		Stop taking drug now	Call doctor now
	Common	Rare	Only if severe	In all cases		
Nausea/vomiting	●		■			
Loss of appetite	●			■		
Weakness/fatigue		●		■		
Unusual bleeding/bruising		●		■		▮
Jaundice		●		■		▮
Rash		●		■		▮
Fever/chills		●		■		▮

INTERACTIONS

Allopurinol Dosage of azathioprine will need to be reduced if you are taking allopurinol.

Co-trimoxazole and trimethoprim may increase the risk of blood problems if taken with azathioprine.

PROLONGED USE

There may be a slightly increased risk of some cancers with long-term use of azathioprine. Blood changes may also occur, but may be corrected by adjusting the dose. During long-term treatment avoidance of exposure to sunlight may help to prevent adverse skin effects.

Monitoring Regular checks on blood composition are usually carried out.

BACLOFEN

Brand name Baclospas, Lioresal
Used in the following combined preparations None

GENERAL INFORMATION

Baclofen is a muscle relaxant drug that acts on the central nervous system, including the spinal cord. It relieves the spasms, cramping, and rigidity of muscles caused by a variety of disorders, such as multiple sclerosis and spinal cord injury. It is also used to treat spasticity due to brain injury, cerebral palsy, or stroke.

Although this drug does not cure these disorders, it increases mobility, and allows other treatment, such as physiotherapy, to be carried out.

Baclofen is less likely to cause muscle weakness than similar drugs, and its side effects, such as dizziness and drowsiness, are usually temporary. Elderly people are more susceptible to side effects, especially during early stages of treatment.

QUICK REFERENCE

Drug group Muscle relaxant (p.120)
Overdose danger rating Medium
Dependence rating Low
Prescription needed Yes
Available as generic Yes

INFORMATION FOR USERS

Your drug prescription is tailored for you. Do not alter dosage without checking with your doctor.

How taken

Tablets, liquid.

Frequency and timing of doses
3 x daily with food or milk.

Adult dosage range
15mg daily (starting dose). Daily dose increased by 15mg every three days as necessary. Maximum daily dose: 100mg.

Onset of effect
Some benefits may appear after 1 – 3 hours, but full beneficial effects may not be felt for several weeks.

Duration of action
Up to 8 hours.

Diet advice
None.

Storage
Keep in a closed container in a cool, dry place away from reach of children.

Missed dose
Take as soon as you remember. If your next dose is due within 2 hours, take a single dose now and skip the next.

Stopping the drug
Do not stop taking the drug without consulting your doctor, who will supervise a gradual reduction in dosage. Abrupt cessation may cause hallucinations, fits, and worsening spasticity.

Exceeding the dose
An occasional unintentional extra dose is unlikely to cause problems. Large overdoses may cause weakness, vomiting and severe drowsiness. Notify your doctor.

SPECIAL PRECAUTIONS

Be sure to tell your doctor if:
▼ You have a long-term kidney problem.
▼ You have had a peptic ulcer.
▼ You have had epileptic fits.
▼ You suffer with breathing problems.
▼ You are taking other medications.

Pregnancy
▼ Safety in pregnancy not established. Discuss with your doctor.

Breast feeding
▼ The drug passes into the breast milk, but at normal doses adverse effects on the baby are unlikely. Discuss with your doctor.

Infants and children
▼ Reduced dose necessary.

Over 60
▼ Increased likelihood of adverse effects. Reduced dose may therefore be necessary.

Driving and hazardous work
▼ Avoid such activities until you have learned how the drug affects you because the drug can cause dizziness and drowsiness.

Alcohol
▼ Avoid. Alcohol may increase the sedative effects of this drug.

Surgery and general anaesthetics
▼ Be sure to inform your doctor or dentist that you are taking baclofen before you have a general anaesthetic.

POSSIBLE ADVERSE EFFECTS

The common adverse effects are related to the sedative effects of the drug. Such effects are minimized by starting with a low dose that is gradually increased.

Symptom/effect	Frequency		Discuss with doctor		Stop taking drug now	Call doctor now
	Common	Rare	Only if severe	In all cases		
Dizziness	●		■			
Drowsiness	●		■			
Nausea	●		■			
Constipation/diarrhoea		●	■			
Headache		●	■			
Confusion		●		■		
Muscle fatigue/weakness		●		■		

INTERACTIONS

Antihypertensives Baclofen may increase the blood-pressure lowering effect of such drugs.

Anti-Parkinson drugs Some drugs taken to treat Parkinson's disease may cause confusion and hallucinations if taken with baclofen.

Sedatives All drugs that have a sedative effect on the central nervous system are likely to increase the sedative properties of baclofen.

Tricyclic antidepressants may increase the effects of baclofen leading to muscle weakness.

PROLONGED USE

No problems expected.

BECLOMETHASONE

Brand names AeroBec, Beclazone, Becloforte, Becodisks, Beconase, Becotide, Filair, Propaderm
Used in the following combined preparations Ventide

GENERAL INFORMATION

Beclomethasone is a corticosteroid drug prescribed to relieve the symptoms of allergic rhinitis (as a nasal spray), and to control asthma (as an inhalant). It controls nasal symptoms by reducing inflammation and mucus production in the nose. It also helps to reduce chest symptoms, such as wheezing and coughing. People who suffer from asthma may take beclomethasone to reduce the severity and frequency of attacks. However, once an attack has started, this drug does not relieve symptoms.

Beclomethasone is given primarily to people whose asthma does not respond to bronchodilators alone (p.92). Beclomethasone is also used as the main ingredient in some skin creams and ointments (see Topical corticosteroids, p.174).

There are few serious adverse effects associated with beclomethasone because it is given *topically* by nasal spray or inhaler or ointment. Fungal infection causing irritation of the mouth and throat is a possible side effect of inhaling beclomethasone. This can, to a certain degree, be avoided by thoroughly rinsing the mouth and gargling with water after each inhalation.

INFORMATION FOR USERS

Your drug prescription is tailored for you. Do not alter dosage without checking with your doctor.

How taken

Ointment, inhaler, nasal spray.

Frequency and timing of doses
2 – 4 x daily.

Dosage range
Adults 1 – 2 puffs 3 – 4 x daily (asthma); 1 – 2 sprays in each nostril 2 – 4 x daily (allergic rhinitis); as directed (skin conditions). *Children* Reduced dose according to age and weight.

Onset of effect
Within 1 week (asthma); 1 – 3 days (allergic rhinitis). Full benefit may not be felt for up to 4 weeks.

Duration of action
Several days after stopping the drug.

Diet advice
None.

Storage
Keep in a closed container in a cool, dry place away from reach of children. Protect from light.

Missed dose
Take as soon as you remember. If your next dose is due within 2 hours, take a single dose now and skip the next.

Stopping the drug
Do not stop the drug without consulting your doctor; symptoms may recur. Sometimes a gradual reduction in dosage is recommended.

Exceeding the dose
An occasional unintentional extra dose is unlikely to be a cause for concern. But if you notice unusual symptoms, or if a large overdose has been taken, notify your doctor. Adverse effects may occur if the recommended dose is regularly exceeded over a prolonged period.

SPECIAL PRECAUTIONS

Be sure to tell your doctor if:
▼ You have had tuberculosis or another respiratory infection.
▼ You are taking other medications.

 Pregnancy
▼ No evidence of risk.

 Breast feeding
▼ No evidence of risk.

 Infants and children
▼ Reduced dose necessary.

Over 60
▼ No known problems.

 Driving and hazardous work
▼ No known problems.

 Alcohol
▼ No known problems.

POSSIBLE ADVERSE EFFECTS

Adverse effects are unlikely as the dose used is low. The main side effects are irritation of the nasal passages and fungal infection of the throat and mouth.

Symptom/effect	Frequency		Discuss with doctor		Stop taking drug now	Call doctor now
	Common	Rare	Only if severe	In all cases		
Nasal discomfort/irritation	●		■			
Cough	●		■			
Sore throat/hoarseness	●				■	
Nosebleed		●			■	

PROLONGED USE

No problems expected.

Monitoring Periodic checks to make sure that the adrenal gland is functioning healthily may be required if large doses are being used.

INTERACTIONS

None.

BENDROFLUAZIDE

Brand names Aprinox, Berkozide, Neo-NaClex
Used in the following combined preparations Centyl-K, Corgaretic, Inderetic, Inderex, Neo-NaClex-K, Prestim

GENERAL INFORMATION

Bendrofluazide belongs to the thiazide group of diuretic drugs that expel water from the body. This makes it useful for reducing oedema caused by heart conditions, and for treating premenstrual oedema. Bendrofluazide is frequently used as a treatment for high blood pressure (see Antihypertensive drugs, p.102).

As with all thiazides, bendrofluazide increases the loss of potassium in the urine which can cause a variety of symptoms (see p.99), and increases the likelihood of irregular heart rhythms, particularly if you are taking drugs such as digoxin for heart failure. To counteract this effect, potassium supplements are often prescribed along with bendrofluazide.

QUICK REFERENCE

Drug group Thiazide diuretic (p.99)

Overdose danger rating Low

Dependence rating Low

Prescription needed Yes

Available as generic Yes

INFORMATION FOR USERS

Your prescription is tailored for you. Do not alter dosage without checking with your doctor.

How taken

Tablets.

Frequency and timing of doses
Once daily, early in the day. (Sometimes 1 – 3 x per week.)

Adult dosage range
2.5 – 10mg daily.

Onset of effect
Within 2 hours.

Duration of action
6 – 12 hours.

Diet advice
Use of this drug may reduce potassium in the body. Eat plenty of fresh fruit and vegetables. Discuss the advisability of reducing salt intake with your doctor.

Storage
Keep in a closed container in a cool, dry place away from reach of children.

Missed dose
No cause for concern, but take as soon as you remember. However, if it is late in the day do not take the missed dose, or you may need to get up during the night to pass urine. Take the next scheduled dose as usual.

Stopping the drug
Do not stop taking the drug without consulting your doctor; symptoms may recur.

Exceeding the dose
An occasional unintentional extra dose is unlikely to be a cause for concern. But if you notice unusual symptoms, or if a large overdose has been taken, notify your doctor.

SPECIAL PRECAUTIONS

Be sure to tell your doctor if:
▼ You have long-term liver or kidney problems.
▼ You have had gout.
▼ You have diabetes.
▼ You suffer from Addison's disease.
▼ You are taking other medications.

Pregnancy
▼ Not usually prescribed. Safety in pregnancy not established. May adversely affect the baby. Discuss with your doctor.

Breast feeding
▼ The drug passes into the breast milk and may reduce your milk supply. Discuss with your doctor.

Infants and children
▼ Not usually prescribed. Reduced dose necessary.

Over 60s
▼ Reduced dose may be necessary.

Driving and hazardous work
▼ No special problems.

Alcohol
▼ No problems expected if consumption is kept low.

POSSIBLE ADVERSE EFFECTS

Some adverse effects are caused by excessive loss of potassium. This can usually be put right by taking a potassium supplement.

In rare cases gout may occur in susceptible people, and certain forms of diabetes may become more difficult to control.

Symptom/effect	Frequency		Discuss with doctor		Stop taking drug now	Call doctor now
	Common	Rare	Only if severe	In all cases		
Leg cramps		●	■			
Impotence		●		■		
Lethargy/fatigue		●	■			
Nausea		●	■			
Rash		●		■		

INTERACTIONS

Non-steroidal anti-inflammatory drugs (NSAIDs) may reduce the diuretic effect of bendrofluazide.

Digoxin The effects of digoxin may be increased if excessive potassium is lost.

Lithium Bendrofluazide may increase lithium levels in the blood.

Corticosteroids These drugs further increase the loss of potassium from the body when taken with bendrofluazide. Potassium supplements are likely to be necessary.

PROLONGED USE

Prolonged use of this drug can lead to excessive loss of potassium and imbalances of other salts.

Monitoring Blood tests may be performed periodically to check kidney function and levels of potassium and other salts.

BENORYLATE

Brand name Benoral
Used in the following combined preparations None

GENERAL INFORMATION

Benorylate is a drug derived from aspirin and paracetamol with analgesic and anti-inflammatory properties. It is mainly used to relieve joint pain and stiffness in osteoarthitis and rheumatoid arthritis. The drug may also be helpful for reducing fever and discomfort in viral illnesses such as flu. Benorylate is occasionally prescribed to treat Still's disease (juvenile rheumatoid arthritis), although treatment is carefully monitored because aspirin is not usually recommended for children.

Benorylate is longer acting than aspirin or paracetamol alone; it needs only to be taken twice a day. It is also less likely to irritate the stomach than aspirin, but irritation may still occur.

INFORMATION FOR USERS

Your drug prescription is tailored for you. Do not alter dosage without checking with your doctor.

How taken

Tablets, liquid, granules.

Frequency and timing of doses
2 – 3 x daily after food.

Adult dosage range
4 – 8g daily.

Onset of effect
Within 30 minutes.

Duration of action
Up to 12 hours.

Diet advice
None.

Storage
Keep in a closed container in a cool, dry place away from reach of children.

Missed dose
If you are taking the drug as a long-term treatment, take as soon as you remember. If your next dose is due within 4 hours, take a single dose now and skip the next. If you are taking the drug for the short-term relief of symptoms, take only when needed.

Stopping the drug
If you have been prescribed the drug for a long-term condition, do not stop taking the drug without consulting your doctor. Otherwise it can be safely stopped as soon as you no longer need it.

OVERDOSE ACTION

 Seek immediate medical advice in all cases. Take emergency action if there is restlessness, vomiting, ringing in the ears or blurred vision.

See Drug poisoning emergency guide (p.470).

SPECIAL PRECAUTIONS

Be sure to tell your doctor if:
▼ You have long-term liver or kidney problems.
▼ You have asthma.
▼ You have nasal polyps.
▼ You have a blood clotting disorder.
▼ You have a stomach ulcer.
▼ You are taking other medications.

 Pregnancy
▼ Not usually prescribed. May cause problems with bleeding. Discuss with your doctor.

 Breast feeding
▼ The drug passes into the breast milk and may affect the baby. Discuss with your doctor.

 Infants and children
▼ Not recommended except for Still's disease. Reduced dose necessary.

 Over 60
▼ Reduced dose necessary.

 Driving and hazardous work
▼ Avoid such activities until you have learned how the drug affects you because the drug can cause dizziness and drowsiness.

 Alcohol
▼ Prolonged heavy intake increases the likelihood of stomach irritation and liver damage with this drug.

PROLONGED USE

There is an increased risk of stomach ulcers with long-term use of this drug.

POSSIBLE ADVERSE EFFECTS

Side effects of benorylate are not usually serious. They are usually due to the aspirin-like effects of the drug.

Symptom/effect	Frequency		Discuss with doctor		Stop taking drug now	Call doctor now
	Common	Rare	Only if severe	In all cases		
Nausea	●		■			
Constipation/diarrhoea	●		■			
Indigestion/heartburn	●		■			
Drowsiness/dizziness		●	■			
Rash		●		■	▲	
Wheezing		●		■	▲	■
Hearing problems		●		■	▲	

INTERACTIONS

Anticoagulants Benorylate may increase the effect of these drugs.

Corticosteroids may reduce the effects of benorylate.

Probenecid and sulphinpyrazone Benorylate may reduce the beneficial effect of these drugs on gout.

Frusemide Benorylate may reduce the effects of frusemide.

BENZOYL PEROXIDE

Brand names Acetoxyl, Acnecide, Acnegel, Benoxyl, Benzagel, Nericur, Panoxyl
Used in the following combined preparations Acnidazil, Quinoderm, Quinoped

GENERAL INFORMATION

Benzoyl peroxide is used in *topical* preparations for the treatment of acne. Available over-the-counter, it comes in concentrations of varying strengths for moderate acne.

Benzoyl peroxide works by removing the top layer of skin and unblocking the sebaceous glands. It also reduces inflammation of blocked hair follicles by killing bacteria that infect them.

It may cause irritation due to its drying effect on the skin, but this generally diminishes with time. The drug should be applied to the affected areas as directed on the label. Washing the area prior to appplication greatly enhances the beneficial effects of benzoyl peroxide. Side effects are less likely if treatment is started with a preparation containing a low concentration of benzoyl peroxide, and changed to a stronger preparation only if necessary. Marked dryness and peeling of the skin, which may occur, can usually be controlled by reducing the frequency of application. Be careful to avoid contact with the eyes, mouth, and mucous membranes. Preparations of benzoyl peroxide may bleach clothing.

QUICK REFERENCE

Drug group Drug for acne (p.177)
Overdose danger rating Low
Dependence rating Low
Prescription needed No
Available as generic No

INFORMATION FOR USERS

Follow instructions on the label. Call your doctor if symptoms worsen.

How taken

Cream, lotion, gel.

Frequency and timing of doses
1 – 2 x daily.

Dosage range
Apply to affected skin sparingly, as instructed on the label.

Onset of effect
Reduces oiliness of skin immediately. Acne usually improves within 4 – 6 weeks.

Duration of action
24 – 48 hours.

Diet advice
None.

Storage
Keep in a closed container in a cool, dry place away from reach of children.

Missed dose
Apply as soon as you remember.

Stopping the drug
Can be safely stopped as soon as you no longer need it.

Exceeding the dose
A single extra application is unlikely to cause problems. Regular over-use may cause extensive irritation, peeling, redness, and swelling.

POSSIBLE ADVERSE EFFECTS

Application of benzoyl peroxide may cause temporary burning or stinging of the skin. Redness, peeling, and swelling may result from excessive drying of the skin and clears up if the treatment is stopped or used less frequently. If severe burning, blistering, or crusting occur, stop using the product and consult your doctor.

Symptom/effect	Frequency		Discuss with doctor		Stop taking drug now	Call doctor now
	Common	Rare	Only if severe	In all cases		
Skin irritation	●		■			
Dryness/peeling	●		■			
Stinging/redness	●		■			
Blistering/crusting/swelling		●		■	▲	▮

INTERACTIONS

Skin-drying preparations Medicated cosmetics, soaps, toiletries, and other anti-acne preparations increase the likelihood of dryness and irritation of the skin with benzoyl peroxide.

SPECIAL PRECAUTIONS

Be sure to consult your doctor or pharmacist before using this drug if:
▼ You have eczema.
▼ You have sunburn.
▼ You are taking other medications.

 Pregnancy
▼ No evidence of risk.

 Breast feeding
▼ No evidence of risk.

 Infants and children
▼ Not recommended under 12 years.

 Over 60
▼ Not usually required.

 Driving and hazardous work
▼ No known problems.

 Alcohol
▼ No known problems.

PROLONGED USE

Benzoyl peroxide should not be used for longer than 6 weeks except on the advice of your doctor.

BETAHISTINE

Brand name Serc
Used in the following combined preparations None

GENERAL INFORMATION

Betahistine, which resembles the naturally-occurring substance histamine in some of its effects, was introduced in the 1970s as a treatment for Ménière's disease, a condition caused by the pressure of excess fluid in the inner ear.

Taken regularly, betahistine reduces the frequency and severity of the attacks of nausea and vertigo that characterize this condition. It is also effective in treating tinnitus (ringing in the ears). Betahistine is thought to work by reducing pressure in the inner ear, possibly by improving blood flow in the small blood vessels. Drug treatment, however, is not successful in all cases; surgery may be needed.

INFORMATION FOR USERS

Your drug prescription is tailored for you. Do not alter dosage without checking with your doctor.

How taken

Tablets.

Frequency and timing of doses
3 x daily after food.

Adult dosage range
24 – 48mg daily.

Onset of effect
Within 1 hour.

Duration of action
6 – 12 hours.

Diet advice
None.

Storage
Keep in a closed container in a cool, dry place away from reach of children.

Missed dose
Take as soon as you remember. If your next dose is due within 2 hours, take a single dose now and skip the next.

Stopping the drug
Do not stop the drug without consulting your doctor; symptoms may recur.

OVERDOSE ACTION

Seek immediate medical advice in all cases. Large overdoses may cause collapse requiring emergency action.

See Drug poisoning emergency guide, p.470.

POSSIBLE ADVERSE EFFECTS

Adverse effects from betahistine are minor and rarely cause problems.

Symptom/effect	Frequency		Discuss with doctor		Stop taking drug now	Call doctor now
	Common	Rare	Only if severe	In all cases		
Nausea	●		■			
Indigestion	●		■			
Headache		●	■			
Rash		●		■		

INTERACTIONS

None

SPECIAL PRECAUTIONS

Be sure to tell your doctor if:
▼ You suffer from asthma.
▼ You have a stomach ulcer.
▼ You have phaeochromocytoma.
▼ You are taking other medications.

Pregnancy
▼ Safety in pregnancy not established. Discuss with your doctor.

Breast feeding
▼ The drug passes into the breast milk, but at normal doses adverse effects on the baby are unlikely. Discuss with your doctor.

Infants and children
▼ Not recommended.

Over 60
▼ No special problems.

Driving and hazardous work
▼ No special problems.

Alcohol
▼ No special problems.

PROLONGED USE

No special problems.

BETAMETHASONE

Brand names Betnelan, Betnesol, Betnovate, Diprosone, Vista-Methasone
Used in the following combined preparations Betnesol N, Betnovate C, Betnovate N, Diprosalic, Fusibet, Lotriderm

GENERAL INFORMATION

Betamethasone is a corticosteroid used to treat a variety of conditions. *Topical* preparations are available for skin complaints, such as eczema and psoriasis. It can be injected directly into the joints to relieve the pain and stiffness of rheumatoid arthritis and other forms of joint inflammation. The drug is also given by mouth or injection to treat certain endocrine conditions

affecting the pituitary and adrenal glands, and some blood disorders.

Low or moderate doses of beta-methasone taken for short periods rarely cause serious side effects. Prolonged use or high dosages can lead to symptoms such as peptic ulcers, weak bones, muscle weak-ness, thin skin, and may retard growth in children.

INFORMATION FOR USERS

Your drug prescription is tailored for you. Do not alter dosage without checking with your doctor.

How taken

Tablets, injection, cream, ointment, lotion, eye ointment/drops, ear drops, nose drops.

Frequency and timing of doses
Varies according to disorder being treated.

Dosage range
Varies; follow your doctor's instructions.

Onset of effect
12 – 48 hours.

Duration of action
Up to 24 hours.

Diet advice
A low sodium and high potassium diet may

be recommended when the oral form of the drug is prescribed for extended periods. Follow the advice of your doctor.

Storage
Keep in a closed container in a cool, dry, place away from reach of children. Protect from light.

Missed dose
Take as soon as you remember. If your next dose is due within 2 hours, take a single dose now and skip the next.

Stopping the drug
Do not stop tablets without consulting your doctor, who may supervise a gradual reduction in dosage. Abrupt cessation after long-term treatment may cause problems with the pituitary and adrenal gland system.

Exceeding the dose
An occasional unintentional extra dose is unlikely to cause problems. If you notice unusual symptoms, or if a large overdose has been taken, notify your doctor.

SPECIAL PRECAUTIONS

Be sure to tell your doctor if:
▼ You suffer from a mental disorder.
▼ You have a heart condition.
▼ You have glaucoma.
▼ You have high blood pressure.
▼ You have a history of epilepsy.
▼ You have had a peptic ulcer.
▼ You have had tuberculosis.
▼ You have any infection.
▼ You have diabetes.
▼ You are taking other medications.

Pregnancy
▼ No evidence of risk with topical preparations. Taken as tablets in low doses, harm to the baby is unlikely. Discuss with your doctor.

Breast feeding
▼ No evidence of risk with topical preparations. Taken by mouth, the drug passes into the breast milk, but in normal doses adverse effects on the baby are unlikely. Discuss with your doctor.

Infants and children
▼ Reduced dose necessary.

Over 60
▼ Reduced dose may be necessary.

Driving and hazardous work
▼ No known problems.

Alcohol
▼ Keep consumption low. Betamethasone tablets increase the risk of adverse effects on the gastrointestinal tract, such as peptic ulcers. No special problems with other dosage forms.

POSSIBLE ADVERSE EFFECTS

Serious adverse effects only occur when high doses are taken by mouth for long periods. Topical preparations are unlikely to cause adverse effects unless overused.

Symptom/effect	Frequency		Discuss with doctor		Stop taking drug now	Call doctor now
	Common	Rare	Only if severe	In all cases		
Indigestion	●			■		
Weight gain		●		■		
Acne		●		■		
Muscle weakness		●		■		
Mood changes		●		■		
Bloody/black stools		●		■	▲	▮

INTERACTIONS

Insulin Betamethasone by mouth or injection may alter insulin requirements.

Oral anticoagulants Betamethasone may alter the effects of these drugs.

Vaccines Serious reactions can occur when certain vaccinations are given during

betamethasone treatment. Discuss with your doctor.

Antihypertensive drugs Betamethasone may reduce the effect of these drugs.

Phenytoin The effects of betamethasone may be reduced by phenytoin.

PROLONGED USE

Prolonged use of betamethasone by mouth can lead to peptic ulcers, thin skin, fragile bones, muscle weakness, and can retard growth in children.

BEZAFIBRATE

Brand name Bezalip, Bezalip Mono
Used in the following combined preparations None

GENERAL INFORMATION

Bezafibrate belongs to a group of drugs that lower lipid levels in the blood. Other drugs in the same chemical group (usually called fibrates) include clofibrate, ciprofibrate, fenofibrate, and gemfibrozil. These drugs are particularly effective in decreasing blood levels of triglycerides. They also reduce levels of cholesterol. Raised levels of lipids (fats) in the blood are associated with atherosclerosis (deposition of fat in blood vessel walls). This can lead to coronary heart disease (e.g. angina and heart attacks) and cerebro-vascular disease (e.g. stroke). When taken with a diet low in saturated fats, there is good evidence that the chances of a heart attack are reduced.

INFORMATION FOR USERS

Your drug prescription is tailored for you. Do not alter dosage without checking with your doctor.

How taken

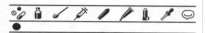

Tablets.

Frequency and timing of doses
1 – 3 x daily with a little liquid after a meal.

Adult dosage range
400 – 600mg daily.

Onset of effect
A beneficial effect on blood fat levels may not be produced for some weeks, and it takes months or years for fat deposits in the arteries to be reduced.

Duration of action
About 6 – 24 hours. This may vary according to the individual.

Diet advice
A low-fat diet may be recommended. Follow the advice of your doctor.

Storage
Keep in a closed container in a cool, dry place away from reach of children.

Missed dose
Take as soon as you remember. If your next dose is due within 4 hours (and you take once daily), take a single dose now and skip the next. If you take 2 – 3 times daily, take the next dose as normal.

Stopping the drug
Do not stop the drug without consulting your doctor.

Exceeding the dose
An occasional unintentional extra dose is unlikely to be a cause for concern. But if you notice unusual symptoms, notify your doctor.

SPECIAL PRECAUTIONS

Be sure to tell your doctor if:
▼ You have long-term liver or kidney problems.
▼ You have a history of gall bladder disease.
▼ You are taking other medications.

 Pregnancy
▼ Safety in pregnancy not established. Discuss with your doctor.

 Breast feeding
▼ The drug may pass into the breast milk and may affect the baby. Discuss with your doctor.

 Infants and children
▼ Not usually prescribed.

 Over 60
▼ No special problems expected.

 Driving and hazardous work
▼ No special problems.

 Alcohol
▼ No special problems.

POSSIBLE ADVERSE EFFECTS

The most common adverse effects are those on the gastrointestinal tract, such as loss of appetite and nausea. These effects normally reduce as treatment continues.

Symptom/effect	Frequency		Discuss with doctor		Stop taking drug now	Call doctor now
	Common	Rare	Only if severe	In all cases		
Nausea	●		■			
Loss of appetite	●		■			
Skin rash		●				
Headache		●		■		
Muscular pain/cramp		●		■		

INTERACTIONS

Anticoagulants Bezafibrate may increase the effect of anticoagulants such as warfarin.

Antidiabetic drugs Bezafibrate may interact with these drugs to lower blood sugar levels.

PROLONGED USE

No problems expected.

Monitoring Blood tests will be undertaken to monitor the effect of the drug on lipids in the blood.

BROMOCRIPTINE

Brand name Parlodel
Used in the following combined preparations None

GENERAL INFORMATION

By inhibiting the secretion of the hormone prolactin from the pituitary gland, bromocriptine is helpful in treating conditions associated with excessive prolactin production. Such conditions include some types of female infertility and occasionally male infertility and impotence. It is effective in treating some benign breast conditions and other symptoms of menstrual disorders. Bromocriptine may be used to suppress lactation in women who do not wish to breast feed.

Bromocriptine also reduces the release of growth hormone. This makes it a useful drug in the treatment of acromegaly (see p.145).

Bromocriptine is also effective for relieving the symptoms of *parkinsonism*. The drug is now widely used to treat those in the advanced stages of parkinsonism when other drugs have failed or are unsuitable.

Serious adverse effects are uncommon when the drug is given in low doses. Nausea and vomiting, the most common problems, can be minimized by taking bromocriptine with meals. Bromocriptine may in rare cases cause ulceration of the stomach.

QUICK REFERENCE

Drug group Drug for parkinsonism (p.87) and pituitary agent (p.145)
Overdose danger rating Low
Dependence rating Low
Prescription needed Yes
Available as generic Yes

INFORMATION FOR USERS

Your drug prescription is tailored for you. Do not alter dosage without checking with your doctor.

How taken

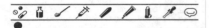

Tablets, capsules.

Frequency and timing of doses
1 – 3 x daily with food or milk.

Adult dosage range
The dose given depends on the condition being treated and your response. In most cases treatment starts with a daily dose of 1 – 1.25mg. This is gradually increased until a satisfactory response is achieved.

Onset of effect
Variable depending on the condition.

Duration of action
About 8 hours.

Diet advice
None.

Storage
Keep in a closed container in a cool, dry place away from reach of children. Protect from light.

Missed dose
Take as soon as you remember. If your next dose is due within 2 hours, take a single dose now and skip the next.

Stopping the drug
Do not stop the drug without consulting your doctor; symptoms may recur.

Exceeding the dose
An occasional unintentional extra dose is unlikely to cause problems. If you notice unusual symptoms, or if a large overdose has been taken, notify your doctor.

POSSIBLE ADVERSE EFFECTS

Adverse effects are usually related to the dose being taken. When used for Parkinson's disease, bromocriptine may cause abnormal movements.

Symptom/effect	Frequency		Discuss with doctor		Stop taking drug now	Call doctor now
	Common	Rare	Only if severe	In all cases		
Confusion/dizziness	●				■	
Nausea/vomiting	●			■		
Constipation		●		■		
Headache		●			■	
Abnormal movements		●			■	
Drowsiness		●		■	▲	■

INTERACTIONS

Antipsychotic drugs These drugs oppose the action of bromocriptine and increase the risk of *parkinsonism*.

Domperidone and metoclopramide These drugs may reduce some of the effects of bromocriptine.

SPECIAL PRECAUTIONS

Be sure to tell your doctor if:
▼ You have poor circulation.
▼ You have a stomach ulcer.
▼ You have a history of psychiatric disorders.
▼ You are taking other medications.

Pregnancy
▼ Safety in pregnancy not established. Discuss with your doctor.

Breast feeding
▼ The drug suppresses milk production, and prevents it completely if given within 12 hours of delivery. If you wish to breast feed, consult your doctor.

Infants and children
▼ Not usually prescribed for children under 15 years.

Over 60
▼ Reduced dose may be necessary.

Driving and hazardous work
▼ Avoid such activities until you have learned how the drug affects you because of the possibility of dizziness and drowsiness.

Alcohol
▼ Avoid. Alcohol increases the likelihood of confusion while taking this drug.

PROLONGED USE

No special problems.

Monitoring Periodic blood tests may be performed to check hormone levels. Gynaecological tests may be carried out annually (or every six months in post-menopausal women).

BUMETANIDE

Brand name Burinex
Used in the following combined preparations Burinex-K, Burinex-A

GENERAL INFORMATION

Bumetanide is a powerful, short-acting loop diuretic. Like other diuretics, it is used to treat oedema (fluid retention) resulting from heart failure, nephrotic syndrome, and cirrhosis of the liver. Bumetanide is particularly useful in the treatment of people with impaired kidney function who do not respond well to thiazide diuretics. Because it is fast-acting, it is often injected in emergencies to relieve pulmonary oedema.

Bumetanide increases the loss of potassium in the urine, which can result in a wide variety of symptoms (see p.99). For this reason, potassium supplements or a diuretic that conserves potassium are often given with the drug.

INFORMATION FOR USERS

Your drug prescription is tailored for you. Do not alter dosage without checking with your doctor.

How taken

Tablets, liquid, injection.

Frequency and timing of doses
Usually once daily in the morning. In some cases, twice daily.

Dosage range
0.5 – 5mg daily. Dose may be increased if kidney function is impaired.

Onset of effect
Within 30 minutes by mouth; more quickly by injection.

Duration of action
2 – 4 hours.

Diet advice
Use of this drug may reduce potassium in the body. Eat plenty of fresh fruit and vegetables.

Storage
Keep in a closed container in a cool, dry place away from reach of children. Protect from light.

Missed dose
No cause for concern, but take as soon as you remember. However, if it is late in the day do not take the missed dose, or you may need to get up during the night to pass urine. Take the next scheduled dose as usual.

Stopping the drug
Do not stop the drug without consulting your doctor; symptoms may recur.

Exceeding the dose
An occasional unintentional extra dose is unlikely to be a cause for concern. But if you notice unusual symptoms, or if a large overdose has been taken, notify your doctor.

SPECIAL PRECAUTIONS

Be sure to tell your doctor if:
▼ You have long-term kidney or liver problems.
▼ You have diabetes.
▼ You have prostate trouble.
▼ You have gout.
▼ You are taking other medications.

 Pregnancy
▼ Not usually prescribed. May cause a reduction in blood supply to the developing baby. Discuss with your doctor.

 Breast feeding
▼ This drug may reduce your milk supply. Discuss with your doctor.

 Infants and children
▼ Not usually prescribed. Reduced dose necessary.

 Over 60
▼ Dosage is often reduced.

 Driving and hazardous work
▼ Avoid such activities until you have learned how the drug affects you because of the possibility of dizziness and faintness.

  Alcohol
▼ Keep consumption low. Bumetanide increases the likelihood of dehydration and hangovers after drinking alcohol.

POSSIBLE ADVERSE EFFECTS

Adverse effects are caused mainly by the rapid fluid loss produced by bumetanide. These diminish as the body adjusts to taking the drug.

Symptom/effect	Frequency		Discuss with doctor		Stop taking drug now	Call doctor now
	Common	Rare	Only if severe	In all cases		
Dizziness/faintness	●		■			
Lethargy/fatigue		●	■			
Cramps		●	■			
Rash		●		■		
Nausea/vomiting		●		■		
Pain in joints		●		■		

PROLONGED USE

Serious problems are unlikely, but levels of certain salts in the body may occasionally become disrupted during prolonged use.

Monitoring Periodic tests may be performed to check on kidney function and levels of body salts.

INTERACTIONS

Non-steroidal anti-inflammatory drugs (NSAIDs) These may reduce the diuretic effect of bumetanide.

Aminoglycoside antibiotics These may increase the risk of hearing problems when taken with high doses of bumetanide.

Lithium Bumetanide may increase the blood levels of lithium, leading to an increased risk of lithium poisoning.

Digoxin The adverse effects of digoxin may be increased if excessive potassium is lost.

CALCIPOTRIOL

Brand name Dovonex
Used in the following combined preparations None

GENERAL INFORMATION

Calcipotriol is a new drug used in the treatment of mild to moderate psoriasis. It is effective in plaque psoriasis affecting up to 40% of the patient's skin area.

Calcipotriol is a derivative of vitamin D and is thought to work by reducing the production of certain skin cells that cause the symptoms of skin thickening and scaling, which are the most common symptoms of psoriasis. Because it is related to vitamin D, excessive

widespread use can lead to a rise in calcium levels in the body; otherwise calcipotriol is unlikely to cause any serious adverse effects.

The drug is applied to the affected areas in the form of an ointment. It should not be used on the face, and it is important that the hands are washed after applying this ointment to avoid accidental transfer to unaffected areas. Local irritation may occur during the early stages of treatment.

INFORMATION FOR USERS

Your drug prescription is tailored for you. Do not alter dosage without checking with your doctor.

How taken

Ointment.

Frequency and timing of doses
2 x daily.

Adult dosage range
Applied twice daily; maximum 100g each week.

Onset of effect
Improvement is seen within a few days.

Duration of action
One application lasts up to 12 hours. Beneficial effects are longer lasting.

Diet advice
None.

Storage
Store at room temperature away from reach of children.

Missed dose
Apply the next dose at the scheduled time.

Stopping the drug
Do not stop taking the drug without consulting your doctor; symptoms may recur.

Exceeding the dose
Excessive prolonged use may lead to an increase in blood calcium levels, causing nausea, constipation, thirst, and frequent urination. Notify your doctor.

SPECIAL PRECAUTIONS

Be sure to tell your doctor if:
▼ You have a metabolic disorder.
▼ You have previously had a hypersensitivity reaction to the drug.
▼ You are taking other medications.

Pregnancy
▼ No evidence of risk, but discuss with your doctor.

Breast feeding
▼ No evidence of risk, but discuss with your doctor.

Infants and children
▼ Not recommended.

Over 60
▼ No problems expected.

Driving and hazardous work
▼ No problems expected.

Alcohol
▼ No problems expected.

POSSIBLE ADVERSE EFFECTS

Adverse effects are rarely a problem. A temporary local irritation may occur during the start of treatment.

Symptom/effect	Frequency		Discuss with doctor		Stop taking drug now	Call doctor now
	Common	Rare	Only if severe	In all cases		
Local irritation	●		■			
Rash on face/mouth		●		■		
Thirst/urination frequency		●		■		
Nausea/constipation		●		■		

INTERACTIONS

None known.

PROLONGED USE

The drug is not normally used for longer than 6 weeks.

CALCITONIN

Brand name Calcitare, Calsynar, Miacalcic
Used in the following combined preparations None

GENERAL INFORMATION

Calcitonin is a hormone produced by the thyroid gland that helps control loss of calcium from bones. It causes a decrease in the blood of calcium and phosphate. Two forms of the drug are available: calcitonin derived from pork thyroid (porcine) and synthetic salmon calcitonin (salcatonin). The dosages of these two forms differ. Both types are used to treat Paget's disease and conditions where there is an abnormally high level of calcium in the blood (hypercalcaemia). Paget's disease can cause bone pain and fractures and may lead to compression of the nerves in the spine and skull, sometimes causing deafness or impaired vision.

Calcitonin, given by injection, halts abnormal bone formation and, within a few months, can relieve pain and other symptoms. Although some symptoms of nerve compression may improve, deafness is not usually helped.

Because some people are allergic to calcitonin, a skin test may be performed before starting treatment.

INFORMATION FOR USERS

Your drug prescription is tailored for you. Do not alter dosage without checking with your doctor.

How taken

Injection.

Frequency and timing of doses
Paget's disease: 3 x weekly or once daily;
Hypercalcaemia: every 24 hours (porcine); 6–8 hourly (salcatonin).

Adult dosage range
Paget's disease: 80 – 160 IU (international units) per dose (porcine); 50 –100 IU per dose (salcatonin).
Hypercalcaemia According to weight and severity.

Onset of effect
Within a week. Full therapeutic effect may not be felt for several months.

Duration of action
Up to 72 hours.

Diet advice
None.

Storage
Follow instructions on container. Keep away from reach of children.

Missed dose
Take as soon as you remember. If your next dose is due within 24 hours (taken on alternate days) or within 6 hours (taken daily), take a single dose now and skip the next. Resume your normal dosage schedule thereafter.

Stopping the drug
Do not stop taking the drug without consulting your doctor; stopping the drug may lead to worsening of the underlying condition.

Exceeding the dose
An occasional unintentional extra dose is unlikely to cause problems. Large overdoses may cause nausea, vomiting, or flushing. Notify your doctor.

SPECIAL PRECAUTIONS

Be sure to tell your doctor if:
▼ You are prone to allergic reactions.
▼ You are taking other medications.

 Pregnancy
▼ Safety in pregnancy not established. Discuss with your doctor.

 Breast feeding
▼ This drug may reduce milk production. Discuss with your doctor.

 Infants and children
▼ Not usually prescribed.

 Over 60
▼ No special problems.

 Driving and hazardous work
▼ No special problems.

 Alcohol
▼ No special problems.

POSSIBLE ADVERSE EFFECTS

Adverse effects occur frequently with calcitonin. Nausea, vomiting, and diarrhoea usually diminish with continued use. Local reactions at the injection site are common.

Symptom/effect	Frequency		Discuss with doctor		Stop taking drug now	Call doctor now
	Common	Rare	Only if severe	In all cases		
Nausea/vomiting	●		■			
Flushing	●		■			
Local irritation at injection site	●		■			
Unpleasant taste		●	■			
Tingling of hands		●	■			

INTERACTIONS

None.

PROLONGED USE

The effectiveness of the porcine form of drug may be partially reduced in some people after about a year. Antibodies to the drug can develop.

Monitoring Periodic checks on blood calcium levels and imaging procedures may be required to assess the effectiveness of the drug.

CAPTOPRIL

Brand names Acepril, Capoten
Used in the following combined preparations Acezide, Capozide

GENERAL INFORMATION

Captopril belongs to the class of drugs called ACE inhibitors and it is used to treat high blood pressure and heart failure. It works by dilating the blood vessels and easing blood flow.

Captopril lowers blood pressure rapidly but may require several weeks to achieve maximum effect. People with heart failure may be given captopril in addition to diuretics. It can achieve dramatic improvement, relieving blood vessel muscle spasm and reducing the workload of the heart.

The first dose is usually very small and should be taken while lying down as there is a risk of a sudden fall in blood pressure. Diuretics are often prescribed with captopril.

A variety of minor side effects may occur. Some people experience upset in their sense of taste, others get a persistent dry cough. A reduction in dose may help minimise these effects.

QUICK REFERENCE

Drug group ACE inhibitor (p.98)
Overdose danger rating Medium
Dependence rating Low
Prescription needed Yes
Available as generic No

INFORMATION FOR USERS

Your drug prescription is tailored for you. Do not alter dosage without checking with your doctor.

How taken

Tablets.

Frequency and timing of doses
2 – 3 x daily.

Adult dosage range
12.5 – 25mg daily initially, gradually increased to 50 – 150mg daily.

Onset of effect
30 – 60 minutes.

Duration of action
6 – 8 hours.

Diet advice
None.

Storage
Keep in a closed container in a cool, dry place away from reach of children.

Missed dose
Take as soon as you remember. If your next dose is due within 2 hours, take a single dose now and skip the next.

Stopping the drug
Do not stop the drug without consulting your doctor; stopping the drug may lead to worsening of the underlying condition.

Exceeding the dose
An occasional unintentional extra dose is unlikely to cause problems. Large overdoses may cause dizziness or fainting. Notify your doctor.

POSSIBLE ADVERSE EFFECTS

Captopril causes a variety of minor adverse effects on the gastrointestinal system.

Rashes, which may occur, usually disappear soon after treatment is begun.

Symptom/effect	Frequency		Discuss with doctor		Stop taking drug now	Call doctor now
	Common	Rare	Only if severe	In all cases		
Dizziness/fainting		●			■	
Loss of taste	●		■			
Rash	●				■	
Mouth ulcers/sore mouth		●			■	
Persistent dry cough	●				■	
Sore throat/fever		●			■	

INTERACTIONS

Non steroidal anti-inflammatory drugs Some of these drugs may reduce the effectiveness of captopril.

Lithium Levels of lithium may be increased by captopril.

Vasodilators may reduce blood pressure even further.

Potassium-sparing diuretics Captopril may increase the risk of high blood levels of potassium with these drugs.

Cyclosporin The risk of high potassium levels in the blood is increased by cyclosporin.

SPECIAL PRECAUTIONS

Be sure to tell your doctor if:
▼ You have long-term kidney problems.
▼ You have coronary artery disease.
▼ You are taking other medications.

Pregnancy
▼ Not usually prescribed. May harm the developing baby. Discuss with your doctor.

Breast feeding
▼ The drug passes into the breast milk, but at normal doses adverse effects on the baby are unlikely. Discuss with your doctor.

Infants and children
▼ Not usually prescribed. Reduced dose necessary.

Over 60
▼ Reduced dose may be necessary.

Driving and hazardous work
▼ Avoid such activities until you have learned how the drug affects you because the drug can cause dizziness and fainting.

Alcohol
▼ Avoid. Alcohol may increase the adverse effects of this drug.

Surgery and general anaesthetics
▼ Captopril may need to be stopped before you have a general anaesthetic. Discuss this before any operation.

PROLONGED USE

No problems expected.

Monitoring Periodic checks on the white blood cell count and the urine are usually performed regularly during the first three months of treatment.

CARBAMAZEPINE

Brand name Tegretol
Used in the following combined preparations None

GENERAL INFORMATION

Chemically related to the tricyclic anti-depressants (see p.84), carbamazepine reduces the likelihood of fits caused by abnormal nerve signals in the brain. Doctors have used it in the long-term treatment of epilepsy since 1960, and it is considered particularly suitable for treating children because side effects are less of a problem compared to some other drugs for epilepsy. Carbamazepine is also prescribed to relieve the intermittent severe pain caused by damage to the cranial nerves – for example, in trigeminal neuralgia. Carbamazepine is also occasionally prescribed to treat certain psychological or behavioural disorders.

QUICK REFERENCE

Drug group Anticonvulsant (p.86) and antipsychotic drug (p.87)
Overdose danger rating Medium
Dependence rating Low
Prescription needed Yes
Available as generic Yes

INFORMATION FOR USERS

Your drug prescription is tailored for you. Do not alter dosage without checking with your doctor.

How taken

Tablets, chewable tablets, liquid.

Frequency and timing of doses
1 – 4 x daily.

Adult dosage range
Epilepsy 100 – 1200mg daily.
Pain relief 100 – 1600mg daily.
Psychiatric disorders 400–1600mg daily

Onset of effect
Within 4 hours.

Duration of action
12 – 24 hours.

Diet advice
None.

Storage
Keep in a closed container in a cool, dry place away from reach of children.

Missed dose
Take as soon as you remember. If your next dose is due within 2 hours, take a single dose now and skip the next.

Stopping the drug
Do not stop the drug without consulting your doctor; symptoms may recur.

Exceeding the dose
An occasional unintentional extra dose is unlikely to cause problems. Large overdoses may cause tremor, convulsions, and coma. Notify your doctor.

POSSIBLE ADVERSE EFFECTS

Most people experience very few adverse effects with this drug, but when blood levels get too high, adverse effects are common and the dose may need to be reduced.

Symptom/effect	Frequency		Discuss with doctor		Stop taking drug now	Call doctor now
	Common	Rare	Only if severe	In all cases		
Dizziness/unsteadiness	●		■			
Drowsiness	●		■			
Nausea/loss of appetite	●		■			
Blurred vision	●			■		
Ankle swelling		●		■		
Rash		●		■	▲	■

INTERACTIONS

Anticoagulants Carbamazepine may reduce the effect of anticoagulant drugs. The anticoagulant dose may need to be adjusted accordingly.

Oral contraceptives Carbamazepine may reduce the effectiveness of oral contraceptives. An alternative form of contraception may need to be used. Discuss with your doctor.

Cimetidine may increase the effects of carbamazepine.

Verapamil and co-proxamol These may increase effects from carbamazepine.

SPECIAL PRECAUTIONS

Be sure to tell your doctor if:
▼ You have long-term kidney or liver problems.
▼ You have heart problems.
▼ You are taking other medications.

Pregnancy
▼ Not usually prescribed. May cause abnormalities in the unborn baby. Discuss with your doctor.

Breast feeding
▼ The drug passes into the breast milk, but at normal doses adverse effects on the baby are unlikely. Discuss with your doctor.

Infants and children
▼ Reduced dose necessary.

Over 60
▼ May cause confused or agitated behaviour in the elderly. Reduced dose may be necessary.

Driving and hazardous work
▼ Discuss with your doctor. Your underlying condition, as well as the possibility of reduced alertness while taking this drug, may make such activities inadvisable.

Alcohol
▼ Avoid. Alcohol may increase the sedative effects of this drug.

PROLONGED USE

There is a slight risk of blood abnormalities occurring during prolonged use.

Monitoring Periodic blood tests may be performed to monitor levels of the drug in the body and the composition of the blood.

CARBENOXOLONE

Brand names Bioplex, Bioral
Used in the following combined preparation Pyrogastrone

GENERAL INFORMATION

Carbenoxolone was widely used to treat gastric and duodenal ulcers. Newer drugs have now largely super-seded carbenoxolone for this purpose. The only oral preparation now available in the UK is a combination of carben-oxolone with antacids used for oesophageal ulcers and inflammation. Carbenoxolone works by stimulating the production of mucus and protecting the mucosal barrier from gastric juices.
   Changes in sodium and potassium levels in the body can cause a number of adverse effects which are not a problem with more modern drugs used to treat gastric and duodenal ulcers. Carbenoxolone is also used to treat mouth ulcers. It is either applied to the ulcers in the form of a gel or used in the form of a mouthwash. When used in accord-ance with the instructions, side effects are very unlikely to occur.

INFORMATION FOR USERS

Your drug prescription is tailored for you. Do not alter dosage without checking with your doctor.

How taken

Mouthwash granules, gel.

Frequency and timing of doses
3 x daily after meals and at bedtime.

Adult dosage range
100mg daily (by mouth).

Onset of effect
Stomach ulcers may take several weeks to heal.

Duration of action
Up to 12 hours.

Diet advice
None.

Storage
Keep in a closed container in a cool, dry place away from reach of children.

Missed dose
Do not take the missed dose. Take the next scheduled dose as usual.

Stopping the drug
When used for mouth ulcers, you can stop when the ulcers have healed.

Exceeding the dose
An occasional unintentional extra dose is unlikely to cause problems.

POSSIBLE ADVERSE EFFECTS

Most of the adverse effects of this drug are caused by loss of potassium and an increase in levels of sodium salts in the body. This is unlikely to occur with the gel and mouthwash preparations.

Symptom/effect	Frequency		Discuss with doctor		Stop taking drug now	Call doctor now
	Common	Rare	Only if severe	In all cases		
Ankle swelling	●		■			
Muscle weakness		●		■		
Numbness and tingling		●		■		

INTERACTIONS

Antihypertensive drugs Carbenoxolone may reduce the beneficial effects of these drugs.

Digoxin Carbenoxolone may cause abnormal heart rhythms when taken with digoxin because of a reduction in potassium levels.

Thiazide diuretics may cause excessive potassium loss with carbenoxolone.

SPECIAL PRECAUTIONS

Be sure to tell your doctor if:
▼ You have long-term liver or kidney problems.
▼ You have heart disease.
▼ You have high blood pressure.
▼ You are taking other medications.

Pregnancy
▼ Safety in pregnancy not established. Discuss with your doctor.

Breast feeding
▼ The drug passes into the breast milk, but at normal doses adverse effects on the baby are unlikely. Discuss with your doctor.

Infants and children
▼ Not recommended.

Over 60
▼ Increased risk of adverse effects. Reduced dose may therefore be necessary.

Driving and hazardous work
▼ No special problems.

Alcohol
▼ Avoid. Alcohol may aggravate the underlying condition and counter the beneficial effects of this drug.

PROLONGED USE

Gastric/duodenal ulcers Courses of longer than 3 months are not normally prescribed because of a risk of fluid retention and high blood pressure.

Monitoring Weight and blood pressure are usually checked at intervals during treatment. Blood levels of *body salts* may also be checked.

Mouth ulcers Used until ulcers have healed.

CARBIMAZOLE

Brand name Neo-Mercazole
Used in the following combined preparations None

GENERAL INFORMATION

Carbimazole is an antithyroid drug used to suppress the formation of thyroid hormones in people with an overactive thyroid gland (thyrotoxicosis). In some people, particularly those with Graves' disease (the commonest form of thyrotoxicosis), drug treatment alone may relieve the disorder.

Carbimazole is also used in more serious cases, for example, to restore the normal function of the thyroid before its partial removal by surgery, or to intensify the absorption of radioactive iodine when that cell-destroying drug is used. Carbimazole also prevents the harmful release of thyroid hormone that can sometimes follow the use of radioactive iodine. Because the full benefits of this medication are not felt for several weeks, beta blockers may be given during this period to help control symptoms. Maintenance treatment may be continued for as long as 18 months unless surgery or radioactive iodine is used. Occasionally the dose of carbimazole is kept high with thyroxine prescribed as well to prevent a goitre developing.

INFORMATION FOR USER

Your drug prescription is tailored for you. Do not alter dosage without checking with your doctor.

How taken

Tablets.

Frequency and timing of doses
2 – 3 x daily.

Adult dosage range
Usually 30mg daily; in severe cases this may have to be increased to 60mg. Once control is achieved, dosage is reduced gradually to a maintenance dose of 5 – 15mg.

Onset of effect
Some improvement is usually felt within 1 – 3 weeks. Full beneficial effects usually take 4 – 8 weeks.

Duration of action
12 – 24 hours.

Diet advice
Your doctor may advise you to avoid foods that are high in iodine.

Storage
Keep in a closed container in a cool, dry place away from reach of children.

Missed dose
Take as soon as you remember. If your next dose is due, take both doses together.

Stopping the drug
Do not stop the drug without consulting your doctor; symptoms may recur.

Exceeding the dose
An occasional unintentional extra dose is unlikely to cause problems. Large overdoses may cause nausea, vomiting and headache. Notify your doctor.

SPECIAL PRECAUTIONS

Be sure to tell your doctor if:
▼ You have long-term liver or kidney problems.
▼ You are taking other medications.

Pregnancy
▼ Not usually prescribed. May cause defects in the baby. Discuss with your doctor.

Breast feeding
▼ The drug passes into the breast milk, but at normal doses adverse effects on the baby are unlikely. Discuss with your doctor.

Infants and children
▼ Reduced dose necessary.

Over 60
▼ No special problems.

Driving and hazardous work
▼ Avoid such activities until you have learned how the drug affects you because it may cause dizziness.

Alcohol
▼ No known problems.

POSSIBLE ADVERSE EFFECTS

Serious side effects are rare. A sore throat or mouth ulcers may indicate adverse effects on the blood and require prompt medical attention.

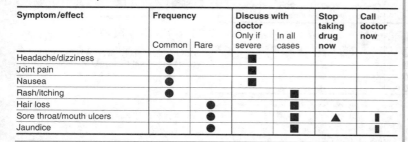

Symptom/effect	Frequency		Discuss with doctor		Stop taking drug now	Call doctor now
	Common	Rare	Only if severe	In all cases		
Headache/dizziness	●		■			
Joint pain	●		■			
Nausea	●		■			
Rash/itching	●			■		
Hair loss		●		■		
Sore throat/mouth ulcers		●		■	▲	▮
Jaundice		●		■		▮

PROLONGED USE

High doses over a prolonged period may reduce the production of blood cells by the bone marrow.

Monitoring Periodic tests of thyroid function are usually required. Blood cell counts may also be carried out.

INTERACTIONS

None.

CEFACLOR

Brand name Distaclor
Used in the following combined preparations None

GENERAL INFORMATION

Cefaclor is an antibiotic given by mouth to treat a variety of bacterial infections, mainly those affecting the respiratory tract, sinuses, skin, soft tissue, urinary tract and middle ear. It has a wider range of effectiveness than many antibiotics against some types of bacteria that are resistant to penicillin.

Sometimes cefaclor is prescribed as follow-up treatment for more severe infections after a different cepha-losporin has been given by injection.

When cefaclor is taken at the same time as a meal, the food may delay its absorption. However, the amount of drug absorbed is not affected.

Diarrhoea is the most common side effect of cefaclor. Some people may suffer from nausea or vomiting, itching, rash, and fever especially if they are sensitive to penicillin. In such cases another drug is substituted.

QUICK REFERENCE

Drug group Cephalosporin antibiotic (p.130)

Overdose danger rating Low

Dependence rating Low

Prescription needed Yes

Available as generic No

INFORMATION FOR USERS

Your drug prescription is tailored for you. Do not alter dosage without checking with your doctor.

How taken

Capsules, sustained-release tablets, liquid.

Frequency and timing of doses
3 x daily.

Dosage range
Adults 750mg – 4g daily.
Children Reduced dose according to age and weight.

Onset of effect
30 – 60 minutes.

Duration of action
Up to 8 hours.

Diet advice
None.

Storage
Keep capsules in a closed container in a cool, dry place away from children. Refrigerate liquid, but do not freeze, and keep for no longer than 14 days. Protect from light.

Missed dose
Take as soon as you remember. If your next dose is due at this time, take both doses now.

Stopping the drug
Take the full course. Even if you feel better the original infection may still be present and may recur if treatment is stopped too soon.

Exceeding the dose
An occasional unintentional extra dose is unlikely to be a cause for concern. But if you notice unusual symptoms, or if a large overdose has been taken, notify your doctor.

POSSIBLE ADVERSE EFFECTS

Most people do not suffer any adverse effects while taking cefaclor. Diarrhoea occurs fairly commonly but it tends not to be severe. Most other adverse effects are due to an allergic reaction that may necessitate stopping the drug.

Symptom/effect	Frequency		Discuss with doctor		Stop taking drug now	Call doctor now
	Common	Rare	Only if severe	In all cases		
Diarrhoea	●		■			
Nausea/vomiting		●	■			
Itching		●		■		
Fever		●		■		
Rash		●		■	▲	
Joint pain/swelling		●		■	▲	

INTERACTIONS

Probenecid This drug increases the level of cefaclor in the blood. The dosage of cefaclor may need to be adjusted accordingly.

Anticoagulants The effects of warfarin may be increased by cefaclor.

Oral contrraceptives Cefaclor may reduce the contraceptive effect of these drugs. Discuss with your doctor.

SPECIAL PRECAUTIONS

Be sure to tell your doctor if:
▼ You have a long-term kidney problem.
▼ You have had a previous allergic reaction to penicillin antibiotics.
▼ You have a history of bleeding disorders.
▼ You are taking other medications.

Pregnancy
▼ No evidence of risk to developing baby.

Breast feeding
▼ The drug passes into the breast milk and may affect the baby. Discuss with your doctor.

Infants and children
▼ Reduced dose necessary. Increased incidence of skin reactions.

Over 60
▼ No special problems.

Driving and hazardous work
▼ No special problems.

Alcohol
▼ No special problems.

PROLONGED USE

Cefaclor is usually given only for short courses of treatment.

CEPHALEXIN

Brand name Ceporex, Keflex
Used in the following combined preparations None

GENERAL INFORMATION

Cephalexin is a cephalosporin antibiotic prescribed for a variety of mild to moderate infections. Cephalexin does not have such a wide range of uses as some other antibiotics, but is helpful in treating bronchitis, cystitis, and certain skin and soft tissue infections. Sometimes it is prescribed as follow-up treatment for severe infections after a more powerful cephalosporin has been given by injection.

Cephalexin comes in a range of oral preparations, including paediatric drops for use in young children.

Diarrhoea is the most common side effect of cephalexin, although it tends to be less severe than with other cephalosporin antibiotics. In addition, some people may find that they are allergic to this drug, especially if they are sensitive to penicillin.

QUICK REFERENCE

Drug group Cephalosporin antibiotic (p.130)
Overdose danger rating Low
Dependence rating Low
Prescription needed Yes
Available as generic Yes

INFORMATION FOR USERS

Your drug prescription is tailored for you. Do not alter dosage without checking with your doctor.

How taken

Tablets, capsules, liquid.

Frequency and timing of doses
2 – 4 x daily.

Dosage range
Adults 1 – 4g daily.
Children Reduced dose according to age and weight.

Onset of effect
Within 1 hour.

Duration of action
6 – 12 hours.

Diet advice
None.

Storage
Keep tablets and capsules in a closed container in a cool, dry place away from reach of children. Refrigerate liquid, but do not freeze and keep for no longer than 10 days. Protect from light.

Missed dose
Take as soon as you remember. If your next dose is due at this time, take both doses now.

Stopping the drug
Take the full course. Even if you feel better the original infection may still be present and may recur if treatment is stopped too soon.

Exceeding the dose
An occasional unintentional extra dose is unlikely to be a cause for concern. But if you notice unusual symptoms, or if a large overdose has been taken, notify your doctor.

SPECIAL PRECAUTIONS

Be sure to tell your doctor if:
▼ You have a long-term kidney problem.
▼ You have had a previous allergic reaction to penicillin or cephalosporin antibiotics.
▼ You have a history of blood disorders.
▼ You are taking other medications.

Pregnancy
▼ No evidence of risk to developing baby.

Breast-feeding
▼ The drug passes into the breast milk, but at normal doses adverse effects on the baby are unlikely. Discuss with your doctor.

Infants and children
▼ Reduced dose necessary.

Over 60
▼ No special problems.

Driving and hazardous work
▼ No known problems.

Alcohol
▼ No known problems.

POSSIBLE ADVERSE EFFECTS

Most people do not suffer serious adverse effects while taking cephalexin. Diarrhoea is common but it tends not to be severe. The rarer adverse effects are usually due to an allergic reaction and may necessitate stopping the drug.

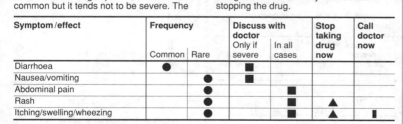

Symptom/effect	Frequency		Discuss with doctor		Stop taking drug now	Call doctor now
	Common	Rare	Only if severe	In all cases		
Diarrhoea	●		■			
Nausea/vomiting		●	■			
Abdominal pain		●		■		
Rash		●		■	▲	
Itching/swelling/wheezing		●		■	▲	■

PROLONGED USE

Cephalexin is usually given only for short courses of treatment.

INTERACTIONS

Probenecid This drug increases the level of cephalexin in the blood. The dosage of cephalexin may need to be adjusted accordingly.

Oral contraceptives Cephalexin may reduce the contraceptive effect of these drugs. Discuss with your doctor.

Aminoglycoside antibiotics Cephalexin may increase the risk of kidney problems when taken in conjunction with aminoglycoside antibiotics.

CHENODEOXYCHOLIC ACID

Brand name Chendol, Chenofalk
Used in the following combined preparations Combidol, Lithofalk

GENERAL INFORMATION

Chenodeoxycholic acid is a chemical that occurs naturally in bile, where it has an important role in controlling the concentration of cholesterol in the blood. As an orally administered drug, it is prescribed as an alternative to surgery in the treatment of gallstones. It acts by reducing levels of cholesterol in the bile, helping gallstones that are made predominantly of cholesterol to dissolve. Chenodeoxycholic acid is ineffective with stones of a high calcium or bile acid content. Its benefits are increased by weight loss and a diet high in fibre, low in fat. Chenodeoxycholic acid dissolves gallstones in 3 to 18 months. The progress of treatment is assessed regularly by ultrasound or X-ray examination. Drug treatment may be continued after the stones have disappeared to prevent recurrence of gallstones.

Diarrhoea is the most common adverse effect. Regular blood tests are usually carried out to check liver function, which may be temporarily affected by the drug.

QUICK REFERENCE

Drug group Drug for gallstones (p.114)
Overdose danger rating Low
Dependence rating Low
Prescription needed Yes
Available as generic No

INFORMATION FOR USERS

Your drug prescription is tailored for you. Do not alter dosage without checking with your doctor.

How taken

Tablets, capsules.

Frequency and timing of doses
1 – 3 x daily with food or milk.

Adult dosage range
According to body weight.

Onset of effect
Within 30 minutes. Full beneficial effects may not be felt for up to 18 months.

Duration of action
Up to 12 hours.

Diet advice
A low cholesterol, high fibre diet is advisable as it enhances gallstone dissolution, prevents new stones forming, and reduces circulating cholesterol levels.

Storage
Keep in a closed container in a cool, dry place away from reach of children.

Missed dose
No cause for concern, but take as soon as you remember. If your next dose is due within 2 hours, take a single dose now and skip the next.

Stopping the drug
Do not stop the drug without consulting your doctor; symptoms may recur.

Exceeding the dose
An occasional unintentional extra dose is unlikely to be a cause for concern. But if you notice unusual symptoms, or if a large overdose has been taken, notify your doctor.

SPECIAL PRECAUTIONS

Be sure to tell your doctor if:
▼ You have long-term liver problems.
▼ You have peptic ulcers.
▼ You have inflammatory bowel disease.
▼ You are taking other medications.

Pregnancy
▼ Not usually prescribed. May adversely affect the baby. Discuss with your doctor.

Breast-feeding
▼ Safety not established. Discuss with your doctor.

Infants and children
▼ Not recommended.

Over 60
▼ No special problems.

Driving and hazardous work
▼ No known problems.

Alcohol
▼ No known problems.

POSSIBLE ADVERSE EFFECTS

Diarrhoea is the most widely experienced adverse effect, particularly at the start of treatment. It can often be minimized by a reduction in dosage.

Symptom/effect	Frequency		Discuss with doctor		Stop taking drug now	Call doctor now
	Common	Rare	Only if severe	In all cases		
Diarrhoea	●		■			
Indigestion		●	■			
Rash		●		■	▲	

INTERACTIONS

Cholestyramine, colestipol, and aluminium antacids These reduce the beneficial effect of chenodeoxycholic acid.

Oral contraceptives Oestrogen-containing preparations may counter the beneficial effects of chenodeoxycholic acid.

PROLONGED USE

Monitoring Blood tests may be performed to check liver function. Ultrasound or X-ray examinations may be carried out to assess the progress of treatment.

CHLORAL HYDRATE

Brand name Noctec (chloral hydrate), Welldorm Elixir (chloral hydrate), Welldorm Tablets (chloral betaine)
Used in the following combined preparations None

GENERAL INFORMATION

Chloral hydrate is one of the oldest sleeping drugs in use. Although it has largely been superseded by the benzodiazepines, it is still prescribed by doctors for the short term treatment of insomnia. Unlike many sleeping drugs, chloral hydrate is suitable for occasional use in the treatment of sleeplessness in children.

Because it loses effectiveness quickly, chloral hydrate is not as commonly used as other sleeping drugs for the long-term treatment of insomnia. The liquid form has an unpleasant taste but the drug is also available in capsules.

INFORMATION FOR USERS

Your drug prescription is tailored for you. Do not alter dosage without checking with your doctor.

How taken

Tablets, capsules, liquid.

Frequency and timing of doses
Once daily 15 – 30 minutes before bedtime. Tablets and capsules should be taken with a full glass of water. Liquid should be well diluted with milk or water.

Dosage range
Adults 500mg – 2g daily.
Children Reduced dose according to age and weight.

Onset of effect
15 – 45 minutes.

Duration of action
4 – 9 hours.

Diet advice
None.

Storage
Keep in a closed container in a cool, dry place away from reach of children.

Missed dose
If you fall asleep without having taken a dose and wake some hours later, do not take the missed dose. If necessary, return to your normal dose schedule the following night.

Stopping the drug
If you have been taking the drug for less than 4 weeks, it can be safely stopped as soon as you feel that you no longer need it. However, if you have been taking the drug for longer than a few weeks, consult your doctor who may supervise a gradual reduction in dosage. Stopping abruptly may lead to withdrawal symptoms (see p.82).

OVERDOSE ACTION

Seek immediate medical advice in all cases. Take emergency action if severe confusion, vomiting or loss of consciousness occur.

See Drug poisoning emergency guide (p.470)

SPECIAL PRECAUTIONS

Be sure to tell your doctor if:
▼ You have long-term kidney or liver problems.
▼ You have heart problems.
▼ You suffer from porphyria.
▼ You have had problems with alcohol or drug abuse.
▼ You have a stomach ulcer.
▼ You are taking other medications.

 Pregnancy
▼ Safety in pregnancy not established. Discuss with your doctor.

 Breast feeding
▼ The drug passes into the breast milk and may affect the baby. Discuss with your doctor.

 Infants and children
▼ Reduced dose necessary.

 Over 60
▼ Reduced dose may be necessary.

 Driving and hazardous work
▼ Avoid such activities until you have learned how the drug affects you. The drug can cause daytime drowsiness.

 Alcohol
▼ Avoid. Alcohol may increase the sedative effects of this drug.

PROLONGED USE

Regular use of this drug over several weeks can lead to a reduction in its effect as the body adapts. It may also be habit-forming when taken for extended periods, especially if larger than average doses are taken.

POSSIBLE ADVERSE EFFECTS

The principal adverse effects of this drug are related to its sedative properties. These effects normally diminish after the first few days of treatment.

Symptom/effect	Frequency		Discuss with doctor		Stop taking drug now	Call doctor now
	Common	Rare	Only if severe	In all cases		
Indigestion	●		■			
Clumsiness/unsteadiness		●	■			
Daytime drowsiness		●	■			
Unusual excitement		●		■		
Headache		●		■		
Rash		●		■	▲	

INTERACTIONS

Sedatives All drugs that have a sedative effect on the central nervous system are likely to increase the sedative properties of chloral hydrate.

Anticoagulants The dosage of anticoagulants such as warfarin may need to be adjusted in patients taking chloral hydrate.

CHLORAMPHENICOL

Brand name Chloromycetin, Kemicetine, Minims Chloramphenicol, Sno-Phenicol
Used in the following combined preparations Actinac, Chloromycetin Hydrocortisone

GENERAL INFORMATION

Chloramphenicol, discovered in 1947, is an antibiotic that is commonly included in topical preparations for eye and ear infections. Given by mouth or injection, it is widely distributed in the body and penetrates the brain effectively, making it useful in the treatment of meningitis and brain abscesses. It is also prescribed for typhoid fever and serious chest infections. It is particularly useful for combating acute infections such as pneumonia, epiglottitis, or meningitis caused by bacteria resistant to other antibiotics. Q fever, Rocky Mountain spotted fever, and similar infections may also be treated with the drug.

Although most people experience few adverse effects, chloramphenicol occasionally causes serious or even fatal blood disorders. For this reason, oral or injectable chloramphenicol is reserved for life-threatening infections that do not respond to safer drugs.

QUICK REFERENCE

Drug group Antibiotic (p.128)
Overdose danger rating Low
Dependence rating Low
Prescription needed Yes
Available as generic Yes

INFORMATION FOR USERS

Your drug prescription is tailored for you. Do not alter dosage without checking with your doctor.

How taken

Capsules, liquid, injection, cream, eye and ear drops, eye ointment.

Frequency and timing of doses
Every 6 hours (by mouth); every 2 – 6 hours (eye preparations); 3 x daily (ear drops).

Adult dosage range
Varies according to preparation and condition. Follow your doctor's instructions.

Onset of effect
1 – 3 days depending on the condition.

Duration of action
6 – 8 hours.

Diet advice
None.

Storage
Keep in closed container in a cool, dry place away from reach of children. Protect from light.

Missed dose
Take as soon as your remember (capsules, liquid). If your next dose is due, double the dose to make up the missed dose. For eye and ear preparations, apply as soon as your remember.

Stopping the drug
Take the full course. Even if you feel better the infection may still be present and may recur if treatment is stopped too soon.

Exceeding the dose
An occasional unintentional extra dose is unlikely to be a cause for concern. But if you notice unusual symptoms, or if a large overdose has been taken, notify your doctor.

SPECIAL PRECAUTIONS

Be sure to tell your doctor if:
▼ You have long-term liver or kidney problems.
▼ You have a blood disorder.
▼ You are taking other medications.

 Pregnancy
▼ No evidence of risk with eye or ear preparations. Safety in pregnancy of other methods of administration not established. Discuss with your doctor.

 Breast feeding
▼ No evidence of risk with eye or ear preparations. Taken by mouth the drug passes into the breast milk and may increase the risk of blood disorders in the baby. Discuss with your doctor.

 Infants and children
▼ Reduced dose necessary.

 Over 60
▼ No problems expected.

 Driving and hazardous work
▼ No known problems.

 Alcohol
▼ No known problems.

POSSIBLE ADVERSE EFFECTS

Transient irritation may occur with eye or ear drops. Sore throat, fever, and unusual tiredness with any form of chloramphenicol may be signs of blood abnormalities and should be reported to your doctor without delay even after treatment has stopped.

Symptom/effect	Frequency		Discuss with doctor		Stop taking drug now	Call doctor now
	Common	Rare	Only if severe	In all cases		
Burning/stinging (drops)		●	■			
Numb/tingling hands/feet		●		■		
Rash/itching		●		■		
Impaired vision		●		■	▲	❚
Sore throat/fever/weakness		●		■	▲	❚
Painful mouth/tongue		●		■	▲	❚

INTERACTIONS (not eye/ear drops)

General note Chloramphenicol may increase the effect of certain other drugs including phenytoin, oral antidiabetics, and oral anticoagulants. Phenobarbitone and rifampicin may reduce the effect of chloramphenicol.

Other antibiotics Chloramphenicol may inhibit the antibacterial effects of penicillin antibiotics.

Paracetamol may prolong the duration of action of chloramphenicol.

PROLONGED USE

Prolonged use of this drug may increase the risk of serious blood disorders and eye damage.

Monitoring Periodic blood cell counts and eye tests may be performed. Blood levels of the drug are usually monitored on babies given chloramphenicol by mouth or by injection.

CHLORDIAZEPOXIDE

Brand names Librium, Tropium
Used in the following combined preparations Limbitrol

GENERAL INFORMATION

Introduced in the mid-1960s, chlordiazepoxide belongs to a group of drugs known as benzodiazepines. These are used to help to relieve nervousness and tension, relax muscles and encourage sleep. The actions and adverse effects of this drug group are described more fully on p.83.

Prescribed primarily to treat anxiety, chlordiazepoxide is also used to relieve the symptoms of alcohol withdrawal.

As a combined preparation with the tricyclic antidepressant amitriptyline, chlordiazepoxide is sometimes used to treat depression associated with anxiety.

Small doses of chlordiazepoxide are sometimes found to be useful in treating cases of muscle spasm.

Addictive if taken regularly over a long period, chlordiazepoxide may also lose effectiveness with time. For those reasons treatment is regularly reviewed.

QUICK REFERENCE

Drug group Benzodiazepine anti-anxiety drug (p.83)
Overdose danger rating Medium
Dependence rating Medium
Prescription needed Yes
Available as generic Yes

INFORMATION FOR USERS

Your drug prescription is tailored for you. Do not alter dosage without checking with your doctor.

How taken

Tablets, capsules, injection.

Frequency and timing of doses
1 – 4 x daily.

Adult dosage range
10 – 100mg daily. The dosage varies considerably from person to person.

Onset of effect
1 – 2 hours.

Duration of action
12 – 24 hours, but some effect may last up to 4 days.

Diet advice
None.

Storage
Keep in a closed container in a cool, dry place away from reach of children.

Missed dose
No cause for concern, but take when you remember. If your next dose is due within 2 hours, take a single dose now and skip the next.

Stopping the drug
If you have been taking the drug for less than 2 weeks, it can be safely stopped as soon as you feel you no longer need it. However, if you have been taking the drug for longer, consult your doctor who may supervise a gradual reduction in dosage. Stopping abruptly may lead to withdrawal symptoms (see p.79).

Exceeding the dose
An occasional unintentional extra dose is unlikely to cause problems. Large overdoses may cause unusual drowsiness or coma. Notify your doctor.

SPECIAL PRECAUTIONS

Be sure to tell your doctor if:
▼ You have long-term kidney or liver problems.
▼ You have a history of breathing problems.
▼ You have had problems with alcohol or drug abuse.
▼ You are taking other medications.

Pregnancy
▼ Safety in pregnancy not established. Discuss with your doctor.

Breast feeding
▼ The drug passes into the breast milk and may affect the baby. Discuss with your doctor.

Infants and children
▼ Not recommended.

Over 60
▼ Reduced dose may be necessary.

Driving and hazardous work
▼ Avoid such activities until you have learned how the drug affects you because the drug can cause reduced alertness and slowed reactions.

Alcohol
▼ Avoid. Alcohol may increase the sedative effects of this drug.

POSSIBLE ADVERSE EFFECTS

The principal adverse effects of this drug are related to its sedative and tranquillizing properties. These effects normally diminish after the first few days of treatment.

Symptom/effect	Frequency		Discuss with doctor		Stop taking drug now	Call doctor now
	Common	Rare	Only if severe	In all cases		
Daytime drowsiness	●		■			
Dizziness/unsteadiness	●		■			
Forgetfulness/confusion		●	■			
Headache		●	■			
Blurred vision		●			■	
Rash		●			■	▲

INTERACTIONS

Cimetidine May cause a build-up of chlordiazepoxide levels in the blood which increases the likelihood of adverse effects.

Sedatives All drugs that have a sedative effect on the central nervous system are likely to increase the sedative properties of chlordiazepoxide.

PROLONGED USE

Regular use of this drug over several weeks can lead to a reduction in its effect as the body adapts. It may also be habit-forming, when taken for extended periods, especially if larger than average doses are taken.

CHLOROQUINE

Brand names Avloclor, Malarivon, Nivaquine
Used in the following combined preparations None

GENERAL INFORMATION

Chloroquine was introduced for the prevention and treatment of malaria. It usually clears an attack of the disease within three days. Injections may be given when an attack is severe. As a preventative treatment, a low dose of chloroquine is given once weekly starting two weeks before visiting a high-risk area and continuing for six weeks after departure. Chloroquine is not suitable for use in all countries because of resistance to the drug. The other main use for chloroquine is in the treatment of autoimmune diseases, including rheumatoid arthritis and lupus erythematosus.

Common side effects include nausea, headache, diarrhoea, and abdominal cramps. Occasionally a rash develops. More seriously, chloroquine can damage the retina during prolonged treatment, causing blurred vision sometimes proceeding to blindness. Regular eye examinations are performed to detect early changes.

QUICK REFERENCE

Drug group Antimalarial drug (p.137) and antirheumatic drug (p.117)

Overdose danger rating High

Dependence rating Low

Prescription needed No (malaria prevention); Yes (other uses)

Available as generic No

INFORMATION FOR USERS

Your drug prescription is tailored for you. Do not alter dosage without checking with your doctor.

How taken

Tablets, liquid, injection.

Frequency and timing of doses
By mouth Once weekly (prevention of malaria); 1 – 4 x daily (treatment of malaria); once daily (arthritis).

Adult dosage range
300mg as a single dose on the same day each week. Start 2 weeks before entering endemic area, continuing for 4 weeks after leaving (prevention of malaria); initial dose 600mg and following doses 300mg (treatment of malaria); 150mg per day (arthritis).

Onset of effect
2 – 3 days. In rheumatoid arthritis, full effect may not be felt for up to 6 months.

Duration of action
Up to one week.

Diet advice
None.

Storage
Keep in a closed container in a cool, dry, place away from reach of children. Protect from light.

Missed dose
Take as soon as you remember. If your next dose is due within 24 hours (once weekly schedule), 6 hours (once or twice daily schedule) take a single dose now and skip the next.

Stopping the drug
Do not stop the drug without consulting your doctor.

OVERDOSE ACTION

Seek immediate medical advice in all cases. Take emergency action if breathing difficulties, fits or loss of consciousness occur.

See Drug poisoning emergency guide (p.470).

POSSIBLE ADVERSE EFFECTS

Side effects such as nausea, diarrhoea, and abdominal pain might be avoided by taking the drug with food. Changes in vision should be reported promptly.

Symptom/effect	Frequency		Discuss with doctor		Stop taking drug now	Call doctor now
	Common	Rare	Only if severe	In all cases		
Nausea	●		■			
Diarrhoea/abdominal pain	●		■			
Headache/dizziness		●	■			
Rash		●		■	▲	▮
Blurred vision		●		■	▲	▮

INTERACTIONS

Antacids and kaolin may reduce the absorption of chloroquine.

Digoxin The level of digoxin in the blood may be increased by chloroquine.

SPECIAL PRECAUTIONS

Be sure to tell your doctor if:
▼ You have liver or kidney problems.
▼ You have glucose 6-phosphate dehydrogenase (G6PD) deficiency.
▼ You have eye or vision problems.
▼ You have psoriasis.
▼ You have a history of epilepsy.
▼ You suffer from porphyria.
▼ You are taking other medications.

Pregnancy
▼ No evidence of risk with low doses. High doses may affect the baby. Discuss with your doctor.

Breast feeding
▼ The drug may pass into breast milk in small amounts. At normal doses effects on the baby are unlikely. Discuss with your doctor.

Infants and children
▼ Reduced dose necessary.

Over 60
▼ No special problems, except that it may be difficult to tell between changes in eyesight due to ageing, and those that are drug induced.

Driving and hazardous work
▼ Avoid such activities until you have learned how the drug affects you since it may cause dizziness.

Alcohol
▼ Keep consumption low.

PROLONGED USE

Prolonged use may cause eye damage and blood disorders.

Monitoring Periodic eye tests and blood counts may be carried out.

CHLORPHENIRAMINE

Brand names Piriton
Used in the following combined preparations Expulin, Expurhin Paediatric, Galpseud Plus, Haymine

GENERAL INFORMATION

Chlorpheniramine, an antihistamine used for over 30 years, is given to treat allergies such as hayfever, allergic conjunctivitis, urticaria (hives), and angioedema (allergic swellings). It is included in several over-the-counter cold remedies (see p.94).

Like other antihistamines, it relieves allergic skin symptoms such as itching, swelling and redness. It also reduces sneezing and runny nose and itching eyes in hayfever. It has a mild *anticholinergic* action, which suppresses mucus secretion.

Chlorpheniramine may also be used to prevent or treat allergic reactions to blood transfusions or X-ray contrast material, and as a supplement to adrenaline injections for acute allergic shock (anaphylaxis).

INFORMATION FOR USERS

Follow instructions on the label. Call your doctor if symptoms worsen.

How taken

Tablets, liquid, injection.

Frequency and timing of doses
4 – 6 x daily (tablets, liquid); single dose as needed (injection).

Dosage range
Adults 12 – 24mg daily (orally); up to 40mg daily (injection).
Children Reduced dose according to age and weight.

Onset of effect
Within 60 minutes (by mouth); within 20 minutes (injection).

Duration of action
4 – 8 hours (tablets, liquid, injection).

Diet advice
None.

Storage
Keep in a closed container in a cool, dry place away from reach of children. Protect from light.

Missed dose
Take as soon as you remember. If your next dose is due within 2 hours, take a single dose now and skip the next.

Stopping the drug
Can be safely stopped as soon as you no longer need it.

Exceeding the dose
An occasional unintentional extra dose is unlikely to cause problems. Large overdoses may cause drowsiness or agitation. Notify your doctor.

SPECIAL PRECAUTIONS

Be sure to consult your doctor or pharmacist before taking this drug if:
▼ You have long-term liver problems.
▼ You have had epileptic fits.
▼ You have glaucoma.
▼ You have urinary difficulties.
▼ You are taking other medications.

Pregnancy
▼ Safety in pregnancy not established. Discuss with your doctor.

Breast feeding
▼ The drug passes into the breast milk, but at normal doses adverse effects on the baby are unlikely. Discuss with your doctor.

Infants and children
▼ Reduced dose necessary.

Over 60
▼ Reduced dose may be necessary. Increased likelihood of adverse effects.

Driving and hazardous work
▼ Avoid such activities until you have learned how the drug affects you because the drug can cause drowsiness, dizziness and blurred vision.

Alcohol
▼ Avoid. Alcohol may increase the sedative effects of this drug.

POSSIBLE ADVERSE EFFECTS

Drowsiness is the most common adverse effect of chlorpheniramine. Other side effects are rare. Some of these, such as dryness of the mouth, blurred vision and difficulty passing urine, are due to its *anticholinergic* effects. Gastrointestinal irritation may be reduced by taking tablets or liquid with food or drink.

Symptom/effect	Frequency		Discuss with doctor		Stop taking drug now	Call doctor now
	Common	Rare	Only if severe	In all cases		
Drowsiness/dizziness	●		■			
Digestive disturbance		●	■			
Urinary difficulties		●	■			
Dry mouth		●	■			
Blurred vision		●	■			
Excitation (children)		●			■	▲
Rash		●			■	▲

INTERACTIONS

Sedatives All drugs that have a sedative effect are likely to enhance the sedative effect of chlorpheniramine.

Phenytoin The effects of phenytoin may be enhanced by chlorpheniramine.

Anticholinergic drugs The anticholinergic effects of chlorpheniramine are likely to be increased by all drugs that have anticholinergic effects, including certain drugs for parkinsonism.

PROLONGED USE

The effect of the drug may become weaker with prolonged use over a period of weeks or months as the body adapts. Transfer to a different antihistamine may be recommended.

CHLORPROMAZINE

Brand name Largactil
Used in the following combined preparations None

GENERAL INFORMATION

Chlorpromazine was the first antipsychotic drug to be marketed. It remains one of the most widely used of this group of drugs, effective in suppressing abnormal behaviour, reducing aggression, and inducing a generally tranquillizing effect.

Chlorpromazine is used in the treatment of schizophrenia, mania, and other disorders where confused, aggressive, or abnormal behaviour

may occur, and a degree of sedation is required. Other uses of chlorpromazine include the treatment of nausea and vomiting, especially when caused by drug or radiation treatment; and treating severe, prolonged hiccoughs.

The main drawback to the use of chlorpromazine is that it can produce many side effects (below) some of which are serious.

INFORMATION FOR USERS

Your drug prescription is tailored for you. Do not alter dosage without checking with your doctor.

How taken

Tablets, liquid, injection, suppositories.

Frequency and timing of doses
1 – 4 x daily.

Adult dosage range
Mental illness 75 – 300mg daily. Dose may be increased in severe illness.
Nausea and vomiting 40 – 150mg daily.

Onset of effect
30 – 60 minutes by mouth; 15 – 20 minutes by injection; up to 30 minutes by suppository.

Duration of action
8 – 12 hours by mouth or injection; 3 – 4 hours by suppository. Some effect may

persist for up to 3 weeks when stopping the drug after regular use.

Diet advice
None.

Storage
Keep in a closed container in a cool, dry place away from reach of children. Protect from light.

Missed dose
Take as soon as you remember. If your next dose is due within 2 hours, do not take the missed dose. Take your next scheduled dose as usual.

Stopping the drug
Do not stop the drug without consulting your doctor; symptoms may recur.

Exceeding the dose
An occasional unintentional extra dose is unlikely to cause problems. Large overdoses may cause unusual drowsiness, fainting, muscle rigidity and agitation. Notify your doctor.

SPECIAL PRECAUTIONS

Be sure to tell your doctor if:
▼ You have kidney or liver problems.
▼ You have had heart problems.
▼ You have had epileptic fits.
▼ You have thyroid disease.
▼ You have Parkinson's disease.
▼ You have glaucoma.
▼ You are taking other medications.

Pregnancy
▼ Not usually prescribed. Taken near the time of delivery it can prolong labour and may cause drowsiness in the newborn baby. Discuss with your doctor.

Breast feeding
▼ The drug passes into the breast milk and may affect the baby. Discuss with your doctor.

Infants and children
▼ Not recommended for children under one year. Reduced dose is necessary for older children.

Over 60
▼ Initial dosage is low, increased as required if there are no adverse reactions, such as abnormal limb movements or low blood pressure.

Driving and hazardous work
▼ Avoid such activities until you have learned how the drug affects you because of the possibility of drowsiness and slowed reactions.

Alcohol
▼ Avoid. Alcohol may increase the sedative effects of this drug.

Surgery and general anaesthetics
▼ Chlorpromazine treatment may need to be stopped before you have a general anaesthetic. Discuss this with your doctor or dentist before any operation.

POSSIBLE ADVERSE EFFECTS

Chlorpromazine has an *anticholinergic* effect which can cause symptoms. The most

significant adverse effect is parkinsonism.

Symptom/effect	Frequency		Discuss with doctor		Stop taking drug now	Call doctor now
	Common	Rare	Only if severe	In all cases		
Drowsiness/lethargy	●		■			
Weight gain	●		■			
Blurred vision	●			■		
Dizziness/fainting	●			■		
Parkinsonism	●			■		
Infrequent periods		●		■		
Rash		●		■	▲	

INTERACTIONS

Sedatives All drugs that have a sedative effect on the central nervous system are likely to increase the sedative properties of chlorpromazine.

Antiparkinson drugs Chlorpromazine may reduce the effect of these drugs.

Anticholinergic drugs The side effects of drugs with *anticholinergic* properties may be increased by chlorpromazine.

PROLONGED USE

If used for more than a few months, it may cause movement disorders. Occasionally, jaundice may occur.

CHLORPROPAMIDE

Brand names Diabinese, Glymese
Used in the following combined preparations None

GENERAL INFORMATION

Chlorpropamide is an oral antidiabetic drug. Given in conjunction with a diet low in carbohydrates and fats, it is used in the treatment of adult (maturity-onset) diabetes mellitus. It lowers blood sugar by stimulating the production and secretion of insulin from the pancreas and by promoting the uptake of sugar into body cells.

The longest acting of the oral anti-diabetic drugs, chlorpropamide need only be taken once daily. It is not given to people with kidney failure and is used with caution in the elderly since it may build up in the body and cause excessive lowering of the blood sugar.

Chlorpropamide is also prescribed for mild forms of diabetes insipidus, in which it reduces the volume of urine produced by increasing water reabsorption in the kidneys.

INFORMATION FOR USERS

Your drug prescription is tailored for you. Do not alter dosage without checking with your doctor.

How taken

Tablets.

Frequency and timing of doses
Once daily with breakfast.

Adult dosage range
100 – 500mg daily.

Onset of effect
Within 1 hour.

Duration of action
1 – 3 days.

Diet advice
For treatment of diabetes mellitus, a low carbohydrate, low fat diet must be maintained. Follow your doctor's advice.

Storage
Keep in a closed container in a cool, dry, place away from reach of children.

Missed dose
Take before your next meal.

Stopping the drug
Do not stop the drug without consulting your doctor; stopping the drug may lead to worsening of your diabetes.

OVERDOSE ACTION

 Seek immediate medical advice in all cases. If symptoms of low blood sugar such as faintness, confusion, sweating or shaking occur, eat or drink something sugary. Take emergency action if fits or loss of consciousness occur.

See Drug poisoning emergency guide (p.470).

SPECIAL PRECAUTIONS

Be sure to tell your doctor if:
▼ You have long-term liver or kidney problems.
▼ You are allergic to sulphonamide drugs.
▼ You have thyroid problems.
▼ You are taking other medications.

 Pregnancy
▼ Not usually prescribed. Insulin is generally used in pregnancy because it gives better diabetic control.

 Breast feeding
▼ The drug passes into the breast milk and may cause low blood sugar in the baby. Discuss with your doctor.

 Infants and children
▼ Not prescribed for diabetes mellitus. Reduced dose necessary for diabetes insipidus.

 Over 60
▼ Not usually prescribed. Other oral antidiabetic drugs are preferred. Reduced dose necessary.

 Driving and hazardous work
▼ Usually no problem. Avoid these activities if you have warning signs of low blood sugar.

 Alcohol
▼ Avoid. Alcoholic drinks may upset diabetic control and react adversely with this drug.

Surgery and general anaesthetics
▼ Surgery may reduce the response to this drug; insulin treatment may need to be substituted.

POSSIBLE ADVERSE EFFECTS

Serious adverse effects are rare. Faintness, sweating, tremor, weakness and confusion may be signs of low blood sugar due to lack of food or too high a dose.

Symptom/effect	Frequency		Discuss with doctor		Stop taking drug now	Call doctor now
	Common	Rare	Only if severe	In all cases		
Faintness/confusion	●			■		
Weakness/tremor	●			■		
Sweating	●			■		
Nausea/vomiting		●	■			
Diarrhoea		●		■		
Headache		●		■		
Rash/itching		●		■		

INTERACTIONS

General note The following drugs may enhance the effects of chlorpropamide leading to low blood sugar levels: aspirin, non-steroidal anti-inflammatory drugs, warfarin, and beta blockers. Some drugs may increase blood sugar levels resulting in loss of control by chlorpropamide; these include: diuretics, corticosteroids, oestrogens, and phenytoin.

PROLONGED USE

No problems expected.

Monitoring If the drug is taken for diabetes mellitus, regular monitoring of urine or blood sugar is required.

CHOLESTYRAMINE

Brand name Questran, Questran A
Used in the following combined preparations None

GENERAL INFORMATION

Cholestyramine is a resin that binds bile acids in the intestine preventing their reabsorption. Cholesterol in the body is normally converted to bile acids, cholestyramine therefore results in a reduction of cholesterol levels in the blood. The action on the bile acids makes bowel movements bulkier, thus creating an antidiarrhoeal effect. The action on cholesterol helps people with hyperlipidaemia (high levels of fat in the blood) who have not responded to dietary measures, or who are at particular risk from heart disease because of diabetes or a family history

of death from heart attacks.

If bile salts accumulate in the bloodstream, as sometimes happens in liver disorders such as primary biliary cirrhosis, cholestyramine may be prescribed to alleviate any accompanying itching that may occur.

In large doses, cholestyramine often causes bloating, mild nausea, and constipation. Cholestyramine may also interfere with the body's ability to absorb fat and certain vitamins dissolved in fat, causing pale, bulky, foul-smelling faeces

QUICK REFERENCE

Drug group Lipid-lowering drug (p.103)
Overdose danger rating Low
Dependence rating Low
Prescription needed Yes
Available as generic No

INFORMATION FOR USERS

Your drug prescription is tailored for you. Do not alter dosage without checking with your doctor.

How taken

Powder mixed with water, juice, or soft food.

Frequency and timing of doses
1 – 4 x daily before meals and at bedtime.

Adult dosage range
4 – 36g daily.

Onset of effect
Full beneficial effects may not be felt for several weeks.

Duration of action
12 – 24 hours.

Diet advice
A low fat, low calorie diet may be recommended for those overweight. Use of this drug may deplete levels of certain vitamins. Supplements may be advised.

Storage
Keep in a closed container in a cool, dry place away from the reach of children.

Missed dose
Take as soon as you remember.

Stopping the drug
Do not stop taking the drug without consulting your doctor.

Exceeding the dose
An occasional unintentional extra dose is unlikely to cause problems. But if you notice unusual symptoms or if a large overdose has been taken, notify your doctor.

SPECIAL PRECAUTIONS

Be sure to tell your doctor if:
▼ You have jaundice.
▼ You have a peptic ulcer.
▼ You suffer from haemorrhoids.
▼ You are taking other medications.

Pregnancy
▼ Safety in pregnancy not established. Discuss with your doctor.

Breast feeding
▼ The drug passes into the breast milk, but at normal doses adverse effects on the baby are unlikely. Discuss with your doctor.

Infants and children
▼ Not recommended under 6 years. Reduced dose necessary in older children.

Over 60
▼ Increased likelihood of adverse effects.

Driving and hazardous work
▼ No special problems.

Alcohol
▼ Although this drug does not interact with alcohol, your underlying condition may make it inadvisable to take alcohol.

POSSIBLE ADVERSE EFFECTS

Adverse effects are more likely if large doses are taken by people over 60. Minor side effects, such as indigestion and abdominal discomfort, are rarely a cause for concern. More serious adverse effects are usually the result of vitamin deficiency.

Symptom/effect	Frequency		Discuss with doctor		Stop taking drug now	Call doctor now
	Common	Rare	Only if severe	In all cases		
Indigestion	●		■			
Abdominal discomfort	●		■			
Nausea/vomiting	●		■			
Constipation	●		■			
Bruising/increased bleeding		●		■		
Diarrhoea (high doses)		●		■		

INTERACTIONS

General note Cholestyramine reduces the body's ability to absorb other drugs. It may be necessary to organize a schedule in consultation with your doctor whereby you take other medications at a fixed time

before you take cholestyramine. Usually, taking other medication 30 – 60 minutes prior to cholestyramine, or 4 – 6 hours after, solves the problem. The dosage of other drugs may need to be adjusted.

PROLONGED USE

As this drug reduces vitamin absorption, supplements of vitamins A, D, and K and folic acid may be advised.

Monitoring Periodic blood checks are usually required to monitor the level of cholesterol in the blood.

CHORIONIC GONADOTROPHIN

Brand names Gonadotraphon LH, Pregnyl, Profasi
Used in the following combined preparations None

GENERAL INFORMATION

Produced by the placenta, human chorionic gonadotrophin (HCG) is a hormone that stimulates the ovaries to produce two other hormones, oestrogen and progesterone, that are essential to the conception and early growth of the fetus. The hormone is extracted from the urine of pregnant women and used for several purposes.

Its principal value is in the treatment of female infertility. Given by injection, usually with another hormone, HCG encourages the ovaries to release an egg (ovulation) so that it can be fertilized. Ovulation usually occurs 18 hours after injection, and intercourse should follow within 48 hours. HCG increases the likelihood of multiple births.

The drug is also in rare cases given to young boys to treat undescended testes.

HCG is also occasionally given to men to improve the production of sperm, which can take up to 6 – 9 months of treatment.

INFORMATION FOR USERS

This drug is given only under medical supervision and is not for self-administration.

How taken

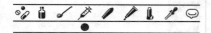

Injection.

Frequency and timing of doses
1 – 3 times per week.

Dosage range
Dosage varies from person to person, and may need adjustment during treatment.

Onset of effect
1 – 8 days (female infertility); 6 – 9 months (male infertility).

Duration of action
2 – 3 days.

Diet advice
None.

Storage
Not applicable. This drug is not kept in the home.

Missed dose
Arrange to receive the missed dose as soon as possible. A delay of more than 24 hours may reduce the chance of conception.

Stopping the drug
Complete the course of treatment as directed. Stopping the drug prematurely will reduce the chance of conception.

Exceeding the dose
The drug is always injected under close medical supervision. Overdose is unlikely.

POSSIBLE ADVERSE EFFECTS

When taken for fertility problems, the more common adverse effects of HCG are rarely severe and tend to diminish with time.

Women who take large doses of the drug may experience abdominal pain or swelling due to overstimulation of the ovaries.

Symptom/effect	Frequency		Discuss with doctor		Stop taking drug now	Call doctor now
	Common	Rare	Only if severe	In all cases		
Headache/tiredness	●			■		
Pain at injection site	●			■		
Mood changes	●			■		
Women only						
Abdominal pain		●		■		
Men only						
Enlarged breasts		●		■	▲	
Swollen feet/ankles		●		■		

INTERACTIONS

None.

SPECIAL PRECAUTIONS

Be sure to tell your doctor if:
▼ You have a long-term kidney problem.
▼ You have asthma.
▼ You have had epileptic fits.
▼ You suffer from migraine.
▼ You have a heart disorder.
▼ You have had a previous allergic reaction to this drug.
▼ You have prostate trouble.
▼ You are taking other medications.

Pregnancy
▼ Not prescribed.

Breast feeding
▼ Not prescribed.

Infants and children
▼ HCG is safely prescribed to treat undescended testes in boys.

Over 60
▼ Not usually required.

Driving and hazardous work
▼ Avoid such activities until you have learned how the drug affects you because the drug can cause tiredness.

Alcohol
▼ Avoid excessive amounts. Alcohol increases tiredness and, in excess, may reduce fertility.

PROLONGED USE

No special problems.

Monitoring Women taking HCG to improve fertility usually have regular pelvic examinations and checks on cervical mucus to confirm that ovulation is taking place. Men may be given regular sperm counts.

CIMETIDINE

Brand name Dyspamet, Tagamet, Galenamet, Zita, Peptimax, Phimetin
Used in the following combined preparations Algitec

GENERAL INFORMATION

Introduced in the 1970s, cimetidine reduces the secretion of gastric acid and of pepsin, an enzyme which helps the digestion of protein. By reducing levels of acid and pepsin, it promotes healing of ulcers in the stomach and duodenum (see p.109). Cimetidine is also used in reflux oesophagitis, a tendency to burp acid stomach contents part way up the oesophagus. Treatment is usually given in courses of four to eight weeks, with further short courses if symptoms recur.

Cimetidine also affects the actions of certain enzymes in the liver where many drugs are broken down. It is therefore prescribed with caution if you are receiving drugs, particularly anticoagulants and anticonvulsants, whose levels need to be carefully controlled. As cimetidine promotes healing of the stomach lining, it may mask the symptoms of stomach cancer, delaying diagnosis. It is usually prescribed only when this disease has been ruled out.

INFORMATION FOR USERS

Your prescription is tailored for you. Do not alter dosage without checking with your doctor.

How taken

Tablets, liquid, injection.

Frequency and timing of doses
1 – 4 x daily (after meals and at bedtime).

Adult dosage range
800 – 2400mg daily.

Onset of effect
Within 90 minutes.

Duration of action
2 – 6 hours.

Diet advice
None.

Storage
Keep in a closed container in a cool, dry place away from reach of children. Protect from light.

Missed dose
Do not take the missed dose. Take your next dose as usual.

Stopping the drug
If prescribed by your doctor, do not stop taking the drug without consulting him or her; symptoms may recur.

Exceeding the dose
An occasional unintentional extra dose is unlikely to be a cause for concern. But if you notice unusual symptoms, or if a large overdose has been taken, notify your doctor.

POSSIBLE ADVERSE EFFECTS

Adverse effects of cimetidine are uncommon. They are usually related to dosage level and almost always disappear when the drug is stopped.

Symptom/effect	Frequency		Discuss with doctor		Stop taking drug now	Call doctor now
	Common	Rare	Only if severe	In all cases		
Diarrhoea		●		■		
Dizziness/confusion		●		■		
Muscle pain		●		■		
Breast enlargement (men)		●		■		
Impotence		●		■		
Rash		●		■	▲	

INTERACTIONS

Benzodiazepines Cimetidine may cause an increase in blood levels of some of these drugs, leading to an increased risk of adverse effects.

Beta blockers Cimetidine may increase blood levels of these drugs.

Anticoagulants Cimetidine may increase the effect of these drugs. The dosage of anticoagulants may need to be reduced.

Anticonvulsants Cimetidine may increase the blood levels of such drugs and the dose may need to be reduced.

SPECIAL PRECAUTIONS

Be sure to tell your doctor if:
▼ You have long-term kidney or liver problems.
▼ You are taking other medications.

Pregnancy
▼ Safety in pregnancy not established. Discuss with your doctor.

Breast feeding
▼ The drug passes into the breast milk, but at normal doses adverse effects on the baby are unlikely. Discuss with your doctor.

Infants and children
▼ Reduced dose necessary.

Over 60
▼ No special problems unless kidney function is reduced, in which case dosage is decreased

Driving and hazardous work
▼ Avoid such activities until you have learned how the drug affects you because the drug may cause dizziness and confusion.

Alcohol
▼ Avoid. Alcohol may aggravate the underlying condition and counter the beneficial effects of cimetidine.

PROLONGED USE

Courses of longer than 8 weeks are not usually necessary.

CINNARIZINE

Brand name Cinaziere, Marzine–RF, Stugeron, Stugeron Forte
Used in the following combined preparations None

GENERAL INFORMATION

Cinnarizine is an antihistamine drug, introduced in the 1970s. It is mainly used to control nausea and vomiting, particularly motion (travel) sickness. It is also used to control the symptoms (nausea and vertigo) of inner ear disorders such as labyrinthitis and Ménière's disease.

In high doses cinnarizine has a *vasodilator* effect and is used to improve circulation in peripheral vascular disease and Raynaud's disease.

Cinnarizine has adverse effects similar to those of most other antihistamines. Drowsiness is the most common problem, but this is usually less severe than with other antihistamine drugs.

INFORMATION FOR USERS

Follow instructions on the label. Call your doctor if symptoms worsen.

How taken

Tablets, capsules.

Frequency and timing of doses
2 – 3 x daily. For the prevention of motion sickness, the first dose should be taken 2 hours before travel.

Dosage range
Adults 45 – 90mg daily (nausea/vomiting); 150 – 225mg daily (circulatory disorders); 30mg, then 15mg every 8 hours as needed (motion sickness).
Children aged 5 – 12, 15mg, then 7.5mg every 8 hours as needed (motion sickness).

Onset of effect
Within 30 minutes. Several weeks (in circulation diseases).

Duration of action
Up to 8 hours.

Diet advice
None.

Storage
Keep in a closed container in a cool, dry place away from reach of children.

Missed dose
Take as soon as you remember. If your next dose is due within 2 hours, take a single dose now and skip the next.

Stopping the drug
If you are taking cinnarizine to treat an inner ear disorder or a circulatory condition, do not stop the drug without consulting your doctor; symptoms may recur. However, when taken for motion sickness, the drug can be safely stopped as soon as you no longer need it.

Exceeding the dose
An occasional unintentional extra dose is unlikely to cause problems. Large overdoses may cause drowsiness or agitation. Notify your doctor.

SPECIAL PRECAUTIONS

Be sure to consult your doctor or pharmacist before taking this drug if:
▼ You have low blood pressure.
▼ You have glaucoma.
▼ You have an enlarged prostate.
▼ You are taking other medications.

Pregnancy
▼ Safety in pregnancy not established. Discuss with your doctor.

Breast feeding
▼ The drug passes into the breast milk, but at normal doses adverse effects on the baby are unlikely. Discuss with your doctor.

Infants and children
▼ Reduced dose necessary.

Over 60
▼ No special problems.

Driving and hazardous work
▼ Avoid such activities until you have learned how the drug affects you because it can cause drowsiness.

Alcohol
▼ Avoid. Alcohol may increase the sedative effects of this drug.

PROLONGED USE

No special problems.

POSSIBLE ADVERSE EFFECTS

Drowsiness is the main adverse effect of this drug. *Anticholinergic* effects such as blurred vision and dry mouth may also occur occasionally.

Symptom/effect	Frequency		Discuss with doctor		Stop taking drug now	Call doctor now
	Common	Rare	Only if severe	In all cases		
Drowsiness/lethargy	●		■			
Blurred vision		●	■			
Dry mouth		●	■			
Rash		●		■	▲	

INTERACTIONS

General note All drugs that have a sedative effect on the central nervous system may increase the sedative properties of cinnarizine. Such drugs include sleeping drugs, anti-anxiety drugs, antidepressants and narcotic analgesics.

CIPROFLOXACIN

Brand name Ciproxin
Used in the following combined preparations None

GENERAL INFORMATION

Ciprofloxacin is a quinolone antibiotic, which was introduced in 1987. It is effective against several types of bacteria that tend to be resistant to other commonly used antibiotics. It is prescribed to treat a wide range of infections, and is particularly useful for infections of the chest, intestine, and urinary tract. It is also used as a single dose in treating gonorrhoea.

When taken in the form of tablets, ciprofloxacin is well absorbed by the body and works quickly and effectively. In more severe systemic bacterial infections, however, it may need to be given by injection.

Ciprofloxacin is convenient to take, as it has a long duration of action and needs to be taken only twice daily. The drug causes few side effects, of which gastrointestinal disturbance is the most common.

QUICK REFERENCE

Drug group Antibiotic (p.128)
Overdose danger rating Medium
Dependence rating Low
Prescription needed Yes
Available as generic No

INFORMATION FOR USERS

Your drug prescription is tailored for you. Do not alter dosage without checking with your doctor.

How taken

Tablets, injection.

Frequency and timing of doses
Twice daily with plenty of fluid.

Adult dosage range
0.5 – 1.5g daily (tablets); 200 – 400mg daily (injection).

Onset of effect
The drug begins to work within a few hours, although full beneficial effect may not be felt for several days.

Duration of action
About 12 hours.

Diet advice
Do not get dehydrated. Ensure that you drink fluids regularly.

Storage
Keep in a closed container in a cool, dry place away from reach of children. The injection must be protected from light.

Missed dose
Take as soon as you remember, and take your next dose as usual.

Stopping the drug
Take the full course. Even if you feel better the original infection may still be present, and symptoms may recur if treatment is stopped too soon.

Exceeding the dose
An occasional unintentional extra dose is unlikely to cause problems. Large overdoses may cause mental disturbance and fits. Notify your doctor.

SPECIAL PRECAUTIONS

Be sure to tell your doctor if:
▼ You have long-term liver or kidney problems.
▼ You have had epileptic fits.
▼ You are taking other medications.

 Pregnancy
▼ Safety in pregnancy not established. Discuss with your doctor.

 Breast feeding
▼ The drug passes into the breast milk and may affect the baby adversely. Discuss with your doctor.

 Infants and children
▼ Not recommended.

 Over 60s
▼ No special problems.

 Driving and hazardous work
▼ Avoid such activities until you have learned how the drug affects you because it can cause dizziness.

 Alcohol
▼ Avoid. Alcohol may increase the adverse effects of this drug.

POSSIBLE ADVERSE EFFECTS

Although ciprofloxacin may cause nausea and vomiting, other side effects are less common, except when very high doses are given for severe infections.

Symptom/effect	Frequency		Discuss with doctor		Stop taking drug now	Call doctor now
	Common	Rare	Only if severe	In all cases		
Nausea/vomiting	●		■			
Diarrhoea	●		■			
Abdominal pain	●		■			
Dizziness		●	■			
Joint pain		●	■			
Headache		●	■			
Rash		●			■	

PROLONGED USE

No problems expected. Blood tests may be necessary to monitor kidney and liver function.

INTERACTIONS

Antacids containing magnesium or aluminium hydroxide interfere with the absorption of ciprofloxacin. Do not take antacids within 2 hours of taking ciprofloxacin tablets.

Iron Oral iron preparations will reduce the absorption of ciprofloxacin.

Theophylline Ciprofloxacin may increase the blood levels of theophylline. Dose adjustment may be necessary, and body levels of theophylline may need monitoring.

Non-steroidal anti-inflammatory drugs These drugs increase the risk of epileptic fits occurring.

CISAPRIDE

Brand names Prepulsid
Used in the following combined preparations None

GENERAL INFORMATION

Cisapride is a new drug that stimulates forward movement in the oesophagus and intestines. It is useful in a number of conditions including the symptoms of gastro-oesophageal reflux, such as dyspepsia, heartburn and regurgitation. Cisparide may be useful when stomach emptying is delayed. This happens in some diabetics and patients suffering from systemic sclerosis and autonomic nueropathy. It is sometimes used for

the short-term treatment of dyspepsia (indigestion) that fails to respond to other remedies.

Cisapride produces its effect by increasing the release of acetylcholine in the gut wall; this in turn increases the contractions of the muscles in the gut wall. Adverse effects on the gastrointestinal tract rarely require discontinuing the drug and tend to reduce in time.

INFORMATION FOR USERS

Your drug prescription is tailored for you. Do not alter dosage without checking with your doctor.

How taken

Tablets, liquid.

Frequency and timing of doses
1 – 4 x daily. 15 – 30 minutes before meals and/or at bedtime (for symptoms during the night).

Adult dosage range
20 – 40mg daily in divided doses.

Onset of effect
15 – 30 minutes.

Duration of action
Up to 10 hours.

Diet advice
None, unless your doctor has advised according to the condition you have.

Storage
Keep in a closed container in a cool, dry place away from reach of children. Protect from light.

Missed dose
Do not take unless you have symptoms. Take the next dose as usual unless you took the last dose less than 2 hours ago.

Stopping the drug
Do not stop the drug without consulting your doctor; symptoms may recur.

Exceeding the dose
An occasional unintentional overdose is unlikely to be a cause for concern. But if you notice unusual symptoms, or if a large overdose has been taken, notify your doctor.

SPECIAL PRECAUTIONS

Be sure to tell your doctor if:
▼ You have long-term liver or kidney problems.
▼ You have a history of gastrointestinal illness.
▼ You are taking other medications.

 Pregnancy
▼ Safety in pregnancy not established. Discuss with your doctor.

 Breast feeding
▼ The drug passes into the breast milk, but at normal doses adverse effects on the baby are unlikely. Discuss with your doctor.

 Infants and children
▼ Not usually prescribed. Occasionally used to treat reflux.

 Over 60
▼ No special problems.

 Driving and hazardous work
▼ Avoid such activities until you have learned how the drug affects you because the drug can cause dizziness.

 Alcohol
▼ No special problems.

POSSIBLE ADVERSE EFFECTS

The most common adverse effects are those on the gastrointestinal system. These usually reduce as treatment continues.

Symptom/effect	Frequency		Discuss with doctor		Stop taking drug now	Call doctor now
	Common	Rare	Only if severe	In all cases		
Abdominal cramps	●		■			
Diarrhoea	●		■			
Dizziness		●			■	
Headaches		●			■	
Tremor		●			■	

PROLONGED USE

Cisapride is normally given for a course of treatment lasting between 4 and 12 weeks depending on the condition being treated.

INTERACTIONS

Strong analgesics Analgesics of the opiate type may reduce the effect of cisapride.

Anticoagulants The effect of anti-coagulants such as warfarin may be increased by cisapride.

CISPLATIN

Brand names Neoplatin
Used in the following combined preparations None

GENERAL INFORMATION

Cisplatin is one of the most effective drugs available to treat cancer of the ovaries or testes. People with cancer of the head, neck, bladder, cervix, and lung have also responded well to cisplatin. Recent research indicates that this drug may be an effective treatment against bone cancer in children. Cisplatin is often given along with other anticancer drugs.

The most common and serious adverse effect of cisplatin is impaired kidney function. To reduce the risk of permanent kidney damage, the drug is usually given only once every four weeks, allowing the kidneys time to recover between courses of treatment. Nausea and vomiting may occur shortly after administration of cisplatin. Because these symptoms may be quite severe, an anti-emetic drug is often given to reduce them.

Damage to hearing is common, and may be more severe in children. Use of this drug may also increase the risk of anaemia, disorders of blood clotting, and infection during treatment.

INFORMATION FOR USERS

This drug is given only under medical supervision and is not for self-administration.

How taken

Injection.

Frequency and timing of doses
Once every 4 weeks (on its own); once daily for 5 days every 3 weeks (in combination with other anticancer drugs).

Adult dosage range
Dosage is determined individually according to body height, weight and response.

Onset of effect
Some adverse effects, such as nausea and vomiting may appear within hours of starting treatment.

Duration of action
Some adverse effects may last for up to 1 week after treatment has stopped.

Diet advice
Prior to treatment it is important that the body is well hydrated. Fluid is usually given by infusion.

Storage
Not applicable. The drug is not normally kept in the home.

Missed dose
Not applicable. The drug is given only in hospital under medical supervision

Stopping the drug
Not applicable. The drug will be stopped under medical supervision.

Exceeding the dose
Overdosage is unlikely since treatment is carefully monitored, and the drug is given intravenously only under close supervision.

POSSIBLE ADVERSE EFFECTS

Most adverse effects appear within a few hours of injection and are carefully monitored in hospital after each dose. Some effects wear off within 24 hours. Nausea and loss of appetite may last for up to a week.

Symptom/effect	Frequency		Discuss with doctor		Stop taking drug now	Call doctor now
	Common	Rare	Only if severe	In all cases		
Nausea/vomiting	●		■			
Loss of appetite/taste	●		■			
Ringing in the ears/hearing loss	●			■		
Breathing difficulties		●		■		▌
Fits		●		■		▌
Wheezing		●		■		▌
Swollen face/rash		●		■		▌

INTERACTIONS

General note A number of drugs increase the adverse effects of cisplatin. Because cisplatin is given only under close medical supervision, these interactions are carefully monitored and the dosage is adjusted accordingly.

SPECIAL PRECAUTIONS

Cisplatin is prescribed only under close medical supervision, taking account of your present condition and medical history.

Pregnancy
▼ Not usually prescribed. Cisplatin may cause birth defects or premature birth. Discuss with your doctor.

Breast feeding
▼ Not advised. The drug passes into the breast milk and may affect the baby adversely. Discuss with your doctor.

Infants and children
▼ Not usually prescribed. The risk of hearing loss is increased.

Over 60
▼ Reduced dose may be necessary. Increased likelihood of adverse effects.

Driving and hazardous work
▼ No known problems.

Alcohol
▼ No known problems.

PROLONGED USE

Prolonged use of this drug increases the risk of damage to the kidneys, nerves, bone marrow and to hearing.

Monitoring Hearing tests and blood checks to monitor kidney function and bone marrow activity are carried out regularly.

CLODRONATE

Brand names Bonefos
Used in the following combined preparations None

GENERAL INFORMATION

Clodronate belongs to the group of drugs called bisphosphonates. It is prescribed to treat high calcium levels that can arise during certain malignant diseases. The drug works by preventing the breakdown of bone, which leads to the excessive levels of calcium in the blood.

Clodronate can be given as an injection (to treat the initially high levels of calcium) and as capsules (as a maintenance treatment). Adverse effects are usually mild and rarely cause significant problems. The effects of the drug are monitored by measuring levels of calcium and other constituents in the blood.

INFORMATION FOR USERS

Your drug prescription is tailored for you. Do not alter dosage without checking with your doctor.

How taken

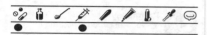

Capsules, injection.

Frequency and timing of doses
1 – 2 x daily. Avoid food for 2 hours before and after taking (capsules).

Adult dosage range
1.6 – 3.2g daily.

Onset of effect
Full effects may not be felt for a few days.

Duration of action
Up to 24 hours. Some effects may persist for several weeks.

Diet advice
Absorption of clodronate is reduced by foods, especially those containing calcium, e.g. dairy products, so the drug should be taken on an empty stomach.

Storage
Keep in a closed container in a cool, dry place out of the reach of children.

Missed dose
Take as soon as you remember. If your next dose is due within 5 hours, take a single dose now and skip the next.

Stopping the drug
Do not stop the drug without consulting your doctor. Stopping the drug may lead to worsening of the underlying condition.

Exceeding the dose
An occasional, unintentional extra dose is unlikely to cause problems. If larger doses have been taken or you notice unusual symptoms, notify your doctor.

SPECIAL PRECAUTIONS

Be sure to tell your doctor if:
▼ You have long-term kidney problems.
▼ You have colitis.
▼ You are taking other medications.

Pregnancy
▼ Safety in pregnancy not established. Discuss with your doctor.

Breast feeding
▼ Safety not established. Discuss with your doctor.

Infants and children
▼ Not recommended.

Over 60
▼ No special problems.

Driving and hazardous work
▼ No special problems.

Alcohol
▼ No special problems.

POSSIBLE ADVERSE EFFECTS

The most common adverse effects are diarrhoea and nausea. However, these symptoms are usually mild. If they are a problem, your doctor may recommend a reduction in dosage.

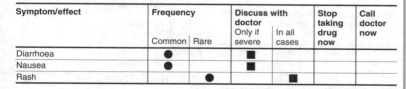

Symptom/effect	Frequency		Discuss with doctor		Stop taking drug now	Call doctor now
	Common	Rare	Only if severe	In all cases		
Diarrhoea	●		■			
Nausea	●		■			
Rash		●		■		

INTERACTIONS

Antacids/iron Antacids and iron should be given at least 2 hours before or after clodronate to minimize effects on absorption.

PROLONGED USE

Monitoring Blood levels of calcium and other constituents will be carried out during treatment.

CLOMIPHENE

Brand names Clomid, Serophene
Used in the following combined preparations None

GENERAL INFORMATION

Clomiphene increases the output of hormones by the pituitary gland, stimulating ovulation (egg release) in women. If hormone levels in the blood fail to rise after the drug is taken, the gland is not working as it should.

For female infertility, tablets are taken for five consecutive days during each menstrual cycle. This stimulates ovulation. If clomiphene fails to stimulate ovulation after several months, other drugs may be prescribed.

Multiple pregnancies (usually twins) occur more commonly in women treated with clomiphene. Adverse effects include an increased risk of ovarian cysts. In rare cases, the ovaries become greatly enlarged, leading to abdominal pain and swelling.

INFORMATION FOR USERS

Your drug prescription is tailored for you. Do not alter dosage without checking with your doctor.

How taken

Tablets.

Frequency and timing of doses
Once daily for 5 days during each menstrual cycle.

Dosage range
50mg daily initially, dose may be increased up to 100mg daily.

Onset of effect
Ovulation occurs 4 – 10 days after the last dose in any cycle. However, it may be several months before this occurs.

Duration of action
5 days.

Diet advice
None.

Storage
Keep in a closed container in a cool, dry place away from reach of children. Protect from light.

Missed dose
Take as soon as you remember. If your next dose is due at this time, take the missed dose and the next scheduled dose together.

Stopping the drug
Take as directed by your doctor. Stopping the drug will reduce the chance of conception.

Exceeding the dose
An occasional unintentional extra dose is unlikely to be a cause for concern. But if you notice unusual symptoms, or if a large overdose has been taken, notify your doctor.

SPECIAL PRECAUTIONS

Be sure to tell your doctor if:
▼ You have long-term liver problems.
▼ You are taking other medications.

Pregnancy
▼ Not prescribed. The drug is stopped as soon as pregnancy occurs.

Breast feeding
▼ Not prescribed.

Infants and children
▼ Not prescribed.

Over 60
▼ Not prescribed.

Driving and hazardous work
▼ Avoid such activities until you have learned how the drug affects you because the drug may cause blurred vision.

Alcohol
▼ Keep consumption low.

POSSIBLE ADVERSE EFFECTS

Most side effects are related to the dose taken. Ovarian enlargement and cyst formation can occur. If this happens the problem usually resolves within a few days or weeks of stopping the drug.

Symptom/effect	Frequency		Discuss with doctor		Stop taking drug now	Call doctor now
	Common	Rare	Only if severe	In all cases		
Hot flushes	●		■			
Abdominal discomfort	●			■		
Breast tenderness		●		■		
Impaired vision		●		■		
Dry skin/hair loss/rash		●	■			
Jaundice		●	■		▲	■

INTERACTIONS

None.

PROLONGED USE

Prolonged use may cause visual impairment.

Monitoring Eye tests may be recommended if symptoms of visual impairment are noticed. Monitoring of body temperature and blood or urine hormone levels are performed regularly to detect signs of ovulation and pregnancy.

CLOMIPRAMINE

Brand names Anafranil, Anafranil SR
Used in the following combined preparations None

GENERAL INFORMATION

Clomipramine belongs to a class of antidepressant drugs known as the tricyclics. It is mainly used in the long-term treatment of depression. It elevates mood, increases physical activity, improves appetite, and restores interest in everyday activities.

Clomipramine is particularly useful in the treatment of irrational fears and obsessive behaviour. Unlike most other tricyclics, clomipramine can be given by injection in severe illness.

In overdose clomipramine may cause coma and dangerously abnormal heart rhythms.

INFORMATION FOR USERS

Your drug prescription is tailored for you. Do not alter dosage without checking with your doctor.

How taken

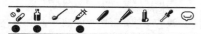

Tablets (SR), capsules, liquid, injection.

Frequency and timing of doses
1 – 4 x daily.

Adult dosage range
10 – 250mg daily.

Onset of effect
Some effects may be felt within a few days, but full antidepressant effect may not be felt for up to 4 weeks.

Duration of action
During prolonged treatment antidepressant effect may last up to 2 weeks.

Diet advice
None.

Storage
Keep in a closed container in a cool, dry place away from reach of children.

Missed dose
Take as soon as you remember. If your next dose is due within 3 hours, take a single dose now and skip the next.

Stopping the drug
An abrupt stop can cause withdrawal symptoms and a recurrence of the original trouble. Consult your doctor, who may supervise a gradual reduction in dosage.

OVERDOSE ACTION

Seek immediate medical advice in all cases. Take emergency action if palpitations are noted or consciousness is lost.

See Drug poisoning emergency guide (p.470).

POSSIBLE ADVERSE EFFECTS

The possible adverse effects of this drug are mainly the result of its *anticholinergic* action, such as dry mouth and constipation. Heart effects occur in some people.

Symptom/effect	Frequency		Discuss with doctor		Stop taking drug now	Call doctor now
	Common	Rare	Only if severe	In all cases		
Drowiness/dizziness	●			■		
Sweating/flushing	●			■		
Dry mouth	●			■		
Blurred vision	●			■		
Constipation	●			■		
Difficulty passing urine		●		■	▲	
Palpitations		●		■	▲	▮

INTERACTIONS

Sedatives All drugs that have sedative effects intensify those of clomipramine.

Anti-epileptic drugs The effects of these drugs can be reduced by clomipramine. The antidepressant effect of clomipramine may be decreased.

Antihypertensive drugs Clomipramine may enhance the effectiveness of some of these drugs.

Monoamine oxidase inhibitors (MAOIs) A serious interaction may occur if these are given with clomipramine.

SPECIAL PRECAUTIONS

Be sure to tell your doctor if:
▼ You have heart problems.
▼ You have had epileptic fits.
▼ You have kidney or liver problems.
▼ You have had glaucoma.
▼ You have thyroid disease.
▼ You have had prostate trouble.
▼ You are taking other medications.

Pregnancy
▼ Safety in pregnancy not established. Discuss with your doctor.

Breast feeding
▼ The drug passes into the breast milk and may affect the baby. Discuss with your doctor.

Infants and children
▼ Not usually prescribed.

Over 60
▼ Increased likelihood of adverse effects. Reduced dose may therefore be necessary.

Driving and hazardous work
▼ Avoid such activities until you have learned how the drug affects you because of the possibility of blurred vision, drowsiness and dizziness.

Alcohol
▼ Avoid. Alcohol may increase the sedative effects of this drug.

Surgery and general anaesthetics
▼ Clomipramine treatment may need to be stopped before you have a general anaesthetic. Discuss this with your doctor or dentist before any operation.

PROLONGED USE

No problems expected.

CLONAZEPAM

Brand name Rivotril
Used in the following combined preparations None

GENERAL INFORMATION

Clonazepam belongs to a group of drugs known as the benzodiazepines, which are mainly used in the treatment of anxiety and insomnia (see p.83). Clonazepam, however, is almost exclusively used as an anticonvulsant to prevent and treat epileptic fits. It is particularly useful for the prevention of brief muscle spasms and absence seizures (petit mal) in children, but other forms of epilepsy, such as sudden flaccidity or fits induced by bright lights, also respond to clonazepam treatment. Being a benzodiazepine, it also has tranquillizing and sedative effects.

Clonazepam is used either on its own or along with other anticonvulsant drugs. Its anticonvulsant effect may begin to wear off after a few months.

INFORMATION FOR USERS

Your drug prescription is tailored for you. Do not alter dosage without checking with your doctor.

How taken

Tablets, injection.

Frequency and timing of doses
1 – 4 x daily

Dosage range
Adults 1mg daily (starting dose), increased gradually to 4 – 8mg daily (maintenance dose).
Children Reduced dose according to age and weight.

Onset of action
Within 1 hour.

Duration of action
Approximately 30 hours.

Diet advice
None.

Storage
Keep in a closed container in a cool, dry place away from reach of children.

Missed dose
No cause for concern, but take as soon as you remember. Take your next dose when it is due.

Stopping the drug
Do not stop the drug without consulting your doctor; symptoms may recur.

Exceeding the dose
An occasional unintentional extra dose is unlikely to cause problems. Larger overdoses may cause unusual drowsiness. Notify your doctor.

SPECIAL PRECAUTIONS

Be sure to tell your doctor if:
▼ You have severe respiratory disease.
▼ You have long-term kidney or liver problems.
▼ You are taking other medications.

 Pregnancy
▼ Safety in pregnancy not established. Discuss with your doctor.

 Breast feeding
▼ The drug passes into the breast milk and may affect the baby. Discuss with your doctor.

 Infants and children
▼ Reduced dose necessary.

 Over 60
▼ Reduced dose may be necessary.

 Driving and hazardous work
▼ Your underlying condition as well as the possibility of drowsiness while taking this drug, may make such activities inadvisable. Discuss with your doctor.

 Alcohol
▼ Avoid. Alcohol may increase the sedative effects of this drug.

POSSIBLE ADVERSE EFFECTS

The principal adverse effects of this drug are related to its sedative and tranquillizing properties. These effects normally diminish after the first few days of treatment and can often be reduced by medically supervised adjustment of dosage.

Symptom/effect	Frequency		Discuss with doctor		Stop taking drug now	Call doctor now
	Common	Rare	Only if severe	In all cases		
Daytime drowsiness	●		■			
Dizziness/unsteadiness	●		■			
Increased salivation	●		■			
Altered behaviour	●			■		
Forgetfulness/confusion		●		■		
Muscle weakness		●		■		

PROLONGED USE

Both beneficial and adverse effects of clonazepam may become less marked during prolonged treatment as the body adapts.

INTERACTIONS

Other anticonvulsants Clonazepam may alter the effects of other anti-convulsants you are taking, and adjustment of dosage or change of drug may be necessary.

Sedatives All drugs that have a sedative effect on the central nervous system are likely to increase the sedative properties of clonazepam. Such drugs include anti-anxiety and sleeping drugs, antihistamines, antidepressants, narcotic analgesics, and antipsychotics.

CLONIDINE

Brand names Catapres, Catapres Perlongets, Dixarit
Used in the following combined preparations None

GENERAL INFORMATION

Clonidine has both central and peripheral actions in the body. It decreases impulses from the brain which keep blood pressure up, and increases activity in nerve pathways which help lower blood pressure.

Clonidine has also been given for other conditions such as migraine, menopausal hot flushes and with-drawal symptoms during drug detoxification. Its main drawback is that when used in the doses required to control blood pressure, there may be a severe rise in blood pressure if doses are missed or if the drug is stopped suddenly. Its use to treat hypertension has largely been superseded by other drugs.

QUICK REFERENCE

Drug group Antihypertensive drug (p.102) and Drug for migraine (p.89)

Overdose danger rating Medium

Dependence rating Low

Prescription needed Yes

Available as generic No

INFORMATION FOR USERS

Your drug prescription is tailored for you. Do not alter dosage without checking with your doctor.

How taken

Tablets, capsules (slow-release), injection.

Frequency and timing of doses
1 – 3 x daily.

Adult dosage range
High blood pressure 0.15 – 1.2mg daily. Doses of up to 2.4mg daily have been used in some resistant cases.
Migraine 100 – 150mcg daily.

Onset of effect
2 – 5 hours (by mouth); 10 minutes (by injection).

Duration of action
6 – 20 hours.

Diet advice
None.

Storage
Keep in a closed container in a cool, dry place away from reach of children. Protect from light.

Missed dose
Take as soon as you remember. If your next dose is due within 2 hours, take a single dose now and skip the next.

Stopping the drug
Do not stop the drug without consulting your doctor, who will supervise a gradual reduction in dosage. Abrupt withdrawal may cause a dangerous rise in blood pressure.

Exceeding the dose
An occasional unintentional extra dose is unlikely to cause problems. You may experience vomiting or drowsiness. Notify your doctor.

SPECIAL PRECAUTIONS

Be sure to tell your doctor if:
▼ You have had depression.
▼ You have poor circulation.
▼ You have coronary artery disease.
▼ You are taking other medications.

Pregnancy
▼ No evidence of risk, but other drugs might be more suitable. Discuss with your doctor.

Breast feeding
▼ The drug passes into the breast milk and may affect the baby. Discuss with your doctor.

Infants and children
▼ Not recommended.

Over 60
▼ No special problems.

Driving and hazardous work
▼ Avoid such activities until you have learned how the drug affects you because the drug can cause drowsiness.

Alcohol
▼ Avoid. Alcohol may increase the sedative effects of this drug.

POSSIBLE ADVERSE EFFECTS

Clonidine may cause drowsiness, dry mouth and constipation. These effects usually decrease after long-term therapy. An adjustment in dosage may help.

Symptom/effect	Frequency		Discuss with doctor		Stop taking drug now	Call doctor now
	Common	Rare	Only if severe	In all cases		
Drowsiness	●		■			
Constipation	●		■			
Dry mouth	●		■			
Dizziness		●			■	
Rash		●			■	
Depression		●			■	
Ankle swelling		●			■	
Cold hands		●			■	
Impotence		●			■	

PROLONGED USE

The more common adverse effects, such as drowsiness, constipation and dry mouth may decrease with long-term use.

INTERACTIONS

Tricyclic antidepressants May reduce the effect of clonidine.

Sedatives The sedating effects of clonidine are likely to be enhanced if other drugs with a sedative effect are taken.

Beta blockers Increased risk of serious rise in blood pressure if clomidine is stopped.

CLOTRIMAZOLE

Brand name Canesten, Masnoderm
Used in the following combined preparations Canesten-HC, Lotriderm

GENERAL INFORMATION

Clotrimazole is an antifungal drug, commonly used for yeast and fungal infections. It is effective for treating tinea (ringworm) infections of the skin, and candida (thrush) infections of the mouth, vagina or penis. The drug is applied in the form of cream, solution or dusting powder to the affected area and inserted as pessaries or cream in vaginal conditions.

Adverse effects from clotrimazole are very rare, although some people may experience burning and irritation on the skin surface where the drug has been applied.

QUICK REFERENCE

Drug group Antifungal drug (p.138)

Overdose danger rating Low

Dependence rating Low

Prescription needed No

Available as generic No

INFORMATION FOR USERS

Your drug prescription is tailored for you. Do not alter dosage without checking with your doctor.

How taken

Solution, pessaries, cream, spray, dusting powder.

Frequency and timing of doses
Vaginal cream 1 – 2 times daily.
Vaginal pessaries Once daily at bedtime.
Solution, skin cream, spray 2 – 3 x daily.

Dosage range
Vaginal cream One applicatorful (5g) per dose.
Pessaries 100 – 500mg per dose.
Skin cream, solution, spray As directed.

Onset of effect
Within 2 – 3 days.

Duration of action
Up to 12 hours.

Diet advice
None.

Storage
Keep in a closed container in a cool, dry place away from reach of children.

Missed dose
No cause for concern, but make up the missed dose or application as soon as you remember.

Stopping the drug
Take the full course. Even if symptoms disappear, the original infection may still be present and symptoms may recur if treatment is stopped too soon.

Exceeding the dose
An occasional unintentional extra dose is unlikely to be a cause for concern. But if a large amount has been swallowed, notify your doctor.

SPECIAL PRECAUTIONS

Be sure to tell your doctor or pharmacist if:
▼ You are taking other medications.

Pregnancy
▼ No evidence of risk to developing baby.

Breast feeding
▼ No evidence of risk.

Infants and children
▼ No special problems.

Over 60
▼ No special problems.

Driving and hazardous work
▼ No known problems.

Alcohol
▼ No known problems.

PROLONGED USE

No problems expected.

POSSIBLE ADVERSE EFFECTS

Clotrimazole rarely causes adverse effects. Skin preparations and vaginal applications may occasionally cause localized burning and irritation.

Symptom/effect	Frequency		Discuss with doctor		Stop taking drug now	Call doctor now
	Common	Rare	Only if severe	In all cases		
Local burning or stinging	●		■			
Skin irritation		●	■			
Rash		●	■		▲	

INTERACTIONS

None known.

CLOZAPINE

Brand name Clozaril
Used in the following combined preparations None

GENERAL INFORMATION

Clozapine is a new type of antipsychotic drug used to treat schizophrenia. It is used only in patients who have not responded to other treatment or who have experienced intolerable side effects with other drugs. The drug helps control severe resistant schizophrenia, helping re-establish a more normal lifestyle. Improvement is gradual, and relief of severe symptoms can take more than three weeks.

Treatment is always started and supervised by a hospital, as all patients must be registered with the Clozaril Patient Monitoring Service (CPMS). This is because the drug can cause a very serious side effect, agranulocytosis (a large fall in the number of white blood cells). Blood tests are performed prior to treatment and regularly thereafter; the drug is supplied only if results are normal.

Clozapine is less likely than other antipsychotics to cause *parkinsonism*.

QUICK REFERENCE

Drug group Antipsychotic (p.85)
Overdose danger rating Medium
Dependence rating Low
Prescription needed Yes
Available as generic No

INFORMATION FOR USERS

This drug is given only under strict medical supervision and continual monitoring.

How taken

Tablets.

Frequency and timing of doses
2 – 3 x daily; a larger dose may be given at night.

Adult dosage range
25 – 900mg daily.

Onset of effect
Gradual. Some effect may appear within 3 – 5 days, but the full beneficial effect may not be felt for over 3 weeks.

Duration of action
Up to 16 hours.

Diet advice
None.

Storage
Keep in a closed container in a cool, dry place away from reach of children.

Missed dose
Take as soon as you remember. If your next dose is due within 2 hours, take a single dose now and skip the next.

Stopping the drug
Do not stop the drug without consulting your doctor; symptoms may recur.

Exceeding the dose
An occasional unintentional extra dose is unlikely to cause problems. Large overdoses may cause unusual drowsiness, fits, and agitation. Notify your doctor.

SPECIAL PRECAUTIONS

Be sure to tell your doctor if:
▼ You have long-term liver or kidney problems.
▼ You have a history of blood disorders.
▼ You have had epileptic fits.
▼ You are taking other medications.

 Pregnancy
▼ Not usually prescribed. Safety not established. Discuss with your doctor.

 Breast feeding
▼ The drug passes into the breast milk and may affect the baby adversely. Discuss with your doctor.

 Infants and children
▼ Not prescribed.

 Over 60s
▼ Adverse effects are more likely. Initial dose is low and is slowly increased.

 Driving and hazardous work
▼ Avoid such activities until you have learned how the drug affects you because the drug can cause drowsiness, dizziness, and blurred vision.

 Alcohol
▼ Avoid. Alcohol may increase the sedative effects of this drug.

POSSIBLE ADVERSE EFFECTS

Clozapine is less likely to cause the parkinsonian side effects (tremor and stiffness) that occur with the use of other antipsychotic drugs. The most serious side effect is agranulocytosis, and strict monitoring is necessary.

Symptom/effect	Frequency		Discuss with doctor		Stop taking drug now	Call doctor now
	Common	Rare	Only if severe	In all cases		
Drowsiness/tiredness	●		■			
Excess saliva	●		■			
Fast heartbeats	●			■		
Dry mouth						
Blurred vision		●		■		
Tremor/muscle rigidity		●	■			
Dizziness/fainting		●	■			
Fever/sore throat		●		■		▌
Fits		●		■		▌

INTERACTIONS

Sedatives All drugs that have a sedative effect on the central nervous system are likely to increase the sedative properties of clozapine.

General note A number of drugs increase the risk of adverse effects on the blood. Do not take other medication without checking with your doctor or pharmacist.

PROLONGED USE

Agranulocytosis may occur, and occasionally liver function may be upset.

Monitoring Blood tests are carried out weekly for the first 18 weeks, and fortnightly thereafter. Liver function tests may also be performed.

CODEINE

Used in the following combined preparations Benylin with Codeine, Codafen-Continus, Codis, Diarrest, Migraleve, Paracodol, Phensedyl, Solpadeine, Solpadol, Syndol, Terpoin, Tylex, Veganin, and others

GENERAL INFORMATION

In common medical use since the beginning of the century, codeine is a mild narcotic analgesic similar to, but weaker than, morphine.

It is primarily used to relieve mild to moderate pain, often in combination with a non-narcotic analgesic, but it is an effective cough suppressant too. It is an ingredient in many non-prescription cough syrups and cold relief preparations.

Like other narcotic drugs, codeine is constipating, a characteristic that sometimes makes it useful in the short-term control of diarrhoea.

Codeine is habit-forming, but addiction seldom occurs if the drug is used for a limited period of time and the recommended dosage followed.

INFORMATION FOR USERS

Follow instructions on the label. Call your doctor if symptoms worsen.

How taken

Tablets, liquid, injection.

Frequency and timing of doses
4 – 6 x daily (pain); every 3 – 4 x daily when necessary (cough); every 4 – 6 hours when necessary (diarrhoea).

Adult dosage range
120 – 240mg daily (pain); 45 – 120mg daily (cough); 30–180mg daily (diarrhoea).

Onset of effect
30 –60 minutes.

Duration of action
4 – 6 hours.

Diet advice
None

Storage
Keep in a closed container in a cool, dry place away from reach of children. Protect from light.

Missed dose
Take as soon as you remember if needed for relief of symptoms. If not needed, do not take the missed dose and return to your normal dose schedule when necessary.

Stopping the drug
Can be safely stopped as soon as you no longer need it.

OVERDOSE ACTION

 Seek immediate medical advice in all cases. Take emergency action if there are symptoms such as slow or irregular breathing, severe drowsiness, or loss of consciousness.

See Drug poisoning emergency guide (p.470).

POSSIBLE ADVERSE EFFECTS

Serious adverse effects are rare with codeine. Constipation occurs especially with prolonged use, but other side effects, such as nausea, vomiting and drowsiness, are not usually troublesome at recommended doses, and usually disappear if the dose is reduced.

Symptom/effect	Frequency		Discuss with doctor		Stop taking drug now	Call doctor now
	Common	Rare	Only if severe	In all cases		
Constipation	●		■			
Nausea/vomiting		●		■		
Drowsiness		●		■		
Dizziness		●		■		
Agitation/restlessness		●		■	▲	
Rash/hives		●		■	▲	
Wheezing/breathlessness		●		■	▲	▮

INTERACTIONS

Sedatives All drugs that have a sedative effect on the central nervous system are likely to increase sedation with codeine.

Such drugs include antidepressants, antipsychotics, sleeping drugs and antihistamines.

SPECIAL PRECAUTIONS

Be sure to consult your doctor or pharmacist before taking this drug if:
▼ You have long-term liver or kidney problems.
▼ You have a lung disorder such as asthma or bronchitis.
▼ You are taking other medications.

 Pregnancy
▼ No evidence of risk, but may adversely affect the baby's breathing if taken during labour.

 Breast feeding
▼ The drug passes into the breast milk, but at normal doses adverse effects on the baby are unlikely. Discuss with your doctor.

 Infants and children
▼ Reduced dose necessary.

 Over 60
▼ Reduced dose may be necessary.

 Driving and hazardous work
▼ Avoid such activities until you have learned how the drug affects you because the drug may cause dizziness and drowsiness.

 Alcohol
▼ Avoid. Alcohol may increase the sedative effects of this drug.

PROLONGED USE

Codeine is normally used only for short-term relief of symptoms. It can be habit-forming if taken for extended periods, especially if higher than average doses are taken.

COLCHICINE

Brand names None
Used in the following combined preparation None

GENERAL INFORMATION

Colchicine, a drug originally extracted from the autumn crocus flower and later synthesized, has been used since the 18th century for gout. Although it has now been to some extent superseded by newer drugs, it is still often used to relieve joint pain and inflammation in acute flare-ups of gout. It is most effective when taken at the first sign of symptoms and almost always produces an improvement. Colchicine is also often given in the first few months of treatment with allopurinol or probenecid (other drugs used for treating gout) because these may at first increase the frequency of gout attacks.

Colchicine is also occasionally prescribed for the relief of symptoms of familial Mediterranean fever (a rare congenital condition).

QUICK REFERENCE

Drug group Drug for gout (p.119)
Overdose danger rating High
Dependence rating Low
Prescription needed Yes
Available as generic Yes

INFORMATION FOR USERS

Your drug prescription is tailored for you. Do not alter dosage without checking with your doctor.

How taken

Tablets.

Frequency and timing of doses
Prevention of gout attacks 2 – 3 x daily.
Relief of gout attacks Every 2 – 3 hours.

Adult dosage range
Prevention of gout attacks 1 – 1.5mg daily.
Relief of gout attacks 1mg initially, followed by 0.5mg every 2 – 3 hours, until relief of pain, vomiting or diarrhoea occurs, or until a total dose of 10mg is reached. This course must not be repeated within 3 days.

Onset of effect
Relief of symptoms in an attack of gout may be felt in 6 – 24 hours. Full effect in gout prevention may not be felt for several days.

Duration of action
Up to 2 hours. Some effect may last longer.

Diet advice
Certain foods are known to make gout worse. Discuss with your doctor.

Storage
Keep in a closed container in a cool, dry place away from reach of children. Protect from light.

Missed dose
Take as soon as you remember. If your next dose is due within 30 minutes, take a single dose now and skip the next.

Stopping the drug
When taking colchicine frequently during an acute attack, stop if diarrhoea or abdominal pain develop. In other cases do not stop without consulting your doctor.

OVERDOSE ACTION

Seek immediate medical advice in all cases; some reactions can be fatal. Take emergency action if severe nausea, vomiting, bloody diarrhoea, severe abdominal pain, or loss of consciousness occur.

See Drug poisoning emergency guide (p.470).

SPECIAL PRECAUTIONS

Be sure to tell your doctor if:
▼ You have long-term liver or kidney problems.
▼ You have heart problems.
▼ You have a blood disorder.
▼ You have stomach ulcers.
▼ You have chronic inflammation of the bowel.
▼ You are taking other medications.

 Pregnancy
▼ Not usually prescribed. May cause defects in the unborn baby. Discuss with your doctor.

 Breast feeding
▼ The drug passes into the breast milk and may affect the baby. Discuss with your doctor.

 Infants and children
▼ Not recommended.

 Over 60
▼ Increased likelihood of adverse effects.

 Driving and hazardous work
▼ No special problems.

 Alcohol
▼ Avoid. Alcohol may increase stomach irritation caused by colchicine.

POSSIBLE ADVERSE EFFECTS

The appearance of any symptom that may be an adverse effect of the drug is a sign that you should stop the drug until you have received further medical advice.

Symptom/effect	Frequency		Discuss with doctor		Stop taking drug now	Call doctor now
	Common	Rare	Only if severe	In all cases		
Nausea/vomiting	●			■	▲	
Diarrhoea/abdominal pain	●			■	▲	
Numbness and tingling		●		■	▲	
Unusual bleeding/bruising		●		■	▲	
Rash		●		■	▲	

INTERACTIONS

Cyclosporin Taking cyclosporin with colchicine may lead to adverse effects on the kidney.

PROLONGED USE

Prolonged use of this drug may lead to hair loss, rashes, tingling in the hands and feet, muscle pain and weakness, and blood disorders.

Monitoring Periodic blood checks are usually required.

CONJUGATED OESTROGENS

Brand name Premarin
Used in the following combined preparations Prempak C

GENERAL INFORMATION

Conjugated oestrogen preparations consist of naturally occurring oestrogens similar to those found in the urine of pregnant mares.

Given by mouth, they are used to relieve menopausal symptoms such as hot flushes and sweating. They are also used to treat and prevent osteoporosis (brittle bones), which may occur after the menopause, and are sometimes used in the treatment of breast cancer.

As replacement therapy, conjugated oestrogens are usually taken on a cyclic dosing schedule, often in conjunction with a progestogen to simulate the hormonal changes of a normal menstrual cycle. They are also prescribed in the form of vaginal cream to relieve pain and dryness of the vagina or vulva after the menopause.

QUICK REFERENCE

Drug group Female sex hormone (p.147) and drug for bone disorders (p.122).
Overdose danger rating Low
Dependence rating Low
Prescription needed Yes
Available as generic No

INFORMATION FOR USERS

Your drug prescription is tailored for you. Do not alter dosage without checking with your doctor.

How taken

Tablets, cream.

Frequency and timing of doses
Tablets 1 – 3 x daily.
Cream Once daily.

Adult dosage range
Replacement therapy 0.625 – 1.25mg daily (tablets); 1 – 2g daily (cream).
Breast cancer up to 30mg daily.

Onset of effect
5 – 20 days.

Duration of action
1 – 2 days.

Diet advice
None.

Storage
Keep in a closed container in a cool, dry place away from reach of children.

Missed dose
Take as soon as you remember.

Stopping the drug
Do not stop the drug without consulting your doctor; symptoms may recur.

Exceeding the dose
An occasional unintentional extra dose is unlikely to be a cause for concern. But if you notice unusual symptoms, or if a large overdose has been taken, notify your doctor.

SPECIAL PRECAUTIONS

Be sure to tell your doctor if:
▼ You have heart failure or high blood pressure.
▼ You have had blood clots or a stroke.
▼ You have liver or kidney problems.
▼ You have diabetes.
▼ You have asthma.
▼ You suffer from migraine or epilepsy.
▼ You are taking other medications.

 Pregnancy
▼ Not prescribed. May adversely affect the baby. Discuss with your doctor.

 Breast feeding
▼ Not prescribed. The drug passes into the breast milk and may inhibit the flow of milk. Discuss with your doctor.

 Infants and children
▼ Not prescribed.

 Over 60
▼ No special problems.

 Driving and hazardous work
▼ No known problems.

 Alcohol
▼ No known problems.

Surgery and general anaesthetics
▼ Conjugated oestrogens may need to be stopped several weeks before you have surgery. Discuss with your doctor.

POSSIBLE ADVERSE EFFECTS

The most common adverse effects of conjugated oestrogens are similar to symptoms that occur in the early stages of pregnancy, and generally diminish or disappear after 2 or 3 months of treatment. Sudden, sharp pain in the chest, groin or legs may indicate an abnormal blood clot and requires urgent medical attention.

Symptom/effect	Frequency		Discuss with doctor		Stop taking drug now	Call doctor now
	Common	Rare	Only if severe	In all cases		
Nausea/vomiting	●		■			
Breast swelling/tenderness	●		■			
Increase or decrease in weight	●		■			
Reduced sex drive		●	■			
Depression		●		■		
Premenstrual-syndrome		●		■		
Pain in chest/groin/legs		●		■		■

INTERACTIONS

Tobacco smoking increases the risk of serious adverse effects on the heart and circulation with conjugated oestrogens.

Oral anticoagulants Conjugated oestrogens reduce the anticoagulant effect of these drugs.

PROLONGED USE

There is a slightly higher risk of breast cancer and cancer of the uterus when oestrogens are used long-term. The risk of gallbladder disease is also increased.

Monitoring Physical examinations and blood pressure checks may be needed.

CO-PROXAMOL

Brand names Cosalgesic, Distalgesic
Used in the following combined preparations (Co-proxamol is a combination of two drugs)

GENERAL INFORMATION

Co-proxamol is the name for a combination of the non-narcotic analgesic drug paracetamol and a mild narcotic analgesic dextropropoxyphene. Co-proxamol is used for the relief of mild to moderate pain that has not responded to paracetamol or other non-narcotic analgesics alone.

Because the drug contains a narcotic, it can cause a variety of side effects common to drugs of that group:

dizziness, nausea, mild euphoria and constipation. Co-proxamol may also be habit-forming if taken regularly for an extended period. Overdose with co-proxamol is dangerous because dextropropoxyphene may interefere with breathing if taken in excess, and overdose of paracetamol may cause irreversible damage to the liver and kidneys.

QUICK REFERENCE

Drug group Narcotic analgesic (p.80)
Overdose danger rating High
Dependence rating Medium
Prescription needed Yes
Available as generic Yes

INFORMATION FOR USERS

Your drug prescription is tailored for you. Do not alter dosage without checking with your doctor.

How taken

Tablets.

Frequency and timing of doses
3 – 4 x daily as necessary.

Adult dosage range
2 tablets per dose, up to a maximum of 8 tablets daily.

Onset of effect
30 – 60 minutes.

Duration of action
6 hours.

Diet advice
None.

Storage
Keep in a closed container in a cool, dry place away from reach of children.

Missed dose
Take as soon as you remember if needed for the relief of pain. Do not take doses less than 4 hours apart.

Stopping the drug
If you have been taking the drug regularly for less than 4 weeks, it can be safely stopped as soon as you no longer need it. If you have been regularly taking the drug longer than this, your doctor may recommend a gradual reduction in dosage.

OVERDOSE ACTION

 Seek immediate medical advice in all cases. Take emergency action if irregular breathing, drowsiness or loss of consciousness occur.

See Drug poisoning emergency guide (p.470).

SPECIAL PRECAUTIONS

Be sure to tell your doctor if:
▼ You have long-term liver or kidney problems.
▼ You have had problems with drug or alcohol abuse.
▼ You have a lung disorder such as asthma or bronchitis.
▼ You suffer from depression.
▼ You are taking other medications.

 Pregnancy
▼ Safety in pregnancy not established. Discuss with your doctor.

 Breast feeding
▼ The drug passes into the breast milk and may affect the baby. Discuss with your doctor.

 Infants and children
▼ Not recommended.

 Over 60
▼ Reduced dose necessary.

 Driving and hazardous work
▼ Avoid such activities until you have learned how the drug affects you because the drug can cause drowsiness and dizziness.

 Alcohol
▼ Avoid. Alcohol may increase the sedative effects of this drug.

POSSIBLE ADVERSE EFFECTS

Serious adverse effects are rare with this drug. Headache, dizziness and nausea may be reduced by lying down after each dose or by reducing the dosage.

Symptom/effect	Frequency		Discuss with doctor		Stop taking drug now	Call doctor now
	Common	Rare	Only if severe	In all cases		
Dizziness/drowsiness	●		■			
Constipation		●	■			
Nausea/vomiting	●		■			
Euphoria		●	■		▲	
Rash		●		■	▲	

PROLONGED USE

Co-proxamol is not usually prescribed long term. It can be habit-forming if taken for extended periods and a higher dose may be needed to have the same effect as your body adapts to the drug.

INTERACTIONS

General note All drugs that have a sedative effect are likely to increase the sedative properties of co-proxamol. Such drugs include sleeping drugs, anti-anxiety drugs and antidepressants .

Carbamazepine Co-proxamol can enhance the effects of carbamazepine.

Oral anticoagulants Co-proxamol may increase the anticoagulant effect of these drugs.

CO-TRIMOXAZOLE

Brand names Bactrim, Chemotrim, Comixco, Comox, Fectrim, Laratrim, Septrin
Used in the following combined preparations (Co-trimoxazole is a combination of trimethoprim and sulphamethoxazole)

GENERAL INFORMATION

Co-trimoxazole is an antibacterial drug that is a combination of one part trimethoprim and five parts sulpha-methoxazole. It is prescribed for the prevention and treatment of urinary tract infections and the treatment of infections of the respiratory tract, gastro-intestinal tract, skin and ear. Co-trimoxazole is also used to treat prostatitis, gonorrhoea and pneumocystis pneumonia. Treatment is usually continued for at least five days and should not be stopped sooner, otherwise the infection is likely to recur.

The side effects of co-trimoxazole are a combination of those caused by the two antibacterial drugs it contains. These can be nausea, vomiting, sore tongue, rash and rarely blood disorders and jaundice.

QUICK REFERENCE

Drug group Antibacterial drug (p.131)

Overdose danger rating Medium

Dependence rating Low

Prescription needed Yes

Available as generic Yes

INFORMATION FOR USERS

Your drug prescription is tailored for you. Do not alter dosage without checking with your doctor.

How taken

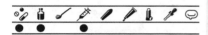

Tablets, liquid, injection.

Frequency and timing of doses
Normally 2 x daily, preferably with food.

Adult dosage range
Usually 4 – 6 tablets daily (each standard tablet is 480mg). Higher doses are required for the treatment of pneumocystis pneumonia.

Onset of effect
1 – 4 hours.

Duration of action
12 hours.

Diet advice
Drink plenty of fluids, particularly in warm weather.

Storage
Keep in a closed container in a cool, dry place away from reach of children. Protect from light.

Missed dose
Take as soon as you remember. If your next dose is due at this time, double the usual dose to make up the missed dose.

Stopping the drug
Take the full course. Even if you feel better the original infection may still be present and symptoms may recur if treatment is stopped too soon.

Exceeding the dose
An occasional unintentional extra dose is unlikely to be a cause for concern. Large overdoses may cause nausea, vomiting, dizziness and confusion. Notify your doctor.

SPECIAL PRECAUTIONS

Be sure to tell your doctor if:
▼ You have long-term liver or kidney problems.
▼ You have a blood disorder.
▼ You have glucose-6-phosphate dehydrogenase (G6PD) deficiency.
▼ You are allergic to sulphonamide drugs.
▼ You suffer from porphyria.
▼ You are taking other medications.

 Pregnancy
▼ Not usually prescribed. May cause defects in the baby. Discuss with your doctor.

 Breast feeding
▼ The drug passes into the breast milk, but at normal doses adverse effects on the baby are unlikely. Discuss with your doctor.

 Infants and children
▼ Not recommended in infants under 6 weeks old. Reduced dose necessary in older children.

 Over 60
▼ Side effects are more likely. Used only when necessary.

 Driving and hazardous work
▼ No known problems.

 Alcohol
▼ No known problems.

POSSIBLE ADVERSE EFFECTS

Side effects can be caused by either the trimethoprim or the sulphamethoxazole ingredient of this preparation. The most common problems are nausea and rash.

Symptom/effect	Frequency		Discuss with doctor		Stop taking drug now	Call doctor now
	Common	Rare	Only if severe	In all cases		
Diarrhoea		●	■			
Nausea/vomiting	●			■		
Rash/itching	●			■	▲	▮
Sore tongue		●		■		
Headache		●		■		
Jaundice		●		■		▮

INTERACTIONS

Warfarin Co-trimoxazole may increase its anticoagulant effect; the dose of warfarin may have to be reduced.

Phenytoin Co-trimoxazole may cause a build-up of phenytoin in the body; the dose of phenytoin may have to be reduced.

Oral antidiabetic drugs Co-trimoxazole may increase the blood sugar lowering effect of these drugs.

Cyclosporin Taking cyclosporin with co-trimoxazole can impair kidney function.

PROLONGED USE

Long-term use of this drug may lead to folic acid deficiency which, in turn, can cause a blood abnormality. Folic acid supplements may be prescribed.

Monitoring Periodic blood tests to monitor blood composition are usually carried out.

CYCLOPENTHIAZIDE

Brand name Navidrex
Used in the following combined preparations Navispare, Trasidrex

GENERAL INFORMATION

Cyclopenthiazide belongs to the thiazide group of diuretic drugs that remove excess water from the body and reduce oedema (fluid retention) in people with congestive heart failure, kidney and liver disorders, and pre-menstrual syndrome.

Cyclopenthiazide is also used to treat high blood pressure (see Antihypertensive drugs, p.102). Cyclopenthiazide increases loss of potassium in the urine which can cause a variety of symptoms (see p.99), and increases the likelihood of irregular heart rhythms, particularly if you are taking drugs such as digoxin. A potassium supplement is often prescribed in combination with cyclopenthiazide.

QUICK REFERENCE

Drug group Thiazide diuretic (p.99)

Overdose danger rating Low

Dependence rating Low

Prescription needed Yes

Available as generic No

INFORMATION FOR USERS

Your drug prescription is tailored for you. Do not alter dosage without checking with your doctor.

How taken

Tablets.

Frequency and timing of doses
Once daily.

Adult dosage range
0.25 – 1.5mg daily.

Onset of effect
Within 2 hours.

Duration of action
6 – 12 hours.

Diet advice
Use of this drug may reduce potassium in the body. Eat plenty of fresh fruit and vegetables.

Storage
Keep in a closed container in a cool, dry place away from reach of children.

Missed dose
No cause for concern, but take as soon as you remember. However, if it is late in the day do not take the missed dose, or you may need to get up during the night to pass urine. Take the next scheduled dose as usual.

Stopping the drug
Do not stop the drug without consulting your doctor; symptoms may recur.

Exceeding the dose
An occasional unintentional extra dose is unlikely to be a cause for concern. But if you notice any unusual symptoms, or if a large overdose has been taken, notify your doctor.

SPECIAL PRECAUTIONS

Be sure to tell your doctor if:
▼ You have long-term kidney or liver problems.
▼ You have had gout.
▼ You have diabetes.
▼ You are taking other medications.

 Pregnancy
▼ Safety in pregnancy not established. Discuss with your doctor.

 Breast feeding
▼ The drug passes into the breast milk, but at normal doses adverse effects on the baby are unlikely. Discuss with your doctor.

 Infants and children
▼ Not usually prescribed. Reduced dose necessary.

 Over 60s
▼ Increased likelihood of adverse effects.

 Driving and hazardous work
▼ No special problems.

 Alcohol
▼ Keep consumption low. Cyclopenthiazide increases the likelihood of dehydration and hangovers after consumption of alcohol.

POSSIBLE ADVERSE EFFECTS

Most effects are caused by excessive loss of potassium. This can usually be put right by taking a potassium supplement. In rare cases gout may occur in susceptible people, and certain forms of diabetes may become more difficult to control.

Symptom/effect	Frequency		Discuss with doctor		Stop taking drug now	Call doctor now
	Common	Rare	Only if severe	In all cases		
Diarrhoea or constipation		●	■			
Loss of appetite	●		■			
Nausea	●				■	
Leg cramp/muscle weakness		●			■	
Headache/dizziness		●			■	
Rash		●			■	▲

INTERACTIONS

Non-steroidal anti-inflammatory drugs Some of these drugs may reduce the diuretic effect of cyclopenthiazide whose dosage may need to be adjusted.

Digoxin The effects of digoxin may be increased if excessive potassium is lost.

Corticosteroids These drugs further increase the loss of potassium from the body when taken with cyclopenthiazide.

Lithium Cyclopenthiazide may increase lithium levels in the blood, leading to a risk of serious adverse effects.

PROLONGED USE

Excessive loss of potassium may result. The drug occasionally causes reduced levels of red blood cells and platelets.

Monitoring Blood tests may be performed periodically to check kidney function and levels of potassium.

CYCLOPHOSPHAMIDE

Brand name Endoxana
Used in the following combined preparations None

GENERAL INFORMATION

Cyclophosphamide belongs to the group of anticancer drugs known as alkylating agents. It is used for a wide range of cancers including leukaemias, lymphomas (lymph gland cancers), and solid tumours particularly of the lung and breast. Cyclophosphamide is also used in certain malignant conditions occurring in children. It is commonly given together with other drugs to treat cancer or with radiotherapy.

Cyclophosphamide causes nausea, vomiting, and loss of hair; it can affect the heart, lungs, liver and bladder. Because cyclophosphamide often reduces blood cell production, the drug may lead to abnormal bleeding and increased risk of infection, and it can reduce fertility in men.

QUICK REFERENCE

Drug group Anticancer drug (p.154)
Overdose danger rating Medium
Dependence rating Low
Prescription needed Yes
Available as generic Yes

INFORMATION FOR USERS

Your drug prescription is tailored for you. Do not alter dosage without checking with your doctor.

How taken

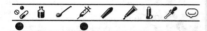

Tablets, injection.

Frequency and timing of doses
Varies from once daily to every 20 days, depending on the condition being treated.

Dosage range
Dosage is determined individually according to the nature of the condition, body weight and response.

Onset of effect
Some effects may appear within hours of starting treatment. Full beneficial effects may not be felt for up to 6 weeks.

Duration of action
Several weeks.

Diet advice
High fluid intake with frequent bladder emptying is recommended. This will usually prevent the drug causing bladder irritation.

Storage
Keep in a closed container in a cool, dry place away from reach of children. Protect from light.

Missed dose
Injections are given only in hospital. If you are taking tablets, take the missed dose as soon as you remember. If your next dose is due within 6 hours, take a single dose now and skip the next. Tell your doctor that you missed a dose.

Stopping the drug
The drug will be stopped under medical supervision (injection). Do not stop taking the drug without consulting your doctor (tablets); stopping the drug may lead to worsening of the underlying condition.

Exceeding the dose
An occasional unintentional extra dose is unlikely to cause problems. Large overdoses may cause nausea, vomiting, and bladder damage. Notify your doctor.

SPECIAL PRECAUTIONS

Cyclophosphamide is prescribed only under close medical supervision, taking account of your present condition and medical history.

Pregnancy
▼ Not usually prescribed. May cause birth defects. Discuss with your doctor.

Breast feeding
▼ Not advised. The drug passes into the breast milk and may affect the baby adversely. Discuss with your doctor.

Infants and children
▼ Reduced dose necessary.

Over 60
▼ No special problems.

Driving and hazardous work
▼ No known problems.

Alcohol
▼ No problems expected, but avoid excessive amounts.

PROLONGED USE

Prolonged use of this drug may reduce the production of blood cells.

Monitoring Periodic checks on blood composition and on all effects of the drug are usually required.

POSSIBLE ADVERSE EFFECTS

Cyclophosphamide often causes nausea and vomiting, which usually diminish as your body adjusts. Also, women often experience irregular periods. Blood in the urine may be a sign of bladder damage and requires prompt medical attention.

Symptom/effect	Frequency		Discuss with doctor		Stop taking drug now	Call doctor now
	Common	Rare	Only if severe	In all cases		
Nausea/vomiting	●		■			
Hair loss	●		■			
Irregular menstruation	●			■		
Mouth ulcers		●		■		
Bloodstained urine		●		■		▮

INTERACTIONS

Allopurinol This drug may increase the risk of toxic effects caused by cyclophosphamide.

CYCLOSPORIN

Brand name Sandimmun
Used in the following combined preparations None

GENERAL INFORMATION

Cyclosporin was introduced in 1984. It belongs to a group of drugs known as immunosuppressants. These drugs suppress the body's natural defences against infection and foreign cells. This action is of particular use following organ transplants, when the immune system may start to reject the transplanted organ unless the immune system is controlled.

Cyclosporin is now widely used following many different types of transplant surgery, including heart, kidney, bone marrow, liver, and pancreas. Its use has considerably reduced the risk of tissue rejection. Cyclosporin is sometimes used to treat severe psoriasis when other treatments have failed.

Because cyclosporin reduces the effectiveness of the immune system, people being treated with this drug are more susceptible than usual to infections. Cyclosporin can also cause kidney damage.

It is important not to make dose changes on your own. Ask your pharmacist for a patient information leaflet printed by the manufacturer.

INFORMATION FOR USERS

Your drug prescription is tailored for you. Do not alter dosage without checking with your doctor.

How taken

Capsules, liquid, injection.

Frequency and timing of doses
1 – 2 x daily.

Adult dosage range
Dosage is calculated on an individual basis according to age and weight.

Onset of effect
Within 12 hours.

Duration of action
Up to 3 days.

Diet advice
Avoid high-potassium foods and potassium supplements.

Storage
Capsules to be left in blister pack until required. Keep in a closed container in a cool, dry place away from reach of children. Do not refrigerate.

Missed dose
Take as soon as you remember. If your dose is more than 36 hours late, consult your doctor.

Stopping the drug
Do not stop taking the drug without consulting your doctor; stopping the drug may lead to transplant rejection.

Exceeding the dose
An occasional unintentional dose is unlikely to cause problems. Large overdoses may cause headaches and affect kidney function. Notify your doctor.

POSSIBLE ADVERSE EFFECTS

The most common adverse effects are gum swelling, excessive hair growth, nausea and vomiting, and tremor. Headache and muscle cramps may also occur. Less common effects are diarrhoea, facial swelling, flushing, "pins and needles" sensations, rash, and itching.

Symptom/effect	Frequency		Discuss with doctor		Stop taking drug now	Call doctor now
	Common	Rare	Only if severe	In all cases		
Increased body hair	●		■			
Nausea	●			■		
Tremor	●			■		
Swelling of gums	●			■		

INTERACTIONS

General note Cyclosporin may interact with a large number of drugs. Check with your doctor or pharmacist before taking any new prescription or over-the-counter medications.

SPECIAL PRECAUTIONS

Cyclosporin is prescribed only under close medical supervision, taking account of your present condition and medical history.

Pregnancy
▼ Not usually prescribed. Safety in pregnancy not established. Discuss with your doctor.

Breast feeding
▼ Not recommended. The drug passes into the breast milk and safety has not been established. Discuss with your doctor.

Infants and children
▼ Safety not established; used only with great caution.

Over 60s
▼ Reduced dose may be necessary.

Driving and hazardous work
▼ No known problems.

Alcohol
▼ No known problems.

PROLONGED USE

Long-term use, especially in high doses, can affect kidney and/or liver function. It may reduce numbers of white blood cells, thus increasing susceptibility to infection.

Monitoring Regular checks on blood samples are normally carried out to measure cyclosporin levels and to monitor blood composition, as well as kidney and liver function.

CYPROTERONE ACETATE

Brand names Androcur, Cyprostat
Used in the following combined preparation Dianette

GENERAL INFORMATION

Cyproterone acetate is a synthetic sex hormone that blocks the action of male sex hormones (p.146). It has effects similar to those of progesterone, a natural female sex hormone (p.147).

The drug is used on its own as part of the treatment of cancer of the prostate gland. It is also occasionally used to alter sexual behaviour in male sexual deviants.

Cyproterone is given in a combined preparation with an oestrogen drug in the treatment of severe acne in women who have not responded to antibiotics. This preparation is also used to reduce excessive hair growth (hirsutism) in women. Combined with oestrogen, cyproterone has a contraceptive effect, but it is not prescribed as an oral contraceptive unless other reasons for taking the drug are present. (See also Oral contraceptives, p.161.)

The drug may reduce sperm production and thus cause infertility in men, but this normally corrects itself after drug treatment is stopped.

QUICK REFERENCE

Drug group Synthetic sex hormone used in the treatment of acne (p.177)
Overdose danger rating Low
Dependence rating Low
Prescription needed Yes
Available as generic No

INFORMATION FOR USERS

Your drug prescription is tailored for you. Do not alter dosage without checking with your doctor.

How taken

Tablets.

Frequency and timing of doses
2 x daily (sexual deviation); 2 – 3 x daily (prostate cancer); once daily for 21 days each month (acne).

Adult dosage range
100mg daily (sexual deviation); 300mg daily (prostate cancer); 2mg daily (acne).

Onset of effect
Beneficial effect may not be noticed for several months.

Duration of action
24 hours.

Diet advice
None.

Storage
Keep in a closed container in a cool, dry place away from reach of children.

Missed dose
Take as soon as you remember. Women relying on the drug for contraception should follow the advice under What to do if you miss a pill (p.163).

Stopping the drug
Do not stop taking the drug without consulting your doctor; stopping the drug may lead to worsening of the underlying condition and contraceptive protection will be lost.

Exceeding the dose
An occasional unintentional extra dose is unlikely to be a cause for concern. But if you notice unusual symptoms, or if a large overdose has been taken, notify your doctor.

POSSIBLE ADVERSE EFFECTS

The most common adverse effects of cyproterone – breast tenderness and weight changes – usually diminish during continued treatment.

Symptom/effect	Frequency		Discuss with doctor		Stop taking drug now	Call doctor now
	Common	Rare	Only if severe	In all cases		
Breast tenderness/enlargement	●		■			
Weight changes	●		■			
Shortness of breath		●	■			
Tiredness/fatigue	●		■			
Changes in hair pattern/growth		●	■			

INTERACTIONS

None.

SPECIAL PRECAUTIONS

Be sure to tell your doctor if:
▼ You have a long-term liver problem.
▼ You suffer from depression.
▼ You have had blood clots.
▼ You have diabetes.
▼ You are taking other medications.

 Pregnancy
▼ Not usually prescribed. May cause female characteristics in a male baby. Discuss with your doctor.

 Breast feeding
▼ The drug passes into the breast milk and may affect the baby. Discuss with your doctor.

 Infants and children
▼ Not prescribed.

 Over 60
▼ No special problems.

 Driving and hazardous work
▼ Avoid such activities until you have learned how the drug affects you because it can cause tiredness.

 Alcohol
▼ Keep consumption low. Alcohol may reduce the beneficial effects of cyproterone.

PROLONGED USE

Cyproterone may occasionally cause *anaemia* or liver damage in long-term use.

Monitoring Blood tests to check levels of blood cells and liver function may be carried out periodically.

DANAZOL

Brand name Danol
Used in the following combined preparations None

GENERAL INFORMATION

Danazol is a synthetic steroid hormone that inhibits certain hormones called pituitary gonadotrophins. It has a number of effects on the endocrine system.

It is used in a range of conditions including endometriosis (a condition where fragments of endometrial tissue grow outside the uterus), menstrual disorders such as menorrhagia, and some cases of breast pain and to reduce breast swelling in men (gynaecomastia). It has also been used, long term, to treat hereditary angioedema (a rare disorder that causes facial swelling).

Danazol is also used to relieve pain, tenderness, and lumpiness in the breast caused by fibrocystic disease.

Danazol treatment commonly disrupts normal menstrual periods and in some cases periods may stop altogether. Other adverse effects include nausea, dizziness, rash, and flushing. Women taking high doses may notice unusual hair growth and deepening of the voice.

INFORMATION FOR USERS

Your drug prescription is tailored for you. Do not alter dosage without checking with your doctor.

How taken

Capsules.

Frequency and timing of doses
2 – 4 x daily.

Adult dosage range
200 – 800mg daily, depending on the condition being treated, its severity, and the response to the drug.

Onset of effect
Some effects occur after a few days. Full beneficial effects may take some months.

Duration of action
1 – 2 days.

Diet advice
None.

Storage
Keep in a closed container in a cool, dry place away from reach of children.

Missed dose
Take as soon as you remember. If your next dose is due within 2 hours, take a single dose now and skip the next.

Stopping the drug
Do not stop the drug without consulting your doctor; symptoms may recur.

Exceeding the dose
An occasional unintentional extra dose is unlikely to cause problems. If you notice unusual symptoms, or if a large overdose has been taken, notify your doctor.

SPECIAL PRECAUTIONS

Be sure to tell your doctor if:
▼ You have long-term liver or kidney problems.
▼ You have heart disease.
▼ You have had epileptic fits.
▼ You suffer from unexplained vaginal bleeding.
▼ You have diabetes mellitus.
▼ You are taking other medications.

 Pregnancy
▼ Not prescribed. May cause masculine characteristics in a female baby. Pregnancy should be avoided for 3 months following cessation of treatment.

 Breast feeding
▼ The drug passes into the breast milk and may affect the baby. Discuss with your doctor.

 Infants and children
▼ Not recommended.

 Over 60
▼ Unlikely to be required.

 Driving and hazardous work
▼ No known problems.

 Alcohol
▼ No known problems.

POSSIBLE ADVERSE EFFECTS

Danazol rarely causes adverse effects in low doses. Adverse effects from higher doses such as acne, weight gain, and nausea are the result of hormonal changes. Voice changes and unusual hair growth in women are largely reversed after treatment.

Symptom/effect	Frequency		Discuss with doctor		Stop taking drug now	Call doctor now
	Common	Rare	Only if severe	In all cases		
Swollen feet/ankles	●		■			
Weight gain	●		■			
Nausea/dizziness	●		■			
Acne/oily skin	●		■			
Women only						
Unusual hair growth and loss	●			■		
Reduced breast size		●	■			
Voice changes		●		■		

INTERACTIONS

Oral anticoagulants Danazol may increase their effects.

Oral antidiabetic drugs Danazol may reduce their effects.

Anticonvulsants The effects of these drugs may be altered by danazol.

PROLONGED USE

This drug is normally taken for 3 to 9 months depending on the condition being treated. There is a slight risk of liver damage. See also Possible adverse effects, left.

Monitoring Periodic liver function tests may be carried out.

DAPSONE

Brand names None
Used in the following combined preparation Maloprim

GENERAL INFORMATION

Dapsone is an effective treatment for leprosy. It is prescribed for all forms of the disease, in combination with other drugs such as rifampicin. For tuberculoid leprosy, treatment should be continued for at least two years. For lepromatous leprosy, lifelong treatment may sometimes be necessary. Another use of dapsone is in combination with pyrimethamine (Maloprim) for the prevention of malaria.

Dapsone is also used to treat dermatitis herpetiformis. This skin condition often occurs with coeliac disease, in which the bowel is abnormally sensitive to gluten (a wheat protein). In combination with a gluten-free diet, dapsone improves the skin condition.

Side effects are rare with dapsone, even during prolonged treatment. The most serious adverse effect is haemolytic anaemia. Periodic blood tests are recommended to detect early signs of this disorder.

INFORMATION FOR USERS

Your drug prescription is tailored for you. Do not alter dosage without checking with your doctor.

How taken

Tablets.

Frequency and timing of doses
Once daily (leprosy); 3 – 4 x daily (dermatitis herpetiformis).

Dosage range
Adults 50 – 100mg daily (leprosy); 50mg initially increased up to 400mg daily. The dose is reduced to a minimum as soon as possible. Sometimes this is as low as 50mg weekly (dermatitis herpetiformis). *Children* Reduced dose according to age and weight.

Onset of effect
Within a few weeks (leprosy); 1 – 3 days (dermatitis herpetiformis).

Duration of action
30 – 150 hours.

Diet advice
A gluten-free diet may be recommended for dermatitis herpetiformis sufferers.

Storage
Keep in a closed container in a cool, dry place away from reach of children. Protect from light.

Missed dose
Take as soon as you remember. If your doses are scheduled 3 – 4 times daily, and your next dose is due within 2 hours, take a single dose now and skip the next. If your doses are scheduled once daily, and your next dose is due within 8 hours, take a single dose now and skip the next.

Stopping the drug
Do not stop the drug without consulting your doctor; symptoms may recur.

Exceeding the dose
An occasional unintentional extra dose is unlikely to cause problems. Large overdoses may cause nausea, vomiting, dizziness, and headache. Notify your doctor.

SPECIAL PRECAUTIONS

Be sure to tell your doctor if:
▼ You have long-term liver or kidney problems.
▼ You have glucose-6-phosphate dehydrogenase (G6PD) deficiency or another blood disorder.
▼ You are allergic to sulphonamides.
▼ You are taking other medications.

 Pregnancy
▼ Safety in pregnancy not established. If dapsone is taken, folate supplements should also be taken by the mother. Discuss with your doctor.

 Breast feeding
▼ The drug passes into the breast milk, but at normal doses adverse effects on the baby are unlikely. Discuss with your doctor.

 Infants and children
▼ Reduced dose necessary.

 Over 60
▼ Reduced dose may be necessary.

 Driving and hazardous work
▼ Problems are unlikely.

 Alcohol
▼ No known problems.

POSSIBLE ADVERSE EFFECTS

Side effects are rare at normal doses. Loss of appetite, tiredness, or weakness may be signs of haemolytic anaemia and should be reported promptly to your doctor.

Symptom/effect	Frequency		Discuss with doctor		Stop taking drug now	Call doctor now
	Common	Rare	Only if severe	In all cases		
Nausea/vomiting		●	■			
Dizziness/headache		●	■			
Palpitations		●		■		
Loss of appetite		●		■		
Nervousness		●		■		
Jaundice		●		■	▲	❚
Rash		●		■	▲	❚

INTERACTIONS

Rifampicin may lower the blood levels of dapsone requiring an increase in dosage.

Probenecid increases the levels of dapsone, and the risk of side effects.

PROLONGED USE

There is a risk of serious blood disorders with prolonged use of dapsone.

Monitoring Periodic blood counts and liver function tests may be performed.

DEXAMETHASONE

Brand names Decadron
Used in the following combined preparations Dexa-Rhinaspray, Maxidex, Maxitrol, Otomize, Sofradex

GENERAL INFORMATION

Dexamethasone is a long-acting corticosteroid prescribed for a variety of skin and soft tissue conditions caused by allergy or inflammation. Dexamethasone can be injected into joints to relieve joint pain and stiffness due to rheumatoid arthritis (see p.118). It can be injected into a vein in the emergency treatment of shock and brain swelling (due to head injury, stroke or a tumour), asthma, and emphysema. Eye drops are available to treat eye inflammation.

Low doses of dexamethasone taken for short periods rarely cause serious side effects. However, as with other corticosteroids, long-term treatment with high doses can cause unpleasant or dangerous side effects.

INFORMATION FOR USERS

Your drug prescription is tailored for you. Do not alter dosage without checking with your doctor.

How taken

Tablets, injection, eye drops.

Frequency and timing of doses
2 – 4 x daily with food (by mouth); 1 – 6 hourly (eye drops).

Dosage range
Usually 0.5 – 10mg daily.

Onset of effect
1 – 4 days.

Duration of action
Some effects may last several days.

Diet advice
None.

Storage
Keep in a closed container in a cool, dry place away from reach of children. Protect from light.

Missed dose
Take as soon as you remember. If your next dose is due within 2 hours, take a single dose now and skip the next.

Stopping the drug
Do not stop taking the drug without consulting your doctor. It may be necessary to withdraw the drug gradually.

Exceeding the dose
An occasional unintentional extra dose is unlikely to be a cause for concern. But if you notice unusual symptoms, or if a large overdose has been taken, notify your doctor.

SPECIAL PRECAUTIONS

Be sure to tell your doctor if:
▼ You have had a peptic ulcer.
▼ You have glaucoma.
▼ You have had tuberculosis.
▼ You have suffered from depression or mental illness.
▼ You have a herpes infection.
▼ You are taking other medications.

 Pregnancy
▼ Safety in pregnancy not established. Discuss with your doctor.

 Breast feeding
▼ The drug passes into the breast milk, but at normal doses adverse effects are unlikely. Discuss with your doctor.

 Infants and children
▼ Reduced dose necessary.

 Over 60
▼ No known problems.

 Driving and hazardous work
▼ No known problems.

 Alcohol
▼ Avoid. Alcohol may increase the risk of peptic ulcer with this drug.

POSSIBLE ADVERSE EFFECTS

The more serious adverse effects only occur when dexamethasone is taken in high doses for long periods of time. These are carefully monitored during prolonged treatment.

Symptom/effect	Frequency		Discuss with doctor		Stop taking drug now	Call doctor now
	Common	Rare	Only if severe	In all cases		
Indigestion	●		■			
Weight gain		●	■			
Acne and other skin effects		●	■			
Fluid retention		●			■	
Muscle weakness		●			■	
Mood changes		●			■	

INTERACTIONS

Antidiabetic drugs Dexamethasone reduces the action of these drugs. Dosage may need to be adjusted accordingly to prevent abnormally high blood sugar.

Barbiturates, phenytoin, and rifampicin These drugs may reduce the effectiveness of dexamethasone. The dosage may need to be adjusted accordingly.

Non-steroidal anti-inflammatory drugs These drugs may increase the likelihood of indigestion from dexamethasone.

Vaccines Dexamethasone can interact with some vaccines. Discuss with your doctor.

PROLONGED USE

Prolonged use of this drug can lead to glaucoma, cataracts, diabetes, fragile bones, thin skin, and can retard growth in children. People receiving long-term treatment with this drug are advised to carry a treatment card.

DEXTROMETHORPHAN

Brand name Cosylan
Used in the following combined preparations Actifed Compound, Day Nurse, Night Nurse, Tancolin, and others

GENERAL INFORMATION

Dextromethorphan is a cough suppressant available over the counter in a number of cough remedies. It is useful for suppressing persistent, dry coughing, especially if sleep is disturbed.

It has little general *sedative* effect and, unlike the stronger narcotic cough suppressants, it is unlikely to lead to *dependence* when taken as recommended.

Like other cough suppressants, it should not be used for phlegm-producing coughs because it may prolong a chest infection by preventing the normal elimination of sputum. Although the drug is less sedative than many similar drugs, drowsiness is the principal adverse effect.

QUICK REFERENCE

Drug group Cough suppressant (p.94)
Overdose danger rating Medium
Dependence rating Medium
Prescription needed No
Available as generic No

INFORMATION FOR USERS

Follow instructions on the label. Call your doctor if symptoms worsen.

How taken

Liquid.

Frequency and timing of doses
Up to 4 x daily as required.

Adult dosage range
Dependent on the preparation used.

Onset of effect
Within 30 minutes.

Duration of action
4 – 8 hours.

Diet advice
None.

Storage
Keep in a closed container in a cool, dry place away from reach of children.

Missed dose
Take as soon as you remember if needed to relieve coughing.

Stopping the drug
Can be safely stopped as soon as you no longer need it.

Exceeding the dose
An occasional unintentional extra dose is unlikely to cause problems. Large overdoses may cause nausea, vomiting, stomach pain, dizziness, drowsiness, and breathing problems. Notify your doctor.

SPECIAL PRECAUTIONS

Be sure to tell your doctor or pharmacist before taking this drug if:
▼ You have a long-term liver problem.
▼ You suffer from asthma or another serious respiratory problem.
▼ You are taking other medications.

Pregnancy
▼ Safety in pregnancy not established. Discuss with your doctor.

Breast feeding
▼ The drug passes into the breast milk, but at normal doses adverse effects on the baby are unlikely. Discuss with your doctor.

Infants and children
▼ Not recommended under 1 year. Reduced dose necessary in older children.

Over 60
▼ No special problems.

Driving and hazardous work
▼ Avoid such activities until you have learned how the drug affects you because the drug may reduce alertness.

Alcohol
▼ Avoid. Alcohol may increase the sedative effects of this drug.

POSSIBLE ADVERSE EFFECTS

Adverse effects are rare when dextromethorphan is taken in recommended doses, and diminish if the dosage is reduced and as your body adjusts to the drug.

Symptom/effect	Frequency		Discuss with doctor		Stop taking drug now	Call doctor now
	Common	Rare	Only if severe	In all cases		
Dizziness/drowsiness		●	■			
Constipation		●	■			
Nausea/vomiting		●	■			
Abdominal pain		●	■			

INTERACTIONS

Sedatives All drugs that have a sedative effect on the central nervous system are likely to increase the sedative properties of dextromethorphan. Such drugs include antihistamines, anti-anxiety drugs, sleeping drugs, antidepressants, narcotic analgesics, and antipsychotics.

Monoamine oxidase inhibitors (MAOIs) These drugs may interact dangerously with dextromethorphan. Do not take any cough medicine without discussing with your doctor or phamacist.

PROLONGED USE

Dextromethorphan should not be taken for longer than 2 days except on the advice of a doctor.

DEXTROMORAMIDE

Brand name Palfium
Used in the following combined preparations None

GENERAL INFORMATION

Dextromoramide is a narcotic analgesic drug which has been used in Britain since 1959. This group of drugs, derived from the unripe seeds of the opium poppy, has powerful painkilling properties. Dextromoramide is used for the relief of severe pain following injury or in long-term illnesses such as cancer. It is often given with a tranquillizing drug which enhances its analgesic effect.

Compared with similar drugs, dextromoramide has a rapid onset of effect, but a short duration of action. It is less likely than morphine, a similar drug, to cause sedation and constipation. Regular use of dextromoramide can produce *dependence; withdrawal symptoms* may occur if treatment is stopped abruptly. However, most people prescribed the drug are able to stop without difficulty.

INFORMATION FOR USERS

Your drug prescription is tailored for you. Do not alter dosage without checking with your doctor.

How taken

Tablets, injection, suppositories.

Frequency and timing of doses
As directed.

Adult dosage range
5 – 20mg per dose (by mouth).

Onset of effect
Within 30 minutes.

Duration of action
2 – 3 hours.

Diet advice
None.

Storage
Keep in a closed container in a cool, dry place away from reach of children.

Missed dose
Take as soon as you remember to control persistent pain.

Stopping the drug
If you have been taking the drug regularly for several days, do not stop taking the drug abruptly without consulting your doctor. Your may need to reduce the dose gradually to avoid withdrawal symptoms.

OVERDOSE ACTION

 Seek immediate medical advice in all cases. Take emergency action if there are symptoms such as irregular breathing, severe drowsiness or loss of consciousness.

See Drug poisoning emergency guide (p.470).

POSSIBLE ADVERSE EFFECTS

The adverse effects of dextromoramide are similar to those of other narcotic analgesics. However, sedation and constipation tend to be less severe. Dizziness and sweating at the start of treatment can be relieved by rest.

Symptom/effect	Frequency		Discuss with doctor		Stop taking drug now	Call doctor now
	Common	Rare	Only if severe	In all cases		
Dizziness/sweating	●		■			
Nausea/vomiting		●		■		
Drowsiness		●		■		
Constipation		●		■		

INTERACTIONS

Sedatives Dextromoramide increases the sedative properties of all drugs that have a sedative effect on the central nervous system. Such drugs include alcohol, antidepressants, antipsychotics, sleeping drugs, and antihistamines.

Monoamine oxidase inhibitors (MAOIs) Dextromoramide may cause a dangerous rise in blood pressure when taken within 3 weeks of taking MAOIs.

SPECIAL PRECAUTIONS

Be sure to tell your doctor if:
▼ You have a long-term liver problem.
▼ You have an underactive thyroid gland.
▼ You have a lung disorder such as asthma or emphysema.
▼ You are taking other medications.

 Pregnancy
▼ Not usually prescribed. Taken near the time of delivery the drug may affect the baby's breathing. Discuss with your doctor.

 Breast feeding
▼ The drug passes into the breast milk and may affect the baby. Discuss with your doctor.

 Infants and children
▼ Rarely required. Reduced dose necessary.

 Over 60
▼ Increased likelihood of adverse effects. Reduced dose may therefore be necessary.

 Driving and hazardous work
▼ People on dextromoramide treatment are unlikely to be well enough to undertake such activities.

 Alcohol
▼ Avoid. Alcohol may increase the sedative effects of this drug.

PROLONGED USE

The effects of the drug usually become weaker during prolonged use as the body adapts. It may also be habit-forming if taken for extended periods.

DIAMORPHINE

Brand names None
Used in the following combined preparations None

GENERAL INFORMATION

Diamorphine (also called heroin) belongs to a group of drugs called the narcotic analgesics (see p.80). These drugs are derived from opium, which in turn is prepared from the unripe seed capsules of the opium poppy. Diamorphine resembles morphine in its actions and uses, but produces better pain relief with less severe side effects when given intravenously.

Diamorphine relieves the severe pain that can be caused by injury, surgery, heart attack or chronic diseases such as cancer. It is used to relieve distress in acute heart failure,

and occasionally as a cough suppressant when other remedies have been ineffective. Its painkilling effect wears off quickly, in contrast to some other narcotic analgesics.

Most patients taking diamorphine for pain relief over brief periods of time do not become *dependent* and are able to stop taking the drug without difficulty. However, people who abuse diamorphine for its euphoric effects, especially by injection, are very likely to become addicted (see p.417).

QUICK REFERENCE

Drug group Narcotic analgesic (p.80)
Overdose danger rating High
Dependence rating High
Prescription needed Yes
Available as generic Yes

INFORMATION FOR USERS

Your drug prescription is tailored for you. Do not alter dosage without checking with your doctor.

How taken

Tablets, liquid, injection.

Frequency and timing of doses
Every 4 hours.

Adult dosage range
5 – 10mg per dose. Some people may need more per dose.

Onset of effect
Depends on method of administration.

Duration of action
Up to 4 hours.

Diet advice
None.

Storage
Keep in a closed container in a cool, dry place away from reach of children. Protect from light.

Missed dose
Take as soon as you remember. Return to your normal dosing schedule as soon as possible.

Stopping the drug
Do not stop taking the drug without consulting your doctor.

OVERDOSE ACTION

 Seek immediate medical advice in all cases. Take emergency action if there are symptoms such as slow or irregular breathing, severe drowsiness, or loss of consciousness.

See Drug poisoning emergency guide (p.470).

POSSIBLE ADVERSE EFFECTS

Nausea, vomiting, and constipation are common, especially with high doses. Other drugs may be needed to counteract these symptoms.

Symptom/effect	Frequency		Discuss with doctor		Stop taking drug now	Call doctor now
	Common	Rare	Only if severe	In all cases		
Drowsiness	●		■			
Nausea/vomiting	●		■			
Constipation	●		■			
Dizziness	●			■		
Confusion		●		■		
Breathing difficulties		●		■		▮

INTERACTIONS

Sedatives Diamorphine increases the sedative effects of other sedating drugs including antidepressants, antipsychotics, sleeping drugs, and antihistamines.

Monoamine oxidase inhibitors (MAOIs) These drugs may produce a severe rise in blood pressure when taken with diamorphine.

SPECIAL PRECAUTIONS

Be sure to tell your doctor if:
▼ You have long-term kidney or liver problems.
▼ You have heart or circulatory problems.
▼ You have a lung disorder such as asthma or bronchitis.
▼ You have thyroid disease.
▼ You are taking other medications.

 Pregnancy
▼ Not usually prescribed. May cause breathing difficulties in the newborn baby. Discuss with your doctor.

 Breast feeding
▼ The drug passes into the breast milk and may affect the baby adversely. Discuss with your doctor.

 Infants and children
▼ Reduced dose necessary.

 Over 60
▼ Increased likelihood of adverse effects. Reduced dose may be necessary.

 Driving and hazardous work
▼ People on diamorphine treatment are unlikely to be well enough to undertake such activities.

 Alcohol
▼ Avoid. Alcohol may increase the sedative effects of this drug.

PROLONGED USE

The effects of the drug usually become weaker during prolonged use as the body adapts. It is likely to be produce *dependence* if taken for extended periods.

DIAZEPAM

Brand names Atensine, Dialar, Diazemuls, Rimapam, Stesolid, Tensium, Valium
Used in the following combined preparations None

GENERAL INFORMATION

Introduced in the early 1960s, diazepam is the best known and most widely used of a group of drugs known as the benzodiazepines. These drugs help relieve nervousness and tension, relax muscles, and encourage sleep. Their actions and adverse effects are described more fully on p.83.

Diazepam has a wide range of uses. Besides being commonly used in the treatment of anxiety and anxiety-related insomnia, it is prescribed as a muscle relaxant, in the treatment of alcohol withdrawal, and for the relief of epileptic seizures. Given intravenously, diazepam is used to sedate people undergoing certain uncomfortable medical procedures.

Diazepam can be habit-forming if taken regularly over a long period. Its effects may also diminish with time. Changing medications or tapering off diazepam for a while may restore desired effects. Treatment with diazepam is usually reviewed frequently.

QUICK REFERENCE

Drug group Benzodiazepine anti-anxiety drug (p.83), muscle relaxant (p.120), and anticonvulsant (p.86)

Overdose danger rating Medium

Dependence rating High

Prescription needed Yes

Available as generic Yes

INFORMATION FOR USERS

Your drug prescription is tailored for you. Do not alter dosage without checking with your doctor.

How taken

Tablets, injection, rectal solution, suppositories.

Frequency and timing of doses
1 – 4 x daily.

Adult dosage range
Anxiety 6 – 30mg daily
Muscle spasm 2 – 60mg daily.

Onset of action
Immediate effect (intravenously); 30 minutes – 2 hours (other methods of administration).

Duration of action
Up to 24 hours. Some effect may last up to 4 days.

Diet advice
None.

Storage
Keep in a closed container in a cool, dry place away from reach of children.

Missed dose
Take as soon as you remember. If your next dose is due within 2 hours, take a single dose now and skip the next.

Stopping the drug
If you have been taking the drug continuously for less than 2 weeks, it can be safely stopped as soon as you feel you no longer need it. However, if you have been taking it for longer, consult your doctor, who will supervise a gradual reduction in dosage. Stopping abruptly may lead to withdrawal symptoms (see p.79).

Exceeding the dose
An occasional unintentional extra dose is unlikely to cause problems. Larger overdoses may cause unusual drowsiness. Notify your doctor.

SPECIAL PRECAUTIONS

Be sure to tell your doctor if:
▼ You have severe respiratory disease.
▼ You have long-term liver or kidney problems.
▼ You have had problems with alcohol or drug abuse.
▼ You are taking other medications.

 Pregnancy
▼ Safety in pregnancy not established. Discuss with your doctor.

 Breast feeding
▼ The drug passes into the breast milk and may affect the baby. Discuss with your doctor.

 Infants and children
▼ Reduced dose necessary.

 Over 60
▼ Increased likelihood of adverse effects. Reduced dose may therefore be necessary.

 Driving and hazardous work
▼ Avoid such activities until you have learned how the drug affects you because the drug can cause reduced alertness and slowed reactions.

 Alcohol
▼ Avoid. Alcohol may increase the sedative effects of this drug.

POSSIBLE ADVERSE EFFECTS

The principal adverse effects of this drug are related to its sedative properties. The effects normally diminish after a few days and can often be reduced by adjustment of dosage.

Symptom/effect	Frequency		Discuss with doctor		Stop taking drug now	Call doctor now
	Common	Rare	Only if severe	In all cases		
Daytime drowsiness	●		■			
Dizziness/unsteadiness	●			■		
Headache		●	■			
Blurred vision		●		■		
Forgetfulness/confusion		●		■		
Rash		●		■	▲	

INTERACTIONS

Sedatives All drugs with a sedative effect on the central nervous system can increase the sedative properties of diazepam.

Cimetidine Breakdown of diazepam in the liver may be inhibited by cimetidine. This can cause a build-up of diazepam in the blood which increases the likelihood of adverse effects.

PROLONGED USE

Regular use of this drug over several weeks can lead to a reduction in its effect as the body adapts. It may also be habit-forming when taken for extended periods, and severe withdrawal reactions can occur.

DICLOFENAC

Brand names Diclozip, Rheumalgan, Valenac, Volraman, Voltarol
Used in the following combined preparations Arthrotec

GENERAL INFORMATION

As a single dose, diclofenac has analgesic properties similar to paracetamol. It relieves mild to moderate headache, menstrual pain, and pain following minor surgery. When diclofenac is given regularly long term, it exerts an anti-inflammatory effect and is used to relieve pain and stiffness in rheumatoid arthritis and osteoarthritis. Diclofenac may also be used to treat acute attacks of gout.

The combined preparation, Arthrotec, is a combination of diclofenac and misoprostol (see p.337). Misoprostol helps prevent gastroduodenal ulceration and may be particularly useful in patients at risk of developing this problem.

QUICK REFERENCE

Drug group Non-steroidal anti-inflammatory drug (p.116), analgesic (p.80), and drug for gout (p.119)

Overdose danger rating Low

Dependence rating Low

Prescription needed Yes

Available as generic Yes

INFORMATION FOR USERS

Your drug prescription is tailored for you. Do not alter dosage without checking with your doctor.

How taken

Tablets, SR tablets, injection, suppositories, gel.

Frequency and timing of doses
2 – 3 x daily with food.

Adult dosage range
75 – 150mg daily.

Onset of action
Around 1 hour (pain relief); full anti-inflammatory effect may take 2 weeks.

Duration of action
Up to 12 hours. Up to 24 hours (SR tablets).

Diet advice
None.

Storage
Keep in a closed container in a cool, dry place away from reach of children.

Missed dose
Take as soon as you remember. If your next dose is due within 4 hours, take a single dose now and skip the next.

Stopping the drug
When taken for short-term pain relief, diclofenac can be safely stopped as soon as you no longer need it. If prescribed for long-term treatment (e.g. for arthritis) speak to your doctor before stopping the drug.

Exceeding the dose
An occasional unintentional extra dose is unlikely to cause problems. But, if you do notice any unusual symptoms or if a large overdose has been taken, notify your doctor.

SPECIAL PRECAUTIONS

Be sure to tell your doctor if:
▼ You have kidney or liver problems.
▼ You have a bleeding disorder.
▼ You have had a peptic ulcer or oesophagitis.
▼ You have porphyria.
▼ You suffer from indigestion.
▼ You are allergic to aspirin.
▼ You suffer from asthma.
▼ You have heart problems or high blood pressure.
▼ You are taking other medications.

 Pregnancy
▼ Not usually prescribed in the last 3 months of pregnancy as it may increase the risk of adverse effects on the baby's heart and may prolong labour. Discuss with your doctor.

 Breast feeding
▼ Small amounts of the drug pass into the breast milk, but adverse effects on the baby are unlikely. Discuss with your doctor.

 Infants and children
▼ Reduced dose necessary.

 Over 60
▼ Increased risk of adverse effects. Reduced dose may therefore be necessary.

 Driving and hazardous work
▼ No problems expected.

 Alcohol
▼ Keep consumption low. Alcohol may increase the risk of stomach irritation.

Surgery and general anaesthetics
▼ Discuss with your doctor or dentist before any surgery.

POSSIBLE ADVERSE EFFECTS

The most common adverse effects are the result of gastrointestinal disturbances. Black or bloodstained faeces should be reported to your doctor without delay.

Symptom/effect	Frequency		Discuss with doctor		Stop taking drug now	Call doctor now
	Common	Rare	Only if severe	In all cases		
Gastrointestinal disorders	●		■			
Headache/dizziness		●	■			
Drowsiness		●	■			
Swollen feet/ankles		●		■		
Rash		●		■	▲	
Wheezing/breathlessness		●		■	▲	■

INTERACTIONS

General note Diclofenac interacts with a wide range of drugs. These include oral anticoagulants, corticosteroids, other non-steroidal anti-inflammatory drugs, and aspirin.

Indigestion remedies These should not be taken at the same time of day as diclofenac preparations that are enteric coated (i.e. coated to resist being broken down in the acid environment of the stomach) as they disrupt this coating.

Lithium, digoxin, and methotrexate Diclofenac may increase the blood levels of these drugs.

Antihypertensive drugs and diuretics The beneficial effects of these drugs may be reduced.

Cyclosporin Diclofenac may increase the risk of kidney problems.

PROLONGED USE

There is an increased risk of bleeding from peptic ulcers and in the bowel with prolonged use of diclofenac.

DICYCLOMINE

Brand name Merbentyl
Used in the following combined preparations Diarrest, Kolanticon

GENERAL INFORMATION

Dicyclomine is an *anticholinergic* antispasmodic drug that relieves painful abdominal cramps caused by spasm in the gastrointestinal tract. Used to treat irritable bowel syndrome, the drug has also been prescribed to treat the condition known as 'evening' colic in babies.

Because dicyclomine has anti-cholinergic properties, it is included in some combined preparations used for flatulence, indigestion, and diarrhoea.

Dicyclomine relieves symptoms, but does not cure the underlying condition. Additional treatment with other drugs and self-help measures may therefore be recommended by your doctor.

QUICK REFERENCE

Drug group Drug for irritable bowel syndrome (p.110)

Overdose danger rating Medium

Dependence rating Low

Prescription needed Yes

Available as generic No

INFORMATION FOR USERS

Your drug prescription is tailored for you. Do not alter dosage without checking with your doctor.

How taken

Tablets, liquid.

Frequency and timing of doses
3 x daily before or after meals.

Dosage range
Adults 30 – 60mg daily.
Children Reduced dose according to age and weight.

Onset of effect
Within 1 – 2 hours.

Duration of action
4 – 6 hours.

Diet advice
None.

Storage
Keep in a closed container in a cool, dry place away from reach of children. Protect from light.

Missed dose
Take as soon as you remember. If your next dose is due within 2 hours, take a single dose now and skip the next.

Stopping the drug
Do not stop the drug without consulting your doctor; symptoms may recur.

Exceeding the dose
An occasional unintentional extra dose is unlikely to cause problems. Large overdoses may cause drowsiness, dizziness, and difficulty in swallowing. Notify your doctor.

SPECIAL PRECAUTIONS

Be sure to tell your doctor if:
▼ You have glaucoma.
▼ You have urinary problems.
▼ You have hiatus hernia.
▼ You are taking other medications.

 Pregnancy
▼ No evidence of risk.

 Breast feeding
▼ The drug passes into the breast milk, but at normal doses adverse effects on the baby are unlikely. Discuss with your doctor.

 Infants and children
▼ Reduced dose necessary.

 Over 60
▼ No special problems.

 Driving and hazardous work
▼ Avoid such activities until you have learned how the drug affects you because the drug can cause drowsiness and blurred vision.

 Alcohol
▼ Avoid. Alcohol may increase the sedative effects of this drug.

POSSIBLE ADVERSE EFFECTS

Most people do not notice any adverse effects when taking dicyclomine. Those that do occur are related to its anticholinergic properties and include drowsiness and dry mouth. Such symptoms may be overcome by an adjustment of dosage, or may pass off after a few days of usage as your body adjusts to the drug.

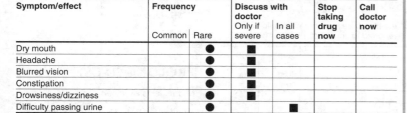

Symptom/effect	Frequency		Discuss with doctor		Stop taking drug now	Call doctor now
	Common	Rare	Only if severe	In all cases		
Dry mouth		●	■			
Headache		●	■			
Blurred vision		●	■			
Constipation		●	■			
Drowsiness/dizziness		●	■			
Difficulty passing urine		●		■		

INTERACTIONS

Sedatives All drugs that have a sedative effect on the central nervous system may increase the sedative properties of dicyclomine.

PROLONGED USE

No problems expected.

DIGOXIN

Brand name Lanoxin
Used in the following combined preparations None

GENERAL INFORMATION

Digoxin is the most widely used form of digitalis, a drug extracted from the leaves of the foxglove plant. It is sometimes given in the treatment of congestive heart failure and certain alterations of heart rhythm.

Digoxin slows down the rate of the heart so that each beat is more effective in pumping blood. In congestive heart failure, it also helps to control tiredness, breathlessness, and fluid retention. Its effects are not as long-lasting as those of other digitalis drugs, and this makes any adverse reactions easier to control.

For digoxin to be effective, the dose must be very near the toxic dose, and treatment must be monitored closely. A number of adverse effects (see below) may indicate the toxic level is being reached and should be reported to your doctor immediately.

INFORMATION FOR USERS

Your drug prescription is tailored for you. Do not alter dosage without checking with your doctor.

How taken

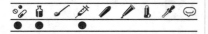

Tablets, liquid, injection.

Frequency and timing of doses
1 – 3 x daily (starting dose); once daily (maintenance dose).

Dosage range
Adults 0.0625 – 0.25mg daily (orally).

Onset of effect
Within a few minutes (injection); within 1 – 2 hours (by mouth).

Duration of action
Up to 4 days.

Diet advice
This drug may be more toxic if potassium levels are depleted. Include fruit and vegetables in your diet.

Storage
Keep in a closed container in a cool, dry place away from reach of children. Protect from light.

Missed dose
Take as soon as you remember. If your next dose is due within 8 hours, take a single dose now and skip the next. If you notice unusual symptoms inform your doctor straight away.

Stopping the drug
Do not stop the drug without consulting your doctor; stopping the drug may lead to worsening of the underlying condition.

OVERDOSE ACTION

 Seek immediate medical advice in all cases. Take emergency action if palpitations, severe weakness, chest pain, or loss of consciousness occur.

See Drug poisoning emergency guide (p.470).

SPECIAL PRECAUTIONS

Be sure to tell your physician if:
▼ You have long-term kidney problems.
▼ You have thyroid trouble.
▼ You are taking other medications.

 Pregnancy
▼ No evidence of risk.

 Breast feeding
▼ The drug passes into the breast milk, but at normal doses adverse effects on the baby are unlikely. Discuss with your doctor.

 Infants and children
▼ Reduced dose necessary.

 Over 60
▼ Increased likelihood of adverse effects. Reduced dose may therefore be necessary.

 Driving and hazardous work
▼ Special problems are unlikely, but do not drive until you know how the drug affects you.

 Alcohol
▼ No special problems.

PROLONGED USE

No problems expected.

Monitoring Periodic checks on blood levels of digoxin and body salts may be advised.

POSSIBLE ADVERSE EFFECTS

The possible adverse effects of digoxin are usually due to increased levels of the drug in the blood. Any symptoms should be reported to your doctor without delay.

Symptom/effect	Frequency		Discuss with doctor		Stop taking drug now	Call doctor now
	Common	Rare	Only if severe	In all cases		
Tiredness	●		■			
Nausea/loss of appetite	●			■		
Confusion	●			■		
Visual disturbance	●			■		
Palpitations	●			■	▲	▌

INTERACTIONS

General note Many drugs interact with digoxin. Do not take any medication without your doctor's or pharmacist's advice.

Diuretics may increase the risk of adverse effects from digoxin.

Antacids may reduce the effects of digoxin. The effect of digoxin may increase when such drugs are stopped.

Anti-arrhythmics may increase blood levels of digoxin.

DILTIAZEM

Brand names Adizem, Angiozem, Britiazim, Dilzem, Tildiem,
Used in the following combined preparations None

GENERAL INFORMATION

Diltiazem belongs to the group of drugs known as calcium channel blockers (p.101). These interfere with the conduction of signals in the muscles of the heart and blood vessels.

Diltiazem is used in the treatment of angina and high blood pressure. When taken regularly, it reduces the frequency of angina attacks but does not work quickly enough to alleviate the pain of an angina attack that is in progress.

Diltiazem does not adversely affect breathing and is of particular value for people who suffer from asthma, for whom other types of anti-angina drug may not be suitable. Possible adverse effects include headache, ankle swelling, and tiredness.

INFORMATION FOR USERS

Your drug prescription is tailored for you. Do not alter dosage without checking with your doctor.

How taken

Tablets, SR-tablets.

Frequency and timing of doses
3 x daily; 1 x daily (SR-tablets).

Adult dosage range
180mg – 480mg daily.

Onset of effect
2 – 3 hours.

Duration of action
6 – 8 hours.

Diet advice
None.

Storage
Keep in a closed container in a cool, dry place away from reach of children.

Missed dose
Take as soon as you remember. If your next dose is due within 2 hours, take a single dose now and skip the next.

Stopping the drug
Do not stop taking the drug without consulting your doctor; symptoms may recur.

Exceeding the dose
An occasional unintentional extra dose is unlikely to be a cause for concern. Large overdoses may cause dizziness. Notify your doctor.

SPECIAL PRECAUTIONS

Be sure to tell your doctor if:
▼ You have long-term kidney or liver problems.
▼ You have heart failure.
▼ You are taking other medications.

 Pregnancy
▼ Not usually prescribed. Discuss with your doctor.

 Breast feeding
▼ The drug passes into the breast milk and may affect the baby. Discuss with your doctor.

 Infants and children
▼ Not recommended.

 Over 60
▼ Increased likelihood of adverse effects. Reduced dose may therefore be necessary.

 Driving and hazardous work
▼ Avoid such activities until you have learned how the drug affects you because the drug may cause dizziness due to lowered blood pressure.

 Alcohol
▼ Avoid. Alcohol may reduce blood pressure causing dizziness.

POSSIBLE ADVERSE EFFECTS

Diltiazem can cause a variety of minor symptoms that are common to other calcium channel blockers. These include headache and nausea. The most serious effect is the possibility of a slowed heart beat, which may cause tiredness or dizziness. These effects can sometimes be controlled by an adjustment in dosage.

Symptom/effect	Frequency		Discuss with doctor		Stop taking drug now	Call doctor now
	Common	Rare	Only if severe	In all cases		
Headache	●		■			
Nausea	●		■			
Dry mouth	●		■			
Leg and ankle swelling	●		■			
Tiredness		●		■		
Dizziness		●		■		
Rash		●		■	▲	

INTERACTIONS

Antihypertensive drugs Diltiazem increases their effects leading to a further reduction in blood pressure.

Anticonvulsants Levels of these drugs may be altered by diltiazem.

Digoxin Blood levels and adverse effects of this drug may be increased if it is taken with diltiazem. The dosage of digoxin may need to be reduced.

Theophylline Diltiazem may increase the levels of theophylline.

PROLONGED USE

No problems expected.

DIPHENHYDRAMINE

Brand names Nytol
Used in the following combined preparations Benylin, Caladryl, Guanor, Histalix, Noradran, Pharmidone, Propain, Uniflu

GENERAL INFORMATION

Diphenhydramine, in use for over 40 years, is one of the oldest antihistamines. Its main use is as an ingredient in a range of cough and cold remedies. Diphenhydramine is also an ingredient in creams and ointments used in the treatment of skin allergies.

When it is taken by mouth, this drug has a marked sedative action and often causes drowsiness.

Diphenhydramine is sometimes given in tablet form to treat temporary sleep disorders.

QUICK REFERENCE

Drug group Antihistamine (p.124), anti-emetic (p.90), and antiparkinson drug (p.87)

Overdose danger rating Medium

Dependence rating Low

Prescription needed No

Available as generic No

INFORMATION FOR USERS

Follow instructions on the label.
Call your doctor if symptoms worsen.

How taken

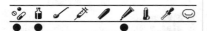

Tablets, lotion, liquid, cream.

Frequency and timing of dose
The frequency varies according to the preparation being used. Follow the instructions on the container.

Adult dosage range
For sleep disorders: 50mg at night.
For other conditions: dosage varies according to the preparation being used.

Onset of effect
Within 45 minutes (by mouth).

Duration of action
4 – 6 hours.

Diet advice
None.

Storage
Keep in a closed container in a cool, dry place away from reach of children.

Missed dose
Take as soon as you remember. If your next dose is due within 2 hours, take a single dose now and skip the next.

Stopping the drug
Can be safely stopped as soon as you no longer need it.

Exceeding the dose
An occasional unintentional extra dose is unlikely to cause problems. Large overdoses may cause drowsiness or agitation. Notify your doctor.

POSSIBLE ADVERSE EFFECTS

Drowsiness is the commonest adverse effect of diphenhydramine. Other side effects, such as dry mouth and blurred vision, are due to its *anticholinergic* action.

Symptom/effect	Frequency		Discuss with doctor		Stop taking drug now	Call doctor now
	Common	Rare	Only if severe	In all cases		
Drowsiness	●			■		
Dry mouth	●			■		
Nausea		●		■		
Blurred vision		●		■		
Urinary difficulties		●			■	
Disorientation/excitation		●			■	

INTERACTIONS

Sedatives These drugs are likely to enhance the sedative effect of this drug.

Anticholinergic drugs These are likely to increase the anticholinergic effects of diphenhydramine.

SPECIAL PRECAUTIONS

Be sure to consult your doctor or pharmacist before taking this drug if:
▼ You have long-term liver problems.
▼ You have myasthenia gravis.
▼ You have glaucoma.
▼ You have urinary difficulties.
▼ You are taking other medications.

Pregnancy
▼ No evidence of risk.

Breast feeding
▼ The drug passes into the breast milk, but at normal doses adverse effects on the baby are unlikely. Discuss with your doctor.

Infants and children
▼ Not recommended in newborn or premature infants. Reduced dose necessary in older children.

Over 60
▼ Reduced dose may be necessary. Increased likelihood of adverse effects.

Driving and hazardous work
▼ Avoid such activities until you have learned how the drug affects you because the drug can cause drowsiness.

Alcohol
▼ Avoid. Alcohol may increase the sedative effects of this drug.

PROLONGED USE

The effect of the drug may become weaker with prolonged use over a period of weeks or months as the body adapts.

DIPHENOXYLATE

Brand names None
Used in the following combined preparations Diarphen, Lomotil

GENERAL INFORMATION

Diphenoxylate is a narcotic antidiarrhoeal drug chemically related to the opiate analgesics. It reduces bowel contractions and consequently the frequency and fluidity of bowel movements. Available as tablets and liquid, it is used for the relief of sudden or recurrent bouts of diarrhoea.

It is not suitable for diarrhoea caused by infection, antibiotics, or poisons because it may delay recovery by slowing down the expulsion of harmful substances from the bowel. Diphenoxylate can cause toxic megacolon, a dangerous dilation of the bowel that shuts off the blood supply to the wall of the bowel and increases the risk of perforation.

At recommended doses, serious adverse effects are rare. To guard against addiction, atropine is added to all diphenoxylate preparations. If these are taken in excessive amounts, the atropine will cause highly unpleasant *anticholinergic* reactions. Diphenoxylate is especially dangerous for young children. Be sure to store the drug out of their reach.

INFORMATION FOR USERS

Your drug prescription is tailored for you. Do not alter dosage without checking with your doctor.

How taken

Tablets, liquid.

Frequency and timing of doses
3 – 4 x daily.

Dosage range
Adults 10mg initially, followed by doses of 5mg.
Children Reduced dose necessary according to age and weight.

Onset of effect
Within 1 hour. Control of diarrhoea may take some hours.

Duration of action
Up to 24 hours.

Diet advice
Ensure adequate fluid intake during an attack of diarrhoea.

Storage
Keep in a closed container in a cool, dry place away from reach of children.

Missed dose
Take as soon as you remember. If your next dose is due within 3 hours, take a single dose now and skip the next.

Stopping the drug
Can be safely stopped as soon as you no longer need it.

Exceeding the dose
An occasional unintentional extra dose is unlikely to cause problems. Large overdoses may cause unusual drowsiness, dryness of the mouth and skin, restlessness, and in extreme cases, loss of consciousness. Notify your doctor.

SPECIAL PRECAUTIONS

Be sure to tell your doctor if:
▼ You have a long-term liver problem.
▼ You have severe abdominal pain.
▼ You have blood-stained diarrhoea.
▼ You have recently taken antibiotics.
▼ You have ulcerative colitis.
▼ You are taking other medications.

 Pregnancy
▼ Safety in pregnancy not established. Discuss with your doctor.

 Breast feeding
▼ The drug passes into the breast milk and may cause drowsiness in the baby. Discuss with your doctor.

 Infants and children
▼ Not recommended in children under 4 years. Reduced dose necessary in older children.

 Over 60
▼ Reduced dose may be necessary.

 Driving and hazardous work
▼ Avoid such activities until you have learned how the drug affects you because the drug may cause drowsiness and dizziness.

 Alcohol
▼ Avoid. Alcohol may increase the sedative effects of this drug.

PROLONGED USE

Not usually recommended.

POSSIBLE ADVERSE EFFECTS

Side effects occur infrequently with diphenoxylate. If abdominal pain or distension, nausea, or vomiting occur, notify your doctor.

Symptom/effect	Frequency		Discuss with doctor		Stop taking drug now	Call doctor now
	Common	Rare	Only if severe	In all cases		
Drowsinesss	●		■			
Restlessness		●	■			
Headache		●	■			
Skin rash/itching		●	■			
Dizziness		●			■	
Nausea/vomiting		●			■	▲
Abdominal discomfort		●			■	▲	■

INTERACTIONS

Sedatives All drugs that have a sedative effect on the central nervous system may increase the sedative effect of diphenoxylate.

Monoamine oxidase inhibitors (MAOIs) There is a risk of a dangerous rise in blood pressure if MAOIs are taken with diphenoxylate.

DIPYRIDAMOLE

Brand name Cerebrovase , Persantin
Used in the following combined preparations None

GENERAL INFORMATION

Dipyridamole was originally introduced in the late 1970s as an anti-angina drug, theoretically improving the capacity of those with angina to exercise. More effective drugs are now available for that purpose, but dipyridamole is still used as an antiplatelet drug. It is given to "thin" the blood in patients who have had surgery to replace a heart valve. This reduces the possibility of blood clotting within the circulation. Dipyridamole is usually given together with other drugs such as warfarin or aspirin. The drug can also be given by injection during certain types of diagnostic tests on the heart.

Side effects may occur, especially during the early days of treatment. If they persist, your doctor may advise a reduction in dosage.

QUICK REFERENCE

Drug group Antiplatelet drug (p.104)

Overdose danger rating Medium

Dependence rating Low

Prescription needed Yes

Available as generic Yes

INFORMATION FOR USERS

Your drug prescription is tailored for you. Do not alter dosage without checking with your doctor.

How taken

Tablets, injection.

Frequency and timing of doses
3 – 4 x daily one hour before meals.

Adult dosage range
300 – 600mg daily.

Onset of action
Within an hour. Full therapeutic effect may not be felt for 2 – 3 weeks.

Duration of action
Up to 8 hours.

Diet advice
None.

Storage
Keep in a closed container in a cool dry place away from reach of children. Protect from light.

Missed dose
Take as soon as you remember. If your next dose is due within 2 hours, take a single dose now and skip the next.

Stopping the drug
Do not stop taking the drug without consulting your doctor; withdrawal of the drug could lead to abnormal blood clotting.

Exceeding the dose
An occasional unintentional extra dose is unlikely to cause problems. Large overdoses may cause dizziness or vomiting. Notify your doctor.

SPECIAL PRECAUTIONS

Be sure to tell your doctor if:
▼ You have low blood pressure.
▼ You suffer from migraine.
▼ You have angina.
▼ You are taking other medications.

 Pregnancy
▼ Safety in pregnancy not established. Discuss with your doctor.

 Breast feeding
▼ The drug passes into the breast milk, but at normal doses adverse effects on the baby are unlikely. Discuss with your doctor.

 Infants and children
▼ Reduced dose necessary.

 Over 60s
▼ No special problems.

 Driving and hazardous work
▼ Avoid such activities until you have learned how the drug affects you because of the possibility of dizziness and faintness.

 Alcohol
▼ No known problems.

POSSIBLE ADVERSE EFFECTS

Adverse effects are rare. Possible symptoms include dizziness, headache, faintness, nausea, and rash. In rare cases, it may aggravate angina.

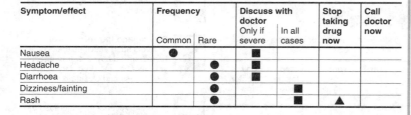

Symptom/effect	Frequency		Discuss with doctor		Stop taking drug now	Call doctor now
	Common	Rare	Only if severe	In all cases		
Nausea	●		■			
Headache		●	■			
Diarrhoea		●	■			
Dizziness/fainting		●			■	
Rash		●		■		▲

PROLONGED USE

No known problems.

INTERACTIONS

Anticoagulants The effects of these drugs may be increased by dipyridamole, so increasing the risk of uncontrolled bleeding. The dosage of the anticoagulant should be reduced accordingly.

Antacids may reduce the effectiveness of dipyridamole.

DISOPYRAMIDE

Brand names Dirythmin-SA, Isomide, Rythmodan
Used in the following combined preparations None

GENERAL INFORMATION

Disopyramide is an anti-arrhythmic drug, used to treat irregular heart rhythms, particularly cases of rapid heart beat.

It has a mild *anticholinergic* action, and some of its less serious adverse effects are connected to this. Because it reduces the force of the heart beat, it can worsen existing heart failure and low blood pressure. These effects may be more common with disopyramide than with other anti-arrhythmics. Since disopyramide can lower blood sugar levels, monitoring may be necessary, and people with diabetes must use the drug with caution.

QUICK REFERENCE

Drug group Anti-arrhythmic (p.100)
Overdose danger rating High
Dependence rating Low
Prescription needed Yes
Available as generic Yes

INFORMATION FOR USERS

Your drug prescription is tailored for you. Do not alter dosage without checking with your doctor.

How taken

Tablets, capsules, injection.

Frequency and timing of doses
3 – 4 x daily or every 12 hours (slow-release capsules).

Adult dosage range
Adults 300 – 800mg daily.

Onset of effect
Within 2 hours.

Duration of action
6 – 7 hours or up to 12 hours (slow-release capsules).

Diet advice
None.

Storage
Keep in a closed container in a cool, dry place away from reach of children.

Missed dose
Take as soon as you remember. If your next dose is due within 2 hours, take a single dose now and skip the next.

Stopping the drug
Do not stop the drug without consulting your doctor; stopping the drug may lead to worsening of the underlying condition.

OVERDOSE ACTION

Seek immediate medical advice in all cases. Take emergency action if consciousness is lost.

See Drug poisoning emergency guide (p.470).

POSSIBLE ADVERSE EFFECTS

Some of the possible adverse effects of this drug are the result of its *anticholinergic* action. These include dry mouth, constipation, and blurred vision. The most serious adverse effect is the possibility of worsening existing heart failure or low blood pressure. Some of these problems can be overcome by an adjustment in dosage.

Symptom/effect	Frequency		Discuss with doctor		Stop taking drug now	Call doctor now
	Common	Rare	Only if severe	In all cases		
Dry mouth	●		■			
Constipation/difficulty urinating	●		■			
Blurred vision	●		■			
Dizziness/feeling faint	●			■		

INTERACTIONS

Phenytoin The effect of disopyramide may be reduced by this drug.

Other anti-arrhythmics These drugs may increase the risk of adverse effects on the heart.

Antihistamines Some antihistamines increase the risk of abnormal heart rhythms; check with your doctor or pharmacist.

Rifampicin The effect of disopyramide may be reduced by this drug.

Erythromycin The effect of disopyramide may be increased by this drug.

Diuretics These drugs may increase the risk of adverse effects.

SPECIAL PRECAUTIONS

Be sure to tell your doctor if:
▼ You have long-term kidney or liver problems.
▼ You have heart failure.
▼ You have low blood pressure.
▼ You have had glaucoma.
▼ You have prostate trouble.
▼ You have diabetes.
▼ You are taking other medications.

Pregnancy
▼ Safety in pregnancy not established. Discuss with your doctor.

Breast feeding
▼ The drug passes into breast milk, but at normal doses adverse effects in the baby are unlikely. Discuss with your doctor.

Infants and children
▼ Not usually prescribed. Reduced dose necessary.

Over 60
▼ Reduced dose may be necessary.

Driving and hazardous work
▼ Avoid such activities until you have learned how the drug affects you because the drug can cause blurred vision and dizziness.

Alcohol
▼ Avoid. Alcohol may increase the adverse effects of this drug.

PROLONGED USE

No problems expected.

Monitoring Periodic checks on blood sugar levels may be advised

DISULFIRAM

Brand name Antabuse
Used in the following combined preparations None

GENERAL INFORMATION

Disulfiram is a drug used to help alcoholics abstain from alcohol. It does not cure alcoholism but provides a powerful deterrent to drinking.

If you are taking disulfiram and drink even a small amount of alcohol, highly unpleasant reactions follow, such as flushing, throbbing headache, breathlessness, nausea, thirst, palpitations, dizziness, and fainting. These may last from 30 minutes to several hours, leaving the person feeling drowsy and sleepy. Because the reactions can also include unconsciousness, it is wise to carry a warning card stating the person

to notify in an emergency.

When a person takes both disulfiram and alcohol, a toxic substance (acetaldehyde) that is manufactured in the body and broken down rises to higher concentrations in the blood, triggering the unwelcome reactions. Many doctors prescribing disulfiram for alcoholism give a small test dose of alcohol a few days after treatment is started to give the patient an idea of what may happen. Many doctors also recommend that disulfiram treatment be combined with alcoholic counselling programmes.

INFORMATION FOR USERS

Your drug prescription is tailored for you. Do not alter dosage without checking with your doctor.

How taken

Tablets.

Frequency and timing of doses
Once daily.

Adult dosage range
800mg initially, gradually reduced over 5 days to 100 – 200mg (maintenance dose).

Onset of effect
Interaction with alcohol occurs within a few minutes of taking alcohol.

Duration of action
Interaction with alcohol can occur for about 6 days after the last dose of disulfiram.

Diet advice
Avoid all alcoholic drinks even in very small amounts. Food, fermented vinegar, mouthwashes, medicines, and lotions containing alcohol should also be avoided.

Storage
Keep in a closed container in a cool, dry place away from reach of children. Protect from light.

Missed dose
Take as soon as you remember. If your next dose is due within 2 hours, take a single dose now and skip the next.

Stopping the drug
Do not stop taking the drug without consulting your doctor.

Exceeding the dose
An occasional unintentional extra dose is unlikely to cause problems. Large overdoses may cause a temporary increase in adverse effects. Notify your doctor.

SPECIAL PRECAUTIONS

Be sure to tell your doctor if:
▼ You have long-term kidney or liver problems.
▼ You have heart problems, coronary artery disease, or high blood pressure.
▼ You have had epileptic fits.
▼ You have diabetes.
▼ You have any breathing problems.
▼ You are taking other medications.

 Pregnancy
▼ Safety in pregnancy not established. Discuss with your doctor.

 Breast feeding
▼ The drug may pass into the breast milk and may affect the baby. Discuss with your doctor.

 Over 60
▼ Reduced dose may be necessary.

 Driving and hazardous work
▼ Avoid such activities until you have learned how the drug affects you because the drug can cause drowsiness and dizziness.

 Alcohol
▼ Never drink while under treatment with disulfiram and avoid food and medicines that contain alcohol. Alcohol may interact dangerously with this drug.

POSSIBLE ADVERSE EFFECTS

Adverse effects from disulfiram usually disappear when you get used to taking the drug. If they persist or become severe, the dosage may need to be adjusted.

| Symptom/effect | Frequency | | Discuss with doctor | | Stop taking drug now | Call doctor now |
	Common	Rare	Only if severe	In all cases		
Drowsiness	●		■			
Reduced libido		●	■			
Nausea/vomiting		●	■			

INTERACTIONS

General note A number of drugs can produce an adverse reaction with disulfiram. You are advised to check with your doctor or pharmacist before taking any other medication.

Phenytoin The effects of this drug are increased when taken with disulfiram.

Anticoagulants Disulfiram increases the anticoagulant effect of these drugs.

Isoniazid Disulfiram may markedly increase the adverse effects of this drug.

Metronidazole A severe reaction can occur if this drug is taken with disulfiram.

PROLONGED USE

Not usually prescribed for longer than 6 months without review. It is wise to carry a card indicating you are taking disulfiram with instructions as to who should be notified in an emergency.

DITHRANOL

Brand names Alphodith, Anthranol, Antraderm, Dithrocream, Exolan
Used in the following combined preparations Dithrolan, Psoradrate, Psorin

GENERAL INFORMATION

Dithranol is the most effective *topical* non-steroidal agent for moderately severe psoriasis. Applied as a cream or ointment, it restores excessive skin growth to normal. It is sometimes accompanied by periodic ultraviolet (PUVA) treatments to boost its effect.

If psoriasis is severe, treatment at a specialized outpatient centre may be recommended. However, most people can use the drug at home, leaving it on either overnight or for periods of up to 30 minutes each day, before washing it off. Since it may stain, clothes and bed linen should be protected.

Dithranol frequently causes irritation or redness of normal skin around the treated areas, especially at high concentrations. A protective coat of petroleum jelly applied to normal skin before using the drug helps to minimize such effects; plastic gloves should be worn during application. Raw, blistered, or oozing areas should never be treated. The drug should not be used on the face, genital area or skin folds such as those of the neck or groin.

INFORMATION FOR USERS

Your drug prescription is tailored for you. Do not alter dosage without checking with your doctor.

How taken

Ointment, cream.

Frequency and timing of doses
Once daily, either low concentration (0.1 – 0.5 per cent) at bedtime for 8 – 12 hours (overnight treatment) or high concentration (1 per cent) during the day for 10 – 30 minutes as directed (short-contact treatment). Remove the medicine by washing as directed after each application.

Adult dosage range
Apply thinly to the affected area as directed. The strength of the ointment or cream is increased if required as treatment continues.

Onset of effect
2 – 3 days. Full beneficial effect of the drug may not be felt for several weeks.

Duration of action
Up to 72 hours.

Diet advice
None.

Storage
Keep in a closed container in a cool, dry place away from reach of children.

Missed dose
Apply as soon as you remember. If not remembered until the next morning (overnight treatment), skip the missed application and apply your next dose as usual. If your next dose is due within 4 hours (short-contact treatment), apply a single dose now and skip the next dose.

Stopping the drug
For best results, apply the full course of treatment as instructed.

Exceeding the dose
An occasional unintentional extra application is unlikely to cause problems. If the cream is left on the skin longer than recommended, irritation and redness may result. If this occurs, notify your doctor.

SPECIAL PRECAUTIONS

Be sure to tell your doctor or pharmacist if:
▼ You have a long-term kidney problem.
▼ You are taking other medications.

Pregnancy
▼ No evidence of risk, but discuss with your doctor.

Breast feeding
▼ No evidence of risk, but discuss with your doctor.

Infants and children
▼ Not recommended under 12 years.

Over 60
▼ No special problems.

Driving and hazardous work
▼ No known problems.

Alcohol
▼ No known problems.

POSSIBLE ADVERSE EFFECTS

Irritation or redness of the skin around the treated areas is fairly common and is usually helped by reducing the amount or frequency of application. Allergic skin rashes are rare.

Symptom/effect	Frequency		Discuss with doctor		Stop taking drug now	Call doctor now
	Common	Rare	Only if severe	In all cases		
Local irritation/burning sensation	●		■			
Redness	●		■			
Rash		●		■	▲	∎

INTERACTIONS

General note Any drug that increases the sensitivity of the skin to light may increase the risk of redness or irritation with dithranol. These include coal tar or coal tar derivatives, and rarely thiazide diuretics, griseofulvin, nalidixic acid, phenothiazine antipsychotics, sulphonamides, and tetracycline antibiotics.

PROLONGED USE

No special problems.

DOMPERIDONE

Brand names Motilium
Used in the following combined preparations None

GENERAL INFORMATION

Domperidone was introduced in the early 1980s for use as an anti-emetic. It is particularly useful for treating nausea and vomiting caused by gastrointestinal disorders such as gastroenteritis, and that occurring as a side effect of treatment with other drugs (especially anticancer drugs) or radiation therapy. It is not, however, an effective treatment for motion sickness or nausea caused by inner ear disorders such as Ménière's disease.

Its main advantage over other anti-emetics is that it does not usually cause sedation or other adverse effects such as abnormal movement. It is not, however, suitable for long-term treatment of gastrointestinal disorders in which alternative drug treatment is usually prescribed.

QUICK REFERENCE

Drug group Anti-emetic (p.90)
Overdose danger rating Medium
Dependence rating Low
Prescription needed Yes
Available as generic No

INFORMATION FOR USERS

Your drug prescription is tailored for you. Do not alter dosage without checking with your doctor.

How taken

Tablets, liquid, suppositories.

Frequency and timing of doses
Every 4 – 8 hours as required.

Adult dosage range
30 – 120mg daily (orally); 90 – 360mg daily (suppository).

Onset of effect
Within 1 hour. The effects of the drug may be delayed if taken after the onset of nausea.

Duration of action
Approximately 6 hours.

Diet advice
None.

Storage
Keep in a closed container in a cool, dry place away from reach of children.

Missed dose
Take the next dose as required.

Stopping the drug
Can be safely stopped as soon as you no longer need it.

Exceeding the dose
An occasional unintentional extra dose is unlikely to cause problems. Large overdoses may cause drowsiness. Notify your doctor.

SPECIAL PRECAUTIONS

Be sure to tell your doctor if:
▼ You have a long-term kidney problem.
▼ You are taking other medications.

 Pregnancy
▼ Safety in pregnancy not established. Discuss with your doctor.

 Breast feeding
▼ The drug may pass into the breast milk, but at normal doses adverse effects on the baby are unlikely. Discuss with your doctor.

 Infants and children
▼ Prescribed only to treat nausea and vomiting caused by anticancer drugs or radiation therapy. Reduced dose necessary.

 Over 60
▼ No special problems.

 Driving and hazardous work
▼ No special problems.

 Alcohol
▼ No special problems, but alcohol is best avoided in cases of nausea and vomiting.

POSSIBLE ADVERSE EFFECTS

Adverse effects from this drug are rare.

Symptom/effect	Frequency		Discuss with doctor		Stop taking drug now	Call doctor now
	Common	Rare	Only if severe	In all cases		
Breast enlargement		●		■		
Milk secretion from breast		●		■		
Muscle spasms		●		■	▲	▮

INTERACTIONS

Anticholinergic drugs These may reduce the beneficial effects of domperidone.

Narcotic analgesics These may reduce the beneficial effects of domperidone.

PROLONGED USE

Not prescribed for long-term treatment.

DOTHIEPIN

Brand name Dothapax, Prepadine, Prothiaden
Used in the following combined preparations None

GENERAL INFORMATION

Dothiepin belongs to the class of anti-depressant drugs known as the tricyclics. It is used in the long-term treatment of depression and is particularly useful when depression is accompanied by anxiety and insomnia. It elevates mood, increases physical activity, improves appetite and restores interest in everyday activities. Taken at night, it encourages sleep and helps to eliminate the need for additional sleeping drugs.

Dothiepin takes several weeks to achieve its full antidepressant effect. It has adverse effects common to all tricyclics, including a risk of causing dangerous heart rhythms, fits, and coma if taken in overdose.

INFORMATION FOR USERS

Your drug prescription is tailored for you. Do not alter dosage without checking with your doctor.

How taken

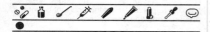

Tablets, capsules.

Frequency and timing of doses
2 – 3 x daily or once at night.

Adult dosage range
75 – 150mg daily.

Onset of effect
Full antidepressant effect may not be felt for 2 – 6 weeks, but adverse effects may be noticed within a few days.

Duration of action
Several days.

Diet advice
None.

Storage
Keep in a closed container in a cool, dry place away from reach of children.

Missed dose
Take as soon as you remember. If your next dose is due within 2 hours, take a single dose now and skip the next.

Stopping the drug
Do not stop taking the drug without consulting your doctor, who may supervise a gradual reduction in dosage. Abrupt cessation may cause a recurrence of the original problem and withdrawal symptoms.

OVERDOSE ACTION

 Seek immediate medical advice in all cases. Take emergency action if palpitations occur or consciousness is lost.

See Drug poisoning emergency guide (p.470).

SPECIAL PRECAUTIONS

Be sure to tell your doctor if:
▼ You have heart problems.
▼ You have had epileptic fits
▼ You have long-term liver or kidney problems.
▼ You have glaucoma.
▼ You have prostate trouble.
▼ You are taking other medications.

 Pregnancy
▼ Safety in pregnancy not established. Discuss with your doctor.

 Breast feeding
▼ The drug passes into the breast milk, but effects on the baby are unlikely. Discuss with your doctor.

 Infants and children
▼ Not recommended.

 Over 60
▼ Reduced dose may be necessary.

 Driving and hazardous work
▼ Avoid such activities until you have learned how the drug affects you because the drug can reduce alertness and may cause blurred vision, dizziness, and drowsiness.

 Alcohol
▼ Avoid. Alcohol may increase the sedative effects of this drug.

Surgery and general anaesthetics
▼ Dothiepin treatment may need to be stopped before you have a general anaesthetic. Discuss this with your doctor or dentist before any operation.

POSSIBLE ADVERSE EFFECTS

The adverse effects of this drug are mainly the result of its *anticholinergic* action. These are more common in the early days of treatment.

Symptom/effect	Frequency		Discuss with doctor		Stop taking drug now	Call doctor now
	Common	Rare	Only if severe	In all cases		
Drowsiness	●		■			
Sweating	●		■			
Blurred vision	●			■		
Dizziness/fainting		●		■		
Rash		●		■	▲	
Difficulty passing urine		●		■	▲	
Palpitations		●		■	▲	■

INTERACTIONS

Sedatives All drugs that have sedative effects intensify those of dothiepin.

Barbiturates These reduce the antidepressant effect of dothiepin.

Heavy smoking This may reduce the antidepressant effect of dothiepin.

Antihypertensive drugs Dothiepin may reduce the effectiveness of such drugs.

Monoamine oxidase inhibitors (MAOIs) In the rare cases where these drugs are given with dothiepin, serious interactions may occur: fever, fits, and delirium.

PROLONGED USE

No problems expected.

DOXORUBICIN

Brand name None
Used in the following combined preparations None

GENERAL INFORMATION

Doxorubicin is one of the most effective anticancer drugs. It is prescribed to treat a wide variety of cancers, usually in conjunction with other anticancer drugs. Doxorubicin is used in acute leukaemia and cancer of the lymph nodes (Hodgkin's disease), lung, breast, bladder, stomach, thyroid, and reproductive organs.

Nausea and vomiting after an injection are the most common side effects of doxorubicin. Although unpleasant, these symptoms tend to be less severe as the body adjusts to treatment. The drug may stain the urine bright red, although this is not harmful. More seriously, because doxorubicin interferes with the production of blood cells, blood clotting disorders, anaemia, and infections may occur. Therefore effects on the blood are carefully monitored. Hair loss is also a common side effect. Dose-dependent changes in heart rhythm and heart failure are a risk.

QUICK REFERENCE

Drug group Cytotoxic anticancer drug (p.154)

Overdose danger rating Medium

Dependence rating Medium

Prescription needed Yes

Available as generic No

INFORMATION FOR USERS

This drug is given only under medical supervision and is not for self-administration.

How taken

Injection.

Frequency and timing of doses
Every 1 – 4 weeks.

Adult dosage range
Dosage is determined individually according to body height, weight, and response.

Onset of effect
Some adverse effects may appear within one hour of starting treatment, but full beneficial effects may not be felt for up to 4 weeks.

Duration of action
Adverse effects can persist for up to 2 weeks after stopping treatment.

Diet advice
None.

Storage
Not applicable. The drug is not normally kept in the home.

Missed dose
The drug is administered in hospital under close medical supervision. If for some reason you skip your dose, contact your doctor as soon as you can.

Stopping the drug
Discuss with your doctor. Stopping the drug prematurely may lead to a worsening of the underlying condition.

Exceeding the dose
Overdosage is unlikely since treatment is carefully monitored and supervised.

SPECIAL PRECAUTIONS

Doxorubicin is prescribed only under close medical supervision, taking account of your present condition and medical history.

Pregnancy
▼ Not usually prescribed. Doxorubicin may cause birth defects or premature birth. Discuss with your doctor.

Breast feeding
▼ Not advised. The drug passes into the breast milk and may affect the baby adversely. Discuss with your doctor.

Infants and children
▼ Reduced dose necessary.

Over 60
▼ Reduced dose may be necessary. Increased risk of adverse effects.

Driving and hazardous work
▼ No known problems.

Alcohol
▼ No known problems.

POSSIBLE ADVERSE EFFECTS

Nausea and vomiting generally occur within an hour or so of injection. Hair loss and loss of appetite are also experienced by many people. Palpitations may be a symptom of an adverse effect of the drug on the heart. Since treatment with this drug is closely supervised in hospital, all adverse effects are monitored.

Symptom/effect	Frequency		Discuss with doctor		Stop taking drug now	Call doctor now
	Common	Rare	Only if severe	In all cases		
Nausea/vomiting	●			■		
Loss of appetite	●			■		
Hair loss	●			■		
Diarrhoea		●		■		
Mouth ulcers		●		■		
Palpitations		●		■		■

INTERACTIONS

Cyclosporin The administration of cyclosporin whilst receiving doxorubicin can lead to adverse effects on the nervous system.

PROLONGED USE

Prolonged use of doxorubicin may reduce the activity of the bone marrow, leading to reduced production of all types of blood cell. It may also affect the heart adversely.

Monitoring Periodic checks on blood composition are usually required. Regular heart examinations are also carried out.

DOXYCYCLINE

Brand names Nordox, Vibramycin
Used in the following combined preparations None

GENERAL INFORMATION

Doxycyline is a member of the tetracycline group of antibiotics. Longer acting than some other drugs in this group, it is mainly used in the treatment of respiratory tract infections, urinary tract infections, and infections of the skin, eye, prostate, and gastrointestinal tract. It is particularly effective against chlamydia infection. Doxycycline is also used in the treatment of acne.

It is less likely to cause diarrhoea as a side effect than other tetracyclines,

and absorption of the drug is not significantly impaired by food. It can therefore be taken with meals to reduce side effects such as nausea or indigestion. Doxycycline is also safe (unlike other tetracyclines) for people with impaired kidney function. Like other tetracyclines, doxycycline can cause staining of developing teeth and is therefore usually avoided in young children or pregnant women.

QUICK REFERENCE

Drug group Tetracycline antibiotic (p.128)
Overdose danger rating Low
Dependence rating Low
Prescription needed Yes
Available as generic Yes

INFORMATION FOR USERS

Your drug prescription is tailored for you. Do not alter dosage without checking with your doctor.

How taken

Tablets, capsules.

Frequency and timing of doses
1 – 2 x daily with water in a sitting or standing position.

Dosage range
50 – 200mg daily.

Onset of effect
4 – 12 hours.

Duration of action
Up to 24 hours.

Diet advice
You may be advised to avoid milk with this drug.

Storage
Keep in a closed container in a cool, dry place away from reach of children.

Missed dose
Take as soon as you remember. If your next dose is due within 6 hours, take a single dose now and skip the next.

Stopping the drug
Take the full course. Even if you feel better the original infection may still be present and symptoms may recur if treatment is stopped too soon.

Exceeding the dose
An occasional unintentional extra dose is unlikely to cause problems. But if you have unusual symptoms, or if a large overdose has been taken, notify your doctor.

POSSIBLE ADVERSE EFFECTS

Adverse effects from doxycycline are rare, although some people may experience nausea, vomiting, or diarrhoea. Other rare

adverse effects include rash, itching, and increased sensitivity of the skin to sunlight, which may cause a rash to develop.

Symptom/effect	Frequency		Discuss with doctor		Stop taking drug now	Call doctor now
	Common	Rare	Only if severe	In all cases		
Nausea/vomiting		●	■			
Diarrhoea		●	■			
Rash/itching		●		■	▲	
Light–sensitive rash		●		■	▲	

INTERACTIONS

Barbiturates, carbamazepine, and phenytoin All these drugs reduce the effectiveness of doxycycline. The doxycycline dosage may need to be increased accordingly.

Oral anticoagulants Doxycycline increases the anticoagulant action of these drugs.

Antacids May impair absorption of this drug. Do not take within 1 hour of doxycycline.

Penicillin Doxycycline interferes with the antibacterial action of penicillin.

Oral contraceptives Doxycycline can reduce the effectiveness of oral contraceptives. Discuss with your doctor.

SPECIAL PRECAUTIONS

Be sure to tell your doctor if:
▼ You have liver impairment.
▼ You have previously suffered an allergic reaction to a tetracycline antibiotic.
▼ You are taking other medications.

Pregnancy
▼ Not usually prescribed. May discolour the teeth of the developing baby. Discuss with your doctor.

Breast feeding
▼ The drug passes into the breast milk and may lead to discoloration of the baby's teeth and have other adverse effects. Discuss with your doctor.

Infants and children
▼ Not recommended under 12 years old. Reduced dose necessary in older children.

Over 60
▼ No special problems.

Driving and hazardous work
▼ No known problems.

Alcohol
▼ No known problems, but avoid excessive amounts.

PROLONGED USE

No problems expected.

DYDROGESTERONE

Brand name Duphaston
Used in the following combined preparations None

GENERAL INFORMATION

Dydrogesterone is a progestogen, a synthetic hormone similar to the natural female sex hormone progesterone. It is widely used to treat a variety of menstrual disorders thought to be caused by a deficiency of this hormone. These include absent, irregular or painful periods, and premenstrual syndrome (see also p.160).
    Dydrogesterone is also prescribed together with an oestrogen as part of

hormone replacement therapy following the menopause. It is sometimes prescribed for endometriosis (p.160), and it is also given to prevent miscarriage in women who have suffered repeated miscarriage.
    The drug is usually taken on selected days during the menstrual cycle depending on the disorder being treated.

QUICK REFERENCE

Drug group Female sex hormone (p.147)

Overdose danger rating Low

Dependence rating Low

Prescription needed Yes

Available as generic No

INFORMATION FOR USERS

Your drug prescription is tailored for you. Do not alter dosage without checking with your doctor.

How taken

Tablets.

Frequency and timing of doses
2 – 3 x daily. In many conditions this drug is taken at certain times in the menstrual cycle.

Adult dosage range
20 – 30mg daily.

Onset of effect
Beneficial effects of this drug may not be felt for several months.

Duration of action
12 hours.

Diet advice
None.

Storage
Keep in a closed container in a cool, dry place away from reach of children. Protect from light.

Missed dose
Take as soon as you remember. If your next dose is due within 2 hours, take a single dose now and skip the next.

Stopping the drug
Do not stop the drug without consulting your doctor; symptoms may recur.

Exceeding the dose
An occasional unintentional extra dose is unlikely to be a cause for concern. But if you notice unusual symptoms, or if a large overdose has been taken, notify your doctor.

SPECIAL PRECAUTIONS

Be sure to tell your doctor if:
▼ You have a long-term liver problem.
▼ You have heart or circulatory problems.
▼ You have diabetes.
▼ You are taking other medications.

 Pregnancy
▼ No evidence of risk.

 Breast feeding
▼ Safety not established. Discuss with your doctor.

 Infants and children
▼ Not prescribed.

 Over 60
▼ No special problems.

 Driving and hazardous work
▼ No special problems.

 Alcohol
▼ No special problems.

POSSIBLE ADVERSE EFFECTS

Irregular periods and "breakthrough" bleeding are the most common adverse effects of this drug. These symptoms may be helped by dosage adjustment.

Symptom/effect	Frequency		Discuss with doctor		Stop taking drug now	Call doctor now
	Common	Rare	Only if severe	In all cases		
Swollen feet/ankles	●		■			
Weight gain	●		■			
Irregular vaginal bleeding	●			■		
Nausea/vomiting		●	■			
Breast tenderness		●	■			
Headache		●		■		

PROLONGED USE

No special problems.

INTERACTIONS

None.

ECONAZOLE

Brand name Ecostatin, Gyno-Pevaryl, Pevaryl
Used in the following combined preparations Econacort, Pevaryl-TC

GENERAL INFORMATION

Econazole is an effective antifungal drug used in treating a range of fungal and yeast infections. These include ringworm (tinea), athlete's foot, fungal nappy rash, and thrush (candida) infections of the vagina, vulva, and skin.

A pessary form of the drug is used to treat vaginal and vulval infection. Other forms are suitable for treating areas of skin. Where possible, the infected area should be clean and dry while being treated.

Serious adverse effects with econazole are rare, although local stinging, burning, and skin irritation can sometimes occur. If there is a lot of inflammation with the infection, econazole is sometimes given in combination with a corticosteroid.

INFORMATION FOR USERS

Your drug prescription is tailored for you. Do not alter dosage without checking with your doctor or pharmacist.

How taken

Powder, pessary, cream, lotion, spray.

Frequency and timing of doses
1 – 3 x daily.

Dosage range
As directed according to the preparation used.

Onset of effect
1 – 2 days.

Duration of action
Up to 24 hours.

Diet advice
None.

Storage
Keep in a closed container in a cool, dry place away from reach of children.

Missed dose
No cause for concern, but apply as soon as you remember.

Stopping the drug
Apply the full course. Even if symptoms disappear, the original infection may still be present and symptoms may recur if treatment is stopped too soon.

Exceeding the dose
An occasional unintentional extra dose is unlikely to be a cause for concern. But if you notice any unusual symptoms, or if a large overdose has been taken, notify your doctor.

SPECIAL PRECAUTIONS

Be sure to tell your doctor or pharmacist if:
▼ You have had a previous allergic reaction to this drug.
▼ You are taking other medications.

 Pregnancy
▼ No evidence of risk to developing baby.

 Breast feeding
▼ No evidence of risk.

 Infants and children
▼ No special problems.

 Over 60
▼ No special problems.

 Driving and hazardous work
▼ No known problems.

 Alcohol
▼ No known problems.

POSSIBLE ADVERSE EFFECTS

Local irritation may occur at the site of application, but disappears when treatment is stopped. More serious adverse effects rarely occur with econazole.

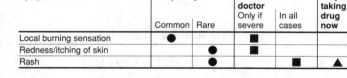

Symptom/effect	Frequency		Discuss with doctor		Stop taking drug now	Call doctor now
	Common	Rare	Only if severe	In all cases		
Local burning sensation	●		■			
Redness/itching of skin		●	■			
Rash		●			■	▲

PROLONGED USE

No problems expected, but rarely needed long term.

INTERACTIONS

None.

ENALAPRIL

Brand name Innovace
Used in the following combined preparations Innozide

GENERAL INFORMATION

Enalapril belongs to the ACE inhibitor group of *vasodilator* drugs (see p.98) prescribed to treat hypertension (high blood pressure) and heart failure. It is sometimes given in conjunction with a diuretic to increase its effect.

The first dose of enalapril may cause a sudden drop in blood pressure. You should be resting at the time and able to lie down afterwards for 2 – 3 hours.

The more common adverse effects, such as dizziness and headache, usually diminish with long-term treatment. Rashes can also occur during treatment. These usually disappear when the drug is stopped. In some cases they clear up on their own despite continued treatment.

QUICK REFERENCE

Drug group Vasodilator (p.98) and Antihypertensive drug (p.102)
Overdose danger rating Medium
Dependence rating Low
Prescription needed Yes
Available as generic No

INFORMATION FOR USERS

Your drug prescription is tailored for you. Do not alter dosage without checking with your doctor.

How taken

Tablets.

Frequency and timing of doses
Once daily.

Adult dosage range
2.5 – 5mg daily (starting dose), increased to 10 – 40mg daily (maintenance dose).

Onset of effect
Within 1 hour.

Duration of action
24 hours.

Diet advice
None.

Storage
Keep in a closed container in a cool, dry place away from reach of children. Protect from light.

Missed dose
Take as soon as you remember. If your next dose is due within 8 hours, take a dose now and skip the next.

Stopping the drug
Do not stop the drug without consulting your doctor; stopping the drug may lead to worsening of the underlying condition.

Exceeding the dose
An occasional unintentional extra dose is unlikely to cause problems. Large overdoses may cause dizziness or fainting. Notify your doctor.

SPECIAL PRECAUTIONS

Be sure to tell your doctor if:
▼ You have long-term kidney problems.
▼ You are taking other medications.

Pregnancy
▼ Not usually prescribed. May cause abnormalities in the unborn baby. Discuss with your doctor.

Breast feeding
▼ The drug passes into the breast milk, but at normal doses adverse effects on the baby are unlikely. Discuss with your doctor.

Infants and children
▼ Not recommended.

Over 60
▼ Reduced dose may be necessary.

Driving and hazardous work
▼ Avoid such activities until you have learned how the drug affects you because the drug can cause dizziness and fainting.

Alcohol
▼ Avoid. Alcohol increases the likelihood of an excessive drop in blood pressure.

POSSIBLE ADVERSE EFFECTS

The more common adverse effects, such as dizziness and headache, usually diminish with long-term treatment. The less common effects may also diminish during long-term treatment, but an adjustment in dosage may be necessary.

Symptom/effect	Frequency		Discuss with doctor		Stop taking drug now	Call doctor now
	Common	Rare	Only if severe	In all cases		
Dizziness/feeling faint	●		■			
Headache	●		■			
Nausea		●		■		
Diarrhoea		●		■		
Rash/urticaria		●		■		
Muscle cramps		●		■		
Persistent cough/voice changes		●		■		

INTERACTIONS

Antihypertensive drugs are likely to add to the blood pressure lowering effect of enalapril.

Lithium Enalapril increases the levels of lithium in the blood, and serious adverse effects from lithium excess may occur.

Potassium supplements and potassium-sparing diuretics Enalapril may add to the effect of these drugs leading to raised levels of potassium in the blood.

Cyclosporin Increased levels of potassium in the blood may result if cyclosporin is taken.

PROLONGED USE

No problems expected.

Monitoring Periodic tests on blood and urine may be performed.

EPHEDRINE

Brand name CAM
Used in the following combined preparations Davenol, Expurhin, Franol, Franol Plus, Haymine, Phensedyl

GENERAL INFORMATION

In use for more than 50 years, ephedrine promotes the release of noradrenaline, a *neurotransmitter,* as well as having a direct effect on receptors in the nervous system. It used to be widely prescribed as a bronchodilator for its action of relaxing the muscles surrounding the airways thereby easing breathing difficulty caused by asthma, bronchitis, and emphysema. Newer and more effective drugs have largely replaced

ephedrine for these purposes. The main use of the drug nowadays is as a decongestant, when it is usually applied as nose drops.

Adverse effects from nose drops used in moderation are unusual, but taken by mouth, ephedrine may stimulate the heart and central nervous system causing palpitations and anxiety.

QUICK REFERENCE

Drug group Bronchodilator (p.92) and decongestant (p.93)
Overdose danger rating Medium
Dependence rating Low
Prescription needed No
Available as generic Yes

INFORMATION FOR USERS

Follow instructions on the label. Call your doctor if symptoms worsen.

How taken

Tablets, syrup, nose drops, injection.

Frequency and timing of doses
By mouth 3 x daily.
Nose drops 3 – 4 x daily.

Dosage range
Adults 45 – 180mg daily (by mouth); 1 – 2 drops into each nostril per dose (nose drops).
Children Reduced dose according to age and weight.

Onset of effect
Within 15 – 60 minutes.

Duration of action
3 – 6 hours.

Diet advice
None.

Storage
Keep in a closed container in a cool, dry place away from reach of children. Protect from light.

Missed dose
Do not take the missed dose. Take your next dose as usual.

Stopping the drug
Can be safely stopped as soon as you no longer need it.

Exceeding the dose
An occasional unintentional extra dose is unlikely to cause problems. Large overdoses may cause shortness of breath, high fever, fits or loss of consciousness. Notify your doctor.

SPECIAL PRECAUTIONS

Be sure to consult your doctor or pharmacist before taking this drug if:
▼ You have long-term kidney problems.
▼ You have heart disease.
▼ You have high blood pressure.
▼ You have diabetes.
▼ You have an overactive thyroid gland.
▼ You have had glaucoma.
▼ You have urinary difficulties.
▼ You are taking other medications.

 Pregnancy
▼ Safety in pregnancy not established. Discuss with your doctor.

 Breast feeding
▼ The drug passes into the breast milk and may affect the baby. Discuss with your doctor.

 Infants and children
▼ Reduced dose necessary.

 Over 60
▼ Not usually prescribed.

 Driving and hazardous work
▼ Avoid such activities until you have learned how the drug affects you because it may cause mental confusion.

 Alcohol
▼ No special problems.

Surgery and general anaesthetics
▼ Ephedrine may need to be stopped before you have a general anaesthetic. Discuss this with your doctor or dentist before any surgery.

POSSIBLE ADVERSE EFFECTS

Adverse effects from ephedrine nose drops are uncommon, although local irritation can occur. When taken by mouth, the drug may have adverse effects on the central nervous system (e.g. insomnia, anxiety) and cardiovascular system (palpitations). Taking the last dose before 4 pm may prevent insomnia.

Symptom/effect	Frequency		Discuss with doctor		Stop taking drug now	Call doctor now
	Common	Rare	Only if severe	In all cases		
Anxiety/restlessness	●		■			
Insomnia	●		■			
Confusion		●	■			
Tremor		●	■			
Urinary difficulties		●		■		
Palpitations/chest pain		●		■	▲	▮

INTERACTIONS

Monoamine oxidase inhibitors (MAOIs) Ephedrine may interact with these drugs to cause a dangerous rise in blood pressure.

Beta blockers Ephedrine may interact with these drugs to cause a dangerous rise in blood pressure.

Antihypertensive drugs Ephedrine may counteract the effects of antihypertensive drugs.

PROLONGED USE

Prolonged use is not recommended except on medical advice. Decongestant effects may lessen and rebound congestion may occur.

EPOETIN (ERYTHROPOIETIN)

Brand names Eprex, Recormon
Used in the following combined preparations None

GENERAL INFORMATION

Epoetin is a form of the naturally occurring hormone called erythropoietin, which is produced by the kidneys. Available as two types (alpha and beta), epoetin stimulates the body to produce red blood cells. It is manufactured by a special technique that uses bacteria to make human erythropoietin.

It is prescribed to treat anaemia in chronic kidney failure patients on dialysis. These patients produce very little erythropoietin themselves so the number of red blood cells is very low. This was previously treatable only by giving regular blood transfusions. When erythropoietin is injected regularly, more red cells will be made by the bone marrow, and this relieves the anaemia, making blood transfusions unnecessary. As it is a natural hormone, erythropoietin has few side effects, but treatment must be carefully monitored or patients may produce too many red blood cells, causing high blood pressure, or the blood may start clotting too easily.

Erythropoietin has also been given to patients with AIDS who have anaemia due to the disease and its treatment; however, this is a trial use and is not widely available. It has also been tried by athletes who wish to improve their performance; this is not a recognized use and would be regarded as an illegal use of drugs by the sports authorities.

INFORMATION FOR USERS

This drug is given only under medical supervision and is not for self-administration.

How taken

Injection.

Frequency and timing of doses
2 – 3 x weekly.

Dosage range
Dosage is calculated on an individual basis according to body weight. The dosage also varies depending on the form of epoetin used.

Onset of effect
Active inside the body within 2 – 3 hours, but effects may not be noted for 2 – 3 months.

Duration of action
4 – 7 hours. Some effects may persist for several days.

Diet advice
None. However, if you have kidney failure, you may have to follow a special diet.

Storage
Store at 2 – 8°C. Do not freeze or shake. Protect from light.

Missed dose
Do not make up any missed doses.

Stopping the drug
Discuss with your doctor.

Exceeding the dose
A single excessive dose is unlikely to cause problems. Too high a dose over a long period can increase the likelihood of adverse effects.

SPECIAL PRECAUTIONS

Be sure to tell your doctor if:
▼ You have high blood pressure.
▼ You have previously suffered allergic reactions to any drugs.
▼ You have peripheral vascular disease.
▼ You have had epileptic fits.
▼ You are taking other medications.

 Pregnancy
▼ Not usually prescribed. Safety in pregnancy not established. Discuss with your doctor.

 Breast feeding
▼ Safety not established. Discuss with your doctor.

 Infants and children
▼ Not recommended.

 Over 60s
▼ No known problems.

 Driving and hazardous work
▼ Not applicable.

 Alcohol
▼ Follow your doctor's advice regarding alcohol.

PROLONGED USE

The long-term effects of the drug are still under investigation, but problems are unlikely if treatment is carefully monitored.

Monitoring Regular blood tests are required to monitor blood composition.

POSSIBLE ADVERSE EFFECTS

The most common effects are increased blood pressure and problems at the site of the injection; all unusual symptoms should be discussed with your doctor immediately.

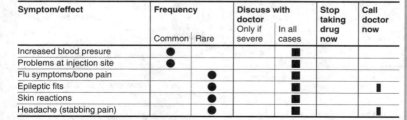

Symptom/effect	Frequency		Discuss with doctor		Stop taking drug now	Call doctor now
	Common	Rare	Only if severe	In all cases		
Increased blood presure	●			■		
Problems at injection site	●			■		
Flu symptoms/bone pain		●		■		
Epileptic fits		●		■		
Skin reactions		●		■		▮
Headache (stabbing pain)		●		■		▮

INTERACTIONS

Iron supplements may increase the effect of erythropoietin if you have a low level of iron in your blood.

ERGOTAMINE

Brand names Lingraine, Medihaler-Ergotamine
Used in the following combined preparations Cafergot, Migril

GENERAL INFORMATION

Ergotamine is used to treat migraine headaches. It constricts blood vessels around the skull and is used only by people for whom *analgesics* (like aspirin or paracetamol) or any anti-inflammatory drugs (like ibuprofen) fail to provide sufficient relief. It is most effective if taken at the first sign of a migraine attack. Once headache and nausea are established, the drug may be less effective and cause a stomach upset and increase the nausea of

migraine. Ergotamine is also available combined with caffeine as tablets and suppositories. These may be more effective in some patients.

Ergotamine causes temporary narrowing of blood vessels throughout the body and therefore is not pre-scribed for those with poor circulation. If it is taken too frequently it can dangerously reduce blood circulation to the hands and feet; ergotamine should never be taken regularly.

QUICK REFERENCE

Drug group Drug for migraine (p.89)

Overdose danger rating Medium

Dependence rating Low

Prescription needed Yes

Available as generic No

INFORMATION FOR USERS

Your drug prescription is tailored for you. Do not alter dosage without checking with your doctor.

How taken

Tablets (held under the tongue or swallowed), suppositories, inhaler.

Frequency and timing of doses
Once (at the onset), repeated if necessary after 30 minutes (tablets) or 5 minutes (inhaler) up to the maximum dose (below).

Adult dosage range
1 – 2mg per dose. Take no more than 6mg in 24 hours or 12mg in 1 week (by mouth), 6 inhalations in 24 hours or 15 inhalations in 1 week (inhaler) or 4mg in 24 hours or 8mg in 1 week (rectally).

Onset of effect
Within 30 minutes.

Duration of action
Up to 36 hours.

Diet advice
Changes in diet are unlikely to affect the action of this drug, but certain foods may provoke migraine attacks in some people (see p.89).

Storage
Keep in a closed container in a cool, dry place away from reach of children. Protect from light.

Missed dose
Regular doses of this drug are not necessary and may be dangerous. Take only when you have symptoms of migraine.

Stopping the drug
Can be safely stopped as soon as you no longer need it.

Exceeding the dose
An occasional unintentional extra dose is unlikely to cause problems. Large overdoses may cause vomiting, dizziness, seizures or coma. Notify your doctor.

SPECIAL PRECAUTIONS

Be sure to tell your doctor if:
▼ You have kidney or liver problems.
▼ You have heart problems.
▼ You have poor circulation.
▼ You have high blood pressure.
▼ You have had a recent stroke.
▼ You have an overactive thyroid gland.
▼ You are taking other medications.

Pregnancy
▼ Not usually prescribed. Ergotamine can cause contractions of the uterus.

Breast feeding
▼ Not recommended during breast feeding. It passes into the milk and may have adverse effects on the baby. It may also reduce your milk supply.

Infants and children
▼ Not usually prescribed.

Over 60
▼ Use with caution. Hidden heart or circulatory problems may be aggravated.

Driving and hazardous work
▼ No special problems.

Alcohol
▼ No special problems, but some drinks may provoke migraine in some people (see p.89).

Surgery and general anaesthetics
▼ Notify your doctor if you have used ergotamine within 48 hours prior to surgery.

POSSIBLE ADVERSE EFFECTS

The more common symptoms of treatment with ergotamine are digestive disturbances and nausea. An anti-emetic drug may be prescribed to relieve nausea.

Symptom/effect	Frequency		Discuss with doctor		Stop taking drug now	Call doctor now
	Common	Rare	Only if severe	In all cases		
Nausea/vomiting	●		■			
Diarrhoea		●	■			
Leg cramps		●			■	
Abdominal pain		●			■	
Tingling in fingers/toes		●		■	▲	

INTERACTIONS

Erythromycin There is an increased likelihood of adverse effects when this drug is taken with ergotamine.

Beta blockers may increase circulatory problems with ergotamine.

Sumatriptan There is an increased risk of adverse effects on blood circulation if sumatriptan (another drug for migraine) is used with ergotamine.

PROLONGED USE

Reduced circulation to the hands and feet may result if doses near to the maximum are taken for a long time. It is important that the dosage and length of treatment are not exceeded.

ERYTHROMYCIN

Brand names Arpimycin, Erycen, Erymax, Erythrocin, Erythromid, Erythroped, Ilosone, Rommix, Stiemycin
Used in the following combined preparations Zineryt

GENERAL INFORMATION

One of the safest and most widely used antibiotics, erythromycin is effective against a wide range of bacteria. It is a useful alternative to penicillins and tetracyclines for people who are allergic to those drugs.

Erythromycin is commonly prescribed for throat, middle ear, and chest infections, including some rare types of pneumonia such as mycoplasma pneumonia and Legionnaire's disease, and in sexually transmitted diseases such as gonorrhoea, chlamydial infections, and syphilis.

Sometimes given to treat and reduce the likelihood of infecting others with whooping cough, erythromycin may also be included as part of the treatment for diphtheria.

Erythromycin taken by mouth may sometimes cause nausea and vomiting. Other possible adverse effects include rash and a rare risk of liver disorders. Local application of erythromycin is sometimes helpful in treating acne.

INFORMATION FOR USERS

Your drug prescription is tailored for you. Do not alter dosage without checking with your doctor.

How taken

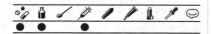

Tablets, capsules, liquid, injection.

Frequency and timing of doses
Every 6 – 12 hours.

Dosage range
1 – 4g daily.

Onset of effect
2 – 4 hours.

Duration of action
6 – 12 hours.

Diet advice
None.

Storage
Keep in a closed container in a cool, dry place away from reach of children.

Missed dose
Take as soon as you remember. If your next dose is due within 2 hours, take a single dose now and skip the next.

Stopping the drug
Take the full course. Even if you feel better the original infection may still be present and symptoms may recur if treatment is stopped too soon.

Exceeding the dose
An occasional unintentional extra dose is unlikely to cause problems. If you notice unusual symptoms, or if a large overdose has been taken, notify your doctor.

POSSIBLE ADVERSE EFFECTS

Nausea and vomiting are the most common adverse effects and are most likely to occur with large doses taken by mouth. Symptoms such as fever, rash, and jaundice may be a sign of a liver disorder and should always be reported to your doctor.

Symptom/effect	Frequency		Discuss with doctor		Stop taking drug now	Call doctor now
	Common	Rare	Only if severe	In all cases		
Nausea/vomiting	●		■			
Diarrhoea	●		■			
Rash/itching	●			■	▲	
Deafness		●		■		▮
Jaundice		●		■	▲	▮
Unexplained fever		●		■	▲	▮

INTERACTIONS

Theophylline Erythromycin increases the risk of side effects with this drug.

Carbamazepine Erythromycin may increase blood levels of this drug.

Warfarin Erythromycin increases the risk of bleeding with warfarin.

Digoxin Erythromycin may increase blood levels of this drug.

Terfenadine and astemizole Erythromycin increases the risk of adverse effects of these antihistamines on the heart.

SPECIAL PRECAUTIONS

Be sure to tell your doctor if:
▼ You have a long-term liver problem.
▼ You have had a previous allergic reaction to erythromycin.
▼ You are taking other medications.

 Pregnancy
▼ No evidence of risk to developing baby.

 Breast feeding
▼ The drug passes into the breast milk, but at normal doses adverse effects on the baby are unlikely. Discuss with your doctor.

 Infants and children
▼ Reduced dose necessary.

 Over 60
▼ No special problems.

 Driving and hazardous work
▼ No known problems.

 Alcohol
▼ No known problems.

PROLONGED USE

Courses of longer than 14 days may increase the risk of liver damage.

ETHAMBUTOL

Brand name Myambutol
Used in the following combined preparations Mynah

GENERAL INFORMATION

Ethambutol is used in the treatment of tuberculosis. Given in conjunction with other antituberculous drugs, it helps to boost their effects.

Occasionally, it may be given early in treatment, when resistance to the more commonly used drugs is suspected. This may apply particularly when people may have caught the disease by contact with a recent immigrant from Africa or Asia where resistance to other drugs has been increasing.

Although the drug has few common adverse effects, it may occasionally cause optic neuritis, a type of eye damage, leading to blurring and fading of vision. Ethambutol is not usually given to children under six. Patients are usually advised to have periodic eye checks.

INFORMATION FOR USERS

Your drug prescription is tailored for you. Do not alter dosage without checking with your doctor.

How taken

Tablets.

Frequency and timing of doses
Once daily.

Adult dosage range
According to body weight.

Onset of effect
It may take several days for symptoms to improve.

Duration of action
Up to 24 hours.

Diet advice
None.

Storage
Keep in a closed container in a cool, dry, place away from reach of children.

Missed dose
Take as soon as you remember. If your next dose is scheduled within 6 hours, take your dose now and skip the next.

Stopping the drug
Take the full course. Even if you feel better the original infection may still be present and may recur if treatment is stopped too soon.

Exceeding the dose
An occasional unintentional extra dose is unlikely to cause problems. Large over-doses may cause headache and abdominal pain. Notify your doctor.

POSSIBLE ADVERSE EFFECTS

Side effects are uncommon with this drug, but are more likely after prolonged treatment at high doses. Blurred vision or eye pain requires prompt medical attention.

Symptom/effect	Frequency		Discuss with doctor		Stop taking drug now	Call doctor now
	Common	Rare	Only if severe	In all cases		
Nausea/vomiting		●	■			
Dizziness		●	■			
Numb/tingling hands/feet		●		■		
Blurred vision		●		■	▲	
Eye pain		●		■	▲	
Loss of colour vision		●		■	▲	■
Rash/itching		●		■	▲	

INTERACTIONS

None.

SPECIAL PRECAUTIONS

Be sure to tell your doctor if:
▼ You have a long-term kidney problem.
▼ You have cataracts or other eye problems.
▼ You have had a previous allergic reaction to this drug.
▼ You are taking other medications.

 Pregnancy
▼ Safety in pregnancy not established. Discuss with your doctor.

 Breast feeding
▼ The drug passes into the breast milk, but at normal doses adverse effects on the baby are unlikely. Discuss with your doctor.

 Infants and children
▼ Not prescribed in children under 6.

 Over 60
▼ Increased likelihood of adverse effects. Reduced dose may therefore be necessary.

 Driving and hazardous work
▼ No special problems unless visual disturbances occur.

 Alcohol
▼ No known problems.

PROLONGED USE

Prolonged use may increase the risk of eye damage.

Monitoring Periodic eye tests may be recommended.

ETHINYLOESTRADIOL

Used in the following combined preparations BiNovum, Brevinor, Eugynon 30, Femodene, Logynon, Marvelon, Microgynon, Ovranette, TriNovum, and many others

GENERAL INFORMATION

Ethinyloestradiol is a synthetic oestrogen similar to the natural female sex hormone, oestradiol. It is widely used in oral contraceptives, combined with a synthetic progesterone drug (progestogen). Ethinyloestradiol is also used to supplement oestrogen when the body's production is low, e.g. during the menopause. In such cases, it is often given with a progestogen.

It is occasionally used to control abnormal bleeding from the uterus and to treat delayed sexual development (hypogonadism) in females. Certain cancers of the prostate respond to ethinyloestradiol. It is sometimes given, in high doses, for post-coital contraception. In conjunction with cyproterone, it is used to treat severe acne in women.

INFORMATION FOR USERS

Your drug prescription is tailored for you. Do not alter dosage without checking with your doctor.

How taken

Tablets.

Frequency and timing of doses
Once daily.

Adult dosage range
Menopausal symptoms 10 – 20 mcg daily.
Hormone deficiency 10 – 50 mcg daily.
Combined contraceptive pills 20 – 50 mcg daily depending on preparation.

Onset of effect
10 – 20 days. Contraceptive protection is effective after 7 days in most cases.

Duration of action
1 – 2 days.

Diet advice
None.

Storage
Keep in a closed container in a cool, dry place away from reach of children.

Missed dose
Take as soon as you remember. If your next dose is due within 4 hours, take a single dose now and skip the next. If you are taking the drug for contraceptive purposes, see p.161.

Stopping the drug
Do not stop the drug without consulting your doctor. Contraceptive protection is lost unless an alternative is used.

Exceeding the dose
An occasional extra dose is unlikely to be a cause for concern. But if you notice unusual symptoms, or if a large overdose has been taken, notify your doctor.

SPECIAL PRECAUTIONS

Be sure to tell your doctor if:
▼ You have heart failure or high blood pressure.
▼ You have had blood clots or a stroke.
▼ You have long-term liver problems.
▼ You are a smoker.
▼ You have diabetes.
▼ You suffer from migraine or epilepsy.
▼ You are taking other medications.

Pregnancy
▼ Not prescribed. May adversely affect the baby. Discuss with your doctor.

Breast feeding
▼ The drug passes into the breast milk; it may also inhibit milk flow. Discuss with your doctor.

Infants and children
▼ Not usually prescribed.

Over 60
▼ No special problems.

Driving and hazardous work
▼ No known problems.

Alcohol
▼ No known problems.

Surgery and general anaesthetics
▼ Ethinyloestradiol may need to be stopped several weeks before you have major surgery. Discuss this with your doctor.

POSSIBLE ADVERSE EFFECTS

The most common adverse effects with ethinyloestradiol are similar to symptoms in the early stages of pregnancy, and generally diminish with time. Sudden, sharp pain in the chest, groin or legs may indicate an abnormal blood clot and needs attention.

Symptom/effect	Frequency		Discuss with doctor		Stop taking drug now	Call doctor now
	Common	Rare	Only if severe	In all cases		
Nausea/vomiting	●			■		
Breast swelling/tenderness	●			■		
Weight gain	●			■		
Headache		●		■		
Depression		●		■		
Pain in chest/groin/legs		●		■	▲	▮

INTERACTIONS

Tobacco smoking increases the risk of serious adverse effects on the heart and circulation with ethinyloestradiol.

Antibiotics may reduce the effectiveness of oral contraceptives containing ethinyloestradiol.

Antihypertensive drugs and diuretics Ethinyloestradiol may reduce the effectiveness of these drugs.

Anticonvulsants Patients taking these drugs may require a higher dose of oral contraceptive. The combination may also make epilepsy less well controlled.

PROLONGED USE

Prolonged use of ethinyloestradiol slightly increases the risk of cancer of the uterus after the menopause when used without a progestogen. The risk of gallstones may also be higher.

Monitoring Periodic checks on blood pressure and physical examinations may be performed.

ETHOSUXIMIDE

Brand name Emeside, Zarontin
Used in the following combined preparations None

GENERAL INFORMATION

Ethosuximide was introduced in 1960. It belongs to a group of drugs known as anticonvulsants, used in the treatment of epilepsy. Ethosuximide is most commonly prescribed for the long-term prevention of absence seizures (daydream-like episodes, also known as petit mal). It is also used to treat myoclonic seizures. Other types of epilepsy do not respond well to ethosuximide. The major drawback to the use of ethosuximide is that it can reduce production of blood cells. Minor adverse effects often occur in the early days of treatment, but diminish with time.

QUICK REFERENCE

Drug group Anticonvulsant (p.86)

Overdose danger rating Medium

Dependence rating Low

Prescription needed Yes

Available as generic No

INFORMATION FOR USERS

Your drug prescription is tailored for you. Do not alter dosage without checking with your doctor.

How taken

Capsules, liquid.

Frequency and timing of doses
Once daily.

Dosage range
Adults 500mg daily (starting dose) gradually increased up to a maximum of 1.5g daily.

Onset of effect
Within 1 hour.

Duration of action
Approximately 2 days.

Diet advice
None.

Storage
Keep in a closed container in a cool, dry place away from reach of children.

Missed dose
Take as soon as you remember. If your next dose is due within 6 hours, take a dose now and skip the next.

Stopping the drug
Do not stop the drug without consulting your doctor; symptoms may recur.

Exceeding the dose
An occasional unintentional extra dose is unlikely to cause problems. Larger overdoses may cause unusual drowsiness. Notify your doctor.

SPECIAL PRECAUTIONS

Be sure to tell your doctor if:
▼ You have long-term kidney or liver problems.
▼ You have porphyria.
▼ You are taking other medications.

Pregnancy
▼ Safety in pregnancy not established. Discuss with your doctor.

Breast feeding
▼ The drug passes into breast milk and may have effects on the baby. Poor suckling may occur. Discuss with your doctor.

Infants and children
▼ Reduced dose necessary.

Over 60
▼ Reduced dose may be necessary.

Driving and hazardous work
▼ Your underlying condition, as well as the sedative effects of this drug, may make such activities inadvisable. Discuss with your doctor.

Alcohol
▼ Avoid. Alcohol may increase the sedative effect of this drug.

POSSIBLE ADVERSE EFFECTS

Most people experience few adverse effects with this drug, but when blood levels get too high, adverse effects are common and the dose may need to be reduced.

Symptom/effect	Frequency		Discuss with doctor		Stop taking drug now	Call doctor now
	Common	Rare	Only if severe	In all cases		
Drowsiness	●		■			
Loss of appetite	●		■			
Dizziness	●		■			
Nausea/vomiting	●		■			
Headache		●	■			
Depression		●			■	
Paranoia		●			■	
Sore throat		●			■	
Easy bruising		●			■	
Rash		●			■	

INTERACTIONS

Sedatives All drugs that have a sedative effect on the central nervous system are likely to increase the sedative properties of ethosuximide. Such drugs include antihistamines, sleeping drugs, narcotic analgesics, antipsychotics, and antidepressants.

Carbamazepine may reduce levels of ethosuximide in the blood.

Phenytoin and sodium valproate may alter levels of ethosuximide in the blood.

PROLONGED USE

There is a slight risk of blood abnormalities occurring.

ETIDRONATE

Brand name Didronel
Used in the following combined preparations None

GENERAL INFORMATION

Etidronate is prescribed for the treatment of bone disorders such as Paget's disease. It acts only on the bones, reducing the activity of the bone cells thus stopping the progress of the disease. This action also stops calcium from being released from bone into the bloodstream, so it reduces the amount of calcium in the blood. Etidronate is also used to treat osteoporosis. Generally, the side effects of etidronate are mild. The most common is diarrhoea, which is more likely to occur with higher doses. If taken at high doses (20mg/kg daily) the drug stops new bone being formed properly, which can lead to thinning of the bones and fractures. For this reason, high doses must be carefully monitored and used for as short a time as possible. The effect is reversed on stopping the drug.

QUICK REFERENCE

Drug group Drug for bone disorders (p.122)
Overdose danger rating Medium
Dependence rating Low
Prescription needed Yes
Available as generic No

INFORMATION FOR USERS

Your drug prescription is tailored for you. Do not alter dosage without checking with your doctor.

How taken

Tablets, injection.

Frequency and timing of doses
Once daily on an empty stomach, 2 hours before and after food.

Dosage range
Paget's disease 5 – 20mg/kg daily for a maximum of 3 – 6 months (tablets). There may be repeated cycles.
Hypercalcaemia 7.5mg/kg daily for 3 days (injection). This may be repeated.
Osteoporosis 400mg daily for 2 weeks (tablets), repeated every 3 months.

Onset of effect
Paget's disease/osteoporosis Beneficial effects may not be felt for several months.
Hypercalcaemia Within several hours, but full beneficial effects may take 4 – 7 days.

Duration of action
Up to 24 hours. Some effects may persist for several days or weeks.

Diet advice
Absorption of etidronate is reduced by foods, especially those containing calcium, e.g. dairy products, so the drug should be taken on an empty stomach. The diet must contain adequate calcium and vitamin D; supplements may be given.

Storage
Keep in a closed container in a cool, dry place away from reach of children.

Missed dose
Take as soon as you remember. If your next dose is due within 6 hours, take a single dose now and skip the next.

Stopping the drug
Do not stop the drug without consulting your doctor. Stopping the drug may lead to worsening of the underlying condition.

Exceeding the dose
An occasional unintentional extra dose is unlikely to cause problems. Large overdoses may cause numbness and muscle spasm. Notify your doctor.

SPECIAL PRECAUTIONS

Be sure to tell your doctor if:
▼ You have long-term kidney problems.
▼ You have colitis.
▼ You are taking other medications.

 Pregnancy
▼ Safety in pregnancy not established. Discuss with your doctor.

 Breast feeding
▼ Safety not established. Discuss with your doctor.

 Infants and children
▼ Not recommended.

 Over 60
▼ No special problems.

 Driving and hazardous work
▼ No special problems.

 Alcohol
▼ No special problems.

POSSIBLE ADVERSE EFFECTS

The most common side effect is diarrhoea. This is more likely if the dose is increased above 5mg/kg daily. In some patients with Paget's disease, bone pain may be increased initially, but this usually disappears with further treatment.

Symptom/effect	Frequency		Discuss with doctor		Stop taking drug now	Call doctor now
	Common	Rare	Only if severe	In all cases		
Diarrhoea	●		■			
Nausea	●		■			
Constipation/abdominal pain		●	■			
Rash/itching		●		■		
Bone pain		●		■		■

INTERACTIONS

Antacids/iron Antacids should be given at least 2 hours before or after etidronate to minimize effects on absorption.

PROLONGED USE

Courses of treatment longer than 3 – 6 months are not usually prescribed, although repeat courses may be required. Continuous use of this drug is not recommended as it may lead to an increased risk of bone fractures.

Monitoring Blood levels of phosphate and alkaline phosphatase (an enzyme found in bones) are sometimes measured. Urine tests for hydroxyproline may also be performed.

FENBUFEN

Brand name Lederfen, Fenbuzip
Used in the following combined preparations None

GENERAL INFORMATION

Fenbufen is prescribed to relieve the pain, stiffness, and inflammation that may accompany a number of disorders. It is similar to aspirin in the way it works; it acts as an analgesic as well as an anti-inflammatory and it is an effective treatment for the symptoms of rheumatoid arthritis, osteoarthritis, and gout. It also relieves pain from soft tissue injuries and following surgery.

Sometimes, fenbufen is prescribed along with slower acting drugs in the treatment of rheumatoid arthritis.

Fenbufen is said to be less likely to cause bleeding in the stomach than some other non-steroidal anti-inflammatory drugs, but is more likely to cause a rash.

INFORMATION FOR USERS

Your drug prescription is tailored for you. Do not alter dosage without checking with your doctor.

How taken

Tablets, effervescent tablets.

Frequency and timing of doses
2 x daily after food.

Adult dosage range
900mg daily.

Onset of effect
Pain relief begins in 1 – 2 hours. Full anti-inflammatory effect in arthritic conditions may not be felt for up to 2 weeks.

Duration of action
10 – 12 hours.

Diet advice
None.

Storage
Keep in a closed container in a cool, dry place away from reach of children.

Missed dose
Take as soon as you remember. If your next dose is due within 4 hours, take a single dose now and skip the next.

Stopping the drug
When taken for short-term pain relief, fenbufen can be safely stopped as soon as you no longer need it. If prescribed for the long-term treatment of arthritis, however, you should seek medical advice before stopping the drug.

Exceeding the dose
An occasional unintentional extra dose is unlikely to be a cause for concern. But if you notice unusual symptoms, or if a large overdose has been taken, notify your doctor.

SPECIAL PRECAUTIONS

Be sure to tell your doctor if:
▼ You have long-term kidney or liver problems.
▼ You have high blood pressure.
▼ You have had a stomach ulcer, oesophagitis or acid indigestion.
▼ You are allergic to aspirin.
▼ You have asthma.
▼ You are taking other medications.

 Pregnancy
▼ Not usually prescribed. May affect the unborn baby and may prolong labour. Discuss with your doctor.

 Breast feeding
▼ The drug passes into the breast milk, but at normal doses adverse effects on the baby are unlikely. Discuss with your doctor.

 Infants and children
▼ Not recommended for children under 14 years.

 Over 60
▼ No special problems.

 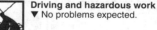 **Driving and hazardous work**
▼ No problems expected.

 Alcohol
▼ Avoid. Alcohol may increase the risk of stomach disorders with fenbufen.

Surgery and general anaesthetics
▼ Discuss with your doctor or dentist before any surgery.

POSSIBLE ADVERSE EFFECTS

The most common adverse effects are the result of gastrointestinal disturbances. Black or bloodstained faeces should be reported to your doctor without delay.

Symptom/effect	Frequency		Discuss with doctor		Stop taking drug now	Call doctor now
	Common	Rare	Only if severe	In all cases		
Nausea/vomiting	●		■			
Rash	●			■	▲	
Heartburn/indigestion	●			■		
Wheezing/breathlessness		●		■	▲	■

INTERACTIONS

General note Fenbufen interacts with a wide range of drugs to increase the risk of bleeding and/or stomach ulcers. Such drugs include oral anticoagulants, corticosteroids, other non-steroidal anti-inflammatory drugs (NSAIDs), and aspirin.

Antibacterial drugs There is a risk of fits occurring if acrosoxacin, nalidixic acid, ciprofloxacin, ofloxacin, cinoxacin or norfloxacin are taken wtih fenbufen.

Antihypertensive drugs and diuretics The beneficial effects of these drugs may be reduced by fenbufen.

PROLONGED USE

There is an increased risk of bleeding from stomach ulcers and in the bowel with prolonged use of fenbufen.

FLAVOXATE

Brand name Urispas
Used in the following combined preparations None

GENERAL INFORMATION

Flavoxate is an antispasmodic drug used to relieve painful urination caused by urinary tract infection or inflammation of the prostate (prostatitis). It is also prescribed for over-frequent or uncontrollable urination.

Having no antibacterial properties of its own, flavoxate is usually administered together with an antibiotic or antibacterial drug to eradicate the underlying infection.

The drug may in rare cases cause nausea and vomiting. It may also produce blurred vision and dry mouth as a result of its mild *anticholinergic* action.

QUICK REFERENCE

Drug group Urinary antispasmodic drug (p.166)

Overdose danger rating Medium

Dependence rating Low

Prescription needed Yes

Available as generic No

INFORMATION FOR USERS

Your drug prescription is tailored for you. Do not alter dosage without checking with your doctor.

How taken

Tablets.

Frequency and timing of doses
3 x daily.

Dosage range
600mg daily.

Onset of effect
Within 2 hours.

Duration of action
6 – 8 hours.

Diet advice
None.

Storage
Keep in a closed container in a cool, dry place away from reach of children.

Missed dose
Take as soon as you remember. If your next dose is due within 2 hours, take a single dose now and skip the next.

Stopping the drug
Do not stop the drug without consulting your doctor; symptoms may recur.

Exceeding the dose
An occasional unintentional extra dose is unlikely to cause problems. Large overdoses may cause dizziness, drowsiness, hallucinations and palpitations. Notify your doctor.

SPECIAL PRECAUTIONS

Be sure to tell your doctor if:
▼ You have had glaucoma.
▼ You have prostate trouble.
▼ You have any form of gastrointestinal disease.
▼ You are taking other medications.

Pregnancy
▼ Safety in pregnancy not established. Discuss with your doctor.

Breast feeding
▼ It is not known whether this drug passes into breast milk. Discuss with your doctor.

Infants and children
▼ Not usually prescribed for children under 12 years.

Over 60
▼ Increased risk of adverse effects.

Driving and hazardous work
▼ Avoid such activities until you have learned how the drug affects you because the drug can cause drowsiness and blurred vision.

Alcohol
▼ No known problems.

POSSIBLE ADVERSE EFFECTS

Flavoxate rarely causes side effects; those that do occur are mainly due to the drug's *anticholinergic* action and can often be reduced by adjustment in dosage.

Symptom/effect	Frequency		Discuss with doctor		Stop taking drug now	Call doctor now
	Common	Rare	Only if severe	In all cases		
Drowsiness/lethargy		●	■			
Dry mouth		●	■			
Nausea/vomiting		●	■			
Headache		●		■		
Confusion		●		■		
Blurred vision		●		■		

INTERACTIONS

None.

PROLONGED USE

No problems expected.

FLUCONAZOLE

Brand names Diflucan
Used in the following combined preparations None

GENERAL INFORMATION

Fluconazole is a relatively new antifungal drug. It is used to treat local candida infections ("thrush") of the vagina and mouth, and also systemic candida infection. In addition, it is used to treat some of the more unusual fungal infections including cryptococcal meningitis. Fungal infections in patients with defective immunity may also be prevented by fluconazole. The dosage and length of course will depend on the condition being treated. Fluconazole is generally well tolerated, the most comon side effects being those affecting the gastrointestinal tract.

INFORMATION FOR USERS

Your drug prescription is tailored for you. Do not alter dosage without checking with your doctor.

How taken

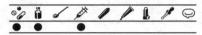

Capsules, liquid, injection.

Frequency and timing of doses
Once daily.

Adult dosage range
50 – 400mg daily.

Onset of effect
It begins to work within a few hours, but full beneficial effects may take several days.

Duration of action
Up to 24 hours.

Diet advice
None.

Storage
Keep in a closed container in a cool, dry place away from reach of children.

Missed dose
Take as soon as you remember. If your next dose is due within 6 hours, take a single dose now and skip the next.

Stopping the drug
Take the full course. Even if you feel better, the original infection may still be present and may recur if treatment is stopped too soon.

Exceeding the dose
An occasional extra dose is unlikely to be a cause for concern. But if you notice any unusual symptoms, or if a large overdose has been taken, notify your doctor.

POSSIBLE ADVERSE EFFECTS

Fluconazole is generally well tolerated. Side effects most commonly affect the gastrointestinal tract.

| Symptom/effect | Frequency | | Discuss with doctor | | Stop taking drug now | Call doctor now |
	Common	Rare	Only if severe	In all cases		
Nausea	●		■			
Abdominal discomfort	●		■			
Diarrhoea	●		■			
Flatulence	●		■			
Rash		●		■	▲	

INTERACTIONS

Anticoagulants Fluconazole may increase the effect of warfarin.

Oral antidiabetic drugs Fluconazole may increase the risk of hypoglycaemia with oral sulphonylureas, e.g. gliclazide, chlorpropamide, glibenclamide, tolbutamide.

Phenytoin Fluconazole may increase the blood level of phenytoin.

Theophylline Fluconazole may increase the blood level of theophylline.

Cyclosporin Fluconazole may increase the blood level of cyclosporin.

Rifampicin The effect of fluconazole may be reduced by rifampicin.

Antihistamines Increased risk of terfenadine and astemizole causing adverse effects on the heart.

SPECIAL PRECAUTIONS

Be sure to tell your doctor if:
▼ You have any liver or kidney problems.
▼ You suffer from epilepsy.
▼ You have previously had an allergic reaction to antifungal drugs.
▼ You are taking other medications.

Pregnancy
▼ Safety in pregnancy not established. Discuss with your doctor.

Breast feeding
▼ Not recommended. The drug passes into the breast milk. Discuss with your doctor.

Infants and children
▼ Not recommended. Dosage reduction required for children in whom fluconazole is used only if there is no alternative.

Over 60
▼ Normal dose used as long as kidney function is not impaired.

Driving and hazardous work
▼ No known problems.

Alcohol
▼ No known problems.

PROLONGED USE

Fluconazole is usually given for short courses of treatment. However, for prevention of relapse of cryptococcal meningitis in patients with defective immunity, it may be administered indefinitely.

FLUOXETINE

Brand name Prozac
Used in the following combined preparations None

GENERAL INFORMATION

Fluoxetine belongs to a relatively new group of antidepressants called specific serotonin re-uptake inhibitors (SSRIs). Drugs of this type tend to cause less sedation and have fewer side effects than older antidepressants. Fluoxetine elevates mood, increases the patient's physical activity, and restores interest in everyday activities.

Fluoxetine is broken down slowly and remains in the body for several weeks after treatment is stopped. Headache, nausea, restlessness, and insomnia are common side effects. As well as being used to treat depression, fluoxetine is used to reduce binge eating and purging activity (bulimia nervosa).

INFORMATION FOR USERS

Your drug prescription is tailored for you. Do not alter dosage without checking with your doctor.

How taken

Capsules, liquid.

Frequency and timing of doses
Once daily in the morning.

Adult dosage range
20 – 60mg daily.

Onset of effect
Some benefit may appear within 14 days, but full benefits may not be felt for 4 weeks or more.

Duration of action
Following prolonged treatment, beneficial effects may last for up to 6 weeks. Adverse effects may wear off within a few days.

Diet advice
None.

Storage
Keep in a closed container in a cool, dry place away from reach of children.

Missed dose
Take as soon as you remember. If your next dose is due within 8 hours, take a single dose now and skip the next.

Stopping the drug
Do not stop the drug without consulting your doctor, who may supervise a gradual reduction in dosage.

Exceeding the dose
An occasional unintentional extra dose is unlikely to cause problems. Large overdoses may cause adverse effects. Notify your doctor.

POSSIBLE ADVERSE EFFECTS

The most common adverse effects are restlessness, insomnia, and intestinal irregularities. Fluoxetine produces fewer *anticholinergic* side effects than tricyclics.

Symptom/effect	Frequency		Discuss with doctor		Stop taking drug now	Call doctor now
	Common	Rare	Only if severe	In all cases		
Headache/nervousness	●		■			
Insomnia/anxiety	●			■		
Nausea/diarrhoea	●			■		
Weight loss	●			■		
Drowsiness		●	■			
Sexual dysfunction		●	■		▲	
Rash		●		■	▲	▮

INTERACTIONS

Sedatives All drugs having a sedative effect on the central nervous system may increase the sedative effects of fluoxetine.

Monoamine oxidase inhibitors (MAOIs) Leave at least 14 days between stopping an MAOI and starting fluoxetine, as serious adverse effects can occur. Leave at least 5 weeks between stopping fluoxetine and starting an MAOI.

Tryptophan Taken together, tryptophan and fluoxetine may produce agitation, restlessness, and gastric distress.

Lithium Changes in serum lithium levels can occur.

Other antidepressants Fluoxetine reduces the breakdown of tricyclic antidepressants and may result in sedation, dry mouth, and constipation.

SPECIAL PRECAUTIONS

Be sure to tell your doctor if:
▼ You have impaired liver or kidney function.
▼ You have heart problems.
▼ You have diabetes.
▼ You have had epileptic fits.
▼ You are taking other medications.

 Pregnancy
▼ Safety in pregnancy not established. Discuss with your doctor.

 Breast feeding
▼ The drug passes into the breast milk. Discuss with your doctor.

 Infants and children
▼ Safety and effectiveness not established.

 Over 60s
▼ Increased likelihood of adverse effects. Reduced dose may therefore be necessary.

 Driving and hazardous work
▼ Avoid such activities until you have learned how the drug affects you because it can cause drowsiness.

 Alcohol
▼ Avoid. Alcohol may increase the sedative effects of this drug.

PROLONGED USE

No problems expected. Side effects tend to decrease with time.

FLUTICASONE

Brand name Flixonase, Flixotide
Used in the following combined preparations None

GENERAL INFORMATION

Fluticasone is a corticosteroid drug used to relieve the symptoms of allergic rhinitis (as a nasal spray – Flixonase) and to control asthma (as an inhalant – Flixotide). It acts mainly by reducing inflammation. Fluticasone does not produce immediate relief, so it is important to take the drug regularly. For allergic rhinitis, treatment needs to begin 2– 3 weeks before the hay fever season commences. People who suffer from asthma should take fluticasone continually to prevent attacks occurring.

There are few serious adverse effects associated with fluticasone as it is administered directly into the lungs (inhalation) and nasal mucosa (nasal spray). However, fungal infection causing irritation of the mouth and throat is a possible side effect of inhaled fluticasone but can be minimised by thoroughly rinsing the mouth and gargling with water after each inhalation.

QUICK REFERENCE

Drug group Corticosteroid (p.141)
Overdose danger rating Low
Dependence rating Low
Prescription needed Yes
Available as generic No

INFORMATION FOR USERS

Your drug prescription is tailored for you. Do not alter dosage without checking with your doctor.

How taken

Inhaler, nasal spray.

Frequency and timing of doses
Allergic rhinitis 1 – 2 x daily; asthma 2 x daily.

Adult dosage range
Allergic rhinitis 2 sprays into each nostril per dose; *asthma* 100 –1,000mcg per dose.

Onset of effect
4 - 7 days (asthma); 3 - 4 days (allergic rhinitis).

Duration of action
The effects can last for several days after stopping the drug.

Diet advice
None.

Storage
Keep in a cool, dry place away from reach of children.

Missed dose
Take as soon as you remember.

Stopping the drug
Do not stop the drug without consulting your doctor. Symptoms may recur.

Exceeding the dose
An occasional unintentional extra dose is unlikely to be a cause for concern. If a large overdose has been taken, notify your doctor. Adverse effects may occur if the recommended dose is regularly exceeded over a prolonged period.

POSSIBLE ADVERSE EFFECTS

Adverse effects are unlikely to occur. The main side effects are irritation of the nasal passages (nasal spray) and fungal infection of the throat and mouth (inhalation).

Symptom/effect	Frequency		Discuss with doctor		Stop taking drug now	Call doctor now
	Common	Rare	Only if severe	In all cases		
Nasal irritation	●		■			
Nose bleeds		●		■		
Taste/smell disturbances		●	■			
Sore throat/mouth/hoarseness	●			■		
Breathing difficulties		●		■		■

INTERACTIONS

None

SPECIAL PRECAUTIONS

Be sure to tell your doctor if:
▼ You have chronic sunusitis.
▼ You have had nasal ulcers or surgery.
▼ You have had tuberculosis or another respiratory infection.
▼ You are taking other medications.

 Pregnancy
▼ Safety in pregnancy not established. Discuss with your doctor.

 Breast feeding
▼ Safety in breast feeding not established. However, fluticasone is unlikely to pass into breast milk. Discuss with your doctor.

 Infants and children
▼ Not recommended under 4 years. Reduced dose necessary in older children.

 Over 60s
▼ No known problems.

 Driving and hazardous work
▼ No known problems.

 Alcohol
▼ No known problems.

PROLONGED USE

No problems expected.

Monitoring Periodic checks to make sure that the adrenal gland is functioning properly may be required if large doses are being taken.

FRUSEMIDE

Brand name Dryptal, Frumax, Lasix
Used in the following combined preparations Diumide-K, Fru-Co, Frumil, Frusene, Lasikal, Lasilactone, Lasipressin

GENERAL INFORMATION

Frusemide is a powerful, short-acting loop diuretic that has been in use for over 20 years. Like other diuretics, it is used to treat the oedema (fluid retention) caused by heart failure, and certain lung, liver, and kidney disorders.

Because it is fast acting, frusemide is often used in emergencies to relieve pulmonary oedema. Frusemide is particularly useful for people with impaired kidney function because they do not respond well to thiazide diuretics.

Frusemide increases the loss of potassium, a condition which can produce a wide variety of symptoms. For this reason, supplements of potassium or a potassium-sparing diuretic are often given with the drug.

QUICK REFERENCE

Drug group Loop diuretic (p.99) and antihypertensive drug (p.102)

Overdose danger rating Low

Dependence rating Low

Prescription needed Yes

Available as generic Yes

INFORMATION FOR USERS

Your drug prescription is tailored for you. Do not alter dosage without checking with your doctor.

How taken

Tablets, liquid, injection.

Frequency and timing of doses
Once daily, usually in the morning. High dose therapy: 4–6 hourly.

Adult dosage range
20 – 80mg daily. Dose may be increased to a maximum of 2g daily if kidney function is impaired.

Onset of effect
Within 1 hour (tablets); within 5 minutes (injection).

Duration of action
Up to 6 hours.

Diet advice
Use of this drug may reduce potassium in the body. Eat plenty of potassium-rich fresh fruit and vegetables.

Storage
Keep in a closed container in a cool, dry place away from reach of children. Protect from light.

Missed dose
No cause for concern, but take as soon as you remember. However, if it is late in the day do not take the missed dose, or you may need to get up during the night to pass urine. Take the next scheduled dose as usual.

Stopping the drug
Do not stop the drug without consulting your doctor; symptoms may recur.

Exceeding the dose
An occasional unintentional extra dose is unlikely to cause concern. But if you notice any unusual symptoms, or if a large overdose has been taken, notify your doctor.

SPECIAL PRECAUTIONS

Be sure to tell your doctor if:
▼ You have long-term kidney or liver problems.
▼ You have gout.
▼ You have diabetes.
▼ You have prostate trouble.
▼ You are taking other medications.

Pregnancy
▼ Safety in pregnancy not established. Discuss with your doctor.

Breast feeding
▼ The drug may reduce milk supply, but amount in the milk is unlikely to affect the baby. Discuss with your doctor.

Infants and children
▼ Reduced dose necessary.

Over 60s
▼ Increased likelihood of adverse effects. Reduced dose may therefore be necessary.

Driving and hazardous work
▼ Do not drive until you know how the drug affects you; it may reduce mental alertness.

Alcohol
▼ Keep comsumption low. Frusemide increases the likelihood of dehydration and hangovers after drinking alcohol.

POSSIBLE ADVERSE EFFECTS

Adverse effects are caused mainly by the rapid fluid loss produced by frusemide. These tend to diminish as the body adjusts to taking the drug. The disturbance in body salts and water balance can result in headaches, dizziness, and muscle cramps.

Symptom/effect	Frequency		Discuss with doctor		Stop taking drug now	Call doctor now
	Common	Rare	Only if severe	In all cases		
Dizziness	●		■			
Lethargy		●	■			
Noise in ears (high dose)		●	■			
Muscle cramps		●	■			
Rash		●		■	▲	

INTERACTIONS

Non-steroidal anti-inflammatory drugs (NSAIDs) may reduce the diuretic effect of frusemide.

Lithium Frusemide may increase the blood levels of lithium, leading to an increased risk of lithium poisoning.

Aminoglycoside antibiotics increase the risk of hearing problems and kidney problems when taken with frusemide.

PROLONGED USE

Serious problems are unlikely, but levels of salts, such as potassium, sodium, and calcium, may occasionally become depleted during prolonged use.

Monitoring Periodic tests may be performed to check on kidney function and levels of body salts.

GAMOLENIC ACID

Brand names Epogam, Efamast, Efamol, EPOC, and others
Used in the following combined preparations Many preparations

GENERAL INFORMATION

Gamolenic acid is an essential fatty acid which is found in evening primrose oil and starflower oil (borage oil). Essential fatty acids are found in some foods and are necessary for full health. Beneficial effects of evening primrose oil include improving the condition of hair and skin, and strengthening the nails. Essential fatty acids have numerous functions and contribute to the manufacture of cells and certain important chemical such as prostaglandins. Administration of gamolenic acid enhances their production in the body.

Gamolenic acid has been investigated for use in a variety of conditions including multiple sclerosis and premenstrual syndrome and it has recently become available on prescription for treating eczema and breast pain.

INFORMATION FOR USERS

Follow instructions on the label. Call your doctor if symptoms worsen.

How taken

Capsules, liquid.

Frequency and timing of doses
If desired, 2 x daily. The capsules may be cut open and the contents swallowed.

Adult dosage range
Epogam 8 – 12 capsules daily (eczema); Efamast 6 – 8 capsules daily (breast pain). For other brands follow the instructions on the packet.

Onset of effect
Normally 8 – 12 weeks, but some effects may take longer.

Duration of action
12 – 24 hours, although the beneficial effects will last longer.

Diet advice
None.

Storage
Keep in a closed container in a cool, dry, place away from reach of children.

Missed dose
Take as soon as you remember.

Stopping the drug
If the drug is stopped, symptoms may eventually recur.

Exceeding the dose
An occasional unintentional extra dose is unlikely to be a cause for concern. Excessive dosage may cause loose stools and abdominal pain. If you notice unusual symptoms, or if a large overdose has been taken, notify your doctor.

POSSIBLE ADVERSE EFFECTS

Gamolenic acid does not usually cause problems with adverse effects.

Symptom/effect	Frequency		Discuss with doctor		Stop taking drug now	Call doctor now
	Common	Rare	Only if severe	In all cases		
Nausea		●	■			
Headache		●	■			

INTERACTIONS

Phenothiazines e.g. chlorpromazine, prochlorperazine. There may be an increased risk of epilepsy in patients taking phenothiazines with gamolenic acid.

SPECIAL PRECAUTIONS

Be sure to tell your doctor if:
▼ You have a history of epilepsy.
▼ You are taking other medications.

Pregnancy
▼ Safety in pregnancy not established. Discuss with your doctor.

Breast feeding
▼ No known problems.

Infants and children
▼ Not recommended under 1 year. Reduced dose necessary in older children.

Over 60
▼ No special problems.

Driving and hazardous work
▼ No known problems.

Alcohol
▼ No known problems.

PROLONGED USE

No problems expected.

GENTAMICIN

Brand names Cidomycin, Garamycin, Genticin, Minims gentamicin
Used in the following combined preparations Gentisone HC

GENERAL INFORMATION

Gentamicin is an aminoglycoside antibiotic. Given by injection, it is generally reserved for hospital treatment of serious or complicated infections. These include lung, bone, joint, wound, and urinary tract infections, peritonitis, septicaemia, and meningitis. It is also used with a penicillin for the prevention and treatment of heart valve infections (endocarditis).

Also available as drops and ointment, gentamicin is commonly given for eye and ear infections. Ointment may also occasionally be prescribed for infected burns or ulcers. The development of resistance is a common problem following treatment with skin preparations.

Gentamicin given by injection can have serious adverse effects on the kidneys and on the ears, leading to damage to the balance mechanism and deafness. Courses of treatment are therefore limited to not more than seven days where possible. Treatment is monitored with special care when high doses are needed or when kidney function is poor.

INFORMATION FOR USERS

Your drug prescription is tailored for you. Do not alter dosage without checking with your doctor.

How taken

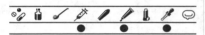

Injection, cream, ointment, eye ointment, eye and ear drops.

Frequency and timing of doses
Every 8 hours (injection); 3 – 4 times daily (skin preparations); every 6 – 12 hours (eye ointment); every 4 – 8 hours (eye and ear drops).

Adult dosage range
According to condition and response (injection); according to your doctor's instructions (eye, ear, and skin preparations).

Onset of effect
Within 1 hour (injection).

Duration of action
8 – 12 hours.

Diet advice
None.

Storage
Keep in a closed container in a cool, dry, place away from reach of children.

Missed dose
Apply skin, eye and ear preparations as soon as you remember.

Stopping the drug
Apply the full course. Even if you feel better, the original infection may still be present and may recur if treatment is stopped too soon.

Exceeding the dose
Overdose by injection is unlikely since treatment is carefully monitored. For other preparations, an occasional unintentional extra dose is unlikely to be a cause for concern. If you notice unusual symptoms, notify your doctor.

SPECIAL PRECAUTIONS

Be sure to tell your doctor if:
▼ You have a long-term kidney problem.
▼ You have a hearing disorder.
▼ You have myasthenia gravis.
▼ You have had a previous allergic reaction to aminoglycosides.
▼ You are taking other medications.

 Pregnancy
▼ No evidence of risk with *topical* preparations. Injections are not prescribed, as they may cause hearing defects in the baby. Discuss with your doctor.

 Breast feeding
▼ No evidence of risk with topical preparations. Given by injection, the drug may pass into the breast milk. Discuss with your doctor.

 Infants and children
▼ Reduced dose necessary for injections.

 Over 60
▼ Increased likelihood of adverse effects. Reduced dose may therefore be necessary.

 Driving and hazardous work
▼ No known problems from preparations for the skin, eye, or ear.

 Alcohol
▼ No known problems.

POSSIBLE ADVERSE EFFECTS

Adverse effects are rare but those that occur with the injectable form may be serious. Dizziness, loss of balance (vertigo), impaired hearing, and changes in the urine should be reported promptly. Allergic reactions, including rash and itching, are symptoms that may occur with all preparations that contain gentamicin.

Symptom/effect	Frequency		Discuss with doctor		Stop taking drug now	Call doctor now
	Common	Rare	Only if severe	In all cases		
Nausea/vomiting		●	■			
Dizziness/vertigo		●		■	▲	❙
Rash/itching		●		■	▲	❙
Ringing in the ears		●		■	▲	❙
Loss of hearing		●		■	▲	❙
Bloody/cloudy urine		●		■	▲	❙

INTERACTIONS

General note A wide range of drugs increase the risk of hearing loss and/or kidney failure with gentamicin. Such drugs include frusemide and vancomycin.

PROLONGED USE

Not usually given for longer than 10 days. There is a risk of adverse effects on hearing, balance and kidney function.

Monitoring Blood levels of the drug are usually checked during injection treatment.

GLIBENCLAMIDE

Brand names Calabren, Daonil, Diabetamide, Euglucon, Libanil, Malix, Semi-Daonil
Used in the following combined preparations None

GENERAL INFORMATION

Glibenclamide is one of the oral anti-diabetic drugs belonging to the class known as sulphanylureas. Like other drugs of this type, it stimulates the production and secretion of insulin from the islet cells in the pancreas and promotes the uptake of sugar into body cells, thereby lowering the level of sugar in the blood.

It is used in the treatment of adult (maturity-onset) diabetes mellitus, in conjunction with a diabetic diet low in carbohydrates and fats.

In conditions of severe illness, injury or stress, the drug may lose its effectiveness in stimulating insulin production in the pancreas, making insulin injections necessary. Adverse effects are generally mild. Symptoms of poor diabetic control will occur if the dosage is not appropriate.

QUICK REFERENCE

Drug group Oral antidiabetic drug (p.142)

Overdose danger rating High

Dependence rating Low

Prescription needed Yes

Available as generic Yes

INFORMATION FOR USERS

Your drug prescription is tailored for you. Do not alter dosage without checking with your doctor.

How taken

Tablets.

Frequency and timing of doses
Once daily in the morning with breakfast.

Adult dosage range
5 – 15mg daily.

Onset of effect
Within 3 hours.

Duration of action
10 – 15 hours.

Diet advice
A low carbohydrate, low fat diet must be maintained in order for the drug to be fully effective. Follow the advice of your doctor.

Storage
Keep in a closed container in a cool, dry place away from reach of children. Protect from light.

Missed dose
Take before your next meal.

Stopping the drug
Do not stop the drug without consulting your doctor; stopping the drug may lead to worsening of your diabetes.

OVERDOSE ACTION

Seek immediate medical advice in all cases. If early warning symptoms of excessively low blood sugar such as faintness, sweating, trembling, confusion or headache occur, eat or drink something sugary. Take emergency action if fits or loss of consciousness occur.

See Drug poisoning emergency guide (p.470).

POSSIBLE ADVERSE EFFECTS

Serious adverse effects with glibenclamide are rare. More common symptoms, often accompanied by hunger, may be signs of low blood sugar due to lack of food or too high a dose of the drug.

Symptom/effect	Frequency		Discuss with doctor		Stop taking drug now	Call doctor now
	Common	Rare	Only if severe	In all cases		
Faintness/confusion	●			■		
Weakness/tremor	●			■		
Sweating	●			■		
Nausea/vomiting		●	■			
Rash/itching		●		■		
Jaundice		●		■		■

INTERACTIONS

General note A variety of drugs may reduce the effect of glibenclamide and so may raise blood sugar levels. These include corticosteroids, oestrogens, diuretics and rifampicin. Other drugs increase the risk of low blood sugar. These include warfarin, sulphonamides, aspirin and beta blockers.

SPECIAL PRECAUTIONS

Be sure to tell your doctor if:
▼ You have long-term liver or kidney problems.
▼ You are allergic to sulphonamide drugs.
▼ You have thyroid problems.
▼ You are taking other medications.

Pregnancy
▼ Not usually prescribed. Insulin is generally substituted in pregnancy because it gives better diabetic control.

Breast feeding
▼ The drug passes into the breast milk, but at normal doses adverse effects on the baby are unlikely. Discuss with your doctor.

Infants and children
▼ Not prescribed.

Over 60
▼ Reduced dose may be necessary.

Driving and hazardous work
▼ Usually no problem. Avoid these activities if you have warning signs of low blood sugar.

Alcohol
▼ Avoid. Alcoholic drinks may upset diabetic control.

Surgery and general anaesthetics
▼ Surgery may alter effect of glibenclamide on diabetes; insulin treatment may need to be substituted.

PROLONGED USE

No problems expected.

Monitoring
Regular monitoring of levels of sugar in the urine or blood is required.

GLYCERYL TRINITRATE

Brand names Deponit, Minitran, Nitrocontin, Nitrolingual, Nitronal, Percutol, Suscard, Sustac, Transiderm-Nitro, Tridil
Used in the following combined preparations None

GENERAL INFORMATION

Introduced in the late 1800s, glyceryl trinitrate is one of the oldest drugs in continual use. It belongs to a group of vasodilator drugs called nitrates which are used to relieve the pain of angina attacks. Glyceryl trinitrate is not a cure for heart disease; it can only relieve symptoms, and it may have to be taken long term. It is available in short-acting forms (sublingual or buccal tablets and spray) and in long-acting forms (slow-release tablets and skin patches). The short-acting forms act very quickly to relieve angina. Glyceryl trinitrate may cause a variety of minor symptoms such as flushing and headache, most of which can be controlled by adjusting the dosage. Glyceryl trinitrate are best taken for the first time while you are sitting, as fainting may follow the drop in blood pressure.

QUICK REFERENCE

Drug group Anti-angina drug (p.101)
Overdose danger rating Medium
Dependence rating Low
Prescription needed No
Available as generic Yes

INFORMATION FOR USERS

Your drug prescription is tailored for you. Do not alter dosage without checking with your doctor.

How taken

Tablets, injection, ointment, spray, skin patches, sublingual patches.

Frequency and timing of doses
Prevention of angina attacks 3 x daily (buccal and slow-release tablets); once daily (skin patches); every 3 – 4 hours (ointment). *Relief of angina attacks* Use spray, buccal or sublingual tablets at the onset of an attack or immediately prior to exercise. Dose may be repeated within 5 minutes if further relief is required.

Adult dosage range
Prevention of angina attacks 5.2 – 30mg daily (slow-release tablets); 3 – 15mg daily (buccal tablets); 2.5 – 15mg daily (skin patches); as directed (ointment). *Relief of angina attacks* 0.3 – 1mg per dose (sublingual tablets); 1 – 3mg per dose (buccal tablets); 1 – 2 sprays per dose (spray).

Onset of effect
Within minutes (buccal and sublingual tablets and spray); 1– 3 hours (slow-release tablets, skin patches and ointment).

Duration of action
20 – 30 minutes (sublingual tablets and spray); 3 – 5 hours (buccal tablets and ointment); 8 – 12 hours (slow-release tablets); up to 24 hours (skin patches).

Diet advice
None.

Storage
Keep tablets in a tightly closed container fitted with a foil-lined, screw-on cap in a cool, dry place away from reach of children. Protect from light. Do not expose to heat. Discard within 8 weeks of opening. Check label of other preparations for storage conditions.

Missed dose
Take as soon as you remember, or when needed. If your next dose is due within 2 hours, take a single dose now and skip the next.

Stopping the drug
Do not stop taking the drug without consulting your doctor.

Exceeding the dose
An occasional unintentional extra dose is unlikely to cause problems. Large overdoses may cause dizziness, vomiting, severe headache, fits, or loss of consciousness. Notify your doctor.

SPECIAL PRECAUTIONS

Be sure to tell your doctor if:
▼ You have any blood disorders.
▼ You have had glaucoma.
▼ You have thyroid disease.
▼ You are taking other medications.

 Pregnancy
▼ Safety in pregnancy not established. Discuss with your doctor.

 Breast feeding
▼ It is not known whether the drug passes into breast milk. Discuss with your doctor.

 Infants and children
▼ Not usually prescribed.

 Over 60s
▼ No special problems.

 Driving and hazardous work
▼ Avoid such activities until you have learned how the drug affects you because the drug can cause dizziness.

 Alcohol
▼ Avoid excess; alcohol may increase dizziness due to lowered blood pressure.

POSSIBLE ADVERSE EFFECTS

The most serious adverse effect is lowered blood pressure, and this may need to be monitored periodically. Other adverse effects usually reduce after regular use and they can also be controlled by an adjustment in dosage.

Symptom/effect	Frequency		Discuss with doctor		Stop taking drug now	Call doctor now
	Common	Rare	Only if severe	In all cases		
Headache	●		■			
Flushing	●		■			
Dizziness	●			■		

PROLONGED USE

The effects of the drug usually become slightly weaker during prolonged use as the body adapts.

Monitoring Periodic checks on blood pressure are usually required.

INTERACTIONS

Antihypertensive drugs These drugs increase the possibility of lowered blood pressure or fainting when taken with glyceryl trinitrate.

GRISEOFULVIN

Brand names Fulcin, Grisovin
Used in the following combined preparations None

GENERAL INFORMATION

Griseofulvin is used to treat forms of fungal skin infection that do not respond to creams and lotions. Given by mouth, it is effective for tinea (ringworm) infections of the scalp, beard, palms, soles of feet, and nails.

Some of these infections may take several months before any noticeable improvement is seen, and during this period a *topical* antifungal drug may also be prescribed. Fingernail infections usually improve after 6 to 9 months. In toenail infections there may

not be any noticeable improvement until a healthy nail has grown, which may take a year.

The most common adverse effects are headache and nausea. Some people may become more sensitive to sunlight. Griseofulvin may in rare cases cause damage to the liver and may affect bone marrow activity adversely. For these reasons it is prescribed only when other treatments have proved ineffective, and never when liver function is impaired.

QUICK REFERENCE

Drug group Antifungal drug (p.138)
Overdose danger rating Low
Dependence rating Low
Prescription needed Yes
Available as generic No

INFORMATION FOR USERS

Your drug prescription is tailored for you. Do not alter dosage without checking with your doctor.

How taken

Tablets, liquid.

Frequency and timing of doses
1 – 4 x daily after meals and at bedtime.

Dosage range
Adults 500mg – 1g daily depending on the condition treated.
Children Reduced dose according to age and weight.

Onset of effect
Full beneficial effect may not be felt for 3 – 4 weeks (skin); 4 – 6 weeks (scalp); 6 – 9 months (fingernails); 8 – 18 months (toenails).

Duration of action
Up to 24 hours.

Diet advice
None.

Storage
Keep in a closed container in a cool, dry place away from reach of children.

Missed dose
Take as soon as you remember. If your next dose is due within 3 hours, take a dose now and skip the next.

Stopping the drug
Take the full course. Even if symptoms disappear, the original infection may still be present and symptoms may recur if treatment is stopped too soon.

Exceeding the dose
An occasional unintentional extra dose is unlikely to cause problems. But if you notice unusual symptoms, or if a large overdose has been taken, notify your doctor.

SPECIAL PRECAUTIONS

Be sure to tell your doctor if:
▼ You have a long-term liver problem.
▼ You suffer from porphyria.
▼ You have previously had a skin rash after taking griseofulvin.
▼ You are taking other medications.

 Pregnancy
▼ Safety in pregnancy not established. Discuss with your doctor.

 Breast feeding
▼ Small amounts may pass into the breast milk, but at normal doses it is unlikely to affect the baby. Discuss with your doctor.

 Infants and children
▼ Reduced dose necessary.

 Over 60
▼ No special problems.

 Driving and hazardous work
▼ Avoid such activities until you have learned how the drug affects you because the drug can cause drowsiness, dizziness, and confusion.

 Alcohol
▼ Avoid. Alcohol may increase the sedative effects of this drug.

POSSIBLE ADVERSE EFFECTS

Most adverse reactions are minor and diminish within a few days of starting treatment. If, however, symptoms do persist, consult your doctor.

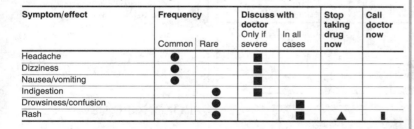

Symptom/effect	Frequency		Discuss with doctor		Stop taking drug now	Call doctor now
	Common	Rare	Only if severe	In all cases		
Headache	●		■			
Dizziness	●		■			
Nausea/vomiting	●		■			
Indigestion		●	■			
Drowsiness/confusion		●		■		
Rash		●		■	▲	▮

INTERACTIONS

Oral anticoagulants Griseofulvin may reduce the effect of these drugs.

Barbiturates These drugs reduce the effect of griseofulvin.

Oral contraceptives When used with griseofulvin, breakthrough bleeding and pregnancies have occurred.

PROLONGED USE

There is a slight risk of liver damage and of reduced bone marrow function causing low levels of white blood cells.

Monitoring Periodic blood tests may be performed to check liver function and blood composition.

HALOPERIDOL

Brand names Dozic, Haldol, Serenace
Used in the following combined preparations None

GENERAL INFORMATION

Introduced in the early 1960s, haloperidol is the most widely used of a group of drugs known as butyrophenones. It is effective in reducing the violent, aggressive manifestations of mental illnesses such as schizophrenia, mania, dementia, and other disorders where hallucinations are experienced. Haloperidol is also used for the short-term management of severe anxiety. It does not cure the underlying disorder, but it does relieve the distressing symptoms. It is also used in the control of Tourette's syndrome and is of benefit in children with severe behaviour problems where other drugs are ineffective.

The main drawback to the use of haloperidol is that it produces disturbing side effects, in particular, abnormal involuntary movements and stiffness of the face and limbs.

QUICK REFERENCE

Drug group Butyrophenone antipsychotic (p.85)
Overdose danger rating Medium
Dependence rating Low
Prescription needed Yes
Available as generic Yes

INFORMATION FOR USERS

Your drug prescription is tailored for you. Do not alter dosage without checking with your doctor.

How taken

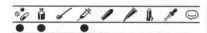

Tablets, capsules, liquid, injection.

Frequency and timing of doses:
2 – 4 x daily.

Adult dosage range:
Mental illness 1.5 – 20mg daily initially. Increased gradually, if necessary, up to a maximum of 200mg daily.
Severe anxiety 1mg daily.

Onset of effect
20 – 30 minutes (by injection); 2 – 3 hours (by mouth).

Duration of action
6 – 24 hours. Up to 4 weeks (depot injection).

Diet advice
None.

Storage
Keep in a closed container in a cool, dry place away from reach of children.

Missed dose
Take as soon as you remember. If your next dose is due within 3 hours take a single dose now and skip the next.

Stopping the drug
Do not stop the drug without consulting your doctor; symptoms may recur.

Exceeding the dose
An occasional unintentional extra dose is unlikely to cause problems. Larger overdoses may cause unusual drowsiness, muscle weakness or rigidity, and/or faintness. Notify your doctor.

SPECIAL PRECAUTIONS

Be sure to tell your doctor if:
▼ You have long-term liver or kidney problems.
▼ You have heart or circulation problems.
▼ You have had epileptic fits.
▼ You have an overactive thyroid gland.
▼ You have Parkinson's disease.
▼ You have had glaucoma.
▼ You have asthma, bronchitis, or another lung disorder.
▼ You are taking other medications.

Pregnancy
▼ Safety in pregnancy not established. Discuss with your doctor.

Breast feeding
▼ The drug passes into the breast milk and may affect the baby. Discuss with your doctor.

Infants and children
▼ Rarely required. Reduced dose necessary.

Over 60
▼ Reduced dose may be necessary.

Driving and hazardous work
▼ Avoid such activities until you have learned how the drug affects you because this drug may cause drowsiness and slowed reactions.

Alcohol
▼ Avoid. Alcohol may increase the sedative effect of this drug.

POSSIBLE ADVERSE EFFECTS

Haloperidol can cause a variety of minor *anticholinergic* symptoms that often become less marked with time. The most significant adverse effect is abnormal movements of the face and limbs (parkinsonism). This may be controlled by dosage adjustment.

Symptom/effect	Frequency		Discuss with doctor		Stop taking drug now	Call doctor now
	Common	Rare	Only if severe	In all cases		
Drowsiness/lethargy	●		■			
Loss of appetite	●		■			
Parkinsonism	●			■		
Dizziness/fainting		●		■		
Rash		●		■	▲	
High fever/confusion		●		■	▲	■

INTERACTIONS

Sedatives All drugs that have a sedative effect are likely to increase the sedative properties of haloperidol.

Antihistamines Terfenadine and astemizole may have adverse effects on the heart if taken with haloperidol.

Anticholinergic drugs The side effects of drugs with anticholinergic properties may be increased by haloperidol.

Anticonvulsants Dosage may need adjustment.

PROLONGED USE

Use of this drug for more than a few months may lead to *tardive dyskinesia*, i.e. abnormal, involuntary movements of the eyes, face and tongue. Occasionally, jaundice may occur.

HEPARIN

Brand names Clexane, Fragmin, Hepsal, Innohep, Logiparin, Minihep, Monoparin, Multiparin, Unihep, Uniparin
Used in the following combined preparations None

GENERAL INFORMATION

Heparin is an anticoagulant used to prevent and aid in the dispersion of blood clots. Because it acts quickly, it is particularly useful during emergencies, for instance, to prevent further clotting when a clot has already reached the lungs or the brain. People undergoing open heart surgery and kidney dialysis are also given heparin to prevent clotting. A low dose of heparin is sometimes given to people after surgery to prevent clots forming in leg veins (i.e. deep vein thrombosis). Often, heparin is given in conjunction with other slower-acting anticoagulants, such as warfarin, until they reach their full beneficial effects.

Its most serious adverse effect, as with all anticoagulants, is the risk of excessive bleeding, so the ability of the blood to clot is watched very carefully under medical supervision. Bruising may occur around the site of the injection.

A new form of heparin called "low molecular weight heparin" (LMWH) may be more effective in preventing blood clots after orthopaedic surgery.

QUICK REFERENCE

Drug group Anticoagulant (p.104)
Overdose danger rating High
Dependence rating Low
Prescription needed Yes
Available as generic Yes

INFORMATION FOR USERS

This drug is given only under medical supervision and is not for self-administration.

How taken

Injection.

Frequency and timing of doses
Every 8 – 12 hours by continuous intravenous infusion.

Dosage range
Treatment 5000 units initially, followed by 40,000 units over 24 hours.
Prevention 5000 units subcutaneously.

Onset of effect
Within 15 minutes.

Duration of action
4 – 12 hours after treatment is stopped.

Diet advice
None.

Storage
Keep in a closed container in a cool, dry place away from reach of children. Protect from light.

Missed dose
Take as soon as you remember.

Stopping the drug
Do not stop taking the drug without consulting your doctor. Stopping the drug may lead to clotting of blood.

OVERDOSE ACTION

 Seek immediate medical advice in all cases. Take emergency action if bleeding, severe headache, or loss of consciousness occur. Overdose can be reversed under medical supervision by a drug called protamine.

See Drug poisoning emergency guide (p.470).

POSSIBLE ADVERSE EFFECTS

As with all anticoagulants, bleeding is the most common adverse effect with heparin.

The less common effects may occur during long-term treatment.

Symptom/effect	Frequency		Discuss with doctor		Stop taking drug now	Call doctor now
	Common	Rare	Only if severe	In all cases		
Bleeding/bruising	●				■	▮
Alopecia		●			■	
Aching bones		●			■	
Rash		●			■	▲

INTERACTIONS

Aspirin Do not take. Aspirin may increase the anticoagulant effect of this drug, and there is an increased risk of bleeding in the intestine or joints.

Dipyridamole The anticoagulant effect of heparin may be increased when taken with this drug. The dosage of heparin may need to be adjusted accordingly.

SPECIAL PRECAUTIONS

Be sure to tell your doctor if:
▼ You have kidney or liver problems.
▼ You have high blood pressure.
▼ You bleed easily.
▼ You have any allergies.
▼ You have stomach ulcers.
▼ You are taking other medications.

 Pregnancy
▼ Careful monitoring is necessary as it may cause the mother to bleed excessively if taken near delivery. Discuss with your doctor.

 Breast feeding
▼ No evidence of risk.

 Infants and children
▼ Reduced dose necessary according to age and weight.

 Over 60
▼ No special problems.

 Driving and hazardous work
▼ Avoid risk of injury, since excessive bruising and bleeding may occur.

 Alcohol
▼ No special problems.

Surgery and general anaesthetics
▼ Heparin may need to be stopped. Discuss this with your doctor or dentist before any surgery.

PROLONGED USE

Osteoporosis and hair loss may occur; tolerance to heparin may develop.

Monitoring Periodic blood checks will be required.

HYDRALAZINE

Brand name Apresoline
Used in the following combined preparations None

GENERAL INFORMATION

Hydralazine was introduced in the 1950s for use as an antihypertensive. It is a vasodilator (see p.98), i.e. a drug that relaxes the muscles of the artery walls and dilates blood vessels. It is used most often to treat moderate to severe high blood pressure.

Although usually given orally, hydralazine has a rapid onset of action when given by injection. This makes it particularly useful in emergencies. Hydralazine is usually given as additional medication together with a diuretic and/or a beta blocker.

The most serious adverse effect is the possibility of drug-induced lupus erythematosus, an autoimmune-like illness, that occurs only with long-term treatment in high doses and disappears when the drug is withdrawn.

QUICK REFERENCE

Drug group Antihypertensive drug (p.102)
Overdose danger rating High
Dependence rating Low
Prescription needed Yes
Available as generic Yes

INFORMATION FOR USERS

Your drug prescription is tailored for you. Do not alter dosage without checking with your doctor.

How taken

Tablets, injection.

Frequency and timing of doses
2 – 3 x daily.

Dosage range
Adults 50 – 100mg daily, up to a maximum of 200mg daily.

Onset of effect
30 minutes – 2 hours (tablets); 10 – 20 minutes (injection).

Duration of action
6 – 8 hours (tablets); 2 – 4 hours (injection).

Diet advice
None.

Storage
Keep in a closed container in a cool, dry place away from reach of children.

Missed dose
Take as soon as you remember. If your next dose is due within 4 hours, take a single dose now and skip the next.

Stopping the drug
Do not stop the drug without consulting your doctor; stopping the drug may lead to worsening of the underlying condition.

OVERDOSE ACTION

Seek immediate medical advice in all cases. Take emergency action if severe nausea and vomiting, rapid heart beat, or loss of consciousness occur.

See Drug poisoning emergency guide (p.470).

SPECIAL PRECAUTIONS

Be sure to tell your doctor if:
▼ You have long-term kidney or liver problems.
▼ You have heart disease.
▼ You have had a stroke.
▼ You have had lupus erythematosus.
▼ You tend to be allergic.
▼ You are taking other medications.

Pregnancy
▼ Safety in pregnancy not established. Discuss with your doctor.

Breast feeding
▼ The drug passes into the breast milk, but at normal doses adverse effects on the baby are unlikely. Discuss with your doctor.

Infants and children
▼ Not usually prescribed. Reduced dose necessary.

Over 60
▼ No special problems.

Driving and hazardous work
▼ Avoid such activities until you have learned how the drug affects you because the drug can cause dizziness.

Alcohol
▼ Avoid. Alcohol may increase the adverse effects of this drug.

POSSIBLE ADVERSE EFFECTS

Many of the common adverse effects diminish during long-term treatment.

Dizziness usually occurs when getting up; rising slowly will help.

Symptom/effect	Frequency		Discuss with doctor		Stop taking drug now	Call doctor now
	Common	Rare	Only if severe	In all cases		
Headache	●		■			
Dizziness		●	■			
Rapid heart beat	●			■		
Nausea/vomiting		●	■			
Diarrhoea		●		■		
Rash		●		■		
Flushing		●		■		
Joint pain		●		■		

INTERACTIONS

Tricyclic antidepressants and monoamine oxidase inhibitors (MAOIs) may increase the effects of hydralazine.

PROLONGED USE

Lupus erythematosus, an autoimmune-like illness, may occur with prolonged use. This usually disappears when the drug is withdrawn.

Monitoring Periodic blood checks may be performed.

HYDROCHLOROTHIAZIDE

Brand names Esidrex, HydroSaluric
Used in the following combined preparations Acezide, Capozide, Co-Betaloc, Dyazide, Kalten, Moduretic, and others

GENERAL INFORMATION

Hydrochlorothiazide belongs to the thiazide group of diuretic drugs that remove excess water from the body and reduce oedema (fluid retention) in people with congestive heart failure, kidney disorders, cirrhosis of the liver, and premenstrual syndrome.

Hydrochlorothiazide is used to treat high blood pressure (see Antihypertensive drugs, p.102). Hydrochlorothiazide increases the loss of potassium in the urine which can cause a variety of symptoms (see p.99), and increases the likelihood of irregular heart rhythms, particularly if you are taking drugs such as digoxin. Potassium supplements are often prescribed with hydrochlorothiazide.

INFORMATION FOR USERS

Your drug prescription is tailored for you. Do not alter dosage without checking with your doctor.

How taken

Tablets.

Frequency and timing of doses
Once daily, or every 2 days, early in the day.

Adult dosage range
25 – 200mg daily.

Onset of effect
Within 2 hours.

Duration of action
6 – 12 hours.

Diet advice
Use of this drug may reduce potassium in the body. Eat plenty of fresh fruit and vegetables. Discuss the advisability of reducing your salt intake with your doctor.

Storage
Keep in a closed container in a cool, dry place away from reach of children. Protect from light.

Missed dose
No cause for concern, but take as soon as you remember. However, if it is late in the day do not take the missed dose, or you may need to get up during the night to pass urine. Take the next scheduled dose as usual.

Stopping the drug
Do not stop the drug without consulting your doctor; symptoms may recur.

Exceeding the dose
An occasional unintentional extra dose is unlikely to be a cause for concern. But if you notice any unusual symptoms, or if a large overdose has been taken, notify your doctor.

SPECIAL PRECAUTIONS

Be sure to tell your doctor if:
▼ You have long-term kidney or liver problems.
▼ You have had gout.
▼ You have diabetes.
▼ You are taking other medications.

 Pregnancy
▼ Not usually prescribed. May cause jaundice in the newborn baby. Discuss with your doctor.

 Breast feeding
▼ The drug passes into the breast milk, but at normal doses adverse effects on the baby are unlikely. Discuss with your doctor.

 Infants and children
▼ Not usually prescribed. Reduced dose necessary.

 Over 60s
▼ Increased likelihood of adverse effects.

 Driving and hazardous work
▼ No special problems.

 Alcohol
▼ Keep consumption low. Hydrochlorothiazide increases the likelihood of dehydration and hangovers after consumption of alcohol.

POSSIBLE ADVERSE EFFECTS

Most effects are caused by excessive loss of potassium. This can usually be put right by taking a potassium supplement. In rare cases gout may occur in susceptible people, and certain forms of diabetes may become more difficult to control.

Symptom/effect	Frequency		Discuss with doctor		Stop taking drug now	Call doctor now
	Common	Rare	Only if severe	In all cases		
Leg cramps	●		■			
Lethargy		●	■			
Dizziness		●	■			
Digestive disturbance		●	■			
Temporary impotence		●	■			
Rash		●		■		▲

INTERACTIONS

Non-steroidal anti-inflammatory drugs Some of these drugs may reduce the diuretic effect of hydrochlorothiazide whose dosage may need to be adjusted.

Digoxin Adverse effects may be increased if excessive potassium is lost.

Corticosteroids These drugs further increase loss of potassium from the body when taken with hydrochlorothiazide.

Lithium Hydrochlorothiazide may increase lithium levels in the blood leading to a risk of serious adverse effects.

PROLONGED USE

Excessive loss of potassium and imbalances of other salts may result.

Monitoring Blood tests may be performed periodically to check kidney function and levels of potassium and other salts.

HYDROCORTISONE

Brand names Colifoam, Corlan, Dioderm, Efcortelan, Efcortesol, Hydrocortistab, Hydrocortone, Solu-Cortef
Used in the following combined preparations Alphaderm, Epifoam, Tarcortin, Xyloproct, and others

GENERAL INFORMATION

Hydrocortisone is chemically identical to the hormone cortisol that is produced by the adrenal glands, and one use of the drug is in the replacement of natural hormones in adrenal insufficiency (Addison's disease).

The main use of hydrocortisone, however, is in the treatment of a variety of allergic and inflammatory conditions. Used in *topical* preparations it provides prompt relief from inflammation of the skin, eye, and outer ear. It is used in oral form to relieve asthma, inflammatory bowel disease and many other rheumatic and allergic disorders. Injected directly into the joints, it relieves pain and stiffness (see p.118). Injections may also be given to relieve severe attacks of asthma.

Overuse of hydrocortisone skin preparations can lead to permanent thinning of the skin. Taken by mouth, long-term treatment with high doses may cause serious side effects.

QUICK REFERENCE

Drug group Corticosteroid (p.141)

Overdose danger rating Low

Dependence rating Low

Prescription needed Yes (except for some topical preparations)

Available as generic Yes

INFORMATION FOR USERS

Your drug prescription is tailored for you. Do not alter dosage without checking with your doctor.

How taken

Tablets, lozenges, injection, enema, cream ointment, eye drops, eye ointment.

Frequency and timing of doses
Varies according to condition.

Dosage range
Varies according to condition.

Onset of effect
Within 1 – 4 days.

Duration of action
Up to 12 hours.

Diet advice
Salt intake may need to be restricted when the drug is taken by mouth. It may also be necessary to take potassium supplements.

Storage
Keep in a closed container in a cool, dry place away from reach of children.

Missed dose
Take as soon as you remember. If your next dose is due within 2 hours, take a single dose now and skip the next.

Stopping the drug
Do not stop taking the drug without consulting your doctor. A gradual reduction in dosage is required following prolonged treatment with oral hydrocortisone.

Exceeding the dose
An occasional unintentional extra dose is unlikely to be a cause for concern. But if you notice unusual symptoms, or if a large overdose has been taken, notify your doctor.

SPECIAL PRECAUTIONS

Be sure to tell your doctor if:
▼ You have had a peptic ulcer.
▼ You have suffered from depression or a mental illness, or epilepsy.
▼ You have glaucoma.
▼ You have had tuberculosis.
▼ You have an infection.
▼ You have diabetes.
▼ You are taking other medications.

 Pregnancy
▼ No evidence of risk with topical preparations. Oral doses may adversely affect the developing baby. Discuss with your doctor.

 Breast feeding
▼ The drug passes into the breast milk and may affect the baby. Discuss with your doctor.

 Infants and children
▼ Reduced dose necessary.

 Over 60
▼ Reduced dose may be necessary.

 Driving and hazardous work
▼ No special problems.

 Alcohol
▼ Avoid. Alcohol may increase the risk of peptic ulcer with this drug taken by mouth.

POSSIBLE ADVERSE EFFECTS

The more serious adverse effects only occur when hydrocortisone is taken by mouth in high doses for long periods of time. These are carefully monitored during treatment.

Symptom/effect	Frequency		Discuss with doctor		Stop taking drug now	Call doctor now
	Common	Rare	Only if severe	In all cases		
Indigestion	●		■			
Weight gain	●		■			
Acne	●		■			
Fluid retention		●		■		
Muscle weakness		●		■		
Mood changes		●		■		

INTERACTIONS (by mouth only)

Barbiturates, anticonvulsants, and rifampicin These drugs reduce the effectiveness of hydrocortisone.

Antidiabetic drugs Hydrocortisone reduces the action of these drugs.

Antihypertensive drugs Hydrocortisone reduces the effects of these drugs.

Vaccines Severe reactions can occur when this drug is taken with certain vaccines.

PROLONGED USE

Depending on method of administration, prolonged high dosage may cause diabetes, glaucoma, fragile bones and thin skin, and may retard growth in children. People on long-term treatment are advised to carry a treatment card.

Monitoring Periodic checks on blood pressure are usually required when the drug is taken by mouth.

HYOSCINE

Brand name Buscopan, Junior Kwells, Kwells, Scopoderm-TTS
Used in the following combined preparations Omnopon-scopolamine

GENERAL INFORMATION

Hyoscine is an *anticholinergic* drug that has an *antispasmodic* effect on the intestine and a calming action on the nerve pathways that control nausea and vomiting. It also dilates the pupil.

There are two forms of the drug. Hyoscine butylbromide is prescribed to reduce spasm of the gastrointestinal tract in irritable bowel syndrome. The hydrobromide form is used to control motion sickness and nausea caused by disturbances of the inner ear (see Vertigo and Ménière's disease, p.90) and is also used as a *premedication* to dry secretions before surgical operations. Eye drops containing hyoscine hydrobromide are used to dilate the pupil during eye examinations and eye surgery.

QUICK REFERENCE

Drug group Drug for irritable bowel syndrome (p.110), drug affecting the pupil (p.170), and drug for nausea/vomiting (p.90)

Overdose danger rating Medium

Dependence rating Low

Prescription needed Yes

Available as generic Yes

INFORMATION FOR USERS

Your prescription is tailored for you. Do not alter dosage without checking with your doctor.

How taken

Tablets, injection, eye drops, skin patch.

Frequency and timing of doses
As required up to 4 x daily by mouth (irritable bowel syndrome) or up to 3 x daily (nausea and vomiting); every 72 hours (skin patch).

Adult dosage range
Irritable bowel syndrome 80mg (hyoscine butylbromide) daily.
Nausea and vomiting 0.3mg (hyoscine hydrobromide) per dose.

Onset of effect
Within 1 hour.

Duration of action
Up to 6 hours by mouth. Up to 72 hours (skin patch).

Diet advice
None.

Storage
Keep in a closed container in a cool, dry place away from reach of children. Protect from light.

Missed dose
Take when you remember. Adjust the timing of your next dose accordingly.

Stopping the drug
Can be safely stopped as soon as you no longer need it.

Exceeding the dose
An occasional unintentional extra dose is unlikely to cause problems. Large overdoses may cause drowsiness or agitation. Notify your doctor.

SPECIAL PRECAUTIONS

Be sure to tell your doctor if:
▼ You have long-term kidney or liver problems.
▼ You have heart problems.
▼ You have had glaucoma.
▼ You have prostate trouble.
▼ You are taking other medications.

Pregnancy
▼ Safety in pregnancy not established. Discuss with your doctor.

Breast feeding
▼ No evidence of risk. Discuss with your doctor.

Infants and children
▼ Not recommended under 6 years. Reduced dose necessary in older children.

Over 60
▼ Reduced dose may be necessary.

Driving and hazardous work
▼ Avoid such activities until you have learned how the drug affects you because the drug can cause drowsiness and blurred vision.

Alcohol
▼ Avoid. Alcohol may increase the sedative effect of this drug.

POSSIBLE ADVERSE EFFECTS

Taken by mouth or by injection, hyoscine has a strong *anticholinergic* effect on the body, causing a variety of minor symptoms. These can sometimes be minimized by a reduction in dosage.

Symptom/effect	Frequency		Discuss with doctor		Stop taking drug now	Call doctor now
	Common	Rare	Only if severe	In all cases		
Drowsiness	●		■			
Dry mouth	●		■			
Blurred vision	●			■		
Constipation		●	■			
Difficulty in passing urine		●		■		

PROLONGED USE

Use of this drug for longer than a few days is unlikely to be necessary.

INTERACTIONS

Sedatives All drugs that have a sedative effect on the central nervous system are likely to increase the sedative properties of hyoscine. Such drugs include anti-anxiety and sleeping drugs, antidepressants, narcotic analgesics, and antipsychotics.

IBUPROFEN

Brand names Apsifen, Arthrofen, Brufen, Cuprofen, Fenbid, Ibugel, Inoven, Junifen, Motrin, Nurofen, Proflex and others
Used in the following combined preparations Codafen

GENERAL INFORMATION

Ibuprofen is available over-the-counter to relieve the pain, stiffness and inflammation that may accompany a number of disorders. It is similar to aspirin in the way it works and in the way it can be used. Because it acts as an analgesic as well as an anti-inflammatory, it is an effective treatment for the symptoms of rheumatoid arthritis, osteoarthritis, and gout. It also relieves mild to moderate headache, menstrual pains, pain from soft tissue injuries and following operations.

Sometimes, ibuprofen is prescribed along with slower acting drugs in the treatment of rheumatoid arthritis.

Ibuprofen has fewer side effects than many of the other non-steroidal anti-inflammatory drugs (NSAIDs). Unlike aspirin, it rarely causes bleeding in the stomach. Ibuprofen can also be applied as a gel for localised musculoskeletal conditions.

QUICK REFERENCE

Drug group Analgesic (p.80) and non-steroidal anti-inflammatory drug (p.116)

Overdose danger rating Low

Dependence rating Low

Prescription needed No

Available as generic Yes

INFORMATION FOR USERS

Follow instructions on the label. Call your doctor if symptoms worsen.

How taken

Tablets, SR tablets, capsules, liquid, cream, granules.

Frequency and timing of doses
4 – 6 x daily (general pain relief); 3 – 4 x daily with food (arthritis); 1 – 2 times daily (SR tablets).

Adult dosage range
600mg – 1.8g daily (general pain relief); 1.2 – 2.4g daily (arthritis).

Onset of effect
Pain relief begins in 1 – 2 hours. Full anti-inflammatory effect in arthritic conditions may not be felt for up to 2 weeks.

Duration of action
5 – 10 hours.

Diet advice
None.

Storage
Keep in a closed container in a cool, dry place away from reach of children.

Missed dose
Take as soon as you remember. If your next dose is due within 2 hours, take a single dose now and skip the next.

Stopping the drug
When taken for short-term pain relief, ibuprofen can be safely stopped as soon as you no longer need it. If prescribed for the long-term treatment of arthritis, however, you should seek medical advice before stopping the drug.

Exceeding the dose
An occasional unintentional extra dose is unlikely to be a cause for concern. But if you notice unusual symptoms, or if a large overdose has been taken, notify your doctor.

SPECIAL PRECAUTIONS

Be sure to consult your doctor or pharmacist before taking this drug if:
▼ You have a long-term kidney problem.
▼ You have high blood pressure.
▼ You have had a peptic ulcer, oesophagitis or acid indigestion.
▼ You are allergic to aspirin.
▼ You have asthma.
▼ You are taking other medications.

Pregnancy
▼ Not usually prescribed. May affect the unborn baby and may prolong labour. Discuss with your doctor.

Breast feeding
▼ The drug passes into the breast milk, but at normal doses adverse effects on the baby are unlikely. Discuss with your doctor.

Infants and children
▼ Reduced dose necessary.

Over 60
▼ Reduced dose may be necessary.

Driving and hazardous work
▼ No problems expected.

Alcohol
▼ Avoid. Alcohol may increase the risk of stomach disorders with ibuprofen.

Surgery and general anaesthetics
▼ Discuss with your doctor or dentist before any surgery.

POSSIBLE ADVERSE EFFECTS

The most common adverse effects are the result of gastrointestinal disturbances. Black or bloodstained faeces should be reported to your doctor without delay.

Symptom/effect	Frequency		Discuss with doctor		Stop taking drug now	Call doctor now
	Common	Rare	Only if severe	In all cases		
Nausea/vomiting		●	■			
Heartburn/indigestion	●		■			
Rash		●		■	▲	
Wheezing/breathlessness		●		■	▲	■

INTERACTIONS

General note Ibuprofen interacts with a wide range of drugs to increase the risk of bleeding and/or peptic ulcers. Such drugs include oral anticoagulants, corticosteroids, other non-steroidal anti-inflammatory drugs (NSAIDs), and aspirin.

Antihypertensive drugs and diuretics The beneficial effects of these drugs may be reduced by ibuprofen.

Lithium Ibuprofen may raise blood levels of lithium.

PROLONGED USE

There is an increased risk of bleeding from peptic ulcers and in the bowel with prolonged use of ibuprofen.

IDOXURIDINE

Brand names Idoxene
Used in the following combined preparations Herpid, Iduridin, Virodox

GENERAL INFORMATION

Idoxuridine, in use for over 25 years, is a *topically* applied drug that is often effective against certain viral infections. Available as eye ointment, it is used to treat herpes simplex infections of the inner eyelids or the cornea of the eye.

In the treatment of deep herpes simplex infections of the eye, for which corticosteroids are prescribed, idoxuridine may also be given to prevent the spread of any viral growth stimulated by the corticosteroid. When high doses of corticosteroids are administered, orally or by eye drops, for other disorders, idoxuridine may be given to prevent the flare-up of a previous herpes eye infection. Idoxuridine is also used on infected areas of skin; it may give some relief when used locally in shingles.

Serious adverse effects are rare with idoxuridine, but the risk of eye damage is increased with prolonged treatment or overuse. For this reason, courses of treatment longer than 21 days are not usually recommended.

QUICK REFERENCE

Drug group Antiviral drug (p.133)
Overdose danger rating Low
Dependence rating Low
Prescription needed Yes
Available as generic No

INFORMATION FOR USERS

Your drug prescription is tailored for you. Do not alter dosage without checking with your doctor.

How taken

Skin application, eye ointment.

Frequency and timing of doses
4 x daily (skin application); every 4 hours (eye ointment).

Dosage range
Apply as directed.

Onset of effect
Within 2 – 4 days.

Duration of action
A few hours after each application.

Diet advice
None.

Storage
Keep in a closed container in a cool, dry place away from reach of children.

Missed dose
Apply as soon as you remember.

Stopping the drug
Take for the length of time directed. The original infection may still be active, and symptoms may recur if treatment is stopped too soon.

Exceeding the dose
An occasional unintentional extra dose is unlikely to be a cause for concern. But if you notice unusual symptoms or if a large overdose has been taken, notify your doctor.

POSSIBLE ADVERSE EFFECTS

Serious adverse effects are uncommon with idoxuridine. If you experience unusual sensitivity to light (photophobia), visual impairment or allergic reactions such as itching, swelling or pain, consult your doctor promptly.

Symptom/effect	Frequency		Discuss with doctor		Stop taking drug now	Call doctor now
	Common	Rare	Only if severe	In all cases		
Eye irritation (eye ointment)	●		■			
Strange taste in mouth	●		■			
Local stinging (skin application)		●			■	
Blurred vision		●			■	
Swollen lids/pain in the eye		●			■	

INTERACTIONS

Boric acid eye preparations increase the risk of irritation and of eye damage.

SPECIAL PRECAUTIONS

Be sure to tell your doctor if:
▼ You have ever had an allergic reaction to iodine or an iodine-containing preparation.
▼ You are taking other medications.

 Pregnancy
▼ Safety in pregnancy not established. Discuss with your doctor.

 Breast feeding
▼ May make milk taste unpleasant. Discuss with your doctor. No evidence of risk.

 Infants and children
▼ Not recommended in children under 12 years old.

 Over 60
▼ No special problems.

 Driving and hazardous work
▼ No known problems.

Alcohol
▼ No known problems.

PROLONGED USE

Rarely required. Treatment is not normally continued for longer than 21 days.

IMIPRAMINE

Brand names Tofranil
Used in the following combined preparations None

GENERAL INFORMATION

Imipramine belongs to a class of anti-depressant drugs known as the tricyclics. It is mainly used in the long-term treatment of depression to elevate mood, increase physical activity, improve appetite, and restore interest in everyday life. Less sedating than some other antidepressants, it is particularly useful when a depressed person is withdrawn or apathetic, though it can aggravate insomnia if taken in the evening.

Imipramine is also given for the treatment of bedwetting in children, though proof of benefits is not conclusive. Imipramine can cause a variety of side effects. In overdose it may cause coma and dangerous heart rhythms.

QUICK REFERENCE

Drug group Tricyclic anti-depressant (p.84) and drug for urinary disorders (p.166)

Overdose danger rating High

Dependence rating Low

Prescription needed Yes

Available as generic Yes

INFORMATION FOR USERS

Your drug prescription is tailored for you. Do not alter dosage without checking with your doctor.

How taken

Tablets, liquid.

Frequency and timing of doses
1 – 4 x daily.

Dosage range
Adults Usually 75 – 200mg daily.
Children Reduced dose according to age and weight.

Onset of effect
Some benefits and effects may appear within hours, but full antidepressant effect may not be felt for 2 – 6 weeks.

Duration of action
Following prolonged treatment, antidepressant effect may persist for up to 6 weeks. Adverse effects may wear off within days.

Diet advice
None.

Storage
Keep in a closed container in a cool, dry place away from reach of children.

Missed dose
Take as soon as you remember. If your next dose is due within 3 hours, take a single dose now and skip the next.

Stopping the drug
Do not stop taking the drug without consulting your doctor, who will supervise a gradual reduction in dosage. Stopping abruptly may cause withdrawal symptoms.

OVERDOSE ACTION

Seek immediate medical advice in all cases. Take emergency action if consciousness is lost.

See Drug poisoning emergency guide (p.470).

SPECIAL PRECAUTIONS

Be sure to tell your doctor if:
▼ You have had heart problems.
▼ You have long-term kidney or liver problems.
▼ You have had epileptic fits.
▼ You have had glaucoma.
▼ You have prostate trouble.
▼ You are taking other medications.

Pregnancy
▼ Safety in pregnancy not established. Discuss with your doctor.

Breast feeding
▼ The drug passes into the breast milk, but at normal doses adverse effects on the baby are unlikely. Discuss with your doctor.

Infants and children
▼ Not recommended under 6 years. Reduced dose necessary in older children.

Over 60
▼ Increased likelihood of adverse effects. Reduced dose may therefore be necessary.

Driving and hazardous work
▼ Avoid such activities until you have learned how the drug affects you because the drug may cause reduced alertness and dizziness.

Alcohol
▼ Alcohol may increase the sedative effect of imipramine.

Surgery and general anaesthetics
▼ Imipramine treatment may need to be stopped before you have a general anaesthetic. Discuss this with your doctor or dentist before any operation.

POSSIBLE ADVERSE EFFECTS

The possible adverse effects of this drug are mainly the result of its *anticholinergic* action and its effect on the normal rhythm of the heart.

Symptom/effect	Frequency		Discuss with doctor		Stop taking drug now	Call doctor now
	Common	Rare	Only if severe	In all cases		
Sweating/flushing	●		■			
Dry mouth/constipation	●		■			
Blurred vision	●			■		
Dizziness/drowsiness		●		■		
Rash		●		■	▲	
Palpitations		●		■	▲	■

INTERACTIONS

Sedatives Imipramine may increase the effects of sedative drugs.

Antihistamines Increased risk of astemizole and terfenadine causing abnormal heart rhythms.

Phenytoin Imipramine may increase levels of phenytoin.

Monoamine oxidase inhibitors (MAOIs) There is a possibility of a serious interaction. Such drugs are prescribed together only under strict supervision.

PROLONGED USE

No problems expected. Imipramine is not usually prescribed for children as a treatment for bedwetting for longer than three months.

INDOMETHACIN

Brand names Artracin, Flexin, Imbrilon, Indocid, Indoflex, Indolar, Indomax, Indomod, Mobilan, Rheumacin SR, Rimacid
Used in the following combined preparations None

GENERAL INFORMATION

Indomethacin, introduced in 1963, is a non-steroidal anti-inflammatory drug (NSAID). Like other NSAIDs, it reduces pain, stiffness and inflammation.

Indomethacin is used to treat many arthritic conditions, including rheumatoid arthritis, ankylosing spondylitis, osteoarthritis, acute attacks of gout, bursitis, and tendinitis. It is sometimes given to treat a heart disorder known as patent ductus arteriosus that occurs in premature infants.

This drug has several potentially serious side effects including gastrointestinal disorders, severe headache, and dizziness, and it may mask the symptoms of infections. It is not given to people with poor kidney function.

QUICK REFERENCE

Drug group Non-steroidal anti-inflammatory drug (p.116) and drug for gout (p.119)

Overdose danger rating Medium

Dependence rating Low

Prescription needed Yes

Available as generic Yes

INFORMATION FOR USERS

Your drug prescription is tailored for you. Do not alter dosage without checking with your doctor.

How taken

Capsules, SR capsules, liquid, injection, suppositories.

Frequency and timing of doses
1 – 2 x daily with food (SR capsules); 2 – 4 x daily with food (standard capsules).

Adult dosage range
50 – 200mg daily.

Onset of effect
Some analgesic effect may be felt within 2 – 4 hours. Full anti-inflammatory effect may not be felt for up to 4 weeks.

Duration of action
5 – 10 hours. Some effect may last for up to 24 hours (slow-release capsules).

Diet advice
None.

Storage
Keep in a closed container in a cool, dry place away from reach of children.

Missed dose
Take as soon as you remember. If your next dose is due within 3 hours, take a single dose now and skip the next.

Stopping the drug
Do not stop the drug without consulting your doctor; symptoms may recur.

Exceeding the dose
An occasional unintentional extra dose is unlikely to cause problems. Large overdoses may cause dizziness, confusion, and nausea. Notify your doctor.

POSSIBLE ADVERSE EFFECTS

Gastrointestinal disturbances, headaches, dizziness and lightheadedness are common. Black or bloodstained bowel movements should be reported promptly.

Symptom/effect	Frequency		Discuss with doctor		Stop taking drug now	Call doctor now
	Common	Rare	Only if severe	In all cases		
Abdominal pain/indigestion	●		■			
Headache	●		■			
Dizziness/lightheadedness	●		■			
Nausea/vomiting	●			■		
Diarrhoea	●			■		
Drowsiness/depression		●		■		
Blurred vision		●		■		
Rash		●		■	▲	
Wheezing/breathlessness		●		■	▲	∎

INTERACTIONS

General note Indomethacin interacts with a wide range of drugs to increase the risk of bleeding and/or peptic ulcers. Such drugs include oral anticoagulants, corticosteroids, other NSAIDs, and aspirin.

Lithium Indomethacin may raise blood levels of lithium.

Antihypertensive drugs and diuretics The beneficial effects of these drugs may be reduced by indomethacin.

Probenecid Blood levels of this drug may be raised by indomethacin.

SPECIAL PRECAUTIONS

Be sure to tell your doctor if:
▼ You have long-term liver or kidney problems.
▼ You have had a peptic ulcer, oesophagitis or acid indigestion.
▼ You have heart problems.
▼ You have high blood pressure.
▼ You have had epileptic fits.
▼ You suffer from asthma.
▼ You have bleeding problems.
▼ You are allergic to aspirin.
▼ You are taking other medications.

Pregnancy
▼ Not usually prescribed. May affect the unborn baby, and taken in late pregnancy, may prolong labour. Discuss with your doctor.

Breast feeding
▼ The drug passes into the breast milk and may affect the baby. Discuss with your doctor.

Infants and children
▼ Not usually prescribed for children under 14 except for patent ductus arteriosus. Given for juvenile arthritis only when possible benefits outweigh risks.

Over 60
▼ Reduced dose necessary. Increased likelihood of adverse effects.

Driving and hazardous work
▼ Avoid such activities until you have learned how the drug affects you; it can cause dizziness and drowsiness.

Alcohol
▼ Alcohol may increase the risk of stomach irritation.

Surgery and general anaesthetics
▼ Discuss this with your doctor or dentist before you are given a general anaesthetic.

PROLONGED USE

There is an increased risk of bleeding from peptic ulcers and in the bowel with prolonged use of indomethacin.

INSULIN

Brand names Human Actraphane, Human Actrapid, Human Initard, Human Insulatard, Human Mixtard, Human Monotard, Human Protophane, Human Ultratard, Humulin, Hypurin, Initard, Mixtard, Rapitard, Semitard, Velosulin, and others

GENERAL INFORMATION

Insulin is a hormone manufactured by the pancreas and vital to the body's ability to use sugar. Introduced as a drug in the 1920s, it is given by injection to supplement or replace natural insulin in diabetes mellitus. It is the only effective treatment in juvenile (insulin-dependent) diabetes and may also be prescribed in adult (maturity-onset) diabetes. It should be used in conjunction with a carefully controlled diet. Illness, vomiting or alterations in diet or in exercise levels may require dosage adjustment.

A wide variety of different insulin preparations are available. These can be short, medium, or long-acting. Combinations of these types are often given together. People receiving insulin should carry a warning card or tag so that in case of accident, the appropriate treatment can be given.

QUICK REFERENCE

Drug group Drug for diabetes (p.142)

Overdose danger rating High

Dependence rating Low

Prescription needed No

Available as generic No

INFORMATION FOR USERS

Your drug prescription is tailored for you. Do not alter dosage without checking with your doctor.

How taken

Injection, infusion pump.

Frequency and timing of doses
1 – 4 times daily. Short-acting insulin is usually given 15 – 30 minutes before meals. However, the exact time of these injections and the times of administration for longer acting preparations will be tailored to your individual needs; follow the instructions you are given.

Dosage range
The dose (and type) of insulin is determined according to the needs of the individual.

Onset of effect
30 – 60 minutes (short-acting); 1 – 2 hours (intermediate and long-acting).

Duration of action
6 – 8 hours (short-acting); 18 – 26 hours (medium-acting); 28 – 36 hours (long-acting).

Diet advice
A low carbohydrate diet is needed. Follow your doctor's advice.

Storage
Refrigerate, but do not freeze. Follow the instructions on the container.

Missed dose
Discuss with your doctor. Appropriate action depends on dose and type of insulin.

Stopping the drug
Do not stop taking the drug without consulting your doctor; stopping the drug may lead to confusion and coma.

OVERDOSE ACTION

 Seek immediate medical advice in all cases. You may notice symptoms of low blood sugar such as faintness, hunger, sweating, trembling, confusion, or headache. If these occur, eat or drink something sugary. Take emergency action if fits or loss of consciousness occur.

See Drug poisoning emergency guide (p.470).

SPECIAL PRECAUTIONS

Be sure to tell your doctor if:
▼ You have had a previous allergic reaction to insulin.
▼ You are taking other medications, or your other drug treatment is changed.

 Pregnancy
▼ No evidence of risk to the developing baby from insulin, but poor control of diabetes increases the risk of birth defects. Careful monitoring is required.

 Breast feeding
▼ No evidence of risk. Adjustment in dose may be necessary while breast feeding.

 Infants and children
▼ Reduced dose necessary.

 Over 60
▼ No special problems.

 Driving and hazardous work
▼ Usually no problem, but strenuous exercise alters your insulin and sugar requirements. Avoid these activities if you have warning signs of low blood sugar.

 Alcohol
▼ Avoid. Alcoholic drinks can upset diabetic control.

Surgery and general anaesthetics
▼ Insulin requirements may increase during surgery and blood glucose levels will need to be monitored during and after an operation. Notify your doctor or dentist that you are diabetic before any surgery.

POSSIBLE ADVERSE EFFECTS

Symptoms such as dizziness, sweating, weakness and confusion indicate low blood sugar. Serious allergic reactions (rash, swelling and shortness of breath) are rare.

Symptom/effect	Frequency		Discuss with doctor		Stop taking drug now	Call doctor now
	Common	Rare	Only if severe	In all cases		
Injection–site irritation	●			■		
Weakness/sweating	●			■		
Dimpling at injection site		●		■		
Rash/facial swelling		●		■		▮
Shortness of breath		●		■		▮

INTERACTIONS

General note 1. Many drugs (some antibiotics, monoamine oxidase inhibitors, oral antidiabetic drugs) increase the risk of low blood sugar.

Corticosteroids and diuretics may oppose the effect of insulin.

General note 2. Check with your doctor or pharmacist before taking ANY medicines; some contain sugar and may upset control of diabetes.

Beta blockers may affect insulin needs and mask signs of low blood sugar.

PROLONGED USE

No problems expected.

Monitoring Regular monitoring of levels of sugar in the urine and/or blood is required.

INTERFERON

Brand names Immukin, Intron-A, Roferon-A, Wellferon
Used in the following combined preparations None

GENERAL INFORMATION

Interferons are a group of substances produced in human and animal cells infected by viruses or stimulated by other substances. They are thought to promote resistance to other types of viral infection (see p.127). Two main types of interferon are used to treat a range of diseases (interferon-alpha and interferon-gamma). Conditions which may respond to interferon treatment include: hairy cell leukaemia, chronic myeloid leukaemia, condyloma acuminata, and chronic active hepatitis-B. It is also used to treat AIDS-related Kaposi's sarcoma. Research is being carried out on the use of interferons in the treatment of life-threatening viral diseases, including those that occur in people who have defective immune systems. Use of interferons is associated with significant adverse effects (see below).

INFORMATION FOR USERS

This drug is given only under medical supervision and is not for self-administration.

How taken

Injection.

Frequency and timing of doses
Once daily or on alternate days.

Adult dosage range
The dosage is calculated taking account of the body surface area of the patient, and the condition being treated.

Onset of effect
Active inside the body within 1 hour, but effects may not be noted for one to two months.

Duration of action
Effects last for about 12 hours.

Diet advice
None.

Storage
Not applicable. The drug is not kept in the home.

Missed dose
Not applicable. This drug is given only in hospital under close medical supervision.

Stopping the drug
Discuss with your doctor.

Exceeding the dose
Overdosage is unlikely since treatment is carefully monitored.

SPECIAL PRECAUTIONS

Be sure to tell your doctor if:
▼ You have long-term kidney or liver problems.
▼ You have heart disease.
▼ You have had epileptic fits.
▼ You have previously suffered allergic reactions to any drugs.
▼ You have had asthma or eczema.
▼ You suffer from depression.
▼ You are taking other medications.

 Pregnancy
▼ Not usually prescribed. Safety in pregnancy not established. Discuss with your doctor.

 Breast feeding
▼ It is not known whether the drug passes into breast milk. Discuss with your doctor.

 Infants and children
▼ Not usually used.

 Over 60
▼ Reduced dose may be necessary. Increased likelihood of adverse effects.

 Driving and hazardous work
▼ Not applicable.

 Alcohol
▼ Avoid. Alcohol may increase the sedative effects of this drug.

POSSIBLE ADVERSE EFFECTS

The symptoms listed below are the most common problems. All unusual symptoms should be brought to your doctor's attention without delay. Some of these symptoms are dose-related; a reduction in dosage may be necessary.

Symptom/effect	Frequency		Discuss with doctor		Stop taking drug now	Call doctor now
	Common	Rare	Only if severe	In all cases		
Headache	●		■			
Lethargy/depression	●		■			
Dizziness/drowsiness	●				■	
Digestive disturbances	●				■	
Fever/chills	●				■	
Hair loss		●			■	

INTERACTIONS

General note A number of drugs increase the risk of adverse effects on the blood, heart or nervous system. This is taken into account when prescribing an interferon with other drugs.

Theophylline The effects of theophylline may be enhanced.

Sedatives All drugs that have a sedative effect on the nervous system are likely to increase the sedative properties of interferons. Such drugs include anti-anxiety and sleeping drugs, antihistamines, antidepressants, narcotic analgesics and antipsychotics.

PROLONGED USE

There may be an increased risk of liver damage. Blood cell production in the bone marrow may be reduced.

Monitoring Frequent blood tests are required to monitor blood composition and liver function.

IPRATROPIUM BROMIDE

Brand names Atrovent, Rinatec
Used in the following combined preparation Duovent

GENERAL INFORMATION

Ipratropium bromide is an *anticholinergic* bronchodilator that relaxes the muscles surrounding the bronchioles (airways in the lungs). It is used mainly in the treatment of reversible airways disorders, particularly chronic bronchitis. It can be given only by inhaler or via a nebulizer for these conditions. The drug has a slower onset of action than the *sympathomimetic* bronchodilators, but the effect lasts longer. For this reason it is not as effective in treating acute attacks of wheezing, or in the emer-gency treatment of asthma. It is usually used together with the faster-acting drugs. Ipratropium is also prescribed as a nasal spray for the treatment of a continually runny nose due to allergy.

Unlike other anticholinergic drugs, side effects are rare. It is not likely to affect the heart, eyes, bowel, or bladder. Ipratropium bromide must be used with caution in people with glaucoma; however, problems are unlikely at normal doses.

QUICK REFERENCE

Drug group Bronchodilator (p.92)
Overdose danger rating Low
Dependence rating Low
Prescription needed Yes
Available as generic No

INFORMATION FOR USERS

Your drug prescription is tailored for you. Do not alter dosage without checking with your doctor.

How taken

Inhaler, nasal spray, liquid for nebulizer.

Frequency and timing of doses
3 – 4 x daily.

Adult dosage range
80 – 320mcg daily (inhaler); 400 – 2000mcg daily (nebulizer); 1 – 2 puffs to the affected nostril up to 4 x daily (nasal spray).

Onset of effect
5 – 15 minutes.

Duration of action
Up to 8 hours.

Diet advice
None.

Storage
Keep in a cool, dry place away from reach of children. Do not puncture or burn the container.

Missed dose
Take as soon as you remember. If your next dose is due within 2 hours, take a single dose now and skip the next.

Stopping the drug
Do not stop taking the drug without consulting your doctor. Symptoms may recur.

Exceeding the dose
An occasional unintentional extra dose is unlikely to be a cause for concern. But if you notice unusual symptoms, or if a large overdose has been taken, notify your doctor.

SPECIAL PRECAUTIONS

Be sure to tell your doctor if:
▼ You have glaucoma.
▼ You have prostate problems.
▼ You have difficulty in urination.
▼ You are taking other medications.

Pregnancy
▼ No evidence of risk, but discuss with your doctor before using in the first 3 months of pregnancy.

Breast feeding
▼ No evidence of risk.

Infants and children
▼ Reduced dose necessary.

Over 60s
▼ No special problems.

Driving and hazardous work
▼ No special problems.

Alcohol
▼ No special problems.

POSSIBLE ADVERSE EFFECTS

Side effects are rare. The most common is dry mouth or throat.

Symptom/effect	Frequency		Discuss with doctor		Stop taking drug now	Call doctor now
	Common	Rare	Only if severe	In all cases		
Dry mouth/throat	●		■			
Constipation		●	■			
Urinary hesitancy		●	■			

INTERACTIONS

None.

PROLONGED USE

No special problems.

ISONIAZID

Brand name Rimifon
Used in the following combined preparations Mynah, Rifater, Rifinah, Rimactazid

GENERAL INFORMATION

In use for over 30 years, isoniazid (also known as INAH) remains an effective drug for tuberculosis. It is given alone to prevent the disease and with other drugs for the treatment of tuberculosis. Treatment usually lasts for 6 months. However, courses lasting 9 months or 1 year may sometimes be prescribed. One of the side effects of isoniazid is the increased loss of pyridoxine (vitamin B_6) from the body. This effect, which is more likely with high doses, is rare in children, but common among people with poor nutrition. Since pyridoxine deficiency can lead to irreversible nerve damage, supplements are usually given.

INFORMATION FOR USERS

Your drug prescription is tailored for you. Do not alter dosage without checking with your doctor.

How taken

Tablets, liquid, injection.

Frequency and timing of doses
Normally once daily.

Dosage range
300mg daily (adults); according to age and weight (children).

Onset of effect
Over 2 – 3 days.

Duration of action
Up to 24 hours.

Diet advice
Isoniazid may deplete pyridoxine (vitamin B_6) levels in the body, and supplements are usually prescribed.

Storage
Keep in a closed container in a cool, dry, place away from reach of children. Protect from light.

Missed dose
Take as soon as you remember. If your next dose is scheduled within 8 hours, take a single dose now and skip the next.

Stopping the drug
Take the full course. Even if you feel better the infection may still be present and may recur if treatment is stopped too soon.

OVERDOSE ACTION

Seek immediate medical advice in all cases. Take emergency action if breathing difficulties, loss of consciousness or fits occur.

See Drug poisoning emergency guide (p.470).

SPECIAL PRECAUTIONS

Be sure to tell your doctor if:
▼ You have long-term liver or kidney problems.
▼ You have had liver damage following isoniazid treatment in the past.
▼ You have diabetes.
▼ You have had epileptic fits.
▼ You are taking other medications.

Pregnancy
▼ Safety in pregnancy not established. Discuss with your doctor.

Breast feeding
▼ The drug passes into the breast milk and may affect the baby. The infant should be monitored for signs of toxic effects. Discuss with your doctor.

Infants and children
▼ Reduced dose necessary.

Over 60
▼ Increased likelihood of adverse effects.

Driving and hazardous work
▼ No special problems.

Alcohol
▼ Avoid excessive amounts. Large quantities may reduce the effectiveness of isoniazid.

POSSIBLE ADVERSE EFFECTS

Although serious problems are uncommon, all adverse effects of this drug should receive prompt medical attention, because of the possibility of nerve or liver damage.

Symptom/effect	Frequency		Discuss with doctor		Stop taking drug now	Call doctor now
	Common	Rare	Only if severe	In all cases		
Nausea/vomiting		●	■			
Fatigue/weakness		●		■		
Numbness/tingling		●		■		
Rash		●		■		
Blurred vision		●		■	▲	
Jaundice		●		■	▲	▮
Twitching/muscle weakness		●		■	▲	▮

INTERACTIONS

Anticonvulsants The effects of these drugs may be increased with isoniazid.

Antacids These may reduce the absorption of isoniazid.

PROLONGED USE

Pyridoxine (vitamin B_6) deficiency may occur with prolonged use and lead to nerve damage. Supplements are usually prescribed. There is also a risk of liver damage.

Monitoring Periodic blood tests are usually performed to monitor liver function.

ISOPRENALINE

Brand names Medihaler-iso, Saventrine
Used in the following combined preparations Intal Compound

GENERAL INFORMATION

Isoprenaline is a *sympathomimetic* drug that dilates the bronchioles (small air passages in the lungs) and improves the transmission of electrical signals in the heart. Given by aerosol inhaler, it is used as a bronchodilator to relieve the brochospasm associated with asthma, bronchitis, and emphysema. In rare cases isoprenaline is given intravenously as an emergency treatment for serious heart disorders and the relief of severe asthma. Because isoprenaline may increase the heart rate, it is not suitable for those with heart disorders such as angina. For the same reason, however, it is used in heart block as an interim treatment before an artificial pacemaker is implanted.

Excessive use may cause insomnia, headaches, agitation and, in extreme cases, dangerous heart rhythms.

QUICK REFERENCE

Drug group Bronchodilator (p.92)
Overdose danger rating High
Dependence rating Low
Prescription needed Yes
Available as generic No

INFORMATION FOR USERS

Your drug prescription is tailored for you. Do not alter dosage without checking with your doctor.

How taken

Tablets, injection, inhaler.

Frequency and timing of doses
As required up to a maximum of 8 doses in 24 hours (inhaler); every 2 – 8 hours (tablets).

Adult dosage range
1 – 3 puffs per dose (inhaler); 90 – 840mg daily (tablets).

Onset of effect
2 – 5 minutes (inhaler).

Duration of action
Up to 6 hours.

Diet advice
None.

Storage
Keep in a closed container in a cool, dry place away from reach of children. Protect from light. Do not puncture or burn inhalers.

Missed dose
Do not take the missed dose. Take the next dose as usual.

Stopping the drug
Do not stop taking the drug without consulting your doctor; symptoms may recur.

OVERDOSE ACTION

 Seek immediate medical advice in all cases. Take emergency action if dizziness, fainting, palpitations or loss of consciousness occur.

See Drug poisoning emergency guide (p.470).

SPECIAL PRECAUTIONS

Be sure to tell your doctor if:
▼ You have heart problems.
▼ You have high blood pressure.
▼ You have an overactive thyroid gland.
▼ You have diabetes.
▼ You suffer from nervous problems.
▼ You are taking other medications.

 Pregnancy
▼ Safety in pregnancy not established.

 Breast feeding
▼ It is not known whether the drug passes into breast milk. Discuss with your doctor.

 Infants and children
▼ Reduced dose necessary. Not recommended for treating respiratory conditions.

 Over 60
▼ Adverse effects are more likely to occur.

 Driving and hazardous work
▼ Avoid such activities until you have learned how the drug affects you because the drug can cause dizziness and nervousness.

 Alcohol
▼ No known problems.

Surgery and general anaesthetics
▼ Inform doctor or dentist that you are taking this drug if you need an anaesthetic.

POSSIBLE ADVERSE EFFECTS

Many of the adverse effects go away during treatment as your body adjusts to the medicine. However, palpitations are a sign of excessive stimulation of the heart and chest pain always requires prompt medical attention.

Symptom/effect	Frequency		Discuss with doctor		Stop taking drug now	Call doctor now
	Common	Rare	Only if severe	In all cases		
Dry mouth	●		■			
Tremor	●		■			
Nervousness	●			■		
Headache		●	■			
Chest pain/palpitations		●		■		▪

PROLONGED USE

The effect of isoprenaline may wear off with prolonged use. However, reduced benefit from the drug may also indicate a worsening of asthma and should be brought to your doctor's attention.

INTERACTIONS

Tricyclic antidepressants These drugs may interact with isoprenaline, causing adverse effects on heart rhythm.

ISOSORBIDE DINITRATE/MONONITRATE

Brand names [Dinitrate] Cedocard, Imtack, Isoket, Isordil, Soni-slo, Sorbichew, Sorbid SA, Sorbitrate, Vascardin [Mononitrate]Elantan, Imdur, Ismo, Isotrate, MCR-50, Monit, Mono-Cedocard

GENERAL INFORMATION

Isosorbide "dinitrate" and isosorbide "mononitrate" are types of vasodilator drugs. Both these nitrates are related to glyceryl trinitrate and are most often used to treat patients suffering from angina. They may also be used to treat certain cases of heart failure.

Unlike glyceryl trinitrate, both forms of isosorbide are stable and can be stored for long periods without losing their effectiveness.

Headache, flushing, and dizziness often occur during the early stages of treatment; small initial doses minimize these symptoms. The effectiveness of isosorbide dinitrate and mononitrate may be reduced after a few months, in which case an alternative treatment may need to be considered.

INFORMATION FOR USERS

Your drug prescription is tailored for you. Do not alter dosage without checking with your doctor.

How taken

Dinitrate Tablets (held under the tongue, chewed, or swallowed), SR tablets, SR capsules, injection, spray.
Mononitrate Tablets, SR-tablets, SR-capsules.

Frequency and timing of doses
Relief of angina attacks Tablets chewed or held under the tongue, or spray, as needed (certain preparations only).
Prevention of angina 2 – 4 x daily; 1 – 2 x daily (SR-tablets, capsules).

Adult dosage range
Relief of angina attacks 5 – 10mg per dose.
Prevention of angina 30 – 120mg daily.

Onset of action
2 – 3 minutes when chewed or held under the tongue or used as spray (certain preparations only); 30 minutes when swallowed.

Duration of effect
Up to 2 hours (chewed); up to 5 hours (swallowed); up to 10 hours (slow-release capsules).

Diet advice
None.

Storage
Keep in a closed container in a cool, dry place away from reach of children. Protect from light.

Missed dose
Take as soon as you remember. If your next dose is due within 2 hours, take a single dose now and miss the next.

Stopping the drug
Do not stop taking the drug without consulting your doctor; stopping the drug may lead to worsening of the underlying condition.

Exceeding the dose
An occasional unintentional extra dose is unlikely to cause problems. Large overdoses may cause dizziness and headache. Notify your doctor.

SPECIAL PRECAUTIONS

Be sure to tell your doctor if:
▼ You have liver or kidney problems.
▼ You have any blood disorders or anaemia.
▼ You have had glaucoma.
▼ You are taking other medications.

Pregnancy
▼ Safety in pregnancy not established. Discuss with your doctor.

Breast feeding
▼ Safety not established. Discuss with your doctor.

Infants and children
▼ Not usually prescribed.

Over 60
▼ No special problems.

Driving and hazardous work
▼ Avoid such activities until you have learned how the drug affects you because the drug can cause dizziness.

Alcohol
▼ Avoid. Alcohol may further lower blood pressure, depressing the heart and causing dizziness and faintness.

POSSIBLE ADVERSE EFFECTS

The most serious adverse effect is excessively lowered blood pressure, and this may need to be monitored on a regular basis. Other adverse effects of both forms of the drug usually improve after regular use; dose adjustment may help.

Symptom/effect	Frequency		Discuss with doctor		Stop taking drug now	Call doctor now
	Common	Rare	Only if severe	In all cases		
Headache	●		■			
Flushing	●		■			
Dizziness	●				■	
Fainting/weakness		●			■	

PROLONGED USE

The initial adverse effects may disappear with prolonged use. The effects of both forms of the drug become weaker as the body adapts, requiring increased dosage or other drugs.

INTERACTIONS

Antihypertensives A further lowering of blood pressure occurs when such drugs are taken with isosorbide dinitrate.

ISOTRETINOIN

Brand name Isotrex, Roaccutane
Used in the following combined preparations None

GENERAL INFORMATION

Isotretinoin, a drug that is chemically related to vitamin A, is used for the treatment of severe acne that has failed to respond to other treatments.

It works by reducing production of the skin's natural oils (sebum) and of the horny protein (keratin) that forms in the outer layers of the skin. This latter effect makes it useful for the treatment of some conditions in which the skin thickens abnormally, causing scaling.

A single course of isotretinoin treatment lasting about 16 weeks often clears acne completely. In the early weeks of treatment, the skin may become unusually dry, flaky and itchy. This usually improves as treatment continues. Serious adverse effects include liver damage, visual impairment, and bowel inflammation.

QUICK REFERENCE

Drug group Drug for acne (p.177)
Overdose danger rating Medium
Dependence rating Low
Prescription needed Yes
Available as generic No

INFORMATION FOR USERS

Your drug prescription is tailored for you. Do not alter dosage without checking with your doctor.

How taken

Capsules, gel.

Frequency and timing of doses
1 – 2 x daily (capsules with food).

Adult dosage range
Dosage is determined individually.

Onset of effect
2 – 4 weeks. Acne may worsen during the first few weeks of treatment in some people.

Duration of action
Effects persist for several weeks after the drug has been stopped. Acne is usually completely cleared.

Diet advice
None.

Storage
Keep in a closed container in a cool, dry place away from reach of children. Protect from light.

Missed dose
Take as soon as you remember. If your next dose is due within 4 hours, take a single dose now and skip the next.

Stopping the drug
Can be safely stopped as soon as you no longer need it, but best results are achieved when the course of treatment is completed as prescribed.

Exceeding the dose
An occasional unintentional extra dose is unlikely to cause problems. Large overdoses may cause headaches, vomiting, abdominal pain, facial flushing, dizziness and incoordination. Notify your doctor.

SPECIAL PRECAUTIONS

Be sure to tell your doctor if:
▼ You have long-term liver or kidney problems.
▼ You suffer from arthritis.
▼ You have diabetes.
▼ You wear contact lenses.
▼ You are taking other medications.

 Pregnancy
▼ Not prescribed. May cause abnormalities in the developing baby. Effective contraception must be used for at least 1 month before, and during treatment, and at least one month after stopping.

 Breast feeding
▼ The drug passes into the breast milk and may affect the baby. Discuss with your doctor.

 Infants and children
▼ Not prescribed.

 Over 60
▼ Not usually prescribed.

 Driving and hazardous work
▼ No special problems.

 Alcohol
▼ Regular heavy drinking may raise blood fat levels with isotretinoin, and thus increase the risk of heart and blood vessel disease.

POSSIBLE ADVERSE EFFECTS

Dryness of the nose and mouth, inflammation of the lips and flaking of the skin occur in most people treated with isotretinoin. If headache accompanied by symptoms such as nausea and vomiting, abdominal pain with diarrhoea or blood in bowel movements, or visual impairment occur, consult your doctor promptly.

Symptom/effect	Frequency		Discuss with doctor		Stop taking drug now	Call doctor now
	Common	Rare	Only if severe	In all cases		
Dry skin/nosebleeds	●		■			
Muscle/joint pain	●		■			
Dryness/inflammation of lips/eyes	●			■		
Headache		●		■		
Impaired vision		●		■		
Nausea/vomiting		●		■		
Abdominal pain/diarrhoea		●		■	▲	■

INTERACTIONS

Tetracycline antibiotics These may increase the risk of high pressure in the skull leading to headaches, nausea, and vomiting.

Skin-drying preparations Medicated cosmetics, soaps, toiletries, and anti-acne preparations increase the likelihood of dryness and irritation of the skin with isotretinoin.

Vitamin A Supplements of this vitamin increase the risk of adverse effects from isotretinoin.

PROLONGED USE

Course of treatment rarely exceeds 16 weeks. Prolonged use may cause a rise in fat levels in the blood, thereby increasing the risk of heart and blood vessel disease.

Monitoring Periodic checks on fat levels in the blood and liver function tests may be recommended.

KETOCONAZOLE

Brand name Nizoral
Used in the following combined preparations None

GENERAL INFORMATION

Ketoconazole is prescribed for severe, internal *systemic* fungal infections. It is also given to treat serious infections of the skin and mucous membranes caused by the candida yeast. People with rare fungal diseases (paracoccidioidomycosis, histoplasmosis, and coccidioidomycosis) may also be given this antifungal drug.

Ketoconazole is applied as a cream to treat fungal skin infections, and as a shampoo for the treatment of scalp infections and seborrhoeic dermatitis.
  The most common side effect with ketoconazole is nausea, which can be reduced by taking the drug at bedtime or with meals. Ketoconazole may also cause liver damage.

INFORMATION FOR USERS

Your drug prescription is tailored for you. Do not alter dosage without checking with your doctor.

How taken

Tablets, liquid, cream, shampoo.

Frequency and timing of doses
Once daily with food (orally); 1 – 2 x daily (skin cream); 1 – 2 x weekly (shampoo used for serborrhoeic dermatitis).

Dosage range
Adults 200 – 400mg daily (by mouth).
Children Reduced dose according to age and weight.

Onset of effect
The drug begins to work within a few hours; full beneficial effect may take several days.

Duration of action
Up to 24 hours.

Diet advice
None.

Storage
Keep in a closed container in a cool, dry place away from reach of children.

Missed dose
Take as soon as you remember. If your next dose is due within 6 hours, take a single dose now and skip the next.

Stopping the drug
Take the full course. Even if you feel better, the original infection may still be present and symptoms may recur if treatment is stopped too soon.

Exceeding the dose
An occasional unintentional extra dose is unlikely to cause problems. Large overdoses may cause gastric problems. Notify your doctor.

SPECIAL PRECAUTIONS

Be sure to tell your doctor if:
▼ You have long-term liver or kidney problems.
▼ You have had stomach ulcers.
▼ You have previously had an allergic reaction to antifungal drugs.
▼ You are taking other medications.

 Pregnancy
▼ Not usually prescribed. May cause defects in the developing baby. Discuss with your doctor.

 Breast feeding
▼ The drug passes into the breast milk and may affect the baby adversely. Discuss with your doctor.

 Infants and children
▼ Reduced dose necessary.

 Over 60
▼ No special problems.

 Driving and hazardous work
▼ No special problems.

 Alcohol
▼ No known problems.

POSSIBLE ADVERSE EFFECTS

Nausea is the most common side effect of this drug; liver damage is a rare but serious adverse effect causing jaundice that may necessitate stopping the drug.

Symptom/effect	Frequency		Discuss with doctor		Stop taking drug now	Call doctor now
	Common	Rare	Only if severe	In all cases		
Nausea/vomiting	●		■			
Headache		●	■			
Abdominal pain		●	■			
Itching/rash		●			■	▲
Painful breasts (men)		●			■	▲
Jaundice		●			■	▲	■

INTERACTIONS

Antacids, cimetidine and ranitidine These drugs may reduce the effectiveness of ketoconazole if they are taken within 2 hours before or after ketoconazole.

Rifampicin reduces the effect of ketoconazole.

Warfarin Ketoconazole increases the effect of warfarin.

Cyclosporin Ketoconazole increases the level of cyclosporin in the blood.

Phenytoin Levels of ketoconazole may be reduced by phenytoin.

Antihistamines Increased risk of terfenadine and astemizole causing adverse effects on the heart.

PROLONGED USE

The risk of liver damage increases with long-term use.

Monitoring Periodic blood tests are usually taken to check the effect of the drug on the liver.

LACTULOSE

Brand names Duphalac, Osmolax
Used in the following combined preparations None

GENERAL INFORMATION

Lactulose is an effective laxative that softens stools by increasing the amount of water in the large intestine. It is useful for the relief of constipation and faecal impaction, especially in the elderly. It is less likely to disrupt normal bowel action than some other types of laxatives.

Lactulose can also prevent and treat the brain disturbance associated with liver failure known as hepatic encephalopathy.

Because lactulose acts locally in the large intestine and is not absorbed into the body, it is safer than many other laxatives. However, it can cause stomach cramps and flatulence at the start of treatment.

QUICK REFERENCE

Drug group Laxative (see p.111)

Overdose danger rating Low

Dependence rating Low

Prescription needed No

Available as generic Yes

INFORMATION FOR USERS

Your drug prescription is tailored for you. Do not alter dosage without checking with your doctor.

How taken

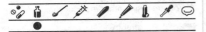

Liquid.

Frequency and timing of doses
2 x daily (chronic constipation);
3 – 4 x daily (liver failure).

Adult dosage range
15 – 30ml daily (chronic constipation);
90 – 150ml daily (liver failure).

Onset of effect
24 – 48 hours.

Duration of action
6 – 18 hours.

Diet advice
It is important to maintain an adequate intake of fluid – up to 8 glasses of water daily.

Storage
Keep in a closed container, in a cool, dry place, away from reach of children. Do not store after diluting.

Missed dose
Take as soon as you remember. If your next dose is due within 3 hours, take a single dose now and skip the next.

Stopping the drug
In the treatment of constipation, the drug can be safely stopped as soon as you no longer need it.

Exceeding the dose
An occasional unintentional extra dose is unlikely to be a cause for concern. But if you notice unusual symptoms, or if a large overdose has been taken, notify your doctor.

SPECIAL PRECAUTIONS

Be sure to consult your doctor or pharmacist before taking this drug if:
▼ You have severe abdominal pain.
▼ You are taking other medications.

Pregnancy
▼ No evidence of risk. Discuss with your doctor.

Breast feeding
▼ No evidence of risk.

Infants and children
▼ Reduced dose necessary.

Over 60
▼ No special problems.

Driving and hazardous work
▼ No known problems.

Alcohol
▼ No known problems.

POSSIBLE ADVERSE EFFECTS

Adverse effects are rarely serious and often disappear when your body adjusts to the medicine. Diarrhoea indicates that the dosage of lactulose may be too high.

Symptom/effect	Frequency		Discuss with doctor		Stop taking drug now	Call doctor now
	Common	Rare	Only if severe	In all cases		
Flatulence/belching	●		■			
Stomach cramps	●		■			
Nausea		●	■			
Abdominal distension		●		■		
Diarrhoea		●		■		

INTERACTIONS

None

PROLONGED USE

No special problems expected.

LEVODOPA

Brand names Brocadopa, Laradopa
Used in the following combined preparations Madopar, Sinemet

GENERAL INFORMATION

The treatment of Parkinson's disease underwent dramatic change in the 1960s with the introduction of levodopa. Because the body can transform levodopa into dopamine, a chemical in the brain whose absence or shortage causes Parkinson's disease (see p.87), pronounced improvements were expected. These focused not so much on a cure as on symptomatic benefits.

However, it was found that, while effective, levodopa produced severe side effects: nausea, dizziness, palpitations. Even when levodopa treatment was initiated gradually, it was difficult to balance the benefits against the adverse reactions. What made the treatment even more difficult was the need for increasingly large dosages.

Today, when levodopa treatment is prescribed, the drug is combined with carbidopa or benserazide, substances that enhance the effects of levodopa in the brain, enabling lower doses to be given. This also helps to reduce the side effects of levodopa.

INFORMATION FOR USERS

Your drug prescription is tailored for you. Do not alter dosage without checking with your doctor.

How taken

Tablets, capsules.

Frequency and timing of doses
3 – 6 x daily with food or milk.

Adult dosage range
125 – 500mg initially, increased until benefits and side effects are balanced.

Onset of effect
Within 1 hour.

Duration of action
2 – 12 hours.

Diet advice
None.

Storage
Keep in a closed container in a cool, dry place away from reach of children. Protect from light.

Missed dose
Take as soon as you remember. If your next dose is due within 2 hours, take a single dose now and skip the next.

Stopping the drug
Do not stop taking the drug without consulting your doctor; stopping the drug may lead to worsening of the underlying condition.

Exceeding the dose
An occasional unintentional extra dose is unlikely to cause problems. Larger overdoses may cause vomiting or drowsiness. Notify your doctor.

POSSIBLE ADVERSE EFFECTS

Adverse effects of levodopa are closely related to dosage levels. At the start of treatment, when dosage is usually low, unwanted effects are likely to be mild. Such effects may increase in severity as dosage is increased to boost the drug's beneficial effects. All adverse effects of this drug should be discussed with your doctor.

Symptom/effect	Frequency		Discuss with doctor		Stop taking drug now	Call doctor now
	Common	Rare	Only if severe	In all cases		
Digestive disturbance	●			■		
Nervousness/agitation	●			■		
Dizziness/fainting		●		■		
Abnormal movement	●			■		
Confusion/vivid dreams		●		■		
Palpitations		●		■	▲	■

INTERACTIONS

Antidepressants Levodopa may interact with MAOIs to cause a dangerous rise in blood pressure. It may also interact with tricyclics.

Iron absorption of levodopa may be reduced by iron.

Antipsychotics may increase the risk of adverse effects.

Pyridoxine (vitamin B_6) Excessive intake of this vitamin may reduce the effect of levodopa.

SPECIAL PRECAUTIONS

Be sure to tell your doctor if:
▼ You have heart problems.
▼ You have long-term kidney or liver problems.
▼ You have a lung disorder such as asthma or bronchitis.
▼ You have an overactive thyroid gland.
▼ You have had glaucoma.
▼ You have a peptic ulcer.
▼ You have diabetes.
▼ You are taking other medications.

Pregnancy
▼ Unlikely to be required.

Breast feeding
▼ Unlikely to be required.

Infants and children
▼ Not normally used in children.

Over 60
▼ No special problems.

Driving and hazardous work
▼ Your underlying condition, as well as the possibility of this drug causing faintness and dizziness, may make such activities inadvisable. Discuss with your doctor.

Alcohol
▼ No known problems.

PROLONGED USE

The effectiveness usually declines in time, necessitating increased dosage. The adverse effects become so severe that ultimately the drug must be stopped.

LEVONORGESTREL

Brand names Microval, Norgeston
Used in the following combined preparations Cyclo-progynova, Eugynon 30, Microgynon, Ovran, Ovranette, and others

GENERAL INFORMATION

Levonorgestrel is a synthetic hormone similar to a natural female sex hormone, progesterone. Its main use is as an ingredient in oral contraceptives. Its contraceptive action is to thicken the mucus at the neck of the uterus (cervix), thereby making it difficult for sperm to enter the uterus.

Levonorgestrel is available in progestogen-only preparations and in combined oral contraceptives with an oestrogen drug.

Levonorgestrel is occasionally given with an oestrogen for emergency, post-coital contraception. Levonorgestrel is also prescribed in combination with an oestrogen drug in hormone replacement therapy to treat menopausal symptoms.

Levonorgestrel rarely causes serious adverse effects. When prescribed without an oestrogen, menstrual irregularities, particularly mid-cycle, or "breakthrough", bleeding are common.

QUICK REFERENCE

Drug group Female sex hormone (p.147) and oral contraceptive (p.161)

Overdose danger rating Low

Dependence rating Low

Prescription needed Yes

Available as generic No

INFORMATION FOR USERS

Your drug prescription is tailored for you. Do not alter dosage without checking with your doctor.

How taken

Tablets.

Frequency and timing of doses
Once daily, at the same time each day.

Adult dosage range
Progestogen-only pills 30 micrograms daily.

Onset of effect
Norgestrel starts to act within 4 hours, but contraceptive protection may not be fully effective for 14 days depending on which day of the cycle the tablets are started.

Duration of action
24 hours. Some effects may persist for up to 3 months after levonorgestrel is stopped.

Diet advice
None.

Storage
Keep in a closed container in a cool, dry place away from reach of children.

Missed dose
See What to do if you miss a pill (p.163).

Stopping the drug
The drug can be safely stopped as soon as contraceptive protection is no longer required. For treatment of menopausal symptoms, consult your doctor before stopping the drug.

Exceeding the dose
An occasional unintentional extra dose is unlikely to be a cause for concern. But if you notice unusual symptoms, or if a large overdose has been taken, notify your doctor.

SPECIAL PRECAUTIONS

Be sure to tell your doctor if:
▼ You have a long-term liver problem.
▼ You have heart failure or high blood pressure.
▼ You have diabetes.
▼ You have had blood clots or a stroke.
▼ You are taking other medications.

Pregnancy
▼ Not prescribed. May cause abnormalities in the developing baby. Discuss with your doctor.

Breast feeding
▼ The drug passes into the breast milk, but at normal doses adverse effects on the baby are unlikely. Discuss with your doctor.

Infants and children
▼ Not prescribed.

Over 60
▼ Not prescribed.

Driving and hazardous work
▼ No known problems.

Alcohol
▼ No known problems.

POSSIBLE ADVERSE EFFECTS

Menstrual irregularities (blood spotting between menstrual periods or absence of menstruation) are the most common side effects of levonorgestrel alone.

Symptom/effect	Frequency		Discuss with doctor		Stop taking drug now	Call doctor now
	Common	Rare	Only if severe	In all cases		
Swollen feet/ankles	●		■			
Weight gain	●		■			
Irregular vaginal bleeding	●			■		
Nausea/vomiting		●	■			
Breast tenderness		●	■			
Depression		●			■	
Headache		●		■		

INTERACTIONS

General note Levonorgestrel may interfere with the beneficial effects of many drugs, including bromocriptine, oral anticoagulants, anticonvulsants, antihypertensive and antidiabetic drugs. Many other drugs may affect the action of oral contraceptives, reducing contraceptive protection. These include anticonvulsants, antituberculous drugs, and antibiotics. Inform your doctor that you are taking this drug before taking additional prescribed medication.

PROLONGED USE

Problems are rare.

LINDANE

Brand names Quellada
Used in the following combined preparations None

GENERAL INFORMATION

Lindane (also called gamma benzene hexachloride) is an insecticide. Used in the treatment of scabies and body lice infestations, it rapidly kills the parasites after being absorbed through their tough outer "skin".

The drug is usually applied as a lotion, but shampoos for head lice are also available.

Adverse effects are rare when recommended doses are applied correctly, although lindane may occasionally cause irritation or a rash. Itching, due to an allergic reaction to residual mite eggs and faeces, may persist for several weeks after the drug has been used for treatment for scabies. Avoid the drug coming into contact with the eyes. Lindane is poisonous if swallowed. Small children are particularly at risk from accidental poisoning.

INFORMATION FOR USERS

Follow instructions on the label. Call your doctor if symptoms worsen.

How taken

Lotion, shampoo.

Frequency and timing of doses
A single treatment, repeated after one week or as instructed.

Dosage range
Apply as directed on the label. For scabies, the whole body except the head and neck needs to be covered.

Onset of effect
Within a few minutes.

Duration of action
Active until washed off.

Diet advice
None.

Storage
Keep in a closed container in a cool, dry place away from reach of children.

Missed dose
Not applicable.

Stopping the drug
Follow the advice of your doctor or pharmacist. A second treatment is sometimes required to clear the parasites completely.

OVERDOSE ACTION

 A single excessive application to the skin or hair is unlikely to cause problems. Frequently repeated applications of the drug may cause agitation, vomiting, muscle cramps and fits, requiring prompt medical attention. If the drug has been swallowed seek immediate medical help.

See Drug poisoning emergency guide (p.470).

SPECIAL PRECAUTIONS

Be sure to tell your doctor or pharmacist before using this drug if:
▼ You have sensitive skin.
▼ You have had epileptic fits.
▼ You are taking other medications.

 Pregnancy
▼ Not usually prescribed. Safety in pregnancy not established. Discuss with your doctor.

 Breast feeding
▼ Safety not established. Discuss with your doctor.

 Infants and children
▼ Not recommended in babies under 1 month old.

 Over 60
▼ No special problems.

 Driving and hazardous work
▼ No known problems.

 Alcohol
▼ No known problems.

POSSIBLE ADVERSE EFFECTS

Used correctly, lindane rarely causes adverse effects. If you develop skin irritation during treatment, wash off the drug and consult your doctor.

Symptom/effect	Frequency		Discuss with doctor		Stop taking drug now	Call doctor now
	Common	Rare	Only if severe	In all cases		
Rash		●		■		▲
Irritation		●		■		▲

INTERACTIONS

None.

PROLONGED USE

Not given for prolonged periods.

LITHIUM

Brand names Camcolit, Li-liquid, Liskonum, Litarex, Phasal, Priadel
Used in the following combined preparations Efalith

GENERAL INFORMATION

A form of the lightest metal we know, the drug lithium has been used since the 1940s to help those suffering from a severe mental disturbance, manic depression. Lithium decreases the intensity and frequency of the episodic swings from extreme excitement to deep depression that are characteristic of that disorder.

A preferred agent for mania alone, it is also sometimes used to prevent and treat severe depression (see p.84). Treatment with lithium may be started in hospital for the more seriously ill. Careful monitoring is required because high levels of lithium in the blood can cause serious adverse effects. Since it may take two to three weeks for any benefit of lithium to become apparent, an antipsychotic drug is often given with lithium until the lithium becomes effective.

(see p.84).

QUICK REFERENCE

Drug group Antimanic drug (p.85)
Overdose danger rating High
Dependence rating Low
Prescription needed Yes
Available as generic No

(p.85)

INFORMATION FOR USERS

Your drug prescription is tailored for you. Do not alter dosage without checking with your doctor.

How taken

Tablets, SR-tablets, liquid.

Frequency and timing of doses
1 – 3 x daily with meals.

Adult dosage range
0.25 – 2g daily. Dosage may vary according to individual response.

Onset of effect
Some effects may be noticed in 3 – 5 days, but full benefits may not be felt for 3 weeks.

Duration of action
18 – 36 hours. Some effect may last for several days.

Diet advice
Lithium levels in the blood are affected by the amount of sodium (present in salt) in the body, so you should be careful not to suddenly increase or reduce the amount of salt in your diet. Be sure to drink adequate volumes of fluids – especially in hot weather.

Storage
Keep in a closed container in a cool, dry place away from reach of children.

Missed dose
Take as soon as you remember. If your next dose is due within 4 hours, take a single dose now and miss the next.

Stopping the drug
Do not stop the drug without consulting your doctor; symptoms may recur.

OVERDOSE ACTION

Seek immediate medical advice in all cases. Take emergency action if consciousness is lost or if convulsions occur.

See Drug poisoning emergency guide (p.470).

(p.470).

SPECIAL PRECAUTIONS

Be sure to tell your doctor if:
▼ You have long-term kidney or liver problems.
▼ You have heart or circulation problems.
▼ You have an overactive thyroid gland.
▼ You have myasthenia gravis.
▼ You are taking other medications.

 Pregnancy
▼ Not usually prescribed. May cause defects in the unborn baby. Discuss with your doctor.

 Breast feeding
▼ The drug passes into the breast milk and may affect the baby. Discuss with your doctor.

 Infants and children
▼ Not recommended.

 Over 60
▼ Increased likelihood of adverse effects. Reduced dose may therefore be necessary.

 Driving and hazardous work
▼ Avoid such activities until you have learned how the drug affects you because of the possibility of reduced alertness.

 Alcohol
▼ Avoid. Alcohol may increase the sedative effects of this drug.

PROLONGED USE

Prolonged use may lead to kidney problems. Treatment for periods of longer than 5 years is not normally advised unless the benefits are significant and tests show no sign of reduced kidney function.

Monitoring Regular monitoring of blood levels of the drug and the composition of the blood is usually carried out. Kidney and thyroid function should also be monitored.

POSSIBLE ADVERSE EFFECTS

Most adverse effects are related to the blood levels of the drug. Your doctor will try to find a dose that is sufficient to control your condition without causing excessive adverse effects. Most of the symptoms below are signs of a high lithium level in the blood. Stop taking the drug and seek medical advice promptly if you notice any of these.

Symptom/effect	Frequency		Discuss with doctor		Stop taking drug now	Call doctor now
	Common	Rare	Only if severe	In all cases		
Nausea/vomiting/diarrhoea	●			■	▲	
Tremor	●			■		
Weight gain		●	■			
Muscle weakness		●		■		
Drowsiness/lethargy		●		■	▲	
Blurred vision		●		■	▲	
Rash		●		■	▲	

INTERACTIONS

General note Many drugs interact with lithium. Do not take any over-the-counter or prescription drug without first consulting your doctor or pharmacist.

LOFEPRAMINE

Brand name Gamanil
Used in the following combined preparations None

GENERAL INFORMATION

Lofepramine belongs to the group of tricyclic antidepressant drugs. It is mainly used in the long-term treatment of depression. It elevates mood, increases physical activity, improves appetite, and restores interest in everyday activities.

Less sedating than some of the other tricyclic antidepressants, lofepramine is useful when depression is accompa-nied by lethargy.

The main advantage of lofepramine over other similar drugs is that it seems to have a weaker *anticholinergic* action and therefore milder side effects. In overdose lofepramine may be less harmful than the older tricyclic drugs.

QUICK REFERENCE

Drug group Tricyclic antidepressant (p.84)

Overdose danger rating Medium

Dependence rating Low

Prescription needed Yes

Available as generic No

INFORMATION FOR USERS

Your drug prescription is tailored for you. Do not alter dosage without checking with your doctor.

How taken

Tablets.

Frequency and timing of doses
2 – 3 x daily.

Adult dosage range
140 – 210mg daily.

Onset of effect
Can appear within hours, though full antidepressant effect may not be felt for 2–6 weeks.

Duration of action
Antidepressant effect may last for six weeks; adverse effects, only a few days.

Diet advice
None.

Storage
Keep in a closed container in a cool, dry place away from reach of children. Protect from light.

Missed dose
Take as soon as you remember. If your next dose is due within 3 hours, take a single dose now and skip the next.

Stopping the drug
An abrupt stop can cause withdrawal symptoms and a recurrence of the original trouble. Consult your doctor, who may supervise a gradual reduction in dosage.

Exceeding the dose
An occasional unintentional extra dose is unlikely to cause problems. But if you notice any unusual symptoms, or if a large overdose has been taken, notify your doctor.

SPECIAL PRECAUTIONS

Be sure to tell your doctor if:
▼ You have heart problems.
▼ You have had epileptic fits.
▼ You have long-term liver or kidney problems.
▼ You have glaucoma.
▼ You have an overactive thyroid.
▼ You have prostate trouble.
▼ You are taking other medications.

Pregnancy
▼ Safety in pregnancy not established. Discuss with your doctor.

Breast feeding
▼ The drug passes into the breast milk and may affect the baby. Discuss with your doctor.

Infants and children
▼ Not recommended.

Over 60
▼ Reduced dose may be necessary.

Driving and hazardous work
▼ Avoid such activities until you have learned how the drug affects you because of the possibility of blurred vision and reduced alertness.

Alcohol
▼ Avoid. Alcohol may increase the sedative effects of this drug.

POSSIBLE ADVERSE EFFECTS

The possible adverse effects of this drug are mainly the result of its mild *anticholinergic* action and its blocking action on the transmission of signals through the heart.

Symptom/effect	Frequency		Discuss with doctor		Stop taking drug now	Call doctor now
	Common	Rare	Only if severe	In all cases		
Sweating/flushing	●		■			
Drowsiness		●	■			
Dry mouth		●	■			
Blurred vision		●		■		
Dizziness/fainting		●		■		
Difficulty in passing urine		●		■		
Palpitations		●		■	▲	▮

INTERACTIONS

Sedatives All drugs that have sedative effects intensify those of lofepramine.

Heavy smoking This may reduce the antidepressant effect of lofepramine.

Antihypertensive drugs Lofepramine may reduce the effectiveness of some of these drugs.

Monoamine oxidase inhibitors (MAOIs) Serious interactions are possible. These drugs are only prescribed together under close medical supervision.

PROLONGED USE

No problems expected.

LOPERAMIDE

Brand names Arret, Diocalm Ultra, Imodium
Used in the following combined preparations None

GENERAL INFORMATION

Loperamide is an antidiarrhoeal drug that is available in capsules or liquid form. It reduces the loss of water and salts from the bowel and slows bowel activity, resulting in the passage of firmer bowel movements at less frequent intervals.

A fast-acting drug, it is widely prescribed for both sudden and recurrent bouts of diarrhoea. However, it is not generally recommended for diarrhoea caused by infection because it may delay the expulsion of harmful substances from the bowel. Loperamide is often prescribed for people with colostomies or ileostomies to reduce fluid loss from the stoma (outlet).

Adverse effects from this drug are rare; unlike the opium-based antidiarrhoeals, there is no risk of abuse. It can be purchased over the counter in a pharmacy.

QUICK REFERENCE

Drug group Antidiarrhoeal drug (p.110)

Overdose danger rating Medium

Dependence rating Low

Prescription needed No

Available as generic Yes

INFORMATION FOR USERS

**Follow instructions on the label.
Call your doctor if symptoms worsen.**

How taken

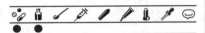

Capsules, liquid.

Frequency and timing of doses
Acute diarrhoea Take a double dose at start of treatment then a single dose after each loose stool up to the maximum daily dose.
Chronic diarrhoea 2 x daily.

Adult dosage range
Acute diarrhoea 4mg (starting dose), then 2mg (maximum 16mg daily).
Chronic diarrhoea 4 – 8mg daily.

Onset of effect
Within 1 – 2 hours.

Duration of action
6 – 18 hours.

Diet advice
Ensure adequate fluid, sugar and salt intake during a diarrhoeal illness.

Storage
Keep in a closed container in a cool, dry place away from reach of children.

Missed dose
Do not take the missed dose. Take your next dose if needed.

Stopping the drug
Can be safely stopped as soon as you no longer need it.

Exceeding the dose
An occasional unintentional extra dose is unlikely to cause problems. Large overdoses may cause constipation, or drowsiness, and affect breathing. Notify your doctor.

SPECIAL PRECAUTIONS

Be sure to consult your doctor or pharmacist before taking this drug if:
▼ You have long-term liver or kidney problems.
▼ You have had recent abdominal surgery.
▼ You are taking other medications.

Pregnancy
▼ Safety in pregnancy not established. Discuss with your doctor.

Breast feeding
▼ The drug passes into the breast milk and may affect the baby. Discuss with your doctor.

Infants and children
▼ Reduced dose necessary. Not to be given to children under 4 years.

Over 60
▼ No special problems

Driving and hazardous work
▼ No known problems.

Alcohol
▼ No known problems.

POSSIBLE ADVERSE EFFECTS

Adverse effects are rare with loperamide and often difficult to distinguish from the effects of the diarrhoea it is used to treat. If symptoms such as bloating, abdominal pain or fever persist or worsen during treatment with loperamide, consult your doctor.

Symptom/effect	Frequency		Discuss with doctor		Stop taking drug now	Call doctor now
	Common	Rare	Only if severe	In all cases		
Constipation		●	■		▲	
Bloating		●	■			
Abdominal pain		●	■			
Itching skin		●		■		
Rash		●		■	▲	

INTERACTIONS

None.

PROLONGED USE

This drug is not usually taken for prolonged periods (except for persons with a medically diagnosed long term gastro-intestinal condition), but special problems are not expected during long-term use.

LORATIDINE

Brand name Clarityn
Used in the following combined preparations None

GENERAL INFORMATION

Loratidine is a long-acting antihistamine drug. It is used for the relief of symptoms associated with allergic rhinitis such as sneezing, nasal discharge, and itching and burning of the eyes. Symptoms are normally relieved within an hour of oral administration. Loratidine is also used for allergic skin conditions such as chronic urticaria (itching). One advantage of loratidine over older antihistamines, such as chlorpheniramine, is that it has fewer sedative and anticholinergic effects and so is less likely to cause drowsiness.

Loratidine should be discontinued about 4 days prior to skin testing for allergy as it may decrease or prevent otherwise positive results.

INFORMATION FOR USERS

Your drug prescription is tailored for you. Do not alter dosage without checking with your physician.

How taken

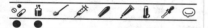

Tablets, liquid.

Frequency and timing of doses
Once daily.

Adult dosage range
10mg daily.

Onset of action
Usually within 1 hour.

Duration of action
Up to 24 hours.

Diet advice
None.

Storage
Keep in a closed container in a cool, dry place away from reach of children.

Missed dose
Take as soon as you remember. If your next dose is due within 6 hours, take a single dose now and skip the next.

Stopping the drug
Can be safely stopped as soon as you no longer need it.

Exceeding the dose
An occasional unintentional extra dose is unlikely to cause problems. But if a large overdose has been taken, notify your doctor.

POSSIBLE ADVERSE EFFECTS

The incidence of adverse effects with loratidine is low.

Symptom/effect	Frequency		Discuss with doctor		Stop taking drug now	Call doctor now
	Common	Rare	Only if severe	In all cases		
Fatigue	●		■			
Nausea	●		■			
Headache	●		■			

INTERACTIONS

None.

SPECIAL PRECAUTIONS

Be sure to tell your doctor or pharmacist if:
▼ You are taking other medications.

 Pregnancy
▼ Safety in pregnancy not established. Discuss with your doctor.

 Breast feeding
▼ The drug passes into the breast milk, but effects on the baby are unlikely.

 Infants and children
▼ Not recommended for children under 2 years. Reduced dose necessary for older children.

 Over 60
▼ No problems expected.

 Driving and hazardous work
▼ Problems are unlikely.

 Alcohol
▼ No known problems, but avoid excessive amounts.

PROLONGED USE

No problems expected.

LYPRESSIN

Brand name Syntopressin
Used in the following combined preparations None

GENERAL INFORMATION

Lypressin is a synthetic form of a hormone called vasopressin, which regulates an important kidney function. Vasopressin deficiency causes diabetes insipidus, a water imbalance arising from the kidneys' inability to concentrate the urine. Frequent urination occurs, and continued thirst.

Used as a nasal spray, it helps correct the hormonal deficiency. Short-acting, it is most helpful in people with milder forms of the disease. In more severely affected individuals, it may not give adequate control of urine production, and longer-acting treatments are usually prescribed.

Side effects are rare. Nasal congestion reduces absorption of the drug, making larger doses necessary to maintain its beneficial effect.

QUICK REFERENCE

Drug group Drug for diabetes insipidus (p.145)

Overdose danger rating Medium

Dependence rating Low

Prescription needed Yes

Available as generic No

INFORMATION FOR USERS

Your drug prescription is tailored for you. Do not alter dosage without checking with your doctor.

How taken

Nasal spray.

Frequency and timing of doses
3 – 7 x daily.

Dosage range
1 – 4 sprays in each nostril per dose.

Onset of effect
Within a few minutes.

Duration of action
3 – 6 hours.

Diet advice
Your doctor may advise you to monitor your fluid intake at the start of treatment.

Storage
Store in a cool, dry place, away from the reach of children. Do not use after one month of starting a bottle. Store any bottles not in use in a refrigerator, but do not freeze.

Missed dose
Take as soon as you remember. Space subsequent doses at equal intervals throughout the day.

Stopping the drug
Do not stop the drug without consulting your physician; symptoms may recur.

Exceeding the dose
An occasional unintentional overdose is unlikely to cause problems. Large overdoses may cause abdominal cramps, headache, and abnormal heart rhythm. Notify your doctor.

SPECIAL PRECAUTIONS

Be sure to tell your doctor if:
▼ You have heart problems.
▼ You have high blood pressure.
▼ You suffer from allergic rhinitis or asthma.
▼ You are taking other medications.
▼ You have kidney problems.
▼ You have epilepsy.

Pregnancy
▼ Has been used in pregnancy without ill effect on the baby. However the drug could impair the blood supply to the uterus. Discuss with your doctor.

Breast feeding
▼ The drug passes into the breast milk, but at normal doses adverse effects on the baby are unlikely. Discuss with your doctor.

Infants and children
▼ No special problems.

Over 60
▼ No special problems.

Driving and hazardous work
▼ No known problems.

Alcohol
▼ No known problems, but your doctor may advise on fluid intake.

Surgery and general anaesthetics
▼ Your treatment may need to be changed before you have a general anaesthetic. Discuss this with your doctor or dentist before any surgery.

POSSIBLE ADVERSE EFFECTS

Adverse effects are rare. The drug may occasionally cause nasal congestion or ulceration. It may also stimulate contraction of the bowel, leading to abdominal cramps and an increased urge to defecate. Coughing and breathing difficulty may be caused by inadvertent inhalation of the spray into the lungs.

Symptom/effect	Frequency		Discuss with doctor		Stop taking drug now	Call doctor now
	Common	Rare	Only if severe	In all cases		
Abdominal cramps	●		■			
Urge to defecate	●		■			
Nausea	●		■			
Headache		●	■			
Shortness of breath		●		■		
Runny/stuffy nose		●		■		
Irritation/sores in nose		●		■		

INTERACTIONS

Chlorpropamide, clofibrate and carbamazepine may increase the effect of lypressin.

Lithium may oppose the effect of lypressin.

PROLONGED USE

No problems expected.

MAGNESIUM HYDROXIDE

Brand names Milk of Magnesia
Used in the following combined preparations Actonorm, Aludrox, Carbellon, Maalox, Mucaine, Mucogel, and others

GENERAL INFORMATION

Magnesium hydroxide is a fast-acting antacid used to neutralize stomach acid. It is available in a number of over-the-counter preparations for the treatment of indigestion and heartburn. Magnesium hydroxide also prevents pain due to stomach and duodenal ulcers, gastritis, and reflux oesophagitis, although other drugs are normally used for this now. It also acts as a laxative by absorbing water into the intestine from surrounding blood vessels to soften the faeces.

Magnesium hydroxide is not often used alone as an antacid because of this laxative effect. However, this is countered when the drug is combined with aluminium hydroxide, which tends to be constipating.

QUICK REFERENCE

Drug group Antacid (p.108) and laxative (p.111)
Overdose danger rating Low
Dependence rating Low
Prescription needed No
Available as generic Yes

INFORMATION FOR USERS

**Follow instructions on the label.
Call your doctor if symptoms worsen.**

How taken

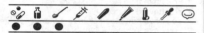

Tablets, liquid, powder.

Frequency and timing of doses
4 x daily with water, preferably an hour after food.

Adult dosage range
Antacid 5 – 20ml per dose (liquid);
1 – 2g per dose (tablets).
Laxative 5 – 20ml per dose (liquid).

Onset of effect
Within 15 minutes (antacid); 2 – 8 hours (laxative).

Duration of action
2 – 4 hours.

Diet advice
None.

Storage
Keep in a closed container in a cool, dry place away from reach of children.

Missed dose
Take as soon as you remember.

Stopping the drug
When used as an antacid, can be safely stopped as soon as you no longer need it. When given as ulcer treatment, follow your doctor's advice.

Exceeding the dose
An occasional unintentional extra dose is unlikely to be a cause for concern. But if you notice unusual symptoms, or if a large overdose has been taken, notify your doctor.

SPECIAL PRECAUTIONS

Be sure to consult your doctor or pharmacist before taking this drug if:
▼ You have a long-term kidney problem.
▼ You have a bowel disorder.
▼ You are taking other medications.

Pregnancy
▼ No evidence of risk.

Breast feeding
▼ No evidence of risk.

Infants and children
▼ Not recommended under 1 year except on the advice of a doctor. Reduced dose necessary.

Over 60
▼ No special problems.

Driving and hazardous work
▼ No known problems.

Alcohol
▼ Avoid excess alcohol as it irritates the stomach and may reduce the benefits of the drug.

POSSIBLE ADVERSE EFFECTS

Diarrhoea is the only common adverse effect of this drug. Dizziness and muscle weakness due to absorption of excess magnesium in the body may occur in people with poor kidney function.

Symptom/effect	Frequency		Discuss with doctor		Stop taking drug now	Call doctor now
	Common	Rare	Only if severe	In all cases		
Diarrhoea	●		■			

INTERACTIONS

General note Magnesium hydroxide interferes with the absorption of a wide range of drugs taken by mouth, including tetracycline antibiotics, iron supplements, diflunisal, phenytoin, and penicillamine.

Enteric-coated tablets As with other antacids, magnesium hydroxide may allow break-up of the enteric coating of tablets, sometimes leading to stomach irritation.

PROLONGED USE

Magnesium hydroxide should not be used for prolonged periods without consulting your doctor. Prolonged use in people with kidney damage may cause drowsiness, dizziness, and weakness, due to accumulation of magnesium in the body.

MEDROXYPROGESTERONE

Brand names Depo-Provera, Farlutal, Provera
Used in the following combined preparations None

GENERAL INFORMATION

Medroxyprogesterone is a progesto-gen, a synthetic female sex hormone similar to the natural hormone, progesterone. It is used to treat menstrual disorders such as mid-cycle bleeding and amenorrhoea (absent periods).

Medroxyprogesterone is often used to treat endometriosis, a condition in which there is abnormal growth of uterine-lining tissue in the pelvic cavity. *Depot* injections of the drug are used as a contraceptive. However, since it may cause serious side effects, including persistent bleeding from the uterus, amenorrhoea, and prolonged infertility, this use remains controversial, and it is recommended only in special circumstances in Britain.

Medroxyprogesterone may be used to treat some types of cancer, such as cancer of the breast or uterus.

QUICK REFERENCE

Drug group Female sex hormone (p.147)

Overdose danger rating Low

Dependence rating Low

Prescription needed Yes

Available as generic No

INFORMATION FOR USERS

Your drug prescription is tailored for you. Do not alter dosage without checking with your doctor.

How taken

Tablets, injection.

Frequency and timing of doses
1 – 3 x daily. (Long-acting injection for contraception: every 3 months.) NB Tablets may need to be taken at certain times during your cycle; follow instructions you have been given.

Adult dosage range
Menstrual disorders 2.5 – 10mg daily; *endometriosis* 30mg daily; *cancer* 100 - 1500mg daily; *contraception* 150mg.

Onset of effect
1 – 2 months (cancer); 1 – 2 weeks (other conditions).

Duration of action
1 – 2 days (by mouth); up to some months after injection.

Diet advice
None.

Storage
Keep in a closed container in a cool, dry place away from reach of children.

Missed dose
Take as soon as you remember. If your next dose is due within 3 hours, take a single dose now and skip the next.

Stopping the drug
Do not stop the drug without consulting your doctor; symptoms may recur.

Exceeding the dose
An occasional unintentional extra dose is unlikely to be a cause for concern. But if you notice unusual symptoms, or if a large overdose has been taken, notify your doctor.

SPECIAL PRECAUTIONS

Be sure to tell your doctor if:
▼ You have high blood pressure.
▼ You have diabetes.
▼ You have had blood clots or a stroke.
▼ You have long-term liver or kidney problems.
▼ You are taking other medications.

 Pregnancy
▼ Not prescribed. May cause abnormalities in the unborn baby. Discuss with your doctor.

 Breast feeding
▼ The drug passes into the breast milk, but at normal doses adverse effects on the baby are unlikely. Discuss with your doctor.

 Infants and children
▼ Not usually prescribed.

 Over 60
▼ No special problems.

 Driving and hazardous work
▼ No known problems.

  Alcohol
▼ No known problems.

POSSIBLE ADVERSE EFFECTS

Medroxyprogesterone rarely causes serious adverse effects. Fluid retention may lead to weight gain, swollen feet or ankles, and breast tenderness. Long-term treatment may cause irregular menstrual bleeding or spotting between periods.

Symptom/effect	Frequency		Discuss with doctor		Stop taking drug now	Call doctor now
	Common	Rare	Only if severe	In all cases		
Weight gain	●		■			
Swollen ankles	●		■			
Breast tenderness		●	■			
Nausea		●	■			
Fatigue/depression		●		■		
Irregular menstruation		●		■		
Rash/itching/acne		●		■	▲	

INTERACTIONS

None

PROLONGED USE

Long term use of this drug may slightly increase the risk of blood clots in the leg veins.

Monitoring Periodic checks on blood pressure, yearly cervical smear tests and breast examinations are usually required.

MEFENAMIC ACID

Brand name Dysman, Ponstan
Used in the following combined preparations None

GENERAL INFORMATION

Mefenamic acid, introduced in 1963, is a non-steroidal anti-inflammatory drug (NSAID). Like other NSAIDs, it relieves pain and inflammation. It is an effective analgesic, and is used to treat headache, toothache, and menstrual pains (dysmenorrhoea) and it reduces excessive menstrual bleeding (menorrhagia).

Mefenamic acid is also used for long-term relief of pain and stiffness in rheumatoid arthritis and osteoarthritis.

The most common side effects of mefenamic acid are gastrointestinal: abdominal pain, nausea and vomiting, and indigestion. Other more serious adverse effects include kidney problems and blood disorders.

QUICK REFERENCE

Drug group Non-steroidal anti-inflammatory drug (p.116)

Overdose danger rating Medium

Dependence rating Low

Prescription needed Yes

Available as generic Yes

INFORMATION FOR USERS

Your drug prescription is tailored for you. Do not alter dosage without checking with your doctor.

How taken

Tablets, capsules, liquid.

Frequency and timing of doses
3 x daily with food.

Adult dosage range
1.5g daily.

Onset of effect
1 – 2 hours.

Duration of action
Up to 6 hours.

Diet advice
None.

Storage
Keep in a closed container in a cool, dry place away from reach of children.

Missed dose
Take as soon as you remember. If your next dose is due within 3 hours, take a single dose now and skip the next.

Stopping the drug
Can be safely stopped as soon as you no longer need it.

Exceeding the dose
An occasional unintentional extra dose is unlikely to cause problems. Large overdoses may cause muscle twitching, poor coordination or fits.

SPECIAL PRECAUTIONS

Be sure to tell your doctor if:
▼ You have long-term liver or kidney problems.
▼ You have had a peptic ulcer, oesophagitis, or acid indigestion.
▼ You have inflammatory bowel disease.
▼ You have asthma.
▼ You have high blood pressure.
▼ You are allergic to aspirin.
▼ You are taking other medications.

 Pregnancy
▼ Not usually prescribed. May affect the unborn baby and, taken in late pregnancy, may prolong labour. Discuss with your doctor.

 Breast feeding
▼ The drug passes into the breast milk, but at normal doses adverse effects on the baby are unlikely. Discuss with your doctor.

 Infants and children
▼ Reduced dose necessary.

 Over 60
▼ Increased likelihood of adverse effects.

 Driving and hazardous work
▼ Avoid such activities until you have learned how the drug affects you because the drug can cause drowsiness and dizziness.

 Alcohol
▼ Avoid. Alcohol may increase the risk of stomach irritation with mefenamic acid.

Surgery and general anaesthetics
▼ Discuss this with your doctor or dentist before any surgery.

POSSIBLE ADVERSE EFFECTS

Gastrointestinal disturbances are the most common side effects of mefenamic acid. The drug should be stopped if diarrhoea or a rash occur, and not used thereafter. Black or bloodstained bowel movements should be reported to your doctor without delay.

Symptom/effect	Frequency		Discuss with doctor		Stop taking drug now	Call doctor now
	Common	Rare	Only if severe	In all cases		
Indigestion	●			■		
Diarrhoea	●			■	▲	
Dizziness/drowsiness		●	■			
Nausea/vomiting		●	■			
Abdominal pain		●				
Rash		●		■	▲	
Wheezing/breathlessness		●		■	▲	■

INTERACTIONS

General note Mefenamic acid interacts with a wide range of drugs to increase the risk of bleeding and/or peptic ulcers. Such drugs include oral anticoagulants, corticosteroids, other non-steroidal anti-inflammatory drugs (NSAIDs), and aspirin.

Lithium Mefenamic acid may raise blood levels of lithium.

Antihypertensive drugs and diuretics The beneficial effects of these drugs may be reduced by mefenamic acid.

Oral antidiabetics Mefenamic acid may increase the blood sugar lowering effect of these drugs.

PROLONGED USE

There is an increased risk of bleeding from peptic ulcers and in the bowel during long-term use. In rare cases the drug may affect the liver and blood. Blood tests should be carried out during prolonged use.

MEGESTROL

Brand name Megace
Used in the following combined preparations None

GENERAL INFORMATION

Megestrol is a synthetic female sex hormone similar to the natural hormone, progesterone. Available as tablets, it is used in the treatment of certain types of advanced cancer of the breast and uterus that are sensitive to hormones. It is often prescribed when the tumour cannot be removed by surgery, or when the disease has recurred after surgery, or when other anticancer drugs or radiation treatment have failed.

Successful treatment reduces the size of the tumour; it may also cause secondary growths to disappear. Improvement usually occurs within two months of treatment. Because the drug does not eradicate the cancer completely, megestrol treatment may need to be continued indefinitely.

QUICK REFERENCE

Drug group Female sex hormone (p.147) and anticancer drug (p.154)
Overdose danger rating Low
Dependence rating Low
Prescription needed Yes
Available as generic No

INFORMATION FOR USERS

Your drug prescription is tailored for you. Do not alter dosage without checking with your doctor.

How taken

Tablets.

Frequency and timing of doses
1 – 4 x daily.

Adult dosage range
Breast cancer 160mg daily.
Cancer of the uterus 40 – 320mg daily.

Onset of effect
Within 2 months.

Duration of action
1 – 2 days.

Diet advice
None.

Storage
Keep in a closed container in a cool, dry place away from reach of children.

Missed dose
Take as soon as you remember.

Stopping the drug
Do not stop the drug without consulting your doctor. Stopping the drug may lead to worsening of your underlying condition.

Exceeding the dose
An occasional unintentional extra dose is unlikely to be a cause for concern. But if you notice unusual symptoms, or if a large overdose has been taken, notify your doctor.

POSSIBLE ADVERSE EFFECTS

Adverse effects are rare with megestrol. It may cause weight gain owing to increased appetite and food intake.

Symptom/effect	Frequency		Discuss with doctor		Stop taking drug now	Call doctor now
	Common	Rare	Only if severe	In all cases		
Weight gain	●		■			
Swollen feet/ankles		●	■			
Nausea		●	■			
Headache		●		■		
Itching		●		■		
Hair loss		●		■		
Rash		●		■	▲	

INTERACTIONS

None known.

SPECIAL PRECAUTIONS

Be sure to tell your doctor if:
▼ You have long-term liver or kidney problems.
▼ You have had thrombosis.
▼ You have high blood pressure.
▼ You have heart problems.
▼ You are taking other medications.

 Pregnancy
▼ Not usually prescribed.

 Breast feeding
▼ Breast feeding is usually discontinued. Discuss with your doctor.

 Infants and children
▼ Not usually required.

 Over 60
▼ No special problems.

Driving and hazardous work
▼ No known problems.

Alcohol
▼ No known problems.

PROLONGED USE

Long-term use of this drug may increase the risk of blood clots in the leg veins.

Monitoring Periodic checks on blood pressure may be performed.

MERCAPTOPURINE

Brand name Puri-Nethol
Used in the following combined preparations None

GENERAL INFORMATION

Mercaptopurine is widely used to prevent the recurrence of certain forms of leukaemia. Prescribed with other anticancer drugs, it is also given to leukaemia victims who have not responded well to other treatment.

Nausea and vomiting, mouth ulcers, and loss of appetite are the most common side effects of mercaptopurine. Such symptoms tend to be milder than those of other cytotoxic drugs, and they often disappear as the body adjusts to the drug. More seriously, mercaptopurine can cause liver damage and interfere with the production of blood cells, causing blood clotting disorders and anaemia. Also, there is an increased likelihood of infections.

INFORMATION FOR USERS

Your drug prescription is tailored for you. Do not alter dosage without checking with your doctor.

How taken

Tablets.

Frequency and timing of doses
Once daily.

Dosage range
Dosage is determined individually according to body weight and response.

Onset of effect
1 – 2 weeks.

Duration of action
Side effects may persist for several weeks after stopping treatment.

Diet advice
None.

Storage
Keep in a closed container in a cool, dry place away from reach of children. Protect from light.

Missed dose
If your next dose is due within 6 hours take a single dose now and skip the next. Tell your doctor that you missed a dose.

Stopping the drug
Do not stop taking the drug without consulting your doctor; stopping the drug may lead to worsening of your underlying condition.

Exceeding the dose
An occasional unintentional extra dose is unlikely to cause problems. Large overdoses may cause nausea and vomiting. Notify your doctor.

POSSIBLE ADVERSE EFFECTS

The most common adverse effects with mercaptopurine are nausea and vomiting, and loss of appetite. Jaundice may also occur, but is reversible on stopping the drug. Because mercaptopurine interferes with the production of blood cells it may cause anaemia and blood clotting disorders, and infections are more likely.

Symptom/effect	Frequency		Discuss with doctor		Stop taking drug now	Call doctor now
	Common	Rare	Only if severe	In all cases		
Nausea/vomiting	●		■			
Loss of appetite	●		■			
Mouth ulcers	●			■		▮
Jaundice		●		■		▮
Black bowel movements		●		■		▮
Bloodstained vomit		●		■		▮

INTERACTIONS

Allopurinol This drug increases blood levels of mercaptopurine.

Warfarin The effects of warfarin may be decreased by mercaptopurine.

SPECIAL PRECAUTIONS

Be sure to tell your doctor if:
▼ You have long-term liver or kidney problems.
▼ You suffer from gout.
▼ You have recently had any infection.
▼ You are taking other medications.

Pregnancy
▼ Not usually prescribed. Discuss with your doctor.

Breast feeding
▼ Not advised. The drug passes into the breast milk and may affect the baby adversely. Discuss with your doctor.

Infants and children
▼ Reduced dose necessary.

Over 60
▼ Reduced dose may be necessary. Increased risk of adverse effects.

Driving and hazardous work
▼ No known problems.

Alcohol
▼ Avoid. Alcohol may increase the adverse effects of this drug.

PROLONGED USE

Prolonged use of this drug may reduce bone marrow activity, leading to a reduction of all types of blood cells.

Monitoring Regular blood checks and tests on liver function are required.

MESALAZINE

Brand name Asacol, Pentasa, Salofalk
Used in the following combined preparations None

GENERAL INFORMATION

Mesalazine is used in patients who have ulcerative colitis and sometimes used in the treatment of Crohn's disease, which affects the large bowel. It is given to relieve symptoms during an acute attack and is also taken as a preventive measure. When taken to treat severe cases, mesalazine is often used together with other drugs such as corticosteroids.

When taken as tablets, the active component is released in the large bowel where it produces its local effect on the inflamed mucosa. Enemas and suppositories are also available and are particularly useful when the disease affects the rectum and lower colon.

Mesalazine produces fewer side effects than some of the older treatments such as sulphasalazine. Patients who are unable to tolerate sulphasalazine may be able to take mesalazine without any problems.

QUICK REFERENCE

Drug group Drug for inflammatory bowel disease (p.112)
Overdose danger rating Low
Dependence rating Low
Prescription needed Yes
Available as generic No

INFORMATION FOR USERS

Your drug prescription is tailored for you. Do not alter dosage without checking with your doctor.

How taken

Tablets, suppositories, enemas.

Frequency and timing of doses
3 x daily, swallowed whole and not chewed (tablets); 3 x daily (suppositories); once daily at bedtime (enema).

Adult dosage range
Acute attack 1.5 – 2.4g daily; maintenance 750mg – 2.4g daily.

Onset of effect
Adverse effects may be noticed within a few days, but full beneficial effects may not be felt for a couple of weeks.

Duration of action
Up to 12 hours.

Diet advice
Your doctor may advise on your diet taking account of the condition you are suffering from.

Storage
Keep in a closed container in a cool, dry place away from reach of children. Protect from light.

Missed dose
Take as soon as you remember. If your next dose is due within 2 hours, take a single dose now and skip the next.

Stopping the drug
Do not stop taking the drug without consulting your doctor; symptoms may recur.

Exceeding the dose
An occasional unintentional extra dose is unlikely to cause problems. But if you notice any unusual symptoms, or if a large overdose has been taken, notify your doctor.

POSSIBLE ADVERSE EFFECTS

The common side effects of mesalazine are on the gastrointestinal tract. Other problems rarely occur.

Symptom /effect	Frequency		Discuss with doctor		Stop taking drug now	Call doctor now
	Common	Rare	Only if severe	In all cases		
Nausea	●		■			
Abdominal pain	●		■			
Diarrhoea	●		■			
Colitis worsening		●		■	▲	
Fever/wheezing		●		■	▲	▮
Skin rash		●		■	▲	

INTERACTIONS

Lactulose Lactulose may reduce the release of mesalazine at its site of action.

SPECIAL PRECAUTIONS

Be sure to tell your doctor if:
▼ You have liver or kidney problems.
▼ You are allergic to aspirin.
▼ You are taking other medications.

Pregnancy
▼ Negligible amounts of drug cross the placenta. However, safety in pregnancy not established. Discuss with your doctor.

Breast feeding
▼ Negligible amounts pass into the breast milk. However, safety not established. Discuss with your doctor.

Infants and children
▼ Not recommended under 15 years.

Over 60
▼ Dosage reduction not normally necessary unless there is kidney impairment.

Driving and hazardous work
▼ No special problems.

Alcohol
▼ No special problems.

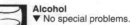

PROLONGED USE

No problems expected.

METFORMIN

Brand names Glucophage, Orabet
Used in the following combined preparations None

GENERAL INFORMATION

Metformin is an antidiabetic drug of the biguanide group. Taken by mouth, it is used to treat adult (maturity-onset) diabetes in which insulin-secreting cells are still active in the pancreas.

It lowers blood sugar by reducing the absorption of glucose from the digestive tract into the bloodstream, by reducing the glucose production by cells in the liver and kidneys, and by increasing the sensitivity of cells to insulin so that they take up glucose more effectively from the blood.

Metformin is administered in conjunction with a special diabetic diet that limits the intake of sugar and fats. It is often prescribed with another antidiabetic drug that stimulates insulin secretion by the pancreas.

QUICK REFERENCE

Drug group Antidiabetic drug (p.142)
Overdose danger rating High
Dependence rating Low
Prescription needed Yes
Available as generic Yes

INFORMATION FOR USERS

Your drug prescription is tailored for you. Do not alter dosage without checking with your doctor.

How taken

Tablets.

Frequency and timing of doses
2 – 3 x daily with food.

Adult dosage range
1.5 – 3g daily.

Onset of effect
Within 2 hours. It may take 2 weeks to achieve control of diabetes.

Duration of action
8 – 12 hours.

Diet advice
An individualized low fat, low sugar diet must be maintained in order for the drug to be fully effective. Follow your doctor's advice.

Storage
Keep in a closed container in a cool, dry place away from reach of children.

Missed dose
Take as soon as you remember. If your next dose is due within 2 hours, take a single dose now and skip the next.

Stopping the drug
Do not stop taking the drug without consulting your doctor; stopping the drug may lead to worsening of the underlying condition.

OVERDOSE ACTION

 Seek immediate medical advice in all cases. Take emergency action if fits or loss of consciousness occur.

See Drug poisoning emergency guide (p.470).

POSSIBLE ADVERSE EFFECTS

Minor gastrointestinal symptoms such as nausea and vomiting and loss of appetite are often helped by taking the drug with food. Diarrhoea usually settles after a few days of continued treatment. Symptoms such as dizziness, sweating, weakness, and confusion require prompt medical attention because they could indicate excessive lowering of blood sugar.

Symptom/effect	Frequency		Discuss with doctor		Stop taking drug now	Call doctor now
	Common	Rare	Only if severe	In all cases		
Loss of appetite	●		■			
Nausea/vomiting	●		■			
Diarrhoea		●	■			
Dizziness/confusion		●		■		
Weakness/sweating		●		■		
Rash		●		■		

INTERACTIONS

General note A number of drugs reduce the effects of metformin. These include corticosteroids, oestrogens, and diuretics.

Other drugs, notably monoamine oxidase inhibitors (MAOIs) and beta blockers, increase its effects.

SPECIAL PRECAUTIONS

Be sure to tell your doctor if:
▼ You have long-term liver or kidney problems.
▼ You have heart failure.
▼ You are a heavy drinker.
▼ You are taking other medications.

 Pregnancy
▼ Not usually prescribed. Insulin is usually substituted because it provides better diabetic control during pregnancy. Discuss with your doctor.

 Breast feeding
▼ Safety not established. Discuss with your doctor.

 Infants and children
▼ Not recommended.

 Over 60
▼ Increased likelihood of adverse effects. Reduced dose may therefore be necessary.

 Driving and hazardous work
▼ Usually no problems. Avoid such activities if you have warning signs of low blood sugar.

  Alcohol
▼ Avoid. Alcohol increases the risk of low blood sugar, and can cause coma by increasing the acidity of the blood.

PROLONGED USE

Prolonged treatment with metformin can deplete reserves of vitamin B_{12} and this may cause anaemia.

Monitoring Regular checks on levels of sugar in the urine and/or blood are usually required. An annual check on vitamin B_{12} levels may also be carried out.

METHOXSALEN

Brand name None (imported products only)
Used in the following combined preparation None

GENERAL INFORMATION

Methoxsalen, introduced in 1953, belongs to a group of substances called psoralens. These occur naturally in plants and have been used historically to correct vitiligo, a condition in which patches of skin lose their colour, or pigmentation. Nowadays, methoxsalen is more often given for severe psoriasis that has failed to improve with other treatments.

Given two hours before treatment with ultraviolet light (UVA), it halts the accelerated growth of skin cells in people with psoriasis. Methoxsalen lotion is used for small areas of vitiligo.

The pigment-promoting effect of methoxsalen has led to its inclusion in some countries in preparations for the promotion of suntanning. This use is prohibited in the United Kingdom because of the risk of burns. After taking methoxsalen, a person should limit his or her exposure to direct sunlight; sunglasses and sun-screening lipstick are recommended for 24 hours.

QUICK REFERENCE

Drug group Psoriasis drug (p.178)
Overdose danger rating Medium
Dependence rating Low
Prescription needed Yes
Available as generic No

INFORMATION FOR USERS

This drug is given only under medical supervision and is not for self-administration.

How taken

Tablets, lotion.

Frequency and timing of doses
By mouth 2 – 3 x weekly 2 hours before UVA treatment.

Dosage range
By mouth 20 – 40mg per dose depending on skin colour (vitiligo); according to body weight (psoriasis).

Onset of effect
Within 1 hour (by mouth).

Duration of action
Sensitivity of the skin to sunlight is increased for 24 hours after taking methoxsalen.

Diet advice
Certain foods, such as limes, figs, parsley, parsnips, mustard, carrots, and celery may increase the sensitivity of the skin to light with methoxsalen.

Storage
Not applicable. The drug is not kept in the home.

Missed dose
No cause for concern. Attend your next scheduled treatment as usual.

Stopping the drug
Can be safely stopped as soon as you no longer need it.

Exceeding the dose
Overdose is unlikely since treatment is carried out under medical supervision.

SPECIAL PRECAUTIONS

Be sure to tell your doctor if:
▼ You have a long-term liver problem.
▼ You are regularly exposed or about to be exposed to intense sunlight, X-rays, industrial or laboratory chemicals.
▼ You have porphyria or systemic lupus erythematosus.
▼ You have had skin cancer.
▼ You have recently received anticancer drugs or radiation therapy.
▼ You are taking other medications.
▼ You have cataracts.

Pregnancy
▼ Not usually prescribed. Safety in pregnancy not established. Discuss with your doctor.

Breast feeding
▼ The drug passes into the breast milk and may affect the baby. Discuss with your doctor.

Infants and children
▼ Not recommended under 12 years.

Over 60
▼ No special problems.

Driving and hazardous work
▼ No known problems.

Alcohol
▼ No known problems.

POSSIBLE ADVERSE EFFECTS

Slight redness of the skin normally occurs for a day or two after treatment. High doses of methoxsalen or overexposure to ultraviolet light may cause severe redness, soreness, blistering, or peeling of the skin, and swelling of the feet or lower legs.

Symptom/effect	Frequency		Discuss with doctor		Stop taking drug now	Call doctor now
	Common	Rare	Only if severe	In all cases		
Redness/soreness	●				■	
Nausea	●			■		
Dizziness/headache		●		■		
Depression		●			■	
Insomnia		●			■	

INTERACTIONS

General note Any drug that increases the sensitivity of the skin to light may increase the risk of redness, blistering, and peeling. Such drugs include coal tar, and rarely griseofulvin, thiazide diuretics, phenothiazines, sulphonamides, and tetracyclines.

PROLONGED USE

Prolonged use may increase the risk of premature ageing of the skin and skin cancer in fair-skinned people, and cataracts are a risk of ultraviolet light treatment.

METHYLCELLULOSE

Brand names Celevac, Cologel
Used in the following combined preparation None

GENERAL INFORMATION

Methylcellulose is a laxative used to treat constipation, diverticular disease, and irritable bowel syndrome. Taken by mouth, it is not absorbed into the bloodstream but remains in the intestine. It absorbs up to 25 times its volume of water thereby softening and increasing the volume of stools. It is also used to reduce the frequency and increase the firmness of stools in chronic watery diarrhoea, and to control the consistency of bowel movements

after colostomies and ileostomies.

Methylcellulose preparations are also sometimes used together with appropriate dieting to treat obesity. The bulking agent swells to give a feeling of fullness, thus encouraging adherence to a reducing diet.

Methylcellulose is found in contact lens irrigation solutions and in a variety of lotions, creams, ointments, and pastes.

QUICK REFERENCE

Drug group Laxative (p.111) and antidiarrhoeal drug (p.110)

Overdose danger rating Low

Dependence rating Low

Prescription needed No

Available as generic No

INFORMATION FOR USERS

Follow instructions on the label. Call your doctor if symptoms worsen.

How taken

Tablets, liquid

Frequency and timing of doses
1 – 4 x daily. Unless otherwise instructed, take with a full glass of water.

Adult dosage range
1.5g – 6g daily.

Onset of effect
Within 24 hours.

Duration of action
Up to 3 days.

Diet advice
If taken as a laxative, drink plenty of fluid, at least 6 – 8 glasses daily.

Storage
Keep in a closed container in a cool, dry place away from reach of children.

Missed dose
Take as soon as you remember. Resume normal dosing thereafter.

Stopping the drug
Can be safely stopped as soon as you no longer need it.

Exceeding the dose
An occasional unintentional extra dose is unlikely to be a cause for concern. But if you notice unusual symptoms, or if a large overdose has been taken, notify your doctor.

SPECIAL PRECAUTIONS

Be sure to consult your doctor before taking this drug if:
▼ You have severe constipation and/or abdominal pain.
▼ You have unexplained rectal bleeding.
▼ You have difficulty swallowing.
▼ You vomit readily.
▼ You are taking other medications.

 Pregnancy
▼ No evidence of risk to developing baby.

 Breast feeding
▼ No evidence of risk.

 Infants and children
▼ Reduced dose necessary.

 Over 60
▼ No special problems.

 Driving and hazardous work
▼ No known problems.

 Alcohol
▼ No known problems.

POSSIBLE ADVERSE EFFECTS

When taken by mouth, methylcellulose may cause bloating and excess wind. Insufficient fluid intake may cause blockage of the oesophagus (gullet) or intestine. Consult

your doctor if you experience severe abdominal pain or if you have no bowel movement for 2 days after taking methylcellulose.

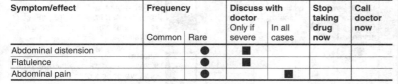

Symptom/effect	Frequency		Discuss with doctor		Stop taking drug now	Call doctor now
	Common	Rare	Only if severe	In all cases		
Abdominal distension		●	■			
Flatulence		●	■			
Abdominal pain		●			■	

INTERACTIONS

None

PROLONGED USE

No problems expected.

METHYLDOPA

Brand names Aldomet, Dopamet, Metalpha
Used in the following combined preparations Hydromet

GENERAL INFORMATION

Methyldopa, introduced in the 1960s, is one of the best known antihypertensive drugs. People take this drug to deal with varying degrees of high blood pressure. A diuretic is usually prescribed along with methyldopa in order to enhance its effect and to reduce fluid retention. Other anti-hypertensive drugs, such as hydralazine, and beta blockers (p.93) are also often prescribed to lower blood pressure more effectively.

Women with high blood pressure in late pregnancy often take methyldopa, as it will not affect the unborn child.

The most common adverse effect of methyldopa is that it often causes drowsiness, and sometimes depression. Methyldopa is less likely than other antihypertensive drugs to cause dizziness due to a fall in blood pressure on standing. Also, because this drug does not reduce blood flow to the kidneys, it is sometimes given to people with kidney disorders.

INFORMATION FOR USERS

Your drug prescription is tailored for you. Do not alter dosage without checking with your doctor.

How taken

Tablets, liquid, injection.

Frequency and timing of doses
2 – 4 x daily.

Dosage range
Adults 500mg – 3g daily.
Children Reduced dose.

Onset of effect
3 – 6 hours. Full effect begins in 2 – 3 days.

Duration of action
6 – 12 hours. Some effect may last for 1 – 2 days after stopping the drug.

Diet advice
None.

Storage
Keep in a closed container in a cool, dry place away from reach of children. Protect from light.

Missed dose
Take as soon as you remember. If your next dose is due within 2 hours, take a single dose now and skip the next.

Stopping the drug
Do not stop the drug without consulting your doctor, who will gradually reduce your dose. Suddenly stopping methyldopa may lead to an increase in blood pressure.

Exceeding the dose
An occasional unintentional extra dose is unlikely to cause problems. Large overdoses may cause drowsiness or palpitations. Notify your doctor.

SPECIAL PRECAUTIONS

Be sure to tell your doctor if:
▼ You have long-term liver or kidney problems.
▼ You have anaemia.
▼ You have angina.
▼ You suffer from depression.
▼ You are taking other medications.

 Pregnancy
▼ No evidence of risk. It is taken during late pregnancy to treat high blood pressure with no serious effects on the baby.

 Breast feeding
▼ The drug passes into the breast milk but at normal doses adverse effects on the baby are unlikely. Discuss with your doctor.

 Infants and children
▼ Reduced dose necessary.

 Over 60
▼ Reduced dose necessary.

 Driving and hazardous work
▼ Avoid such activities until you have learned how the drug affects you because the drug can cause drowsiness.

 Alcohol
▼ Avoid. Alcohol may increase the sedative effects of this drug.

Surgery and general anaesthetics
▼ Discuss the possibility of stopping methyldopa with your doctor or dentist before any surgery.

POSSIBLE ADVERSE EFFECTS

Most adverse effects are uncommon and diminish in time. The fluid retention that occurs during treatment with methyldopa is counteracted by taking a diuretic.

Symptom/effect	Frequency		Discuss with doctor		Stop taking drug now	Call doctor now
	Common	Rare	Only if severe	In all cases		
Drowsiness	●		■			
Depression/headaches	●			■		
Fever		●		■		
Stuffy nose		●		■		
Dizziness/fainting		●		■		
Nausea/vomiting		●		■		
Rash		●		■	▲	
Jaundice		●		■	▲	▮

INTERACTIONS

Lithium Levels of lithium may be increased by methyldopa.

Tricyclic antidepressants may reduce the effect of methyldopa.

Levodopa The effects of methyldopa may be enhanced by levodopa.

PROLONGED USE

Liver and blood problems may occur rarely.

Monitoring Periodic checks on blood and urine are usually required.

METOCLOPRAMIDE

Brand names Gastrobid, Gastromax, Gastroflux, Maxolon, Metramid, Parmid, Primperan
Used in the following combined preparation Migravess, Paramax

GENERAL INFORMATION

Metoclopramide has a direct action on the gastrointestinal tract. It is used for conditions in which there is a need to encourage normal propulsion of food through the stomach and intestine.

It has powerful anti-emetic properties and its most common use is in the prevention and treatment of nausea and vomiting. It is especially helpful for the relief of the nausea that sometimes accompanies migraine headaches and the nausea caused by treatment with anticancer drugs. Metoclopramide is also prescribed to alleviate symptoms of hiatus hernia caused by acid reflux into the oesophagus.

One unusual side effect of metoclopramide, muscle spasm of the face and neck, is more likely to occur in children and young adults under 20 years. Other side effects are not usually troublesome.

INFORMATION FOR USERS

Your drug prescription is tailored for you. Do not alter dosage without checking with your doctor.

How taken

Tablets, SR tablets/capsules, liquid, injection.

Frequency and timing of doses
Usually 3 x daily; 1 – 2 x daily (sustained-release products).

Adult dosage range
15 – 30mg daily.

Onset of effect
Within 1 hour.

Duration of action
6 – 8 hours.

Diet advice
Fatty and spicy foods and alcohol are best avoided if nausea is a problem.

Storage
Keep in a closed container in a cool, dry place away from reach of children.

Missed dose
Take as soon as you remember. If your next dose is due within 3 hours, take a single dose now and skip the next.

Stopping the drug
Can be safely stopped as soon as you no longer need it.

Exceeding the dose
An occasional unintentional extra dose is unlikely to be a cause for concern. Large overdoses may cause drowsiness and muscle spasms. Notify your doctor.

POSSIBLE ADVERSE EFFECTS

The main adverse effects of metoclopramide are drowsiness and, less commonly, uncontrolled muscle spasm. Other symptoms rarely occur.

Symptom/effect	Frequency		Discuss with doctor		Stop taking drug now	Call doctor now
	Common	Rare	Only if severe	In all cases		
Drowsiness		●	■			
Restlessness		●		■		
Diarrhoea		●		■		
Muscle tremor/rigidity		●		■		
Muscle spasm of face		●		■	▲	■

INTERACTIONS

Sedatives All drugs that have a sedative effect on the central nervous system increase the sedative properties of metoclopramide. Such drugs include anti-anxiety and sleeping drugs, antidepressants, antihistamines, narcotic analgesics, and antipsychotics.

Phenothiazine antipsychotics Metoclopramide increases the likelihood of adverse effects from these drugs.

Lithium Metoclopramide increases the risk of central nervous system side effects.

SPECIAL PRECAUTIONS

Be sure to tell your doctor if:
▼ You have long-term kidney or liver problems.
▼ You are taking other medications.

Pregnancy
▼ Safety in pregnancy not established. Discuss with your doctor.

Breast feeding
▼ The drug passes into the breast milk but at normal doses adverse effects on the baby are unlikely. Discuss with your doctor.

Infants and children
▼ Reduced dose necessary.

Over 60
▼ Reduced dose may be necessary.

Driving and hazardous work
▼ Avoid such activities until you have learned how the drug affects you because the drug may cause drowsiness.

Alcohol
▼ Avoid. Alcohol may oppose the beneficial effects and increase the sedative effects of this drug.

PROLONGED USE

Not normally used long term, except under specialist supervision for certain gastrointestinal disorders.

METRONIDAZOLE

Brand names Flagyl, Metrogel, Metrolyl, Metrotop, Metrozol, Vaginyl, Zadstat
Used in the following combined preparations None

GENERAL INFORMATION

Metronidazole is prescribed to fight protozoal infections and a variety of bacterial infections.

It is widely used in the treatment of trichomonas infection of the vagina. Because the organism responsible for this disorder is sexually transmitted and may not cause any symptoms, a simultaneous course of treatment is usually advised for the sexual partner.

Certain infections of the abdomen, pelvis, and gums also respond well to metronidazole. It is also used to treat septicaemia and infected leg ulcers

and pressure sores. Metronidazole may be given to prevent or treat infections following surgery. Because metronidazole in high doses can penetrate the brain, it is also used to treat abscesses occurring there.

Metronidazole is available in the form of a gel for local application.

The drug is also prescribed for amoebic dysentery and giardiasis, a rare protozoal infection.

The most common adverse effects that occur with metronidazole are nausea and loss of appetite.

INFORMATION FOR USERS

Your drug prescription is tailored for you. Do not alter dosage without checking with your doctor.

How taken

Tablets, liquid, injection, suppositories, gel.

Frequency and timing of doses
3 x daily for 5 – 10 days, depending on condition. Sometimes a single large dose is prescribed.

Adult dosage range
600 – 1200mg daily (by mouth); 3g daily (suppositories); 1.5g daily (injection).

Onset of effect
The drug starts to work within an hour or so; beneficial effects may not be felt for 1 – 2 days.

Duration of action
6 – 12 hours.

Diet advice
None.

Storage
Keep in a closed container in a cool, dry place away from reach of children. Protect from light.

Missed dose
Take as soon as you remember. If your next dose is due within 2 hours, take a single dose now and skip the next.

Stopping the drug
Take the full course. Even if you feel better the infection may still be present and symptoms may recur if treatment is stopped too soon.

Exceeding the dose
An occasional unintentional extra dose is unlikely to be a cause for concern. But if you notice unusual symptoms, especially numbness or tingling, or if a large overdose has been taken, notify your doctor.

SPECIAL PRECAUTIONS

Be sure to tell your doctor if:
▼ You have long-term liver or kidney problems.
▼ You have a blood disorder.
▼ You have a disorder of the central nervous system such as epilepsy.
▼ You are taking other medications.

 Pregnancy
▼ Safety in pregnancy not established. Discuss with your doctor.

 Breast feeding
▼ The drug passes into the breast milk, but at normal doses adverse effects on the baby are unlikely. However, metronidazole may give a bitter taste to the milk. Discuss with your doctor.

 Infants and children
▼ Reduced dose necessary.

 Over 60
▼ No special problems.

 Driving and hazardous work
▼ Avoid such activities until you have learned how the drug affects you because the drug can cause dizziness and drowsiness.

 Alcohol
▼ Avoid. Taken with metronidazole alcohol may cause flushing, nausea, vomiting, abdominal pain and headache.

POSSIBLE ADVERSE EFFECTS

Minor gastrointestinal disturbances are common but tend to diminish with time. It may cause a darkening of the urine, which is of no concern. More serious adverse effects on the nervous system, causing numbness or tingling, are extremely rare.

Symptom/effect	Frequency		Discuss with doctor		Stop taking drug now	Call doctor now
	Common	Rare	Only if severe	In all cases		
Nausea/loss of appetite	●		■			
Dark urine	●		■			
Dry mouth/metallic taste		●	■			
Headache/dizziness/drowsiness		●	■			
Numbness/tingling		●		■		

INTERACTIONS

Oral anticoagulants Metronidazole may increase the effect of oral anticoagulants.

Lithium Metronidazole increases the risk of adverse effects on the kidneys.

Phenytoin Metronidazole may increase the effects of phenytoin.

Cimetidine may increase levels of metronidazole in the body.

PROLONGED USE

Not usually prescribed for longer than 10 days. Prolonged treatment may cause temporary loss of sensation in the hands and feet, and may also reduce production of white blood cells.

MIANSERIN

Brand names Bolvidon, Norval
Used in the following combined preparations None

GENERAL INFORMATION

Mianserin is an antidepressant drug that has been available for over 10 years. It is used in the treatment of severe depression, in which it elevates mood, increases physical activity, improves appetite, and restores interest in everyday activities. Because mianserin also has a sedative effect, it is useful when depression is accompanied by anxiety and insomnia. Taken at night, it encourages sleep and helps to eliminate the need for additional sleeping drugs.

Unlike many other antidepressants, mianserin has only weak *anti-cholinergic* effects. It is therefore less likely to cause dry mouth, blurred vision, constipation, and urinary difficulties. It is also less dangerous in overdose. Serious adverse effects are rare, but include reduced blood cell production in the bone marrow.

INFORMATION FOR USERS

Your drug prescription is tailored for you. Do not alter dosage without checking with your doctor.

How taken

Tablets.

Frequency and timing of doses
Once at night or 3 – 4 x daily.

Adult dosage range
30 – 90mg daily. Higher doses may be necessary occasionally.

Onset of effect
It may take 2 – 4 weeks for beneficial effects to be felt. Adverse effects may be noticed within a few days.

Duration of action
Antidepressant effect may last for several weeks, but adverse effects wear off within a few days.

Diet advice
None.

Storage
Keep in a closed container in a cool, dry place away from reach of children. Protect from light.

Missed dose
Take as soon as you remember. If your next dose is due within 4 hours, take a single dose now and skip the next.

Stopping the drug
Do not stop taking the drug without consulting your doctor, who may supervise a gradual reduction in dosage. Abrupt cessation may cause a recurrence of the original problem.

Exceeding the dose
An occasional unintentional extra dose is unlikely to cause problems. Large overdoses may cause dizziness, drowsiness, vomiting, and loss of coordination. Notify your doctor.

SPECIAL PRECAUTIONS

Be sure to tell your doctor if:
▼ You have long-term liver or kidney problems.
▼ You have heart problems.
▼ You have had epileptic fits.
▼ You have diabetes.
▼ You have prostate trouble.
▼ You have had glaucoma.
▼ You are taking other medications.

Pregnancy
▼ Safety in pregnancy not established. Discuss with your doctor.

Breast feeding
▼ The drug passes into breast milk, but at normal doses adverse effects on the baby are unlikely. Discuss with your doctor.

Infants and children
▼ Not recommended.

Over 60
▼ Reduced dose may be necessary.

Driving and hazardous work
▼ Avoid such activities until you have learned how the drug affects you because the drug can reduce alertness and cause drowsiness.

Alcohol
▼ Avoid. Alcohol may increase the sedative effects of this drug.

POSSIBLE ADVERSE EFFECTS

Serious adverse effects are rare. Fever, persistent sore throat, or inflammation in the mouth may in rare cases indicate that blood cell production has been affected. Such symptoms should be brought to your doctor's attention.

Symptom/effect	Frequency		Discuss with doctor		Stop taking drug now	Call doctor now
	Common	Rare	Only if severe	In all cases		
Drowsiness/dizziness	●		■			
Tremor		●	■			
Sweating		●	■			
Joint pain		●		■		
Rash		●		■		
Jaundice		●		■	▲	■

INTERACTIONS

Sedatives All drugs that have sedative effects intensify those of mianserin.

Phenytoin Mianserin may alter levels of this drug in the blood.

Monoamine oxidase inhibitors (MAOIs) In the rare cases where these drugs are given with mianserin, dangerously high blood pressure, fever, fits, and delirium may sometimes occur.

PROLONGED USE

There is a risk of reduced blood cell production in the bone marrow. Liver function may also be affected adversely.

Monitoring Regular blood counts and liver function tests may be recommended.

MINOXIDIL

Brand name Loniten, Regaine
Used in the following combined preparations None

GENERAL INFORMATION

Minoxidil is a vasodilator drug (see p.98). These relax the muscles of artery walls and dilate blood vessels. It is effective in controlling dangerously high blood pressure and that which is rising very rapidly. Because it is stronger acting than many other antihypertensive drugs, it is particularly useful for people whose blood pressure has not been controlled by other treatment. Because minoxidil, like other vasodilators, can cause fluid retention and increased heart rate, it is usually prescribed with a diuretic and a beta blocker to increase effectiveness and counteract side effects. Unlike many other antihypertensives, minoxidil rarely causes dizziness and fainting. Its major drawback is that, if taken for longer than two months, it increases hair growth, especially on the face. Although this can be controlled by shaving or depilatories, some find the abnormal hair growth distressing. Use is made of this effect in treating baldness in men and women. For this purpose it is applied locally as a solution.

QUICK REFERENCE

Drug group Antihypertensive drug (p.102) and treatment for hair loss (p.179)

Overdose danger rating Medium

Dependence rating Low

Prescription needed Yes

Available as generic No

INFORMATION FOR USERS

Your drug prescription is tailored for you. Do not alter dosage without checking with your doctor.

How taken

Tablets, solution for local application.

Frequency and timing of doses
Once or twice daily.

Adult dosage range
5mg daily initially, increasing gradually to a maximum of 50mg daily.

Onset of effect
Within 1 hour.

Duration of action
Up to 24 hours. Some effect may last for 2 – 5 days after stopping the drug.

Diet advice
None.

Storage
Keep in a closed container in a cool, dry place away from reach of children.

Missed dose
Take as soon as you remember. If your next dose is due within 5 hours, take a single dose now and skip the next.

Stopping the drug
Do not stop the drug without consulting your doctor; stopping the drug may lead to worsening of the underlying condition.

Exceeding the dose
An occasional unintentional extra dose is unlikely to cause problems. Large overdoses may cause nausea, vomiting, palpitations and or dizziness. Notify your doctor.

SPECIAL PRECAUTIONS

Be sure to tell your doctor if:
▼ You have long-term kidney problems.
▼ You have heart problems.
▼ You retain fluid.
▼ You are taking other medications.

Pregnancy
▼ Safety in pregnancy not established. Discuss with your doctor.

Breast feeding
▼ The drug passes into the breast milk, but at normal doses adverse effects on the baby are unlikely. Discuss with your doctor.

Infants and children
▼ Reduced dose necessary.

Over 60
▼ Reduced dose may be necessary.

Driving and hazardous work
▼ Avoid such activities until you have learned how the drug affects you because the drug can cause dizziness and lightheadedness.

Alcohol
▼ Avoid, alcohol may further reduce blood pressure.

POSSIBLE ADVERSE EFFECTS

Fluid retention is a common adverse effect of minoxidil and this may lead to an increase in weight. Diuretics are often prescribed to control this adverse effect.

Symptom/effect	Frequency		Discuss with doctor		Stop taking drug now	Call doctor now
	Common	Rare	Only if severe	In all cases		
Increased hair growth	●		■			
Fluid retention/ankle swelling	●		■			
Nausea		●	■			
Breast tenderness		●		■		
Dizziness/lightheadedness		●		■		
Rash		●		■		
Palpitations		●		■	▲	▮

INTERACTIONS

Antidepressants The hypotensive effects of minoxidil may be enhanced by antidepressant drugs.

PROLONGED USE

Prolonged use of this drug may lead to swelling of the ankles and increased hair growth.

MISOPROSTOL

Brand name Cytotec
Used in the following combined preparations Arthrotec, Napratec

GENERAL INFORMATION

Misoprostol reduces the amount of acid secreted in the stomach and promotes healing of gastric and duodenal ulcers. It is related to naturally occurring chemicals called prostaglandins. Gastric and duodenal ulcers may be caused by aspirin (p.199) and non-steroidal anti-inflammatory drugs (p.116) that block certain prostaglandins, and misoprostol can be used to prevent or cure these ulcers. The ulcers heal after a few weeks' treatment with misoprostol. Sometimes misoprostol is given during treatment with these drugs as a preventive measure, and combined preparations are available that reduce the likelihood of ulcers occurring. Diarrhoea and indigestion are the most likely adverse effects. If they are severe it may be necessary to stop treatment with the drug. Diarrhoea can be made worse by antacids containing magnesium; these should therefore be avoided.

INFORMATION FOR USER

Your drug prescription is tailored for you. Do not alter dosage without checking with your doctor.

How taken

Tablets.

Frequency and timing of doses
2 – 4 x daily.

Adult dosage range
400 – 800 mcg daily.

Onset of effect
Within 24 hours.

Duration of action
Up to 24 hours; some effects may be longer lasting.

Diet advice
None

Storage
Keep in a closed container in a cool, dry place away from reach of children.

Missed dose
Take as soon as you remember. If your next dose is due within 3 hours, take a single dose now and skip the next.

Stopping the drug
Do not stop the drug without consulting your doctor; symptoms may recur.

Exceeding the dose
An occasional unintentional extra dose is unlikely to cause problems. But if you notice any unusual symptoms, notify your doctor.

POSSIBLE ADVERSE EFFECTS

Adverse effects on the gastrointestinal tract can occur. These may be reduced by spreading the doses out during the day. Taking the drug with food may be recommended.

Symptom/effect	Frequency		Discuss with doctor		Stop taking drug now	Call doctor now
	Common	Rare	Only if severe	In all cases		
Diarrhoea	●		■			
Abdominal pain		●				
Nausea/vomiting		●				
Indigestion	●					
Vaginal/intermenstrual bleeding		●				
Skin rashes		●				

SPECIAL PRECAUTIONS

Be sure to tell your doctor if:
▼ You are pregnant or intending to become pregnant.
▼ You have had a stroke.
▼ You have heart or circulation problems.
▼ You have high blood pressure.
▼ You are taking other medications.

Pregnancy
▼ Misoprostol should not be taken during pregnancy since it can cause the womb to contract before the baby is due.

Breast feeding
▼ Safety not established. Discuss with your doctor.

Infants and children
▼ Not recommended.

Over 60
▼ No special problems.

Driving and hazardous work
▼ No problems expected.

Alcohol
▼ No problems expected, but excessive amounts may undermine the desired effect of the drug.

Surgery and general anaesthetics
▼ Discuss this with your doctor or dentist before any surgery.

INTERACTIONS

None.

PROLONGED USE

No problems expected.

MOCLOBEMIDE

Brand name Manerix
Used in the following combined preparations None

GENERAL INFORMATION

Moclobemide is the first of a new class of antidepressant known as reversible inhibitors of monoamine oxidase A (RIMA). By relieving depressive illness, moclobemide helps to elevate mood and restore interest in everyday activities. Like all antidepressants, it takes at least one to two weeks before moclobemide starts to lift depression.

Unlike traditional MAOIs, such as phenelzine and tranylcypromine, moclobemide is unlikely to interact with foods that contain tyramine, e.g. matured cheeses and yeast extracts. However, it is advisable to avoid large quantities of tyramine rich foods as some people may be particularly sensitive.

Moclobemide is well tolerated, although nausea and dizziness may be experienced early in treatment. These should soon wear off.

INFORMATION FOR USERS

Your drug prescription is tailored for you. Do not alter dosage without checking with your doctor.

How taken

Tablets.

Frequency and timing of doses
2 – 4 x daily.

Adult dosage range
150 – 600mg daily.

Onset of effect
1 – 4 weeks.

Duration of action
Up to 24 hours.

Diet advice
Avoid very large amounts of tyramine rich foods (e.g. matured cheeses, yeast extracts, fermented soya bean products).

Storage
Keep in a closed container in a cool, dry place away from reach of children.

Missed dose
Take as soon as you remember. If your next dose is due within 2 hours, take a single dose now and skip the next.

Stopping the drug
Do not stop the drug without consulting your doctor; symptoms may recur.

Exceeding the dose
An occasional unintentional extra dose is unlikely to be a cause for concern. If a large overdose has been taken, seek immediate medical advice.

POSSIBLE ADVERSE EFFECTS

Moclobemide is generally well tolerated. Adverse side effects such as sleep disturbances, nausea, and headache usually disappear after a while.

Symptom/effect	Frequency		Discuss with doctor		Stop taking drug now	Call doctor now
	Common	Rare	Only if severe	In all cases		
Sleep disturbances	●		■			
Dizziness	●				■	
Nausea	●					
Headache	●		■			
Confusion		●			■	
Restlessness/agitation		●			■	

INTERACTIONS

General note A number of drugs interact with moclobemide. If you take other medications, discuss this with your doctor or pharmacist.

Cimetidine The levels of moclobemide may be increased by cimetidine, requiring an adjustment in dosage.

Opiate analgesics Drugs such as pethidine, codeine, morphine, and fentanyl have enhanced effects if taken with moclobemide.

Antidepressants Other antidepressants are not normally taken together with moclobemide. In some cases a time lapse is required before moclobemide is taken.

Ephedrine, pseudoephedrine, phenylpropanolamine These are contained in certain cold remedies. They should not be taken whilst on moclobemide.

SPECIAL PRECAUTIONS

Be sure to tell your doctor if:
▼ You have liver or kidney problems.
▼ You have phaeocromocytoma.
▼ You have an overactive thyroid.
▼ You are taking other medications.

Pregnancy
▼ Safety in pregnancy not established. Discuss with your doctor.

Breast feeding
▼ Small amounts of the drug pass into breast milk. Discuss with your doctor.

Infants and children
▼ Not recommended.

Over 60
▼ No special problems.

Driving and hazardous work
▼ Avoid such activities until you have learned how the drug affects you because the drug can cause dizziness and confusion.

Alcohol
▼ Avoid excessive amounts.

Surgery and general anaesthetics
▼ Discuss this with your doctor or dentist before any surgery.

PROLONGED USE

No problems expected.

MORPHINE

Brand names MST Continus, Oramorph, Sevredol, SRM-Rhotard
Used in the following combined preparations Cyclimorph, Omnopon

GENERAL INFORMATION

In use since the 19th century, morphine belongs to a group of drugs called the *narcotic analgesics* (see p.80). These drugs are derived from opium, which comes from the unripe seed capsules of the opium poppy.

Morphine relieves the severe pain that can be caused by injury, surgery, heart attack, or chronic diseases such as cancer. It is sometimes given as a *premedication* before surgery.

Its painkilling effect wears off quickly, in contrast to some other narcotic analgesics, and it may be given as a special sustained-release (long-acting) formulation to relieve continuous, severe pain.

It is habit-forming; dependence and addiction can occur. However, most patients taking morphine for pain relief over brief periods of time do not become dependent and are able to stop taking the drug without difficulty.

QUICK REFERENCE

Drug group Narcotic analgesic (p.80)

Overdose danger rating High

Dependence rating High

Prescription needed Yes

Available as generic Yes

INFORMATION FOR USERS

Your drug prescription is tailored for you. Do not alter dosage without checking with your doctor.

How taken

Tablets, liquid, granules, injection, suppositories.

Frequency and timing of doses
Every 4 hours; every 12 hours (sustained-release preparations).

Adult dosage range
5 – 25mg per dose; however, some patients may need 75mg or more per dose. Doses vary considerably for each individual.

Onset of effect
Within 1 hour; within 4 hours (sustained-release preparations).

Duration of action
4 hours. Up to 12 hours (slow-release tablets).

Diet advice
None.

Storage
Keep in a closed container in a cool, dry place away from reach of children.

Missed dose
Take as soon as you remember. Return to your normal dosing schedule as soon as possible.

Stopping the drug
If the reason for taking the drug no longer exists, you may stop the drug and notify your doctor.

OVERDOSE ACTION

 Seek immediate medical advice in all cases. Take emergency action if there are symptoms such as slow or irregular breathing, severe drowsiness, or loss of consciousness.

See Drug poisoning emergency guide (p.470).

SPECIAL PRECAUTIONS

Be sure to tell your doctor if:
▼ You have long-term kidney or liver problems.
▼ You have heart or circulatory problems.
▼ You have a lung disorder such as asthma or bronchitis.
▼ You have thyroid disease.
▼ You are taking other medications.
▼ You have a history of epileptic fits.

 Pregnancy
▼ Not usually prescribed. May cause breathing difficulties in the newborn baby. Discuss with your doctor.

 Breast feeding
▼ The drug passes into the breast milk, but at low doses adverse effects in the baby are unlikely. Discuss with your doctor.

 Infants and children
▼ Reduced dose necessary.

 Over 60
▼ Reduced dose may be necessary. Increased likelihood of adverse effects.

 Driving and hazardous work
▼ People on morphine treatment are unlikely to be well enough to undertake such activities.

 Alcohol
▼ Avoid. Alcohol may increase the sedative effects of this drug.

POSSIBLE ADVERSE EFFECTS

Nausea, vomiting, and constipation are common, especially with high doses. Anti-nausea drugs or laxatives may be needed to counteract these symptoms.

Symptom/effect	Frequency		Discuss with doctor		Stop taking drug now	Call doctor now
	Common	Rare	Only if severe	In all cases		
Drowsiness	●		■			
Nausea/vomiting	●		■			
Constipation	●		■			
Dizziness	●			■		
Confusion		●		■		
Breathing difficulties		●		■	▲	▌

INTERACTIONS

Sedatives Morphine increases the sedative effects of other sedating drugs including antidepressants, antipsychotics, sleeping drugs, and antihistamines.

Monoamine oxidase inhibitors (MAOIs) These drugs may produce a severe change in blood pressure when taken with morphine.

PROLONGED USE

The effects of the drug usually become weaker during prolonged use as the body adapts. Dependence may occur if taken for extended periods.

NALIDIXIC ACID

Brand names Negram, Uriben
Used in the following combined preparations Mictral

GENERAL INFORMATION

Nalidixic acid is an antibacterial drug used in the treatment of lower urinary tract infections (cystitis). It is also sometimes given for the prevention of recurrent urinary tract infections.

Taken by mouth, it does not accumulate in the body tissues but is concentrated in the urine. It is effective against almost all the species of bacteria that commonly infect the urinary tract. However, because some organisms rapidly develop resistance,

a second course of treatment is less likely to be as effective.

Nalidixic acid is fast acting and usually clears acute outbreaks of infection completely within a few days, though the full prescribed course should be completed.

Though generally safe, nalidixic acid sometimes causes serious side effects. The drug may interfere with some urine tests and can give a false high reading of urine sugar level.

QUICK REFERENCE

Drug group Antibacterial drug (p.131)

Overdose danger rating Medium

Dependence rating Low

Prescription needed Yes

Available as generic Yes

INFORMATION FOR USERS

Your drug prescription is tailored for you. Do not alter dosage without checking with your doctor.

How taken

Tablets, liquid, granules.

Frequency and timing of doses
4 x daily.

Dosage range
Adults 4g daily for one week for acute infections, reduced to 2g daily during longer courses of treatment.
Children Reduced dose according to age and weight.

Onset of effect
12 – 14 hours.

Duration of action
Up to 12 hours.

Diet advice
None.

Storage
Keep in a closed container in a cool, dry place away from reach of children.

Missed dose
Take as soon as you remember. If your next dose is due within 2 hours, take a single dose now and skip the next.

Stopping the drug
Take the full course. Even if you feel better, the infection may still be present and symptoms may recur if treatment is stopped too soon.

Exceeding the dose
An occasional unintentional extra dose is unlikely to be a cause for concern. Large overdoses may cause nausea and vomiting, lethargy, mental disturbance (psychosis), and fits. Notify your doctor.

SPECIAL PRECAUTIONS

Be sure to tell your doctor if:
▼ You have long-term liver or kidney problems.
▼ You have had epileptic fits.
▼ You have Parkinson's disease.
▼ You are taking other medications.

 Pregnancy
▼ Safety in pregnancy not established. Discuss with your doctor.

 Breast feeding
▼ The drug passes into the breast milk and may affect the baby. Discuss with your doctor.

 Infants and children
▼ Reduced dose necessary. Not recommended in children under 3 months.

 Over 60
▼ No special problems.

 Driving and hazardous work
▼ Avoid such activities until you have learned how the drug affects you because the drug may cause dizziness, drowsiness, and blurred vision.

 Alcohol
▼ Avoid. Alcohol may increase the sedative effects of this drug.

POSSIBLE ADVERSE EFFECTS

Nalidixic acid does not usually cause adverse effects. The most common side effects are nausea, vomiting, and rashes.

In some people it increases the sensitivity of the skin to sunlight. It can also cause visual disturbances, drowsiness, and dizziness.

Symptom/effect	Frequency		Discuss with doctor		Stop taking drug now	Call doctor now
	Common	Rare	Only if severe	In all cases		
Nausea/vomiting	●		■			
Rash/itching/joint pain	●			■		
Dizziness/drowsiness/headache		●	■			
Diarrhoea		●	■			
Light-sensitive rash		●		■		
Blurred vision		●		■		

INTERACTIONS

Oral anticoagulants Nalidixic acid may increase the anticoagulant effect of these drugs; dosage adjustment may be necessary.

Nitrofurantoin Nitrofurantoin interferes with the effectiveness of nalidixic acid.

Probenecid increases the risk of adverse effects with this drug.

PROLONGED USE

No problems expected, though blood tests may be carried out periodically to monitor any effects on the blood, liver, or kidneys.

NAPROXEN

Brand names Arthrosin, Arthroxen, Laraflex, Naprosyn, Nycopren, Pranoxen, Rheuflex, Synflex, Valrox
Used in the following combined preparations Napratec

GENERAL INFORMATION

Naproxen is a non-steroidal anti-inflammatory drug (NSAID) used to reduce pain, stiffness and inflammation.

It relieves symptoms of adult and juvenile rheumatoid arthritis, osteoarthritis and ankylosing spondylitis, although it does not cure the underlying disease.

Naproxen is also used to treat acute attacks of gout, and may sometimes be prescribed for the relief of migraine and of pain following orthopaedic surgery, dental treatment, strains, and sprains. It is also effective for treating painful menstrual cramps.

Gastrointestinal side effects are fairly common and there is an increased risk of bleeding. However, it is safer than aspirin, and in long-term use it needs to be taken only once or twice daily.

INFORMATION FOR USERS

Your drug prescription is tailored for you. Do not alter dosage without checking with your doctor.

How taken

Tablets, liquid, granules, suppositories.

Frequency and timing of doses
Every 6 – 8 hours as required (general pain relief); 1 – 2 x daily (muscular pain and arthritis); every 8 hours (gout). All doses should be taken with food.

Adult dosage range
Mild to moderate pain, menstrual cramps 500mg (starting dose), then 250mg every 6 – 8 hours as required. *Muscular pain and arthritis* 500 – 1250mg daily. *Gout* 750mg (starting dose), then 250mg every 8 hours until attack has subsided.

Onset of effect
Pain relief begins within 1 hour. Full anti-inflammatory effect may take 2 weeks.

Duration of action
Up to 12 hours.

Diet advice
None.

Storage
Keep in a closed container in a cool, dry place away from reach of children. Protect from light.

Missed dose
Take as soon as you remember. If your next dose is due within 4 hours, take a single dose now and skip the next.

Stopping the drug
When taken for short-term pain relief, naproxen can be safely stopped as soon as you no longer need it. If prescribed for long-term treatment, however, you should seek medical advice before stopping the drug.

Exceeding the dose
An occasional unintentional extra dose is unlikely to be a cause for concern. But if you notice any unusual symptoms, or if a large overdose has been taken, notify your doctor.

SPECIAL PRECAUTIONS

Be sure to tell your doctor if:
▼ You have liver or kidney problems.
▼ You have heart problems.
▼ You have a bleeding disorder.
▼ You have high blood pressure.
▼ You have had a peptic ulcer, oesophagitis or acid indigestion.
▼ You are allergic to aspirin.
▼ You suffer from asthma.
▼ You are taking other medications.

Pregnancy
▼ Not usually prescribed. When taken in the last three months of pregnancy, may increase the risk of adverse effects on the baby's heart and may prolong labour. Discuss with your doctor.

Breast feeding
▼ The drug passes into the breast milk, but at normal doses adverse effects on the baby are unlikely. Discuss with your doctor.

Infants and children
▼ Reduced dose necessary.

Over 60
▼ Increased likelihood of adverse effects. Reduced dose may therefore be necessary.

Driving and hazardous work
▼ Avoid such activities until you have learned how the drug affects you because it may reduce your ability to concentrate.

Alcohol
▼ Keep consumption low. Alcohol may increase the risk of stomach irritation with naproxen.

Surgery and general anaesthetics
▼ Naproxen may prolong bleeding. Discuss with your doctor or dentist before surgery.

POSSIBLE ADVERSE EFFECTS

Most adverse effects are not serious and may diminish with time. Black or bloodstained bowel movements should be reported to your doctor without delay.

Symptom/effect	Frequency		Discuss with doctor		Stop taking drug now	Call doctor now
	Common	Rare	Only if severe	In all cases		
Gastrointestinal disorders	●		■			
Headache		●	■			
Inability to concentrate		●	■			
Ringing in the ears		●		■		
Swollen feet/ankles		●		■		
Rash/itching		●		■	▲	
Wheezing/breathlessness		●		■	▲	■

INTERACTIONS

General note Naproxen interacts with a wide range of drugs to increase the risk of bleeding and/or peptic ulcers. It may also alter the blood levels of lithium.

Antihypertensive drugs and diuretics The beneficial effects of these drugs may be reduced by naproxen.

PROLONGED USE

There is an increased risk of bleeding from peptic ulcers and in the bowel if naproxen is used long term.

NEFOPAM

Brand name Acupan
Used in the following combined preparations None

GENERAL INFORMATION

Nefopam is an analgesic drug with a strong and rapid effect. It is used for the relief of moderate to severe pain caused by injury, surgery, and cancer. It may also be used for severe toothache. This drug reduces the perception of pain by the brain, but its precise mechanism of action is unclear. Unlike most analgesics that act on the brain, nefopam does not interfere with breathing or cause dependence or abuse.

The drug does, however, have *anticholinergic* and *sympathomimetic* actions that may produce nausea, nervousness, and dry mouth. Because nefopam has a stimulatory effect on the heart, it is not used to treat pain from heart attacks. A pink discoloration of the urine may occur; this is harmless.

QUICK REFERENCE

Drug group Non-narcotic analgesic (p.80)

Overdose danger rating Medium

Dependence rating Low

Prescription needed Yes

Available as generic No

INFORMATION FOR USERS

Your drug prescription is tailored for you. Do not alter dosage without checking with your doctor.

How taken

Tablets, injection.

Frequency and timing of doses
3 x daily when necessary.

Adult dosage range
90 – 270mg daily.

Onset of effect
Within 1 hour.

Duration of action
4 – 8 hours.

Diet advice
None.

Storage
Keep in a closed container in a cool, dry place away from reach of children.

Missed dose
Take as soon as you remember for persistent pain.

Stopping the drug
Can be safely stopped as soon as you no longer need it.

Exceeding the dose
An occasional unintentional extra dose is unlikely to cause problems. Large overdoses may cause drowsiness or fits. Notify your doctor.

SPECIAL PRECAUTIONS

Be sure to tell your doctor if:
▼ You have long-term liver or kidney problems.
▼ You have had epileptic fits.
▼ You have a heart condition.
▼ You have glaucoma.
▼ You have urinary difficulties.
▼ You are taking other medications.

 Pregnancy
▼ Safety in pregnancy not established. Discuss with your doctor.

 Breast feeding
▼ The drug passes into the breast milk, but at normal doses adverse effects on the baby are unlikely. Discuss with your doctor.

 Infants and children
▼ Not recommended.

 Over 60
▼ Increased likelihood of adverse effects. Reduced dose may therefore be necessary.

 Driving and hazardous work
▼ Avoid such activities until you have learned how the drug affects you because the drug can cause drowsiness, dizziness, and blurred vision.

 Alcohol
▼ Avoid. Alcohol may increase the sedative effects of this drug.

POSSIBLE ADVERSE EFFECTS

The adverse effects of this drug are mainly the result of its *anticholinergic* and sympa-thomimetic actions. They can sometimes be alleviated by dosage reduction.

Symptom/effect	Frequency		Discuss with doctor		Stop taking drug now	Call doctor now
	Common	Rare	Only if severe	In all cases		
Nausea	●		■			
Nervousness	●		■			
Dry mouth	●		■			
Dizziness/drowsiness		●	■			
Blurred vision		●	■			
Urinary retention		●	■			
Palpitations		●		■	▲	▮

INTERACTIONS

Monoamine oxidase inhibitors (MAOIs) These drugs may produce a dangerous rise in blood pressure when taken with nefopam.

Anticholinergic drugs Nefopam increases the risk of side effects from drugs that also have anticholinergic effects. Such drugs include tricyclic antidepressants, some antihistamines, and some drugs for parkinsonism.

Sympathomimetic decongestants Nefopam may increase the adverse effects of these drugs.

PROLONGED USE

No problems expected.

NEOSTIGMINE

Brand name Prostigmin
Used in the following combined preparations Robinul-Neostigmine

GENERAL INFORMATION

Shorter acting and more potent than some other drugs in its field, neostigmine has been used for over 50 years to treat myasthenia gravis, a rare autoimmune condition (see p. 121). The disorder involves muscle weakness caused by faulty transmission of nerve impulses. By prolonging these impulses, neostigmine improves muscle strength, though it does not cure the disease. In severe cases it may be prescribed in conjunction with corticosteroids or other drugs.

The injectable form of neostigmine is also used to relieve urinary retention or temporary paralysis of the bowel (paralytic ileus).

QUICK REFERENCE

Drug group Drug for myasthenia gravis (p.121)
Overdose danger rating High
Dependence rating Low
Prescription needed Yes
Available as generic No

INFORMATION FOR USERS

Your drug prescription is tailored for you. Do not alter dosage without checking with your doctor.

How taken

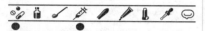

Tablets, injection.

Frequency and timing of doses
Every 3 – 4 hours initially. Thereafter according to the needs of the individual.

Dosage range
Adults 75 – 300mg daily (by mouth); 5 – 20mg daily (by injection).
Children Reduced dose necessary according to age and weight.

Onset of effect
45 – 75 minutes (by mouth); within 20 minutes (by injection).

Duration of action
2 – 4 hours.

Diet advice
None.

Storage
Keep in a closed container in a cool, dry place away from reach of children. Protect from light.

Missed dose
Take as soon as you remember. If your next dose is due within 2 hours, take a single dose now and skip the next.

Stopping the drug
Do not stop the drug without consulting your doctor; symptoms may recur.

OVERDOSE ACTION

Seek immediate medical advice in all cases. You may experience severe abdominal cramps, diarrhoea, vomiting, increased salivation, weakness, and tremor. Take emergency action if unusually slow heartbeat, troubled breathing, fits, or loss of consciousness occur.

See Drug poisoning emergency guide (p. 470).

SPECIAL PRECAUTIONS

Be sure to tell your doctor if:
▼ You have heart problems.
▼ You have had epileptic fits.
▼ You have asthma.
▼ You have difficulty passing urine.
▼ You have Parkinson's disease.
▼ You are taking other medications.

Pregnancy
▼ No evidence of risk to developing baby with neostigmine taken in the first 6 months of pregnancy. Large doses near the time of delivery may lead to temporary muscle weakness in the newborn baby. Discuss with your doctor.

Breast feeding
▼ No evidence of risk.

Infants and children
▼ Reduced dose necessary.

Over 60
▼ Increased likelihood of adverse effects.

Driving and hazardous work
▼ Your underlying condition may make such activities inadvisable. Discuss with your doctor.

Alcohol
▼ No special problems.

Surgery and general anaesthetics
▼ Neostigmine may interact with some anaesthetics. Make sure your treatment is known to your doctor or dentist before any surgery.

POSSIBLE ADVERSE EFFECTS

Most of the common adverse effects of neostigmine are dose-related and due to overstimulation of the parasympathetic nervous system (see p.79).

Symptom/effect	Frequency		Discuss with doctor		Stop taking drug now	Call doctor now
	Common	Rare	Only if severe	In all cases		
Increased salivation	●		■			
Diarrhoea	●			■		
Abdominal cramps	●			■		
Nausea/vomiting	●			■		
Blurred vision/sweating	●			■		
Muscle cramps/twitching		●		■		
Rash		●		■	▲	■

INTERACTIONS

General note Drugs that suppress the transmission of nerve signals in muscles may aggravate myasthenia gravis and oppose the effect of neostigmine. Such drugs include quinidine, propranolol, lithium, and aminoglycoside antibiotics.

PROLONGED USE

No problems expected.

NICOTINE

Brand names Nicabate, Nicorette, Nicotinell-TTS
Used in the following combined preparations None

GENERAL INFORMATION

Smoking is a difficult habit to stop because of the addiction to nicotine and also because of the psychological attachment to the use of cigarettes or a pipe. Taking nicotine by a different route can help the smoker to deal with the two parts of the habit separately.

Nicotine is available both as chewing gum and as transdermal patches for the relief of withdrawal symptoms on giving up smoking.

The gum should be chewed when the urge to smoke occurs. It is chewed slowly for up to 30 minutes, by which time all of the available nicotine in the gum has been released.

The patches are applied every 24 hours to dry, non-hairy skin on the trunk or upper arm. The same area of application should be avoided for several days. The strength of the patch applied is gradually reduced and abstinence is generally achieved within three months.

QUICK REFERENCE

Overdose danger rating Medium
Dependence rating Low
Prescription needed No
Available as generic No

INFORMATION FOR USERS

Your drug prescription is tailored for you. Do not alter dosage without checking with your doctor.

How taken

Chewing gum, transdermal patch.

Frequency and timing of doses
When the urge to smoke is felt (chewing gum); every 24 hours (transdermal patches) but one brand has to be removed after 16 hours to leave a gap before reapplication.

Adult dosage range
Will depend on previous smoking habits. 7 – 30mg over 24 hours (transdermal patches); 5 – 15mg over 16 hours (transdermal patches); 1 x 2mg piece to 15 x 4mg pieces per day (chewing gum).

Onset of effect
Within minutes (chewing gum); a few hours (transdermal patches).

Duration of action
Up to 24 hours (transdermal patches); 30 minutes (chewing gum).

Diet advice
None.

Storage
Keep in a cool, dry place away from reach of children.

Missed dose
Change your patch as soon as you remember, and keep the new patch on for the required amount of time before changing it again.

Stopping the drug
The dose of nicotine is normally tailed off gradually.

Exceeding the dose
Application of several nicotine patches at the same time could result in serious overdosage. Seek immediate medical help. Overdosage with chewing gum can only occur if many pieces are chewed simultaneously. In this case seek immediate medical help.

SPECIAL PRECAUTIONS

Be sure to tell your doctor if:
▼ You have long-term liver or kidney problems.
▼ You have diabetes mellitus.
▼ You have thyroid disease.
▼ You have circulation problems.
▼ You have heart problems.
▼ You have a peptic ulcer.
▼ You have phaeochromocytoma.
▼ You have any skin disorders.
▼ You are taking other medications.

 Pregnancy
▼ Nicotine should not be used (in any form) during pregnancy.

 Breast feeding
▼ Nicotine should not be used (in any form) while breast feeding.

 Infants and children
▼ Nicotine products should not be administered to children.

 Over 60
▼ No special problems.

 Driving and hazardous work
▼ Usually no problems.

 Alcohol
▼ No special problems.

POSSIBLE ADVERSE EFFECTS

The chewing gum may cause slight irritation of the throat and increased salivation. The patches may cause similar side effects to smoking but these will probably be less marked. Any skin reaction to the patch will usually disappear in a couple of days.

Symptom/effect	Frequency		Discuss with doctor		Stop taking drug now	Call doctor now
	Common	Rare	Only if severe	In all cases		
Local irritation	●		■			
Headache	●		■			
Dizziness		●	■			
Nausea		●	■			
Cold/flu-like symptoms		●	■			
Insomnia		●	■			
Indigestion		●	■			

PROLONGED USE

The patches and chewing gum should not normally be used for more than three months.

INTERACTIONS

General note Nicotine patches or chewing gum should not be used with other nicotine-containing products including cigarettes.

Stopping smoking may increase the blood levels of some drugs (e.g. theophylline, warfarin). Discuss with your doctor or pharmacist.

NICOTINIC ACID

Brand names None
Used in the following combined preparations (Derivatives used in a number of vitamin products.)

GENERAL INFORMATION

Nicotinic acid is a form of niacin, a B vitamin (see p.426). Apart from its use as a vitamin supplement in the treatment of niacin deficiency, nicotinic acid is also prescribed in the treatment of a number of disorders. High doses of the drug are used to treat certain types of hyperlipidaemia (high levels of fat in the blood), which may increase the risk of heart disease.

Nicotinic acid also has a vasodilator effect, improving circulation to the fingers and toes. It may be prescribed in the treatment of chilblains and Raynaud's disease. Although it has also been used in peripheral vascular disease (narrowing of blood vessels causing poor circulation), there is little proof of its value in this disorder.

Adverse effects are a problem mainly when high doses of the drug are used.

QUICK REFERENCE

Drug group Vasodilator (p.98), lipid-lowering drug (p.103) and vitamin supplement (p.149)

Overdose danger rating Medium

Dependence rating Low

Prescription needed No

Available as generic Yes

INFORMATION FOR USERS

Your drug prescription is tailored for you. Do not alter dosage without checking with your doctor.

How taken

Tablets, capsules, injection.

Frequency and timing of doses
3 x daily after food.

Adult dosage range
300mg – 6g daily (hyperlipidaemia). See p.426 for dosages for treating vitamin deficiency.

Onset of effect
Adverse effects may be felt within a few hours, but beneficial effects may not be apparent for several weeks.

Duration of action
About 8 hours.

Diet advice
A low fat diet may be recommended in the treatment of hyperlipidaemia.

Storage
Keep in a closed container in a cool, dry place away from reach of children.

Missed dose
Take as soon as you remember. If your next dose is due within 2 hours, take a single dose now and skip the next.

Stopping the drug
Do not stop taking the drug without consulting your doctor; stopping the drug may lead to worsening of the underlying condition.

Exceeding the dose
An occasional unintentional extra dose is unlikely to cause problems. Large overdoses may cause dizziness and collapse. Notify your doctor.

SPECIAL PRECAUTIONS

Be sure to tell your doctor if:
▼ You have long-term liver or kidney problems.
▼ You have diabetes mellitus.
▼ You have gout.
▼ You have a stomach ulcer.
▼ You are taking other medications.

 Pregnancy
▼ Not usually prescribed. Discuss with your doctor.

 Breast feeding
▼ The drug passes into the breast milk and may affect the baby. Discuss with your doctor.

 Infants and children
▼ Reduced dose necessary.

 Over 60
▼ Reduced dose may be necessary.

 Driving and hazardous work
▼ Avoid such activities until you have learned how the drug affects you because the drug can cause dizziness.

 Alcohol
▼ No special problems.

POSSIBLE ADVERSE EFFECTS

Adverse effects (notably marked flushing) generally occur only with the high doses used to treat hyperlipidaemia. Development of a rash may require withdrawal of the drug.

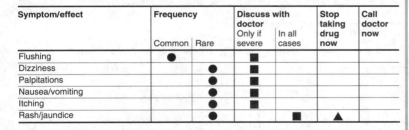

Symptom/effect	Frequency		Discuss with doctor		Stop taking drug now	Call doctor now
	Common	Rare	Only if severe	In all cases		
Flushing	●		■			
Dizziness		●	■			
Palpitations		●	■			
Nausea/vomiting		●	■			
Itching		●	■			
Rash/jaundice		●		■	▲	

PROLONGED USE

This drug may occasionally alter liver function in long-term use.

Monitoring Regular blood tests of liver function are usually carried out. When the drug is used to treat hyperlipidaemia, levels of fat in the blood are also monitored.

INTERACTIONS

Antihypertensive drugs Nicotinic acid may increase the effects of these drugs.

NIFEDIPINE

Brand names Adalat, Adalat IC, Adalat LA, Adalat Retard, Angiopine, Calcilat, Coracten, Nifensar XL
Used in the following combined preparations Beta-Adalat, Tenif

GENERAL INFORMATION

Nifedipine belongs to a group of drugs known as calcium channel blockers (p.101) which interfere with the conduction of signals in the muscles of the heart and blood vessels.

Nifedipine is used in the treatment of angina, both as a regular medication to help prevent attacks and for the immediate relief of pain during an attack (see p.101). Unlike some other anti-angina drugs (i.e. beta blockers), it can be used safely by asthmatics.

Nifedipine is also widely used to reduce raised blood pressure and is often helpful in improving circulation to the limbs, for example, in the treatment of Raynaud's disease.

In common with other drugs of its class, it may cause blood pressure to fall too low, and may occasionally cause disturbances of heart rhythm. In rare cases, angina worsens as a result of taking nifedipine.

INFORMATION FOR USERS

Your drug prescription is tailored for you. Do not alter dosage without checking with your doctor.

How taken

Tablets, capsules, sustained-release tablets/capsules, injection.

Frequency and timing of doses
3 x daily; 1 – 2 x daily (sustained-release preparations). For angina attacks: a capsule may be bitten and the liquid kept in the mouth or swallowed.

Adult dosage range
15 – 90mg daily.

Onset of effect
30 – 60 minutes. When capsules are bitten effects may be felt within minutes.

Duration of action
8 – 12 hours (capsules).

Diet advice
None.

Storage
Keep in a closed container in a cool, dry place away from reach of children. Protect from light.

Missed dose
Take as soon as you remember, or when needed. If your next dose is due within 3 hours, take a single dose now and skip the next.

Stopping the drug
Do not stop the drug without consulting your doctor; symptoms may recur.

Exceeding the dose
An occasional unintentional extra dose is unlikely to cause problems. Large overdoses may cause dizziness. Notify your doctor.

SPECIAL PRECAUTIONS

Be sure to tell your doctor if:
▼ You have long-term kidney or liver problems.
▼ You have heart failure.
▼ You have diabetes.
▼ You are taking other medications.

 Pregnancy
▼ Not usually prescribed. May cause abnormalities in the developing baby and delay labour. Discuss with your doctor.

 Breast feeding
▼ The drug passes into the breast milk and may affect the baby. Discuss with your doctor.

 Infants and children
▼ Not recommended.

 Over 60
▼ Increased likelihood of adverse effects. Reduced dose may therefore be necessary.

 Driving and hazardous work
▼ Avoid such activities until you have learned how the drug affects you because the drug can cause dizziness owing to lowered blood pressure.

 Alcohol
▼ Avoid. Alcohol may further reduce blood pressure causing dizziness or other symptoms.

POSSIBLE ADVERSE EFFECTS

Nifedipine can cause a variety of minor symptoms. Dizziness, especially on rising, may be caused by an excessive reduction in blood pressure. Patients with angina may notice an increase in the severity or frequency of attacks after starting nifedipine treatment. This should always be reported to your doctor. Sometimes an adjustment in dosage or a change of drug may be necessary.

Symptom/effect	Frequency		Discuss with doctor		Stop taking drug now	Call doctor now
	Common	Rare	Only if severe	In all cases		
Headache	●		■			
Dizziness/fatigue	●		■			
Flushing	●		■			
Ankle swelling	●		■			
Frequency in passing urine		●	■			
Increased angina		●		■	▲	▮

INTERACTIONS

Antihypertensive drugs Nifedipine may increase the effects of these drugs.

Phenytoin Nifedipine may increase levels of phenytoin.

Digoxin Blood levels of digoxin may be increased when it is taken with nifedipine.

PROLONGED USE

No problems expected.

NITRAZEPAM

Brand names Mogadon, Remnos, Somnite, Unisomnia
Used in the following combined preparations None

GENERAL INFORMATION

Nitrazepam belongs to a group of drugs known as the benzodiazepines. The actions and adverse effects of this group of drugs are described more fully under Anti-anxiety drugs (p.83).

Nitrazepam is used in the short-term treatment of insomnia. Because it is a long-acting drug compared with some other benzodiazepines, it is more likely to cause drowsiness and/or light-headedness the following day. For this reason, the drug is effective for preventing early wakening, but hangover is more common than with other benzodiazepine drugs.

Like other benzodiazepines, nitrazepam can be habit-forming if taken regularly over a long period. Its effects may also grow weaker with time. For these reasons treatment with nitrazepam is usually reviewed at least every two weeks.

INFORMATION FOR USERS

Your drug prescription is tailored for you. Do not alter dosage without checking with your doctor.

How taken

Tablets, capsules, liquid.

Frequency and timing of doses
Once daily, immediately before bedtime.

Adult dosage range
5 – 10mg daily.

Onset of effect
30 – 60 minutes.

Duration of action
6 – 8 hours. Some effects may persist for 24 – 36 hours.

Diet advice
None.

Storage
Keep in a closed container in a cool, dry place away from reach of children. Protect from light.

Missed dose
If you fall asleep without having taken a dose and wake some hours later, do not take the missed dose. If necessary, return to your normal dose schedule the following night.

Stopping the drug
If you have been taking the drug continuously for less than 2 weeks, it can be safely stopped as soon as you feel you no longer need it. However, if you have been taking the drug for longer, consult your doctor who may supervise a gradual reduction in dosage. Stopping abruptly may lead to withdrawal symptoms (see p.82).

Exceeding the dose
An occasional unintentional extra dose is unlikely to cause problems. Large overdoses may cause unusual drowsiness. Notify your doctor.

SPECIAL PRECAUTIONS

Be sure to tell your doctor if:
▼ You have severe respiratory disease.
▼ You have long-term liver or kidney problems.
▼ You have had problems with alcohol or drug abuse.
▼ You are taking other medications.

 Pregnancy
▼ Safety in pregnancy not established. Discuss with your doctor.

 Breast feeding
▼ The drug passes into the breast milk and may affect the baby. Discuss with your doctor.

 Infants and children
▼ Not usually prescribed.

 Over 60
▼ Increased likelihood of adverse effects. Reduced dose may therefore be necessary.

 Driving and hazardous work
▼ Avoid such activities until you have learned how the drug affects you because the drug can cause reduced alertness and slowed reactions (even the following day).

 Alcohol
▼ Avoid. Alcohol may increase the sedative effects of this drug.

POSSIBLE ADVERSE EFFECTS

The principal adverse effects of this drug are related to its sedative and tranquillizing properties. These effects normally diminish after the first few days of treatment.

Symptom/effect	Frequency		Discuss with doctor		Stop taking drug now	Call doctor now
	Common	Rare	Only if severe	In all cases		
Daytime drowsiness	●		■			
Dizziness/unsteadiness	●			■		
Forgetfulness/confusion	●			■		
Headache		●		■		
Blurred vision		●		■		
Rash		●		■	▲	

INTERACTIONS

Sedatives All drugs that have a sedative effect on the central nervous system are likely to increase the sedative properties of nitrazepam.

PROLONGED USE

Regular use of this drug over several weeks can lead to a reduction in its effect as the body adapts. It may also be habit-forming when taken for extended periods, especially if larger than average doses are taken.

NITROFURANTOIN

Brand names Furadantin, Macrobid, Macrodantin
Used in the following combined preparations None

GENERAL INFORMATION

Nitrofurantoin is a fast-acting anti-bacterial drug that is prescribed to treat urinary tract infections. The drug reaches high levels in the urinary tract where the bacteria are concentrated. Nitrofurantoin usually cures an infection within days.

Unfortunately, this drug produces adverse effects in about 10 per cent of people taking it, the most common of which is irritation of the stomach. This can be alleviated to a certain extent by taking the drug with food. Nitrofurantoin occasionally causes toxic effects in the lungs and/or nervous system; it may also affect liver function, leading to jaundice. Serious adverse effects are much more likely in people with reduced kidney function, which causes drug levels to build up in the body.

QUICK REFERENCE

Drug group Antibacterial drug (p.131)
Overdose danger rating Low
Dependence rating Low
Prescription needed Yes
Available as generic Yes

INFORMATION FOR USERS

Your drug prescription is tailored for you. Do not alter dosage without checking with your doctor.

How taken

Tablets, capsules, sustained-release capsules, liquid.

Frequency and timing of doses
3 – 4 x daily with food; once daily (prevention); twice daily (sustained-release capsules).

Dosage range
Adults 50 – 100mg daily at bedtime (prevention); 200 – 400mg daily (treatment). *Children* Reduced dose necessary according to age and weight.

Onset of effect
4 – 6 hours.

Duration of action
6 – 12 hours.

Diet advice
None.

Storage
Keep in a closed container in a cool, dry place away from reach of children. Protect from light.

Missed dose
Take as soon as you remember. If your next dose is due within 3 hours, take a single dose now and skip the next.

Stopping the drug
Take the full course. Even if you feel better the original infection may still be present and symptoms may recur if treatment is stopped too soon.

Exceeding the dose
An occasional unintentional extra dose is unlikely to be a cause for concern. But if you notice unusual symptoms, or if a large overdose has been taken, notify your doctor.

SPECIAL PRECAUTIONS

Be sure to tell your doctor if:
▼ You have long-term liver or kidney problems.
▼ You have diabetes.
▼ You have anaemia.
▼ You have a lung disorder.
▼ You have glucose 6 phosphate dehydrogenase (G6PD) deficiency.
▼ You are taking other medications.

 Pregnancy
▼ Safety in pregnancy not established. Discuss with your doctor.

 Breast feeding
▼ The drug passes into the breast milk and may cause anaemia in G6PD-deficient infants. Discuss with your doctor.

 Infants and children
▼ Reduced dose necessary.

 Over 60
▼ No special problems.

 Driving and hazardous work
▼ No known problems.

 Alcohol
▼ No known problems.

POSSIBLE ADVERSE EFFECTS

Nitrofurantoin has a number of serious adverse effects that may make it necessary to stop taking the drug. The more common adverse effects, such as loss of appetite and nausea and vomiting, tend to diminish as your body adjusts to the drug.

Symptom/effect	Frequency		Discuss with doctor		Stop taking drug now	Call doctor now
	Common	Rare	Only if severe	In all cases		
Loss of appetite	●		■			
Nausea/vomiting	●		■			
Jaundice		●		■	▲	▮
Headache		●		■		
Rash		●		■	▲	
Numb/tingling face		●		■	▲	
Unexplained fever		●		■	▲	
Shortness of breath		●		■	▲	▮

PROLONGED USE

Nitrofurantoin is not usually prescribed for long periods. If it is taken long term as a preventative measure, signs of toxic effects should be watched for.

INTERACTIONS

Probenecid Probenecid may increase the risk of adverse effects when taken in conjunction with nitrofurantoin.

Nalidixic acid This reduces the antibacterial effect of nitrofurantoin.

NORETHISTERONE

Brand names Menzol. Micronor, Noriday, Noristerat, Primolut N, Utovlan
Used in the following combined preparations Brevinor, Loestrin, Norinyl, Ortho-Novin, Synphase,TriNovum, and others

GENERAL INFORMATION

Norethisterone is a progestogen, a synthetic hormone similar to a natural female sex hormone, progesterone. It has a wide variety of uses including the postponement of menstruation and the treatment of menstrual disorders such as endometriosis (p.160). In these disorders the drug is only taken on particular days during the menstrual cycle. One of the major uses for norethisterone is as an ingredient of oral contraceptive preparations, either on its own or in combination with an oestrogen drug. It is also available in an injectable contraceptive preparation for use in special circumstances. It is also prescribed in the treatment of certain types of breast cancer.

Adverse effects from this drug are rare, but contraceptive preparations containing this drug may cause "breakthrough" bleeding. (See also p.161.)

QUICK REFERENCE

Drug group Female sex hormone (p.147)
Overdose danger rating Low
Dependence rating Low
Prescription needed Yes
Available as generic No

INFORMATION FOR USERS

Your drug prescription is tailored for you. Do not alter dosage without checking with your doctor.

How taken

Tablets, injection.

Frequency and timing of doses
1 – 3 x daily.

Adult dosage range
10 – 15mg daily (menstrual disorders); 15mg daily (postponement of menstruation); 350 micrograms daily (progestogen-only contraceptives); 30 – 60mg daily (cancer).

Onset of effect
The drug starts to act within a few hours.

Duration of action
24 hours.

Diet advice
None.

Storage
Keep in a closed container in a cool, dry place away from reach of children. Protect from light.

Missed dose
Take as soon as you remember. If you are taking the drug for contraception, see What to do if you miss a pill (p.163).

Stopping the drug
The drug can be safely stopped as soon as contraceptive protection is no longer required. If prescribed for an underlying disorder, do not stop taking the drug without consulting your doctor.

Exceeding the dose
An occasional unintentional extra dose is unlikely to be a cause for concern. But if you notice unusual symptoms, or if a large overdose has been taken, notify your doctor.

POSSIBLE ADVERSE EFFECTS

Adverse effects of norethisterone are rarely troublesome and are generally typical of drugs of this type. Prolonged treatment may cause jaundice due to liver damage.

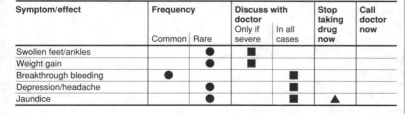

Symptom/effect	Frequency		Discuss with doctor		Stop taking drug now	Call doctor now
	Common	Rare	Only if severe	In all cases		
Swollen feet/ankles		●	■			
Weight gain		●	■			
Breakthrough bleeding	●			■		
Depression/headache		●		■		
Jaundice		●		■	▲	

INTERACTIONS

General note Norethisterone may interfere with the beneficial effects of many drugs, including oral anticoagulants, anticonvulsants, antihypertensives, and antidiabetic drugs. Many other drugs may reduce the contraceptive effect of norethisterone-containing pills. These include anticonvulsants, antituberculous drugs, and antibiotics. Be sure to inform your doctor that you are taking norethisterone before taking additional prescribed medication.

Cyclosporin Levels of cyclosporin may be raised by norethisterone.

SPECIAL PRECAUTIONS

Be sure to tell your doctor if:
▼ You have long-term liver or kidney problems.
▼ You have diabetes.
▼ You have had epileptic fits.
▼ You suffer from migraines.
▼ You have heart or circulatory problems.
▼ You are taking other medications.

 Pregnancy
▼ Not usually prescribed. May cause defects in the baby. Discuss with your doctor.

 Breast feeding
▼ The drug passes into the breast milk, but at normal doses adverse effects on the baby are unlikely. Discuss with your doctor.

 Infants and children
▼ Not prescribed.

 Over 60
▼ Not usually prescribed.

 Driving and hazardous work
▼ No special problems.

 Alcohol
▼ No special problems.

PROLONGED USE

Prolonged use may in rare cases cause liver damage.

Monitoring Blood tests to check liver function may be carried out.

NYSTATIN

Brand names Nystan
Used in the following combined preparations Dermovate NN, Mysteclin, Nystaform, Timodine, Tinaderm-M, and others

GENERAL INFORMATION

Nystatin is an antifungal drug named after the New York State Institute of Health, where it was developed in the early 1950s.

It is effective against candidiasis (thrush), an infection caused by the Candida yeast. Available in a variety of dosage forms, it is used to treat infections of the skin, mouth, throat,

intestinal tract, oesophagus, and vagina. Poorly absorbed from the digestive tract into the bloodstream, it is of no use against *systemic* infections. It is not given by injection.

It rarely causes adverse effects and can be used during pregnancy to treat vaginal candidiasis.

QUICK REFERENCE

Drug group Antifungal drug (p.138)
Overdose danger rating Low
Dependence rating Low
Prescription needed Yes
Available as generic Yes

INFORMATION FOR USERS

Your drug prescription is tailored for you. Do not alter dosage without checking with your doctor.

How taken

Tablets, pastilles, liquid, pessaries, ointment, cream, gel.

Frequency and timing of doses
Mouth or throat infections 4 x daily. Liquid should be held in the mouth for several minutes before swallowing.
Intestinal infections 4 x daily.
Skin infections 2 – 4 x daily.
Vaginal infections Once daily for 2 weeks.

Adult dosage range
2 – 4 million units daily (by mouth); 100,000 – 200,000 units at night (pessaries); 1 – 2 applicatorfuls (vaginal cream); as directed (skin preparations).

Onset of effect
Full beneficial effect may not be felt for 7 – 14 days.

Duration of action
Up to 6 hours.

Diet advice
None.

Storage
Keep in a closed container in a cool, dry place away from reach of children. Protect from light.

Missed dose
Take as soon as you remember. Take your next dose as usual.

Stopping the drug
Take the full course. Even if the affected area seems to be cured, the original infection may still be present and symptoms may recur if treatment is stopped too soon.

Exceeding the dose
An occasional unintentional extra dose is unlikely to be a cause for concern. But if you notice unusual symptoms, or if a large overdose has been taken, notify your doctor.

SPECIAL PRECAUTIONS

Be sure to tell your doctor if:
▼ You are taking other medications.

Pregnancy
▼ No evidence of risk to developing baby.

Breast feeding
▼ No evidence of risk.

Infants and children
▼ Reduced dose necessary.

Over 60
▼ No special problems.

Driving and hazardous work
▼ No known problems.

Alcohol
▼ No known problems.

PROLONGED USE

No problems expected. Usually given for a course of treatment until the infection is cured.

POSSIBLE ADVERSE EFFECTS

Adverse effects are uncommon, and are usually mild and transient. Nausea and vomiting may occur with high doses of nystatin taken by mouth.

Symptom/effect	Frequency		Discuss with doctor		Stop taking drug now	Call doctor now
	Common	Rare	Only if severe	In all cases		
Diarrhoea		●	■			
Nausea/vomiting		●	■			
Rash		●		■		

INTERACTIONS

None.

OESTRADIOL

Brand name Climaval, Estraderm, Estrapak, Evorel, Progynova, Vagifem, Zumenon
Used in the following combined preparations Climagest, Cyclo-Progynova, Estracombi, Hormonin, Nuvelle, Trisequens

GENERAL INFORMATION

Oestradiol is a naturally occurring oestrogen (a female sex hormone). It is mainly used as hormone replacement therapy (HRT) to treat menopausal and post menopausal symptoms such as hot flushes, night sweats, and vaginal atrophy. Other beneficial effects of HRT include prevention of the loss of bone tissue, which occurs in osteoporosis, and reduction of the risk of heart attacks. Oestradiol is often given with a progestogen either as separate medication or as a combined product. Treatment is sometimes only taken for a set number of days each month; instructions should be followed carefully.

In addition to being taken as tablets, oestradiol skin patches and implants are available. Implants of oestradiol need replacing only after four to eight months. Skin patches of the drug may cause a local rash and itching at the site of application.

INFORMATION FOR USERS

Your drug prescription is tailored for you. **Do not alter dosage without checking with your doctor.**

How taken

Tablets, skin patches, implants, pessaries.

Frequency and timing of doses
Once daily (tablets); every 24 hours (skin patches); every 4 – 8 months (implants); once daily to twice weekly (pessaries).

Adult dosage range
1 – 4mg daily (tablets); 25 – 100 micrograms daily (skin patches); 25 – 100mg per dose (implants); 25 micrograms per dose (pessaries).

Onset of effect
10 – 20 days.

Duration of action
up to 24 hours; some effects may be longer lasting.

Diet advice
None.

Storage
Keep in a closed container in a cool, dry place away from reach of children.

Missed dose
Take as soon as you remember. If your next dose is due within 4 hours, take a single dose now and skip the next.

Stopping the drug
Do not stop the drug without consulting your doctor; symptoms may recur.

Exceeding the dose
An occasional unintentional extra dose is unlikely to be a cause for concern. But if you notice unusual symptoms, or if a large overdose has been taken, notify your doctor.

POSSIBLE ADVERSE EFFECTS

The most common adverse effects with oestradiol are similar to symptoms in the early stages of pregnancy, and generally diminish with time. Sudden sharp pain in the chest, groin, or legs may indicate an abnormal blood clot that needs attention.

Symptom/effect	Frequency		Discuss with doctor		Stop taking drug now	Call doctor now
	Common	Rare	Only if severe	In all cases		
Nausea/vomiting	●		■			
Breast swelling/tenderness	●		■			
Weight gain	●		■			
Headache		●	■			
Depression		●		■		
Pain in chest/groin/legs		●		■	▲	■

INTERACTIONS

Tobacco smoking This increases the risk of serious adverse effects on the heart and circulation with oestradiol.

Rifampicin This may reduce the effects of oestradiol.

Anticonvulsants Phenobarbitone, phenytoin, and carbamazepine reduce the effects of oestradiol.

SPECIAL PRECAUTIONS

Be sure to tell your doctor if:
▼ You have impaired liver function.
▼ You have heart or circulation problems.
▼ You have had blood clots or a stroke.
▼ You have diabetes.
▼ You are a smoker.
▼ You suffer from migraine or epilepsy.
▼ You are taking other medications.

Pregnancy
▼ Not prescribed.

Breast feeding
▼ Not prescribed. The drug passes into breast milk and may inhibit its flow. Discuss with your doctor.

Infants and children
▼ Not usually prescribed.

Over 60s
▼ No special problems.

Driving and hazardous work
▼ No problems expected.

Alcohol
▼ No known problems.

Surgery and general anaesthetics
▼ Oestradiol may need to be stopped several weeks before you have major surgery. Discuss this with your doctor.

PROLONGED USE

In some circumstances prolonged use of oestradiol may slightly increase the risk of cancer of the womb. The risk of gallstones may also be higher.

Monitoring Physical examinations and blood pressure checks may be performed.

OMEPRAZOLE

Brand name Losec
Used in the following combined preparations None

GENERAL INFORMATION

Omeprazole is an anti-ulcer drug which was introduced in 1989. It is used mainly to treat stomach and duodenal ulcers that have not responded to other treatment. It reduces (by about 70 per cent) the amount of acid produced by the stomach and works in a different way from other anti-ulcer drugs which reduce acid secretion. Omeprazole is very effective for treating pain and inflammation caused by reflux oesophagitis.

Treatment is usually given for four to eight weeks, depending on where the ulcer is situated. The drug is not used long term to prevent ulcers developing.

Most people do not have serious side effects with omeprazole. However, it may affect the actions of enzymes in the liver, where many drugs are broken down, so treatment should be monitored if it is used with phenytoin or warfarin. As with other anti-ulcer drugs, it may mask signs of stomach cancer, so it is used only when the possibility of this disease has been ruled out.

INFORMATION FOR USER

Your drug prescription is tailored for you. Do not alter dosage without checking with your doctor.

How taken

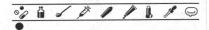

Capsules.

Frequency and timing of doses
Once daily.

Adult dosage range
20 – 40mg daily and sometimes up to 120mg daily.

Onset of effect
2 – 5 hours.

Duration of action
24 hours.

Diet advice
None.

Storage
Keep in a closed container in a cool, dry place away from reach of children. Omeprazole is very sensitive to moisture. It must not be transferred to another container and must be used within 3 months of opening.

Missed dose
Take as soon as you remember. If your next dose is due within 8 hours, take a single dose now, and skip the next.

Stopping the drug
Do not stop the drug without consulting your doctor. Symptoms may recur.

Exceeding the dose
An occasional unintentional extra dose is unlikely to be a cause for concern. But if you notice unusual symptoms or if a large overdose has been taken, notify your doctor.

POSSIBLE ADVERSE EFFECTS

Adverse effects are usually mild, and often diminish with continued use of the drug.

Symptom/effect	Frequency		Discuss with doctor		Stop taking drug now	Call doctor now
	Common	Rare	Only if severe	In all cases		
Nausea		●	■			
Headache	●		■			
Diarrhoea	●		■			
Constipation		●	■			
Rash		●		■		

INTERACTIONS

Warfarin The effects of warfarin may be increased by omeprazole.

Phenytoin The effects of phenytoin may be increased by omeprazole.

Cyclosporin Blood levels of cyclosporin are raised by omeprazole.

SPECIAL PRECAUTIONS

Be sure to tell your doctor if:
▼ You have long-term kidney or liver problems.
▼ You have epilepsy.
▼ You are taking other medications.

 Pregnancy
▼ Safety in pregnancy not established. Discuss with your doctor.

 Breast feeding
▼ The drug may pass into the breast milk. Safety of breast feeding not established. Discuss with your doctor.

 Infants and children
▼ Not recommended.

 Over 60s
▼ No special problems.

 Driving and hazardous work
▼ No special problems.

 Alcohol
▼ Avoid. Alcohol may aggravate your underlying condition and reduce the beneficial effects of this drug.

PROLONGED USE

Courses of longer than eight weeks are not usually prescribed.

ONDANSETRON

Brand name Zofran
Used in the following combined preparations None

GENERAL INFORMATION

Ondansetron is an anti-emetic particularly useful for treating nausea and vomiting associated with anti-cancer drugs, such as cisplatin, and radiotherapy. It may also be used for nausea and vomiting that occurs after an operation.

The dose given and frequency will depend on which anti-cancer drug you are having and what the dose of that drug is. Generally, you will have a dose either by mouth or by injection before infusion of your anti-cancer agent and then tablets for up to five days after your treatment has finished.

Sometimes, other drugs, such as dexamethasone, are taken with ondansetron as this can enhance its effectiveness. Serious adverse effects are unlikely to occur.

INFORMATION FOR USERS

Your drug prescription is tailored for you. Do not alter dosage without checking with your doctor.

How taken

Tablets, injection.

Frequency and timing of doses
Normally 2 x daily but the frequency will depend on the reason for which it is being used.

Adult dosage range
4 – 32mg daily depending on the reason for which it is being used.

Onset of effect
Within 1 hour.

Duration of action
Approximately 12 hours.

Diet advice
None.

Storage
Keep in a closed container in a cool, dry place away from reach of children.

Missed dose
Take as soon as you remember. If your next dose is due within 2 hours, take a single dose now and skip the next.

Stopping the drug
Can be safely stopped as soon as you no longer need it.

Exceeding the dose
An occasional unintentional extra dose is unlikely to be a cause for concern. But if you notice unusual symptoms, or if a large overdose has been taken, notify your doctor.

SPECIAL PRECAUTIONS

Be sure to tell your doctor if:
▼ You have liver problems.
▼ You are taking other medications.

 Pregnancy
▼ Safety in pregnancy not established. Discuss with your doctor.

 Breast feeding
▼ The drug passes into the breast milk. Discuss with your doctor.

 Infants and children
▼ Reduced dose necessary.

 Over 60
▼ No special problems.

 Driving and hazardous work
▼ No problems expected.

 Alcohol
▼ No known problems.

POSSIBLE ADVERSE EFFECTS

Ondansetron is generally well tolerated. It is less likely to cause sedation and movement disorders than some other anti-emetics.

Symptom/effect	Frequency		Discuss with doctor		Stop taking drug now	Call doctor now
	Common	Rare	Only if severe	In all cases		
Constipation	●		■			
Headache	●		■			
Warm feeling in head/stomach		●	■			

PROLONGED USE

Not generally prescribed for long-term treatment.

INTERACTIONS

None.

ORPHENADRINE

Brand names Biorphen, Disipal, Norflex
Used in the following combined preparation None

GENERAL INFORMATION

Orphenadrine is an *anticholinergic* drug that is used to treat all forms of Parkinson's disease. Although it is less effective than other drugs used in the treatment of this disorder, its adverse effects tend to be less severe. It is particularly valuable for relieving the muscle rigidity that often occurs in Parkinson's disease; it is less helpful for improving slowing of movement that also commonly affects sufferers.

Orphenadrine possesses significant muscle relaxant properties. It produces this effect by blocking nerve pathways responsible for muscle rigidity and spasm. It is prescribed for the relief of muscle spasm caused by muscle injury, prolapsed ("slipped") disc, and whiplash injuries.

QUICK REFERENCE

Drug group Anticholinergic muscle relaxant (p.120) and Drug for parkinsonism (p.87)

Overdose danger rating High

Dependence rating Low

Prescription needed Yes

Available as generic Yes

INFORMATION FOR USERS

Your drug prescription is tailored for you. Do not alter dosage without checking with your doctor.

How taken

Tablets, liquid, injection.

Frequency and timing of doses
2 – 3 x daily.

Dosage range
150 – 400mg daily.

Onset of effect
Within 60 minutes (by mouth); within 5 minutes (by injection).

Duration of action
8 – 12 hours.

Diet advice
None.

Storage
Keep in a closed container in a cool, dry place, away from reach of children. Protect from light.

Missed dose
Take as soon as you remember. If your next dose is due within 2 hours, take a single dose now and skip the next.

Stopping the drug
Do not stop the drug without consulting your doctor; symptoms may recur.

OVERDOSE ACTION

Seek immediate medical advice in all cases. Take emergency action if palpitations, fits, or loss of consciousness occur.

See Drug poisoning emergency guide (p.470)

SPECIAL PRECAUTIONS

Be sure to tell your doctor if:
▼ You have long-term liver or kidney problems.
▼ You have heart problems.
▼ You have had glaucoma.
▼ You have difficulty passing urine.
▼ You have myasthenia gravis.
▼ You are taking other medications.

 Pregnancy
▼ Safety in pregnancy not established. Discuss with your doctor.

 Breast feeding
▼ The drug passes into the breast milk, but at normal doses adverse effects on the baby are unlikely. Discuss with your doctor.

 Infants and children
▼ Not usually prescribed.

 Over 60
▼ Increased likelihood of adverse effects. Reduced dose may therefore be necessary.

 Driving and hazardous work
▼ Avoid such activities until you have learned how the drug affects you because the drug can cause dizziness, lightheadedness, and blurred vision.

 Alcohol
▼ Avoid. Alcohol may increase the sedative effects of this drug.

POSSIBLE ADVERSE EFFECTS

The adverse effects of orphenadrine are similar to those of other anticholinergic drugs. The more common symptoms, such as dryness of the mouth and blurred vision, can often be overcome by an adjustment in dosage.

Symptom/effect	Frequency		Discuss with doctor		Stop taking drug now	Call doctor now
	Common	Rare	Only if severe	In all cases		
Dry mouth/skin	●		■			
Difficulty passing urine	●		■			
Constipation	●		■			
Dizziness	●		■			
Blurred vision	●			■		
Confusion/agitation		●		■		
Rash/itching		●		■	▲	
Palpitations		●		■	▲	■

INTERACTIONS

Anticholinergic drugs The anticholinergic effects of orphenadrine are likely to be increased by these drugs.

Dextroproxyphene and co-proxamol Confusion, anxiety, and tremors may occur if these are taken with orphenadrine.

Sedatives The effects of all drugs that have a sedative effect on the central nervous system are likely to be increased by orphenadrine.

PROLONGED USE

No problems expected. Effectiveness in treating Parkinson's disease may diminish with time.

OXPRENOLOL

Brand names Apsolox, Slow-Trasicor, Trasicor
Used in the following combined preparation Trasidrex

GENERAL INFORMATION

Oxprenolol belongs to the class of drugs known as beta blockers. These drugs reduce the heart rate, and are used in the treatment of angina, abnormal heart rhythms, and hypertension (high blood pressure).

For hypertension, oxprenolol is often prescribed together with a diuretic. It is also used to reduce palpitations and tremor caused by anxiety and to control the symptoms of overactivity of the thyroid gland such as fast heart rate, tremor, anxiety, and tension.

In common with other beta blockers, it has a number of side effects such as dizziness and cold hands and feet. It should not be used by people with breathing problems such as asthma, chronic bronchitis, or emphysema. It is not generally prescribed for people with diabetes or peripheral vascular disease.

INFORMATION FOR USERS

Your drug prescription is tailored for you. Do not alter dosage without checking with your doctor.

How taken

Tablets.

Frequency and timing of doses
2 – 3 x daily (tablets); 1 – 2 x daily (slow-release tablets).

Dosage range
Adults 60 – 480mg daily (tablets). *Children* Reduced dose according to age and weight.

Onset of effect
Within 1 – 2 hours. Full antihypertensive effect may not be felt for 2 – 3 weeks.

Duration of action
6 – 12 hours (tablets, injection);
12 – 24 hours (slow-release tablets).

Diet advice
None.

Storage
Keep in a closed container in a cool, dry place away from reach of children.

Missed dose
Take as soon as you remember. If your next dose is due within 2 hours (tablets) or 6 hours (slow-release tablets), take a single dose now and skip the next.

Stopping the drug
Do not stop the drug without consulting your doctor, who may supervise a gradual reduction in dosage. Stopping abruptly may lead to worsening of the underlying condition.

Exceeding the dose
An occasional unintentional extra dose is unlikely to cause problems. Large overdoses may cause breathing difficulties and serious effects on the heart. Notify your doctor.

POSSIBLE ADVERSE EFFECTS

The adverse effects of this drug include cold hands and feet. Asthma and heart failure may occasionally be provoked or worsened on starting treatment.

Symptom/effect	Frequency		Discuss with doctor		Stop taking drug now	Call doctor now
	Common	Rare	Only if severe	In all cases		
Lethargy/fatigue	●		■			
Cold hands and feet	●			■		
Nightmares/vivid dreams		●	■			
Nausea		●	■			
Drowsiness/dizziness		●		■		
Rash/dry eyes		●		■		
Breathing difficulties		●		■		▮
Slow pulse and fainting		●		■		▮

INTERACTIONS

Corticosteroids These drugs may reduce the blood pressure lowering effect of oxprenolol.

Ergotamine Oxprenolol may increase the adverse effects of this drug.

Insulin/oral antidiabetic drugs The action of these drugs may be strengthened by oxprenolol.

SPECIAL PRECAUTIONS

Be sure to tell your doctor if:
▼ You have liver problems.
▼ You have a lung disorder such as asthma, bronchitis, or emphysema.
▼ You have diabetes.
▼ You have poor circulation in the legs.
▼ You have heart problems.
▼ You are taking other medications.

Pregnancy
▼ May affect the developing baby. Discuss with your doctor.

Breast feeding
▼ The drug passes into the breast milk, but at normal doses adverse effects on the baby are unlikely. Discuss with your doctor.

Infants and children
▼ Reduced dose necessary.

Over 60
▼ No special problems.

Driving and hazardous work
▼ Do not undertake such activities until you have learned how the drug affects you because it can sometimes cause drowsiness and dizziness.

Alcohol
▼ Avoid excessive amounts.

PROLONGED USE

No problems expected.

PARACETAMOL

Brand names Alvedon, Calpol, Disprol, Hedex, Panadol, Panaleve, and others
Used in the following combined preparations Anadin Extra, Migraleve, Panadeine, Solpadeine, Tylex, and others

GENERAL INFORMATION

Although paracetamol has been known since the early 1900s, it has been widely used as an analgesic only since the 1950s. One of a group of drugs known as the non-narcotic analgesics, it is kept in the home to relieve occasional bouts of mild pain and to reduce fever. It is suitable for children as well as adults.

One of the advantages of taking paracetamol is that it does not cause stomach upset or bleeding problems. This makes it a particularly useful

alternative for people who suffer from peptic ulcers or who cannot tolerate aspirin. Occasional doses can also be safely taken if you are receiving treatment with anticoagulants.

An overdose of paracetamol is dangerous, capable of causing serious damage to the liver and kidneys. Large doses of paracetamol may also be toxic if you are a regular consumer of even moderate amounts of alcohol.

QUICK REFERENCE

Drug group Non-narcotic analgesic (p.80)
Overdose danger rating High
Dependence rating Low
Prescription needed No
Available as generic Yes

INFORMATION FOR USERS

Follow instructions on the label.
Call your doctor if symptoms worsen.

How taken

Tablets, capsules, liquid, suppositories.

Frequency and timing of doses
Every 4 – 6 hours as necessary, but not more than 4 doses per 24 hours in children.

Dosage range
Adults 500mg – 1g per dose up to 4g daily.
Children 60 – 120mg per dose (3 months – 1 year); 120 – 250mg per dose (1 – 5 years); 250 – 500mg per dose (6 – 12 years).

Onset of effect
Within 15 – 60 minutes.

Duration of action
Up to 6 hours.

Diet advice
None.

Storage
Keep in a closed container in a cool, dry place away from reach of children.

Missed dose
Take as soon as you remember if required to relieve pain. Otherwise do not take the missed dose, and only take a further dose when you are in pain.

Stopping the drug
Can be safely stopped as soon as you no longer need it.

OVERDOSE ACTION

 Seek immediate medical advice in all cases. Take emergency action if nausea, vomiting, or stomach pain occur.

See Drug poisoning emergency guide (p.470).

SPECIAL PRECAUTIONS

Be sure to consult your doctor or pharmacist before using this drug if:
▼ You have long-term liver or kidney problems.
▼ You are taking other medications.

 Pregnancy
▼ No evidence of risk with occasional use.

 Breast feeding
▼ No evidence of risk.

 Infants and children
▼ Children under 3 months on doctor's advice only. Reduced dose necessary up to 12 years.

 Over 60
▼ No special problems.

 Driving and hazardous work
▼ No special problems.

 Alcohol
▼ Prolonged heavy intake of alcohol in combination with paracetamol may substantially increase the risk of injury to the liver.

POSSIBLE ADVERSE EFFECTS

Paracetamol has rarely been found to produce any side effects when taken as recommended.

Symptom/effect	Frequency		Discuss with doctor		Stop taking drug now	Call doctor now
	Common	Rare	Only if severe	In all cases		
Nausea		●	■			
Rash		●		■	▲	

PROLONGED USE

You should not normally take this drug for longer than 48 hours except on the advice of your doctor.

INTERACTIONS

Cholestyramine inhibits the absorption of paracetamol.

Anticoagulants such as warfarin may need dosage adjustment if paracetamol is taken regularly in high doses.

Zidovudine The risk of adverse effects with this drug is increased by paracetamol.

PENICILLAMINE

Brand names Distamine, Pendramine
Used in the following combined preparations None

GENERAL INFORMATION

Penicillamine has two principal uses. It is an antirheumatic drug, given to adults and children to slow or even halt the progression of rheumatoid arthritis. Because of its potentially serious side effects on the blood and kidneys, it is used only when the inflammation of the joints is disabling or when other drugs have proved ineffective.

Penicillamine is also a *chelating* agent, used in cases of metal poisoning to eliminate copper, mercury, lead, or arsenic from the body. Penicillamine binds (i.e. combines) with those substances, forming a chemical compound that the body can excrete. It is also prescribed in Wilson's disease, a rare disorder involving copper deposits in the liver and brain, and prevents a certain rare type of urinary stone. Penicillamine is sometimes used in the treatment of chronic active hepatitis.

INFORMATION FOR USERS

Your drug prescription is tailored for you. Do not alter dosage without checking with your doctor.

How taken

Tablets.

Frequency and timing of doses
Once daily one hour before meals (rheumatoid arthritis); 4 x daily one hour before meals (Wilson's disease, kidney stones, metal poisoning).

Dosage range
Adults 125 – 250mg daily (starting dose), increasing to 500 – 750mg daily over 6 –12 months (rheumatoid arthritis); 1.5 – 2g daily (starting dose) reducing to 750mg – 1g (Wilson's disease).
Children Reduced dose necessary according to age and weight.

Onset of effect
Full effect may not be felt for 6 – 12 weeks.

Duration of action
Some effect may last for 1 – 3 months after the drug has been stopped.

Diet advice
People with Wilson's disease may be advised to follow a low-copper diet. Discuss with your doctor.

Storage
Keep in a closed container in a cool, dry place away from reach of children.

Missed dose
Take as soon as you remember.

Stopping the drug
Do not stop the drug without consulting your doctor; symptoms may recur.

Exceeding the dose
An occasional unintentional extra dose is unlikely to cause problems. If large doses have been taken consult your doctor.

POSSIBLE ADVERSE EFFECTS

Adverse effects are frequent. Allergic rashes and itching, gastrointestinal disturbances (such as nausea), and loss of taste are common and often dose-related. More serious, life-threatening reactions may occur.

Symptom/effect	Frequency		Discuss with doctor		Stop taking drug now	Call doctor now
	Common	Rare	Only if severe	In all cases		
Digestive disturbance	●		■			
Loss of taste/appetite	●		■			
Rash/itching	●				■	▲	■
Fever		●		■		
Blood in urine		●			■	▲	■

INTERACTIONS

Iron preparations These may reduce the absorption of penicillamine.

Antacids may reduce the absorption of penicillamine.

Digoxin Penicillamine may reduce the effect of digoxin.

SPECIAL PRECAUTIONS

Be sure to tell your doctor if:
▼ You have long-term liver or kidney problems.
▼ You have a blood disorder.
▼ You have a skin disorder.
▼ You are taking other medications.

 Pregnancy
▼ Not usually prescribed. May cause defects in the baby. Discuss with your doctor.

 Breast feeding
▼ Safety not established. Discuss with your doctor.

 Infants and children
▼ Reduced dose necessary.

 Over 60
▼ Increased likelihood of adverse effects. Reduced dose usually necessary.

 Driving and hazardous work
▼ No known problems.

 Alcohol
▼ No known problems.

PROLONGED USE

In rare cases, blood disorders or impaired kidney function may develop.

Monitoring Blood and urine are regularly tested for kidney damage or blood abnormalities.

PENTAZOCINE

Brand name Fortral
Used in the following combined preparation Fortagesic

GENERAL INFORMATION

Pentazocine is a narcotic analgesic with actions and uses similar to those of morphine. It is prescribed in the treatment of moderate and severe pain caused by injury, surgery, and chronic illnesses such as cancer. Because pentazocine may sometimes increase blood pressure, thereby putting a strain on the heart, it is not used to relieve the pain of heart attacks.

Pentazocine is a short-acting drug and doses usually need to be repeated every four hours. It is less likely to cause breathing difficulty and drowsiness than some other narcotic drugs, but it may occasionally cause confusion and hallucinations. As with other drugs of this group, *dependence* may develop in people who take high doses of the drug for prolonged periods.

INFORMATION FOR USERS

Your drug prescription is tailored for you. Do not alter dosage without checking with your doctor.

How taken

Tablets, capsules, injection, suppositories.

Frequency and timing of doses
Every 3 – 4 hours when necessary after food.

Adult dosage range
25mg – 100mg per dose (by mouth).

Onset of effect
Within 1 hour.

Duration of action
About 4 hours.

Diet advice
None.

Storage
Keep in a closed container in a cool, dry place away from reach of children.

Missed dose
Take as soon as you remember, if needed for the relief of persistent or recurrent pain.

Stopping the drug
If you have been taking the drug regularly for more than a few days, do not stop taking the drug abruptly without consulting your doctor. You may need to reduce the dose gradually to avoid *withdrawal symptoms*.

OVERDOSE ACTION

Seek immediate medical advice in all cases. Take emergency action if fits, breathing difficulty, or loss of consciousness occur.

See Drug poisoning emergency guide (p.470).

POSSIBLE ADVERSE EFFECTS

Adverse effects of pentazocine are usually only minor, but a number of people have to change to another drug because they experience dizziness or confusion.

Symptom/effect	Frequency		Discuss with doctor		Stop taking drug now	Call doctor now
	Common	Rare	Only if severe	In all cases		
Dizziness/confusion	●		■			
Drowsiness	●		■			
Nausea/vomiting	●		■			
Flushing/sweating		●		■		
Disturbed vision		●		■		
Hallucinations/nightmares		●		■	▲	

INTERACTIONS

General note Pentazocine may cause increased drowsiness with all drugs that have a sedative effect on the central nervous system. These include sleeping drugs, anti-anxiety drugs, antidepressants, and antihistamines.

Monoamine oxidase inhibitors (MAOIs) These drugs may produce a dangerous rise in blood pressure if taken with pentazocine.

SPECIAL PRECAUTIONS

Be sure to tell your doctor if:
▼ You have liver or kidney problems.
▼ You have heart failure.
▼ You have a lung disorder such as asthma or emphysema.
▼ You have high blood pressure.
▼ You have had problems with drug or alcohol abuse.
▼ You have had epileptic fits.
▼ You are taking other medications.

 Pregnancy
▼ No evidence of risk.

 Breast feeding
▼ Safety not established. Discuss with your doctor.

 Infants and children
▼ Reduced dose necessary.

 Over 60
▼ Increased likelihood of adverse effects. Reduced dose may therefore be necessary.

 Driving and hazardous work
▼ Avoid such activities until you have learned how the drug affects you because the drug can cause dizziness, drowsiness, and confusion.

 Alcohol
▼ Avoid. Alcohol may increase the sedative effects of this drug.

PROLONGED USE

Prolonged treatment with high doses of pentazocine is likely to cause dependence.

PETHIDINE

Brand names None
Used in the following combined preparations Pamergan

GENERAL INFORMATION

Similar to morphine, pethidine is a strong *narcotic* analgesic. It is used almost exclusively in hospitals to relieve the severe pain felt during labour, and to relieve pain after an operation. Pethidine is sometimes given as *premedication* before surgery. It takes effect quickly but its effect lasts for a short time compared to some other analgesics. This means that doses can be timed during labour to minimize adverse effects on the baby.

Pethidine can be habit-forming. Both *tolerance* and dependence can develop if the drug is used inappropriately or excessively. When taken for pain relief of the appropriate conditions for brief periods of time, it is unlikely that drug dependence will occur.

INFORMATION FOR USERS

Your drug prescription is tailored for you. Do not alter dosage without checking with your doctor.

How taken

Tablets, injection.

Frequency and timing of doses
Every 4 hours as needed for pain.

Adult dosage range
50 – 150mg per dose.

Onset of effect
Within 1 hour (by mouth); within 15 minutes (by injection).

Duration of action
2 – 4 hours.

Diet advice
None.

Storage
Keep in a closed container in a cool, dry place away from reach of children.

Missed dose
Take only if required for pain relief.

Stopping the drug
If you have been given the drug for short-term pain relief it can be safely stopped as soon as you no longer need it. In other cases, discuss with your doctor.

OVERDOSE ACTION

 Seek immediate medical advice in all cases. Take emergency action if there are symptoms such as muscle twitching, nervousness, shallow breathing, severe drowsiness, or loss of consciousness.

See Drug poisoning emergency guide (p.470).

POSSIBLE ADVERSE EFFECTS

Adverse effects of pethidine are common but may wear off with continued use of the drug as your body adjusts.

Symptom/effect	Frequency		Discuss with doctor		Stop taking drug now	Call doctor now
	Common	Rare	Only if severe	In all cases		
Dizziness	●		■			
Nausea/vomiting	●		■			
Drowsiness	●		■			
Constipation		●	■			
Confusion/faintness	●			■		
Shortness of breath		●		■		■

INTERACTIONS

Phenothiazine tranquillizers Severe lowering of blood pressure can occur if these drugs are taken with pethidine.

Monoamine oxidase inhibitors (MAOIs) If taken within 14 days of these drugs, pethidine may cause dangerous toxic reactions.

Sedatives All drugs that have a sedative effect on the central nervous system may increase the sedative properties of pethidine.

SPECIAL PRECAUTIONS

Be sure to tell your doctor if:
▼ You have long-term liver or kidney problems.
▼ You have heart problems.
▼ You have had epileptic fits.
▼ You have a lung disorder such as asthma or bronchitis.
▼ You have a thyroid disorder.
▼ You have prostate problems.
▼ You are taking other medications.

 Pregnancy
▼ Not usually prescribed before the onset of labour. Safety in pregnancy not established. Pethidine is often used to relieve pain during labour, but is given with care as it may cause breathing difficulties in the newborn baby.

 Breast feeding
▼ The drug passes into the breast milk and may affect the baby. Discuss with your doctor.

 Infants and children
▼ Reduced dose necessary.

 Over 60
▼ Increased likelihood of sedation. Reduced dose may therefore be necessary.

 Driving and hazardous work
▼ It is unlikely that someone requiring this drug will be engaging in these activities.

 Alcohol
▼ Avoid. Alcohol may increase the sedative effects of this drug.

PROLONGED USE

The effects of the drug usually become weaker during prolonged use as the body adapts. It may also be habit-forming if taken for extended periods.

PHENELZINE

Brand name Nardil
Used in the following combined preparations None

GENERAL INFORMATION

Phenelzine belongs to a group of antidepressant drugs known as the monoamine oxidase inhibitors (MAOIs). These drugs elevate mood, improve appetite and sleep, and restore interest in life in general. Phenelzine is most commonly used to relieve depression, especially when accompanied by irrational fears (phobias), or exaggerated emotional reactions.

The main problem associated with the use of phenelzine is the risk of dangerous interactions with a wide range of other drugs and many foods. Since these interactions can be life-threatening, the drug is usually reserved for people who have not responded to all other types of antidepressant. People on phenelzine should carry a warning card.

INFORMATION FOR USERS

Your drug prescription is tailored for you. Do not alter dosage without checking with your doctor.

How taken

Tablets.

Frequency and timing of doses
1 – 4 x daily (occasionally on alternate days).

Adult dosage range
45 – 90mg daily (starting dose). When full benefit is felt, dosage is gradually reduced to a lower maintenance dose.

Onset of effect
1 – 4 weeks.

Duration of action
Up to 14 days after treatment is begun or discontinued.

Diet advice
Certain foods with a high tyramine content must be avoided while taking this drug and for at least 14 days after treatment finishes. When phenelzine is dispensed, the

pharmacist should provide a card listing foods and medicines to avoid. These include cheese, pickled herring, red wine, meat and yeast extracts, and broad bean pods.

Storage
Keep in a closed container in a cool, dry place away from reach of children.

Missed dose
Take as soon as you remember. If your next dose is due within 3 hours, take a single dose now and skip the next.

Stopping the drug
Do not stop the drug without consulting your doctor; symptoms may recur.

OVERDOSE ACTION

 Seek immediate medical advice in all cases. Symptoms may be delayed for many hours. Sweating, fever, and rigid muscles may occur. Take emergency action if breathing difficulty or collapse occur.

See Drug poisoning emergency guide (p.470).

SPECIAL PRECAUTIONS

Be sure to tell your doctor if:
▼ You have long-term liver problems.
▼ You have heart problems.
▼ You have diabetes.
▼ You have had epileptic fits.
▼ You have had a stroke.
▼ You are taking other medications.

 Pregnancy
▼ Safety in pregnancy not established. Discuss with your doctor.

 Breast feeding
▼ The drug passes into the breast milk, but at normal doses adverse effects on the baby are unlikely. Discuss with your doctor.

 Infants and children
▼ Not recommended.

 Over 60
▼ Used only when potential benefits outweigh risks. Increased likelihood of adverse effects.

 Driving and hazardous work
▼ Avoid such activities until you have learned how the drug affects you because of the possibility of loss of concentration, dizziness, drowsiness, and blurred vision.

 Alcohol
▼ Never drink heavy red wines, particularly chianti, when taking this drug. These may cause a dangerous reaction. Other forms of alcohol should also be avoided.

Surgery and general anaesthetics
▼ Phenelzine treatment should be withdrawn at least 2 weeks before general anaesthetics and some dental treatments. Discuss this with your doctor or dentist before any operation or dental procedure.

POSSIBLE ADVERSE EFFECTS

Phenelzine can cause a range of adverse effects. If you experience severe headache, nausea and/or vomiting, or unexplained sweating, seek medical advice at once. Such symptoms may be a sign of rising blood pressure.

Symptom/effect	Frequency		Discuss with doctor		Stop taking drug now	Call doctor now
	Common	Rare	Only if severe	In all cases		
Dizziness/fainting/drowsiness	●			■		
Dry mouth	●			■		
Blurred vision	●			■		
Difficulty in passing urine		●		■		
Jaundice		●		■	▲	▮
Rash		●		■	▲	

INTERACTIONS

General note Phenelzine interacts with a large number of prescription drugs, over-the-counter medicines, and foods. Do not

take **any** type of medicine without prior consultation with your doctor or pharmacist.

PHENOBARBITONE

Brand names Gardenal
Used in the following combined preparations None

GENERAL INFORMATION

Introduced over 70 years ago, pheno-barbitone belongs to the group of drugs known as barbiturates. It is mainly used in the treatment of epilepsy. Before the development of safer drugs, it was also used as a sleeping drug and sedative.

In the treatment of epilepsy, pheno-barbitone is often given together with other anticonvulsant drugs such as phenytoin.

The main disadvantage of pheno-barbitone is that it often causes unwanted sedation. However, in children and the elderly it may occasionally cause excessive excitement.

QUICK REFERENCE

Drug group Barbiturate anticonvulsant drug (p.86)
Overdose danger rating High
Dependence rating High
Prescription needed Yes
Available as generic Yes

INFORMATION FOR USERS

Your drug prescription is tailored for you. Do not alter dosage without checking with your doctor.

How taken

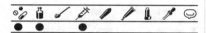

Tablets, liquid, injection.

Frequency and timing of doses
1 – 3 x daily.

Dosage range
Adults 60 – 180mg daily.

Onset of effect
30 – 60 minutes (by mouth).

Duration of action
24 – 48 hours (some effect may persist for up to 6 days).

Diet advice
None.

Storage
Keep in a closed container in a cool, dry place away from reach of children.

Missed dose
Take as soon as you remember. If you take once daily and the next dose is due within 10 hours, take a single dose now and skip the next. If you take 2 – 3 times daily and the next dose is due within 2 hours, take a single dose now and skip the next.

Stopping the drug
Do not stop taking the drug without consulting your doctor, who may supervise a gradual reduction in dosage. Abrupt cessation may cause fits, or lead to restlessness, trembling, and insomnia.

OVERDOSE ACTION

Seek immediate medical advice in all cases. Take emergency action if unsteadiness, severe weakness, confusion, or loss of consciousness occur.

See Drug poisoning emergency guide (p.470).

SPECIAL PRECAUTIONS

Be sure to tell your doctor if:
- ▼ You have long-term liver or kidney problems.
- ▼ You have heart problems.
- ▼ You have poor circulation.
- ▼ You have porphyria.
- ▼ You have breathing problems.
- ▼ You are taking other medications.

Pregnancy
▼ May affect the baby and increase the tendency of bleeding in the newborn. Discuss with your doctor.

Breast feeding
▼ The drug passes into the breast milk and could cause drowsiness in the baby. Discuss with your doctor.

Infants and children
▼ Reduced dose necessary.

Over 60
▼ Reduced dose may be necessary. Increased likelihood of confusion.

Driving and hazardous work
▼ Your underlying condition, as well as the possibility of reduced alertness while taking this drug, may make such activities inadvisable. Discuss with your doctor.

Alcohol
▼ Never drink while under treatment with phenobarbitone. Alcohol may interact dangerously with this drug.

POSSIBLE ADVERSE EFFECTS

Most of the adverse effects of pheno-barbitone are the result of its sedative effect.

They can sometimes be minimized by medically supervised reduction of dosage.

Symptom/effect	Frequency		Discuss with doctor		Stop taking drug now	Call doctor now
	Common	Rare	Only if severe	In all cases		
Drowsiness	●		■			
Clumsiness/unsteadiness	●		■			
Dizziness/faintness	●		■			
Confusion		●			■	
Rash/localized swellings		●			■	

INTERACTIONS

Sedatives All drugs that have a sedative effect on the central nervous system are likely to increase the sedative properties of phenobarbitone.

Corticosteroids Phenobarbitone may reduce the effect of corticosteroid drugs.

Anticoagulants The effect of these drugs may be reduced when they are taken with phenobarbitone.

Oral contraceptives Phenobarbitone may reduce the effectiveness of oral contraceptives. Discuss with your doctor.

PROLONGED USE

The sedative effect of phenobarbitone can build up during prolonged use, causing excessive drowsiness and lethargy. However, *tolerance* may develop, so reducing these effects.

Monitoring Blood samples may be taken periodically to test blood levels of the drug.

PHENOXYMETHYLPENICILLIN

Brand names Apsin, Distaquaine V-K, Stabillin V-K
Used in the following combined preparations None

GENERAL INFORMATION

Phenoxymethylpenicillin is a synthetic penicillin-type antibiotic prescribed for a wide range of infections.

Various commonly occurring respiratory tract infections – for example, some types of tonsillitis and pharyngitis, and ear infections – often respond well to phenoxymethylpenicillin. It is also effective for the treatment of the gum disease known as Vincent's gingivitis.

Less common infections caused by the Streptococcus bacterium, such as scarlet fever and erysipelas (a skin infection), may also be treated with phenoxymethylpenicillin. It is also prescribed long term to prevent the recurrence of rheumatic fever, a rare, though potentially serious condition.

As with other penicillin antibiotics, the most serious possible adverse effect that may rarely occur is an allergic reaction that may cause collapse, wheezing, and a rash in susceptible people.

QUICK REFERENCE

Drug group Penicillin antibiotic (p.128)

Overdose danger rating Low

Dependence rating Low

Prescription needed Yes

Available as generic Yes

INFORMATION FOR USERS

Your drug prescription is tailored for you. Do not alter dosage without checking with your doctor.

How taken

Tablets, liquid.

Frequency and timing of doses
2 – 4 x daily, at least 30 minutes before food.

Dosage range
Adults 1 – 2g daily.
Children Reduced dose according to age.

Onset of effect
1 – 2 days.

Duration of action
Up to 12 hours.

Diet advice
None.

Storage
Keep in a closed container in a cool, dry place away from reach of children.

Missed dose
Take as soon as you remember. If your next dose is due within 2 hours, take a single dose now and skip the next.

Stopping the drug
Take the full course. Even if you feel better the original infection may still be present and may recur if treatment is stopped too soon.

Exceeding the dose
An occasional unintentional extra dose is unlikely to be a cause for concern. But if you notice unusual symptoms, or if a large overdose has been taken, notify your doctor.

SPECIAL PRECAUTIONS

Be sure to tell your doctor if:
▼ You have a long-term kidney problem.
▼ You have had a previous allergic reaction to a penicillin or cephalosporin antibiotic.
▼ You have an allergic disorder such as asthma or urticaria.
▼ You are taking other medications.

Pregnancy
▼ No evidence of risk.

Breast feeding
▼ The drug passes into the breast milk, but at normal doses adverse effects on the baby are unlikely. Discuss with your doctor.

Infants and children
▼ Reduced dose necessary.

Over 60
▼ No special problems.

Driving and hazardous work
▼ No known problems.

Alcohol
▼ No known problems.

POSSIBLE ADVERSE EFFECTS

Most people do not experience any serious adverse effects when taking phenoxymethyl-penicillin. However, this drug may provoke an allergic reaction in susceptible people.

Symptom/effect	Frequency		Discuss with doctor		Stop taking drug now	Call doctor now
	Common	Rare	Only if severe	In all cases		
Nausea/vomiting	●		■			
Diarrhoea	●		■			
Rash/itching		●		■	▲	▮
Breathing difficulties		●		■	▲	▮

INTERACTIONS

Probenecid Probenecid increases the level of phenoxymethylpenicillin in the blood.

Tetracycline antibiotics may reduce the effectiveness of phenoxymethylpenicillin.

Oral contraceptives
Phenoxymethylpenicillin may reduce the contraceptive effect of these drugs.

PROLONGED USE

Prolonged use may increase the risk of Candida infections and diarrhoea.

PHENYLBUTAZONE

Brand names Butacote
Used in the following combined preparation None

GENERAL INFORMATION

Phenylbutazone is one of the oldest (and strongest) non-steroidal antiinflammatory drugs (NSAIDs).

Formerly used to treat a variety of arthritic conditions, including rheumatoid arthritis, it is now prescribed only for reducing pain, stiffness, and inflammation in the treatment of ankylosing spondylitis when other forms of treatment have been found unsuitable.

Phenylbutazone has several potentially serious adverse effects, including a rare risk of blood disorders. For this reason it is prescribed only under specialist supervision in hospital where monitoring facilities are available.

QUICK REFERENCE

Drug group Non-steroidal anti-inflammatory drug (p.116)
Overdose danger rating High
Dependence rating Low
Prescription needed Yes
Available as generic No

INFORMATION FOR USERS

Your drug prescription is tailored for you. Do not alter dosage without checking with your doctor.

How taken

Tablets.

Frequency and timing of doses
2 – 3 x daily swallowed whole after food.

Adult dosage range
200 – 600mg daily.

Onset of effect
Pain relief may be noticed after 2 hours. Full beneficial effect may not be felt for 3 – 4 days.

Duration of action
Some effect may last for 3 – 4 days.

Diet advice
None.

Storage
Keep in a closed container in a cool, dry place away from reach of children.

Missed dose
Take as soon as you remember. If your next dose is due within 2 hours, take a single dose now and skip the next.

Stopping the drug
Can be safely stopped as soon as you no longer need it.

OVERDOSE ACTION

Seek immediate medical advice in all cases. Take emergency action if fits or loss of consciousness occur.

See Drug poisoning emergency guide (p.470).

SPECIAL PRECAUTIONS

Be sure to tell your doctor if:
▼ You have liver or kidney problems.
▼ You have heart problems.
▼ You have high blood pressure.
▼ You have had a blood disorder.
▼ You have thyroid disease.
▼ You have had a peptic ulcer, oesophagitis or acid indigestion.
▼ You are allergic to aspirin.
▼ You are taking other medications.

 Pregnancy
▼ Not usually prescribed. When taken in the last 3 months of pregnancy, may cause adverse effects on the baby's heart and prolong labour. Discuss with your doctor.

 Breast feeding
▼ The drug passes into the breast milk and may affect the baby. Discuss with your doctor.

 Infants and children
▼ Not recommended under 14 years.

 Over 60
▼ Increased likelihood of adverse effects. Reduced dose may therefore be necessary.

 Driving and hazardous work
▼ No special problems.

 Alcohol
▼ Avoid. Alcohol may increase the risk of stomach irritation with phenylbutazone.

Surgery and general anaesthetics
▼ Phenylbutazone may prolong bleeding. Discuss this with your doctor or dentist before any surgery.

POSSIBLE ADVERSE EFFECTS

Nausea, water retention, and rashes may occur. Black or bloodstained bowel movements, sore throat, or fever should be reported to your doctor without delay.

Symptom/effect	Frequency		Discuss with doctor		Stop taking drug now	Call doctor now
	Common	Rare	Only if severe	In all cases		
Nausea/vomiting		●		■		
Abdominal pain	●				■	
Swollen feet/ankles	●				■	
Rash/bruising/mouth ulcers		●		■	▲	▮
Fever/sore throat		●		■	▲	▮
Wheezing/breathlessness		●		■	▲	▮

INTERACTIONS

General note Phenylbutazone interacts with a wide range of drugs to increase the risk of bleeding and/or peptic ulcers. Such drugs include oral anticoagulants, corticosteroids, and aspirin.

Lithium Phenylbutazone may raise blood levels of lithium.

Antihypertensive drugs and diuretics The beneficial effects of these drugs may be reduced by phenylbutazone.

Oral antidiabetics Phenylbutazone may increase the blood sugar lowering effect of these drugs.

PROLONGED USE

Blood disorders may occur during long-term use.

Monitoring Regular blood tests are carried out.

PHENYLEPHRINE

Brand names Minims phenylephrine
Used in the following combined preparations Betnovate-Rectal, Dimotapp, Isoptofrin, Uniflu, Vibrocil

GENERAL INFORMATION

Phenylephrine is one of the most common nasal decongestants, and is included in a variety of *topical* preparations to relieve the symptoms of hay fever and head colds. It is also included as an ingredient in some tablets used to relieve the symptoms of colds and flu.

By constricting blood vessels in the lining of the eye, small doses of the drug can also reduce the pain of conjunctivitis. Phenylephrine is also used to dilate the pupil during eye examinations and eye surgery.

Care should be taken not to exceed the dose, because this may cause increased eye irritation (eye drops) and produce congestion and swelling in the nasal passages. High or prolonged doses of phenylephrine are liable to cause a rebound of nasal stuffiness and a rise in blood pressure and heart rate, and should be avoided by people with heart trouble or high blood pressure.

QUICK REFERENCE

Drug group Decongestant (p.93)
Overdose danger rating Medium
Dependence rating Low
Prescription needed No
Available as generic Yes

INFORMATION FOR USERS

Your drug prescription is tailored for you. Do not alter dosage without checking with your doctor.

How taken

Tablets, injection, nasal drops, spray, eye drops.

Frequency and timing of doses
As directed according to the preparation.

Dosage range
As directed according to preparation.

Onset of effect
Within a few minutes.

Duration of action
4 – 6 hours.

Diet advice
None.

Storage
Keep in a closed container in a cool, dry place away from reach of children. Protect from light.

Missed dose
Take as soon as you remember. If your next dose is due within 2 hours, take a single dose now and skip the next.

Stopping the drug
Can be safely stopped as soon as you no longer need it.

Exceeding the dose
An occasional unintentional extra dose is unlikely to cause problems. Large overdoses may cause irritation of the eyes or palpitations. Notify your doctor.

SPECIAL PRECAUTIONS

Be sure to tell your doctor or pharmacist if:
▼ You have angina or another heart problem.
▼ You have diabetes.
▼ You have asthma.
▼ You have high blood pressure.
▼ You have had glaucoma.
▼ You are taking other medications.

Pregnancy
▼ Not usually prescribed. Discuss with your doctor.

Breast feeding
▼ The drug passes into the breast milk but at normal doses adverse effects on the baby are unlikely. Discuss with your doctor.

Infants and children
▼ Not usually recommended in infants.

Over 60
▼ Increased likelihood of adverse effects. Reduced dose may therefore be necessary.

Driving and hazardous work
▼ Avoid such activities until you have learned how the drug affects you because when used in the eye the drug can cause blurred vision.

Alcohol
▼ No known problems.

POSSIBLE ADVERSE EFFECTS

Phenylephrine has fewer adverse effects than many other drugs of the same group because it has little stimulating effect on the central nervous system. Most of the symptoms are related to frequent use, and should be reported promptly.

Symptom/effect	Frequency		Discuss with doctor		Stop taking drug now	Call doctor now
	Common	Rare	Only if severe	In all cases		
Blurred vision	●			■		
Headache	●			■		
Rebound nasal stuffiness	●			■		
Eye pain (eye drops)		●		■	▲	
Chest pain		●		■	▲	▮
Palpitations		●		■	▲	▮

INTERACTIONS

Monoamine oxidase inhibitors (MAOIs)
There is a risk of a dangerous rise in blood pressure if phenylephrine is used with these drugs. It should not be taken during or within 14 days of MAOI treatment.

Antihypertensive drugs Phenylephrine may interact with these drugs to reverse their effect.

PROLONGED USE

Prolonged continuous use should be avoided because a rebound of symptoms may occur on stopping.

PHENYLPROPANOLAMINE

Used in the following combined preparations Contac 400, Day Nurse Capsules, Dimotapp, Eskornade, Mucron, Sinutab, Triogesic, Triominic, Vicks Coldcare, and others.

GENERAL INFORMATION

Phenylpropanolamine belongs to a group of drugs known as *sympatho-mimetics*. It is used as a decongestant in many over-the-counter cold relief preparations. By reducing inflammation and swelling of blood vessels in the nose, it relieves nasal congestion in colds, hay fever, and sinusitis.

Phenylpropanolamine mimics some of the actions of the sympathetic nervous system (p.75), and as a consequence it can produce undesir-able stimulant side effects. It may raise the heart rate and severely elevate blood pressure; and can also cause palpitations and wakefulness.

QUICK REFERENCE

Drug group Decongestant (p.93)
Overdose danger rating High
Dependence rating Low
Prescription needed No
Available as generic No

INFORMATION FOR USERS

Follow instructions on the label. Call your doctor if symptoms worsen.

How taken

Tablets, SR-tablets, capsules, liquid.

Frequency and timing of doses
3 – 4 x daily; twice daily (slow-release).

Dosage range
75 – 100mg daily.

Onset of effect
Within 30 minutes.

Duration of action
4 – 6 hours. Up to 12 hours (slow-release preparations).

Diet advice
None.

Storage
Keep in a closed container in a cool, dry place away from reach of children. Protect from light.

Missed dose
Take as soon as you remember if needed. If you take the medication twice daily, and your next dose is due within 12 hours, take a single dose now and skip the next. If you take 3 – 4 times daily and your next dose is due within 2 hours, take a single dose now and skip the next.

Stopping the drug
Can be safely stopped as soon as you no longer need it.

OVERDOSE ACTION

Seek immediate medical advice in all cases. Take emergency action if delirium, convulsions, or loss of consciousness occur.

See Drug poisoning emergency guide (p.470).

POSSIBLE ADVERSE EFFECTS

High doses may be associated with anxiety, nausea, dizziness, and, rarely, with a marked rise in blood pressure, causing palpitations, headache, and breathlessness.

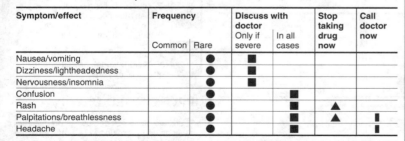

Symptom/effect	Frequency		Discuss with doctor		Stop taking drug now	Call doctor now
	Common	Rare	Only if severe	In all cases		
Nausea/vomiting		●	■			
Dizziness/lightheadedness		●	■			
Nervousness/insomnia		●	■			
Confusion		●		■		
Rash		●		■	▲	
Palpitations/breathlessness		●		■	▲	■
Headache		●		■		■

INTERACTIONS

Other sympathomimetics increase the risk of adverse effects with this drug.

Beta blockers A severe rise in blood pressure can occur if beta blockers are taken.

Monoamine oxidase inhibitors (MAOIs) dangerously increase the risk of high blood pressure with phenylpropano-lamine. It should not be taken during or within 14 days following MAOI treatment.

SPECIAL PRECAUTIONS

Be sure to consult your doctor or pharmacist before taking this drug if:
▼ You have high blood pressure.
▼ You have heart problems.
▼ You have had glaucoma.
▼ You have an overactive thyroid gland.
▼ You have diabetes.
▼ You have urinary difficulties.
▼ You are taking other medications.

 Pregnancy
▼ Safety in pregnancy not established. Discuss with your doctor.

 Breast feeding
▼ The drug passes into the breast milk and may affect the baby. Discuss with your doctor.

 Infants and children
▼ Not recommended for children under 8 years.

 Over 60
▼ Increased likelihood of adverse effects. Reduced dose may therefore be necessary.

 Driving and hazardous work
▼ Do not undertake such activities until you know how the drug affects you because it may cause dizziness.

 Alcohol
▼ No known problems.

PROLONGED USE

Phenylpropanolamine should not be taken for long periods without medical supervision because it may raise the blood pressure and put a strain on the heart.

PHENYTOIN

Brand name Epanutin, Pentran
Used in the following combined preparations None

GENERAL INFORMATION

By reducing abnormal electrical discharges within the brain, phenytoin reduces the likelihood of convulsions. Introduced in the 1930s, it has been widely prescribed for the long-term treatment of epilepsy, including grand mal and temporal lobe epilepsy.

Over the years, various other uses for phenytoin have been found: for migraine, trigeminal neuralgia, and for the correction of certain abnormal heart rhythms.

Because some adverse effects of phenytoin (such as overgrowth of the gums) are more pronounced in children, it is prescribed for children only when other drugs are unsuitable, and is avoided if possible in young women because it can affect a developing baby.

INFORMATION FOR USERS

Your drug prescription is tailored for you. Do not alter dosage without checking with your doctor.

How taken

Tablets, capsules, liquid, injection, chewable tablets.

Frequency and timing of doses
1 – 3 x daily with food or water.

Dosage range
Adults 150 – 600mg daily.
Children According to age and weight.

Onset of effect
Full anticonvulsant effect may not be felt for 7 – 10 days.

Duration of action
24 hours.

Diet advice
Folic acid and vitamin D deficiency may occasionally occur while taking this drug. Make sure you eat a balanced diet containing fresh, green vegetables.

Storage
Keep in a tightly closed container in a cool, dry place away from reach of children.

Missed dose
Take as soon as you remember.

Stopping the drug
Do not stop the drug without consulting your doctor; symptoms may recur.

Exceeding the dose
An occasional unintentional extra dose is unlikely to cause problems. You may notice unusual drowsiness, slurred speech, or confusion. Notify your doctor.

SPECIAL PRECAUTIONS

Be sure to tell your doctor if:
▼ You have long-term liver or kidney problems.
▼ You have diabetes.
▼ You have porphyria.
▼ You are taking other medications.

Pregnancy
▼ May be associated with malformation and a tendency to bleeding in the newborn baby. Folate supplements should be taken by the mother. Discuss with your doctor.

Breast feeding
▼ The drug passes into breast milk, but at normal doses adverse effects on the baby are unlikely. Discuss with your doctor.

Infants and children
▼ Reduced dose necessary. Increased likelihood of overgrowth of the gums and excessive growth of body hair.

Over 60
▼ Reduced dose may be necessary.

Driving and hazardous work
▼ Your underlying condition, as well as the effects of this drug, may make such activities inadvisable. Discuss with your doctor.

Alcohol
▼ Avoid. Alcohol may alter the effects of this drug.

POSSIBLE ADVERSE EFFECTS

Phenytoin has a number of adverse effects, many of which only appear after prolonged use. If they become severe, your doctor may prescribe a different anticonvulsant.

Symptom/effect	Frequency		Discuss with doctor		Stop taking drug now	Call doctor now
	Common	Rare	Only if severe	In all cases		
Dizziness/headache	●		■			
Confusion	●		■			
Nausea/vomiting	●		■			
Insomnia	●		■			
Overgrowth of gums		●		■		
Increased body hair		●	■			
Rash		●		■		

INTERACTIONS

General note Many drugs may interact with phenytoin, causing either an increase or a reduction in the blood level of phenytoin. The dosage of phenytoin may need to be adjusted while you are taking other medications. Consult your doctor.

Warfarin The anticoagulant effect of warfarin may be altered. Dosage adjustment may be necessary.

Oral contraceptives Phenytoin may reduce the effectiveness of oral contraceptives. A higher dose contraceptive is usually required. Oral contraceptives may also make phenytoin less effective as an anticonvulsant.

Cyclosporin The levels of cyclosporin in the blood may be reduced.

PROLONGED USE

There is a slight risk of blood abnormalities occurring. Prolonged use may also lead to adverse effects on skin, gums, and bones. It may also disrupt control of diabetes.

Monitoring Periodic blood tests may be performed to monitor levels of the drug in the body and composition of the blood cells and chemistry.

PILOCARPINE

Brand names Minims pilocarpine, Ocusert Pilo, Sno Pilo
Used in the following combined preparation Isopto Carpine

GENERAL INFORMATION

Pilocarpine, in use since 1875, is a pupil-constricting drug (miotic) used to treat glaucoma. Obtained from the leaves of a plant, *Pilocarpus*, it is frequently prescribed for chronic glaucoma and, less often, for emergency treatment of severe glaucoma prior to surgery. It may also be given to counteract the dilation of the pupil induced by drugs given during surgery or eye examination.

It is prescribed most frequently in the form of eye drops. These are quick-acting but have to be re-applied every four to eight hours in chronic glaucoma. A slow-release formulation inserted under the eyelid (Ocusert), once weekly, may be more convenient for long-term use.

Like other similar drugs, pilocarpine frequently causes blurred vision. Excessive spasm of eye muscles may cause headaches, particularly at the start of treatment. However, serious adverse effects are rare.

QUICK REFERENCE

Drug group Miotic drug for glaucoma (p.168)

Overdose danger rating Medium

Dependence rating Low

Prescription needed Yes

Available as generic Yes

INFORMATION FOR USERS

Your drug prescription is tailored for you. Do not alter dosage without checking with your doctor.

How taken

Eye drops, slow-release inserts (Ocuserts).

Frequency and timing of doses
Eye drops 3 – 6 x daily (chronic glaucoma). In acute glaucoma, pilocarpine is given at 5 minute intervals until the condition is controlled.
Ocusert Once every 7 days at bedtime.

Dosage range
According to formulation and condition. In general, 1 – 2 eye drops are used per application.

Onset of effect
15 – 30 minutes.

Duration of action
3 – 8 hours (eye drops); about 7 days (Ocusert).

Diet advice
None.

Storage
Keep in a closed container in a cool, dry place away from reach of children (eye drops). Discard eye drops 1 month after opening.

Missed dose
Use as soon as you remember. If not remembered until 2 hours before your next dose (eye drops), skip the missed dose and take your next dose now.

Stopping the drug
Do not stop the drug without consulting your doctor; symptoms may recur.

Exceeding the dose
An occasional unintentional extra application is unlikely to cause problems. Excessive use may cause facial flushing, an increase in the flow of saliva, and sweating. If accidentally swallowed, seek medical attention immediately.

SPECIAL PRECAUTIONS

Be sure to tell your doctor if:
▼ You have asthma.
▼ You have inflamed eyes.
▼ You wear contact lenses.
▼ You are taking other medications.

Pregnancy
▼ No evidence of risk at the doses used for chronic glaucoma.

Breast feeding
▼ The drug passes into the breast milk, but at normal doses adverse effects on the baby are unlikely. Discuss with your doctor.

Infants and children
▼ Not usually prescribed.

Over 60
▼ Reduced night vision is particularly noticeable.

Driving and hazardous work
▼ Avoid such activities, especially in poor light, until you have learned how the drug affects you because the drug may cause nearsightedness and poor night vision.

Alcohol
▼ No known problems.

POSSIBLE ADVERSE EFFECTS

Alteration in vision is common. Ocuserts may cause irritation if they move out of position. Brow ache and eye pain are common at the start of treatment, but usually wear off after a few days.

Symptom/effect	Frequency		Discuss with doctor		Stop taking drug now	Call doctor now
	Common	Rare	Only if severe	In all cases		
Blurred vision	●		■			
Poor night vision	●		■			
Headache/brow ache	●		■			
Eye pain/irritation	●			■		▮
Twitching eye lids		●		■		
Red/watery eyes		●	■			

PROLONGED USE

The effect of the drug may occasionally wear off with prolonged use as the body adapts, but may be restored by changing temporarily to another antiglaucoma drug.

INTERACTIONS

None.

PIPERAZINE

Brand names Expelix
Used in the following combined preparation Pripsen

GENERAL INFORMATION

Piperazine is a drug used to treat infestation of the gastrointestinal tract by threadworms or roundworms. It works by paralysing the worms so that they can be eliminated from the body.

Roundworm infestation is usually cleared by a single dose. A laxative may be given by mouth or enema to speed the expulsion of the worms.

Threadworm infestation may require seven days' treatment accompanied by scrupulous attention to personal hygiene to reduce the risk of reinfection. All members of the family are usually treated. A further course may be prescribed after a week.

Adverse effects from this drug are uncommon, and it is safe for both adults and children. Piperazine is available without prescription, but worm infestations are best treated under medical supervision.

QUICK REFERENCE

Drug group Anthelmintic (p.139)
Overdose danger rating Medium
Dependence rating Low
Prescription needed No
Available as generic Yes

INFORMATION FOR USERS

Follow instructions on the label. Call your doctor if symptoms worsen.

How taken

Liquid, powder.

Frequency and timing of doses
Roundworm A single dose.
Threadworm Once daily for 7 days (sometimes taken as a single dose).

Adult dosage range
Roundworm 4g per dose.
Threadworm 2g per dose (4g if taken as a single dose).

Onset of effect
Roundworm infestations may be cleared within 24 hours. Threadworms may take several days to eliminate.

Duration of action
24 – 48 hours.

Diet advice
None.

Storage
Keep in a closed container in a cool, dry place away from reach of children.

Missed dose
Take as soon as you remember. If your next dose is due within 4 hours, take a single dose now and skip the next.

Stopping the drug
Take the full course. Even if you have no symptoms, the worms may still be present and symptoms may recur if treatment is stopped too soon.

Exceeding the dose
An occasional unintentional extra dose is unlikely to cause problems. Large overdoses may cause dizziness, drowsiness, and abdominal pain. Notify your doctor.

SPECIAL PRECAUTIONS

Be sure to consult your doctor or pharmacist before taking this drug if:
▼ You have long-term liver or kidney problems.
▼ You have had epileptic fits.
▼ You have had a mental illness.
▼ You have a nervous system disease.
▼ You are taking other medications.

Pregnancy
▼ Safety in pregnancy not established. Discuss with your doctor.

Breast feeding
▼ The drug may pass into the breast milk, but at normal doses adverse effects on the baby are unlikely. Discuss with your doctor.

Infants and children
▼ Reduced dose necessary.

Over 60
▼ No special problems.

Driving and hazardous work
▼ Avoid such activities until you have learned how the drug affects you because the drug can cause dizziness and loss of coordination.

Alcohol
▼ No special problems.

POSSIBLE ADVERSE EFFECTS

Adverse effects are rare when piperazine is taken at the recommended doses.

Symptom/effect	Frequency		Discuss with doctor		Stop taking drug now	Call doctor now
	Common	Rare	Only if severe	In all cases		
Abdominal pain		●	■			
Nausea/vomiting		●	■			
Diarrhoea		●	■			
Dizziness		●	■			
Loss of coordination		●	■			
Drowsiness/confusion		●	■			
Rash/itching		●		■		

INTERACTIONS

Phenothiazine antipsychotic drugs
Piperazine increases the risk of abnormal movements with these drugs.

PROLONGED USE

Not usually prescribed continuously for longer than 7 days. You may be advised to repeat the course after a week or longer.

PIROXICAM

Brand name Feldene, Larapram, Pirozip
Used in the following combined preparations None

GENERAL INFORMATION

Piroxicam, introduced in 1980, is a non-steroidal anti-inflammatory drug (NSAID). Like other drugs of this group, it reduces pain, stiffness, and inflammation. Blood levels of the drug remain high for many hours after a dose, so that it need only be taken once daily.

It is prescribed for rheumatoid arthritis, osteoarthritis, ankylosing spondylitis, and acute attacks of gout. Although it gives lasting relief of the symptoms of arthritis, it does not cure the disease. It is sometimes prescribed in conjunction with slow-acting drugs in rheumatoid arthritis to relieve pain and inflammation while these drugs take effect. It may be given for pain relief in bursitis and tendinitis or after minor surgery.

It is less likely than aspirin to cause stomach ulcers and is generally considered safe for long-tem use.

QUICK REFERENCE

Drug group Non-steroidal anti-inflammatory drug (p.116) and drug for gout (p.119)

Overdose danger rating Medium

Dependence rating Low

Prescription needed Yes

Available as generic Yes

INFORMATION FOR USERS

Your drug prescription is tailored for you. Do not alter dosage without checking with your doctor.

How taken

Tablets, capsules, injection, suppositories, gel.

Frequency and timing of doses
1 – 3 x daily with food.

Adult dosage range
10 – 40mg daily.

Onset of effect
Pain relief begins in 3 – 4 hours. Used for arthritis, the full anti-inflammatory effect develops over 2 – 4 weeks. Used for gout, this effect develops over 4 – 5 days.

Duration of action
Up to 2 days. Some effect may last for 7 – 10 days after treatment has been stopped.

Diet advice
None.

Storage
Keep in a closed container in a cool, dry place away from reach of children. Protect from light.

Missed dose
Take as soon as you remember. If your next dose is due within 4 hours, take a single dose now and skip the next.

Stopping the drug
When taken for short-term pain relief, piroxicam can be safely stopped as soon as you no longer need it. If prescribed for the long-term treatment of arthritis, however, you should seek medical advice before stopping the drug.

Exceeding the dose
An occasional unintentional extra dose is unlikely to cause problems. Large overdoses may cause nausea and vomiting. Notify your doctor.

SPECIAL PRECAUTIONS

Be sure to tell your doctor if:
▼ You have liver or kidney problems.
▼ You have heart problems.
▼ You have had a peptic ulcer, oesophagitis, or acid indigestion.
▼ You have porphyria.
▼ You have asthma.
▼ You are allergic to aspirin.
▼ You are taking other medications.

 Pregnancy
▼ Not usually prescribed. When taken in the last three months of pregnancy, may increase the risk of adverse effects on the baby's heart and may prolong labour. Discuss with your doctor.

 Breast feeding
▼ The drug passes into the breast milk, but at normal doses adverse effects are unlikely. Discuss with your doctor.

 Infants and children
▼ Not recommended in children under 6 years. Reduced dose necessary.

 Over 60
▼ Increased likelihood of adverse effects. Reduced dose may therefore be necessary.

 Driving and hazardous work
▼ Avoid such activities until you have learned how the drug affects you because it can cause dizziness.

 Alcohol
▼ Avoid. Alcohol may increase the risk of stomach disorders with piroxicam.

Surgery and general anaesthetics
▼ Piroxicam may prolong bleeding. Discuss this with your doctor or dentist before any surgery.

POSSIBLE ADVERSE EFFECTS

Gastrointestinal side effects, dizziness, and headache are not generally serious. Black or bloodstained bowel movements should be reported to your doctor immediately.

Symptom/effect	Frequency		Discuss with doctor		Stop taking drug now	Call doctor now
	Common	Rare	Only if severe	In all cases		
Nausea/indigestion	●		■			
Abdominal pain	●			■		
Dizziness/headache		●	■			
Swollen feet/ankles		●		■		
Rash/itching		●		■	▲	
Wheezing /breathlessness		●		■	▲	■

INTERACTIONS

General note Piroxicam interacts with a wide range of drugs to increase the risk of bleeding and/or peptic ulcers. Such drugs include oral anticoagulants, corticosteroids, other non-steroidal anti-inflammatory drugs (NSAIDs), and aspirin.

Lithium Piroxicam may raise blood levels of lithium.

Antihypertensive drugs and diuretics The beneficial effects of these drugs may be reduced by piroxicam.

PROLONGED USE

There is an increased risk of bleeding from peptic ulcers and in the bowel with prolonged use of piroxicam.

PIZOTIFEN

Brand name Sanomigran
Used in the following combined preparations None

GENERAL INFORMATION

Pizotifen is an antihistamine drug that has a chemical structure similar to that of the tricyclic antidepressants (p.84) and also has similar *anticholinergic* effects. It is used to prevent migraine headaches in people who suffer frequent, disabling attacks. The exact mechanism by which it works is not known, but it is thought to be due to its blocking action on chemicals (histamine and serotonin) that act on the blood vessels in the brain.

Pizotifen has also been used to relieve the symptoms of carcinoid syndrome, a disorder in which excess production of serotonin causes attacks of flushing and diarrhoea.

The main disadvantage of prolonged use of pizotifen is that it stimulates appetite, and as a result often causes weight gain. It is usually prescribed only for people for whom other measures for the prevention of migraine – for example, avoidance of stress and foods that trigger attacks – have failed.

QUICK REFERENCE

Drug group Drug for migraine (p.89)

Overdose danger rating Medium

Dependence rating Low

Prescription needed Yes

Available as generic No

INFORMATION FOR USERS

Your drug prescription is tailored for you. Do not alter dosage without checking with your doctor.

How taken

Tablets, liquid.

Frequency and timing of doses
Once at night or 3 x daily.

Adult dosage range
1.5 – 4.5mg daily. Maximum single dose 3mg.

Onset of effect
Full beneficial effects may not be felt for several days.

Duration of action
Effects of this drug may last for several weeks.

Diet advice
Migraine sufferers may be advised to avoid foods that trigger headaches in their case.

Storage
Keep in a closed container in a cool, dry place away from reach of children. Protect from light.

Missed dose
Take as soon as you remember. If your next dose is due within 4 hours, take a single dose now and skip the next.

Stopping the drug
Do not stop the drug without consulting your doctor; symptoms may recur.

Exceeding the dose
An occasional unintentional extra dose is unlikely to cause problems. Large overdoses may cause drowsiness, nausea, palpitations, and fits. Notify your doctor.

SPECIAL PRECAUTIONS

Be sure to tell your doctor if:
▼ You have a long-term kidney problem.
▼ You have glaucoma.
▼ You have prostate trouble.
▼ You are taking other medications.

Pregnancy
▼ Safety in pregnancy not established. Discuss with your doctor.

Breast feeding
▼ The drug passes into the breast milk, but at normal doses adverse effects on the baby are unlikely. Discuss with your doctor.

Infants and children
▼ Reduced dose usually necessary.

Over 60
▼ No special problems.

Driving and hazardous work
▼ Avoid such activities until you have learned how the drug affects you because it can cause drowsiness.

Alcohol
▼ Avoid. Alcohol may increase the sedative effects of this drug.

POSSIBLE ADVERSE EFFECTS

Drowsiness, a common adverse effect, can often be minimized by starting with a low dose that is gradually increased.

Symptom/effect	Frequency		Discuss with doctor		Stop taking drug now	Call doctor now
	Common	Rare	Only if severe	In all cases		
Weight gain/increased appetite	●		■			
Drowsiness	●		■			
Nausea/dizziness		●	■			
Muscle pains		●	■			
Dry mouth		●	■			
Blurred vision		●	■			

INTERACTIONS

Anticholinergic drugs The weak anticholinergic effects of pizotifen may be increased by other anticholinergic drugs including tricyclic antidepressants.

Monoamine oxidase inhibitors (MAOIs) A dangerous rise in blood pressure may occur if pizotifen is taken with these drugs.

Sedatives All drugs that have a sedative effect on the central nervous system are likely to increase the sedative properties of pizotifen. These include sleeping drugs, anti-anxiety drugs, narcotic analgesics, and antihistamines.

PROLONGED USE

Pizotifen often causes weight gain during long-term use.

PRAZOSIN

Brand name Alphavase, Hypovase
Used in the following combined preparations None

GENERAL INFORMATION

Prazosin is an antihypertensive drug that relieves high blood pressure by relaxing the muscles in the walls of the blood vessels, dilating them, and easing the flow of blood. For the same reason, it is also sometimes given to those suffering from Raynaud's disease, characterized by poor circulation to the hands and feet. In moderate to severe high blood pressure, it may be given with beta blockers or other antihypertensive drugs. Another use for prazosin, when it is given in low doses, is to relieve symptoms caused by an enlarged prostate gland.

Dizziness and fainting are common at the onset of treatment with prazosin because the first dose may cause a dramatic drop in blood pressure. For this reason the initial dose is usually low and given when the person is lying down. Dosage levels may later be increased as necesssary.

INFORMATION FOR USERS

Your drug prescription is tailored for you. Do not alter dosage without checking with your doctor.

How taken

Tablets.

Frequency and timing of doses
2 – 3 x daily.

Adult dosage range
High blood pressure 0.5mg (starting dose), increased as necessary to 20mg daily.
Enlarged prostate up to 4mg daily.

Onset of effect
Within 2 hours.

Duration of action
6 – 8 hours.

Diet advice
None.

Storage
Keep in a closed container in a cool, dry place away from reach of children.

Missed dose
Take as soon as you remember. If your next dose is due within 2 hours, take a single dose now and skip the next.

Stopping the drug
Do not stop taking the drug without consulting your doctor; stopping the drug may lead to a rise in blood pressure.

Exceeding the dose
An occasional unintentional extra dose is unlikely to cause problems. Large overdoses may cause dizziness or fainting. Notify your doctor.

SPECIAL PRECAUTIONS

Be sure to tell your doctor if:
▼ You have long-term liver or kidney problems.
▼ You are taking other medications.

 Pregnancy
▼ Safety in pregnancy not established. Discuss with your doctor.

 Breast feeding
▼ The drug passes into the breast milk, but at normal doses adverse effects on the baby are unlikely. Discuss with your doctor.

 Infants and children
▼ Not recommended in children under 12.

 Over 60
▼ Reduced dose may be necessary.

 Driving and hazardous work
▼ Avoid such activities until you have learned how the drug affects you because the drug can cause drowsiness, dizziness, and fainting.

 Alcohol
▼ Avoid. Alcohol may increase the adverse effects of this drug.

POSSIBLE ADVERSE EFFECTS

Prazosin may cause dizziness and fainting on rising, so it is important that the first dose is taken at bedtime. You should remain in bed for at least 3 hours after taking the drug. Some of the minor symptoms, such as headache and nausea, will diminish with long-term therapy, although this may take up to 3 months.

Symptom/effect	Frequency		Discuss with doctor		Stop taking drug now	Call doctor now
	Common	Rare	Only if severe	In all cases		
Nausea	●		■			
Headache	●		■			
Dizziness/faintness	●		■			
Weakness/drowsiness	●		■			
Dry mouth		●	■			
Stuffy nose		●	■			
Rash		●		■		

PROLONGED USE

No problems expected.

INTERACTIONS

Diuretics Diuretics enhance the blood pressure lowering effect of prazosin.

Beta blockers Beta blockers may enhance the blood pressure lowering effect of prazosin.

PREDNISOLONE

Brand names Deltacortril, Deltastab, Minims prednisolone, Precortisyl, Predenema, Predfoam, Prednesol, Predsol, Pred Forte
Used in the following combined preparations Predsol-N, Scheriproct

GENERAL INFORMATION

Prednisolone is a powerful corticosteroid. It is given by mouth and by injection for a wide range of conditions, including rheumatic disorders, certain skin diseases, allergic states, and some blood disorders. Given as eye drops, it reduces eye inflammation in conjunctivitis or iritis. Prednisolone enemas may be given to treat inflammatory bowel disease. The drug can be injected into joints to relieve rheumatoid and other forms of arthritis.

With fludrocortisone, prednisolone is also prescribed for pituitary or adrenal gland disorders.

Low doses taken short term by mouth or topical applications rarely cause serious side effects. However, long-term treatment with large doses can cause fluid retention, indigestion, acne, hypertension, and diabetes. Enteric coated tablets reduce the effects on the stomach.

INFORMATION FOR USERS

Your drug prescription is tailored for you. Do not alter dosage without checking with your doctor.

How taken

Tablets, injection, suppositories, enema, foam, eye and ear drops.

Frequency and timing of doses
1 – 2 x daily or on alternate days (tablets/injection); 2 – 4 x daily, more frequently initially (eye/ear drops).

Adult dosage range
Considerable variation. Follow your doctor's instructions.

Onset of effect
2 – 4 days.

Duration of action
12 – 72 hours.

Diet advice
A low sodium and high potassium diet is recommended when the oral or injected form of the drug is prescribed for extended periods. Follow the advice of your doctor.

Storage
Keep in a closed container in a cool, dry place away from reach of children. Protect from light.

Missed dose
Take as soon as you remember. If your next dose is due within 6 hours, take a single dose now and skip the next.

Stopping the drug
Do not stop the drug without consulting your doctor. Abrupt cessation of long-term treatment by mouth or injection may be dangerous.

Exceeding the dose
An occasional unintentional extra dose is unlikely to cause problems. If you notice unusual symptoms, or if a large overdose has been taken, notify your doctor.

SPECIAL PRECAUTIONS

Be sure to tell your doctor if:
▼ You have had a peptic ulcer.
▼ You have had glaucoma.
▼ You have had tuberculosis.
▼ You suffer from depression.
▼ You have any infection.
▼ You have diabetes.
▼ You have osteoporosis.
▼ You are taking other medications.

 Pregnancy
▼ No evidence of risk with drops or joint injections. Given by tablets in low doses, harm to the baby is unlikely. Discuss with your doctor.

 Breast feeding
▼ No evidence of risk with drops or joint injections. Taken by mouth, the drug passes into the breast milk, but at low doses adverse effects on the baby are unlikely. Discuss with your doctor.

 Infants and children
▼ Only given when essential. Reduced dose may be necessary.

 Over 60
▼ Increased likelihood of adverse effects. Reduced dose may therefore be necessary.

 Driving and hazardous work
▼ No known problems.

 Alcohol
▼ Alcohol may increase the risk of peptic ulcers with prednisolone by mouth or injection. No special problems with other dosage forms.

POSSIBLE ADVERSE EFFECTS

The rare, but more serious adverse effects occur only when prednisolone is taken by mouth or injection in high doses or for long periods of time.

Symptom/effect	Frequency		Discuss with doctor		Stop taking drug now	Call doctor now
	Common	Rare	Only if severe	In all cases		
Indigestion	●			■		
Acne	●			■		
Weight gain		●		■		
Muscle weakness		●		■		
Mood changes/depression		●		■		
Bloody/black stools		●		■	▲	▮

INTERACTIONS

Anti-epileptics Carbamazepine, phenytoin, and phenobarbitone can reduce the effects of prednisolone.

Vaccines Serious reactions can occur when vaccinations are given with this drug. Discuss with your doctor.

Insulin and antidiabetic drugs Prednisolone by mouth or injection reduces the actions of these drugs.

Antihypertensive drugs Prednisolone by mouth or injection may reduce the effect of antihypertensive drugs.

PROLONGED USE

Prolonged use of prednisolone by mouth or injection is only recommended when essential because it can lead to adverse effects such as diabetes, glaucoma, cataracts, and fragile bones, and may retard growth in children.

PRIMIDONE

Brand name Mysoline
Used in the following combined preparations None

GENERAL INFORMATION

Introduced in the 1950s, primidone belongs to a group of drugs known as the anticonvulsants. It is chemically related to the barbiturates (see Anticonvulsant drugs, p.86) and is partially converted to phenobarbitone in the body. But it is mainly used for its effect in suppressing epileptic fits. However, it is also occasionally prescribed to treat people who suffer from certain types of tremor.

Though it may be prescribed on its own, it is more frequently taken with another anticonvulsant. Its major adverse effects are due to its sedative action on the central nervous system.

QUICK REFERENCE

Drug group Anticonvulsant (p.86)
Overdose danger rating High
Dependence rating Medium
Prescription needed Yes
Available as generic No

INFORMATION FOR USERS

Your drug prescription is tailored for you. Do not alter dosage without checking with your doctor.

How taken

Tablets, liquid.

Frequency and timing of doses
1 – 3 x daily.

Adult dosage range
Initially 125mg, increased gradually up to a maximum of 1.5g daily.

Onset of effect
Within 1 hour.

Duration of action
Up to 24 hours.

Diet advice
None.

Storage
Keep in a closed container in a cool, dry place away from reach of children.

Missed dose
Take as soon as you remember. If you normally take once daily, and your next dose is due within 8 hours, take a single dose now and skip the next. If you normally take 2 – 3 times daily, and your next dose is due within 2 hours, take a single dose now and skip the next.

Stopping the drug
Do not stop the drug without consulting your doctor; symptoms may recur, and withdrawal reactions can result.

OVERDOSE ACTION

 Seek immediate medical advice in all cases. Take emergency action if consciousness is lost.

See Drug poisoning emergency guide (p.470).

POSSIBLE ADVERSE EFFECTS

Most people experience very few adverse effects with this drug, but when blood levels get too high, adverse effects are common and the dose may need to be reduced.

Symptom/effect	Frequency		Discuss with doctor		Stop taking drug now	Call doctor now
	Common	Rare	Only if severe	In all cases		
Drowsiness	●		■			
Clumsiness/unsteadiness	●		■			
Dizziness/lightheadedness	●		■			
Headache		●	■			
Nausea/vomiting		●	■			
Rash		●		■		

INTERACTIONS

Sedatives All drugs that have a sedative effect are likely to increase the sedative properties of primidone. Such drugs include antihistamines, sleeping drugs, narcotic analgesics, antipsychotics, and antidepressants.

Anticoagulants Primidone may reduce the effect of anticoagulant drugs. The anticoagulant dose may need to be adjusted accordingly.

Oral contraceptives Primidone may reduce the effectiveness of oral contraceptives. An alternative form of contraception may need to be used. Discuss with your doctor.

Corticosteroids Primidone may reduce the effect of some of these drugs. The corticosteroid dose may need to be adjusted accordingly.

SPECIAL PRECAUTIONS

Be sure to tell your doctor if:
▼ You have long-term liver or kidney problems.
▼ You have heart problems.
▼ You have poor circulation.
▼ You have a lung disorder such as asthma or bronchitis.
▼ You have porphyria.
▼ You are taking other medications.

 Pregnancy
▼ Not usually prescribed. May cause abnormalities in the unborn baby. Discuss with your doctor.

 Breast feeding
▼ The drug passes into the breast milk and may affect the baby. Discuss with your doctor.

 Infants and children
▼ Reduced dose necessary, depending on weight.

 Over 60
▼ Reduced dose may be necessary.

 Driving and hazardous work
▼ Your underlying condition, as well as the possibility of reduced alertness while taking this drug, may make such activities inadvisable. Discuss with your doctor.

 Alcohol
▼ Avoid. Alcohol may dangerously increase the sedative effects of this drug.

PROLONGED USE

Continued use of this drug may sometimes lead to dependence.

Monitoring Regular blood tests may be performed to measure blood levels and to check the blood cells.

PROBENECID

Brand name Benemid
Used in the following combined preparations None

GENERAL INFORMATION

Probenecid is prescribed for people who suffer from recurrent attacks of gout. It reduces the level of uric acid in the body by increasing the amount excreted in the urine. It is used for the long-term prevention of gout attacks, not for the inflammation and pain once an attack has begun. During the first six months of treatment, attacks may even be more frequent, and another drug may be given in addition to probenecid during this period. It is occasionally prescribed to boost the effect of penicillin or cephalosporin antibiotics in the treatment of certain infections, since it blocks their excretion by the kidneys, thereby increasing their levels in the blood.

Serious adverse reactions are rare, though by increasing uric acid secretion, probenecid can increase the risk of uric acid kidney stones.

QUICK REFERENCE

Drug group Uricosuric drugs for gout (p.119)

Overdose danger rating Medium

Dependence rating Low

Prescription needed Yes

Available as generic No

INFORMATION FOR USERS

Your drug prescription is tailored for you. Do not alter dosage without checking with your doctor.

How taken

Tablets.

Frequency and timing of doses
2 – 4 x daily with food (gout); 4 x daily or as a single-dose treatment (with penicillin).

Dosage range
Gout 0.5g daily for 1 week then 1 – 2g daily. *With penicillin and similar antibiotics* 1 – 2g daily.

Onset of effect
Within 2 – 4 hours. Full beneficial effects in gout may not be seen for some weeks.

Duration of action
4 – 16 hours.

Diet advice
Ensure adequate fluid intake, at least 2 litres daily.

Storage
Keep in a closed container in a cool, dry place away from reach of children. Protect from light.

Missed dose
Take as soon as you remember. If your next dose is due within 3 hours, take a single dose now and skip the next.

Stopping the drug
Do not stop the drug without consulting your doctor; symptoms may recur.

Exceeding the dose
An occasional unintentional extra dose is unlikely to cause problems. Large overdoses may cause nausea, vomiting, or tremors. Notify your doctor.

SPECIAL PRECAUTIONS

Be sure to tell your doctor if:
▼ You have long-term kidney problems.
▼ You have had a blood disorder.
▼ You have had kidney stones.
▼ You have had a peptic ulcer.
▼ You are taking other medications.

Pregnancy
▼ Safety in pregnancy not established. Discuss with your doctor.

Breast feeding
▼ The drug passes into the breast milk, but at normal doses adverse effects on the baby are unlikely. Discuss with your doctor.

Infants and children
▼ Not recommended under 2 years. Reduced dose necessary in older children.

Over 60
▼ Reduced dose may be necessary.

Driving and hazardous work
▼ No expected problems.

Alcohol
▼ Avoid excessive amounts.

POSSIBLE ADVERSE EFFECTS

Most people do not feel any severe adverse effects when taking probenecid. The more common ones usually diminish as your body adjusts to the medicine. However, excretion of uric acid crystals can lead to the passing of blood and painful urination.

Symptom/effect	Frequency		Discuss with doctor		Stop taking drug now	Call doctor now
	Common	Rare	Only if severe	In all cases		
Nausea/vomiting	●		■			
Headache/dizziness	●		■			
Flushing	●			■		
Blood in urine	●			■	▲	
Painful urination	●			■		
Rash/itching	●			■	▲	

PROLONGED USE

No problems expected.

Monitoring Periodic blood tests may be carried out to ensure that anaemia does not occur.

INTERACTIONS

General note Many drugs affect the action of probenecid and may require an adjustment of dosage. Some may reduce the effect of probenecid (for example, aspirin); and others may have their effects increased by probenecid (for example, oral antidiabetic drugs, indomethacin and other non-steroidal anti-inflammatory drugs, acyclovir, and methotrexate).

PROCHLORPERAZINE

Brand names Buccastem, Prozière, Stemitil, Vertigon
Used in the following combined preparations None

GENERAL INFORMATION

Prochlorperazine, introduced in the late 1950s, belongs to a group of drugs called the phenothiazines, which act on the central nervous system.

In small doses, it controls nausea and vomiting, especially when they occur as side effects of medical treatment by drugs or radiation, or of anaesthesia. Prochlorperazine is also used to treat the nausea that occurs with inner ear disorders. In large doses, it is effective as an antipsychotic, suppressing abnormal behaviour, reducing aggressiveness, and producing tranquillization (see p.85). It thus minimizes and controls the abnormal behaviour associated with schizophrenia, mania, and other mental disorders. It does not cure these diseases but helps to relieve symptoms.

QUICK REFERENCE

Drug group Phenothiazine antipsychotic (p.85) and anti-emetic (p.90)

Overdose danger rating Medium

Dependence rating Low

Prescription needed Yes

Available as generic Yes

INFORMATION FOR USERS

Your drug prescription is tailored for you. Do not alter the dosage without checking with your doctor.

How taken

Tablets, capsules, SR-capsules, liquid, powder, injection, suppositories.

Frequency and timing of doses
2 – 4 x daily (tablets); 2 – 3 x daily (suppositories); 1 – 2 x daily (slow-release capsules); 2 – 3 x daily (injection).

Adult dosage range
Nausea and vomiting 20mg initially, then 5 – 10mg per dose (tablets); 25mg per dose (suppositories); 10 – 15mg per dose (slow-release capsules). *Mental illness* 15 – 40 mg daily. Larger doses may be given.

Onset of effect
Within 60 minutes (by mouth or suppository); 10 – 20 minutes (by injection).

Duration of action
3 – 6 hours (up to 12 hours in slow-release form).

Diet advice
None.

Storage
Keep in a closed container in a cool, dry place away from reach of children. Protect from light.

Missed dose
Take as soon as you remember. If your next dose is due within 2 hours, take a single dose now and skip the next.

Stopping the drug
Do not stop the drug without consulting your doctor; symptoms may recur.

Exceeding the dose
An occasional unintentional extra dose is unlikely to cause problems. Large overdoses may cause unusual drowsiness, and may affect the heart. Notify your doctor.

SPECIAL PRECAUTIONS

Be sure to tell your doctor if:
▼ You have heart problems.
▼ You have long-term liver or kidney problems.
▼ You have epileptic fits.
▼ You have Parkinson's disease.
▼ You have an underactive thyroid gland.
▼ You have prostate problems.
▼ You have glaucoma.
▼ You are taking other medications.

Pregnancy
▼ Safety in pregnancy not established. Discuss with your doctor.

Breast feeding
▼ The drug passes into the breast milk and may affect the baby. Discuss with your doctor.

Infants and children
▼ Not recommended in children weighing less than 10kg. Reduced dose necessary.

Over 60
▼ Increased likelihood of adverse effects. Reduced dose may therefore be necessary.

Driving and hazardous work
▼ Avoid such activities until you have learned how the drug affects you because the drug may cause drowsiness and reduced alertness.

Alcohol
▼ Avoid. Alcohol may increase and prolong the sedative effects of this drug.

POSSIBLE ADVERSE EFFECTS

Prochlorperazine has an *anticholinergic* effect, which can cause a variety of minor symptoms that become less marked with time. The most significant adverse effect with high doses is abnormal movements of the face and limbs (*parkinsonism*) caused by changes in the balance of brain chemicals.

Symptom/effect	Frequency		Discuss with doctor		Stop taking drug now	Call doctor now
	Common	Rare	Only if severe	In all cases		
Drowsiness/lethargy	●		■			
Dry mouth	●		■			
Dizziness/fainting	●			■		
Parkinsonism	●			■		
Rash		●		■	▲	
Jaundice		●		■		■

PROLONGED USE

Use of this drug for more than a few months may lead to the development of involuntary, potentially irreversible movements of the eyes, mouth, and tongue (*tardive dyskinesia*). Occasionally jaundice may occur.

Monitoring Periodic blood tests may be performed.

INTERACTIONS

Sedatives All drugs that have a sedative effect are likely to increase the sedative properties of prochlorperazine.

Antiparkinsonism drugs Prochlorperazine may block their beneficial effect.

Antihistamines Increased risk of abnormal heart rhythms occurring with perfenadine and astemizole.

Anticholinergic drugs Side effects of these drugs may be increased by prochlorperazine.

PROCYCLIDINE

Brand names Arpicolin, Kemadrin
Used in the following combined preparations None

GENERAL INFORMATION

Introduced in the 1950s, procyclidine is an *anticholinergic* drug that is used to treat Parkinson's disease. It is particularly helpful in the early stages of the disorder for treating muscle tremor and rigidity. It also helps to reduce excess salivation. However, it has little effect on the shuffling gait and slow muscular movements that are also characteristic of Parkinson's disease.

Procyclidine is also frequently used to treat parkinsonism resulting from treatment with antipsychotic drugs.

The drug may cause a number of minor adverse effects (see below). But these are rarely sufficiently serious to warrant stopping treatment.

INFORMATION FOR USERS

Your drug prescription is tailored for you. Do not alter dosage without checking with your doctor.

How taken

Tablets, liquid, injection.

Frequency and timing of doses
2 – 3 x daily.

Adult dosage range
7.5 – 30mg daily, exceptionally up to 60mg daily. Dosage with this drug has to be determined individually, in order to find the best balance between effective relief of symptoms and the occurrence of adverse effects.

Onset of effect
Within 30 minutes.

Duration of action
8 – 12 hours.

Diet advice
None.

Storage
Keep in a closed container in a cool, dry place away from reach of children.

Missed dose
Take as soon as you remember. If your next dose is due within 2 hours, take a single dose now and skip the next.

Stopping the drug
Do not stop the drug without consulting your doctor, who may reduce the dose gradually.

OVERDOSE ACTION

 Seek immediate medical advice in all cases. Take emergency action if palpitations, fits, or unconsciousness occur.

See Drug poisoning emergency guide (p.470).

POSSIBLE ADVERSE EFFECTS

The possible adverse effects of procyclidine are mainly the result of its *anticholinergic* action. Some of the more common symptoms, such as dry mouth, constipation, and blurred vision may be overcome by adjustment of dosage.

Symptom/effect	Frequency		Discuss with doctor		Stop taking drug now	Call doctor now
	Common	Rare	Only if severe	In all cases		
Dry mouth	●		■			
Constipation	●		■			
Nervousness	●		■			
Drowsiness/dizziness	●		■			
Blurred vision	●			■		
Confusion		●		■		
Difficulty in passing urine		●		■		
Palpitations		●		■	▲	▮

INTERACTIONS

Anticholinergic drugs and antihistamines These drugs may increase the adverse effects of procyclidine.

Ketoconazole The absorption of this drug may be reduced by procyclidine.

Phenothiazine antipsychotics Procyclidine may increase the adverse effects of these drugs.

SPECIAL PRECAUTIONS

Be sure to tell your doctor if:
▼ You have long-term liver or kidney problems.
▼ You have had glaucoma.
▼ You have high blood pressure.
▼ You suffer from constipation.
▼ You have prostate trouble.
▼ You have had peptic ulcers.
▼ You are taking other medications.

 Pregnancy
▼ Safety in pregnancy not established. Discuss with your doctor.

 Breast feeding
▼ The drug passes into the breast milk and may affect the baby. Discuss with your doctor.

 Infants and children
▼ Not recommended.

 Over 60
▼ Reduced dose may be necessary.

 Driving and hazardous work
▼ Avoid such activities until you have learned how the drug affects you because the drug can cause drowsiness, dizziness, blurred vision, and mild confusion.

 Alcohol
▼ Avoid. Alcohol may increase the adverse effects of this drug.

PROLONGED USE

Prolonged use of this drug may provoke the onset of glaucoma.

Monitoring Periodic eye examinations are usually advised.

PROGUANIL

Brand name Paludrine
Used in the following combined preparations None

GENERAL INFORMATION

Proguanil is an antimalarial drug that has been used for over 30 years. It is used to prevent the development of malaria in people visiting parts of the world where the disease is prevalent. Treatment with the drug needs to be started one week before travel and should be continued for four weeks after your return. In some parts of the world the malaria parasite is resistant to proguanil and it may need to be taken with another drug such as chloroquine to ensure adequate protection. Always seek expert advice on malaria preven-tion in good time before travelling. It is important that the drug is taken regularly to be effective. See your doctor immediately if you become ill within 3 months of returning.

Adverse effects from this drug are rare and usually subside with continued treatment. It is very important also to provide personal protection against being bitten, such as keeping well covered and using mosquito nets, repellants etc.

QUICK REFERENCE

Drug group Antimalarial drug (p.137)

Overdose danger rating Medium

Dependence rating Low

Prescription needed No

Available as generic No

INFORMATION FOR USERS

Follow instructions on the label.

How taken

Tablets.

Frequency and timing of doses
Once daily after food.

Adult dosage range
200mg daily.

Onset of effect
Within 24 hours.

Duration of action
24 – 48 hours.

Diet advice
None.

Storage
Keep in a closed container in a cool, dry place away from reach of children.

Missed dose
Take as soon as you remember. If your next dose is due at this time, take both doses together.

Stopping the drug
Do not stop taking the drug within 4 weeks of leaving a malaria-infected area, otherwise there is a risk that you may develop the disease.

Exceeding the dose
An occasional unintentional extra dose is unlikely to cause problems. Large overdoses may cause abdominal pain and vomiting. Notify your doctor.

SPECIAL PRECAUTIONS

Be sure to tell your doctor if:
▼ You have a long-term kidney problem.
▼ You are taking other medications.

Pregnancy
▼ Safety in pregnancy not established, although benefits generally considered to outweigh risks. Folate supplements should be taken. Discuss with your doctor.

Breast feeding
▼ The drug passes into the breast milk, but at normal doses adverse effects on the baby are unlikely. Discuss with your doctor.

Infants and children
▼ Reduced dose necessary.

Over 60
▼ No known problems.

Driving and hazardous work
▼ No known problems.

Alcohol
▼ No special problems.

POSSIBLE ADVERSE EFFECTS

Adverse effects from proguanil are rare. Stomach irritation is the most common problem, but this usually settles as treatment continues.

Symptom/effect	Frequency		Discuss with doctor		Stop taking drug now	Call doctor now
	Common	Rare	Only if severe	In all cases		
Nausea/vomiting		●	■			
Abdominal pain/indigestion		●	■			

INTERACTIONS

Warfarin The effects of warfarin may be enhanced by proguanil.

PROLONGED USE

No known problems.

PROMAZINE

Brand name Sparine
Used in the following combined preparations None

GENERAL INFORMATION

Promazine was introduced in the late 1950s and is a member of a group of drugs called phenothiazines. These drugs act on the brain to regulate abnormal behaviour (see Antipsychotics, p.85).

Promazine is primarily used to calm agitated and restless behaviour. It is also prescribed as a sedative for the short-term treatment of severe anxiety, especially in the elderly and during terminal illness.

In theory, promazine may cause the unpleasant side effects common to most other phenothiazine drugs, particularly shaking and abnormal movements of arms and legs (parkinsonism). In practice, the drug is rarely used for periods long enough to produce these problems.

INFORMATION FOR USERS

Your drug prescription is tailored for you. Do not alter dosage without checking with your doctor.

How taken

Tablets, liquid, injection.

Frequency and timing of doses
4 x daily.

Adult dosage range
100mg – 800mg daily.

Onset of effect
30 minutes – 1 hour.

Duration of action
4 – 6 hours.

Diet advice
None.

Storage
Keep in a closed container in a cool, dry place away from reach of children. Protect from light.

Missed dose
Take as soon as you remember. If your next dose is due within 2 hours, take a single dose now and skip the next.

Stopping the drug
Do not stop the drug without consulting your doctor; symptoms may recur.

Exceeding the dose
An occasional unintentional extra dose is unlikely to cause problems. Large overdoses may cause drowsiness, dizziness, unsteadiness, fitting, and coma. Notify your doctor.

POSSIBLE ADVERSE EFFECTS

The more common adverse effects of promazine, such as drowsiness, dry mouth, and blurred vision, may be helped by an adjustment of dosage. Parkinsonism is rare.

Symptom/effect	Frequency		Discuss with doctor		Stop taking drug now	Call doctor now
	Common	Rare	Only if severe	In all cases		
Drowsiness/lethargy	●		■			
Dry mouth	●		■			
Constipation	●		■			
Blurred vision	●			■		
Parkinsonism		●		■		
Jaundice		●		■		■
Rash		●	■		▲	

INTERACTIONS

Anticonvulsants Promazine may reduce the effectiveness of anticonvulsants.

Drugs for parkinsonism Promazine may reduce the effectiveness of these drugs.

Sedatives All drugs that have a sedative effect are likely to increase the sedative properties of promazine.

Antihistamines There may be an increased risk of abnormal heart rhythms occurring with terfenadine and astemizole.

SPECIAL PRECAUTIONS

Be sure to tell your doctor if:
▼ You have heart problems.
▼ You have long-term liver or kidney problems.
▼ You have had epileptic fits.
▼ You have breathing problems.
▼ You have prostate problems.
▼ You have glaucoma.
▼ You have Parkinson's disease.
▼ You have thyroid disease.
▼ You are taking other medications.

Pregnancy
▼ Safety in early pregnancy not established. The drug is sometimes injected during labour. Discuss with your doctor.

Breast feeding
▼ The drug passes into the breast milk, but at normal doses adverse effects on the baby are unlikely. Discuss with your doctor.

Infants and children
▼ Not recommended.

Over 60
▼ Increased likelihood of adverse effects. Reduced dose may therefore be necessary.

Driving and hazardous work
▼ Avoid such activities until you have learned how the drug affects you, because the drug may cause drowsiness and reduced alertness.

Alcohol
▼ Avoid. Alcohol may increase the sedative effect of this drug.

PROLONGED USE

Use of this drug for more than a few months may be associated with *jaundice*. Abnormal movements of the face and limbs may also occur. Sometimes a reduction in dosage may be recommended.

Monitoring Periodic blood tests may be performed.

PROMETHAZINE

Brand names Avomine, Phenergan, Sominex
Used in the following combined preparations Medised, Pamergan, Phensedyl, Tixylix

GENERAL INFORMATION

Promethazine is one of the pheno-thiazines, a class of drugs developed in the 1950s for their beneficial effect on abnormal behaviour arising from mental illnesses (see Antipsychotics, p.85). Promethazine was, however, found to have effects more like the antihistamines used to treat allergies (see p.124) and some types of nausea and vomiting (see Anti-emetics, p.90). Promethazine is widely used to reduce itching in a variety of skin conditions including urticaria (hives), chickenpox, and eczema. It can also relieve the nausea and vomiting caused by inner ear disturbances such as motion sickness and Ménière's disease. Because of its sedative effect, promethazine is sometimes used as a sleeping medicine for short periods and given as *premedication* before surgery.

Promethazine is sometimes combined with narcotic cough suppressants for the relief of allergy-related coughs and nasal congestion.

INFORMATION FOR USERS

Follow instructions on the label. Call your doctor if symptoms worsen.

How taken

Tablets, liquid, injection.

Frequency and timing of doses
Allergic symptoms 1 – 3 x daily or as a single dose at night.
Motion sickness 1 – 2 hours before travel, then every 6 – 8 hours as necessary.
Nausea and vomiting Every 4 – 6 hours as necessary.

Dosage range (promethazine hydrochloride)
Adults 20 – 75mg per dose.
Children Reduced dose according to age.

Onset of effect
Within 1 hour. If dose is taken after nausea has started, the onset of effect is delayed.

Duration of action
8 – 16 hours.

Diet advice
None.

Storage
Keep in a closed container in a cool, dry place away from reach of children. Protect from light.

Missed dose
No cause for concern, but take as soon as you remember. Adjust the timing of your next dose accordingly.

Stopping the drug
Can be safely stopped as soon as symptoms disappear.

Exceeding the dose
An occasional unintentional extra dose is unlikely to cause problems. Large overdoses may cause drowsiness, unsteadiness, or agitation, fitting, and coma. Notify your doctor.

SPECIAL PRECAUTIONS

Be sure to consult your doctor or pharmacist before taking this drug if:
▼ You have long-term liver or kidney problems.
▼ You have had epileptic fits.
▼ You have heart disease.
▼ You have glaucoma.
▼ You suffer from asthma.
▼ You have Parkinson's disease.
▼ You have urinary difficulties.
▼ You are taking other medications.

Pregnancy
▼ Safety in pregnancy not established. Discuss with your doctor.

Breast feeding
▼ The drug passes into the breast milk, but at normal doses adverse effects on the baby are unlikely. Discuss with your doctor.

Infants and children
▼ Reduced dose necessary.

Over 60
▼ No special problems.

Driving and hazardous work
▼ Avoid such activities until you have learned how the drug affects you because the drug can cause drowsiness.

Alcohol
▼ Avoid. Alcohol may increase the sedative effects of this drug.

POSSIBLE ADVERSE EFFECTS

Promethazine usually causes only minor *anticholinergic* effects. More serious adverse effects generally occur only during long-term use or with abnormally high doses.

Symptom/effect	Frequency		Discuss with doctor		Stop taking drug now	Call doctor now
	Common	Rare	Only if severe	In all cases		
Drowsiness/lethargy	●		■			
Dry mouth	●		■			
Blurred vision	●		■			
Light–sensitive rash		●			■	▲

INTERACTIONS

Sedatives All drugs that have a sedative effect are likely to increase the sedative properties of promethazine. Such drugs include other antihistamines, sleeping drugs, and antipsychotics.

Monoamine oxidase inhibitors (MAOIs) Avoid promethazine if MAOIs have been taken in the last 14 days.

Antihistamines There may be an increased risk of abnormal heart rhythms occurring with terfenadine and astemizole.

PROLONGED USE

Use of this drug for extended periods is rarely necessary, but may sometimes cause abnormal movements of the face and limbs (parkinsonism). This problem usually disappears when the drug is stopped.

PROPRANOLOL

Brand names Angilol, Apsolol, Berkolol, Beta-Prograne, Betadur, Cardinol, Inderal, Inderal La, Propanix, and others
Used in the following combined preparations Inderetic, Inderex

GENERAL INFORMATION

Propranolol, introduced in 1965, was the first of the beta blockers to become widely available in the United Kingdom. Most often used to treat hypertension, angina, and abnormal heart rhythms, it is also helpful in controlling the fast heart rate and other symptoms caused by overactivity of the thyroid gland and in reducing the palpitations, sweating, and tremor caused by severe anxiety.

It is also used to prevent migraine headaches.

Because propranolol can cause breathing difficulties, it is not prescribed to anyone suffering from asthma, chronic bronchitis or emphysema. Like all beta blockers, propranolol affects the body's response to low blood sugar; it should be used with caution by diabetics.

INFORMATION FOR USERS

Your drug prescription is tailored for you. Do not alter dosage without checking with your doctor.

How taken

Tablets, SR-capsules, liquid, injection.

Frequency and timing of doses
2 – 4 x daily. Once daily (slow-release capsules).

Adult dosage range
Abnormal heart rhythms 30 – 160mg daily.
Angina 80 – 240mg daily.
Hypertension 160 – 320mg daily.
Migraine prevention and anxiety 80 – 160mg daily.

Onset of effect
1 – 2 hours (tablets); after 4 hours (slow-release capsules). In hypertension and migraine, it may be several weeks before full benefits of this drug are felt.

Duration of action
6 – 12 hours. 24 – 30 hours (slow-release capsules).

Diet advice
None.

Storage
Keep in a closed container in a cool, dry place away from reach of children. Protect from light.

Missed dose
Take as soon as you remember. If your next dose is due within 2 hours (tablets), or 12 hours (slow-release capsules), take a single dose now and skip the next.

Stopping the drug
Do not stop the drug without consulting your doctor. Abrupt cessation may lead to worsening of the underlying condition.

OVERDOSE ACTION

Seek immediate medical advice in all cases. Take emergency action if breathing difficulties, collapse, or loss of consciousness occur.

See Drug poisoning emergency guide (p.470).

POSSIBLE ADVERSE EFFECTS

Propranolol has adverse effects that are common to most beta blockers. Symptoms such as fatigue and nausea are usually temporary and diminish with long-term use. Fainting may be a sign that the drug has slowed the heart beat excessively.

Symptom/effect	Frequency		Discuss with doctor		Stop taking drug now	Call doctor now
	Common	Rare	Only if severe	In all cases		
Lethargy/fatigue	●		■			
Cold hands and feet	●		■			
Nausea		●	■			
Nightmares/vivid dreams		●		■		
Rash/dry eyes		●		■		
Fainting/breathlessness		●		■		■

INTERACTIONS

Indomethacin and NSAIDs These may reduce the antihypertensive effect of propranolol.

Antihypertensive drugs Propranolol may enhance the lowering effect on blood pressure of these drugs.

SPECIAL PRECAUTIONS

Be sure to tell your doctor if:
▼ You have long-term liver or kidney problems.
▼ You have a lung disorder such as asthma, bronchitis, or emphysema.
▼ You have heart failure.
▼ You have diabetes.
▼ You have poor circulation in the legs.
▼ You are taking other medications.

Pregnancy
▼ May affect the baby. Discuss with your doctor.

Breast feeding
▼ The drug passes into breast milk, but at normal doses adverse effects on the baby are unlikely. Discuss with your doctor.

Infants and children
▼ Reduced dose necessary.

Over 60
▼ Increased risk of adverse effects.

Driving and hazardous work
▼ No special problems.

Alcohol
▼ No special problems.

Surgery and general anaesthetics
▼ Propranolol may need to be stopped before you have a general anaesthetic. Discuss this with your doctor or dentist before any surgery.

PROLONGED USE

No problems expected.

PROPYLTHIOURACIL

Brand names None
Used in the following combined preparations None

GENERAL INFORMATION

Propylthiouracil is an antithyroid drug used to manage an overactive thyroid gland (thyrotoxicosis). In some people, particularly those with Graves' disease (the commonest form of the disorder), drug treatment alone may bring on a remission. It may also be prescribed for long-term treatment of the disease in those who may be at special risk from surgery, such as children and pregnant women.

Propylthiouracil is also employed to restore the normal functioning of the gland before its partial removal by surgery.

Propylthiouracil is sometimes given together with thyroxine to prevent the development of hypothyroidism (low thyroid hormone levels). Propylthiouracil is preferred to other antithyroid drugs when treatment is essential during pregnancy.

The most important adverse effect that sometimes occurs is a reduction in white blood cells leading to the risk of infection. If you develop a sore throat or mouth ulceration, see your doctor immediately; this might be a sign that your blood is being affected.

QUICK REFERENCE

Drug group Antithyroid drug (p.144)

Overdose danger rating Medium

Dependence rating Low

Prescription needed Yes

Available as generic Yes

INFORMATION FOR USERS

Your drug prescription is tailored for you. Do not alter dosage without checking with your doctor.

How taken

Tablets.

Frequency and timing of doses
1 – 3 times daily.

Dosage range
Initially 300 – 600mg daily. Usually the dose can be reduced to 50 – 150mg daily.

Onset of effect
10 – 20 days. Full beneficial effects may not be felt for 6 – 10 weeks.

Duration of action
24 – 36 hours.

Diet advice
Your doctor may advise you to avoid foods that are high in iodine (see p.425).

Storage
Keep in a closed container in a cool, dry place away from reach of children. Protect from light.

Missed dose
Take as soon as you remember. If your next dose is due within 3 hours, take a single dose now and skip the next.

Stopping the drug
Do not stop the drug without consulting your doctor; stopping the drug may lead to a recurrence of thyrotoxicosis.

Exceeding the dose
An occasional unintentional extra dose is unlikely to cause problems. Large overdoses may cause nausea, vomiting, and headache. Notify your doctor.

SPECIAL PRECAUTIONS

Be sure to tell your doctor if:
▼ You have long-term liver or kidney problems.
▼ You are taking other medications.

 Pregnancy
▼ Prescribed with caution. May cause goitre and thyroid hormone deficiency (hypothyroidism) in the newborn infant if too high a dose is used. Discuss with your doctor.

 Breast feeding
▼ The drug passes into the breast milk, and may affect the baby. Discuss with your doctor.

 Infants and children
▼ Reduced dose necessary.

 Over 60
▼ No special problems.

 Driving and hazardous work
▼ No problems expected.

 Alcohol
▼ No known problems.

PROLONGED USE

High doses of propylthiouracil over a prolonged period may reduce the number of white blood cells.

Monitoring Periodic tests of thyroid function are usually required, and blood cell counts may also be carried out.

POSSIBLE ADVERSE EFFECTS

Serious side effects are rare with propylthiouracil. Skin rashes and itching are fairly common. Sore throat or fever may indicate adverse effects on the blood. If these occur inform your doctor straight away.

Symptom/effect	Frequency		Discuss with doctor		Stop taking drug now	Call doctor now
	Common	Rare	Only if severe	In all cases		
Nausea/vomiting	●		■			
Joint pain	●			■		
Headache	●			■		
Rash/itching	●			■		
Jaundice		●		■	▲	▌
Sore throat		●		■	▲	▌

INTERACTIONS

Anticoagulants Propylthiouracil may increase the effects of these drugs, making an adjustment in dosage necessary.

PYRIDOSTIGMINE

Brand name Mestinon
Used in the following combined preparations None

GENERAL INFORMATION

Pyridostigmine is used to treat myasthenia gravis, a rare autoimmune condition involving the faulty transmission of nerve impulses to the muscles (p.121). By prolonging nerve signals, pyridostigmine improves muscle strength, though it does not cure the disease. In severe cases it may be prescribed with corticosteroids or other drugs. Pyridostigmine may also be given to reverse temporary paralysis of the bowel and urinary retention following operations.

Side effects such as abdominal cramps, nausea, and diarrhoea generally disappear when the dose of pyridostigmine is reduced.

INFORMATION FOR USERS

Your drug prescription is tailored for you. Do not alter dosage without checking with your doctor.

How taken

Tablets.

Frequency and timing of doses
Every 3 – 4 hours initially. Thereafter, according to the needs of the individual.

Adult dosage range
Adults 150mg – 1.2g daily (by mouth); *Children* Reduced dose necessary according to age and weight.

Onset of effect
30 – 60 minutes.

Duration of action
3 – 6 hours.

Diet advice
None.

Storage
Keep in a closed container in a cool, dry place away from reach of children. Protect from light.

Missed dose
Take as soon as you remember. If your next dose is due within 2 hours, take a single dose now and skip the next.

Stopping the drug
Do not stop the drug without consulting your doctor; symptoms may recur.

OVERDOSE ACTION

 Seek immediate medical advice in all cases. You may experience severe abdominal cramps, vomiting, weakness, and tremor. Take emergency action if unusually slow heartbeat, troubled breathing, fits, or loss of consciousness occur.

See Drug poisoning emergency guide (p.470).

SPECIAL PRECAUTIONS

Be sure to tell your doctor if:
▼ You have heart problems.
▼ You have had epileptic fits.
▼ You have asthma.
▼ You have difficulty passing urine.
▼ You have Parkinson's disease.
▼ You are taking other medications.

 Pregnancy
▼ No evidence of risk to the developing baby in the first 6 months. Large doses near the time of delivery may lead to temporary muscle weakness in the baby. Discuss with your doctor.

 Breast feeding
▼ No evidence of risk.

 Infants and children
▼ Reduced dose necessary.

 Over 60
▼ Increased likelihood of adverse effects.

 Driving and hazardous work
▼ Your underlying condition may make such activities inadvisable. Discuss with your doctor.

 Alcohol
▼ No special problems.

Surgery and general anaesthetics
▼ Pyridostigmine may interact with some anaesthetic agents. Make sure your treatment is known to your doctor, dentist, and anaesthetist before any surgery.

POSSIBLE ADVERSE EFFECTS

Adverse effects of pyridostigmine are usually dose-related. In rare cases, hypersensitivity may occur leading to an allergic skin rash.

Symptom/effect	Frequency		Discuss with doctor		Stop taking drug now	Call doctor now
	Common	Rare	Only if severe	In all cases		
Nausea/vomiting	●			■		
Increased salivation	●			■		
Sweating	●			■		
Abdominal cramps/diarrhoea	●			■		
Watery eyes/small pupils		●		■		
Headache		●			■	
Rash		●			■	

INTERACTIONS

General note Drugs that suppress transmission of nerve signals may oppose the effect of pyridostigmine. Such drugs include digoxin, aminoglycoside antibiotics, procainamide, quinidine, lithium.

PROLONGED USE

No problems expected.

PYRIMETHAMINE

Brand name Daraprim
Used in the following combined preparations Fansidar, Maloprim

GENERAL INFORMATION

Pyrimethamine is an antimalarial drug generally used against types of malaria resistant to other drugs. Although it does not cure malaria, pyrimethamine is valuable as a preventive measure, and it effectively relieves the chills-and-fever symptoms of malarial attacks.

Because malaria parasites can readily develop resistance to pyrimethamine, the drug is usually given in a combination tablet with sulfadoxine, an antibacterial drug. The activity of the two greatly exceeds that of either drug alone.

Pyrimethamine is prescribed with other sulphonamides to treat toxoplasmosis, another protozoal infection. Because blood disorders can arise during prolonged use, regular blood counts are made and vitamin supplements administered.

INFORMATION FOR USERS

Follow instructions on the label. Call a doctor if you become ill.

How taken

Tablets.

Frequency and timing of doses
Once weekly starting 1 week before travel and continuing for at least 4 weeks after leaving malarial area (prevention of malaria).

Dosage range
Adults 25mg per dose (prevention of malaria).
Children Reduced dose necessary according to age.

Onset of effect
24 hours.

Duration of action
Up to 1 week.

Diet advice
None.

Storage
Keep in a closed container in a cool, dry place away from reach of children. Protect from light.

Missed dose
Take as soon as you remember. If your next dose is due within 24 hours, take a single dose now and skip the next.

Stopping the drug
Take the full course. If stopped too soon treatment may fail.

Exceeding the dose
An occasional unintentional extra dose is unlikely to cause problems. Large overdoses may cause trembling, breathing difficulty, and fits. Notify your doctor.

POSSIBLE ADVERSE EFFECTS

Side effects of pyrimethamine occur only rarely with the low doses given for prevention of malaria. Unusual tiredness, weakness, bleeding, bruising, and sore throat may be signs of a blood disorder. Notify your doctor promptly if they occur.

Symptom/effect	Frequency		Discuss with doctor		Stop taking drug now	Call doctor now
	Common	Rare	Only if severe	In all cases		
Loss of appetite	●		■			
Insomnia	●		■			
Gastric irritation	●			■		
Rash	●			■		▮
Unusual bleeding/bruising	●			■		▮
Sore throat/fever	●			■		▮

INTERACTIONS

General note Drugs that suppress the bone marrow or cause folic acid deficiency may increase the risk of serious blood disorders. Such drugs include anticancer drugs, antirheumatics, phenylbutazone, sulphasalazine, co-trimoxazole, and phenytoin.

SPECIAL PRECAUTIONS

Be sure to consult your doctor or pharmacist before using this drug if:
▼ You have long-term liver or kidney problems.
▼ You have had epileptic fits.
▼ You have anaemia.
▼ You are taking other medications.

Pregnancy
▼ No evidence of risk, but pregnant women receiving this drug should also take a folic acid supplement. Discuss with your doctor.

Breast feeding
▼ The drug passes into the breast milk, but at normal doses adverse effects on the baby are unlikely. Discuss with your doctor.

Infants and children
▼ Reduced dose necessary.

Over 60
▼ No special problems.

Driving and hazardous work
▼ No special problems.

Alcohol
▼ No known problems.

PROLONGED USE

Prolonged use of this drug in high doses may cause folic acid deficiency, leading to serious blood disorders. Supplements of folic acid may be recommended.

Monitoring Regular blood cell counts may be required during high dose treatment for toxoplasmosis.

QUININE

Brand names None
Used in the following combined preparations None

GENERAL INFORMATION

Quinine, obtained from the bark of the cinchona tree, is the earliest anti-malarial drug. Introduced in the last century, it is no longer widely used because it frequently causes side effects (see below). However, it is still occasionally given for malaria that is resistant to safer treatments. In some of these cases, it is administered by mouth in conjunction with other drugs. Quinine is also prescribed in low doses for prevention of painful night-time leg cramps, and this is now its commonest use in many countries.

At the high doses used to treat malaria, quinine may cause ringing in the ears, headaches, nausea, hearing loss, and blurred vision, a group of symptoms known as cinchonism. In rare cases, the drug may also cause subcutaneous bleeding due to a reduction in blood platelets.

QUICK REFERENCE

Drug group Drug for muscle disorders (p.120) and antimalarial drug (p.137)

Overdose danger rating High

Dependence rating Low

Prescription needed Yes

Available as generic Yes

INFORMATION FOR USERS

Your drug prescription is tailored for you. Do not alter dosage without checking with your doctor.

How taken

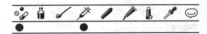

Tablets, injection.

Frequency and timing of doses
Malaria Every 8 hours.
Muscle cramps Once daily at bedtime or 2 x daily after evening meal and at bedtime.

Adult dosage range
Up to 1.8g daily (malaria);
200 – 300mg daily (cramps).

Onset of effect
2 – 3 hours (cramps); 1 – 2 days (malaria).

Duration of action
Up to 24 hours.

Diet advice
None.

Storage
Keep in a closed container in a cool, dry place away from reach of children. Protect from light.

Missed dose
Take as soon as you remember. If your next dose is due within 4 hours, skip the missed dose and resume your normal dosing schedule thereafter.

Stopping the drug
If prescribed for malaria, take the full course. Even if you feel better, the original infection may still be present and may recur if treatment is stopped too soon. If taken for muscle cramps, the drug can safely be stopped as soon as you no longer need it.

OVERDOSE ACTION

 Seek immediate medical advice in all cases. Take emergency action if breathing problems, fits, or loss of consciousness occur.

See Drug poisoning emergency guide (p.470).

SPECIAL PRECAUTIONS

Be sure to tell your doctor if:
▼ You have a long-term kidney problem.
▼ You have tinnitus (ringing in the ears).
▼ You have optic neuritis.
▼ You have myasthenia gravis.
▼ You have glucose-6-phosphate dehydrogenase (G6PD) deficiency.
▼ You have heart problems.
▼ You are taking other medications.

 Pregnancy
▼ Not usually prescribed. May cause defects in the unborn baby. Discuss with your doctor.

 Breast feeding
▼ The drug passes into the breast milk, but at normal doses adverse effects on the baby are unlikely. Discuss with your doctor.

 Infants and children
▼ Reduced dose necessary.

 Over 60
▼ No special problems.

 Driving and hazardous work
▼ Blurring of vision, an uncommon side effect, may impair these activities.

 Alcohol
▼ No known problems.

PROLONGED USE

No problems expected with low doses used to control night-time leg cramps.

POSSIBLE ADVERSE EFFECTS

Adverse effects are unlikely with low doses. At antimalarial doses hearing disturbances, headache, and blurred vision are more common. Nausea may occur.

Symptom/effect	Frequency		Discuss with doctor		Stop taking drug now	Call doctor now
	Common	Rare	Only if severe	In all cases		
Nausea	●		■			
Headache	●			■		
Ringing in the ears	●			■		
Rash/itching	●			■	▲	
Loss of hearing	●			■	▲	▌
Disturbed vision	●			■	▲	▌

INTERACTIONS

Digoxin Quinine increases the blood level of digoxin.

Cimetidine This drug increases the blood levels of quinine.

RANITIDINE

Brand name Zantac
Used in the following combined preparations None

GENERAL INFORMATION

Ranitidine is mainly used in the prevention and treatment of stomach and duodenal ulcers and gastrointestinal bleeding. It acts by reducing the amount of acid produced by the stomach, allowing the ulcers to heal.

Ranitidine also reduces discomfort and inflammation from reflux oesophagitis. Treatment is usually given in courses lasting from four to eight weeks, with further short courses if symptoms recur.

Unlike cimetidine, a similar drug, ranitidine does not affect the actions of certain enzymes in the liver, where many drugs are broken down. This means that ranitidine can be taken with other drugs like anticoagulants and anticonvulsants, without causing an interaction that may reduce the effectiveness of treatment.

Most people do not experience any serious effects during a course of treatment with ranitidine. As ranitidine promotes healing of the stomach lining, there is a risk that it may mask stomach cancer, delaying diagnosis. It is therefore usually prescribed only when the possibility of stomach cancer has been ruled out.

INFORMATION FOR USERS

Your drug prescription is tailored for you. Do not alter dosage without checking with your doctor.

How taken

Tablets, soluble tablets, liquid, injection.

Frequency and timing of doses
Once daily at bedtime or 2 x daily.

Adult dosage range
150 – 600mg daily.

Onset of effect
Within 1 hour.

Duration of action
12 hours.

Diet advice
None.

Storage
Keep in a closed container in a cool, dry place away from reach of children.

Missed dose
Take as soon as you remember. If your next dose is due within 3 hours, take a single dose now and skip the next.

Stopping the drug
Do not stop the drug without consulting your doctor; symptoms may recur.

Exceeding the dose
An occasional unintentional extra dose is unlikely to be a cause for concern. But if you notice unusual symptoms, or if a large overdose has been taken, notify your doctor.

SPECIAL PRECAUTIONS

Be sure to tell your doctor if:
▼ You have long-term liver or kidney problems.
▼ You are taking other medications.

 Pregnancy
▼ Safety in pregnancy not established. Discuss with your doctor.

 Breast feeding
▼ The drug passes into the breast milk, but at normal doses adverse effects on the baby are unlikely. Discuss with your doctor.

 Infants and children
▼ Reduced dose necessary.

 Over 60
▼ No special problems.

 Driving and hazardous work
▼ No known problems. Dizziness can occur in a very small proportion of patients.

 Alcohol
▼ Avoid. Alcohol may aggravate your underlying condition and reduce the beneficial effects of this drug.

POSSIBLE ADVERSE EFFECTS

The adverse effects of ranitidine, of which headache is the most common, are usually related to dosage level and almost always disappear when treatment finishes.

Symptom/effect	Frequency		Discuss with doctor		Stop taking drug now	Call doctor now
	Common	Rare	Only if severe	In all cases		
Headache/dizziness	●		■			
Rash	●			■	▲	
Jaundice	●		■		▲	▮

INTERACTIONS

None.

PROLONGED USE

No problems expected.

RIFAMPICIN

Brand names Rifadin, Rimactane
Used in the following combined preparations Rifater, Rifinah, Rimactazid

GENERAL INFORMATION

Rifampicin is an antibacterial drug that is highly effective in the treatment of tuberculosis. Taken by mouth, it is well absorbed in the intestine and widely distributed throughout the body, including the brain. It is therefore very useful in tuberculous meningitis.

It is always prescribed with other antituberculous drugs; this enhances its effect and prevents the development of resistance to the drug.

Rifampicin is also used for leprosy and other serious infections, including artificial heart valve infections (endocarditis) and bone infections (osteomyelitis). Rifampicin is never used alone to treat such infections because of the rapid emergence of resistance in some of the bacteria present. A harmless red-orange coloration may be imparted to urine, saliva, and tears.

INFORMATION FOR USERS

Your drug prescription is tailored for you. Do not alter dosage without checking with your doctor.

How taken

Tablets, capsules, liquid, injection.

Frequency and timing of doses
By mouth Once daily in the morning 30 minutes before food (tuberculosis); 1 – 2 x daily (prevention of meningitis, treatment of endocarditis); once daily or once monthly (leprosy).
By injection once daily (tuberculosis).

Adult dosage range
According to weight, usually 450 – 600mg daily (tuberculosis); 600mg – 1.2g daily (prevention of meningitis, treatment of endocarditis); 600mg per dose (leprosy).

Onset of effect
Over several days.

Duration of action
Up to 24 hours.

Diet advice
None.

Storage
Keep in a closed container in a cool, dry, place away from reach of children. Protect from light.

Missed dose
Take as soon as you remember. If your next dose is due within 6 hours, take both doses now and return to normal dosing thereafter.

Stopping the drug
Take the full course. Even if you feel better the original infection may still be present and symptoms may recur if treatment is stopped too soon. In rare cases stopping the drug suddenly after high-dose treatment can lead to a severe flu-like illness.

Exceeding the dose
An occasional unintentional extra dose is unlikely to cause problems. Large overdoses may cause nausea and vomiting and lethargy. Notify your doctor.

SPECIAL PRECAUTIONS

Be sure to tell your doctor if:
▼ You have a long-term liver problem.
▼ You are taking other medications.
▼ You wear contact lenses.

 Pregnancy
▼ Safety in pregnancy not established. Discuss with your doctor.

 Breast feeding
▼ The drug passes into the breast milk, but at normal doses adverse effects on the baby are unlikely. Discuss with your doctor.

 Infants and children
▼ Reduced dose necessary.

 Over 60
▼ Increased risk of adverse effects. Reduced dose may therefore be necessary.

 Driving and hazardous work
▼ No problems expected.

 Alcohol
▼ No special problems. Avoid excessive amounts.

PROLONGED USE

Rifampicin may cause liver damage.

Monitoring Periodic blood tests may be performed to monitor liver function.

POSSIBLE ADVERSE EFFECTS

Rifampicin normally causes a harmless orange-red discoloration of the urine and other body fluids. Serious adverse effects are rare. Jaundice usually improves during treatment but should nevertheless be reported to your doctor. Symptoms such as headache and breathing difficulties may occur after stopping high-dose treatment.

Symptom/effect	Frequency		Discuss with doctor		Stop taking drug now	Call doctor now
	Common	Rare	Only if severe	In all cases		
Muscle cramps/aches		●		■		
Nausea/vomiting/diarrhoea		●	■			
Jaundice		●		■	▲	▮
Flu–like illness		●		■	▲	▮
Rash/itching		●		■		

INTERACTIONS

General note Rifampicin may reduce the effectiveness of a wide variety of drugs. Such drugs include phenytoin, oral contraceptives, corticosteroids, oral antidiabetics, disopyramide, and oral anticoagulants.

RISPERIDONE

Brand name Risperdal
Used in the following combined preparations None

GENERAL INFORMATION

Risperidone is used to treat patients with schizophrenia. Although it will not cure the underlying disorder, risperidone will help alleviate the distressing symptoms. It is effective in relieving both "positive" symptoms (e.g. hallucinations, thought disturbances, and hostility) and "negative" symptoms (e.g. emotional and social withdrawal). It may also help other symptoms associated with schizophrenia such as depression and anxiety. Risperidone is less likely to cause movement disorders as a side effect than some other antipsychotics.

QUICK REFERENCE

Drug group Anti-psychotic (p.85)
Overdose danger rating Medium
Dependence rating Low
Prescription needed Yes
Available as generic No

INFORMATION FOR USERS

Your drug prescription is tailored for you. Do not alter dosage without checking with your doctor.

How taken

Tablets.

Frequency and timing of doses
2 x daily.

Adult dosage range
2mg daily (starting dose) increasing to 6mg – 16mg daily (maintenance dose).

Onset of effect
Within 2 – 3 days.

Duration of action
Approximately 2 days.

Diet advice
None.

Storage
Keep in a closed container in a cool, dry place away from reach of children. Protect from light.

Missed dose
Take as soon as you remember. If your next dose is due within 3 hours, take a single dose now and skip the next.

Stopping the drug
Do not stop taking the drug without consulting your doctor, symptoms may recur.

Exceeding the dose
An occasional unintentional extra dose is unlikely to cause problems. If larger doses have been taken, notify your doctor.

SPECIAL PRECAUTIONS

Be sure to tell your doctor if:
▼ You have liver or kidney problems.
▼ You have heart or circulation problems.
▼ You have had epileptic fits.
▼ You have Parkinson's disease.
▼ You are taking other medications.

 Pregnancy
▼ Safety in pregnancy not established. Discuss with your doctor.

 Breast feeding
▼ The drug probably passes into breast milk. Discuss with your doctor.

 Infants and children
▼ Not recommended under 15 years.

 Over 60
▼ Reduced dose necessary.

 Driving and hazardous work
▼ Avoid such activities until you have learned how the drug affects you because of the possibility of drowsiness and slowed reactions.

 Alcohol
▼ Avoid. Alcohol may increase the sedative effects of this drug.

Surgery and general anaesthetics
▼ Risperidone treatment may need to be stopped before you have a general anaesthetic. Discuss this with your doctor or dentist before any operation.

POSSIBLE ADVERSE EFFECTS

Risperidone is generally well tolerated with a low incidence of movement disorders. It is less sedating than some other antipsychotics.

Symptom/effect	Frequency		Discuss with doctor		Stop taking drug now	Call doctor now
	Common	Rare	Only if severe	In all cases		
Insomnia	●		■			
Anxiety/agitation	●		■			
Headache	●		■			
Dizziness		●		■		
Shakiness/tremor		●		■		
Rash		●		■		
High fever/rigid muscles		●		■	▲	▮

INTERACTIONS

Antiparkinson drugs Risperidone may reduce the effect of these drugs.

Sedatives All drugs that have a sedative effect on the central nervous system are likely to increase the sedative properties of risperidone.

PROLONGED USE

If used long term, serious movement disorders (*tardive dyskinesia*) may occur.

RITODRINE

Brand name Yutopar
Used in the following combined preparations None

GENERAL INFORMATION

Ritodrine is a *sympathomimetic* drug that relaxes the muscles of the uterus. It is used to prevent premature labour. After contractions are initially stopped by injections of the drug, tablets are then substituted. These continue to be administered until the doctor considers it safe for the baby to be born, usually at or before 36 weeks. Ritodrine may also be used to halt labour temporarily while corticosteroid drugs are given to help development of the baby's lungs and lessen the risk of breathing problems after delivery.

Stimulation of the heart leading to palpitations is the commonest side effect of ritodrine. Given by injection, it may also increase blood sugar levels and aggravate diabetes.

QUICK REFERENCE

Drug group Uterine relaxant used in labour (p.165)

Overdose danger rating Medium

Dependence rating Low

Prescription needed Yes

Available as generic No

INFORMATION FOR USERS

Your drug prescription is tailored for you. Do not alter dosage without checking with your doctor.

How taken

Tablets, injection.

Frequency and timing of doses
By continuous intravenous infusion or by intramuscular injection. Then by mouth every 2 hours for 24 hours, followed by doses every 4 – 6 hours.

Dosage range
Up to 120mg daily (by mouth).

Onset of effect
Within a few minutes (injection); 30 – 60 minutes (by mouth).

Duration of action
6 – 8 hours.

Diet advice
Eat nothing and drink only clear fluids until drug treatment has halted contractions.

Storage
Keep in a closed container in a cool, dry place away from children. Protect from light.

Missed dose
Take as soon as you remember. If your doses are scheduled every 4 – 6 hours and your next dose is due within 2 hours, take a single dose now and skip the next.

Stopping the drug
Do not stop taking the drug without consulting your doctor; stopping the drug may lead to the onset of labour.

Exceeding the dose
An occasional unintentional extra dose is unlikely to cause problems. Large overdoses may cause palpitations and breathing difficulty. Notify your doctor.

POSSIBLE ADVERSE EFFECTS

Adverse effects are dose-related and are more severe when ritodrine is given by injection. By mouth, adverse effects other than palpitations are rare. Breathlessness due to fluid in the lungs may occasionally occur.

Symptom/effect	Frequency		Discuss with doctor		Stop taking drug now	Call doctor now
	Common	Rare	Only if severe	In all cases		
Trembling/sweating	●		■			
Palpitations	●			■		
Nausea/vomiting		●		■		
Chest pain/breathlessness		●		■	▲	▮
Rash/flushing		●		■	▲	▮

INTERACTIONS

Antidepressant drugs may increase the likelihood of adverse effects from ritodrine.

Beta blockers These drugs reduce the effect of ritodrine.

Other sympathomimetic drugs Ritodrine may increase the effects of these drugs.

Corticosteroids There is an increased risk of breathing problems when ritodrine is taken with corticosteroids.

Antidiabetic drugs Ritodrine may raise blood sugar. Antidiabetic drug dosage may need to be increased.

SPECIAL PRECAUTIONS

Be sure to tell your doctor if:
▼ You have heart problems.
▼ You have pre-eclampsia (high blood pressure, swollen ankles, protein in urine).
▼ You have an overactive thyroid.
▼ You have diabetes.
▼ You are taking other medications.

 Pregnancy
▼ Used in pregnancy of over 16 weeks, there is no proven risk to the health of the baby. It is not prescribed in pregnancies of less than 16 weeks, since its safety is not established.

 Breast feeding
▼ Not applicable. Ritodrine is not used during breast feeding.

 Infants and children
▼ Not prescribed.

 Over 60
▼ Not prescribed.

 Driving and hazardous work
▼ Your underlying condition may make such activities inadvisable. Discuss with your doctor.

 Alcohol
▼ Not advisable during pregnancy.

Surgery and general anaesthetics
▼ Ritodrine may increase the risk of adverse effects on the heart with a general anaesthetic. Discuss with your doctor before any surgery.

PROLONGED USE

No special problems.

SALBUTAMOL

Brand names Aerolin, Cyclocaps, Maxivent, Salamol, Salbulin, Ventodisks, Ventolin, Volmax
Used in the following combined preparations Aerocrom, Ventide

GENERAL INFORMATION

Salbutamol is a *sympathomimetic* bronchodilator that relaxes the muscle surrounding the bronchioles (airways in the lung).

It is used mainly in the treatment of asthma, chronic bronchitis and emphysema. Although salbutamol can be taken by mouth, inhalation is considered to be more effective because the drug is delivered directly to the bronchioles, giving rapid relief, allowing smaller doses and creating fewer side effects.

Compared with some similar drugs, it has little stimulant effect on the heart rate and blood pressure, making it safer for those with heart problems or high blood pressure. Because salbutamol relaxes the muscles of the uterus, it is also used in prevention of premature labour.

The most common side effect of salbutamol is fine tremor of the hands, which may interfere with precise manual work. Anxiety, tension, and restlessness may also occur.

QUICK REFERENCE

Drug group Bronchodilator (p.92) and drug used in premature labour (p.165)

Overdose danger rating Low

Dependence rating Low

Prescription needed Yes

Available as generic Yes

INFORMATION FOR USERS

Your drug prescription is tailored for you. Do not alter dosage without checking with your doctor.

How taken

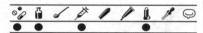

Tablets, SR-tablets, liquid, injection, inhaler.

Frequency and timing of doses
1 – 2 inhalations 3 – 4 x daily (inhaler);
3 – 4 x daily (tablets/liquid); twice daily (SR-tablets).

Dosage range
400 – 800 mg daily (inhaler);
8 – 32mg daily (orally).

Onset of effect
Within 5 – 15 minutes (inhaler); within 30 – 60 minutes (orally).

Duration of action
Up to 6 hours (inhaler); up to 8 hours (orally).

Diet advice
None.

Storage
Keep in a closed container in a cool, dry place away from reach of children. Protect from light. Do not puncture or burn inhalers.

Missed dose
Take as soon as you remember if you need to, and skip the next dose if it is due within 2 hours. Otherwise take your next dose as usual.

Stopping the drug
Do not stop the drug without consulting your doctor; symptoms may recur.

Exceeding the dose
An occasional unintentional extra dose is unlikely to be a cause for concern. But if you notice any unusual symptoms, or if a large overdose has been taken, notify your doctor.

SPECIAL PRECAUTIONS

Be sure to tell your doctor if:
▼ You have heart problems.
▼ You have high blood pressure.
▼ You have an overactive thyroid gland.
▼ You have diabetes.
▼ You are taking other medications.

Pregnancy
▼ Sometimes used to prevent premature labour. Discuss with your doctor.

Breast feeding
▼ The drug passes into the breast milk, but at normal doses adverse effects on the baby are unlikely. Discuss with your doctor.

Infants and children
▼ Reduced dose necessary.

Over 60
▼ Increased likelihood of adverse effects. Reduced dose may therefore be necessary.

Driving and hazardous work
▼ Avoid such activities until you have learned how the drug affects you because the drug can cause tremors.

Alcohol
▼ No known problems.

POSSIBLE ADVERSE EFFECTS

Muscle tremor, especially of the hands, anxiety and restlessness are the most common adverse effects. Palpitations and headache are rare.

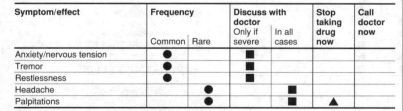

Symptom/effect	Frequency		Discuss with doctor		Stop taking drug now	Call doctor now
	Common	Rare	Only if severe	In all cases		
Anxiety/nervous tension	●		■			
Tremor	●		■			
Restlessness	●		■			
Headache		●			■	
Palpitations		●			■	▲

PROLONGED USE

No problems expected.

INTERACTIONS

Other sympathomimetics may increase the effects of salbutamol, so increasing the risk of adverse effects.

Beta blockers Drugs in this group may reduce the action of salbutamol.

Theophylline There is a risk of low potassium levels in blood occurring if taken with salbutamol.

SERTRALINE

Brand name Lustral
Used in the following combined preparations None

GENERAL INFORMATION

Sertraline belongs to the relatively new group of antidepressants called specific serotonin re-uptake inhibitors (SSRIs). It elevates mood, increases physical activity, and restores interest in everyday life. Sertraline is generally well tolerated and any gastrointestinal adverse effects, such as nausea or diarrhoea, are usually dose-related and decrease with continued use. It is less sedating and causes fewer anticholinergic side effects than tricyclic antidepressants.

QUICK REFERENCE

Drug group Antidepressant (p.84)
Overdose danger rating Medium
Dependence rating Low
Prescription needed Yes
Available as generic No

INFORMATION FOR USERS

Your drug prescription is tailored for you. Do not alter dosage without checking with your doctor.

How taken

Tablets.

Frequency and timing of doses
Once daily with food.

Adult dosage range
50 – 200mg daily. Doses of 150mg or greater are generally not used for more than 8 weeks.

Onset of effect
Some benefit may appear within 7 days although 2 to 4 weeks are usually necessary for full antidepressant activity.

Duration of action
Following prolonged treatment, antidepressant effects may persist for some weeks. Adverse effects may wear off within a few days.

Diet advice
None.

Storage
Keep in a closed container in a cool, dry place away from reach of children.

Missed dose
Take as soon as you remember. If your next dose is due within 8 hours, take a single dose now and skip the next.

Stopping the drug
Do not stop taking the drug without consulting your doctor. Symptoms may recur.

Exceeding the dose
An occasional unintentional extra dose is unlikely to cause problems. But if you notice any unusual symptoms, or if a large overdose has been taken, notify your doctor.

SPECIAL PRECAUTIONS

Be sure to tell your doctor if:
▼ You have impaired liver or kidney function.
▼ You have had epileptic fits.
▼ You are receiving electroconvulsive (ECT) therapy.
▼ You are taking other medications.

Pregnancy
▼ Safety in pregnancy not established. Discuss with your doctor.

Breast feeding
▼ The drug may pass into the breast milk. Discuss with your doctor.

Infants and children
▼ Not recommended.

Over 60s
▼ No special problems.

Driving and hazardous work
▼ Avoid such activities until you have learned how the drug affects you because the drug can cause drowsiness.

Alcohol
▼ Avoid. Alcohol may increase the sedative effects of this drug.

Surgery and general anaesthetics
▼ Sertraline may need to be stopped before you have a general anaesthetic. Discuss with your doctor or dentist before any operation.

POSSIBLE ADVERSE EFFECTS

Adverse effects on the gastrointestinal tract, such as nausea, indigestion, and diarrhoea may decrease with a reduction in dosage. Other adverse effects are rarely a problem.

Symptom/effect	Frequency		Discuss with doctor		Stop taking drug now	Call doctor now
	Common	Rare	Only if severe	In all cases		
Dry mouth		●	■			
Nausea/diarrhoea	●		■			
Sexual difficulty		●	■			
Tremor		●	■			
Indigestion	●		■			
Increased sweating		●	■			
Drowsiness		●	■			

PROLONGED USE

No problems expected.

INTERACTIONS

Monoamine oxidase inhibitors (MAOIs)
At least 14 days should elapse between stopping MAOIs and starting sertraline, and at least 7 days should elapse between stopping sertraline and starting MAOIs.

Tryptophan Taken together, tryptophan and sertraline may cause agitation and nausea.

Lithium Taken with sertraline, lithium can increase the risk of unwanted effects.

Sumatriptan Taken with sertraline, sumatriptan may increase the risk of unwanted effects.

Sedatives These may increase any sedative effect of sertraline.

SIMVASTATIN

Brand name Zocor
Used in the following combined preparations None

GENERAL INFORMATION

Simvastatin is a lipid-lowering drug, which was introduced in 1989. It blocks the action of an enzyme that is needed for cholesterol to be manufactured in the liver, and as a result the blood levels of cholesterol are lowered. It is prescribed for people with hyper-cholesterolaemia (high levels of cholesterol in the blood) who have not responded to other forms of therapy, such as a special diet, and are at risk of developing heart disease. At present it is used only for patients with a high cholesterol level that is not caused by another disease; these high levels are often hereditary.

Side effects are usually mild and often wear off with time. In the body, simvastatin is found mainly in the liver, and it may upset the levels of various liver enzymes. This effect does not usually indicate serious liver damage.

QUICK REFERENCE

Drug group Lipid-lowering drug (p.103)
Overdose danger rating Medium
Dependence rating Low
Prescription needed Yes
Available as generic No

INFORMATION FOR USERS

Your drug prescription is tailored for you. Do not alter dosage without checking with your doctor.

How taken

Tablets.

Frequency and timing of doses
Once daily at night.

Adult dosage range
10 – 40mg daily.

Onset of effect
Within 2 weeks; full beneficial effects may not be felt for 4 – 6 weeks.

Duration of action
Up to 24 hours.

Diet advice
A low-fat diet is usually recommended.

Storage
Keep in a closed container in a cool, dry place away from reach of children. Protect from light.

Missed dose
Take as soon as you remember. If your next dose is due within 8 hours, do not take the missed dose, but take the next dose on schedule.

Stopping the drug
Do not stop taking the drug without consulting your doctor. Stopping the drug may lead to worsening of the underlying condition.

Exceeding the dose
An occasional unintentional extra dose is unlikely to cause problems. Large overdoses may cause liver problems. Notify your doctor.

SPECIAL PRECAUTIONS

Be sure to tell your doctor if:
▼ You have long-term liver problems.
▼ You have eye or vision problems.
▼ You have muscle weakness.
▼ You are taking other medications.

Pregnancy
▼ Not usually prescribed. Safety in pregnancy not established. Discuss with your doctor.

Breast feeding
▼ The safety of use during breast feeding has not been established. Discuss with your doctor.

Infants and children
▼ Not recommended.

Over 60s
▼ No special problems.

Driving and hazardous work
▼ No special problems.

Alcohol
▼ Avoid excessive amounts. Alcohol may increase the risk of developing liver problems with this drug.

POSSIBLE ADVERSE EFFECTS

Side effects are usually mild and do not last long. The most common are those affecting the gastrointestinal system. Simvastatin very rarely may cause muscle problems, and any muscle pain or weakness should be reported at once.

Symptom/effect	Frequency		Discuss with doctor		Stop taking drug now	Call doctor now
	Common	Rare	Only if severe	In all cases		
Abdominal pain	●			■		
Constipation/diarrhoea	●			■		
Nausea	●			■		
Flatulence	●			■		
Headache	●			■		
Rash	●				■	▲
Muscle pain/weakness	●				■	∎

PROLONGED USE

Prolonged treatment can adversely affect liver function.

Monitoring Regular liver function tests are recommended. Periodic eye tests may also be performed.

INTERACTIONS

Anticoagulants Simvastatin may increase the effect of anticoagulants. Dosage adjustment may be necessary, and prothrombin time should be monitored regularly.

Cyclosporin Simvastatin nay increase the incidence of some adverse effects.

SODIUM AUROTHIOMALATE

Brand name Myocrisin
Used in the following combined preparations None

GENERAL INFORMATION

Sodium aurothiomalate is a gold-based drug used in the treatment of adult and juvenile rheumatoid arthritis. Unlike other anti-arthritic drugs, it may slow or even halt the progression of the disease, although it does not repair joint damage that has already occurred.

This drug is usually prescribed when conventional drug treatment, rest, and physiotherapy have failed, but may also be given in the early stages if the disease is severe. It is given by intramuscular injection, usually in the buttocks. Since it has no immediate therapeutic effect, but may take 4 – 6 months to produce its full response, non-steroidal anti-inflammatory drugs (NSAIDs) are generally given concurrently for the first few months.

Treatment may continue indefinitely if side effects are not troublesome. However, adverse effects such as blood disorders, rashes, and impaired kidney function may necessitate stopping the drug.

INFORMATION FOR USERS

This drug is given only under medical supervision and is not for self-administration.

How taken

Injection.

Frequency and timing of doses
Once a week (starting dose), reduced to once every 2 – 4 weeks (maintenance dose).

Dosage range
Adults 10mg (starting dose), increased to a maximum dose of 50mg weekly according to response.
Children Reduced dose necessary according to age and weight.

Onset of effect
Between 6 weeks and 6 months, according to the individual.

Duration of action
Up to 2 months. Adverse effects may last for several months after stopping the drug.

Diet advice
None.

Storage
Not applicable. This drug is not kept in the home.

Missed dose
No cause for concern. Treatment can be resumed when possible.

Stopping the drug
Do not stop treatment without consulting your doctor.

Exceeding the dose
This drug is only administered on expert advice and therefore overdose is extremely unlikely.

POSSIBLE ADVERSE EFFECTS

Potentially serious skin reactions are relatively common. Medical advice should be sought immediately if mouth ulcers, soreness, metallic taste, cloudy urine, or a rash occur. Flushing, dizziness, or joint pain may last for 1 or 2 days after injections.

Symptom/effect	Frequency		Discuss with doctor		Stop taking drug now	Call doctor now
	Common	Rare	Only if severe	In all cases		
Metallic taste	●			■		▮
Local irritation at injection site	●		■			
Mouth ulcers/soreness/fever	●			■		▮
Rash/itching	●			■	▲	▮
Diarrhoea/stomach pain		●		■		
Cloudy urine		●		■		
Shortness of breath		●		■		▮
Jaundice		●		■		▮

INTERACTIONS

None.

SPECIAL PRECAUTIONS

Be sure to tell your doctor if:
▼ You have long-term liver or kidney problems.
▼ You have heart or blood problems.
▼ You have a blood disorder.
▼ You have a skin disease.
▼ You are taking other medications.

Pregnancy
▼ Not usually prescribed. Safety in pregnancy not established. Discuss with your doctor.

Breast feeding
▼ The drug passes into the breast milk and may affect the baby. Discuss with your doctor.

Infants and children
▼ Reduced dose necessary.

Over 60
▼ No special problems.

Driving and hazardous work
▼ No known problems.

Alcohol
▼ No known problems.

PROLONGED USE

Prolonged use may rarely lead to eye problems, skin rashes, numbness in the hands or feet, or discoloration of the skin.

Monitoring Periodic blood and urine checks should be performed regularly, usually 1 – 2 weeks before each injection.

SODIUM BICARBONATE

Used in the following combined preparations Alka Seltzer, Bismag, Bisodol, Carbalax, Dioralyte, Gaviscon, Gastrocote, Mictral, Roter, and many others

GENERAL INFORMATION

Sodium bicarbonate is available without prescription on its own or in multi-ingredient preparations for the relief of occasional episodes of indigestion and heartburn. It may also relieve discomfort caused by peptic ulcers. It is now seldom recommended by doctors because other drugs are safer and more effective.

Because it also reduces the acidity of the urine, relieving painful urination, it is sometimes recommended for cystitis. Given by injection, it is effective in reducing the acidity of the blood and body tissues in metabolic acidosis, a potentially fatal condition that may occur in life-threatening illnesses or following cardiac arrest. It should be avoided by people with heart failure and a history of kidney disease. Sodium bicarbonate ear drops, are sometimes used for the removal of ear wax.

QUICK REFERENCE

Drug group Antacid (p.108)

Overdose danger rating Medium

Dependence rating Low

Prescription needed No

Available as generic Yes

INFORMATION FOR USERS

Follow instructions on the label. Call your doctor if symptoms worsen.

How taken

Tablets, capsules, liquid, powder (dissolved in water), injection, ear drops.

Frequency and timing of doses
Indigestion As required (orally).

Adult dosage range
Dependent on the condition being treated. As an antacid: 1 – 5g each dose.

Onset of effect
Within 15 minutes as an antacid.

Duration of action
30 – 60 minutes as an antacid.

Diet advice
None

Storage
Keep in a closed container in a cool, dry place away from reach of children.

Missed dose
No cause for concern.

Stopping the drug
When taken for indigestion, it can be safely stopped. When taken for other disorders, consult your doctor.

Exceeding the dose
An occasional unintentional extra dose is unlikely to cause problems. Large overdoses may cause unusual weakness, dizziness, or headache. Notify your doctor.

SPECIAL PRECAUTIONS

Be sure to consult your doctor or pharmacist before taking this drug if:
▼ You have long-term liver or kidney problems.
▼ You have heart problems.
▼ You have high blood pressure.
▼ You have severe abdominal pain or vomiting.
▼ You are on a low sodium diet.
▼ You are taking other medications.

Pregnancy
▼ No evidence of risk, but it is not likely to help morning sickness, and can encourage fluid retention.

Breast feeding
▼ No evidence of risk.

Infants and children
▼ Not usually prescribed. Not recommended in children under 6 years except on the advice of a doctor. Reduced dose necessary.

Over 60
▼ Reduced dose may be necessary.

Driving and hazardous work
▼ Do not take if you are flying. The gas produced expands and may increase stomach distension and belching.

Alcohol
▼ Avoid. Alcohol irritates the stomach and may counter the beneficial effects of this drug.

POSSIBLE ADVERSE EFFECTS

Belching and stomach pain may arise from the carbon dioxide produced as sodium bicarbonate neutralizes stomach acid, and can be caused by a single dose. The other effects result from the long term regular use of sodium bicarbonate.

Symptom/effect	Frequency		Discuss with doctor		Stop taking drug now	Call doctor now
	Common	Rare	Only if severe	In all cases		
Belching	●		■			
Abdominal pain		●	■			
Swollen feet/ankles		●		■	▲	
Muscle cramps		●		■	▲	
Tiredness/weakness		●		■	▲	
Nausea/vomiting		●		■	▲	▮

INTERACTIONS

General note Sodium bicarbonate interferes with the absorption or excretion of a wide range of drugs taken by mouth. Consult your doctor if you are taking oral anticoagulants, tetracycline antibiotics, phenothiazine antipsychotics, oral iron preparations, or lithium, and wish to take more than an occasional dose of sodium bicarbonate.

Diuretics The beneficial effects of these drugs may be reduced by use of sodium bicarbonate.

Corticosteroids Large amounts of sodium bicarbonate may hasten potassium loss, and increase fluid retention and high blood pressure.

PROLONGED USE

Severe weakness, fatigue, irritability, and muscle cramps may occur when this drug is taken regularly for extended periods. It should not be used daily for longer than 2 weeks without consulting your doctor.

Monitoring Blood and urine tests may be performed during prolonged use.

SODIUM CROMOGLYCATE

Brand names Intal, Cromogem, Eye-Crom, Nalcrom, Opticrom, Rynacrom
Used in the following combined preparations Aerocrom, Intal Compound, Rynacrom Compound

GENERAL INFORMATION

Sodium cromoglycate, introduced in the 1970s, is used primarily to prevent asthma and allergic conditions.

Taken by inhaler as a powder (spinhaler) or a spray, it is commonly prescribed to prevent mild to moderate asthma. It also reduces the frequency and severity of asthma attacks induced by exercise or cold air. Sodium cromoglycate has a slow onset of action, taking from a few days to up to six weeks of regular dosage to produce its anti-asthmatic effect. It is not effective for the relief of an asthma attack in progress.

Aside from its use in asthma, sodium cromoglycate is also given as eye drops to prevent allergic conjunctivitis. Taken as a nasal spray, it is also used to prevent allergic rhinitis (hayfever). It is also given for food allergy in the form of capsules.

Side effects are mild. Coughing and wheezing on inhalation may be prevented by using a *sympathomimetic* bronchodilator (p.82) first. Hoarseness and throat irritation can be avoided by rinsing the mouth with water after inhalation.

QUICK REFERENCE

Drug group Anti-allergy drug (p.125)

Overdose danger rating Low

Dependence rating Low

Prescription needed No (some preparations)

Available as generic No

INFORMATION FOR USERS

Your drug prescription is tailored for you. Do not alter dosage without checking with your doctor.

How taken

Capsules, inhaler (various types), eye and nose drops, nasal spray, eye ointment.

Frequency and timing of doses
Capsules 4 x daily before meals. Capsules may be swallowed whole or their contents dissolved in water. *Inhaler, nasal preparations* 4 – 8 x daily. *Eye preparations* 4 x daily (drops); 2 – 3 x daily (eye ointment).

Dosage range
Inhaler As directed. *Eye drops* 1 – 2 drops per dose (apply to each eye). *Capsules* 800mg daily. *Nasal preparations* Apply to each nostril as directed.

Onset of effect
Varies with dosage, form, and condition treated. Eye conditions and allergic rhinitis may respond after a few days' treatment with drops, while asthma and chronic allergic rhinitis may take take 2 – 6 weeks to show improvement.

Duration of action
4 – 6 hours. Some effect persists for several days after treatment is stopped.

Diet advice
Capsules: you may be advised to avoid certain foods. Follow your doctor's advice.

Storage
Keep in a closed container in a cool, dry place away from reach of children. Protect from light.

Missed dose
Take as soon as you remember. If your next dose is due within 2 hours, take a single dose now and skip the next.

Stopping the drug
Do not stop the drug without consulting your doctor; symptoms may recur.

Exceeding the dose
An occasional unintentional extra dose is unlikely to be a cause for concern. But if you notice unusual symptoms, or if a large overdose has been taken, notify your doctor.

SPECIAL PRECAUTIONS

Be sure to tell your doctor if:
▼ You are taking other medications.

Pregnancy
▼ No evidence of risk.

Breast feeding
▼ No evidence of risk.

Infants and children
▼ Reduced dose necessary.

Over 60
▼ No special problems.

Driving and hazardous work
▼ No known problems.

Alcohol
▼ No known problems.

POSSIBLE ADVERSE EFFECTS

Coughing and hoarseness are common with inhalation of sodium cromoglycate. Nasal spray may cause sneezing. These symptoms usually diminish with continued use.

Symptom/effect	Frequency		Discuss with doctor		Stop taking drug now	Call doctor now
	Common	Rare	Only if severe	In all cases		
Coughing/hoarseness	●		■			
Local irritation	●		■			
Nausea/vomiting (capsules)		●		■		
Joint pain		●		■		
Wheezing/breathlessness		●		■		
Rash (capsules)		●		■	▲	

PROLONGED USE

No problems expected.

INTERACTIONS

None.

SODIUM VALPROATE

Brand name Convulex (valproic acid), Epilim, Orlept
Used in the following combined preparations None

GENERAL INFORMATION

Sodium valproate is an anticonvulsant drug. It is often used along with other drugs for the treatment of a range of different types of epilepsy. Its action, however, is similar to that of other anticonvulsant drugs (see p.86), reducing electrical discharges in the brain.

Beneficial in long-term treatment, it does not have a sedative effect. This makes it particularly suitable for children who suffer from atonic epilepsy (a sudden relaxing of the muscles throughout the body) or absence seizures (during which the person appears to be daydreaming).

QUICK REFERENCE

Drug group Anticonvulsant (p.86)
Overdose danger rating Medium
Dependency rating Low
Prescription needed Yes
Available as generic Yes

INFORMATION FOR USERS

Your drug prescription is tailored for you. Do not alter dosage without checking with your doctor.

How taken

Tablets, liquid, injection.

Frequency and timing of doses
2 x daily.

Dosage range
600mg – 2.5g daily, adjusted as necessary.

Onset of effect
Within 60 minutes.

Duration of action
12 hours or more.

Diet advice
None.

Storage
Keep in a tightly closed container in a cool, dry place away from reach of children. Protect from light.

Missed dose
Take as soon as you remember. If your next dose is due within 2 hours, take a single dose now and skip the next.

Stopping the drug
Do not stop the drug without consulting your doctor; symptoms may recur.

Exceeding the dose
An occasional unintentional extra dose is unlikely to cause problems. Large overdoses may lead to coma. Notify your doctor.

POSSIBLE ADVERSE EFFECTS

Most serious adverse effects of sodium valproate are rare. They include liver failure, and platelet and bleeding abnormalities.

Symptom/effect	Frequency		Discuss with doctor		Stop taking drug now	Call doctor now
	Common	Rare	Only if severe	In all cases		
Temporary loss of hair		●	■			
Weight gain		●	■			
Nausea/indigestion		●		■		
Rash		●		■		▮
Drowsiness		●		■		▮
Jaundice		●		■		
Vomiting		●		■	▮	

INTERACTIONS

Other anticonvusant drugs may reduce blood levels of sodium valproate.

Antidepressants/antipsychotics These drugs may reduce the effectiveness of sodium valproate.

SPECIAL PRECAUTIONS

Be sure to tell your doctor if:
▼ You have long-term liver or kidney problems.
▼ You are taking other medications.

Pregnancy
▼ Not usually prescribed. May cause abnormalities in the unborn baby. Discuss with your doctor.

Breast feeding
▼ The drug passes into the breast milk, but at normal doses adverse effects on the baby are unlikely. Discuss with your doctor.

Infants and children
▼ Reduced dose necessary.

Over 60
▼ Reduced dose may be necessary.

Driving and hazardous work
▼ Your underlying condition, as well as the possibility of reduced alertness while taking this drug, may make such activities inadvisable. Discuss with your doctor.

Alcohol
▼ Avoid. Alcohol may increase the sedative effects of this drug.

PROLONGED USE

Use of this drug may cause liver damage, which is more likely in the first 6 months of use.

Monitoring Periodic checks on blood levels of the drug are usually required. Blood tests of liver function and blood composition may also be carried out.

SOMATROPIN

Brand name Genotropin, Humatrope, Norditropin, Saizen
Used in the following combined preparations None

GENERAL INFORMATION

Growth hormone is produced by the pituitary gland. In children and adolescents it promotes the normal growth and development of the body. But if it is not produced in sufficient quantities, growth is slowed and abnormally short stature results.

A synthetic form of growth hormone known as somatropin, produced by genetic engineering techniques, is administered regularly by injection to children who have a deficiency of the natural hormone to promote normal growth. Treatment is continued throughout childhood until the expected height is reached in late adolescence.

The earlier treatment is started, the greater the chance of complete success. Somatropin is not effective as a means of increasing height when hormone levels are normal. In spite of condemnation by doctors and sports authorities, the drug has occasionally been abused by athletes for its muscle-building properties, similar to those of anabolic steroids (p.146).

Treatment with this drug rarely causes adverse effects. Careful monitoring of growth is carried out. There is a slight risk of provoking diabetes mellitus, and sometimes thyroid function may be reduced.

INFORMATION FOR USERS

The drug is given only under medical supervision and is not for self-administration.

How taken

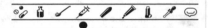

Injection.

Frequency and timing of doses
2 – 7 x weekly.

Dosage range
Dosage is adjusted according to age, weight, and individual response.

Onset of effect
1 – 2 months.

Duration of action
Up to 1 week.

Diet advice
Drug treatment for growth needs to be accompanied by a nourishing, balanced diet. Excessive intake of protein may rarely cause a build-up of nitrogen waste in the body. Your doctor will give detailed advice.

Storage
To be stored in a refrigerator between 2˚ and 8˚C.

Missed dose
Arrange for a missed injection to be administered as soon as possible.

Stopping the drug
Treatment can be safely stopped when the child has reached mature adult height. Stopping the drug prematurely may prevent full growth from being achieved.

Exceeding the dose
Overdosage is unlikely since treatment is carefully monitored.

POSSIBLE ADVERSE EFFECTS

Somatropin rarely causes adverse effects if taken in normal doses. Excessive growth of bones may occur if the drug is given in too high a dosage.

Symptom/effect	Frequency		Discuss with doctor		Stop taking drug now	Call doctor now
	Common	Rare	Only if severe	In all cases		
Injection site pain/swelling		●		■		

INTERACTIONS

Corticosteroids These may reduce the effect of somatropin.

SPECIAL PRECAUTIONS

Be sure to tell your doctor if:
▼ Your child has diabetes.
▼ Your child has a thyroid problem.
▼ Your child is taking other medications.

 Pregnancy
▼ Not prescribed.

 Breast feeding
▼ No evidence of risk. Discuss with your doctor.

 Infants and children
▼ Safe for use throughout childhood.

 Over 60
▼ Not prescribed.

 Driving and hazardous work
▼ No special problems.

 Alcohol
▼ No problems expected.

PROLONGED USE

Rate of growth may decrease during prolonged treatment. Treatment may be stopped for a few months and then restarted.

Monitoring Regular checks on height, bone growth, thyroid function, and urine glucose levels are usually carried out.

SPIRONOLACTONE

Brand names Aldactone, Laractone, Spiroctan, Spirolone, Spirospare
Used in the following combined preparations Aldactide, Lasilactone

GENERAL INFORMATION

Spironolactone belongs to the class of drugs known as potassium-sparing diuretics. Combined with thiazide or loop diuretics, it is used in the treatment of oedema (fluid retention) resulting from congestive heart failure. On its own or, more commonly, in combination with a thiazide diuretic, it may be used to treat oedema associated with cirrhosis of the liver, nephrotic syndrome (a kidney disorder), and a rare disease called Conn's syndrome, caused by a tumour in one of the adrenal glands.

Spironolactone is relatively slow to act, and its effects may appear only after several days of treatment. As with other potassium-sparing diuretics, there is a risk of unusually high levels of potassium in the blood if the kidneys are functioning abnormally. For this reason spironolactone is prescribed with caution for people with kidney failure. The drug does not worsen diabetes or gout, as do some other diuretics. The major side effect is nausea; abnormal breast enlargement may sometimes occur in men if high doses are given.

QUICK REFERENCE

Drug group Potassium-sparing diuretic (p.99)

Overdose danger rating Low

Dependence rating Low

Prescription needed Yes

Available as generic Yes

INFORMATION FOR USERS

Your drug prescription is tailored for you. Do not alter dosage without checking with your doctor.

How taken

Tablets, liquid.

Frequency and timing of doses
Once daily, usually in the morning with food.

Dosage range
50 – 200mg daily.

Onset of effect
Within 1 – 3 days, but full effect may take up to 2 weeks.

Duration of action
2 – 3 days.

Diet advice
Avoid foods that are high in potassium, e.g. dried fruit and salt substitutes.

Storage
Keep in a closed container in a cool, dry place away from reach of children.

Missed dose
Take as soon as you remember.

Stopping the drug
Do not stop the drug without consulting your doctor; symptoms may recur.

Exceeding the dose
An occasional unintentional extra dose is unlikely to be a cause for concern. But if you notice unusual symptoms, or if a large overdose has been taken, notify your doctor.

POSSIBLE ADVERSE EFFECTS

Spironolactone has few adverse effects; the main problem is the possibility that potassium may be retained by the body, causing muscle weakness and numbness.

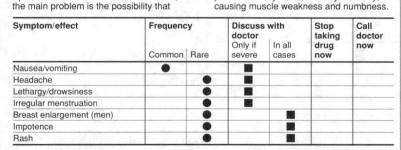

Symptom/effect	Frequency		Discuss with doctor		Stop taking drug now	Call doctor now
	Common	Rare	Only if severe	In all cases		
Nausea/vomiting	●		■			
Headache		●	■			
Lethargy/drowsiness		●	■			
Irregular menstruation		●	■			
Breast enlargement (men)		●		■		
Impotence		●		■		
Rash		●		■		

INTERACTIONS

Lithium Spironolactone may increase blood levels of lithium.

Digoxin Adverse effects may result from increased digoxin levels.

ACE Inhibitors These drugs increase the risk of raised blood levels of potassium.

SPECIAL PRECAUTIONS

Be sure to tell your doctor if:
▼ You have long-term liver or kidney problems.
▼ You have Addison's disease.
▼ You have a metabolic disorder.
▼ You are taking other medications.

 Pregnancy
▼ Not usually prescribed. May have adverse effects on the baby. Discuss with your doctor.

 Breast feeding
▼ The drug passes into the breast milk, but at normal doses adverse effects on the baby are unlikely. Discuss with your doctor.

 Infants and children
▼ Not usually prescribed. Reduced dose necessary.

 Over 60
▼ Reduced dose may be necessary. Increased likelihood of adverse effects.

 Driving and hazardous work
▼ Avoid such activities until you have learned how the drug affects you because this drug may occasionally cause drowsiness.

 Alcohol
▼ No known problems.

PROLONGED USE

Long-term use in the young is avoided if possible.

Monitoring Blood tests may be performed to check on kidney function and levels of body salts.

STILBOESTROL

Brand names Apstil
Used in the following combined preparations Tampovagan

GENERAL INFORMATION

Stilboestrol is a powerful synthetic oestrogen. Although it has been used for many years for a range of conditions including hormone deficiency and menopausal symptoms, its main use these days is in the treatment of prostate cancer and post-menopausal cancer of the breast. In these conditions it works by suppressing the effects of male sex hormones. Newer drugs are now used for treating the other conditions previously treated with stilboestrol.

Side effects are common with the drug, and it is because of these potential risks that it is now less widely used. In men, impotence is often a problem and abnormal breast development (gynaecomastia) can occur. Withdrawal bleeding often occurs in women.

QUICK REFERENCE

Drug group Female sex hormone (p.147)
Overdose danger rating Low
Dependence rating Low
Prescription needed Yes
Available as generic Yes

INFORMATION FOR USERS

Your drug prescription is tailored for you. Do not alter dosage without checking with your doctor.

How taken

Tablets, pessaries.

Frequency and timing of doses
Tablets Once daily.
Pessaries Once daily.

Adult dosage range
Prostate cancer 1 – 3mg daily.
Breast cancer 10 – 20mg daily.

Onset of effect
10 – 20 days.

Duration of action
Up to 24 hours. Some effects may last a few weeks.

Diet advice
None

Storage
Keep in a closed container in a cool, dry place away from reach of children.

Missed dose
Take as soon as you remember. If your next dose is due within 6 hours, take a single dose now and skip the next.

Stopping the drug
Do not stop the drug without consulting your doctor.

Exceeding the dose
An occasional unintentional extra dose is unlikely to be a cause for concern. But if you notice unusual symptoms, or if a large overdose has been taken, notify your doctor.

SPECIAL PRECAUTIONS

Be sure to tell your doctor if:
▼ You have long-term liver problems.
▼ You have heart failure or high blood pressure.
▼ You have had blood clots or a stroke.
▼ You have diabetes.
▼ You suffer from migraine or epilepsy.
▼ You are taking other medications.

Pregnancy
▼ Not prescribed.

Breast feeding
▼ The drug passes into the breast milk and may affect the baby. The drug may also have adverse effects on lactation. Discuss with your doctor.

Infants and children
▼ Not recommended.

Over 60
▼ No special problems.

Driving and hazardous work
▼ No known problems.

Alcohol
▼ No known problems.

POSSIBLE ADVERSE EFFECTS

The most common adverse effects are similar to symptoms in early pregnancy, but improve after 2 – 3 months of treatment. A sudden, sharp pain in the chest, groin, or legs may indicate an abnormal blood clot and requires urgent medical attention.

Symptom/effect	Frequency		Discuss with doctor		Stop taking drug now	Call doctor now
	Common	Rare	Only if severe	In all cases		
Nausea/vomiting	●		■			
Tender/enlarged breasts	●		■			
Swollen feet/ankles	●		■			
Impotence (men only)	●			■		
Pain in chest/groin/legs		●		■	▲	▌

INTERACTIONS

Tobacco smoking Smoking increases the risk of serious adverse effects on the heart and circulation with stilboestrol.

Anticonvulsants, rifampicin, and certain antibiotics These drugs may reduce the effectiveness of stilboestrol.

Antihypertensives and diuretics Stilboestrol may reduce the blood pressure lowering effect of these drugs by causing fluid retention.

PROLONGED USE

The risk of gallstones is increased with long-term use of this drug.

Monitoring Periodic general physical examinations and checks on blood pressure are usually required.

STREPTOKINASE

Brand names Kabikinase, Streptase
Used in the following combined preparation Varidase

GENERAL INFORMATION

Streptokinase, an enzyme produced by Streptococcus bacteria, is used in hospitals to dissolve the fibrin (see p.105) of blood clots, especially those in the arteries of the heart and lungs. It is also used on the clots formed in shunts during kidney dialysis.

A fast-acting drug, streptokinase is most effective in dissolving newly-formed clots, and it is often released at the site of the clot via a catheter inserted into an artery. Administered in the early stages of a heart attack to dissolve a clot in the coronary arteries (thrombosis), it can reduce the amount of damage to heart muscle. Because excessive bleeding is a common side effect, treatment is closely supervised.

Streptokinase is also used to treat wounds and ulcers in combination with another enzyme called streptodornase. For this use, it is applied locally.

QUICK REFERENCE

Drug group Thrombolytic agent (p.105)

Overdose danger rating Medium

Dependence rating Low

Prescription needed Yes

Available as generic No

INFORMATION FOR USERS

This drug is given only under medical supervision and is not for self-administration.

How taken

Injection.

Frequency and timing of doses
By a single injection or continuously over a period of 24 – 72 hours.

Dosage range
Dosage is determined individually by the patient's condition and response.

Onset of effect
As soon as streptokinase reaches the blood clot, it begins to dissolve within minutes. Most of the clot will be dissolved within a few hours.

Duration of action
Effect disappears within a few minutes of stopping the drug.

Diet advice
None.

Storage
Not applicable. This drug is not normally kept in the home.

Missed dose
Not applicable. This drug is given only in hospital under close medical supervision.

Stopping the drug
The drug is usually given for a period of 3 days.

Exceeding the dose
Overdosage is unlikely since treatment is carefully monitored.

SPECIAL PRECAUTIONS

Streptokinase is only prescribed under close medical supervision, usually only in life-threatening circumstances.

Pregnancy
▼ Not usually prescribed. If used during the first 18 weeks of pregnancy there is a risk that the placenta may separate from the wall of the uterus.

Breast feeding
▼ No evidence of risk.

Infants and children
▼ Reduced dose necessary.

Over 60
▼ No special problems.

Driving and hazardous work
▼ not applicable.

Alcohol
▼ Not applicable.

POSSIBLE ADVERSE EFFECTS

Streptokinase is given only under strict supervision and all adverse effects are closely monitored so that any of the symptoms below can be quickly dealt with.

Symptom/effect	Frequency		Discuss with doctor		Stop taking drug now	Call doctor now
	Common	Rare	Only if severe	In all cases		
Excessive bleeding	●			■		
Rash/itching		●		■		
Fever		●		■		
Wheezing		●		■		
Abnormal heart rhythms		●		■		
Collapse		●		■		

PROLONGED USE

Streptokinase is never used long-term.

INTERACTIONS

Anticoagulants There is an increased risk of bleeding when these are taken at the same time as streptokinase.

Antiplatelet drugs increase the risk of bleeding if given with streptokinase.

SUCRALFATE

Brand name Antepsin
Used in the following combined preparations None

GENERAL INFORMATION

Sucralfate, a drug partly derived from aluminium, is prescribed to treat gastric and duodenal ulcers. It does not neutralize stomach acid, but it forms a protective barrier over the ulcer that prevents it from being attacked by digestive juices, thus giving the ulcer time to heal.

If it is necessary during treatment to take antacids to relieve pain, they should be taken at least half an hour after taking sucralfate.

Apart from constipation, sucralfate does not have many common adverse effects. However, the safety of the drug in long-term use has not yet been confirmed. Therefore courses of more than 12 weeks are not recommended.

INFORMATION FOR USERS

Your drug prescription is tailored for you. Do not alter dosage without checking with your doctor.

How taken

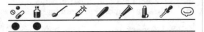

Tablets, liquid.

Frequency and timing of doses
2 – 4 x daily, 1 hour before each meal and at bedtime. The tablets may be dispersed in a little water before swallowing. Occasionally up to 6 x daily.

Dosage range
4 – 8g daily.

Onset of effect
Some improvement may be noted after one or two doses, but it takes a few weeks for an ulcer to heal.

Duration of action
Up to 5 hours.

Diet advice
None

Storage
Keep in a closed container in a cool, dry place away from reach of children.

Missed dose
Do not make up the dose you missed. Take your next dose on your original schedule.

Stopping the drug
Do not stop the drug without consulting your doctor; symptoms may recur.

Exceeding the dose
An occasional unintentional extra dose is unlikely to be a cause for concern. But if you notice any unusual symptoms, or if a large overdose has been taken, notify your doctor.

SPECIAL PRECAUTIONS

Be sure to tell your doctor if:
▼ You have long-term kidney problems.
▼ You are taking other medications.

Pregnancy
▼ Safety in pregnancy not established. Discuss with your doctor.

Breast feeding
▼ No evidence of risk.

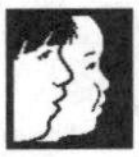

Infants and children
▼ Not usually prescribed. Reduced dose necessary.

Over 60
▼ No special problems.

Driving and hazardous work
▼ No known problems.

Alcohol
▼ Avoid. Alcohol may counteract the beneficial effect of this drug.

POSSIBLE ADVERSE EFFECTS

Most people do not feel any adverse effects while they are taking sucralfate. The most common is constipation, which diminishes as your body adjusts to the drug.

Symptom/effect	Frequency		Discuss with doctor		Stop taking drug now	Call doctor now
	Common	Rare	Only if severe	In all cases		
Constipation	●		■			
Diarrhoea		●	■			
Nausea		●		■		
Indigestion	●		■			
Dry mouth		●	■			
Rash/itching		●		■		
Dizziness/vertigo		●		■		
Insomnia		●		■		

PROLONGED USE

Not usually prescribed for periods longer than 12 weeks at a time.

INTERACTIONS

Antacids and other ulcer-healing drugs These reduce the effectiveness of sucralfate and should not be taken half an hour before or after sucralfate.

Phenytoin The effect of this drug may be reduced if taken with sucralfate.

Tetracyclines, ceprofloxacin, norfloxacin, ofloxacin Sucralfate may reduce the effects of these antibiotics.

Warfarin The effects of warfarin may be reduced.

Digoxin The effects of digoxin may be reduced.

SULPHASALAZINE

Brand name Salazopyrin
Used in the following combined preparations None

GENERAL INFORMATION

Sulphasalazine, chemically related to the sulphonamide antibacterial drugs, is used to treat two inflammatory disorders of the bowel. One is ulcerative colitis (which mainly affects the large intestine): the other is Crohn's diseas (which typically affects the small intestine). In recent years, sulphasalazine has also been found to be effective in the treatment of rheumatoid arthritis.

Adverse effects such as nausea, loss of appetite, and general discomfort are more likely when higher doses are taken. Side effects caused by stomach irritation may be avoided by a change to a specially coated formulation of the drug. Allergic reactions such as fever and skin rash may be avoided or minimized by low initial doses and gradual increases. Maintenance of adequate fluid intake is important while taking this drug. In rare cases among men, temporary sterility may occur.

QUICK REFERENCE

Drug group Drug for inflammatory bowel disease (p.112) and antirheumatic drug (p.117)
Overdose danger rating Low
Dependence rating Low
Prescription needed Yes
Available as generic Yes

INFORMATION FOR USERS

Your drug prescription is tailored for you. Do not alter dosage without checking with your doctor.

How taken

Tablets, liquid, suppositories, enema.

Frequency and timing of doses
4 x daily after meals with a glass of water (tablets); 2 x daily (suppositories); once daily (enema).

Adult dosage range
2 – 4g daily (Crohn's disease/ulcerative colitis); 500mg – 3g daily (rheumatoid arthritis).

Onset of effect
Adverse effects may be noticed within a few days, but full beneficial effects may take 1 – 3 weeks depending on the condition's severity.

Duration of action
Up to 24 hours.

Diet advice
It is important to drink plenty of fluids (at least 1.5 litres a day) during treatment. Sulphasalazine may reduce the absorption of folic acid from the intestine, leading to a deficiency of this vitamin. Eat plenty of green vegetables.

Storage
Keep in a closed container in a cool, dry place away from reach of children.

Missed dose
Take as soon as you remember. If your next dose is due within 2 hours, take a single dose now and skip the next.

Stopping the drug
Do not stop the drug without consulting your doctor; symptoms may recur.

Exceeding the dose
An occasional unintentional extra dose is unlikely to be a cause for concern. But if you notice unusual symptoms, or if a large overdose has been taken, notify your doctor.

SPECIAL PRECAUTIONS

Be sure to tell your doctor if:
▼ You have long-term liver or kidney problems.
▼ You have glucose-6-phosphate dehydrogenase (G6PD) deficiency.
▼ You have a blood disorder.
▼ You suffer from porphyria.
▼ You are allergic to sulphonamides or salicylates.
▼ You wear contact lenses.
▼ You are taking other medications.

Pregnancy
▼ No evidence of risk to developing baby. Folic acid supplements may be required.

Breast feeding
▼ The drug passes into the breast milk and may affect the baby. Discuss with your doctor.

Infants and children
▼ Not recommended under 2 years. Reduced dose necessary in older children, according to body weight.

Over 60
▼ No special problems.

Driving and hazardous work
▼ No special problems.

Alcohol
▼ No known problems.

POSSIBLE ADVERSE EFFECTS

Adverse effects are common with high doses, but may disappear with a reduction in the dose. Symptoms such as nausea and vomiting may be helped by taking the drug with food. Orange or yellow discoloration of the urine is no cause for alarm.

Symptom/effect	Frequency		Discuss with doctor		Stop taking drug now	Call doctor now
	Common	Rare	Only if severe	In all cases		
Nausea/vomiting	●		■			
Malaise/loss of appetite	●		■			
Ringing in the ears		●	■			
Headache	●			■		
Joint pain	●			■		
Fever/rash		●		■		■

INTERACTIONS

General note Sulphasalazine may increase the effects of a variety of drugs, including oral antidiabetics, anticonvulsants, and methotrexate.

Digoxin Sulphasalazine may reduce the absorption of this drug.

Iron absorption may be impaired by sulphasalazine.

PROLONGED USE

Blood disorders may occur with prolonged use of this drug.

Monitoring Periodic tests of blood composition and liver function are usually required.

SUMATRIPTAN

Brand name Imigran
Used in the following combined preparations None

GENERAL INFORMATION

Sumatriptan is a highly effective new drug for migraine generally used when people fail to respond to analgesics (e.g. aspirin, paracetamol). It is of considerable value in the treatment of acute migraine attacks, with or without aura, but it is not meant to be taken regularly to prevent attacks. Sumatriptan is also used for the acute treatment of cluster headache (a form of migraine headache). It should be taken as soon as possible after the onset of the attack, although, unlike other drugs used in migraine, it will still be of benefit at whatever stage of the attack it is taken.

Sumatriptan relieves symptoms by preventing the dilation of blood vessels in the brain, which causes the migraine attack.

QUICK REFERENCE

Drug group Anti-migraine drug (p.89)

Overdose danger rating Medium

Dependence rating Low

Prescription needed Yes

Available as generic No

INFORMATION FOR USERS

Your drug prescription is tailored for you. Do not alter dosage without checking with your doctor.

How taken

Tablets, injection.

Frequency and timing of doses
Should be taken as soon as possible after the onset of an attack. However, it is equally effective at whatever stage it is taken. DO NOT take a second dose for the same attack. The tablets should be swallowed whole with water.

Adult dosage range
Tablets 100mg (one tablet) per attack. This can be repeated if another attack occurs up to a maximum of 300mg (three tablets) in 24 hours. *Injection* 6mg per attack. For a second attack the injection may be repeated after at least 1 hour. Maximum 12mg (two injections) in 24 hours.

Onset of effect
Tablets 30 mins. *Injection* 10 – 15 mins.

Duration of action
Tablets The maximum effect occurs after 2 – 4 hours. *Injection* The maximum effect occurs after 1½ – 2 hours.

Diet advice
None unless otherwise advised.

Storage
Keep in a closed container in a cool, dry place away from reach of children. Protect from light.

Missed dose
Not applicable. Taken only to treat a migraine attack.

Stopping the drug
Only taken to treat a migraine attack.

Exceeding the dose
An occasional unintentional extra tablet/injection is unlikely to be a cause for concern. But if you notice unusual symptoms, or if a large overdose has been taken, notify your doctor.

SPECIAL PRECAUTIONS

Be sure to tell your doctor if:
▼ You have liver or kidney problems.
▼ You have heart problems.
▼ You have high blood pressure.
▼ You have had a heart attack.
▼ You have angina.
▼ You are taking other medications.

 Pregnancy
▼ Safety in pregnancy not established. Discuss with your doctor.

 Breast feeding
▼ Safety not established. Discuss with your doctor.

 Infants and children
▼ Not recommended.

 Over 60
▼ Over 65 years not as yet recommended.

 Driving and hazardous work
▼ Avoid such activities until you have learned how the drug affects you because the drug can cause drowsiness.

 Alcohol
▼ No special problems, but some drinks may provoke migraine in some people (see p.85).

Surgery and general anaesthetics
▼ Notify your doctor if you have used sumatriptan within 48 hours prior to surgery.

POSSIBLE ADVERSE EFFECTS

Many of the adverse effects will disappear after about 1 hour as your body becomes adjusted to the medicine.

Symptom/effect	Frequency		Discuss with doctor		Stop taking drug now	Call doctor now
	Common	Rare	Only if severe	In all cases		
Pain at injection site	●		■			
Tingling/heat sensation	●		■			
Tightness/pressure sensation		●		■		
Flushing	●		■			
Dizziness		●	■			
Heaviness/weakness sensation	●		■			
Fatigue/drowsiness		●	■			
Chest pain		●		■	▲	▌

INTERACTIONS

Antidepressants Monoamine oxidase inhibitors (MAOIs) and some other antidepressants, such as fluvoxamine, fluoxetine, paroxetine, and sertraline increase the risk of adverse effects with sumatriptan.

Lithium Sumatriptan should not be given to patients taking lithium, due to an increased risk of adverse effects.

Ergotamine There is an increased risk of adverse effects on the blood circulation if ergotamine is used with sumatriptan.

PROLONGED USE

Sumatriptan should not be used continuously to prevent migraine but only to treat migraine attacks.

TAMOXIFEN

Brand names Emblon, Noltam, Nolvadex, Oestrifen, Tamofen
Used in the following combined preparations None

GENERAL INFORMATION

Tamoxifen is an anti-oestrogen drug (oestrogen is a naturally-occurring female sex hormone). It is used for two conditions. In the treatment of certain types of infertility, tamoxifen is taken only on certain days of the menstrual cycle. In the treatment of breast cancer, it is used before and after the menopause; it can slow the growth of the tumour and even shrink it. It is also being tested in large trials to see whether it prevents breast cancer.

Because its effect is specific, tamoxifen has fewer adverse effects than most other drugs that can be used to treat breast cancer. However, it may cause eye damage if high doses are taken for long periods. When used to treat cancer that has spread to the bone, tamoxifen may cause pain in the affected site at first.

INFORMATION FOR USERS

Your drug prescription is tailored for you. Do not alter dosage without checking with your doctor.

How taken

Tablets.

Frequency and timing of doses
2 x daily.

Adult dosage range
20 – 40mg daily. Dosage may occasionally be increased.

Onset of effect
Side effects may be felt within days, but beneficial effects may take 4 – 10 weeks.

Duration of action
Effects may be felt for several weeks after stopping the drug.

Diet advice
None.

Storage
Keep in a closed container in a cool, dry place away from reach of children. Protect from light.

Missed dose
Take as soon as you remember. If your next dose is due within 2 hours, take a single dose now and skip the next.

Stopping the drug
Do not stop the drug without consulting your doctor; stopping the drug may lead to worsening of your underlying condition.

Exceeding the dose
An occasional unintentional extra dose is unlikely to be a cause for concern. But if you notice unusual symptoms, or if a large overdose has been taken, notify your doctor.

SPECIAL PRECAUTIONS

Be sure to tell your doctor if:
▼ You have cataracts or poor eyesight.
▼ You suffer from porphyria.
▼ You are taking other medications.

 Pregnancy
▼ Not usually prescribed. May have effects on the developing baby. Discuss with your doctor.

 Breast feeding
▼ Not usually prescribed. Discuss with your doctor.

 Infants and children
▼ Not prescribed.

 Over 60
▼ No special problems.

 Driving and hazardous work
▼ Do not drive until you have learnt how the drug affects you; it can cause dizziness and blurred vision.

 Alcohol
▼ No known problems.

POSSIBLE ADVERSE EFFECTS

These are rarely serious and do not usually require treatment to be stopped. Nausea and hot flushes are the most common reactions.

Symptom/effect	Frequency		Discuss with doctor		Stop taking drug now	Call doctor now
	Common	Rare	Only if severe	In all cases		
Hot flushes	●		■			
Irregular vaginal bleeding	●			■		
Nausea	●		■			
Swollen feet/ankles		●	■			
Bone and tumour pain		●		■		
Dizziness		●		■		
Blurred vision/visual disturbances		●		■		

PROLONGED USE

There is a risk of damage to the eye with long-term high dose treatment.

Monitoring Eyesight may be tested periodically.

INTERACTIONS

Anticoagulants People treated with anticoagulants such as warfarin will usually need a lower dose of the anticoagulant.

TEMAZEPAM

Brand name Normison
Used in the following combined preparations None

GENERAL INFORMATION

Temazepam belongs to a group of drugs known as the benzodiazepines. The actions and adverse effects of this group of drugs are described more fully under Anti-anxiety drugs (p.83).

Temazepam is used in the short-term treatment of insomnia. Because it is a short-acting drug compared with some other benzodiazepines, it is less likely to cause drowsiness and/or lightheadedness the following day.

For this reason, the drug is not usually effective for preventing early wakening, but hangover is less common than with other benzodiazepine drugs.

Like other benzodiazepines, temazepam can be habit-forming if taken regularly over a long period. Its effects may also grow weaker with time. For those reasons treatment with temazepam is usually reviewed every two weeks.

INFORMATION FOR USERS

Your drug prescription is tailored for you. Do not alter dosage without checking with your doctor.

How taken

Capsules, tablets, liquid.

Frequency and timing of doses
Once daily, half an hour before bedtime.

Adult dosage range
10 – 60mg.

Onset of effect
15 – 40 minutes.

Duration of action
6 – 8 hours.

Diet advice
None.

Storage
Keep in a closed container in a cool, dry place away from reach of children. Protect from light.

Missed dose
If you fall asleep without having taken a dose and wake some hours later, do not take the missed dose. If necessary, return to your normal dose schedule the following night.

Stopping the drug
If you have been taking the drug continuously for less than 2 weeks, it can be safely stopped as soon as you feel you no longer need it. However, if you have been taking the drug for longer, consult your doctor who may supervise a gradual reduction in dosage. Stopping abruptly may lead to withdrawal symptoms (see p.82).

Exceeding the dose
An occasional unintentional extra dose is unlikely to cause problems. Large overdoses may cause unusual drowsiness. Notify your doctor.

SPECIAL PRECAUTIONS

Be sure to tell your doctor if
▼ You have severe respiratory disease.
▼ You suffer from depression.
▼ You have long-term liver or kidney problems.
▼ You have had problems with alcohol or drug abuse.
▼ You are taking other medications.

 Pregnancy
▼ Safety in pregnancy not established. Discuss with your doctor.

 Breast feeding
▼ The drug passes into the breast milk, but at normal doses adverse effects on the baby are unlikely. Discuss with your doctor.

 Infants and children
▼ Not recommended.

 Over 60
▼ Reduced dose may be necessary. Increased likelihood of adverse effects.

 Driving and hazardous work
▼ Avoid such activities until you have learned how the drug affects you because the drug can cause reduced alertness and slowed reactions.

 Alcohol
▼ Avoid. Alcohol may increase the sedative effects of this drug.

POSSIBLE ADVERSE EFFECTS

The principal adverse effects of this drug are related to its sedative and tranquillizing properties. These effects normally diminish after the first few days of treatment.

Symptom/effect	Frequency		Discuss with doctor		Stop taking drug now	Call doctor now
	Common	Rare	Only if severe	In all cases		
Daytime drowsiness		●		■		
Dizziness/unsteadiness		●		■		
Headache		●		■		
Dry mouth/throat		●		■		
Vivid dreams/nightmares		●		■		
Rash		●		■	▲	

INTERACTIONS

Sedatives All drugs that have a sedative effect on the central nervous system are likely to increase the sedative properties of temazepam.

PROLONGED USE

Regular use of this drug over several weeks can lead to a reduction in its effect as the body adapts. It may also be habit-forming, when taken for extended periods, especially if larger than average doses are taken. Temazepam should not normally be used for longer than 4 weeks.

TERFENADINE

Brand name Seldane, Triludan
Used in the following combined preparations None

GENERAL INFORMATION

Terfenadine is a long-acting antihistamine. Its main use is in the treatment of allergic rhinitis, particularly hay fever. Taken as tablets or liquid, it reduces sneezing and irritation of the eyes and nose. Allergic skin conditions such as urticaria (hives) may also be helped by terfenadine.

The main difference between this drug and the older, traditional antihistamines is that it has little sedative effect on the central nervous system. It is therefore particularly suitable for people who need to avoid drowsiness – for example, at work. Terfenadine can rarely produce dangerous changes in heart rhythm. If palpitations develop or you feel faint, seek medical help without delay.

QUICK REFERENCE

Drug group Antihistamine (p.124)
Overdose danger rating Medium
Dependence rating Low
Prescription needed No
Available as generic No

INFORMATION FOR USERS

Follow instructions on the label. Call your doctor if symptoms worsen.

How taken

Tablets, liquid.

Frequency and timing of doses
1 – 2 x daily.

Dosage range
Adults 120mg daily.
Children Reduced dose according to age.

Onset of effect
1 – 3 hours. Some effects may not be felt for 1 – 2 days.

Duration of action
Up to 12 hours.

Diet advice
None.

Storage
Keep in a closed container in a cool, dry place away from reach of children.

Missed dose
No cause for concern, but take as soon as you remember. If your next dose is due within 5 hours, take a single dose now and skip the next.

Stopping the drug
Can be safely stopped as soon as you no longer need it.

Exceeding the dose
An occasional unintentional extra dose is unlikely to cause problems. Large overdoses may cause nausea or drowsiness and have adverse effects on the heart. Notify your doctor.

SPECIAL PRECAUTIONS

Be sure to consult your doctor or pharmacist before taking this drug if:
▼ You have long-term liver problems.
▼ You have any heart problems.
▼ You have had epileptic fits.
▼ You have glaucoma.
▼ You are taking other medications.

Pregnancy
▼ Safety in pregnancy not established. Discuss with your doctor.

Breast feeding
▼ No evidence of risk.

Infants and children
▼ Not recommended for children under 3 years old. Reduced dose necessary in older children.

Over 60
▼ No problems expected.

Driving and hazardous work
▼ Problems are unlikely. However, avoid such activities until you have learned how the drug affects you because the drug can cause drowsiness in some people.

Alcohol
▼ Avoid excessive amounts.

POSSIBLE ADVERSE EFFECTS

Indigestion and abdominal pain occur occasionally with terfenadine; other side effects are very unusual. Terfenadine can have adverse effects on the heart; if you have palpitations and/or feel faint, seek medical help without delay.

Symptom/effect	Frequency		Discuss with doctor		Stop taking drug now	Call doctor now
	Common	Rare	Only if severe	In all cases		
Indigestion		●	■			
Headache		●	■			
Drowsiness		●	■			
Dizziness		●		■	▲	▮
Fainting/palpitations		●		■	▲	▮

INTERACTIONS

Antifungal drugs Ketoconazole, itraconazole, and possibly other antifungal drugs increase levels of terfenadine and may lead to adverse effects on the heart.

Antidepressants/ antipsychotics These drugs increase the possibility of abnormal heart rhythms.

Anticholinergic drugs The anticholinergic effects of terfenadine may be increased by all drugs that have anticholinergic effects, including antipsychotics and tricyclic antidepressants.

Erythromycin This drug may increase levels of terfenadine and lead to adverse effects on the heart.

Sedatives Terfenadine may increase the sedative effects of anti-anxiety drugs, sleeping drugs, antidepressants, and antipsychotics.

PROLONGED USE

No problems expected.

TESTOSTERONE

Brand name Primoteston, Restandol, Sustanon, Virormone
Used in the following combined preparations None

GENERAL INFORMATION

Testosterone is a male sex hormone produced by the testes and, in small quantities, by the ovaries in women. It encourages bone and muscle growth in both men and women and stimulates sexual development in men. A shortage of testosterone may be caused by a disorder of the testes or pituitary gland. When this happens, synthetic or animal testosterone supplements may be given by injection, by mouth, or as an implant.

Testosterone is used to initiate puberty in male adolescents if it has been delayed because of a hormone deficiency. The drug may help to increase fertility in men who suffer from pituitary or testicular disorders. It does not, however, increase sperm production in men with normally developed testes. Rarely, testosterone is used to treat breast cancer.

Testosterone has a number of adverse effects. Dosages for treating delayed puberty in adolescents need to be controlled carefully because testosterone can interfere with growth or cause over-rapid sexual development. High doses may cause deepening of the voice or excessive hair growth.

INFORMATION FOR USERS

Your drug prescription is tailored for you. Do not alter dosage without checking with your doctor.

How taken

Capsules, injection, implanted pellets.

Frequency and timing of doses
Once daily (by mouth); twice weekly to every 3 weeks depending on condition (injection); every 6 months (implant).

Dosage range
Varies with method of administration.

Onset of effect
2 – 3 days.

Duration of action
1 - 2 days (by mouth); 1 – 3 weeks (injection); approximately 6 months (implant).

Diet advice
None.

Storage
Keep in a closed container in a cool, dry place away from reach of children. Protect from light.

Missed dose
No cause for concern, but take as soon as you remember. If your next dose (by mouth) is due within 3 hours, take a single dose now and skip the next.

Stopping the drug
Do not stop taking the drug without consulting your doctor.

Exceeding the dose
An occasional unintentional extra dose is unlikely to be a cause for concern. But if you notice unusual symptoms, or if a large overdose has been taken, notify your doctor.

POSSIBLE ADVERSE EFFECTS

Most of the more serious adverse effects are only likely to occur with long-term treatment with testosterone, and may be helped by a reduction in dosage.

Symptom/effect	Frequency		Discuss with doctor		Stop taking drug now	Call doctor now
	Common	Rare	Only if severe	In all cases		
Jaundice		●		■	▲	
Men only						
Difficulty in passing urine		●		■		
Abnormal erection	●			■		
Women only						
Unusual hair growth		●	■			
Voice changes		●		■		
Enlarged clitoris		●		■		

INTERACTIONS

Anticoagulants Testosterone may increase the effect of these drugs. Dosage may need to be adjusted accordingly.

Anti-epileptics Phenobarbitone, phenytoin, and carbamazepine may reduce the effects of testosterone.

SPECIAL PRECAUTIONS

Be sure to tell your doctor if:
▼ You have long-term liver or kidney problems.
▼ You have heart problems.
▼ You have prostate trouble.
▼ You have high blood pressure.
▼ You have epilepsy.
▼ You are taking other medications.

Pregnancy
▼ Not prescribed.

Breast feeding
▼ Not prescribed.

Infants and children
▼ Not prescribed for young children. Reduced dose necessary in adolescents.

Over 60
▼ Rarely required. Increased risk of prostate problems in elderly men.

Driving and hazardous work
▼ No special problems.

Alcohol
▼ No special problems.

PROLONGED USE

Prolonged use of this drug may lead to reduced growth in adolescents.

Monitoring Regular checks of the effects of testosterone treatment are required.

TETRACYCLINE

Brand names Achromycin, Sustamycin, Tetrabid, Tetrachel, Topicycline
Used in the following combined preparations Deteclo, Mysteclin

GENERAL INFORMATION

Tetracyclines were a very widely used group of antibiotics. However, the development of strains of bacteria resistant to the drugs has reduced their effectiveness in many types of infection. Tetracycline is still used for chest infections caused by chlamydia (e.g. psittacosis) and mycoplasma micro-organisms. It is used in non-specific urethritis and a number of rarer conditions, which include Q-fever, Rocky Mountain spotted fever, cholera, and brucellosis.

Acne improves following long-term treatment with tetracycline drugs either taken by mouth or applied to the skin as a solution.

Common side effects are nausea and vomiting and diarrhoea. Rashes may also occur. Tetracycline may discolour developing teeth if taken by children or by the mother during pregnancy. It is not prescribed for people with poor kidney function as it can cause further deterioration.

QUICK REFERENCE

Drug group Tetracycline antibiotic (p.128)

Overdose danger rating Low

Dependence rating Low

Prescription needed Yes

Available as generic Yes

INFORMATION FOR USERS

Your drug prescription is tailored for you. Do not alter dosage without checking with your doctor.

How taken

Tablets, capsules, SR-capsules, injection, ointment, ear/eye ointment.

Frequency and timing of doses
By mouth Every 6 hours, at least 1 hour before or 2 hours after meals; every 12 hours (sustained release). *Topical preparations* As directed.

Adult dosage range
1 – 2g daily.

Onset of effect
4 – 12 hours. Improvement in acne may not be noticed for up to 4 weeks.

Duration of action
Up to 12 hours.

Diet advice
Milk products should be avoided for 1 hour before and 2 hours after taking the drug, since they may impair its absorption.

Storage
Keep in a closed container in a cool, dry place away from reach of children.

Missed dose
Take as soon as you remember. If your next dose is due within 2 hours, take a single dose now and skip the next.

Stopping the drug
Take the full course. Even if you feel better the original infection may still be present and may recur if treatment is stopped too soon.

Exceeding the dose
An occasional unintentional extra dose is unlikely to be a cause for concern. But if you notice unusual symptoms, or if a large overdose has been taken, notify your doctor.

SPECIAL PRECAUTIONS

Be sure to tell your doctor if:
▼ You have long-term liver or kidney problems.
▼ You have previously suffered an allergic reaction to a tetracycline antibiotic.
▼ You are taking other medications.

 Pregnancy
▼ Not usually prescribed. May discolour the teeth of the developing baby. Discuss with your doctor.

 Breast feeding
▼ The drug passes into the breast milk and may lead to discoloration of the baby's teeth. Discuss with your doctor.

 Infants and children
▼ Not recommended under 12 years old. Reduced dose necessary in older children.

 Over 60
▼ No special problems.

 Driving and hazardous work
▼ No known problems.

 Alcohol
▼ No known problems.

POSSIBLE ADVERSE EFFECTS

Adverse effects from tetracycline skin preparations are rare. When given by mouth or injection, the drug may cause nausea and vomiting or diarrhoea.

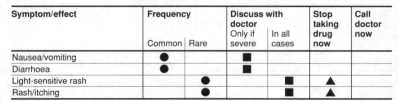

Symptom/effect	Frequency		Discuss with doctor		Stop taking drug now	Call doctor now
	Common	Rare	Only if severe	In all cases		
Nausea/vomiting	●		■			
Diarrhoea	●		■			
Light-sensitive rash		●		■	▲	
Rash/itching		●		■	▲	

PROLONGED USE

No problems expected.

INTERACTIONS

Oral contraceptives Tetracycline can reduce the effectiveness of oral contraceptives.

Iron may reduce the effectiveness of tetracycline.

Penicillins Tetracycline interferes with the antibacterial action of penicillins.

Antacids Antacids interfere with the absorption of tetracycline and may reduce its effectiveness.

Oral anticoagulants Tetracycline may increase the action of these drugs.

THEOPHYLLINE/AMINOPHYLLINE

Brand names Lasma, Nuelin, Slo-Phyllin, Theo-Dur, Uniphyllin (theophylline)/ Pecram, Phyllocontin (aminophylline)
Used in the following combined preparations Anestan, Do-Do Tablets, Franol, Labophylline, and others (theophylline)

GENERAL INFORMATION

Theophylline (and aminophylline, which breaks down to theophylline in the body) is used to treat bronchospasm (constriction of the air passages) in patients suffering from asthma, bronchitis, and emphysema.

It is usually taken continuously as a preventative measure, but it is also used to treat acute attacks.

Slow-release preparations produce beneficial effects lasting for up to 12 hours. These preparations may be prescribed twice daily, but they are also useful as a single dose taken at night to prevent night-time asthma and early morning wheezing.

Treatment with theophylline must be monitored because the effective dose is very close to the toxic dose. Some adverse effects, such as indigestion, nausea, headache, and agitation can be controlled by regulating the dosage and checking blood levels of the drug.

INFORMATION FOR USERS

Your drug prescription is tailored for you. Do not alter dosage without checking with your doctor.

How taken

Tablets, capsules, liquid, injection.

Frequency and timing of doses
3 – 4 x daily (tablets, liquid); every 12 or 24 hours (slow-release tablets or capsules). Medication should be taken at the same time each day in relation to meals.

Dosage range
Adults 375 – 1000mg depending on which product is used.

Onset of effect
Within 30 minutes (by mouth); within 90 minutes (slow-release tablets or capsules).

Duration of action
Up to 8 hours (by mouth); 12 – 24 hours (slow-release tablets or capsules).

Diet advice
Avoid barbecued foods and sudden changes in your regular diet.

Storage
Keep in a closed container in a cool, dry place away from reach of children.

Missed dose
Take as soon as you remember. If your next dose is due within 2 hours, take half the dose now (short-acting preparations) or forget about the missed dose and take your next dose now (long-acting preparations). Return to your normal dose schedule thereafter.

Stopping the drug
Do not stop taking the drug without consulting your doctor; stopping the drug may lead to worsening of the underlying condition.

OVERDOSE ACTION

 Seek immediate medical advice in all cases. Take emergency action if confusion, chest pains, or loss of consciousness occur.

See Drug poisoning emergency guide (p.470).

SPECIAL PRECAUTIONS

Be sure to tell your doctor or pharmacist if:
▼ You have long-term liver problems.
▼ You have angina or irregular heart beat.
▼ You have epilepsy.
▼ You have gastrointestinal ulcers.
▼ You smoke.
▼ You are taking other medications.

 Pregnancy
▼ Safety in pregnancy not established. Discuss with your doctor.

 Breast feeding
▼ The drug passes into the breast milk and may affect the baby. Discuss with your doctor.

 Infants and children
▼ Reduced dose necessary according to age and weight.

 Over 60
▼ Reduced dose may be necessary.

 Driving and hazardous work
▼ No known problems.

 Alcohol
▼ Avoid excess as this may alter levels of the drug.

PROLONGED USE

No problems expected.

Monitoring Periodic checks on blood levels of this drug are usually required.

POSSIBLE ADVERSE EFFECTS

Most adverse effects of this drug are related to dosage. Other effects are related to the drug's action on the central nervous system.

Symptom/effect	Frequency		Discuss with doctor		Stop taking drug now	Call doctor now
	Common	Rare	Only if severe	In all cases		
Agitation		●		■		
Headache	●			■		
Nausea/vomiting	●		■			
Diarrhoea		●	■			
Insomnia		●	■			
Palpitations		●		■	▲	■

INTERACTIONS

Erythromycin, ciprofloxacin, cimetidine, and corticosteroids may increase the level of theophylline in the blood.

Carbamazepine, phenytoin, barbiturates and tobacco smoking may reduce blood levels of theophylline.

THIORIDAZINE

Brand name Melleril
Used in the following combined preparations None

GENERAL INFORMATION

Thioridazine, belonging to the pheno-thiazine antipsychotic group of drugs (see p.85), was introduced in 1959.

This important tranquillizer is widely used to treat a variety of psychotic conditions. Its tranquillizing effect suppresses abnormal behaviour and reduces aggression. It is used in the treatment of schizophrenia, mania, dementia, and other disorders where confused or abnormal behaviour may occur. Thioridazine has a similar action to chlorpromazine, but it is less sedating and does not produce movement disorders to the same extent. Because of this, thioridazine is particularly suitable for treating the elderly.

The main drawback to the use of thioridazine is that when given in high doses it can cause eye problems. If large doses are required for long periods, another antipsychotic drug is usually substituted.

INFORMATION FOR USERS

Your drug prescription is tailored for you. Do not alter dosage without checking with your doctor.

How taken

Tablets, liquid.

Frequency and timing of doses
2 – 4 x daily.

Adult dosage range
50 – 800mg daily.

Onset of effect
2 – 3 hours.

Duration of action
4 – 10 hours. Some effects may last as long as 36 hours.

Diet advice
None.

Storage
Keep in a closed container in a cool, dry place away from reach of children.

Missed dose
Take as soon as you remember. If your next dose is due within 3 hours, take a single dose now and skip the next.

Stopping the drug
Do not stop the drug without consulting your doctor; symptoms may recur.

Exceeding the dose
An occasional unintentional extra dose is unlikely to cause problems. Large overdoses may cause unusual drowsiness, muscle rigidity, fainting, and agitation. Notify your doctor.

POSSIBLE ADVERSE EFFECTS

Thioridazine has a strong *anticholinergic* effect that can cause a variety of minor symptoms (see p.79). These often become less marked with time. The most significant adverse effect is eye problems. This can occasionally be controlled by medically supervised adjustment of dosage, or a change of drug.

Symptom/effect	Frequency		Discuss with doctor		Stop taking drug now	Call doctor now
	Common	Rare	Only if severe	In all cases		
Drowsiness	●		■			
Dry mouth	●		■			
Stuffy nose	●			■		
Blurred vision		●		■		
Muscle stiffness/tremor		●		■		
Unsteadiness		●		■		
Dizziness/fainting		●		■		▲

INTERACTIONS

Sedatives All drugs that have a sedative effect are likely to increase the sedative properties of thioridazine.

Antiparkinsonism drugs Thioridazine may counter the beneficial effect of these drugs.

Anticholinergic drugs The side effects of drugs with *anticholinergic* properties may be increased by thioridazine.

Antihistamines The risk of terfenadine and astemizole producing abnormal heart rhythms is increased by thioridazine.

SPECIAL PRECAUTIONS

Be sure to tell your doctor if:
▼ You have long-term liver or kidney problems.
▼ You have had epileptic fits.
▼ You have had glaucoma.
▼ You have a heart condition.
▼ You have Parkinson's disease.
▼ You are taking other medications.

Pregnancy
▼ Safety in pregnancy not established. Discuss with your doctor.

Breast feeding
▼ The drug passes into the breast milk, but at normal doses adverse effects on the baby are unlikely. Discuss with your doctor.

Infants and children
▼ Not usually prescribed. Reduced dose necessary.

Over 60
▼ Increased likelihood of adverse effects. Reduced dose may therefore be necessary.

Driving and hazardous work
▼ Avoid such activities until you have learned how the drug affects you because of the possibility of drowsiness and blurred vision.

Alcohol
▼ Avoid. Alcohol may increase the sedative effects of this drug.

PROLONGED USE

Use of this drug for more than a few months may lead to the development of eye problems and abnormal movements of the face and limbs known as *tardive dyskinesia*. Occasionally jaundice may occur.

Monitoring Eye examinations should be carried out at intervals if the drug is taken long term.

THYROXINE

Brand name Eltroxin
Used in the following combined preparations None

GENERAL INFORMATION

Thyroxine is the major hormone produced by the thyroid gland. A synthetic preparation is used to replace the natural hormone when this is deficient, causing hypothyroidism and sometimes leading to myxoedema, characterized by puffiness of the face. Certain types of goitre (enlarged thyroid) are helped by thyroxine, and it may be given to prevent the development of goitre during treatment with antithyroid drugs. It is also prescribed for thyroid cancer and its prevention in people undergoing radiation therapy in the neck.

Because adults with severe thyroid deficiency are sensitive to thyroid hormones, treatment is introduced gradually to prevent adverse effects (see below). Particular care is required in those with heart problems.

INFORMATION FOR USERS

Your drug prescription is tailored for you. Do not alter dosage without checking with your doctor.

How taken

Tablets.

Frequency and timing of doses
Once daily.

Dosage range
Adults Doses of 50 – 100 micrograms daily, increased at 3 – 4 week intervals as required. The maximum dose is 200 micrograms daily.
Children Reduced dose according to age and weight.

Onset of effect
Within 48 hours. Full beneficial effects may not be felt for several weeks.

Duration of action
1 – 3 weeks.

Diet advice
None.

Storage
Keep tablets in a closed container in a cool, dry place away from reach of children. Protect from light.

Missed dose
Take as soon as you remember. If your next dose is due within 8 hours, take a single dose now and skip the next.

Stopping the drug
Do not stop the drug without consulting your doctor; symptoms may recur.

Exceeding the dose
An occasional unintentional extra dose is unlikely to cause problems. Large overdoses may cause palpitations during the next few days. Notify your doctor.

SPECIAL PRECAUTIONS

Be sure to tell your doctor if:
▼ You have high blood pressure.
▼ You have heart problems.
▼ You are taking other medications.

 Pregnancy
▼ No evidence of risk.

 Breast feeding
▼ The drug passes into the breast milk, but at normal doses adverse effects on the baby are unlikely. Discuss with your doctor.

 Infants and children
▼ Dosage depends on age and weight.

 Over 60
▼ Reduced dose usually necessary.

 Driving and hazardous work
▼ No known problems.

 Alcohol
▼ No known problems.

POSSIBLE ADVERSE EFFECTS

Adverse effects are rare with thyroxine and are usually the result of overdosage causing thyroid overactivity. These effects diminish as the dose is lowered. Too low a dose of thyroxine may cause signs of thyroid underactivity.

Symptom/effect	Frequency		Discuss with doctor		Stop taking drug now	Call doctor now
	Common	Rare	Only if severe	In all cases		
Anxiety/agitation		●		■		
Diarrhoea		●		■		
Weight loss		●		■		
Sweating/flushing		●		■		
Muscle cramps		●		■		
Palpitations/chest pain		●		■		■

PROLONGED USE

No special problems.

Monitoring Periodic tests of thyroid function are usually required.

INTERACTIONS

Oral anticoagulants Thyroid hormone may increase the effect of these drugs.

Cholestyramine This drug may reduce the absorption of thyroxine.

Salbutamol The side effects of salbutamol may be increased by thyroxine.

Sucralfate The absorption of thyroxine may be reduced by sucralfate.

TIBOLONE

Brand names Livial
Used in the following combined preparations None

GENERAL INFORMATION

Tibolone is used for treating symptoms of natural or surgical menopause such as hot flushes, sweating, depressed mood, and decreased sex drive. It is taken continuously and, unlike most other hormone replacement therapies, does not require a cyclical course of progestogen to be taken.

Tibolone has a low incidence of side effects and does not cause withdrawal bleeding in post-menopausal women.

QUICK REFERENCE

Drug group Hormone replacement therapy (page 147)
Overdose danger rating Low
Dependence rating Low
Prescription needed Yes
Available as generic No

INFORMATION FOR USERS

Your drug prescription is tailored for you. Do not alter dosage without checking with your doctor.

How taken

Tablets.

Frequency and timing of doses
Daily, preferably at the same time each day. Swallow whole – do not chew.

Adult dosage range
2.5mg daily.

Onset of effect
You may notice improvement of symptoms within a few weeks but the best results are obtained when taken for at least 3 months.

Duration of action
A few days.

Diet advice
None.

Storage
Keep in a closed container in a cool, dry place away from reach of children. Protect from light.

Missed dose
Take as soon as you remember.

Stopping the drug
Do not stop the drug without consulting your doctor, as symptoms may recur.

Exceeding the dose
An occasional unintentional extra dose is unlikely to be a cause for concern. If several tablets are taken together, they may cause a stomach upset. Notify your doctor.

SPECIAL PRECAUTIONS

Be sure to tell your doctor if:
▼ You have liver or kidney problems.
▼ You suffer from epilepsy or migraine.
▼ You have diabetes.
▼ You have a tumour.
▼ You have a history of cardiovascular or cerebrovascular disease.
▼ You have a high cholesterol level.
▼ You have vaginal bleeding.
▼ You have had a period in the last 12 months.
▼ You are taking other medications.

 Pregnancy
▼ Not prescribed.

 Breast feeding
▼ Not prescribed.

 Infants and children
▼ Not prescribed.

 Over 60
▼ No special problems.

 Driving and hazardous work
▼ No problems expected.

 Alcohol
▼ No known problems.

POSSIBLE ADVERSE EFFECTS

Tibolone is well tolerated and the incidence of adverse effects low. Vaginal bleeding is more likely if it is less than one year since the menopause. For this reason, the drug is not recommended if it is less than 12 months from your last period.

Symptom/effect	Frequency		Discuss with doctor		Stop taking drug now	Call doctor now
	Common	Rare	Only if severe	In all cases		
Weight increase		●	■			
Ankle swelling		●	■			
Dizziness		●	■			
Acne		●		■		
Vaginal bleeding		●		■		
Headache		●	■			
Stomach upset		●	■			
Facial hair growth		●	■			
Jaundice		●		■	▲	∎

PROLONGED USE

Periodic examination by your doctor is advised.

INTERACTIONS

Some anti-convulsants Phenytoin, phenobarbitone, primidone and carbamazepine can accelerate the metabolism of tibolone and so decrease blood levels of the drug.

Anticoagulants The effects of warfarin may be enhanced by tibolone.

Rifampicin This can accelerate the metabolism of tibolone and so decrease blood levels of the drug.

TIMOLOL

Brand names Betim, Blocadren, Timoptol
Used in the following combined preparations Moducren, Prestim

GENERAL INFORMATION

Timolol is a beta blocker prescribed to treat hypertension (high blood pressure) and angina (pain due to narrowing of the coronary arteries). It may also be given after a heart attack to prevent further damage to the heart muscle. When used for hypertension, timolol may be given with a diuretic. Timolol is commonly administered as eye drops to people suffering from certain types of glaucoma. It is also occasionally given to prevent migraine.

Taken as tablets, timolol can cause breathing difficulties, especially in people with asthma, chronic bronchitis, or emphysema. As with other beta blockers, timolol may mask the body's response to low blood sugar and, for that reason, is prescribed with caution to diabetics.

Serious side effects are unusual with timolol eye drops; some people may experience eye irritation, blurring of vision, and headache.

INFORMATION FOR USERS

Your drug prescription is tailored for you. Do not alter dosage without checking with your doctor.

How taken

Tablets, eye drops.

Frequency and timing of doses
1 – 3 x daily.

Adult dosage range
By mouth 10 – 60mg daily (hypertension); 10 – 45mg daily (angina); 10 – 20mg daily (after a heart attack); 10 – 20mg daily (migraine prevention).

Onset of effect
Within 30 minutes (by mouth).

Duration of action
Up to 24 hours.

Diet advice
None.

Storage
Keep in a closed container in a cool, dry place away from reach of children.

Missed dose
Take as soon as you remember. If your next dose is due within 3 hours, take a single dose now and skip the next.

Stopping the drug
Do not stop the drug without consulting your doctor; stopping the drug may lead to worsening of the underlying condition.

OVERDOSE ACTION

 Seek immediate medical advice in all cases of overdose by mouth. Take emergency action if palpitations, breathing difficulties, or loss of consciousness occur.

See Drug poisoning emergency guide (p.470).

POSSIBLE ADVERSE EFFECTS

Timolol taken by mouth can occasionally provoke or worsen asthma and heart problems. Fainting may be a sign that the drug has slowed the heartbeat excessively. Eye drops cause these problems only rarely; headache or blurred vision are more likely.

Symptom/effect	Frequency		Discuss with doctor		Stop taking drug now	Call doctor now
	Common	Rare	Only if severe	In all cases		
Lethargy/fatigue	●		■			
Blurred vision (drops)	●		■			
Headache/dizziness	●		■			
Cold hands/feet		●	■			
Eye irritation (drops)		●	■			
Nightmares/vivid dreams		●		■		
Fainting/breathlessness		●		■	▲	■

INTERACTIONS

Salbutamol The effects of this drug may be reduced by timolol

Non-steroidal anti-inflammatory drugs These drugs may reduce the anti-hypertensive effect of timolol.

SPECIAL PRECAUTIONS

Be sure to tell your doctor if:
▼ You have a lung disorder such as bronchitis or emphysema.
▼ You have diabetes.
▼ You have poor circulation.
▼ You are taking other medications.

 Pregnancy
▼ May have effects on the baby. Discuss with your doctor.

 Breast feeding
▼ The drug passes into the breast milk, but at normal doses adverse effects on the baby are unlikely. Discuss with your doctor.

 Infants and children
▼ Not usually prescribed.

 Over 60
▼ Reduced dose may be necessary.

 Driving and hazardous work
▼ Avoid such activities until you have learned how the drug affects you because tablets may cause dizziness and eye drops may cause blurred vision.

 Alcohol
▼ May enhance lowering of blood pressure; avoid excessive amounts.

PROLONGED USE

No problems expected.

TOLBUTAMIDE

Brand names Rastinon
Used in the following combined preparations None

GENERAL INFORMATION

Tolbutamide is an antidiabetic agent that lowers blood sugar by stimulating insulin secretion from the pancreas. Taken by mouth, it is used to treat adult (maturity onset) diabetes in which active insulin-secreting cells are still present. Where these are lacking, as in juvenile diabetes, the drug is ineffective.

Tolbutamide does not work in isolation, but is given in conjunction with a special diabetic diet that limits carbohydrate intake.

Shorter acting than many oral antidiabetic drugs, tolbutamide may help in the initial control of diabetes. It may also be used in those with impaired kidney function because it is less likely to build up in the body and cause excessive lowering of blood sugar. As with other oral antidiabetic drugs, it may need to be replaced with insulin during serious illness, injury, or surgery, when diabetic control is lost.

QUICK REFERENCE

Drug group Antidiabetic drug (p.142)
Overdose danger rating High
Dependence rating Low
Prescription needed Yes
Available as generic Yes

INFORMATION FOR USERS

Your drug prescription is tailored for you. Do not alter dosage without checking with your doctor.

How taken

Tablets.

Frequency and timing of doses
Taken with meals either once daily in the morning, or 2 x daily in the morning and evening.

Adult dosage range
500mg – 2g daily.

Onset of effect
Within 1 hour.

Duration of action
6 – 10 hours.

Diet advice
A low fat, low carbohydrate diet must be maintained for the drug to be fully effective. Follow the advice of your doctor.

Storage
Keep in a closed container in a cool, dry place away from reach of children. Protect from light.

Missed dose
Take as soon as you remember. If your next dose is due within 2 hours, take a single dose now and skip the next.

Stopping the drug
Do not stop the drug without consulting your doctor; stopping the drug may lead to worsening of the underlying condition.

OVERDOSE ACTION

 Seek immediate medical advice in all cases. You may notice symptoms of low blood sugar, such as faintness, confusion or headache. If these occur eat something sugary. Take emergency action if fits or loss of consciousness occur.

See Drug poisoning emergency guide (p.470)

POSSIBLE ADVERSE EFFECTS

Serious adverse effects are rare with tolbutamide. Symptoms such as dizziness, sweating, weakness and confusion may indicate low blood sugar levels.

Symptom/effect	Frequency		Discuss with doctor		Stop taking drug now	Call doctor now
	Common	Rare	Only if severe	In all cases		
Dizziness/confusion	●			■		
Weakness/sweating	●			■		
Headache		●	■			
Nausea/vomiting		●		■		
Jaundice		●		■	▲	▮
Rash/itching		●		■	▲	

INTERACTIONS

General note A variety of drugs may oppose the effect of tolbutamide and so may raise blood sugar levels. Such drugs include corticosteroids, oestrogens, diuretics and rifampicin. Other drugs increase the risk of low blood sugar. These include warfarin, sulphonamides, beta blockers and aspirin.

SPECIAL PRECAUTIONS

Be sure to tell your doctor if:
▼ You have long-term liver or kidney problems.
▼ You are allergic to sulphonamides.
▼ You have thyroid problems.
▼ You are taking other medications.

 Pregnancy
▼ Not usually prescribed. May cause birth defects if taken in the first 3 months of pregnancy. Discuss with your doctor.

 Breast feeding
▼ The drug passes into the breast milk and may affect the baby. Discuss with your doctor.

 Infants and children
▼ Not prescribed.

 Over 60
▼ Increased risk of low blood sugar. Reduced dose is therefore usually necessary.

 Driving and hazardous work
▼ Usually no problem. Avoid these activities if you have warning signs of low blood sugar.

 Alcohol
▼ Avoid. Alcohol may upset diabetic control.

PROLONGED USE

No problems expected.

Monitoring Regular monitoring of urine and/or blood sugar is required.

TRAZODONE

Brand name Molipaxin
Used in the following combined preparations None

GENERAL INFORMATION

Trazodone is one of many drugs used to treat depression. It helps to elevate mood and restore interest in everyday activities. But because it has a strong sedative effect, it is particularly useful when the depression is accompanied by anxiety or insomnia or both. Taken at night, it helps to reduce the need for additional sleeping drugs.

Trazodone is less likely to cause adverse effects than the tricyclic antidepressants. It is also somewhat safer for people with heart problems and is therefore used to treat depression among the elderly.

INFORMATION FOR USERS

Your drug prescription is tailored for you. Do not alter the dosage without checking with your doctor.

How taken

Tablets, capsules, liquid.

Frequency and timing of doses
1 – 3 x daily with food.

Adult dosage range
150mg daily (starting dose), increased to 200 – 300mg daily (maintenance dose). Occasionally up to 600mg daily.

Onset of effect
Some benefits and adverse effects may appear within a few days of starting treatment, but full antidepressant effect may not be felt for 2 – 4 weeks.

Duration of action
Adverse effects may last up to 24 hours after stopping the drug. Following cessation of prolonged treatment, the antidepressant effect may persist for up to 6 weeks.

Diet advice
None.

Storage
Keep in a closed container in a cool, dry place away from reach of children. Protect from light.

Missed dose
Take as soon as you remember. If your next dose is due within 3 hours, take a single dose now and skip the next.

Stopping the drug
Do not stop the drug without consulting your doctor; symptoms may recur.

Exceeding the dose
An occasional unintentional extra dose is unlikely to cause problems. Large doses may cause unusual drowsiness. Notify your doctor.

SPECIAL PRECAUTIONS

Be sure to tell your doctor if:
▼ You have had epileptic fits.
▼ You have long-term kidney or liver problems.
▼ You have heart disease or are recovering from a recent heart attack.
▼ You are taking other medications.

Pregnancy
▼ Safety in pregnancy not established. Discuss with your doctor.

Breast feeding
▼ The drug passes into the breast milk, but at normal doses adverse effects on the baby are unlikely. Discuss with your doctor.

Infants and children
▼ Not recommended.

Over 60
▼ Increased likelihood of adverse effects. Reduced dose may therefore be necessary.

Driving and hazardous work
▼ Avoid such activities until you have learned how the drug affects you because the drug can cause drowsiness.

Alcohol
▼ Avoid. Alcohol may increase the sedative effects of this drug.

POSSIBLE ADVERSE EFFECTS

Trazodone has fewer common adverse effects than some of the other antidepressants, mainly because it has a much weaker *anticholinergic* action.

Symptom/effect	Frequency		Discuss with doctor		Stop taking drug now	Call doctor now
	Common	Rare	Only if severe	In all cases		
Drowsiness	●		■			
Constipation/diarrhoea		●	■			
Dry mouth		●	■			
Dizziness/fainting		●		■		
Headache		●		■		
Rash		●		■	▲	
Painful/prolonged erection		●		■	▲	▮

INTERACTIONS

Sedatives All drugs that have a sedative effect on the central nervous system are likely to increase the sedative properties of trazodone. Such drugs include antihistamines, sleeping drugs, narcotic analgesics, and antipsychotics.

Anti-epileptic drugs Trazodone may reduce the effects of these drugs.

TRIAMTERENE

Brand name Dytac
Used in the following combined preparations Dyazide, Dytide, Frusene, Kalspare, Triam-Co

GENERAL INFORMATION

Triamterene belongs to the class of drugs known as potassium-sparing diuretics. In combination with thiazide or loop diuretics, it is used in the treatment of hypertension and oedema (fluid retention). On its own, or more commonly in combination with a thiazide diuretic, it may be used to treat oedema as a complication of heart failure, nephrotic syndrome or cirrhosis of the liver.

Triamterene is quick to act; its effect on urine flow is apparent within two hours. For this reason, avoid taking it after about 4 p.m. As with other potassium-sparing diuretics, there is a risk of unusually high levels of potassium building up in the blood if the kidneys are functioning abnormally. Consequently, triamterene is prescribed with caution for people with kidney failure.

INFORMATION FOR USERS

Your drug prescription is tailored for you. Do not alter dosage without checking with your doctor.

How taken

Capsules.

Frequency and timing of doses
1 – 2 x daily after meals or on alternate days.

Dosage range
50 – 250mg daily.

Onset of effect
Within 2 hours.

Duration of action
9 – 12 hours.

Diet advice
Avoid foods that are high in potassium, e.g. dried fruit and salt substitutes.

Storage
Keep in a closed container in a cool, dry place away from reach of children.

Missed dose
Take as soon as you remember. However, if it is late in the day, do not take the missed dose, or you may need to get up at night to pass urine. Take the next scheduled dose as usual.

Stopping the drug
Do not stop the drug without consulting your doctor; symptoms may recur.

Exceeding the dose
An occasional unintentional extra dose is unlikely to be a cause for concern. But if you notice unusual symptoms, or if a large overdose has been taken, notify your doctor.

SPECIAL PRECAUTIONS

Be sure to tell your doctor if:
▼ You have long-term liver or kidney problems.
▼ You have had kidney stones.
▼ You have gout.
▼ You are taking other medications.

 Pregnancy
▼ Not usually prescribed. May cause a reduction in the blood supply to the developing baby. Discuss with your doctor.

 Breast feeding
▼ The drug passes into the breast milk and may affect the baby. It could also reduce your milk supply. Discuss with your doctor.

 Infants and children
▼ Not usually prescribed. Reduced dose necessary.

 Over 60
▼ Increased likelihood of adverse effects. Reduced dose may therefore be necessary.

 Driving and hazardous work
▼ No special problems.

 Alcohol
▼ No known problems.

POSSIBLE ADVERSE EFFECTS

Triamterene has few adverse effects; the main problem is the possibility that potassium may be retained by the body, causing muscle weakness and numbness. The drug may colour your urine blue.

Symptom/effect	Frequency		Discuss with doctor		Stop taking drug now	Call doctor now
	Common	Rare	Only if severe	In all cases		
Digestive disturbance	●		■			
Headache	●		■			
Muscle weakness	●			■		
Rash	●			■		
Dry mouth	●		■			

INTERACTIONS

Lithium Triamterene may increase the blood levels of lithium.

Non-steroidal anti-inflammatory drugs NSAIDs may increase the risk of potassium building up in the blood.

ACE Inhibitors These drugs increase the risk of raised blood levels of potassium with triamterene.

Cyclosporin This drug may increase levels of potassium with triamterene.

PROLONGED USE

Serious problems are unlikely, but levels of salts such as sodium and potassium may occasionally become disrupted during prolonged use.

Monitoring Blood tests may be performed to check on kidney function and levels of body salts.

TRIMETHOPRIM

Brand names Ipral, Monotrim, Trimogal, Trimopan
Used in the following combined preparations Bactrim, Chemotrim, Comox, Fectrim, Polytrim, Septrin, and others

GENERAL INFORMATION

Trimethoprim is an antibacterial drug that has been used for many years in combination with another anti-bacterial drug, sulphamethoxazole, in a preparation known as co-trimoxazole (see p. 248). In the 1970s trimethoprim alone became a popular drug for the prevention and treatment of infections of the urinary and respiratory tracts. It has fewer adverse effects than co-trimoxazole, and is equally effective in many conditions. In severe infections it can be given by injection.

Although side effects of trimethoprim are not usually troublesome, tests to monitor blood composition are often advised when the drug is taken for prolonged periods.

INFORMATION FOR USERS

Your drug prescription is tailored for you. Do not alter dosage without checking with your doctor.

How taken

Tablets, liquid, injection.

Frequency and timing of doses
1 – 2 x daily.

Adult dosage range
300 – 400mg daily (treatment);
100 – 200mg daily (prevention).

Onset of effect
1 – 4 hours.

Duration of action
Up to 24 hours.

Diet advice
None.

Storage
Keep in a closed container in a cool, dry place away from reach of children. Protect from light.

Missed dose
Take as soon as you remember.

Stopping the drug
Take the full course. Even if you feel better, the original infection may still be present and symptoms may recur if treatment is stopped too soon.

Exceeding the dose
An occasional unintentional extra dose is unlikely to be a cause for concern. But if you notice unusual symptoms, or if a large overdose has been taken, notify your doctor.

POSSIBLE ADVERSE EFFECTS

Trimethoprim taken on its own rarely causes side effects. However, additional adverse effects of the drug sulphamethoxazole may occur when trimethoprim is taken in combination with this drug.

Symptom/effect	Frequency		Discuss with doctor		Stop taking drug now	Call doctor now
	Common	Rare	Only if severe	In all cases		
Rash/itching	●		■			
Nausea/vomiting	●		■			

INTERACTIONS

Phenytoin The antifolate effect of phenytoin may be enhanced by trimethoprim.

Warfarin The effects of this drug may be increased by trimethoprim.

SPECIAL PRECAUTIONS

Be sure to tell your doctor if:
▼ You have long-term liver or kidney problems.
▼ You have a blood disorder.
▼ You are taking other medications.

Pregnancy
▼ Safety in pregnancy not established. Discuss with your doctor.

Breast feeding
▼ The drug passes into the breast milk, but at normal doses adverse effects on the baby are unlikely. Discuss with your doctor.

Infants and children
▼ Reduced dose necessary.

Over 60
▼ No special problems.

Driving and hazardous work
▼ No known problems.

Alcohol
▼ No known problems.

PROLONGED USE

Long-term use of this drug may lead to folate deficiency, which, in turn, may lead to blood abnormalities. Folate supplements may be prescribed.

Monitoring Periodic blood tests to monitor blood composition are usually advised.

URSODEOXYCHOLIC ACID

Brand names Destolit, Ursofalk
Used in the following combined preparations Combidol, Lithofalk

GENERAL INFORMATION

Ursodeoxycholic acid is a chemical that occurs naturally in bile, where it has an important role in controlling the concentration of cholesterol in the blood. As an orally administered drug, it is prescribed as an alternative to surgery in the treatment of gallstones. It acts by reducing levels of cholesterol in the bile, helping gallstones that are made predominantly of cholesterol to dissolve. Ursodeoxycholic acid is ineffective with stones of a high calcium or bile acid content. Its benefits are increased by weight loss and a diet high in fibre and low in fat. Ursodeoxycholic acid dissolves gallstones in 3 to 18 months. The progress of treatment is assessed regularly by ultrasound or by X-ray. Drug treatment is continued for at least 3 months after the stones have disappeared in order to prevent a recurrence. Recurrence of gallstones still occurs in about 25 per cent of people within a year of stopping treatment. Prolonged treatment may then be required.

INFORMATION FOR USERS

Your drug prescription is tailored for you. Do not alter dosage without checking with your doctor.

How taken

Tablets, capsules.

Frequency and timing of doses
2 x daily after food.

Adult dosage range
According to body weight.

Onset of effect
Within 30 minutes. Full beneficial effects may not be felt for up to 18 months.

Duration of action
Up to 12 hours.

Diet advice
A low cholesterol, high fibre diet is advisable since it enhances gallstone dissolution, prevents new stones forming and reduces circulating cholesterol levels.

Storage
Keep in a closed container in a cool, dry place away from reach of children.

Missed dose
No cause for concern but take as soon as you remember. If your next dose is due within 2 hours, take a single dose now and skip the next.

Stopping the drug
Do not stop the drug without consulting your doctor; symptoms may recur.

Exceeding the dose
An occasional unintentional extra dose is unlikely to be a cause for concern. But if you notice unusual symptoms or if a large overdose has been taken, notify your doctor.

SPECIAL PRECAUTIONS

Be sure to tell your doctor if:
▼ You have a long-term liver problem.
▼ You have peptic ulcers.
▼ You are taking other medications.

 Pregnancy
▼ Not usually prescribed. The drug may affect the baby. Discuss with your doctor.

 Breast feeding
▼ Safety not established. Discuss with your doctor.

 Infants and children
▼ Rarely needed. When used, dose is based on body weight.

 Over 60
▼ No special problems.

 Driving and hazardous work
▼ No known problems.

 Alcohol
▼ No known problems.

POSSIBLE ADVERSE EFFECTS

Adverse effects from ursodeoxycholic acid are rare.

Symptom/effect	Frequency		Discuss with doctor		Stop taking drug now	Call doctor now
	Common	Rare	Only if severe	In all cases		
Diarrhoea		●	■			
Indigestion		●	■			
Rash		●		■	▲	

INTERACTIONS

Cholestyramine, colestipol, and aluminium antacids These reduce the beneficial effect of ursodeoxycholic acid.

Oral contraceptives Oestrogen-containing preparations may counter the beneficial effects of ursodeoxycholic acid.

PROLONGED USE

No problems expected.

Monitoring Ultrasound or X-ray examinations may be carried out to assess the progress of treatment.

VERAPAMIL

Brand names Berkatens, Cordilox, Geangin, Securon, Univer
Used in the following combined preparations None

GENERAL INFORMATION

Verapamil belongs to a group of drugs known as calcium channel blockers, which interfere with the conduction of signals in the muscles of the heart and blood vessels. Used in the treatment of hypertension and arrhythmias, verapamil is also frequently given for angina. It reduces the frequency of attacks but does not, as other calcium channel blockers can, work quickly enough to help relieve pain while an attack is in progress. Verapamil increases your ability to tolerate physical exertion, and since it does not affect breathing, it can be used safely by asthmatics.

Because of its effects on the heart, verapamil is also prescribed for certain types of abnormal heart rhythm. For such disorders it can be given by injection as well as in tablet form.

It is not generally prescribed for people with low blood pressure, slow heart beat, or heart failure because it may make these conditions worse. It may be constipating.

QUICK REFERENCE

Drug group Anti-angina drug (p.101), anti-arrhythmic drug (p.100), and antihypertensive drug (p.102)

Overdose danger rating Medium

Dependence rating Low

Prescription needed Yes

Available as generic Yes

INFORMATION FOR USERS

Your drug prescription is tailored for you. Do not alter dosage without checking with your doctor.

How taken

Tablets, liquid, injection.

Frequency and timing of doses
2 – 3 x daily. Slow-release tablets are taken 1 – 2 x daily.

Adult dosage range
120 – 480mg daily.

Onset of effect
1 – 2 hours (tablets); 2 – 3 minutes (injection).

Duration of action
6 – 8 hours. During prolonged treatment some beneficial effects may last for up to 12 hours. Slow-release tablets act for 12 – 24 hours.

Diet advice
None.

Storage
Keep in a closed container in a cool, dry place away from reach of children.

Missed dose
Take as soon as you remember. If you normally take the drug once daily and your next dose is due within 8 hours, take a single dose now and skip the next. If you normally take it 2 – 3 times daily and your next dose is due within 3 hours, take a single dose now and skip the next.

Stopping the drug
Do not stop the drug without consulting your doctor; symptoms may recur.

Exceeding the dose
An occasional unintentional extra dose is unlikely to be a cause for concern. Large overdoses may cause dizziness and fainting. Notify your doctor.

SPECIAL PRECAUTIONS

Be sure to tell your doctor if:
▼ You have long-term liver or kidney problems.
▼ You are taking other medications.

 Pregnancy
▼ Not usually prescribed. May inhibit labour if taken during later stages of pregnancy. Discuss with your doctor.

 Breast feeding
▼ The drug passes into the breast milk, but at normal doses adverse effects on the baby are unlikely. Discuss with your doctor.

 Infants and children
▼ Reduced dose necessary.

 Over 60
▼ No special problems.

 Driving and hazardous work
▼ Avoid such activities until you have learned how the drug affects you because the drug can cause dizziness.

 Alcohol
▼ Avoid. Alcohol may further reduce blood pressure, causing dizziness or other symptoms.

POSSIBLE ADVERSE EFFECTS

Verapamil can cause minor symptoms such as constipation and headache.

Symptom/effect	Frequency		Discuss with doctor		Stop taking drug now	Call doctor now
	Common	Rare	Only if severe	In all cases		
Constipation	●		■			
Headache	●		■			
Nausea/vomiting	●		■			
Ankle swelling	●		■			
Flushing		●	■			
Dizziness		●		■		

PROLONGED USE

No problems expected.

INTERACTIONS

Beta blockers When verapamil is taken with these drugs there is a slight risk of abnormal heart beat and heart failure. Therefore, they are not usually prescribed together.

Carbamazepine The effects of this drug may be enhanced by verapamil.

Digoxin The effects of this drug may be increased if it is taken with verapamil. The dosage of digoxin may need to be reduced.

Antihypertensives Blood pressure may be further lowered when these drugs are taken with verapamil.

WARFARIN

Brand name Marevan
Used in the following combined preparations None

GENERAL INFORMATION

Warfarin is an anticoagulant used to prevent blood clots, mainly where blood flow is slowest, particularly in the leg and pelvic veins. Such clots can break off and travel through the bloodstream to lodge in the lungs, where they cause pulmonary embolism. Warfarin is also used to reduce the risk of clots forming in the heart in people with atrial fibrillation, or after the insertion of artificial heart valves. Such clots may travel to the brain and cause a stroke.

A widely used oral anticoagulant, warfarin requires regular monitoring to ensure proper maintenance dosage. As full beneficial effects of warfarin are not felt for 2 – 3 days, a faster-acting drug, such as heparin, is often used to complement the effects of warfarin at the start of treatment.

Like all anticoagulants, the most serious adverse effect is the risk of excessive bleeding, usually from excessive dosage.

QUICK REFERENCE

Drug group Anticoagulant (p.104)
Overdose danger rating High
Dependence rating Low
Prescription needed Yes
Available as generic Yes

INFORMATION FOR USERS

Your drug prescription is tailored for you. Do not alter dosage without checking with your doctor.

How taken

Tablets.

Frequency and timing of doses
Once daily, taken at the same time each day.

Dosage range
10 – 15mg daily according to age and weight and reduced to a daily maintenance dose, normally between 3 and 9mg, as determined by blood tests.

Onset of effect
Within 24 – 48 hours, with full effect after several days.

Duration of action
2 – 3 days.

Diet advice
None.

Storage
Keep in a closed container in a cool, dry place away from reach of children. Protect from light.

Missed dose
Take as soon as you remember. Take your next dose at the time it is due.

Stopping the drug
Do not stop the drug without consulting your doctor; stopping the drug may lead to worsening of the underlying condition.

OVERDOSE ACTION

Seek immediate medical advice in all cases. Take emergency action if severe bleeding or loss of consciousness occur.

See Drug poisoning emergency guide (p.470).

POSSIBLE ADVERSE EFFECTS

Bleeding is the most common adverse effect with warfarin. Any bruising, dark stools, dark urine, or unusual bleeding should be reported to your doctor straight away.

Symptom/effect	Frequency		Discuss with doctor		Stop taking drug now	Call doctor now
	Common	Rare	Only if severe	In all cases		
Fever		●		■	▲	▌
Nausea/vomiting		●		■	▲	▌
Abdominal pain/diarrhoea		●		■		
Rash		●		■		
Hair loss		●		■		
Bleeding/bruising	●			■	▲	▌

INTERACTIONS

General note A wide variety of drugs interact with warfarin, either by increasing or decreasing the anticlotting effect. These include barbiturates, cimetidine, oral antidiabetic drugs, certain laxatives, and certain antibiotics. Consult your pharmacist before you use over-the-counter medicines.

Aspirin Aspirin may significantly prolong or intensify the effect of warfarin.

SPECIAL PRECAUTIONS

Be sure to tell your doctor if:
▼ You have long-term liver or kidney problems.
▼ You have high blood pressure.
▼ You have peptic ulcers.
▼ You bleed easily.
▼ You are taking other medications.

 Pregnancy
▼ Not usually prescribed. Given in early pregnancy the drug can cause malformations in the unborn child. Taken near the time of delivery may cause the mother to bleed excessively. Discuss with your doctor.

 Breast feeding
▼ The drug passes into the breast milk, but at normal doses adverse effects on the baby are unlikely. Discuss with your doctor.

 Infants and children
▼ Reduced dose necessary.

 Over 60
▼ No special problems.

 Driving and hazardous work
▼ Use caution. Even minor bumps can cause bad bruises and excessive bleeding.

 Alcohol
▼ Avoid excessive amounts. Alcohol may increase the effects of this drug.

Surgery and general anaesthetics
▼ Warfarin may need to be stopped before surgery. Discuss with your doctor or dentist. In an emergency, its effect can be reversed by giving vitamin K by injection or by giving fresh frozen plasma.

PROLONGED USE

No special problems.

ZIDOVUDINE (AZT)

Brand name Retrovir
Used in the following combined preparations None

GENERAL INFORMATION

Zidovudine, formerly known as azidothymidine (AZT), is an antiviral agent used in the treatment of AIDS (acquired immune deficiency syndrome) or ARC (AIDS-related complex).

Zidovudine is used for people with serious AIDS-related illnesses, such as pneumocystis pneumonia and AIDS-virus infection of the brain cells. It reduces the frequency and severity of infections.

More recently, zidovudine has been approved for use in those infected with HIV, but who have no symptoms of the disease. It is possible that zidovudine delays the onset of severe symptoms.

The most common adverse effect of zidovudine is reduction in bone marrow activity, leading to blood disorders that may necessitate stopping the drug. For this reason, regular blood checks are performed. Zidovudine is not a lasting cure for AIDS, but it has dramatically improved the prospects for many of those treated.

INFORMATION FOR USERS

Your drug prescription is tailored for you. Do not alter dosage without checking with your doctor.

How taken

Capsules, liquid, injection.

Frequency and timing of doses
Every 4 hours.

Adult dosage range
0.5 – 1.5g daily.

Onset of effect
Within 48 hours.

Duration of action
About 4 hours.

Diet advice
None.

Storage
Keep in a tightly closed container in a cool, dry place away from reach of children. Protect from light.

Missed dose
Take as soon as you remember. If your next dose is due within 2 hours, take a single dose now and skip the next.

Stopping the drug
Do not stop taking the drug without consulting your doctor; symptoms may recur.

Exceeding the dose
An occasional unintentional extra dose is unlikely to cause problems. Serious adverse effects from large overdoses are unusual, but notify your doctor.

POSSIBLE ADVERSE EFFECTS

The most common adverse effect of zidovudine is anaemia. Symptoms include pallor, fatigue, and shortness of breath; sore throat and fever are less frequent effects.

Some adverse effects such as insomnia and fever may occur with too high a dose. These effects may be overcome by reducing the frequency of dosing.

Symptom/effect	Frequency		Discuss with doctor		Stop taking drug now	Call doctor now
	Common	Rare	Only if severe	In all cases		
Nausea/vomiting	●		■			
Headache	●		■			
Pallor/fatigue	●			■		
Breathlessness	●			■		▮
Insomnia		●		■		
Loss of appetite	●		■			
Aching muscles		●		■		
Sore throat/fever		●		■		

INTERACTIONS

General note A wide range of other drugs may increase the risk of harmful effects with zidovudine. These include drugs that act on the kidneys or affect blood production. Take no other medications without consulting your doctor or pharmacist.

Paracetamol significantly increases the risk of blood disorders.

Probenecid increases blood levels of zidovudine and the risk of toxic effects.

SPECIAL PRECAUTIONS

Be sure to tell your doctor if:
▼ You have long-term liver or kidney problems.
▼ You have had a previous allergic reaction to zidovudine.
▼ You have a history of blood disorders.
▼ You are taking other medications.

 Pregnancy
▼ Safety in pregnancy not established. Discuss with your doctor.

 Breast feeding
▼ The drug passes into the breast milk and may affect the baby. Discuss with your doctor.

 Infants and children
▼ Not recommended in infants less than 3 months old. Reduced dose necessary.

 Over 60
▼ Increased likelihood of adverse effects. Reduced dose may therefore be necessary.

 Driving and hazardous work
▼ No special problems.

 Alcohol
▼ No known problems.

PROLONGED USE

There is an increased risk of serious blood disorders with prolonged use of zidovudine.

Monitoring Regular blood checks are required during treatment.

A – Z OF VITAMINS AND MINERALS

The section on individual vitamins and minerals gives detailed information on the 24 major chemicals that are required by the body for good health – chemicals that are essential, but which the body is unable to manufacture itself. These include the main vitamins – A, C, D, E, K, H (biotin), and the six B vitamins – together with twelve essential minerals.

The section on Vitamins in Part 3 (p.149) describes in general terms the main sources of the major vitamins and minerals, their roles in the body and their primary uses, while the following profiles discuss each vitamin and mineral in closer detail.

The following pages may be particularly useful as a guide for those who think their diet lacks sufficient amounts of a certain vitamin or mineral, and for those with disorders of the digestive tract or liver, who may need extra vitamins. If you think that you may be deficient in a particular vitamin or mineral, refer to the table on p.150 to check that your diet includes good sources of each vitamin and mineral.

The vitamin and mineral profiles

For ease of reference, the vitamin and mineral profiles are arranged in alphabetical order and give information under standard headings. These include the different names by which each chemical is known; whether it is available over the counter or by prescription only; its role in body maintenance; specific foods in which it can be found; the recommended daily amounts; how to detect a deficiency; how and when to supplement your diet, and the risk of excessive intake of a particular vitamin or mineral.

Normal daily vitamin and mineral requirements are usually based on recommended daily dietary allowances (RDA). Dosages for treating deficiency are usually considerably higher, but need to be determined individually by a doctor.

HOW TO UNDERSTAND THE PROFILES

Each vitamin and mineral profile contains information arranged under standard headings to enable you to find the information you need.

Availability
Tells you whether the vitamin or mineral is available over the counter or only by prescription.

Other names
Lists the chemical and non-chemical names by which the vitamin or mineral is also known.

Dietry and other natural sources
Tells you how the vitamin or mineral is obtained naturally.

When supplements are helpful
Suggests when your doctor may recommend that you take supplements.

Dosage range for treating deficiency
Gives you a usual recommended dosage of vitamin and mineral supplements.

Actions on the body
Explains the role played by each vitamin and mineral in maintaining healthy body funtion.

Normal daily requirement
Gives you a guide to the recommended daily allowance (RDA) of each vitamin and mineral.

Symptoms of deficiency
Describes the common signs of deficiency to look out for.

Symptoms and risks of excessive intake
Describes the risks that may accompany excessive intake of each vitamin or mineral and warning signs to look out for.

PYRIDOXINE

Other names Pyridoxine hydrochloride, vitamin B$_6$

Availability
Pyridoxine and pyridoxine hydrochloride are available without prescription in a variety of single ingredient and multivitamin and mineral preparations.

Actions on the body
Pyridoxine plays a vital role in the activities of many enzymes. It is essential for the breakdown and utilization of proteins, carbohydrates and fats from food, for the release of carbohydrates stored in the liver and muscles for energy, and for the manufacture of niacin (vitamin B$_3$). It is needed for the production of red blood cells and antibodies, for a healthy skin and for healthy digestion. It is also important for normal function of the central nervous system and several hormones.

Dietary and other natural sources
Liver, chicken, fish, wholemeal cereals, wheat-germ and eggs are rich in this vitamin. Bananas, avocados and potatoes are also good sources.

Normal daily requirement
The daily reference nutrient intakes (RNI) for pyridoxine are: 0.2mg (birth – 6 months); 0.3 mg (7 – 9 months); 0.4mg (10 months – 1 year); 0.7mg (1 – 3 years); 0.9mg (4 – 6 years); 1mg (males aged 7 – 10 years and females aged 7 – 14); 1.2mg (males aged 11 – 14 years); 1.5mg (males aged 15 – 18); 1.2mg (females aged 15 years and over); and 1.4mg (males aged 19 years and over). There are no extra requirements in pregnancy or breast feeding.

When supplements are helpful
Most balanced diets contain adequate amounts of pyridoxine, and it is also manufactured in small amounts by bacteria that live in the intestine. However, breast fed infants may require additional pyridoxine. Elderly adults may also require supplements. Supplements may be given on medical advice together with other B vitamins to people with certain conditions in which absorption from the intestine is impaired. Supplements may also be recommended to prevent or treat deficiency caused by alcoholism and treatment with drugs such as penicillamine and hydralazine. Supplements may also help relieve depression caused by a deficiency of the vitamin in women taking oestrogen-containing oral contraceptives, and may prevent morning sickness in pregnancy. Supplements may help relieve premenstrual depression, irritability and breast tenderness.

Symptoms of deficiency
Pyridoxine deficiency may cause weakness, irritability, nervousness, depression, skin disorders, inflammation of the mouth and tongue and cracked lips. In adults, it may cause anaemia (abnormally low levels of red blood cells). Convulsions may occur in infants.

Dosage range for treating deficiency
Depends on the individual and the nature and severity of the disorder. In general, deficiency is treated with 5 – 25mg daily for three weeks followed by 1.5 – 2.5mg daily in a multivitamin preparation. Deficiency resulting from genetic defects that prevent use of the vitamin is treated with doses of 2 – 15mg daily in infants and 10 – 250mg daily in adults and children. Daily doses of 50mg given with other B vitamins from day 10 of a menstrual cycle to day 3 of the following cycle may help relieve the premenstrual syndrome.

Symptoms and risks of excessive intake
Daily doses of over 500mg taken over a prolonged period may damage the nervous system resulting in unsteadiness, numbness and awkwardness of the hands.

RIBOFLAVIN

Other names Vitamin B$_2$, vitamin G

Availability
Riboflavin is available without a prescription, alone and in a wide variety of multivitamin and mineral preparations.

Actions on the body
Riboflavin plays a vital role in the activities of several enzymes. It is involved in the breakdown and utilization of carbohydrates, fats and proteins and in the production of energy in cells using oxygen. It is needed for utilization of other B vitamins and for production of hormones by the adrenal glands.

Dietary and other natural sources
Riboflavin is found in most foods. Good dietary sources are liver, milk, cheese, eggs, leafy, green vegetables, wholemeal cereals and pulses. Brewer's yeast is also a rich source of the vitamin.

Normal daily requirement
The daily reference nutrient intakes (RNI) for riboflavin are: 0.4mg (birth – 1 year); 0.6mg (1 – 3 years); 0.8mg (4 – 6 years); 1mg (7 – 10 years); 1.2mg (males aged 11 – 14 years); 1.1mg (females aged 11 years and over); and 1.3mg (males aged 15 years and over). Daily requirements rise by 0.3mg in pregnancy and by 0.5mg when breast feeding.

When supplements are helpful
A balanced diet generally provides adequate amounts of riboflavin. Supplements may be beneficial in people on very low calorie diets. Requirements may also be increased by prolonged use of phenothiazine antipsychotics, tricyclic antidepressants and oestrogen-containing oral contraceptives. Supplements are required for riboflavin deficiency associated with certain conditions in which absorption of nutrients from the intestine is impaired. Riboflavin deficiency is also common among alcoholics. As with other B vitamins, the need for riboflavin is increased by injury, surgery, severe illness and psychological stress. In all cases, supplements work best in a complete B-complex formulation.

Symptoms of deficiency
Prolonged deficiency may lead to chapped lips, cracks and sores in the corners of the mouth, a red, sore tongue, and skin problems in the genital area. The eyes may itch, burn, and may become unusually sensitive to light. Twitching of the eyelids and blurred vision may also occur.

Dosage range for treating deficiency
Usually treated with 5 – 25mg daily in combination with other B vitamins.

Symptoms and risks of excessive intake
Excessive intake does not appear to have harmful effects. However, prolonged use of large doses of riboflavin alone may deplete other B vitamins and it is therefore best taken together with other B vitamins.

421

BIOTIN

Other names Coenzyme R, vitamin H

Availability
Biotin is available without a prescription, alone and in a wide variety of multivitamin and mineral preparations.

Actions on the body
Biotin plays a vital role in the activities of several *enzymes*. It is essential for the breakdown of fatty acids and carbohydrates in the diet for conversion into energy, for the manufacture of fats, and for excretion of the products of protein breakdown.

Dietary and other natural sources
Traces of biotin are present in a wide variety of foods. Dietary sources rich in this mineral include liver, nuts, beans, egg yolks and cauliflower.

Normal daily requirement
A daily reference nutrient intake (RNI) has not been established, but 10 – 200 micrograms (mcg) is both safe and adequate.

When supplements are helpful
Most diets provide adequate amounts of biotin, and it is also manufactured in relatively large amounts by bacteria that live in the intestine. The need for supplements is rare. However, deficiency can occur with prolonged, excessive consumption of raw egg whites (as in eggnogs), since these contain a protein – avidin – that prevents absorption of the vitamin in the intestine. The risk of deficiency is also increased during long-term treatment with antibiotics or sulphonamide antibacterial drugs, which may destroy the biotin-producing bacteria in the intestine. However, additional biotin is not usually necessary with a balanced diet.

Symptoms of deficiency
Symptoms of biotin deficiency include weakness, tiredness, poor appetite, hair loss and depression. Severe deficiency may cause eczema of the face and body, and inflammation of the tongue.

Dosage range for treating deficiency
Depends on the individual and on the nature and severity of the disorder. In general, dietary deficiency is treated with 150 – 300mcg of biotin daily. Deficiency of biotin resulting from a genetic defect that limits use of the vitamin by body cells is treated with doses of 5mg given once or twice daily.

Symptoms and risks of excessive intake
None known.

CALCIUM

Other names Calcium amino acid chelate, calcium carbonate, calcium chloride, calcium citrate, calcium glubionate, calcium gluconate, calcium gluceptate, calcium lactate

Availability
Oral forms are available over the counter. Injectable forms of calcium are available only under medical supervision.

Actions on the body
The most abundant mineral in the body, calcium makes up more than 90 per cent of the hard matter in bones and teeth. It is essential for the formation and maintenance of strong bones and healthy teeth, for blood clotting, the transmission of nerve impulses, and the contraction of muscle.

Dietary and other natural sources
The main dietary sources of calcium are milk and dairy products, sardines, dark green, leafy vegetables, dried beans and nuts. Calcium may also be obtained by drinking water in hard water areas.

Normal daily requirement
The recommended daily nutrient intakes (RNI) for calcium are: 525mg (birth – 1 year); 350mg (1 – 3 years); 450mg (4 – 6 years); 550mg (7 – 10 years); 1,000mg (males aged 11 –18 years); 800mg (females aged 11 – 18 years); and 700mg (19 years and over). Daily requirements do not increase during pregnancy, but rise by 550mg during breast feeding.

When supplements are helpful
Unless a sufficient amount of dairy products are consumed – a pint of milk contains approximately 600mg – the diet may not contain enough calcium, and supplements may be needed. Women are especially vulnerable to calcium deficiency because pregnancy and breast feeding demand large amounts of calcium which may be extracted from the skeleton if intake is not adequate. Osteoporosis (fragile bones) has been linked to dietary calcium deficiency in some cases, but may not be helped by supplements in all women. Hormone replacement therapy may also be necessary (see Drugs for bone disorders, p.122).

Symptoms of deficiency
Symptoms of deficiency do not develop because, when dietary intake is inadequate, the body obtains the calcium it needs from the skeleton. Long-term lack of calcium can lead to softening of the bones, which in children leads to abnormal bone development (rickets), and in adults to osteoporosis and osteomalacia, causing backache, muscle weakness, bone pain and fractures of the long bones. Severe deficiency, resulting in low levels of calcium in the blood, causes abnormal stimulation of the nervous system resulting in cramp-like spasms in the hands, feet and face.

Dosage range for treating deficiency
Oral supplements of up to 800mg daily may be advised for children with rickets, and up to 1,000mg daily may be given for osteoporosis and osteomalacia. Severe deficiency is treated in hospital by intravenous injection of calcium. Vitamin D is usually given together with calcium to increase its absorption from the intestine.

Symptoms and risks of excessive intake
Excessive intake of calcium may reduce the amount of iron and zinc absorbed and also may cause constipation and nausea. There is an increased risk of palpitations and, for susceptible people, of calcium deposits in the kidneys leading to kidney stones and kidney damage. These symptoms do not usually develop unless calcium is taken with large amounts of vitamin D.

CHROMIUM

Other names Chromium amino acid chelate, glucose tolerance factor (GTF)

Availability
Chromium supplements are available without prescription.

Actions on the body
Chromium plays a vital role in the activities of several *enzymes*. It is involved in the breakdown of sugar for conversion into energy and in the manufacture of certain fats. It works together with insulin and is thus essential to the body's ability to use sugar. It may also be involved in the manufacture of proteins in the body

When supplements are helpful
Most people who eat a healthy diet containing plenty of fresh or unprocessed foods receive adequate amounts of chromium. However, supplements may be advised in malnourished children and elderly people (who retain less of the mineral). Diabetics and those with diabetes-like symptoms may also benefit from additional chromium. Supplements may also be helpful if symptoms show chromium deficiency.

Dietary and other natural sources
Traces of chromium are present in a wide variety of foods. Meat, dairy products and wholemeal cereals are good sources of this mineral.

Normal daily requirement
Only minute quantities of chromium are required. A recommended daily nutrient intake (RNI) has not been determined, but a safe intake for adults is about 25mcg.

Symptoms of deficiency
Chromium deficiency is not very common in Britain. A diet of too many processed foods may contribute to chromium deficiency. Inadequate intake of chromium over a prolonged period may impair the body's ability to use sugar, leading to high blood sugar levels. However, in most cases, this is symptomless. In some people, there may be diabetes-like symptoms such as tiredness, mental confusion and numbness or tingling of the hands and feet. Deficiency may worsen pre-existing diabetes and may depress growth in children. Chromium deficiency may also contribute to the development of atherosclerosis (narrowing of the arteries).

Dosage range for treating deficiency
Severe chromium deficiency may be treated with daily doses of up to 10mcg.

Symptoms and risks of excessive intake
Chromium is poisonous in excess. Levels producing symptoms are usually obtained from exposure to industrial waste in drinking water or the atmosphere, not from excessive dietary intake. Symptoms include inflammation of the skin and, if inhaled, damage to the nose. People who are repeatedly exposed to chromium fumes have a greater-than-average risk of developing lung cancer.

COPPER

Other names Copper amino acid chelate, cupric chloride, copper chloride dihydrate, copper gluconate, copper sulphate

Availability
Copper gluconate, copper sulphate and copper amino acid chelate are available in oral preparations without a prescription. Cupric chloride is an injectable form and is available only on prescription. Copper chloride dihydrate is part of a multiple ingredient preparation for hospital use.

Actions on the body
Copper is an essential constituent of several proteins and *enzymes*. It plays an important role in the development of red blood cells, helps to form the dark pigment that colours hair and skin and helps the body to use vitamin C. It is essential for the formation of collagen and elastin – proteins found in ligaments, blood vessel walls and the lungs – and for the proper formation and maintenance of strong bones. It is also required for central nervous system activity.

Dietary and other natural sources
Most unprocessed foods contain copper. Liver, shellfish, nuts, mushrooms, wholemeal cereals, and dried pulses are particularly rich sources. Soft water may dissolve copper from pipes.

Normal daily requirement
Recommended daily intakes are: 0.2mg (birth – 3 months); 0.3mg (4 months – 1 year); 0.4mg (1 – 3 years); 0.6mg (4 – 6 years); 0.7mg (7 – 10 years); 0.8mg (11 – 14 years); 1.0mg (15 – 18 years); and 1.2mg (19 years and over). Daily requirements do not change during pregnancy, but rise by 0.3mg when breast feeding.

When supplements are helpful
A diet that regularly includes a selection of the foods mentioned above provides sufficient copper. Supplements are rarely necessary. However, doctors may advise additional copper for malnourished children and infants.

Symptoms of deficiency
Copper deficiency is very rare. The major change is anaemia due to failure of production of red blood cells, the main symptoms of which are pallor, fatigue, shortness of breath and palpitations. In severe cases, abnormal bone changes may occur. An inherited copper deficiency disorder called Menke's syndrome (kinky hair disease) results in brain degeneration, retarded growth, sparse and brittle hair, and weak bones.

Dosage range for treating deficiency
This depends on the individual and on the nature and severity of the disorder.

Symptoms and risks of excessive intake
As little as 10 – 15 mg of copper taken by mouth can produce toxic effects. Symptoms of poisoning include nausea, vomiting, abdominal pain, diarrhoea, and general aches and pains. Large overdoses of copper may cause destruction of red blood cells (haemolytic anaemia), and liver and kidney damage. In Wilson's disease, an inherited disorder, the patient cannot excrete copper and suffers from long-term copper poisoning. The disease is treated with *chelating agents*, such as penicillamine, p.357.

FLUORIDE

Other names Calcium fluoride, sodium fluoride, sodium monofluorophosphate, stannous fluoride

Availability
Sodium fluoride is added to drinking water and is available on prescription in single or multiple ingredient preparations. Mouth rinses and toothpastes containing sodium fluoride, stannous fluoride or sodium monofluorophosphate are available over the counter. Calcium fluoride is the naturally occurring form of the mineral.

Actions on the body
Fluoride helps to prevent tooth decay and contributes to the strength of bones. It is thought to work on the teeth by strengthening the mineral composition of the tooth enamel, making it more resistant to attack by acid in the mouth. Fluoride is most effective when taken during the formation of teeth in childhood, since it is then incorporated into the tooth itself. It may also strengthen developing bones.

Dietary and other natural sources
Fluoride is added to drinking water in many areas, and water is therefore a prime source of this mineral (fluoride levels in water vary from area to area and untreated water also contains a small amount of fluoride). Foods and beverages (especially tea) grown or prepared in areas with fluoride-treated water may also contribute fluoride.

Normal daily requirement
No recommended daily intake has been established, but around 0.15mg is a safe level for infants (under 3 months), and about 0.5mg up to 2 years.

When supplements are helpful
Most diets typically provide 0.9 – 2.6mg of fluoride per day, depending on whether or not the water supply contains fluoride. Drinking water containing fluoride at 1 part per million (ppm) provides an additional 1.4 – 1.8mg per day for adults and 0.4 – 0.8mg per day for young children. If the level is inadequate, children may be given fluoride drops or tablets. The use of fluoride supplements is currently under investigation for the prevention and treatment of osteoporosis (fragile bones).

Symptoms of deficiency
Fluoride deficiency increases the risk of tooth decay, especially in children.

Dosage range for treating deficiency
Dietary supplements may be given to children when the concentration of fluoride in the water supply is less than 0.7ppm. When fluoride is present at less than 0.3ppm, the recommended daily dose is: 0.25 micrograms (mcg) (birth – 2 years); 0.5mcg (2 – 4 years); and 1mcg (over 4 years). When the fluoride concentration is 0.3 – 0.7ppm, supplements are not recommended in infants under 2, and the recommended daily dose in older children is 0.25mcg (2 – 4 years) and 0.5mcg (over 4 years).

Symptoms and risks of excessive intake
In large quantities, fluoride may cause slow poisoning – termed fluorosis. Prolonged intake of water containing more than 2ppm fluoride may lead to mottled or brown discoloration of the enamel in developing teeth. Very high levels (over 8ppm) may also lead to bone disorders and degenerative changes in the kidneys, liver, adrenal glands, heart, central nervous system and reproductive organs. Suggestions of a link between fluoridation of the water supply and cancer are without foundation. A child who has taken a number of fluoride tablets may vomit and lose consciousness. Give milk if the child is conscious, while urgent medical help is sought.

FOLIC ACID

Other names Folacin, vitamin M, folate sodium, leuco-vorin calcium (folinate calcium, citrovorum factor), folates

Availability
Folic acid is available without prescription, alone and in a variety of multivitamin and mineral preparations. Strengths of 500mcg and over are available only on prescription.

Actions on the body
Folic acid is essential for the activities of several *enzymes*. It is required for the manufacture of nucleic acids – the genetic material of cells – and thus for the processes of growth and reproduction. It is vital for the formation of red blood cells by the bone marrow and the development and proper function of the central nervous system.

Dietary and other natural sources
The best sources are green, leafy vegetables, mushrooms and liver. Root vegetables, oranges, nuts, dried pulses, and egg yolks are also rich sources.

Normal daily requirement
The recommended daily nutrient intakes (RNI) for folic acid, as folate, in micrograms (mcg), are: 50mcg (birth – 1 year); 70mcg (1 – 3 years); 100mcg (4 – 6 years); 150mcg (7 – 10 years); and 200mcg (11 years and over). In pregnancy and breast feeding, requirements are increased by 100mcg and 60mcg respectively.

When supplements are helpful
A varied diet containing fresh fruit and vegetables usually provides adequate amounts. However, minor deficiency is fairly common, and can be corrected by the addition of one uncooked fruit or vegetable or a glass of fruit juice daily. Supplements are often given during pregnancy and breast feeding, and may also be needed in premature or low birthweight infants and those fed on goat's milk (breast and cow's milk contain adequate amounts of the vitamin). Doctors may recommend additional folic acid for people on haemodialysis, with certain blood disorders or psoriasis, or certain conditions in which absorption of nutrients from the intestine is impaired, severe alcoholism, or liver disease. Supplements may be helpful if you are a heavy drinker or if you are taking certain drugs that deplete folic acid. These include anticonvulsants, antimalarial drugs, oestrogen-containing contraceptives, certain analgesics, corticosteroids and sulphonamide antibacterial drugs. In women who are at risk of having a baby with spina bifida, folic acid supplements, if started before conception and continued throughout the pregnancy, may reduce the risk.

Symptoms of deficiency
Folic acid deficiency leads to abnormally low numbers of red blood cells (anaemia). The main symptoms include fatigue, loss of appetite, nausea, diarrhoea, and hair loss. Mouth sores are common and the tongue is often sore. Deficiency may also cause poor growth in infants and children.

Dosage range for treating deficiency
Symptoms of anaemia are usually treated with 15mg of folic acid daily, together with vitamin B$_{12}$. A lower maintenance dose may be substituted after symptoms have subsided.

Symptoms and risks of excessive intake
Excessive folic acid is not toxic. However, it may worsen the symptoms of a coexisting vitamin B$_{12}$ deficiency and should never be taken to treat anaemia without a full medical investigation of the cause of the anaemia.

IODINE

Other names Calcium iodide, potassium iodide, sodium iodide

Availability
Iodine supplements are available without prescription, as kelp tablets and in several multivitamin and mineral preparations. Iodine skin preparations are also available without a prescription for antiseptic use. Treatments for thyroid suppression and expectorant cough medicines containing iodine are available only on prescription.

Actions on the body
Iodine is essential for the formation of thyroid hormone which regulates the body's energy production, promotes growth and development, and helps burn excess fat.

Dietary and other natural sources
Seafood is the best source of iodine, but bread and dairy products are the main sources of this mineral in most diets. Iodized table salt is also a good source. Iodine may also be inhaled from the atmosphere in coastal regions or from pollution produced by automobile exhaust fumes.

Normal daily requirement
The recommended daily nutrient intakes (RNI) for iodine in micrograms (mcg) are: 50mcg (birth – 3 months); 60mcg (4 months – 1 year); 70mcg (1 – 3 years); 100mcg (4 – 6 years); 110mcg (7– 10 years); 130mcg (11 – 14 years); and 140mcg (15 years and over). Requirements do not increase during pregnancy or breast feeding.

When supplements are helpful
Most diets contain adequate amounts of iodine and use of iodized table salt can usually make up for any lack. Supplements are rarely necessary except on medical advice. However, excessive intake of raw cabbage or nuts may reduce uptake of iodine into the thyroid gland and lead to deficiency if iodine intake is otherwise low. Kelp supplements may be helpful.

People exposed to radiation from radioactive iodine released into the environment may be given sodium iodide at 10 – 100mg per day (adults and children over 1 year) or 15mg per day (children under 1 year) for 3 – 10 days.

Symptoms of deficiency
Deficiency may result in a goitre (enlargement of the thyroid gland) and hypothyroidism (deficiency of thyroid hormone). Symptoms of hypothyroidism include tiredness, physical and mental slowness, weight gain, facial puffiness and constipation. Babies born to iodine-deficient mothers are lethargic and difficult to feed. Left untreated, they develop cretinism, with poor growth and mental retardation.

Dosage range for treating deficiency
Deficiency may be treated with doses of 150mcg of iodine daily, often as iodized table salt (4g or 1teaspoon daily).

Symptoms and risks of excessive intake
Iodine that occurs naturally in food is non-toxic, but iodine taken as a drug can be harmful in excess. Large overdoses of iodine compounds may cause abdominal pain, vomiting, bloody diarrhoea, and swelling of the thyroid and salivary glands. The safe upper limit of iodine intake is 1,000mcg daily.

IRON

Other names Ferrous fumarate, ferrous gluconate, ferrous sulphate, iron dextran, iron-polysaccharide complex

Availability
Ferrous sulphate, ferrous fumarate, ferrous gluconate and iron-polysaccharide complex are available without prescription, alone and in multivitamin and mineral preparations. Iron dextran, an injectable form, is available only on prescription.

Actions on the body
Iron has an important role in the formation of red blood cells and is a vital component of the oxygen-carrying pigment, haemoglobin. It is involved in the formation of myoglobin, a pigment which stores oxygen in muscles for use during exercise. It is also an essential component of several *enzymes*, and is involved in the uptake of oxygen by the cells and the conversion of blood sugar to energy.

Dietary and other natural sources
Liver is the best dietary source of iron. Meat (especially offal), eggs, chicken, fish, green, leafy vegetables, dried fruit, enriched or wholemeal cereals, breads or pastas, nuts and dried pulses are also rich sources. Iron from meat, eggs, chicken and fish is better absorbed than from vegetables.

Normal daily requirement
The recommended daily intakes (RNI) for iron are: 1.7mg (birth – 3 months); 4.3mg (4 – 6 months); 7.8mg (7 months – 1 year); 6.9mg (1 – 3 years); 6.1mg (4 – 6 years); 8.7mg (7 – 10 years); 11.3mg (males aged 11– 18 years); 14.8mg (females aged 11– 50 years); and 8.7 mg (males aged 19 and over, and females aged 51 and over). Requirements are increased during pregnancy and for two to three months after childbirth.

When supplements are helpful
Most average diets supply adequate amounts of iron. However, larger amounts are necessary during pregnancy. Supplements are therefore given throughout pregnancy and for 2 to 3 months after childbirth to maintain and replenish adequate iron stores in the mother. Premature babies may be prescribed supplements soon after birth (breast fed) or after 6 months of age (formula fed) to prevent deficiency. Supplements may be helpful in young vegetarians, women with heavy menstrual periods and people with chronic blood loss due to disease (for example, peptic ulcer).

Symptoms of deficiency
Iron deficiency causes *anaemia*, symptoms of which are pallor, fatigue, shortness of breath and palpitations. Apathy, irritability, and lowered resistance of the body to infection may also occur.

Dosage range for treating deficiency
Depends on the individual and the nature and severity of the condition. In adults, iron deficiency anaemia is usually treated with 30 – 100mg of iron two or three times daily. In children the dose is reduced according to age and weight. Iron supplements of 30 – 60mg daily are prescribed throughout pregnancy.

Symptoms and risks of excessive intake
Iron poisoning is extremely dangerous. Abdominal pain, nausea and vomiting may be followed by fever, abdominal bloating, dehydration and dangerously lowered blood pressure. Immediate medical attention is vital.

Excessive intake, especially when taken with large amounts of vitamin C, may cause iron to accumulate in organs causing congestive heart failure, cirrhosis of the liver and diabetes mellitus.

MAGNESIUM

Other names Magnesium amino acid chelate, magnesium gluconate, magnesium oxide, magnesium oxide dolomite, magnesium sulphate

Availability
Magnesium is available without prescription in a variety of multivitamin and mineral preparations. Magnesium is also an ingredient of numerous over-the-counter antacid and laxative preparations, but it is not absorbed well from these sources.

Actions on the body
About 60 per cent of the body's magnesium is found in bones and teeth. It is essential for the formation of healthy bones and teeth, the transmission of nerve impulses, and the contraction of muscles. It activates several *enzymes* , and is important in the conversion of blood sugar into energy. It also helps to regulate body temperature.

Dietary and other natural sources
The best dietary source of magnesium is green, leafy vegetables. Nuts, wholemeal cereals and soya beans are also rich in magnesium. Drinking water in hard water areas may also be a source of this mineral.

Normal daily requirement
The recommended daily intakes (RNI) for magnesium are: 55mg (birth – 3 months); 60mg (4 – 6 months); 75mg (7 – 9 months); 80mg (10 – 12 months); 85mg (1 – 3 years); 120mg (4 – 6 years); 200mg (7 – 10 years); 280mg (11 – 14 years); 300mg (males aged 15 and over, and females aged 15 – 18); and 270mg (females aged 19 and over). Daily requirements do not increase during pregnancy, but rise by 50mg during breast feeding.

When supplements are helpful
A varied diet provides adequate amounts of magnesium, particularly in hard water areas. Supplements are usually only necessary on medical advice for magnesium deficiency associated with certain conditions in which absorption from the intestine is impaired, such as from repeated vomiting or diarrhoea, advanced kidney disease, severe alcoholism or prolonged treatment with certain diuretic drugs.

Oestrogens and oestrogen-containing oral contraceptives may reduce blood magnesium levels, but women on adequate diets do not need supplements.

Symptoms of deficiency
Symptoms include anxiety, restlessness, tremors, confusion, palpitations, depression, irritability and dis-orientation. Severe magnesium deficiency causes marked overstimulation of the nervous system, resulting in cramp-like spasms of the hands and feet and fits. Inadequate intake may be a possible factor in the development of coronary heart disease, and may also lead to calcium deposits in the kidneys, resulting in kidney stones.

Dosage range for treating deficiency
This depends on the individual and on the nature and severity of the disorder. Severe deficiency is usually treated in hospital by injection of magnesium sulphate.

Symptoms and risks of excessive intake
Magnesium toxicity (hypermagnesaemia) is rare, but can occur in people with impaired kidney function with prolonged intake of large amounts (more than 3,000mg daily) found in antacid or laxative preparations. Symptoms include nausea, vomiting, dizziness (due to a drop in blood pressure) and muscle weakness. Very large increases in magnesium in the blood may cause fatal respiratory failure or heart arrest.

NIACIN

Other names Niacinamide, nicotinamide, nicotinic acid, nicotinyl alcohol tartrate, vitamin B_3

Availability
Niacin is available without prescription in a wide variety of single ingredient and multivitamin and mineral preparations. However, high doses of nicotinic acid are available only on prescription.

Actions on the body
Niacin plays a vital role in the activities of many *enzymes*. It is important in the production of energy from blood sugar and in the manufacture of fats. Niacin is essential for the proper functioning of the nervous system, for a healthy skin and digestive system and for the manufacture of sex hormones (oestrogens, progesterone and testosterone).

Dietary and other natural sources
Liver, lean meat, poultry, fish, wholemeal cereals, nuts and dried pulses are the best dietary sources of niacin.

Normal daily requirement
The recommended daily intakes (RNI) for niacin are: 3mg (birth – 3 months); 4mg (7 – 9 months); 5mg (10 –12 months); 8mg (1 – 3 years); 11mg (4 – 6 years); 12mg (males aged 7 – 10 and females aged 7 – 14); 15mg (males aged 11 – 14); 18 mg (males aged 15 – 18); 14mg (females aged 15 – 18); 17mg males aged 19 – 50); 13mg (females aged 19 – 50); 16mg (males aged 51 and over); and 123mg (females aged 51 and over); Daily requirements do not increase during pregnancy, but rise by 2mg during breast feeding.

When supplements are helpful
Most British diets provide adequate amounts of niacin, and dietary deficiency is rare. Supplements are required for niacin deficiency associated with bowel disorders in which absorption from the intestine is impaired, also liver disease and severe alcoholism. Large doses of niacin (up to 9g daily) lower the levels of certain fats in the blood, including cholesterol, and are used in the treatment of hyperlipid-aemia (raised blood fat levels).

Symptoms of deficiency
Severe niacin deficiency causes pellagra (literally, rough skin). Symptoms include sore, red, cracked skin in areas exposed to sun, friction or pressure, inflammation of the mouth and tongue, abdominal pain and distension, nausea, diarrhoea and mental disturbances such as anxiety, depression and dementia.

Dosage range for treating deficiency
For severe pellagra, adults are usually treated with 100 – 500mg niacinamide daily by mouth, and children are usually given 100 – 300mg daily. For less severe deficiency, doses of 25 –50mg are given.

Symptoms and risks of excessive intake
At doses of over 50mg, niacin (nicotinic acid) may cause transient itching, flushing, tingling or headache. The synthetic form of niacin, niacinamide (nicotinamide) is free of these effects. Large doses of niacin may cause nausea and may aggravate a peptic ulcer. This can be prevented by taking the drug on a full stomach. At doses of over 2g daily (which have been used to treat hyperlipidaemia), there is a risk of gout, liver damage and high blood sugar levels leading to nervousness and extreme thirst.

PANTOTHENIC ACID

Other names Calcium pantothenate, panthenol, pantothenol, vitamin B$_5$

Availability
Pantothenic acid, calcium pantothenate and panthenol are available without prescription in a variety of multivitamin and mineral preparations.

Actions on the body
Pantothenic acid plays a vital role in the activities of many *enzymes*. It is essential for the production of energy from sugars and fats, for the manufacture of fats, cortico-steroids and sex hormones, for the utilization of other vitamins, for the proper function of the nervous system and the adrenal glands, and for normal growth and development.

Dietary and other natural sources
Pantothenic acid is present in almost all vegetables, cereals and animal foods. Liver, kidney, heart, fish and egg yolks are good dietary sources. Brewer's yeast, wheat-germ and royal jelly (the substance on which queen bees feed) are also rich in the vitamin.

Normal daily requirement
No recommended daily intake has been established, but requirements are met by 3 – 7mg daily.

When supplements are helpful
Most diets provide adequate amounts of pantothenic acid. Any deficiency is likely to occur together with other B vitamin deficiency diseases such as pellagra (see niacin), beriberi (see thiamine) or in alcoholics, and will be treated with B complex supplements. There is no firm evidence that large doses help, as some believe, in the prevention of greying hair, nerve disorders in diabetes, or psychiatric illness. As with other B vitamins, the need for pantothenic acid is increased by injury, surgery, severe illness and psychological stress.

Symptoms of deficiency
Pantothenic acid deficiency may cause low blood sugar levels, duodenal ulcers, respiratory infections and general ill-health. Symptoms include fatigue, headache, nausea, abdominal pain, numbness and tingling in the limbs, muscle cramps, faintness, confusion and lack of coordination.

Dosage range for treating deficiency
Usually 5 – 20mg per day.

Symptoms and risks of excessive intake
In tests, doses of 1,000mg or more of pantothenic acid have not caused toxic effects. The risk of toxicity is considered to be very low since pantothenic acid is a water-soluble vitamin which does not accumulate in the tissues. Any excess is eliminated rapidly in the urine. Very high intakes of 10 – 20g can cause diarrhoea.

POTASSIUM

Other names Potassium acetate, potassium chloride, potassium citrate, potassium gluconate, Slow K

Availability
Salts of potassium in small doses are available in a number of multivitamin and mineral supplements. They are available at higher doses in prescription-only drugs given as dietary supplements and in some diuretics to offset the loss of potassium in the urine (e.g. Burinex-K). Potassium salts are also widely available in sodium-free salt (salt substitute).

Actions on the body
Potassium works together with sodium in controlling the body's water balance, conduction of nerve impulses, contraction of muscle, and maintenance of a normal heart rhythm. It is essential for storage of carbohydrate and its breakdown for energy.

Dietary and other natural sources
The best dietary sources of potassium are green, leafy vegetables, oranges, potatoes and bananas. Lean meat, pulses and milk are also rich in the mineral. Many methods of food processing may lower potassium levels found in fresh food.

Normal daily requirement
The daily reference nutrient intakes (RNI) for potassium are: 0.8g (birth – 3 months); 0.85g (4 – 6 months); 0.7g (7 months – 1 year); 0.8g (1 – 3 years); 1.1g (4 – 6 years); 2g (7 – 10 years); 3.1g (11 – 14 years); 3.5g (15 years and over). There are no extra requirements in pregnancy or breast feeding.

When supplements are helpflul
Most diets contain adequate amounts of potassium, and supplements are rarely required in normal circumstances. However, people who drink large amounts of coffee or alcohol or eat lots of salty foods may become marginally deficient. People with diabetes or certain types of kidney disease may be deficient in potassium but the commonest cause is prolonged treatment with diuretics. Long-term use of corticosteroids may also deplete the body's potassium. Prolonged vomiting and diarrhoea also cause this, and people who abuse laxatives may have potass-ium deficiency. Supplements are usually only advised when symptoms suggest deficiency, or for people at particular risk.

Symptoms of deficiency
Early symptoms of potassium deficiency may include muscle weakness, fatigue, dizziness, and mental con-fusion. Impairment of nerve and muscle function may progress to cause disturbances of the heart rhythm, and paralysis of the skeletal muscles and those of the bowel, leading to constipation.

Dosage range for treating deficiency
Depends on the preparation, individual and the cause and severity of deficiency. In general, daily doses equivalent to 4 – 6g of potassium chloride are given to prevent deficiency – for example, in people treated with diuretics that deplete potassium. Doses equivalent to 3.0 – 7.2g of potassium chloride daily are used to treat deficiency.

Symptoms and risks of excessive intake
Blood potassium levels are normally regulated by the kidneys and any excess is rapidly eliminated in the urine. Doses of over 18g may cause serious disturbances of the heart rhythm and muscular paralysis. In people with impaired kidney function, excess potassium may build up and the risk of potassium poisoning is increased. People on haemodialysis treatment need to take a carefully controlled low potassium diet.

PYRIDOXINE

Other names Pyridoxine hydrochloride, vitamin B_6

Availability
Pyridoxine and pyridoxine hydrochloride are available without prescription in a variety of single ingredient and multivitamin and mineral preparations.

Actions on the body
Pyridoxine plays a vital role in the activities of many *enzymes*. It is essential for the breakdown and utilization of proteins, carbohydrates and fats from food, for the release of carbohydrates stored in the liver and muscles for energy, and for the manufacture of niacin (vitamin B_3). It is needed for the production of red blood cells and *antibodies*, for a healthy skin and for healthy digestion. It is also important for normal function of the central nervous system and several hormones.

Dietary and other natural sources
Liver, chicken, fish, wholemeal cereals, wheat-germ and eggs are rich in this vitamin. Bananas, avocados and potatoes are also good sources.

Normal daily requirement
The daily reference nutrient intakes (RNI) for pyridoxine are: 0.2mg (birth – 6 months); 0.3 mg (7 – 9 months); 0.4mg (10 months – 1 year); 0.7mg (1 – 3 years); 0.9mg (4 – 6 years); 1mg (males aged 7 – 10 years and females aged 7 – 14); 1.2mg (males aged 11 – 14 years); 1.5mg (males aged 15 – 18); 1.2mg (females aged 15 years and over); and 1.4mg (males aged 19 years and over). There are no extra requirements in pregnancy or breast feeding.

When supplements are helpful
Most balanced diets contain adequate amounts of pyridoxine, and it is also manufactured in small amounts by bacteria that live in the intestine. However, breast fed infants may require additional pyridoxine. Elderly adults may also require supplements. Supplements may be given on medical advice together with other B vitamins to people with certain conditions in which absorption from the intestine is impaired. Supplements may also be recommended to prevent or treat deficiency caused by alcoholism and treatment with drugs such as penicillamine and hydralazine. Supplements may also help relieve depression caused by a deficiency of the vitamin in women taking oestrogen-containing oral contraceptives, and may help prevent morning sickness in pregnancy. Supplements may help relieve premenstrual depression, irritability and breast tenderness.

Symptoms of deficiency
Pyridoxine deficiency may cause weakness, irritability, nervousness, depression, skin disorders, inflammation of the mouth and tongue and cracked lips. In adults, it may cause anaemia (abnormally low levels of red blood cells). Convulsions may occur in infants.

Dosage range for treating deficiency
Depends on the individual and the nature and severity of the disorder. In general, deficiency is treated with 5 – 25mg daily for three weeks followed by 1.5 – 2.5mg daily in a multivitamin preparation. Deficiency resulting from genetic defects that prevent use of the vitamin is treated with doses of 2 – 15mg daily in infants and 10 – 250mg daily in adults and children. Daily doses of 50mg given with other B vitamins from day 10 of a menstrual cycle to day 3 of the following cycle may help relieve the premenstrual syndrome.

Symptoms and risks of excessive intake
Daily doses of over 500mg taken over a prolonged period may damage the nervous system resulting in unsteadiness, numbness and awkwardness of the hands.

RIBOFLAVIN

Other names Vitamin B_2, vitamin G

Availability
Riboflavin is available without a prescription, alone and in a wide variety of multivitamin and mineral preparations.

Actions on the body
Riboflavin plays a vital role in the activities of several *enzymes*. It is involved in the breakdown and utilization of carbohydrates, fats and proteins and in the production of energy in cells using oxygen. It is needed for utilization of other B vitamins and for production of hormones by the adrenal glands.

Dietary and other natural sources
Riboflavin is found in most foods. Good dietary sources are liver, milk, cheese, eggs, leafy, green vegetables, wholemeal cereals and pulses. Brewer's yeast is also a rich source of the vitamin.

Normal daily requirement
The daily reference nutrient intakes (RNI) for riboflavin are: 0.4mg (birth – 1 year); 0.6mg (1 – 3 years); 0.8mg (4 – 6 years); 1mg (7 – 10 years); 1.2mg (males aged 11 – 14 years); 1.1mg (females aged 11 years and over); and 1.3mg (males aged 15 years and over). Daily requirements rise by 0.3mg in pregnancy and by 0.5mg when breast feeding.

When supplements are helpful
A balanced diet generally provides adequate amounts of riboflavin. Supplements may be beneficial in people on very low calorie diets. Requirements may also be increased by prolonged use of phenothiazine antipsychotics, tricyclic antidepressants and oestrogen-containing oral contraceptives. Supplements are required for riboflavin deficiency associated with certain conditions in which absorption of nutrients from the intestine is impaired. Riboflavin deficiency is also common among alcoholics. As with other B vitamins, the need for riboflavin is increased by injury, surgery, severe illness and psychological stress. In all cases, supplements work best in a complete B-complex formulation.

Symptoms of deficiency
Prolonged deficiency may lead to chapped lips, cracks and sores in the corners of the mouth, a red, sore tongue, and skin problems in the genital area. The eyes may itch, burn, and may become unusually sensitive to light. Twitching of the eyelids and blurred vision may also occur.

Dosage range for treating deficiency
Usually treated with 5 – 25mg daily in combination with other B vitamins.

Symptoms and risks of excessive intake
Excessive intake does not appear to have harmful effects. However, prolonged use of large doses of riboflavin alone may deplete other B vitamins and it is therefore best taken together with other B vitamins.

SELENIUM

Other names Selenious acid, selenium sulphide, selenium yeast, sodium selenite

Availability
Selenium is available without a prescription in single ingredient tablets (50 and 200 micrograms) and in capsules in combination with vitamin E. It is also available on prescription in a number of multivitamin and mineral preparations. Selenium sulphide is the active ingredient of several antidandruff shampoos.

Actions on the body
Selenium works in association with vitamin E to preserve elasticity in the tissues, thus slowing down the processes of ageing. It also increases endurance by improving the supply of oxygen to the heart muscle. It is necessary for the formation of a group of substances called prostaglandins that give protection against high blood pressure, help to prevent abnormal blood clotting in arteries which|may lead to a stroke or heart attack, and stimulate contractions of the uterus in pregnancy.

Dietary and other natural sources
Meat, fish, wholemeal cereals and dairy products are good dietary sources. The amount of selenium found in vegetables depends on the content of the mineral in the soil where they were grown.

Normal daily requirement
The daily reference nutrient intakes (RNI) for selenium are: 10mcg (birth – 3 months); 13mcg (4 – 6 months); 10mcg (7 months – 1 year); 15mcg (1 – 3 years); 20mcg (4 – 6 years); 30mcg (7 – 10 years); 45mcg (11 – 14 years); 70mcg (males aged 15 – 18 years); 60mcg (females aged 15 years and over); and 75mcg (males aged 19 years and over). There is no extra requirement in pregnancy, but 15mcg extra daily is required when breast feeding.

When supplements are helpful
Most normal diets provide adequate amounts of selenium, and supplements are, therefore, rarely necessary. At present, there is no conclusive medical evidence in support of some claims that selenium may provide protection against cancer or that it prolongs life. A daily intake of more than 150mcg is not recommended, except on the advice of a doctor.

Symptoms of deficiency
Long-term lack of selenium may result in loss of stamina and reduced elasticity of tissues, leading to premature ageing. Severe deficiency may cause muscle pain and tenderness, and can eventually lead to a fatal form of heart disease in children in areas where selenium levels in the diet are very low.

Dosage range for treating deficiency
Depends on the individual and on the nature and severity of the disorder. Severe selenium deficiency may be treated with doses of up to 200mcg daily.

Symptoms and risks of excessive intake
Selenium is the most poisonous of dietary minerals. Excessive intake may cause baldness, loss of nails and teeth, fatigue, nausea, vomiting, and sour-milk breath. A massive overdose of this may be fatal, and total daily intake should not exceed 450mcg.

SODIUM

Other names Sodium bicarbonate (baking soda), sodium chloride (table salt), sodium lactate, sodium phosphate

Availability
Sodium is widely available in the form of common table salt (sodium chloride). Sodium lactate is a prescription-only drug used in intravenous feeding. Sodium phosphate is a laxative available only on prescription. Sodium bicarbonate is used in many over-the-counter antacids.

Actions on the body
Sodium works with potassium in controlling the water balance in the body, conduction of nerve impulses, contraction of muscle, and maintenance of a normal heart rhythm.

Dietary and other natural sources
Sodium is present in almost all foods as a natural ingredient, or as an extra ingredient added during processing. The main sources are table salt, processed foods, cheese, breads and cereals, and smoked, pickled or cured meats and fish. High concentrations are found in pickles and snack foods, including potato crisps and olives. Sodium is also present in water that has been treated with water softeners.

Normal daily requirement
The daily reference nutrient intakes (RNI) for sodium are: 0.21mg (birth – 3 months); 0.28g (4 – 6 months); 0.32g (7 - 9 months); 0.35g (10 months – 1 year); 0.5g (1 – 3 years); 0.7g (4 – 6 years); 1.2g (7 – 10 years); and 1.6g (11 years and over). Most British diets contain far more sodium than this: the average consumption of sodium is 3 – 7g daily. One teaspoon of table salt contains about 2g of sodium.

When supplements are helpful
The need for supplementation is rare in temperate climates, even with "low salt" diets. In tropical climates, however, sodium supplements may help prevent heat stroke occurring as a result of sodium loss caused by excessive perspiration during heavy work. Supplements may be given on medical advice to replace salt lost due to prolonged diarrhoea and vomiting, particularly in infants, and to prevent or treat deficiency due to certain kidney disorders, cystic fibrosis, adrenal gland insufficiency, use of diuretics or severe bleeding.

Symptoms of deficiency
Sodium deficiency caused by dietary insufficiency is rare. It is usually a result of conditions that increase loss of sodium from the body such as diarrhoea, vomiting and excessive perspiration. Early symptoms include lethargy, muscle cramps and dizziness. In severe cases, there may be a marked drop in blood pressure leading to confusion, fainting and palpitations.

Dosage range for treating deficiency
Depends on the individual and on the nature and severity of symptoms. In extreme cases intravenous sodium chloride may be required.

Symptoms and risks of excessive intake
Excessive sodium intake is thought to contribute to the development of high blood pressure. In people whose blood pressure is already raised, it may increase the risk of heart disease, stroke, and kidney damage. Other adverse effects include abnormal fluid retention leading to dizziness and swelling of the legs and face. Large overdoses, even of table salt, may cause fits or coma, and could be fatal. Table salt should never be used as an emetic.

THIAMIN

Other names Thiamin hydrochloride, thiamin mononitrate, thiamine, vitamin B₁

Availability
Thiamin is available without prescription in a variety of multivitamin and mineral preparations and as single ingredient tablets.

Actions on the body
Thiamin plays a vital role in the activities of many *enzymes*. It is essential for the breakdown and utilization of carbohydrates. It is important for a healthy nervous system, healthy muscles, and normal heart function.

Dietary and other natural sources
Thiamin is present in all unrefined food. Good dietary sources include pork, wholemeal or enriched cereals and breads, brown rice, pasta, liver, kidneys, meat, fish, pulses, nuts, eggs, and most vegetables, Wheat-germ and bran are excellent sources.

Normal daily requirement
The daily reference nutrient intakes (RNI) for thiamin are: 0.2mg (birth – 9 months); 0.3mg (10 months – 1 year); 0.5mg (1 – 3 years); 0.7mg (males aged 4 – 10 years and females aged 4 – 14 years); 0.9mg (males aged 11 – 14 years); 1.1mg (males aged 15 – 18 years); 0.8mg (females aged 15 years and over); 1mg (males aged 19 – 50 years); and 0.9mg (males aged over 50). Daily requirements rise by 0.1mg in the last three months of pregnancy and by 0.2mg when breast feeding.

When supplements are helpful
A balanced diet generally provides adequate amounts of thiamin. However, supplements may be helpful in those with high energy requirements, for example, caused by overactivity of the thyroid or during heavy manual work. As with other B vitamins, requirements of thiamin are increased during severe illness, surgery, serious injury and prolonged psychological stress. Additional thiamin is usually necessary on medical advice for deficiency associated with conditions in which absorption of nutrients for the intestine is impaired, prolonged liver disease or severe alcoholism.

Symptoms of deficiency
Mild deficiency may cause fatigue, irritability, loss of appetite, and disturbed sleep. Severe deficiency may cause confusion, loss of memory, depression, abdominal pain, constipation, and beriberi, a disorder that affects the nerves, brain and heart. Symptoms of beriberi include tingling or burning sensation in the legs, cramps and tenderness in the calf muscles, incoordination, palpitations, fits, vomiting, and heart failure. In chronic alcoholics and narcotic addicts with malnutrition, thiamin deficiency may lead to a characteristic deterioration of central nervous system function known as Wernicke's syndrome, which results in paralysis of the eye muscles, severe memory loss and dementia, for which urgent treatment is needed.

Dosage range for treating deficiency
Varies, but in general , 5 – 25mg is given three times daily by mouth. Injections of the vitamin are some times given when deficiency is very severe or when symptoms have appeared suddenly.

Symptoms and risks of excessive intake
The risk of adverse effects is very low since any excess is rapidly eliminated in the urine. However, prolonged use of large doses of thiamin may deplete other B vitamins and should therefore be taken in a vitamin B complex formulation. Allergic reactions have occurred in rare cases after intravenous injection of large doses of this vitamin.

VITAMIN A

Other names Beta-carotene, carotenoids, etretinate, isotretinoin, retinoic acid, retinoids, retinol, retinol palmitate, tretinoin

Availability
Retinol, retinol palmitate, and beta-carotene are available without prescription in various single-ingredient and multi-vitamin and mineral preparations. Etretinate, tretinoin, and isotretinoin are related to vitamin A and are available only on prescription for skin disorders such as acne and psoriasis.

Actions on the body
Vitamin A is essential for normal growth and strong bones and teeth in children. It is necessary for normal vision and healthy teeth structure. It helps keep skin healthy and protects the linings of the mouth, nose, throat, lungs, and digestive and urinary tracts against infection. Vitamin A is also necessary for fertility in both sexes.

Dietary and other natural sources
Liver (the richest source), fish liver oils, eggs, milk and dairy products, orange and yellow vegetables and fruits (carrots, tomatoes, apricots, and peaches), and green vegetables are all good sources. Vitamin A is also added to margarine.

Normal daily requirement
Recommended daily intake (RNI) is: 350mcg (up to 1 year); 400mcg (1 – 3 years); 500mcg (4 – 10 years); 600mcg (males aged 11 – 14, females aged 11 and over); 700mcg (males aged 15 years and over, also pregnant women); 950mcg (breast feeding).

When supplements are helpful
Most diets provide adequate amounts of vitamin A. But diets very low in fat or protein can lead to deficiency. Supplements may be necessary in people with certain intestinal disorders, cystic fibrosis, obstruction of the bile ducts, diabetes mellitus, and overactivity of the thyroid gland, and for people on long-term treatment with lipid-lowering drugs, since these reduce absorption of the vitamin from the intestine.

Symptoms of deficiency
Night blindness (difficulty seeing in dim light) is the earliest symptom. Others include dry, rough skin, loss of appetite, and diarrhoea. Resistance to infection is decreased. Eyes may become dry and inflamed. Severe deficiency may lead to corneal ulcers and weak bones and teeth.

Dosage range for treating deficiency
Severe deficiency in adults and children over 8 years is treated initially with 15mg daily.

Symptoms and risks of excessive intake
Prolonged excessive intake in adults can cause headache, nausea, diarrhoea, dry, itchy skin, hair loss, and loss of appetite. Fatigue and irregular menstruation are common. In extreme cases, bone pain and enlargement of the liver and spleen may occur. High doses of beta-carotene may turn the skin orange, but are not dangerous. Excessive intake in pregacy may lead to birth defects (see box, below).

VITAMIN A AND PREGNANCY

Very large doses of vitamin A taken in the early weeks of pregnancy can, rarely, cause defects in the baby, damaging the face, eyes, ears, or palate. Pregnant women and those intending to become pregnant should keep to the dose prescribed by their doctor and not take extra vitamin A or eat liver (one serving may contain 4 – 12 times the recommended dose for a pregnant woman). No other dietary restrictions are necessary.

VITAMIN B12

Other names Cobalamin, cobalamins, cyanocobalamin, hydroxocobalamin

Availability
Vitamin B_{12} is available without prescription in a wide variety of preparations. Hydroxocobalamin is given only by injection under medical supervision.

Actions on the body
Vitamin B_{12} plays a vital role in the activities of several *enzymes*. It is essential for the manufacture of the genetic material of cells and thus for growth and development. The formation of red blood cells by the bone marrow is particularly dependent on this vitamin. It is also involved in the utilization of folic acid and carbohydrates in the diet, and is necessary for maintaining a healthy nervous system.

Dietary and other natural sources
Liver is the best dietary source of vitamin B_{12}. Almost all animal products, and seaweed, are also rich in the vitamin, but vegetables are not.

Normal daily requirement
Only minute quantities of vitamin B_{12} are required. Daily reference nutrient intakes (RNI) are: 0.3mcg (birth – 6 months); 0.4mcg (7 months – 1 year); 0.5mcg (1 – 3 years); 0.8mcg (4 – 6 years); 1mcg (7 – 10 years); 1.2mcg (11 – 14 years); 1.5mcg (15 years and over); 2mcg (breast feeding). Requirements are unchanged in pregnancy.

When supplements are helpful
A balanced diet usually provides more than adequate amounts of the vitamin, and deficiency is generally due to impaired absorption from the intestine rather than a low dietary intake. However, a strict vegetarian or vegan diet lacking in eggs or dairy products is likely to be deficient in vitamin B_{12}, and supplements are usually needed. The commonest cause of deficiency is pernicious anaemia, in which absorption of the vitamin is impaired due to inability of the stomach to secrete a special substance – intrinsic factor – that normally combines with the vitamin so that it can be taken up in the intestine. Supplements are also prescribed on medical advice in certain bowel disorders such as coeliac disease and steatorrhoea, after surgery to the stomach or intestine, and in tapeworm infestation.

Symptoms of deficiency
Vitamin B_{12} deficiency usually develops over months or years – the liver can store up to 6 years' supply. It leads to *anaemia*. The mouth and tongue often become sore. Deficiency of the vitamin also affects the brain and spinal cord, leading to numbness and tingling of the limbs, memory loss and depression.

Dosage range for treating deficiency
Depends on the individual and on the type and severity of deficiency. Pernicious anaemia (deficiency due to impaired absorption of B_{12}) is treated in adults with 1,000mcg twice during the first week, followed by 100 – 200mcg monthly by injection until anaemia disappears. Higher doses of up to 1,000mcg of B_{12}, together with folic acid, may be given if deficiency is severe. Children are treated with doses of 30 – 50mcg daily. Dietary deficiency is usually treated with oral supplements of 6mcg daily (2 – 3mcg in infants). Deficiency resulting from a genetic defect that prevents use of the vitamin is treated with 250mcg every three weeks throughout life.

Symptoms and risks of excessive intake
Harmful effects from high doses of vitamin B_{12} are unknown. Allergic reactions may occur rarely with impure preparations given by injection.

VITAMIN C

Other names Ascorbic acid, calcium ascorbate, sodium ascorbate

Availability
Vitamin C is available without prescription in a wide variety of single ingredient and multivitamin and mineral preparations. Sodium ascorbate is given only by injection under medical supervision.

Actions on the body
Vitamin C plays an essential role in the activities of several *enzymes*. It is vital for the growth and maintenance of healthy bones, teeth, gums, ligaments and blood vessels, and is an important component of all body organs. It is important for the manufacture of certain *neurotransmitters* and adrenal hormones. It is also required for the utilization of folic acid and absorption of iron. Vitamin C is also necessary for normal immune responses to infection and for wound healing.

Dietary and other natural sources
Vitamin C is found in most fresh fruits and vegetables. Citrus fruits, tomatoes, potatoes, and green, leafy vegetables are good dietary sources. Strawberries and cantaloupe melons are also rich in the vitamin.

Normal daily requirement
Recommended daily intake (RNI) is 25mg (birth – 1 year); 30mg (1 – 10 years); 35mg (11 – 14 years); 40mg (over 14 years); 50mg (pregnancy); and 70mg (breast feeding).

When supplements are helpful
A healthy diet generally contains sufficient quantities of vitamin C. However, it is used up more rapidly after a serious injury, major surgery, burns and in extremes of temperature. Because inhalation of carbon monoxide destroys the vitamin, city dwellers need more than people who live in the countryside, and smokers are likely to be deficient. Supplements may be necessary to prevent or treat deficiency in the elderly and chronically sick, and in severe alcoholism. Women taking oestrogen-containing contraceptives may also require supplements. There is no convincing evidence that vitamin C in large doses prevents colds, although it may reduce the severity of symptoms.

Symptoms of deficiency
Mild deficiency may cause weakness, aches and pains, swollen gums and nosebleeds. Severe deficiency results in scurvy, the symptoms of which include inflamed, bleeding gums, excessive bruising, and internal bleeding. In adults, bones fracture easily and teeth become loose. In children there is abnormal bone and tooth development. Wounds fail to heal and become infected. Deficiency often leads to *anaemia* (abnormally low levels of red blood cells), symptoms of which are pallor, fatigue, shortness of breath and palpitations. Untreated scurvy may cause fits, coma and death.

Dosage range for treating deficiency
For scurvy, 300mg of vitamin C is given daily for several weeks. Addition of a good source of vitamin C, such as a glass of orange juice, to the diet daily is also recommended.

Symptoms and risks of excessive intake
The risk of harmful effects is low as excess vitamin C is excreted in the urine. However, doses of over 1g daily may cause, diarrhoea, nausea and stomach cramps. Kidney stones have been known to develop.

VITAMIN D

Other names Alfacalcidol, calcefediol, calciferol, calci-triol, cholecalciferol, ergocalciferol, vitamin D_2, vitamin D_3

Availability
Vitamin D is available without prescription in various single ingredient and multivitamin and mineral preparations. Injections are given only under medical supervision.

Actions on the body
Vitamin D (together with parathyroid hormone) helps regulate the balance of calcium and phosphate in the body. It aids the absorption of calcium from the intestinal tract, and is essential for strong bones and teeth.

Dietary and other natural sources
Fortified milk is the best dietary source of vitamin D. Oily fish (sardines, herring, salmon and tuna), liver, milk, dairy products and egg yolks are good sources of this vitamin. It is also formed by the action of ultraviolet rays in sunlight on chemicals naturally present in the skin.

Normal daily requirement
Recommended daily intake (RNI) is 8.5mcg (birth – 6 months); 7mcg (7 months – 3 years); 10mcg (over 65 years, and pregnant and breast feeding women). Most people outside these groups do not require dietary vitamin D. 1mcg vitamin D equals 40 international units (IU).

When supplements are helpful
Vitamin D requirements are small, and usually adequately met by dietary sources and normal exposure to sunlight. However, a poor diet and inadequate sunlight may lead to deficiency; dark-skinned people, (particularly those living in smoggy urban areas) and night-shift workers are more at risk. In areas of moderate sunshine, supplements may be given to infants. Premature infants, strict vegetarians and the elderly may benefit from supplements. Supplements are usually necessary on medical advice to prevent and treat vitamin D deficiency-related bone disorders, for conditions in which absorption from the intestine is impaired, deficiency due to liver disease, certain kidney disorders, prolonged use of certain drugs and genetic defects. It is also used in treatment of hypoparathyroidism.

Symptoms of deficiency
Long-term deficiency leads to low blood levels of calcium and phosphate, which results in softening of the bones. In children, this causes abnormal bone development (rickets), and in adults, osteomalacia, causing backache, muscle weakness, bone pain and fractures.

Dosage range for treating deficiency
In general, rickets caused by dietary deficiency is treated initially with 5,000 – 10,000 IU of vitamin D daily, followed by a maintenance dose of 400 IU. Osteomalacia caused by vitamin D deficiency is treated initially with 3,000 – 50,000 IU daily, followed by a daily maintenance dose of 400 IU. Deficiency caused by impaired intestinal absorption is treated with doses of 10,000 – 50,000 IU daily (adults) and 10,000 – 25,000 IU daily (children).

Symptoms and risks of excessive intake
Doses of over 400 IU of vitamin D daily are not beneficial in most people, and may increase the risk of adverse effects such as weakness, unusual thirst, increased urination, gastrointestinal disturbances and depression. Prolonged, excessive use disrupts the balance of calcium and phosphate in the body and may lead to abnormal calcium deposits in the soft tissues, blood vessel walls and kidneys, and retarded growth in children. Daily intakes of over 25mcg (1,000 IU) in infants and 1.25mg (50,000 IU) in adults and children are considered excessive.

VITAMIN E

Other names Alpha tocopheryl acetate, tocopherol, tocopherols

Availability
Vitamin E is available without prescription in many single ingredient and multivitamin and mineral preparations. It is also included in skin creams. Alpha tocopherol is the most powerful form.

Actions on the body
Vitamin E is vital for healthy cell structure, for slowing the effects of the ageing process on cells and for maintaining the activities of certain *enzymes*. Vitamin E protects the lungs and other tissues from damage by pollutants, and protects red blood cells against destruction by poisons in the bloodstream. It also helps to form red blood cells, and is involved in the production of energy in the heart and muscles. There is some evidence it may protect against coronary heart disease and cancer, but this remains unproven at present.

Dietary and other natural sources
Vegetable oils are good sources. Other sources rich in this vitamin include green, leafy vegetables, wholemeal cereals and wheat-germ.

Normal daily requirement
Vitamin E is measured in milligrams of alpha-Tocopherol Equivalents (mg alpha-TE). No UK recommendations have been made as Vitamin E requirement depends on intake of polyunsaturated fatty acid, which varies widely. Recommended daily allowances (RDA) in the USA are: 3mg alpha-TE (birth – 6 months); 4mg alpha-TE (7 months – 1 year); 6mg alpha-TE (1 – 3 years); 7mg alpha-TE (4 – 10 years); 10mg alpha-TE (males of 11 and over); 8mg alpha-TE (females of 11 and over); 10mg alpha-TE (pregnancy); 12mg alpha-TE (first 6 months of breast feeding); and 11mg alpha-TE (second 6 months of breast feeding).

When supplements are helpful
A normal diet supplies adequate amounts of vitamin E, and supplements are rarely necessary. However, people consuming large amounts of polyunsaturated fats in vegetable oils, especially if used in cooking at high temperatures, may need supplements. Supplements of vitamin E are also recommended for premature infants and people with impaired intestinal absorption, liver disease or cystic fibrosis.

Symptoms of deficiency
Vitamin E deficiency leads to destruction of red blood cells (haemolysis) and eventually *anaemia* (abnormally low levels of red blood cells), symptoms of which are pallor, fatigue, shortness of breath and palpitations. In infants, deficiency causes irritability and fluid retention.

Dosage range for treating deficiency
Doses are generally four to five times the recommended dietary allowance (RDA) in adults and children.

Symptoms and risks of excessive intake
Harmful effects are rare, but prolonged use of over 250mg daily may lead to nausea, abdominal pain, vomiting and diarrhoea. Large doses may also reduce the amounts of vitamin A, D, and K absorbed from the intestines.

VITAMIN K

Other names Menadione, phytomenadione, vitamin K_1, vitamin K_2, vitamin K_3

Availability
Vitamin K is available without prescription as a dietary supplement in several multivitamin and mineral preparations. Injectable and oral preparations used to treat bleeding disorders are available only on prescription.

Actions on the body
Vitamin K is necessary for the formation in the liver of several substances that promote the formation of blood clots (blood clotting factors) including prothrombin (clotting factor II).

Dietary and other natural sources
The best dietary sources of vitamin K are green, leafy .vegetables and root vegetables, alfalfa, fruits, seeds, cow's milk, and yoghurt. In adults and children the intestinal bacteria manufacture a large part of the vitamin K that is required.

Normal daily requirement
The recommended safe daily intake of vitamin K in newborn infants is 10mcg. No reference nutrient intake (RNI) has been set for other age groups, but in the USA the recommended daily allowance (RDA) is: 10mcg (6 months – 1 year); 15mcg (1 – 3 years); 20mcg (4 – 6 years); 30mcg (7 – 10 years); 45mcg (11 – 14 years); 65mcg (males aged 15 – 18); 55 mcg (females aged 15 – 18); 70mcg (males aged 19 – 24); 60mcg (females aged 19 – 24); 80mcg (males aged 25 and over); and 65mcg (females aged 25 and over). There are no extra requirements in pregnancy or breast feeding.

When supplements are helpful
Vitamin K requirements are generally met adequately by dietary intake and by manufacture of the vitamin by bacteria that live in the intestine. Supplements are given routinely to newborn infants, since they lack intestinal bacteria capable of producing the vitamin and are therefore more at risk of deficiency. In adults and children, additional vitamin K is usually necessary only on medical advice for deficiency associated with prolonged use of antibiotics or sulphonamide antibacterials that destroy bacteria in the intestine, or where absorption of nutrients from the intestine is impaired. These conditions include liver disease, obstruction of the bile duct and intestinal disorders causing chronic diarrhoea. Vitamin K may also be given to reduce blood loss during labour or after surgery in people who have been taking aspirin or oral anticoagulants, and also reverses the effect of overdose with oral anticoagulants.

Symptoms of deficiency
Vitamin K deficiency leads to low levels of prothrombin (hypoprothrombinaemia) and other clotting factors, resulting in delayed blood clotting and a tendency to bleed. This may cause oozing from wounds, nosebleeds and bleeding from the gums, intestine, urinary tract, and rarely in the brain.

Dosage range for treating deficiency
Depends on the individual and on the nature and severity of the disorder.

Symptoms and risks of excessive intake
Excess dietary intake of vitamin K has no known harmful effects. Synthetic vitamin K (menadione) may cause liver damage and rupture of red blood cells (haemolysis) at large doses and in people with glucose-6-phosphate dehydrogenase (G6PD) deficiency. This may lead to reddish brown urine, jaundice and, in extreme cases, to *anaemia*. Adverse effects are extremely rare with vitamin K preparations taken by mouth.

ZINC

Other names Zinc acetate, zinc chloride, zinc oxide, zinc sulphate

Availability
Zinc supplements are available without prescription in single ingredient and multivitamin and mineral preparations. Zinc chloride is an injectable preparation given only under medical supervision during intravenous feeding. Because of its local soothing effect, zinc is also included in many topical formulations used for treating minor skin irritations, dandruff, haemorrhoids (piles), and fungal infections. It is also used in certain eye drops to reduce tear flow.

Actions on the body
Zinc plays a vital role in the activities of over 100 *enzymes*. It is essential for the manufacture of proteins and nucleic acids (the genetic material of cells), and is involved in the function of the hormone insulin in the utilization of carbohydrates. It is necessary for a normal rate of growth, development of the reproductive organs, normal function of the prostate gland and healing of wounds and burns.

Dietary and other natural sources
Zinc is present in small amounts in a wide variety of foods. Zinc from animal sources is better absorbed than that from plants. Protein-rich foods such as lean meat and seafood are the best sources of the mineral. Wholemeal breads and cereals, and dried pulses are good dietary sources.

Normal daily requirement
Recommended daily intake (RNI) is: 4mg (birth – 6 months); 5mg (7 months – 3 years); 6.5mg (4 – 6 years); 7mg (7 – 10 years); 9mg (11 – 14 years); 9.5mg (males over 14); and 7mg (females over 14). There is no extra requirement during pregnancy, but RNI is 13mg in the first 4 months of breast feeding and 9.5mg thereafter.

When supplements are helpful
A balanced diet containing natural, unprocessed foods usually provides adequate amounts of zinc. Dietary deficiency is rare in Britain, and is likely only in people who are generally malnourished such as debilitated elderly people on poor diets. Supplements are usually recommended on medical advice for those with reduced absorption of the mineral due to certain intestinal disorders, such as cystic fibrosis, for those with increased zinc requirements due to sickle cell disease or major burns and in people with liver damage occurring, for example, as a result of excessive alcohol intake.

Symptoms of deficiency
Deficiency may cause loss of appetite and impair the sense of taste. In children, it may also lead to poor growth and in severe cases, to delayed sexual development and dwarfism. Severe, prolonged lack of zinc may result in a rare skin disorder involving hair loss, rash, inflamed areas of skin with pustules, inflammation of the mouth, tongue, eyelids and around the fingernails.

Dosage range for treating deficiency
Depends on the individual and on the cause and severity of the deficiency. In general, 30 – 50mg daily, usually in the form of zinc sulphate.

Symptoms and risks of excessive intake
The risk of harmful effects is low with excess zinc intake. However, prolonged use of large doses may interfere with the absorption of iron and copper, leading to deficiency of these minerals, and may cause nausea, vomiting, headache, fever, malaise and abdominal pain.

DRUGS OF ABUSE

The purpose of these pages is to clarify the medical facts concerning certain drugs (or classes of drugs) that are commonly abused in Britain. Their physical and mental effects, sometimes combined with dangerous habit-forming potential, have led to their use outside a medical context. Some of the drugs listed here are illegal, others have legitimate medical uses – for example, sleeping drugs and anti-anxiety drugs – and are also discussed elsewhere in the book. Alcohol, nicotine and solvents, although not medical drugs, are all substances with drug-like effects and high abuse potential. They are also listed for the sake of completeness.

The individual profiles are designed to instruct and inform the reader so that he or she may become more aware of the hazards of drug abuse and be able to recognize signs of abuse in others. Since a large proportion of drug abusers are young people, the following pages may serve as a useful source of reference for parents and teachers concerned that young people in their charge may be taking drugs.

The drugs of abuse profiles

The profiles are arranged in alphabetical order under their medical names, with street names, drug categories and cross-references to other sections of the book where appropriate. Each profile contains information on that drug under standard headings. Topics covered include the various ways it is taken, its habit-forming potential, its legitimate medical uses, effects and risks, the signs of abuse and interactions with other drugs.

HOW TO UNDERSTAND THE PROFILES

Each drug of abuse profile contains standard headings under which you will find information covering important aspects of the drug.

Drug category
Categorizes the drug according to its principal effects of the body, with cross-references to other parts of the book where relevant.

Other common names
Lists the various alternative and street names of each drug.

How taken
Tells you the various forms in which each substance is taken.

Short-term effects
Tells you about the immediate mental and physical effects of the drug.

Signs of abuse
Describes the outward effects of taking the drug, both short-and long-term, that concerned observers may notice.

Pratical points
Gives tips on how to avoid abuse of the drug and suggests ways to stop or reduce intake.

Habit forming potential
Explains to what extent the drug is likely to produce physical or psychological *dependence.*

Legitimate uses
Describes the accepted medical uses of the substance, if any.

Long-term effects and risks
Explains the serious long-term effects on health and the risks involved with regular use of the drug.

Interactions
Tells you about interactions that may occur with other drugs.

NICOTINE

Other common names Found in tobacco products
Drug category Central nervous system stimulant

Habit-forming potential
The nicotine in tobacco is largely responsible for tobacco addiction in over one third of the population who are cigarette smokers. Most are also probably psychologically dependent on the process of smoking. Most people who start to smoke go on to do so regularly and most become physically dependent on nicotine. Stopping can produce temporary *withdrawal symptoms* that include nausea, weight gain, drowsiness, fatigue, insomnia, irritability, inability to concentrate, depression and craving for cigarettes.

How taken
Usually smoked in the form of cigarettes, cigars and pipe tobacco. Sometimes chewed (chewing tobacco) or sniffed (tobacco snuff). Nicotine is also available in chewing gum.

Legitimate uses
There are no legal restrictions on tobacco use. Its sale, however, is restricted to those over the age of 16. Nicotine chewing gum or slow-release patches may be prescribed on a temporary basis along with behaviour modification therapy to help people who want to give up smoking.

Short-term effects
Nicotine stimulates the sympathetic nervous system (see p.79). In regular tobacco users, it increases concentration, relieves tension and fatigue, and counters boredom and monotony. These effects are short lived, thus encouraging frequent use. Physical effects include narrowing of blood vessels, increase in heart rate and blood pressure, and reduction in urine output. First-time users often feel dizzy and nauseated, and may vomit.

Long-term effects and risks
Nicotine taken regularly may cause a rise in fatty acids in the bloodstream. This effect, combined with the effects of the drug on heart rhythm and blood vessel size, increases the risk of diseases of the heart and circulation, including angina, high blood pressure, peripheral vascular disease, stroke and coronary thrombosis. In addition, its stimulatory effects may lead to excess production of stomach acid, thereby increasing the risk of peptic ulcers.

Other well-known risks of tobacco smoking, such as chronic lung diseases, adverse effects on pregnancy, and cancers of the lung, mouth, and throat, may be due to other harmful ingredients, like tar and carbon monoxide, in the smoke.

Signs of abuse
Regular smokers often have yellow, tobacco-stained fingers and teeth, and bad breath. The smell of tobacco may linger on hair and clothes. A smoker's cough or shortness of breath are early signs of lung damage or heart disease.

Interactions
Cigarette smoking reduces the blood levels of a variety of drugs and reduces their effects. Such drugs include theophylline, propranolol, heparin, tricyclic antidepressants, phenothiazine antipsychotics, benzodiazepines, and caffeine. Diabetics may require larger doses of insulin. The health risks involved in taking oral contraceptives are increased by smoking.

Practical points
▼ Don't start smoking; nicotine is highly addictive.
▼ If you smoke already, give up now even if you have not yet suffered adverse effects.
▼ Ask your doctor for advice and support.
▼ Inquire about self-help groups in your neighbourhood for people trying to give up smoking. For relief from withdrawal symptoms, see p.344.

NITRITES

Other common names Amyl nitrite, butyl nitrite, poppers, snappers
Drug category Vasodilators (see also p.98)

Habit-forming potential
Nitrites do not seem to cause physical *dependence*; major *withdrawal symptoms* have never been reported. However users may become psychologically dependent on the stimulant effect of these drugs.

How taken
By inhalation, usually from small bottles with screw or plug tops or from small glass ampoules that are broken.

Legitimate uses
Amyl nitrite was originally introduced as a treatment for angina, but has now largely been replaced by safer, longer-acting drugs. It is still used as an antidote for cyanide poisoning. Butyl and isobutyl nitrites are not used medically.

Short-term effects
Nitrites increase the flow of blood by relaxing blood vessel walls. They give the user a rapid high, felt as a strong rush of energy. Less pleasant effects include an increase in heart rate, intense flushing, dizziness, pounding headache, nausea and coughing. High doses may cause fainting, and regular use may produce a blue discoloration of the skin due to alteration of haemoglobin in the red blood cells.

Long-term effects and risks
Nitrites are very quick-acting drugs. Their effects start within thirty seconds of inhalation and last for about five minutes. Regular users may become tolerant to these drugs, thus requiring higher doses to achieve the desired effects. Lasting physical damage, including cardiac problems, can result from chronic use of these drugs, and deaths have occurred.

The risk of toxic effects is increased in those with low blood pressure. Nitrites may also precipitate glaucoma in susceptible people, by increasing pressure inside the eye.

Signs of abuse
Nitrites have a pungent, fruity odour. They evaporate quickly: the contents of a small bottle left uncapped in a room usually disappear within two hours. Unless someone is actually taking the drug or is suffering from an overdose, the only sign of abuse is a bluish skin discoloration.

Interactions
The blood pressure-lowering effects of these drugs may be increased by alcohol, beta blockers, calcium channel blockers and tricyclic antidepressants, thus increasing the risks of dizziness and fainting.

440

ALCOHOL

Other common names Booze, drink (includes beer, wine and spirits)
Drug category Central nervous system depressant, sedative

Habit-forming potential
Because individual responses vary so widely, it is difficult to measure the habit-forming potential of alcohol. But there is certainly a disease called alcoholism, characterized by a person's inability to control intake. Regular drinking and heavy drinking do not cause alcoholism so much as indicate that it may be present. Alcoholism involves psychological and physical *dependence*, evidenced by large daily consumption, heavy weekend drinking, or long episodic binges.

How taken
By mouth, usually in the form of wines, beers and spirits.

Legitimate uses
There are no legal restrictions on the consumption of alcohol, but the sale of alcoholic drinks is restricted to those over the age of 18.

Medically, surgical spirit (which contains isopropyl, or denatured ethyl alcohol) is widely used as an *antiseptic* before injections to minimize the risk of infection. It is also used to harden the skin and thus prevent pressure sores in bedridden people, and foot sores in hikers or runners.

Short-term effects
Alcohol acts as a central nervous system depressant, thus reducing anxiety, tension, and inhibitions. In moderate quantities, it creates a feeling of relaxation and confidence and increases sociability and talkativeness, but does not improve mental performance. Moderate amounts also dilate small blood vessels, particularly in the skin, leading to flushing and a feeling of warmth. Increasing amounts progressively impair concentration and judgement, and the body's reactions are increasingly slowed. Accidents, particularly driving accidents, are more likely. As blood alcohol levels rise, violent or aggressive behaviour is possible. Speech is slurred, and the person becomes unsteady, staggers, and may experience double vision and loss of balance. Nausea and vomiting are frequent; incontinence may occur. Loss of consciousness may follow if blood alcohol levels continue to rise, and there is a risk of death from inhalation of vomit or from stopped breathing.

Long-term effects and risks
A large number of heavy drinkers develop liver diseases, including alcoholic hepatitis, cirrhosis, liver cancer or fatty liver (excess fat deposits that may lead to cirrhosis). Coronary heart disease, high blood pressure and strokes are also possible consequences of heavy drinking. Inflammation of the stomach (gastritis) and peptic ulcers are also more common. Alcoholics have an above average risk of developing dementia (irreversible mental deterioration).

Long-term heavy drinking is usually associated with physical dependence. An alcoholic may appear to be sober, even after heavy drinking, because of built-up tolerance. But a reverse tolerance effect is often seen in long-time alcoholics, where relatively little alcohol will cause signs of overt intoxication. In addition to health problems, alcohol dependence is associated with a range of personal and social problems. Alcoholics may suffer from anxiety and depression, and since they often eat poorly they are at risk of nutritional deficiency diseases, particularly thiamin deficiency (see p.430).

Drinking during pregnancy can cause fetal abnormalities and poor physical and mental development in infants; even taking moderate amounts of alcohol can lead to miscarriage, low birth weight, and mental retardation.

Signs of abuse
Signs that alcohol consumption is becoming out of control include any or all of the following: changes in drinking pattern (for example, early morning drinking or a switch from beer to spirits); changes in drinking habits (such as drinking alone or having a drink before an appointment or interview); personality changes; neglect of personal appearance; poor eating habits; furtive behaviour; increasingly frequent or prolonged bouts of intoxication with memory lapses ("blackouts") of events that occurred during drinking episodes. Physical symptoms may include nausea, vomiting or shaking in the morning, abdominal pain, cramps, weakness in the legs and hands, redness and enlarged blood vessels in the face, unsteadiness, poor memory and incontinence. Sudden discontinuation of heavy drinking, if untreated, can lead to delirium tremens (severe shaking, hallucinations and occasionally fatal convulsions) beginning after one to four days of abstinence and lasting for up to three days. Withdrawal symptoms can be controlled by drugs such as chlormethiazole or benzodiazepines, such as diazepam, given short term under medical supervision.

Interactions
Alcohol interacts with a wide variety of drugs. In particular, it increases the risk of sedation with any drug that has a *sedative* effect on the central nervous system. These include anti-anxiety drugs, sleeping drugs, *general anaesthetics*, *narcotic analgesics*, antipsychotics, tricyclic antidepressants, antihistamines, and certain antihypertensive drugs (methyldopa and clonidine). Taking alcohol with other depressant drugs of abuse, particularly narcotics, barbiturates, or solvents, can lead to coma, which may be fatal.

Taken with aspirin and similar analgesics, alcohol increases the risk of bleeding from the stomach, particularly in people who have had stomach ulcers.

People taking disulfiram (Antabuse), a drug used to help people stay in an alcohol-free state, will experience highly unpleasant reactions if they then take even a small amount of alcohol. The results include flushing of the face, throbbing headache, palpitations, nausea, and vomiting.

Alcohol may inhibit the breakdown of some oral anti-diabetic drugs and oral anticoagulants, and thus increase their effects.

Taken with monoamine oxidase inhibitors (MAOIs), alcohol, particularly in the form of red wine, may cause a dangerous rise in blood pressure.

Practical points
If you drink, know what your limits are. They vary from person to person, and capacity depends a good deal on body weight, age, experience, and mental and emotional state. If you are a woman and are pregnant, or are planning to have a baby soon, the safest course is abstinence. If you are planning to drive, don't drink. If you find that you are having trouble controlling your drinking, seek help and advice from your doctor or from an organization, such as Alcoholics Anonymous, dedicated to helping people with this problem. Even if you don't have a control problem, don't drink heavily – remember that alcohol can have harmful effects on many parts of your body, including your liver and your brain.

AMPHETAMINES

Other common names Speed, uppers, bennies
Drug category Central nervous system stimulant
(see p.88)

Habit-forming potential
Regular use of amphetamine or methamphetamine rapidly leads to *tolerance*, so that higher and higher doses are required to achieve the same effect. Users become psychologically *dependent* on the effects of the drug.

How taken
Usually swallowed as tablets. Sometimes sniffed or mixed with water and injected.

Legitimate uses
In the 1950s and 1960s, amphetamines were widely prescribed as appetite suppressants. This use has largely been abandoned because of the risk of dependence and abuse. They are still prescribed for hyperactivity and narcolepsy (see also Nervous system stimulants, p.88). Amphetamines are classified under Schedule II of the Misuse of Drugs Act. Possession is illegal without a prescription.

Short-term effects
In small doses, amphetamines increase mental alertness and physical energy. Breathing and heart rate speed up, the pupils dilate, appetite decreases, and dryness of the mouth is common. As these effects wear off, depression and fatigue may follow. At high doses, the drugs may cause tremor, sweating, anxiety, headache, palpitations, and chest pain. Very large doses may cause delusions, hallucinations, delirium, convulsions, coma, and death.

Long-term effects and risks
Regular use frequently leads to weight loss and constipation. Regular users may also become emotionally unstable. Severe depression and suicide are associated with withdrawal. Heavy long-term use reduces resistance to infection. Use of amphetamines in early pregnancy may increase the risk of birth defects, especially in the heart. Taken throughout pregnancy, amphetamines lead to premature birth and low birth weight.

Signs of abuse
The amphetamine user may appear unusually energetic, cheerful, and excessively talkative while under the influence of the drug. Restlessness and agitation are also characteristic. There is a lack of interest in food and unusual sleeping patterns; regular users may use the drug to stay awake for two or three nights at a stretch, then sleep for up to forty-eight hours afterwards. Mood swings are common.

Interactions
Amphetamines interact with a variety of drugs. Taken with monoamine oxidase inhibitors (MAOIs), they may lead to a dangerous rise in blood pressure. They also increase the risk of abnormal heart rhythms with digitalis drugs, levodopa, and certain anaesthetics given by inhalation. Amphetamines tend to counteract the *sedative* effects of drugs that depress the central nervous system.

ECSTASY (MDMA)

Modifications to the structure of amphetamines have produced several *designer drugs*. One of these, "ecstasy", is frequently abused and has no medical uses. In low doses, it produces mental relaxation, tense muscles, increased sensitivity to stimuli, and sometimes hallucinations. Higher doses have amphetamine-like effects. It can rarely produce severe and sometimes fatal reactions, even after a single dose, and it is under Schedule I of the Misuse of Drugs Act.

BARBITURATES

Other common names Barbs, downers
Drug category Central nervous system depressant
(see also Sleeping drugs, p.82), sedative

Habit-forming potential
Long-term, regular use of barbiturates can be habit-forming. Both physical and psychological *dependence* may occur.

How taken
By mouth in the form of capsules or tablets. Occasionally mixed with water and injected.

Legitimate uses
In the past barbiturates were widely prescribed as sleeping drugs. Since the 1960s, however, they have been increasingly replaced by benzodiazepines, which may also be addictive, but are less likely to cause death from overdose.
  The widest uses of barbiturates today are in anaesthesia (thiopentone) and for epilepsy (phenobarbitone).
  Most barbiturates are listed under Schedule III of the Misuse of Drugs Act.

Short-term effects
Short-term effects are similar to those of alcohol. A low dose produces relaxation, while larger amounts make the user more intoxicated and drowsy. Coordination is impaired and slurred speech, clumsiness and confusion may occur. Increasingly large doses may produce loss of consciousness, coma and death caused by depression of the breathing mechanism.

Long-term effects and risks
The greatest risk of long-term barbiturate use is physical dependence. In an addicted person, sudden withdrawal of the drug precipitates a withdrawal syndrome that varies in severity depending partly on the type of barbiturate, its dose and the duration of use, but primarily on the availability and administration of supportive treatment, including appropriate medication. Symptoms may include irritability, disturbed sleep, nightmares, nausea, vomiting, weakness, tremors and extreme anxiety, and abrupt withdrawal after several months of use may cause convulsions, delirium, fever and coma lasting for up to one week. Long-term, heavy use of barbiturates also increases the risk of accidental overdose, and also of chest infections, since these drugs suppress the cough reflex.
  Taken in pregnancy, barbiturates may cause fetal abnormalities and, used regularly in the last three months, may lead to *withdrawal symptoms* in the newborn baby.

Signs of abuse
Signs of long-term heavy use include prolonged bouts of intoxication with memory lapses ("blackouts"), neglect of personal appearance and responsibilities, personality changes and episodes of severe depression.

Interactions
Barbiturates interact with a wide variety of drugs and increase the risk of sedation with any drug that has a *sedative* effect on the central nervous system. These include anti-anxiety drugs, narcotic analgesics, antipsychotics, tricyclic antidepressants and antihistamines. High doses taken with alcohol can lead to a fatal coma.
  Barbiturates also increase the activity of certain enzymes in the liver, leading to an increase in the breakdown of certain drugs, thus reducing their effects. Tricyclic antidepressants, phenytoin, griseofulvin and corticosteroids are affected in this way.

BENZODIAZEPINES

Other common names Tranquillizers
Drug category Central nervous system depressants
(see Sleeping drugs, p.82 and Anti-anxiety drugs, p.83)

Habit-forming potential
The addictive potential of benzodiazepines is much lower than that of some other central nervous system depressants such as barbiturates. However, regular, long-term use of these drugs can lead to psychological and physical *dependence* on their *sedative* effects.

How taken
By mouth as tablets or capsules or by injection.

Legitimate uses
Benzodiazepines are commonly prescribed, mainly for short-term treatment of anxiety and stress and for relief of sleeplessness. They are also used in anaesthesia, both as premedication and for induction of *general anaesthesia*. Other medical uses include the management of alcohol withdrawal, control of epileptic fits, and relief of muscle spasms. Benzodiazepines are classified under Schedule IV of the Misuse of Drugs Act.

Short-term effects
Benzodiazepines can reduce mental activity along with anxiety. In moderate doses, they may also cause unsteadiness, reduce alertness and slow the body's reactions, thus impairing driving ability and increasing the risk of accidents. Any benzodiazepine in a high enough dose induces sleep. Very large overdoses may cause depression of the breathing mechanism.

Long-term effects and risks
Benzodiazepines tend to lose their sedative effect with long-term use. This may lead the user to increase the dose progressively, a manifestation of *tolerance* and physical dependence. Older people may become apathetic or confused when taking these drugs. On stopping the drug, the chronic user may develop *withdrawal symptoms* that may include anxiety, panic attacks, palpitations, shaking, insomnia, headaches, dizziness, aches and pains, nausea, loss of appetite and clumsiness. This can last for days or weeks. Babies born to women who use benzodiazepines regularly may suffer withdrawal symptoms during the first week of life.

Signs of abuse
Abuse can occur by injection in young people. Another type of abuser is a middle-aged or elderly person who may have been taking these drugs on prescription for months or years. He or she is usually unaware of the problem, and may freely admit to taking "nerve" or sleeping pills in normal or large quantities. As long as moderate drug intake continues, general health is not noticeably affected.

Interactions
Benzodiazepines increase the risk of sedation with any drug that has a sedative effect on the central nervous system. These include other anti-anxiety and sleeping drugs, alcohol, narcotic analgesics, antipsychotics, tricyclic antidepressants and antihistamines.

Practical points
Benzodiazepines should normally be used for courses of two weeks duration or less. If these drugs have been taken for longer than two weeks, it is usually best to reduce the dose gradually to reduce the risk of withdrawal symptoms. If you have been taking benzodiazepines for many months or years, it is best to consult your doctor to work out a dose reduction programme. If possible, it will help to tell your family and friends and enlist their support.

COCAINE

Other common names Coke, crack, nose candy, snow
Drug category Central nervous system stimulant and local anaesthetic

Habit-forming potential
Taken regularly, cocaine is habit-forming. Users may become psychologically *dependent* on its physical and mental effects, and may step up their intake to maintain or increase these effects or to prevent the feelings of severe fatigue and depression that may follow after the drug is stopped. The risk of dependence is especially pronounced with the form of cocaine known as "freebase" or "crack" (see below).

How taken
Smoked, sniffed or occasionally injected.

Legitimate uses
Cocaine was formerly widely used as a local anaesthetic. It is still sometimes given for *topical* anaesthesia in the mouth and throat prior to minor surgery or other procedures. Because of its side effects and potential for abuse, cocaine has now largely been replaced by safer local anaesthetic drugs. Cocaine is classified under Schedule II of the Misuse of Drugs Act.

Short-term effects
Cocaine is a central nervous system stimulant. In moderate doses it overcomes fatigue and produces feelings of well-being and elation. Appetite is reduced. Physical effects include an increase in heart rate and blood pressure, dilation of the pupils, tremor and increased sweating. Large doses can lead to agitation, anxiety, paranoia and hallucinations. Paranoia may cause violent behaviour. Very large doses may cause convulsions and death due to heart attacks or heart failure.

Long-term effects and risks
Heavy, regular use of cocaine can cause restlessness, anxiety, hyperexcitability, nausea, insomnia and weight loss. Continued use may lead to increasing paranoia and psychosis. Repeated sniffing also damages the membranes lining the nose and may eventually lead to the destruction of the septum, the structure that separates the nostrils.

People with heart disease, high blood pressure and overactive thyroid gland run the risk of heart problems.

Signs of abuse
The cocaine user may appear unusually energetic and exuberant under the influence of the drug and show little interest in food. Heavy, regular use may lead to disturbed eating and sleeping patterns. Agitation, mood swings, aggressive behaviour and suspiciousness of other people may also be signs of a heavy user.

Interactions
Cocaine can increase blood pressure, thus opposing the effect of antihypertensive drugs. Taken with monoamine oxidase inhibitors (MAOIs), it can cause a dangerous rise in blood pressure. It also increases the risk of adverse effects on the heart when taken with certain general anaesthetics.

CRACK

This potent form of cocaine is taken in the form of crystals that are smoked. Highly addictive, it has more intense effects than other forms of cocaine and there is an increased risk of abnormal heart rhythms, high blood pressure, stroke and death. Long-term consequences include coughing of black phlegm, wheezing, irreversible lung damage, hoarseness and parched lips, tongue and throat from inhaling the hot fumes. Mental deterioration, personality changes, social withdrawal, paranoia or violent behaviour, and attempts at suicide may occur.

LSD

Other common names Lysergic acid, acid, haze, microdots
Drug category Hallucinogen

Habit-forming potential
Although it is not physically addictive, LSD may cause psychological *dependence*. After several days of regular use, a person develops a resistance to its actions. A waiting period must pass before resumption of the drug will produce the original effects.

How taken
By mouth, as tiny coloured tablets, or absorbed on to small squares of paper (known as "microdots"), gelatine sheets or sugar cubes.

Legitimate uses
None. Early interest of the medical profession in LSD focused on its possible use in psychotherapy, but additional studies suggested that it could lead to psychosis in susceptible people. It is listed under Schedule I of the Misuse of Drugs Act.

Short-term effects
The effects of usual doses of LSD last for about 12 hours, beginning almost immediately after taking the drug. Initial effects include restlessness, dizziness, a feeling of coldness with shivering and an uncontrollable desire to laugh. Subsequent effects include distortions in perception of sound and vision; true hallucinations are rare. Introspection is often increased and mystical, pseudo-religious experiences may occur. Unpleasant or terrifying hallucinations, loss of emotional control, and overwhelming feelings of anxiety, despair or panic may occur, particularly if the user is suffering from underlying anxiety or depression. Suicide may be attempted. Driving and other hazardous tasks are extremely dangerous. Some people under the influence of this drug have fallen off high buildings, mistakenly believing they could fly.

Long-term effects and risks
Long-term LSD use increases the risk of mental distur-bances, including severe depression. In those with existing psychological difficulties, it can lead to lasting mental problems. In addition, some frequent users experience brief but vivid recurrences of LSD's effects ("flashbacks") for months or years after last taking the drug, causing anxiety and disorientation. There is no evidence of lasting physical ill-effects from LSD use.

Signs of abuse
A person under the influence of LSD may feel strange, but rarely shows outward signs of intoxication. Occasionally, a user drugged with LSD may seem over-excited, or appear withdrawn or confused.

Interactions
Chlorpromazine reduces the effects of LSD, and so can be used in treating a person who is acutely disturbed.

MARIJUANA

Other common names Cannabis, grass, pot, dope, weed, hash, ganja
Drug category Central nervous system depressant, hallucinogen, anti-emetic

Habit-forming potential
There is evidence that regular users of marijuana can become physically and psychologically *dependent* on its effects.

How taken
Usually smoked. May be eaten, often in cakes or biscuits, or brewed like tea and drunk.

Legitimate uses
Preparations of the leaves and resin of the cannabis plant (marijuana) have been in medical use for over two thousand years. Introduced into western medicine in the mid-nineteenth century, marijuana used to be taken for a wide variety of complaints including anxiety, insomnia, rheumatic disorders, migraine, painful menstruation, strychnine poisoning and opiate withdrawal. Today, marijuana derivatives can be prescribed with certain restrictions for the relief of nausea and vomiting caused by treatment with anticancer drugs. Marijuana itself is listed under Schedule I of the Misuse of Drugs Act.

Short-term effects
These partly depend on the effects expected by the user as well as on the amount and strength of the preparation used. In small doses, it promotes a feeling of relaxation and well being, enhances auditory and visual perception, and increases talkativeness. Appetite is usually increased. In some individuals the drug may have little or no effect.

Under the influence of the drug, short-term memory may be impaired and driving ability and coordination are dis-rupted. Loss of the sense of time, confusion, and emotional distress can result. Hallucinations may occur in rare cases. The effects last for one to three hours after smoking marijuana and for up to twelve hours or longer after it is eaten. Death from overdose is unknown.

Long-term effects and risks
Marijuana smoking, like tobacco smoking, is likely to increase the risk of bronchitis and lung cancer. Regular users may become apathetic and lethargic, and neglect their work or studies and personal appearance. In sus-ceptible people, heavy use may trigger a temporary psychiatric disturbance. Marijuana is thought by some doctors to increase the likelihood of experimentation with other drugs.

Since marijuana may lower blood pressure and increase the heart rate, people with heart disorders may be at risk from adverse effects of this drug. Regular use of marijuana may reduce fertility in both men and women, and used during pregnancy, may contribute to premature birth.

Signs of abuse
The marijuana user may appear unusually talkative or drunk under the influence of the drug. Appetite is increased.

Marijuana smoke has a distinct herbal smell that may hang on the hair and clothes of those who use it.

Interactions
Marijuana may increase the risk of sedation with any drugs that have a *sedative* effect on the central nervous system. These include anti-anxiety drugs, sleeping drugs, general anaesthetics, narcotic analgesics, antipsychotics, tricyclic antidepressants, antihistamines and alcohol.

MESCALINE

Other common names Peyote, cactus buttons, big chief
Drug category Hallucinogen

Habit-forming potential
Mescaline has a low habit-forming potential; it does not cause physical *dependence* and does not usually lead to psychological dependence. After several days of taking mescaline, the user is resistant to further doses of the drug, thus discouraging regular daily use.

How taken
By mouth as capsules, or in the form of peyote cactus buds, eaten fresh or dried, drunk as tea or ground up and smoked with marijuana.

Legitimate uses
The peyote cactus has been used by Mexican Indians for over 2,000 years, both as a religious sacrament and as a herbal remedy for various ailments ranging from wounds and bronchitis to failing vision. Mescaline is classified under Schedule I of the Misuse of Drugs Act.

Short-term effects
Mescaline alters visual and auditory perception, although true hallucinations are rare. Appetite is reduced under the influence of this drug. There is also a risk of unpleasant mental effects, particularly in people who are anxious or depressed.

Peyote may have additional effects caused by several other active substances (beside mescaline) in the plant. Strychnine-like chemicals may cause nausea, vomiting and, occasionally, tremors and sweating, which usually precede the perceptual effects of mescaline by up to two hours.

Long-term effects and risks
The long-term effects of mescaline have not been well studied. It may increase the risk of mental disturbances, particularly in people with existing psychological problems. Studies have shown that after taking mescaline most of the drug concentrates in the liver rather than in the brain, and it may therefore have special risks for people with impaired liver function.

Signs of abuse
Signs of mescaline or peyote abuse may not be obvious. Users might sometimes appear withdrawn, disoriented or confused.

Interactions
The combination of alcohol and peyote is recognized to be dangerous. There is a risk of temporary derangement, leading to disorientation, panic and violent behaviour. Vomiting is likely to occur.

NARCOTICS (HEROIN)

Other common names Horse, junk, smack, scag, H
Drug category Central nervous system depressant

Habit-forming potential
Narcotic analgesics include not only drugs that are derived from the opium poppy (opium, morphine) but also synthetic drugs whose medical actions are similar to those of morphine (pethidine, methadone, dextropropoxyphene). Their frequent use leads to *tolerance,* and all have potential for producing *dependence.* Among them, heroin (diamorphine, p.258) is the most potent, widely abused, and dangerous.

After only a few weeks of use *withdrawal symptoms* may occur when the drug is stopped; fear of such withdrawal effects may be a strong inducement to carry on using the drug. In heavy users, the drug habit is often coupled with a lifestyle revolving around its use.

How taken
A white or speckled brown powder, heroin is either sniffed or injected. Other narcotics may be taken by mouth.

Legitimate uses
Heroin is widely used in Britain and in Belgium for the treatment of acute severe pain, such as following a heart attack. It is not used medically in most other countries. Other narcotics are used as analgesics. Most narcotics are listed under Schedule II of the Misuse of Drugs Act. Mild narcotics such as codeine are also sometimes included in cough suppressant and antidiarrhoeal medications and are listed under Schedule V.

Short-term effects
Strong narcotics induce a feeling of well-being and contentment. Pain is dulled and the activity of the nervous system is depressed: breathing and heart rate are slowed and the cough reflex is inhibited. First-time users often feel nauseated and vomit. With higher doses, there is increasing drowsiness, sometimes leading to coma and possibly death from stopped breathing.

Long-term effects and risks
Long-term regular use of narcotics leads to constipation, reduced sexual drive, disruption of menstrual periods and poor eating habits. Poor nutrition and personal neglect may lead to general ill-health.

Street drugs are often mixed ("cut") with other substances such as caffeine, quinine, talcum powder and flour, that can damage blood vessels and clog the lungs. There is also a risk of abscesses at the injection site. Dangerous infections, such as hepatitis, syphilis and AIDS may be transmitted via unclean or shared needles.

After several weeks of regular use, sudden withdrawal of narcotics produces a flu-like withdrawal syndrome beginning 6 – 24 hours after the last dose. Symptoms may include runny nose and eyes, hot and cold sweats, sleeplessness, aches, tremor, anxiety, nausea, vomiting, diarrhoea, muscle spasms and abdominal cramps. These effects are at their worst 48 – 72 hours after withdrawal and fade after 7 – 10 days.

Signs of abuse
Signs of abuse include apathy, neglect of personal appearance and hygiene, loss of appetite and weight, loss of interest in former hobbies and social activities, personality changes and furtive behaviour. Signs of intoxication include pinpoint pupils and a drowsy or drunken appearance.

Interactions
Narcotics dangerously increase the risk of sedation with any drug that has a sedative effect on the central nervous system, including barbiturates and alcohol.

NICOTINE

Other common names Found in tobacco products
Drug category Central nervous system stimulant

Habit-forming potential
The nicotine in tobacco is largely responsible for tobacco *addiction* in over one third of the population who are cigarette smokers. Most are also probably psychologically *dependent* on the process of smoking. Most people who start to smoke go on to do so regularly and most become physically dependent on nicotine. Stopping can produce temporary *withdrawal symptoms* that include nausea, weight gain, drowsiness, fatigue, insomnia, irritability, inability to concentrate, depression and craving for cigarettes.

How taken
Usually smoked in the form of cigarettes, cigars and pipe tobacco. Sometimes chewed (chewing tobacco) or sniffed (tobacco snuff). Nicotine is also available in chewing gum.

Legitimate uses
There are no legal restrictions on tobacco use. Its sale, however, is restricted to those over the age of 16. Nicotine chewing gum or slow-release patches may be prescribed on a temporary basis along with behaviour modification therapy to help people who want to give up smoking.

Short-term effects
Nicotine stimulates the sympathetic nervous system (see p.79). In regular tobacco users, it increases concentration, relieves tension and fatigue, and counters boredom and monotony. These effects are short-lived, thus encouraging frequent use. Physical effects include narrowing of blood vessels, increase in heart rate and blood pressure, and reduction in urine output. First-time users often feel dizzy and nauseated, and may vomit.

Long-term effects and risks
Nicotine taken regularly may cause a rise in fatty acids in the bloodstream. This effect, combined with the effects of the drug on heart rhythm and blood vessel size, increases the risk of diseases of the heart and circulation, including angina, high blood pressure, peripheral vascular disease, stroke and coronary thrombosis. In addition, its stimulatory effects may lead to excess production of stomach acid, thereby increasing the risk of peptic ulcers.

Other well-known risks of tobacco smoking, such as chronic lung diseases, adverse effects on pregnancy, and cancers of the lung, mouth, and throat, may be due to other harmful ingredients, like tar and carbon monoxide, in the smoke.

Signs of abuse
Regular smokers often have yellow, tobacco-stained fingers and teeth, and bad breath. The smell of tobacco may linger on hair and clothes. A smoker's cough or shortness of breath are early signs of lung damage or heart disease.

Interactions
Cigarette smoking reduces the blood levels of a variety of drugs and reduces their effects. Such drugs include theophylline, propranolol, heparin, tricyclic antidepressants, phenothiazine antipsychotics, benzodiazepines, and caffeine. Diabetics may require larger doses of insulin. The health risks involved in taking oral contraceptives are increased by smoking.

Practical points
▼ Don't start smoking: nicotine is highly addictive.
▼ If you smoke already, give up now even if you have not yet suffered adverse effects.
▼ Ask your doctor for advice and support.
▼ Inquire about self-help groups in your neighbourhood for people trying to give up smoking. For relief from withdrawal symptoms, see p.344.

NITRITES

Other common names Amyl nitrite, butyl nitrite, poppers, snappers
Drug category Vasodilators (see also p.98)

Habit-forming potential
Nitrites do not seem to cause physical *dependence*; major *withdrawal symptoms* have never been reported. However, users may become psychologically dependent on the stimulant effect of these drugs.

How taken
By inhalation, usually from small bottles with screw or plug tops or from small glass ampoules that are broken.

Legitimate uses
Amyl nitrite was originally introduced as a treatment for angina, but has now largely been replaced by safer, longer-acting drugs. It is still used as an *antidote* for cyanide poisoning. Butyl and isobutyl nitrites are not used medically.

Short-term effects
Nitrites increase the flow of blood by relaxing blood vessel walls. They give the user a rapid high, felt as a strong rush of energy. Less pleasant effects include an increase in heart rate, intense flushing, dizziness, pounding headache, nausea and coughing. High doses may cause fainting, and regular use may produce a blue discoloration of the skin due to alteration of haemoglobin in the red blood cells.

Long-term effects and risks
Nitrites are very quick-acting drugs. Their effects start within thirty seconds of inhalation and last for about five minutes. Regular users may become *tolerant* to these drugs, thus requiring higher doses to achieve the desired effects. Lasting physical damage, including cardiac problems, can result from chronic use of these drugs, and deaths have occurred.

The risk of *toxic* effects is increased in those with low blood pressure. Nitrites may also precipitate glaucoma in susceptible people, by increasing pressure inside the eye.

Signs of abuse
Nitrites have a pungent, fruity odour. They evaporate quickly: the contents of a small bottle left uncapped in a room usually disappear within two hours. Unless someone is actually taking the drug or is suffering from an overdose, the only sign of abuse is a bluish skin discoloration.

Interactions
The blood pressure-lowering effects of these drugs may be increased by alcohol, beta blockers, calcium channel blockers and tricyclic antidepressants, thus increasing the risks of dizziness and fainting.

PHENCYCLIDINE

Other common names PCP, angel dust, crystal, ozone
Drug category General anaesthetic, hallucinogen

Habit-forming potential
There is little evidence that phencyclidine causes physical *dependence*. Some users become psychologically dependent on this drug and *tolerant* to its effects.

How taken
May be sniffed, used in smoking mixtures (in the form of angel dust), eaten (as tablets) or, rarely, injected.

Legitimate uses
Although it was once used as an anaesthetic, it no longer has any medical use. Its only legal use now is in veterinary medicine. It is classified under Schedule II of the Misuse of Drugs Act. Phencyclidine's effects on behaviour (see below) make it one of the most dangerous of all drugs of abuse. Fortunately, it is rarely abused in Europe.

Short-term effects
Phencyclidine taken in small amounts generally produces a "high", but sometimes leads to anxiety or depression. Co-ordination of speech and movement deteriorates. Thinking and concentration are impaired. Hallucinations and violent behaviour may occur. Other effects include increase in blood pressure and heart rate, dilation of the pupils, dryness of the mouth, tremor, numbness and greatly reduced sensitivity to pain, which may make it difficult to restrain a person who has become violent under the influence of the drug. Shivering, vomiting, muscle weakness and rigidity may occur. Higher doses lead to coma or stupor. The recovery period is often prolonged, with alternate periods of sleep and waking, usually followed by memory blackout of the whole episode.

Long-term effects and risks
Repeated phencyclidine use may lead to paranoia, auditory hallucinations, violent behaviour, anxiety and severe depression. While depressed, the user may attempt suicide by overdosing on the drug. Heavy users may also develop brain damage, causing memory blackouts, disorientation, visual disturbances and speech difficulties.

Deaths due to prolonged convulsions, cardiac or respiratory arrest, and ruptured blood vessels in the brain have been reported. After high doses or prolonged coma, there is also a risk of mental derangement, which may be permanent.

Signs of abuse
The phencyclidine user may appear drunk while under the influence of the drug. Hostile or violent behaviour and mood swings with bouts of depression may be more common with heavy use.

Interactions
May inhibit effects of *anticholinergic* drugs, as well as beta blockers and antihypertensive drugs.

SOLVENTS

Other common names Includes sniffing of glue and other volatile substances
Drug category Central nervous system depressant

Habit-forming potential
There is a low risk of physical *dependence* with solvent abuse, but regular users may become psychologically dependent. Young people with family and personality problems are particularly at risk of becoming habitual users.

How taken
By breathing in the fumes, usually from a plastic bag placed over the nose and/or mouth or from a cloth or handkerchief soaked in the solvent.

Legitimate uses
Solvents are used in a wide variety of industrial, domestic and cosmetic products. They function as aerosol propellants for spray paints, hair lacquer, lighter fuel and deodorants. They are used in adhesives, paints, paint stripper, lacquers, petrol and cleaning fluids. Most products containing solvents may not be sold to people under the age of 18.

Short-term effects
The short-term effects of solvents include lightheadedness, dizziness, confusion, and progressive drowsiness and loss of coordination with increasing doses. Accidents of all types are more likely. Heart rhythm might be disturbed, sometimes fatally. Large doses can lead to disorientation, hallucinations and loss of consciousness. Nausea, vomiting, and headaches may also occur. There are over 150 deaths every year in Britain from solvent abuse.

Long-term effects and risks
One of the greatest risks of solvent abuse is accidental death or injury while intoxicated. Some products, particularly aerosol gases, butane gas, and cleaning fluids, may seriously disrupt heart rhythm or cause heart failure and sometimes death. Aerosols and butane gas can also cause suffocation by sudden cooling of the airways and are particularly dangerous if squirted into the mouth. Butane gas has been known to ignite in the mouth. Aerosol products, such as deodorants and paints, may suffocate the user by coating the lungs. People have also suffocated while sniffing solvents from plastic bags placed over their heads. There is also a risk of death from inhalation of vomit and depression of the breathing mechanism.

Long-term misuse of solvent-based cleaning fluids can cause permanent liver or kidney damage, while long-term exposure to benzene (found in plastic cements, lacquers, paint remover, petrol, and cleaning fluid) may lead to blood and liver disorders. Hexane-based adhesives may cause nerve damage leading to numbness and tremor. Repeated sniffing of leaded petrol may cause lead poisoning.

Regular daily use of solvents can lead to pallor, fatigue, and forgetfulness. Heavy use may affect school performance and lead to weight loss, depression, and general deterioration of health.

Signs of abuse
Most abusers are adolescents between the ages of 10 and 17, although the average age is thought to be falling.

Obvious signs of solvent abuse include a chemical smell on the breath and traces of glue or solvents on the body or clothes. Others include furtive behaviour, uncharacteristic moodiness, unusual soreness or redness around the mouth, nose, or eyes, and a persistent cough.

Interactions
Sniffing solvents increases the risk of sedation with any drug that has a sedative effect on the central nervous system, such as anti-anxiety drugs, sleeping drugs, narcotics, antipsychotics, tricyclic antidepressants, and alcohol.

DRUGS IN SPORT

The use of drugs to improve athletic performance has been universally condemned by sporting authorities. The deliberate use of certain drugs gives the user an unfair advantage, and may also endanger health. For these reasons, certain substances have been prohibited by organizations such as the International Olympic Committee and other national authorities. If traces of a prohibited substance are found by means of a urine test, the athlete is banned from the competition and risks lifelong exclusion from the sport.

Not only strong, prescribed medications affect athletic performance; everyday items such as cigarettes, alcohol, tea, and coffee can also have an effect. Drugs of any kind should be taken by athletes only under strict medical supervision. Anyone wishing to embark on a strenuous programme of activity is advised to consult a doctor for advice about the effects any current medication may have, or how the underlying condition for which the drugs are prescribed may affect the body's ability to cope with exertion.

Many drugs affect athletic performance. Some are medications prescribed by doctors to treat specific medical conditions but abused by athletes who want to benefit from the body-building and general performance-improving effects of these drugs. Others are everyday non-prescribed substances – caffeine and nicotine, for example – which have a relatively minor effect on performance. If taken in excess, however, even these substances can raise drug levels in the athlete's body to a point at which detection is possible.

Detecting drugs
Drugs can be detected in urine, and tests for prohibited substances are performed frequently in most sports during competitions, and at other times during training.

Prohibited substances
The International Olympic Committee recognizes six classes of "doping" drugs: stimulants, narcotic analgesics, androgenic anabolic steroids, beta blocking drugs, diuretics, and peptide hormones and analogues. As well as abusing certain pharmacological or chemical substances, some athletes also engage in illegal blood doping (see below).

Legitimate medications
Certain prescribed drugs may be taken legitimately by athletes for medical disorders such as asthma or epilepsy. Other prescribed drugs such as antibiotics may not make any appreciable difference to athletic performance, but the underlying disorder for which they are being taken may mean that strenuous exercise is inadvisable. Care should be taken when using certain over-the-counter preparations because many contain low doses of prohibited substances.

TYPES OF DRUGS
Antibiotics
Antibiotics may occasionally impair ability by causing nausea or diarrhoea.

Antihistamines
Preparations containing chlorphenamine or diphenhydramine may cause drowsiness, dizziness, or blurred vision.

Anti-inflammatory drugs (NSAIDs)
Using anti-inflammatory drugs to relieve pain in muscles, tendons, or ligaments can be dangerous; masking pain may result in aggravation of an injury.

Asthma drugs
An asthma drug should not contain isoprenaline, ephedrine, or phenylephrine as these are prohibited stimulants.

Blood doping
This illegal practice, condemned by international sporting authorities, involves removing a pint of blood from an athlete during training and replacing it shortly before a competition. After blood is removed, the volume and number of red cells in the remaining blood is naturally replenished. When the pint is reinfused shortly before a competition, the haemoglobin content of the blood is increased, enhancing the blood's ability to deliver oxygen to muscles. A similar effect is achieved by taking erythropoietin (epoetin) to stimulate extra blood production.

Caffeine
Although caffeine is listed as a prohibited stimulant, disqualification results only if large quantities are found in a urine sample.

Cocaine
Cocaine is an illegal and highly addictive stimulant prohibited in sport. It has a number of dangerous side effects including heart arrhythmias, negative personality changes, and damage to the nasal lining after regular inhalation. High doses can trigger convulsions or psychosis, and may cause death, even in a first-time user. See also Stimulants (table).

Cough and cold remedies
Avoid preparations containing codeine, ephedrine, pseudoephedrine, phenylephrine, or phenylpropanolamine for 12 hours before a competition.

Diarrhoea remedies
Any preparation containing codeine must be avoided.

Dieting drugs
Most non-prescribed diet drugs contain a prohibited stimulant and diuretic. See also Stimulants and Diuretics (table).

Hay fever remedies
Many hay fever remedies contain the prohibited stimulants ephedrine, pseudoephedrine, phenlyephrine, or phenlypropanolamine. See also Stimulants (table) and Antihistamines.

Liniment
Liniment acts as a counter irritant on pain receptors in the skin. It is important that its application does not mask pain to the point where further damage to an injury may result after exertion.

Nicotine
Nicotine reduces the flow of blood through the muscles. Carbon monoxide from smoking decreases the available oxygen carried round the body, reducing the capacity for exercise.

Painkillers
Strong painkillers such as codeine and morphine, known as narcotic analgesics, are prohibited in sport (table). Weaker painkillers, such as aspirin and paracetamol, and local anaesthetic preparations in spray, ointment, or cream form, are not prohibited but their use can mask pain, resulting in the aggravation of an injury.

Sleeping drugs
Many sports authorities ban sedative drugs completely, so a sleeping drug should not be taken within 24 hours of a competition.

DRUGS BANNED BY THE OLYMPIC COMMITTEE

DRUG	EFFECT	RISK
Anabolic steroids Anabolic steroids consist of a group of substances that produce an effect similar to that of the male sex hormone testosterone. They increase the production of muscle protein and speed the recovery of muscles after a period of exercise.	The use of anabolic steroids permits a more demanding training schedule and allows an increase in muscle bulk and strength. They are also believed to increase aggressive tendencies and competitiveness. Until they were banned, anabolic steroids were commonly used by body builders, weight lifters, and athletes in field events.	Abuse of anabolic steroids may cause liver damage, liver tumours, and adrenal gland damage. Anabolic steroids are also linked with psychological changes, particularly aggressiveness and impulsiveness, and users have an increased risk of suicide. In men they may cause infertility or impotence. In women, they may result in the acquisition of male characteristics. Taken in childhood, anabolic steroids may cause short stature by affecting the growing areas of bone.
Beta blockers Beta blocking drugs are prescribed to treat angina, cardiac arrhythmias, high blood pressure, migraine, over-active thyroid, and the physical symptoms of anxiety.	Taking beta blockers results in a steadier, slower heart beat and lower blood pressure. Competitors in some sports formerly used beta blockers to reduce the physical symptoms of anxiety such as sweating, shaking, and palpitations, and to increase their sense of physical calm and stability. In particular, they were used to reduce tremor in sports where a steadiness of hand is vital – shooting and archery for example.	Beta blockers reduce blood flow to muscles and make exertion more difficult. There may also be slight constriction of the airways which may cause breathlessness in asthmatics or those with chronic bronchial disorders. Beta blockers are prohibited universally in the absence of a specific medical disorder that requires them.
Diuretics Diuretics are prescribed as a treatment for heart failure and high blood pressure.	In the past, athletes used diuretics to flush out traces of other banned substances – particularly anabolic steroids, narcotic analgesics, and stimulants – from their bodies. They have also been abused by wrestlers, weight lifters, boxers, and jockeys attempting to shed weight to achieve a target for a competition or race.	The use of diuretics as an aid to short-term weight loss is extremely dangerous as there is insufficient time between the "weigh in" and the competition for lost body fluids and salts to be replaced. This results in fatigue, dehydration, and muscle weakness with a consequent impairment of performance.
Growth hormone A synthetic version of growth hormone is prescribed to stimulate normal body growth and development where the pituitary gland produces too little of the natural substance.	Athletes have abused growth hormone to stimulate unnatural growth and development of muscle.	Abuse of the drug may ultimately cause muscle weakness. Other side effects include coarsening of the skin, and deepening of the voice. Prolonged use may lead to high blood pressure.
Painkillers Only the strongest pain-killers – narcotic analgesics such as codeine and morphine – are prohibited. They are banned to protect athletes from their dangerous pain-masking qualities.	By dulling the pain, painkillers enable athletes to continue to exercise beyond the point where they would normally be prevented by pain.	The use of painkillers greatly increases the risk of an injury being aggravated by further exercise. Even weak painkillers should be avoided during exercise, and activity resumed only when the pain has disappeared.
Stimulants There are two categories of stimulant that have an effect on athletic perform-ance: non-prescribed substances, such as caffeine found in tea and coffee, and powerful prescribed medications, such as amphetamines, some of which are illicit abused drugs.	Stimulants have been used in sport to inhibit fatigue and increase self-confidence, particularly in endurance sports. They are also believed to reduce appetite and increase aggression.	The use of amphetamines may lead to an increase in blood pressure, cardiac arrhythmia, hyperthermia (heatstroke), and convulsions. In high doses they may cause altered perception and hallucinations. Prolonged use may cause heart failure and increase the risk of brain haemorrhage. Because of the heightened aggressiveness they provoke, stimulants increase the risk of injury to both user and opponent. Many stimulants are addictive.

GLOSSARY

The following pages contain definitions of drug-related terms whose technical meanings are not explained in detail elsewhere in the book, or for which an easily-located precise explanation may be helpful. These are words which may not be familiar to the general reader, or that have a slightly different meaning in a medical context than in ordinary use. Some of the terms included refer to particular drug actions or effects, others describe methods of drug administration. A few medical conditions that may occur as a result of drug use are also defined. All words printed in italics within the main text are included as entries in this glossary.

The glossary is arranged in alphabetical order. Each entry has a bold heading. In order to avoid unnecessary repetition, where relevant, entries include cross-references to further information on that topic in sections elsewhere in the book, or to another glossary term.

A

Addiction
An imprecise term that can cover anything from intense, habitual cravings for coffee, tea or tobacco, to physical and psychological dependence on more potent agents such as narcotics. See also *Dependence*.

Adjuvant
A drug that enhances the therapeutic effect of another drug, but that does not necessarily have a beneficial effect when used alone. An example is aluminium, which is added to certain vaccines to enhance the immune response, thereby increasing the protection given by the vaccine.

Adrenergic
See *Sympathomimetic*.

Adverse reaction
An unexpected or unpredictable reaction to a drug that is unrelated to the drug's usual effects. The cause may sometimes be an allergic reaction or a genetic disorder, such as the lack of an enzyme that normally inactivates the drug. See also The effects of drugs (p.15).

Agonist
A term meaning to have a positive, stimulating effect. An agonist drug is one that binds to a *receptor*, thereby triggering or increasing a particular activity in that cell.

Amoebecide
A drug that kills amoebae (single-celled micro-organisms). See also Antiprotozoal drugs (p.136).

Anaemia
A condition in which the concentration of the oxygen-carrying pigment of the blood, haemoglobin, is below normal. Many different disorders may cause anaemia, and it may sometimes occur as a result of drug treatment. Severe anaemia may cause fatigue, pallor and, occasionally, breathing difficulty.

Anaesthetic, general
A drug or drug combination given to produce unconsciousness before and during surgery or potentially painful investigative procedures. General anaesthesia is usually induced initially by injection of a drug such as thiopentone, and maintained by inhalation of the fumes of a volatile liquid such as halothane or a gas such as nitrous oxide mixed with oxygen. See *Premedication*.

Anaesthetic, local
A drug applied topically or injected to numb sensation in a small area. See Local anaesthetics (p.80).

Analeptic
A drug given in hospital to stimulate breathing. See also Respiratory stimulants (p.88).

Analgesia
Relief of pain, usually by administration of drugs. See also Analgesics (p.80).

Anaphylaxis
A severe reaction to an allergen such as a bee sting or a drug (see Allergy, p.123). Symptoms may include rash, swelling, breathing difficulty and collapse. See also Anaphylactic shock (p.472).

Antagonist
A term meaning to have a negative effect. An antagonist drug (often called a "blocker") is one that binds to a *receptor* without stimulating cell activity and prevents any other substance from occupying that receptor.

Antibody
A protein manufactured by lymphocytes (a type of white blood cell) to neutralize an antigen (foreign protein) in the body. The formation of antibodies against an invading micro-organism is part of the body's defence against infection. Immunization carried out to increase the body's resistance to a specific disease involves either injection of specific antibodies or administration of a vaccine that stimulates antibody production. See also Vaccines and immunization (p.134).

Anticholinergic
A drug that blocks the action of acetylcholine, or a term that refers to the *parasympathomimetic* effects of such a drug. Acetylcholine is a *neurotransmitter* secreted by the endings of nerve cells that allows certain nerve impulses to be transmitted, including those that relax some involuntary muscles, tighten others and affect the release of saliva. Anticholinergic drugs are used to treat urinary incontinence because they relax the bladder's squeezing muscles while tightening those of the sphincter. Anticholinergic drugs also relax the muscles of the intestinal wall, helping to relieve irritable bowel syndrome (p.110). See also Autonomic nervous system (p.79).

Antidote
A substance that neutralizes or counter-acts the effects of a poison. Very few poisons have a specific antidote.

Antineoplastic
An anticancer drug (p.154).

Antiperspirant
A substance applied to the skin to reduce excess sweating. Antiperspirants work by reducing the activity of the sweat glands or by blocking the ducts that carry sweat to the skin surface.

Antipyretic
A drug that reduces fever. The most commonly used antipyretic drugs are aspirin and paracetamol.

Antiseptic
A chemical that destroys bacteria. Antiseptics may be applied to the skin or to other areas to prevent infection. See Anti-infective skin preparations (p.175).

Antispasmodic
A drug that reduces spasm (abnormally strong or inappropriate contraction) of the muscles of the gastrointestinal tract, airways and blood vessels. Antispasmodic drugs are most commonly prescribed to relieve irritable bowel syndrome (p.110).

Antitussive
A drug that prevents or relieves a cough. See also Drugs to treat coughs (p.94).

Aperient
A mild laxative. See Laxatives (p.111).

Astringent
A substance that causes tissue to dry and shrink by reducing its ability to absorb water. Astringents are used in a number of antiperspirants and skin tonics because they remove excessive moisture from the skin surface. They are also used in ear drops for outer-ear inflammation because they promote healing of the inflamed tissue.

B

Bactericidal
A term used to describe a drug that kills bacteria. See also Antibiotics (p.128) and Antibacterials (p.131).

Bacteriostatic
A term used to describe a drug that stops the growth or multiplication of bacteria. See also Antibiotics (p.128) and Antibacterials (p.131).

Balm
A soothing or healing preparation applied to the skin.

Bioavailability
The amount of a drug that enters the bloodstream and so reaches tissues throughout the body, usually expressed as a percentage of the dose given. Injection of a drug directly into a vein produces 100 per cent bioavailability. Drugs given by mouth generally have a much lower bioavailability because only a proportion of the drug can usually be absorbed through the digestive system. Furthermore, some of the drug may be broken down in the liver before reaching the main circulation.

Body salts
Also known as electrolytes, these are compounds of various minerals that are present in such body fluids as blood, urine, and sweat, and within cells. These salts play an important role in regulating water balance, acidity of the blood, conduction of nerve impulses, and muscle contraction. The balance between the various salts can be upset by such conditions as diarrhoea and vomiting. The balance may also be altered by the action of drugs such as diuretics (p.99).

Brand name
See *Generic* name.

Bronchoconstrictor
A substance that causes the airways in the lungs to narrow. An attack of asthma may be caused by the release of bronchoconstrictor substances such as histamine or certain prostaglandins.

Bronchodilator
A drug that widens the airways. See Bronchodilators (p.92).

C

Capsule
See p.19.

Cathartic
A drug that stimulates bowel action to produce a soft or liquid bowel movement. See also Laxatives (p.111).

Chelating agent
A chemical used in the treatment of poisoning by metals such as iron, lead, arsenic, and mercury. It acts by combining with the metal to form a less poisonous substance and in some cases increases excretion in the urine. Penicillamine is a commonly-used chelating agent.

Chemotherapy
The treatment of cancer or infections by drugs. *Cytotoxic* drugs (p.154) and antibiotics (p.128) are examples of drugs used in chemotherapy.

Cholinergic
A drug, also called *parasympathomimetic*, that stimulates the parasympathetic nervous system. See also Autonomic nervous system (p.79).

Coma
A state of unconsciousness and unresponsiveness to external stimuli such as noise and pain. Coma results from disturbance of, or damage to part of the brain (often by drug overdose).

Contraindication
A factor in a person's current condition, medical history, or genetic make-up that may increase the risks of an adverse effect from a drug, to the extent that the drug should not be prescribed.

Counter-irritant
Another term for *rubefacient*.

Cycloplegic
The action of paralysing the ciliary muscle in the eye. This muscle alters the shape of the lens when it contracts, enabling the eye to focus on objects. A cycloplegic drug prevents this action, and by doing so makes both examination of, and surgery on, the eye easier. See also Drugs affecting the pupil (p.170).

Cytotoxic
A drug that kills or damages cells. Drugs with this action are most commonly used to treat cancer. Although they primarily affect abnormal cells, they may also kill or damage healthy cells. See also Anti-cancer drugs (p.154).

D

Dependence
A term that relates to physical or psychological dependence on a substance, or both. Psychological dependence involves intense mental cravings if a drug is unavailable or withdrawn. Physical dependence produces physical withdrawal symptoms (sweating, shaking, abdominal pain, and convulsions) if the substance is not taken. Dependence also implies loss of control over intake. See also Drug dependence (p.23).

Depot injection
Injection into a muscle of a drug that has been specially formulated to provide for a slow, steady absorption of its active ingredients by the surrounding blood vessels. The drug may be mixed with oil or wax. The release period can be made to last up to several weeks. See also Methods of administration (p.17).

Designer drugs
A group of unlicensed substances whose only purpose is to duplicate the effects of certain illegal drugs of abuse or to provide even stronger ones.

Designer drugs differ chemically in some minor degree from the original drug, enabling the user and supplier to evade prosecution for dealing in, or possession of, an illegal drug. They are very dangerous because their effects are unpredictable, they are often highly potent, and they may contain impurities.

Double-blind
A type of test used by drug companies to measure the effectiveness of a new drug against an existing medicine or a *placebo*. Neither the patients nor the doctors administering the drug know who is receiving what substance. Only after the test is complete and the patients' responses are recorded is the identity of those who received the new drug revealed. Double-blind trials are carried out for almost all new drugs. See also Testing and approving new drugs (p.12).

Drip
A non-medical term for *intravenous infusion*.

E

Electrolyte
See *Body salts*.

Elixir
A clear, sweetened liquid often containing alcohol that forms the base for many liquid medicines such as those used to treat coughs.

Embrocation
An ointment rubbed on to the skin to relieve joint pain, muscle cramp or muscle injury. An embrocation usually contains a *rubefacient*.

Emetic
Any substance that causes a person to vomit. An emetic may work by irritating the lining of the stomach and/or by stimulating the part of the brain that controls vomiting. An emetic, such as ipecac (ipecacuanha), may be used in the treatment of drug overdose. See also Drug poisoning emergency guide (p.470).

Emollient
A substance that has a soothing, softening effect when applied to the skin. An emollient also has a moisturising effect, preventing loss of water from the skin surface, by forming an oily film. See also Bases for skin preparations (p.175).

Emulsion
A combination of two substances that normally do not mix together properly but remain as particles of one suspended in the liquid form of the other. Many lotions are emulsions; they need to be shaken before use in case the constituent substances have separated.

Endorphins
A group of substances that occur naturally in the brain. Released in response to pain, they bind to specialized *receptors* and reduce perception of pain. Narcotic anal-/gesics such as morphine work by mimicking the action of endorphins. See also Analgesics (p.80).

Enzyme
A protein that controls the rate of one or more chemical reactions in the body. There are thousands of enzymes active in the human body. Each type of body cell produces a specific range of enzymes. Cells in the liver contain enzymes that stimulate the breakdown of nutrients and drugs; cells in the digestive tract release enzymes that help digest food. Some drugs work by altering the activity of enzymes – for example, certain anticancer drugs halt tumour growth by altering enzyme function in cancer cells.

Excitatory
A term meaning having a stimulating or enhancing effect. A chemical released from a nerve ending that causes muscle contraction is having an excitatory effect. See also *inhibitory*.

Expectorant
A type of cough remedy that enhances the production of sputum (phlegm) and is used in the treatment of a productive (sputum-producing) cough. See also Drugs to treat coughs (p.94).

F

Formula, chemical
A way of expressing the constituents of a chemical in symbols and numbers. Every known chemical substance has a formula. Water, for instance, has the formula H_2O, indicating that it is composed of two hydrogen atoms (H_2) and one oxygen atom (O). Drugs all have more complicated formulas.

Formulary
See *Pharmacopeia*.

G H

Generic name
The official name for a single, therapeutic-/ally active substance. It is distinct from a brand name, a term chosen by a manufacturer for a product containing a generic drug. For example: diazepam is a generic name; Valium is a brand-name product that contains diazepam.

Half-life
A term used in pharmacology for the time the body takes to reduce the blood level of a drug by half. Knowledge of the half-life of a drug helps to determine frequency of dosage.

Hallucinogen
A drug that causes hallucinations (unreal perceptions of surroundings and objects). Common hallucinogens include the drugs of abuse LSD and marijuana (p.438). Alcohol taken in large amounts may also have an hallucinogenic effect; hallucinations may also occur during withdrawal from alcohol. Certain prescribed drugs may in rare cases cause hallucinations.

Hormone
A chemical released directly into the bloodstream by a gland or tissue. The body produces numerous hormones each of which has a specific range of functions such as controlling the *metabolism* of cells, growth, sexual development, and the body's response to stress or illness. Hormone-producing glands make up the endocrine system (see Hormones and endocrine system, p.140); the kidneys, intestine, and brain also release hormones.

I

Immunization
The process of inducing immunity (resistance to infection) as a preventive measure against the spread of infectious diseases. See Vaccines and immunization (p.134).

Indication
The term used to describe a disorder, symptom, or condition for which a drug or treatment may be prescribed. For example, indications for the use of beta blockers include angina and high blood pressure.

Infusion pump
A machine for administering a continuous, controlled amount of a drug or other fluid through a needle inserted into a vein or under the skin. It consists of a small battery powered pump that controls the flow of fluid from a syringe into the attached needle. The pump may be strapped to the patient and preprogrammed to deliver the fluid at a constant rate. See also Methods of administration (p.17).

Inhaler
A device used for administering a drug in powder or vapour form. Inhalers are used principally in the treatment of respiratory disorders such as asthma and chronic bronchitis. Among the medications administered in this way are corticosteroids and bronchodilator drugs. See also Methods of administration (p.17) and inhalers (p.92).

Inhibitory
A term meaning to have a blocking effect on cell activity, e.g. a chemical released from a nerve ending that prevents muscle contraction has an inhibitory effect. See also *Antagonist*.

Inoculation
A method of administering microorganisms or other biological substances to produce immunity to disease by scratching the vaccine into the skin. See Vaccines and immunization (p.134).

Intramuscular injection
Injection of a drug into a muscle, usually in the upper arm or buttock. The drug is absorbed from the muscle into the bloodstream.

Intravenous infusion
Prolonged, slow injection of fluid (often a solution of a drug) into a vein. The fluid flows at a controlled rate from a bag or bottle through a fine tube inserted into an opening into a vein. An intravenous infusion may also be administered via an *infusion pump*.

Intravenous injection
Direct injection of a drug into a vein, which puts the drug immediately into the circulation. Because it has a rapid effect, intravenous injection is useful in an emergency.

J L

Jaundice
A condition in which the skin and whites of the eyes take on a yellow coloration.

Jaundice can be caused by an accumulation in the blood of the pigment bilirubin. Jaundice is a sign of many disorders of the liver. A drug may cause jaundice as an adverse effect either by damaging the liver or by causing an increase in the breakdown of red blood cells in the circulation.

Lotion
A liquid preparation that may be applied to large areas of skin. See also Bases for skin preparations (p.175).

M

Medication
Any substance prescribed to treat illness.

Medicine
A medication or drug that maintains, improves, or restores health.

Metabolism
The term for all chemical processes in the body that involve the formation of new substances or the breakdown of substances to release energy. Metabolism provides energy required to keep the body functioning at rest – to maintain breathing, heart beat, and body temperature and to replace worn tissues. It also provides energy needed during exertion. Metabolism produces this energy from the breakdown of digested foods.

Miotic
A drug that constricts (narrows) the pupil. Opiate drugs such as morphine have a miotic effect, and someone who is taking one of these drugs has pinpoint pupils. The pupil is sometimes deliberately narrowed by other miotic drugs in the treatment of glaucoma. See also Drugs for glaucoma (p.168) and Drugs affecting the pupil (p.170).

Mucolytic
A drug that liquefies mucus secretions in the airways. See also Drugs to treat coughs (p.94).

Mydriatic
A drug that dilates (widens) the pupil. *Anticholinergic* drugs, such as atropine, have this effect and may cause *photophobia* as a consequence. Mydriatic drugs may occasionally provoke the onset of glaucoma. See also Drugs affecting the pupil (p.170).

N

Narcotic
Stemming from the Greek word for numbness or stupor and once applied to drugs derived from the opium poppy, the word narcotic no longer has a precise medical meaning. Doctors today use the term narcotic analgesics to refer to opium-derived and synthetic drugs that have pain-relieving properties and other effects similar to those of morphine (see Analgesics, p.80). See also Narcotics (p.439).

Nebulizer
A method of administering a drug to the airways and lungs in aerosol form through a face mask. The apparatus includes an electric or hand-operated pump that sends a stream of air or oxygen through a length of tubing into a small canister containing the drug in liquid form. This inflow of gas causes the drug to be dispersed into a fine mist which is then carried through another tube into the face mask. Inhalation of this drug mist is much easier than inhaling from a pressurized aerosol (see also *Inhaler*).

Neuroleptic
A drug used to treat psychotic illness. See Antipsychotic drugs (p.85).

Neurotransmitter
A chemical released from a nerve ending after receiving an electrical impulse. A neurotransmitter may carry a message from the nerve to another nerve so that the electrical impulse passes on, or to a muscle to stimulate contraction, or to a gland to stimulate secretion of a particular hormone. Acetylcholine and noradrenaline are examples of neurotransmitters . Many drugs either mimic or block the action of neurotransmitters. See also Brain and nervous system (p.78).

O

Orphan drug
A drug that is effective for a rare condition, but that may not be marketed by a drug manufacturer because of the small profit potential compared with the high costs of development and production.

OTC
The abbreviation for over-the-counter. Over-the-counter drugs can be bought from a chemist's shop without a prescription.

P

Parasympathomimetic
A drug that stimulates the parasympathetic nervous system (see Autonomic nervous system, p.79). These drugs (also called cholinergic drugs) are used as *miotics* and to stimulate bladder contraction in urinary retention (see Drugs used in urinary disorders, p.166).

Parkinsonism
Neurological symptoms including tremor of the hands and muscle rigidity that resemble Parkinson's disease. It may be caused by prolonged treatment with an antipsychotic drug.

Pharmacist
A licensed, trained health professional (often called a "chemist") concerned with the preparation and dispensing of drugs. Pharmacists may advise on the correct use of non-prescription drugs and may answer many questions about the use of prescribed medication.

Pharmacodynamics
A word used to describe the effects or actions that a drug produces in the body. For example, pain relief or bronchoconstriction are pharmacodynamic effects that stem from the chemical make-up of the drug concerned.

Pharmacokinetics
The term used to describe how the body deals with a drug, including how it is absorbed into the bloodstream, distributed to different tissues, broken down, and finally excreted from the body.

Pharmacologist
A scientist concerned with the study of drugs and their actions. Pharmacologists are responsible for research into new drugs. Clinical pharmacologists are usually qualified doctors. They are primarily concerned with the actions of drugs in the treatment of specific disorders and with monitoring their effects on patients in clinical trials and in medical practice.

Pharmacopeia
A publication, also known as a formulary, that lists and describes drugs used in medicine. The term pharmacopeia usually refers to an official national publication such as the British Pharmacopeia (BP). Used as a reference book by doctors and pharmacists, a pharmacopeia describes sources, preparations, doses and tests that can be used to identify individual drugs and to determine their purity. It may also contain information about mechanisms of action, possible adverse effects, comments about the relative effectiveness and safety of a drug in treating a particular disorder, and price comparisons between similar drugs.

Pharmacy
A term used to describe the practice of preparing drugs and making up prescriptions. It is also used to refer to the place where these activities are carried out.

Photophobia
Dislike of bright light. Photophobia may be induced by certain drugs (notably *mydriatics*) and diseases.

Placebo
A "medicine," often in tablet or capsule form, that contains no medically active ingredient. Placebos are frequently used in clinical trials of new drugs (see *Double-blind*). A physician may sometimes administer a placebo because of the emotional or psychological uplift it may give to a patient convinced that his or her condition calls for some form of drug treatment. See also Placebo response (p.15).

Poison
A substance that, in relatively small amounts, disrupts the structure and/or function of cells, causing harmful and sometimes fatal effects. Many drugs are poisonous if taken in overdose.

Premedication
The term applied to drugs given between one and two hours before an operation to prepare a person for surgery. Premedication usually contains a narcotic analgesic to help relieve pain and anxiety and to reduce the dose of anaesthetic needed to produce unconsciousness (see also *Anaesthetic, general*). An *anticholinergic* drug is also sometimes included to reduce secretions in the airways.

Prescription
A written instruction from the doctor to the pharmacist, detailing the name of the drug to be dispensed, the dosage, how often it has to be taken, and other instructions as necessary. A prescription is written and signed by a doctor and carries the name and address of the patient for whom the drug is prescribed. The pharmacist keeps a record, often computerized, of all prescriptions dispensed. See also Managing your drug treatment (p.25).

Prophylactic
A drug, procedure, or piece of equipment used to prevent disease. For example, a course of drugs given to a traveller to prevent malarial infection, is termed malaria prophylaxis.

Proprietary
A term now generally applied to a drug that is sold over the counter, its name being registered to a private manufacturer, i.e. a proprietor.

Purgative
A drug that helps eliminate faeces from the body, either to relieve constipation or to empty the bowel/intestine before surgery. See also *Cathartic*.

R

Receptor
A specific site on the surface of a cell with a characteristic chemical and physical structure. Natural body chemicals such as *neurotransmitters* bind to cell receptors to initiate a response in the cell. Many drugs also have an effect on cells by binding to a receptor. They may promote cell activity or may block it. See also *Agonist* and *Antagonist*.

Replication
The duplication of genetic material (DNA or RNA) in a cell as part of the process of cell division which enables a tissue to grow or a virus to multiply.

Rubefacient
A preparation, also known as a counter-irritant, that, when applied to an area of skin, causes it to redden by increasing blood flow in vessels in that area. A rubefacient such as methyl salicylate may be included in an *embrocation*.

S

Sedative
A drug that dampens the activity of the central nervous system. Sleeping drugs (p.82) and anti-anxiety drugs (p.83) have a sedative effect, and many other drugs such antihistamines (p.124) and antidepressants (p.84) can produce sedation as a side effect.

Side effect
A reaction to a drug that can be explained by the established effects of the drug itself. A side effect may be a predictable effect such as dry mouth caused by an *anticholinergic* drug, or an exaggeration of the normal

therapeutic effect, such as bleeding caused by an anticoagulant drug. The term is distinct from *adverse reaction*.

Subcutaneous injection
A method of administering a drug by which the drug is injected just beneath the skin. The drug is then slowly absorbed over a few hours into the surrounding blood vessels. Insulin is given in this way. See also Methods of administration (p.17).

Sublingual
A term meaning under the tongue. Some drugs are administered sublingually in tablet form. The drug is then very rapidly absorbed through the lining of the mouth into the bloodstream within a few seconds. Nitrate drugs may be given this way to provide rapid relief of an angina attack. See also Methods of administration (p.17).

Suppository
A bullet-shaped pellet usually containing a drug for insertion into the rectum. See also Methods of administration (p.17).

Sympatholytic
A term meaning blocking the effect of the sympathetic nervous system. Sympatholytic drugs work either by reducing the release of the stimulatory *neurotransmitter* noradrenaline from nerve endings, or by occupying the *receptors* that the neurotransmitters adrenaline and noradrenaline normally bind to, thereby preventing their normal actions. Beta blockers are examples of sympatholytic drugs. See also Autonomic nervous system (p.79).

Sympathomimetic
Having the same effect as stimulation of the sympathetic nervous system to cause, say, an increase in the heart rate and widening of the airways. A drug with a sympathomimetic action may work either by causing the release of the stimulatory *neurotransmitter* noradrenaline from nerve endings or by mimicking the action of neurotransmitters. See Autonomic nervous system (p.79). Sympathomimetic drugs include certain bronchodilators (p.92) and decongestants (p.93).

Systemic
Having a generalized effect, causing physical or chemical changes in tissues throughout the body. For a drug to have a systemic effect it must be absorbed into the bloodstream, usually via the digestive tract, by injection or by rectal suppository.

T

Tablet
See p.19.

Tardive dyskinesia
Abnormal, uncontrolled movements mainly of the face, tongue, mouth, and neck, that may be caused by prolonged treatment with antipsychotic drugs. This condition is distinct from *parkinsonism* that may also be caused by such drugs. See also antipsychotic drugs (p.85).

Tolerance
The need to take a higher dosage of a specific drug to maintain the same physical or mental effect. Tolerance occurs during prolonged treatment with narcotic analgesics and benzodiazepines. See also Drug dependence (p.23).

Tonics
A diverse group of remedies prescribed or bought over the counter for relieving vague symptoms such as malaise, lethargy, and loss of appetite, for which no obvious cause can be found. Tonics sometimes contain vitamins and minerals, but there is no scientific evidence that such ingredients have anything other than a *placebo* effect. Nevertheless, many individuals feel better after taking a tonic for a few weeks, and this does no harm.

Topical
The term used to describe the application of a drug to the site where it is intended that it should have its effect. Disorders of the skin, eye, outer ear, nasal passages, anus, and vagina are often treated with drugs applied topically.

Toxic reaction
Unpleasant and possibly dangerous symptoms caused by a drug, the result either of an overdose or an *adverse reaction*.

Toxin, toxic
A toxin is a poisonous substance such as a harmful chemical released by bacteria or created by a drug interaction. Drugs that are usually safe in normal doses may produce toxic effects when taken in overdose. An *adverse reaction* may be produced by a toxin. See The effects of drugs (p.15).

Tranquillizer, major
A drug used to treat psychotic illness such as schizophrenia. See Antipsychotic drugs (p.85).

Tranquillizer, minor
A sedative drug used to treat anxiety and emotional tension. See Antianxiety drugs (p.83).

Transdermal patch
A method of administering a drug in which an adhesive patch impregnated with the drug is placed on the skin. The drug is slowly absorbed through the skin into the underlying blood vessels. Drugs administered in this way include nitrates, remedies for travel sickness, and oestrogens. See also Methods of administration (p.17).

V W

Vaccine
A substance administered to induce active immunity against a specific infectious disease (see Vaccines and immunization, p.134).

Vasoconstrictor
A drug that narrows blood vessels, often prescribed to reduce nasal congestion. See Decongestants (p.93). Vasoconstrictors are also frequently given with injected local anaesthetics (p.80). Ephedrine is a commonly-prescribed vasoconstrictor.

Vasodilator
A drug that widens blood vessels. See Vasodilators (p.98).

Withdrawal symptom
Any symptom caused by abrupt stopping of a drug. These symptoms occur as a result of physical *dependence* on a drug. Drugs that may cause withdrawal symptoms after prolonged use include narcotics, benzodiazepines, and nicotine. Withdrawal symptoms vary according to each drug, but common examples include sweating, shaking, anxiety, nausea, and abdominal pain. See also Drug dependence (p.23).

THE GENERAL INDEX

This General Index contains references to the information in all areas of the book. It can be used to look up topics such as groups of drugs, diseases, and conditions. References for generic and brand-name drugs are also listed, with references to either the appropriate drug profile or the listing in the Drug Finder (pp.48-75). For those brand-name drugs pictured in the Colour Identification Guide (pp.34-47), there is also an italicized reference to the page number and grid letter where the photograph will be found. Entries that contain a page reference followed by the letter "g" indicate a reference to the Glossary (pp.446-451).

Azidothymidine 420
Azithromycin 50
Azlocillin 50
AZT 420
Aztreonam 50

B

Babies, drug treatment in 20
Bacampicillin 50
Back pain *see* Non-steroidal
  anti-inflammatory drugs
  116
Baclofen 204
Baclospas 204
Bacteria 126
Bacterial infections, drugs for
  antibacterial drugs 131
  antibiotics 128
  antituberculous drugs 132
Bactericidal 447g
Bacteriostatic 447g
Bactrim 248, 416
Bactroban 50
Balantidiasis 136
Baldness, male pattern 179
Balm 447g
Bambec 50
Bambuterol 50
Baratol 50
Barbiturates 82
  as drugs of abuse 436
Barrier creams 175
Bases for skin preparations
  175
Baxan 50
BCG *see* Tuberculosis
  prevention 132
Beclazone 205
Becloforte 205
Beclomethasone 205
Becodisks 205
Beconase 205
Becosym 50
Becotide 205
Becotide Rotacaps *illus.*
  40M, 40N
Bedsores infected *see*
  Anti-infective skin
  preparations 175
Bedwetting *see* Enuresis
Beechams CoughCaps
  illus. 40J
Beechams Pills 50
Beechams Powders 50
Beechams Powders
  Capsules 50
Belladonna 50
Benadon 50
Bendrofluazide 206
Benemid 50; *illus. 42D*
Benethamine penicillin 50
Benoral 207
Benorylate 207; *illus. 46 I*

Benoxyl 208
Benperidol 50
Benserazide 50
Benylin Children's Cough 50
Benylin Expectorant 50
Benylin Paediatric 50
Benylin with Codeine 50
Benzagel 208
Benzalkonium chloride 50
Benzathine penicillin 50
Benzhexol 50
Benzocaine 50
Benzodiazepines 83
  as drugs of abuse 437
  as sleeping drugs 78
Benzoin tincture 50
Benzoyl peroxide 208
Benztropine 50
Benzydamine 50
Benzyl benzoate 176
Benzylpenicillin 50
Berkamil 193
Berkaprine 203
Berkatens 418
Berkmycen 50
Berkolol 380
Berkozide 206
Berotec 50
Beta-Adalat 200, 346
Beta blockers 97
  as anti-anxiety drugs 83
  in glaucoma 169
  use in sport 443
Beta-Cardone 50
Beta-carotene 430
Betadur 380
Betagan 51
Betahistine 209
Betaloc 51
Betamethasone 210
Beta-Prograne 380
Beta receptors, types of 97
Betasept shampoo 51
Betaxolol 51
Bethanechol 51
Betim 412
Betnelan 210; *illus. 45J*
Betnesol 210
Betnesol-N 210
Betnovate 210
Betnovate-C 210
Betnovate-N 210
Betnovate Rectal 364
Betoptic 51
Bezafibrate 211
Bezalip 211
Bezalip Mono 211; *illus. 42P*
Bicillin 51
BiNovum 282
Bioavailability 447g
Biogastrone 51
Biophylline 408
Bioplex 218
Bioral 218
Bioral Gel 51
Biorphen 354

Biotin 422
Biperiden 51
Bipolar (manic) depression
  see Antimanic drugs 85
Bisacodyl 51
Bismag 393; *illus. 43J*
Bismuth 51
Bisodol 393
Bisoprolol 51
Bites, allergic reaction to
  see Antihistamines 124
Bladder
  cancer, drugs for *see*
  Anticancer drugs 154
  disorders *see* Drugs used
  for urinary disorders 166
Bleeding, control of *see*
  Blood clotting
Bleomycin 51
Blocadren 412; *illus. 38B*
Blood
  cancer *see* Leukaemias
  cells 152
  circulation 95
  clotting, drugs that affect 104
  doping 442
  glucose, monitoring of 143
  used in labour 165
  pressure, high *see*
  Hypertension
  transfusions, allergic
  reactions to *see*
  Antihistamines 124
Body salts 447g
Boils *see* Infection, bacterial
Bolvidon 335; *illus. 45R*
Bone 115
  cancer, drugs for *see*
  Anticancer drugs 154
  disorders, drugs for 122
  infections 129
  pain *see* Non-steroidal
  anti-inflammatory drugs
  116
  wasting disorders 122
Bonefos 51; *illus. 39 I*
Bone marrow
  blood cell production in 152
  cancer, drugs for *see*
  Anticancer drugs 154
Bonjela gel 51
Bonjela pastilles 51
Bowel
  disease, inflammatory 112
  infections, drugs for
  antibiotics 128
  antifungal drugs 138
  antiprotozoal drugs 136
Bradilan 51
Brain 78
  cancer, drugs for *see*
  Anticancer drugs 154
  infections, drugs for
  antibiotics 128
  antifungal drugs 138
  antiprotozoal drugs 136

Brand-name drugs *see*
  Generic name 448g
Breast cancer, drugs for *see*
  Anticancer drugs 154
Breast discomfort,
  premenstrual *see* Drugs
  used to treat menstrual
  disorders 160
Breast feeding, drug
  treatment during 21
Breathing, drugs to improve
  bronchodilators 92
  respiratory stimulants 88
  See also Respiratory
  system 91
Breathlessness *see*
  Bronchodilators 92
Brelomax 51
Bretylate 51
Bretylium tosylate 51
Brevibloc 51
Brevinor 282, 349
Bricanyl 51
Britiazim 263
Britlofex 51
Brocadopa 315; *illus. 39N*
Broflex 51
Brolene 51
Bromocriptine 212
Brompheniramine 51
Bronchitis, drugs for
  antibacterials 131
  antibiotics 128
  bronchodilators 92
Bronchoconstrictor 447g
Bronchodil 51
Bronchodilator 447g
Bronchodilators 92
Brufen 302
Brufen Retard *illus. 46F*
Buccastem 375
Buclizine 51
Budesonide 51
Bufexamac 51
Bulk-forming agents
  as antidiarrhoeal drugs 110
  as laxatives 111
Bumetanide 213
Bupivacaine 51
Buprenorphine 51
Burinex 213; *illus. 44C*
Burinex-A 213
Burinex-K 213
Burneze 51
Burns, infected
  drugs for *see* Anti-infective
  skin preparations 175
  relieving pain of *see* Local
  anaesthetics 80
Bursitis, drugs for
  locally-acting cortico-
  steroids 118
  non-steroidal anti-
  inflammatory drugs 116
Buscopan 301; *illus. 44Q*
Buserelin 51

Q

U

DRUG POISONING EMERGENCY GUIDE

The information on the following pages is intended to give practical advice for dealing with a known or suspected drug poisoning emergency. Although many of the first aid techniques described can be used in a number of different types of emergency, instructions apply only to drug overdose or poisoning.

Emergency action is necessary in any of the following circumstances:
● If a person has taken an overdose of any of the high danger drugs listed in the box on p.472.
● If a person has taken an overdose of a less dangerous drug, but has one or more of the danger symptoms listed below.
● If a person has taken, or is suspected of having taken, an overdose of an unknown drug.
● If a child has swallowed, or is suspected of having swallowed, any prescription or non-prescription drug.

What to do

If you are faced with a drug poisoning emergency, it is important to carry out first aid and arrange immediate help in the right order. The Priority action decision chart (below) will help you to assess the situation and to determine your priorities. The following information should help you to remain calm in an emergency if you ever need to deal with a case of drug poisoning.

DANGER SYMPTOMS

Take emergency action if the person has one or more of the following symptoms:
● Drowsiness or unconsciousness
● Shallow, irregular or stopped breathing
● Vomiting
● Fits or convulsions

PRIORITY ACTION DECISION CHART

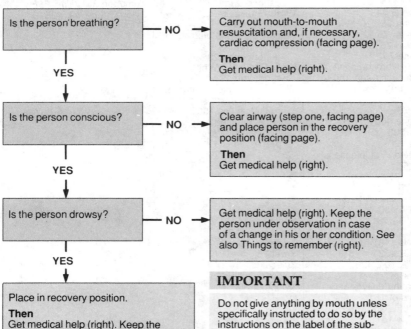

Is the person breathing? — **NO** → Carry out mouth-to-mouth resuscitation and, if necessary, cardiac compression (facing page).
Then Get medical help (right).

↓ **YES**

Is the person conscious? — **NO** → Clear airway (step one, facing page) and place person in the recovery position (facing page).
Then Get medical help (right).

↓ **YES**

Is the person drowsy? — **NO** → Get medical help (right). Keep the person under observation in case of a change in his or her condition. See also Things to remember (right).

↓ **YES**

Place in recovery position.
Then Get medical help (right). Keep the person under observation in case of a change in his or her condition. See also Things to remember (right).

IMPORTANT

Do not give anything by mouth unless specifically instructed to do so by the instructions on the label of the substance or by a doctor. Fluids may hasten absorption of the drug thereby increasing the danger.

GETTING MEDICAL HELP

In an emergency, a calm person who is competent in first aid should stay with the victim, while others summon help. However, if you have to deal with a drug poisoning emergency on your own, use first aid (see the Priority Action Decision Chart, left) before getting help.

Calling an ambulance may be the quickest method of transport to hospital. Then call your doctor or a hospital accident and emergency department for advice. If possible, tell them what drug has been taken and how much, and the age of the victim. Follow the doctor's or hospital's instructions precisely.

THINGS TO REMEMBER

Effective treatment of drug poisoning depends on the doctor making a rapid assessment of the type and amount of drug taken. Collecting evidence that will assist the diagnosis will help. After you have carried out first aid, look for empty or opened medicine containers. Keep any of the drug that is left together with its container (or syringe), and give these to the nurse or doctor. Save any vomit for analysis in the hospital.

ESSENTIAL FIRST AID

MOUTH-TO-MOUTH RESUSCITATION

When there is no rise and fall of the chest and you can feel no movement of exhaled air, immediately commence mouth-to-mouth resuscitation.

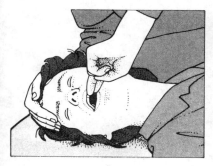

1 Lay the victim on his or her back on a firm surface. Clear the mouth of vomit or any other foreign material that might otherwise block the airways, and remove false teeth.

2 Place one hand under the neck and lift gently to tip the head back and raise the chin, while pressing down on the forehead. This should allow the mouth to drop open.

3 Pinch the victim's nostrils closed with the hand that is placed on the forehead and use the other to grip his or her chin firmly to keep the mouth open. Take a deep breath, seal your mouth over that of the victim and give two quick breaths. Continue to give further breaths every 5 seconds.

4 After each breath, turn to watch the chest falling while you listen for the sound of air leaving the victim's mouth. Continue until the victim starts to breathe regularly on his or her own, or until medical help arrives.

CARDIAC COMPRESSION

This is a technique used in conjunction with mouth-to-mouth resuscitation to restart a stopped heart beat. It is a procedure that should normally be undertaken only by someone who has received training.

Cardiac compression involves putting repeated, strong pressure on the centre of the chest with the heels of both hands, at a rate of 80 compressions per minute (right). After every 15 compressions, two breaths should be given using mouth-to-mouth resuscitation (above).

CHECKING PULSE

If the victim does not start breathing after two breaths of mouth-to-mouth resuscitation, check the pulse in the neck. If there is no pulse, start cardiac compression if you have been trained in this technique.

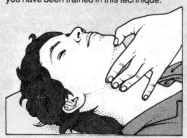

This sequence should be continued until breathing restarts.

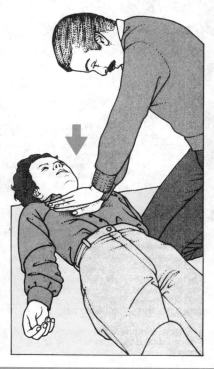

THE RECOVERY POSITION

The recovery position is the safest position for an unconscious or drowsy person. It allows the person to breathe easily and will help prevent choking if vomiting occurs. A victim of drug poisoning should be placed in the recovery position when more urgent first aid such as mouth-to-mouth resuscitation has been carried out and when shock (p.472) is not suspected. Place the victim on his or her front with one leg bent and the arm on that side raised. Turn the head to the same side. Tilt the head back so that the chin juts forward. Cover the person with a blanket or clothing for warmth.

DEALING WITH A FIT

Certain types of drug poisoning may provoke fits. These may occur whether the person is conscious or not. The victim usually falls to the ground twitching or making uncontrolled movements of limbs and body. If you witness a fit, remember the following points:

● Do not try to hold the person down.

● Do not put anything into their mouth.

● Try to ensure that the person does not suffer injury by keeping them away from dangerous objects or furniture.

● Once the fit is over, place the person in the recovery position (p.471).

HIGH DANGER DRUGS

The following is a list of drugs given a high overdose rating in the drug profiles. If you suspect that someone has taken an overdose of one of these drugs, immediate medical attention must be sought.

Adrenaline	Hydralazine	Primidone
Amitriptyline		Procyclidine
Aspirin	Imipramine	Propranolol
Atropine	Insulin	Pyridostigmine
	Isoniazid	
Benorylate	Isoprenaline	Quinine
Chloral hydrate	Lithium	Theophylline/
Chloroquine		aminophylline
Chlorpropamide	Metformin	Timolol
Clomipramine	Moclobemide	Tolbutamide
Codeine	Morphine	
Colchicine		Warfarin
Co-proxamol	Neostigmine	
Dextromoramide	Orphenadrine	
Diamorphine		
Digoxin	Paracetamol	
Disopyramide	Pentazocine	
Dothiepin	Pethidine	
	Phenelzine	
Glibenclamide	Phenobarbitone	
	Phenylbutazone	
Heparin	Phenylpropanolamine	

DEALING WITH ANAPHYLACTIC SHOCK

Anaphylactic shock occurs as the result of a severe allergic reaction to a drug. Blood pressure drops dramatically and the airways may become narrowed. The reaction usually occurs within minutes of taking the drug. The main symptoms are:

● Pallor
● Tightness in the chest
● Breathing difficulty
● Rash
● Facial swelling
● Collapse

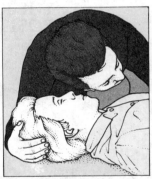

1 First ensure that the person is breathing. If breathing has stopped, immediate mouth-to-mouth resuscitation should be carried out as described on p.471.

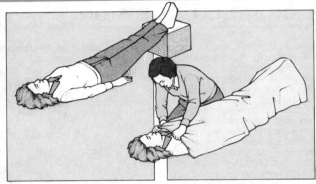

2 If the person is breathing normally, lay him or her down, face upwards, with legs raised above the level of the heart to ensure the adequate circulation of the blood. Use a footstool, carton, or a similar item to support the feet.

3 Cover the person with a blanket or articles of clothing while waiting for medical help. Do not attempt to administer anything by mouth.

HOW TO INDUCE VOMITING

In certain circumstances you may be advised to make the person vomit in order to expel the drug from the stomach, so preventing it from being absorbed. This should be attempted only when specifically advised, and never when the person is unconscious. The simplest method of inducing vomiting is to give syrup of ipecac, a drug that should be kept among the regular medical supplies of those living a long way from hospital.

Recommended dosages are 10ml for children under 18 months; 15ml for those aged 18 months - 12 years and 30ml for adults. This stimulates vomiting within 20 - 30 minutes. Do not push fingers down the throat. When vomiting occurs, remember the points listed below.

1 Ensure that the victim leans well forward to avoid choking or inhalation of vomit.

2 Keep the vomit for later analysis (see Things to remember, p.470)

3 Give water to rinse the mouth. This should be spat out, not swallowed.

040-604-1